TAGISH
INLAND TLINGIT
TAHLTAN
Klukwan
Chilkoot
Haines
Yandestaki
AUK
Taku River
Glacier Bay
Auke Bay
Juneau
TAKU
Grouse Fort
Hoonah
SUMDUM
Sumdum
Stikine River
HUTSNUWU
Angoon
Kake Village
Neltushkin
Frederick Sound
SITKA
Sitka
Chatham Strait
Kake
STIKINE
KAKE
Wrangell
Kuiu
KUYU
Tuxekan
SANYA
Portland Canal
NISKA
HENYA
Klawock
KLAWAK
Ketchikan
Nass River
GITKSAN
TSIMSHIAN
Cape Fox
New Metlakatla
Bucareli Bay
Tongass
TONGASS
KAIGANI
CARRIER
Prince Rupert
Skeena River
Dixon Entrance
HAIDA
KWAKIUTL
BELLA COOLA

THE TLINGIT INDIANS

Dear Yukie,
Thank you always for your
beautiful art. The reflections
of your gentle soul are throughout
our house.
David & Beth
Levine

THE TLINGIT INDIANS

George Thornton Emmons

Edited with additions by
Frederica de Laguna
and a biography by Jean Low

UNIVERSITY OF WASHINGTON PRESS *Seattle and London*
AMERICAN MUSEUM OF NATURAL HISTORY *New York*

THE TLINGIT INDIANS IS PUBLISHED AS NUMBER 70
IN THE ANTHROPOLOGICAL PAPERS OF THE
AMERICAN MUSEUM OF NATURAL HISTORY.

The preparation of this edited volume was made possible in part by grants from the Program for Editions of the National Endowment for the Humanities, an independent federal agency. Publication of the book has also been supported by a grant from the National Endowment for the Humanities.

Colleagues, friends, and former students of Frederica de Laguna have also contributed to the book's publication through a special fund; their names are listed in the back of the book.

Printed in the United States of America
Design by Corinna Campbell

Library of Congress Cataloging-in-Publication Data

Emmons, George Thornton.
The Tlingit Indians / George Thornton Emmons ; edited with additions by Frederica de Laguna and a biography by Jean Low.
p. cm. — (Anthropological papers of the American Museum of Natural History ; v. 70)
Includes bibliographical references and index.
ISBN 0-295-97008-1
1. Tlingit Indians—Social life and customs. 2. Alaska—Social life and customs. 3. Emmons, George Thornton. I. De Laguna, Frederica, 1906– . II. Title. III. Series.
E99.T6E46 1991
979.8′004972—dc20 90-46274
CIP

The paper used in this publication meets the minimum requirements of American National Standard for Information Sciences—Permanence of Paper for Printed Library Materials, ANSI Z39.48-1984.

∞

To the Tlingit People

George Thornton Emmons, your friend, would have wanted this book dedicated to you, to the greatness of your ancestors, and to the bright hopes of your children. If you should read here statements made by visitors among you which you feel are unfair or discourteous, remember no people are perfect and no observers free of bias, no matter how hard they may try.

So from George Thornton Emmons
and Frederica de Laguna,
G̲unalchéesh, ax̲ x̲ooní!
[G̣unalčí·š, ˀax̣ x̣u·ní!]

"Copper" drawn by Bill Holm, based on a 1787 sketch by James Colnett. Colnett labeled the sketch "underarmour" (see pages 179–83 for discussion of coppers).

Contents

ABBREVIATIONS

American Museum of Natural History, New York	AMNH
British Association for the Advancement of Science	BAAS
Bureau of American Ethnology, Smithsonian Institution, Washington, D.C.	BAE
British Columbia Provincial Archives, Victoria	BCPA
Field Museum of Natural History, Chicago	FMNH
Museum of the American Indian, New York	MAI
Portland Art Museum	PAM
Princeton University Museum	PUM
Smithsonian Institution, Washington, D.C.	SI
Thomas Burke Memorial Washington State Museum, Seattle	TBMM
United States National Museum	USNM
University Museum, University of Pennsylvania, Philadelphia	UM

PREFACE

Editing The Tlingit Indians

It was about a century ago (1888?) that Lieutenant George Thornton Emmons, USN, set about writing a monograph on the Tlingit Indians, urged by the directors and anthropologists at the American Museum of Natural History in New York, to whom he had just sold a magnificent ethnographic collection from the Tlingit with full accompanying notes. When he died in 1945, his book was still unfinished, although he had worked on it for over thirty years, leaving several drafts in the American Museum and also in the British Columbia Provincial Archives in Victoria, where he had been writing during the last decade of his life. I have been no faster than Emmons in preparing this "final draft" for publication, for it has been some thirty-odd years since I undertook this work. But if we have been so slow, Emmons and I, it is because we each had other claims on our time, and also because Emmons had amassed such a wealth of ethnographic data and left so many notes, drawings, sketches, and manuscripts that to sort them out and to organize them into coherent form proved to be a Herculean task.

In December 1955, when Harry L. Shapiro, then chairman of the Department of Anthropology at AMNH, asked me to edit this work for publication in the museum's *Anthropological Papers,* I jumped at the chance, confident that four seasons of fieldwork among the Tlingit had equipped me for the job. I realized then neither the magnitude of the undertaking nor the extent of my ignorance, but shortly began to work, with the editorial assistance of Bela Weitzner, then associate curator of ethnology at the museum.

In the fall of 1959, as visiting professor at the University of California for a semester, I found many books and periodicals in the incomparable Berkeley libraries that were useful to this undertaking. During the summer of 1962 in Victoria, British Columbia, I was able to work in the same room in the Provincial Archives in which Emmons had worked, surrounded by the volumes he had consulted. There I went over its collection of Emmons's manuscripts and notes, arranging them for the archives, and referred to the sources in the library. Through the kindness of Dr. Willard E. Ireland, then director of BCPA, and later of Frances Gundry, I procured photocopies of important portions of the notebooks and other manuscripts, and photographic copies of the pictures. I also took full notes on the differences between the BCPA typescript of *The Tlingit Indians* and the typed version in AMNH. During a sabbatical in 1962–63, I made full use of the library facilities at Berkeley. Later, the libraries of Bryn Mawr College and Haverford College secured additional material for me through interlibrary loan.

I therefore had the following manuscripts with which to work: At AMNH I had the original handwritten text and a typescript of both *The Tlingit Indians* and the *History of Tlingit Clans and Tribes,* a typed copy of the famous catalogue of 1887 which had won approval from Boas (1888a, 1888b), many sketches in pencil and pen and ink made by Emmons of Tlingit artifacts and activities, and photographs taken by him and by others which he wished to use as illustrations. In addition, there were tables, notes, and other documents, including an account by Shukoff—a half-Russian, half-Tlingit ("creole")—about Tlingit customs and beliefs, recorded in Russian in 1882 and translated into English in 1884, from which Emmons had clearly drawn information.

At BCPA, there was another (older?) typed version of *The Tlingit Indians* and of the *History,* handwritten versions of different chapters and of different topics, ten notebooks of field notes, lists and tables, questionnaires with answers (often in different hands, not all of which were identifiable), clippings from magazines and newspapers with Emmons's notations, and more photographs and sketches.

Lastly, there were the publications of Emmons himself on the Tlingit, to many of which he referred in his unpublished manuscripts. The correspondence of Emmons in these two repositories, as well as in other museums to which he had offered his collections, has been studied by my friend and collaborator, Jean Low, who prepared the biography of Emmons for this volume. (See also Low 1977.)

Since the typists who had copied the various manuscripts and the original catalogue at AMNH often could not read Emmons's writing, it was necessary to check the typescripts against manuscripts, a difficult task because Emmons made his "*u*" indistinguishable from "*ee*" and "*n,*" and I often had to rely on what I believed the words were likely to have been in Tlingit. His transliterations of Tlingit words were inconsistent and idiosyncratic, and despite the efforts of Dr. Pliny E.

Goddard, himself a linguist, and Miss Weitzner, Emmons clung stubbornly to his own spellings, even though these changed through the years, especially after Boas published *Grammatical Notes on the Language of the Tlingit Indians* in 1917. Using this work, as well as the first dictionary of Tlingit by Constance Naish and Gillian Story (1963; see also the second edition of 1976, and their Tlingit verb dictionary, 1973), and what I myself knew of Tlingit, I attempted to work out a more rational system of spelling for the words recorded by Emmons. The system used by Naish and Story, which was later developed into the modern Popular Orthography, did not fit my purposes, since it was intended to be used by someone already familiar with Tlingit phonetics and not the ordinary reader, even though an anthropologist. I soon found that my linguistic efforts were not good enough.

I then had the great good fortune of meeting Jeff Leer, a linguist at the Alaska Native Language Center, University of Alaska, Fairbanks, who is an expert on Tlingit. At my request he worked out a phonetic orthography for Northern Tlingit which a nonlinguistic anthropologist could pronounce. It is not completely phonemic, since the anthropological reader would probably not bother to read and remember a linguistic introduction explaining the phonetic rules. Jeff Leer generously went over all my files of Tlingit words and phrases with Emmons's spellings culled from manuscripts, plus all the names of persons, clans, tribes, houses, and places mentioned in the manuscripts, and supplied the correct Tlingit forms for these—omitting only proper names for persons and places with which he, and his Tlingit informants at hand, were unfamiliar. To have gathered the spellings of all Tlingit proper names would have necessitated a season's field trip or more. I am most grateful for this help and for Leer's expertise. In all cases, the original spellings by Emmons have been left in the text, usually in italics, followed by the phonetic correction in square brackets [ ]. The table on page xiv gives the phonetic values of the symbols I have used, as well as their equivalents in the Popular Orthography used by the Tlingit today. The translations given by Emmons for native words and expressions are in quotation marks, but when these "translations" are really only explanations of the words, such as the Tlingit often give, and a more correct or literal translation can be supplied, this is given in quotation marks within the brackets.

Although we may think of the Tlingit as primarily hunters and fishermen, they had a rich botanical lore, relying on plants for medicinal cures and magical ingredients, as well as for use in manufactures. I was again very fortunate to meet and make friends with Alix (Mrs. M. P.) Wennekens, an ethnobotanist with years of experience in Yukon Territory and Alaska, at the time living in Anchorage. She went over all the references by Emmons to plants used by the Tlingit, and carefully identified them, using Eric Hultén's *Flora of Alaska* (1968) as a standard for the scientific designations.

Since Emmons had used the current Alaska place names of his day, and frequently failed to make clear the location of settlements, especially those abandoned, it was necessary to check every place name in English with Donald J. Orth's *Dictionary of Alaska Place Names* (1967), the bible for such information. This gives the variants of the names, degrees of latitude and longitude, and origins of the designations. With this, and with the *U.S. Coast Pilot* of Alaska, especially the older editions, I was often able to identify places for which Emmons had given only the native designation. (In Orth's work I also learned that Lieutenant Commander E. K. Moore, U.S. Navy, had named Emmons Island and its southeastern point, Emmons Point, for our Lieutenant George Thornton Emmons. The island is in Hoonah Sound.)

One difficult task was to organize the data Emmons had left, since there was an embarrassment of riches in the various manuscripts and notes, often with several versions of the same topic. And it was evident that Emmons himself had also worried over the organization of his materials, for in the wavering hand of old age he had drawn up various lists of chapter and section titles, without solving the problem of their arrangement. There were, I found, many duplications of the same pieces of information or different treatments of the same topic, or the same incident might be described several places in the manuscript, in different contexts. There were often more complete and more vivid descriptions in what I took to be his older notes, made in the field or copied from his field notebooks, than in the more "polished" version of his ethnography. Therefore, I substituted these older and more specific passages from the notebooks in place of the more generalized or "literary" account.

It finally became clear that I should have to depart from the strict order of the "Table of Contents" in the typed manuscript from AMNH on which I was working, in some cases to shift a section or paragraph from one chapter to another, in others to divide a lengthy chapter in two, or to change chapter titles after combining sections. In this way, "Chapter V, Domestic Life" completely disappeared, the sections of which it had been originally composed being assigned to more logical places. These shifts were the more easily accomplished because it was evident that Emmons had written each section separately. The most drastic change was to eliminate the *History of Tlingit Clans and Tribes* from Chapter 2, and to substitute my own sketch of the kinship system, since this was a topic that Emmons had hardly touched. I was, however, spared the task of dealing with the chapter on myths and folktales, since Emmons decided to omit this after he became acquainted with Swanton's *Tlingit Myths and Texts,* published in 1909.

Emmons had made use of the excellent libraries of the Provincial Archives in Victoria, and earlier in the American Museum in New York. He had clearly planned to support or amplify his own observations with passages from the eighteenth- and early nineteenth-century explorers, traders, and other visitors to the Tlingit, but had given up before this task was completed. Since he had usually mentioned only the author's name as reference, and was often inaccurate in quoting, the job of checking and correcting these passages was not easily accomplished. I usually found that I had to use Emmons's references only as a guide and that I had to discover and extract the pertinent passage to which he had made a vague allusion. In addition, I surveyed all the available publications that Emmons might have used, were he familiar with them, including sources in foreign languages (French, German, Spanish, and Russian), many of which had not been translated when Emmons was writing. I have therefore attempted to carry out his intentions by securing additional information from these sources, and adding such quotations to his text. The most important of the early sources which I included were von Langsdorff, von Kotzebue, Khlebnikov, Veniaminov, Tikhmenev, Lütké, Holmberg, Crespi, Sierra, Mourelle, Riobo, Malaspina, Suría, Beresford, Portlock, and Fleurieu. Emmons had also made references to some of these, as well as to Dixon, Lisiansky, La Pérouse, and Vancouver, but a number of selections from these last are also mine. I have also included some of Emmons's contemporaries: Aurel Krause, Reverend S. Hall Young, Caroline (Mrs. Eugene M.) Willard, Ivan Petroff, Franz Boas, H. H. Bancroft, Ensign Albert Niblack, and the official reports of naval officers in Alaska (chiefly those of Commander Beardslee and Commander Glass). It is curious that Emmons made no use of these reports, with which he must have been familiar, and that he ignored Niblack's important ethnological survey of the Northwest Coast Indians (chiefly their material culture, 1890). Was Emmons guilty of this neglect because he was jealous of his reputation as an authority on the Tlingit and did not wish to share it? Lastly, I have included references to later works on the Tlingit which I thought would be particularly useful, such as those by Philip Drucker, Viola Garfield, Erna Gunther, Edward L. Keithahn, Kalervo Oberg, R. L. Olson, John R. Swanton, and my own publications. In this, I have not attempted to be comprehensive, but rather to illuminate the text and guide readers to important sources. In adding citations I have tried usually to place these in chronological order, for in this way some insight into Tlingit cultural history is given. Usually the introductory remarks to such quotations are mine, as may be summaries of passages from the authors cited.

My additions and corrections of substantive material are indicated by enclosure within square brackets, and by the notes that accompany each chapter. The latter point out not only which quotations I have supplied and my introductory and concluding remarks for them, but also other liberties I have taken with the text, such as transferring sections from one place to another. I have also added punctuation where needed, and have simplified the phrasing of sentences that were hard to follow because Emmons often wrote in an awkward manner; but minor stylistic changes I have not bothered to indicate, preferring a smoother text with a minimum use of brackets.

Because this is George Emmons's book, I asked Jean Low, who had been studying his life and had already published an article on him (1977), to write his biography for this volume, showing how he became a naval officer and was stationed in Alaska where he collected Indian artifacts for many great museums. Then in my own introduction, I discuss his contributions to ethnography and how he became an authority on the Tlingit. It has been a pleasure to work with Jean Low.

Frederica de Laguna
Bryn Mawr College, Pennsylvania

TRANSLITERATION OF TLINGIT

Emmons had his own way of writing Tlingit. It did not form a system, since the same sound might be rendered by different letters or combinations of letters approximating their value in English, but inadequate to reflect Tlingit sounds. To him, his spelling was perfectly clear, and when Miss Bella Weitzner attempted to secure a consistent system of orthography from him, he brushed this aside as unnecessary. In the following pages I have made no attempt to introduce consistency into Emmons's text, and it will be seen that he has spelled the same word or name differently in different places and at different times. I have only given a phonetic spelling in brackets [ ], following Emmons's forms.

The accompanying chart showing the system of phonetic transcription has been prepared by Jeff Leer for use in this book. It should be noted that as often as possible the initial sound of a proper name has been rendered by a capital letter, to conform to familiar usage. This applies to the vowel following an initial glottal stop, and the initial fricative l, /ł/, is given as Ł, not to be confused with the L used by some writers (see Swanton) to represent ƛ (tł).

SYSTEM OF PHONETIC TRANSCRIPTION OF TLINGIT

Tlingit Consonants

		Affricative Series			Velars		Uvulars		
	Dental	Lateral	Sibilant	Shibilant	Unrounded	Rounded	Unrounded	Rounded	Glottal*
Plain stops	d	λ (dl)	ʒ (dz)	ǯ (j)	g	g^w (gw)	g̣ (g̲)	g̣^w (g̲w)	ʔ (.)
Aspirated stops	t	ƛ (tl)	c (ts)	č (ch)	k	k^w (kw)	q (k̲)	q^w (k̲w)	
Glottalized stops	t̓ (t´)	ƛ̓ (tl´)	c̓ (ts´)	č̓ (ch´)	k̓ (k´)	k̓^w (k´w)	q̓ (k̲´)	q̓^w (k̲´w)	
Plain fricatives		ł (l)	s	š (sh)	x	x^w (xw)	x̣ (x̲)	x̣^w (x̲w)	h
Glottalized fricatives		ł̓ (l´)	s̓ (s´)		x̓ (x´)	x̓^w (x´w)	x̣̓ (x̲´)	x̣̓^w (x̲´w)	
Sonants	n			y	ỵ (y̲)	w			

Tlingit Vowels

a	a·	i	i·	e	e·	u	u·
	(aa)		(ee)		(ei)		(oo)

Only high pitch /´/ need be indicated in Northern Tlingit

Note: I am deeply indebted to Jeff Leer, Alaska Native Language Center, University of Alaska, Fairbanks, for help in making this chart for the phonetic transcription of Tlingit. In addition, he has gone over the entire list of Tlingit words and names in the text and rendered them according to this system. The format for the table of consonants is taken from Leer's *Tongass Texts* (in Frank and Emma Williams 1978:7). The symbols used in the Popular Orthography (devised for the Tlingits' own use) are given below the phonetic symbol, except when they are alike: d, g, h, k, n, s, t, w, x, y.

*The glottal stop /ʔ/ occurs before any syllable-initial vowel, as in words beginning with a vowel. (This slight glottalization occurs regularly in English, although we are not aware of it.) The Popular Orthography does not indicate this at the beginning of words, but does put a period /./ between vowels that begin and end syllables within words.

Acknowledgments

In addition to the many individuals and staffs of institutions who helped us in our research, we should like to mention especially Harry L. Shapiro and Bella Weitzner, who started this project, and also Florence Baumer, Joseph Sedacca, Anna Marie Lunsford, Anibal Rodriguez, David Hurst Thomas, Stanley A. Freed, and Craig Morris, all of the American Museum of Natural History, who provided help in editing, archival research, and administrative matters; Willard E. Ireland and Frances Gundry of the British Columbia Provincial Archives, who generously provided photocopies of materials; and Donald N. Abbott of the British Columbia Provincial Museum. Also for archival and historical help we thank Donald Baird of Princeton University, Mary Jane Lenz and Nancy Henry of the Museum of the American Indian, William S. Hanable and Robert DeArmond of the Alaska Historical Society, Ted Hinckley of San Jose State College, California, Mary Elizabeth Ruwell of the University Museum, Philadelphia, and lastly Ira Jackniss and Douglas Cole of Simon Fraser University, Burnaby, B.C., who shared their spoils with us.

Michael Krauss (for Eyak) and Jeff Leer (for Tlingit) of the Alaska Native Language Center rendered invaluable linguistic assistance. David Galloway of the British Museum (Natural History), J. C. H. King of the British Museum (Mankind), Lynn Maranda of Richmond, B.C., and Stephen Wilson of London tracked down Captain Colnett's unpublished manuscript with the first description of a "copper." Adrienne L. Kaeppler of the Bishop Museum, Honolulu, Judi Miller of the Canadian Conservation Institute, Ottawa, and Cheryl Samuel of Victoria, B.C., dispelled myths about the provenience of certain geometric style "Raven's Tail" robes and about Tlingit dyes and paints. Alix Wennekens of Sequim, Washington, identified the plants mentioned by Emmons, with the help of Karen Workman of Anchorage for native tobacco. Catharine McClellan of the University of Wisconsin, Madison, shared field work among the Tlingit with the editor, and supplied information about Indians of Yukon Territory.

As the editor of the volume, I am especially grateful to Bill Holm of the Burke Museum, University of Washington, for his careful reading of the text, his correction of some errors, and his generous sharing of his expert knowledge of the whole Northwest Coast. Helen Fogg also read the entire manuscript, checking facts and references. In addition, I very much appreciate the contributions made by current and former students, colleagues, and friends to the publication fund for this book.

Preparation of the edited manuscript was supported in part by a research grant from the National Endowment for the Humanities. For this support and subsequent generous support for publication, as well as for a small grant from the Rosalyn R. Schwartz Fund of Bryn Mawr College, I am most grateful.

We both thank everyone at the American Museum of Natural History and at the University of Washington Press, especially Naomi Pascal, Marilyn Trueblood, Leila Charbonneau, and Corinna Campbell, who helped to see this venture through to publication and distribution. We hope that Bella Weitzner, who saw the beginning of this enterprise, will approve of its ending.

Frederica de Laguna and Jean F. Low

George Thornton Emmons, Lt., USN, ret., 1904. (AMNH.)

EDITOR'S INTRODUCTION

George Thornton Emmons As Ethnographer

George Thornton Emmons carried out his ethnographical investigations of the Tlingit Indians primarily during the 1880s and 1890s when he was assigned to U.S. naval vessels in southeastern Alaska. He had opportunities for ethnographic work even when on active duty, and during his numerous sick leaves seems to have spent as much time as possible with the Tlingit. After his retirement from the service in 1899 because of ill health, he frequently returned to Alaska, usually for the summer months. Recalled to temporary government service in 1902 for the U.S. Boundary Commission, he investigated, with the help of the Chilkat Tlingit, the alleged Russian boundary markers on the Chilkat Pass. In 1904 he studied the condition of the Alaska natives, and his report was forwarded to the Senate by President Theodore Roosevelt, who supported Emmons's suggestions in his recommendation for legislation. Emmons made his last trip to Alaska in 1926, as a tourist, with his wife.

In a letter of March 28, 1903, to the Alaska Boundary Tribunal (1904, 2:402–3), Emmons testified about his naval service in Alaska:

> . . . the men-of-war to which I was attached cruised continually along the mainland coast of Alaska and the outlying islands of the Alexander Archipelago, from Portland Canal to Dixons [*sic*] Entrance, to the head of Lynn Canal, and through Icy Straits and Cross Sound, and seaward as far west as Yukatat [Yakutat] or Bering Bay, visiting all of the settlements, anchorages, and inlets along the coast in order to render assistance to those in need, to preserve order among both whites and natives, and to enforce the statutory laws of the United States at the discretion of the commanding officer.
>
> Prior to the establishment of civil government in Alaska, in 1885, the commanding officer of the naval vessel stationed in those waters represented the law supreme; he touched at the native villages, received the chiefs, listened to the complaints of the people, arbitrated and judged the cases, and punished the guilty. Under the orders of the commander, the medical officer of the man-of-war inspected the natives, prescribed for them, and dispensed Government medical stores free. When necessity required, armed detachments were landed from the vessel to preserve order or make arrests. After the establishment of civil law in the Territory the naval commander cooperated with the Government officers to enforce the law and to police the country. . . .
>
> My duty and investigations among the natives of Alaska have, through twenty years, frequently brought me in connection with the Chilkat and Chilkoot people. I have visited all of their villages many times. I have traveled through their country from the head of the Kar-arlth to the head of the Thlehini rivers [tributaries of the Chilkat River]. I have made a study of their history, and I have lived with them on the most intimate terms, until they have given me one of their family names and look upon me as one of themselves. . . .

But nowhere among his papers or notes did Emmons indicate who had given him his Indian name or what it was, or to what clan ("family") it belonged. Did he acquire it through an exchange of names, like that between Lieutenant Schwatka, USA, and In-da-Yonk (the brother of the defrocked shaman Skundoo)? Was it through a more formal type of "adoption," when a traditional clan name, in disuse at the time, was given him? Or was it when the Sitka Wolf 1 clan (Ka·g^{w}a·nta·n) "adopted the Navy" (de Laguna 1972:268), and all the Ka·g^{w}a·nta·n women wore middy blouses at a potlatch and called themselves yenua-ša· ("man-of-war women")? Because of the friendship between Emmons and members of the Chartrich-Shotridge group at Klukwan, the name may well have come from them, even though we do not know whether it was from the Wolf 1 clan or the Raven 3 clan, both represented in that group (see Tables 9 and 10 for listing of clans).

During his service in Alaska, which frequently involved leading shore parties to deal with trouble cases ("wars") between native groups or between the Tlingits and the whites, or breaches of the law, Lieutenant Emmons made friends among the Indians, a people with whom he came to enjoy a long, satisfying relationship. The Indians admired anyone in naval uniform, but they liked Emmons because he was one of the few white men of his day to show a serious interest in their culture and to learn, or try to learn, their language. On his many trips with the Tlingit, ashore or afloat, on duty or on leave, he evidently took careful notes of what he saw and heard, and systematically gathered information on native arts and crafts, hunting and fishing, tribal social customs, magico-religious practices and beliefs, and folklore.

Emmons became noted as the foremost collector of Tlingit Indian artifacts. In this, he may have been spurred by rivalry with Professor William S. Libbey of Princeton, with whom he shared the spoils of a shaman's grave at Yakutat in 1886 (see Jean Low's biography, this volume). On this occasion the two men evidently discovered the grave themselves (at least there is no mention of guide or informant) and they simply removed the contents, including the skull of the shaman. But they did not know the name of the dead doctor or to what clan he belonged (de Laguna 1972:686–87, pls. 170–77). For many other collections of shamanistic paraphernalia, Emmons was able to list in his catalogue the name of the shaman, his clan, location of his gravehouse, and, more important, the identities of the spirits represented by his masks and other objects. How was this possible? The person who approached a shaman's grave or handled his things was believed by the natives to risk serious illness or death. Yet a knowledgeable native must have been with Emmons when the latter was labeling or cataloguing the specimens. This problem has bothered many scholars.

It should be remembered that during the period when Emmons was collecting Tlingit artifacts, the Navy and the missionaries were making their strongest efforts to eradicate the belief in and practice of shamanism, especially since the shaman was guilty of causing the torture and sometimes the death of accused witches. Emmons himself was present and may even have taken an active part in apprehending and punishing such shamans, done by publicly cutting off their long hair. Later, shamans were tried and imprisoned in penitentiaries. A shaman so disgraced would certainly have to lie low until his hair grew out again. Some were apparently able to revive a clandestine practice; others were unable or did not try. This left a number of "doctor's outfits" available for the collector on the spot. Emmons seems to have kept track of doctors with valuable things he hoped to get. Thus a note in the British Columbia Provincial Archives (BCPA), which acquired many of his papers, reports: "old Neltooskin [Neltushkin, Admiralty Island] Dr. whose hair was cut by *Adams* has fine outfit" (see Chapter 15, the section "Shaman and Witch"). Fearing worse to come, such a disgraced shaman might be willing to part with his outfit, and to identify the spirits represented. The death of a shaman, when no successor was in sight, was also a favorable time for the collector (see Chapter 14, the section "Death of a Shaman").

At this period also, missionary work was flourishing, and Tlingit communities vied for missions and schools. Many persons, including elders and chiefs, were converted to Christianity, and young people also were ready to turn away from all "heathen" practices, and so escape the heavy burden of emulating their ancestors' potlatches and the hardships and dangers of the shaman's profession. Yet it was obligatory for the potential inheritors of a shaman's powers to expose themselves to his spirits after his demise, and failure to take up his profession when the spirits came was believed to risk death. These spirits were especially associated with the dead shaman's grave and the paraphernalia cached there. Thus one method of avoiding the call would be to have a white man, who apparently could not be injured by the spirits, take away the dangerous things (as one might clean up a dump of toxic waste). And the money paid by the collector was welcome.

The Indian who wanted to be respected by the Christian whites renounced his belief in the shaman, yet could not rid himself of it. He fearfully carried the shamanistic charms in moss, to avoid touching them, when he brought them to Emmons (see Chapter 14, the section "Death of a Shaman"). He must have sighed with relief when Emmons packed them up and shipped them off to the States.

We suspect that it was sometimes prudent or necessary for such transactions or for collecting items from a shaman's grave or cache to be carried out in secret. Yet if so, how could Emmons justify such acts, since he was always so ready to defend the property rights of the Tlingit? Was he not here acting out of character? It should be noted that Emmons was objective and fair in all his writings about Tlingit character and culture, except when it came to the cruelties inflicted by the shamans upon those whom they denounced as witches. Here he stood firmly on the side of the missionaries and the authorities. For him the "victim" was the witch, not the dying patient or the defrocked "doctor." No doubt the removal of shamanistic paraphernalia, insofar as this could help in suppressing the practice of shamanism, could be justified as the removal of evil, whereas appropriation of totem poles from an "abandoned" village was a violation of clan property rights, and like grave robbery (Emmons to W. H. Holmes, August 23, 1906, SI Archives).

Emmons was just thirty years old in September 1882 when he came to Sitka on the USS *Adams*, under Captain Merriman, having sailed from San Francisco. That year (if we can trust his often faulty memory for dates) he witnessed the cremation of a Tlingit chief at Sitka, and in September met Cowee or Kowee, chief and shaman of the Ł̓i˙ne˙dí, Raven clan 15, at what is now Juneau (Emmons 1911c). These experiences must have kindled in Emmons the desire to know more about the Tlingit.

In 1888, Emmons sold his first collection of 1,351 specimens to the American Museum of Natural History (AMNH) in New York. In December 1891 he received orders detaching him from his regular duties on the USS *Pinta* (the former Navy tug which had replaced the *Adams*), and assigning him to duty under the secretary of the interior, to represent the Navy at the World's Columbian Exposition in Chicago. He spent months in collecting, shipping, and organizing a display of Tlingit specimens for the fair (which he sold to AMNH after the fair closed). He was in charge of the Alaska Exhibit at the fair, serving in that capacity until March 1894, when he returned to Alaska as executive officer of the *Pinta*. In 1909, after his retirement from the Navy, Emmons held a similar position at the Alaska-Yukon-Pacific Exposition in Seattle (although he managed to spend most of the summer of 1909 in the field). To both expositions Emmons supplied important collections, later sold to museums, and from each received a medal in recognition of his contributions.

His collections were made for sale. Through direct purchase from him, or by exchange between institutions, there is not now a major museum in this country or abroad that does not have specimens collected by Emmons. These were primarily from the Tlingit, although in 1899, 1904, and 1906 he visited the Tahltan, later made small collections from the Niska and Gitksan Tsimshian, and also acquired small lots from other groups. His Tlingit collections, especially the two major ones in AMNH, are documented by the most meticulous notes on provenience, function, materials of manufacture, and other information about each piece, including the Tlingit designation. The catalogues of these collections are ethnographies in miniature.

The extent of Emmons's collections may be judged from the fact that AMNH now owns "about 5,200 objects collected by him; many are the finest specimens of their kind" (Wardwell 1978:26). And Clark Wissler, in a letter to Henry Fairfield Osborne, president of the Museum, on October 14, 1910, in which he urged the purchase of a Tsimshian collection from Emmons, wrote of him: "I may say that Lieutenant Emmons is one of our best collectors and does his work with a thoroughness that may well be envied by many who profess to be anthropologists" (quoted in Wardwell 1978:28).

While the largest collections from Emmons, and probably the finest on the Tlingit, are in AMNH, other important collections made by him are in the Thomas Burke Memorial Washington State Museum in Seattle, the Royal Ontario Museum of Archaeology (Toronto), the Museum of the American Indian (New York), the U.S. National Museum of Natural History (Smithsonian Institution, Washington, D.C.), the Field Museum of Natural History (Chicago), and the University (of Pennsylvania) Museum (Philadelphia), with a few specimens in the British Provincial Museum (Victoria), the Alaska State Museum (Juneau), and the Sheldon Jackson Museum (Sitka). The total is probably more than 11,000.

In 1888, Franz Boas called attention (in the first volume of the *Journal of American Folk-Lore,* pp. 215–19) to the great value of the catalogue that accompanied the collection made by Emmons in 1882–87 and sold in 1888 to AMNH. And in *Science* Boas (1888b:199) termed the collection itself "one of the most complete, systematic, and consequently valuable, brought from the Northwest Coast to the museums of our country."

Undoubtedly exhilarated by such praise, Emmons began that year to plan something of a scientific kind for publication, as revealed in a letter of July 2, 1888, to Albert Bickmore (AMNH Archives). In this, Emmons reported that he had a year's leave from the Navy and planned to spend it in preparing "a creditable monograph of the 'Tlinkit' tribes illustrated largely from my collection," to include the new material which he hoped to gather "during my canoe travel through the Alexandra [*sic*] Archipelago. . . ." This suggests that he contemplated a book dealing with Tlingit material culture, although he wrote to J. W. Powell (February 29, 1889, SI Archives) that he had "spent the last year working out the history, legends, customs, and manners of the Tlingit people . . ." and that he had secured another year's leave in which he could continue the project. This ethnographic writing was more difficult and time-consuming than Emmons had anticipated, for in July 1896 and again in December of that year, the report was not yet finished, and he was still "six months" from completion (letters to Morris K. Jesup, AMNH Central Archives).

In May 1897, after a series of sick leaves, Emmons was sent on special duty to AMNH, until March 1898. Here he was presumably working on his writing. On January 13, 1898, Emmons wrote to Jesup, president of the museum, on the progress of his work (AMNH Central Archives). He had found it necessary to make a rather extended comparative examination of writings of a similar nature to determine what form was best suited to the subject matter. Then he arranged and classified his field notes and illustrations, collected during the past fifteen years, and made the "necessary extracts from Russian, French, and English sources." These were evidently the quotations from the early explorers and traders which he planned to include in his ethnographic monograph. "All this labor has been extremely tedious and confusing," he wrote. But he was "fairly well launched" on the writing and expressed himself "very well satisfied with the progress made."

In a letter the same day to John Winser, secretary of the American Museum, Emmons, obviously dispirited, complained that he did not know what progress he was making, because what he had written one day might have to be rewritten the next, but he had done his best; and "had I known beforehand the labor entailed in such work . . . I would never have undertaken it. I find the work very confusing and attribute my ill health wholly to that cause, but I shall continue to a finish and hope to make a creditable report when finished."

Emmons placed his manuscripts and field notes in AMNH for safekeeping when his special leave ended in March 1898. He was found unfit for duty and in January 1899 was placed on the Navy's Retired List, and returned to Sitka for reasons of health. Soon the directors of AMNH and Franz Boas were pressuring him to get busy on his writing again. This pressure was easier to apply after Emmons had moved to Princeton in the fall of 1899. The museum staff was particularly anxious that his notes and manuscripts not be lost. Thus Winser wrote to him November 23, 1900, to suggest that he return these documents to the museum if he was not working on them, inquired how his work was progressing, reminded him that "all documents belong to us," and tried to ensure that they would come to the museum in the event of his death (letters in AMNH Central Archives).

It is not clear on exactly what topic Emmons tried to write when he resumed his ethnographic work in 1899 or 1900. Was he trying to arrange his materials for a general ethnography, as suggested by his letters of 1899 and by his notebooks of that period, or was it on some specific topic? He began publishing at first on the Tlingit, later on other tribes, and became known as the foremost authority on the Tlingit, with the possible exception of Dr. John R. Swanton at the Bureau of American Ethnology in Washington. It is evident that Emmons soon concentrated on Tlingit basketry. His first ethnological monographs were published in the *Memoirs* of AMNH: *The Basketry of the Tlingit* (1903) and *The Chilkat Blanket, with Notes on the Blanket Designs by Franz Boas* (1907). Emmons had a falling out with Boas because the latter had included Swanton's interpretations of the designs, and Emmons had no wish to share the credit. Later writings appeared in *The American Museum Journal* (later titled *Natural History*), and in the museum's *Anthropological Papers;* in *Indian Notes and Monographs* of the Museum of the American Indian; in the *Handbook of American Indians North of Mexico* (Bulletin 30, Bureau of American Ethnology), and in the *American Anthropologist.* There is no doubt that Emmons was considered as something of an anthropologist (though without diploma). He became honorary member and patron of AMNH in May 1899, and honorary fellow in February 1912; he was elected a corresponding member of the American Ethnological Society in December 1905; and became a member of the American Anthropological Association in March 1906. These were honors that Emmons treasured, listing them in the same memorandum (ca. 1916, or later ?, left with Miss Katherine Ross, Victoria, B.C.) in which he recorded his promotions in the Navy and the vessels, with their commanding officers, on which he had served.

The Basketry of the Tlingit (1903) was reviewed by Otis T. Mason, expert in primitive technology at the U.S. National Museum and himself the author of an impressive monograph on aboriginal basketry (1904). His review appeared in the *American Anthropologist,* the principal journal of the profession, and hailed this contribution by Emmons: "This is a model of intensive ethnographic work, of a kind that makes extensive studies of value possible" (Mason 1903:700). That this delighted the author may be judged from the fact that Emmons left three or four copies of the review among his papers at his death (in BCPA). *The Chilkat Blanket* (1907) was also reviewed by Mason, at greater length, but with equal praise: "This is a book that every lover of the textile art would be proud to own and to which every student of its history should have access" (Mason 1908:296). Emmons had five copies of this review from the *American Anthropologist* at the time of his death. Emmons's next monograph, *The Tahltan Indians* (1911a), was published by the University (of Pennsylvania) Museum, and its author was delighted with the little book, sending one hundred copies of it to friends and persons of distinction in anthropological and naval circles. It was reviewed by Pliny E. Goddard, linguist and curator in the Department of Anthropology at AMNH (Goddard 1912). While praising the presentation of Tahltan material culture and the illustrative plates, Goddard took Emmons to task for his treatment of shamanism and religion: In the matter of shamanistic practices, ". . . it seems that our author has lacked the point of view and perhaps also sufficient sympathy and interest to secure and present the information. One feels that this may also have been the case in regard to religious beliefs and practices generally. . . . with a primitive people it is necessary to cultivate a broad and tolerant sympathy. Aside from some phases of material culture, the key to such a people's whole view of life lies in their religious conceptions" (p. 111).

He also found Emmons in error in confounding folklore about the origins of clans with "reliable historical traditions." Since Emmons evidently prided himself on his ability to understand American Indians, this criticism must have cut deeply, and may, perhaps, in the long run have made it more difficult for him to write a comprehensive monograph on the Tlingit.

Boas had voiced a similar criticism of Emmons as an ethnographer in a letter of June 20, 1903, to Livingston Farrand, collaborator with Boas in some of his early work on the Northwest Coast (quoted at greater length by Jean Low, this volume): "We shall never get from Emmons good material on religion, mythology, and language; while his industrial and historical material is, I believe, good."

It is uncertain at what date Emmons began working on this, his great monograph, *The Tlingit Indians.* He probably had something like it in mind, but vaguely conceived, by 1889, as is suggested by his letters and notes of the succeeding decade. He was evidently overwhelmed by the bulk and richness of his materials. The preparation of his basketry and blanket papers may have been suggested by Boas to break this writer's block. He clearly expected to write more on the Tlingit (Emmons to M. K. Jesup, president of AMNH, January 19, 1907); and in 1909 agreed to write on "the life of the Tlingit," based on his twenty-seven years of duty in Alaska and his life among these people (letter to Osborne, then president of AMNH, February 1909; both letters in AMNH Central Archives).

After his monograph on the Tahltan (1911a), Emmons again returned to the Tlingit; and Clark Wissler, head of the Department of Anthropology at AMNH, exerted pressure and offered support for his efforts, both financial and psychological. The outcome was the paper, "The Whale House of the Chilkat" (1916a), which appeared both in the *Anthropological Papers* of AMNH (professional publication) and in popular form in *The American Museum Journal* (1916b). Yet Emmons was displeased because the plates were run at the end of the article instead of in the text, as Wissler had promised. "It seems to me all work I do for Museums is a disappointment in some way and I question whether I will not discontinue all writing," he complained in a letter of October 10, 1916, to his friend Dr. C. F. Newcombe (in BCPA). But in August, Emmons had reported to Wissler: "I have finished the history of the 60-odd Tlingit families [clans] on which I have been working for 20 odd years" (August 20, 1916, AMNH Central Archives). This was undoubtedly the manuscript of the *History of Tlingit Clans and Tribes* (to use my title for this unnamed work, which he later proposed to add to Chapter 2 of *The Tlingit Indians,* an impossibly awkward arrangement).

It was Pliny E. Goddard, curator of ethnology at AMNH, who finally goaded Emmons into making more effective efforts on the great monograph, as evidenced by a letter from Goddard to Emmons on February 14, 1924 (in AMNH). Miss Bella Weitzner, then associate curator of ethnology, remembers discussions about the book in 1927 between Emmons and Goddard (Weitzner, pers. comm.). But again, on January 18, 1928 (letter in BCPA), Emmons wrote to William Newcombe of Victoria that he was getting to the end of his writing, on which he had worked for forty years (since the laudatory note by Boas in the *Journal of American Folk-Lore* in 1888?), but that he was now tired of it. In the spring of that year (1928), however, and shortly before Goddard's death, Miss Weitzner remembers that Emmons began to bring to the museum the first handwritten chapters, together with various notes, as well as sketches and photographs to be used as illustrations.

These chapters were submitted one at a time, as they were written. This continued after Emmons had moved to Victoria, B.C., in 1932. As each chapter was typed, it was sent back to the author with Miss Weitzner's queries and suggested revisions. A number of these letters have survived in BCPA, and some of the author's indignant responses in AMNH (Anthropology files). Emmons intermittently revised the manuscript, almost up to the time of his death, adding materials that he found in the library of BCPA, where he worked. In 1945, Emmons received letters from Miss Weitzner in February, March, and April, and was obviously greatly concerned over the fate of his monograph. After his death, his manuscript, notes, and photographs that he had in Victoria came to BCPA.

Emmons took seriously his avocation as ethnologist. The better to fit himself to describe the Tlingit, he read such publications (in English) of the early explorers to the Northwest Coast as were available to him in the libraries of AMNH and BCPA. (I doubt that he had enough command of foreign languages to use those in French, German, Spanish, and Russian.) It is interesting that he should first have worked at collecting the names and histories of the over sixty clans of the Tlingit, since this was a subject almost entirely neglected by his predecessors and by his contemporaries. Although Lewis Henry Morgan had certainly made the study of matrilineal clans and of kinship terminology familiar to the academic community, there is no evidence in Emmons's notes or writings that he was aware of Morgan's work or of Morgan's interests; if he had been, Emmons would certainly have collected Tlingit kin terms, which he neglected, and would have corrected Morgan's views of what a society based on matrilineal clans had to be, which he did not do. Among the early writers on the Tlingit, it was only Veniaminov who had come close to understanding the structure of Tlingit society ([1840]

Top. *A man believed to be Lieutenant Emmons purchasing baskets, Sitka. (Date and photographer unknown. AMNH.)* Bottom. *Chief "Nah-kane" at home with his wife. She poses in a button blanket; he in a Chilkat robe and crest hat, with a rattle in his hand. Their treasures are in the chests and bags behind them. Hoonah. (Courtesy of the Bancroft Library, University of California, Berkeley.)*

Three Kagwantan, Wolf 1, house chiefs, Sitka, 1900. All wear Chilkat blankets, secured with cedar bark shoulder rings. The man on the left wears the Brown Bear Hat with seven cylinders, the man in the middle the Killerwhale Hat, and the man on the right the Murrelet Hat. (Photograph by Winter and Pond. AMNH.)

1984:383–86), with its division into the "two main clans" of Wolf and Raven (those "opposites" of each other who intermarried); each of these subdivided again into "clans" associated with some animal, bird, fish, and so forth; and these again into "lesser clans or families," named according to their houses. The popular designation of the clans, in Veniaminov's day as well as today, in European languages and sometimes in Tlingit, was by reference to their major totemic crests (i.e., as Bear clan, Frog clan). But Veniaminov went beyond this and recorded the true names of eight clans in the Wolf division, regretting that he had been unable to learn the names of the Raven clans. But even had he done so, no translation of his work had been published, and thus could not have been read by Emmons. It is all the more remarkable, therefore, that the latter systematically collected the names of some sixty-odd clans, some extinct, and recorded their histories and their distributions among the local tribes, even including their house names (see Tables 9–11, 14). In this, Emmons evidently anticipated Swanton's researches in 1904 (1908:389–407). Emmons had the obvious advantage in that his naval duties took him to every major Tlingit settlement and he could spend his free time with the natives, whereas Veniaminov was confined by Tlingit hostility to the fortified posts at Sitka and Wrangell, and Swanton was limited by the short time available for his research (three months). Still, this does not diminish Emmons's accomplishments. Since Tlingit activities can be fully understood only in terms of clan membership and participation, it can be seen from this book the extent to which Emmons supplied such necessary information, even though I have had to defer the text of his *History of Tlingit Clans and Tribes* to a later publication.

No one can question the value of Emmons's ethnographic collections and the meticulous details with which they are documented. This documentation became more comprehensive in the course of time, as shown by the entries in the AMNH catalogues. What is particularly impressive is that Emmons did not limit his interests to the artistically fine or the spectacular, although he was sensitive to the values and style of Tlingit art, but also collected the lowly objects of ordinary domestic use and the improvisations of the temporary camp. In this holistic concept of material culture and its place in the total life of a people, Emmons's contributions show genuine insight.

Although Boas had doubted that Emmons could provide adequate information on shamanism and religion, because of his linguistic deficiencies, Emmons was able to contribute the fullest descriptions of Tlingit ceremonies, including potlatches, peacemaking, funerals, and shamanistic performances, of any anthropologist to visit the Tlingit, except for Olson (1967). His discussion of shamanism and of Tlingit beliefs in spirits is of great value and all the more remarkable considering that he had to work with an interpreter.

Emmons gathered information in a fairly systematic way. His field notebooks contain jottings on ethnographic items as he heard about them, but other notebooks show that these items were later copied out and organized according to topic, while a list of queries (preserved with the answers) served as memoranda of points he needed to cover. He systematically gathered Tlingit words and names, recording the native vocabulary under the English equivalents in an address book with alphabetical index. He copied the geographical headings from the *U.S. Coast Pilot* for southeastern Alaska, and added to it as many Tlingit designations as he had gathered. He made out questionnaires on a number of topics and consulted knowledgeable individuals for answers, such as K. J. Hendrickson, missionary at Yakutat; Eugene Willard, missionary at Haines; William Paul, educated Tlingit of Wrangell; and Dr. John Swanton of the Smithsonian. Evidence of such correspondence becomes more conspicuous when Emmons was no longer traveling to Alaska. It is, however, significant that Emmons apparently did not correspond with or cite in his manuscripts his contemporaries who were writing on the Tlingit, such as Reverend S. Hall Young (1927) or Mrs. Willard (1884), and the numerous reports by naval officers.

The wide range of information gathered by Emmons indicates a generous view of anthropology and a holistic understanding of culture. Again, he is not reporting simply the exotic or the spectacular, but includes homely, everyday matters. One of his notebooks that has been preserved in BCPA was probably purchased and begun in 1896 (because it resembles so closely one so dated). In it is a good part of the outline for a monograph on the Tlingit, beginning with "Chapter III, Tribal Organization," and running through to an unnumbered chapter, presumably XIII, on "Myths of the Thlingets." Under each heading are numbered topics, phrased as queries. For example, Chapter III ranges from "1. Meaning of Thlinget?" to "35. Could clans of a tribe go to war without involving the whole tribe?" The chapter headings, after the missing I and II, were: Tribal Organization; Habitations; People; Domestic Life (ranging from division of labor, preparation of foods, to treatment of ailments, and methods of driving away fog); Birth, Courtship, Marriage, & Death; Arts and Industries; Fishing and Hunting; War and its Customs; Feasts, Dances, & Amusements; Shamanism; and Myths of the Thlingets. This was practically the outline of the manuscript he actually wrote.

The form and content of this outline suggest that Emmons may have been following some formal guide, like the *Notes and Queries on Anthropology,* which had been published by the British Association for the Advancement of Science (BAAS) in 1874 and 1892, as well as more recently. There was nothing novel about such scientific questionnaires for travelers and explorers, since La Pérouse had sailed to Alaska in 1785 with such documents (Chinard 1937:x–xviii), as had Malaspina in 1791 (see de Laguna 1972:139). Lewis and Clark had one from Jefferson in 1804 (Hallowell 1960:37–39), but I have not been able to discover the guide that Emmons was following. It may have been indirectly the "Circular of Inquiry," which Horatio Hale had prepared to instruct Boas in his first fieldwork on the Northwest Coast (1888–91), when the latter was working for E. B. Tylor's committee of the BAAS (Gruber 1967). Hale had been a scientist on the United States Exploring Expedition, 1838–40, on which Emmons's father, the future admiral, had won distinction and perhaps his taste for collecting ethnographic curiosities, and so Hale's holistic approach and his insistence on "describing the total range of human traits," may have impinged upon Emmons from Boas, and also, but less likely, from his father. As Gruber suggested (1967:32): "It is not as the result of simple coincidence that the standard monographs in general anthropology [of the late nineteenth and early twentieth centuries] followed closely the outline of desiderata provided by Hale's 'Circular of Inquiry'" which Boas followed. Emmons's closest association with Boas was during the time that the latter was planning and directing the individual researchers who made up the Jesup North Pacific Expedition and who contributed separate monographs to its publication series. In spirit, *The Tlingit Indians* of George T. Emmons belongs in their company.

Both Hale and Boas emphasized the value of native linguistic material for ethnology: comparative philology as a clue to the past, and information in the native language as a means of penetrating the native's understanding of his or her world. Emmons lacked linguistic training and did not attempt to record Tlingit texts. He did, however, record in his notes and manuscripts a fairly large vocabulary of Tlingit nouns and short phrases, unfortunately in a transliteration of his own devising. Its greatest shortcoming was a lack of consistency in spelling. He probably could use certain simple phrases and words in speaking Tlingit, and undoubtedly recognized more. He seems to have been familiar with the names for most things in which he was interested, from material objects to shamanistic spirits and basketry designs, but there is no evidence that he could dispense with an interpreter, unless the Indian with whom he was conversing understood English. Despite this handicap, his understanding of Tlingit concepts is impressive.

If this book could have been finished and published within his lifetime, Emmons might have received the fuller scholarly recognition he craved. He was working on this book up to within a few months of his death. Was his inability to finish it in part due to his reluctance to shut off forever this reminder of the happiest period of his life?

Introduction

The material of this writing describes the life of the Tlingit as seen in 1882 and through twenty-five years. In the early eighties they were yet a comparatively primitive people living together in the large old communal houses: depending upon the natural products of the country; practising cremation and the elaborate death ceremonies akin to ancestral worship; still under the superstition of witchcraft and dominated by shamanistic fears, but withal an independent intelligent, industrious, honest race and very friendly when fairly met.

Later after their exodus to the salmon canneries and mines their desertion of the old villages rendered communal life impossible and they became transients between the past and the future with every hope and indication of the development of a superior native population to replace that of earlier days

G. T. Emmons.

Tlingit myths are not included in this writing as they have already been so completely and interestingly presented by Doctor Swanton in "Bulletin No 39. of the Bureau of American Ethnology

Text in G. T. Emmons's own hand, with a later addition. (AMNH.)

A BIOGRAPHY by JEAN LOW

Lieutenant George Thornton Emmons, USN 1852–1945

George Thornton Emmons was born in his grandmother's house in Baltimore on June 6, 1852. Franklin Pierce had been nominated the day before as the Democratic Party's candidate for president, and, though there were disagreements between the states, the Civil War was still nine years away. Outside the old brick house at 142 Fayette Street, all was quiet that Sunday, the celebrations of the political convention over, and the usual bustle of commerce still. Inside, a baby boy was welcomed by Lieutenant George Foster Emmons and Frances Antonia Thornton Emmons, their first son and third child. (The daughters were Antonia Thornton, born in 1846, and Frances Antonia, born in November 1850 but lived only until September 1851.)

George's maternal grandfather, Francis Anthony of Virginia, was a chief purser in the Navy and his father was well on his way to a brilliant naval career. Having entered the New York Naval School at seventeen, George Foster Emmons later distinguished himself on the Wilkes Exploring Expedition when he and one companion routed ten Fiji war canoes, again when he rescued his captain from the sinking USS *Peacock* by rowing for five hours through tumultuous surf at the mouth of the Columbia River, and still again when he led an exploring expedition through wild and uncharted country from Astoria to Sutter's Fort on the Sacramento River. He was twice a member of the Brazil Squadron, at one time commanding its flagship, and he took many prizes while on blockade duty during the Civil War.

As captain of the USS *Ossipee* he took part in the ceremonies transferring Alaska to the United States in October 1867, and in 1872 was promoted to the rank of rear admiral. He was devoted to the Navy, and it was only natural that his dreams and ambitions focused on a Navy career for his son. He could not have foreseen, on that happy summer's day in 1852, that his plans and dreams would bring to him nothing but disappointment, and to his son almost overwhelming conflicts.

The house on Fayette Street, where the family lived, was presided over by young George's maternal grandmother, Sally Donaldson Thornton, and was shared with his aunts, their husbands (mostly Navy men), and their children, until George was fourteen.

Baltimore, during those years, became steadily more turbulent, torn between North and South, and when a troop train, going through the city from the North, was fired upon, President Lincoln placed the city under martial law. George Emmons had his first formal education in the public schools here.

After the Civil War, the family, having been joined by two more boys, Thornton and Horace, moved to Princeton where Captain Emmons (as he then was) bought at auction a boys' school which he converted into the family home. Called Edgehill Place, it was complemented by stables and a carriage house and surrounded by thirteen acres of grounds. His father was acquainted with a group of naval officers in Princeton, and again, as in Baltimore, young George was surrounded by talk of the sea.

From Princeton George was sent for his education first to a boarding school in Pennsylvania and then to the Cheshire Academy in Connecticut, an Episcopalian boys' school, which he particularly disliked.

On one occasion, when George Foster Emmons took his son to visit Abraham Lincoln, young George, then about thirteen, spent the time plotting, and was successful in wresting a button from the president's coat.[1] His first important trophy?

In 1870 he applied to Annapolis. Failing to get an appointment from his congressman, Haight of New Jersey, he did secure one from President Grant, whom his father was then serving as naval attaché. He entered the academy in the fall of 1870 and graduated in 1874, ranking twenty-eighth out of a class of thirty; his highest grade was in law, his lowest in seamanship.[2]

With the exception of one and one-half years' service on the USS *Trenton* in European waters, his other assignments were brief, and the first six years of his Navy records show a total of three years and two months of absence due to illness.[3]

On February 1, 1878, Emmons married Jessie Claude of Annapolis, with whom he had probably been acquainted before his graduation from the Naval Academy. They lived, part of the time, at Edgehill Place. His father's will, written in February 1883, indicated a strong disapproval of Jessie. The marriage was made, according to George Foster Emmons, "contrary to my wishes and advice," and the will went on to stipulate that George's wife be "debarred from the usual hospitalities of Edgehill Place."[4]

After six and one-half years, Emmons obtained a divorce from Jessie on the grounds of adultery. Since she had given birth to a boy on April l, 1884, but had not seen her husband since May 1882, the charges were uncontestable. Jessie did not appear at the divorce hearings, and the thirty-nine pages of testimony consist of depositions from the proprietress of the boarding house in which Jessie was staying when the baby was born, the nurse in attendance, Emmons, and others, including a bizarre bit of testimony from his brother, Thornton. The latter stated that in the late fall of 1881, when Emmons was away from home, he had apprehended Jessie in Lover's Lane "in the act of criminal intercourse with a man." Thornton returned home, a family conference was called, and it was decided *not* to tell Emmons, who resumed living with Jessie on his return home a few days later. He was not told of the incident until his return from Alaska in 1884. A final decreė of divorce was granted in November 1884.[5] Emmons has left no record of his feelings about Jessie, and his matter-of-fact deposition gives no clue.

Having been promoted to lieutenant, junior grade, in 1881,[6] Emmons was ordered to the USS *Adams* in June 1882, and he accompanied his ship from San Francisco to Alaska. One of his first assignments there, from Captain Merriman, was to quell a riot in the old Auk village near what was to become Juneau. He told of this in a letter written to the *Alaska Magazine,* many years later:

> In 1882 upon reaching Juneau at four a.m. in Sept. I was ordered to take an armed boat crew ashore and avert a supposed murder in the Auk village. Having first arrived in the sloop of war *Adams* for two years service in Alaska', I had no idea in what house in the ranch the man lived or as to his identity so I took the old Chief Kowee and required him to guide me to the house. This was the beginning of friendly relations with "Kowie" who was a very fine old type and some years later in 1886 just one hundred years after La Perouse entered Lituya he gave me the full account of the first meeting of several canoe parties of his Tlingit forbears who were in the bay at that time and their astonishment at seeing the ships and white men and their old legend of the spirit of the tide bore that enters the bay and I later got at Hoonah a large old carved feast pipe that illustrated the spirit. I had a copy of La Perouse with me in Alaska and was familiar with the catastrophe but Kowie's account that had been handed down by word of mouth through a century proved the accuracy of native history and was most interesting.[7]

The meeting with the Auk chief marked the begining of a new career for Emmons, one he would pursue the rest of his life.

In his subsequent dealings with the natives he continued to seek the most prestigious among them to become his teacher-informants. In Klukwan, home of the Chilkat tribe, he became acquainted with Chief Chartrich, with Louis Shotridge, his grandson, and with George Shotrich, Louis's father. In 1886 Emmons received a letter from Louis,[8] who was then a small boy:

> Chilkat Alaska Sept 10
> Lt. G.T.E.
> Sitka Alaska
> Dear friend,
> I will tell you all about misilf.
> I am ready to go down to Sitka. But I wish you talk to the captin first. and send a load to me & I will give it to the Captin in Rustler. And please write me if you want me.
> I like to stay down in sitka Mission. and the steamer is up here today. But you don't write to me so I don't go down and I am hurry to write the steamer will start now and you excuse me if I don't the words right.
> friend
>
> Louis G. Shotrich
> Stoo-woo-kah
>
> I will say good by for the present.

On the bottom of this letter is a comment in Emmons's handwriting: "In 1902 Louis G. Shotrich 'Stoo-woo-ka-lo' became the chief of the 'karquanton' family [Ka•g^{w}a•nta•n clan] of the Chilkat tribe at the age of 22 years."

When George Shotrich was in trouble with the local authorities, Emmons put up his bail, and it was Emmons whom the old chief designated to buy his ceremonial robe (Chilkat blanket) upon his death.[9]

At that time the Navy was an authority to the natives, and Emmons was respected by them for his uniform, and welcomed for his sincere and flattering interest in their old customs. His attitude and interest in the natives was not understood by his shipmates, who tended to ignore or overlook him, nor was it condoned by his family in Princeton. The approval he sought so eagerly all his life was denied him by all except his native friends, but he continued in his work.

In addition to his quest for knowledge of the Tlingits' customs and history, Emmons had an insatiable appetite for collecting their artifacts and soon began to amass them in enormous quantities.

His assignment to the USS *Adams* was followed two years later by a transfer to the small Navy gunboat, the USS *Pinta,* which he joined on its first trip to Alaska. The home port was Sitka, the old Russian capital (its name changed from New Archangel to the Tlingit tribal name). Sitka was a small town with a mixture of inhabitants—Americans and Russians, and the Tlingits who lived in their segregated quarters known as the Ranch. Sitka is a place of great physical beauty but dreary climate, where the incessant rain feeds the lush growth of the rain forest and dampens the spirit, and it was to be home to Emmons for sixteen years.

The duties of the *Pinta* were those of a police ship, for although civil government had come to Alaska in some measure with the arrival of its first governor, John Kinkead, there was very little organized law enforcement. Accordingly, the little gunboat patrolled the southeastern Alaskan waters, trying to bring a semblance of order out of the chaos created by the transfer from one governing power to another. It was an ideal assignment for an officer interested in the culture, history, and artifacts of the natives.

Although at this time of his life Emmons was quiet and unassuming, he was outspoken in defense of the natives. From Chilkoot he wrote a long letter to the Sitka newspaper, *The Alaskan,* defending the Indian guides against the miners, who claimed, in an earlier petition to the same paper, that their native packers were getting rich by overcharging for packing supplies over the trail to the interior lakes. Emmons's letter was a spirited one in which he described the rigors of the trip over the mountains, the heavy packs the natives were required to carry, and the fact that the members of this tribe (Chilkat and Chilkoot) were alone able to carry the enormous weight over the thirty miles of the rough and precipitous trail.[10]

In another incident, in May 1887, Emmons's persuasiveness prevailed upon some Chilkoot guides who had refused to pack a Canadian surveying party over the Chilkoot Pass. In his words:

> After the fur-trade of the littoral was leased by the Hudson's Bay Co., three ships visited Pyramid Harbor each spring where they met the natives who once overpowered the crew and took possession of the "Labouchere," either then or upon another occasion some shots were fired into an encampment and several Chilkoots of the lower [Chilkat River] village killed. But a life taken is never forgotten and although all the participants in the affair were dead when the Canadian Survey party under Ogilvie reached Dyea in 1887 enroute to the Interior, the Chilkoots absolutely refused to pack them over the Divide and would give no reason for their stand. From my intimate acquaintance with the people I was asked to intervene and calling the tribe together we met in a clearing in the willows. The men in many colored blankets sat in a circle, and listened in silence as I told them that it was our wish that they should assist the party instead of suffering the loss of over a thousand dollars by refusing to handle the hundred-odd packers. I asked them why they made an exception of Ogilvie when they would pack any other party. For some minutes they sat with their heads down in their blankets, then the chief arose and made a fiery speech saying that King George men [Englishmen] in the days of their fathers had fired on their camp and killed three of their people and as no compensation had ever been made they refused to have any relations with them. This was the recognized law of the coast—a life taken either accidentally or intentionally required a life or an equivalent in property in return. In the end I persuaded them to forego the blood atonement and accept the benefit that this work would bring them.[11]

This dramatic description, recorded by Emmons in one of his notebooks, is not mentioned in other eyewitness accounts of Ogilvie's dilemma. These give no credit to Emmons, cite only the role of Lieutenant Commander H. E. Newell of the *Pinta* in solving Ogilvie's problem, and report that the Chilkoots packed for him just to the summit of the Chilkoot Pass, where the "Stick" Indians of the interior took over.

In these first years on the *Pinta,* the Lieutenant's eyes were always open to the possibilities of collecting. This was the case in 1886, for example, when the *Pinta* conveyed to Yakutat a mountain climbing expedition, financed by the *New York Times* and Princeton College, and led by the articulate explorer, Army Lieutenant Frederick Schwatka. While waiting at Port Mulgrave, Yakutat, for native canoes and Indians to take them to Icy Bay, from which they planned to make their assault on Mount Saint Elias, the climbers and members of the ship's company were busy purchasing specimens of native manufacture. Competing with Professor William Libbey, a geologist from Princeton University (then "College"), Emmons lost no time in gathering together as much as he could. Their most valuable treasures, however, came from a shaman's grave they found near Port Mulgrave. Seton-Karr, an English alpinist with Schwatka, described the scene on the *Pinta:*

> Someone went out in a canoe and made a great "find" of some boxes in the grave of a medicine-man in a retired part of the bay. Whenever a "shawaan" dies his charms and other articles that he has used are placed in boxes, buried with him, and left to rot unless rescued as curios, for no Indian will touch them. As no Indian even dares to approach the grave of a medicine-man, the abstractions can never be discovered or lamented. In the evening the two sacksfull were spread out on the floor in the captain's cabin for inspection, and comprised, among other things, a quantity of masks of painted wood, a leather shawl, ornamented with sea-parrots' bills, and a crown of wild-goats' horns.[12]

According to Emmons's catalogues and accession notes sent to museums, many of the artifacts he collected were taken from shamans' graves. Although some of the members of the Sitka Ethnological Society were critical of Emmons for robbing graves, their first field trip was to an island near Sitka where they helped themselves to the contents of a grave.[13]

By March 1887 Emmons had a large ethnological collection and had written about it to Heber R. Bishop, a wealthy friend of the American Museum of Natural History (AMNH). On March 11 of that year Bishop reported to the Executive Committee that he had corresponded with Lieutenant Emmons regarding this collection, and the committee directed Bishop to ask Emmons to send his collection to the museum for display while the members raised the purchase money by subscription.[14] By August, Emmons had assembled on the dock in Sitka three tons of material, packed in twenty cases, to be shipped to the New York museum.[15] The collection was accompanied by a catalogue in which Emmons described each piece, its provenience, and its use.

The cases arrived in New York on August 22, and by January 6, 1888, there was an authorization to purchase. Emmons wanted $12,000 for the lot, and the committee raised this amount by subscription—not easily, nor before Emmons had issued a deadline, saying that he had a private buyer in Chicago.[16] This was just the beginning of deadlines and buyers waiting in the wings to spur anyone who lagged in making the decision to buy. In this case, however, the deadline was extended, and Emmons expressed the hope that the New York museum would purchase his collection: ". . . for I wish the Museum to obtain the collection as I can make it the finest Indian collection *from one people* that is known, and in your Museum I can always have access to it which would not be the case should it become the property of an individual."[17]

On the first day of May 1888, Albert Bickmore, who managed the Department of Anthropology, wrote to the president of the Museum, Morris K. Jesup, commenting on the collection: "They are all old and original specimens and have a standard and increasing value. They have not been brought together by chance but in regular and thoughtful sequence. Each specimen is carefully numbered and a description, generally very full and of permanent value is given in the catalogue."[18]

Soon afterward, the trustees, recognizing the value of Emmons's catalogue notes as well as his general knowledge of the Tlingit, began urging him to write up his notes for publication. In an article entitled "Gleanings from the Emmons Collection of Ethnological Specimens from Alaska," Franz Boas summed up his remarks in his last paragraph: "It will be seen from these brief remarks that the collection embodies a vast amount of new information regarding the folk-lore and customs of the Tlingit and we wish through these lines to call attention of ethnologists to the rich source of information laid open to them."[19]

Shortly after his first collection was shipped, Emmons married again: on August 11, 1887, Kitty May Baker of Sitka became his wife in a Presbyterian ceremony in Sitka.[20] His choice of a wife this time was felicitous. Kitty (Emmons later had her name changed to Katherine) had come to Alaska with her parents the year before, when she was seventeen. Her father, Orris Baker, ran the Baranof Hotel; and Kitty, who loved music, played the organ at the Protestant church, gave recitals, and had a dancing class. Although tiny in stature, she had tremendous inner strength, and she adored George Emmons. She was lonely during his long absences, but she cheerfully attended to the household chores, to the raising of their children (Thornton, born in 1890, and Frances, born in 1895), and to community activities.

Shortly after they were married, Emmons, having been granted a leave from the Navy, started traveling among the natives from village to village, recording and collecting, this time with the blessings and encouragement of the American Museum of Natural History. *The Alaskan* of December 1, 1888, reported his return to Sitka from a four-week trip to several native villages (Kake, Killisnoo, and Hoonah among them), with the added information that his purpose had been to add to his curio collection and his Tlingit studies for a work, "*shortly* to be published."[21] Leave from the Navy was extended until 1891 while he continued his travels, but the manuscript did not materialize.

By the following year Emmons had learned a great deal more about the Tlingit and had amassed another large collection. At the end of 1891 he was told to report to the secretary of the interior to be a representative at the World's Columbian Exposition to be held in Chicago in 1893.[22] Accordingly, he left for that city, having first shipped 2,700 curios, which he spent many months arranging after their arrival. They were installed in the Government Building in the 3,000 square feet of space allotted to him. A review of this display appeared in *Kate Field's Washington*. In part: "One of the most interesting corners of the great Fair which one jots down mentally as 'worth seeing' for the benefit of inquiring friends is the Emmons collection. . . . The owner of this most attractive exhibit, Lt. G. T. Emmons, U.S. Navy, who, through a continuance of ten years duty in Alaska has devoted his energies to the study of the native tribes. Such an extensive and complete ethnological history of a single people has probably never been made on this continent. . . ."[23]

In 1894 he returned to Alaska as executive officer of the *Pinta*. He wished, however, to have the Navy assign him to the American Museum of Natural History for a regular tour of duty.

Accordingly, on September 8 he wrote to Morris K. Jesup, president of the Museum:

> I write regarding procuring command of the Pinta. My return to Alaska was practically in the interests of the Museum, as I desired to continue my study of Tlingit ethnology, as well as to gather for the Museum any valuable and desirable material that I might meet with, so the Museum receives every benefit without expense, and I want the Museum to place me in a more advantageous position where I can regulate my own movements and accomplish the most good, while carrying on my legitimate duties in the Government's interests. At present I am Executive Officer of the Pinta but my duties so continuous and my time so occupied that I find no opportunity to carry on my Indian work. All would be changed were I in command—then I could go where I pleased.
>
> It will take a very strong endorsement if someone connected with the Museum who is very close to the Administration could request the command for me it might be arranged, but unless there was an absolute certainty of the granting of the request I would prefer that nothing be done in the matter, as a failure could only result in injuring me. I have already procured some fine specimens for the Museum and hope to get 30 odd pieces of jade.
>
> Do not let my letter go beyond yourself as it would only injure me with the Department.[24]

Letters requesting a leave with pay or an assignment to the Museum were sent to the Navy on Emmons's behalf, by Jesup and John Winser, secretary of AMNH. All requests were denied, and it was not until 1897 that he was assigned this special duty.[25]

Shortly after the world's fair was over, Emmons offered his second collection to the American Museum. A letter from Winser to trustee Percy R. Pyne on October 31, 1894, gives an indication of the value the museum placed on this acquisition: "The second Emmons collection from Alaska was offered last December for $25,000. Of exceptional value, over 2900 objects. Its intrinsic value more than double the first collection and bought in the face of a cash offer from the Field Columbian Museum. Only one course was open, and that, to buy it."[26]

Once again the American Museum bought a collection, this time for $15,000, and once again they were threatened with another buyer, the fledgling Field Columbian Museum of Chicago, founded after the world's fair, its nucleus some of the magnificent collections it had obtained at the close of the exposition. It was the beginning of competition among the three largest natural history museums—New York, Chicago, and the Smithsonian (U.S. National Museum)—for Northwest Coast material. Emmons was quick to capitalize on the rivalry.

Unfortunately, Emmons has not left a great deal of information on his sources of supply, and appeared, in many cases, to be secretive. We have seen that he robbed graves, that he dealt with the most important men of the village, and that he bought large numbers of things. It is usually possible to trace only a few pieces from their native sources to their final resting places in museums, or to know *how* they were acquired and from *whom*. Emmons collected vast numbers of things personally, but as time went on his sources became more diffuse.

After his second sale, Emmons built his own house in Sitka, a square unadorned structure which still stands on Lincoln Street. The first plaster house ever built there, it was ready for the birth of Frances Antonia, George and Katherine's daughter, in 1895.

As executive officer of the *Pinta,* Emmons continued to study and collect until, in December 1896, he was assigned to the USS *Michigan* (a shore station) and was sent to the New York and Illinois areas. Again, as in his early career in the Navy, he became ill and was declared by the Medical Examining Board to be unfit for duty.[27] On May 29, 1897, he reported for special duty at AMNH, his assignment there granted at last. His letters indicate that he did most of his museum work, as well as selling and trading, from Princeton. He had returned with his family to Edgehill Place, where they joined his mother, his brothers, his sister Antonia, her husband, and their two children. It was not a very happy move for the little family, used to a house of their own. Antonia Emmons White (now married to career Navy officer Edwin White) was the head of the household; Admiral Emmons (who died July 2, 1884) had designated her to be the inheritor of Edgehill Place, its furniture, carriages, horses, cow, stables, and grounds, with the wish that it remain in the family as their home.[28] Antonia, very conscious of her role as a Navy wife (Edwin White rose to the rank of admiral), lost no opportunity to remind her brother that he had become "just a dirty old Indian"; he responded by locking her out of his quarters.[29] Her father had anticipated friction among the family members and stipulated in his will that they should resolve their differences among themselves without resorting to lawyers.

Although Emmons found the work on his proposed manuscript tedious, he reported to Jesup that he was "fairly

Left. *Jim Kitch-Kook, chief of the Bison House People, Kharse-hit-tan* (Xa·s-hit-ta·n), *a branch of the Kuse-ka-dee* (Qu·ske·di), *Raven 8, wearing a woven sleeveless shirt with a Bison design. Sitka, 1900. (Photograph by Winter and Pond. AMNH.)* Right. *Joe Kennelku, chief of the Da-she-ton* (De·ši·ta·n), *Raven 13, wearing a sleeveless shirt with the clan Beaver design. Killisnoo, 1902. (Photograph by Vincent Soboleff. BCPA.)*

Top left. *Spruce root basket with false embroidery of colored grass, collected by G. T. Emmons before 1888. (AMNH.)* Top right. *Henya grave poles, south end of Tuxekan village, west coast of Prince of Wales Island, 1888. (Photographer unknown. BCPA.)* Bottom. *Chilkat blanket with a design representing the Raven, the crest of the owner. (Photographed at Yakutat by Frederica de Laguna, 1949.)*

well launched on writing."[30] In 1898 Emmons was called back to active service and detailed to the USS *Minneapolis*. A stream of letters back and forth from the ship to the museum followed, making arrangements for the sale of artifacts and for the disposition of his notes, in which the museum had a proprietary interest, and payments.[31] However, this duty, like so many others, was short, and in May he was detached, his health failed, and he was granted sick leave. He wrote to Winser from Wisconsin, where he had gone to recuperate, expressing the wish that his health would permit him to work on the manuscript later.[32]

In October he was reassigned to the USS *Wheeling*, again detached in two months, and, for the second time that year, declared unfit for service.[33] Writing to Boas later in May 1899, he stated that he had "suffered a complete collapse," and "I can give you no assurance of the publication of a portion of my notes."[34] Forty-eight years old, ill, and forced to retire, he found his days of active service in the Navy and his residence in Alaska were both at an end. His Navy career, though far from illustrious, had served as a stable base for his second career of collecting, far more important to him. He suffered from both psychological and physical ill health and was plagued by recurring bouts of both the rest of his life.

Although one phase of life came to an end, another began, and Emmons was now free to devote all his energies to collecting and writing. Later in 1899 he made the first of many collecting and study trips to British Columbia to visit the Tahltan Indians of the Stikine River. When this trip was over, he wrote to his friend and fellow collector, Dr. C. F. Newcombe of Victoria, that he had "cleaned out the Tahltan village."[35] Earlier he had told Morris Jesup that in his second collection (referring to Alaska) he had "gleaned the country, and no other collections can be made."[36] Yet, despite his avowedly thorough culling of the country, we find him going again and again to Alaska and British Columbia and offering collections from both places.

Boas, who was becoming more and more critical of Emmons as the years went by and the manuscript failed to appear, suggested that he write an article on Tlingit basketry.[37] For Emmons, this was the more comfortable path, and although the other museum officials continued to exhort and cajole him about his major work, he began his study of Tlingit basketry. In 1900, in an interview with *The Alaskan* (Sitka), he stressed that he was not being paid for this effort, another theme he was to emphasize again and again during the coming years.[38] Yet he continued to write articles, publishing twenty in all, most of them on Indian culture and artifacts. He found writing tedious, he labored at it, and the results were mixed. The basketry monograph, published in 1903 by AMNH, received a favorable review by Otis T. Mason, who was the author of a definitive work on Indian baskets.[39] His monograph on the Chilkat blanket, edited and added to by Boas, and also published by AMNH, received another favorable review from Mason.[40] During the writing of the blanket work, Emmons came into serious conflict with Boas, who had called upon John Swanton of the Bureau of American Ethnology to interpret the blanket designs. Emmons regarded this as an interference, and polite but chilly letters were exchanged. Earlier, Boas had written to Livingston Farrand, an anthropologist on the staff of the museum:

> In regard to Emmons I feel that it would be best to have no further dealings with him and to demand all his notes, which, I understand, belong to us. He is a very slippery customer. On the other hand, I presume that he knows so much about the Tlingit that we have to stand him for the sake of the Museum. My own preference would be to send a man who knows ethnology to Alaska and let him do the whole thing over. We shall never get from Emmons good material on religion, mythology, and language, while his industrial and historical material is, I believe, good.[41]

Later, Emmons wrote to Newcombe expressing his dislike of Boas in strong, anti-Semitic terms.[42] There was fault on both sides. Boas, deep in his rivalry with George Dorsey of the Field Museum, was intensely annoyed that Emmons collected for both institutions. Emmons was overly sensitive and jealous of his work and undoubtedly felt threatened by the brilliant German's training and reputation.

Despite the difficulties, *The Chilkat Blanket*, written by Emmons and edited by Boas with the latter's "Notes on the Blanket Designs," was published in 1907 as a memoir by AMNH, and for more than half a century remained the definitive work on the subject.

In 1911 Emmons published the story he had learned from the Auk chief, Kowee or Cowee, about the meeting between La Pérouse and the Tlingit, and in the article explained some Tlingit beliefs:

> Like all primitive peoples elsewhere the Tlingit endowed all nature with spirit life, and so accounted for the many mysteries that compassed them about. In their imagination, the glacier was the child of the mountains, born in regions of eternal snow, and, when its arch-enemy the sun looks down to destroy it, the parents tear the rocks from their sides and scatter them over the surface for protection; in the scintillating aurora they saw the warrior spirits at play in the highest heaven; and when nature was at its best the spirit of the tree and the rock came forth as the shadow and slept the calm waters.[43]

Emmons continued to write articles until 1939, when, at the age of eighty-seven, he collaborated with G. P. L. Miles of England in publishing "Shamanistic Charms."[44]

All his life Emmons was an avid collector. "The spirit of collecting is born in us, we are not free agents," he wrote to Dr. Newcombe.[45] He was, aside from a few assignments, a free-lance collector who liked to gather together large lots of specimens for sale. His first two collections, gathered almost entirely by him before the turn of the century, were his best. Although he preferred to sell to the American Museum in New York, he was soon forced to turn elsewhere, and significant sales were made to Chicago's Field Museum, whose Department of Ethnology was under the direction of the ambitious George Dorsey. Dorsey and Boas (at AMNH, 1880–1905) were competitive in the extreme regarding their acquisitions, a help to an ambitious entrepreneur. In 1902 Emmons sold a large lot to the Field Museum, mostly Tlingit materials, and in 1903 another large lot of baskets.

Once again Boas was displeased, and wrote to Dorsey: "Lieutenant Emmons has agreed not only to work for your museum but offers to work for our museum also. I take it that he is simply trying to get as much as he can from both of us."[46] Dorsey, however, was delighted and wrote to Newcombe that he "had finally concluded the terms of purchase for his [Emmons] Tlingit collection, numbering 1400 specimens. It is a remarkably complete collection and contains many magnificent specimens of great interest and value."[47]

Emmons also sold to the Smithsonian, although the lots were smaller. A letter sent within the Smithsonian from Hodge, an assistant, to Rathbun, the assistant secretary, recommending a purchase, commented on Emmons's collections: "Coming from such a source I think it is hardly necessary to examine the collections offered inasmuch as purely aboriginal Alaska articles have grown so scarce as to be unobtainable now."[48]

Collecting was always a competitive business, and when it came to obtaining collections, friendships came second. Emmons and Newcombe were friends and rivals. Newcombe, writing to Dorsey, by whom he was employed for several years, said, of collecting in the Tlingit village of Klukwan, that he would not let friendship with Emmons interfere with the purchase, for "I take this to be an open field."[49] And Emmons wrote to the Smithsonian:

> . . . [I] came across on the Fraser river in B.C. an ethnological and archaeological collection of one man gathered in the past eight or nine years from old village sites. It illustrates the archaeology of Lytton as described by Harlan Smith [1900]. I bought it knowing that someone would take it for I have no use for it but I did not like to pass it by. B.C. has at last aroused itself to the fact that it has lost its opportunity to gather a necessary collection to illustrate the native tribes and now Dr. Newcombe has been given ample funds and every means to gather everything remaining but it is too late.[50]

All through his years of collecting Emmons had a curious habit of trading. No sooner would he sell a collection than he would request to have some of the pieces back and would offer others in trade. It was an incessant shuffle by means of which Emmons managed never to relinquish his hold on any collection completely. Some of his requests were granted, others denied, and the curators were puzzled in handling the problem, as is illustrated in a letter sent within the Smithsonian, from Otis T. Mason to W. H. Holmes:

> Lying on the floor of your room are a number of Tlingit specimens selected by Lt. Emmons which he wishes to exchange for material collected for the groups in Buffalo. Under ordinary circumstances the giving of precious treasure of this institution on any plea whatever would not be thought of. Even granting that the pieces in this lot are duplicates in a loose sort of way, we know very well that no such thing as a duplicate exists in ethnological material. He is wise enough and knows Tlingit well enough to pick out the very rarest and most precious objects. The average value of the Museum would be lowered by parting with these specimens. On the other hand I am aware that the Lieutenant's friendship is worth a great deal to us, and that he is a mine of information, though he seems to be as deep as he is profound. I shall be governed by your advice in the matter of recommending the exchange. The Lieutenant is in a great hurry to have some of them sent on to Princeton at once, before he leaves for Alaska. If we decline to enter into this exchange with him we run into the risk of losing his good will, and it seems to be a question of an apothecary's balance in which the precious objects are in one scale and the Lieutenant is in the other.[51]

Holmes replied that he would not consider an exchange, since the material was too valuable.

Gradually the "Big Three" museums of natural history began to turn their attention to other parts of the world, and the competition among them for Northwest Coast artifacts subsided, all but ending a large part of Emmons's market. Soon, however, a new wave of collecting began on the part of newer and smaller museums that wished to have representative collections from these tribes.

Before 1909 Emmons had gathered, despite his prophecies that it could never be done again, another representative collection. His old customers were cool, but he was invited to exhibit his things at the Alaska-Yukon-Pacific Exposition in Seattle in 1909.[52] Emmons did not like to ship his collection across the country, nor did he want to attend the exposition, but, lured by an offer to buy, he consented to ship and then arrange his collection in Seattle. Once again he received favorable reviews and a gold medal. Negotiations for the sale, however, were protracted. He wanted $14,000 for the lot of 1,900 pieces, and the sale, paid for in installments and with interest, was not concluded with Washington State Museum (TBMM) until 1913.[53]

Another large customer was George Heye, who established his own museum, formally called the Museum of the American Indian (MAI), and informally known as "The Heye," in New York. Heye was himself an avid collector who picked up Indian materials of all kinds. Emmons first sold to Heye in 1905 and continued to sell to him thoughout the 1930s. A recent computer readout would indicate that MAI has 1,650 specimens from Emmons.[54]

Although Emmons had lengthy dealings with the University Museum of the University of Pennsylvania in Philadelphia, its director, George Byron Gordon, "wanted everything he saw but didn't have the funds to buy," and sales to this institution were not large.[55] In subsequent years there was a long correspondence about Emmons's monograph on the Tahltan Indians, which the museum had published in 1911.

As Emmons continued to sell, his sources of supply became increasingly scattered. He made his last field trip to British Columbia in 1925, but long before that time he would buy large or small lots from a variety of sources, including Victoria and Alaska curio dealers, Miss Sally Ball (former postmistress of Sitka), and L. L. Bales, a prospector who was responsible for most of his Arctic pieces. He tried many times to buy Dr. Newcombe's collection without success, although he did get a few pieces in trade. In addition to artifacts, he sold geological specimens, the most prominent of which were jade. His sources of supply were far-flung, and small collections and single pieces represent a bewildering array. He had, at various times, a set of Fiji war clubs, a Japanese suit of armor, and the trappings of Red Cloud, the Sioux chief. He sold to Governor Clark of Alaska an Eskimo collection, very likely gathered by Bales, and a smaller one of baskets. Other collections went to Harvard's Peabody Museum and to A. C. Bossom, a private collector of New York and New England.[56]

His relationships with the curators varied. As we have seen, Boas distrusted him and he disliked Boas. He sparred with the pugnacious Dorsey, who told him in one letter that if he didn't like an Eskimo spear sent to him in trade, he could "always use it for kindling."[57] He liked Pliny Goddard at the American Museum, with whom he exchanged jocular letters; Otis T. Mason of the Smithsonian was another favorite.

Emmons never seemed to understand why curators would not buy from him, apparently not able to see the situation from their point of view. He was particularly hard on F. W. Hall of the Washington State Museum (now TBMM). Hall, busy with many museum chores, was desperately trying to raise money for a small British Columbia collection, but Emmons pressed him mercilessly, at one time threatening to have the collection sent to Heye.[58]

As anthropology became more of a university discipline, Emmons grew increasingly scornful of "armchair anthropologists" and any new theory. In a series of letters to the Newcombes, Emmons made scathing comments about anthropologists, curators, and museums. In one bitter-sad letter to Willy Newcombe (Dr. Newcombe's son), written in 1929, he expressed his feelings:

> As to Louis Shotridge he is a lacky of Gordon. He should know something more than he does. I have seen a notice of Barbeau's book but have not seen it. Barbeau is a nice fellow and a close student but too scientific and his painter friend who made portraits of the Upper Skeena and Nass people was awful. I always wanted to see the Ottawa material. There is nothing new in the Eastern Museums. No one knows or cares anything about the N.W. Coast. Asia, Africa, and the South-Sea people are the rage today. I do not think that Goddard's place will be filled. Wissler takes it over with his other work and has no knowledge of the coast but there is little left on the coast for anyone. It is all in Museums and no one to care for it—largely stored. I cannot look ahead to the summer and really do not know if I will come out to the coast, Indian life has so departed.[59]

Although the curators many times grumbled over Emmons's prices and his trading requests, they all respected his knowledge, particularly of the Tlingit.

In 1928, Katherine Emmons died following an operation. Emmons's grief was profound and prolonged as he tried to immerse himself in his work, trading, selling, and mending things in his workshop. She had been a stable force in his life, always his staunch supporter, and her loss was a heavy blow. For a few years he stayed in Princeton, then in 1932, having lost heavily in the stock market, he sold his house and moved to Victoria.

Emmons was never a rich man, although the enormous volume of his dealings sometimes made him seem to be one. Dorsey, writing to Willy Newcombe in 1911, remarked: "Emmons is the champeen dealer—he should be a millionaire by this time."[60] But he was far from being a millionaire.

Although he had been extremely acquisitive, it was not for money, a fact not understood by his contemporaries. He loved the artifacts for themselves, and wanted to possess them. His acumen in the business world did not match his shrewdness as a trader, and in later life his income was reduced to his Navy pension and whatever his son, Thornton, could send him.

Emmons had two commissions of a similar nature, from the Smithsonian and the American Museum. W. H. Holmes of the Smithsonian asked him to put together a Chilkat life group, and for this Emmons traveled to Alaska and procured a Chilkat blanket in the process of being woven, as well as other things illustrative of Tlingit life. The group was exhibited at Buffalo's Pan-American Exposition in 1901, after which it was placed on permanent display at the Smithsonian. Although Holmes and the other officials were pleased with his work, Emmons felt slighted, and, in a letter to Newcombe, criticized Holmes for taking all the credit when he had done all the work.[61]

Another life group was done at the request of the American Museum, to be exhibited in their huge Haida canoe. Again Emmons traveled to Alaska, where he met the photographer and sculptor making observations and plans for a potlatch group. Under Emmons's direction, the sculptor executed a group representing a Chilkat chief and his followers in ceremonial dress arriving at a potlatch. These figures, installed in the canoe, make a dramatic entrance to the Northwest Coast Hall of the museum.

In the early 1900s Emmons had a number of assignments from President Theodore Roosevelt, with whom he was personally acquainted, and by whom he was called to the White House from time to time for consultation on Alaskan matters. The first of these assignments, made through the Department of Agriculture, was for a study of the forests of southeastern Alaska, and for this Emmons prepared, in February 1902, a sixteen-page handwritten document, "Woodlands of Alaska," in which he discussed various trees, their growth patterns, and their use.[62] He recommended setting aside five islands of the Alexander Archipelago as a forest reserve. It was a thorough and meticulous document, and Roosevelt commented on it in a letter to Secretary of the Interior E. A. Hitchcock on April 15: "This Alaska Forest reservation strikes me favorably. Let us look into it and if it is proper have it done. . . ."[63] And on August 9, 1902, William Loeb, personal secretary to the president, sent a note to the Department of the Interior: "The President wishes to know what has been done with reference to the forest reserves of Alaska, which reserves were indicated on the map which he forwarded to the Department with the full report of Lt. Emmons. It is the President's desire that those reserves be established at once."[64]

On August 20 the Alexander Archipelago Forest Reserve was established by Presidential Proclamation, eventually to become part of the largest forest reserve in the nation, Tongass National Forest. Although Roosevelt was pleased, Emmons's role in the creation of this forest reserve received little attention.

Again in 1902, Roosevelt sent Emmons to find the reputed Russian boundary markers above Klukwan, whose position it was hoped would strengthen the case of the United States against Canada in the Boundary Dispute. Emmons interviewed natives at Sitka and Klukwan, among whom was a very old Chilkat woman, who said that, as a small child, she had accompanied her father and a Russian party halfway to where they set up a marker, several stone slabs set tentlike together, forming what the Tlingit called a "Stone House." Emmons set out from Klukwan with Chilkat guides on July 30, traveling first by canoe, then on foot, and finally on horseback with his friend, Jack Dalton. Two days later they reached the "Stone House," in Rainy Hollow, below the summit of the Chilkat Pass.[65]

The third request from Roosevelt in 1904 was for a report on the condition of the natives of Alaska. After a trip as far north as Valdez, Emmons submitted his report to the president, and again it was favorably received and incorporated into the president's fourth annual message to Congress, as a Senate document.[66] In this report Emmons divided the native tribes into two groups: the Tlingit, Haida, and Tsimshian in the south, and the Aleut, Eskimo, and Athabaskan in the north. The first group, he found, fared far better in its adaptation to the white man than the second. These Indians had a more independent spirit as well as a willingness and aptitude for learning, while the second group, more docile by nature, the victims of the Russian paternalistic system, were less able to take care of themselves. The needs of the first group were great, but those of the second, dire. He was emphatic about the need for schools and hospitals, as well as the granting of citizenship and the right to own property. Although Roosevelt gave far more than cursory attention to Emmons's recommendations, Congress appropriated only $25,000, far less than was needed to accomplish his program. Alaska was still "Seward's Icebox" in the eyes of Congress, its importance diminished by its distance.

On all of his government trips, Emmons took the opportunity to collect, and corresponded with the museums wherever he went. As he wrote to Newcombe, "when in Indian country it would be impossible to help picking up things.[67]

In the early 1930s Emmons was involved in a minor but revealing controversy with Princeton University. He had long had his eye on a collection made by the missionary and educator of Alaska, Sheldon Jackson, and given to Jackson's alma mater, the Princeton Theological Seminary. Later, this collection was given to Princeton University by the Seminary. Emmons proposed to the trustees of the Seminary that they retrieve the collection, and he offered them $1,000 for it. The trustees of Princeton University were not at all pleased with the scheme and pointed out that the collection had been an outright gift and would not be returned. Unfortunately for Emmons, he had, as expressed by Princeton professor Donald Baird, rendered himself "persona non grata" with Princeton University.[68]

In the same year (1930), articles appeared in two of the British Columbia papers, accusing "an American Navy Lieutenant" of taking more than his share of carved native spindle whorls from British Columbia.[69] Emmons was furious and fired off letters to Willy Newcombe and to Diamond Jenness of the National Museum of Canada, wishing to know who was responsible for what he considered unjust accusations.[70] Jenness wrote him a polite letter and the controversy faded.[71] In his burst of self-righteousness Emmons appears to have overlooked the thousands of artifacts he had taken from British Columbia.

As we have seen, Emmons moved to Victoria in 1932. Now in his eighties, he lived first in a hotel and then in an apartment with his nurse, Miss Katherine Ross. Between them was a deep and abiding affection, and she was confidante, nurse, and mother as he became completely dependent on her.

In these final years he would rise early and write every day until noon, still trying to finish the Tlingit manuscript. He had a few friends in the city that he had visited so often, one of whom was Willy Newcombe, with whom he enjoyed sparring over the meaning and provenience of their beloved masks, rattles, and bones. These discussions would grow loud and argumentative as, with great glee, they disagreed over everything.

Although Miss Ross took good care of Emmons, his health grew worse as he was plagued by forgetfulness and fainting spells. The police would bring him home from the streets of Victoria, where they would find him wandering aimlessly, calling for "Katherine" but not able to remember his own name. By the next day he had usually recovered and was able to resume his activities.

On a smaller scale, he still carried on his trading. He liked to spread his precious remaining artifacts along the narrow stairway entrance to his apartment, prompting his landlady to refer to them as his "toys."[72] Nearly ninety, he wrote to William Hanlon, former mayor of Sitka: ". . . now in the next house to that of Annahootz in the Ranch or it might be the second house years ago on the upstairs loft there were two long native made boards about 12 or 15 feet long painted red and blacked in the old Raven design that had once been on the side wall of an older house as a picture when put together. If you can locate them would you see if you can buy them for me?"[73] At ninety-one he was still trying to sell a jade collection and he startled the adoring Miss Ross by selling a silver bracelet, given as a gift from him, from her wrist.[74]

Collecting, selling, and trading were over on June 11, 1945, when Emmons died of pneumonia in St. Joseph's hospital in Victoria, at the age of ninety-three. He left to Katherine Ross his watch, a small collection of artifacts, and less than $2,000 in other assets.

If at times he seemed misanthropic and self-righteous, Emmons also appears to have been tireless in his two pursuits: to learn about tribal lore and customs and to find the finest of Indian objects. For a man without formal training in anthropology, his perceptions were acute, and his persistence in the face of ill health and disapproval is astonishing. Whatever his motive, he saved thousands upon thousands of priceless pieces of Indian art from disintegration—pieces that can be seen and enjoyed in museums throughout the United States and abroad. A strong part of his motivation came from a reverence for the old ways, as expressed in a passage from *The Chilkat Blanket:*

> The end of weaving is near at hand, and, as the art has disappeared from the home of its birth [the Tsimshian], so it will soon be lost to the Chilkat. To-day but fifteen weavers remain, and the majority of them are well advanced in years. The younger generation is not attracted by this work. Time becomes of more value every day, and the possibility of making an increased wage in the canneries and fisheries is much more attractive. Then the days of the dance are over, the old ceremonial houses are falling to pieces, and the use of the blanket is past. Another generation will know it only as a memory.[75]

Notes

About the sources: Although there were many letters left by Lieutenant Emmons, there were no diaries, and no letters to his family and friends which might have given a more personal perspective to this biography. I was fortunately able to interview several persons who knew him, among them his daughter, the late Frances Emmons Peacock, his granddaughter, Virginia Emmons Kalthoff, and his step-granddaughter, Sally Contant. Friends included Ainslee Helmcken and Katherine Ross of Victoria, and Hugh Brady and William Paul of Seattle. These four have since died. Miss Ross, in particular, was able to tell me much about Emmons from an intimate, personal perspective.

1. Personal correspondence and conversation with the late Katherine Ross.

2. G. T. Emmons's academic record, courtesy of W. W. Jeffries, archivist and professor of history, U.S. Naval Academy.

3. Records of the Bureau of Naval Personnel, "Records of Officers," 7:401–5, record group 24. This lists all ship assignments, promotions, leaves, and special orders.

4. Last Will and Testament of George Foster Emmons, Rear Admiral, U.S. Navy, February 1, 1883. Archives and History Bureau, New Jersey State Library, Trenton, New Jersey.

5. Final Decree and Testimony, *Emmons v. Emmons,* Superior Court of New Jersey, Office of the Clerk, Trenton, New Jersey, November 24, 1884. (Jessie Emmons was not a Tlingit woman, as stated by Carpenter in *The Far North,* 1973, p. 288 and note 12.)

6. Although "promoted" to lieutenant junior grade on October 15, 1881, he still held only his commission as master, as of that date, and was not "commissioned Lt. Jr. Grade from 3 March '83" until June 1, 1883, the day that he was transferred to the *Pinta* (see note 3). The actual commissioning was dependent, we believe, on his ability to pass the necessary physical examination.

7. Unpublished letter, Emmons to the *Alaska Magazine,* Feb. 19, 1927. Anthropology Archives, Thomas Burke Memorial Washington State Museum. For Kowee's story and a picture of the pipe, see Emmons 1911c, and figure on page 315 herein.

8. Letter courtesy of Frances Emmons Peacock, daughter of G. T. Emmons.

9. Information from handwritten memorandum by G. T. Emmons, courtesy of Katherine Ross.

10. Letter to *The Alaskan,* Sitka, June 19, 1886, p. 1.

11. In a notebook of Emmons's, filed with the Newcombe papers, BCPA. See the reference to this case (below) in Chapter 2, section entitled "Law," and in testimony from John J. Healey of Dyea, Sol Ripinski of Haines, and William Ogilvie himself, in *Proceedings of the Alaskan Boundary Tribunal,* vol. 4, part 2, 1903, Appendix to the Counter Case of the United States, etc., pp. 215–17, 217–20, 233–36. The Chilkoot had to put down their loads at the summit of the pass, because beyond that the Athabaskans had the right to pack.

12. Seton-Karr 1887:59–60. See also de Laguna 1972:187, 189, 192, 686–87, and pls. 170–77.

13. "Report of the Halleck Island Committee." Unpublished notes of the Sitka Ethnological Society, Sept. 9, 1895. Alaska Society of Natural History and Ethnology, Sheldon Jackson Museum Archives, Sitka.

14. Minutes of the Executive Committee, AMNH Central Archives.

15. *The Alaskan* (Sitka), Aug. 13, 1887, p. 4.

16. Bishop to Bickmore, Jan. 30, 1888, AMNH Central Archives.

17. Emmons to Bickmore, Dec. 2, 1888, AMNH Central Archives.

18. Bickmore to Jesup, May 1, 1888, AMNH Central Archives.

19. Boas, 1888a, p. 219.

20. *The Alaskan* (Sitka), Aug. 13, 1887.

21. *The Alaskan* (Sitka), Dec. 1, 1888, p. 3.

22. Edwin Willits (chairman of the Department of Agriculture) to Emmons, Dec. 22, 1891. Uncatalogued materials of Admiral G. F. Emmons, Beinecke Room, Yale University.

23. "Alaskan Curios at the Fair," *Kate Field's Washington,* as quoted in *The Alaskan* (Sitka), Oct. 21, 1893, pp. 1, 3–4.

24. Emmons to Jesup, Sept. 8, 1894, AMNH Central Archives.

25. Winser to Emmons, Dec. 17, 1896; Jesup to John D. Kong, Secretary of the Navy, May 14, 1897, AMNH Central Archives.

26. Winser to Pyne, Oct. 31, 1894, AMNH Central Archives.

27. Report of Medical Survey, Department of the Navy, Dec. 6, 1896.

28. See note 4.

29. G. T. Emmons, as told to Katherine Ross.

30. Emmons to Jesup, Jan. 13, 1898, AMNH Central Archives.

31. Winser to Emmons, March 11, 1898; Emmons to Winser, March 13, 1898; Emmons to Boas, March 17, 1898; Winser to Emmons, March 21, 1898; Winser to Emmons, April 19, 1898, AMNH Central Archives.

32. Emmons to Winser, July 8, 1898, AMNH Central Archives.

33. See note 27.

34. Emmons to Boas, May 21, 1899, AMNH Department of Anthropology Files.

35. Newcombe to Dorsey, July 24, 1900, BCPA.

36. Emmons to Jesup, July 25, 1896, AMNH Central Archives.

37. Emmons to Boas, July 19, 1900, AMNH Department of Anthropology Files.

38. *The Alaskan* (Sitka), Aug. 18, 1900, p. 1.

39. Emmons 1903; Mason 1903.

40. Emmons 1907; Mason 1908.

41. Boas to Farrand, June 20, 1903, AMNH Central Archives.

42. Emmons to Newcombe, Feb. 9, 1917, and Sept. 1918, BCPA.

43. Emmons 1900c:294–95.

44. Emmonds [*sic*] and Miles 1913. [It looks as if Miles hastily threw together notes from Emmons.—FdeL]

45. Emmons to Newcombe, Feb. 22, 1903, BCPA.

46. Boas to Dorsey, June 19, 1902, AMNH Department of Anthropology Files.

47. Dorsey to Newcombe, March 14, 1902, BCPA.

48. Hodge to Rathbun, Sept. 1, 1904, National Anthropological Archives, General Correspondence Files, SI.

49. Newcombe to Dorsey, May 8, 1902, AMNH Archives.

50. Emmons to Smithsonian, July 22, 1913, Smithsonian Archives, record unit 192, USNM, Permanent Administration Files, box 21, folder 10, no. 44522.

51. Mason to Holmes, April 5, 1901, National Anthropological Archives, SI, no. 87889.

52. Emmons to Gordon, Oct. 13, 1908, UM Archives, University of Pennsylvania.

53. Anthropology Archives, TBMM, accession no. 42, August 1913.

54. Personal communication, Mary Jane Lenz, Research Department, MAI, June 1985.

55. Emmons to Newcombe, Nov. 6, 1917, BCPA.

56. Cole 1985, esp. pp. 241–43.

57. Dorsey to Emmons, Jan. 15, 1903, AMNH Archives.

58. Emmons to Hall, March 4, 1914, Anthropology Archives, TBMM.

59. Emmons to William A. Newcombe, Jan. 23, 1929, BCPA.

60. Dorsey to W. Newcombe, July 19, 1911, BCPA.

61. Emmons to C. F. Newcombe, 1917, BCPA.

62. Navy Orders, Feb. 11, 1902, to proceed to Washington and report to Secretary of Agriculture, Feb. 13, 1902, for conference with Chiefs of the Bureau of Forestry and of Biological Survey, respecting the forests and game of southeastern Alaska. At Yale University is a copy of "Woodlands of Alaska," with a penciled notation in G. T. Emmons's hand: "Written for the U.S. Department of Agriculture, February 1902." (This corrects some information in Conrad 1977.) Western Americana Collection, Beinecke Rare Book and Manuscript Library, Yale University.

63. Roosevelt to Hitchcock, April 15, 1902, Roosevelt Letters, Stanford University.

64. Loeb to Department of the Interior, Aug. 9, 1902, Roosevelt Letters, Stanford University.

65. Emmons, field notebook of the trip, BCPA; Emmons, *History of Tlingit Clans and Tribes,* chapter on the Chilkat, AMNH. Although Emmons believed these piles of stone to be old Russian boundary markers, there is still considerable doubt as to what they were. The Canadians believed them to be put there by the natives. Had they been Russian they gave the United States a claim to the mineral resources believed to exist in Rainy Hollow and along the headwaters of the Chilkat River. However, these "markers" were never mentioned in the final hearings in London, and the boundary was drawn just above the confluence of the Tlehini and Porcupine Creek, which left the goldmining claims on the creek in United States territory, to the chagrin of the Canadians.

66. Emmons 1905.

67. Emmons to Newcombe, Feb. 22, 1903, BCPA.

68. W. B. Scott to the Honorable Board of Trustees of Princeton University, Feb. 21, 1930. Memorandum on the Sheldon Jackson Collection sent to the Clerk of the Board of Trustees, by V. L. Collins, Secretary, Princeton University, March 1, 1930, Guyot Hall, Princeton. Personal correspondence with Dr. Donald Baird, Professor Emeritus of Geology, Princeton University.

69. *Daily Province* (Vancouver), Jan. 12, 1930; *Victoria Colonist* (Victoria), Feb. 1, 1930.

70. Emmons to W. Newcombe, Jan. 24, 1930.

71. Jenness to Emmons, Feb. 19, 1930, BCPA.

72. See note 1.

73. Emmons to Hanlon, Feb. 6, 1942, Sitka National Historical Park Files, Sitka, Alaska.

74. See note 1.

75. Emmons 1907:350.

The Tlingit Indians

CHAPTER 1

The Land and the People

PHYSICAL FEATURES OF TLINGIT TERRITORY*

Southeastern Alaska, the home of the Tlingit, comprises the narrow coastal strip of the continental shore, extending northward from Portland Canal for six hundred miles to the Copper River delta, and includes the Alexander Archipelago and the Kayak Islands. [By "Kayak Islands" Emmons means Kayak, Wingham, Kanak, and Martin islands in Controller Bay.] There are traditions that the Tlingit formerly occupied the coast as far as the Skeena River, from which territory they were driven north by the Tsimshian.

[Emmons uses "southeastern Alaska" to refer not only to the panhandle south of Cape Spencer, to which the Tlingit themselves restrict the designation, but also to the shores of the Gulf of Alaska. In the last quarter of the eighteenth century, from which dates our earliest historical information, the Tlingit held the Gulf Coast only as far west as Cape Fairweather, just beyond Lituya Bay. In the Dry Bay–Akwe River area the population was mixed Tlingit and Athabaskan; at Yakutat and Icy Bay it was predominantly Tlingit with Eyak remnants; and from Cape Yakataga through Controller Bay the population was Tlingitized Eyak. The Eyak occupied the mouth of the Copper River and the present site of Cordova in Prince William Sound. Although the Eyak or Tlingitized Eyak held the mainland shores of Controller Bay, the islands in the bay belonged to the Chugach Eskimo. (Birket-Smith and de Laguna 1938; de Laguna 1972:15–16)].

The mainland area consists of a succession of lofty mountains extending inland from fifty to a hundred miles in confused masses rather than as a consistent range. It is a forbidding country of rugged rock and snow-covered peaks, separated by narrow, precipitous, ice-choked valleys. The interior is virtually inaccessible except along the three great rivers that have cut through the coastal ranges to the sea, or over the low divide at the head of the Chilkat River which leads to the headwaters of the Alsek and Yukon rivers and which separates the waters that flow into the Pacific from those that reach Bering Sea. [The major river routes linking the interior and coast are, of course, the Skeena and Nass in Tsimshian country, British Columbia; the Unuk River (emptying into Behm Canal), the Stikine, and the Taku in southeastern Alaska proper; the Alsek River to Dry Bay on the Gulf Coast; and the Copper River to the Gulf Coast Eyak.]

From Dixon Entrance to Cross Sound the coast of southeastern Alaska is broken by deep fjords and innumerable bays. The mountains rise directly from the water, except where alluvial flats and narrow beaches have been formed by the wash of the rivers and streams at the mouths of the valleys, or where the receding glaciers have left broad moraines. [*U.S. Coast Pilot 8* (1962:17) characterizes the panhandle as "a 30-mile-wide strip of mainland bordered by an 80-mile-wide compact chain of islands."]

The Alexander Archipelago, with its thousand islands extending seaward for fifty miles, forms a mighty breakwater along this shore. It is actually an outer submerged fringe of the mountain range that has been separated from the mainland through erosion [and subsidence], and differs in no way from the littoral, except in the generally lower altitude and more limited glaciers. The resulting network of channels constitutes the highways of travel and supplies the main sources of food for the natives.

Above Cross Sound, and especially above Lituya Bay, there is a marked change. Here the shores of the Gulf of Alaska, sweeping northwestward to Controller Bay, are for the most part low and unbroken. They consist of sands and gravels derived from the great glaciers of the Fairweather and Saint Elias mountains, either left behind as moraines after the ice, or washed down by the streams. The shoreline is interrupted only by Lituya Bay, Dry Bay at the mouth of the Alsek River, Yakutat Bay, Icy Bay, and by the small

---

Editor's note: In this and following footnotes to chapter and section titles, I attempt to explain the changes I have made in editing the manuscripts left by Emmons. This chapter was originally titled "Introduction," despite the short two-paragraph "Introduction" which has been reproduced on p. xvi in Emmons's own handwriting. The photograph is a composite—the main part written in the 1920s, and the postscript added in the 1940s (to the typed version of the text)—and demonstrates the deterioration of Emmons's handwriting in his old age. I have therefore given the chapter its present title.

My additions and comments added to the text are set in a lighter weight typeface than Emmons's material and are set off by square brackets to maintain a clear distinction between Emmons's voice and my voice.

**Editor's note:* This section combines what had been originally written under "Territory" and "Physical Features."

estuaries of glacier-fed streams. In former times the ice front of the great Malaspina Glacier reached the sea between Yakutat and Icy Bay.

CLIMATE*

The climatic conditions of the Northwest Coast are very similar to those of the British Isles and the adjacent shores of Europe. A warm ocean current from Japan crosses the Pacific to the Aleutian Islands and follows the southeastward trend of the coast. [It would be more accurate to say that the Kuroshio or west wind drift from Japan, strikes the North American coast about the Queen Charlotte Islands, where the larger branch of the current moves southeasterly down the coast. The smaller branch swings northwest up the Alaska coast and west along the Alaska Peninsula before turning southeast to rejoin the main current in a giant spiral. See Bartholomew 1942:16 map.] Its moisture is carried landward by the prevailing winds where it condenses on striking the high mountains, giving an annual precipitation of about eighty-four inches in most of southeastern Alaska. But paradoxically, the atmosphere is rather dry. Wet articles hung out of actual contact with the rain dry readily, and although offshore fog occasionally drives in, humidity like that prevailing on the Atlantic seaboard is unknown.

[The figures in Table 1 give some idea of the range of climatic conditions from Annette Island and Ketchikan near the southern end of the panhandle to Haines and Skagway at the head of Lynn Canal, and to Yakutat on the Gulf Coast. The inner islands, the mainland, and especially the inner fjords have a climate that is more continental in character, with greater fluctuations in temperature, but somewhat less precipitation, than along the outer coast. In general, "high humidity, fogs, heavy cloud cover, small temperature range, and abundant precipitation are characteristic of the maritime zone" (*U.S. Coast Pilot 8* 1962:18).]

FLORA AND FAUNA†

The effect of this excessive precipitation is apparent in the luxuriant vegetation that clothes the mountains up to the snow line. Hemlock, spruce, red and yellow cedar [western red cedar and yellow cypress] are the dominant woods. Cottonwood, willow, the Oregon (red) and the shrubby (Sitka) alder are found along the streams and river bottoms, with a stunted growth of maple, shore pine [Pacific silver fir], and crab apple of rare occurrence. Hemlock is the most abundant of the woods, but because of its weight and coarse grain is of least value. Spruce is second in quantity, but is economically the most important wood in the life of the people. The houses are built of it; the general service canoe is fashioned from its trunk; the root serves for baskets, cordage, and fishing gear; and the inner bark is eaten. The cedars are unquestionably the most valuable, though the least abundant, and are found only sporadically. The red cedar, from which the great traveling and war canoes are made, occurs only in the southern district [south of Frederick Sound, and the largest red cedar only south of Dixon Entrance], whereas the yellow cedar [cypress] is more generally distributed. Both are fine-grained and used for carvings and household decoration, for chests, boxes, and other domestic purposes. Mats, baskets, cordage, and clothing are made from the inner bark. To a lesser degree, all other woods serve a useful purpose. [The most important trees are listed, with Tlingit and species names, in Table 2.]

Bushes and plant life are still more varied. Berries of every species common to these latitudes are found in greatest abundance. Blueberries, huckleberries, salmonberries, cranberries, strawberries, and raspberries are the most important. All of these are eaten fresh, while most of them are also preserved in grease, or mashed, cooked, and pressed into cakes for winter use.

Animal life is not at all abundant and the number of species is limited. The rugged character of the country, combined with the climatic conditions, bespeak a limited food supply. Black-tailed deer are numerous on the islands and mainland as far north as Cross Sound, where the greater glaciers seem to bar their further distribution. Brown (Kodiak) grizzly, black bear, and glacier bear [the last discovered by, and named for Emmons: *Ursus americanus emmonsii* (Hall and Kelson 1959:866)], mountain goat, wolf, red fox (through cross to black), land otter, beaver, marten, mink, ermine, marmot, porcupine, several varieties of rodents, and a few squirrels, rabbits, and muskrats are found in limited numbers on the mainland and fewer varieties flourish on the islands.

But if nature is niggardly with her gifts to the land, she is most generous to the water, both in animal and fish life.

**Editor's note:* I compiled the figures in Table 1.

†Editor's note: Two sections in the original manuscript are here combined. I have checked and corrected the reference to the number of sea otter pelts obtained by La Pérouse; the last paragraph has been compiled from modern sources.

Lutak Inlet near the mouth of the Chilkoot River, 1949. (Photograph by Frederica de Laguna. Emmons had chosen similar illustrations of Tlingit country but the negatives had deteriorated.)

The sea otter, the most valuable of all fur-bearing animals, was originally numerous along these shores. In ten days in 1786 La Pérouse procured upwards of a thousand skins in Lituya Bay [and could easily have obtained five or six thousand by visiting other bays. Yet the majority of these skins, obtained in trade, were in rags. (Chinard 1937:xxxix, xl–xli, summarizing La Pérouse 1797, vol. 4.)] In fact, it was largely the quest for this fur that influenced the Russians to extend their operations from the Aleutian Islands to the continent, and then eastward along the coast to southeastern Alaska. Greed and lack of government regulations [until early in the twentieth century] have rendered this animal virtually extinct. [The herds are reappearing again, especially since 1950.] The fur seal, in its spring migration northward, passes close along the outer shore. Hair seal are abundant in all the waters, particularly where glacial ice flows exist. Sea lions are found on the offshore islands.

But the major wealth of the waters and the major dependence of the people are the salmon that in summer crowd into the inland streams to spawn. The five varieties are all taken and constitute the bulk of native food throughout the year. Halibut, herring, eulachon, cod, and rock fish of several varieties, sculpin, squid, crabs, mussels, clams, abalone [haliotis], and other smaller varieties of marine life are also utilized at different seasons.

Waterfowl include varieties of saltwater ducks, gulls, puffin, tern, grebe, guillemot, cormorant, petrel, albatross, murre, and smaller shore birds, also the oyster catcher, crane, and snipe. These, together with swans, geese, and freshwater ducks, are more abundant than the land birds. The latter include the bald eagle, a number of hawks and owls, grouse, ptarmigan, raven, crow, thrushes, flicker, woodpecker, sparrows, bluejay, crossbill, wren, robin, snowbird (snow bunting), and hummingbirds.

[The flora and fauna of Tlingit country are that of Merriam's "Canadian zone," or Nelson's "Sitkan district," or the "Coastal Spruce-Hemlock forests" as defined by the U.S. Forest Service (Gabrielson and Lincoln 1959:42–44). Tlingit country is, in fact, practically coterminous with the boundaries of the Tongass National Forest, which Emmons was himself instrumental in creating (Conrad 1977), plus its presently excluded enclaves (national parks and monuments, town sites, Indian-held areas), but including the coastal stretch northwest to the boundary of the Chugach National Forest. A detailed report on Alaska trees and bushes can be found in Viereck and Little (1972), and plants are described by Hultén (1968), the authoritative source.

[Animals of Alaska are covered by the extensive studies of North American mammals by Hall and Kelson (1959); the sea mammals are further detailed in the Alaska Geographic Society's *Alaska Whales and Whaling* (1978). In addition to Gabrielson and Lincoln (1959) on birds, Armstrong's handy guide (1980), with colored photographs for each species (except for a few illustrated by colored paintings), may be consulted, as may Peterson's field guide (1941, and subsequent editions). Although dealing especially with the freshwater fish of Alaska, Morrow's study (1980), with illustrations by Dalen, includes anadromous species like the Pacific salmon that breed in fresh water, and primarily marine species like the herring and cod that may sometimes be found in brackish water. The ranges of the fishes of coastal Canada, described by Clemens and Wilby (1961), in many cases include southeastern Alaska.]

THE TLINGIT*

The Tlingit occupied southeastern Alaska when it was discovered by Europeans in 1741, and are found there today, although in greatly diminished numbers. [It was presumably Hoonah Tlingit who were seen by Chirikov in the vicinity of Lisianski Strait, where Emmons believes that he lost two boats and their crews in 1741 (Golder 1922–25, 1:311 note, citing Emmons for identification of the scene of this tragedy, and pp. 344–46). But the native houses on Kayak and Wingham islands in Controller Bay which were visited by Bering's men apparently belonged to the Chugach Eskimo (Birket-Smith and de Laguna 1938:345–52).]

While early traditions of the Tlingit connect them with the coast about the mouth of the Skeena River, their territory as settled and claimed through many generations included the coast and contiguous islands of the Alexander Archipelago, from Dixon Entrance [including Zayas, Dundas, and probably parts of Wales and Pearce islands in British Columbia] up to and including Controller Bay. [The latter was, rather, the northernmost limit of direct Tlingit influence.] About the early part of the eighteenth century the Tlingit were driven out of the southern portion of Prince of Wales Island by Haida from Masset on the Queen Charlotte Islands. [See Table 3 for the major divisions of the Tlingit tribes.]

[Emmons here evidently refers to the report of G. M. Dawson for 1878–79 in which Dawson (1880:104B) mentioned a Haida tradition ". . . of internecine wars as a result of which a portion of the Haidas of the northern part of the Queen Charlotte Islands were driven to seek new homes on the Prince of Wales group. Their story is borne out by other circumstances, and the date of the migration cannot be more than 150 years ago [i.e., about 1730, or shortly before Bering's voyage of discovery]. These Haidas living beyond the Queen Charlotte group are generally known collectively as *Kai-ga-ni,* which name is also among the Indians applied to the country they inhabit." Kaigani territory includes all of Dall and Prince of Wales islands and the adjacent smaller islands south of Meares Passage on the west and Narrow Point on the east, with the possible exception of Forrester and Lowrie islands, which were in part claimed by the Henya Tlingit, and the Moira Sound region on the east coast of Prince of Wales Island, which was disputed by the Tongass Tlingit.]

In 1891, Annette Island in the southern area [which had been deserted by the Tongass Tlingit] was set aside by Act of Congress as a home for those Tsimshians who crossed over from Metlakatla under Father Duncan.

Owing to the almost impenetrable barrier formed by the coastal mountains, and to the fact that the Tlingit were a canoe-using people who looked to the sea for almost all their food, the Tlingit attached little importance to the more inland country, the boundary of which was never clearly defined, except along the trade routes to the interior. At the head of Lynn Canal where a comparatively low divide forms a gateway to the Yukon River basin, the line of demarcation was drawn at the summit of Chilkat Pass, and although the Chilkat Tlingit dominated the less aggressive interior [Athabaskan] tribes, they acknowledged the territorial rights of the latter beyond this line. This was clearly demonstrated when the gold fields of the interior were discovered, and the Tlingit who were employed as packers from the coast surrendered their loads at this point.

*Editor's note: This section was originally the first in Chapter 4, but had been transferred by Bella Weitzner, with Emmons's approval, to the beginning of Chapter 2, and from there to this chapter. I checked and amplified the reference to Dawson. Information on the Inland Tlingit is taken from McClellan, and that on the Tahltan was compiled from the original manuscript and from Emmons (1911a).

[The same rule applied to the summit of the Chilkoot Pass farther east, beyond which the Chilkoot Tlingit refused to carry packs for the party under William Ogilvie in 1887, because Tagish lands began here.

[The upper Taku River basin, currently uninhabited, was formerly the home of the Inland Taku Tlingit, who now live about Lakes Atlin and Teslin. The former boundary between the coastal Taku Tlingit and the Inland Tlingit seems to have been near the present International Boundary, probably below King Salmon River and Tulsequah Landing on the Taku (McClellan 1975, 1:58, 63). Emmons believed that the coastal Taku Tlingit were a relatively "recent" tribe, made up of Athabaskans from the Stikine and Taku rivers and coastal Tlingit who had maintained their relations with the interior through extended visits and intermarriage.]

But notwithstanding this close relationship and association, the coastal Taku were just as arbitrary as all other Tlingit in their methods of excluding their interior neighbors from visiting or trading on the coast. After the establishment of Juneau, in the early summer when the river was high, the up-river people came down with their furs and lived as guests with their coast relatives. In trading with the stores, they were carefully supervised by their hosts who took part in every transaction to their own advantage. [See McClellan 1975, 1:50.]

On the Stikine River, over one hundred miles within the acknowledged territory of the Tahltan Athabaskans, there is a strange overlapping of Tlingit and Tahltan territorial rights. Here, for a distance of some fifteen miles, from just below Glenora to Telegraph Creek, the Tlingit claimed exclusive fishing rights on all the tributaries along the northern shore, as well as ownership of the adjacent berry patches, but not the hunting rights in the area, nor fishing rights on the Stikine itself. The value of these privileges to the coast people was of more importance than is readily apparent, for while salmon were more abundant on the coast, the wetter climate of the coast rendered the curing uncertain, whereas success was guaranteed by the dry atmosphere and continuous sunshine of the interior. Here, also, there was an abundance of berries, especially of the soapberry and cranberry, so esteemed for winter use, and not indigenous to the coast.

In addition to the Tlingit territorial claims, certain clans of the Stikine Tlingit tribe monopolized trade with the Tahltan, whom they used to meet at prearranged times at or above Telegraph Creek, when they exchanged products of the coast for interior furs and caribou skins. This mutually profitable trade helped to preserve peace between the two groups. Yet the stronger Tlingit would not permit the Tahltan to descend to the coast. Thus, a Tahltan chief who wanted to see a ship which was near the mouth of the Stikine had to pay five hundred beaver skins to a Stikine chief for safe conduct. This was while the Hudson's Bay Company was leasing the littoral from the Russians, 1840–67. [See Emmons 1911a:6–7.]

The encroachment on their territory was resented by the Tahltan, but they had no power to oppose it. It remained in force until some time after the Dominion authorities were established at Glenora, to whom the Tahltan appealed for justice, and then the river was declared open to all.

NAME*

The name "Tlingit" [Łingít] was first used by the Tlingit themselves in a general sense to distinguish a human being from an animal. They believed that little difference existed in the earliest days between men and animals except in form. But with extended intercourse and a knowledge of other people, it became a specific or national name.

The term "Kolosh" or "Kalushian," variously spelled, appears on all the early charts and was the official designation of this people for more than a century. Veniaminov ascribed it to the Aleuts who accompanied the earliest Russian expeditions to the coast, and who were so impressed by the similarity in shape between the cumbersome ornament [labret] worn in the lower lip by the older Tlingit women and their own wooden dishes, called *kaluga,* that they characterized the Tlingit people as "those of the *kaluga,*" or of the diminutive, *kalushka.* This name was adopted by the Russians as expressively appropriate [Veniaminov (1840) 1984:381; Hodge 1907–10, 1:723, 2:764–65]. It is only within relatively recent years [post 1880?] that their proper name, Tlingit, has been used.

To the neighboring people they are variously known, and in like manner to the latter they gave their own suitably descriptive names. The Haida called them *Tlingit haada* [Łəʒgəs xa·dá·], "Tlingit people." The Tlingit named the Haida *Da-kee-nar,* "outside or far away people" from their

**Editor's note:* This section followed "The Tlingit" in "Chapter II" of the version edited by Miss Weitzner. A good deal of correction and reorganization of the manuscript was necessary, in order to include the native names for the Tlingit and theirs for other peoples, but I have preserved Emmons's original intent. His etymologies are definitely suspect.

The Russians distinguished between the Tlingit (Koliush) and similar northwestern tribes (Kolosh), but in transliteration these terms become confused (Lydia Black, pers. comm.).

seaward home [de·kina·, "way-out-to-sea people"]. To the (Coast) Tsimshian, the Tlingit were *Git kaneets,* "people of the north," perhaps from *nee,* "to see" [?], for the country of the southernmost Tlingit, the Sanya, could be seen far away to the northeast. The Tlingit, in turn, called the Tsimshian people *Tuts kwan* or *Tsuts-hun* [Ċu·cxán]. The *Nish-ka* [Niska or Nisqa] called the Tlingit *Kiti-kans,* "people (among) trees" [possibly Git-gan-s, from (Tsim.) gan, "tree"]. The name *Nishka,* "men of Nass," is said to be of Tlingit origin, from *nas* [na·s, -na·sí], "intestine," for the Nass River was referred to as "food belly," from the abundance of fish life at the mouth of the river.

The Déné [Tahltan Athabaskans] of the interior called the Tlingit *To-tee-heen,* "people of the stinking (salt) water" [?]. The interior people were generally designated by the Tlingit as *Gu-na-nar* [Gunana·], "stranger people," but those with whom they traded were known by specific local names.

Their direct neighbors of Eskimo [*sic!,* Eyak] stock, living to the westward at the mouth of Eyak Lake, call themselves *Eak-tella,* but are known to the Tlingit as *Yat Kwan* [Yá·t Qʷá·n, "this-place dwellers," or "local tribe"]. The Copper River people [Atna Athabaskans] were called *Eek Kwan,* "Copper tribe" [ʔIqkaha· Qʷá·n, or ʔIqka· Qʷá·n, from ʔí·q ka-ha· qʷá·n, "copper digging people"].

[It should be noted that the people living at the mouth of the Copper River and on Eyak Lake were not Eskimo, but were the Eyak Indians. Their own name for themselves was ʔí·ya·qədəlahgəyu· (Krause 1970a, 1970b). The Tlingit term, yá·t qʷá·n, means simply "local people," and is used by the Gulf of Alaska Tlingit to designate the aboriginal groups they found in the area, the Eyak-speakers of Yakutat and Controller bays, and this designation was extended to the Eyak living farther west, who were never absorbed by the Tlingit. The Chugach Eskimo were known to the Yakutat Tlingit as Guté·x̌, which was perhaps originally an Eyak word.]

The "Flatheads" of Vancouver Island and the adjacent mainland [Kwakiutl, Nootka, Bella Bella, Bella Coola, and Salish] the Tlingit called *Tow-yat* [Ṫaw-yá·ṫ, "feather(s)-long"].

The general name for whites was *Goots-ka-yu Kwan,* "sky or cloud faced tribe" [Guṡk̓iyí· Qʷá·n, from guṡ-ki-(ya) qʷá·n, "clouds-base face people," i.e., people of the horizon, usually shortened to guṡk̓i qʷá·n. Another common term is "white or snow man," ƛe·t qá·.]. The Tlingit also distinguished between the different nationalities, such as *Anushi* [ʔAnú·ši], for the Russians; "King George Men" [Kinǯiċwá·n] for Canadians and also British, and an older name *Nanginan* [Nanginán or ʔInginán, "England"] for the English. Americans were "Boston Men" [Wa·šdan Qʷá·n].

ORIGIN OF THE TLINGIT*

The Tlingit are unquestionably of interior origin, and came down the rivers to the coast in early days as small families or bands in search of better food conditions than those afforded by their own country. The older and more important clans that constitute the Tlingit of southeastern Alaska unanimously refer to the Tsimshian territory as their former home from which they wandered north. The continuous northward migration that for years had been peopling the islands and coasts of southeastern Alaska, and extending Tlingit territory, was suddenly arrested toward the close of the eighteenth century, when it met the counter movement of the Russian invasion along the Mount Saint Elias shore. [See Tribe XVII in Table 3 for what was apparently the westernmost and most recent Tlingit group to be formed.]

[In speculating on the origin of the clans and of the two matrilineal moieties, Raven and Wolf, which Emmons included in his unfinished *History of Tlingit Clans and Tribes,* he suggested that these two exogamous bodies may have originated from the meeting and intermarriage of "two divisions . . . possibly two ethnic stocks. . . ." (See Chapter 2 under "Phratry or Moiety" and "Clan.") This is, of course, a problem that involves not simply the Tlingit but all peoples of the Northwest Coast and adjacent interior who have matrilineal kin groups (de Laguna 1975). Swanton had earlier discussed the origin of the Tlingit people and of their clan-moiety system, and since Emmons was obviously influenced by him, it is surprising that he did not quote Swanton (1908:407–8) in this connection:

> The Tlingit quite uniformly trace the origin of nearly all their clans to the Tsimshian coast "below Port Simpson"; that is, to the neighborhood of the mouth of the Skeena river. It is said by some that nearly all of the present clans immigrated in this manner, and that most of the "old Alaskans," those whom they found in possession, have died out. . . . The only point that may have significance is the fact that nearly all [the small clans or lineages] so enumerated [as "old Alaskans"] were of the Raven clan. There are several other bits of evidence which seem to show that the distinction between the two phratries was of more importance historically than would at first appear. . . . This suggests the

**Editor's note:* This section has been taken from *The History of Tlingit Clans and Tribes.* I have added a discussion of the origin of clans and moieties, including a passage from Swanton, a brief paragraph on the center of Northwest Coast cultural development, and have corrected and included the references to Davis and Brooks on the Japanese current, and added the opinions of Knapp and Childe, and the Reverend Jones, to indicate popular opinion about the alleged Asian affinities of the Tlingit.

question whether distinction of phratry could have been associated originally with a racial difference, and such a possibility again presents itself when we come to consider the origins of the separate clan divisions.

[Swanton then presented synopses of the traditional histories of the major clans, demonstrating, like Emmons in his unpublished *History of Tlingit Clans and Tribes,* that most clan histories refer either to an origin within what is now Tsimshian territory or to more recent migrations from the Athabaskan interior. The older and more extensive migrations of the Tlingit moved northward from an area that included the mouth of the Skeena River and Prince of Wales Island. In other words, the origins of the Tlingit were to be found close to the present homes of the Tsimshian and the Haida.]

The center of primitive culture was on the Northwest Coast about the shores of Dixon Entrance and the adjacent mainland where met the Tlingit, Haida, and Tsimshian. Among these three people is found the highest degree of intelligence, artistic sense, and the strict observance of well-established laws. Beyond their confines in every direction the inferiority of their neighbors is very pronounced, and it seems barely possible that descent from them alone could have produced such superior results. We have abundant evidence that many of the Tlingit families are of interior origin, and the Haidas likewise have family traditions that connect them with the mainland, while the Tsimshian, including the *Nishka* [Niska] of the Nass River, from their history, came in part from the *Kitekshan* [Gitksan of the upper Skeena]. But for one who has any personal acquaintance with the interior people and knows their limitations, it is difficult to understand how, in their poverty and with their want of initiative, they could have been so transformed unless under some strong foreign influences. This suggests the question: Could there have existed hereabouts the nucleus of a more advanced race that, upon absorption by the greater number of interior people that constantly reached the coast, imposed upon the latter their higher culture? Did such a union produce the Tlingit, Haida, and Tsimshian, who in social organization, folklore, and customs are much alike?

[Here Emmons quoted Swanton's conclusions concerning the similarities between the Tlingit and Haida languages (Swanton 1908:485):

> They [the similarities] seem to the writer to be the faint echo of a time when the ancestors of some of the people now represented by the Haida and Tlingit spoke one tongue, and there is certainly nothing in the structure of stems, words, or sentences to contradict this view. At the same time, in order to bring about the differences which now exist, the two peoples must have lived long apart and have been subjected to very different influences.

[We would now include the Tlingit, Haida (?), Eyak, and Athabaskan in a common Na-Déné linguistic stock (Sapir 1915b; Krauss 1982:13). But linguistic evidence alone will not explain the rise of northern Northwest Coast culture. In discussing the origin of the Tongass or *Tan-ta Kwan* (Tribe I), Emmons suggested the possibility of Asian influence:]

Something to this effect was told me by a very intelligent older man of the Tlingit tribe of Tongass, who said that in the earliest days a few people from seaward were driven ashore and settled on Dall Island off the southwestern coast of Prince of Wales Island. The name of these foreign people was given as *Wish-shun-a-de,* "something very old, either man or animal" [i.e., animate; wudiša·ne·dí, "old-age beings"?]. These people are supposed to have been the ancestors of the *Ta-qway-de* [Te·qʷe·dí, Wolf 32; see the lists of clans, Tables 9 and 10], now one of the most important Wolf clans among the Tlingit and the oldest clan among the *Tan-ta Kwan* [Tongass tribe]. There is a curious belief prevalent among the older natives that these people came from over the sea and were the first to reach the coast. They settled on Dall Island, and in time increased and were joined by other people from the interior who had come to the coast, and this combination formed the nucleus from which the Tlingit, Haida, and Tsimshian were derived.

According to the tradition, there were two parties, each represented by one of two sisters. The younger sister and her party crossed over to the Queen Charlotte Islands, where their descendants became the Haida, while the older sister and her party remained behind, and combined with immigrants from the interior to form the Tlingit. The descendants of the older sister later acquired the clan name *Ta-qway-de* [Te·qʷe·dí, Wolf 32]. When descendants of the two parties now meet at death feasts, the Haida branch accord the Tlingit clan first place, in recognition of the seniority of the line.

This claim opens up the interesting possibility of a strain of oriental blood in these people, and would explain how the superior qualities of the Tlingit, Haida, and Tsimshian were developed in so short a period, for these three people have not lived in the vicinity of Dixon Entrance so very long, and nothing archaeologically important has been discovered [when Emmons wrote], that tells of an earlier race, possessed of superior culture, whom they might have absorbed.

[Emmons obviously did not consider the possibility that the center of cultural development on the Northwest Coast may have once been farther south among the Kwakiutl, Nootka, and Bella Coola (Kroeber 1939:28–31), or indeed, that these peoples may never have lost their cultural preeminence (Drucker 1955b:76).]

An ocean current, the *Kora Sowa* (Black Water) [Kuroshio, "black stream"] flows steadily east from Japan along the Aleutian Islands, through the Gulf of Alaska, and along the continental shore to California where it spreads oceanward. It approaches the coast more closely at Dixon Entrance where the Queen Charlotte Islands stand out to meet it, in consequence of which, drift material from the Asiatic shore is often stranded here, especially on the northern part of Graham Island. Hereabouts I have seen in use by the people some very old pieces of coconut, bamboo, and sea beans that were believed to have been found along the shore. But more direct evidence is contained in the record of Japanese derelicts that have been rescued off shore or that have been wrecked on the coast. Horace Davis (1872), also speculating on the likelihood of an admixture of Japanese blood among the Northwest Coast Indians, gave the following data concerning such wrecks of Japanese vessels that, through stress of weather and loss of propelling power [loss of their masts and rudders], have been carried by this stream to our shores (Davis 1872:21):

1815, Junk boarded at Sea, lat. 32° 45′ N., lon. 166° 57′ W.
1813, " " about " 49° " " 131° "
1820, " stranded on Point Adams.
1833, " " " Cape Flattery.
1805, " " near Sitka.
1782, " " on an Aleutian Island.
1862, " " " Attou "
1871, " " " Adakh "
1832, " " " Oahu, Hawaiian Islands.

In January 1916, a Japanese fishing boat, caught off the harbor of Shimoda, Japan, by a storm in which her mainmast and rudder were carried off, drifted helplessly for twenty-four days across the Pacific, and finally landed about Dixon Entrance.

While none of these incidents confirms the native theory that some of the earlier settlers at this point were Oriental, yet it shows how reasonably this might have occurred, and how a center of Asiatic culture might account for much that is problematical today.

[Charles Wolcott Brooks, connected for many years with the Japanese consulate in San Francisco, collected all available information about disabled Japanese junks carried eastward, "as Furnishing Evidence of a constant infusion of Japanese Blood among the Coast Tribes of Northwestern Indians" (1876, title page). His explanation of the course of the Japanese warm current was more comprehensive and he offered more details about the history of Japanese navigation that led to the loss of so many vessels, but I do not know if his paper was consulted by Emmons. Nor, apparently, was the latter familiar with the account of wrecked Japanese junks, with a few surviving members of the crew, in Captain Belcher's narrative (1843, 1:303–6).

[Speculation about Asian origins for the Northwest Coast Indians has been recurrent and popular, as the following citations will indicate.

[Knapp and Childe (1896:18) in their popular book about the Tlingit, wrote:

> [The "Thlinkets"] are part something else and the rest just plain Indian. In our opinion that something else is Mongolian, Japanese, or Chinese.

[The missionary, Reverend Jones (1914:34), speculated at greater length about the Tlingit:

> We believe that both the [Pacific] Islanders and the Alaskans are of Mongolian origin, chiefly Japanese, and that the Alaskans were the first scion from this stock, and the Islanders, for the most part at least, indirectly of the same through the Alaskans. . . . After studying the problem for years we believe the racial flow was along the Asiatic coast to Kamchatka, thence to Alaska, and from Alaska to the islands of the Pacific. This would account for the similarity of the many customs observed by the two peoples. [The "Thlingets" he felt, were now inferior to the Japanese because they have suffered centuries of isolation.] Until a more plausible theory of the origin of our Alaskans is advanced, supported by stronger arguments than the foregoing, we shall continue to believe that our neighbor, Japan, is responsible for the existence of this aboriginal people.]

PHYSICAL APPEARANCE*

The Tlingit are of medium height, but among the Chilkats and other mainland people who trail [travel] inland and intermarry more or less with those of the interior a noticeably larger percentage of taller men is found. In weight they are far heavier than light, and while fat men weighing over 250 pounds occur among the Tsimshian and

**Editor's note:* This section was at one time included in "Chapter IV. The Tlingit People." References have been checked and a few added. These include Shukoff, Beresford, Marchand in Fleurieu, La Pérouse, Lisiansky, von Kotzebue, Krause, Young, Petroff, and Boursin. The introductory phrases for such quotations are mine, as are comments or summaries after the citation.

Natives of Sitka, 1827. (Lütké 1835, pl. 6. Courtesy of Columbia University Library.) Free translation of plate legend by Frederica de Laguna: "The men let their hair fall carelessly, or confine it with a narrow band; a few make a knot on top of the head. They often dress it with long plumes, and on festival days powder it with eagle down. Women wear long tresses on each side, ornamented with ribbons or cords. The dress is a short tunic, and a fur robe fastened at the neck with two strings. They are beginning 'o wear a shirt and trousers, but their favorite dress is a woolen blanket from the Russians or British. On festivals, the chiefs wear blankets of goat wool, ornamented with long fringes, and on the head a flat bonnet of sealskin, surmounted by a point to which they attach feathers, walrus whiskers, or other similar ornaments. Women wear strings of shells as necklaces and ear ornaments. Children are generally naked. Both sexes normally paint the face, mostly using red ochre. They now get vermilion from the Europeans, which they keep carefully wrapped up in cloth."

Haida, I have never met one among the Tlingit, although with increased age the women grow quite heavy.

The men show a splendid bodily development, with broad chest and muscular arms, but from constant life in a cramped posture in the canoe, the legs are crooked and disappointingly weak; the Chilkat who hunt on land and make long trips inland are equally well proportioned. The hands and feet of both sexes are small and finely formed, the fingers long and tapering with well-shaped nails, notwithstanding constant usage in rough work.

The head is abnormally large. The face is broad with pronounced cheekbones, the forehead receding, the nose large, straight, often aquiline and broad at the nostrils, the mouth large, the lips full, the eyes small, dark and deep set, the eyebrows heavy and black, the lashes long. The teeth are strong, even and white, with no sign of disease in the older people, but are often worn down even with the gums from the amount of sand and grit that gets into all their food that is cured in the open. That is because the salmon streams [where they catch and dry their staple food] more often than not flow through old glacier moraines where the continuous winds are laden with fine silt that covers the fish, berries, and seaweed curing in the sun.

The complexion darkens with increasing age, and noticeably so in the men, from exposure. The ancient custom of covering the face with a coating of grease and powdered hemlock fungus, which is allowed to remain for weeks at a time, counteracts the effects of exposure, particularly in canoes on the water, and when removed reveals a comparatively pale color. Children are very little darker than Europeans, and, in fact, the people as a whole differ but slightly in this respect from the out-of-doors people of the Mediterranean shores, although their skin coloring is muddier.

The hair is coarser than ours and that of the men black, while the women's shows a reddish shade and is finer. In age it becomes grizzled, but never white.

[Hair dressing styles, ear and nose ornaments, labrets, bracelets, face painting, and tattooing are subjects originally discussed here; these topics have been transferred to Chapter 9, "Dress and Decoration."

[Emmons consulted the deposition made by Shukoff, a half-Russian, half-Tlingit Sitkan, on the customs of the Tlingit. This had been given in Tlingit to a Russian interpreter and later translated into English (Shukoff manuscript):

> The present race of Tlingits are far from looking like their ancestors, also in their customs and everyday life and dress and home arts and manufactures. The old Tlingits were very tall and much healthier race than present people, also color of skin much darker, more of a yellowish color, hair black and straight and coarse like horse's tail, eyes dark, all men and women pigeon-toed, if the Tlingit stands straight the big toes come together and heels are far apart, and this is caused by midwife not knowing how to strap children in board cradles. [The wooden cradle is evidently a (Russian?) substitute for the basketry cradle, but the notion that a deformed body would result from a crooked cradle or one improperly used is Tlingit.] Most of the Tlingit do not have beards, if beard comes they pull out with copper or iron pinchers, those who do not have pinchers use fingers.

[Beresford, with Captain Dixon in 1787, wrote (1789:238) about the Northwest Coast Indians in general, although his observations would apply well to the Tlingit of Yakutat and Sitka:

> The people in general are about the middle size, their limbs straight, and tolerably well-shaped; many of the older people are rather lean, but I never saw one person who could be called corpulent amongst them: both sexes are remarkably distinguished by high prominent cheek bones and small eyes. A love of dirt and filth is universally predominant all over the coast. . . . if I may judge from the few people I saw tolerably clean, these Indians are very little darker than the Europeans in general.
>
> The hair of both sexes is long and black, and would be an ornament to them, were it not for the large quantities of grease and red oker constantly rubbed into it, which not only gives it a disgusting appearance, but affords a never-failing harbour for vermin. Sometimes, indeed, the women keep their hair in decent order, parting it from the forehead to the crown, and tying it behind after the manner of a club.
>
> The young men have no beards . . . [but] all the men we saw, who were advanced in years, had beards all over the chin, and some of them whiskers on each side [of] the upper lip. . . . [I] was given to understand, that the young men got rid of their beards by plucking them out, but that as they advance in years, the hair is suffered to grow.

[La Pérouse, who visited Lituya Bay in 1786, described the Tlingit he found there (1799, 1:404–5):

> The stature of these Indians is much the same as ours. Their features vary considerably, and exhibit no characteristic marks except in the expression of their eyes, to which gentleness is an utter stranger. The colour of their skin is very brown, because it is incessantly exposed to the air: but their children are born as fair as ours. They have, it is true, less beard than Europeans . . . [but, like other American Indians,] are accustomed to eradicate the hair. The frame of their body is slight. The weakest of our seamen would have thrown the strongest of the Indians in wrestling. I saw some whose swelled legs seemed to indicate the scurvy, though their gums were sound. I suspect they never arrive at any very old age; but I saw one woman that appeared to be

Interior of a Tlingit cabin, Sitka, 1827. (Lütké 1835, pl. 4. Courtesy of Columbia University Library.) Free translation of plate legend by Frederica de Laguna: "This is the interior of a native hut near Sitka, finished with planks and showing Russian influence in construction. The old way was to sink several posts in the ground and cover them with bark, leaving only a low entrance and smokehole. The present house is of planks, with a plank floor except for the central square place for the hearth. Here the family gathers, passing the time in complete inactivity. [Two cedar-bark mats, some fish, and seaweed hang on the drying racks.] Fish sliced thin is roasting on spits in front of the fire. A child and a dog are eating from the same wooden dish. A screen of mats or planks separates a sleeping room or storeroom from the main room. One can also see a small axe. The men and women are muffled in fur robes and cloth. A girl wears a small labret; the woman a larger one."

sixty; and she enjoyed no privileges, but was obliged like the rest, to submit to the various labours imposed on her sex.

[Captain Marchand left us a fuller description of the Sitka Tlingit whom he visited in 1791 (Fleurieu 1801, 1:322–24):

The natives who occupy the environs of TCHINKITÂNAY Bay are of a stature below the middle size; none of five feet four inches (French) are to be seen: their body is thick, but tolerably well-proportioned; their round and flat face, is not set off by their snub but sharp nose, little watery eyes, sunk in the head, and prominent cheek-bones. It is no easy matter to determine the colour of their complexion; it might be imagined to be red or light brown, but a coat of natural dirt, thickened by a foreign mixture of red and black substances with which they smear their visage, suffers no remnant of their primitive skin to be discovered. . . . Their coarse, thick hair, covered with ochre, down of birds, and all the filth which neglect and time have accumulated in it, contributes to render their aspect still more hideous. They wear their beard only at a certain age; the youths carefully eradicate it: adults suffer it to grow. . . . It is probable that the face of those at TCHINKITÂNAY Bay would be less disgusting, if they preserved that which nature has given them; for the young boys have an agreeable, and even an interesting countenance; but age and still more the trouble which they take to make themselves ugly by wishing to embellish themselves, end in giving them hard, coarse, and even ferocious features: Surgeon ROBLET attributes their air of ferocity to the frequent expression of the passions by which they are agitated. . . . [pp. 322–23]

The women, more fair, or less dark than the men, are still more ugly: a big and clumsy head; a circular face; a nose squeezed in about the middle of its length; eyes small and inanimate; cheek-bones very prominent; hair, or rather a mane, thick, bushy and coarse, tied behind with strips of leather, either in the form of a cue or a club; the shoulders strong and broad; the neck low, tolerably firm and well rounded in those who are not sixteen, but extremely flabby and pendent in those who have suckled; a waist short and thick; knees and feet turned in, subject to strike against each other in walking; and to complete the whole, a filthiness truly disgusting. [pp. 323–24]

[Lisiansky (1814:237), wrote of the Tlingit at Sitka in August 1805:

The population here [Sitka area] is estimated at eight hundred males; the females amount probably to a greater number: of the males, about a hundred reside in the isle of Jacobi, and the rest on that of Chichagoff, in Chatham's Strait. They are of a middling stature, have a youthful appearance, and are active and clever. Their hair is lank, strong, and of a jet black; the face round, the lips thick, and the complexion dark, or copper-colour: some of them, and especially the women, if they did not daub themselves with different paints, which injure the skin, would be much fairer. Painting the face, and powdering the hair with eagle's down, are considered as the necessary appendages of beauty.

[Von Kotzebue (1830:49–50) described the Sitka Tlingit in 1825; against whom he was certainly prejudiced:

The Sitka Islanders, as well as their neighbours on the continent, are large and strongly built, but have their limbs so ill-proportioned, that they all appear deformed. Their black, straight hair hangs dishevelled over their broad faces, their cheekbones stand out, their noses are wide and flat, their mouths large, their lips thick, their eyes small, black, and fiery, and their teeth strikingly white.

Their natural colour is not very dark; but they appear much more so than is natural to them, from the custom of smearing themselves daily over the face and body with ochre and a sort of black earth. Immediately after the birth, the head of the child is compressed, to give it what they consider a fine form, in which the eyebrows are drawn up, and the nostrils stretched asunder. [This is only molding with the hands, not deformation by binding the head in the cradle as is practiced farther south.] In common with many other nations, they tear the beard out by the roots as soon as it appears. This is the business of the women. . . . [Clothing is only a little apron and a cloak or a blanket or bearskin. Only in heavy rain is the head covered with a "grass" (spruce root) hat. Women wear "linen shifts" to the ankles or grass mats.]

. . . I believe there is not a people in the world so hardened against the weather. In the winter, during a cold of 10° of Reaumur, the Kalushes walk about naked, and jump into the water as the best method of warming themselves. At night they lie without any covering, under the open sky, near a great fire, so near indeed as to be sometimes covered by the hot ashes.

[Krause ([1885] 1956:92–95) gave a rather complete description of the Chilkat whom he had visited in 1881–82, including measurements of two adults and a boy. He, like Emmons, found the best physical types among the Chilkat, probably because they used their canoes less than other Tlingit. The men "have a proud and erect posture and a springy step," but the older women become bent over and develop "a waddling walk" (p. 93).

[S. Hall Young, missionary at Wrangell during 1878–88, and later in other parts of Alaska, wrote at length about the Tlingit (1927:159):

One thing we noticed with surprise was the great number of lame women, whose one leg sagged; and their walk had that peculiar flop and swing that gave them the designation of "side-wheelers." There were so many of them that we often wondered at the cause. We laid it to impurity of blood causing hip disease. It was long before we found the truth about it, which was this: When a baby girl was born, especially if she belonged to a family of high caste, the midwife immediately dislocated one or both hips of the poor infant in order, as they said, that they might be good and prolific mothers! This horrible practice, which peopled those tribes with hundreds of hopeless cripples, was put down only with great difficulty.

[It has been impossible to verify this extraordinary statement. Petroff (1884:170), citing Holmberg (1855:40–41), also noted the lameness in women:

All observers and visitors at Sitka have noticed that the Thlinket women have a waddling, crooked, and sometimes even a limping gait, which seems all the more remarkable in view of the proud and erect bearing of the men. It would be a natural conclusion to ascribe this defect to this long period of imprisonment [seclusion at puberty] at a time when the female body is developing most rapidly; but we find the same custom to exist among Eskimo tribes, with even stricter rules, without causing a similar change in gait and bearing of the women. [Holmberg did not specify the Eskimo among the tribes having stricter puberty confinement.]

[Lameness in women, especially those in middle age, has been noticeable even in the last half of the present century. Osteoarthritis of the hip, initiated perhaps by the long confinement at puberty and aggravated by sitting on the floor to work, would seem to be the better explanation.

[Henry Boursin (1893:54), special agent for the Eleventh Census (1890) in Alaska, offered a description of the Tlingit, similar to that given by Emmons:

The typical Thlingit is lighter colored than the Indian [of the interior?], varying from yellow-white to light brown. His weight is about 145 pounds, and height about 5 feet 5 inches. Owing to the prominent cheek bones, wide jaws, and low, broad nose, the face is flat and wide. His black or brown eyes are small, and with orbits which rise in an oblique line from the nose to the temple. The mouth is large, with heavy lips and large white teeth. The facial expression, though varying much in different persons, is, as a rule, good natured and submissive. His form is badly proportioned, a long deep-chested body, and short, misshapen legs making him physically an unprepossessing person. He walks in a slow, ungainly fashion with the feet "toed in".

The primitive native passed much of his time in a canoe, hence his defective legs and awkward movements. At the present time the canoe is no longer a necessity to a considerable number of the Thlingits, who have learned to make a better living as laborers, and these are appreciably improved in form. The members of the different tribes possess certain physical and mental characteristics peculiar to the tribe. The Sitkas having been influenced by civilization for a longer time than any of the others are of the lightest color, best dressed, and most intelligent. The Chilkats and Takus are taller, better featured, and more self-assertive than the average, and the former are particularly shrewd traders. The Auks are badly formed and unintelligent. The Yakutats are the darkest colored and most primitive. The Hutznahu [Hutsnuwu] are the largest in stature.

CHARACTER*

The early explorers described the Tlingit as courageous, warlike, and arrogant, ready to avail themselves of the slightest opportunity to attack with advantage. They destroyed the first Russian posts established in their midst [Sitka in 1802 and Yakutat in 1805], as well as the Hudson's Bay Company factory far in the interior [Fort Selkirk on the Yukon in 1852] because it interfered with what they considered as their legitimate trade. Throughout Russian occupation of Alaska, and including the early years of our occupation up to 1875, military control was necessary, and the white man lived within stockaded walls.

[Thus, Golovnin ([1822] 1861:58 Petroff translation), writing of conditions at Sitka in 1817–19, warned that one could not trust the Kolosh promises of peace: "They never let an opportunity go by of killing a Russian if they can do it without much risk to themselves." Therefore, hunters could leave the fort only in large armed parties. This hostility he ascribed to the instigation of foreigners, especially the American traders who were prejudiced against the Russians and supplied the Tlingit with the guns and ammunition to be used against the Russians.

[And von Kotzebue (1830, 2:41–42) reported as of 1825 that although the Kolosh had made peace with the Russians after the latter had retaken Sitka: "The savages thirsted for revenge; and, notwithstanding the treaties concluded with them, unceasingly sought to gratify it by secret arts and ambushes; so that the Russians, unless well armed, and in considerable numbers, could not venture beyond the shelter of their fortress without imminent danger of being murdered."

[Even as late as the middle of the century, Golovin could write ([1862] 1979:27): "Until recently no Russian dared to go fifty paces out from the New Arkhangel fortress unarmed. At present this hostility does not exist, but trade relations are carried on only with the Sitka Kolosh who live only ten *sazhens* [seventy feet] from New Arkhangel. The Kolosh who live in the straits are not hostile to us, but neither are they friendly. They themselves say that they 'tolerate the Russians.'" Golovin characterized the Tlingit as savage, brave, accustomed to enduring pain and privation, cunning, and unscrupulous. To them, stealing from strangers is virtuous; they have a passion for haggling, are excellent shots, love drinking, and carry on interclan feuds for generations.

[Veniaminov ([1840] 1984:427–38) had a good deal to say about the character and abilities of the Tlingit, based on his observations of them at Sitka and Wrangell. He also knew the Aleut well, and was acquainted with Eskimo from Bering Sea, the Koniag, and Indians from California, with all of whom he compared the Tlingit. He was so much impressed with the latter that he believed that they "could be, and probably in time will be, the dominant people of all the North Americans, from Bering Sea to the California Sound and perhaps even beyond" (p. 427). Although the Tlingit lacked some good qualities of the Aleuts, they excelled them in enterprise, acumen, and trading. Veniaminov predicted that with education the Tlingit would surpass all their neighbors. He stressed their intelligence, shown by the perfection of their crafts, their ability to think, and the accomplishments of the few Tlingit children who had been to school. Their enterprise and ability in trade was illustrated by this example:

> For instance, one of the children of a chief (Toen), having begun to trade with (a capital of) only several sea otters, in the course of three or four years acquired eight slaves, an excellent canoe, a wife, several guns and a multitude of items—in short, he became a rich man. [Footnote: Recently, having come to know Russians better and having learned the Russian language, he, on his own wish, was christened. He came to Sitkha especially for this purpose.—Translator] [p. 429]

**Editor's note:* This section has been transferred from the original "Chapter IV. The Tlingit People." I have added quotations and data from V. M. Golovnin, von Kotzebue, P. N. Golovin, Veniaminov, Boursin, Khlebnikov, and Lütké. The last four paragraphs are taken from the original "Chapter V. Domestic Life." Fort Selkirk was stripped clean, not destroyed, but this ended it.

[The men were active and indefatigable in matters of importance to them, but almost never helped with domestic tasks, deemed appropriate only to women and slaves. The Tlingit women were diligent in home tasks and in small-scale trading, decent and even loving to their mates and children. They learned the Russian language more quickly than the Aleuts, and some became skilled in Russian dressmaking. The Tlingit showed far more foresight than the Aleuts in putting up winter supplies, and were thrifty, calculating, and acquisitive of wealth, storing their expensive things in imported Canton chests. They had physical endurance to withstand whippings and immersion in cold water (part of the training of boys and men), but lacked patience in suffering an injury or insult, and displayed a passion for vengeance. They were reputed to be "beastly and bloodthirsty," because custom demanded blood for blood, and the killing of slaves at funerals and memorial potlatches was "for love of their kin" (p. 432). Although boasting of their bravery in war, and "audacious to the point of insolence" in dealing with a weak-appearing Russian, they could be put to flight by one who fearlessly stood his ground. What might appear to be vanity was not. Rather, the Tlingit had a sense of their own dignity, which they showed through endurance of bodily suffering, brave posturing, and independence. They felt infinitely superior to the Aleuts whom they considered to be cowards and almost slaves to the Russians. So wrote Veniaminov.

[Boursin (1893:54) gave a very unflattering account of the Tlingit, with which Emmons would not have agreed:

> The strongest trait in the character of the Thlingit is imitativeness, and it is chiefly this faculty which has enabled him to quickly adopt the easily acquired and plainly apparent features of civilization. A willingness to work and handiness with tools, shrewd bargain driving, and quick observation complete the list of his good qualities.
>
> Their faults are many and glaring. They are born liars and grossly immoral; drunkenness is the rule and not the exception, and all these vices have been strengthened, not checked, by contact with civilization. I have never known a Thlingit to act as if he possessed a conscience or to exhibit the least sign of gratitude. Theft is natural, but this propensity has been considerably modified by fear of the law. Gambling is usual among men, and both sexes of all ages use tobacco.
>
> Nearly all of their barbarous customs are less strictly observed than formerly, and some have been abandoned . . . but in the most remote villages a considerable number retain the primitive beliefs. Their belief in witchcraft and shamanism, with their attendant superstitions, is also dying out, although much more slowly.]

The Tlingit has little fear of death, either from disease or in warfare. This disregard is best illustrated in the readiness with which anyone would offer his life in payment for a family [clan] debt and, unarmed, calmly walk to his execution and die without a murmur. When discovered, the Tlingit were constantly at war with their neighbors and each other, and for protection in the villages the different families [clans, or lineages] surrounded their houses with stockades or built them as forts.

They have always been an active, industrious, accumulative people. Climatic conditions induced activity, and their system of the potlatch necessitated saving. They were illiberal, selfish, and avaricious. Every act required a return. The great potlatch, for which they saved during a lifetime, [the accumulated property] to be distributed in a day, was not prompted by generous motives. It was the event of their lives, religious in the sense that the dead were honored, [and an occasion for] a glorification of family and individual prestige, [for] a discharge of obligations, and [for establishing] a credit for the future. No smallest article was given away without a purpose. I believe that this system of saving for the potlatch, in which they constantly denied themselves, was responsible for such unfortunate traits of character. For in my many years of intimate relations with them as an alien, I made many friends among them and experienced much kindness at their hands which I prefer to feel was not wholly prompted by selfishness.

While the early explorers speak of a tendency to pilfer, yet with their neighbors and among themselves the Tlingit were strictly honest, and the property of a guest was inviolable. This I can state from my own experience through many years among all of the tribes. Traveling alone, with considerable money, food, and personal belongings, none of which was ever under lock, and living in the communal houses with many people, I never lost the smallest article. [See corroboration by explorers at Yakutat (de Laguna 1972:192–93).] Again, on a man-of-war we had some thirty natives for several years and never throughout their enlistment was there a single instance of theft. [Emmons refers here to the USS *Adams,* on which he served from June 15, 1882, to August 1884, when he was transferred to the USS *Pinta,* also based at Sitka, serving on the latter until August 28, 1896, except for extended periods of leave.] In summer, when the village was deserted for fishing camps, the houses with all of their property intact were left unlocked with perfect impunity. I have seen several hundred dollars worth of blankets, clothing, and goods, covered by a canoe sail and left for days at a time, in perfect security, though in the open near a well-traveled trail. Wood may be cut and corded, or a deer might be hung in a tree, and no one would disturb them. But all this has changed since the settlement of the country by the whites, who have cheated them in trade, pillaged their caches, and generally demoralized them.

Though dignified, reticent, and suspicious with strangers, their relations with each other are marked by good nature and sociability. The relations between husband and wife are characterized by constancy and affection, and suffer only when clan differences occur [i.e., quarrels between their respective clans], which, if bitter and resulting in unsettled feuds, may cause permanent separation. This was the case of Chartrich [anglicized as Shotridge, Łša·dux̣íčx̣], the old chief of the *Kargwantan* [Ka·gʷa·nta·n, Wolf 1] of Chilkat, whose wife, a Stikine, *Khar-tu-kwan-snee* [probably from qa·-tu-ka·náx̣-š-tu·s-ni·, Raven 17] was sent back to her people and never returned [because of such a quarrel between their clans]. The affection for children is very marked and is returned by them as long as they remain in the household; but after marriage, clan duties, different associations and surroundings so separate them from their early life that they seem to become indifferent to their parents. This indifference is more noticeable in the treatment of those who have outlived their usefulness, and, while they are provided for, they occupy the poorest places in the house and have little or no voice in family affairs, unless in the case of someone of the highest class who is still accorded honor upon ceremonial occasions.

The Tlingit is exceedingly sensitive to slights or ridicule. Pride, vanity, and jealousy are the causes of quarrels, wars, and feuds that in the past kept the whole country in a turmoil. In quarrels, they seldom resort to personal force, unless under the influence of liquor, when they would not strike, but grapple and bite, but under great provocation they did not hesitate to kill. This was a last resort that entailed trouble for the whole body [of kin groups], for there could be nothing personal between individuals of different clans, and a death had to be paid for [by the clan of the slayer to that of the victim] even if it [the blood debt] went on for generations. Friendly relations could never be restored until due compensation was made, and the value of a life was reckoned according to the social standing of the person [slain or injured].

Their system of destroying their own property to shame the aggressor served as a restraining influence and made for self-control. In this act they not only regained prestige, but made it necessary for the aggressor to destroy a much greater amount, or else to make amends by means of a feast and compensation. [Examples of this "peculiar system" will be found in Chapter 2, the section "Law."]

No diplomat was ever more jealous of precedence at ceremonials than a Tlingit of high caste, and this was not wholly personal, for in public the individual was merged in the family [clan], and it was at feasts that most feuds originated through jealousy or want of tact.

Some of the early explorers credit [accuse] the Tlingit with brutality and cruelty. But while warfare was carried on by raids, ambuscades, and treachery, common to all primitive people, yet, aside from the sacrifice of slaves, I do not believe that they were temperamentally cruel. [Emmons may have been thinking of a passage by Lisiansky, based on notes made at Sitka in August 1805, describing the attack of the Tlingit on the Russian post. This is quoted in Chapter 12, the section on "Aboriginal Warfare."

[Khlebnikov described the aftermath of the Tlingit storming of the Russian fort in June 1802, when some of the Russians attempted to hide in the woods (Khlebnikov [1833] 1861b:47–49, Petroff translation):

> But the Koloshi, full of rage, ran after them with hideous cries, thrust their lances through them and dragged them about for a long time to increase their suffering, and then they slowly cut off the heads of the half-dead men with threats and abuse. . . . [Eglevsky and Kotchessof] severely wounded and half dead, were seized and carried off to the village of the Koloshi. . . . They were mutilated and suffered cruel tortures. The barbarians, not at once, but slowly cut off their noses, ears, and other parts of the body, struck their mouths and maliciously smiled at the sufferings of their victims. [One of the men, a Creole,] could not long withstand the tortures and was relieved soon by death, but the unfortunate Eglevsky existed under terrible suffering for over twenty-four hours.

[Lütké (1835:201, 217, 219), however, commented on the kindness and consideration shown by the Tlingit to members of their own family: children, the aged, orphans, which he had observed at Sitka in 1826, and added that slaves were treated almost like the children of the house, although they still sometimes would sacrifice slaves at potlatches, even though the Kolosh maintained that they had abandoned slave sacrifice at the funerals of great chiefs.]

In general relations with each other, the Tlingit were kindly and courteous, and dignified with strangers. Mentally they are alert, imaginative, artistic, musical, and possessed of great technical and artistic skill in weaving and carving.

Old Hutsnuwu man in front of stockaded "Fort House," Angoon, 1889. (Photograph by G. T. Emmons? AMNH.)

Judging from their legends and their practices, as a primitive people, they must have been fairly moral [in sexual matters]. But with the advent of the whites, they did not hesitate to go and live with them, which really differed little from their own system of marriage as long as such relations continued. In time, however, this led to more or less prostitution.

The character of the Tlingit is the natural result of their communal life [in the large lineage houses] where many families were in such intimate contact that self-control in daily intercourse became a necessity for the peace of the household, and consequently moderation and quiet prevailed. Each family lived independently with a general regard for others. When working, the Tlingit talked sparingly, whether engaged in household duties or when hunting, fishing, or traveling in the open. Few unnecessary words were spoken. I have traveled day after day in canoes when absolute silence prevailed, except to answer a question that might be asked. But when the day's work was over, around the fire in the house or camp, conversation became general and the mutes of the day indulged in stories of the occurrences of the day, particularly any humorous incidents that may have been observed. It was at such times that the children were taught the old legends and trained in the family [clan] songs.

In the presence of strangers, speech was restrained, which may be attributed to a natural suspicion common to all primitive people, as well as to the feeling that a loose tongue indicated want of character. In this connection, I remember the case of *Wawa,* "Talking Back" [a Chinook jargon word], of the Chilkat, who naturally should have succeeded to the chieftainship of his clan, but who was passed over because of his loquacity. But let his vanity be hurt, and the Tlingit loses all sense of control and breaks forth in impassioned speech. This occurs more with women than with men, for when greatly incensed they will go out of the house and on the common roadway shout their feelings to the whole community.

Public speaking was an art greatly appreciated and was a feature of all feasts. It required not only eloquence, but extreme tact, for at this time the people were keyed up to the highest pitch of excitement. The slightest indiscrete reference or word might recall old injuries, feuds, and jealousies, and so precipitate bloodshed.

I often found that when talking for any length of time the Tlingit became really tired, and, even though being paid for the information, would refuse to talk further. The fatigue was physical, not mental, for they were interested in the subject.

HEALTH AND DISEASE*

Before the advent of the whites, the Tlingit led a perfectly natural life in a moderate climate with an abundance of nourishing food and were a strong healthy race. [According to] family traditions they were fairly prolific, but through exposure and ignorance, infant mortality was excessive, and this continued until medical assistance reached them. [It is still much higher than that of white Alaskans (1980).]

Eruptive diseases were unknown among them and when introduced proved very fatal. Smallpox, the scourge of native peoples, was brought by the Spaniards about 1775.

[Emmons here referred to Captain Portlock (1789:271–72, 276), who, in 1787, at Portlock Harbor on the west coast of Chichagof Island in Sitka territory, saw an old man and a girl of fourteen, both marked with smallpox. The man indicated that he had lost ten children to the disease, and had ten strokes tattooed on his arm, presumably in their memory. No children under ten or twelve were pockmarked, so Portlock concluded that this disease had been brought about 1775 or 1777, probably by the Spaniards who were on the coast in 1775. A number of Indians visiting the ship were marked, as were many people on Sitka Sound.]

In 1835–38, smallpox decimated the whole Northwest Coast, depopulating whole villages, at the sites of which the rotted timbers of the houses may still be seen [1900?] Again in 1862 it appeared with extreme virulence.

Syphilis was brought by the early Russians and traders, and ran its course, weakening the constitution and rendering the people easy subjects to tuberculosis. This too must have been brought to them [by Europeans], and was fostered by modernized conditions of life when they exchanged fur for cotton clothing, oil and grease for flour, and the continuous out-of-doors life for the small house, unventilated and heated by stoves, and, still more fatal, the immoderate use of liquor, which was considered a necessary and legitimate article of trade until it became a menace to the trader himself. [In 1842 Russian and Hudson's Bay Company officials agreed to attempt to prohibit the sale of liquor to the Tlingit.] At least twenty-five percent of every village community today [1900?] is tubercular to some degree. [Modern methods of diagnosis and especially the immunization against tuberculosis, introduced by the Public Health Service in 1950, have greatly cut these figures, and the Tlingit population is now increasing (1980).]

Diabetes is of common occurrence, probably from the effect of climate. Rheumatism from exposure, though general, is seldom seen in a severe form. Pneumonia must always have existed, but has been aggravated by predisposition to tuberculosis and by the confined [modern] house. Eye troubles were prevalent from smoke in the old houses, and most old people were so afflicted and partly blind. Indigestion was very common from gorging themselves with grease and oil during winter feasts when they led a physically inactive life.

[We can also mention measles, mumps, diphtheria, scarlet fever, and influenza among the diseases introduced by the white man, and these often assumed almost unrecognizable and fatal forms along Indians who had no immunity to them. As a rule, diseases which occur among us as relatively mild afflictions of childhood attack the Indians in epidemics which kill a large proportion of the adult population. The following incident was recounted in Emmons's notes in the British Columbia Provincial Archives (BCPA): "When the Hoonah *Tuck-tain-tons* [Ṫaqde·nta·n, Raven 16] came to Sitka, in January 1892, soon after their arrival the grippe reached Sitka, and their enemies, the *Cut-cow-ee* [X̣at̓kaʔa·yí, Raven 7], spread the report that they brought the disease to Sitka." Was this, perhaps, an accusation of witchcraft?

[Although Emmons wrote little about venereal disease, it was recognized by the Russians as a serious problem, even after they believed that smallpox had been conquered by vaccination. Thus Lieutenant P. N. Golovin ([1862] 1979:

**Editor's note:* This section was originally in "Chapter IV. The Tlingit People," then was transferred to this chapter. The sections on Surgery, Disease, Wounds, Treatment, which were then combined with it, I have shifted to form the bulk of the present Chapter 13: "Illness and Medicine." I added to this section the references to Portlock, and Golovin on venereal disease and the Russian attempts to control it, and incorporated into the text some notes by Emmons in BCPA.

63–64) reported about it at some length in his review of Russian America in 1860. At that time, syphilis was almost gone from the Aleuts, but was very common at Novo-Arkhangelsk, where the Russians became infected by the local Kolosh, who had acquired it from the other Tlingit who carried on the forbidden trade with foreign ships.

> The Kolosh are not concerned about this disease; they consider it an unavoidable evil, and take no measures to treat it. Almost all the women who are engaged in clandestine debauchery in the area around New Arkhangel are afflicted with this disease. At one time syphilis was so widespread among the workers and soldiers in New Arkhangel that when the present Chief Manager arrived in the colonies he had to resort to forceful measures in an attempt to wipe it out. [p. 64]

[He had all the huts near the port where prostitution was carried on torn down, and built a special brothel close to Swan Lake (near Sitka), and posted a sentry there. From time to time he had the Kolosh women who came there rounded up and taken to the hospital for examination. The diseased were kept there for treatment. This confinement was so irksome that the women would run away after two or three days.

> Consequently the Chief Manager has announced that any woman who runs away from the infirmary will have half of her head shaved, which the Kolosh consider very humiliating. At first this measure aroused dissatisfaction among the Kolosh, but when they finally became convinced that the Chief Manager would carry through this threat, and when they finally realized the benefits of medication, they capitulated; now, not only do they not run away from the infirmary, they come voluntarily to request medical treatment.
>
> Some of the laborers and soldiers, who are afraid of becoming infected buy women slaves from the toions [chiefs], [and] keep them at their own expense [in spite of the priests]. It is quite expensive to support a Kolosh woman; it costs from 25 to 30 paper rubles a month, which not everyone can afford. As a result, most of the laborers and soldiers look for easier alliances, and there is no possible way one can watch over them. [These men did not mind the disease; and some even contracted it on purpose to get out of work, until the Chief Manager ordered that all pay and allowances should be docked for all being treated for venereal disease, while they were in the hospital. This cut down on the avowed cases considerably.] [p. 64]

[Tlingit beliefs and practices concerning illness and cure are found in the first sections of Chapter 13.]

POPULATION*

Although Emmons occasionally made references to the numbers of Tlingit at particular places, especially in describing the villages in his unfinished manuscript, *History of Tlingit Clans and Tribes,* he nowhere included specific census figures. Tables 4 through 8 represent the estimates of the Tlingit population made in 1835 by Veniaminov, in 1839 by Sir James Douglas (for that part leased by the Hudson's Bay Company), in 1861 by Lieutenant Verman of the Russian Navy, and in 1880 and 1890 by the U.S. Bureau of the Census. They are included in the belief that this is what Emmons wished. The totals have been recalculated to include only the known Tlingit among the "Kolosh," excluding the Kaigani Haida. The Tlingit tribes and their names are listed as given in Table 3. Where Tlingit settlements are listed as clan villages or as chief's villages, an attempt has been made to identify the clans represented according to the listings in Tables 9 and 10.

---

*_Editor's note:_ This section is mine. Emmons had evidently planned a similar section to run at the end of his "Chapter II. The Tlingit," for a note specifies that the text is "incomplete—see also census and other notes in original." I have not found this "original."

CHAPTER 2

Social Organization

INTRODUCTION

The Tlingit are geographically divided into seventeen tribes. [Emmons usually lists only sixteen, omitting the Klawak, which he seems to have recognized as a separate tribe rather late in his writing.] Socially, they are separated into two exogamous parties, matriarchal in descent [matrilineal], which might be termed phratries [matri-moieties]. These consist of an indeterminate number of consanguineal families or clans [matri-sibs], made up of households [matrilineages, or house lines].

[In addition to the two major phratries or moieties, there was also the clan of "Eagle People" among the Sanya (Tribe II, Table 3). This was a clan that belonged to neither the Wolf side nor the Raven side, but could marry into either.]

Two classes were recognized: an aristocracy at the head of which were the chiefs, and the [common] people. Slaves were property without standing [in Tlingit society]. Shamans and witches were individuals [and did not form organizations or special classes]. There were no secret societies and no special class of warriors.

[It could probably be argued now that the Tlingit recognized rank but not class, since the "commoners" were the putative junior relatives of the chiefs, so in theory there could not have been sharp class lines between the lowliest bastard or good-for-nothing and the leading chief or "great man" (łingít ƛe·n) of the most wealthy and prestigious clan in the region; yet the distinction between the nobles and the commoners was clear. (See also Olson 1967:47.)

[As to the secret societies, Emmons may be technically in error, since Swanton (1908:436) reported: "Secret society dances were imported from the south, as the name łuqᴀna´, evidently from Kwakiutl Lū´koala, testifies, but their observance had by no means reached the importance attained among the Kwakiutl and Tsimshian."

[Although there was one man at Sitka (in the 1870s and later) who imitated the Kwakiutl dog-eaters and taught special dances to his Kiksʔádi clanmates, even the more elaborate performances among the Southern Tlingit (Tongass, Sanya, Stikine tribes) were treated like clan prerogatives, to be staged in connection with potlatches and requiring the assistance of certain guests "in the know" who were specially paid for their services (Swanton 1908:436; Olson 1967:98–100, 118–21). Emmons himself (see Chapter 10, "Afterlife, Spirits, Souls, Reincarnation") described what must have been such a performance involving Land Otter Men impersonation, given at a potlatch in Sitka in 1887, but he did not realize the nature of the show, a yé·k ṡa·tí or "master of spirit" performance.]

TLINGIT TRIBES

When the United States purchased Alaska from Russia in 1867 the Tlingit occupied the narrow coastal strip and the outlying islands from Dixon Entrance [almost] to the Copper River, except for the southern portion of Prince of Wales Island that had been taken from them by the Haida. They comprised sixteen or seventeen tribal divisions as enumerated from the south northward, in Table 11.

That the Tlingit regarded the tribal groups as geographical or territorial divisions is indicated by the compound word *-kwan*, *-qwan*, or *-qoan* [qʷá·n], as variously given by different writers, which followed the specific group's name, and this, as will be seen later, corresponds to that of the country inhabited, and had been given as descriptive of some prominent feature, natural condition, or tribal characteristic. The word for tribe or people is *na* [na·].

[Emmons was mistaken in trying to derive the word *kwan*, or qʷá·n, from "man," *ka* or qá·, and "country or village," *an*

Editor's note: The original Chapter 2 was titled "The Tlingit," or "The Tlingit People," but Miss Weitzner persuaded Emmons to shift the introductory section "The Tlingit" and the next, "Name," to Chapter 1, whereupon this chapter was given its present designation. Emmons intended it to include the following sections: "Phratry, Crest (Crest-kinds, Display of Crest, Crest animals), Painting of face (see accompanying book of sketches), Names (personal), House names, Household, Social Classes, Chief succession, Chief authorities, Councils, Slaves, Laws (N.B.—incomplete see also census and other notes in original), Clans listed: Raven Clans, Wolf clans, Tlingit Tribes," and then apparently he planned to introduce the whole manuscript of *The History of Tlingit Clans and Tribes*. Emmons had no section on kinship, so this I have written, adding to it the scattered remarks on kin relations originally in "Chapter V. Domestic Life." From the latter, I also introduced the section he called "Trading." See Table 31.

or ʔa·n. Qʷá·n, "tribe," means "inhabitants of," a contraction of -qu-há·n, "to dwell." Note that -qwá·ni or -qu-há·ni refers to indwelling souls or spirits, so that while Sitka-qʷá·n would mean "Sitka tribe," Sitka-qwá·ni would mean the "spirits of Sitka." Emmons here was misled by Eugene S. Willard, the missionary at Haines in the early 1880s.]

The tribe consists of one or more clans of each of the two phratries which have come together accidentally through migration or through continued intermarriage, and have combined for mutual protection and for social and economic advantages, and supplement each other upon all family and ceremonial occasions. Each clan remains an independent body under its own chief, and acknowledges no central governing body or tribal authority beyond that which may be voluntarily given under abnormal circumstances. In the case of an attack by a foreign people all might combine under an elected leader, the clan chiefs forming his council. The same clan might be a member of several tribes, so it can be seen that this made it practically impossible for [whole] tribes to war with each other, although clan disputes and feuds were of constant occurrence.

Each tribe has one or more permanent winter villages and well defined territorial limits. The open waterways and certain less productive hunting and fishing grounds, together with sufficient area around the village for the gathering of daily foods and wood, are free to all. But the country as a whole is divided among the clans, and subdivided by each clan among the house groups and families [lineages]. Salmon streams, hunting and berrying grounds are inalienable family [clan] possessions. Travelers through another [clan's] territory could kill for food, but not for pelt or profit. Otherwise, the rights of territory were duly respected and strictly enforced. This was clearly illustrated when the first salmon canneries were established here, as payment was [had to be] made to the separate families [clans] owning the streams, for the privilege of fishing thereabouts.

[Since territories were owned by clans (or lineages), and the same clan might have branches in neighboring tribes, exact tribal boundaries are often difficult to draw (see de Laguna 1960:67–68, with respect to Sitka and Hutsnuwu [Angoon] territories in Peril Strait). Territories were, furthermore, alienable, through sale or surrender after warfare (Swanton 1909:356; Garfield 1947:441; de Laguna 1960: 133–34; de Laguna 1972: 232–33, 252.) Territorial rights usually included even fresh drinking water and firewood (see Olson 1967:55, 70; Oberg 1973:106–7; de Laguna 1983:79–80.)]

Today the old barriers of prejudice and superstition upon which native law and territorial rights were based are fast breaking down, as the people with no legally organized land title, and harassed by governmental laws restricting their hunting and fishing and lumbering activities, are compelled to desert their own homes and seek industrial centers in order to gain a living, and in the course of a generation or so tribal limits will be but a memory.

PHRATRY OR MOIETY

The social organization of the Tlingit is matriarchal, based on the existence of two parties or phratries, [each] made up of an indeterminate number of independent consanguineal clans or totemic families, any member of which can marry in any clan of the opposite phratry, but never in his or her own. These phratral divisions have neither head nor authority [i.e., lack political organization and a moiety chief]. They are primarily marriage groups. The relationship that exists between the different families [clans and lineages] in a phratry is wholly imaginary, regardless of the beginning [i.e., of how they may actually have originated].

The phratral crests are the Raven and the Wolf. Every member [of the Tlingit nation] is born with the absolute right to one or the other. Some writers have claimed that the Eagle takes the place of the Wolf, but this is a mistake. [Swanton (1908:398) said that while one phratry was known as Raven through all the tribes, "the other was usually called Wolf and in the north also Eagle." The name Eagle is now (1980) often heard at Sitka and Juneau.] Each phratry has many minor crests and sometimes one of these is highly honored by a family [clan], but either the Raven or the Wolf alone belongs to one or the other of the phratries. The Eagle would seem to be a most honored crest of later days, but it is the right of only certain families. In the principal Wolf families the chief's house at *Kook nu-ou* [Kax̌nu·wú, "Female Grouse Fort"] of the Hoonah was named Wolf House; the chief's house in Sitka was likewise so named, with the front painted in the Wolf figure, while a minor chief's house was painted in the Eagle design. At Chilkat [Klukwan] the principal houses were named for the Wolf or Brown Bear. I believe that the Eagle crest came through intermarriage with the Haida and Tsimshian.

[Although it is not mentioned in this section, Emmons was fully aware of a third group among the Sanya (Tribe II), the *Na-ah-de,* "people of *Na-ah,*" or *Na-ut-de,* supposedly contracted from *Na-ah ut de,* a name derived from their ancient home in Naha Bay, on the west arm of Behm Canal. These people, the Ne·x̣ˀádi (Swanton's NēxAʹdî, "people of Nēx"), were like a third phratry, although their small numbers and restriction to one Tlingit tribe gave them the status of a clan. They intermarried with both Raven and Wolf moieties, and had the Eagle as a crest and Eagle personal names. This group is discussed below.]

The Raven phratry generally, but particularly in the north, is known as *Klaye-de-na* [Ła·y(a)ne·dí], or *Thlar-a-dee-nar,* "one party." This phratry claims precedence from their mythical connection with Raven, the Creator.

[In a notebook (BCPA) Emmons wrote: "Thlar-ho-na tee meaning of? a cultus [secret?] term means place from which water comes (privates)." The feminine form, Ła·yi-ša·, was explained at Yakutat as "sitting down (Raven) ladies," evidently meaning "urinating Raven women" (see de Laguna 1972:450); but Swanton (1908:407) was told that there was no one name for all the Ravens.]

The Wolf phratry seems to be more divided, and is known under several names referring to different living places: such as *Shen-ku-ka-de,* "coming from *Shenk*" [Šankukʷe·dí, "beings of Shenk"], referring to a living place on a small island off the west coast of Prince of Wales Island; or *Hook-nu-ka-de* [Xúkʷnu·wkʷe·dí], "coming from or living at *Hook-nu-wu,*" referring to "Dry Fort" [Xúkʷ Nu·wú], reported on Dundas Bay, Cross Sound; and *Seet-ka-de* [Ṡitqʷe·dí], "belonging to *Seet,*" which is a more general name and is said to have been given to those who survived the Flood and settled at a small stream on the mainland, called *Seet* [a glacial stream near Sumdum is called Ṡi·ṫ-qu]. [These designations would appear to be clan names that have been applied to the whole moiety; at least, that is true of the first word and the third, Wolf 8 and 24, see Tables 9 and 10.]

[There seems to be no word for moiety, corresponding to qʷá·n for "tribe."]

People referred to their own phratry as *Haye-ka-naye,* "our side man party" [probably ha·yi kana·yí], and to members of the opposite phratry as *Gonet-ka-naye,* "different man party" [gune·tkana·yí; omit "man" from the translations].

On meeting a stranger, one would ask, "*Da su see tee?*" or "What are you?" [da·t na· sá waˀé?, "What clan are you?"; or da·t na·x̣ sá ˀisiti·?]. And he would answer "*Yehlh hut*" [Yé·ł x̣át], "Raven I," or "*Goutch hut*" [G̣u·č x̣át], "Wolf I."

The origin of the phratries is lost in the maze of tradition and is accounted for only in the childlike myths that surround the Creation, and tell of the wanderings of *Yehlh* [Yé·ł], the Raven Creator, in his efforts to wrest from the supernatural beings the elements that would make the world habitable for man, and his transformations into and relations with animals that were alternately human or animal in form under different conditions. All such as Raven addressed as "*Cho-ka,*" "my fellow men," were of his, the Raven phratry, while those whom he called "*Cho,*" or "*Ka-nee,*" "brothers-in-law," or "*Art,*" "aunt on the father's side," were established in the opposite moiety for all time.

[Emmons may here have transposed the meanings for "Cho-ka" and "Cho," for Jeff Leer informs me that ča· means "fellow clansmen," and ča·qá· means "affinal relatives." Olson (1967:14) gives the terms *tcakaʹh* as a greeting between men of "the same" moiety, and *tcagwaʹtsguh,* "opposite small" (i.e., ča· gatsgux), between men of opposite moieties. Ka·ni is "sibling-in-law of same sex as speaker"; ˀa·t is "paternal aunt" extended to other women in the paternal line. See below.]

Thus the male and female Bears that Raven deceived [Swanton 1909:6–7; de Laguna 1972:868–69], *Kun-nook* [G̣anu·kʷ, "Petrel"; de Laguna 1972:857], and even the Killerwhale that Raven is supposed to have married [when Raven assumed the form of a woman (de Laguna 1972:873)], were all called by Raven by the kin terms appropriate to relatives in the opposite phratry.

[According to a Yakutat native, there was a myth that told how Raven, having made women for men to marry, then tried to create a "brotherhood" of all the creatures of the world, assigning major crest animals to one moiety or the other. But the Wolf was against him, and destroyed this harmonious scheme, so Raven doomed the latter to wander, howling for help. While a general patterning of crests, animals, birds, fish, other beings and entities, can be traced, which suggests that potentially everything in the universe might be assigned to the two moieties, in balanced pairs or groups, this has not been worked out into a completely coherent or comprehensive arrangement (de Laguna 1972:833–34; 1975:73). This is illustrated in the list of crests tentatively drawn up by Emmons: see Table 13.]

CLAN

As has been shown, the tribe is but an accidental geographical grouping of independent clans, without power or authority [of its own]. The phratry is an imaginary relationship from a distant past whose only function is [to regulate] marriage, but the clan is the active principle of life, the law, and the religion of the Tlingit. It takes precedence over every other organization. It is [felt as] a blood relationship through all ages that binds together all of its members in the closest union. Within it, all individualism is merged. The act of one is accepted by all, and each person is the defender of its honor, ready to sacrifice property and life in its cause, even though contrary to all personal interest. The membership of the body can never be in doubt [because it is established] through maternal descent, and no substitution is permitted [that is, clan membership cannot be changed]. While this system cuts sharply across [biological] family arrangements, arraying the children against the father, yet it binds its members so closely together that widely separated branches, in different tribes, that have no personal knowledge of one another, are considered as closely related as those who live together. I knew of an instance when the accidental killing of one of another clan called for an indemnity which was beyond the means of the immediate family [the local branch of the slayer's clan], so members of the clan who lived far distant in another tribe came to their assistance and discharged the indebtedness in full. [See the section "Law" below, this chapter.]

Each clan being an absolutely independent body is a unit in itself and regulates its own internal affairs. Its phratral connection simply relates to marriage. The important functions of the clan have altogether to do with its opposites [i.e., the gune·tkana·yí, the clan or clans in the opposite moiety with which it has affinal ties. Their members are, therefore, those called the "fathers," "paternal aunts," "siblings-in-law," and "sib-children" of the clan or clan member (or members) in question. In performing these functions, the closest biological relatives in the given category are involved.] All services are performed by them [i.e., by or for these "opposites"], such as house construction, raising of the carved poles, preparation for cremation, and complementary ceremonies, for which they are compensated and feasted. These close relations, formed through marriage and association, cut across the matriarchal system of descent and inheritance which divides the family and which cannot eliminate the parental [paternal] affection which is human. And so, when not in actual conflict with each other, a better feeling exists between opposites than between subdivisions of the same party that may never render any assistance to one another and whose relationship is so distant that it is imaginary. This is illustrated by the bitter feuds that exist or have lately existed between clans of the same phratry, with like crests, such as the *Kik-sat-de* [Kiksʔádi, Raven 10], and *Thluke-nuh-ut-di* [Łukʷnax̣ʔádi, Raven 16] of Sitka; the *Con-nuh-ut-di* [Ǫa·nax̣ʔádi, Raven 1] and the *Thlu-qwoir-ut-di* [Łukʷa·x̣ʔádi, Raven 17] of Chilkat; and the *Da-she-tan* [De·šî·ta·n, Raven 13] and *An-kark-hit-tan* [ʔA·nx̣a·k hít-ta·n, Raven 14] of *Hootzahta* [Hutsnuwu, Tribe XII].

In attempting to explain the evolution of the clan system in its relation to the phratry, and selecting such incidents in its history as seem most dependable, it is suggested that originally there were but two divisions, phratries or clans, possibly two ethnic stocks, that met and married, and adopted the exogamic system with matriarchal descent.

[In one version of his argument, Emmons showed that he was aware of Boas's belief that "the older form of social organization of the Athapascan, Tsimshian, Haida, Tlingit, and perhaps also of the Bellabella, was based on a threefold division . . ." (Boas 1916:487), and that the data "are rather in favor of the assumption that the twofold division of the Haida and the apparently twofold division of the Tlingit are of recent origin, and that in former times there were at least three well-defined exogamic groups among them" (Boas 1916:526). Emmons rejected this opinion, writing: "In the earliest days, if we accept [the thesis of] the two clan system, a natural clan relationship existed. . . ." In his final version of the argument, he does not even question this assumption. I have also argued that dual organization is ancient among the western Na-Déné, and that the Tlingit Ne·x̣ʔádi of Sanya, traditionally cited as evidence of a third Tlingit phratry, represents only an imperfectly assimilated foreign group, like the "middle" clans so common among the Alaskan Athabaskans (de Laguna 1975:133–34), in effect, supporting Emmons's position.]

In the beginning, the two phratral divisions were practically clans in their relations to each other. In time, with increasing numbers and dissensions, bodies separated and sought new homes, and their relations to the parent phratry became more distant as the independent clans came into existence. This disintegration, as well as the addition of foreign elements, increased the number of clans and resulted not only in the settlement of southeastern Alaska by the Tlingit, but in the transformation of the phratries into exogamous marriage bodies, with no further functions.

A clan thus had its origin when it separated from the main body on its northward or seaward migration [north from the Tsimshian coast, or west from the interior]. And with this severance of tribal [geographical] ties, it proclaimed its complete independence by taking a name [or receiving one]. In most instances this referred to the place where the independent group was first supposed to have settled [or camped]. That the clan names were derived from those of localities is shown by the possessive suffix *dee, ee, tee, de, di,* from *otde, ut-tee, ut-de,* "belonging to," that

Emmons's sketch map of Wrangell, showing the location of clan houses. (AMNH.)

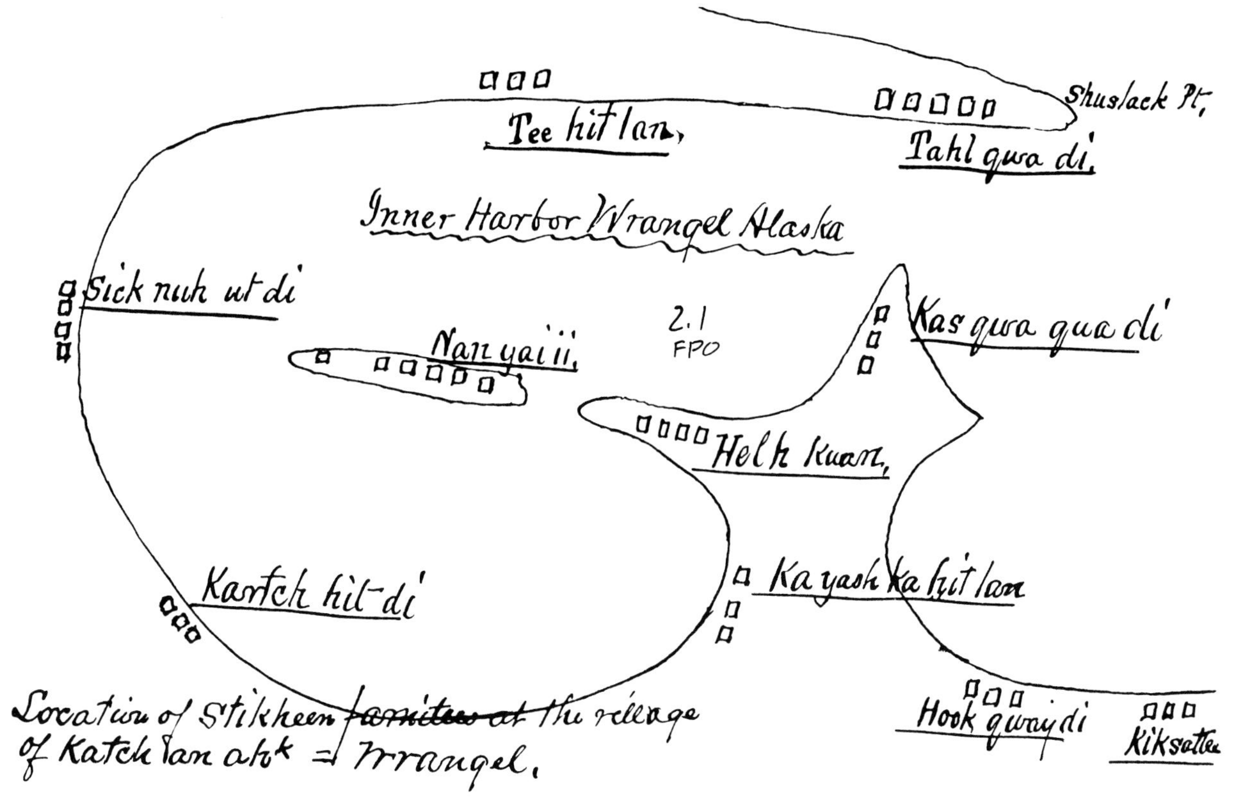

follows the distinctive name of forty-three of the divisions (see Tables 9 and 10). [Actually the forms -ʔádi, -e·dí mean "beings of," or "people of," while -a·yí means "the ones (who . . .)", but the reference is always to a place.]

In the case of eighteen clans, the word *tan, ton* [ta·n], "company or family," ends the clan name, but it is always preceded by *hit* [hít], "house," indicating that it was originally a house group. [The ending, hít-ta·n, is often contracted in speaking; see Raven 14 and Wolf 1. Emmons originally tried (erroneously) to derive *tan* from ʔa·n, "land, country, town."]

Three of the clans are unquestionably of foreign origin since their names end with the tribal designation *kwan* [q^wá·n]. This can be explained by the fact that they lived separately at first and, being strangers, considered themselves, or were considered, as tribes. Later, when they entered the corporate body of a neighboring [Tlingit] tribe, they took their places as clans, although they retained their tribal designation. [See Raven 19, Wolf 10, and Wolf 31. Note that the last, the "Foam Tribe," appears in the census of 1839, Table 5, as the independent "Ahialt" of Port Stewart, Behm Canal, not yet having joined the Stikine.]

One clan, *Tuck-es-te-na* [Dagisdina·, Wolf 7], has the termination *-na,* "people or nation," although they were simply a band, closely related to others, having the same status as other clans among the Chilkat-Chilkoot. [The term, na·, although usually translated by the Tlingit as "tribe, people, nation," really means "clan, sib" when applied to themselves. It probably implies the type of internal unity or "patriotism" which the Tlingit associate with their own clans.]

An indefinite idea seems to have pervaded the minds of the older generation of Tlingit that they were preceded in Alaska by an earlier race, yet if there ever were such previous inhabitants of southeastern Alaska, these people have long since been driven out, exterminated or absorbed by the Tlingit clans, which, as independent wandering bands, met, combined and settled to form the Tlingit tribes. These clans came from two distinct localities. The older, more extensive and important migration was from Prince of Wales Island and the adjacent mainland shores as far south

Members of the Na·nya·ʔa·yí *(Wolf 18) clan in ceremonial costume, in front of Ground Shark House, Wrangell, 1895. (Photographer unknown. AMNH.)*

as the Skeena River, and at different periods moved northward through the inland channels and along the outer coast to the Copper River delta, where their progress was arrested by the Russian invasion. All of the clans of the two southernmost tribes [Tongass and Sanya], save the one mentioned as standing outside of the phratries [the Eagles, *Na-ut-de, Na-ah-tee,* or *Na-hut-tee,* or Ne·x̣ʔádi], are found among the northern people, and constitute the most prominent divisions that form the aristocracy of the Tlingit. This is accentuated in the case of some clans that, though few in numbers and very poor, are accorded that consideration and respect that speaks of a recognized past.

[According to Swanton (1908:409), the NēxA´dî Eagles of the Sanya are believed to have come from "below Port Simpson." They are named for Nēx, a stream in their country. Swanton suggested that they may once have been Athabaskans from Naha Bay in Behm Canal, whose relatives are now at Kincolith among the Niska Tsimshian of the Nass River. Olson (1967:24) believed them to have been most certainly Tsimshian in origin, as Emmons argued in most versions of his manuscript. According to Boas (1916:483, 522), the NexA´dî correspond to the Gun-hū´°t division of the Tsimshian Eagles, a group of "runaways," or Tlingit from Alaska.]

The other and later migration was from the interior, down the Stickheen [Stikine] and Taku rivers and across the mountains to the coast. This movement was very circumscribed in its distribution, being limited almost entirely to the littoral on either side of and between the two rivers. The coastal prejudice against the interior tribes has always militated against these later arrivals, and only in one or two cases, where they have acquired wealth and have intermarried with the older clans, have they attained a higher position, and even then they are referred to as "half *Gu-na-na* (strangers)." [Ģunana· is a term applied especially to the interior peoples, even to the Inland Tlingit who live like the Athabaskans (McClellan 1953:48).] In the beginning, this feeling was unquestionably more political and selfish than racial or personal, and was motivated by the desire to exclude the interior peoples from the coast and from the fur trade, the monopoly of which was so profitable to the Tlingit. With greater opportunity and association with other nations, the coast tribes increased in wealth and intelligence, while they kept their neighbors dependent and primitive, and so their feeling of superiority increased.

HOUSE AND HOUSEHOLD

The clan is made up of households, consisting of closely related families living together under one roof, numbering sometimes over fifty and presided over by a house chief [hít s̓̇a·tí, "master of the house"] whose position and authority within the body was relatively the same as that of the chief toward the clan.

[Emmons here is using "household" in two senses. First, as the "house" (hít), which, in Tlingit thought, is the matrilineage (hít-ta·n) as well as the building it occupies. This group of consanguineal relatives may grow so large that a new building may have to be built to accommodate their resident members; but the "house" endures, until, perhaps, the new "daughter houses" become lineages in their own right, and the parent "house" becomes a clan. For Emmons, "household" also means the persons who actually reside in a lineage-owned house, a group that includes the married-in wives and children of the male "owners," but excludes their sisters—lineage members who live in the houses of their fathers or of their husbands.]

The men of the house constitute the governing power, and, together with unmarried female relatives, were of the same lineage and clan, but the wives and their children were necessarily opposites. In case of war with their clan, the wives and children would be compelled to leave the house and return to their own people. [It is clear from instances cited by Emmons that the women of the lineage, though married into other houses in the opposite moiety, had a good deal to say about the affairs of their "own house."]

The clan houses were grouped about that of the chief and were sometimes enclosed within a stockade. Each household had its own salmon streams, or fishing and hunting grounds, and berrying grounds. [The larger territorial rights seem to have been owned by the clan, while specific fishing places were owned by houses (de Laguna 1983:79; Oberg 1973:106–7).]

Each [biological] family within the household was a self-supporting unit in the economy of ordinary life, while the younger single men were expected to contribute to the support of the house chief. [The latter was usually their "maternal uncle."] At feasts and ceremonial occasions all would assist the household and the clan. [Even the women of the lineage who had married into other households in the village would assist their own lineage chief; all the men and women of the clan would assist their clan chief in preparation for a potlatch. And the married-in wives also made important but informal contributions to their husbands' feasts.]

While the house chief was accorded much respect and represented the communal body at all [public] functions, his authority was very limited. His power depended more upon his personality and strength of character than on his own [official] position.

[We should also remember that slaves, although legally chattels, were members of wealthy Tlingit households.]

KINSHIP*

[Although Emmons did not write a specific section on kinship, he occasionally used Tlingit kin terms in his manuscripts; it therefore seems necessary to include this section to make the chapter more complete. Further information on Tlingit kinship terms and usages may be found in Swanton (1908:424–25); Durlach (1928:17–67); de Laguna (1952; 1972: 475–96); McClellan (1954; 1975, 2:418–38), Olson (1967, esp. pp. 11–17, 19–23); Oberg (1973, esp. pp. 23–38). The Tlingit system is that called "Crow," or "avuncu-Crow" (Murdock 1949:245–48).

[Kin terms are employed in reference, and in direct address except where avoidance rules forbid intercourse between respect relatives. Although two given individuals may be related to each other in a number of ways, the kin terms implying the closest consanguineal relationship should be employed, unless the speaker wishes to establish a greater "social distance." A number of affinal kin terms listed in Table 12 are therefore used only in reference. While the basic terms seem relatively simple, in use they may be widely extended to cover all the clan-mates of the person to whom the term most closely applies. All parallel cousins are, of course, classed as siblings. In formal oratory, groups of relatives, designated by collective plurals, are customarily addressed, and some terms are perhaps never encountered except on such ceremonial occasions.

[All Tlingit kin terms (except for a few vocative forms) are used with possessive prefixes, like ʔax̣ "my," du "his/hers," or qa· "someone's." I have omitted them in the following discussion.

[The term "grandparent" (łí·łk̓ʷ) included one's actual grandparents on both sides, and their siblings. Of these, the

**Editor's note:* Because Emmons did not cover this important topic, I have supplied all of this section, with the exception of the four paragraphs near the end.

Chilkat woman and child, Klukwan, 1900. (Photograph by Winter and Pond? AMNH.)

most important were the father's father and the mother's mother's brother, the latter being the senior male relative in one's own clan. Because of preferred marriages, the paternal grandfather was often the same individual as the mother's mother's brother, or was a member of the same lineage and clan. The term "grandparent" was extended to all consanguineal relatives in the second and third ascending generations, and by courtesy to any old person. The reciprocal term "grandchild" (dačx̣ank̓) implied great affection and intimacy. On ceremonial occasions, members of the mother's father's clan (in the opposite moiety) were collectively addressed as "grandparents" (ha ƚí·ƚk̓ʷ-hás, "our grandparents"); so were the members of the father's father's clan (if different from one's own, though in the same moiety). At a potlatch, any "grandparent" of the same moiety, but in a different clan, might confer an honorable name on a "grandchild," lending his or her clan crest for the occasion.

[The term "father" (ʔí·š) might be extended in collective form to address all members of the father's clan, although the more common usage was "father's brother" (sáni). This term included the paternal male parallel cousins, sons of the paternal aunts, any clansman of the father, and the stepfather. A "father's brother" was a woman's potential spouse or sweetheart, and was a boy's confidant.

[The term "mother" (ƛá·) included the mother's co-wife. The "mother's sister" or "little mother" (ƛá·k̓ʷ) included the mother's female parallel cousins, and her (one's own) fellow clanswomen of her generation. The term was also applied to a stepmother.

[The reciprocals of these terms, "son" (yí·t) and "daughter" (sí·), were used by both the father and his brother and by the mother and her sister, but had very different connotations. For a man, they were applied to his child, his stepchild, his brother's child, the child of a fellow clansman, and the child of his wife's fellow clanswoman. If she was not his own offspring, a man might marry a woman he called "daughter" (even a stepdaughter or brother's daughter), for she was in the opposite moiety. For a woman, these terms were applied to her child, her stepchild, the child of a co-wife, her sister's child, the child of her fellow clanswoman, and the child of her husband's fellow clansman—all children in her own moiety and usually in her own clan. While the mother (or mother's sister, as co-wife or stepmother) took charge of her daughter's education and protected her from boys before marriage, the father and father's brother were not the disciplinarians of their sons and brother's sons. Children were very proud of their fathers and of his clan. As "clan-children" (na·-yátx̣i) they were joking relatives of each other.

[The term for "father's sister" (ʔa·t) included her daughter and daughter's daughter, the father's female parallel cousin, and in fact any of his fellow clanswomen. The reciprocal term "brother's child" (ká·ƚk̓ʷ) made no distinction as to sex. The paternal aunt performed practical and magico-religious rites at the life crises of her brother's children. She was the boy's sweetheart until he married, when she might become his wife, or his sister-in-law, or his mother-in-law to be respectfully avoided. She was her niece's confidante. She was the mother of other "father's sisters" and "father's brothers" (cross-cousins), and was often the wife of a "mother's brother."

[The term "mother's brother" (ká·k) included the male parallel cousins of the mother, and all one's older male fellow clansmen who were not "grandfathers" or "older brothers." In oratory, it referred to one's clan elders and ancestors. The mother's brother was the supreme authority over his "sister's children" (ké·ƚk̓), responsible for the discipline and education of his nephew, who usually came to live with him while still a small boy (eight to ten years old). His nephews had to work for him, though they might use his property, and have access to his wife. At his death, one of the maternal nephews was usually his heir, inheriting his wife, property, and title. If the nephew married his daughter, the mutual respect between maternal uncle and nephew was changed to avoidance.

[Sibling terms were extended to half brothers and half sisters, stepsiblings, parallel cousins regardless of clan, and even to clan- and moiety-mates. Co-wives called each other "sister." Girls cared for small siblings, and small boys and girls played together; but at puberty strict avoidance was enjoined between them, behavior that was also observed between grown members of the same moiety. Communication between grown brother and sister had to be via the spouse of one of them, in spite of the great affection felt for each other. A sister rendered services to her brother's wife and children, and brought gifts of food, to be reciprocated by handsome return presents from the brother to his sister and her husband, even including economic assistance at the latter's potlatches. Yet a brother had authority over his sister, and was especially responsible for her chastity.

[The reciprocal terms, "brother" (ˀí·k) and "sister" (ƛa·k̓), were probably used more often in reference than in address, because of the avoidance rules. There were also special terms by which a man distinguished his "older brother" (húnx̣ʷ) and a woman her "older sister" (šátx̣). Both sexes addressed their younger sibling of like sex by the same term (kí·k̓). It should be noted that sibling terms were extended to the children of one's father's clansmen, one's joking relatives if of like sex. A further extension was made in favor of children of men of a clan that was felt to be especially closely related to that of one's father; these linked "clan-children" were also each others' joking relatives. As the fathers were all moiety "brothers," so also the sons were joking "brothers" in the same moiety.

[The reciprocal terms, "husband" (x̣úx̣ʷ) and "wife" (šát), were sometimes extended by the woman to her husband's brother or fellow clansman, or to the husband of her own fellow clanswoman; and similarly, the man might extend the term "wife" to his wife's sister or clanswoman, or to the wives of his own fellow clansmen. Since these persons belonged to opposite moieties, considerable freedom in social intercourse between them was permitted.

[The "father-in-law" (wú·) and "mother-in-law" (ča·n) were the parents of one's spouse, or of anyone termed husband or wife. The man treated his father-in-law with great deference, even avoidance, and the latter might give instructions to his son-in-law via his daughter, also out of respect. The son-in-law and mother-in-law always avoided each other with the greatest care. Although of the same moiety, or even of the

Two old, aristocratic women, wearing labrets, with their cat, in Wrangell, ca. 1895. (Photograph by Winter and Pond. AMNH. Identified by Emmons as taken at Sitka, 1900.)

same clan and house, "fathers-in-law" and "daughters-in-law" (including the wives of the man's "clan-children") were on terms of great intimacy; they were joking relatives on ceremonial occasions, even though the man might be a reverend "mother's brother." The daughter-in-law treated her mother-in-law as she might a father's sister (which she often was), or like her own mother. Terms for "son-in-law" (sí·-x̣úx̣ʷ) and "daughter-in-law" (yí·t-šát) were purely descriptive, like those for sibling-in-law of opposite sex, and were used only in reference. In every case possible, a consanguineal term would be preferred.

[The "sibling-in-law" of same sex as speaker was ká·ni, a reciprocal term. For a man, it was applied to the husband of a sister, the husband of a sister's daughter, or the husband of any fellow clanswoman; it also included the brother of a wife, the brother of the wife's mother, and might be extended to any fellow clansman of the wife. For a woman, it included the wife of her brother, the wife of her mother's brother, or the wife of any fellow clansman; it also included the sister of her husband, the daughter of her husband's sister, and might be extended to any clanswoman of the husband.

[The levirate and sororate prolonged or renewed these alliances after the death of a spouse.

[The most important sibling-in-law was the person, man or woman, who might be chosen to represent his or her spouse's clan in dealings with his or her own clan. Thus the man who had married a high-ranking woman of a particular clan might be designated by her clan chief as the "clan-brother-in-law" (na·-ká·ni), to act as go-between in affairs involving the two clans. The same term would be applied to the chief's wife when she was serving in the same capacity. The na·-ká·ni should be of noble rank in order to function efficiently as master of ceremonies or peacemaker. Potlatch hosts would send their na·-ká·ni to invite and escort their guests, while each of the two rival groups of guests also had their own na·-ká·ni (members of the host's clan) to protect them.

[Spouses of siblings of the same sex were supposedly rivals but joking relatives (ʔa·ťašá·).

[A partner or relative in one's own clan (ʔi·n ʔa·) was someone close, upon whom one could rely. The term is descriptive, and appears especially in describing children whose fathers are of the same clan (ʔi·n (ʔa·) na·-ỵátx̣ʼi). The term "friend, relative" (x̣u·ní) seems to have been employed in address when one was not certain of the exact relationship. Other terms for clan-mates, moiety-brothers and -sisters, and so forth, are perhaps encountered only in oratory, where one also finds special honorific designations for ancestors and descendants, used in addressing whole clans.

[The trade partner (yaqá·wu) was a member (of another clan?) of the speaker's own moiety, with whom there was a formal relation of reciprocal hospitality and gift-exchange. This relationship has been advantageously employed in dealing with the Athabaskans, among whom the Tlingit established specific alliances between the head men of certain Athabaskan clans and villages and the chiefs of certain Tlingit clans and lineages. The term implies a "matching together."

[Preferred marriages were between a man and a woman he called "father's sister" (ʔa·t); that is, his wife might be an actual paternal aunt, or her parallel female cousin, or her daughter—indeed, any woman of his father's clan. Or he might marry his own brother's daughter, mother's brother's daughter, or the daughter of his wife by a previous marriage—all women he had previously called "daughter" (sí·). Every attempt was made, especially for aristocrats, to perpetuate marriage alliances between two lineages (or two clans), so that the spouses would be each other's "clan-children"; often the chiefs of the two house groups in question stood in the relationship of father and son to each other. In the ideal marriage, the father's sister's daughter was the same as the mother's brother's daughter. The preferred form of residence after marriage was avunculocal, which meant that the couple lived in the house of the groom's maternal uncle; if he were the bride's father, she did not have to move to another house. But even if a man married a woman whose father did not belong to his own lineage or clan, it was not uncommon for the husband and his bride to live for a time in the household of his father-in-law, working for him. In any given household, it should be pointed out, there were usually not only married-in wives from several clans in the same moiety, but the resident males, though not all of the same lineage and clan, were likely to be "children-of" two or perhaps more clans.

[When a married person died, the nearest relative of the deceased was supposed to take his or her place as spouse of the widowed. Suitable younger relatives might be designated in advance as "reserved husband" or "future wife" (du x̣úx̣ʷ-sakʷ, or du šát-sakʷ). Emmons noted that a widower could take an unmarried sister of his dead wife without making a further payment of bride-price. A man often took the widow of his deceased brother as an extra wife. If a young man had been chosen by his uncle to succeed him as house chief, he had to marry his uncle's widow, but he might speak for, or be assigned, a young girl who would be his wife when the old woman died, or when the girl came of age.

[In the old days, polygyny was not uncommon among the wealthy house heads, and even polyandry for aristocratic women was not unknown—"Princess Thom," Raven 17, of Sitka, had two brothers as husbands, for example. Although Captain Portlock (1789:290) was mistaken in believing polygamy was foreign to Tlingit custom, he probably gave a reasonably accurate impression of domestic relations among the Sitkans in 1787:

> POLYGAMY I think is not practiced here, as I never observed any one of them to have more than one woman whom he seemed to consider as his wife, to whom they pay very strict attention and treat with a great deal of affection and tenderness: you cannot affront them more than by attempting to make advances to their wives. They likewise are very fond of, and remarkably affectionate to, their children. The women are the keepers of their treasures or riches, which they generally have in a box or basket, and always take the lead in fashions, which they shew by the placing of their ornaments, or fixing such a curiosity to be the favourite of the day. It is not the custom with those people, as with the South Sea islanders, for the men and women to eat separately, nor are the women confined to eat meats of a particular description; but for men, women, and children, to sit down indiscriminately at their meals. . . .

[This section may be concluded by some observations made by Emmons:]

Relations between husband, wife, and children were most satisfactory, and while not marked by any demonstration of feeling, were consistently thoughtful and extremely affectionate, particularly in dealing with children. The latter in turn were patient, obedient, and helpful. Girls were brought up by their mother and in some cases by their maternal aunt. Boys ordinarily learned from their father. They remained in the household until they married, when they went to the house of their wife and worked for their father-in-law, unless they had a house of their own. Children learned through observation more than through any system of instruction. All persons married upon reaching maturity.

If the maternal nephew of a clan chief or subchief [house head] was in the direct line of succession, he left his father [as a small boy], and was trained by his mother's brother, and upon succeeding him, must marry the widow. A break in the family might result from war between the opposite clans, when the wife and children might be sent out of the house and back to her own people.

A Tlingit man or woman marrying a stranger, whether a Haida, Tsimshian, or interior native, would select or be taken in by one of the clans recognized as opposite to his [or her] own. And the stranger coming into the Tlingit takes his or her place in the totem recognized: [that is,] the neighboring people, Haida, Stick, [Athabaskan] and Tsimshian, are divided into clans, the Raven and the Wolf, similar to the Tlingit, and these are recognized by the Tlingit. The children take the clan of the mother, whether she is a Tlingit or a stranger, and are accorded the same rights as the others of that same division. The woman as a rule goes with the husband to his people, a Tlingit man bringing his Stick or Haida wife to his *kwan* [qʷá·n], and vice versa. In the case of Klanot [Łuná·ṫ, Raven 17], who married a Stick wife, the children were of the mother's totem. [Emmons reports elsewhere that he had three wives, two of whom were interior Athabaskans, mother and daughter. This was a common business arrangement, so the Tlingit traders could secure the best furs from their interior "brothers-in-law." The "wives" never came to the coast.] The Chilkats and Chilkoots, as well as the Takus and Stikines, marry quite frequently with the women of interior tribes, and again the Stikines, Henyas, Tongass, and Sanya intermarry with the Haidas and Tsimshians, and I have seen one instance in which a man of one of the tribes of eastern Oregon had married a Stikine woman. These intertribal marriages gave the husband the privileges of the wife's people and country, in trading, fishing, or hunting.

Dick [*Satan*?, or Se·tá·n?, Raven 6 of Sitka] said: "Children follow the mother's clan, and if she is a foreigner belong truly to her people or tribe. They are called 'half-breeds,' ***ar-shu*** 'half' [ˀa šu·wú, "part of it"], ***-Gun-nar-nar,*** 'Stick' [G̣unana·, "Athabaskan"], or ***-Da-kee-nar,*** 'Haida' [De·kina·, literally "people far out to sea"], if they live among the Tlingits, and have all the privileges of the opposite totem [from that] of the [Tlingit] father."

[It is traditionally reported that the Tsimshian (Coastal, Niska, and Gitksan) have a four-phratry rather than a dual system. These four are Wolf, Eagle, a third called Raven or Frog, and a group known variously as Killerwhale, Bear, and Fireweed. The Haida have two moieties, Raven and Eagle, subdivided into clans, as are the phratries of the Tsimshian. Each of these clans has its own crests, not necessarily ones that would be associated with their moiety according to the Tlingit pattern. But for purposes of intermarriage, the Tsimshian phratries and Haida moieties are equated with Tlingit moieties only on the basis of their clan crests:

Tsimshian	*Haida*	*Tlingit*
Wolf and Bear	Raven	Wolf (or Eagle)
Raven and Eagle	Eagle (or Gɪtɪ´ns)	Raven

See Boas (1916:519–22); and de Laguna (1975). The present four-phratry system of the Tsimshian is apparently a modern development, for at an earlier period only two intermarrying "phratries" would have been found in any Tsimshian town. Among the Coast Tsimshian these pairs were: Killerwhale and Raven, Killerwhale and Eagle, or Wolf and Raven; but never Killerwhale and Wolf or Raven and Eagle. In other words, the moieties were Killerwhale and Wolf on one side and Raven and Eagle on the other. Among the Gitksan, there was the same dual arrangement in the village, but the pairings were different, since at Kitwanga Eagle and Wolf "form a single Crest," and both married Frog, while at Kispiox Fireweed and Wolf were in the same moiety and both married Frog. As Dunn (1984:36–38) has explained (p. 38): "All four submoiety totems are present in Port Simpson and in Metlakatla because these post-contact villages are amalgamations of people from many older villages. . . . It is evidently in these later towns that the quadripartite exogamy developed."]

CRESTS

The crest is the distinctive feature of the life of the Northwest Coast of America. It is the basic principle of the

Brown Bear [hu·c] *screen in front of Ground Shark House, Wrangell. (Photographer unknown. AMNH.)*

well-established code of laws that governs the relations of people with one another and regulates their social functions.

[The crest is usually the symbolic representation of some species of living creature, or entity, which we may call the totem. This emblem or crest (ʔat ʔú·wu) almost always designates a kin group. Crest symbolism pertains not simply to art (though it is best displayed in carved and painted forms, ku·tí·ya̤·), or to religion, but serves primarily to mobilize and channel sentiments and behavior involved in interpersonal relations.]

Tlingit crests may be classified as belonging to the phratry, the clan [and also to the lineage or house], or to the individual, but under certain conditions all may become the property of the clan. The phratral crests, the Raven and the Wolf, may be considered as basic, since they stem from the dual grouping of the Tlingit, and are the inalienable birthright of every member of the phratry. They cannot be exchanged, renounced, or taken away.

[McClellan (1954:84–85) and Oberg (1973:43–48) have pointed out that the two moiety crests are not on an equal footing, since there is no one mythical Wolf like the mythical Raven; not all clans of the Wolf moiety use the Wolf as their main crest; or they may base their claims to the Wolf on different origin stories, or stress the importance of the crest to different degrees. But the Raven clans all derive their Raven crest from the Raven Creator-Transformer, and esteem it more uniformly.]

The crest is coexistent with the spirit which, upon reincarnation, would return to one born in the clan within the phratry. [While familiar with Tlingit notions of reincarnation within the maternal line, we have never encountered any idea linking reincarnation to the crest, or with ravens or wolves, and do not know how to interpret this statement. Perhaps Emmons means that the dual organization and its symbolism are conceived by the Tlingit to be as old and as enduring as humanity, and that all the Tlingit alive today are the reincarnations of the first Tlingit.] But as the phratry is an imaginary body [abstract entity], under which are grouped a number of independent clans that acknowledge neither head nor [central] authority, it is impractical to represent the phratry as such. The crest, though acknowledged, is not really exhibited unless it has been assumed by a clan [in some special way, over and above, or] independent of its phratral significance.

A clan may claim any number of crests in proportion to its recognized position. Although several may be highly esteemed, one is given first place. Older Tlingit say that originally each clan had but one crest and only in time was this number increased. This statement would offer evidence for an original two-clan system of the Tlingit that later, through separation and addition, resulted in many subdivisions, each of which retained the crest belonging to one of the two original clans. In most instances, the [moiety] crest is honored above the others. Although all clans in the phratry share in the common phratral crest, each claims it in a particular way, since each cites its own story or local tradition of origin. When one clan, however, is simply an offshoot of another, it shares with the parent body the common crest and the same origin legend. [Even in such cases there is a tendency for the new group to develop a special version or even a new story to justify its particular claims, and the crest may be depicted in a particular way.] Other crests, of which each clan may possess several, are attributed to supernormal encounters of human beings with supernatural beings or animals. These are often contests or sexual associations with an animal, but with an animal of an older type [than any found today] that possessed the power of transformation or of appearing in human form. [It may be significant that in the stories about what seems to be fairly recently acquired crests the animal or bird does not assume human form, although it may speak or sing or behave in some other way like a human person.] All such events are supposed to have occurred after the clan [or lineage] was formed, and the resultant crests originated in a later period than did the phratry.

A few crests are local in character and are not used beyond tribal limits.

[It is not clear whether Emmons means that the crests are local because they belong to clans that are restricted to only one tribe, or because they refer to some locality: mountain, rock, stream, etc., which has been claimed as a crest. Just as clans themselves tend to be named for places featured in clan histories, so there is a strong tendency to localize all the events of mythology, even though peoples living in different parts of the country may set the same event in totally different spots. Landmarks easily become clan symbols.]

Individual crests are those given [to a "grandchild"] at feasts by the maternal great-grandfather [mother's father's father] or the paternal grandfather, both being of the same phratry as the recipient although in a different clan, or clans, and thus possessing different crests. In the course of successive generations, these crests would [could?] become more widely disseminated and would take their place as additional emblems of other clans. [There is some question as to exactly what could be transferred by a "grandparent" to a "grandchild" under such conditions, and to what extent this was a temporary honor for the occasion, might be limited to the lifetime of the recipient, or might be an outright gift. (Cf. Swanton 1908:423.)]

No transfer of crests outside the phratry was permitted, although for the nonpayment of a debt, the crest of another clan, either of the same or the opposite moiety, could be assumed [by the creditors] and publicly displayed to shame the debtors.

[McClellan (1954:88) has suggested that crests may originally have been bestowed on a clan by its "opposites," perhaps in the form of the manufactured object which portrayed it, especially since such physical representations of the crest must be made by the "opposites" and have no value unless the latter are compensated as makers and witnesses at the potlatches in which these objects are displayed. Crest emblems may also be captured in war, and McClellan (1954:92) has commented on the war symbolism in Tlingit ceremonialism. Any heirloom (ł-s̓a·ti ʔát, "ownerless thing"), even though it does not carry the representation of the crest, may, through display at potlatches, become valuable and function as a crest object. (See Oberg 1973:44–45; de Laguna 1972:450–61).]

Animal crests prevail almost to the exclusion of others and hold the first place, although no difference in value exists between crests of mammal, bird, and fish. A few, miscellaneous in character, include planetary bodies, mythical beings, and natural objects, all of which are [believed] endowed with spirit life, but these are of secondary importance. The relative value of crests depends upon the prominence given them by the more important clans. While this may have varied at different periods, the Raven, Frog, Whale, Beaver and [different species of] Salmon on the one side, and the Wolf, Brown Bear, Killerwhale, and Eagle on the other, are now the most esteemed.

[Emmons attempted to make lists of the crests belonging to the two moieties (see Table 13) but neglected to indicate to which particular clans each crest belonged. Perhaps this would have been impossible, for claims have evidently changed over the years. For example, the crest of one clan might be appropriated by a stronger rival, and, in theory at least, a new crest might even now be obtained and validated. Not only does a single clan possess several crests, but a single crest may be claimed by several clans in the same moiety. In some cases these claims are respected by both parties; in others they are violently disputed. Some crests, like the Beaver, and the Golden Eagle or Fish Hawk (Kiǯu·k / Giǯu·k), are claimed by certain Wolf clans at Yakutat, but belong to

Raven clans in southeastern Alaska. But this has caused no difficulties, probably because the owners do not meet on ceremonial occasions. Table 13, by Emmons, may be compared with that assembled by de Laguna (1975:70–72), to show the tendency to assign, to one moiety or the other, almost all classes of living creatures, celestial and cosmic phenomena, heroes, spirits and supernatural beings, landmarks, and other natural or artificial features.]

There is no idea of actual descent from the crest animal [totem]. The several supposed instances when sexual intercourse took place between human beings and animals are considered to have been merely individual unions, with no bearing on the origin of the clan as such, since all such occurrences are represented as having taken place after the formation of the clan [although such stories are usually cited to justify the clan's claim to the crest]. Often the adoption of the crest was brought about by some assistance rendered [to?] or some expression of friendship on the part of the crest object. [Emmons mentions contests between human beings and animals as justifying crest claims. In other cases, an extraordinary animal may simply have been found or killed; or, a man may have rendered assistance to an animal, in return for which he was given a song, and thereby the right to represent the animal as a crest.] In commemoration of [such an event], the crest was displayed and honored to the mutual advantage of both parties. While not considered an object of religious veneration, yet it [crest, totem] was appealed to in time of need. [Emmons may here be referring to funeral oratory in which the crest may be likened to a "fort" or "refuge," to protect and comfort the bereaved (see McClellan 1954:89; Kan 1983; de Laguna 1983:75–77; Swanton 1909:374–89). Or Emmons may refer to the kinship terms employed in addressing bears, wolves, or killerwhales, begging them not to harm people. Here the totem animal is treated as if it were a member of the clan that claims it as a crest (see de Laguna 1972:824–33).]

One of the oldest myths accounting for the origin of clan emblems goes back to that period when the earth was in darkness and all of the people and animals lived together in human form as separate families [clans] in one village. The sudden release of the sun [daylight] by Raven so frightened them that they scattered in all directions. Those fleeing to the woods, water, and air became the animals, fish, and birds, while those remaining retained their human personality, but took as their crests the changed forms of their former relatives. [While this familiar story of the Theft of Daylight is often told to explain the origin of the various species of animals (see Swanton 1909:5, 83), it is unusual to find it used as an explanation for the clan crests.]

What the attitude of the individual was to the crest animal in the earliest days is a matter of conjecture, but if we accept [the theory of the antiquity of] the dual clan [moiety] system, it is probable that the Raven and the Wolf were held in such high respect that they were never molested. Indeed this feeling still [1900?] prevails regarding the raven, which is an object of superstition, but this may be accounted for by the assumption of bird form by the Creator, *Yehlh* [Yé·ł, "Raven"]. The Tlingit idea of nature is very different from ours. He credits all species and natural objects as possessing a spirit and [interprets] phenomena as the manifestation of spiritual life in the elements, and these spirits may be propitiated by certain speeches, conventional observances, or gifts. But even when animal forms were taken as the crest, these ideas did not interfere with killing the animals for food or useful purposes, since the salmon, halibut, and hair seal form the principal food products, while the bear, land otter, and beaver are the most valued pelts. [Neither the hair seal nor the land otter was common or important as a crest animal.] It would seem that the crest animals and the actual animals are alike only in form, but are both associated with an indefinite being that existed in the far distant past.

DISPLAY OF THE CREST

The display of the crest in the form of carving, painting, or weaving in naturalistic or conventional designs was an end to which Tlingit artistic efforts were directed. The totemic crest was shown on the house front, the heraldic and mortuary columns [totem poles and grave posts], the interior house decorations [posts and rear screen], the war canoe, the warrior's dress and weapons, ceremonial costumes and personal ornaments, articles for feasts and household use [dishes, spoons, pipes, and so forth], and even on the most common tools. The most valuable and significant crest objects, however, were the carved wooden hat or the highly ornamented hat of finely woven spruce root. Such hats, *sach* [ṡ̓á·xʷ], were shown only upon occasions of the greatest importance, when the clan was represented as a whole and large amounts of property were distributed. Or, the hat was placed beside the dead chief as he lay in state. A clan might own one or several such hats, representing only the principal crests, and each time they were exhibited their value would be increased by the amount of property given away. [A distribution of property to invited "opposites" was necessary to validate the owners' claims to the crests displayed.] The wealth was contributed by the whole clan, so, although the hats themselves descended from the clan chief to his successor, the chief was only the custodian, and the hats were actually the property of all the clan.

Similar hats were possessed by the heads of households [lineages], and were used upon like occasions to represent these lesser bodies, but they did not have the same significance [importance] as the clan hats.

Almost as important as a clan emblem, although more a personal possession, was the war knife which was a part of the equipment of every man. On these, the handle or the upper blade often represented the crest. The war knives owned by the chiefs were very elaborate and were greatly esteemed as family [clan or lineage] possessions.

[For other physical embodiments of the crest, see sections on houses in Chapter 3, canoes in Chapter 4, Chapter 9 ("Dress and Decoration"), Chapter 11 ("Ceremonies"), and the sections on totem poles, painting, and art in Chapter 7. Crests were also represented in immaterial form, especially in clan mourning songs or in the cries uttered by warriors facing death. These subjects are not treated by Emmons, but see de Laguna (1972:451–58).]

PAINTING OF THE FACE

Although the styles of face painting varied according to the occasion, for ceremonies it was customary for such paintings to symbolize or represent the clan crest. In former days, the face of the corpse was painted with special designs of this type. The Raven clans used the design known as "Raven's Nose" almost exclusively, but among the Wolf clans there was not as much uniformity of pattern. Thus, while clans of the Wolf moiety generally used the figure, "Wolf's Ears," several clans preferred the "Bear's Den" or a Killerwhale design. [For more on facial painting and tattooing in crest designs, see Chapter 9 ("Dress and Decoration").]

NAMES

Personal names are the property of the clan, and generally refer directly or indirectly to the crest. While the same crest may belong to several clans, the personal names are different, and indicate not only the clan but the social position of the individual.

[The same personal names, even ones referring to the crest, may, in fact, be found among different clans in the same moiety, but are interpreted by the Tlingit as proof of a common origin; persons with the same name, "namesakes," consider themselves as bound by closer ties than even those between siblings, and each acquires as his or her own all the other's close relatives. (See de Laguna 1972:781–90.)]

When children are born and named, the father may afterwards be known as the "father of So-and-so," as in Jack's case, "*Donawalk-ish*" [Dá·na·wa·q-ʔí·š].

[The teknonymous name could also be applied to the mother, as for example, Dá·na·wa·q-ƛá·. Nicknames based on this model were given to men and women, derived from what they liked most: nuk^{w}šiyá·n-ʔí·š, "father of minks," for a trader, carrying a derogatory connotation, and dú·š-ƛá·, "mother of pussy cat," for a woman with a pet cat.]

Other personal names may be given upon a particular occasion, [an honorable name by a "grandparent" to a "grandchild" at a potlatch, if both belonged to the same moiety], or to mark some incident [as the peace name given by the captors to their peace-hostage in the peace ceremony, a name which referred to some possession of the captors], but, under such conditions where ancestral names are continually used, it will be seen that their number is very restricted and that they are jealously guarded.

It was the custom in the past to designate the larger communal houses by names, the most honored of which referred to the clan crest, or to some incident in the legendary history of the family. [Lineage houses might have names of the same kind, but of lesser importance. See Table 14 for the lineage house names recorded by Emmons.] These names were symbolized by the painted house front, or by the decorative interior features. Other names of lesser importance, referring to the position of the house, its ornamentation, material, or form of construction were often common to both phratries.

[Emmons offered a list of house names according to moiety. Since it could not be verified from any of his notes, and seemed, in part, to have been copied from Swanton (1908:400–407), Table 14 has been substituted, since it was compiled from the names actually recorded by Emmons at the native villages described in his unpublished manuscript, *The History of Tlingit Clans and Tribes*.]

A house was named at its dedication potlatch [see Chapter 11, the section "House Building Ceremonies"]. Such naming was not permitted to all, especially not to the smaller and poorer kin groups. The privilege of naming a house was not a right inherent in a household [lineage], however

Ceremonial face painting designs of the Tlingit clans, shown on pages 36 and 37, are used on most solemn occasions: when facing death in war, after death, or sometimes at potlatches. G. T. Emmons copied these designs from his field notebooks (in AMNH and BCPA) onto what he intended to be one long chart, with Raven moiety designs above and Wolf and Eagle designs below. The faces are outlined in India ink, the designs in black or in red ink according to the colors of the paint used, and the dark areas filled in with pencil. Emmons entitles the whole: "After each character of design is added 'Ou-she-nai' simply meaning paint," [ʔawsiná·(?), *"dampened"*]. *Instead of repeating the clan names in the legends, the clan numbers used in Tables 9, 10, and 11 are used. (Sketches by G. T. Emmons, AMNH.)*

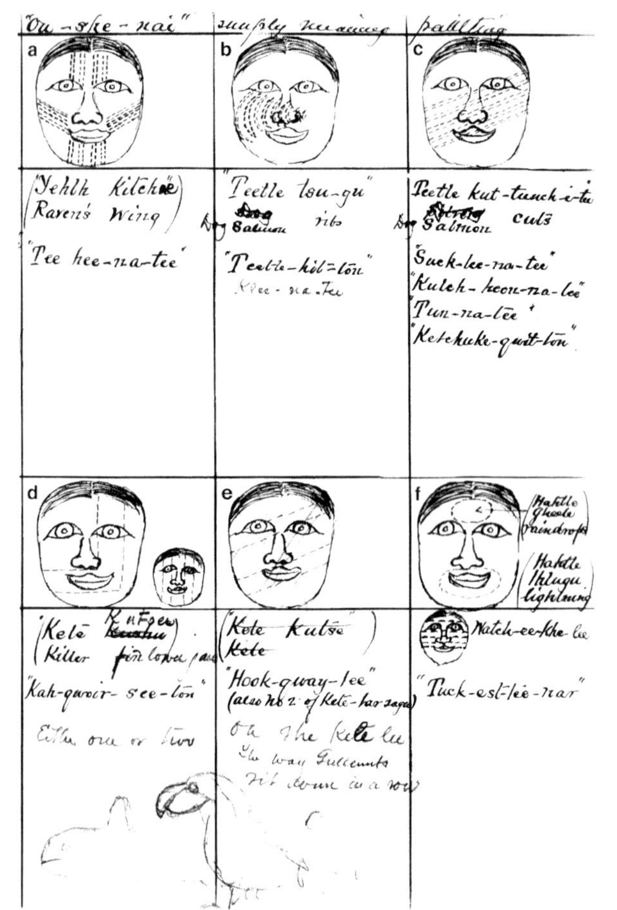

Top. (*a*) *Raven's Nose,* Yehlh lhlu-u [yé·ł ɬu·wú]. *Raven 1, 3, 11, 13, 15, 16, 17, 19, 28, 33.* (*b*) *Water Fall Down Raven,* Heen ho-kah-tsee-ge-tee Yehlh [hí·n x̣u-kʷá·-wʒigi·di yé·ł]. *Raven 6, 7, 8.* (*c*) *Halibut,* Chartle woo [čá·ł-wú (?), *"halibut white"*]. *Raven 32, 28.* [*Emmons adds in pencil: "Ka gha (face) ou-she-na (paint)"*; qa· yá, *"someone's face,"* ʔawsiná(?), *"dampened"*].

Bottom. (*d*) *Wolf's Ears,* Goutch kugu [gu·č gúgu]. *Wolf 1, 4, 5, 6, 8, 15, 16, 17, 18, 20.* (*e*) *Eagle's Nest,* Chark quaddy [čǎ·k kúdi]. *Eagle clan of the Sanya.* (*f*) *Killerwhale's Breath [spout],* Kete tar-sa-qu [kí·t dasé·kʷ]. *Three designs are given, but "1" is crossed out and corrected in Fig. 10d as "2." Wolf 8, 22, 27, and 28.*

Top. (*a*) *Raven's Wing,* Yehlh kitchee [yé·ł kíǯi]. *Raven 12.* (*b*) *Dog Salmon Ribs,* Teetle tsu-gu [tí·ł ṡu·gú]. *Raven 15, 24.* (*c*) *Dog Salmon Cuts,* Teetle kut-tuuch-e-tee [tí·ł ka(ł)dú·č̓ ʔi·tí(?), *"remnants of cut chunks of dog salmon"?*]. *Raven 9, 25, 26, 27.*

Bottom. (*d*) *Killerwhale's Lower Jaw,* Kete kutsee [kí·t x̣aš-yi·, *"jaw under"*], *corrected from Killerwhale's Dorsal Fin,* Kete kushu [kí·t gu·ší]. [*The larger face, "2," is the corrected design of Killerwhale's Breath in Fig. 9f.*] *Wolf 14.* [*Emmons has added "Either one or two."*] (*e*) *Both the design and the title,* Kete kutsee, *"Killerwhale's lower jaw," are crossed out in pencil, but the name of Wolf 26 is left. This clan uses "also No. 2 of* Kete tar-sa-qu*" [Killerwhale's Breath, Fig. 9f].* [*Below in pencil Emmons has sketched a killerwhale with tail fin and two birds, and writes:* "Ou she kete lu," *referring to the Killerwhale's Nose,* kí·t-ɬú *or* kí·t ɬu·wú?, *and "The way Guillemots sit down in a row," although the birds resemble puffins*]. (*f*) *Raindrops,* Hathle gheete [xé·ƛ x̣i·t *or* xé·ƛ gi·t, *"thunder sprinkle" or "downpour"?*], *and Lightning,* Xahtle lhlugu [xé·ł ƛugu]. *Wolf 7. The small face below is "Watch-ee-khe-lee."*

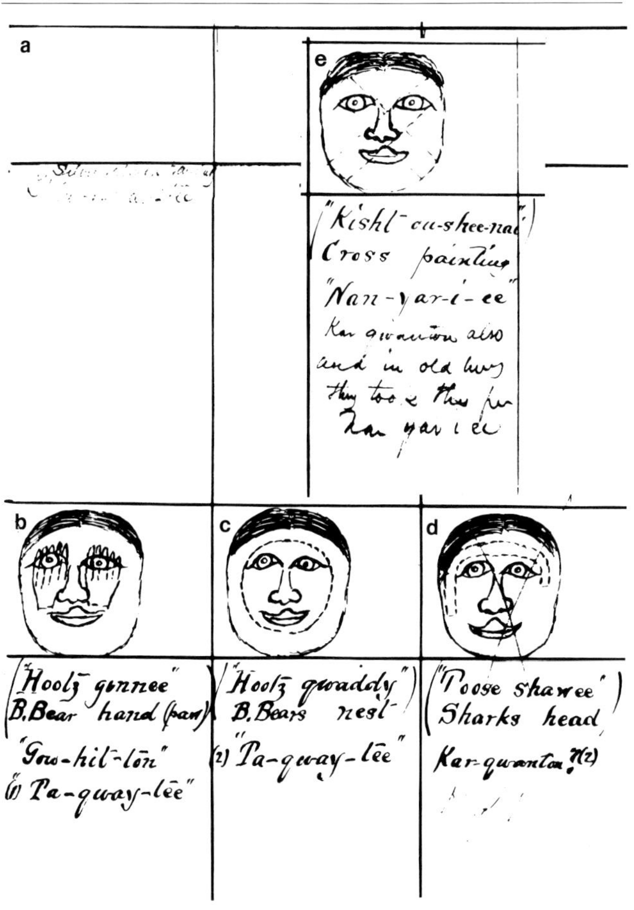

Top. *(a) Design not attempted, probably because the clan, actually Wolf 30 of Yakutat, Emmons had here erroneously identified as a Raven clan.*

Bottom. *(b) Bear's Hand (paw),* Hootz ginnee [x̣ú·č ǯíni]. *Wolf 29, 32. (c) Bear's Nest,* Hootz qwaddy [x̣úč kúdi]. *Wolf 32. (d) Shark's Head,* Toose shawee [tú·s̓ ša·yí *(the design is crossed out in pencil, but Emmons has written "Right" below the entry)*]. *Wolf 1. (e) (Originally on the lower row, to the right of d, but placed here to save space.) Cross Painting,* Kisht ou-she-nai [kané·st, *"cross," from Russian* krest *(?),* ʔawsiná·, *"dampened"*]. *"*Kar-qwanton *[Wolf 1] also, and in old times they took this from* Nan-yar-i-ei *[Wolf 18]."*

large the house or expensive the potlatch. It was a concession made by the clan. Since the most prominent characteristics of the Tlingit are pride, vanity, and a dread of criticism, the failure of others to sanction this act would place the house group in such a humiliating position that the stigma would forever attach to the house name. For example, when a house of the *Kar-qwan-tan* [Ka·gʷa·nta·n, Wolf 1] of Chilkat was built at *Indarstahka* [Yandestake, or Ỵánde·s̓taqyé, a Chilkoot village], Chartrich [Shotridge, or Łša·dux̣íčx̣], the head chief of the clan living at Klukwan, was requested to sanction the naming by being present. All succeeding houses built upon the same site took the original name without ceremony. After the disappearance of a house, the ground could never be appropriated by anyone, even a member of the same clan, as long as a single descendant of the house remained alive.

[I believe, however, that any rebuilding of a named house involved a potlatch, like the original dedication, and that wealthy chiefs rebuilt or repaired their houses to make suitable occasions for potlatching, thus raising their own status.]

SOCIAL CLASSES

The Tlingit among all the clans are divided into two social classes. The first is an hereditary aristocracy: *An-yut-di,* "land children" [ʔa·nỵádi, "children of the town or land," or ʔa·nqá·wu, "man of the town, noble, rich man"], or *Ga,* "noble or good"; [ga is an adverb meaning "all right, acceptable"]. The second is comprised of the people in general: *Eshon-yut-di,* "poor children" [ʔiˀša·n yadí], or *Chuh-ku-gha-yee,* "just anything" [čakugʷé·yi, "any old thing or person"].

The aristocracy consists of the subchiefs [hít s̓a·tí] and their families [i.e., the house or lineage chiefs and their immediate biological relatives]. But standing almost in a class by themselves are the principal clan chief [łingít ƛé·n, "big man," or na· šá·de háni, "clan head"] and his family. Succession to this chieftainship is hereditary within his lineage. Through generations of authority, greater wealth, and a strict observance of established etiquette, these aristocrats have become distinguished by their dignity, intelligence, and address. Their social position is inherited but must be maintained by the giving of elaborate feasts, distributions of property, and by marriage only with their equals. Thus in 1885, when *Anna hootz* [ʔAnaxú·c, "-?-brown bear"], the chief of the Sitka *Karqwantan* [Ka·gʷ-a·nta·n, Wolf 1], contracted what was considered to be a mesalliance with a woman of the lower class, the two chiefs,

Chilkat aristocrats, Klukwan, 1900. (Photograph by Winter and Pond? BCPA.) Ykeeshar [Wux̣í-šá?], *"Wish Head," and his wife with the* Ka·gʷa·nta·n, *Wolf 1, family heirlooms. The man holds the Killerwhale Hat (a wooden helmet), his wife the Murrelet Hat (also wooden). Behind them are two Chilkat blankets with crest designs and the Bear Hat (wooden, with seven woven cylinders).*

Katlean and *Satan,* of the opposite phratry [Katlian or Q̓áƛya·n of Raven 10, and *Satin* or Se·tá·n of Raven 6], who were invited to attend him as the marriage was in the Russian church, refused, saying that "No good could come of mating a chief with a clam digger."

The second social class, constituting the majority of the people, might really be subdivided into a middle and a lower class. From time to time, men of exceptional personality, through prowess in war, the accumulation of means, the giving of feasts, and marrying with those above them in social rank, might compel or be accorded such recognition as would advance them socially. Once they had been accepted into the aristocracy, their position and that of their descendants was fixed forever, although for generations such humble origins would be remembered, and the women might be reminded of it in their quarrels. Those who through want of ambition, misfortune, or extreme poverty became dependent upon others really constituted the lowest class.

The greatest difference between the two main classes was manifest in the value placed upon the lives of their members when compensation was exacted for a killing or an injury, or on ceremonial occasions when precedence, honor, and gifts were given according to rank. At such times the aristocrat or chief might be counted as worth two or more persons of the lower class.

CHIEFS

Each clan recognized a head chief, hereditary in the principal family [lineage], but elected or approved in council by all the adult males of the clan. In every clan there might be one or more subchiefs who were the heads of other important households [lineages]. All the other house heads were similarly selected, and had the same authority and duties relative to their households, as the head chief had to the clan. [Conversely, the clan chief was the house chief of his own lineage.] In some cases, the head of a lesser house might, through personality, wealth, and the number of his followers, come to possess greater power than the clan chief, but he would nevertheless hold a subordinate position, for the clan chief never abdicated nor could he be superseded. [In the course of time, there is no doubt that lineages shifted in relative importance, and in consequence, the position of clan chief probably shifted from one house to another.]

Succession to the chieftainship followed this line: brother, sister's son, mother's sister's son, sister's daughter's son, and sister. Illegitimacy, if known, was a bar to succession.

[We also commonly hear of a son's son succeeding to a chieftainship. This was possible if he were also the chief's sister's son or sister's daughter's son, owing to the rules that required or encouraged marriage of a man with a woman of his father's maternal line. It was felt very fitting if the heir was both the chief's "maternal nephew" and his paternal grandson. Note that women were not debarred from the chieftainship.]

Among those eligible for succession, the senior was apt to be chosen, but seniority could be passed over for cause. This was what happened after the death of *Chartrich* [Shotridge, or *Kloh-kutz*], the chief of the *Ka-gwan-tan* [Wolf 1] of Chilkat. The choice of his successor lay between three nephews, and the office was not filled for two years. Finally the second one was chosen, because the oldest was considered dissipated and lacking in force, and the youngest was too talkative, a trait considered ill-becoming in one of

A native chief of Sitka, 1837. (Belcher 1843, 1:102 figure. Courtesy of the Library of the University of California, Berkeley.)

high caste. If there were no eligible male heirs, a sister of the deceased chief might be selected, as was the case after the killing of Chief *Klan-ot* or *Clan-ott* [Ł ʔuna·t̓, "They never die," Raven 17] at Chilkoot in 1886. However, a child who would properly succeed might be chosen, and his mother or an old man be delegated to act as regent during his minority. In such a case, all the personal property of the deceased chief would be kept intact until the heir reached the proper age to assume full responsibility. If the chief had no brothers, he might himself select a sister's son, who, from six to eight years of age, would be given to him to bring up, and who, upon attaining the succession, would be obliged to marry his widow, his paternal aunt. The same would be required of any unmarried successor. If he were already married, he could take the widow as an extra wife. This custom may have originated as a way of providing for the widow who could not inherit from her husband, because all his property remained in his clan. Very often, and particularly in the case of the nephew, the chief was permitted to name his successor, but even then the candidate had to be approved by the clan in council. As soon as possible, when sufficient property had been accumulated, the successor had to give a feast, sometimes rebuild the [lineage?] gravehouse, [or later, finance the chief's grave and tombstone], erect a carved pole, [build or repair the lineage house], and distribute property to members of the opposite moiety in honor of the dead chief, when the new chief took the latter's name [title].

AUTHORITY OF CHIEFS*

Although the office of chief was the most honorable among the Tlingit, the holder was possessed of limited authority. His power was more moral than real, for the people constituted the governing body. He presided over them in council and represented them in dealing with outsiders, but he governed only through their consent. [Some clan chiefs and lineage heads were also shamans, and as such had considerable influence.]

Character, wealth, and a large family following were factors that might greatly increase his power. While each clan was an independent body, and no such office as tribal or village chief ever existed, yet in time of war, if it involved the whole tribe, a chief of recognized ability would, through common consent, be the leader. This was the case in 1852, when Chartrich, the *Kar-qwan-tan* [Wolf 1] chief of the Chilkat, led a war party of all the tribe to destroy the Hudson's Bay Company's post at Fort Selkirk.

[Our impression is that even such raids as this, or the attacks on the Russian posts at Sitka and Yakutat, were undertaken primarily as an affair of one clan, although other clans, in the same or the opposite moiety, might become allied because of personal interests or relationships. We do not believe that the Tlingit ever conceived of warfare in tribal terms. (See de Laguna 1983; Olson 1967:69–72.)]

The duties of the chief were to lead his clan in war, to represent the clan at all functions, to preside over its councils, to entertain strangers, to assist the needy and provide the death feast for those clansmen who had nothing, to arbitrate disputes and settle differences within the clan.

The authority of a chief did not extend beyond his village or tribe, although precedence might be accorded to a very prominent chief of the same clan who lived in another tribe, if it were a question concerning the clan as a whole. I believe that in primitive days the chief exercised more authority than he did after the arrival of Europeans. Today, with the passing of the old customs, the office has come to receive only social recognition.

**Editor's note:* I have added the quotations from Golovnin and Lütké.

[It seems that, on the contrary, the expectations and attitudes of Europeans and Americans, as well as the clear policy of the Russian and United States administrators to create and make use of "Head Chiefs" and "Sub Chiefs," for a brief time actually strengthened the power of the Tlingit chiefs. It was never, however, extended over any but their fellow clan members. (See de Laguna 1983:80.)]

Councils were not assembled at fixed times, but were called by the chiefs when the occasion required. They were presided over by him, and were attended by the subchiefs and other household heads in his clan. After discussing the subject and agreeing upon a course to pursue, a general meeting of all the adult males of the clan was called and the proposition stated. Every person present had an equal right to speak, and the sentiment of the majority was followed, but generally the prior decision of the house heads was accepted.

[We suspect there may also have been meetings of all the house chiefs in the village, perhaps on an informal basis, even before this became common in the late nineteenth and early twentieth centuries. It is very interesting that Emmons overlooked the political and economic authority of women, especially of old women of high rank, although he was certainly familiar with the reports of the early explorers who had experienced this (see Douglas in Meares 1790:323–24; Vancouver 1801, 4:170–77, 254–55; 5:435), and he must have encountered instances of it himself, to judge by Major Wood's experience in 1877 (Wood 1882:325, 333; see also Sessions 1890:110).

[Golovnin, who was at Sitka in 1818 on a voyage around the world, reported ([1822] 1979:125):

> A few months before our arrival [at Sitka] the Kolyuzh killed two *promyshlenniks* [hunters], even though they were carrying guns, when they went outside to cut lumber, some 3 or 4 versts from the Fort.
>
> However, since the local savages do not belong to one integral society under a single headman, but are divided into different clans that wander around separately and independently, and are even frequently at war among themselves, it is impossible to take revenge on them, for one cannot determine to which clan the culprits belong. The only solution would be to avenge each crime as a matter of policy, without distinction, but in that case they might all join forces to attack the Company settlement, which would make them a real threat, especially if they managed to penetrate the Fort.

[Lütké, who was at Sitka in 1827, sums up the position of the Tlingit chiefs (1835:194, free translation):

> The government of the Kaloshes, like that of all societies still in infancy, is patriarchal. The oldest in the tribe [clan] is chief, whom the Russians call *taïon* [or *toyon*], a word coming from Siberia. He does not have the right to command any but his own family [clan]. The more numerous his descendants, the richer he is, the more slaves he has [Footnote: The most rich have from thirty to forty slaves], the more he is considered. One listens to his counsels, but he can order nothing of anyone, and one serves him only through goodwill, or for a salary.]

SLAVES*

Slavery was a well-established institution throughout the Northwest Coast and played a large part in the life of the Tlingit. Most slaves were captives taken in war, and the Haida were the principal slavers. These fearless marauders in their great cedar canoes harried the coast from the Straits of Juan de Fuca to Sitka, and Haida parties even penetrated [inland] for two hundred miles, plundering the villages and seizing the people whom they enslaved and sold to others. An old chief of the *Kitikshan* [Gitksan, Tsimshian-speakers] at Kispiox told me that the Haida had ascended the Skeena, passed through the canyon of Kitselas, the most dreaded water passage of the western watershed, and, surprising the village when most of the men were absent, had taken upward of two hundred of the younger women as captives. In corroboration of this statement, we find totem poles at Kispiox and Kitwangach [Kitwanga] on the Skeena River that illustrate the escape of one of these women from the Queen Charlotte Islands. Again, Kincolith ("place," or more properly speaking, "rock of scalps"), at the mouth of the Nass, was so named because a raiding party of Haida, after plundering the upper river villages, was forced to land here and kill their captives, to prevent their canoes from being overturned. They hung the scalps on the rocks as a warning to their pursuers.

Most of the slaves, *gough* [gu·x̣ʷ], among the Tlingit were purchased from the Haida and were natives of Vancouver Island, *Towyot* or "Flatheads" [t̓awyá·t̓]. Some Coast Tsimshian and Niska [Nass River Tsimshian-speakers], a few Haidas, and even other southern people were enslaved by the Tlingit when taken in warfare. Their neighbors of the interior, the Athabaskans, were not enslaved, although they

**Editor's note:* I identified the letter by B. E. Bennett to *The Alaskan* as the source of the story about Klan-tach's slave, and added the relevant portion of this letter, as well as information from Beardslee, certain eighteenth-century observers, and Lütké, Bancroft, Simpson, Golovin, Tikhmenev, Petroff, Young, and Sessions, to support Emmons's argument.

were completely dominated. [Dick Sat-in or Satan, Emmons's informant, said that the "Stick Indians" were not taken for slaves, because they "were friends of the Tlingits," but Emmons rejected this explanation.] Their trade was the most valuable asset of the Coast Tlingit, who were not sentimentalists when it was a question of economic values. The only exception is said to have occurred among the Taku [who were sometimes enslaved], but this hardly seems reasonable, since the Coast and Interior Taku were so intimately related and intermarried.

Under certain conditions the Tlingit also enslaved their own people. These were women and children of other Tlingit *kwans* [q˙ʷá·n] or tribes, taken in war, or members of their own families [lineages]. Their social system could never permit the shame of leaving a member of one's own family [lineage or clan] to be held captive by another family [without attempting ransom or revenge]. Orphans with no near relatives were often taken as slaves by members of their own family [lineage], but they were not actually slaves, for upon reaching manhood they could assert themselves and could no longer be held except by force. As late as 1886, three young boys were taken at Killisnoo by older relatives, but all were later released.

[Moses Jamestown, a very old Raven 14 man at Angoon in 1950, said that when he was an orphan boy, living at Whitewater Bay, the large family of his grandfather abused him. He ran away to Sitka, where Captain Glass of the USS *Jamestown* took care of him onboard his ship, the name of which Moses adopted as his own (de Laguna and McClellan, field notes, June 21, 1950). Moses may have been one of the boys mentioned by Emmons.]

At Wrangell one man killed another. To save the slayer's life, the chief paid for the crime, but since the slayer had not discharged the debt by the time he died, the chief took his mother as a slave, although she was never sold [to collect the money owed]. An old Stikine Tlingit told me that the *Kartch-ut-dee* family [Qa·č̓ʔádi, Raven 28], to their great shame, were in the habit of enslaving the poor and orphans of their own blood, and that a chief so held a widow in bondage. Her duty was to care for the large canoe, but it cracked because she neglected to keep it wet and covered. She was so badly punished that she ran away, and married among the Tahltan of the upper Stikine. Even to this day, the coastal Tlingit clan reproach their fellow clansmen in the interior as being the children of a slave.

Witches and also those who had disgraced their clan might be taken as slaves, but only by their own family [i.e., lineage or clan]. Charley *Gun-wok* [Gú·n wà·q, "yellow" or "golden eyes"], a man of some standing and means among the *Tsar-tee-na-dee* [Saqʷti·ne·dí, Raven 25] of the Kakes, refused to make any contribution toward rebuilding the house of his own direct family [lineage]. His family declared him a slave and put him up for sale, and thirty blankets were paid by the tribe [clan?] for him, which his family contributed to the potlatch dedicating the house. He escaped to Wrangell and lived among the Stikine for many years, but later when he returned to the Kakes, he had to redeem himself by a liberal potlatch to remove his shame.

[Emmons's notes and manuscripts do not make clear to whom Charley Gun-wok gave his potlatch. Any face-saving potlatch must surely have been given to members of the opposite moiety, for even if the repayment of the debt to his own lineage or clan had been done in a formal manner, this could not correctly be called a "potlatch" and would not remove a public disgrace.]

The children of slaves were likewise slaves. Even if a freeman married a slave woman, their children were free only during his life, for they might be claimed as slaves or sold by his successor. At Sitka long ago a *Kik-sa-dee* [Kiksʔádi, Raven 10] chief married his slave, and although he requested that his children might be cared for after his death, his sister sold them immediately.

The life of a slave depended entirely upon the character of the master. Under ordinary circumstances, aside from the uncertainty of life, their condition differed little from that of the poorer class. They hunted, fished, packed, handled the canoe, and did all kinds of manual labor, as did all others, and in turn were fed, clothed, and housed. The Tlingit did not practice corporal punishment, and as they were to some degree dependent on, or profited from the slaves' labor, they had no reason to abuse them. When there were only a few slaves they lived in the house with the family, occupying the front platform near the door, but if a chief had many slaves he housed them together and took precautions to prevent their escape. In 1882 the slaves that still remained among the Tlingit were treated like members of the family.

The hard feature of slavery was the uncertainty of life. A slave was the absolute property of the owner, and it was the custom to sacrifice slaves upon the building of a new house, to wipe out an insult, to enhance one's position by the destruction of such valuable property, and upon the death of the master to provide him with spirit servants in the world beyond. To this last end, slaves would be killed as nearly as possible after the manner of the master's death, but if he had died from natural causes, they would be suffocated. When slaves were sacrificed for display, they might be killed by a club, pick, knife, or spear. The most spectacular and possibly the most primitive method was to lay the victim on the ground with his head resting on a stone. Then a stout sapling was placed across his neck and several men would bear their weight down upon each end of the pole, strangling him or breaking his neck. After death from any cause, the body of a slave was not cremated, but was dragged down to the shore and thrown in the water to be carried off by the tide. I was told by an old Hudson's Bay Company man who was in Wrangell in the early sixties that when Shakes [Šé·kš, the principal Wolf 18 chief] died, twenty-three slaves were killed to attend him in the spirit world. When the glaciers bore down upon the Hoonah village in Glacier Bay, it is said that a slave was cast alive into the crevass to appease the ice spirit. At Taku a slave was killed and the scalp given to the ice to stay its course. [The Tlingit believe that the corpse of a human being or of a dog is so offensive to the glacier that it will retreat. (See de Laguna 1972:97, 239, 286, 818, 819.)]

But on the other hand, slaves were often freed at potlatch ceremonies. Upon such occasions, those who had dressed the chief and his children were called before the assemblage, and the chief, giving them the end of his dance wand, would proclaim their freedom. Then they could return to their own people or remain with the tribe and marry a free person. In such an event, however, although their children would be free, the latter would always be despised, as would the one who had married a former slave. Again, slaves or their friends [relatives?] could purchase their freedom at the option of their masters.

As I have stated, the slaves held by the Tlingit were principally Vancouver Islanders purchased from the Haida. Their value depended upon their age and sex. A man was worth more than a woman, and a woman with child or capable of bearing children was proportionately more valuable [than a little girl or a woman past menopause?]. Values seem to have been generally standardized. The following were quoted to me by old people who remembered an earlier period when the traffic in slaves was carried on:

At Yakutat a man was worth 20 pounds of copper, or 6 prime sea otter pelts. A woman was worth 10 pounds of copper, or 5 ordinary sea otter skins.

At Angoon, among the *Hootz-ah-ta* [Hutsnuwu, Tribe XII], a man was worth 30 fox skins, or 10 moose skins, or 2 martin skin blankets, or 1 Chilkat blanket. A woman was worth the same, less 10 fox skins.

At Sitka, a man was worth 15 moose skins, and a woman 10 moose skins (Dick Sat-in).

Among the Stikine in 1860, a man was worth 40 blankets or $200. A woman was worth 20 blankets or $100.

A jade adz was worth from one to three slaves. A "copper," *tinneh* [tiná·], that in length reached from the tip of the finger to the elbow, *glee-shu-kh-ye kat-tin* [possibly t̓ï·y̨-šúx ye-katï·n, "at-the-elbow measure"?], was worth 20 slaves; one that reached from the tip of the finger to the hollow of the neck, *kar-thla-outh ka-tin* [probably qá· ła-wu·ł katï·n, "someone's hold-in-neck measure"?], was valued at 40 slaves. (Dick Sa-tin).

If a slave died within a year or two from the time of transfer, a portion of the purchase price was returned or demanded. A curious case occurred in Sitka in 1896: Forty years before, during a fight at Angoon on Admiralty Island, a Sitka woman, *Kah-shtet-shik*, was accidentally killed. She was the aunt [mother's sister] of *Klan-tach* [Ła·ntï·č], a sub-chief of the *Kar-qwan-tan* [Ka·gʷa·ta·n, Wolf 1] of Sitka. Her family [lineage] demanded compensation, and received in payment a male slave, *Ea-how*, then twenty years old, who had been purchased from the Haida. He died at the age of sixty years from natural causes. Whereupon, the family of the slain woman claimed that they then held nothing in lieu of her life, and demanded another payment of 100 blankets, then worth $150 or $175.

[Emmons is basing this account largely on a letter by U.S. District Attorney Burton E. Bennett, to *The Alaskan*, Sitka, February 8, 1896, to whom Klan-tach had appealed. He wanted:

> . . . a letter to the Killisnoo Indians, ordering them to pay 100 blankets. Of course he was refused, and told that the Killisnoo Indians owed him nothing, and that, moreover, he had no right to own slaves in this country. He explained by saying that he had freed this slave years ago, but he would not leave. It seems that in 1879, when Capt. Glass, of the Jamestown, was here, the Sitka tribe, as well as all other Alaska tribes, had a great many slaves, and he had freed them all, but this man Ea-how concluded to stay with Klan-tach. Klan-tach went away, but it seems that he and his warriors are all determined to get pay for the squaw that was killed forty years ago, as the next morning after leaving my office, he, with five canoes, started for Killisnoo to enforce his claim. I do not know the result yet. This is the last Sitka slave, and probably the last instance of Slave holding in the United States.]

During the Russian regime the question of slavery was not considered [not of concern], nor did the Hudson's Bay

Company take any action against it, although it is claimed that slave sacrifice was often prevented by an appeal or presents. Upon American possession of the Territory, freedom for all slaves was proclaimed but no enforced action was taken until 1880 [1881], when Captain Glass of the Navy called the Sitka Tlingit together and freed their slaves, some twenty in number, to each of whom he gave a paper.

[Commander Glass (1882:28) reported on May 9, 1881, that he had freed seventeen persons held as slaves at Sitka, and sent letters to the leading chiefs of all the tribes that slaves should be freed at once.

[Commander Beardslee (1882:181), Glass's predecessor, had reported: "There is another custom among them [the Tlingit] against which I could make no headway, and therefore did not try, viz: that of owning slaves, which is quite common. As the possession of these slaves gave much importance to the owners—an importance which it was thought best to foster—this problem was for civil law to solve." Commander Beardslee saw his first task as establishing orderly and peaceful relations among the whites and Indians of Alaska, while Glass could build on these.]

By this time [1881] the barter in slaves had long since ceased, and, while a number of slaves were to be found in each tribe, these were older people whose servitude was voluntary, and who lived as poor members of the family [as clan-mates of their owners], and so remained until they died. I saw several of these among the Chilkat as late as 1885, and they went as they pleased and seemed perfectly contented with their lot. [See, however, the case of the Salish slave liberated by Governor Swineford in 1890, at the end of this section.]

As to the number of slaves held, exaggerated estimates placed them beyond all reason. The only approximation worthy of consideration might be derived from the census of the Tlingit made in 1839 under Sir James Douglas for the Hudson's Bay Company, when the latter leased the continental shore from Lynn Canal to Dixon's Entrance for a period of ten years. This was directly after the smallpox epidemic that had raged for three years and had greatly depleted the native population. Not including Sitka and the coastal tribes from the Alsech [Alsek] River to Controller Bay, the total Tlingit population was given as 5,455, including 630 slaves [Table 5]. Another enumeration made by Lieutenant Wehrman [Verman] in 1861, which did not include the Auk and Henyeh [Henya] tribes, gave a total population of 7,641, of which the same number, 630, were slaves [Table 6; recalculated total of Tlingit, including their slaves, is 7,839].

But too much reliance cannot be placed upon these figures, for the Hudson's Bay Company had no jurisdiction over the island population, and because of the hostility of the natives, the Russians confined their activities largely within the limits of their posts. A number of discrepancies appear in these counts. In the first, the Chilkat, who are the largest Tlingit tribe, are credited with a population of 420 freemen, and 78 slaves, while in the second, the number of freemen is increased to 1,456, and the slaves to 160. [An equally unlikely shift in the opposite direction can be noted for the Stikine.] It is very certain that slavery declined along with the decrease in the native population. After the transfer of Alaska from Russia, slavery gradually died out as the condition of native life changed with civilizing influences.

[Eighteenth-century sources report little about Tlingit slaves. This is probably because the slaves worked alongside their masters and mistresses and were usually treated like members of the family. The only exception seems to have been Malaspina's observations on female slaves used as prostitutes at Yakutat in 1791. Malaspina also reported that a Filipino sailor was believed by the Yakutat natives to be a slave (see Malaspina 1885:161, 347, in de Laguna 1972:147, 474–75). Traffic in slaves was evidently well established among the Tlingit at this period, for Mourelle reported that the Spanish in 1779 purchased three boys from the Indians (Henya, presumably) of Bucareli Bay, and from the account by Father Riobo, these boys were probably abandoned orphans (Mourelle in La Pérouse 1799:250; Riobo in Thornton 1918:227). In 1788, the Yakutat Tlingit sold to the Russians, Ismailov and Bocharov, a Koniag slave and a Sitkan slave, both boys about twelve years old, and in 1794 the Russians under Purtov and Kulikalov learned that the Yakutat Tlingit had sold some Chugach captives to the Tlingit in southeastern Alaska (de Laguna 1972:470). Since slavery was known in Europe in the eighteenth century, its existence among the Tlingit seemed to cause little comment. Our first informative accounts date from the nineteenth century.

[Lütké (1835, free translation) wrote:

> The Kaloches believe that the soul lives on after death in another world, but without receiving recompense for good, or punishment for evil. The souls of chiefs do not mingle there with those of their inferiors, but the souls of the slaves who were sacrificed on the tomb of their master remain eternally the slaves of his (soul). [p. 193] [Lütké goes on to mention what is evidently slave sacrifice at potlatches, although he did not understand the purpose of the ceremony, calling it by the Siberian term *igrouchka*, or "public game"] . . . celebrated from time to time, now in this

tribe [clan], now in another. . . . A short time before our arrival at Sitka, such a game was held in the tribe of the taïon Naouchket [Raven 10] who live near the fort, to which came all the neighboring tribes, and in which a *kalga* (slave) was sacrificed. They suffocated the victim by putting a plank across his neck. Doctor Mertens, who was making a collection of skulls from the peoples we visited, found, from the descriptions given him, the place of sacrifice, deep in the woods, and also the corpse of the victim, from which he removed the skull, at the risk of his own life. [pp. 193–94]

The slaves of the Kaloches are prisoners taken from the enemy. Wars are now scarce in the vicinity of our colonies; that is why the Kaloches of these countries have to purchase their slaves from those who live opposite the Queen Charlotte Islands [Kaigani Haida of southwestern Alaska], and beyond. Each owner has full power of life and death over his slave, and in addition to the ceremony of which we have spoken, one sometimes puts slaves to death on the occasion of fetes, of commemorations, of the death of chiefs, etc. It is understood that one always chooses those who are no longer good for anything, and whom one can neither sell nor give away. Sometimes, on the contrary, in similar circumstances, one liberates the slaves. [pp. 195–96]

[As an indication of slightly improved Tlingit-Russian relations, Lütké (1835:143) cited the following:

According to the latest news, two slaves, condemned to be sacrificed in a ceremony, having found the means to escape, took refuge in the fort. The governor took them under his protection and refused to give them up to the chiefs, yet they were not offended by this.

[Von Kotzebue reported from Sitka as of 1825 (1830:54):

The richer a Kalush is, the more powerful he becomes; he has a multitude of wives who bring him a numerous family, and he purchases male and female slaves who must labour and fish for him, and strengthen his force when engaged in warfare. These slaves are prisoners of war, and their descendants. The master's power over them is unlimited, and he even puts them to death without scruple. When the master dies, two of his slaves are murdered on his grave, that he may not want attendance in the other world; these are chosen long before the event occurs, but meet the destiny that awaits them, very philosophically.

[Bancroft (1884, 2:649), in describing Finlayson's difficulties with the Taku Tlingit when the Hudson's Bay Company was establishing "Fort Tako" in their midst, gave this report:

In those days every chief worthy the name possessed from fifty to one hundred slaves, worth thirty blankets each, generally purchased from the natives of Queen Charlotte Island [*sic*], the great slave-mart of the Northwest Coast. The chiefs took no small delight in killing their slaves at their feasts, which was a mark of greatness. While Finlayson was at Fort Tako the savages assembled at Tako Gulf one day in the summer of 1840, and having finished their trading they held a great feast. Warmed to a proper pitch of egotism by the white man's rum, one of the chiefs arose and made a speech: "I am a mighty man, a most valiant chief, and wealthy withal, having so much property I know scarcely what to do with it. So rich am I that often I amuse myself thus"—with which words he drew a pistol and shot dead one of his slaves. Another chief not to be outdone made a longer, braver speech, and shot two slaves. Catching the cruel mania others followed, until ten poor wretches lay dead. Next day Finlayson with a well armed *posse* went out and buried them, for the lordly savage would not touch a dead slave, but would leave him to rot where he fell. Then he told them that those who indulged in such dastardly acts in the future should not be allowed to trade at the fort.

[In the same period, Sir George Simpson (1847:125–26), on his voyage around the world, 1841–42, visited the Hudson's Bay Company post at Fort Stikine (Wrangell), and reported of the Stikine and their neighbors:

One full third of the large population of this coast are slaves of the most helpless and abject description. Though some of the poor creatures are prisoners taken in war, yet most of them have been born in their present condition. These wretches, besides being constantly the victims of cruelty, are often the instruments of malice or revenge. If ordered by his master to destroy red or white man, the slave must do so, however dangerous may be the service, for, if he either refuse or fail, his own miserable life must play the forfeit. [p. 125]

. . . [Chief Shakes, Wolf 18] was said to be very cruel to his slaves, whom he frequently sacrificed in pure wantonness in order to show how great a man he was. On the recent occasion of a house-warming, he exhibited, as part of the festivities, the butchery of five slaves; and at another time, having struck a white man in a fit of drunkenness and received a pair of black eyes for his pains, he ordered a slave to be shot by way at once of satisfying his own wounded honor and of apologizing to the person whom he had assaulted. His rival, [Quatekay, "the second chief of the tribe," unidentified, but probably Raven 32], on the contrary, was possessed of such kindness of heart, that, on grand holidays, he was more ready to emancipate his slaves than to destroy them. Yet, strange to say, many bondmen used to run away from Quatekay, while none attempted to escape from Shakes,—an anomaly which, however, was easily explained, inasmuch as the one would pardon the recaptured fugitives and the other would torture and murder them. [pp. 125–26]

[With respect to the fur trade carried on now at "Fort Tako," Simpson stated that before its establishment in 1840, most of the Tlingit furs "used to be devoted to the purchasing of slaves from the Indians of Kygarnie and Hood's Bay" (Simpson 1847:128).

[Captain P. N. Golovin ([1862] 1979:28) had been ordered to make a survey of the Russian colonies in North America, and he reported on slavery among the Tlingit:

> Usually all the toions [chiefs] have slaves who are called *kalgas*. A kalga is the property of his owner and can be disposed of at will; he is considered a chattel, not a human being. During certain ceremonies and special occasions it is the custom to kill kalgas. For example, when a toion dies one or two of his kalgas are killed so that the toion will have the service he needs in his next life. This kind of killing is no longer done on Sitka. The Chief Managers have been working at this constantly, and have finally succeeded in persuading the toions that instead of killing a kalga they should sell him to the Company or free him. But if the killing is no longer in vogue next to the walls of the fortress in view of the Russians, this does not mean that this barbaric custom has been completely abandoned by the Sitka Kolosh. They say with total assurance that whenever a toion wants to kill a kalga he takes him to one of the settlements of a friendly tribe and kills him there in accordance with custom. The custom of killing kalgas is universal among all the other Kolosh.

[Tikhmenev ([1861–63] 1978:354, 432–33) confirmed much of the above information. Apparently the ransoming of slaves destined to be sacrificed had become customary at Sitka by 1861, and even some of the other tribes gave them to the Russian-American Company for a return. The bodies of dead slaves were, however, simply thrown out on the beach or in the woods, not cremated. On some public occasions slaves were freed. Most slaves were obtained in trade from the Kaigani Haida and from the Haida of Queen Charlotte Islands, or the Southern Tlingit obtained them on raids to British Columbia and Oregon Territory. In Sitka (?) a male slave was worth 60 blankets, plus other goods totaling 100 paper rubles; a female slave was worth only 40 blankets and 75 rubles worth of other goods. The Tlingit measured their prosperity by the number of their slaves.

[Ivan Petroff, in a note to his translation of Tikhmenev, (1863, 2:59), reported that in 1868, when the "head chief of the Sitkans" died, General Davis, who was at Sitka with a force of 250 men armed with breechloaders and a battery of 10-lb. guns, did not attempt to prevent by force the sacrifice of slaves at the chief's funeral, but instead bribed the Indians with whiskey and tobacco to spare the slaves.

[Reverend S. Hall Young, Protestant missionary at Wrangell during the early years of American occupation, protested against Tlingit slavery and the indifference of the U.S. military at Fort Wrangell to slave sacrifice and the torture of witches (Young 1927):

> [Fort Wrangell, on the site of the earlier Russian Redoubt St. Dionysius and of the Hudson's Bay Company Fort Stikine, was built between the town of the Stikine and the area where the foreign Tlingit tribes camped when they came to trade at the fort.] But for the most part the officers of the Fort knew nothing of what was going on in either camp. . . . Murders, robberies, torturing of witches and even sacrifice of slaves might go on—and did—without the officers knowing or inquiring about these occurrences.
>
> Four or five years after the building of the Fort, at the erection of a large new community house and big totem pole to make good the name of the new chief who had taken the place of the deceased Shustaak [Raven 33], ten slaves were brained at one time with the same greenstone ax and sent to wait upon the deceased chief in "Sickagow" [šigi̢· qá·wu ʔa·ní, "dead people's land"], the Happy Hunting Ground of the Thlingits. Of this massacre the commanding officer of the Fort knew nothing or, if it was reported to him, no investigation was made. [pp. 83–84]
>
> [The Stikine were a wealthy and arrogant tribe.] Before the American occupation of Alaska their great war canoes made frequent raids down the Coast, attacking the villages of the Queen Charlotte group of islands, those on the shores of Vancouver Island and the islands in the Gulf of Georgia. They possessed slaves, who were taken from the Puyallups and Neah Bays, and a few who were said to be descendants of the Chinooks at the mouth of the Columbia River. I estimated that there were at least forty slaves held by the Stickeens when I arrived at Wrangell [July 10, 1878]. [p. 87]
>
> [In 1879] the slavery question became acute. There were many slaves in and about Fort Wrangell, some of them held by the Stickeen chiefs and others brought there by the "Foreign Indians" [Kake, Hutsnuwu, and other Tlingit]. These slaves were obtained in two ways by the Thlingits and the Hydas. The manner in which most of them were procured was by the great war parties, which, from thirty to a hundred years before our arrival, went down the coast in their large canoes, attacked the Flatheads of Puget Sound and the natives of Vancouver Island, killing the men and making captives of the women and children. The slaves thus procured and their children, for they frequently married in captivity, were held as property in all the tribes.
>
> The other method was by self-surrender. A man would become so deeply involved in debt that neither he nor his immediate kin could see any prospect of payment. His creditors were persistent in their demands. At last, after much talk he would give himself up, with as many children of his family as were necessary to satisfy the long-standing obligation, and they would go to the house of the creditor family and become slaves. [p. 127]
>
> However, while those obtained by foray were counted as mere chattels, the master having the power of life and death over them,

those taken for debt within the same tribe stood on a different footing; and there was always the hope in their hearts that they could serve out their time and purchase their freedom. They were part of the family in the community house, and often their masters had a real affection for them and treated them well. [pp. 127–28]

But the slaves captured from foreign tribes were despised, slighted and bartered at the will of their masters. Frequently they were sacrificed at the death of a chief, or to propitiate the spirits of the glaciers which were swallowing up their salmon streams, or the spirits of the mountains which precipitated landslides upon the camps, or the spirits of the ice which overturned huge icebergs to the destruction of unwary canoeists. When they died, instead of their bodies being cremated they were thrown out in the woods to rot or be devoured by the wolfish dogs.

So far as I could ascertain, no real effort had been made by the officers at Fort Wrangell and Sitka to abolish slavery [despite orders that the President's Proclamation of Emancipation should apply to Alaska]. Of course, I instituted a vigorous campaign against this evil. [The collector of customs at Wrangell, Colonel Crittenden, a Southerner who did not want the "Siwashes" to have slaves when his people had to give them up, assisted Young in this.] [p. 128]

Although the masters objected, and often pretended to liberate their slaves while still holding them in servitude, we soon effected practical freedom. We sent back to Nanaimo in British Columbia, to Tacoma and Port Townsend and to the west coast of Vancouver Island upward of twenty men and women who wished to return to their native tribes. [Others seem to have chosen to remain with their former masters.]

[Among the notes left by Emmons in BCPA was an unsigned newspaper article, probably written by a missionary attached to the Presbyterian Mission Home in Hoonah. Emmons evidently intended to make use of this material, for the clipping is labeled "Slaves" in his hand. It reads in part: "Orphan children among the Kling-gets are virtually slaves, and this is as true to-day as it was ten years ago." Then follows the account of how a native woman at Hoonah found the little son of her deceased friend being treated as a slave, and how she brought him away, and placed him in the Mission Home at Hoonah. His "relative-owners" attempted to take him from the Home by force, intending to profit from the wages he might earn, but were prevented from doing so only by the woman writer of the account. The frightened child begged to be sent to Sitka, but the writer was afraid that even there he would not be safe, unless the court could prove him to have been a slave and make him ward of the Sitka Training School.

[To this account Emmons had penciled: "Orphans we liberated at Angoon were held as slaves 1884" (corrected to "1886").

[Perhaps the very last slave to be freed in Alaska was a Salish (?) man, who had been captured at Victoria when a boy of nine, and was owned by a Wrangell Tlingit. According to Sessions (1890:59–60):

> his master had sent him with a canoe, gun and blankets on some errand to his fishing-place, and he escaped, and was overtaken by his master from Wrangell. The Justice of the Peace [at Sitka? or at Wrangell?] took the master prisoner, knowing the governor was coming, and this delightful Sunday morning he was given his emancipation papers, with the great seal of the Government attached, which the Indians always respect; they gave him the canoe, gun and blankets, and sent him free about one thousand miles to Victoria where he was captured so many years ago.]

LAW*

[As will be seen, the Tlingit made no distinction between a lawsuit or dispute between two clans and a war or feud between clans, although we would be inclined to distinguish between them on the basis, perhaps, of ferocity. Both were settled by the same kind of peace ceremony (see Chapter 12). Troubles between individuals within a clan or lineage might lead to violence or a killing, but were private affairs, not the concern of Tlingit law.]

Although the Tlingit were living in a very primitive state when discovered by Europeans, they were by no means savages, since they had formulated and were following a code of exact laws which regulated in detail their relations with each other and which were generally accepted by the neighboring coastal tribes. Property rights were strictly observed, and compensations were made for injuries or killings according to the rank of the victim.

The clan was the unit of social organization, and its property was held in common. Its territory, however, was

---

**Editor's note:* My separation of specific cases into those here classified as legal disputes and those treated as wars in Chapter 12, is rather arbitrary. Emmons sometimes discussed the same episode in this section on Law and in Chapter 12 ("War and Peace"), and the Tlingit used only the single term "war" to refer to both minor disputes and bloody conflicts. In this section I have supplied paragraphs on the Tlingit sense of honor, territorial rights (including monopolies on trade routes, trading, and packing), fishing rights, and settlements involving the sacrifice of human lives. I have also included an account of the trouble at Klukwan in 1881 which began as a drunken brawl and escalated into a "war" between Raven 3 and Wolf 27, finally settled by the Navy. A case of suicide reported by Lull, "trouble" cases described by Young, Louthan's statement on Tlingit methods of compensation, Beardslee's policy in settling disputes, and lastly how Emmons put up bail for George Shotridge have been added because these all illustrate Tlingit notions about the lawful and proper.

to a large degree divided among the individual families or households [lineages], as an inalienable right, which they could not dispose of and which was inherited in the direct maternal line. These possessions consisted particularly of the fishing streams, since salmon constituted their main food. Camping grounds and spheres of activity on the larger rivers were recognized as family [clan or lineage?] rights, as were seal and sea otter camp sites, together with the contiguous waters, and hunting and trapping grounds. The house site was likewise a distinct family [lineage] possession, and even if unoccupied would remain inviolate. The privilege of taking food when traveling through the country was free to all, but pelts belonged to its occupants [the owners of the territory]. Children inherited nothing from their father. While they were young and remained with him, they assisted him and had the right of hunting and fishing in his country, but when they married, these rights would be exercised in their mother's or wife's territory [i.e., in the territory belonging to the maternal uncle or to the father-in-law of the man].

[It is not completely accurate to say that land was inalienable, since the traditions of the Tlingit refer to transfers of territory. Thus the G̣a·nax̣ʔádi, Raven 1, at Angoon surrendered their territorial claims in the Hutsnuwu area to the Raven 13, De·šï·ta·n, in settlement of a dispute (Garfield 1947:441). Clan traditions at Yakutat also refer to gifts and sales of territories, and Swanton (1909, Tale 105:355–56) describes such a sale. (See also de Laguna 1972:232–33, 252–53, 254.)]

Legal settlements were based upon fact and not on intent, and laws recognized only the clan and not the individual. This is most forcibly illustrated in the matter of death, where no distinction was made between accidental and premeditated killing. In both cases, a life of equal value or a proportional indemnity (in slaves, furs, blankets, or other property) was exacted. If the social position of the killer was not equal to that of the victim, the life of another person, or of two or more of a lower social rank, wholly innocent of the offense, might have to be given as an equivalent. Thus, Dick [*Satan*?] reported that high-class people's lives were of more value than the lives of the people at large. The value of a chief's life could not be atoned for by the life of another. While a chief's life might be worth ten or fifteen slaves, a common person's life might be about five slaves, or four hundred blankets. Adjustments for an injury might be made by a consultation in which both families were equally represented and agreed upon an award. [In case of a killing] the aggressor or one of his family might offer his life in atonement, but if no reparation were made, the result would be a feud which would never be forgotten, but would be inherited as a duty for generations. These feuds greatly influenced the social relations of the whole people. They may slumber for a generation, but when the opportunity occurs to press for payment, the question springs to life as fresh and as warmly espoused by the descendants as if it had occurred only that day. This demonstrates the tenacity with which the Tlingit cling to a feud. It is this practice that restricted their lives, rendering them supersensitive, suspicious, revengeful and never wholly at rest.

[It should be noted that it was impossible to make atonement or recompense if the case involved two members of the same clan. The only settlement possible seems to have been for the principals and their close relatives to separate, perhaps one lineage moving to another place. Garfield (1947:445–46) recorded a number of examples of this kind, especially that which split the Te·qʷe·dí, Wolf 32, at Todd on Peril Strait.]

When offended or injured, the Tlingit never offered bodily violence unless he might kill the offender. In all other cases he would shame the latter by destroying his own property, an act which would free him [from the disgrace of the insult] and would cast onus on the other party, requiring the latter to make a still further sacrifice or remain an object of reproach. [The following cases illustrate this principle.]

At Killisnoo [in Hutsnuwu territory, XII], a quarrel occurred between a subchief of Angoon [the main village near by] and the woman he was engaged to marry. She went out in front of the houses in the middle of the village and in a loud, angry harangue heaped words of insult upon him. This brought great shame to him and so hurt his honor that he sat in his house, covered with his blanket, until her tirade was ended. Then he picked up his ax, went down to the shore, and completely demolished his canoe, valued at $200 or $250. This satisfied his honor, and placed the shame forever on the woman, since she could not destroy an equal, or still greater amount of property. And a similar case occurred at *Gau da kan* [Ga·w-t̓aq-ʔa·n, "town beside drum/bell," Hoonah].

Again at Killisnoo, in 1887, a native was knocked down by a white man during an altercation. Since both were employed in the factory [the whaling station or herring factory of the Northwest Trading Company], the Indian went to the superintendent and tried to give him $5, since, according to native ideas, the offender would be compelled to give away a greater sum. When the superintendent would not accept it, he felt very badly and could not understand his position.

In the same village, Killisnoo, a woman, "Kinzie," was accused of being a witch. Although witchcraft [punishment for witchcraft?] had been abolished by law, yet, to right herself in the eyes of the people and put her accusers to confusion, she came out in the road and tore up ten to twenty blankets, which shifted the shame to her accusers.

At Sitka in 1899, Henry [*Satan*, Se·tá·n], a subchief of the *Thluke nuh ut di* [Łʼukʷnax̣ʔádi, Raven 6], quarreled with his brother Dick. A nephew who sided with the latter bit off the end of Henry's finger [and Henry evidently held Dick responsible for the injury]. When the clan gave their great potlatch that winter, Dick made no contribution to it, but at the feast Henry announced, holding up his mutilated finger, "I have been injured to the amount of $600, and this sum I now give away." This put Dick to shame, and in order to regain his standing in the family [clan], and before the guests, he would have to make an even greater contribution, or destroy the same amount. [It is not clear from the account what he did.]

[The most striking examples of this kind are furnished by Chief Shakes (Šé·kš), the chief of the Na·nya̱·ʔa·yí, Wolf 18, of Wrangell. As reported by Sir George Simpson (1847:126), based on his observations in 1841, in the passage already quoted above in the section "Slaves," Shakes seems to have had no compunction in ordering a slave killed to satisfy his honor, when he felt shamed or embarrassed. And Emmons reported a similar incident:]

During the early occupation of Wrangell by our military forces, the principal chief, "Shakes," was knocked down in a drunken row by a soldier. This so hurt his pride that he sacrificed thirteen slaves, thus restoring his honor and supposedly placing the offender in a very humiliating position until the latter should destroy an even greater amount of his own property.

Just as "caste" could be obtained by great feasts and potlatches, so it could be lost if the person involved could not meet his obligations, if a claim for injury was made against him, or if his family would not aid him [in the settlement]. In such a case the whole family [clan] might become involved, and the other family [the claimant clan] might appropriate the crest or totem [of the delinquent clan] and display it in derision, [on a hat, house post, or pole. Presumably the crest or crest object would be surrendered when the debt was paid.] Thus, *Kahjocktee* [Qá· ǯáqʷti, "Man's Slain Body," or perhaps "Manslayer," chief of the Middle-of-the-Town House of Raven 14, at Angoon] used an eagle head on a wooden hat because the *Kar-gwantan* [Wolf 1] owed him a debt and had not paid it. [He also used a face stamp with a bear design, presumably another crest of his debtors; this was purchased by Emmons, see Figure 127d.]

An Indian of the Bear group at Tongass [Wolf 32?] gave a great feast and invited the Killerwhale chief from Wrangell [Wolf 18]. Since the Wrangell chief never gave a return feast or potlatch, when the Tongass man's nephew erected a pole to him [to his dead uncle], he showed the crest of the Brown Bear biting the tail of the Killerwhale to mortify the Wrangell chief.

A Taku chief came to Killisnoo to trade in 1895. He bought considerable whiskey, and after a spree on shore was drowned when going to his boat. His family immediately claimed compensation, since he had gotten drunk on shore with the *Hootz ah ta* [Hutsnuwu tribe], and some property was given them. [Angoon informants remarked, years later: "Lots of trouble in the old days. If someone tipped over in a canoe, they would blame the local people"; de Laguna and McClellan field notes, 1950.] Years afterwards they complained that they had not been paid enough and returned in three large canoes to demand more. This was refused, so they loaded their canoes and prepared to embark. But before doing so, they stuffed a brown bearskin and, throwing it out of their camp, kicked it along the beach in front of the village as an insult to the Brown Bear family [Wolf 32, Te·qʷe·dí] who claim the Brown Bear crest. This humiliation brought the *Hootz ah ta* [Hutsnuwu] quickly to terms and the demand was paid.

In Sitka, some natives broke into a house and stole some whiskey and three died from the effects of the spree. The family [clan? lineage?] demanded the full value of their lives, claiming that the whiskey that had belonged to the white man had killed them and that therefore he was responsible.

In 1887, a Taku man, while packing for white men over the Chilkoot trail, fell and broke his leg. This mishap was wholly accidental. Although the Chilkoot Tlingit claimed the sole right to pack on this trail which they had made themselves and were absolutely opposed to its use by other natives, yet claim for compensation for this accident was made by the family [clan?] of the Taku man, on the ground that it occurred in Chilkoot country and that therefore the Chilkoot were responsible. It was paid, according to native law.

[It seems clear from these and other examples that the Tlingit had a strong sense of honor. It was honorable to pay one's debts. And it was also a matter of honor to press a claim. Many of the cases that led to bloodshed arose from the use of liquor, which inflamed the claimants and defendants. Such feuds, or threatened feuds, were among the important cases with which the U.S. naval authorities in Sitka had to deal. The eagerness with which the wiser, more sober leaders sought Navy arbitration is testimony to their desire for peace as well as to the fairness of Commanders Beardslee and Glass, 1879–82.

Territorial rights were among those which the Tlingit zealously defended, and which they were ready to respect. Such rights included control over the trade routes into the interior, monopolies that were originally linked with exclusive rights to trade with the Athabaskans, but which later came to include the sole right to earn money by packing over the passes for the miners. Thus, when Commander Beardslee in 1879–80 succeeded in persuading the Chilkat and Chilkoot to permit a group of miners to go into the interior, the latter had to promise that they would not trade with the Athabaskans. When two other men who had not made this pledge joined the party and did trade, the Chilkat and Chilkoot were incensed at what they interpreted as a breach of faith. Yet the Chilkat chief, Chartrich (Ka·gʷa·nta·n, Wolf 1), begged Commander Beardslee to take the men away, fearing murder, and himself tried earnestly to keep the peace. (See Beardslee 1882:60–68). Later, when the Chilkoot refused to pack for Ogilvie's survey party in 1887 and would have caused trouble if he had hired Athabaskans to do so on the Tlingit side of the Chilkoot Pass, the Chilkoot themselves, when they finally agreed to do the job, carried the packs only to the summit, for beyond was Athabaskan country where the owners had the exclusive right to pack for the whites.

[Whites and Indians clashed over fishing rights, because the former did not recognize the Indians' exclusive rights to fish in waters claimed by clans. Ensign J. O. Nicholson (in Glass 1882:44–45) reported on what was evidently an invasion of Indian fishing grounds near the cannery town of Klawock in 1881, when the Indians (Klawak and Henya?) drove off the cannery seiners who were taking fish too near their summer village. One drunken Indian organized a strike among the native cannery workers and threatened the cannery cook. When the frightened whites appealed to Commander Glass in Sitka for protection, he sent Ensign Nicholson with twenty men. The latter persuaded the assembled leaders to destroy the Indians' stills, for drunkenness had aggravated the trouble, and at their request gave the chiefs official "papers" recognizing their status. In 1890, the Hutsnuwu were protesting fishing by the whites in Sitkoh Bay, claimed by the De·šiˀta·n, Raven 13, as their exclusive territory. Again an appeal was made by the cannery personnel to the naval authorities in Sitka, and Ensign Robert Coontz (1930:152–55) was sent with six marines and an interpreter to explain the whites' view of their rights and to arrest any Indians who might interfere with them. Coontz was able to secure the surrender of 125 Indians, and took 20 of their leaders to Sitka. In both of these cases, even when the Indians felt that they were in the right, and bitterly resented the intrusion of the whites, they were anxious to keep the peace.

[Honorable settlement of serious disputes often necessitated the sacrifice of one or more lives, as Emmons explains:]

In the spring of 1888, during the traveling of prospectors over the Chilkoot Pass, the question of permitting others than members of the Chilkoot tribe to pack over the trail that had been made by and was rightfully the property of the resident tribe was more than questioned, when Clan-ot [Łˀuna·ṫ, Raven 17], the second chief of the Chilkoots, attacked [Sitka Jim] a chief of the Sitkans who was packing. In the encounter, Clan-ot was killed and the Sitkan severely wounded. Recognizing the law that his life must be given, he [Sitka Jim] made no effort to escape, but went to his tent, was dressed by his relatives, the *con goush* [gangú·š] or "bear's ears" headdress was put on, his face was blackened with coal from the fire [the bear's ears and black face paint were signs of warrior courage], and with his war knife lashed to his hand, he went forth alone to meet his fate. As he rested in the open trail, he saw a number of Chilkoots with rifles approaching. He rose and danced to meet them, singing his death chant and brandishing his knife. Shot through by many bullets, he fell, and was carried to his tent where he died during the night without complaint, knowing that his death fulfilled the law and that no reprisals would follow, for the two men were of equal social position.

At a potlatch at Klukwan about 1895, a young man who was making a disturbance was put out of the house. He returned shortly and shot the man who had ejected him. He then went to his home, dressed in festival attire, and returning to the scene of the trouble, called to the friends of his victim, who killed him immediately. As the two lives were [judged] of equal value, the law was satisfied and the matter was closed. The corpse of the murdered man was dressed, the face painted, and was set up in the corner of the house, and the festivities continued as if nothing had happened.

At Hoonah, as the result of a drunken row, a man in protecting his friend killed the assailant. Although he might have delivered himself to the [United States] authorities with every possibility of being cleared, he followed the custom of his people. In the morning, dressed in festival attire, he walked out of his house, down to the beach, where the friends of the slain man were assembled, and died without a murmur.

Such cases might be indefinitely continued, so strict was the observance of their own laws even after ours had been imposed upon them. While obliged to conform to the latter they continued to follow their own even when greatly to their detriment.

[It is clear, however, from the record and the observations made by Emmons that some individuals tried to evade these terrible obligations. This may be illustrated by the troubles as Klukwan, where, in 1881, long-standing grudges flared up in a "war" between the Ģa·naxte·dí, Raven 3, known to the whites as "Crows," and admittedly high-class, and the Daqławe·dí, Wolf 27, the reputedly lower-class "Whales" [Killerwhales]. (See reports by Hanus, July 1, 1881, in Glass 1882:41–44, and reprinted in the Eleventh U.S. Census of Alaska, 1893:44–46; the report by Lull 1882:47; and Mrs. Willard 1884:79–81.)

[The trouble was precipitated by a drunken brawl, largely provoked by some Ģa·naxte·dí women. It may be summarized as follows:

[At the end of the brawl, Toohokees, a minor Wolf 27 chief, and two of his clansmen had been slashed by Chilcat Charley of Raven 3, a nephew of Toohokees's mother-in-law and clan brother of Toohokees's Raven 3 wife. But Toohokees had killed a young chief of the Raven 3. And as Hanus [in Glass 1882:42] reported:

> According to the Indian custom, it was now necessary that a [Killer]Whale of equal rank should be killed to make things even; so Toohokees detailed his nephew to die for his family. The young man accordingly dressed in his best clothes, and commenced dancing the peculiar death dance the people indulge in when they die for glory, as they consider death under such circumstances; but the Crows refused to shoot him, saying he had done nothing, and demanded the life of his uncle, Toohokees, but the latter would not show himself; both parties commenced firing at one another, and one of the Crows was badly wounded.

[The trouble may have been that the nephew was not of high enough rank. The Ravens now kept calling for Toohokees to come out, but whenever he made a move to do so, his Raven wife, by now sober, protected him with her body—behavior that infuriated her clansmen. Finally, next morning when Toohokees was ready to die, his wife came out of the house with him, and begged her clansmen not to shoot until he had descended the steps, fearing that his body would be bruised in the fall. But she herself was shot, because her Raven clansmen interpreted her behavior as treason.

[Then Toohokees and all the Killerwhales retired, to permit the Ravens to carry off the dead woman. An armistice was agreed until her body should be cremated. (This seems to have been the usual practice.)

[The next morning "Shatevich" (Chartrich, Wolf 1, and married to Raven 3), the highest ranking chief in Klukwan, returned from a trading trip inland; with him were Sidnootz and his sister, both Raven 3. Chartrich tried to halt the fighting, but was unsuccessful. (In this, and other instances, this high chief of the "Cinnamon Bears" was playing the role of the neutral peacemaker and "clan-brother-in-law," since his wife was a Raven 3 woman, like the slain young chief and Toohokees's wife.)

[Sidnootz's sister tried to entice Toohokees out of his house, by reminding him of an old feud between Raven 3 and Wolf 27, and taunted him to come out and kill her. But he shot at her from inside the house. When her brother rushed up, he was wounded and had to be carried off.

[Now at last, Toohokees emerged, dancing the death dance, and several Ravens shot at him. He fell feigning death, but when Sidnootz approached, Toohokees sprang up and shot him through the heart. Toohokees then retired to the woods, well armed, threatening to kill every Raven 3 person before he died. He shot at their houses and wounded another woman. As Hanus (in Glass 1882:42) continued: "Toohokees's mother, sister, and uncle, who were left in the house alone, considered that he was a coward not to die after having killed so many people; so, for the credit of the family [clan], and that it might not be permanently disgraced, they dressed up in their best clothes, came out one at a time and were killed one after another." Shortly after this Toohokees himself was killed.

[G. C. Hanus, master, U.S. Navy, was sent by Commander Glass from Sitka to investigate and settle this trouble. Since the Wolf 27 people were afraid to come out of their homes at the upper end of Klukwan to meet Hanus at Yandestake at the mouth of the Chilkat River, Hanus went to Klukwan, where he was royally received by Chartrich and the Wolf 1. After diplomatic discussions, the Raven 3 said they would make peace if the Wolf 27 would pay one thousand blankets, later reducing their demands to $1,000 and finally to $500, the exact amount depending on whether a seriously wounded Raven 3 man lived or died. Although four Ravens and four Killerwhales had been killed, and several Indians (clans not specified) had been wounded, the extra amount was needed to make the loss on both sides even. Finally, when Commander Lull, who replaced Glass, visited "Chilcot" in August, he found that the Killerwhales and Ravens had settled their differences by the Killerwhales paying one hundred blankets. Leaders of both clans shook hands and promised to live at peace with each other and with the whites. (It is interesting that although the molasses to make the liquor, the real cause of the trouble, had been obtained from a white man, none of the whites in the area had been threatened.) Emmons reported a similar case:]

At Klukwan in the Chilkat country in 1890, a head man of the *Con-nuh-ta-de* [Ǥa·naxte·dí, Raven 3] was killed by the elder of two sons of *Ka-gwan-tan* family [Ka·gʷa·nta·n, Wolf 1; Emmons would seem to say that the two brothers were Ka·gʷa·ta·n]. The murderer escaped into the interior. The mother then called upon the second son to give his life. When he refused, she went into the interior to persuade the murderer [her older son] to return and make the blood atonement. But failing in this, and since she was of the same clan as the murderer, she offered her own life and that of her daughter. Decked out in festival attire, mother and daughter presented themselves and were killed. But, as women, their lives did not compensate for that of the murdered chief. So later, the second son, who was in no ways responsible for the crime, gave himself up, and his life, together with the lives of his mother and sister, were accepted as equal to that of the slain man.

In some instances clan difficulties might be settled by duels in which the contestants were selected, for they had to be of the same social position. They were completely clad in armor and stood foot to foot, thrusting and cutting with long knives, until one or both fell, exhausted from loss of blood or mortally wounded.

As previously stated, the question of compensation in the case of injury or death was in no wise dependent upon the intent; the act and result alone were considered. In the summer of 1890 two Hoonah clans were camped on a salmon stream in Cross Sound. Early one morning the dogs trailed a bear and the men went in pursuit. After some time, two half-grown boys were sent to their assistance with a rifle. On the return trip, the gun in the hands of one of the boys was discharged, killing the other. While this was recognized as an accident, full payment was demanded for the life. As the Hoonah clan acknowledging the debt was very poor, the Sitka branch, though distantly related, willingly made payment in full, as a clan obligation.

Even an accident or self-imposed injury in alien territory called for compensation. In 1890 a Yakutat chief visiting Sitka to dispose of his furs went on a debauch that ended in pneumonia, causing his death. His successor immediately demanded compensation for his life, claiming that if he had not visited Sitka he would not have died. [This seems to have been "Chief Minaman" (Merriman), also known as Daquseč, Wolf 32, 1810–90, of Yakutat. Both he and his daughter died of bad liquor at Sitka, where "seven tribes" were entertained at a potlatch on December 9, 1904, when a tombstone was erected on his grave. (See de Laguna 1972:200–201, pls. 210–11.)]

In the case of a Taku chief who drowned when his canoe tipped over off Killisnoo in 1895, the claim for compensation was made partly on the basis of the fact that the Hutsnuwu had given him the liquor which made him drunk, and partly because he died in foreign territory. Such a law made a host very cautious in the treatment of any guest. In my own case I recall visiting Klukwan in 1885 when relations between the several clans were strained. I was never permitted to approach the upper end of the village without some member of the family of my host in attendance.

[If someone committed suicide, the person who had driven him to this act was held responsible, as Emmons has indicated. For example, a Chilkoot Indian, a Raven man from Yandestake, visiting Sitka in 1881, attempted to kill his wife because he suspected her of infidelity with a Sitka man. He was arrested, but hanged himself in jail. According to custom, his clansmen held the alleged lover responsible. To avoid a feud, Commander Glass held a meeting of the two families concerned, and they agreed to settle the matter by a payment of blankets for the injury. Commander Lull, who temporarily replaced Glass, did not approve of this settlement, but acknowledged it to be just according to Indian law and did not interfere except to restrain the exorbitant demands made by one of the Chilkoot chiefs. When the news of the suicide first reached Yandestake, Danawak (Dá·na·wa·q, "Silver/Dollar Eyes"), the leading chief of the dead man's clan (Łukʷa·x̣ʔádi, Raven 17), is reported to have blamed the commander for not punishing the man who had caused the suicide. But when he learned of the payment, he was satisfied. (See Glass 1882:29–30; Lull 1882:47.)

[S. Hall Young (1927:101–2), the Wrangell missionary, held that the Tlingit were derived from the same stock as the ancient Jews because of their

> ready acceptance of the doctrine of blood-atonement. When we preached the vicarious sacrifice of Christ for sin they exclaimed, "Why, that is just like the death of our So-and-so," naming certain persons who had given their lives for the sake of their fellow-tribesmen.
>
> The unwritten law of the Thlingits demands payment *in like* for every wrong committed against one of their family [clan]. The

doctrine is the old Jewish one, "An eye for an eye and a tooth for a tooth"; but the eye must be of the same colour and the tooth of the same size. In other words, if a murder was committed, a life of the same dignity and tribal value as that of the murdered man must be exacted from the family of his slayer. If a chief is killed by a man of low degree belonging to another family, the chief of that man's family must be the one to pay the forfeit. Caste was very distinct, and there was endless debate concerning the relative prominence of different families. [p. 101]

[Shortly before Young's arrival at Wrangell in 1878, a member of "Tow-a-att's family" (Ṫawyá·ṫ, Wolf 25 or 26) had murdered a member of Shakes' people (Šé·kš, Na·nya̩·ʔa·yí̩, Wolf 18), the most prestigious clan in Wrangell (Young 1927:101–3).

> The two families fortified their houses, which were not far apart, the men of the Shakes family gathering on the little High-Tide-Island on which was the head chief's house. After much debating, many orations shouted back and forth, much recital of the dignity and wealth of the slain man and many demands for life and blankets, the quarrel had become so fierce that there was danger of a general war which would involve scores of natives and cost many lives. The trouble was ended, however, by the voluntary sacrifice of one of Tow-a-att's brothers, who had had no part in the killing of the murdered man.
>
> He dressed up in his best Chilcat blanket, put his chieftain's hat on his head, took in his hand an ancient spear, which was the emblem of his position as chief, went out in front of his stockade, made a speech in which he recalled the trouble and named himself as equal in rank to the man who was killed, and then gallantly walked out, with extended arms, half-way between the two stockades, and there was shot by a volley from the family of Shakes. Then there were feasts and mutual speeches, and the trouble was settled.

[A year later, in 1879, Young (1927:102–3) reported another killing. A Wrangell man killed his wife in a drunken quarrel while they were at their fish camp. He tied the body to his canoe by the neck, and towed it back to Wrangell. Then he called in the six or seven members of his clan or lineage, and fortified his house. The wife's clan was large and proud. They came to Reverend Young to ask what to do:

> The two families were at war, and shots were being fired back and forth from the different houses. [The headmen of Wrangell rejected the idea of bringing the murderer himself to justice, according to white man's law, and the murderer also objected.] "It is not right that my life should pay forfeit for that of my wife, who was a woman; there is my sister; you can take her and kill her, and justice will be satisfied." [The sister took refuge in the fort, and did not venture out for three months] during which time bullets were flying over the town. [Meanwhile, relatives of the dead wife waited outside the murderer's house. In January 1880, when the Hutsnuwu and Stikine were fighting, the murderer came out to fight the Hutsnuwu.] The murderer said, "Let me not die by the hands of my Stickeen friends; let me be killed by our enemies, the Hoochenoos." [But his wife's people shot him anyway.]

[For an account of this last trouble, see Chapter 12, the section "Interclan Warfare."

[F. K. Louthan (in Colyer 1870b:16–17) wrote on October 28, 1869:

> . . . [The Tlingit] are tractable and kind when kindly treated, but vindictive and exacting full compensation for wrongs inflicted, come from what quarter they may. All difficulties, even that of killing one of their number, is [*sic*] measured by an *estimated value,* "so many blankets," or the equivalent in money, or what they may elect. The failure to promptly pay for a real or supposed injury is at once the signal for retaliation. I can but look with great favor upon the system on the part of the government, of adapting itself to the one idea, *immediate settlement* with their people for all wrongs of magnitude, (whether on the part of the military or the individual,) entirely upon *estimated value.* This is the time-honored custom of the red man in Alaska, and pertains to all alike, wherever dispersed throughout the vast Territory.
>
> At present it is more than folly to attempt to induct him into any other way of looking at a wrong or injury.

[Louthan went on to tell how he had dealt with the problem caused by the shooting by a sentry of a Chilkat Indian who was visiting Sitka in the winter of 1868–69. For five months the Chilkats had remained at home and the trade at Sitka suffered, so Louthan paid them a visit with his little schooner. He found them sullen and listless. On the fourth day, his vessel was boarded by seventy-five armed men, bent on satisfaction for the man killed at Sitka. Louthan was able to avoid trouble by giving them a letter to the commanding general at Sitka, asking him to pay for the man killed, and promising himself to pay if the general refused. General Jefferson C. Davis would not even listen to the delegation. Louthan therefore went back to the Chilkats and "promptly paid the price asked—thirteen blankets and one coat, amounting in value, all told, to about fifty dollars, coin. I feel quite sure that in this simple settlement I arrested serious trouble to myself and to the government." Failure to follow this policy resulted in the "Kake War" (see "Encounters with Americans" in Chapter 12).

[When Commander Beardslee was sent with the USS *Jamestown* to Sitka (May 1879 to November 1880), to keep order there after the withdrawal of the Army, he saw it as his duty to learn the laws and customs of the Tlingit. There were no treaties with the Indians, and federal law recognized in such cases that local tribal law was competent to deal with cases between Indians. Of Tlingit law, he wrote (Beardslee 1882:45):

The Indians have a code of laws based upon their ideas of strict justice. If one Indian inflicts a blow or any other injury upon another the matter can be, and frequently is, adjusted at a consultation in which both families are represented[,] either by the inflicting of an equal injury or by the payment to the injured party of an equivalent. Even a life taken can be settled for in this way, payments being made, according to the amount assessed, in slaves, furs, or blankets. By the unwritten but thoroughly established provisions of this law a man who sells or gives to another liquor, from the effects of which death ensues, is responsible for the death, and must pay the assessed value. If an Indian dies while in the house of another, or if killed in any way while in the employ of another, the house-owner or employer is responsible. The Indians seldom fail to yield to this, the very foundation of their laws, and a refusal to make equitable reparation is always a cause of war.

[That was the situation at Sitka. Five Kiksʔádi (Raven 10) had been drowned while serving on a schooner which was lost in Bering Strait. Through their chief, Katlian (Q̓ałyá·n), the Indians were pressing for compensation of $200 for each man lost. The Collector of Customs at Sitka explained that under the U.S. laws of that time no payment could be made, so the claim was reduced to one for the wages of the dead men. The wages were collected at San Francisco, but were swallowed up by lawyers' fees and expenses; the Indians got nothing, and in consequence felt wronged. "As chief of the tribe," Beardslee wrote (1882:45), "it was the duty of Katlaan [Katlian] to act for them in this matter, and he, being angered by what he and they considered injustice, made threats against the whites 'to get even.'" The whites in Sitka, fearing the Indians, appealed for protection, and this caused Beardslee to be sent to Alaska with the *Jamestown*. But actually, he reported, it was Katlian and Annahootz (the Ka·gʷa·nta·n chief) who quieted the inflamed and drunken Indians, and so prevented a massacre.

[In a later passage Beardslee (1882:50) added:

Every person in every family is bound to assist any member of it who has received injury from any member of another family in obtaining compensation from the injurer, or failing in that, from his family. . . .

The most sacred duty is retaliation; the word in their language which expresses it is "to get even." Their code would necessarily involve them in endless feuds, were it not that all injuries have their prices, and can be paid for.

After due consultation at a *pow-wow* between the leaders of the two families, a certain price is fixed, which is paid either in slaves, furs, or blankets, according to its amount. I have been called upon several times to investigate and act as arbiter, and have permitted this atonement, which satisfied all parties, in preference to inflicting punishments, which would make all parties dissatisfied.

[Beardslee's own policy was to refuse to act as judge, telling the Tlingit who had appealed to him that they all knew their laws and could settle their disputes, but that it must be done peacefully. Glass and Lull who succeeded him, both willingly settled disputes for the Indians, even to making peace between the Auks and Stikines, between the Sitkas and the Stikines, and between the Hutsnuwus and the Stikines (the clans actually involved were not identified), and settled some cases between Indians and whites. This "lenient" policy was reversed by Captain Merriman in 1882, leading to the shelling of Angoon (see de Laguna 1960:158–72, and sources cited).

[Curiously enough, Emmons failed to cite one instance that testified to the Tlingit's sense of honor and willingness to comply with the law, even the white man's. This incident is recounted by Eliza R. Scidmore in the Eleventh Census report on Alaska (1893:46).

George, the son of Chartrich, was arrested and taken to Sitka to be tried for some trifling charge. As it was in the height of the salmon season, and 6 weeks would elapse before his trial, George was released on bail, Lieutenant G. T. Emmons pledging $1,000 for his return when wanted for trial. When the government steamer, upon which George was to go back to Sitka, reached Chilkat, one of the fearful windstorms peculiar to Lynn canal was drafting down the long canyon and fiord and lashing the water to a foam. George made three attempts to reach the ship and each time was swamped or upset and obliged to swim back to shore. The ship sailed away without him, but George, paddling for a day and two nights through the lulling storm, managed to overtake the ship at Juneau and reach Sitka in time for trial.

[This episode was important for Emmons, because he listed "Baled Chartrich 1892" (*sic*) in a memorandum of the important events and accomplishments of his life.]

TRADE*

The Tlingit is a born trader. If there were any tricks he did not know originally, he learned them from the early whites whose methods were universally questionable and

**Editor's note:* I have introduced statements on the use of liquor in trade (from Williams in Colyer, and General Davis), on trade goods and their value (from Mahoney), and on the economic power of women (from Wood). The section concludes with a passage from *The History of Tlingit Clans and Tribes*, and a comment on trade partners. Localities and tribes in the interior have been identified by Dr. Catharine McClellan.

often dishonest. It is on record that trading vessels sold the natives muskets with the lock-spring partly sawed through, which shortly broke and rendered the guns useless. Upon the return trip of the vessel, these were repurchased for a trifle, and after being repaired and again tampered with, were resold to the Indians.

[Liquor was also used by the traders as a means of cheating the Indians, who soon became so addicted to it that they were willing to pay outrageous prices to secure it. As Harry G. Williams wrote Vincent Colyer from Wrangell, October 30, 1869 (Williams in Colyer, 1870b:11):

> They are very fond of coffee, sugar, and molasses, and like all other Indians easily become fond of ardent spirits, to obtain which they will sometimes sacrifice nearly everything in their possession. In this manner they are imposed upon by those who know no principle or law, who have been known to sell them essence of peppermint, Stoughton's bitters, and absinthe, charging them four dollars a bottle, (holding one pint). Absinthe is a compound which, if used as a constant beverage, soon unseats the mind, produces insanity, and sometimes death.

[General Jefferson Davis (1869:136) also wrote:

> At present, competition in trade along the coast of Alaska is very great, and the Indians are getting good prices for all commodities they have to sell; when not drugged with liquor, the Indian looks out very well for himself in making bargains.
>
> He cannot, however, withstand the temptations of strong drink, and when under its influence he is easily cheated and robbed of all he has. The great desire the Indians have for strong drinks, and the immense profits derived from the sale of it among them, induces the unscrupulous traders to resort to every trick possible to introduce it into the country. The spurious and poisonous character of the liquors frequently attempted to be smuggled into the country is difficult to describe; it is probably beyond chemical analysis; its effects upon the Indians are little better than strychnine. What the character of the trader is, can be readily inferred.

Despite the law of Congress, July 27, 1868, attempting to regulate the importation of liquor into the Territory, there remained plenty of bootleggers, and the program was no more successful than Prohibition.]

As late as 1885, and even later, trade was carried on with paper tickets, redeemable only where issued, at a profit ranging from 100% to 500%, the latter being on molasses and brown sugar that were used in the distillation of *hootchanoo* [or "hootchenoo," derived from Xú·c-nu·wú, "Brown Bear Fort," the name given by the Hutsnuwu tribe to their homeland on northern Admiralty Island, where home brew was first made by the Tlingit]. These paper tickets, being flimsy, were easily destroyed, and so the trader made a further gain. Until competition became keen and currency came into use, the native received little justice in trade.

Silver as a medium of exchange hardly came into use by the natives before 1880, and then circulated only in the white settlements where there were stores. In the summer of 1883, when at Yakutat, I wished to purchase a canoe, but the native owner would not accept silver, and I had to draw blankets from the ship's stores to pay for it. Before the advent of Europeans, native food products and worked objects had certain relative values for trade purposes, although it is difficult to learn that there were any absolute fixed standards. [See Oberg 1973, chap. 7, "Trade," especially pp. 111–13.] An old Chilkat stated that a Tsimshian who executed the fine carvings in the Whale House at Klukwan received in payment ten slaves, fifty dressed moose skins, and a number of blankets. The Hudson's Bay Company established the beaver skin as the standard of value throughout Canada, but owing to the scarcity of beaver along the coast of British Columbia and Alaska, this could not be maintained. To some extent the land otter pelt replaced the beaver skin, for in 1840, when the Hudson's Bay Company leased the littoral of Alaska from the Russian American Company for ten years, the principal annual payment consisted of three thousand land otter skins. Later, the Hudson's Bay Company's "three-point" blanket became a unit of value that was accepted by all the tribes of the coast and held its place as long as the old communal life lasted. Around the walls of the old houses could be seen piles of chests filled with blankets, representing the wealth of the occupants. Blankets were universally worn by both sexes, distributed at potlatches, exchanged for canoes, or paid in settlement of obligations. [The same blankets were not, however, used for both wearing and for payment. The blanket for wear was called x̣̓ú·w; the new blanket for potlatching and payment was ƚ̓í·.] The establishment of commercial industries in southeastern Alaska and the employment of native labor revolutionized the life of the people. Not only did the blanket lose both its relative and its intrinsic values, but exchange came to be reckoned on a dollar basis.

As the European had imposed on him, the Tlingit in turn dominated the interior people, for it was only through his position as a middleman that arms and ammunition, so necessary to the hunting life, could be obtained. In very early days, the Tlingit procured copper, moose and caribou skins, and smaller furs from the interior, which he traded to the Haida for great red cedar canoes and to the Tsimshian for carved wooden dishes, boxes, and woven fabrics. After the advent of Europeans, the increased demand for furs made the interior trade so much more profitable that the Tlingit discouraged and threatened any white competition, and absolutely prohibited the interior people from coming to the coast, except under Tlingit escort. It is told that during the Hudson's Bay Company's lease of the coast, a Tahltan chief wished to come down the Stikine River to see a trading vessel, then at its mouth, but his passage was permitted only upon payment to a Stikine chief of Wrangell of five hundred beaver skins, and even then, he was kept under surveillance. Unquestionably, the number of beaver skins is greatly exaggerated in the story [see Emmons 1911a:7].

Trade with other Tlingit or with the neighboring coastal peoples was on an individual basis, but with the interior tribes it was a hereditary right in the hands of certain Tlingit chiefs and headmen who traded for themselves and their followers. Their privileges were respected by all parties. This arrangement, based on mutual consent and the dominance of the more powerful Tlingit, seems to have originated from the continued advantages derived by the Tlingit in marrying interior (Athabaskan) women. The Chilkat went on these trading expeditions in the spring (about May) before the salmon fishing season, in midwinter [end of January and February, according to Emmons's notes in BCPA], and sometimes also in the fall [October]. They signaled their approach by firing a large tree, and they met the Athabaskans at some appointed place. The ordinary trip consumed a month. Only the men went on the longest journeys.

The only trade routes into the interior were up the Stikine and Taku rivers, and over the Chilkoot and Chilkat passes. [There was also a route via the Alsek River which empties into Dry Bay on the Gulf Coast of Alaska.] On the rivers they employed canoes, but over the mountains they trailed with back packs and used dogs as pack animals. Both men and women carried packs. The average pack of the man weighed one hundred pounds, although some carried over two hundred pounds, in addition to snowshoes and food. All this they carried over three thousand feet of steep mountain trail, and then several hundred miles beyond, taking advantage of all available water. The woman's pack weighed from fifty to eighty pounds, and dogs carried as much as twenty-five pounds in each saddle bag. The Chilkat were trained to this work from early childhood. I have seen a boy of five playing with a single dried salmon strapped on his back, which he carried throughout the day, and I have met boys a few years older with regular packs containing their own outfits.

Domestic barter was carried on in such products as might be in excess of the needs of the particular tribes involved. The Yakutat were the hair seal hunters and made quantities of oil which they traded, together with pressed strawberry cakes, spruce root baskets (of their own manufacture), and native copper which they procured in trade from the interior natives of the White and Copper rivers. [Commander Beardslee (1882:57) reported the arrival at Sitka of a trading party of Hoonah, bringing skins of sea otters, seals, bears, minks, and also oil from stranded whales. Whale and seal oil, put up in bladders of one to five gallons, or in "oil-tight tubs which they carve out of solid blocks of wood," was worth twenty-five cents a gallon.] The *Hootz-ah-tas* [Hutsnuwu] were the herring grease makers. The Chilkats, Stickines, and Takus, with their trails and river routes to the interior, were the fur traders. The island tribes put up herring spawn and seaweed and had the monopoly of the sea otter grounds. [To protest the intrusion of Tsimshian Indians on their sea otter hunting grounds was the principal reason for the visit of the Hoonah men to Commander Beardslee at Sitka. The Yakutat also came to resent Tsimshian encroachment on theirs (see de Laguna 1972:284–86).] The Tongass and Sanya traded on the Nass for eulachon grease which they exchanged with the more northern people.

Standards of value changed from time to time and increased with each exchange [as products were traded farther and farther from their point of origin]. The following list was obtained at Sitka about 1890. [See Table 15.]

[Frank Mahoney, a trader for some sixteen years, wrote to Vincent Collier in 1870 from Sitka (Mahoney 1870:20):

> [The Chilkats] catch some furs about their own grounds, but the greater portion comes from the interior, or where they go to trade twice a year, spring and fall. There is no doubt but they make a big profit on the skins they bring down.
>
> . . . They will allow no whites to pass up the rivers. The trade which the coast Indians take into the interior consists of dry goods, blankets, tobacco, powder, shot, and light flint-lock muskets, if they can get them. Although the ammunition and muskets are a prohibited trade in this Territory, still the Indians get them from the Hudson's Bay Company of Fort Simpson. Steel traps, knives, hatchets, needles and thread, and a little cheap jewelry, form their principal trade, for which they get in exchange, marten, mink, silver, cross and red fox, black, brown, and grizzly bear, lynx, wolverine, ermine, beaver, land otter, and some inferior skins. . . . [In addition to yard goods and blankets, powder and shot, tobacco and molasses (for making hootch), the traders

sell] Steel traps, knives, vermillion, flour, hard bread, beans, rice, and some few articles in the way of clothing, pants, shirts, (cotton and woolen,) blue cloth caps with glazed covers, shoes, and some minor articles.

[Although Mahoney summarized the trade of all the Tlingit groups, his information on the other tribes was not as complete as for the Chilkat. For the cost to the Chilkat of the furs they obtained and for the prices these fetched from the traders, as well as for the costs of some trade articles, see Table 16, compiled from information in Mahoney's letter.

[A note among Emmons's papers at AMNH indicates: "Beads were valued at so much according to color: Yellow 30 cents; Red 40 cents; Blue 50 cents. Chilkat."]

In exchange and sale, the husband depended upon his wife's judgment, and she had an equal voice. Indeed, if a sale had been consummated in her absence, she might repudiate the transaction and demand the money back. I personally know of an instance when a man purchased a pair of trousers, which, not meeting the approval of his wife, they were taken back and the money had to be refunded. If a surplus of any kind of food were found in the spring, the period of food shortage, the wife selected it and placed it on the outer platform [front porch] in front of the owner, for the attention of passers-by [and traded it].

[Major E. S. Wood, who was traveling in Alaska in the summer of 1877, was both provoked and amused at the way the Tlingit made and revoked bargains. Of the Alaskan women he wrote (1882:333):

> Their authority in all matters is unquestioned. No bargain is made, no expedition set on foot, without first consulting the women. Their veto is never disregarded. I bought a silver-fox skin from Tsa-tate, but his wife made him return the articles of trade and recover the skin. In the same way I was perpetually being annoyed by having to undo bargains because "his wife said *clekh* [ƛ̣ék!]," that is, "no." I hired a fellow to take me about thirty miles in his canoe, when my own crew was tired. He agreed. I paid him the tobacco, and we were about to start when his wife came to the beach and stopped him. He quietly unloaded the canoe and handed me the tobacco. The whole people are curious in the matter of trade. I was never sure that I had done with a bargain, for they claimed and exercised the right to undo a contract at any time, provided they could return the consideration received. This is their code among themselves. For example: I met at the mouth of the Chilkáht a native trader who had been to Fort Simpson, about six hundred miles away, and failing to get as much as he gave in the interior of Alaska for the skins, was now returning to the interior to find the first vendor and revoke the whole transaction. Among themselves their currency is a species of wampum [dentalia], worth about twenty dollars a string, beaver-skins worth about a dollar a skin, and sable or marten worth about two dollars a skin. From the whites they get blankets worth four dollars apiece, and silver dollars; gold they will not touch (except around Sitka and Wrangell), but they accept copper and silver.

[A great deal of domestic and foreign trade was carried on ceremonially by the Tlingit, as a form of gift exchange. This is made clear by the accounts of the eighteenth-century traders, who chafed at the delays caused by Tlingit ceremonialism, and by the reports of Oberg (1973, especially pp. 91–113) and Olson (1936), who described the trade between the Tlingit and their Athabaskan trade partners. (See also de Laguna 1972:346–57.) Emmons had this to say about Chilkat trade in his *History of Tlingit Clans and Tribes:*]

While the Chilkat, like all other Tlingit, looked to the water for their staple food supply, their wealth was derived from the land in their trade with the interior peoples, the products of which they both used and exchanged with more southern coast tribes. Before the advent of Europeans, they procured caribou and moose skins and the pelts of smaller mammals for clothing from the Yukon and Alsek basins, and float copper from the White River valley. Upon the coming of trading vessels, the value of furs greatly increased, and this trade was proportionately augmented while the acquisition of iron and steel made copper valuable only for ornamental purposes. Their first foreign market was Sitka. After the lease of the littoral to the Hudson's Bay Company [in 1840], the exchange was carried on both with the Company's vessels at "Labouchere" or Pyramid Harbor [near the mouth of the Chilkat River], and at Port Simpson. With the American acquisition of Alaska [1867], Wrangell became the center of trade, and later Juneau [about 1883]. The chief industry of the Chilkat-Chilkoot was trading. They made from two to three trips annually over their mountain trails to the interior, each of which consumed from ten to thirty-odd days. The first journey was made in mid-winter when the snow was hard and travel was more certain. This was a preliminary trip to make arrangements for the most important spring trade when the winter catch of furs had been taken. This trip was made in April, before the arrival of the eulachon; the trying out of its oil was of supreme importance, for the grease was the greatest dietetic luxury known to the coast people. The trading journeys were made by family [clan, or lineage] parties and included most or all of the able bodied men of the village. They paddled, poled, and tracked by canoe for days along the rivers to the great glacier which they crossed, and then inland, along rivers, over lakes, and by trail for some two hundred miles, to the native village of *Hootchyee* [Hutshi, on the Yukon headwaters, Southern Tutchone], where, by appointment or through smoke signals, they met the interior people. Another trip, taken in August when the salmon catch had been made, was by way of the Klaheen [Klehini River, the large eastern tributary to the Chilkat, which enters the latter a short distance above Klukwan], to *Kluck shu* [Klukshu], where they traded with the Alsek people [i.e., with the Southern Tutchone of the Alsek headwaters].

In early days they followed down the Alsek in winter to the coast and traded with the *Gu nah ho* [Ģuna·x̣u· qʷá·n, Dry Bay tribe] and Yakutat. Trading was not an individual affair in which each person could follow his own wishes; it was systematized and was carried on by the chiefs and principal men for themselves and their followers, and the right to trade with certain families was the exclusive privilege of some Chilkats. The Chilkat made the prices and dominated these more helpless interior people who were absolutely dependent on them for arms, ammunition, and all European products, as they were excluded from the coast except under escort and surveillance.

The following list of *Gu na nah* or interior [Ģunana·, "Athabaskan"] tribes with whom the Chilkat traded, and the families [clans or moieties] in each corresponding with the Tlingit families [clans] was given me by an old Chilkat at Klukwan:

Thluke shuck, "where the salmon stop in the midst of a log jam in the river" [Klukshu, or Ł̓u·kʷ šú· "coho salmon end," on the headwaters of the Alsek]—[No clans listed].

Huts cut te heen Kwan [probably Neskatahin or Weskatahin, also called "Old Dalton Post," below Klukshu on the Alsek River]—Three corresponding families: *Con nuh ta de* [Ģa·nax̣te·dí, Raven 3], *Shen ku qway de* [Šankukʷe·dí, Wolf 8], *Tuck cla way de* [Daqł̓awe·dí, Wolf 27].

Alsek Kwan [ʔA·łsé·x qʷa·n, perhaps the people from Nuqʷaʔik, originally Tlingit, whose survivors joined the Alsek River Athabaskans]—Two corresponding families: *Con nuh ta de* [Raven 3], *Shen ku qway de* [Wolf 8].

Thlu tchur Kwan, "big fish lake people" [perhaps Kluane Lake]—Three corresponding families: *Con nuh ta de* [Raven 3], *Shen ku qway de* [Wolf 8], *Tuck cla way de* [Wolf 27].

Ah sha eek Kwan [Aishihik]—Two corresponding families: *Con nuh ta de* [Raven 3], *Shen ku qway de* [Wolf 8].

Thluke dah siya Kwan, "salmon lake tribe" [perhaps Ł̓u·kʷ dasiy̨ ʔá·, Lake Laberge?]—Two corresponding families: *Con nuh ta de* [Raven 3], *Shen ku qway de* [Wolf 8].

Eeak heene Kwan, "copper river tribe" [perhaps the Atna of the Copper River, more likely the Northern Tutchone of the White River, from both of whom native copper was traded]—Two corresponding clans: *Con nuh ta de* [Raven 3], *Shen ku qway de* [Wolf 8].

The corresponding families, as given, would in the case of the "*Con nuh ta de*" mean a Raven family, and in the case of the "*Shen ku qway de*" mean a Wolf family [i.e., refers only to the moiety], but in the case of the *Tuck cla way de* which is a Wolf family [a specific Wolf clan], would rather refer to a distinct branch of this family within the Wolf phratry.

[Trade partners, wu·š yaqá·wu, "mutually joined-together," should belong to the same moiety, but to different clans, according to the Yakutat (de Laguna 1972:355); to the same clan, or its equivalent (Olson 1936:212); "Ideally the two men were always of the same sib and were 'best friends'" (McClellan 1975, 2:506). For a vivid description of Southern Tutchone trade relations with the Chilkat, see McClellan 1975, 2:501–9, and for the clans among them, see 439–45. I am indebted to McClellan for tentative identification of the places or peoples listed above by Emmons, all in Southern Tutchone territory but the last. (See McClellan 1975, vol. 1, map 2 and table 1.)]

CHAPTER 3

Villages, Houses, Forts, and Other Works

VILLAGES*

Each Tlingit tribe had at least one permanent settlement that might more aptly be termed the winter village, since it was largely deserted throughout the remainder of the year when its semi-nomadic inhabitants were scattered over their country in families and larger groups, gathering and preparing their subsistence for the winter. The early explorers who skirted the outside coast for a month or two in summer saw only small parties at their fishing camps, and unfortunately there is no fair description of any single permanent village as observed in the eighteenth century. Nor can we get any idea of the population of southeastern Alaska at that time. In later days, the establishment of trade centers, missions, and so forth, have drawn the people away from their old settlements, which have gradually disappeared. So the numerous living sites marked by the absence of trees and by the luxuriant growth of berry bushes and fireweed cannot be taken to indicate the coexistence of so many villages and a proportionately large population of natives [for we cannot assume that all these sites were simultaneously occupied]. Unquestionably, the whole Northwest Coast has suffered a great diminution of population since its discovery, but from the careful records of Vancouver and other early visitors there is nothing to indicate an excessive population, or even one commensurate with the food possibilities of the area.

[From notes in BCPA, it is evident that Emmons went carefully through Vancouver's account and listed all the Tlingit whom Vancouver or his exploring parties had met in 1793 and 1794. The total is surprisingly low. On the basis of archaeological work in the Angoon area, we may conclude that the evidence suggests that "in the past the northern Tlingit were anything but numerous, although the area in which they lived could apparently have supported much greater numbers" (de Laguna 1960:205).]

Each tribe usually had one permanent village, but when two or more villages are found within the same tribal territory, one is the main village, and the others were usually established because of internal differences [or because of other misfortunes]. The Tlingit are naturally wanderers, as their history proves.

Thus, the Chilkat proper have lived at Klukwan from their beginning as a tribe, while the Chilkoot branch originally settled on Chilkoot Lake. Later, because of family dissensions, [some of] the Chilkoot crossed over the divide to the Chilkat River and established *Yundastahka* [Yandestake; Y̨ánde·sť aqyé; Orth 1967:359, "Gandesgastaki"] and *Katqwaltu* [Kutwaltu; from -łutú, "nostril"?; Orth 1967:491, "Kalwatta"]. Again, Angoon on Admiralty Island was the center for the *Hoots-ah ta Kwan* [Hutsnuwu tribe] until trouble arose between the *Dashetan* [De·šï·ta·n, Raven 13] and their nearest relations, the *An-kark-hit-tan* [ˀA·nx̣a·kíta·n, Raven 14], when the latter left and established *Nel-toosk-an* [Neltushkin, Nałdú·šgánt] on Whitewater Bay, south of Angoon. [According to Garfield (1947: 441–42), the Raven 13 claim that their ancestors settled at Whitewater Bay before Angoon was founded. This town was still inhabited until early in the present century, but was deserted before 1950.]

The village of *Klem-sha-shick-ian* [Łʼéw-ša·-šaki-ˀa·n, "sand-mountain-top-town"] in Glacier Bay on the north side of Cross Sound was the home of the *Hoonah Kow* [Xuna·qá·wu, or Hoonah tribe] until it was destroyed by an advancing glacier [see Swanton 1909:337–38 for the story]. The tribe then separated and founded both *Kook nu-ou* [Kax̓-nu·wú, "Grouse Fort"] and *Gaudakan* [Ga·w-ṫaq-ˀa·n, "town beside the drum or bell," which became the modern Hoonah]. Grouse Fort was visited by a fatal disease, and when it was deserted, the inhabitants went to Sitka and settled there.

In 1888, when I was passing through the seaward channels of Prince of Wales Island, I stopped at *Tche-qwan* (or *Tchuqwan*) [?] on a small island about twelve miles

---

Editor's notes: This chapter remains much as Emmons had planned it, except that a section, "Domestic Life," has been transferred here from the original "Chapter V: Domestic Life." The section on "Totem Poles" has been transferred from this chapter to Chapter 7 and descriptions of shamans' graves and gravehouses to Chapter 10 (the latter is found in the section "Recent Graveyards").

**Editor's note:* I added the last paragraph to summarize this section and to introduce the specialized buildings and other features to be described.

above Tuxekan [in Henya territory]. It was a veritable city of the dead from which the survivors had fled en masse after a visitation of small pox [1862]. The houses with their interior carvings and totem poles still stood intact, left to weather and decay, but passing canoes avoided that shore, while the occupants propitiated the evil spirits with an offering of tobacco or food.

The rugged coast of southeastern Alaska with its countless islands, labyrinth of channels, and deep fiords offered living places at every hand that fulfilled such essential requirements as sloping beaches and sheltered waters for the landing of canoes, protection from the winter winds, and fresh water. Less importance than has often been claimed was attached to the immediate proximity of local food-producing areas, for the Tlingit left the winter village and spent the period from early spring to late fall gathering supplies for the winter. The later season was regarded as a period of relaxation and feasting. In fact, the whole social structure was built upon the winter [festivities and ceremonies], for which the work of the rest of the year had provided. Furthermore, the shores and waters were everywhere sufficiently rich in marine life to support the natives in extremities.

Villages were more often situated in shallow bights, easy of access, than at the head of deep bays. The houses faced the beach in one or two parallel rows following the trend of the shore, and were far enough above the reach of the tide to allow for a roadway [path] in front and for the hauling up of canoes. Where space permitted, the old village consisted of a single row of houses, for in these large communal dwellings there were fifty or more inmates, and the house frontage was, in consequence, crowded with canoes, fish-drying frames, etc., and this space became too restricted if it had to be shared with other houses in the rear. So far as I have observed, the addition of a second or even a third row has only come about in recent years with the breaking up of the old communal system and the building of separate family houses. In every village there were two or more totemic families [clans], each occupying a number of houses that originally were grouped about that of their [own clan] chief. With the increase in village population, this plan could not always be followed, as the houses stood fairly close to each other, and new houses had to take their places at either end of the village or in the rear of the others. Sometimes whole villages were protected by stockades or other defenses, as was done by the Sitka people after they destroyed the Russian post and feared the retaliation of the Russians (see below "Forts"). Again, the houses of one particular family in a village might be enclosed within a stockade [as at Wrangell in 1878], or even a single house might be so guarded. Generally, however, the villages were unprotected, while natural defensive positions on nearby bluff headlands or rocky islands were fortified, to which the villagers might flee in time of danger.

[On the beach in front of the houses, there might be ditches into which the large canoes could be drawn and where they were protected from the sun by shelters of bark or brush. If the beach was rocky, the larger stones or boulders would be rolled aside to make smooth lanes (ya·k^{w} de·yí, "canoe road") up which the canoes could be dragged. Behind or at one end of the village, occasionally on an island opposite, was the graveyard, with small houses or mortuary columns to hold the ashes of the dead. Other mortuary columns, or totem poles in towns where Haida or Tsimshian influences were strong, stood in front of the houses. Other structures in the village might be smokehouses for curing fish, cache houses for storing provisions, and shelters behind the houses to which women retired during menstruation or child-bearing. According to Emmons, these shelters were temporary, and the other structures were not necessarily found in every village.

[The Reverend Young's description of the native village at Wrangell in 1878 is not flattering (1927:93):

> A walk through the Stickeen town was both interesting and revolting to our civilized tastes. The houses were all built on the beach, which was slimy and filthy with decayed fish, meat and offal, carcasses of dead dogs, skeletons of deer and other animals and even human bones—those of slaves who had died and, of course, had been refused cremation, strewed the pebbly beach. There were no sidewalks or beaten paths. Many of the community houses were set up on posts, and under them came swashing the higher tides at time of full moon.]

HOUSES*

Tlingit houses, large and small, were structurally alike but differed materially in interior arrangements. The larger

Editor's note: Emmons wanted to include the full description of the Whale House, plus all its illustrations, copied "*exactly*" from his publication (1916a), despite Bella Weitzner's protests. The text that follows here I have based on that printed description, checked against the illustrations, but shortened wherever possible. My additional observations are enclosed in square brackets. I have added information about houses seen by Malaspina and members of his expedition, and the descriptions by Louis and Florence Shotridge of a typical Chilkat house. The last six paragraphs (rebuilding on an old site, and modern houses) are mine. The house-building ceremonies originally included in this section by Emmons have been shifted to Chapter 11.

Two views of Bear House, Ka·gʷa·nta·n, *Wolf 1, Klukwan, 1885. (Photographs by G. T. Emmons. BCPA.)*

Decorated house fronts. (Pencil sketches by G. T. Emmons, probably 1888. AMNH.) Top. *Painting representing a Whale with a Raven's head as the dorsal fin (probably the Whale House of the* Tá·kʷʔa·ne·dí, *Raven 2), Henya, Tuxekan, Prince of Wales Island.* Bottom. *Painting representing the Brown Bear crest of the* Te·qʷe·dí, *Wolf 32, Tongass Island.*

and more important houses were partly subterranean, with one or two steplike platforms descending to a central square enclosure, from four to six feet below the surface of the ground. Such houses were ornamented with carved posts and screens, heraldic in character and illustrating important events in the life of the clan, while the small houses stood directly on the ground [lacking the excavated floor], and were crude and plain. Spruce was uniformly used by the Northern Tlingit, while red cedar was sometimes used by the southern tribes. The carvings were of cedar. Hemlock, the most abundant wood, was sometimes used, especially for the outer planks, but only when other woods were not to be had. The primitive house rested on the ground, but later houses copied from the whites have been built on piles.

The old type of house was rectangular in plan, with a depth greater than the frontage. For example, an old Chilkat house had a frontage of fifty feet, and was fifty-five feet in depth. [The house had a low-pitched gable roof; the gable end with doorway faced the water.] The house front was often painted with animal figures [crests], or was ornamented with carved figures on either side of the entrance [sometimes above it]. The doorway was oval and low, and was reached by several steps. It was itself a means of defense, since one stooping to enter was in no position to attack [the inmates] or to defend himself. The door was heavily built and could be barred from the inside. [Krause ([1885] 1956:87) confirms this description, but indicates that in 1880–81 most doorways were small square openings, not oval; this is, in fact, shown by most of the photographs taken by Emmons a few years later.] Windows that are seen on modern Tlingit houses [1900?] had no place in the past; the doorway and smokehole in the roof were the only openings. To present intelligibly the methods of house construction, I will describe in detail one of the principal old family houses of the Chilkat at Klukwan.

This was *Yough-hit* [Yá·y̨ hít], "Whale House," of the hereditary chief of the *Con-nuh-ta-di* [G̨a·nax̱te·dí, Raven 3]. [See Emmons 1916a.]

The Whale House was built about 1835 and was torn down in 1899 to make way for a half-modern structure which was never finished. It represented the best type of Tlingit architecture: a broad, low building, of heavy hewn spruce timbers, carefully united through groove, tenon,

"Chief Killerwhale Dorsal Fin House," Tle goushi hit [łi-gu·ší, *"it has a dorsal fin"*], *belonging to the chief of the* Ka·gʷa·nta·n, *Wolf 1, Klukwan, 1885. (Pen and ink sketch by G. T. Emmons. AMNH.) The house was built about 1830. It had a frontage of 46 feet and a depth of 50 feet. The front, below the gable, consisted of two heavy hewn spruce timbers, A, one above the other, neatly adzed and fitted into the corner posts, B. On the side nearest the other family houses was a very narrow door to receive supplies or reinforcements.*

and mortise, to support each other without extraneous fastening.

It has a frontage of 49 feet 10 inches, and a depth of 53 feet. At each corner, set firmly in the ground, was a broad, neatly adzed post [shaped like a heavy plank], grooved along the edges to receive the reduced ends of the heavy bed pieces and wall planks. [The tops of the corner posts rose a foot or more above the height of the eaves.] Midway along each of the two sides and in the middle of the back wall was an intermediate upright, correspondingly grooved along both edges to take the other ends of the horizontal wall planks. Across the front, two heavy timbers or planks, one resting on the other, extended from corner post to corner post and built up the front wall to the height of the door sill. The upper member of this pair was grooved along its upper edge to hold the lower ends of the vertical planks that formed the house front. [The rear of the house had horizontal planking up to the eaves; above this, the wall in the gable end was of vertical planks.] The cornice capping [that formed the gable at each end] fitted over the upper ends of the vertical planks, and was notched to fit over a groove or shoulder on the inside of the corner posts. The doorway, some three feet above the ground, was reached by two steps. [It was cut through a very wide plank in the house front.]

The roof structure, wholly independent of the walls, was supported by four heavy interior posts, *gars* [gá·ṡ̓]. These were firmly planted in the ground, in pairs equidistant from the side walls, but nearer to the front wall than the back. Resting in shallow grooves on top of these were the two great roof beams, made from neatly adzed tree trunks, two feet in diameter, that ran the length of the house. On these were placed a series of cross beams that, in turn, supported two similar, but smaller, longitudinal beams, set closer to the center of the house than the larger beams below. These smaller timbers likewise carried cross beams, upon which rested the ridgepole. The last was in two sections, to make space for the central smokehole. On this cribwork that gave the desired pitch to the roof rested the smaller rafters and cross beams on which split boards were overlapped, as shingles are laid, and these were kept in place by small tree trunks that extended the length of the roof and were weighted with heavy boulders at either end. [Krause ([1885] 1956:87) reported that the house roof usually rested on four longitudinal beams, and consisted of two to three courses of planks, overlapped like shingles.]

The smokehole in the center of the roof both lighted and ventilated the interior. It had a movable shutter, working on a crossbar that rested in the notch of cross sticks at either end. It was so nicely balanced that it could be tilted to either side, depending on the direction of the wind. The roof could be reached by a ladder consisting of a small tree trunk notched to make steps.

In the interior of the house was an excavation five feet below ground level, that was reached by descending two steplike platforms that enclosed an open space about twenty-six feet square. This served as the living and work room of the household during the day. The portion in the rear of the fireplace, directly opposite the entrance, was, however, reserved for the head of the house, his immediate family, and guests.

A flooring of heavy smoothed planks of varying widths was laid directly on the earth around the six-foot square fireplace. In the floor on one side was a trapdoor leading to a small cellar that was used as a steambath, the vapor being generated by pouring water on boulders that had been heated in the nearby fire.

The lower platform, that extended around the main floor at an elevation of 2¾ feet, was comparatively narrow. It was about 2½ feet wide along the sides and about 3 feet wide at the front and back. It served both as a lounging place and as a step to the platform or bench above. The retaining walls of the lower platform consisted of four heavy hewn spruce planks, approximately 27 feet long, 3 feet wide, and 5 inches thick. They were so mortised together that they supported each other. The faces of these lower walls were beautifully finished in the finest adzing. Those forming the sides and back were carved in low relief to represent a remarkable figure [painted red] that was neither wholly human nor animal, with widely extended arms and legs. [At Yakutat, it was said that this decoration had been copied from the house of the chief of Ki·waʔá·, the land in the sky to which go the souls of those who have been slain. It is called the "Man Cooking Eels." After this was painted at Klukwan, the town had "nothing but killings, nothing but killings." (See de Laguna 1972:772–73; Holm 1983, no. 195, p. 115).]

Tlingit houses, Klukwan. (Photographs by G. T. Emmons. AMNH.) Top. *The Whale House of the* G̣a·nax̣te·dí, *Raven 3, 1888.* Bottom. *Row of houses, 1889.*

The upper, broader platform, rising two feet above the lower, was at the level of the ground, and was also floored with heavy planks. On the sides it had a width of ten feet, which was greatly increased at the back and correspondingly diminished at the front of the house. The four heavy retaining timbers forming the walls and supporting the platform were 33 feet long at the sides, 31 feet long at the front and rear, 2 feet wide, and 5 inches thick. They were interlocked at the ends. On the carefully adzed faces, carved in low relief and arranged in echelon, were represented three ceremonial "coppers," or *tinneh* [tiná·]. One of the names or titles of the house chief was *Tinneh Sarta,* "Keeper of the Copper" [Tiná· S̓a·ti, "master of the copper." (See Emmons 1916a, pl. 1.)]

The upper platform provided the sleeping places, or bedrooms, of the different families, for while these were not partitioned off, they were separated from each other by old canoe sails, mats, or piles of boxes. Each family owned and occupied such a space, according to their relative importance, the poorer members and slaves being along the front. [Krause ([1885] 1956:88, fig. on p. 92) indicated that the partitioning of boards or blankets on the upper platform might make a vestibule just inside the front door. This entrance was sometimes flanked by carved posts, facing the center of the house, the posts having evidently been taken from an older house.]

At the level of this upper platform were the posts that supported the roof structure. They stood 9¼ feet high and were 2½ feet wide. They were elaborately carved in high relief on the sides facing the interior of the house, with a mixture of animal and human forms, and were painted in red, black, and blue-green. Each post illustrated a legend of the clan or a story of the early wanderings of Raven, a family [lineage, clan] crest. Between the two rear posts was a partition, twenty feet long by ten feet high, made of thin split red cedar boards, of varying widths, neatly fitted vertically and sewn together with finely twisted spruce root. The latter was countersunk to make the whole appear like a single board. The smooth front surface was intricately carved in low relief and painted to represent the Spirit of Rain, *Su* [Sú·w/Sí·w], which was symbolized by a great crouching figure with outstretched arms; the elaborate border of miniature figures represented the splashing of the heavy drops as they struck the ground. This screen was known as "Rain Screen," *Su kheen* [Sú·w x̣̓í·n], and formed the front wall of the sleeping chamber of the master of the house, and was entered by a round hole in the body of the central figure.

There seems to be a difference of opinion as to who executed this work. *Yehlh-kok* [Yé·ł xá·ł, "Raven's Odor"], its "owner," said that it was done by *Kate-tsu* [?], the chief who built the house, and that the painting was the work of *Skeet-lah-ka* [Škiˀƛiqá·?], a later chief, artist, the father of Chartrich, and one who accompanied the Russians up the Chilkat River in 1834. [If so, he would have been himself Raven 3, so his wife (as the official "opposite") would have been paid for his work.] Others claim that the carving was designed and executed by a Tsimshian, while the conventionalized design, and particularly the multiplicity of small figures around the principal one, is essentially Tsimshian in character and entirely different from the realism of Tlingit art. It is unquestionably the finest example of native art.

[Jonaitis (1986:113–15) has suggested that the central figure in the screen may not be the Spirit of Rain, but Raven who stole fresh water from Petrel for the benefit of mankind. Despite Keithahn's denial (1963:113) that Rain was a crest, I think it more likely that it was a crest of the G̣a·nax̣te·dí; for this Chilkat clan was probably, like the Wolf 18 of Wrangell, "so rich that they could use anything" (Swanton 1908:415).]

Interior of the Whale House, Raven 3, Klukwan, ca. 1895. (Photograph by Winter and Pond. Courtesy of William Paul.) The Rain Screen is in the background between the Wormwood Post on the left and the Raven Post on the right. The anthropoid face in the center is carved on the retaining plank of the lowest bench and is the face of the red-painted "Man Cooking Eels," with arms extended. This is repeated on the sides of the house. Clan and house treasures, including the Wormwood Dish (on the upper platform) and the Mother Basket (left foreground), include costumes, masks, hats, boxes, a spy glass, and a blunderbuss.

The house posts were carved in high relief and also painted with red and the [expensive] blue-green pigment. Each illustrates an adventure of Raven or of some ancestor of the clan. [I believe they are the work of a different artist from the maker of the screen, because they are different in style.]

Flanking the Rain Screen were the Woodworm Post, *Thluke-ass-a-Gars* [ƛ̓úk̓ʷx̣ʷ gá·ṡ] on the left, and the Raven Post, *Yehl-Gars* [Yé·ł gá·ṡ] on the right, both representing crests of the Ǫa·nax̣te·dí [Raven 3] owners. The first shows their ancestress holding the Woodworm in front of her body, while two worms crawl on her head. The lower figures are a Crane holding a Frog in its bill. Raven is represented on the other post by the main [anthropomorphic] figure holding a head, the jade adz, *Tsu-hootar* [Ṡú·w x̣út̓a·] with which Raven tricked the King Salmon into coming ashore. Raven stands on the fish, and the small raven issuing from his mouth represents his lies. [This is a pun, since the root for "to lie, deceive" and "raven" are the same: yé·ł. And the carver, therefore, a Tlingit. (See Emmons 1916a, pl. 4.)]

The post to the right of the door is the *Gonakatate-Gars* [Ǫuna·kade·t gá·ṡ]. This wealth-bringing water monster is represented by the central [anthropomorphic] figure, biting the tail of the Whale, the head of which is at the bottom of the post. On top is "Gonakatate's child" [Ǫuna·kade·t yádi], holding a Hawk, a Raven 3 crest. [Since Ǫuna·kade·t is a crest of the Wolf moiety, his child could also be a Raven crest.]

Posts in Frog House, Raven 3, Klukwan, ca. 1895. (Photographs by Winter and Pond. AMNH.) Left. *Giant cannibal of the Yukon valley, killed by a Raven 3 shaman, and so claimed as a clan crest.* Right. *"Brown Bear Friend,"* hootz hun [xú·c x̣u·n], *also a clan crest.*

The Whale is the one entered and killed by Raven, for his head is peeping from the blowhole. On the back is the figure of a woman, *Stah-ka-dee-Shawut* [Stax̣ˀadi ša·wát, "woman of the ———," using an older name for a branch of the Raven 19 clan that lived east of Yakutat, to indicate the locale of Raven's adventure. (See Emmons 1916a:25, pl. 3a).]

The post to the left [pl. 3b], *Duck-Toolh-Gars* [Dukʷ t̓u·x̣̓, "Black Skin"], represents the legendary [Raven 3] hero, tearing in two a Sea Lion. The head on which he stands is the island. [The figures at the top of these two posts are decorated with (human?) hair.]

This description of the Whale House can be applied in general to any of the larger old community houses, except for the few that were elaborately ornamented inside, and no fixed rule was followed in the arrangement of the wall planks. Sometimes those on the sides were perpendicular, or those forming the front wall might be horizontal, and in a very old house at Klukwan the front was built of two immense hewn timbers, 40 feet long, 3 feet 4½ inches wide, and 6 inches thick, and the corner posts were correspondingly thick.

[Emmons is describing the Killerwhale's Dorsal Fin House, of Wolf 27 at Klukwan. Krause ([1885] 1956, illustrations on pp. 86 and 87) shows variations in the arrangements of wall planks. Jonaitis (1986) has published views of the interiors of the Frog House (figs. 1, 7, 9, 10, 11), Whale House (figs. 5, 8, 12, 13), and Killerwhale House (figs. 6, 15) at Klukwan.

[Perhaps the oldest substantial winter houses described and sketched were those seen by members of Malaspina's expedition at Yakutat in 1791. That there were at least the frameworks of two houses is suggested by the discrepancies between that described by Malaspina and by the artist Suría of the house he sketched (the picture is lost) and the drawing signed by Cardero (described below). The first is of an older and more widely distributed type, like that of the Eyak (Birket-Smith and de Laguna 1938:23) and allied to that of the Kwakiuti and Nootka ("Wakashan type," Stewart 1984:65–68), with single ridgepole and two main side beams supported by decorated house posts. That rendered by Cardero has the double ridgepole or two beams near the center of the house, as well as the two main side beams, of the classic "northern style" of the Tsimshian, Haida, and Tlingit (Stewart 1984:71–73, figs. on pp. 68–69). The walls of both structures were structurally independent of the framework, and the planks of roof and walls had been removed to make shelters at the summer fish camps.

[Cardero's drawing (Vaughan et al. 1977:12–13, fig. 13; Engstrand 1981, pl. following p. 50) shows four sets of plain stout houseposts supporting the central pair of beams and the two heavy beams between them and the eaves. What looks like a fence is simply the framework for the walls, and is made of lighter poles. Along one side, the lower roof planks are still in place and a small shelter of boards has been built.

[According to Malaspina (1885:161), a party of officers and Suría went to see the grave monuments on Ankau Point, and near there saw a house frame. "After first measuring them,

D. Tomás Suría drew in perspective the posts and beams that supported [enclosed] a large dwelling that seemed to be intended for the winter." Malaspina (1849:290) also wrote:

> [Near the sepulchers] . . . there was a piece of squared ground, enclosed (fenced) by some very heavy timbers, forming what was like a house without an opening. There were in it some very robust pillars. On these were painted with red ocher the faces of men of extraordinary size; we observed likewise that they had several cracks (splits) from top to bottom . . . . [The "Ankau" (ʔa·n qa·wu, "chief")] indicated by signs that it [the house] was covered on all sides with *telas* [probably planks, or bark] as the high roof was also made; that various men were placed each at the foot of a pillar, and dancing all to the same beat, each drove his knife into it [the pillar].

[Suría (in Wagner 1936:258) also described the house:

> [It is] a skeleton house which is reduced to three frames, each one of three sticks [poles, beams] placed parallel to each other at a proportionate distance, the one in the middle being higher than the other two. On the base of the poles which face inside there are various designs. The chief whom we found there made various signs to us which nobody could understand, but what we thought was that either before or after the funeral ceremonies they have a dance in this place, which must be of some particular significance, as after pointing out that they covered these poles with something he took out his knife and stuck it into the stick [post] and at once began to dance with a very happy gesture, making various movements and emitting an "O" with his throat.

[Although puzzled as to the meaning of this dance, the Spanish were inclined to think it was a religious rite in celebration of some victory over the chief's enemies. I (de Laguna 1972:312) suggest that the chief was acting out the dedicatory potlatch given when the house was built, probably involving the sacrifice of one or more slaves (six, for each post?). That there were two houses sketched is made more likely by the fact that three years later, in July 1794, Vancouver's (1801, 5:396) Lieutenant Puget in the *Chatham,* when exploring the area, found near Ankau Creek "an Indian village, that had the appearance of having been very recently deserted; not one of its former inhabitants was to be seen, excepting about fifty dogs that were making a most dreadful howling." The Indians had simply gone to their summer camps, leaving their dogs behind in the usual way.

[Plans and sketches of a typical Chilkat house with a single bench have been published by Louis and Florence Shotridge (1913:86–89, figs. 68–76). These clearly indicate the same type of structure as Emmons described. In this case, the main roof beams were 44½ feet long and 2 feet in diameter. Spruce was used for the main timbers, and hemlock for the planking because it can be easily split. Wealthy people might import red cedar. It was further explained that the sunken floor was free from drafts, and that all the flooring was smoothed with an adz after the planks had been laid. The doorway was raised in order to be above the average level of the snow in winter. Some families might partition off their sleeping places with board screens, and some of these sleeping rooms were built with an upper story. (By this is probably meant the ceiling on top of the sleeping rooms, which constituted a high platform that could be used for sleeping or storage.) Noted warriors were permitted to decorate the front wall of their sleeping rooms with carvings symbolic of their exploits. See Stewart (1984:60–73) for the making of such houses, and for other types of Northwest Coast houses.]

The primitive house as seen and mentioned by the earliest explorers was built entirely with stone implements, and was unquestionably inferior to its successor built with iron tools. Yet such buildings as that described above [the Whale House] must represent the height of production, both in structure and ornamentation. The evolution of the house to that found today has resulted from trade and association with the whites. The use of nails and sawed lumber did away with the necessity of broad corner posts that were characteristic of Tlingit architecture. Then followed the introduction of windows and doors. With the use of stoves, when stones were no longer used for boiling, the central fireplace and smokehole disappeared. Rooms were partitioned off, and instead of an excavated interior, the building was raised on a foundation of piles. A broad porch was added in front, and only the original proportions remained. Finally these two disappeared, to give place to such modern structures as might be found in any American village.

[During the prosperous last decade of the nineteenth century and the first decade of the twentieth, relatively large, multifamily houses were built of commercial lumber, replacing the old style lineage houses. These were rather tall, gaunt structures, with high-pitched gable roofs. Often carvings or crest paintings made with commercial paints adorned the facades, and the old house posts and decorated screens, taken from earlier houses of the lineage, were placed inside. Thus the carved posts shown in Krause ([1885] 1956, figs. on pp. 89 and 92) were preserved in modern houses in Klukwan. Sometimes the shape and arrangement of the windows were supposed to suggest the lineage crest, as, for example, the eyes of the whale on the present Whale House of the Raven 6 at Sitka. Or the windows might give the name to the

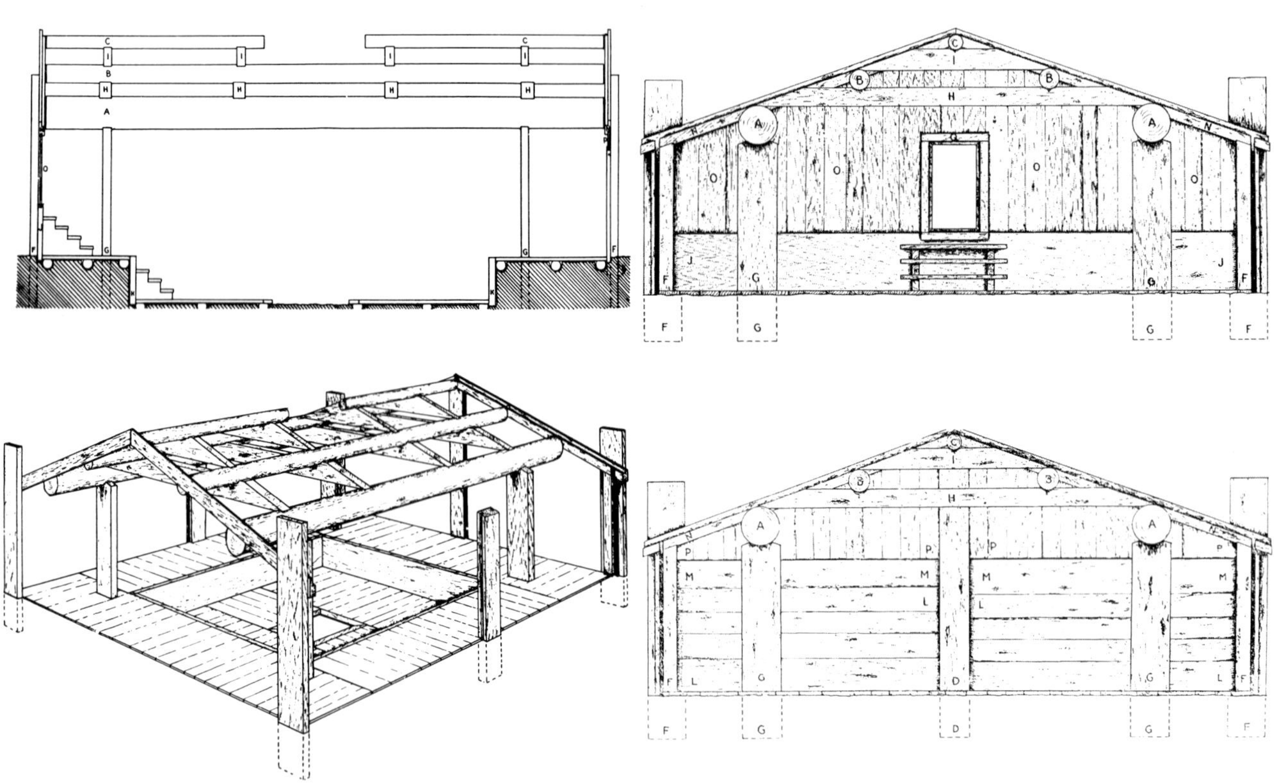

Diagrams of a Chilkat house, Klukwan. (L. and F. Shotridge 1913, figs. 69 to 71. Courtesy of the University of Pennsylvania Museum.) Left. Top. *Longitudinal section.* Bottom. *Basic framework of house.* Right. Top. *Interior of front wall and framework.* Bottom. *Interior of rear wall and framework.*

building, as in the case of Looking Out House (Raven 1 at Tongass, Raven 3 at Klukwan, and Raven 28 at Kake). There was always one large room at the front, and sometimes two or more bedrooms at the back, or even on a second floor, but some houses consisted simply of one large room. In any case, one or two stoves (one for heating, the other for cooking) were placed in the main room, while the bedrooms were unheated. Elderly natives who have lived in the old style houses complain of the cold in the newer, drafty frame structures. After World War I, a number of the latter were abandoned, torn down, or remodeled to make more comfortable, single-family dwellings. Most of the old carvings and screens were sold to museums, or were discarded or painted over when the Alaska Native Brotherhood was founded and there was a movement to abolish clans and their symbolism. In some cases the interior decorations were simply covered with sheets. Sooty stove pipes and faulty oil heaters have been responsible for fires that destroyed many of the early twentieth-century multifamily houses and the native heirlooms they contained.]

The principal houses in the old villages were given names upon their dedication, when those who assisted in their construction were feasted and compensated. [These workers were members of the opposite moiety from the owners of the house.] The highest and most honored house names were those that referred to the totemic emblems or crests of the lineage. Other less valued names referred to the position, shape, or material of the house. [See Table 14 for a list of all the house names recorded by Emmons.] In any case, a name once given survived the mere structure. The naming of a house was more, in a sense, the dedication of the ground, and without further ceremony the house name automatically belonged to all future houses built on it, and even though every member of the household should cease to exist, no other family of the clan could build on the ground without the consent of all, and another clan would never think of doing so.

[It might be more accurate to say that the building of a new house on the same site, even the repairing of an old house, required a potlatch to reward the workers. In this way,

Floor plan of a Chilkat house, Klukwan. (L. and F. Shotridge 1913, fig. 68. Courtesy of University of Pennsylvania Museum.)

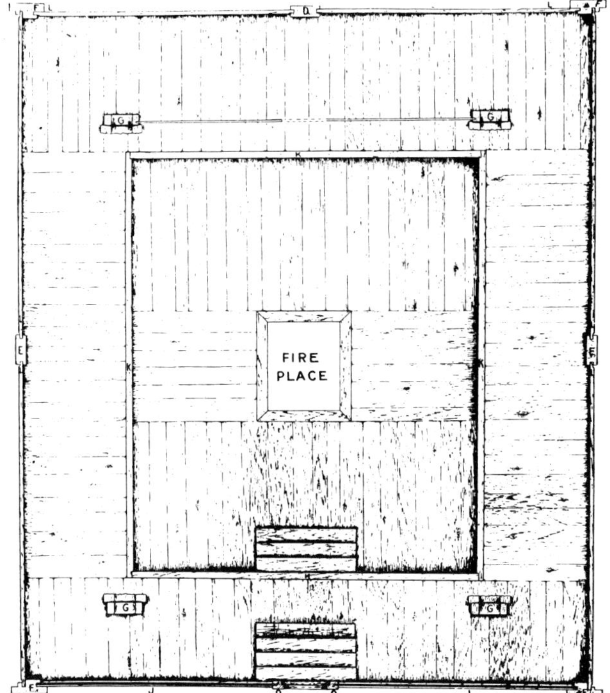

Key to diagrams (page 66) and floor plan:

A. *Two main roof beams*
B. *Two supplementary roof beams*
C. *Ridgepole in two sections, interrupted by smokehole*
D. *Vertical support plate in rear wall*
E. *Vertical support plates in side walls*
F. *Vertical support plates at corners*
G. *Main support posts for roof beams, usually decorated*
H. *Lower cross beams (or planks)*
I. *Upper cross beams (or planks) to support ridgepole*
J. *Heavy base plank at front, grooved to receive vertical wall planks*
K. *Retaining planks of platform*
L. *Two heavy base planks at side and rear walls, fitted into slots in D, E, and F*
M. *Two heavy planks in rear wall, fitted into slots in D and F, and grooved to receive the butt ends of vertical planks, P*
N. *Small rafters at ends of the house, probably also in other places*
O. *Vertical wall planks at front of house, fitted into slot in J*
P. *Vertical wall planks at rear of house, fitted into slot in M*
Q. *Frame for doorway*

the old house name was validated again, or what was essentially the same structure might acquire a new name. But perhaps duplicate naming was a feature of more recent times (late nineteenth, early twentieth century?) when lineages were dying out and attempts were made to perpetuate traditional house names. In any case, when people moved to a new village, it was customary for them to name the new houses after those they had abandoned, and if possible to transfer the old carvings to the new buildings.

[The old multifamily houses were lineage houses, and the building of one was one of the most important events in the life of the Tlingit. This was not simply because of the labor involved, but because the work was done by members of the opposite moiety, who had to be paid at the potlatch given to dedicate the new house. As we shall see (Chapter 11), every stage of the work was celebrated by an appropriate ceremony, in which the spirits of the trees and the ghosts of the lineage were fed, and the workers feasted and rewarded. All this involved the expenditure of wealth in which the house owner or lineage head was assisted by all the members of his clan. Emmons had inserted here a long description of these ceremonies, but they seemed to belong more appropriately to a discussion of potlatches and ceremonies in general.

[The building or refurbishing of a lineage house was usually undertaken by a new house chief when he succeeded to his position, and was given to honor the memory of his dead predecessor. The building or repairing of a gravehouse and the raising of a totem pole were also done in honor of the dead and were often carried out at the same time, or in connection with building a house. All these structures stood not only as memorials to the dead but as evidence of family loyalty and the social standing of the house chief responsible for their construction.

[House building was thus a social and religious event, and should properly be described under life-crisis ceremonials. It is sufficient to report here that Emmons states that the trees to be used for the main supports and beams of the house were cut down by alternately charring and adzing the trunks, and were usually towed to the village for final shaping. He does not describe, however, how the postholes were dug, how the posts were erected, or how the heavy beams were hoisted into place.

[Perhaps it was only in more recent decades, when sawed lumber and carpenter's tools made the labor easier, and when the fur trade and commercial fishing brought wealth to the Tlingit, that it became customary for a wealthy and socially ambitious chief to rebuild his house several times, ideally eight times (but no more), and thereby enhance his prestige through a series of potlatches. Such potlatching was nevertheless still done in memory of the lineage dead and therefore remained associated with funeral ceremonies.

[Descriptions of native houses at Sitka in 1865 (Dall 1895:126) and 1867 (Howard 1868: 262), and at Wrangell in 1869 (Colyer 1870b:2–5, and figs. 1–4) confirm the descriptions given by Emmons.]

DOMESTIC LIFE*

In the large old houses, fifty or more feet square, lived many families, often numbering fifty or more persons. The older men of the house were all of the same clan, presided over by an acknowledged hereditary house chief. The sons were of the opposite moiety, and until grown would remain as children in their fathers' house, but after marriage would establish their own household or go to the house of their wife's father, who was also a member of their phratry. [Some boys, especially those who were likely to be heirs to a house chief, were sent to his house when quite young.] The women and their children in a house were all of the phratry opposite to that of their husbands and might be from several different clans.

Each family occupied an allotted space about the walls of the house, partitioned off by rows of chests, baskets, or side curtains of bark mats or old canoe sails. This space constituted their sleeping place and the storeroom for their personal effects. The open central space around the fireplace formed a common meeting place where all the housemates sat, worked, and ate. The house places were apportioned according to rank. The house head and his family occupied the section in the rear, and the seat of honor was directly behind the fire. Poor dependents and slaves lived inside the entrance on either side. Each family was an independent in its life, occupations, and food supply as if it occupied a separate house, although each, in turn, provided wood for the common fire. [The women often or usually took turns in feeding the whole group, especially when they had some special delicacies.]

During the day the people occupied the open central space around the fire square or lounged on the narrow platforms. When working, the women sat with knees drawn up to the chin or knelt, bent over, with back almost horizontal. The men at work sat upright with legs stretched out straight in front.

At night each family retired to its allotted space around the walls, and slept on skins of caribou, moose, mountain sheep, goat, or bear, or on cedar-bark mats, covered by blankets of ground squirrel, marmot, lynx, or fox skins. A much prized blanket used both as a cover and a robe was made of the fur of the paws of the lynx or fox, procured in trade from the interior. Trade blankets later took the place of furs, both for bedding and general wear. When not working, the Tlingit spent much time sleeping. All retired early, and by eight o'clock the village was quiet; they slept late, rising by nine or after. Formerly they used no headrests, but later adopted the pillow. The central fire provided the only artificial light, for although small stone lamps containing seal oil with a wick of twisted moss were used, these were both ineffective and rare.

Houses were clean or dirty, according to the occupants, but in this respect a great improvement has taken place of late years. In the larger houses, greater order prevailed, which was a necessity for the comfort of the inmates. The bedding was rolled up after rising, and the main floor swept with eagle wings. The greatest disorder was on the inner platforms on either side of the doorway, where fresh-killed meat and fish, water, firewood, and large articles not in general use were thrown. [Here also were placed the watertight baskets or boxes used for urine, collected at night and saved for washing or for fixing dyes.] In some villages, particularly those of the *Hootz ah tah* [Hutsnuwu tribe], small storehouses received the overflow of extra and used articles; or these might be kept in the smokehouse, as at Klukwan; but ordinarily such things were piled on the inner front platform.

[Although it has been customary for whites to comment unfavorably on the dirtiness and smells in native houses, Captain Howard (1868:262) remarked of the Tlingit houses at Sitka in 1867: "Some of them have pretensions to comfort and cleanliness inside, having well-scrubbed boards laid for a floor, round the centre space of six or seven feet square, which is filled in with pebbles and used as a fireplace." Tlingit informants report that these pebbles were frequently changed

**Editor's note:* This section has been taken from the original "Chapter V: Domestic Life." I have added the observations of Captain Howard, Mrs. Shepard, and Mrs. Willard.

and that even the streets of the winter villages were swept. Even if the last is an exaggeration, there seems to be no question that housekeeping in the winter villages contrasted with the dirty conditions in the temporary summer camps.

[Mrs. Shepard (1889:234–35) described a Saturday morning in the Indian part, or "Ranche," of Sitka in 1889:

> . . . [it was] a bright, warm day. Saturday was employed in much the same way as in the more civilized part of our country, namely, as cleaning day. The whole Ranche had a certain air and smell of cleanliness and soapsuds. We met Indian women with streaming locks, and a fresh, clean look about the face, betokening a recent but perhaps only the weekly wash, in readiness for Sunday. Many a papoose was receiving a thorough scrubbing in the clear light of day under the warm rays of the September sun—sixty degrees Fahrenheit.

[Mrs. Willard (1884:53–55) described her trip to Chilkoot village in August of 1881, escorted by Chief Don-a-wok (Dá·na·wa·q, "Silver Dollar Eyes"), Raven 17 of Yandestake, and their gracious reception there by the leading chief, also a shaman and Dona-wak's younger brother, Karskarz:

> We were conducted to the house of the head-chief, who is also a medicine-man, and were received with the greatest kindness.
>
> The house was exceedingly neat, the hard, burnished boards of the floor being white and clean. Sand was sprinkled over the fireplace, in the centre. We mounted the high steps outside to a low-arched doorway, passing through which we found ourselves on a little platform, from which two or three steps led down to a second platform, of greater breadth, extending around the entire building. Two or three feet from its edge was hung tent-cloth, curtaining in sleeping- and store-rooms on the two sides. The end of the room opposite the door, back of the fireplace, is the seat of honor. In this case it consisted of chests of some kind covered with white muslin. Back of it, ranged on a platform, were the treasures in crockery, some half a dozen large washbowls and a neat platter.
>
> [The chief was] robed in a pair of blue pantaloons, a clean pink calico shirt, and falling in graceful folds about him a navy-blue blanket with a border of handsome crimson cloth edged with a row of large pearl buttons. In his hair, which is quite crimped and curling about his high forehead and hangs down his back like the tail of a horse (for they [shamans] are not permitted ever to comb or to plait it), was arranged the whole skin of a little white ermine . . . . [His wife wore] a similar blanket . . . and a great many silver bracelets on her arms. [The guests were served bowls of "beautiful" salmonberries, which they ate with their fingers after saying grace.

If anyone was likely to find a native house dirty, it would be the wife of a missionary!]

Top. *Traditional smokehouse, Klukwan, 1883. (Photograph by G. T. Emmons.)* Bottom. *Killerwhale House of the* Daqławe·dí, *Wolf 27, and Bear Pole of the adjacent Bear House, of the* Te·qʷe·dí, *Wolf 32, Angoon, 1890. (Courtesy of the California State Museum, Sacramento.)*

OTHER HOUSES AND SHELTERS*

Summer houses were smaller and more roughly built structures [than the winter lineage houses]. They were often without flooring, built directly on the ground, and covered with slabs of bark instead of boards. Single families lived in them during the fishing season, for they served both as smokehouse and dwelling. In the better structures the frame was permanently put together; in others, it was lashed with withes of spruce root.

While these summer houses at fish camps were used for smoking and curing of fish, at Klukwan smaller, substantially built smokehouses stood on the river bank in front

**Editor's note:* Information from the Shotridges has been added, and I have included quotations from La Pérouse, Beresford, Portlock, Suría, and von Langsdorff. The last paragraph in the section is mine.

Diagrams of Chilkat smokehouse, Klukwan. (L. and F. Shotridge 1913, figs. 77, 79, and 80. Courtesy of University of Pennsylvania Museum.) Left. *Floorplan, showing two fireplaces for smoking food, in addition to the ordinary central fireplace.* Right. Top. *Basic framework, showing two racks for smoking food.* Bottom. *Interior of front wall, with racks for hanging fish on each side.*

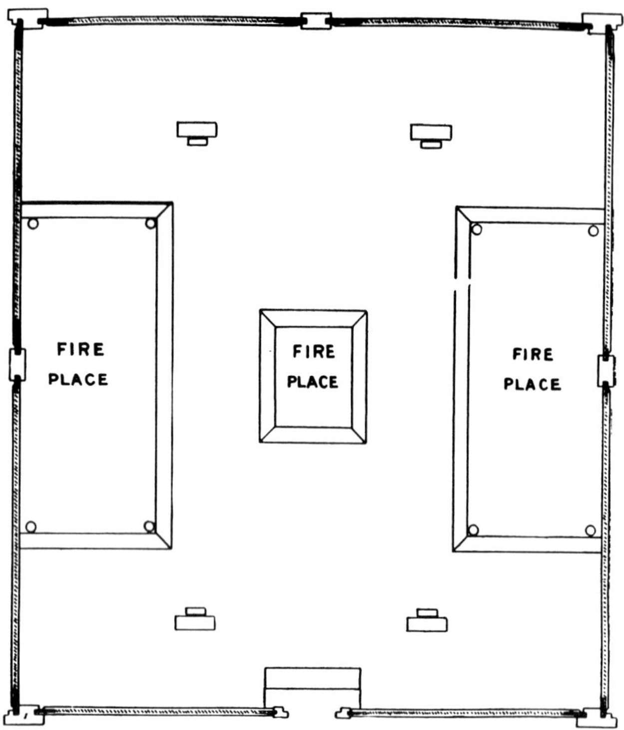

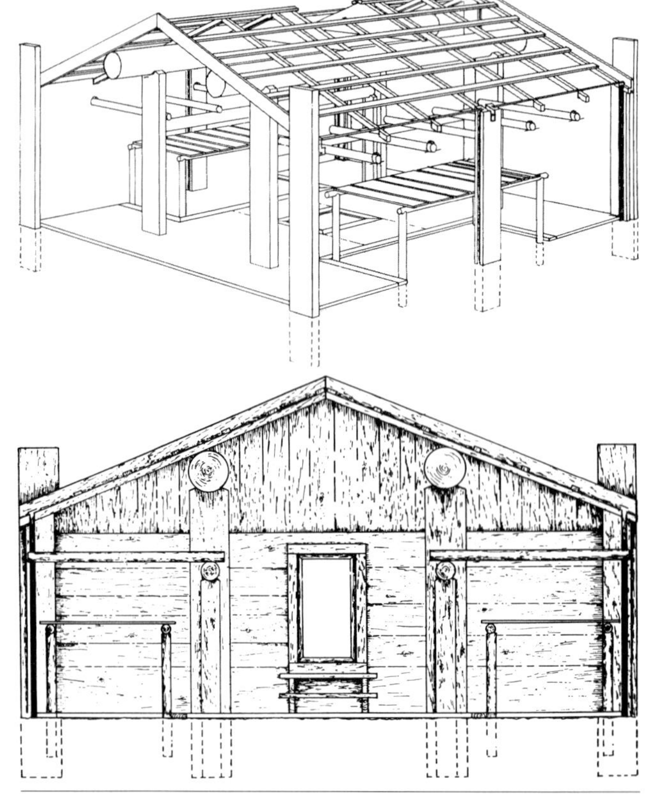

of the dwellings. They had no special features except for a central open fireplace, and also one on each side, over each of which a square broad platform, resting on uprights, served to intercept and spread the smoke of the smoldering fire below, so that it might be diffused among the rows of salmon hung on the rods above.

[The Shotridges (1913:89–94, figs. 77–82) illustrate and describe a Chilkat smokehouse of this type. The construction is similar to that of the larger winter house, except that the roof of shingles, rafters, and poles rested on only a single pair of heavy beams. The floor was not excavated, but had a small central fireplace for cooking and two larger fireplaces at each side for smoking fish. Above the later were tablelike platforms of planks for spreading the smoke, and above these in turn were horizontal poles across which the sticks carrying the split fish were placed.

[Other smokehouses, including modern ones, had either one or two fireplaces. Tables for spreading smoke are known from Angoon (de Laguna and McClellan, field notes, 1950) and Yakutat. See Stewart (1984:75) for sketches of smokehouse and raised cache.]

Hunting camps which were occupied in the winter months were often built of logs.

[La Pérouse (1799, 1:399–400) described a summer camp of Hoonah in Lituya Bay, July 1786, and domestic arrangements in it:

> I have given the appellation of village to three or four sheds of wood, twenty-five feet long, by fifteen or twenty wide, and closed with planks or bark of trees only on the side exposed to the wind. In the middle was a fire, over which hung salmon and halibut drying in the smoke. Eighteen or twenty persons lodged under each of these sheds, the women and children on one side, and the men on the other [no doubt to ensure continence, which had to be observed for safety and success on hazardous or chancy undertakings]. It appeared to me, that each hut contained a small tribe unconnected with it's neighbours; for each had it's canoe, and a sort of chief; each departed, left the bay, and took away it's fish and it's planks, without the rest of the village appearing to take the least concern in the business.
>
> I think I may venture to affirm, that this place is inhabited only in the summer, and that the Indians never pass the winter here. I did not see a single hut, that afforded shelter from the rain; and though there were never three hundred Indians collected in the bay at one time, we were visited by seven or eight hundred others.

Smokehouse with fixed (Russian type) screen for smoke outlet along ridge of roof, Turn Point, near Angoon, 1950. (Photographs by Frederica de Laguna.) Top. *Front end with door and windows.* Bottom. *Interior.*

[As to the condition of these camps, La Pérouse (1799, 1:400) wrote:

> . . . their huts, which are so filthy and stinking, that the den of no known animal can be compared to them. They never go two steps distant to obey the calls of nature, of which they make no mystery, and for which they seek no shade; continuing the conversation in which they were engaged, as if they had not a moment to lose; and if it happen at meal-time, they quickly resume their place, from which they do not retire even a couple of yards.

[Beresford (1789:172–73), who was with Dixon at Yakutat in June 1787, described the summer huts at Port Mulgrave:

> Their habitations are the most wretched hovels that can possibly be conceived; a few poles stuck in the ground, without order or regularity, enclosed and covered with loose boards, constitute an Indian hut, and so little care is taken in their construction, that they are quite insufficient to keep out the snow or rain: the numerous chinks and crannies serve, however, to let out the smoke, no particular aperture being left for that purpose.
>
> The inside of these dwellings exhibits a compleat picture of dirt and filth, indolence and laziness; in one corner are thrown the bones, and remaining fragments of victuals left at their meals; in another are heaps of fish, pieces of stinking flesh, grease, oil, etc., in short, the whole served to shew us, in how wretched a state it is possible for human beings to exist; and yet these people appear contented with their situation, and probably enjoy a much greater portion of happiness and tranquility, than is to be found under the gilded roofs of the most despotic monarch.
>
> 'Tis probable, that the chief reason why these Indians take no greater pains in the structure of their habitations is, that their situation is merely temporary: no sooner does the master of a tribe find game begin to grow scarce, or fish not so plentiful as he expected, than he takes down his hut, puts the boards into his canoe, and paddles away to seek out for a spot better adapted to his various purposes, which, having found, he presently erects his dwelling in the same careless manner as before.

[Portlock (1789:292), who was at the harbor which now bears his name, at the northern edge of Sitka territory, in August 1787, observed:

> Their huts are made of a few boards, which they take away with them when they go to their winter quarters. It is very surprising to see how well they will shape their boards with the shocking tools they employ; some of them being a full ten feet long, two and a half broad, and not more than an inch thick.

[While the planks or materials for the roofs and sides of summer huts are often taken away, the framework of upright posts and beams may remain as a permanent structure at many fishing camps to which the owners may return season after season.

[At a camp in Portlock Harbor, there were three men, three women, three girls, two boys of twelve, and two infants, the survivors of the smallpox epidemic of about 1775. Captain Portlock (1789:272) wrote about it:

> I found men, women, and children, all huddled together in a close house near a large fire, and entirely surrounded with stinking fish. Round the house for at least one hundred yards, and all along the banks of a little creek that ran down by this miserable dwelling, were strewed stinking fish; and in several places were beds of maggots a foot deep, and ten or twelve feet in circumference: nay, the place had really such a dreadfully offensive smell, that the young Indian himself [Captain Portlock's guide], though habituated to such wretched scenes from his earliest infancy, . . . could not bear it, but entreated me very earnestly to leave the place. . . .

[A little later, at a camp in Sitka Sound, Captain Portlock (1789:284–85) found similar conditions:

Hoonah family at sea otter and seal camp, Tuck-kah-ah *[possibly* ṫika-ʔa·, *"one to the landward side"], on George Island, at mouth of Port Althorp, Cross Sound, 1889. Note dark sunburn protection on the women's faces. (Photograph by G. T. Emmons. AMNH and BCPA.)*

Their filth and nastiness were beyond conception; their food, which consisted chiefly of fish, was mixed up with stinking oil, and other ingredients equally disagreeable, and the remains of every meal were thrown into a corner of their hut, upon a heap of the same kind that was in a state of putrefaction, which, together with large quantities of fat and stinking oil, caused a very loathsome and offensive smell; and what rendered it still worse, the same apartment served both to eat and sleep in.

[The artist Suría (in Wagner 1936:253), who was with Malaspina in 1791, also gave a graphic description of Yakutat summer huts:

Their dwellings or habitations are very poor. Here can be seen their disorderly filth, for they are more like pigsties than the habitations of human beings. This causes such a fetid and disagreeable odor on their belongings and persons that you cannot stand it. The houses are on the bank of the sea at the point which the channel for leaving the port forms. They are of boards placed over the trunk of a tree without any order. This traverses it and forms the ridge pole on which the boards rest on one side and the other, the tree trunk being held up by others, perpendicular ones, sunk in the ground. On top of the roof all their belongings can be seen, canoes made, others in skeleton [i.e., wooden frames for skin boats], skins half-cured, wood, and various rubbish. Inside you see the same. What cannot be put outside is put inside. . . . [There is a central fire indoors for cooking and for curing fish.]

[Von Langsdorff, in October 1805, visited what was apparently a combination smokehouse and summer dwelling, although one also occupied in winter by a single family of Tlingit who had presumably fled from Sitka after the return of the Russians. He described it (1814, 2:122–23):

We found a small boarded hut, somewhat longer than it was broad, and covered with a thin coat of the bark of trees: in the midst was a large fire, at which we warmed ourselves very comfortably. The door, and some little openings in the roof, were the only vents for the smoke, so that we seemed rather in a place for smoking fish or meat than a habitation: this resemblance was increased by the number of fish that were hanging about, and the total absence of all cleanliness. The chief, whose habitation it was, had a sort of recess directly opposite to the entrance, where he slept, and round about were several divisions made with beams for the other members of his family, and for the persons belonging to him, who were altogether fifteen in number. We had a place assigned us directly before the chief's apartment, and behind the fire, and after partaking of a repast, consisting of fresh fish cooked, and berries, we laid ourselves down, and enjoyed a very refreshing sleep.]

Bark hut at sealing camp, Disenchantment Bay, Yakutat, 1899. Note sealskins in drying frames, and skin bucket on wooden frame for seal blubber. (Photograph by the Harriman Alaska Expedition. Courtesy of Robert F. Heizer, University of California, Berkeley.)

Temporary shelters were simple lean-to's. Two forked poles were stuck in the ground, six or more feet apart. A cross rod rested in the forks and supported the upper ends of several long poles, the lower ends of which rested on the ground. For these, canoe poles and spears were often used. Across these were laid two or three slender poles, over which wide slabs of bark and brush were placed. The frame was lashed together with spruce root or twisted cedar-bark rope. The sloping back was set to windward and the fire built in front. [Emmons saw such a structure at *Thlakoukqwan* (?), a village on the "upper Chilkat River," perhaps at the mouth of the Klehini.] Among the Chilkat I found two sets of carved camp poles that took the place of the usually plain forked sticks. These were carried in the canoe when traveling and were used to increase the importance of the chief. In later years the temporary camp was made with the canoe sail [photographed by Emmons in 1903, at Portage Bay, near Haines]. Then followed the ordinary canvas wall tent.

[When von Langsdorff was traveling through Peril Strait in October, 1805, some friendly Tlingit saw his campfire and asked permission to join his party for the night. Thus he saw how they made a temporary shelter, which he described as follows (1814, 2:120–21):

> It consisted of two poles forked at the upper ends, and stuck into the earth, with a third pole laid across within the forks. Against this a number of boughs of trees, which they cut down, were stuck up, sloping towards the ground, and over them were laid thin planks, or bark of trees, which they had brought with them. This sloping wall of the half-open tent was turned towards the wind, and a large fire was made in front: by this contrivance, with the assistance of some coarse woolen cloth and skins, they were sufficiently protected from the weather during the night, though the cold was between two and three degrees below the freezing point.

[This lean-to was evidently like that described by Emmons. The latter's notes in BCPA include a sketch and description of the prepared bark sheets that were carried in canoes, for this and other purposes, as given below:]

Slabs of cedar bark of any size [presumably as wide as the girth of the tree permitted, and a convenient length to handle] were used for covering goods in traveling, for covering fish frames, for covering sides and roof of temporary houses and shelters, and for a variety of purposes. To keep the bark from curling up, small flat, half-round rods of split spruce wood were secured on both sides of the bark, opposite each other and near both ends, by means of split root [stitches].

Storehouses were not necessarily found in all villages. In fact, aside from those of the Chilkat and *Hootz ah tah* [Hutsnuwu], where the smoking of fish and the trying out of oil was done in the village, these were the exceptions. Generally the Tlingit left their villages during the period of food gathering, separating into households and individual families, to occupy summer camps on their salmon streams where they prepared their winter supplies. On their return to the winter village, these were stored in the big houses. Where storehouses existed, they were small, rude, log or board structures with earth floors, in which boxes, tools, baskets, and the overflow from the house accumulated in a confused mass. In early days when warfare generally prevailed, supplies of food were cached in caves, on adjacent islands, or in small log houses hidden away in the woods, so that if the village were destroyed, the winter's food would not be lost. After the cultivation of potatoes became customary, cellarlike root houses were built for their storage near the gardens where they were raised.

The Tlingit have always used the natural hot sulphur and soda springs that are found at "Hot Springs" [or Goddard], twelve miles south of Sitka on Baranof Island, or at "Hoonah Hot Springs," at Tenakee Inlet on the east coast of Chichagof Island. They hollowed out bathing places in the rocks. They well understood the curative properties of these waters and greatly enjoyed their effect. In cold weather I have known them to sit in the bath all night, submerged to the neck, and even go to sleep propped up in them, but this was because they were too lazy to cut firewood.

They were very fond of steam baths, and used them universally, especially after long canoe or hunting trips. The

Temporary shelters. (Sketched by G. T. Emmons. AMNH.) Top. *Bark lean-to at a summer camp.* Center. *Tent made with canoe spritsail and paddle, probably the same tent that Emmons photographed at Portage Bay, near Haines, in 1902 or 1903.* Bottom. *Framework of bent saplings for a temporary sweatbath house, Chichagof Island, 1888. (Pen and ink sketch by G. T. Emmons, AMNH.)*

bathhouse was sometimes permanently built within the house, consisting of a small, square, board compartment under the floor or in one corner. Or, it might be a separate structure, built of closely fitted logs with a roof of boards covered with earth. A bathhouse of this type was seen at the old *Kar-qwan-ton* village of *Kluckt-sut-ton-an* [Ka·g^{w}a·nta·n, Wolf 1, village ?], in Necker Bay on the outer coast of Baranof Island. [This village could not be identified, since notes in BCPA place it on the west shore of Chichagof Island.] The structure was 6 feet square, 3½ feet high, built of logs 6 to 8 inches in diameter. A sealskin hung over the doorway. The more common type of bathhouse used at summer camps as well as in villages consisted of a rounded framework of arched saplings, bent over, the ends stuck in the ground, and secured at their crossings with spruce root. The whole was covered with skins, blankets, or a sail. In all cases, stones were heated outside and piled in a corner inside the bathhouse, and steam was generated by throwing water on the stones. After bathing, the Tlingit plunged into cold sea water.

[Gravehouses were placed directly behind the lineage winter houses, if the ground permitted, or were placed at one end of the village, or even on an island opposite. The uncremated bodies of shamans were placed in gravehouses farther away, if possible on a point overlooking the water, or in a cave. Carved posts and poles were another characteristic feature of Tlingit villages. Most of these were mortuary poles, hollowed out or fitted to receive the ashes of the dead. In addition, there were carved posts through which the doorway of the house had been cut (portal poles), and lastly, free-standing memorial poles that served no other function than to exhibit the crests of the owner. All of these posts are commonly called "totem poles," and were far more common in Southern Tlingit villages than in villages of the Northern Tlingit, although a few mortuary poles (or grave markers) were found as far north and west as the Dry Bay and Yakutat areas. For further details, see the sections "Totem Poles," in Chapter 7, and "Various Older Forms of Disposal of the Dead" and "Shamans' Graves," in Chapter 10. This information had been scattered by Emmons in various places, including this chapter, but it seems more appropriate to place it later in the monograph.]

FORTS*

A number of the names for older living places end with the word *nu,* "fort" [nu·w], which indicates that these were defensive positions. Such names are *Kook nu ou* [Kax̌-nu·wú], "Grouse Fort," inside Point Couverden, at "Groundhog Bay," on Icy Strait; *Hootz nu ou* [Xú·c- nu·wú],

**Editor's note:* The citations from Vancouver and Lisiansky have been checked and corrected; and I have added information from Mourelle (Maurelle), von Kotzebue, MacDonald, Young, and Krause.

"Brown Bear Fort," the name for Admiralty Island and also for a fort at Point Hayes, or Point Craven, on Chichagof Island at the eastern end of Peril Strait; and *Chartle con nu* [Čá·ƛ-ka nu·w, "Halibut-on Fort"], at or near Point Craven or Point Hayes, near the eastern end of Peril Strait. Furthermore, family [lineage] houses were often named *Nu hit* [nu·w hít], "Fort House" [either because the house was fortified or because the original house from which the name was taken had been fortified]. Forts are frequently mentioned in the old stories, since these legendary histories indicate that the Tlingit were continually in conflict with each other. From the first, they also fiercely resented the settlements of Europeans in their midst, as is shown by the destruction of the first Russian posts at Sitka and Yakutat. [In both areas, the Indians built fortified villages in anticipation of Russian reprisals.]

The early explorers who visited the Northwest Coast referred to fortified rocks and headlands. [What may be the earliest mention of a Tlingit fortification was made by Maurelle, or Mourelle, second pilot of the *Sonora,* on the Second Bucareli Expedition, August 18, 1775, in Kalinin Bay, Salisbury Sound, in Sitka territory. He wrote (1920, pp. 43–44):

> Here we cast another at a pistol's shot from the land, where we saw, on the bank of the river, a high house, and a parapet of timber supported by stakes drove into the ground, where we observed ten Indian men, besides women and children. [The original editor of this journal, Daines Barrington (1781), suggested in a footnote: "Probably this was a stage for curing fish, of which these Indians soon offered a present to the Spaniards," but it is unlikely that a fish rack would have been called a "parapet."]

[In May and June 1779, this same Mourelle (in La Pérouse, 1799, 1:245) surveyed Port Santa Cruz, Bucareli Bay, in Klawak territory, for the Third Bucareli Expedition:

> Don Maurelle observed but few habitations in the course of his expedition. He saw only one village, on the top of a steep hill; at which there was no way of arriving but by a wooden stair, or rather ladder, so that if a person's foot slipped, he must infallibly tumble down the precipice.]

Vancouver [1801, 6:46–47] described in more detail eight defensive positions, visited by the party under Lt. Johnstone in July 1794, near the entrance to "Kake" [Keku] Strait, at Hamilton Bay on Kupreanof Island:

> . . . Mr. Johnstone states, that the remains of no less than eight deserted villages were seen; some of them were more decayed than the others, but they were all uniformly situated on the summit of some precipice, or steep insular rock, rendered by nature almost inaccessible, and by art and great labour made a strong defense; which proved, that the inhabitants had been subject to the incursions of hostile visitors. These fortified places were well constructed with a strong platform of wood, laid on the most elevated part of the rock, and projecting so far from its sides as to overspread the declivity. The edge of the platform was surrounded by a barricade raised by logs of wood placed on each other. In the vicinity of these ruins were many sepulchres or tombs, in which dead bodies were deposited. [For a description of these, see "Various Older Forms of Disposal of the Dead" in Chapter 10.]

After the destruction in 1802 of the first Russian post at Old Sitka, the natives established themselves at the mouth of Indian River just beyond the present Sitka, to await the coming of their foes, whose attack they repulsed with considerable loss, and only deserted their fort after their ammunition had been exhausted and their food caches in the nearby woods had been taken. Lisiansky [1814:163 and pl. II] described and illustrated this fortified settlement:

> The fort was an irregular square, its longest side looking towards the sea. It was constructed of wood, so thick and strong, that the shot from my guns could not penetrate it at the short distance of a cable's length [100 to 120 fathoms, or 608 feet]. As represented in Plate II, it had a door, *a,* and two holes, *b,* for cannon in the side facing the sea, and two large gates, *c,* in the sides towards the wood. Within were fourteen houses, or barabaras, *d,* as they are called by the natives. Judging from the quantity of dried fish, and other sorts of provision, and the numerous empty boxes and domestic implements which we found, it must have contained at least eight hundred male inhabitants. [The plate shows the enclosure to have been an irregular parallelogram, about one hundred fathoms, or six hundred feet long in the largest dimension; the lower part of the walls was made of four courses of horizontal logs, above which rose a palisade of vertical logs set close together. The latter were connected near their tops, on the outside only (?), by a horizontal beam, and braced at intervals by posts on the outside, leaning against the wall.]

[Von Kotzebue (1830, 2:40–41) also described this fortified place, although he was not in Sitka until 1825:

> When the Kalushes heard that the warrior Nonok, as they called Baronof, had returned, terror prevented their attempting to oppose his landing; and they retired in great haste to their fortification, consisting of a great quadrangle closely set round with thick, high beams, broken only by one very small and strong door. The pallisadoes were furnished with loop-holes, for the firing of muskets and falconets, with which the besieged were amply supplied. This wooden fortress, enclosing about three hundred fighting men with their families, held out several days; but no sooner had the heavy guns of the Russians effected a breach, than

Tlingit Fort, Sitka, 1802–4. (Lisiansky 1814, pl. II and p. 163. Courtesy of the Bancroft Library, University of California, Berkeley.) Plan, and exterior view of ramparts facing the sea. (Scale in fathoms.)

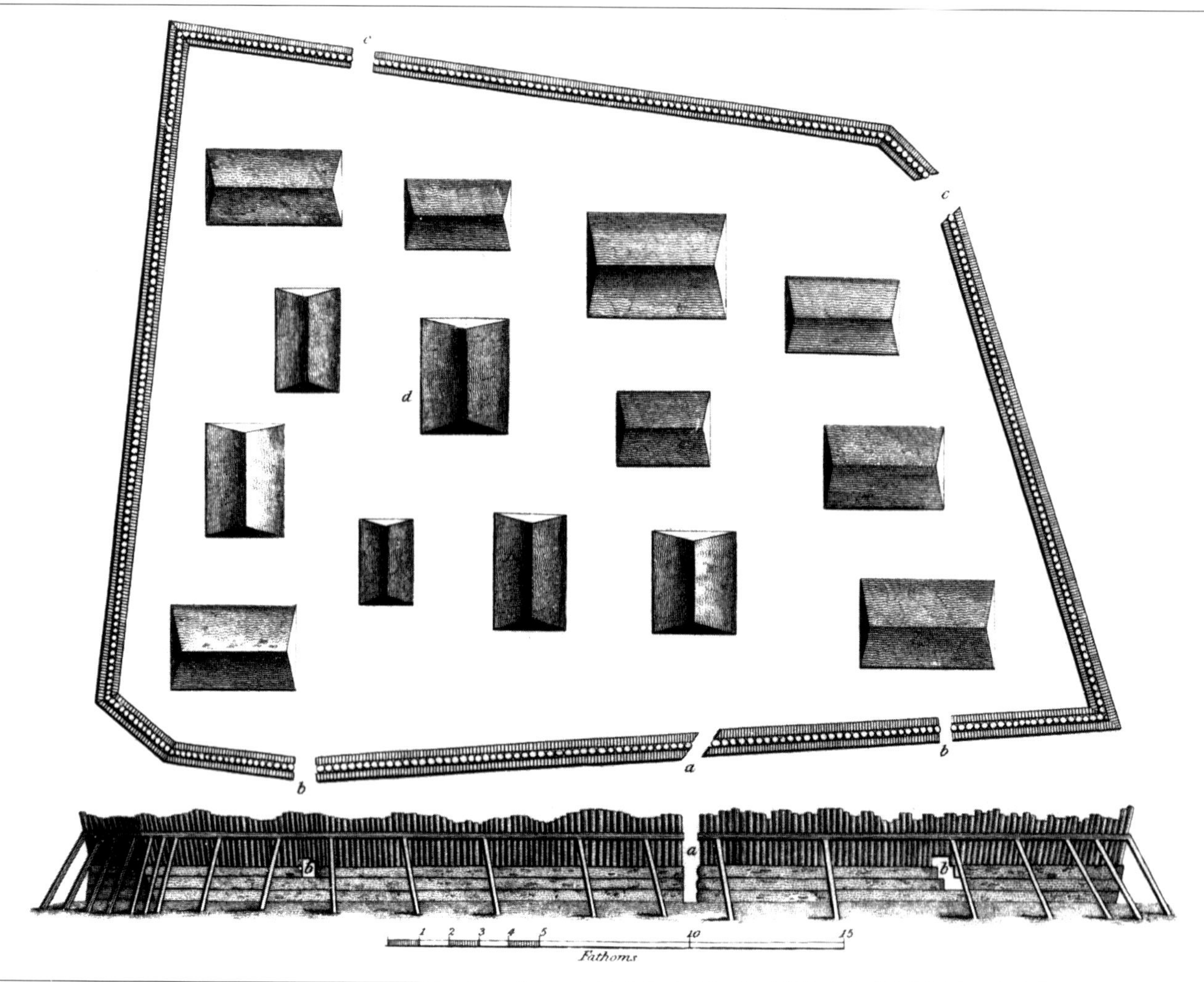

the besieged, finding their position no longer tenable, surrendered at discretion, and delivered over the sons of their chiefs as hostages for their submission [the occupants actually fled in the night to the eastern end of Peril Straits; the surrender and giving of hostages occurred considerably later].]

This was probably the most extensive fortification ever erected by the Tlingit and, as far as I have been able to learn, the only instance where the whole tribe united to live within one fort, except that which this people built later on Chatham Strait, at Point Hayes on the southeastern shore of Chichagof Island.

[The location of this fort Emmons has variously described as at Point Hayes or Point Craven (possibly at one of the small islands nearby), or at Lindenberg Head within Peril Strait. Von Langsdorff visited this fort in October 1805, and described the position (1814, 2:128–29):

> Expelled from Norfolk [Sitka] Sound, they have fortified themselves here, upon a rock which rises perpendicularly to the heighth of some hundred feet above the water. The only possible access to it is on the north-west side, and they have rendered this extremely difficult by strewing it all over with very large trunks of trees which they have cut down. The rock itself is secured against the attack of an enemy by a double palisade of large trunks of trees stuck close together, measuring from twelve to fifteen feet in heighth, and from three to four feet in thickness. A high natural wall of earth beyond the palisading, on the side towards the sea, conceals the habitations effectually, so that they cannot be discerned by any ship.

The houses within the fortress are in the form of parallellograms [*sic*], of various sizes, placed in regular rows at some toises distance from each other. [A *toise* is the equivalent of a fathom, or some six feet.] The roof, which consists of several layers of bark, rests upon ten or twelve thick posts driven into the ground, and the sides of the house are composed of broad thick planks fastened to the same posts. The entrance is at the gable-end, and is often painted with different coloured earths. The interior is extraordinarily dirty, as indeed are the people themselves. The smoke, the stink of fish and train-oil, the countenances besmeared with earths, coal, and ochres, and the lips of the women distorted by their wooden ornaments [labrets], with many habits that appear almost incredible, excite absolute repugnance and disgust: it is by no means uncommon to see the people seeking for the loathsome vermin that inhabit their dirty skin-garments, and carrying the living booty immediately to their mouths.

[Von Langsdorff also reported (pp. 126–27) that the house of Chief Dlchaetin (unidentified), had a raised hearth in the center of the large open space in the house, where several hundreds of persons gathered to gaze at von Langsdorff and his companion, Captain D'Wolf. The night was cold, and the fire was built up so high that the flames roared through the smokehole, yet the bark roof luckily did not catch fire.]

This stronghold was known as *Tchartle nu ou,* or *Chartle con nu,* "Halibut Fort" or "Fort on the Halibut," the exact location of which is in doubt. [See de Laguna 1960: 64, 147–48. Emmons's field notes in BCPA indicate that the dispossessed Sitkans built forts in 1804 both at Lindenberg Harbor, just west of Lindenberg Head, and near Point Hayes.]

Ordinary Tlingit forts were smaller affairs, not surrounding the village, but adjacent to it on some rocky island or precipitous headland, and belonged to a single family [clan], where the members might find refuge upon a sudden attack. For the strategy of coast warfare consisted of surprise attacks, ambuscades, the cutting off of canoe parties, and rapid retreats, so that these strongholds were not calculated to stand sieges, and were but temporarily occupied when necessity might require.

In 1869 Captain Meade, commanding the USS *Saginaw,* destroyed several villages and two forts of the Kake in Security Bay on Kuiu Island, in retaliation for the murder of two white men. The forts were described as stockades "about 100 feet square and from 15 to 17 feet high, and built of logs from 9 to 15 inches thick" [Beardslee 1882:54, from Meade's report of February 24, 1869].

I saw the remains of a similar stockade on a small rocky island in the northern entrance to Kake [Keku] Strait in 1900. It was 50 by 35 feet, of logs 1 foot in diameter and 12 feet high; set firmly in the ground and held together by means of horizontal stringers on the inside [not outside as at Sitka], and braced at the corners. Forked uprights were driven into the ground at regular intervals around the interior, 4 feet from the walls. These supported horizontal beams extending to the walls, on which a platform was built on which the defenders could stand. A heavy door, opening outward and fitted with rude hinges and a bar, was the only opening in the walls.

Remains of old Kake fort on the northwest shore of Kupreanof Island, near the northern entrance to Keku Strait, ca. 1888. (Photograph by Jim Blain, probably James C. Blaine, of Killisnoo, Admiralty Island. BCPA.)

The remains of several old stockades about the eastern entrance of Peril Strait were still visible in 1900. They were generally small and all of the same character, consisting of a palisade of upright tree trunks from twelve to fifteen feet high, the upper ends often pointed. A platform extended around the interior of the walls. On the seaward face of Kruzof Island, one mile or more up a stream entering Sea Lion Cove, were the remains of a small stockade some twenty-odd feet square, of well-joined, adzed timbers, ten feet high, placed perpendicularly, and pointed at the top. Within were forked uprights with cross poles, indicating that it was a former fish camp which had been so protected. On both banks of the lower Chilkat River the fishing camps of the different families [clans of the Chilkat and Chilkoot] were generally protected, as is implied by the addition of *-nu* [nu·w, or nu·wú, "fort of"] to the names of the camps. At one point where the main channel narrows along a precipitous mountainside, a rocky ledge behind one of these camps was fortified by a breastwork of stone, and from a high bluff that extended into the river, passing canoes were destroyed by dropping heavy rocks on them.

While it was exceptional to surround entire villages with defensive walls, groups of family [clan, lineage] houses were often enclosed within palisades, as could be seen as late as

1885 at Angoon on Admiralty Island, and at *Gau da kan* [Hoonah] on Chichagof Island. At the latter village, as late as 1880, the houses of the *Tuck tane tan* [Ṫaqde·nta·n, Raven 16], in the center of the village, were protected in front by a stockade of heavy tree trunks, twelve feet high, pointed at the top, standing perpendicularly and strung together with heavy cross pieces on the inside near the top. From the center, in front of the chief's house, projected a large carved and painted wooden Raven's head, the crest of this clan.

[MacDonald (1979, figs. 13 and 14, p. 34) has described and published illustrations of this fort, the only complete, or standing Tlingit fort to be photographed. It protected only five houses in the village of a dozen or more houses: "The startling feature of these photographs, confirmed by period drawings, is that the palisades always have external supports for the vertical posts. It appears that it would be relatively easy to pull away these supports with ropes and hooks, even under fire, reducing the strength of the palisade wall very considerably." The palisade had heavy cross beams on the inside, and light poles as stringers on the outside, against which the supports were braced.]

Single houses were sometimes protected in this manner [with a stockade], as was seen at Angoon in 1889, but the primitive house with its thick walls was a fortress of defense in itself, even against the firearms of the early Europeans.

[Reverend Young (1927:82), describing Wrangell in 1878, wrote: "In some cases tall stockades had been erected between these groups of family houses [the houses of the clan grouped around those of their chief], behind which and through port-holes piercing them family feuds had been fought out." Krause ([1885] 1956:90) also mentioned palisades around single houses at Klukwan in 1881–82.

[For a further discussion of Tlingit forts, especially in the Hutsnuwu area, see de Laguna 1960:97–98, and 142–43 for Grouse Fort in Hoonah territory.]

PETROGLYPHS*

Most permanent but least intelligible of all of the earlier works of the Tlingit are the petroglyphs which are of frequent occurrence on the shore in the vicinity of old living sites, throughout the inland waters of southeastern Alaska. The present generation, even the oldest natives, have no knowledge of their origin or use, and even deny that they are the work of their ancestors, attributing them to a stranger people who preceded them and left such signs to mark their movements or to guide others who might follow.

But this explanation is not worthy of consideration, for the petroglyphs are more often in secluded bays away from the open channels, and, aside from an occasional indistinguishable figure, they are too characteristic of Tlingit art to be disowned. While some are found on ledges overlooking the water, others are on beach boulders, but all are directly on the shore, and often mark fishing village sites where families assembled for the summer to put up their winter supply of salmon. During this season they had no ceremonies, amusements, or visitors, and probably time hung heavy on the hands of the men, who simply caught the fish in their great abundance, so they employed their leisure in ornamenting the rocks after their style of art. I do not believe that these glyphs have any ethnological value or meaning beyond their artistic conception.

[Keithahn (1940:129–30) found that petroglyphs were almost invariably located below high-tide mark on beaches near the mouths of salmon (sockeye) streams, so oriented that they faced the water, and so he argued that the carvings were made for the purpose of attracting the salmon. The figures, however, represent clan crests or supernatural beings—in many cases, proprietary clan totemic designs—and so, directly or indirectly, would indicate the clan that claimed the territory where they were located, just as do the designs painted or carved on houses and other crest objects. Any of these designs or symbols may both illustrate the event through which the clan acquired the rights to the design and serve as an efficacious token of the supernatural powers thus obtained. Natives have also indicated that rock pictures (carvings and paintings) were made to commemorate victories in war, transfer of wealth or territory in settlement of a feud, important potlatches, and shamanistic exploits, or were only the work of visiting Tsimshian or of the Tlingit themselves, to pass idle hours (de Laguna 1960:71–73).]

In those petroglyphs examined and illustrated [Emmons 1908b, pls. XII, XIII, figs. 44–66], the grooves are from one-half to three-fourths inch in width, and from one-eighth to one-fourth inch deep, according to their state of preservation through age and wear. They were unquestionably made by pecking, as the marks of the hammerstone are still clearly visible on the most recent ones, while the weathered grooves of the older ones are smooth and indistinct.

Editor's note: I have added a paragraph on the meaning of petroglyphs (with a reference to Keithahn). To the descriptions by Emmons of petroglyphs at Wrangell and other sites, I have added information from H. I. Smith and Keithahn, necessitating the rephrasing of several paragraphs.

Petroglyphs on a boulder at the mouth of a stream in Nakwasina Sound, four miles north of Sitka, Baranof Island, illustrating a Raven myth. (Sketched by G. T. Emmons, July 5, 1888. See Emmons 1908b.) (a) Raven carrying fire in his bill (?). (b) "Where the sun comes from" (the Box of Daylight?). (c) The Earth. (d) The North Wind. (e) Ǫa·nu·kʷ ("Petrel"), guardian of fresh water, in the form of a Wolf (the moiety crest).

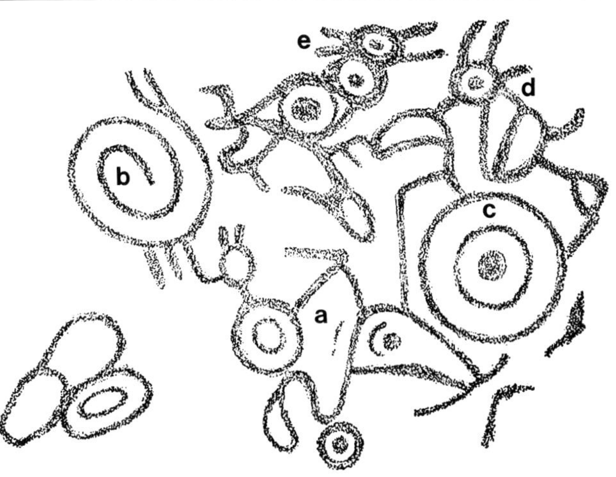

Generally, they are independent figures, having no clear connection or relation to one another, either in design or position, but on July 5, 1888, on a trip to "Katliansky," in Katlian Bay, eight miles north of Sitka, on Baranof Island, I met an old man [Kiksʔádi, Raven 10] who claimed the locality as his hereditary right. He showed me a very remarkable glyph of connected conventional figures, quite old and different from any other known. It marked the site of the former summer fishing village, *Kla-yark* (or *Kla-yask*?, "Katleansky Village") of the *Kik sadi* [Kiksʔádi, Raven 10] chief, *Katlean* [Q̓ałyá·n], who led the attack that destroyed the first Russian fort at Old Sitka in 1802, so this petroglyph was certainly in situ at that date, as all of these nearby villages were deserted in the following years of warfare with the Russian invaders.

[The site was described by Emmons, in manuscript notes, as marked by a clearing and abundant bushes, grass, and a potato garden; but the house sites in 1888 were at least two hundred yards from the mouth of the main stream, which had probably changed its course, and once flowed by the houses.]

At the edge of the rocks was a carved boulder, irregular in shape, about three feet by three feet, by two and one-half feet, just above the high-tide mark. It was wholly covered by a decayed tree trunk and beach growth, which with difficulty we could remove from only one face. Another face seems also to have been worked, but was buried. The grooves were shallow, smooth, and almost obliterated in places, but by filling them with black mud, the outline was sufficiently clear to permit a reasonably fair sketch [in his field notebook, BCPA].

This shows five connected figures, each one of which the old man named as he remembered them from his childhood, and which, from their context and a knowledge of the folktales of this people, told clearly the oldest story of mankind—the Creation. In the legend common to the Northwest Coast tribes, in the beginning the earth was a chaotic mass of rock and ocean, enveloped in darkness and inhabited by a few supernatural beings who controlled and jealously guarded those elements necessary to human life. A benign spirit known as *Yehlh* [Yé·ł], the Transformer, who assumed many guises but more often appeared in the form of a Raven, came and wrestled from these spirits light, fresh water, fire, and the control of the winds, made man, and taught him the use of natural objects, and then disappeared.

In the carving, *Yehlh*, Raven, is shown in the lower figure, distinguished by the raven head and bill, with an oval body, a curved line to represent a leg and a foot; above this is an eye for the joint of the tail. In the bill is a line which may represent the fire that Raven stole and dropped on the rocks and trees, from both of which fire is produced: by the strike-a-light and the twirling stick [fire drill]. A spiral connected with the Raven's tail, the interpreter named *Una-kana-hihkh,* "Where the Sun comes from" [probably ʔanax̣ ke· naxíx, "(sun) is coming up," or gaga·n ʔana·x̣ ke·xíxč, "where the Sun comes up"]. It will be remembered that, in the legend, Raven released the Sun and lighted up the Earth. Joined with the Raven, above and to the right, is a figure made up of three concentric circles, representing the Earth, and above this is a very sketchy animal figure which the Indian identified as *Hoon* [Xú·n], the North Wind, the spirit of cold that sweeps down from the glaciers and snow-covered mountains in winter. To the left, and over the center, is a highly conventionalized figure, *Kun-nook* [Ǫa·nu·kʷ, "Petrel"], the guardian of the well of fresh water, on an island far off in the ocean, from whom Raven stole the fresh water. He carried it away in his bill, and as he flew over the earth, he dropped it here and there, forming the lakes and rivers. This being is here, as often in painting and carving, represented in the form of a Wolf, as is shown by the extended nose or mouth, the long ears, legs, feet, and tail. [This is probably because this character is associated with the Wolf moiety, opposed to the Raven.] As far as I have seen, this is the only connected set of figures in petroglyphs in southeastern Alaska that conveys any definite meaning beyond merely indicating the clan crest.

[Keithahn (1940:132) wrote: "At Wrangell, several boulders collectively illustrate the story of how 'Raven' caught a spring salmon through the use of a stone with a face on it

Tlingit petroglyphs, localities unknown. (Sketched by G. T. Emmons. See Emmons 1908b.) (a and b) Raven. (c) Line of faces and circles. (d) Face (sidewise). (e) Face. (f) Eagle's head. (g) Eagle's nest. (h) Group of figures on a boulder, consisting of a human face, starfish, and two unidentified creatures. (i) Face with large ear ornament (?). (j) Wolf's head. (k) Salmon. (l) Wolf's head. (m) Killerwhale. (n, o, and p) The sun. (q) Spiral. (r) Wolf's head. (s) Shark. (t) Head of sandhill crane. (u) Ceremonial rattle. (v) Unknown figure and "copper."

and which he gave magical power by sprinkling it with eagle down." A complex design was found on a boulder at Sitkoh Bay, Peril Strait (see de Laguna 1960, fig. 8).]

About two hundred yards away, on a smooth split in front of the old village site at the head of Lisiansky Bay, was an oblong boulder some two and one-half feet long, grooved down the middle, and cut the length of one side as a Raven, and on the other a Frog, both of which were important clan crests of the Kiksadi [Raven 10]. The carving was exceptionally deep and well executed and entirely different from other rock carvings.

[Emmons also noted carved rocks by the water's edge, just south of Salisbury Sound in the Sitka area, at the north end of the dry passage (Sukoi Inlet) between Kruzof and a small island to the east (Partofshikof Island). This is probably near the reported site of "Little Clam Fort," *Truke noo-ou* (ʒú·k̓ʷ nu·wú), on Partofshikof Island.]

[There are many sites with petroglyphs in the Stikine area.] Near the northwestern extremity of Etolin Island [Emmons evidently meant Wrangell Island] is a sand beach between two jutting rocky points, and scattered along, just above the high-tide level, are numerous smoothed, dark-gray rocks, seldom exceeding three feet in dimensions, irregularly shaped but generally offering a flattened surface suitable for petroglyphs. Nearly all of these bear single figures, pecked in shallow grooves, representing a variety of natural subjects that are in most instances so realistic that the artist's meaning is unmistakable. Parts of some have been obliterated by the elements and the ash of the tides, or have never been finished. Animal figures, complete in profile, largely predominate, representing those common to the region and totemic in character, while circles, spirals, and faces make up the others. Within the choice of subjects, it would appear that the rock surface determined the selection of the design to be employed, that it might better conform to the decorative field and cover the greater space.

[The subjects include the Raven, Eagle, Crane, Wolf, Salmon, Shark, Killerwhale, Starfish, faces (human or anthro-

Top. *Painted rock on Chilkat River, at* Kuw-tcha-tche-hit ka-ya [kawǯixidi qa· yá·], *"painted face," where the Raven 3 of Klukwan commemorated their victory over the Raven 6 of Hoonah and Yakutat, in a war over the rights to the Raven Hat. (Sketched by G. T. Emmons, "1905" (1902?). AMNH.)* Bottom. *Rock carved to represent a Bear, the crest of Wolf 30, the clan credited with the destruction of the Russian fort at Yakutat in 1805, and said to commemorate that event. It was found in the Ankau lagoons, near the site of the Russian fort, and brought to Yakutat in 1949, but disappeared soon afterward. (Photographed by Frederica de Laguna.)*

pomorphic), the Sun, circles, a spiral, and a frame for a rattle with puffin beaks; see Emmons, 1908b. Harlan I. Smith (1909:598–99, pls. XXVII and XXVIII, and fig. 102) also visited and described this site:

> North of Wrangel, along the beach below high-water mark, from near the limit of the settlement here and there for about a mile to near the northern end of Wrangel island, may be seen petroglyphs on the fragments of beach rock. . . . Some of these have been figured by Lieut. George T. Emmons. [Footnote reference to Emmons 1908b, figs. 53, 62.] A few of them consist of two concentric circles, others apparently were designed to represent the human face, and some of these tend to be square rather than circular. One apparently represents the finback whale [killerwhale]. The plainest of the grooves probably do not exceed a quarter of an inch in depth; others are shallower, or the surface of the rock is weathered away so that they can scarcely be seen. Some of the pictures remind us of those at Yellow island in Baynes sound, near Comox, and at Nanaimo. The type of art shown, while not so characteristic of the Northwest Coast as that expressed in paintings and in carvings in wood, is typical and can be recognized as from this region; and I am of the opinion that these Wrangel petroglyphs are more typical of the Northwest Coast as a whole than are those near Comox and Nanaimo [Vancouver Island, B.C.].]

These carvings are unquestionably of two distinct periods. In the older ones the grooves are worn and smooth and in parts are almost obliterated by time and the action of high tides. Others of a later date show the pits of the pecking stone very distinctly. I can only say in explanation of this difference that the old living site had been reoccupied at different periods, which was not uncommon among the Tlingit in early days. The resident natives offer no explanation of these carvings or their age; they simply say that they were there in their fathers' day, which means nothing. The illustrations [in Emmons 1908b] are from rough outlines that are sufficiently accurate to give the figures, many of which the natives explained.

[Emmons also mentioned petroglyphs in a shallow bight just below "Shustack Point" (Point Shakesti), south of Wrangell. This site was also visited by Harlan Smith (1909:598), who wrote: "Along the beach near Wrangel, Alaska, between Mr. Smith's house and the burial ground about two miles south of the town, below high-water mark, are a number of angular fragments of rock, bearing petroglyphs. These are rather faint and consist of circles about six inches in diameter."

[Keithahn (1940, fig. 14-5) illustrated a Woodworm from this site, a crest of the G̣a·nax̣ʔádi, Raven 1. Most of the other illustrations in his article are of petroglyphs at the larger site north of Wrangell.

[Emmons photographed a petroglyph on the beach, at the airport, one mile south of Wrangell.]

Another site with petroglyphs was at the old fishing village of Tchukass, on the mainland shore of the channel back of Etolin Island [read Wrangell Island. This is apparently "Waterfall Town," Ču-x̌á·s ʔa·n, five miles below the mouth of the Stikine, at "Charley Brown's ranch," at or near Virginia Lake, Mill Creek, on the eastern or mainland shore of Eastern Passage, the pass east of Wrangell Island, and about seven miles northeast of Wrangell.]

Another site was at *Shuk-thu-an,* just south of the mouth of the Stikine. [The name may be Ša·x̣-łu-ʔa·n, "gray currant-point village," or Šák^{w}-łu-ʔa·n, "strawberry-point village."]

[Keithahn (1940:129) wrote in reference to petroglyphs in this area:

> Large streams such as the Stikine River or a famous salmon stream such as Anan Creek in the Wrangell district [on Ernest

Tlingit petroglyphs. Top. *Detail of petroglyphs on Fritz Cove Road, Auke Bay, ten miles from Juneau. (Photograph by S. R. Capps, USGS.)* Bottom. *Petroglyph at the airport, on the beach, one mile south of Wrangell. (Photograph by G. T. Emmons (?). BCPA.)*

> Sound, east of Wrangell Island] have more glyphs than streams in which the salmon run was small. A small stream near Wrangell, barren of salmon at present, boasts many petroglyphs at its mouth. The oldest natives remember when it was an excellent salmon stream.

[Emmons also noted petroglyphs at Hyta, or Hetta, on the east side of Hetta Inlet, north of Howkan, on the southwest side of Prince of Wales Island. It is in territory that was abandoned by the Tongass to the Kaigani Haida, and the carvings are presumably Tlingit. Keithahn (1940, figs. 14-*3c,* 14-*4f,* 14-*6b,* 15*a,* 15*b*) has illustrated two faces, a bird, and two sea monsters from Hetta Inlet, perhaps from the same site. He also reported (p. 123) petroglyphs at Hydaberg Creek, one-half mile from Sukkwan, also on the southwest coast of Prince of Wales Island. One of these (Keithahn, 1940:130, pl. XIb) represents Salmon Boy, and is duplicated by a carving at Wrangell and another at Karta Bay on the east coast of Prince of Wales Island, near Kasaan.

[Emmons wrote of petroglyphs "across from Killisnoo, on Admiralty Island," but these were not found by de Laguna's field party in 1950. He also noted petroglyphs "at the head of Sitkoh Bay, at the southeastern point of Chichagof Island," that is, at the village site of Sitkoh (Sit̓x̣u, "among the glaciers"?); both are sites in Hutsnuwu territory. (For a description of the second site and pictures of the carvings there, see de Laguna 1960:65–67, figs. 6, 8, and pl. 11.) Other known or reported petroglyphs on Admiralty Island were at Angoon, Hood Bay, Chaik Bay, and Whitewater Bay, including Head Island; and red pictographs were also seen one-half mile south of Angoon, and on a cliff near Whitewater Bay (see de Laguna 1960:73–75, figs. 7*a,* 7*b,* 7*c*).

[The list above is not exhaustive, for Emmons speculated that petroglyphs would also be found at other village and fishing sites, as yet undiscovered on the coasts and islands of southeastern Alaska, and Keithahn (1940:128) reported that "at the mouths of all major salmon streams on the West Coast of Prince of Wales Island petroglyphs abound."

[Emmons reported and sketched a red "painted face," *Kuw-tche-hit kah-yah* (kawǯixidi qa· ỵá), on rocks on the west side of the Chilkat River. This seems to be at or near the place known as "Skull Point," or "Painted with blood place," *Kaudjihit kiya'h,* as reported by Olson (1967:26). This was where the bodies and severed heads of the attacking Łʼukʷnax̣ʔádi (Raven 6) from Yakutat drifted, after they were slain by the Chilkat G̣a·nax̣te·dí (Raven 3), in a war over claims to the Raven Hat. The victors are said to have painted the face with the blood of their dead enemies.]

STONE CAIRNS

More baffling than petroglyphs and stone carvings are cairns of piled stones to be found on the mountains well above timberline, both on the mainland and on offshore islands. They have no relation to the Russian occupation, and are not boundary marks. They are away from any trails or lines of travel, at altitudes of from two to three thousand feet, located on clear stretches, generally on mountain tops. The oldest natives can give no explanation of them, beyond the story that when the great Flood covered the earth, those who survived in canoes floated up and moored their craft here with great bark ropes, the decayed ends of which it is claimed can still be seen.

[Cairns like these were said by the Tlingit of Angoon and Yakutat to be "nests" or forts made by survivors of the Flood to protect themselves from the bears that were driven to the summits of mountains by the rising waters (de Laguna and McClellan, field notes, 1950, 1952). Stone piles have been noted by some members of the U.S. Geological Survey, who offered no explanation for them. My archaeological party of 1935 explored a pile of stones on a high ridge above the middle Yukon River, between Nulato and Holy Cross; this "cairn" was due to frost action, according to our geologist, Jack Eardley. But this explanation may not apply to all such piles.]

The following locations of such cairns are known, others may still be discovered: On a mountain 2,500 feet high, above Union Bay and Ernest Sound, on Cleveland Peninsula, there are four or five pyramidal or circular piles of stones. Watson, half-breed, knows about this. On a mountain on Etolin Island is a cairn of boulders. At Gambier Bay, on Admiralty Island, on a mountain about 2,000 feet high, there are five piled stone monuments, three to four feet high: one is about eight feet long, one somewhat in the shape of a J, two are pyramidal, and one is oblong. Cook of Juneau, a prospector, knows about two piles of stone, J-shaped and pyramidal, on a mountain about 2,500 feet high, above Pybus Bay, Admiralty Island. [These may possibly be some of those reported back of Gambier Bay.]

On the mountains on the eastern shore of Lynn Canal, some thirty miles from tidewater, following the valley of the "Katzheen river" [Katzehin River, Łi-ga·si Hí·n, "Tabooed River"], and overlooking the glacier from which the river flows, are two pyramidal cairns, carefully constructed of slate, for the most part. This was evidently for durability, since the rock in the immediate vicinity is softer sandstone. These cairns are some four hundred feet apart, bearing north and south from each other. They are respectively 3½ and 4½ feet high, and 3½ feet wide at the base, and taper to a point. While these cairns are known to the Chilkat, the latter have no knowledge of their origin or use, except that they are similar to others found on islands to the southward which certainly had no connection with the Russian occupation. These cairns above Lynn Canal might be considered as boundary monuments to define the inland limit of Russian territory, since they are thirty miles inland, which marked the extent of the coastal strip of southeastern Alaska claimed by the Russians.

On the Chilkat divide, near the summit of the coastal mountains, overlooking Rainy Hollow, and about ten marine leagues [about forty-four statute miles on a direct line] from tidewater, is what the natives term *Ta hit* [Té hít], "Stone House." This is just beyond the summit, on a level, moss-covered plain, free from any obstructions, and visible for all directions. It originally consisted of three great slabs of granite placed on end, and inclined toward one another to form a pyramid. One of these in time has disintegrated, as is attested by the broken pieces at the base. The two remaining stones still support each other. They are 5 feet high, 4 inches thick, and respectively 4 and 6½ feet wide at the base. Such unwieldy stones must have been transported at great labor from an old streambed several hundred feet distant. This must have been the work of a party of Russians who visited the Chilkat in 1838 and placed such a monument to mark the boundary of southeastern Alaska ["Russian America"], preparatory to leasing the littoral to the Hudson's Bay Company in 1840. This is the belief of the Chilkat people, as attested by the affidavits of some eighteen of the older Tlingit of Klukwan which I took in 1902 when acting as Boundary Commissioner under the Secretary of State. From the character of this monument it does not seem to be related in any way to the piled rock cairns found at other places.

[Just what Emmons found, or did not find, is a puzzle. No "boundary marker" or "stone house" was mentioned in the testimony published by the Boundary Tribunal. What Emmons described may have been an emergency shelter built by natives (or white prospectors?) for anyone caught in a storm on the pass. Shelters in the cracks of "a loose mass of huge boulders piled over each other" on the Chilkoot Pass were called by the Tlingit "stone houses," but Schwatka (1893:81) did not indicate whether these were man-made or natural piles. Also not mentioned in the testimony to the Boundary Tribunal, as well as in Emmons's notebook, were the half-dozen postlike stones, about three feet high (?), set in a line (or lines)—an arrangement that would suggest "boundary markers." Were they set by the Tlingit to define the "boundary" beyond which Athabaskan traders might not come? Or were they "scarecrows," built in connection with a caribou fence? Emmons was certainly anxious that the reputed mineral riches of Rainy Hollow should go to the United States. Although this did not happen, the Boundary was set farther down the Klehini River (at the Canadian Dalton Trail post, "Pleasant Camp") but above the Provisional Boundary of 1899, thereby assuring to the United States the gold placers on "Porcupine Creek," to the indignation of the Canadians (see Wheeler 1929; Green 1982:75–78). Emmons's notebook of the trip to Rainy Hollow (July 23–August 2, 1902), with its curious duplications and omissions, is in BCPA.]

CHAPTER 4

Travel and Transportation

CANOES*

The Tlingit, as well as the other Northwest Coast peoples, were woodworkers. They lived at the edge of dense forests of great cedar, spruce, and hemlock. Their insular surroundings, their life as marine hunters, fishermen, and traders, required a means of transportation which was furnished by the dugout canoe, *york* [ya·kʷ], an unsurpassed model of marine architecture.

The Haida of the Queen Charlotte Islands were acknowledged as the most expert canoe makers, in which they were aided by the exceptionally large red cedars that their islands produced. The Southern Tlingit also had access to this wood in their own territory, but the tribes north of Frederick Sound were dependent upon the spruce, except on the Chilkat River [and at Dry Bay] where inferior canoes were made of cottonwood. Paddles were preferably of cedar, although spruce, alder, and willow were also used. The steering paddle was a third larger and heavier than the others. [When available, yellow cedar might be used for paddles.]

Sail was carried with the wind well abaft the beam, since the canoe lacked keel, centerboard, or sideboard. For over a century a spritsail of cotton cloth has been used. The primitive sail is claimed to have been made of cedar-bark matting. It was a square sail permanently attached to a yard that was hoisted to the masthead, and possibly to another yard at the foot, but of this we know little, since none of the early explorers mentions it. The board [plank] sail used by the Kwakiutl was unknown to the north. Indeed, the Tlingit seem to have had no knowledge or tradition of the use of a sail before the coming of Europeans [see Howay 1941; Drucker 1950:255].

The typical Tlingit canoe used for hunting, fishing, and ordinary travel was made of spruce, and was called *seete* [si·t] or "spruce," and to the whites was the "Sitka canoe." It was fitted with crossbars or thwarts, sewn with spruce root to the sides to strengthen and prevent their collapse, since they had been artificially spread beyond the natural diameter of the tree trunk from which the canoe had been hollowed out. For the stepping of the mast, two horizontal thwarts, one several inches below the other, were fitted well forward. The mast was stepped through holes in the middle of these thwarts, and its foot was fitted into a corresponding mortise in a small block fastened in the bottom of the canoe. Small, removable, triangular platforms, raised several inches above the bottom, rested on cleats in the bow and stern and served as seats. Sometimes a thin strip some three inches high was sewn with spruce root along the gunwale to increase its height. This type of canoe was uniformly painted black outside. Often there was a narrow diagonal red stripe across the rise of the bow and stern.

[A canoe of this type sketched by Emmons at Sitka had an overall length of 22 feet and a beam of 3 feet 3½ inches. The bottom was 17 feet long. The bow had a height of 2 feet 7½ inches, the stern a height of 2 feet 5½ inches, while the height of the sides amidships was only 1 foot 4½ inches.]

The canoe used by the Yakutat of the Mount Saint Elias region is peculiar to them and is not found elsewhere [except among the Eyak-speaking natives of the Gulf of Alaska to the westward and at the mouth of the Copper River (Birket-Smith and de Laguna 1938: 45–52, pls. 9, 10, 11-8; de Laguna 1963, fig. 3, "forked-prow canoe"; de Laguna, 1972, figs. 26*c* and 27, pp. 337–38)]. It was made of spruce and was called *tch yosh* [čiyá·š], a word in a forgotten language [later corrected to "in Copper River language," i.e., Atna]. It was used for sea otter and seal hunting in the open water off the coast where the larger canoe could not live, and for travel through the narrow inland waters between Yakutat and Dry bays where there were many portages. [It

Editor's note: This chapter had to be created from items Emmons had planned to include in his original Chapter VII, under "Wood Carving," or "Wood Working," and "Bags." It was this chapter that gave Emmons the most trouble and which he was never able to put together, possibly because his descriptions were largely written first from the point of view of manufacture, whereas he also had texts dealing with the functions and uses of the articles. The problem was how or even whether to combine them. Here we attempt to do both, but the functions of canoes, sleds, and so on are primary; hence the title.

**Editor's note:* In this section I tried to fit together the numerous descriptions and pictures (sketches and photographs) of the various types of canoe Emmons wanted to include. This necessitated rewriting the text slightly. I have also included a few references.

was light, and could be easily carried, besides being very seaworthy in rough water.] Its notable feature was the projecting ram-shaped bow, which not only gave extra deadwood and strength in rough water but broke the force of the waves ahead. The average length of the canoe was about sixteen feet. It carried two men, both of whom knelt [or squatted] in the bottom amidships, and paddled together two strokes on one side and then two on the other. [This was the Chugach Eskimo style of paddling their kayak and two-holed bidarka, although they usually paddled three times on each side.] The Yakutat made no attempt to steer with a stern paddle, which in fact they could not do from their midship position. In kneeling, they [straddled] and were really seated on a block of wood or narrow bench, some six inches high [and completely hollowed out from end to end], which stabilized their position. When hunting, the man ahead used the weapon. The canoe was uniformly painted black outside, with an inch-wide red band along the gunwale, about two inches below the edge. The paddles were of yellow cedar, longer and with sharper and narrower blades than other paddles used on the coast, and were painted black with a diagonal stripe across the blade. The end of the handle was formed like a hand without the fingers [that is, it was carved to a grip shaped like a clenched fist, hollowed out on one side].

[Emmons sketched a hunting canoe of this Yakutat type that had an overall length of 16 feet 9 inches, and a length of 16 feet on the bottom. The beam was 2 feet 6 inches. The height of the bow was 2 feet ¼ inch; the height of the stern 2 feet 2¼ inches, and the height amidships 13 inches.]

Another type of canoe, found only among the Yakutat, was the ice canoe [gudí·yi], used in hunting hair seal among the ice flows of Yakutat Bay [and Icy Bay]. It was also of spruce, small in size, and intended for two occupants. The bow was rounded and strengthened with a knoblike projection above the waterline as a fender and safeguard among the floating bergs. No specimen of this type was to be found as late as 1883 when I first visited Yakutat, but several small models remained.

[These canoes were 12 to 15 feet long, and about 3½ feet wide. They were paddled stern-first in open water, but when the floating ice was reached, the ends were reversed. The hunter in the bow sneaked up on his quarry by using a small paddle only 18 inches long which he could operate with one hand. (See "heavy prow sealing canoes" in de Laguna 1972:339–40.)]

The Southern Tlingit, particularly the Stikine, had a small canoe for fishing and hunting, of spruce or cedar, which was called *dise york* [dís ya·kʷ], "moon canoe," from

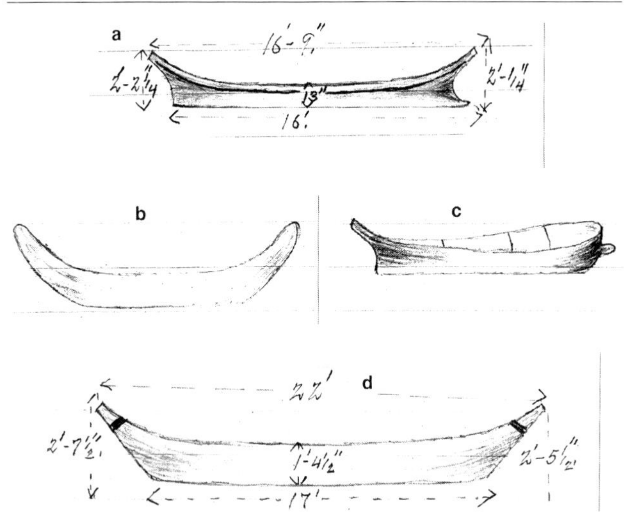

Tlingit canoes with measurements in feet and inches. (Sketched by G. T. Emmons. AMNH.) (a) Hunting canoe, Yakutat. (b) "Moon canoe," Stikine. (c) Ice hunting canoe, Yakutat, 1883. (d) Ordinary spruce canoe, Sitka.

its crescentic shape. It was also called *yucktche york* [yúxʷč̓(i) ya·kʷ], "sea otter canoe." It was alike at both ends and was quite heavy.

The Chilkat [and Dry Bay people] utilized the cottonwood tree that grew to good size on the riverbanks for a small canoe used in fishing and travel on the river. The wood had the advantage of not checking in the heat of the sun, although it warped. When not in use, the canoe was turned bottom up. It was seldom if ever painted. [See "cottonwood canoes," dúqʷ, in de Laguna 1972:336–37.]

The Haida traded their expertly made canoes to all the other Northwest Coast peoples from Vancouver to the Copper River. From the huge red cedars of the Queen Charlotte Islands they fashioned canoes which attained a [cargo] capacity of six to eight tons, and a length of over sixty feet. As late as 1900 I saw such canoes brought north and sold at Killisnoo for $250. Haida canoes varied in size from the small two-man fishing canoe, through the medium size for family use, to the very large canoe for transportation, which was also, in old times, the chief's war canoe. The type was the same, with long projecting spur bow, straight cutwater, and high curving stern. The larger canoes were proportionately heavy, and the raised ends were separate pieces scarfed to the main body. The bow projection was broad and had a groove in the center in which the masts and spars rested [when unshipped]. These canoes were therefore called *shur-ku see-high-ee york*, "bow piece-put-on canoe" [possibly šaka-sihá·yi ya·kʷ, "canoe having skirting on the bow"]. The thwarts were heavy and wide, placed horizontally, and served as seats for the paddlers. A false cutwater, consisting of a rod bridging the sharp angle

Canoe seen by La Pérouse in Lituya Bay in 1786. (After Chinard 1937, pl. opp. p. 42.)

between the curve of the projecting spur of the bow and the keel line, was often attached, permitting the floating [mass of] kelp and seaweed, so abundant in the inland channels, to disengage itself instead of catching on the vertical cutwater. The large canoes were fitted for two masts.

[At Yakutat the large Haida "war canoe" was ironically called "baby canoe," ya·kʷ yádi. Emmons did not record this name. The type is probably the same as that described above, under the name "bow piece-put-on canoe."]

Models of very old canoes indicate that the bow or cutwater was but slightly inclined from the perpendicular, and elderly Haida claim that this was the earliest type of canoe. But in a beam wind, it made so much leeway and was so clumsy that it was first modified by cutting a large hole through the deadwood of the bow. Later the whole lower portion of the deadwood was cut away to form the long projecting graceful bow of the modern Haida canoe. This type was usually called "long tail," *tle-de-kla-ott* [ƛ̓í·dí-kʷɬayáṭ̓], and was perhaps the kind most commonly traded to the Tlingit.

[B. Durham (1960:56) has illustrated the type of canoe with a large hole through the bow. Canoes with two holes through the bow and stern were observed by La Pérouse at Lituya Bay in 1786 (de Laguna 1972, pl. 27 from the engraving; original drawing in Henry 1984, pl. on p. 144). A canoe seen by Malaspina at Yakutat in 1791 (Henry 1984, pl. on p. 164) has stitched-on sideboards, two holes cut through the stern and one through the bow. It was used by the chief, but we note a woman with large labret was steering. Emmons noted the Haida canoe sketched in 1792 by Ingraham (1971, pl. opposite p. 179) that had two holes through the bow; the stern is unpierced.]

In addition to the forms of canoes already described and that were in general use throughout the past century, some models have been observed or collected that represent quite different canoe forms for which older informants have given names.

A very large canoe made by the Haida and traded to the Tlingit was called "wide nose," *thlu-kah-ku-uke* or *thlu ku uke* [ɬukuwúx̣̓ʷ or ɬu· qu-wúx̣̓ʷ], because of the great width of the projecting spur of the bow.

Alongside a shaman's grave at the Chilkat village of Klukwan in 1885, I saw a very old large canoe with bow and stern almost perpendicular, a type of dugout which corresponds rather closely to the primitive, wide-nosed Haida type.

Several models in the AMNH collections represent an old type of large canoe, said to have been used by and procured from southern people. Some suggest a type resembling the Vancouver Island canoe used by the Nootka and others. [See B. Durham 1960:47–52.] This last was called *kokh-tar-geek-geen york* [probably qux̣ʷ-da-gí·gin ya·kʷ, "stern-backwards canoe"] because of its high stern. This was the next to largest type of old canoe. [Although a Kaliakh chief at Controller Bay owned a canoe named "Bac̣k-wards Canoe," presumably the same Tlingit word, this type of Nootka canoe was known at Yakutat as a "goose canoe," ṭ̓a·wáq ya·kʷ, because of the shape of the bow. It seems to correspond to the so-called southern type of canoe.]

Tlingit chiefs prided themselves on the size and ornamentation of their canoes. These have been called "war canoes," but they differed in no wise from those of equal size used for traveling or freighting. They were ornamentally painted along the sides, generally in the bow and stern, with the central portion black. Again, carved figures might be placed at or over the bow, and sometimes at the stern. The canoe was named for the painting or figure, which was generally totemic in character or might refer to some incident in the family [clan or lineage] history. The canoe name was hereditary, like the house name [and the named canoe was a crest object].

One of these canoes was the property of Chief Shakes [Še·kš], of the *Nan-ya-i-ee* [Na·nỵa·ʔa·ỵí, Wolf 18] of the Stikine tribe. It has three names: "Brown Bear Canoe," *Hootz York* [Xú·c Ya·kʷ], from the carved bear figures surmounting the bow and stern. The male bear leaning over the bow was the watchman looking ahead, and the female bear was shown rising out of the stern. The second name was "Killerwhale Canoe," *Kete York* [Kí·t Ya·kʷ], because a killerwhale was painted on either side, and the canoe was reckoned as a great killerwhale whose natural food is the seal. At the extreme bow, on either side, is painted a small killerwhale [pilot whale], known as the "killerwhale's

Chief Shakes's Haida canoe. (Obtained by G. T. Emmons for the World's Fair of 1893, and now in the collections of the Smithsonian Institution. Smithsonian Institution photographs, nos. 4813 and 34375.) Top. *Bow with carved bear and painted "blackfish" (pilot whale) which has caught a seal.* Bottom. *Stern, with carved bear and painted raven.*

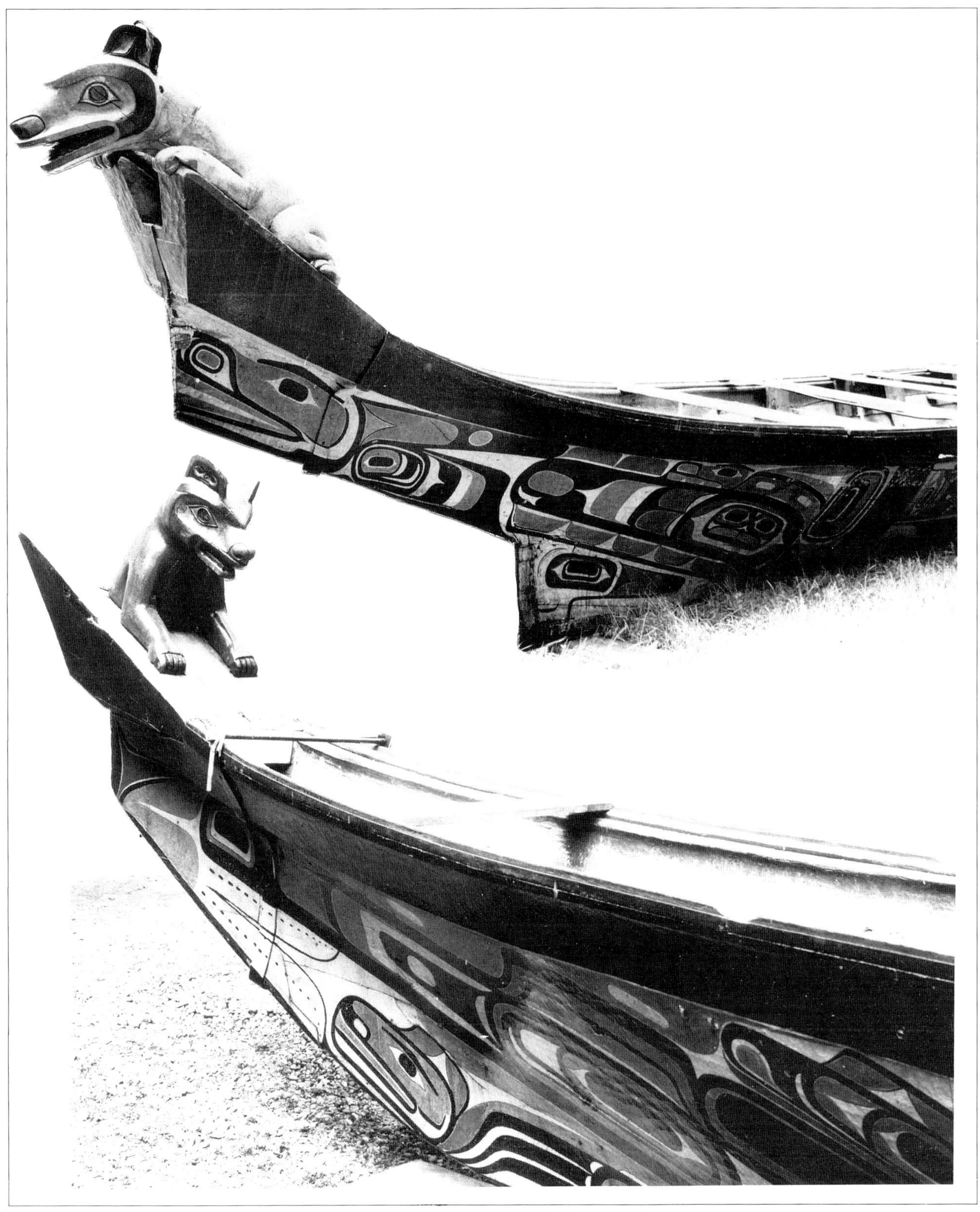

Large Haida canoe, owned by [James] Brady, Sitka. It was painted by Jim [?] in black, red, and blue to represent a Killerwhale near the bow, with a seal in its mouth, preceded by the "killerwhale's spear" (pilot whale). At the stern is an Eagle and still farther astern the head of a wolf or bear. It was called the Killerwhale Canoe. (Photograph by G. T. Emmons. BCPA.)

spear," *kete woo sonnee* [kí·t wu·sá·ni], because it is supposed to swim quickly, like a hunting spear that pierces the seal, as the canoe flies through the water. The small killerwhale casts the seal to the large killerwhale. In the mouth of the latter is painted a seal which has been so taken. On either side of the stern was painted a raven, known as *Kete tah-woo-gor-tee Yehlh* [kí·t -?- yé·ł, "killerwhale -?- raven"], and so the canoe was also named "Raven Canoe," *Yehlh York* [Yé·ł Ya·k^{w}]. The Killerwhale and Brown Bear were both family crests of the chief's clan; the Raven was the crest of the wife's clan. This canoe was procured by me for the U.S. Government exhibition at the World's Fair at Chicago, 1893, and is in the U.S. National Museum in Washington, D.C. [catalogue number 168,115]. The measurements are: overall length 46 feet, beam 5 feet 8 inches, height at bow 5 feet, height amidships 3 feet.

A very fine canoe that belonged to a Haida chief was taken to Sitka [and there apparently sold to a white man, Brady]. It had been elaborately painted in black, red, and blue to represent a killerwhale with a seal in its mouth. Ahead of it was a small killerwhale [pilot whale], "The killerwhale's spear," which is supposed to drive the seals or catch them for the large killerwhale. At the stern is an eagle, and astern [of that] the head of a wolf or of a bear [Emmons is inconsistent in his notes]. This canoe was called "Killerwhale Canoe," *Kete York* [Kí·t Ya·k^{w}]. It was of the type called *ah shuck kus see har ee* [ʔa šaka-sihá·ỵi ya·k^{w}, the type of canoe with built-up bow].

On the bow of a Haida canoe seen in 1900 at the Taku village just below Juneau was a figure pointing ahead, known as "the watchman."

At Wrangell in 1892, in the house of the *Nan-ya-i-ee* chief [presumably Chief Shakes of the Na·nỵa·ʔa·yí, Wolf 18], who had the Brown Bear as one of his crests, was quite a large miniature canoe, painted with black at the bow to represent the head of a brown bear and at the stern the hind quarters of the bear. The painting and ornamentation of these models, which were generally children's toys, were exact copies of the designs on the chief's canoes.

At Killisnoo the model of a Haida war canoe had the figure of a beaver at the bow, since this was the crest of the *Da-she-ton* chief [De·ší·ta·n, Raven 13]. The sides had been painted, but [in 1900] little of the design could be traced.

The *Ka-ghan-tan* [Ka·g^{w}a·nta·n, Wolf 1] of Chilkat had attached to the bow of a chief's canoe the figure of an [anthropomorphic] owl [?] with [a human head, and with hands on the] outstretched wings that were hinged to open and close. [The Owl is not a crest of this clan, but belongs to several clans of the Raven moiety. Perhaps the canoe had been captured or the crest appropriated by the Wolf clan.]

The *Tuck-clar-way-de* [Daqławe·dí, Wolf 27] of the same tribe [Chilkat], when going to a potlatch in another village,

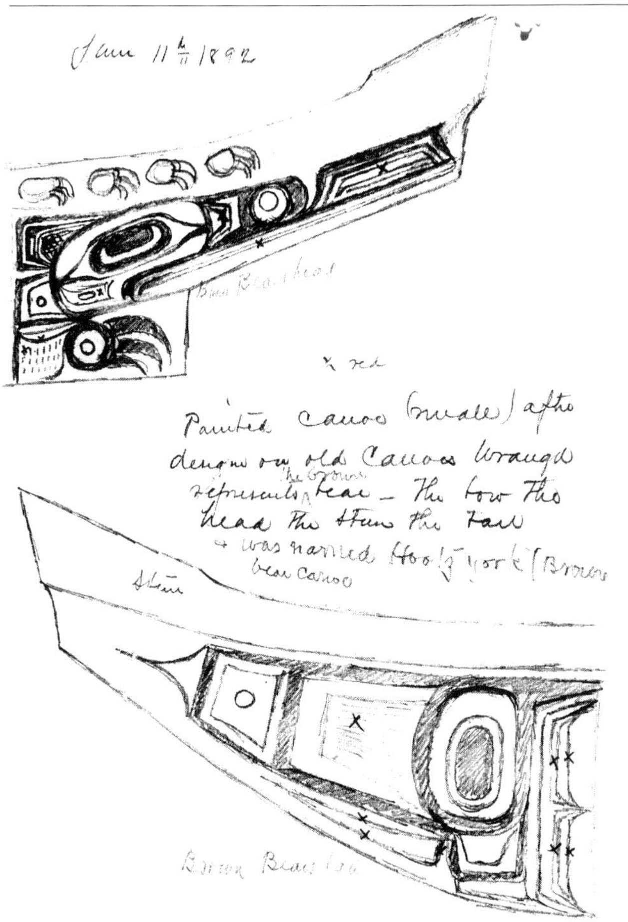

A small or model canoe, Brown Bear Canoe. (Sketched by G. T. Emmons, January 11, 1892, at Wrangell. AMNH.) Bow above; stern below. X indicates red paint; the rest is black.

*Canoe of the chief of the Ka·g*ʷ*a·nta·n, Wolf 1, of the Chilkat. In the bow is the figure of an anthropomorphic owl (?) with hinged wings, and human arms. The canoe was displayed at a potlatch at Klukwan. (Photograph by Blankenberg, no. 182. BCPA.)*

would attach to their canoe, on either side of the bow, the cutout head and forefeet of a bear with the body of a whale, [the mythical] "Sea Bear," ***Heen tark Hootz ee*** [hi·n ta·k xú·ʒi, "bear at the bottom of the water"]. The figure was of wood, painted red, yellow, and white.

[Surveys of Northwest Coast canoes and their appurtenances, including types made by and traded to the Tlingit, may be found in Olson 1927; Drucker 1950:252–55; G. Durham 1955; B. Durham 1960:39–82; de Laguna 1963; 1972:330–45.]

MANUFACTURE AND REPAIR OF CANOES

In making a canoe, the first requirement was to select a tree that had grown slowly in dry soil, since the larger trees that grew abundantly in wet ground were spongy in fiber and would always absorb moisture. Sometimes chips from several trees were tested for checking by drying them near the fire. The grain should be straight and the wood free from knots. Generally the canoe maker camped on the working ground, for if it were any distance from the water, a large log would be difficult to transport, but the partly made or finished dugout could be more easily carried or skidded to the shore.

The tree was felled usually in November or March when the sap was down. [Presumably the winter months, December to February, were too cold for the work.] Before the acquisition of iron, this was a long, tedious task, since the tree had to be scored and worked around by means of the stone adz, wedges, and fire. There is a tradition that this method was learned from the beaver.

When felled, the trunk was cut the required length. The upper surface of the log was cut off [split off with wedges] to a quarter or so of the diameter. Then the log was turned over, the flat surface resting on the ground to give steadiness. The log was now worked down with the adz, first on

Making a canoe. Top. Partly adzed Kaigani canoe, Kasaan. Rough state, not ready to bore. (Photograph by Dr. C. F. Newcombe, BCPA, chosen by Emmons for illustration.) Bottom. *Pen and ink sketch by G. T. Emmons of adzing down a canoe, showing the method of holding the adz. (AMNH.)*

one side, then on the other. The appearance, when finished, was that of an inverted canoe.

[This whole description of canoe making was obviously based both on direct observation, to judge from the sketches made by Emmons, and from an article by J. D. Simpson (1907). This was found in his notes (BCPA) with the notation, "The article is by an Indian who knows the work."]

Around the bottom from gunwale to gunwale, for the entire length of the canoe, many parallel lines were drawn with charcoal, along which were bored tiny holes with the hand drill, an inch or two apart and increasing in depth from the top to the bottom of the canoe, the depths depending on its size. In a small canoe, the sides of the gunwale might be half an inch or so thick, which would be increased to one and one-half inches at the bottom. These holes were filled with a mixture of powdered charcoal and seal oil, or with tiny spruce or cedar roots, and when the inside of the canoe was being worked out, the discolored wood or the root served to show the exact thickness of the wall to be preserved. The depth of the boring was regulated by using drills of different lengths, or by partly capping a longer drill point with a cylinder of wood or by wrapping it with bark or root. These very small holes closed after the wood was wet and swelled.

The shaped log was then turned over and well braced with side stakes, preparatory to hollowing it out, which was done either by burning [and adzing] or by chopping alone. The first method was the more primitive and was considered the better, since the fire hardened the wood. Furthermore, all of the chips cut from the log were used in the burning, which was believed to give back to the log all its full strength. The fire was built along the center and carefully tended night and day. Wet moss was placed outside the area to be burned and kept wet, so that the fire should not extend too far. By this process, the log was charred rather than burned, and the hollowing out was completed with the adz and knife. The canoe, then in the rough, might be finished on the spot or taken to the village.

In working down the canoe, the man kneels alongside. The adz, *hootar,* "chipper" [x̣úťa·, "chopper"], is grasped in both hands not far from the blade, the left hand near the body, the right hand nearer the blade. [The sketch by Emmons shows the left hand gripping the adz, palm up; the right hand, palm down.]

Great care was taken in adzing that the marks should be of exactly the same size and depth, and parallel to each other the length of the canoe without a break. Indeed, this tooled finish was considered most ornamental. I saw it in Sitka in 1888, when the canoe maker with his adz commenced at the gunwale at one end, and worked in the direction of the grain of the wood for a distance of a foot or more, always cutting toward himself. Then he adzed a row below, and so on to the bottom. Commencing again at the gunwale, another foot or more in length was adzed, and the whole process was continued to the other end. In the large canoes the adz marks remained, but in the smaller ones those on the outside were rubbed out and the outer surface was smoothed with dogfish skin.

Since the greatest diameter of the log was less than that required for the sides of the canoe, these had to be spread throughout the midship section. A fire was built alongside [in which stones were heated]. Sand, gravel, and pieces of hemlock bark were placed in the bottom of the canoe, and it was partly filled with water. Then boulders of moderate size, when heated, were picked up with split wooden tongs and dropped into the water in the canoe. This was continued until steam was produced, which was confined by a covering of mats until the wood became pliable. Then the sides were gently stretched apart and crosspieces were inserted. As the wood cooled, it set as it had been stretched.

Making a canoe. (Photographs by W. Newcombe, BCPA, Kaigani, but selected by Emmons for illustration.) Top. *Nearly finished canoe, adzed inside and out, sides ready to be steamed and spread.* Bottom. *Partly finished canoe, showing small pegs driven into the sides as guides to adzing out the interior.*

Later, these temporary stretchers were replaced by permanent thwarts, which were sewed to the sides by twisted spruce root withes, countersunk on the outside in the case of the larger canoes. In sewing with spruce root, a hole was made with the hand drill, and the smaller end of the root was drawn through this until the larger end jammed on the outside. Then the rest of the root was drawn through the corresponding holes and the end knotted about its own parts.

The widths of the gunwale, or side of the canoe, was regulated or marked off by means of a native-made wooden gauge with a shouldered step near each end. Along this step, were a line of small holes for the insertion of a drill or awl. To test the width or thickness of the gunwale, the shoulder of the gauge was pressed against the outside of the canoe, and at the desired thickness the point of an awl was set through the proper hole. The gauge was then drawn along the top of the gunwale and the point of the awl marked the desired width. All canoes had a shallow groove inside that ran the length of the sides, an inch or so below the top of the gunwale. To mark the depth of this groove, the gauge was then placed perpendicularly, resting on top of the gunwale, and the awl inserted in the hole at the required depth, so that as the gauge was drawn along, the awl point marked the line.

Before blackening the outside of a canoe with a mixture of powdered charcoal and seal oil, the vessel was put into the water, filled, and soaked thoroughly for several days. It was found in practice that there were sometimes soft spots in the wood, and it was believed that the covering of black and oil would keep them expanded after they had swelled. [According to Simpson, Emmons's knowledgeable Indian (1907:173), filling the new canoe with water was an "old custom originated from the belief that the water having failed would not try again."]

The spreading of the walls, together with the delicate construction of the canoe, rendered it liable to check when exposed to the sun. It was necessary, therefore, that it should be kept damp and sheltered from the sun's rays. The large war or traveling canoe, used only at intervals, was sometimes placed in a ditch on the shore under a permanent tentlike shelter of boards, cedar bark, and brush, but any canoe hauled up on the beach was covered with bark mats, blankets, or an old sail, and was dampened every morning. When traveling in bright weather, the outside of the canoe was constantly splashed with a deft stroke of the paddle and the inside sprayed with the bailer.

Checks, which quickly extended into splits and imperiled the life of the canoe, were generally treated by soaking the wood and drawing the parts together with twisted withes of spruce root. Tiny holes, one-eighth inch in diameter, were bored with the hand drill on either side of the split. The smaller end of the moistened root was pointed and drawn through from the outside until the larger end jammed in the hole. Then it was passed through the opposite hole from the inside out, and cut off flush with the outside, if but a rough turn was taken. Sometimes the root was carried through again, countersunk on the outside below the waterline, and seized to its own part on the inside. The sewing could be tightened by driving a small half-rounded wedge between the root and the side of the canoe.

To make the withe used for sewing, a spruce limb was cut, and the small branches cut off. These were barked by twisting the little branch until it became a series of bights. The loosened bark was stripped off with the thumbnail. The resultant thong tapered from a maximum diameter of slightly greater than one-eighth inch, so that the larger end would jam in the drilled holes. [If spruce root was used, it apparently had to be heated before the bark could be loosened.] The hand drill, ***tuthl-ku*** or ***tuhlku*** [túɬx̓u], had a flat-faced bitt, mounted in a handle. The thong used in sewing was called *ssu* [s̓ú, "thin root or branch"].

Splits were also caulked with moss or filled with melted spruce gum. In large canoes where the wood was several inches thick, splits were drawn together with a root and then were more permanently secured by means of a number of hardwood dovetails, about three inches long and one-half inch thick, with the grain running lengthwise. These were fitted into corresponding mortises cut on the inside of the canoe, and from their ["figure 8"] shape firmly held the wood on either side of the crack. The split was also sewn with root between these chocks.

[At Sitka, December 14, 1888, Emmons saw a red cedar Haida canoe being mended, from which this description is taken. He noted that the dovetails were 1¾ inches wide at the widest parts of the "figure 8," and ¾ inch wide at the narrowest part, or neck, which was placed at the crack. These dovetails were made of a hardwood, like oak, which was called *shaskh* (probably šís̓q, or šás̓q), traded from the south-east. The distances between the dovetails varied from 13½ to 16 inches. At Chilkat he saw dovetails shaped like an hour-glass.]

Sometimes canoes were strengthened by thin, bent, pliable ribs, but this I have seen only in older canoes after weakness had developed.

When the bottom of the canoe became roughened from constant beaching or grounding in shallow rivers, the canoe was placed on logs or crosspieces at the bow and stern, sufficiently raised to get at the bottom and bilge. A little fire of green yellow cedar [cypress], containing much resinous sap, was built on a small, light board covered with sand or gravel, and this was carefully moved along the outside of the canoe to singe or burn off the fringelike projections on the bottom. The canoe was then turned bottom up and gone over with the curve-bladed [crooked] knife, smoothed with dogfish skin, and rubbed with oil and charcoal.

[See the excellent discussion and illustrations by Stewart (1984:48–60) of the making and mending of Northwest Coast canoes.]

APPURTENANCES OF THE CANOE*

The appurtenances of the canoe were the paddle [ʔax̣á·], mast, sail [s̓ísa· from -s̓i·s "be blown by the wind"], bailer [ší·n], skids or bottom boards, stone anchor "*gu-war-ta*" [gu·waté], and line.

The paddles were made of cedar, alder, willow, or spruce. They were of moderate size, the blade more rounded than pointed, and the handle terminated in a crossbar at the end. Those used for steering the large canoe were much larger and heavier than the others, and all of those belonging to the canoes of chiefs were apt to be painted in conventional crest designs on both sides of the blade.

The primitive sail is said to have been of cedar-bark matting, but of this we know nothing definite, although it is reasonable to believe that so ingenious a people would employ some labor-saving device in their constant travel. But the Tlingit have no tradition of a primitive sail. With the coming of European trading vessels, cotton cloth was immediately traded and used for sails. The smaller canoe carried only one sail, well forward; the larger canoes two sails, the first near the bow, the second a little abaft amidships. Poole speaks of three masts, but I never saw or heard of three among the Tlingit.

[Emmons refers here to the report by Francis Poole (1872:269) about a canoe trip he took in a large Haida canoe, in April 1864: "[The dugout] carried three jury-masts and a considerable show of canvas, not to mention a main staysail. A proud and truly inspiring sight was it to view all this canvas spread on the breeze, and to see thirty-seven human beings all paddling together, with regularity, precision, and force."] A third sail would be of little practical use, since the canoe, without keel or centerboard, could sail only with the wind well abaft the beam. [According to B. Durham (1960:74), however, "Early-19th-century canoes had as many as four masts, with bark-mat sails."]

[Although Emmons believed that the sail was an aboriginal feature on the Northwest Coast, this is debatable. B. Durham wrote (1960:74):

> The possibly-(but probably not-) aboriginal sail of early canoes was a tall and narrow squaresail, laced to upper and lower yards and simply rigged with halyard and braces. Coarsely woven cedar-bark mats usually served as sailcloths, and sometimes animal skins or thin cedar shakes, lashed together, were used. The sail was small in relation to the size of the canoe, and neither the sail-plan nor the hull was suited to sailing with any but a favoring wind. By the last quarter of the 19th century the white man's spritsail had supplanted the tall squaresail.

[And Drucker wrote, in connection with his survey of culture elements on the Northwest Coast (1950:255, Trait 408):

**Editor's note:* I have added the quotations from Captain Ingraham, Bill Durham, and Drucker on native sails.

Sailing the canoe. Top. *Chilkat canoe bound up river with a fair wind, the sails carried wing-and-wing, 1900. (Photograph by G. T. Emmons. AMNH and BCPA.)* Bottom. *Pencil sketch by G. T. Emmons to show how the mast is stepped and the sail rigged. (AMNH.) "A – mast, steps through holes in crosspiece and thwart C and D, and into mortise in block E in bottom of canoe. G – sail, to the leech are seized a number of travelers, B, B, B, B, through which the mast goes. H – halliards made fast to nook of sail, I, with clove hitch, reeve through F hole at masthead and come down on windward side and tie around outer part of thwart with slip hitch and so act as a stay to support mast. K – sprit, the upper end goes through the loop of the upper sheet – L at the peak of the sail and is carried aft and hitched around thwart aft. The lower end of the sprit fits in a loop of a grommet that goes around the mast. The lower sheet makes fast to clew of sail at M and is carried aft and made fast with the other sheet L. The sail is seized or tied to the mast at F."*

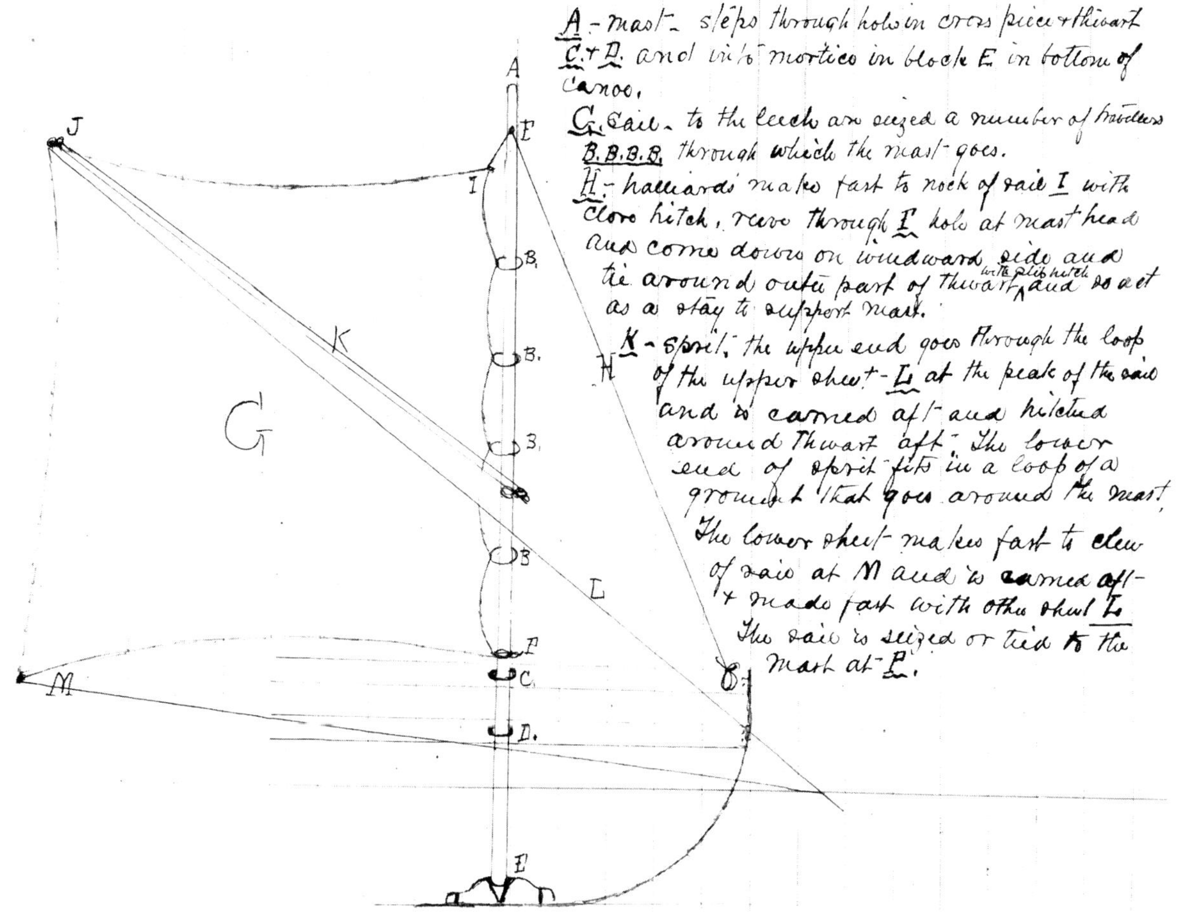

Despite the universal affirmation [by the natives] of the use of sails, there is some doubt in the writer's mind as to such wide use aboriginally. Nootkans also maintain they always had sails, yet we have Cook's definite statement that "sails are no part of their navigation," and Meares' account of ordering his sailmaker to rig a sail on the canoe of a Clayoquot chief and to teach the proud owner its use. The statements of modern informants cannot be taken literally in every instance. Furthermore, there is no mention of sails anywhere in the journals of the early navigators.

[From Meares's introduction of the sail at the end of the 1780s, it seems to have been adopted immediately by the Nootka; for in 1792, when only one day from Friendly Cove, Ingraham (1971:211) encountered many canoes, all with sails, "which was a new thing to me as I never saw them make any use of any in this part before." Presumably the use of the sail spread from the Nootka to other tribes, but evidently did not reach the Tlingit of Sitka until after 1827. (See Lütké, quoted below.)]

The mast and sprit [of the Tlingit canoe] were of small cedar or spruce trees, of almost uniform size throughout their length. The mast was stepped through two thwarts [yax̣ak'á·wu], or crossbars, the beveled foot fitting into a chock in the bottom of the canoe. When loading the canoe, a false piece was stepped in the place of the mast to keep this space clear of the cargo.

The sail was of the sprit rig, and was attached to the mast by means of travelers seized to the leech. To set the sail, these hoops of spruce or willow withes were placed over the stepping hole in the thwart, the halyards were rove through a hole in the head of the mast and tied to the nock of the sail, the sheets made fast to the clews, and the sail hoisted. The halyards were tied with a slipknot around the windward outboard end of the mast-thwart, and so acted as a backstay to support the mast. The head of the sprit spar was fitted through a loop in the sheet at the peak, and the lower end was fitted into the loop of a grommet going about the mast about one-fourth of its height above the thwart. Both sheets led aft and were carried around the after crosspiece with a slipknot, in easy reach of the steersman. With the wind direct aft, the sails were carried wing-and-wing.

The Chilkats always sail upstream when possible. In river work [where the water was swift], tacking was resorted to against the current, and in shallow water poles were used.

The bailer was a short-handled wooden scoop [like a large spoon, both called by the same name, ší·n], but often a small, old, spruce root basket was used.

Bottom boards, to keep the cargo dry from any water that might leak or wash into the canoe, were half sections of small tree trunks, rounded on one side. These likewise served as skids to facilitate beaching and launching, and to protect the bottom of the canoe [from rubbing on gravel or rocks].

The anchor was generally an improvised affair, consisting of a suitably shaped boulder tied around with rope, to which the line of twisted two-strand spruce root was attached. There was, however, little resort to anchoring, owing to the great rise and fall of the tides [which would have made it difficult to secure the canoe properly, or conveniently]. The canoe was generally hauled up on shore, when the Indians were camping for the night.

HANDLING THE CANOE*

The canoe was loaded about amidships, to bring her down slightly by the stern when all the goods and people were in. Only light things were placed in the bow. The people with oars or paddles sat well aft. The headman sat in the stern, the seat of honor, and steered. In blowing weather under sail, two men in the stern might steer, with paddles on each side, or both on the lee side.

When seal hunting in the ice flows, false sides, consisting of single boards, were hung to a projection over the bow, or false prow. Further to disguise the canoe and its occupants, and give all the appearance of the surrounding bergs, a sail was thrown over the bow, and the hunters wore white overshirts.

When friends or guests were leaving, the hosts and their friends would come down to the shore and watch the departing canoe until it was out of sight, as they say they may never see them again.

[When honored guests arrived, it was proper for the hosts to wade out into the water and haul the canoes up onto the beach, and lift out the occupants so they would not get wet. Needless to say, the Tlingit did not attempt to visit villages where they had no relatives, clansmen, or trade partners, and before approaching or attempting to land, notified the residents and identified themselves by singing or hailing.

[Emmons seems to have been particularly impressed by the Yakutat canoe with forked prow, and left several descrip-

**Editor's note:* This section has been put together from pieces of text and notes left by Emmons, to which I have added the quotations from Marchand (in Fleurieu), Portlock, Lisiansky, and Lütké, and summaries of information in Vancouver and Krause.

Top. *Haida canoe on the beach near Sitka, Baranof Island. (Photograph by De la Sablier. AMNH.)* Bottom. *Tom and Paddy poling Tlingit canoe up the Chilkat River on a trip back of the Chilkat Mountains, 1902. (Photograph by G. T. Emmons. AMNH.)*

Top. *Vancouver Island (Nootka) canoe on the beach at Killisnoo. (Photograph by G. T. Emmons. BCPA.)* Bottom. *Yakutat canoe for hunting seal and sea otter. Bow to the right. (Photograph by G. T. Emmons. AMNH.)*

tions in his notes and manuscripts about how it was handled. He had witnessed one brilliantly paddled through the surf by a Yakutat Indian in 1886, when the USS *Pinta* was landing Schwatka's party at Icy Bay for an unsuccessful attempt to climb Mount Saint Elias (see de Laguna, 1972:343).]

The Yakutat canoe is entirely different in design from any other coast canoe. The bow is ram-shaped as if to break the sea ahead of the canoe and to cut the water with the deadwood before it strikes the canoe proper, for the seas are stormy in these regions, and the people have to go well out to hunt the sea otter. These canoes are models of marine architecture, as light as a seabird, but they require good handling, for the projecting bow seems to make them rather cranky. They carry from one to four people, but generally in hunting only one or two men. These sit just forward and abaft amidships, as close together as possible, and rest on their knees, having under them a small seat cut out of a solid piece of wood, about eighteen inches long, five to six inches wide, and about four to five inches high. If a single man is in the canoe, he sits amidships and paddles first on one side and then on the other. I do not recall having ever seen a sail used in these canoes, although the forward crosspiece is always fitted for a mast to step through. The Yakutats use these small canoes for hunting the sea otter in rough water far out to sea, and also for landing on the open shore, where large canoes would be unsuitable. In landing at Icy Bay the most skillful canoe man goes in first. He goes in on the roller and it is quick work. After effecting a landing, he can greatly assist the others by steadying and holding their canoe until the occupants can jump out. The ram-shaped bow is to break the water ahead and not strain the body of the canoe when tossing in a seaway. Also it resists the turning power of the paddle, for the paddler sits in the middle of the canoe and gives two strokes on either side [and cannot steer from the stern]. The idea in a Yakutat canoe is to keep it level fore and aft.

[Fleurieu (1801, 1:346–49) gave a vivid description of the Tlingit canoes seen at Sitka by Captain Marchand in 1791:

Hoonah sealers dressed in white, with canoe covered by white canvas, as camouflage when hunting seals in the ice. (Photograph by Harriman Alaska Expedition, 1899. Courtesy of Robert F. Heizer, University of California, Berkeley.)

Their genius and industry are displayed principally in the construction of their canoes: those which are intended for the use of a single family, composed in general, of seven or eight individuals, are fifteen or sixteen feet in length by two and a half or three feet in width; others have much larger dimensions, and carry from fifteen to twenty persons: they are all cut out of a single trunk of a tree, and have a similar form; their two extremities do not differ from each other, which must give these canoes the advantage of being never obliged to put about: they are very sharp, and terminate in a cut-water, projecting fifteen or eighteen inches, which is not more than an inch in thickness; these two extremities, raised by planks neatly fitted, are higher than the rest of the canoe: seats fixed very near the bottom, are so disposed as to receive the rowers, who, when they are seated, serve, in some measure, as ballast: the provisions, the clothes, and all the baggage, are arranged in the middle part, where they are covered with skins of beasts and strips of bark, which serve also for covering the temporary settlements that are formed on the sea-shore, when the fishing-season is arrived, for drying fish, and furnishing the supply that is to make part of their subsistence during the winter months. Although the lading of the canoes is considerable, since, independently of the men, they carry women, children, provisions, all the household utensils, all the fishing implements, all the moveables belonging to the family (for it appears, that according to the example of the sage, the Americans take all their property with them), these boats are so thin and so light, that they preserve a surprising velocity. We are not less astonished at their stability: notwithstanding the lightness and the small breadth of their hull, they have no need of being supported by outriggers, and they are never coupled together. The Tchinkitanayans [Sitkans] have not the use of the sail; but we doubt not that, having learned, from the example of the Europeans, how useful a help this is for gaining time and saving trouble, they will shortly attempt to apply it to their canoes: they are already versed in the art of weaving: one step more is sufficient for them to add to their canoes a mast and a yard, and to adapt a sail to them.

Although the natives of TCHINKITÂNAY [Łingít ʔa·ní, "Tlingit country," in this case Sitka territory] have long been in possession of European hatchets, they do not yet make use of this instrument for felling the tree which they intend for the construction of a canoe; they have preserved their ancient method of undermining its foot by means of fire: it is by the assistance of this same agent that they contrive to hollow it out; it is also with this instrument,

Large canoe in a trench and covered with blankets to prevent cracking in the sun; a bear dog rests with her puppies. Sitka, 1889. (Photograph by G. T. Emmons. BCPA.)

which is docile in their hands, and the action of which they know how to direct and regulate, that they fashion the tree on the outside, so as to give it the form best calculated for being supported by the water, and for dividing the fluid by either of its extremities indifferently. We shall cease to be surprised that, since they are acquainted with the hatchet, which seems to afford both facility and dispatch, they have not preferred the use of it to the laborious and long proceeding which they continue to employ, if we do not forget that fire has the property of hardening the wood to which it has been applied, consequently of procuring it greater density, and of rendering it more impervious to the water. It cannot be doubted that they have discovered in fire this property of rendering wood more compact, and of prolonging its duration, when it is to be exposed to moisture, since, when they make a point to a stake which they intend to be driven into the ground, they take great care to harden, by means of fire, all the part that is to be buried.

[Captain Portlock, in August 1787, in the harbor that bears his name (1789:257–58), encountered a large Tlingit canoe, carrying twelve persons, three of whom were men, the rest women and children. It was apparently of the same type as that described by Marchand, for he wrote (1789:259):

> Their boat was the body of a large pine tree, neatly excavated, and tapered away towards the ends, until they came to a point, and the fore-part somewhat higher than the after-part; indeed, the whole was finished in a neat and very exact manner.

[Canoes of apparently the same kind, carrying from four to seven natives, were encountered by Vancouver in Behm Canal, near New Eddystone rock, in August 1793, as shown in his illustration (Vancouver 1801, vol. 4, pl. opposite p. 160). A little later, at Traitor's Cove, on the western arm of Behm Canal, Vancouver's party was attacked by natives in small, middle-sized, and large canoes, the numbers of occupants not given. One large canoe was steered by a redoubtable old woman with an enormous labret, who seems to have directed not only the crew but the young chief in the bow (pp. 169–77). Later in the same month, the same group of Indians attempted to make peace, and appeared in four canoes, (each?) containing ten natives (p. 217), and still later, at Port Stewart, Vancouver received friendly visits from the Stikine Tlingit, some twenty-five natives in three canoes one day (p. 223), and a trading party of about sixty persons, in at least five large canoes, led by Chief Ononnistoy, and five other chiefs. One large canoe, at least, was handled by an exclusively male crew, who all paddled with great regularity, and sang (Vancouver 1801, 4:223–30). Unfortunately, no description is given of the canoes. In July 1794, Lieutenant Whidbey's exploring party in Lynn Canal encountered the Chilkat Indians. One large canoe held about twenty Indians, and a chief of most impressive appearance (Vancouver 1801, 5:429); and this party was joined the next day by three more large canoes, and several smaller ones, totaling at least two hundred men, intent on robbing the Europeans. With this party of fighting men, there were three chiefs, out of the eight reported among the Chilkat, but "five principal ladies, each of whom, agreeably to the fashion of the nations of this part of America, steered and conducted one of the five large canoes, the station allotted to them on all warlike occasions, as has been described on a former occasion" (Vancouver 1801, 5:434–35).

[Captain Lütké, who was at Sitka in 1827, was much impressed by the Tlingit canoes and their decorations. He wrote (1835, 1:212, free translation):

> Some of the arts are pushed by the Kaloches to a remarkable point. The principal is the construction of dugouts [pirogues], or, as they are called here, *battes* (a Siberian expression), of which the largest carry from forty to sixty men. The hull is made of a single hollow tree trunk, to which are fastened additional pieces of wood to heighten the sides. They are moved by paddles on both sides, and their progress is so light that no other bark could contest with them. The large ones are each given a name, as for example, the Sun, the Moon, the Stars, the Earth, the Island, the Shaman, the Whale, the Otter, the Eagle, the Raven, etc., and figures analogous to the names are carved on the bow and stern. This last work is executed by special artists, among whom some are very skilled. Sometimes one gives a slave as payment for a little canoe statue.

[Lisiansky, who was at Sitka in 1805, has reported (1814:240):

> The canoes of these people are made of a light wood, called *chaha* [ɬa·x̣, "red cedar"], which grows to the southward. A canoe is formed out of a single trunk, and is, in some instances, large enough to carry sixty men. I saw several that were forty-five feet long; but the common ones do not exceed thirty feet. When paddled, they go fast in smooth water. The largest are used for war, or for transporting whole families from place to place. The smallest serve for fishing, or other purposes that require but few hands. They are ingeniously constructed.

[Krause ([1885] 1956:118–20) has given an excellent description of the Tlingit canoes he knew in 1880–81, but one which adds little to what has been reported by Emmons and the previous observers. He noted, however, that canoe making was done mostly in the winter, and that the tree to be felled had a hole chopped with an ax on the windward side, in which the fire was built, until it fell after several days. If a canoe was damaged, a new piece of wall might be mortised into the side. The Tlingit were averse to travel in stormy weather, but skilled when caught in a storm. They would strike down on an incoming wave in order to push the canoe over its crest. Although the sail was formerly unknown, it was common in 1880.]

SNOWSHOES

The snowshoe, *Tchar-tchee* [ǯá·ǯi], was not original with the Tlingit, but was unquestionably borrowed from the Athabaskans of the interior. [It is likely that most were made in the interior and traded to the coast.]

Snowshoes were worn by the Chilkat in winter in their country where the fall of snow is much deeper than nearer the coast or on the islands, and particularly on their trading trips over the mountain passes to the interior.

Although the snowshoe was used by all the tribes of the mainland, it was rarely or never employed by those of the islands, whose winter climate and activities did not require such a means of travel. The typical snowshoe used by the Chilkat [described below] had a rounded toe; that of the Stikine had a pointed, turned-up end. [The latter may be the snowshoe for breaking trail, q̇aɬuɬk̓í·n, and not a local type.]

The frame, *Tchar-tchee ko-to-yuk* [ǯá·ǯi gu-tu-ẏík, "snowshoe stump inside"?], was best made of the small maple that grows on the drier mountainside, but spruce and a light pliable willow were also used. The typical shoe was of good size, the toe rounded or oval, and turned up, and the heel wedge-shaped. The frame was in two pieces, neatly scarfed, filled and seized with fine sinew at the toe, and drawn together and secured with hide at the heel. The lashing at the toe was called *ar-yat-su-tee* [possibly ʔa ya-ṡ̓í·di, "its face lashing"]; that at the heel *ka-sha-u-gut-tee* [?]. The frame was perforated vertically on the inside around the toe and heel spaces, for the lacing to which the netting was attached. The lacing or reeving was *tchar-tchee yu-har-du-ku* [ǯá·ǯi yuwa·-du·gú, "shoeshoe belly-skin"]. The netting, *i-yar-ar-kee* [ʔa ẏaʔá·gi], was preferably made of caribou babiche, though sometimes it was of sheep or

Chilkat man ready to pack into the interior, Klukwan, 1890. Note the staff, snowshoes of Athabaskan make, high-top moccasin-boots, and pack supported by breast strap and tumpline, with blanket over the shoulders and a hat for padding. (Photograph by G. T. Emmons. AMNH.)

Chilkat snowshoes, Klukwan, probably of Athabaskan make, 1949. (Photograph by Frederica de Laguna.)

moose hide or twisted sinew, and was diagonal in weave. The netting in the middle space, *i-yar-keek-tu* [?], under the foot, was of coarse rawhide of moose, bear, or hair seal, quadrangular in mesh, the fore and aft filaments passing around the crossbars and the transverse ones going through holes in the frame and countersunk on the outside. Some shoes show a hexagonal weave under the foot. The frame had three crossbars. The life of a pair of snowshoes, or rather of the filling, is one season, although the frames can be used again and again. The value of a pair of snowshoes in the fall and winter is $5 to $6.

The Yakutat used a small, roughly made shoe with a filling of wide strips of untanned hair seal skin. [Some of these were the peculiar Eyak type with filling only under the foot (Birket-Smith and de Laguna 1938, pl. 8; de Laguna 1972:345).] The Stikine used both the rounded and the pointed toe snowshoes of the Tahltan with whom they have traded and intermarried for generations.

A brake attachment to prevent slipping on hard, crusted snow or ice, was used, particularly in hilly country. This consisted of the tip of a mountain goat horn lashed to one or both sides of the frame abreast of the foot space, inclining inward and backward, and projecting an inch or so below the frame. While sometimes found on the coast, this device was wholly of interior origin.

The snowshoe frame was made by the man, and the netting was furnished and worked by the woman with a bone or wooden netting needle. The tools used to make the snowshoe were the adz, *hootar* [x̣úṫa˙]; hand drill, *tuhlku* [túłx̣̓u]; snowshoe awl *tsu-ar* [possibly ṡúwa˙]; netting needle, *tchar-tchee ug-gah* [ǯá˙ǯi ʔá˙ga˙]; and knife, *kleta* [łíta˙].

BAGS, PACKS, BOXES, AND SLEDS*

Bags were little used, except by the Chilkat for packing on their trading trips into the interior.

The pack bag was a large, square sack of moose, caribou, mountain sheep, or hair seal skin, partly tanned, with the hair left on the outside to render it waterproof, and a long flap covering the mouth. It was fitted with loops on each side for the attachment of the head and breast straps. These were made of the hard tanned legskin of moose or caribou, with the hair left on. The head strap [tumpline] was somewhat diamond shaped, increasing in width from the ends toward the middle; it was eighteen inches long and three inches wide in the middle, with single or double hide lines, or tails, sewn to each end. These were made fast to the loops at the sides of the pack. The breast strap was a straight strip about fifteen inches long and two inches wide. A V was cut out at each end, beyond which was sewn a bone toggle. A long hide line was rove through the loops of the bag and around the toggle, with several turns, and was tied in front. When resting, the man could slip off the head strap, and release the rope around the toggle. When carrying a heavy weight, the coat or an extra shirt was thrown over the back and shoulders to provide a padding where the straps came;

**Editor's note:* This section has been put together from rather disorganized pieces of text, and I had to rewrite the notes on the sled.

Sled and pack dog, Klukwan. (BCPA.) Top. *Hand-drawn sled, used in travel into the interior, 1885. (Pencil sketch by G. T. Emmons.)* Bottom. *Dog with pack, 1889 or 1890. (Photograph by G. T. Emmons.)*

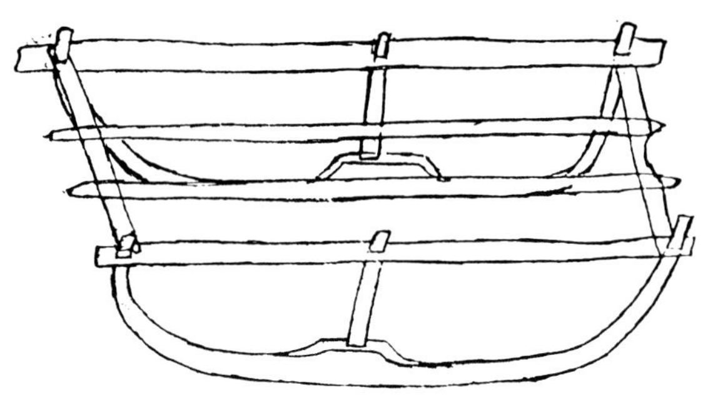

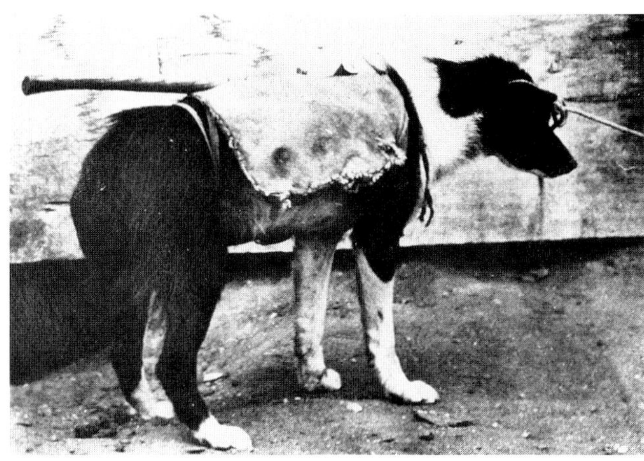

sometimes a small feather pillow was fastened to the pack bag at the hollow of the back. The head strap was used with a heavy pack, and went over the head, just above the forehead, to ease the weight on the back.

Children were taught to pack by carrying a light pack about every day for an hour or so. On the trading trips, the Chilkat carried not only trade goods, but dried salmon and tea, the only food carried for the journey. These trips consumed between twenty-five to thirty-five days, but were calculated at one "moon." The load might weigh from one hundred to two hundred pounds.

[Slaves, of course, did a good deal of heavy packing. Dogs carried lighter loads.]

The dog's pack saddle was made of a single broad strip of tanned caribou skin, later of stout canvas, the ends brought up to form pockets on each side, which were laced across the mouth. It was lashed around under the dog just forward of the hind legs and over the neck to keep it from shifting. A good sized dog would carry a twenty-five pound bag of shot in each pocket. The dog followed his master and seldom strayed.

When the island Tlingit were packing firewood or game for short distances, they used only a cord of twisted hide or cedar bark, passed over the shoulders, and around the pack [or load]. The ends were drawn under the arms and made fast to the parts going over the shoulders.

Wood and game were packed by the man, but berries, roots, shellfish, etc., were packed by the woman in spruce root baskets. A man never packed a basket on his back. [Some of the heavier baskets or boxes might, however, be carried by a pair of men who lifted them by a pole or pair of poles slipped through loops on the basket or under the lashing of the box.]

The Tlingit used wooden chests and boxes, and baskets of spruce root and cedar bark for storing clothing. Those of bark were more like bags than baskets, for they were large and pliable, with loop handles and ropelike borders, and openwork below, through which lacings were rove when they were packed. They were used more by the Southern Tlingit as receptacles for clothing and household articles, both in the house and in canoe travel.

A very primitive type of large storage bag was made of halibut skins sewn with sinew. It was a stiff, crude affair, but absolutely waterproof. I saw several such bags at Sitka and Yakutat that were used principally to pack clothing for canoe travel. [See de Laguna 1972:426.]

Although dogs were used to carry packs and also for assistance in hunting, they were not hitched to sleds. The sled [xáƛ̓a· or ku·x̣íƛ̓a· ỵe·t, from -k-x̣iƛ̓, "to become slippery"] was hand drawn.

[Emmons sketched a built-up sled, with two runners that curved up evenly at both ends, and with an upright at the middle of each side. The four ends of the runners and the two ends of the uprights were narrowed to fit through holes made in the two side slats and in the two crosspieces at the top of the frame. In addition, there were two more longitudinal slats to support the load. The sled is of the so-called Kutchin type. Emmons noted that "the sledge seen at Kloqwan in 1885 was hauled by man going into interior in winter." The last few words are almost illegible.

[Schwatka (1893:53–89) gives an excellent account of his Tlingit packers and their methods of handling canoes and burdens, when they were taking him over the Chilkoot Pass, from Dyea, in 1883.]

CHAPTER 5

Fishing and Hunting

INTRODUCTION*

The Tlingit was primarily a fisherman, sea hunter, and canoeman. Living at the edge of the tide, he looked to the water for his food. Hunting and trapping [of land animals] were side issues due both to the physical difficulties of land travel and to the limited fauna.

[Emmons did not prepare a systematic account of the annual cycle of activities (see Oberg 1973:65–78), perhaps because the traditional seasonal activities varied from tribe to tribe, depending on their location (south, north, open coast or islands, or mainland), so that no one scheme would be valid for all. But he did leave a number of scattered notes on the subject, here brought together.]

In spring, the Tlingit on the mainland coast hunt and trap bear, marten, and mink. Those on the island shores hunt fur seals in April and May. They also catch and dry halibut in April and May, and gather herring spawn. According to Captain Beardslee, they hunt sea otter for six weeks early in the spring. When the salmon come, they devote themselves wholly to this industry as long as the fish run. The king salmon run in April and May. [Other ?] salmon run from June through September.

In the fall there is a short sea otter hunting season. The salmon season is well over by the close of September. Then the people [especially the Southern Tlingit] go to their potato grounds and dig the potatoes for the winter. They also hunt mountain goat for their leaf fat (suet), or bear. Goats and bears are hunted in September, October, November, when they are fattest. By the middle of October the people have assembled in some numbers at the winter villages and have commenced to settle down and get ready for winter. [For the Yakutat annual cycle, see de Laguna 1972:360–61. This is probably typical of the Gulf Coast Tlingit.]

Editor's note: This chapter is much as Emmons originally planned it, although (at one time) he placed it late in the book, as Chapter VIII. In it he included information from what I call his "Game Diary," an excellent record of Alaskan fauna together with the native designations, which Emmons began in April 1894 and continued until September 1896.

**Editor's note:* For this section I have tried to put together scattered notes of Emmons to indicate the annual cycle of Tlingit life.

RELIGIOUS ASPECTS OF THE FOOD QUEST†

The Tlingit never took life unnecessarily, having a positive belief in the existence of a spirit [spirits?] in all nature. Even inanimate objects possessed for him something more than the mere material form. The shadow cast by the tree in the sunshine [was its spirit], and the winter wind, *hoon* [xú·n], was the breath of the ice spirit. Animal species formed families [clans] like those of men, and in the early days of the world, all living beings were much closer to one another. The old legends are full of the intimate relations that existed between animals and men; through capture [of men by animals, and sometimes of animals by men], transformation [from animal to human form and the reverse], and union [between them]. In these stories, the progeny of such mixed unions were generally of the mother's species.

Animals were always treated with great respect. The hunter or fisherman appealed to them before capture; and after their death, followed certain observances that were supposed to propitiate their spirits. The folktales tell of punishment of those who even spoke disrespectfully or slightingly of the animals. One of the oldest legends, supposed to go back to the childhood of the world when darkness reigned, recounts how the "night people," who seem to have been the only inhabitants of the earth, refused to give food to the Raven Creator, so he punished them by opening the box he had stolen, which contained the Sun. This flooded the earth with light, which so frightened the people that they fled in all directions. Those seeking the woods became land animals; others plunging into the sea were transformed into fish, seals, etc.; some jumping upward flew away as birds; while those remaining retained their human form. So it was reasoned that all humans and animals have the same attributes, and differ only in form. Even this might change, or at least appear different under certain conditions, as when the Bear, Sea Lion, or other animals, appeared as men when they approached and car-

†*Editor's note:* This section has been compiled from notes and texts by Emmons on ritual observances, to which I have added information from Shukoff. It cannot, however, be taken as a definitive statement on this important and complicated subject.

ried off women whom they took to wife. [Stories of such encounters between men and animals are told to justify the claims to clan and lineage crests, or to account for the acquisition of certain powers by shamans.]

[A number of ritual observances were followed to ensure success in hunting, fishing, or any undertaking that might involve real or supernatural dangers or an uncertain outcome. Emmons left only a few scattered notes about these. We may summarize as follows: Before such an undertaking, the Tlingit rose before dawn, bathed in the sea, and often fasted, or at least did not eat until midday or later, and had no relations with his wife. These rules had to be observed for four days (according to one note). While he was hunting or fishing, his wife was usually obliged to remain quiet, to do no work, to refrain from any angry act, and possibly to fast also, since her behavior was supposed to influence that of the quarry her husband was pursuing. The same kind of rules pertained to the war party. Some of these regulations were explained by the half-breed Tlingit at Sitka, Shukoff 1882, manuscript among the Emmons papers, AMNH. Simple corrections have been made in the text (punctuation, articles, word order, etc.) to make for easier reading.

> When an Indian goes out hunting, his wife has to wash herself and put a clean shirt on and tie a band around her waist. He also has to wash himself before starting out and put on clean clothes. All those things are observed very strictly when hunting sea otter. During his absence, his wife can't change her clothes or untie the string around her waist until his return, notwithstanding those trips last three or four months and probably longer. [At that time, sea otter were hunted in the open Gulf of Alaska off Yakutat and Icy bays. The belt worn by the wife symbolized the life of her husband.] If he was not very successful on his trip, upon his return he will blame his wife, that she did not fulfill all the requirements of custom. . . .
>
> Before he goes out hunting or fishing, he fasts two days. He will not eat, especially on the day he goes out, for should he swallow a small piece of fish he might swallow his luck. During his absence neither his wife nor children can comb their hair. If his wife should comb her hair while he is away, and take some hair out, he will surely be very unlucky, and his fish hook rope will break. They can't sweep the room out during his absence. In case he takes his hook out and finds it tangled in seaweed, he will at once blame his wife that she combed her hair and brought him bad luck. [Shukoff here was thinking especially of halibut fishing.]
>
> The present race don't follow their ancestors with the same force. Now a great many know Lord's Pray[er], and before going hunting they ask God to help them and bring them luck, and whenever they sit down to gamble they would pray God to give them good luck to win lots of money, and they pray in this way for everything they wish, whether good or bad. And when a man sees anything in a store he wants and can't buy, he goes home and prays for it, that God will help him to steal it if he can't buy it.

[Observances connected with the hunting of specific creatures will be mentioned in the appropriate context. Emmons also has a note about "Hunting Charms"]:

The Tlingit carried charms when hunting which were believed to make him invisible to the prey and to prevent the bear from attacking him. Those I examined consisted of small bundles of odds and ends, principally plant roots and stems. One package contained one small package of roots and another of leaves and small pieces of shells. Much like the articles in the *Don nok* "personal medicine box" [da·ná·k^{w}, "body medicine," or charm, but not the box that contains it]. Such articles were individual charms having special spirit power.

[Any abuse of a living being, especially needless killing or harming a helpless creature, or insulting an animal or bird, was likely to bring bad luck, as is illustrated by an incident recounted by Shukoff:

> In 1881, near Hot Springs [Baranof Island], some six Indian women and a boy were starting out after berries. Before they left the beach, one of the women found a frog, and she commenced to stone him, abusing him all the time. And after killing him, she threw him in the water. They then went across to the other shore and gathered baskets full of berries. And one woman began to mimic a loon as it calls and crooks its neck. They laughed at her [with her?], and they got in the canoe. The water was [then] very smooth and fair weather, when suddenly wind came and upset the canoe. All the women drowned, except one. And the boy got hold of one and tried to save her, but could not. But he reached the shore, came and told the husbands, and they found only one [woman]. The Indians believe they were lost because they killed the frog and mimicked the loon.]

SALMON FISHING*

Salmon constituted the most valuable natural product of the Northwest Coast and formed the staple food of the Tlingit. *Khart* [x̣á·t] was the name applied to fish, and especially to the salmon, but each one of the five species was recognized and separately named:

King, tyee, chinook, or spring salmon (*Oncorhynchus tshawytscha*), called *ta* [ṫá].

**Editor's note:* I have corrected Emmons's confusions of trout and salmon, relying on Morrow 1980; and have added observations by La Pérouse and also the last paragraph.

Indian fish trap, Tamgas River, Annette Island, 1910. (Photograph by J. N. Cobb. AMNH.)

Coho or silver salmon (*O. kisutch*), called *thluke* [ł̓u·kʷ].

Sockeye or red salmon (*O. nerka*), called *khart, gart,* or *ghart* [g̣a·t].

Humpbacked or pink salmon (*O. gorbuscha*), called *tcharse* [čá·s̓; at Yakutat, kʷá·sk̓, from Eyak].

Dog or chum salmon (*O. keta*), called *teetle* [tí·ł̓].

The steelhead or Gardner trout, *ah shut* [ʔa·šát], is [the same] as the rainbow trout (*Salmo gairdneri*), [but in a saltwater phase].

The salmon is a saltwater fish that seeks fresh water only for reproduction. The different varieties follow each other in quick succession, the runs often overlapping, beginning in May and continuing through September. The salmon return to the mother stream [where they were hatched] with great regularity about the same time each year, although the runs vary in size from year to year. When the fish reach the mouth of the stream they school around, really to accustom themselves to the change of water, but appearing to hesitate before committing themselves to the final act of elimination, for on entering fresh water they cease feeding, and after spawning, die. Some salmon turn red in fresh water, when they are called *khark* [x̣á·kʷ]. The old salmon that has spawned and is covered with scabs and fungus is called *kheene* [xe·n; and the dead floating fish is nú·š].

The first three varieties (king, coho, and sockeye), the most valuable commercially, run only in rivers and streams that head in lakes, in the tributaries of which they spawn. The humpbacked and dog salmon are not so particular, and spawn anywhere, in any stream that carries sufficient water, even depositing their eggs within reach of the tide, where they are lost. The first-run dog salmon is preferred to all others for curing, since it has the least fat and keeps the best.

The Tlingit believed that the salmon constituted a numerous and powerful tribe, organized into five separate families or clans [the five species], that lived at *Se eete* [?], somewhere in the ocean [probably the horizon, siʔí·t]. Their country, far away to the westward, was surrounded by an ever opening and closing ring, through which they had to jump quickly to preserve their clean silver sides. Those that were caught, were cut or marked, which accounts for the stripes on their sides. [The dog salmon is supposed to owe its name, *teetle* (tí·ł̓), to the stripe on its side.] Salmon were believed to travel in invisible canoes. The chiefs of the different families [clans] stood in the stern to direct their movements landward. When spring came, a great meeting was called, and all wanted to start at once for their streams, but the dog salmon, through jealousy, broke up the canoes of the cohoes, which accounts for the later appearance of the latter. It is often called the "Fall Silver Salmon." The first run of the dog salmon is called "Seal Head Salmon," *tsar ut ka teetle* [ca·-ʔat-ka (?) tí·ł̓, "seal-something-on (?) dog salmon"], because the young seals are born when these salmon first run.

[The king salmon were the largest; Emmons noted that they run only in the largest rivers, although they run all year round at Killisnoo, where they live on herring. Those caught at the head of Silver Bay, on the west coast of Baranof Island, five miles east of Sitka, weighed 75, 90, and 105 pounds; though in Sitka Harbor they weighed only 30 to 65 pounds.]

The steelhead or Gardner trout, *ah shut* [ʔa·šát], "lake's wife," are salmon trout that live in the lake all winter under the ice, and come down to salt water in early spring. Their flesh then is white and soft, not good to eat. They run up into the lake again about June and spawn in July. [After being in fresh water for a time, their markings change, and they are known as rainbow trout.]

Tlingit fish dams. Top. *At outlet of lake, Redfish Bay, Prince of Wales Island. (Photograph by "H.C.F., A1908." BCPA.)* Bottom. *Second barricade in a stream, Helm Bay, Cleveland Peninsula, to prevent salmon from ascending to the lake. (Photograph by "H.C.F., A1953." AMNH.)*

The most valuable property of the Tlingit was the fishing ground or salmon stream, which was a family [lineage] possession, handed down through generations, and never encroached upon by others. In the case of a poor family that lacked a stream sufficient for their needs, or if they had suffered a failure of the run, another lineage might extend an invitation to fish in their stream, but only after the owner had satisfied his needs.

Late in the spring, after the bear and seal hunting, and the herring and eulachon seasons were over, the people left their permanent villages in single families or in bands of two or more families, and repaired to their fishing camps, where they remained until the pack was put up in October. [The season for this removal to the fish camps varied from district to district. In some regions, the people went to spring camps for hunting, and did not move to the salmon fishing camps until summer. Some villages were located on salmon streams so no removal was necessary.] At the fish camps, the summer house was at the mouth of the stream; in some cases a group of such houses formed a small village. The house, whether temporary or permanent, was of the same form as that in the winter village, though loosely constructed, and it generally served the double purpose of a shelter and a smokehouse.

[Emmons evidently made an effort to discover if any taboos had to be observed during the salmon catching season, but his notes contain no answer to this question. He did record, however, in answer to a query about how the first salmon was treated, that the head was cut off first, then the tail, using a mussel shell knife—the primitive fish knife. No stone or iron knife was permitted. Part of the salmon (unspecified) was thrown in the fire, and water was drunk after eating salmon. No reasons for these last rules were given. It is evident that the Tlingit lacked a true First Salmon Ceremony.]

Salmon were taken in traps, with spear or gaff, or with hook and line, depending upon the variety and the water in which they were caught. The lake streams through which the king, sockeye, and coho passed quickly to their spawning grounds were generally barricaded to hold the fish so they could be more readily taken, and also to delay their spawning, since the flesh remained firmer and in better condition [if the fish were caught before they were ready to spawn]. The obstruction [qíʼt, "dam"] consisted of a heavy tree trunk, from two to three feet in diameter, that was dropped across the stream not far from the mouth, if possible just above a pool. Such a pool was called *Ish ka* [ʔíš ká, "on deep water"]. The log was wedged on either bank, about five feet above the water, sometimes supported in midstream by uprights, and braced on the downstream side by smaller tree trunks to resist the pressure of water and drift [debris] at flood. Small saplings, four or more inches in diameter and ten to fifteen feet long, were laid upstream, side by side and far enough apart to permit the flow of water but sufficiently close together to prevent the passage of the fish. The lower ends of these saplings were embedded in the bottom of the stream, and the upper ends rested against the log which served both as a bridge and as a platform. The fish, running in and meeting the obstruction, would school and were easily speared.

In connection with this barricade, traps were also employed. These consisted of cylindrical or semi-conical baskets of split spruce rods, seized to hoops with spruce roots at the mouth, along the body, and at the closed end. Just within the mouth was a short funnel of similar construction, sufficiently large to permit the fish to enter but not to leave. These traps were placed at openings in the barricade, their mouths downstream, for the fish always head up against the current.

In the Chilkoot River, a short rapid steam, stakes were driven into the bed to mark the hereditary fishing place of

Tlingit fish traps, 1898? (BCPA). Top. *Trap and artificial channel in stream, first inlet south of Moira Sound, Prince of Wales Island. (Photograph by "H.F.C., no. A2427.")* Bottom. *Kuyu fish trap in sections, Kutlaku Creek, at head of Bay of Pillars, Kuiu Island. (Probably photographed by H.C.F., "no. A2604.")*

each family. To these, a canoe was attached, or over them a temporary platform was built. At another point, runways were constructed by piling boulders in parallel lines, in which were set net-shaped traps of spruce rods, so arranged that they could be raised or lowered to conform to the stage of the water. In other streams, runways were similarly constructed in which long narrow baskets were placed and weighted down or staked. Carvings, like miniature totem poles representing human figures, fish, etc., were sometimes secured to the barricades overlooking the traps, in the belief that these would encourage or force the fish to enter. [It will be remembered that Keithahn believed that petroglyphs on the shores were made to attract the salmon.]

[La Pérouse (1799, 1:389), describing a salmon stream just above Lituya Bay which was visited by his officers in 1786, wrote:

> . . . they discovered an Indian village on the banks of a small river, which was staked quite across for the salmon fishery. We had long suspected that this fish [which the Indians were trading to the French] came from that part of the coast, but we were not certain of it, till this adventure satisfied our curiosity. Mr Duché de Vancy made a drawing, which will explain the particulars of this fishery. [The drawing was lost.] In this it will be seen, that the salmon, coming up the river, are stopped by the stakes: unable to leap over them, they turn back towards the sea; in the angles of the dike are placed very narrow wicker baskets, closed at one end, into which they enter, and being unable to turn in them, they are thus caught. This fishery is so abundant, that the crews of both vessels had plenty of salmon during our stay, and each ship salted two casks.]

Short cylindrical basket traps were called ***khike*** [ḱí·tx or ť́í·tx]; long boxlike traps were ***khoukt*** [probably qú·k^{w}]. [Another name for fishtrap, type unspecified, is šá·ƚ.]

Another kind of trap, *tihku* [?], constructed near the mouth of a stream, consisted of a series of artificial basins

Indian Charley gaffing salmon in creek at Freshwater Bay, Chichagof Island, 1901. (Photograph by V. I. Soboleff, no. 520. Courtesy of the Alaska Historical Library, Juneau.)

enclosed by walls of boulders reaching to about the half-tide line. The fish, running in with the flood, entered the basins, but were confined when the tide fell, and so were easily caught. [This type of stone trap or weir was probably that called ʔú·t̓.]

The Chilkats say that, at the mouths of the streams where the fish congregated, they drove stakes in the ground, about three feet apart. The tops were shaped to a sharp point, and I believe notched or barbed. They stood three inches above high water, and the salmon, jumping as they do at the mouth of a stream, impaled themselves upon them. This arrangement is called *nah-har kahtan,* "jump on" [ná·x̣ ʔagata·n]. [Such stakes were also used in the Angoon area; de Laguna and McClellan, field notes, 1950.]

The fisherman, however, relied chiefly on the gaff and spear. Several types of spear were used in clear water where the fish could be seen. The gaff, however, while also used in clear water, was a necessity in glacial streams where the fish were invisible and could only be felt.

The spear or harpoon [ʔá·da·] universally used had a neatly rounded shaft of young fir or spruce, from ten to fifteen feet in length, with its greatest diameter, from one and one-fourth to one and one-half inches, at about one-third the distance from the fore end. It tapered toward both ends, but more gradually toward the fore end, thus placing the center of gravity at the point of greatest diameter and giving the spear a perfect balance. For strength and protection [against splitting], the fore end was served with twisted sinew, hide, or spruce root for a distance of one or two inches. In this end was hollowed out a socket to receive the butt of a barbed head, *kut* [kát]. This was commonly of bone, that of the bear being considered the best. The finest spear heads were of walrus ivory or copper. [Both of these materials were obviously obtained in intertribal trade.] Sometimes a copper blade was fitted into the split point of an ivory spear head. Later, iron superseded all other materials. [See Drucker 1955a, fig. 9d.]

Spear heads were of varying lengths, from three to eight inches, and averaged a quarter inch in thickness. They were oval in cross section, pointed at the tip, and flattened and rounded at the butt. In the thickest part of the butt was a small hole, through which was passed the line that attached the head to the shaft. The heads had from one to four barbs [x̣a·n/-x̣a·ní] on one edge, but some of the short specimens showed evidence of having been worked down from longer broken heads [and therefore might have fewer than three or four barbs (see de Laguna et al. 1964, pl. 13*m*)].

The head was attached to the shaft [sáxʷti, "handle"] by a short length of hide or plaited sinew. This was secured to the shaft with a clove hitch or half turn from eighteen inches to two feet from the fore end. Sometimes it was carried down the shaft and hitched once or twice more, to strengthen the shaft and to distribute the weight of the struggling fish. [The line was called kát ke·t.]

With the introduction of iron, while the old form of barbed head remained the favorite, other more elaborate forms with bilateral barbs were used, and bone heads were equipped with metal blades. The unilaterally barbed head was called *kut-klake da-hon,* "spear-point one-side" [kát ƛe·kdé x̣a·n, "spear-point to-one-side barbs"]; the bilaterally barbed head was *kut woush-ka da-hon,* "spear-point one on each side" [kát wu·š ka·dé x̣a·n, "point both on-side barbs"]. This same spear was used also in seal and sea otter hunting, with the addition of several fathoms of line and a sealskin buoy [kacï·s].

The spear was used in shallow water where the fish were visible and near enough to be reached. The spear was thrust rather than cast, although under certain conditions I have seen it thrown at a distance and wholly released from the hands. The head automatically detached itself upon entering the fish and hung by the short length of line, thus saving the shaft from the strain that would be brought on it if the head were permanently fixed in the end. [This is the "Salmon spear, kat," illustrated by Krause (1885) 1956, pl. II, 5.]

Another type of spear, now obsolete, was used by the Southern Tlingit, but was rarely found north of Frederick Sound. This was called *de nar* [dï·ná·; heard at Yakutat as dé·na·]. It consisted of a toggle [harpoon] head on a loose [fore]shaft that was set into the end of the spear shaft. The head was made in three parts: the blade, and two leaf-shaped, outward curving spurs or barbs that were seized

Fishing and hunting gear. (Pen and ink sketches by G. T. Emmons. AMNH.) (a) Northern Tlingit gaff hook, "koh-da *(come back)* kehk kah" [qúx̣ʷ-de k̓éx̣a·], *as held when about to use. (b) Eulachon net,* go qte [gúqʷč]. *(c) Chilkat three-pronged spear,* tha qwor [ƛa·gwá·]. *(d) Toggle-head harpoon, with loose foreshaft, used especially by the Southern Tlingit,* de nar [di·ná·]. *(e) Head for the above, with single spur. (f) Common type of harpoon or spear with detachable barbed head, used for salmon, seal, and sea otter.*

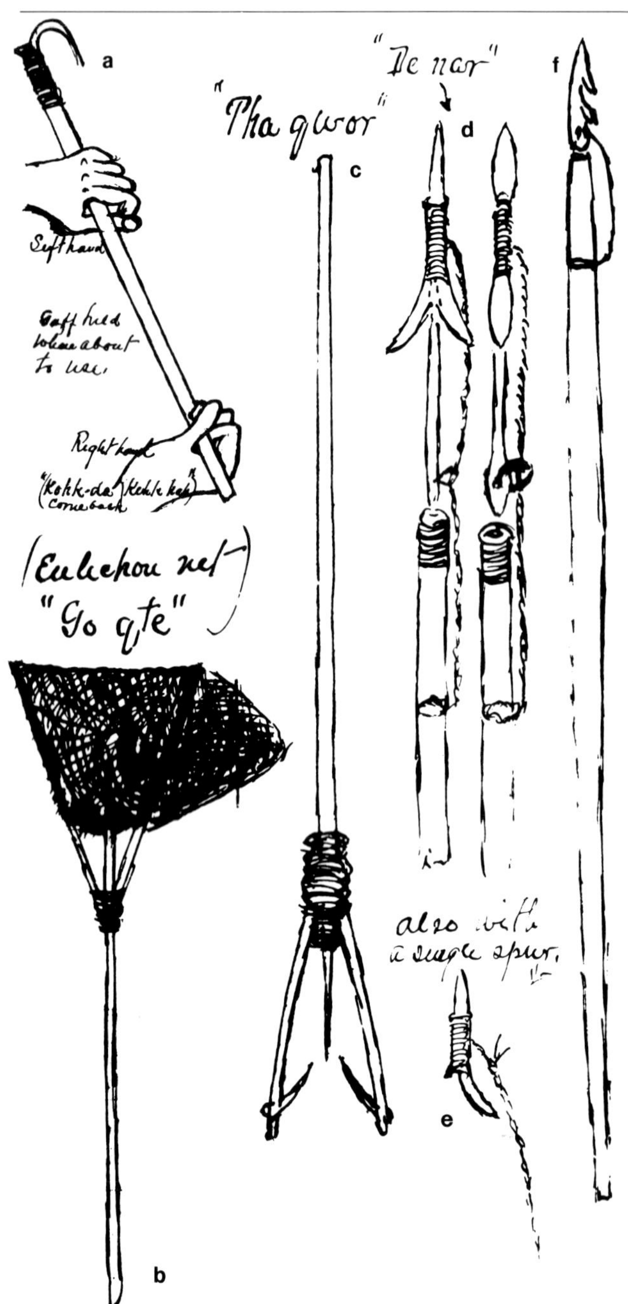

together with sinew or hide. [This lashing was put on] over the end of the short length of line that attached the head to the loose shaft, and this seizing was smoothed over with spruce gum [Drucker 1955a, fig. 9c]. In primitive times the blade and spurs were of mountain goat horn, but later were made of copper and iron. In some, the blade was of metal and the spurs of bone. Again there might be only one spur which was made in one piece with the blade. [Bone parts of such heads were excavated in the Angoon area (de Laguna 1960:111–12, pl. 8b and c), although barbed harpoon heads with butts were far more common (pp. 112–13).]

The loose shaft [foreshaft] was of alder or maple or other hardwood, about eight inches long and oval in cross section. The fore end fitted into the hollow [socket] formed by the flanged spurs of the head. The butt of the foreshaft was expanded and rounded at the base, to fit the socket in the fore end of the spear shaft. Through a hole in the foreshaft was a loop of hide, through which passed, or was attached, the line connecting the harpoon head with the shaft. The foreshaft was called *yat see* "guide" to the *de nar* [possibly ya-č̓i·x̣, "to point (with finger)"].

The Tlingit claim to have borrowed this type of harpoon for fish and fur seals from the more southern tribes. It is used by the Salish, Athabaskans, and Kwakiutl, but without the loose foreshaft [which is perhaps of Eskimo origin].

For lake fishing, especially through the ice, a three-pronged fish spear [leister] was used, called *tha quor* or *klark-war* [ƛa·gwá·]. The shaft was a spruce sapling, ten or more feet long. To the end was lashed a bone point, on either side of which was an outstanding arm [side prong] of wood or bone, about fifteen inches long, with a barb at the end pointing inward and backward. The fish were struck from directly above, so that when the central point entered its back, the side arms were forced out, and, springing back, their barbs caught the sides of the fish. [See Drucker 1950:238, no. 47; Krause (1885) 1956, pl. II, 4.] I have never seen this spear used by any group of Tlingit other than the Chilkat, but it was an old type among the interior people. [With the acquisition of metal, the central point and barbs were no longer made of bone, but of iron nails and spikes.]

Some three miles from Klukwan, across the Chilkat River flats, is a considerable lake with salmon and trout. In winter the Chilkat fish here through the ice, using a small net bag of dried salmon eggs which exuded an oil that attracted the trout to the surface where they could be speared. The fisherman sat over the hole in the ice, covered with a blanket that enabled him to see down into the water.

Tlingit salmon spears or harpoons. (Pencil sketches by G. T. Emmons. Scale in centimeters. AMNH.) (a) Salmon spear shaft, 10 feet 9 inches long, of spruce, with hide wrapping around the slot into which the iron barbed head fits. (b) Assembled. From Angoon. (c) Salmon harpoon from Wrangell, with loose "head" or foreshaft of alder wood, over which, at A, fits the socket or "hollow," B, between the two parts of the iron harpoon head.

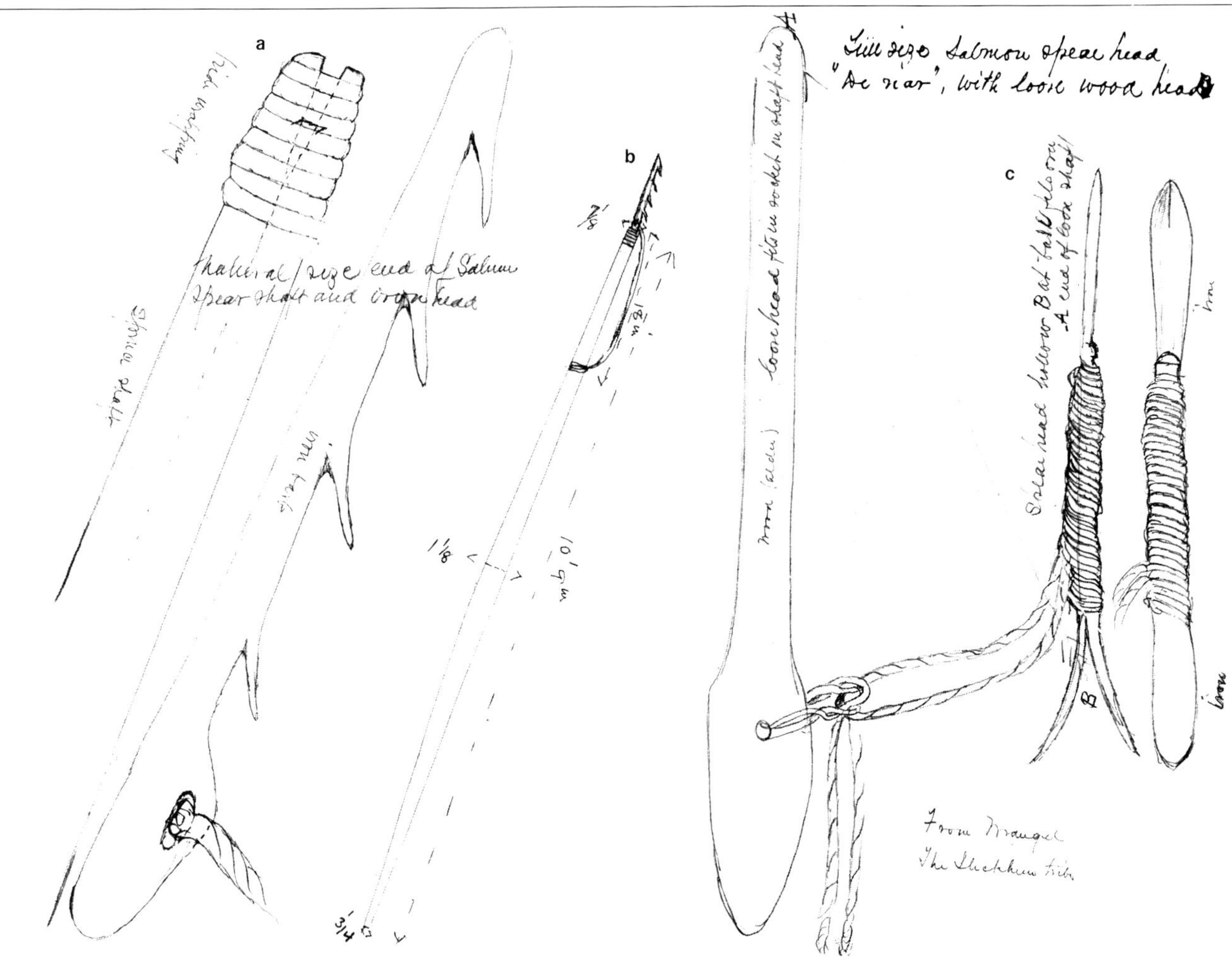

The Chilkat were very superstitious about this lake and never remained there overnight. They claimed that little babies were seen diving from the rocky shore, and headless bodies swimming about, and that at times when the surface of the water was perfectly smooth, a great wave would rise and salmon as large as whales would suddenly appear. At night strange lights danced over the water as a drum sounded from a precipitous rock on the shore. Yet they had no prejudice against fishing there in daylight, since the spirits appeared only at night.

[Was this "Chilkat Lake"? At the foot of the lake was a village called *Taki'n* (? daqí·n) or *Tliktaka't*, "No Sockeyes" (probably ł-yik-dax̣á·t, "not-in-has fish"); Olson 1967:29). At the head of Chilkat Lake, Emmons placed a village for winter fishing through the ice and salmon fishing in summer, called "Under the Rock," *Ta-yi-ee* (probably té ỵéyí·, "rock place-under").]

More important than the spear was the gaff, ***kehk-kah*** "hook" [k̓éx̣a· or k̓íx̣a·], for while equally efficient [as the harpoon] in clear water, it was absolutely necessary in glacial streams and in deep holes under the banks or log-jams. The shaft was often longer than that of the spear, being fully eighteen feet in length, and not so carefully selected, indeed being sometimes quite bent, and was little more than a sapling with the limbs removed. At the end was fitted an iron hook that superseded the older one of deer antler or wood, and that was called *chak-har-gu*, "eagle's claw" [čá·k x̣a·gú]. The iron hook itself was from three to eight inches long. Its shank was longer, and the width of the opening was about three inches. The hook was

Barbed spear or harpoon heads for taking seals. (Pencil sketches by G. T. Emmons. AMNH.) (a and b) Of iron, from Wrangell. (c) Of bone, provenience not given. (d) Of iron, from Sitka. (e) Of iron, from Wrangell.

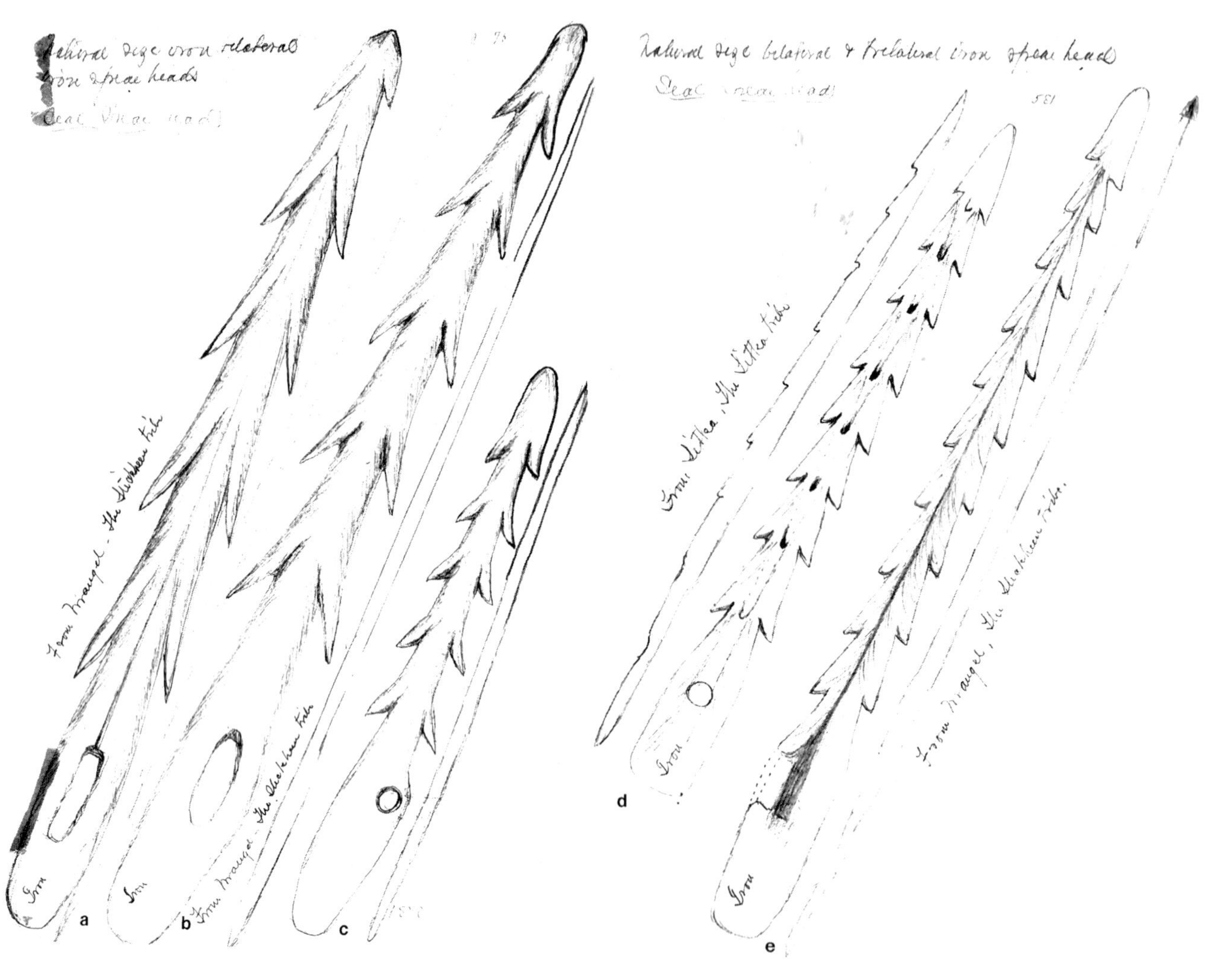

rounded [in cross section], the shank more often flattened, with a lip [formed by bending up the butt end] to prevent its slipping from the lashing that attached it to the shaft. [See Krause (1885) 1956, pl. II, 2.]

The Northern Tlingit lashed the hook permanently to the end of the pole with a hide or spruce root. A shoulder near the end of the pole prevented the lashing from slipping. The Southern Tlingit seldom lashed the hook fast to the shaft, but fitted it into a shallow groove in the end of the pole that was wrapped around with hide for a distance of six or eight inches. The shank of the hook was round and tapered slightly at the end, without a lip. Around the middle of the shank was secured a line of hide, some two feet in length, the other end of which was hitched around the pole, so that the hook detached itself upon entering the fish, and hung to the pole. In using the gaff, it was grasped by the right hand near the butt end, the thumb of the right hand on top. [The left hand was near the fore end], with the thumb underneath. The pole was thrown out with the right hand, directed by the left, and drawn back in a series of short quick jerks.

The extreme Southern Tlingit used this implement as a gaff, and also as a spear [harpoon] by reversing the hook and fitting the end of the shank in the upper part of the

Detachable barbed heads for seal or fish harpoons. (Pencil sketches by G. T. Emmons. AMNH.) (a) Of bone (about 7 inches long), from Wrangell. (b and c) Of bone, dug up near Angoon. (d) Of iron, from Killisnoo. (e) Of iron, from Angoon. (f) Of copper, from Sitka.

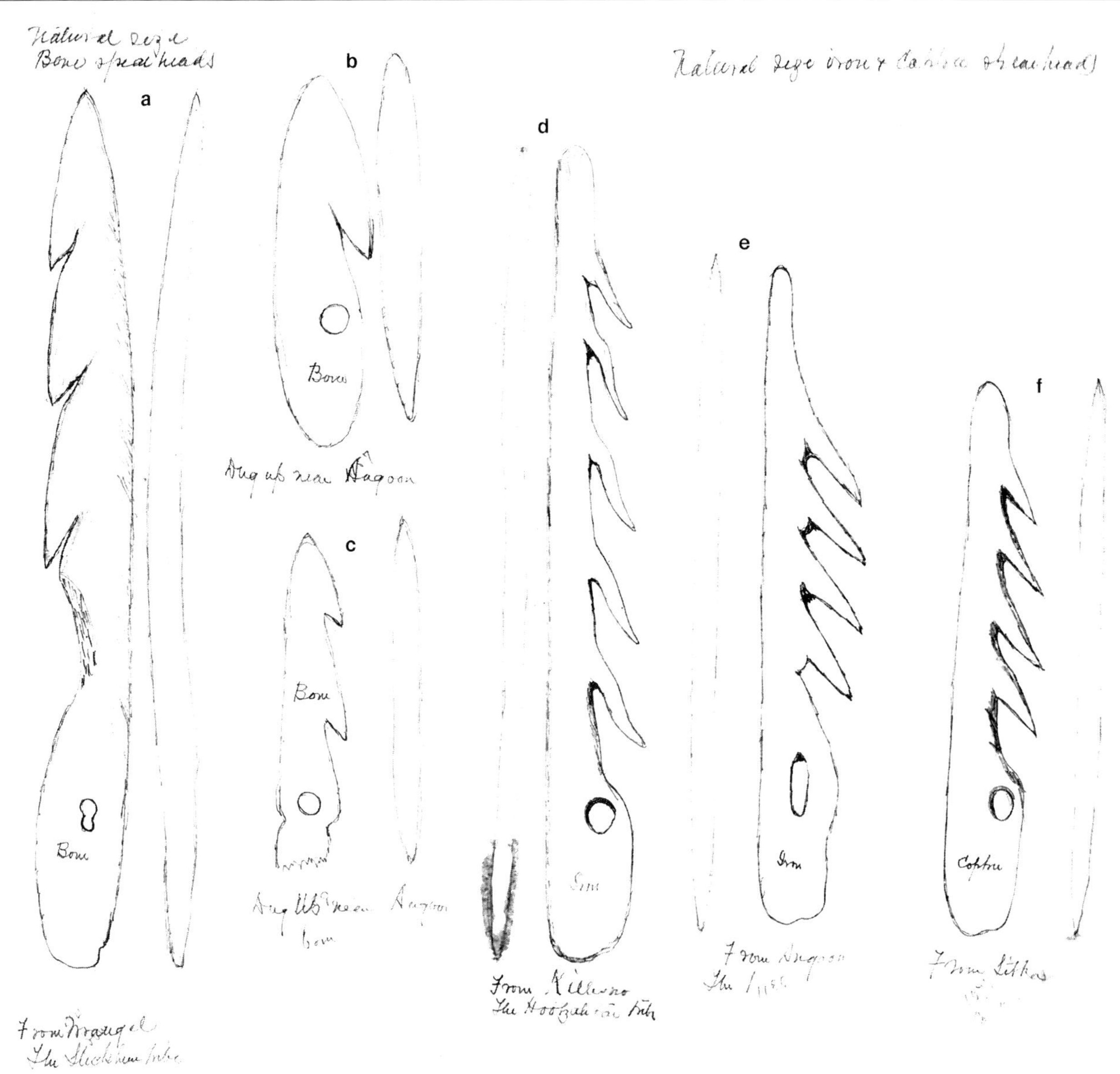

groove under the seizing. I saw a boy of the *Tanta Qwan* [Tongass] at Ketchikan with a gaff in which a section of mountain sheep horn was fitted over the fore end of the pole, and the shank of the reversed hook was slipped into the groove in the shaft. [This piece of horn apparently served as a cap in place of the usual lashing that held the shank of the hook in the groove of the shaft.] This type of implement was used both as a thrusting harpoon that was retained in the hand, and as a spear that was cast at a distance and wholly released, being recovered by a line several fathoms in length that was secured to the butt end of the pole. I have seen it cast as a spear from a high rocky shore when the salmon were in schools in a deep pool at the base. This type of gaff is called ***kohk-da kehk-kah***, "come-back hook" [probably qúx̣de k̓éx̣a·, "backwards gaff"], since the hook reverses itself when the fish is struck.

Trout spear. (Pencil sketch by G. T. Emmons. AMNH.) The spruce shaft is fifteen feet long; the assembled head, with three points of iron and two side prongs of oak, is 8½ inches long. This spear was used by the Chilkat for spearing trout under the lake ice in winter.

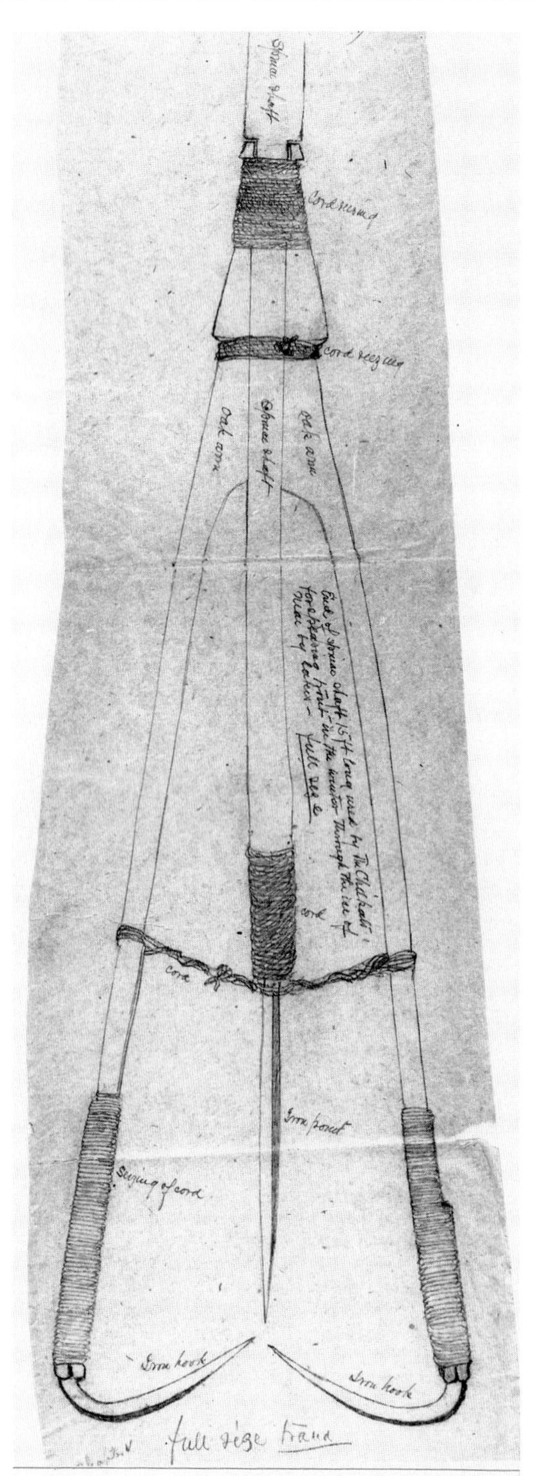

[Drucker 1950:238, Trait 49, observed that he did not believe the gaff to be aboriginal on the Northwest Coast, nor did most of his informants, who ranged from the Nootka to the Northern Tlingit.]

A very old type of gaff, long ago obsolete, was like an enlarged trout hook. At the end of the pole a bone point was lashed at an angle with split spruce root. [Except that the bone point or barb was sharp, this hook resembled that used for taking devilfish, and was called *tar-nar* (tá·na·). Some of the latter were fitted with a curved iron hook at the end, apparently rather blunt, according to the sketch by Emmons.]

Fishing in the rivers and lake streams for the king, sockeye, and coho salmon was done chiefly at night when they ran upstream; and the Yakutat [and Sitka] used torches. For the humpbacked and dog salmon, fishing at night was not necessary, since they spawned in the shallow streams and could be taken at any time.

Fishing for salmon in fresh water with hook and line was not practiced since the fish did not feed when running in to spawn. In salt water the king and coho salmon readily take artificial or natural bait and are today caught by trolling. But in primitive times, the only Tlingit who fished with hook and line were the *Hootz ah tah* [Hutsnuwu] on Admiralty Island, who used an ingenious method of still fishing with herring bait on a set line. This was made possible because they lived at the entrance of a series of lagoons [at Angoon, on the entrance to Kootznahoo Inlet], where the herring ran in great schools and were followed by the salmon. Their gear comprised a wooden float [kací·s], generally in bird form, and a main line of two-stranded, right-handed [S-twist] spruce root, about twenty feet long, that was attached to a hole in the rear end of the float. A sinker, *goo war ta* [gu·waté], when used, consisted of a small oblong stone permanently lashed to the line near the end that terminated in a knot. When prepared for use, the line was coiled around the float from forward aft, and was fastened with a slipknot, leaving out about four feet, at the end of which was a knot. Around the latter was hitched a small line of twisted sinew or hide, five feet long. To this was attached a short wooden hook, *tahk* [ṫe·x̣ or ṫe·x̣á·], with a barb of bone or hardwood, the parts secured with a lashing of split spruce root. The bait used was a fresh herring, strung on the line by means of a wooden needle with an eye at the larger end, made of quill or split root. The line was carried through the eye, like a thread through a needle. The needle was poked into the gill and forced through the flesh of the herring along the backbone, coming out at the small of the tail. The bight of the line was singled and drawn

Southern Tlingit gaff hooks for fish. (Pencil sketches by G. T. Emmons. AMNH.) (a) "Kehk kah" [k̓éx̣a·], set and released. (b) Southern type of gaff with loose head. (c) Southern type with guard of sheep horn. (d) Spruce shaft with groove for the end of the gaff hook, with wrapping of hide or laid up sinew rope. (e) Salmon gaff or spear of the Southern Tlingit, Stikine River. Iron hook (about 9 inches long) with hide line. (f) Small sketches of the hook used as a spear and as a gaff.

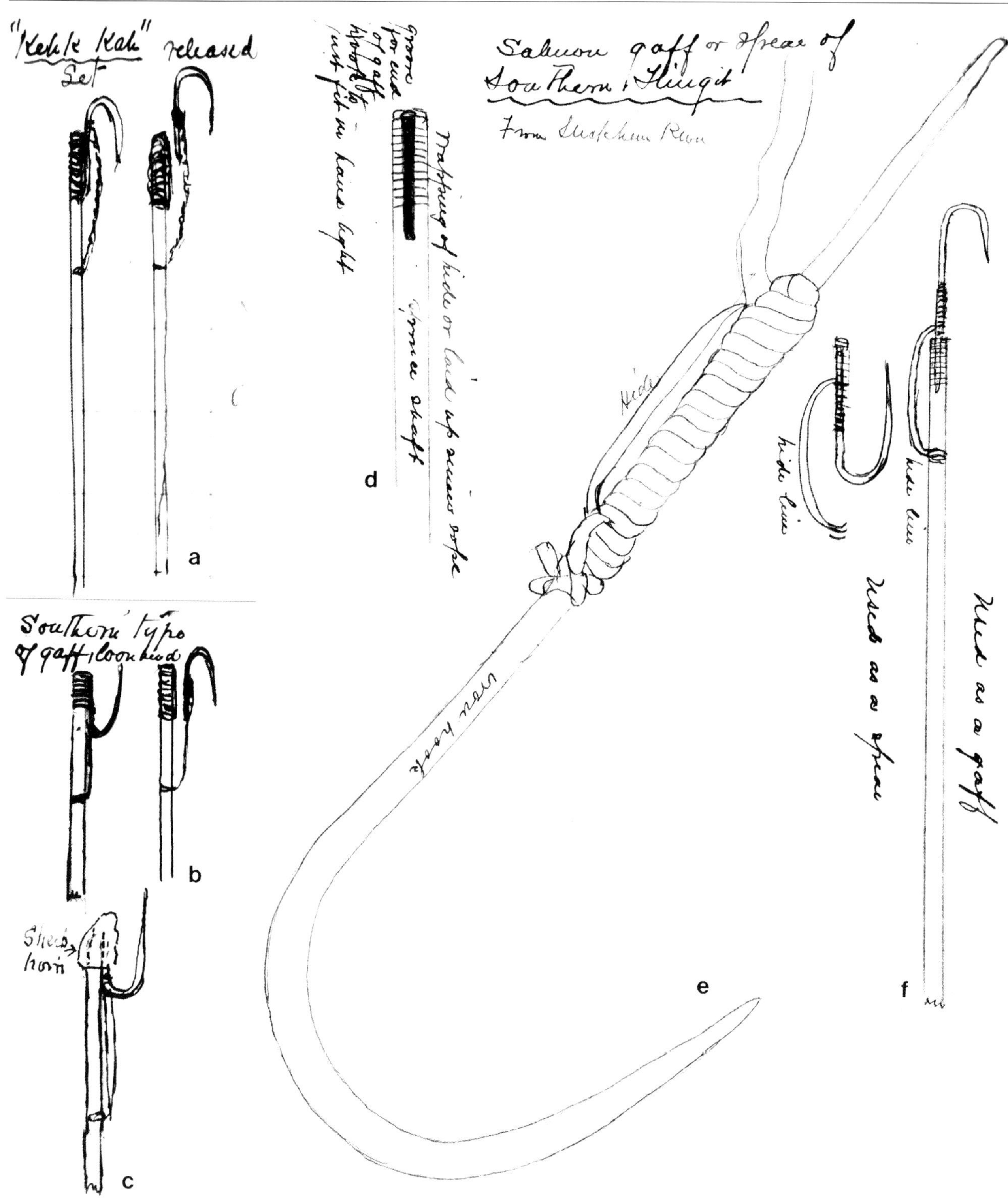

Trolling gear for king and coho salmon, Hutsnuwu of Admiralty Island. (Pen and ink sketches by G. T. Emmons. AMNH.) Right. *Sketches showing the method of baiting the hook by drawing it with a wooden needle through a herring, in through the gill and out at the tail.*

Left. *Wooden float with the main line wrapped around it, secured with a slipknot, and ready to be thrown overboard. The line from the float is fastened to a stone sinker, to which is also attached the secondary line from the baited hook.*

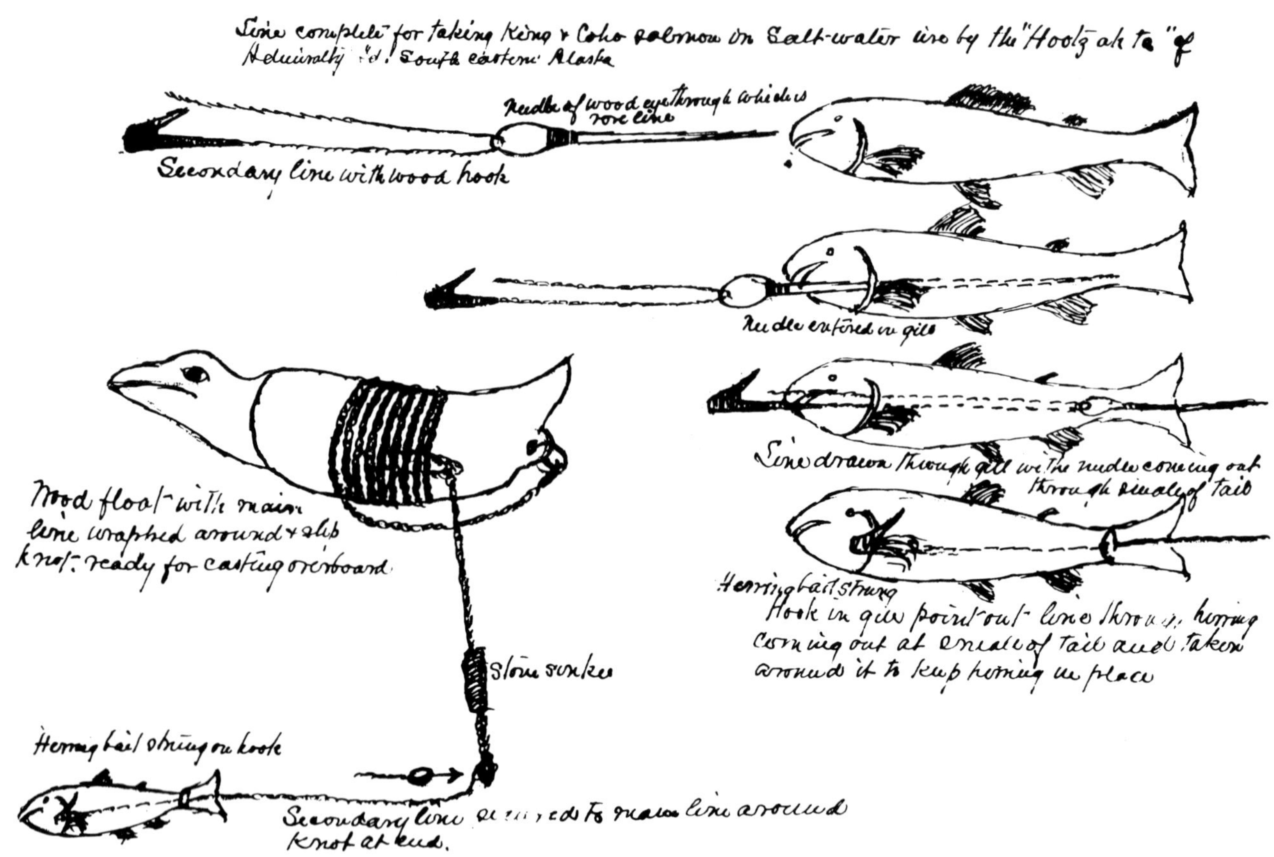

through until the shank of the hook entered the gill, the point [barb] standing out alongside the herring's head. The small line was now secured to the larger one by doubling the loop over the knot at the end of the main line and drawing it taut. The fisherman used one or more of these complete sets, casting them over from the canoe when the salmon were running. When the fish struck and ran away with the hook, the slipknot released the line wound around the buoy and so caused the latter to turn over and over. The fisherman standing by in his canoe would see the movement of the buoy, paddle to it, haul in the line, and kill the fish with a club, *khootz, kutz* [x̣úš]. Then he would set the line again. [The club was presumably a wooden one, like that used for killing halibut.] The Tlingit believed that to kill any fish with a stone would bring rain and storm.

Seines and drift nets were unknown to the Tlingit until after their introduction by Europeans. [At one time] a primitive salmon seine was made of twisted cedar-bark rope, but this has long since been replaced by one of commercial twine. [The seine is called ge·wú.]

Salmon caught at a distance and that had to be packed on the back were laid head to tail, wrapped in skunk cabbage leaves, and tied together. If caught in the stream a short distance from the house, they were strung on a tree limb and dragged through the water.

[For Emmons, just as for George Hunt who wrote such long, full texts on Kwakiutl culture for Franz Boas, the curing of salmon or the preparation for eating is all part of the process that begins with the manufacture of the salmon harpoon, and includes the catching, the bringing home, the cutting up, and even the serving of the fish. But, like Boas, I have decided to cut this account here, and defer to Chapter 6 the description of how women cut and cured the fish. The same arrangement will be followed for all the products of the chase. In a rough way this separates the contributions made by men from those made by women in the food quest.]

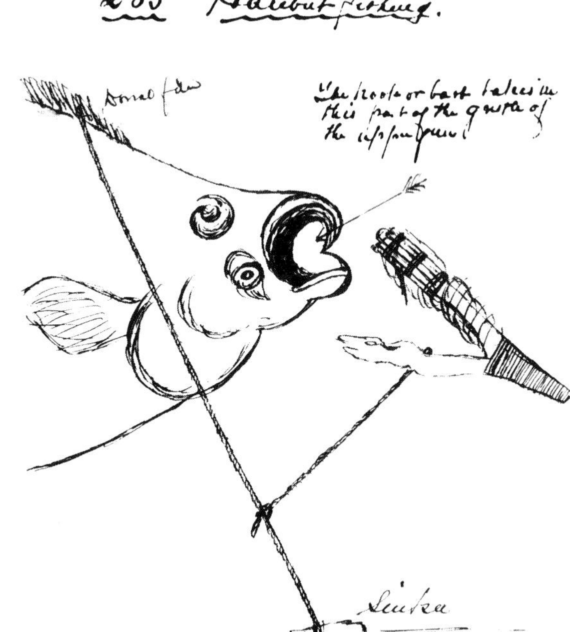

Halibut fishing. (Pen and ink sketch by G. T. Emmons. AMNH.) The sketch shows the halibut hook, attached to a weighted line, floating up, the decorated arm facing the bottom (where the halibut will see it). The other arm has the barb and bait. The heavier line attached to the sinker is here shown rising up to a float on the surface, the float not visible in the picture. The number "283" refers to a set of numbered topics Emmons had prepared in order to cover Tlingit ethnography in a systematic way. The notebook with numbered topics is in BCPA.

HALIBUT FISHING*

Halibut, *tchartl* [čá·ƛ], are most abundant in spring, before the salmon come, but they followed salmon closely in economic value, both as a fresh and as a cured food product. In fact, the largest halibut were called *narlh* [ná·łx̣, or "riches"]. The general distribution of the halibut, its abundance, ease of capture, and the fact that it could be had at all seasons, gave it its importance. It was taken with hooks of amost ingenious pattern, attached by snoods [leaders] of twisted spruce root to a line of two-strand, right-handed [S-twist] spruce root, and set in the tideways where the fish fed. [Such a site was called ʔí·t.] The halibut is a bottom fish and not a great traveler, preferring to have its food brought to it. The line was set by means of a boulder of suitable size and shape, picked up anywhere on the beach. This sinker was fastened directly to the end of the line, or was wrapped around with rope to which the line was secured. The line was buoyed with floats, which also served to mark its position. These were made of an inflated seal bladder or of wood, the latter generally shaped like a seabird. Sometimes two buoys were used, depending on the weight of the line, the strength of the tide, and the depth of the water.

The true Tlingit halibut hook, *nuh* [náx^{w}], consisted of two arms of wood, fitted together at an angle of thirty degrees, and seized with split spruce root set in a groove about an inch above the pointed end of the juncture. The two arms were almost always of different kinds of wood, which was supposed to please the fish. [The hook is arranged so that it floats up from the weighted line on the bottom; the upper arm of the hook carries the barb and bait; the lower arm is carved on the underside, facing the bottom.] The plain [upper] arm, *nuh-whor-wee* [náx^{w} ẋú·wu], "pin of the hook," was of spruce or preferably of yellow cedar, and was fitted at the upper end with a barb of bone (later of iron), that was inclined inward at a sharp angle, and lashed with spruce root. About the outside of the end [opposite the barb] were seized a number of small wooden wedges to give the arm greater buoyancy. [As bait] the tentacle of a squid ["octopus"] was tied around the barb with a narrow string of spruce root. Sometimes a piece of skunk cabbage leaf was added, since the fish was supposed to like its odor. The other arm of the hook, *tchartl kha-ku* [čá·ƛ x̣a·gú], "claw of the halibut," was of alder or yew, and was always carved [on its lower surface] in human or animal form, believed necessary to attract the fish. [The figure faced the bottom so that the halibut could see it. (See Lisiansky 1814, pl. I *d*, where the bottom of the hook is to the left; de Laguna 1972, figs. 44, 45, pp. 388–91.)] Through a hole in the middle of this [carved] arm, secured on the inside by a single knot, the snood is led to the main line and was made fast. This snood or leader was called "its fastener," *uh-har-ta* [probably ʔa xada·]; the lashing about the base [angle] of the hook was "hook's covering," *nuh-uh-seeta* [probably náx^{w} šída·]; the lashing about the barb was "the covering of its end," *uh-shu-see-ta* [probably ʔašu šída·].

The line was set from the canoe. Two, three, or more hooks could be attached to one line at intervals of ten or more feet. The hooks floated with the baited [barbed] arm up. The halibut, swimming fast in the water, belly down, would take the barb through the gristle of the upper jaw, and as he felt the point of the barb, would force his nose

**Editor's note:* I have added information from Beresford, Shukoff, La Pérouse, and von Langsdorff.

Rigging of halibut hooks. (Pencil sketches by G. T. Emmons.) Left. Two iron hooks attached to the ends of a small tree limb by means of a hide line. The main line is secured at A. (Measurements in inches.) Right. Iron halibut hook attached to a hide line, 5 inches long, at the end of a 10-foot-long T-shaped alder branch.

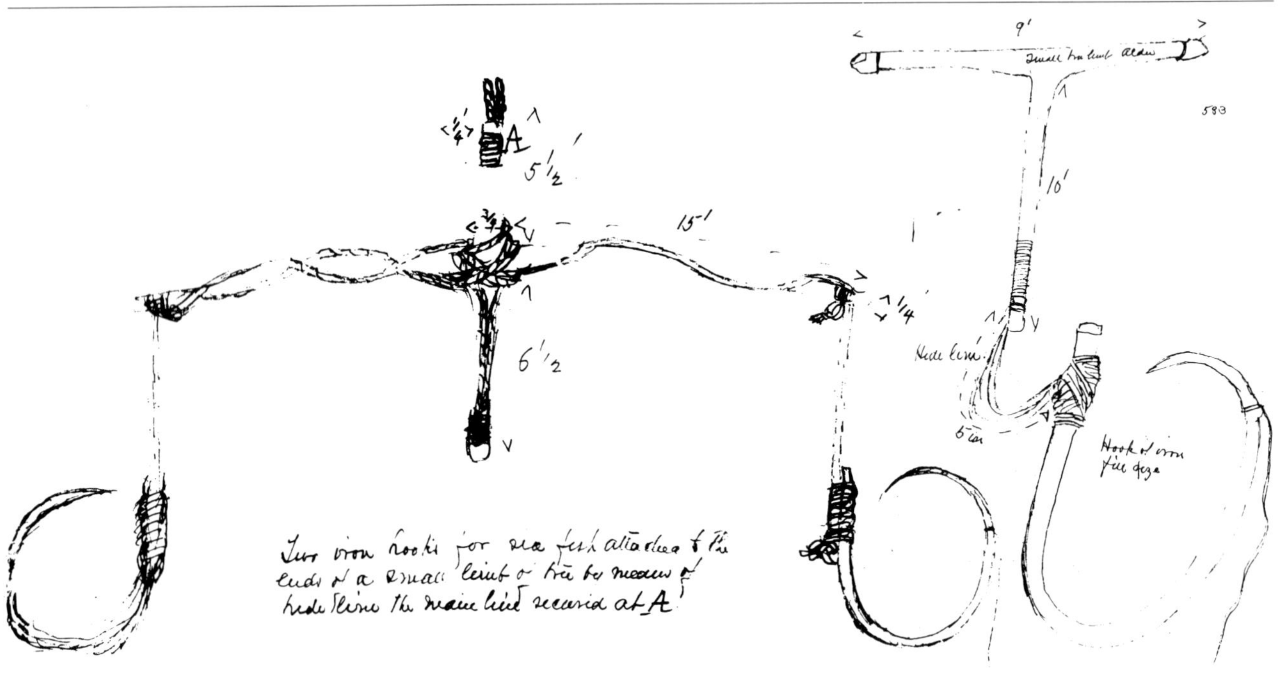

down deeper and the point in farther, making it impossible for him to get free.

[Actually, the halibut's jaws hinge sidewise as he swims. He sucks in the baited hook, the flat underside of his mouth sliding between the barb and the lower arm of the hook. Unable to swallow the bait, he tries to eject the hook with such force that the barb stabs through what would be the "lower jaw" in an ordinary fish (Stewart [1977] 1982:54). Teeth marks on the barbed arms of old hooks corroborate Stewart's description (Bill Holm, pers. comm.).]

No hook known is as certain as this. For the capture of the halibut this device is superior to any invention of the white man, and was so conceived by the early explorers.

[Emmons here refers to the account by William Beresford (1789:174–75), who was with Captain Dixon at Port Mulgrave, Yakutat Bay, in June 1787, and wrote:

> Our whale-boat was one day sent with seven hands to this place [the halibut grounds just off the entrance to Yakutat Bay], on a fishing party; but their success was greatly inferior to that of *two* Indians, who were fishing at the same time, which is rather extraordinary, if we consider the apparent inferiority of their tackle to our's [*sic*]. Their hook is a large simple piece of wood, the shank at least half an inch in diameter; that part which turns up, and which forms an acute angle, is considerably smaller, and brought gradually to a point: a flat piece of wood, about six inches long, and near two inches wide, is neatly lashed to the shank, on the back of which is rudely carved the representation of an human face.
>
> I cannot think that this was altogether designed as an ornament to their hooks, but that it has some religious allusion, and possibly is intended as a kind of Deity, to ensure their success in fishing, which is conducted in a singular manner. They bait their hook with a kind of fish, called by the sailors *squids,* and having sunk it to the bottom, they fix a bladder to the end of the line as a buoy and should that not watch sufficiently, they add another. Their lines are very strong, being made of the sinews or intestines of animals.
>
> One man is sufficient to look after five or six of these buoys; when he perceives a fish bite, he is in no great hurry to haul up his line, but gives him time to be well hooked; and when he has hauled the fish up to the surface of the water, he knocks him on the head with a short club, provided for that purpose, and afterwards stows his prize away at his leisure: this is done to prevent the halibut (which sometimes are very large) from damaging, or perhaps upsetting his canoe in their dying struggles. Thus were we fairly beat at our own weapons, and the natives constantly bringing us plenty of fish, our boat was never sent on this business afterwards.]

In late years a curved iron hook, based on the same principle, has been used, particularly at Yakutat, but has now been abandoned. To the shank of the hook was attached a short hide or sinew snood which was made fast to a T-shaped limb of alder, which was secured to the main line.

The fisherman might attach the end of the line to his canoe and stand by, or he might go ashore and watch the float, or leave it entirely and return later. The striking of the fish was indicated by the movement of the buoy. Then the fish was struck on the head with a short wooden club to kill it before taking it into the canoe. It was a delicate operation to get a hundred-pound halibut over the gunwale. This was done by canting the side of the canoe to the water's edge; the head of the fish was brought to the gunwale, and, by a quick motion, while it was really underwater, the fish was jerked in. If the halibut were of too great size, however, it could always be towed ashore and landed without difficulty.

The primitive fisherman spat on the hook before dropping it overboard, and as he lowered it, he talked to it continually. [Emmons here paraphrased the account given by Shukoff in 1882, which is perhaps better quoted in full, except for slight grammatical corrections:

> When native goes out after halibut and he finds place where there are plenty, he at once begins to bait his fishhook, *nar-hoo-oo ta-hah* [náxʷ x̣̓ú·wu ṫe·x̣̣á·, "pin of the halibut hook"]. They generally use devilfish. When he begins to lower hook, he begins to talk to fishhooks, telling them to be watchful and catch his game, and when once caught, not to let it go. And then [he] ties float carved to represent some sea bird, as shag [cormorant] and seagull, and he watches buoys. And when he pulls line with fish on, he talks to himself, or rather to hook, and when he gets halibut up he talks to halibut: "Look out, you will tear your mouth! [if you struggle]. Your bones were in the fire long ago!" [This meant: "You were caught before in a previous incarnation, and your bones were burned in the correct manner."] Then he strikes halibut in head with heavy club, and at the same time apologizes to the halibut, saying it is not him that strikes, but his hunger. And he pulls it in canoe *always* white side up [belly up]. The reason is that if accidentally put dark side [back] up, he will have no luck next time. [Emmons added: The fish must be so placed preparatory to cutting it.]

[At Yakutat, it was said that each halibut hook was given an individual name, appropriate to the decoration on it. The latter, as Jonaitis (1981:18–19) has pointed out, is "shamanistic" in the choice of figures represented. I do not believe, however, that they are to protect the man who has ventured into "the dangerous sacred domain" of the sea (p. 34), for protection against the dangers of the open sea is provided by the magic acts and prohibitions observed by the hunter or fisherman and his wife. The decorations on the hook are to influence the fish, and so face downward. They also give the hook a kind of life, as does the individual hook's personal name. The fisherman would warm his hands in the sunshine and put them on his rig, and address the buoy, the line, and especially the hooks, telling the latter, "Go down to halibut land and fight!" Or he would tell them to go for the halibut's wife so that the husband would become angry and bite the hook (using a ruse similar to that employed by Raven when he made the king salmon so angry at the greenstone that the fish jumped ashore). And the hook answers the fisherman. In effect, the hook is equipped with magic to lure and capture the fish. (See de Laguna 1972:389–90.)]

In old times when fishing for halibut, sometimes a shark took the hook. They did not kill it with the club [because] this would bring bad luck. [Yakutat informants said that it was impossible to kill a shark with a club, but Raven had discovered that it could be killed with snot from the nose (de Laguna 1972:391). The shark, tú·s̓, was a crest of several Wolf clans.] "*Klate Shart-to-which,*" abbreviated for convenience to "Chartrich" [Shotridge], means "never hit a shark with a club" [ł-ša·du-x̣íč-x̣]. This name was given to Chartrich by his grandfather [Wolf 18, Na·nyạ·ʔa·ỵí, presumably a Stikine chief, since his wife was the "daughter of the great chief of the Stikines." The Shark was one of the crests of the Wolf 18.] The name was given to Chartrich because he was powerful and it would be better not to trouble him, as he would resent it. The abbreviated name means "Very powerful, not to be trifled with." [He was the chief of Wolf 1, Ka·gʷa·nta·n, of Klukwan. His name was sometimes spelled "Shartrich."]

[La Pérouse (1799, 1:406) described fishing with hook and line in Lituya Bay in July 1786, presumably for halibut:

> Their mode of angling is very ingenious. Each line is fastened to a large seal's bladder, and set adrift. One canoe has twelve or fifteen of them. When a fish is caught, he drags along the bladder, and the canoe rows after it. Thus a couple of men can attend twelve or fifteen lines, without the trouble of holding them in the hand. [Presumably there was only one hook on each line.]

[Von Langsdorff (1814, 2:131) reported of the Sitka Tlingit of 1805–6: "the fishing-lines are chiefly woven from a sort of dried sea-weed, which furnishes strings sometimes even twenty yards in length." This was kelp, and the kelp fishing line was called ƛeỵani.]

HERRING FISHING

The Alaska herring, *yow, yar* [ya·w; ỵa·w at Yakutat], though a small fish, is extremely rich in oil and was greatly

Gathering herring spawn with hook, Sitka, 1889. (Photograph by G. T. Emmons? BCPA.)

valued by the natives on this account, as well as for its spawn. Its distribution is limited, and it cannot be depended upon from year to year except in a few localities, of which the chain of lagoons penetrating the western shore of Admiralty Island at Kootznahoo Inlet was the most favored. Vancouver's surveying party [Vancouver 1801, 5:422] mentioned the great abundance of this fish found here in July 1894, and this abundance has continued to this day.

In April, vast schools enter the bays and inlets among the islands to spawn, and they deposit their eggs, *khouk* [gá·x̣ʷ], in countless millions on every growth of sea plant and on the rocks in comparatively shallow water. Taking advantage of this, the natives cut hemlock boughs which they placed on the shore at low water, and weighted down with boulders. Or, still better, the branches were anchored with a rock tied to the butt ends, so that in standing up they would present more surface for the deposit of the eggs which adhered in great clusters. A broad-leafed seaweed, *dow* [ťa·w], "feather," and a long black skeleton moss [or sea grass], *nh* [né, "hair in the water"], seemed equally desirable to the fish to spawn upon, and for the natives to gather when so covered. These were fished for from the canoe with a long spruce pole with a small crosspiece seized at the end, called "sea moss catcher," *nh heetar* [né xíťa·, "sea-hair broom"]. This was entangled in the moss, with a sudden twist the root was detached, and it was brought to the surface and deposited in the canoe. [Preparation of the herring eggs is discussed in Chapter 6.]

After spawning, the herring disappear into deep water, and about September, following their food, a tiny crustacean, they again school in myriads in the inland waters, but not necessarily on their spawning grounds nor in the same localities from year to year, but always about Kootznahoo Roads. For this reason the resident natives of Angoon are the herring fishermen of the coast. At this season and extending through the fall, the fish are very fat and are valued most highly as oil producers, although also enjoyed as a fresh food. They were sun dried in limited quantities.

Fishing was done in small canoes. The steersman in the stern paddled to where he saw the fish jump or the seabirds

Chilkoot River, with native fish weirs and traps, 1900. (Moser, 1901, pl. XXIV. Courtesy of the University of California Library, Berkeley.)

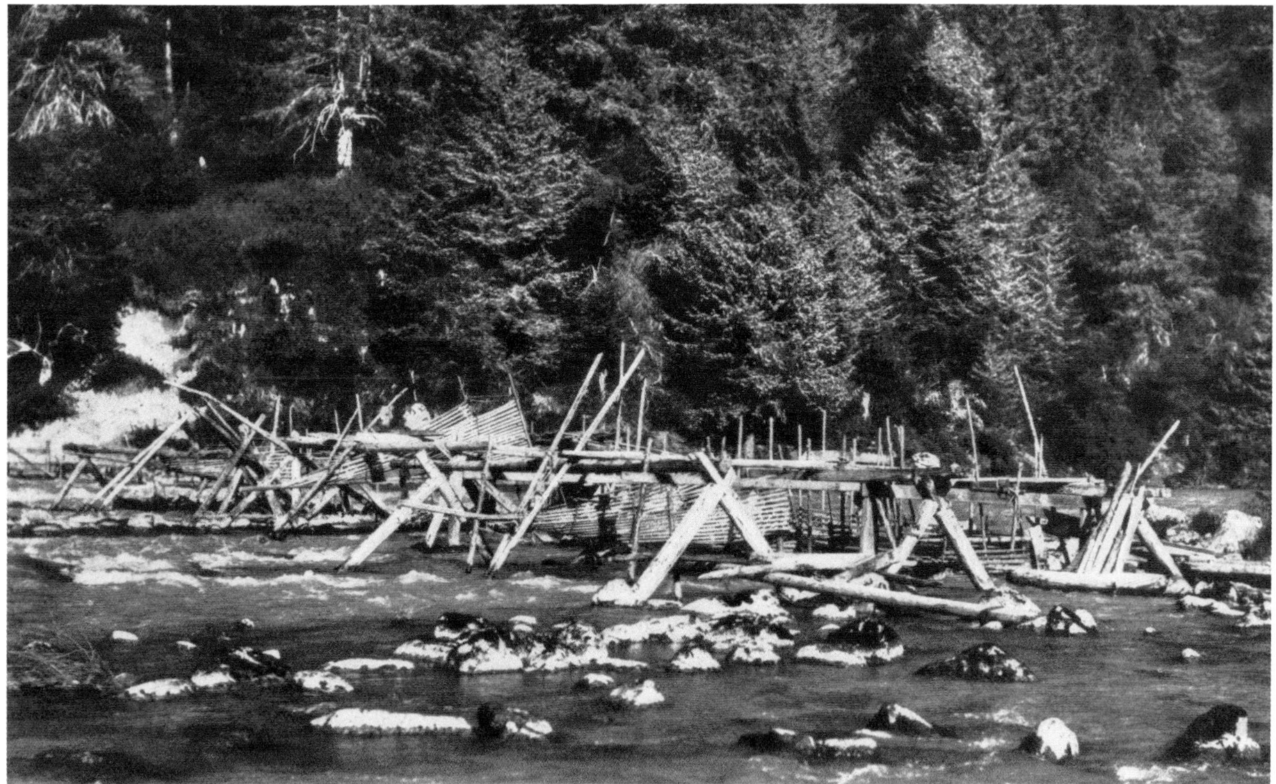

gather, since birds, larger fish, and men were all equally alive to the abundance that nature offered them. The bowman used a rake, ***heet lar*** [xíƛa· or xíλa·]. This was a spruce staff about twelve feet long, oval at the handle and flattened at the other end to a thickness of two or more inches. Along one edge [of the flattened end], for a distance of three feet, were inserted sharpened nails, an inch or so long, and from one-half to one inch apart. Iron has taken the place of older bone teeth. This implement was driven down into the water with a long paddle stroke and brought up with its teeth up. With a quick turn and jerk over the canoe, the impaled fish were shaken off.

[Sitka was also a center for catching herring and for obtaining herring eggs. Thus Lütké (1835:111–12), who was at Sitka in 1827, reported that in spring, during the herring season, the natives used to gather near the fortress of New Archangel up to a thousand strong, and an equal number were on the nearby islands. In summer, there were often five to six hundred natives. At first, no native was permitted to camp near the fort, but Governor Mouraviev (1821–27) finally changed this policy, thinking it more advantageous to have the natives and their families under the guns of the fort. From that time on, the Tlingit became more peaceful. Tikhmenev ([1861–63] 1978:368, 422), reporting on conditions of about 1860, mentioned that the herring fishery at New Archangel was very good, and that in February and March, when most herring were taken, the water became milky from the spawn and milt, and that it was easy to catch the fish with a rake. They were also caught sometimes in the fall.]

EULACHON FISHING

Eulachon, ***sak*** [sa·k], might be termed the luxury fish of the North Pacific coast, for its delicacy of flesh and the high grade of oil extracted from it. It appears in the mouths of the larger rivers from March to May. The run in the Nass was the greatest, and used to engage the Tsimshian to the exclusion of everything else [during the eulachon season], as the trade in grease was a source of great profit to them. The runs in the Alaskan rivers were quite limited; that in the Chilkat River was alone worthy of notice. [Shukoff, however, in discussing potlatches, mentioned that eulachon

Fishing gear. (Pen and ink sketches by G. T. Emmons. AMNH.) (a) Obsolete type of gaff, made like a large trout hook. The hook for octopus and herring spawn, tar-nar [tá·na·], *is similar. (b) Herring rake,* heet-lar [xíƛa·]. *(c) Obsolete type of spear,* klark-war [ƛa·gʷa·], *used for seal and otter in rivers.*

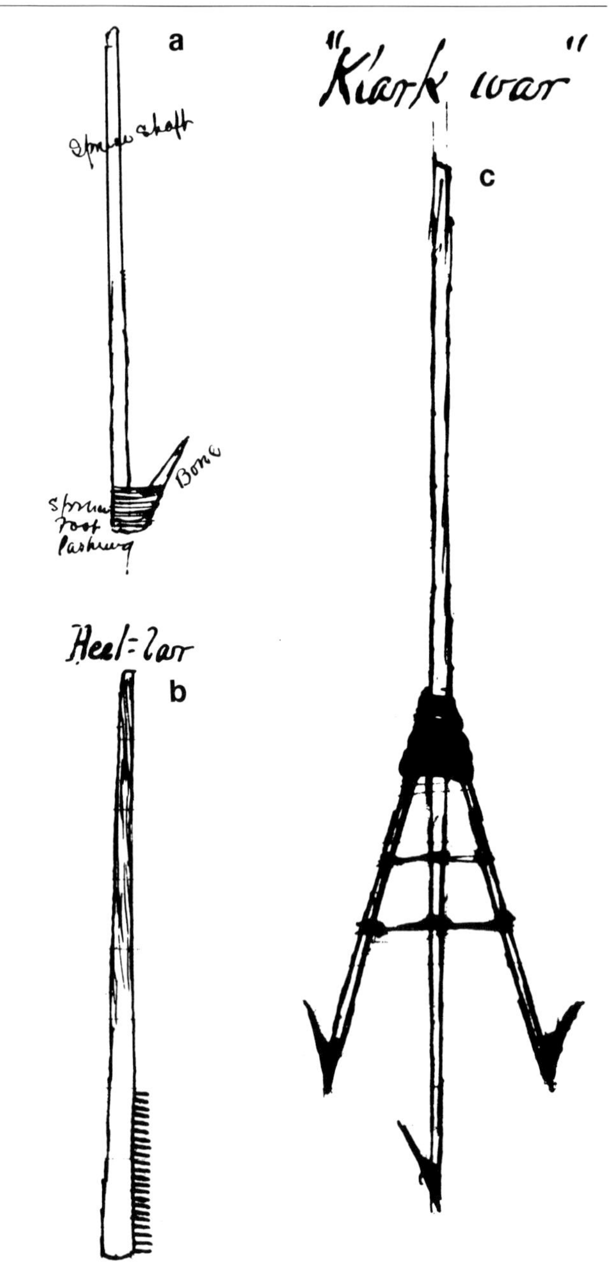

grease was also brought from Yakutat, as well as from Port Simpson. The eulachon were probably caught in the Alsek River.]

Here [on the Chilkat River] the people went into camp on the lower river by villages. The run continued about two weeks. The fish were taken with long-handled scoop nets, *go qte* [gúqʷč], about eighteen inches wide at the mouth and three feet deep, woven of fireweed fiber, nettle, or sinew. The twine of twisted two-strand cord was laid up and knotted with the aid of mesh sticks to form the required mesh. The net was strung on a line or hoop that was laced to the two extended arms of the pole, forming a quadrangle with the longer side between the ends of the two arms. The net might be used from shore, but was generally dipped from the bow of a canoe drifting broadside to the current. It was forced down to the bottom, and drawn up against the current. By a quick twist of the wrist, the contents were emptied into the canoe.

In the Chilkoot River, semi-conical baskets of split spruce rods, set in the runways [of the fish weir] were also used to take eulachon. [The same type of cylindrical basket trap, with a funnel inside, called k̓í·tx or t̓í·tx, was used for eulachon at Dry Bay and the lower Alsek River. The rendering of fish oil is described in Chapter 6.]

TROUT FISHING

There were four well-recognized varieties of trout, and possibly several more, in southeastern Alaska. The "Gardner" or steelhead, *ah shut* [ʔa·šát, "lake's wife," *Salmo gairdneri*], the cutthroat [*S. clarkii*], and the rainbow [actually another name for the steelhead], are all lake fish that run into the streams in the spring. The Dolly Varden, *qwat* [x̣ʷá·t̓, *Salvelinus malma*], comes in from the sea with the salmon. The Tlingit set little store by trout when the more important salmon were abundant.

[Brook trout, *S. fontinalis,* were introduced into southeastern Alaska in 1920 (Morrow 1980:54), but lake trout, *S. namaycush,* are native to the Gulf of Alaska and northern Hoonah and Chilkat-Chilkoot territories (p. 79). The last should be Emmons's "fourth variety," and is evidently that taken in the winter.]

At Chilkat in winter they speared trout through the ice on the lakes. At Chilkoot they took them [Dolly Varden?] in April and May in baskets [traps], set in the rapids [of the Chilkoot River]. At Klukwan, on the upper Chilkat River, they set lines made fast to posts on the banks. To these were attached by means of snoods of twisted goat's wool, small wooden hooks, *tahk* [t̓e·x̣ or t̓e·x̣á], of the usual type [i.e., compound V-shaped hooks], baited with dried eulachon. The fish, on taking the bait, swallowed the whole hook, and were held fast. The lines were taken in and set in the morning and in the evening.

OTHER FISH AND MARINE INVERTEBRATES*

All varieties of saltwater fish, such as cod, *sarkh* [s̓á·x̣̓], rock cod [ʔišqi·n], bass [łitʔisdúkʷ], flounder [ǯánti], sculpin, *wake* [wé·x̣̓], eel [łú·t̓], caplin or stickleback, *kaghun* [k̓a·gán], were taken with a simple compound V-shaped hook, made with a wooden shank and a barb of sharpened bone or wood. The line was of twisted spruce root, and the sinkers, *go-war-ta* [gu·waté], were unworked stones, generally oblong or of a convenient shape for the attachment of the line. [It is curious that Emmons did not mention the fishing line of kelp, ƛ̓eyani.]

In later years, curved iron hooks were employed and these were often secured with hide to a small branch. Sometimes two hooks were used, one at each end of the branch. [This rig was called q̓išt̓.]

Sharks, *toos, toose* [tú·s̓], and dogfish or ground sharks, *kutku* [x̣̓átgu], were taken for the oil in their livers, which was sold for commercial purposes. They were speared [harpooned], but were never hit with a club. [See "Halibut Fishing."]

The Tlingit believed that to kill any fish with a stone would bring rain and storm.

Marine invertebrates were easily gathered by the women. Only the devilfish (squid) presented more of a problem and these were caught by the men. They were considered the best bait for halibut, and so were called "bait" [ná·qʷ]. They were taken with a dull hook, formerly of deer horn and later of iron, lashed to the end of a pole. [At Yakutat this was described as being of wood, like a huge V-shaped trout hook.] This hook, *tar-nar* [tá·na·], was thrust under submerged rocks and into underwater holes, and twisted around, entangling the tentacles of the devilfish, so that it could be drawn to the surface.

SEAL HUNTING

Next to salmon, the hair seal, *tsar* [ca·], had the greatest economic value. The blubber was converted into oil, the flesh was eaten fresh as well as dried, and the flippers were esteemed as great delicacies. The skin was used for leggings, moccasins, and clothing, for packs and other bags, for cradle covers, gun cases, and for cord, and the teeth for ornamentation.

The Yakutat and Hoonah were the most expert seal hunters, although all Tlingit hunted the seal in the spring when they came into the bays to breed and to feed on herring and salmon. They were found in greatest numbers about the floating ice that was discharged from the glaciers in Disenchantment Bay (at the head of Yakutat Bay), Glacier Bay (in Cross Sound), and in Icy Bay, west of Yakutat.

The hunter, in a small canoe painted white, or more often covered with a sail, and himself clothed in white, used both the bow and arrow and the spear [harpoon], but firearms were employed later. The canoe was put among the bergs and in its white covering was almost indistinguishable from the floating ice. The seal was speared when asleep on the ice, or when diving, and it might be called by imitating the cry of the young seal. Whenever it rose to the surface, paddling ceased. When among the ice fields, the hunter continually talked to the spirits inhabiting the bergs, offering snuff or tobacco for their protection and good offices.

The spear [harpoon] was similar to that used for salmon, although the barbed head of bone, ivory, or later of metal, was longer. [Sometimes the same weapon was used for both salmon and seals.] The head was detachable, but was secured to the shaft of hemlock, spruce, or fir by a short length of laid-up sinew or hide cord. Or, instead of being attached to the shaft, the line, several fathoms long, was often secured to an inflated sealskin buoy. In either case, the seal, when struck, was buoyed up by the shaft or the skin float. The spear was thrust or cast, depending on the distance. Even after the introduction of firearms, the spear was retained in order to recover the seal, for, if shot and killed, it quickly sank. Before being taken into the canoe, it was struck on the head with a stout short killing club, usually carved to represent a seal, sea lion, or killerwhale.

An obsolete spear, *klark-war* [λa·gwá·], used for both seal and sea otter, had three arms at the end of the shaft, each with a single barb lashed on. [This spear is called by the same name as the three-pronged fish spear or leister, used for catching fish under the winter ice on lakes, although it is made differently.]

On rivers in which the seals came after the salmon, the hunter concealed himself behind a blind of rock or brush from which he shot. The spear [harpoon] was retained as an extra precaution.

[Emmons sketched] a barbed harpoon head, reportedly used by the Hoonah and Yakutat for sea otter principally, and also for the hair seal and the fur seal. The detachable barbed head was fitted with a moveable arm that had two sharp points. The line from the head was secured to a ten-foot shaft at two places. When the animal was struck

**Editor's note:* This section has been compiled from notes left by Emmons.

and the head detached from the shaft, the weight of the shaft acted as a drag and would draw the hinged arm back so that the sharp points would clutch the animal. This was called *see-kar-qu kut* [perhaps sika·yị kát], "barbed head that never misses its mark."

The fur seal [x̣ú·n] were hunted in the spring, during their northward migration to the Pribilof Islands in Bering Sea. The island Tlingit who hunted them camped on the outer coast and went out in their canoes when weather permitted, following the same method as in hunting the hair seal. In addition to the ordinary harpoon [ʔá·da·], with barbed head [kát], a harpoon with a toggling head, made in two parts plus the blade, was used. This was the *de-nar* [di·ná·], already described as used for salmon by the Southern Tlingit, and rarely seen farther north. [It was, however, reported by Malaspina (1848:287) at Yakutat, where it was used in 1791 for catching salmon; and Yakutat informants in 1950 remembered hearing about it (de Laguna 1972:384–85).]

PORPOISE, SEA LION, AND WHALE*

The large jumping porpoise was called *tcheech* or *cheech* [čí·č], and the smaller gray "puffing pig" or dolphin was *ghan* [q̇a·n]. [Emmons did not mention that the porpoise and the sea lion were both hunted with harpoons similar to those used for seals. At Yakutat the porpoise was valued chiefly for its sinew, since eating the flesh was said to produce an unpleasant body odor. Sea lion flippers were considered good food, and the hide made very strong lines. Emmons reported only:] The sea lion, *tan* [ta·n], was found on the outer rocks and islands, and like the seal, was hunted industriously in the spring.

Whales were not hunted by the Tlingit. Large whales, or whales in general, were called *yah-eh,* or *yai* [yá·ỵ]. The killerwhale [and also the blackfish with which it is often confused] was *keet* or *kete* [kí·t]. The younger or smaller killerwhale [actually the pilot whale, a different species], that often run in front of the school when chasing seals, were called *kete woo-sor-nee,* or *yu-sa-neh* [kí·t wu·sá·ni], "killerwhales' hunting spear."

[A note left by Emmons, in BCPA, is titled "292, The Blackfish 'Kete,'" and reads: "In old days the Thlingits greatly feared the Kete, for if wounded or angered they would make for the canoe. When they encountered them at sea, they would commence to praise them, and if on shore they saw them in the distance they would beg them to drive the seal to them, which they do."

[It would appear that the statement that the Tlingit never hunted whales may not be strictly correct. Undoubtedly they were unable to hunt the largest whales, although they sometimes ate the flesh if they found a dead whale on the shore—especially if there was little else to eat. But they may have hunted some baleen whales, if the report of Marchand's voyage to Sitka in 1791 is correct (Fleurieu 1801, 1:344):

> They have not changed the instrument with which they arm themselves for whale-fishing [for the traded musket]: this instrument is a harpoon of bone, bearded, and mounted on a long pole. Relying on this weapon, which they handle with uncommon dexterity, two Tchinkitanayans [Sitkans] boldly attack the whale. When they are arrived near the place where they have seen him dive for the last time, they slacken the progress of their canoe, play, as it were, with their paddles on the surface of the water; and as soon as he re-appears, the harpooner seizes his harpoon, and drives it at the monster. According to their account, the dart thrown never fails to make its way, through one of the eyes, into the inside of the head: and the animal is soon lifeless. The fat of the whale furnishes the Americans with an oil, which they preserve in guts of a large capacity, and which, as I have said, is a great dainty among them; the beard [baleen] is converted into combs, of which, however, they make little use, and likewise into spoons and other household utensils.

This is the only account of whaling by the Tlingit that we have encountered.]

SEA OTTER HUNTING†

The sea otter, *yuckth* [yúxʷč̓], the most valuable of all fur-bearing animals, was the objective of the early Russian and European traders, and it might readily be said that the sea otter was the primary reason for the exploitation of Alaska that resulted in its settlement [by white men], for the whole trade was in furs, of which the sea otter was the most valuable.

The sea otter is found only in the North Pacific, along the shores from California through Alaska and the Aleutian Islands to Japan, but its area of greatest abundance was from Dixon Entrance to Unalaska. That it was not overhunted before the Russians appeared is evidenced by the incredible numbers that the earliest Europeans procured in trade in

*Editor's note: This section was put together from scraps left by Emmons and from the extraordinary report in Fleurieu.

†Editor's note: I verified the references to La Pérouse and Dixon (Beresford), and added the account from Beardslee about Tsimshian "poachers" on Hoonah hunting grounds.

Sea otter harpoon. (Sketched in pencil by G. T. Emmons. AMNH.) "A spear barb used by the Yakutat and Hoonah tribes for taking the sea otter principally, *also the hair and fur seal, known as* 'See-kar-qu kut' *[probably* sika'yi kát, *"barbed head that never misses its mark"]. The iron barb is fitted with a movable arm B, fitted with two sharp pointed jaws, pivoted at D. The barb, A [about 7 inches long], is hand fitted in end of 10 foot shaft at C, a line of twisted sinew secured through B at C is secured to shaft at E and F. When the prey is struck the barb detaches itself from the shaft or is detached by the strain on shaft, and the weight of shaft acting as a drag, draws the arm B parallel to barb, and the points T T are driven into the animal and clutch it."*

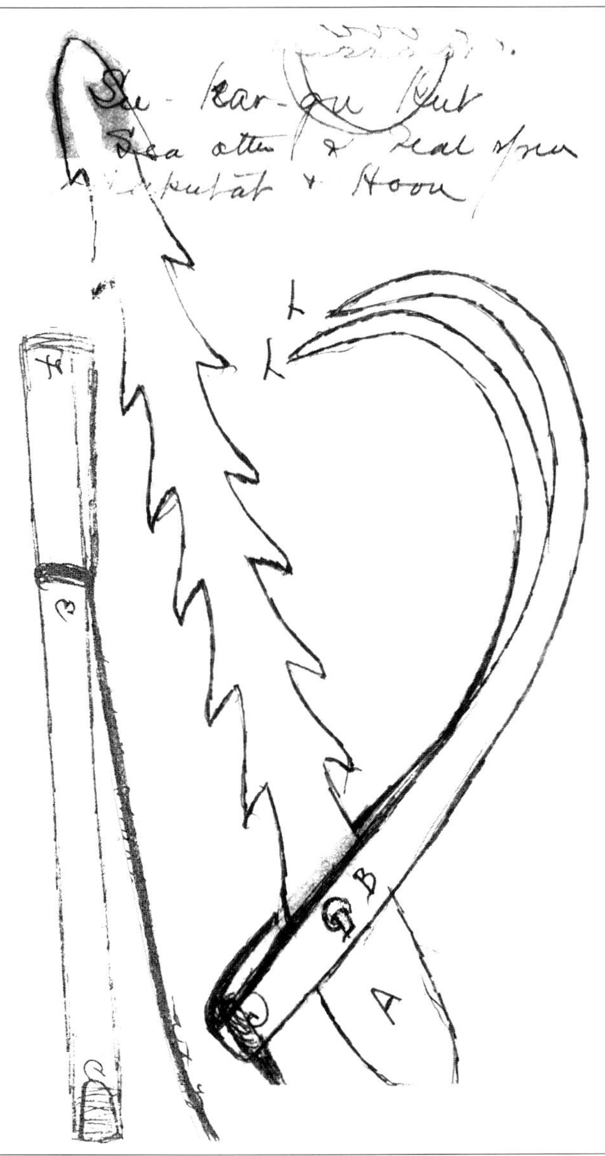

single localities within a few days. With the increased demand, however, the incessant slaughter depleted the western grounds [Aleutian Islands] and then the coast [of southeastern Alaska], until today [1930?] the sea otter is almost extinct.

[The sea otter trade had already become unprofitable by 1821, however. Protection of the herds in Alaska and in California, where two different varieties are represented, has led to an increase in their numbers, quite noticeable since 1937.]

La Pérouse, one of the most exact of the early narrators, estimated that in 1786 [letter of 19 September 1786 to the French Minister of the Navy, from vol. 4 of the original edition of his *Voyages,* 1797, in Chinard 1937:134–35], the Spanish Presidio could procure and supply for the China trade ten thousand skins annually, though of inferior quality to the Alaskan skins, while the Spaniards by expanding to the north could easily procure up to fifty thousand a year. In Lituya Bay, La Pérouse obtained one thousand skins in a fortnight, which he proposed to sell in Canton for the benefit of his crew, all the officers and others onboard feeling that glory was sufficient reward for them [Chinard 1937:xxxix, xl–xli]. From 13 to 21 June, 1787, Dixon anchored off Cape Edgecombe in Sitka Sound, where, according to Beresford (1789, p. 191): "We purchased about two hundred excellent sea otter skins, a good quantity of inferior pieces of sea otter, together with a large parcel of indifferent pieces and slips; about one hundred good seals, and a great number of fine beaver tails."

The incessant pursuit of the sea otter not only tended to its extinction but changed its habits by making it doubly shy and solitary and keeping it far from the shore, which accounts for the fact that a few still remain. Thus in 1892, the Hoonah took sixty sea otter in Lituya Bay, and in 1889 when I was traveling with the Tlingit I saw four newly killed sea otter in a hut at the entrance to Cross Sound. The destruction of the first Russian settlement at Sitka was due largely to [Tlingit resentment at] the hunting of the sea otter by the Aleuts under Russian protection, for the Tlingit law with respect to the inviolability of family [clan] and tribal hunting and fishing rights was most exact, and this infringement by the Aleuts spurred them to action.

[In 1880, according to the reports by Commander Beardslee (1882:57–77), the Hoonahs deeply resented the presence of several canoes of Tsimshian hunters from Fort Simpson, British Columbia, who were shooting sea otters on the Hoonah hunting grounds. The Tlingit appealed to Commander Beardslee to prevent such poaching, predicting that it would lead to war. A miner named Willoughby who was living with the Hoonah sent the Tsimshian a letter (which they could read), reminding them of the treaty which prohibited their intrusion in Alaska, but the Tsimshian, who were supported by the Hudson Bay Company's factor and by a Methodist minister at Port Simpson, vowed to return with sixty canoes, prepared to fight the Tlingit, the "Bostons" and their warship, the USS *Jamestown.* Only the personal intervention of Commander Beardslee prevented trouble, for he obtained a promise from Colonel Powell, R.A., at Port

Yakutat bow for hunting sea otter: longitudinal side and back views, and cross sections. (Pen and ink sketches by G. T. Emmons. AMNH.)

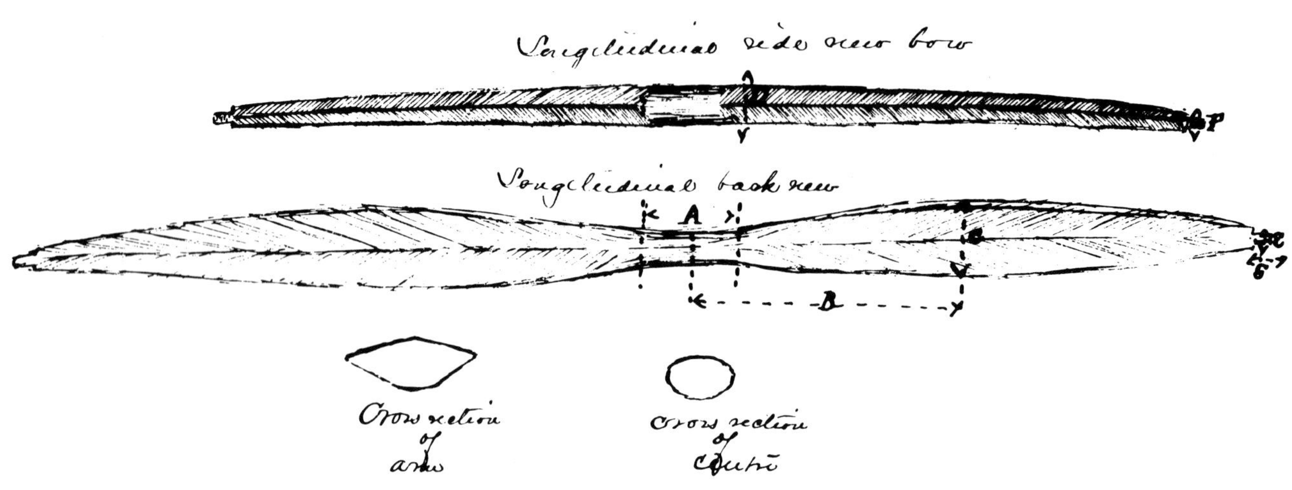

Townsend to prohibit such an expedition, and also a promise from the Hoonah chiefs not to fight. The matter was reported both to Washington and Ottawa, and we gather that no confrontation took place.]

For a century after the introduction of firearms, the natives generally carried on the sea otter hunt with spear [harpoon] and bow and arrow, although they might carry a gun in the canoe. The Yakutat, as late as 1885, hunted in the primitive manner with these implements, in the belief that firearms tended to drive away the animals. The [main] hunting season was from March to June, although individuals might hunt at any time. Preparatory to hunting, the man and his wife bathed and put on clean clothes. The wife tied a band around her waist which she was not permitted to remove until the hunters returned. Women never went in the canoe in hunting or in preparation for the hunt, for everything connected with the sex was believed to be offensive to the sea otter.

The Yakutat were the last of the Tlingit to hunt in the primitive manner. They went out in the ocean, ten and twenty miles offshore, while the other Tlingit kept well inshore. They hunted in parties of ten to twenty canoes, stretching out in a line two to three hundred yards apart. When someone sighted a sea otter, he raised his paddle to indicate the direction, and the canoes would close in, encircling the prey. The sea otter then became a target for the arrows [of the whole fleet]. The object was not to inflict a mortal wound, but simply to penetrate the skin with the tiny, barbed copper head of the arrow. This was detachable, but secured by a line to the shaft in such a way that the latter acted as a drag and impeded the movements of the sea otter underwater, bringing it quickly to the surface. When, with many arrows attached, the animal was exhausted and unable to dive, it was killed with a club and taken into the canoe. The arrows of each hunter were distinguished by private marks on the bone [socket piece] or [by colored yarns] interwoven in the sinew cord. By an agreement as to the [winning] location of the arrowhead in the body of the sea otter, the owner [or winner] would take the whole skin and pay a given number of blankets to the others. [The arrowhead nearest the tail was usually the winner.] The spear [ordinary harpoon] was always carried, and if the animal approached sufficiently near, it was used. Also the gun might be employed if the sea otter should break out of the circle.

Before starting out on the hunt, the weather was carefully considered, and the shaman might be consulted. In landing from the hunt on the open shore, which was always fraught with danger from the line of heavy breakers, the most expert canoeman would make the attempt first. If he were successful, it would be easy for the others to follow, since those on shore could handle the other canoes as they landed. This storm-swept, steep, boulder-strewn shore of the Malaspina Glacier [west of Yakutat Bay] is photographed on my memory, for I made two landings here in 1885. [This may have been in the summer of 1886, when Emmons, then with the *Pinta,* landed Schwatka and Seton-Karr, the members of their expedition to climb Mount Saint Elias, and their baggage, through the surf on the shore near what was then "Icy Bay" (de Laguna 1972:189). Emmons not infrequently

Harpoon arrows and spear heads. (Pencil sketches by G. T. Emmons. AMNH.) (a) Six copper sea otter harpoon arrowheads, Yakutat. (b) Bone salmon spear head, Sitka. (c) Cedar shaft of harpoon arrow. (d) Whale bone foreshaft [socket piece] for harpoon arrow. (e) Assembled sea otter harpoon arrow with copper head. (f) Ivory head of sea otter spear, Yakutat. (g) Quiver (greatly reduced) for sea otter harpoon arrows, Yakutat.

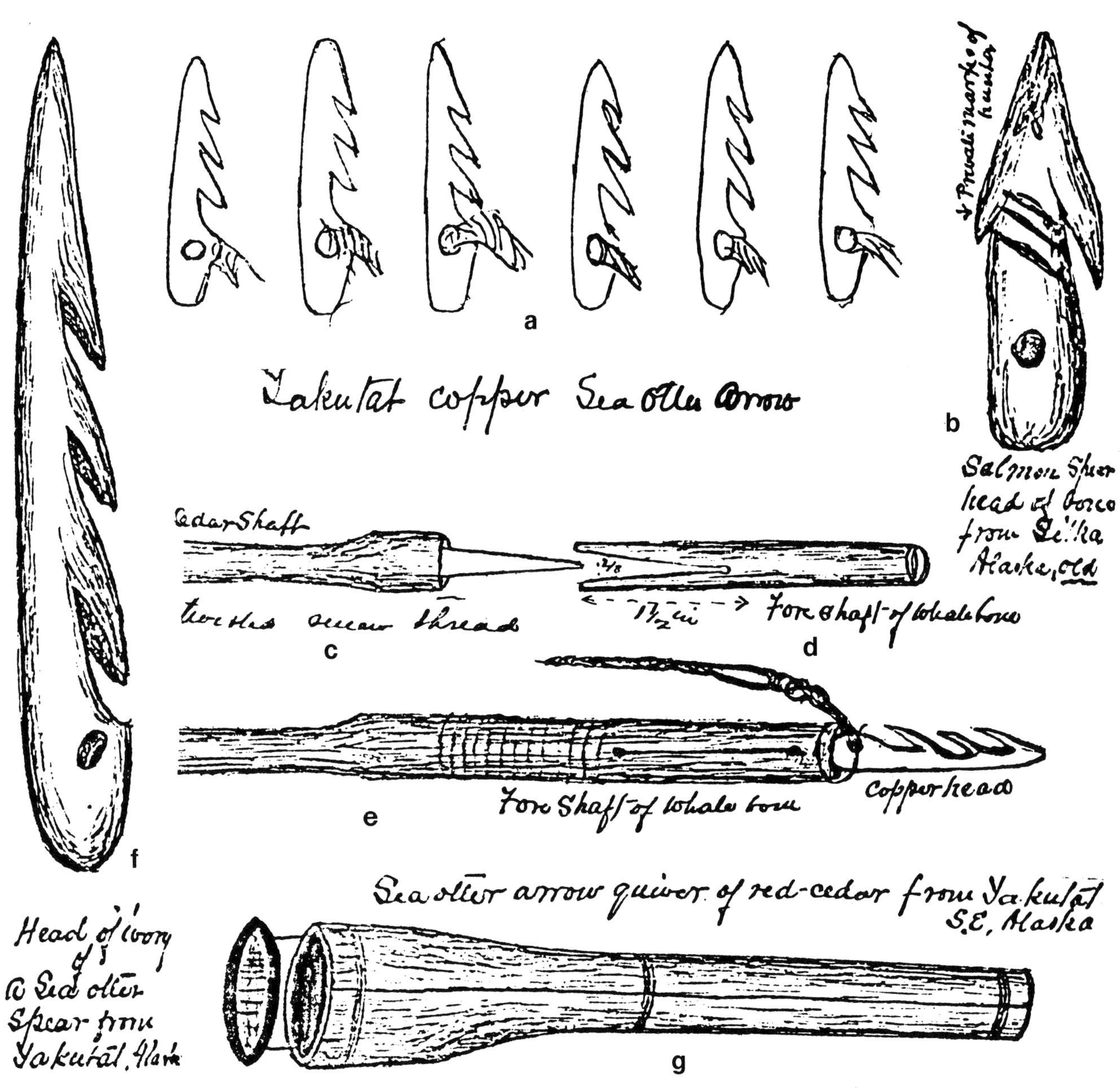

has made a mistake of a year in his dates.] The spirit, *Na goot ku* [?], birdlike in form, that lives in the Fairweather Range [Saint Elias Range?], is the friend of the sea otter hunters, and is invoked to send offshore breezes and calms.

The whole hunting paraphernalia of the Yakutat [used for sea otter hunting] differed from that of the other Tlingit. The canoe was the *tch-yosh* [čiyá·š], large enough for only two or three occupants, very narrow and sharp at both ends, with the projecting ramlike [forked] bow, not found in any other type on the Pacific Coast [except among the Eyak]. The hunters knelt amidships and paddled together, two strokes on one side and then two on the other, using long paddles with narrow pointed blades. The whole outfit was designed for rough water in an open seaway.

The bow, *sucks* [ṡáqs], was made of a single piece of spruce: plain, straight, broad, and from four to four and one-half feet long. The belly was rounded and the back flattened, the latter usually shaped with two inclined planes that met along the center [line] and formed a slight ridge. The grip [in the middle of the bow] was rounded for a distance of some three inches. The nocks were short and straight. The bowstring was of porpoise or whale sinew, made of many fine strands twisted and laid up in square or flat sennit. An eye was formed at one end, and the standing part was passed through this to form a loop which was passed over a nock at one end of the bow. The other end of the bowstring, sometimes reduced in size, was half-hitched around its own part after passing around the other nock.

The arrow, *tchunet* [ču·ne·t], was the most ingenious, most delicately proportioned and elaborately fitted of any on the continent. It was of the same type [harpoon arrow] as that found to the westward as far as the Aleutian Islands, and since the Tlingit were latecomers to the northern [Gulf] coast, it seems probable that this was borrowed, and not original with them. The Yakutat arrow is more uniform in its proportions, however, and more carefully made [than other Tlingit arrows], and the barbed head was always of copper.

[Although sea otter bones were very common in early historic sites in the Angoon area (de Laguna 1960:93), no small barbed heads suitable for harpoon arrows were found there (p. 112), while such small heads were common at Yakutat sites (de Laguna et al. 1964:135–36), where the sea otter harpoon arrow seems to have been in use in prehistoric times. Bone heads were more common than metal, however, even though the prehistoric Yakutat people had native copper.]

The arrow was about thirty inches long, and composed of two principal parts: a shaft of yellow cedar (sometimes of pine or spruce), and a foreshaft [socket piece] of whale bone. The shaft was very delicately formed, tapering to a bell-shaped nock with a rounded notch. It was uniformly painted with red-brown ochre. Three eagle feathers, symmetrically cut and evenly spaced, were seized at both ends with very fine twisted sinew thread. The fore end of the shaft expanded to a shoulder, the diameter of the bone foreshaft [socket piece], and the latter was cut out to fit over a wedge-shaped projection [or tongue] on the end of the wooden shaft. When [these two parts were] fitted together, a thin strip of intestine or bark was wrapped about the juncture, over which a seizing of sinew was passed. The socket piece was about one-fourth the length of the shaft. Its head was hollowed out to receive a peg of wood, split in halves, and in the split thus formed, was fitted a very sharp copper head with three barbs, seldom exceeding one and one-fourth inches in length. Through a perforation in the base of the head was rove a sinew line, laid up round or flat, about five feet long. This terminated in a span [the two ends of which were] attached to the shaft [at widely spaced places]. When prepared for use, the span and line were closely coiled around the shaft, the barbed head fitted in place, and a slip-loop hitch was taken in the slack, under the last turn around the shaft. When the barbed head entered the sea otter, it was automatically detached from the shaft; the slightest pull loosened the line, this uncoiled,

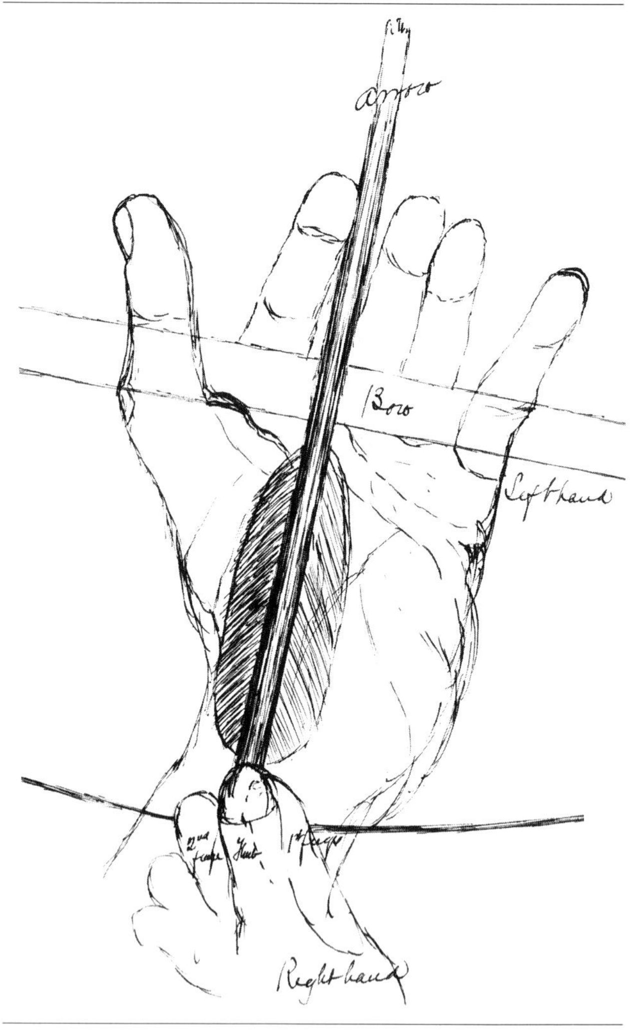

Tlingit bow and arrow. (AMNH.) Sketch by Emmons to indicate how the bow is held by the left hand and the arrow with bowstring by the right hand.

and the arrow acted both as a drag and a buoy. [The heavy bone socket piece steadied the arrow in flight, and after the sea otter was harpooned, it made the shaft float vertically in the water, with the feathered butt sticking up above the surface.] An arrow that had taken a sea otter was considered lucky, and was consequently prized. [Yakutat sea otter bows and arrows are illustrated in de Laguna 1972, pls. 108–12. Compare the harpoon arrows with the arrows used for hunting on land, pl. 108 left, and with the barbed seal spear head, pl. 112 top.]

In shooting, the bow was held horizontally in the left hand, with the thumb and little finger in front and the other fingers in the rear, so that the bow rested in the hollow of the hand. The nock of the arrow was held between the thumb and the second joint of the forefinger of the right hand, but some hunters held it between the first joint of the first and second fingers. The shaft was steadied between the first and second fingers of the left hand [which served as a sight]. The arrow described a curve in flight, unless the sea otter came up alongside, when it was fired direct.

[In southeastern Alaska, the Indians are said to have hunted sea otter in fleets of canoes, each holding two to four men. This surround method was evidently introduced by the Russians and their Aleut or Pacific Eskimo hunters. The Tlingit arrowhead was detachable, but not barbed; it was not a harpoon arrow. Probably most sea otter were taken with a barbed harpoon, like those used for seals (de Laguna 1960:112).]

The quiver, *tchunet tar-kate* [čuˑneˑt daˑkeˑt], "arrow cover," was a cylindrical case of cedar, enlarged at the mouth [to accommodate the feathered ends of the arrows]. It was made by splitting a small log in two, hollowing out the halves, and joining them together with seizings of spruce root, hide, or sinew, in countersunk grooves about each end and at the middle. A neatly fitted top was attached on a sliding loop, the ends of which were knotted through holes near the edge of the mouth. The quiver was often colored dark red-brown. The arrows are put in head-first.

[The wooden quiver was used only (?) in the canoe. When hunting on land, the Tlingit probably used a quiver and bow case of hide, like those of the Athabaskans.]

The hunter often carried in his canoe box the right humerus of a sea otter. Before going out, he would hold it up to his mouth and talk through the tiny hole at the [distal] end, asking what his luck would be. Then he took it between his thumb and forefinger and flipped it up in the air. If it fell and stood with the ridge up, he would be successful. [If it landed on the flatter side, he would get nothing.] In later years, seal hunters used the seal humerus in the same way. [See "The Dice Game" in Chapter 16.]

The skin of the sea otter was opened at the rear, drawn [whole] over the body and head, and stretched on a drying board the shape of the pelt.

LAND ANIMAL HUNTING: ABORIGINAL WEAPONS*

The trapping and hunting of such fur-bearing animals as the bear, wolf, fox, marten, mink, and land otter, was carried on in the spring when the pelts were prime. Beaver were taken in the winter when the lakes were frozen. Deer and mountain goat were hunted in the fall, when they had taken on fat. Southeastern Alaska is not a game country, except for the abundance of deer and bear, and the people have always looked to the water for food and clothing.

In the pursuit of land animals, deadfalls and snares played a more important part than the arrow and spear, and early in the nineteenth century these primitive weapons were discarded for firearms.

The bow used for war and hunting land animals was given up after the introduction of guns, but a few old specimens found here and there seem to be of the same type as that used by the Yakutat for sea otter: a plain stick of spruce or hemlock. Its manufacture was described to me by an old Sitka hunter, who explained that the old-time bow was made of hemlock from the cold (north) side of the tree, which had the greater degree of toughness. The wood was cut in winter when the sap was down, and was well seasoned by hanging under the roof near the smokehole. The outer side of the wood formed the back of the bow. When shaped, it was tempered by wrapping it in damp seaweed and placing it over heated stones from which the fire had been removed, where it remained an hour or two. When removed, it was plunged in cold water for a few minutes, then rubbed down with the hand and tested. If it sprung easily, it was considered a success. The bowstring was of twisted or laid-up whale sinew. Another old man said that the bow was made of spruce selected from a tree growing on high land, and from a branch or young tree that curved in its growth. The outside wood was used.

**Editor's note:* I verified references to La Pérouse and Vancouver, and added additional information from them, as well as from Mourelle, Riobo, Marchand, field notes of de Laguna and McClellan (1950), and the letter from Emmons to his son, describing the whip sling.

[That the bow was preferably made of yew is suggested by the fact that both tree and bow are called ṡáqs. The same word, ṡáqs, may be used to cover both the bow and the arrow.]

La Pérouse (1799, 1:407), who was at Lituya Bay on the Gulf Coast of Alaska in July 1786, described the weapons of the Tlingit as a dagger, wooden lance, and bow and arrows. "The arrows are commonly headed with copper; but the bow has nothing particular, and is much weaker than those of many other nations."

Vancouver (1801, 4:136–37) encountered some Indians, presumably Sanya (?), in Portland Canal in July 1793, who seemed to have been prepared either to trade or to loot. "Their bows were well constructed, and their arrows, with which they were plentifully supplied, appeared but rude, and were pointed with bone or iron."

Several older arrows [collected by Emmons] confirm this statement. They consist of wooden shafts with iron or copper leaf-shaped heads with long tangs, plain or slightly barbed at the base of the blade. Slate and bone heads were also employed, but few of these heads have been collected.

[See de Laguna et al. 1964:138–47, figs. 14, 17, pl. 14 *a* to *e*, for discussions of Tlingit stone, bone, and copper arrowheads; and de Laguna 1972, pl. 108 left, for arrows with iron heads, from Yakutat. Whether barbed or plain, Tlingit arrowheads are said to have been detachable, so that they would remain in the wound when the animal was struck. The arrow shaft could then be retrieved and fitted with another head. The bow and arrow do not seem to have been much used in fighting.

[Mourelle (in La Pérouse 1799, 1:247), who was at Bucareli Bay in 1779, described the Klawak Tlingit bows as having a string "twisted like the base-strings of our best musical instruments," and Father Riobo, who was on the same expedition, wrote (in Thornton 1918:224): "Their arrows are very finely made: some of them are pointed with flint, some with bone, but most of them have heads of copper and iron and they are very sharp."]

Arrowheads are called *tsar-kuth* [possibly ṡa·q kát, "bone barbed-head"], or *tlark* [ƛá·q, the more common word]. Blunt bone heads [gúƛ, or qáš gał at Yakutat] for stunning birds and small animals were fitted to the shaft with sinew seizing. Many of the bone heads, variously shaped and some tipped with metal, have been collected among the Tlingit, but these are predominantly of Athabaskan workmanship and have been brought out by trading parties [of Tlingit]. Ptarmigan feathers were considered best for this type of arrow, for the ptarmigan is so swift in flight, but the feathers of the hawk, eagle, and other birds were also used. [Arrows at Angoon were described as being without feathers (de Laguna 1960:114) on the shaft, ču·ne·t.]

Spears, used either for war or for hunting, had stout shafts of hemlock, spruce, or of some heavy piece of driftwood found on the shore. They were from six to eight feet long, with a [blade] of slate or copper, and later of iron. The metal blade was shaped like the older one of stone. [See also de Laguna et al. 1964, pp. 124–27, fig. 13 *a* and *d*.] The most primitive spear was of wood with the end hardened by burning, and then pointed [as described by La Pérouse (1799, 1:407)]. Vancouver (1801, 4:136) described the spears of natives he met in Portland Canal: ". . . their spears, about sixteen feet long, were pointed with iron, wrought in several simple forms, amongst which some were barbed." [The last may have been harpoons for salmon or seal; it is uncertain whether the other spears were for hunting or war. One Indian (p. 134) was armed with six or eight spears, as well as with bow and arrow, dagger, and armor.]

[Mourelle (in La Pérouse 1799, 1:247) wrote that the "offensive weapons" of the Tlingit (Klawak) of Bucareli Bay in 1779, included "lances, four yards long, headed with iron." Father Riobo (in Thornton 1918:224) wrote of these: "Their lances are very well made and are very straight and regular in form; some having a spear head twenty-four inches in length with a very long and well made staff."

[Marchand (Fleurieu 1801, 1:342–43) saw what were evidently two kinds of spears at Sitka Sound in 1791. (Neither was the harpoon he described on p. 344.)

> Their pikes, which, no doubt, were, at first, tipped with a hard stone, tapering to a point, or with a fish-bone, are at this day armed with an iron head of European manufacture. Their lances, the ancient shape of which is not known, are at present composed of two pieces; of the staff, about fifteen or eighteen feet long, and of the iron, nowise inferior to that of the halbert of parade with which our parish-beadles used to be equipped.

Vancouver and Marchand [see above] give the length of spears as from sixteen to eighteen feet, but I think they referred to the long fish and seal spear [harpoon, ʔá·da·], for the spear used for war and for bear was never over eight feet in length. The shafts were sometimes ornamentally carved in low relief.

[The Tlingit may formerly have had spears or lances of two lengths: the shorter, used for ordinary hunting and close-in fighting, called *woo-son-nee* (wu·sá·ni); and the longer, used especially in hunting bears when they emerged from their

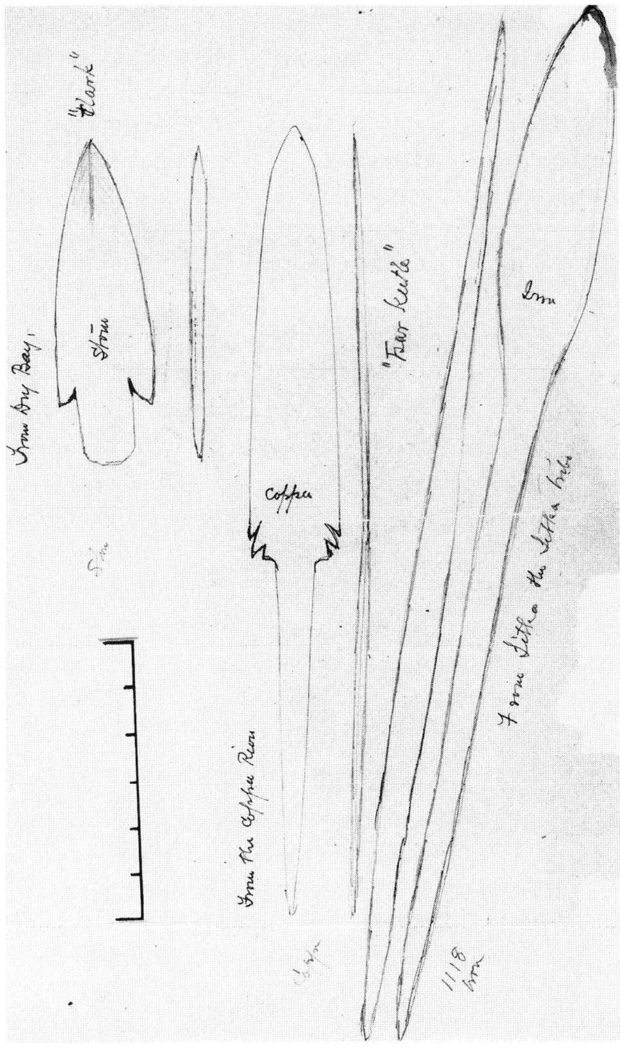

Stone (slate?) arrowhead, tlark [ƛá·q], *from Dry Bay. Copper arrowhead,* tsar kutle [ca· kát, *"seal spear head"*], *from the Copper River. Iron spear or arrowhead from Sitka. (Pencil sketches by G. T. Emmons. AMNH.)*

dens in the spring and were induced to impale themselves on it. This longer spear, ca·g̣áɬ, seems to have been used when fighting from a canoe.]

Even with the acquisition of firearms, the spear was retained, but except for bear hunting, it was essentially a weapon of war.

[Emmons described the whip sling in a letter to his son, Thornton (letter in BCPA). He thought of it only as a toy, not a real hunting weapon, although it was described by the Angoon natives as formerly used in hunting deer, or even bear (de Laguna and McClellan, field notes, 1950):

> My dear Tonta:
>
> All the little Indian boys here are playing with an arrow-thrower. The game is called "arrow game," *Tchu-qwon* [ǯúx̣ʷa·, "whip sling"]; and I am going to tell you how you can make it. First you want a stick about 2 feet long, and from ½ to ⅝ inch in diameter, smaller at one end than the other. It had best be a little hickory stick that has a good spring to it, and not too heavy. At the smaller end tie a small piece of cord, smaller than top cord, and this must be about 6 inches shorter than the stick. In the other end [of the cord] put a knot.
>
> Now this is the throwing stick complete. [At Angoon the whip sling had a handle of spruce wood, and a deerskin thong tied to one end, with a knot at the other end of the thong.]
>
> Now the arrow is made of a piece of shingle, pointed at one end and flat on the other end, like the feather end of the arrow. [The sketch in the letter shows the arrow as 15 inches long, with a notch in the plane of the flattened end, 7 inches from the butt end and 8 inches from the point.] At [blank] inches from the point of the arrow, cut a notch just deep enough to fit the string so that the notch will catch. Then it is all ready.
>
> To throw it, put string with knot in notch. The arrow, from the head being heavy, will swing point down. Then bring stick back and swing it forward like throwing a stone, and as the stick goes forward, it casts the arrow a long distance. [Sketch of man throwing the dart from the whip sling.]
>
> Do not throw near anyone.

[According to Angoon informants (1950), the arrow or dart, ču·ne·t, was of wood with an expanded, flattened butt, notched like an arrow for a bow. Sometimes a single feather was attached, to enable the hunter to spot his dart, but it was not used to aid it in flight. The rest of the arrow or dart shaft was circular in cross section, slightly expanding toward the head. In it were cut two notches to engage the knot of the whip sling: that nearer the middle of the arrow was used for close range shooting; that nearer the head for longer ranges. (In the Alaska State Museum, Juneau, an exhibit of the whip sling has two separate darts, with notches differently placed for the two ranges, not two notches on one dart, as was the case of a model carved at Angoon.) The hunter carried a skin quiver, da·ke·t, to hold six darts. The dart had a head of bone, with a socket, but was not barbed. Since no model of the head was made, we do not know exactly what was meant by this description. The informant may have been describing a common type of arrow on which the wooden shaft expands at the fore end, into which is inserted a plain pinlike point of bone or hardwood, four to six inches long. This is detachable. The end of the arrow is expanded so that when the animal is hit, the whole shaft will not penetrate, but will fall off, to be retrieved. The point or head is unbarbed.]

Hunting gear. (Sketches by G. T. Emmons. AMNH.) Top. *Deer call, made of two pieces of stick, A, A′, lashed together at the ends, with a blade of grass, B, between them.* Middle. *Bullet mold, with "iron die which is heated in fire, then placed in slot between halves of wooden bullet mould, to burn holes for shot."* Bottom. *Musket guard, to which are attached three pieces of leather for caps, and a pricker for the primer.*

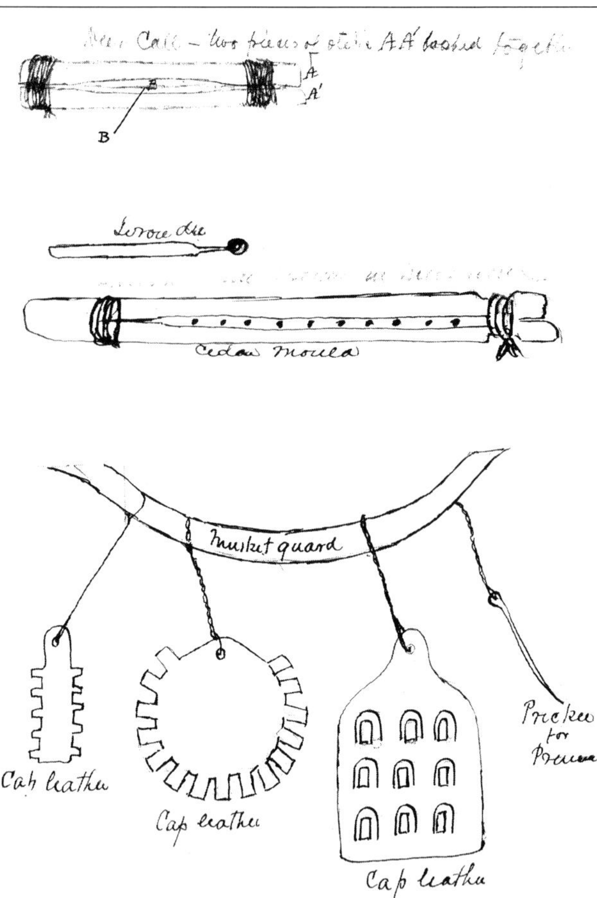

FIREARMS*

The earliest guns were of the flintlock type, followed by the percussion cap musket. These were still to be found in use as late as 1885, although breech-loading rifles were more in demand. The accessories used with these early firearms were carried in a hunting bag. It contained a powder pouch of intestines, with a mouthpiece of bone or wood. Attached to it was a measure or charger of horn, which, for convenience, was often the stopper. There was also a small double basket containing shot, *ut-tu-qwu´n-see tar-ka´te* [ʔat tux̣únši da·ke·t], a leather case for bullets and wadding, and a section of goat horn for caps. To charge the pan of the flintlock, a bone tube for powder was carried suspended around the neck, and attached to the [trigger] guard by a string was a metal pricker to clean the touch hole or nipple. A convenient method of carrying caps was by fitting them over corresponding lugs cut in a piece of leather which was tied to the guard. A thin, paperlike fungus growth, found in rotten wood, and shredded inner bark of the cedar served as wadding. When manufactured bullets were not to be had, pieces of lead or native copper were beaten into slugs, and these were often preferred for bear hunting.

The ingenuity of the Tlingit is shown in the manufacture of shot. The mold consisted of a piece of cedar split in half for a certain distance like a pair of native tongs. At the meeting of the upper edges, a groove extended the length of the split, [in which were deep holes] at short intervals. [To make these holes], a small iron spike with a narrow neck and a knob at the end, the size of the proposed shot, was put into the fire, and when sufficiently heated was placed between the halves of the mold to burn out the hollows. To run the shot, the halves of the mold were drawn together and lashed at the open end. The mold was held at a slight inclination and the molten lead ran down the groove to fill the holes through the openings [that had been formed by the neck of the iron spike].

[Emmons gives the word for a stone bullet mold, *kuk-qwart-kli-ate* (probably kaq^{w}á·ƛ̣i ye̥·t, "[metal] melting receptacle"). This would have been equally appropriate for the wooden mold.]

**Editor's note:* To this section I have contributed a discussion of the introduction of firearms to the Tlingit and the growth of the Indians' dependence on them, based on the reports of Marchand, Malaspina, Vancouver, von Langsdorff, and Lütké, and the statement quoted by Okun about cannon.

When traveling by canoe, the Tlingit kept the gun at hand in a case of hard tanned sealskin, the hair intact on the outside. Wooden boxes were also used as gun cases. In the house, the gun was usually kept loaded, standing against the wall of the sleeping place.

[The first guns (ʔú·na·, from -ʔun, "to shoot") were already in the hands of the Tlingit before the end of the eighteenth century. During the 1780s, the European explorers found no guns among the Tlingit, nor were the Indians eager to obtain them in trade; iron seems to have been the article most desired. During that period, however, the Tlingit often saw the effects of guns in the hands of the whites, and were surprised that bullets could pierce their native wooden and hide armor.

[Marchand (Fleurieu 1801, 1:343), who was at Sitka Sound in August 1791, saw only a few muskets, but those were without ammunition. He believed:

. . . the English, in their visits, distributed a few muskets on the part of the coast which borders on TCHINKITÂNAY Bay [Sitka Sound] . . . . Yet it seems that the English, in giving them muskets, have not furnished the mover and the *primum mobile* which render them formidable; for a native of TCHINKITÂNAY who had possessed one, gave the French to understand he had broken it in a passion, because, said he, the musket always went *crik,* and would never go *pouhou.*

[In July 1793, Vancouver (1801, 4:134–43) found the natives of Portland Canal (presumably Sanya?) apparently without firearms, and using spears to kill bears. They wanted to trade their furs, but rejected everything that was offered: iron, copper, blue cloth, a looking glass, and other trinkets, demanding only guns and ammunition, which Vancouver would not furnish. Later, at Traitor's Cove on the western arm of Behm Canal (pp. 169–83), the Tlingit (Sanya) first began to trade, then attacked Vancouver's boats, and succeeded in stealing whatever they could snatch up, including three muskets and a fowling piece. Although they apparently had some firearms of their own, they attacked with spears, and when one man tried to shoot Vancouver, his gun misfired. They were driven away finally and Vancouver's party escaped. Vancouver was convinced that the Indians had planned the attack, pretending an interest only in trade, but became aggressive when the British seemed to be weak or unsuspecting. Vancouver (1801, 4:179–81) summed up his impressions as to the causes for the attack:

It was manifestly evident that they [the Indians] had been acquainted with civilized commercial people, by the muskets and other European commodities in their possession; and when we considered the peculiar behaviour of the first man who visited us, we had reason to suspect that they had been ill-treated in their traffic with white men. This Indian, by means of signs and words too expressive to be mistaken, gave us clearly to understand, that they had reason to complain of one or more muskets that they had purchased, which burst into pieces on being fired: a fraud which I know has been practiced too frequently, not only on this coast, but at the Sandwich [Hawaiian], and other islands in the Pacific Ocean. These defects have not arisen from ignorance or mismanagement on the part of the Indians, but from the baseness of the metal and imperfect workmanship of the firearms. [These traders were not only dishonest in selling defective goods, but stirred up trouble, to increase the demand for weapons.]

. . . They have been likewise eager to instruct the natives in the use of European arms of all descriptions; and have shewn by their own example, that they consider gain as the only object of pursuit; and whither [*sic*] this be acquired by fair and honorable means, or otherwise, so long as the advantage is secured, the manner how it is obtained seems to have been, with too many of them, but a very secondary consideration.

Under a conviction that repeated acts of such injustice had taken place, it was not unreasonable to suppose, that these people, who had experienced the like frauds, should be of opinion that our muskets, and the other arms that we carried for our protection, were of a superior quality to those they had procured from the traders. This, indeed, was proved by their praising ours and comparing them with those in their possession; and they might possibly from thence have been tempted to trespass on the laws of honesty, in order to acquire by force those really valuable commodities, which, by fair commercial dealings on their part, they could only procure in a defective state. [Vancouver also speculated that they may have wanted to get revenge.]

[Near Bell Island, at the head of Behm Canal, one of Vancouver's boat parties met a small party of suspicious Indians who seemed ready to oppose their landing. One had a musket, another a pistol; the remaining five only bows and arrows (Vancouver 1801, 4:219–20). These were perhaps the X̣e·ł-qʷa·n, Wolf 31, of the Stikine, at that time an independent group. When Vancouver was anchored a little later in August 1793, in Port Stewart on the western arm of Behm Canal, and was trading with a party of Indians (Stikine), a large canoe appeared, conveying the great Stikine chief, Ononistoy, rendered by Emmons as *Kho-na-nest-ta,* "Wandering in a Strange Country" (G̣una·ne·stí), referring to Raven's wanderings. His party was "armed with pistols or blunderbusses, very bright, and in good order." At first it looked as if the two groups might fight, but soon "their arms were again returned to their proper places; their pistols and ammunition were carefully wrapped up, and a perfect reconciliation seemed to have taken place on both sides" (Vancouver 1801, 4:226–27). It is evident that these Indians, presumably all Stikine, knew how to care for their arms. They wanted more firearms and ammunition, but when these were refused, continued an amicable trade with the British for blue cloth, files, tin kettles, and other goods.

[In 1791, Malaspina saw no guns at Yakutat. In 1794, however, when Vancouver's ship, the *Chatham,* under Lieutenant Puget, visited Yakutat Bay, he reported (Vancouver 1801, 5:403) that the natives had "six excellent muskets, kept in the highest order." Later that month, Vancouver's exploring party under Lieutenant Whidbey was ambushed in Lynn Canal by a large force of Chilkat Indians (Vancouver 1801, 5:433), who were

well provided not only with spears, but with seven muskets, and some brass blunderbusses, all in most excellent order. [A chief in one of the canoes] hailed the yawl with a speaking trumpet, which he held in one hand, and had a spying glass in the other; a powder horn was flung across his shoulders, and a clean bright brass blunderbuss was lying near him, which he frequently took up and pointed at Mr. Whidbey, in such a manner as evidently shewed he was no stranger to the use and management of such weapons. [He was also adroit in his use of telescope and trumpet.]

It would appear, therefore, that the Tlingit must have obtained their first firearms about 1790, but that within a very few years had become skilled in their use. This led naturally to the inevitable obsolescence of the aboriginal weapons: whip sling, bow and arrow, and short spear for war and for most hunting; armor and wooden helmets came to be used only as ceremonial garments. Although Marchand believed that the muskets he saw at Sitka had come from the British, we should not rule out the possibility that they may have been obtained from the fearless "Boston" skippers, who left few records of their exploits, and who seemed to care very little about the dangers of their trade to other whites, provided they could make their fortunes in one or two voyages. According to Howay (1973:2), who compiled lists of vessels engaged in the fur trade on the Northwest Coast, from the first records of 1785: "At the outset the trade was entirely British; but from 1789 onward the American traders, principally from Boston, gradually absorbed it, until about 1800 it had become the practical monopoly of the city of Boston." It had already begun to dwindle by 1805, as the sea otter became scarce. The Russians (Tikhmenev [1861–63] 1978:66) blamed the British for encouraging the Tlingit destruction of their fort at Sitka, and for providing the natives with guns and powder. Certainly, the Yakutat and Sitka Tlingit acquired rich booty in firearms, even including cannon, and in ammunition, when they overran the Russian posts at Sitka (1802) and Yakutat (1805). Captain D'Wolf (1861:48) observed at Sitka in 1805–6: "Both sexes are expert in the use of fire-arms, and are excellent judges of their quality." Von Langsdorff (1814, 2:131–32), whom D'Wolf accompanied to visit the displaced Sitka Tlingit living at or near Chatham Strait, wrote:

> Their arms consist principally of bows and arrows; but since their trade with the American States, they have acquired so large a stock of guns, powder, and shot, that they scarcely use their arrows except in hunting sea-otters and sea-dogs [seals]. Captain Dwolf assured me that the best English guns may now be bought cheaper upon the north-west coast of America than in England: if the lock be the least injured, as there is no one who can repair it, the weapon becomes useless to them: it has therefore been found very advantageous, in the latter years, to send a gunsmith with every vessel that comes to trade here, and buy up the useless guns in one place, which are repaired and sold as new ones in another. The Kaluschians nevertheless understand the qualities of a good gun so well, that it is impossible to impose a bad one upon them: even the women are accustomed to the use of fire-arms, and often go out on the hunting parties.

[Within little more than a generation after the first introduction of firearms, the Tlingit hunters had become dependent on them for subsistence. Lütké (1835, 1:128–30) recognized that the Russians had made a great mistake in not excluding foreign traders from Russian America from the very beginning, while there were still plenty of sea otter, and more important, the civilized Americans would then not have been able to supply the savages with the guns that made them so dangerous to the Russians. But now (1827) it was too late: the otters had been destroyed, and the Tlingit had become so dependent on firearms that they could not kill a single animal without them. He therefore deplored the Russian policy of refusing to sell guns to the natives, who were thus forced to turn to the foreigners for trade; whereas if the Russians would provide the necessary guns, they would be able to secure the benefits of the natives' furs, and could give up the futile efforts to keep the foreign traders away. The governor of the company, Muravyov (in his report of 1832) was quoted in Okun 1951:87. "It is well known . . . that cannon may be found in many of the sections inhabited by the Kolosh. Members of the crew of the royal frigate 'Apollo,' which is cruising along the coast of the colonies, have reported that during their stay in the Kaigani [southern Prince of Wales Island], they had seen a small fortress with cannon, under the American flag, and that every day they fire a cannon at sunset and raise the flag. Exceedingly large stores of rifles and gunpowder may be seen in that fortress." But this exaggerated statement is more proof of Russian fears than of the reality.]

LAND ANIMAL HUNTING: TRAPS AND SNARES*

[The bear was the most revered animal hunted by the Tlingit, and its hunting was surrounded by religious observances. Before going hunting, the man should fast and remain continent for four days, and also wash daily in cold water. After a bear had been killed, the hunter sang (presumably a special song for bears) and red ochre was put on the skin. In addition to the following rather fragmentary notes about the treatment of bears, Emmons kept a game diary in 1896, in which information about bears was entered (BCPA). There

Editor's note: I wrote the first paragraph on bears, and to the description by Emmons of bear hunting added data from his notes, from his "Game Diary" of 1896, and from a clipping he had saved (in BCPA). The description of the deadfall for mice I based on the sketch made by Emmons.

are essentially two species of bear known to the Tlingit: the large brown grizzly, "Kodiak bear," or "cinnamon bear," *Ursus horribilis* according to some naturalists, although there is great disagreement over the proper classification of the many varieties in Alaska. This is *the* bear for the Tlingit, *hootz* or *hutz* (xú·c). In addition there is the common black bear, *Ursus americanus*, with a black and a brown variant even in the same litter, as well as several recognized varieties. This is called *tseek* (s̓i·k); while the name for any kind of bear is ci·ne·t. One variety of Alaskan black bear is the so-called glacier bear, *Ursus americanus emmonsii, klate-utardy tseek* or *klate-ukah-tseek* (λe·t -?- s̓i·k), "snowlike blackbear," or *tseek noon* (s̓i·k nú·n), "gray blackbear." Emmons failed to distinguish between the large, true brown bear and the brown variant of the black bear.]

Both black and brown bear are found everywhere on the mainland shore, the glacier bear only about the snow and ice fields. On the islands the distribution is not so general, for while both brown and black bear may be found on some islands, on others only one species exists, and the glacier bear is confined to the mainland. The brown bear, *hootz* [xú·c], has all the attributes of the grizzly, and while ordinarily shy, is most dangerous when cornered or with young, and was seldom if ever hunted in early days with the primitive weapons, although it was snared and trapped. When found hibernating in winter, it was killed with the spear. [This is because the fur is in prime condition in February, before the bears emerge from their dens. Later in the season, the big brown bear commences to rub the fur off the middle of the back of the neck and to scratch bare the underparts and side of the stomach. Also exposure to the sun makes the fur of any bear lifeless and it loses its deep color. These observations were recorded by Emmons from Paul Riddell, Juneau, June 1896, BCPA.]

If a Tlingit were killed by a [brown] bear, it was incumbent on the men of his family [lineage, clan] to form a party and go to the vicinity and kill a bear, since the bears were considered to form a family like those of human beings, and the law of a life for a life had to be carried out.

The brown bear was looked upon with great consideration, not only as a dangerous antagonist, but because of the belief of his connection with man in early days [clan myths about a man who mated with a she-bear, and of a woman who married a male bear], and possibly from the fact that the bear constituted one of the principal clan crests [obtained through these supernatural encounters]. When met, the bear was addressed as if almost human [that is, by the kin terms the speaker would use to the member of a clan that had the Bear totem], and after it was killed certain observances were carried out in its honor so that its spirit might be appeased. In 1894 at Sitka, two brown bears were killed, and when the skins were stretched to dry, eagle down was put on the heads so that their spirits would feel honored. The bones of the head and the feet were either buried deep in the ground, or cast into the sea. But withal, its flesh was eaten and its pelt was used like that of any other animal.

[Some of this information was taken from a newspaper story, which Emmons had clipped from a Sitka paper, date unknown. It continued:

> One boy said: "The bear is the biggest animal in the woods and we call him chief, chief o' the woods, for he is a brave fighter and has power over his mates." When a bear is killed the head and feet are roasted and while the savory meal is cooking the successful Nimrod and his partners adorn themselves with emblems of their tribe [clan crest regalia?], and joining hands around the fire dance and sing appropriately to the joyous occasion. [Does this refer to the special song for a dead bear?] All the bones of the head and claws of the feet are carefully collected and buried deep or thrown into the ocean. "If this is not done the bears will all know it and then they all get mad, and the bullets cannot kill them and they will eat up the hunters. This is why sometimes a bear is very cross."

Despite the "literary" tone of the story, the information from the boy sounds genuinely Tlingit.]

The black bear, *tseek* [s̓i·k], received no more consideration than was paid to any other animal. [It should be remembered that all animals were treated with "respect" by the Tlingit when hunted.] It was trapped, snared, hunted with dogs, and shot.

[Observations recorded in the "Game Diary" (1896), based on information from Paul Riddell, Juneau, indicate that the skull of the black bear is rounded, showing little or no ridge on top, unlike that of the large brown bear. Riddell believed that the two species can crossbreed:

> for in 1890, Regstad a north country man shot an old bear, female about 3 or 4 years old with two yearling cubs. One was black with the skull of a black bear, and the other was brown with the skull peculiar to the brown bear. [This was probably the brown variant of the common black bear. Many interior Indians call them "crossbreed bears," sharing the same belief.]

[An entry made in the same "Game Diary" at Yes Bay, in Sanya territory near the head of Behm Canal (July 1896), reports:

> Black bear will readily climb a tree if pursued by dogs and if they can get a comfortable notch or large limb will remain, but if the

> tree is straight and they can only hold on they will descend and run or take to another tree. Brown bear [grizzly] one, two, and three years old (not too heavy), will also take to the tree, but large brown bear are too heavy for climbing and their claws which [are sharp when they emerge from hibernation] are well worn down very soon in the spring from digging for roots and digging out groundhogs from their holes, are dulled and they are not climbers.]

The glacier bear was thought to belong to the black bear family and was named accordingly: ***klate*** "snow or white," *utardy* "like," *tseek* "black bear" [λe·t -?- ṡiˑk]. It lived about the glaciers and was found from Mount Saint Elias to the Skeena River. It varied greatly in color, from black with every hair tipped with silver white, to the more common pale bluish white, but the distinct rufous of the feet and about the nose marked it. It was most abundant in the Saint Elias and Fairweather ranges. It was not especially hunted by the natives, but was shot when found.

[Entries in the 1896 "Game Diary" and notes evidently taken at Yakutat indicate:

> The greater numbers [of glacier bears] are taken from Lituya Bay to above Dry Bay and about Disenchantment Bay [at the head of Yakutat Bay]. [In addition, specimens have been killed in] Glacier Bay country, about the snow among glaciers near Dyea, about Eagle Glacier [northwest of Juneau], and in the basin near Juneau in 1893.
>
> This bear in character and habits more nearly resembles the black bear. It climbs trees; its foreclaws are but little longer than the hind claws, like the black bear. It lives directly on the glaciers and about them, and lies on the ice and snow. I would say from comparison that the winter skin was much lighter in color than the summer skin. It is not feared by the Tlingits like the brown bear, and from its color is believed to be a chief among bears. Have heard of one white bear seen by an Auk native which had two white cubs [albinos?].
>
> Mrs. Andrews husband who is from Dry Bay says he killed two, both in winter time when the bears were in their holes. Both were very light in color. They hibernate as the black and brown bears, and in habits and characteristics they resemble the black bear. . . . They dig a hole under the roots of fallen trees on the foothills [for their winter dens].
>
> Tom and Percy say the Tlingit believe that this bear was a cross between the mountain goat and the black bear originally, and took the white coat from the goat and the form and habits from the bear.]

The snare was preferred by the mainland tribes [for taking bears], the deadfall by those of the islands. I believe that the snare, *da-sa* [dá·ṡa·], originated with the interior people, and the article itself was generally procured in trade

Snare for bear, set in animal's trail, noose and line of moose hide. (Sketched by G. T. Emmons. AMNH.)

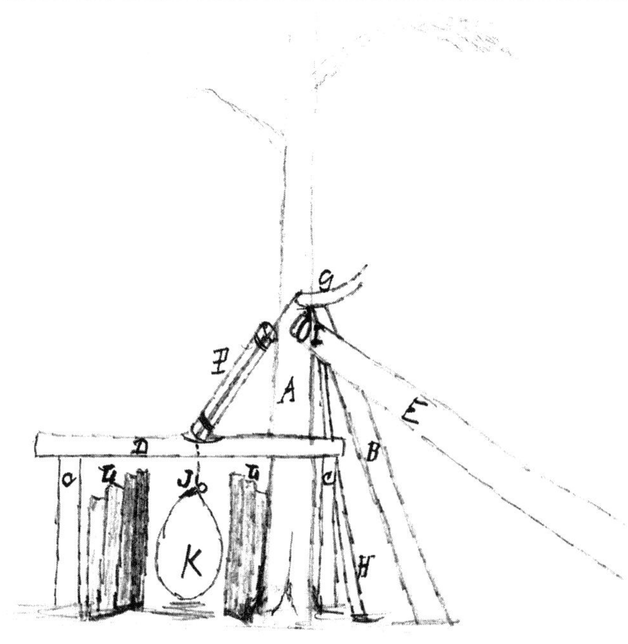

from them. It was best made of a number of strands of moose hide which had been soaked in water for three days, then wrung out and cut in narrow strips. These were twisted together when wet by making an eye in each end, securing one end to a stake or tree, and then twisting by hand. Then both ends were stretched between two stakes, and, by means of a cross stick stuck through the middle, it was still further twisted, and so allowed to set and harden. Some snares were wrapped with bark, and greased to make them slip more easily. For large bears, they were doubled by passing one end through the loop in the other end, which was looped over the end of a heavy tree trunk. This log was nicely balanced over a crotch of a tree, or artificially supported, at a height to take the head of the bear. It was placed in the bear trail and concealed by brush. When the bear's head entered the noose, a slight pull released the log, and as it fell, its weight lifted the bear [the hind paws dangling just free of the ground]. The animal's struggles tightened the noose, and the bear thus finally strangled itself. [A sketch made by Emmons shows the fall log leaning against a standing tree, apparently supported in part by a sapling. The noose itself hangs in front of a "gate," which ensures that the animal will put its head in the noose. The cord from the noose runs through a hollowed-out log, which slides down on the neck of the trapped animal and prevents it from biting or tearing through the rope.]

Tlingit deadfall for bears. (Pencil sketch by G. T. Emmons, made from model. AMNH.) "Bear trap, salmon bait. The heavy trunk D weighted by F F F is held up by a twisted bark or hide thong secured around the head of A, and A is held in place by the strain brought on the toggle B at the end of the rope H when the toggle B is placed between the cross stick C and the fixed stake K. When the bear treads on C entering the trap the toggle is released and the weighted tree trunk falls on its back."

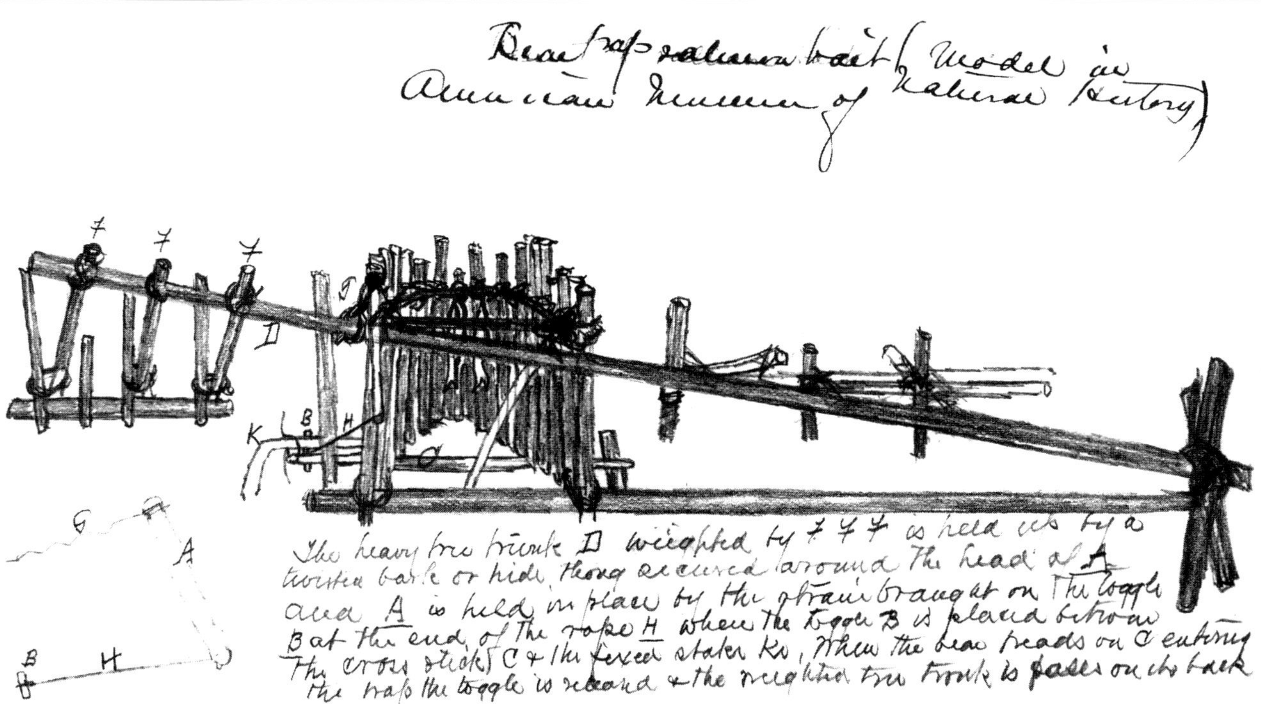

[Notes in AMNH record:] Snares are used by the Chilkats, Yakutats, and *Gu-nah-ho qwans* [Dry Bay people], and as the same snare is in general use by the interior nations and the snares are manufactured by these people, it is reasonable to believe that this system of capture of bears has been taken from these people.

[The same notes describe a different kind of snare:] The Chilkats snare the black and brown bear. A bear trail is selected to set the snare by some convenient tree. A sapling (generally poplar), from five to six inches in diameter, is selected, and this is bent at right angles alongside of another tree. The snare is secured to the bent portion of the sapling by passing the end through the eye and hauling taut the noose which hangs within a few inches of the ground. The snare is sprung by a stick which is placed just in the footprint of the bear (as he always follows in an old track), and it springs the trap, and releases the bent sapling, which springs up, and the bear is swinging with the hind legs just touching or clear of the ground. It is very necessary to have two full turns around the bear's neck, as he most always works one turn loose, the second turn strangling him.

Wolves, lynx, and foxes were snared, but with smaller animals the snare [ʒí·ná·] was fastened to a bent sapling.

The same type of deadfall [yé·x̣ or sí·n] was used not only for bear, but for wolf, fox, marten, mink, and marmot. It was heavier and weighted when intended for the larger animals. It consisted of a partial enclosure of stakes or small tree trunks driven into the ground, with a bait of salmon or dried marten hung at the back. Between the two uprights at the entrance, the heavy trunk of a hemlock tree was held up at one end by a delicate trigger which was connected to a crosspiece within the enclosure. The crosspiece was held in place by the tension on the lower end of the trigger, or by a toggle. When the crosspiece was touched by the entering animal, it fell and released the trigger; this let the suspended log fall on the back of the animal above the shoulders, and crushed it down on a ground log, thus breaking its neck or back. A heavy stake, driven at an angle halfway within the enclosure, confined the body of the animal laterally and permitted little movement. In the case of the heavier trap, the deadfall log was weighted with heavy cross logs.

With the introduction of steel traps, the snare and deadfall for bear were given up, although marten, mink, ermine, and marmot were taken in the primitive manner up to the time of the settlement of the coast by whites. The steel trap

Two additional types of deadfall. Bottom. *Emmons notes that ". . . the tree trunk is held up by* B *which at the head is lashed to* A. *The lower end of* B *presses against the cross stick* C. *The animal entering presses* C *down releasing the end of* B *when the tree trunk drops on its back pressing it down on the ground beam* D."

was set in the bear's trail, carefully covered with leaves and earth. It was attached by a fathom or more of heavy chain to a medium-sized green log, some six to eight feet long, which not only acted as a drag to the struggling animal, but ultimately stopped his progress by being caught between trees or rocks. Traps were visited every five days, those for smaller animals more often. Trapping and snaring were carried out principally in the early spring when the fur was prime, but also to a limited degree in the fall.

The gray and black wolf, *goutch* [gu'č], was snared and trapped. Within the last thirty years [1900–1930?] it has increased greatly in numbers and has crossed some of the broader channels to islands where many deer formerly lived, [and the latter, in consequence] have become extinct. It is a tradition with the Tlingit that their dog came directly from the wolf. The Wolf was the crest of one of the phratries, but that did not prevent its being killed, although its flesh was not eaten and its pelt not greatly valued.

The red fox, *na-kart-sa* [na·gas̀é·], and its variants: the cross, *hahr-kou* [x̣a-ká·x̣, "fur ptarmigan, or spotted"], and the silver and black, *na-kar-sa tooch* [na·gas̀é· t̓u·č, "fox black"] and the Canada lynx, *kark* [ga·q], are rarely met with on the mainland shore and are not found on the islands. They were little sought, but constituted a valuable article of trade received from the interior people.

The land otter, *koush-ta* [kú·šda·], marten, *kouh* [k̓ú·xʷ], mink, *nukshean* [nukʷšiyá·n, łukʷšiyá·n], and weasel or ermine, *da* [dá·], were taken with the deadfall. All of these were more or less connected with the practice of the shaman and none of them was eaten. The marmot, *sark* [hoary marmot, s̀a·x̣], was most abundant on the mainland mountains and was trapped in the deadfall. It was eaten, and the skin used for blankets. [For some reason, not mentioned by Emmons, the sticks used for the marmot traps were carved with magically effective designs or figures, not considered necessary in trapping other animals.] The porcupine, *klar-kutch* [x̣ałakáč, "spiny fur"], was likewise confined to the mainland, and was eaten fresh or dried. The rabbit, *kuh* [gáx̣, probably the snowshoe rabbit], was rare, and was not considered.

The gray squirrel, *khurl-sark* [kałšá·k, kanałša·k], and the flying squirrel, *tsin-ka* [possibly ci'n-x̣é], were few in numbers and attracted no attention, but the ground squirrel, *tsalkh* [cáłk, *Spermophilius*], was most abundant on the Chilkat divide and in the interior. It was much prized for its fur, gray in winter and reddish in summer, and its flesh was also esteemed. Trading parties going inland would set numberless snares when camping for the night and pick them up again in the morning. The snare was set directly in the mouth of the animal's hole, and consisted of a quill noose which passed through an eye at one end. To the other end was attached a short tail of hide with a small wooden toggle near the noose end. A short spur of quill projected at the end, and when set, the noose was held over this, but so lightly that a slight pull would permit it to tighten with the natural spring of the quill. The hide tail was secured to a bent sapling or stake, and the little toggle held it between two light cross sticks. The animal strangled itself when the noose was tightened. A trapper carried fifty or more of these snares hung to his belt.

The black-tailed deer, *kawakon* [quwaka·n or guwaka·n], was most abundant on the mainland as far north as Juneau and on all of the offshore islands. It was originally hunted with the bow and arrow [and also with the whip sling and dart], but later was shot with the musket. When with young, it was decoyed by imitating the call of the fawn. The call consisted of two small sticks bound together and slightly separated in the middle where a blade of grass or thin piece of cedar bark was secured. When blown through, it made much the same noise as a blade of grass placed between the thumbs [and used as a whistle]. In the early fall before the bucks shed the velvet from the horns, deer were hunted above the timberline; later, when driven down by the heavy snow, they were hunted with dogs that were put ashore inside of headlands. The canoe followed along the edge of the shore, guided by the cry of the dogs, and when the quarry was driven into the water, it was easily taken. Deer were eaten fresh, and the liver was most esteemed. The skin was dressed for clothing; the horn was used for tool handles, charms [amulets], toggles, pipes, spear and arrowheads, hooks, etc.; the dew hoofs as rattles and as ornaments for robes and leggings.

The mountain goat, *genou* [ǯánwu], was found only on the mainland mountains, and was more abundant in the vicinity of ice and snow fields, but even came down to the shore when there were heavy snowfalls. It was hunted in the fall when it was in prime condition both as to pelt and fat, but was valued principally for the wool which was woven into Chilkat blankets and twisted into cords, while the pelt with its heavy coat of hair and wool was preferred for bedding. The leaf fat was run into cakes and greatly esteemed both as food and for trade purposes. From the horns, spoons were made, and also charms, personal ornaments, tool handles, cap boxes, and containers for powder and shot. The best drumhead was of goatskin.

The tops of the mountains are honeycombed with the holes of small field mice, ***kutesin*** [kuči·n] or ***kok karkh*** [kagá·k]. [It is uncertain which designation is correct, for there were two species, a rat and a mouse, to which these terms applied.] These mice were very destructive in the houses, eating into the grease boxes. They were taken with a very effective trap of native design. Two flat boards about eighteen inches square (A and B), are hinged together at C and C. Two uprights (D and D) support a crosspiece (E). A flat stick (F), secured and working loose at G, has in the other end a small hole (H). From this hole a string goes over the crosspiece (E) and is secured to the upper board (B) at K. To the string is fastened a small pointed stick (M). When the trap is set, the upper board (B) is raised and held up by the pressure of the pointed stick (M) in the hole (H) at the end of the flat stick (F). Fat of any kind is smeared on top of the flat stick (F), and when the mouse presses on this trigger, it goes down, releasing the pointed stick (M), and the board (B) falls, crushing the mouse.

Tlingit mouse trap. See explanation of the apparatus in text, below. (Sketched by G. T. Emmons. AMNH.)

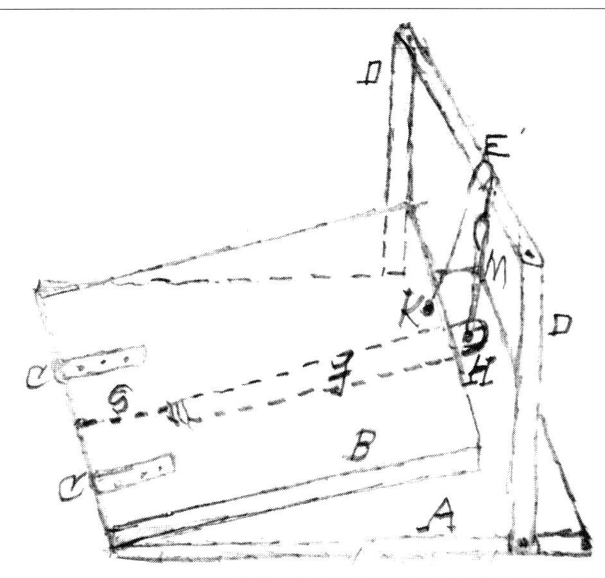

[It is interesting that Emmons reported nothing about the Dall mountain sheep (tawé·), since there was a "Sheep Camp" on the Chilkoot Pass into the interior. Nor is there anything said about the moose, *tsiskw* (císk̓^{w}), or moose cow, *khars* (xa·s), although the animal was certainly known to the Tlingit. There seems to be some confusion here between the moose cow, the domestic cow introduced by the Russians, and the woodland buffalo. Whatever the correct meaning of xa·s, the animal was taken as a clan and as a house crest (Tables 13 and 14), and while often translated as "Moose," the usual representation of the animal is certainly bovine. The buffalo was perhaps found as far west as the Pelly River, and the Tlingit were probably acquainted with it from stories of their Athabaskan neighbors, and perhaps from traded horns and hide. (See McClellan 1975, 1:119.)

[Nor did Emmons mention the beaver, *sigadi* (śige·dí), among the local fur-bearers. It was a crest animal of some importance, at Controller Bay (Kaliakh, Tribe XVII), Yakutat, Hutsnuwu, and among the Eagles at Cape Fox (Sanya), as well as a valuable item of trade. Other animals he omitted to mention were the wolverine (nú·sk^{w}), woodchuck or gopher (cáƚk), and muskrat (cín), probably because they are interior animals of no great commercial value.]

BIRD HUNTING

[Emmons neglected to state that large birds, such as geese, swans, and ducks, were formerly shot with the bow and

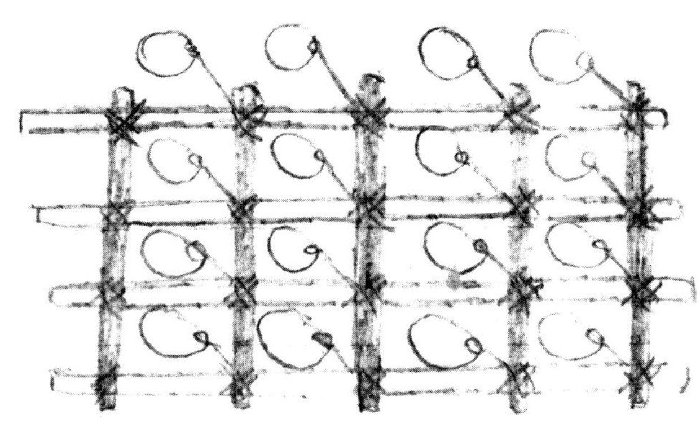

Snares for gulls and saltwater ducks. (Pencil sketch by G. T. Emmons. AMNH.) A wooden framework, with baleen snares, weighted with stones in shallow water, and baited with salmon eggs, is used to catch gulls and saltwater ducks.

arrow. Their flesh was eaten and their feathers utilized, the downy skins of swans making very soft robes. He did mention that bird arrows were equipped with blunt heads (gúƛ̓), but I believe that such arrows were intended for smaller birds. Eagles were obviously hunted, since eagle wings were used for brooms, eagle feathers for arrows (at Yakutat), and eagle down was scattered on all peaceful, ceremonial occasions. At Yakutat, at any rate, ducks and seagulls were taken by means of baited gorges (nú·ṫa·), a barbless double-pointed piece of bone, secured to a line in the middle, which lodged crosswise in the bird's throat when swallowed.]

Gulls and other seabirds were taken in snares, *da-sa* [dá·ṡa·], made of whalebone [baleen], secured to a framework of wooden slats, baited with salmon eggs and weighted down by heavy stones in shallow water at the feeding grounds. When walking or feeding, the feet or head of the bird became entangled in the snare. [The "Game Diary" for 1896 includes this note:] At Yakutat about 20 May great quantities of geese, mallard, teal, curlew (*I-yi-ho-yaw* [ʔayahí·yá·]), snipe, plover; the inland lakes still frozen over and shore above tidewater covered with snow, and birds in a starving condition.

Boys caught hummingbirds on a network of string, smeared over with the slime of snails, to which the birds were attracted by flowers. [A note further reports:] Boys catch hummingbirds by using the slime exuded from a large wood slug and spread on outstanding twigs which will hold a hummingbird. Then they take it, and tie a string to its foot, and play with it. They also took small birds by baiting a hole in the ground with fish spawn, above which was placed a light, close, lattice-work, held up by a small stick to which a long line was attached. When the bird entered [the space below the lattice], the line was pulled and the lattice fell and covered the hole.

Snares were used to catch ptarmigan, ***kate-so-war*** [x̣e·ṡawá]. [A note in the "Game Diary" for April 1896 reports:] "Corta" says ptarmigan make nests of small twigs on ground under small, low, flat juniper.

HUNTING DOGS*

[Few of the early visitors to the Tlingit bothered to mention or describe their dogs, and we can assume that the native breed or breeds were soon lost through mixture with imported animals. The Tlingit called the dog *katle* (ke·ƛ̓), and recognized the coyote as a "dog of the interior" (ha·da· ke·ƛí). A long-eared dog like a spaniel was called sawá·k (presumably a white man's introduction), and this word was sometimes used as a nickname for a man with large ears. Dogs had personal names, sometimes made up especially for them or perhaps traditional dog names; and sometimes dogs were given the name of a son the owner could not father, because, even though he himself had inherited its teknonymous derivative, he had no son by a woman of the clan that owned the name. Although the Tlingit in general seem to have been fond of their dogs, boasted proudly of their achievements, and mourned them when dead, they appear to have treated them very casually. Much of the time the animals had to scavenge for themselves, and the Tlingit did not hesitate to abandon them when they deserted a village for the summer fish camp, or to throw them overboard if they were preparing their canoes for swift attack (Vancouver 1801, 5:396, 4:181). Yet they would not kill a dog. In addition to carrying packs, and assisting in the hunt, dogs were regarded as good protection against Land Otter Men, because they were never fooled by the friendly appearance which these evil creatures might assume to lure intended victims. A Dog Spirit often assisted the shaman in detecting witches. Witches themselves were said to use the pelt or carcass of a dog in their diabolical work. There is some evidence for the belief that the souls of dogs went with the wicked to Dog Heaven, or that the wicked might be transformed into dogs in Dog Heaven (see de Laguna 1972:784, 832–33.)

[La Pérouse (1799, 1:401) described the dogs owned by the Tlingit of Lituya Bay in July 1786:

> Dogs are the only animals with which they have formed any alliance. Of these each hut has commonly three or four. They are

**Editor's note:* I am responsible for the first paragraph on Tlingit dogs, the descriptions from La Pérouse and Marchand, the paragraph on the Tahltan bear dogs, and the last of all on the cats seen at Wrangell by my aunt (de Laguna, Sr.) in 1892, the only reference of this kind in the sources consulted.

small; resembling the shepherd's dog of Buffon; scarcely ever bark, but make a whistling noise much like that of the jackal of the Carnatic; and are so savage, that they seem to be to other dogs what their masters are to civilized people.

[Captain Marchand and his surgeon, Dr. Roblet, observed dogs at Sitka in 1791 (Fleurieu 1801, 1:306):

> The only quadruped that our voyagers saw alive, is the domestic dog. It is of the race of the *shepherd's dog;* but his hair is longer and softer. His feet are extremely large; the tail is bushy, the muzzle long and pointed, the ear erect, the eye sharp, the body thick; and his height may be about eighteen inches. He barks little, and appears timid with strangers. He welcomes and caresses his master, but caresses him alone. The Tchinkitanayans [Sitka Tlingit] boast much of the attachment, the intelligence, and the courage of this animal, excellent for the chace [*sic*], and bold in the water. Surgeon ROBLET remarks, however, that a young dog which he had purchased, on seeing from the ship some Americans [Indians] on the shore, at a very little distance from the SOLIDE, never durst jump into the water, although, by his motions, he manifested the greatest eagerness to go and join them.]

The origin of the dog is attributed to the wolf. Native tradition goes back to the taking of a wolf's nest in the interior and the training of the young to hunt. From this beginning was developed the dog. The young wolf learned to talk, and so today the dog understands everything he is told to do. The wolfish strain in the dog is seen in its form and actions, but in time the breed has become smaller and is every color from white to black, through browns and grays. In character, the dog is rather cowardly, but obedient and long-suffering. It is keen of scent and is used in hunting bear, deer, goat, and land otter. Puppies and even older dogs may be seen with a bear claw or tooth, a land otter foot, or a deer dew hoof secured about the neck to make them good hunters. To give the dog a keen scent, the nostrils of a young dog may be slit with a bear bone, and the blood from the nose caught on a bear's paw or mixed with bear hair. A bear's tooth may be rubbed off on a stone and the powder put in water, and this poured down the nose of the dog. [These, and similar forms of magic, were used to make the dog useful in hunting; Emmons mentioned no magic to make the dog stronger at carrying a loaded pack.]

Besides hunting, the dog was used for packing, particularly by the Chilkat who made long trips inland.

Dogs lived out-of-doors, often burrowing under the house, and were fed principally on fish, but also hunted on their own account. [A few parts of animals were tabooed to dogs.] The Tlingit disliked to kill even the most worthless dogs, and so they accumulated until a village presented a sorry spectacle of many mangy, useless dogs.

[This last is still true, as of 1950 at least, for it is believed that to shoot or drown a dog means that one would lose one's own life, or that of a close relative, in the same manner, or at least "always have bad luck." But the Indians relied on the white man or Asian who was not afraid to dispatch unwelcomed dogs for the community. (See de Laguna 1972:832–33.)

[There was also a special breed of "Tahltan bear dogs," small, quick, terrierlike animals, quite different from the larger wolflike dogs used for ordinary hunting and carrying packs. These small dogs, with quick, fearless nips and yapping, could immobilize a bear, dodging his ferocious bites and cuffs, and holding him at bay until the hunter could arrive and kill him. These animals were highly prized, and perhaps limited to the Tlingit who were in close contact with the Athabaskans. It is curious that they are not mentioned by Emmons.

[Cats were pets of the Tlingit in the 1880s and 1890s, if not earlier. A photograph of about 1900, taken at Sitka (by Winter and Pond, AMNH), shows two elderly women (wearing labrets) with their cats. The cat was called dú·š, and the nickname "cat's mother" was applied to the owner of such a pet, dú·š-ƛá·; there was a woman known by this name at Yakutat (see de Laguna 1972:741). De Laguna, Sr. (1894:35) thus described the dogs and cats of Wrangell in 1892:

> Not an attractive, but a most notable feature of Fort Wrangel, are the dogs. Less beautiful specimens of this generally recognized noble animal we never have seen. Within the huts and without they huddled, starved, piteous in their gaunt length of body and legs. There was surely a dog apiece to every member of the community, and then, perhaps, some to spare. Cats, too, flourished as in an Egyptian temple. But the cats, dishonest like all of their tribe, were kept ignominiously tied by short ropes. They stole the fish, we were told; which fish, by the way, hung like portières all about the cabins.]

CHAPTER 6

Food and Its Preparation

INTRODUCTION*

The Tlingit lived in a land of plenty, and needed to provide only for the winter. He looked to the water for his staple food, but supplemented this with berries, roots, plant stems, tree bark, and land animals. Under ordinary conditions he had only a normal appetite, but gorged himself at the winter feasts. [Von Langsdorff (1814, 2:111), who was at Sitka in 1805–6, was astonished at the amount of food the visiting Tlingit could eat when entertained by Baranov.] Formerly they ate but twice daily: the morning meal upon rising, ***ka-ga ut-ha-ye,*** "morning eating" [qe·x̣̓é· ʔat x̣a·yí, "morning food"], and ***ki-ne ut-ha-ye,*** "evening eating" [x̣á·na· ʔat x̣a·yí, "evening food"]. The latter was the substantial meal. This custom is still observed when traveling, hunting, and working, but generally in the villages the Tlingit have learned from us to eat three times a day. [Fasting when engaged in some chancy, dangerous, or arduous undertaking was believed to be virtuous and magically efficacious; this would explain why the hunter or traveler would not eat until he was safe in camp, or the day's work done.]

[Information about mealtimes is not very full. Thus Suría, at Yakutat in 1791 (Wagner 1936:254), observed that the Indians "are always eating and heating themselves at the fire in the middle of the hut," eating a kind of mush, made of fish (fresh or dried?), cooked in seawater. On the other hand, Beresford (1789:188), when at Norfolk (Sitka) Sound in 1789, noted that the Indians who were trading with the ship regularly left at noon to stay for about an hour on shore, where they could be seen eating: "This evidently shews, that they have at least one *fixed* meal in the day, and that it is regulated by the sun. They likewise frequently left us about four in the afternoon; but this time was not so exactly observed as at noon." He wrote that in the evening, when the trade was almost always done, great numbers of Indians came out to visit and to sing: "[They] never leave off until the approach of night; thus beginning and ending the day in the same manner."]

Salmon constituted the principal article of diet. The Tlingit ate it fresh from spring to mid-fall, and dried and smoked through the remainder of the year. So fond was he of the dried fish that I have seen him carry it in summer when the fresh fish could be had without effort. [It is so convenient and light to carry, and so nourishing, that dried salmon was and still is taken on hunting, fishing, and berrying expeditions and picnics.]

In preparation for the meal, the mother filled a dish with grease [ʔï·x̣/ʔe·x̣] around which the family gathered. She held a dried fish [ʔat x̣̓í·ši/ʔat x̣̓é·ši] before the fire until the oil exuded, when she broke it in pieces which she placed in a flat platter. These pieces were taken by members of the family, dipped in the grease, and skillfully conveyed to the mouth without spilling a drop.

The Tlingit ate no raw fish or meat, except the sea-soaked salmon head, fish spawn, and shellfish. They boiled, roasted, steamed, and baked their food. Boiling was done by means of heated rocks in boxes or woven spruce root baskets. Fish and meat were spitted in front of the fire or hung from a roof beam just to the side of the fire and turned from time to time; if the food were very fat, a dish was placed beneath to catch the grease. Steaming or baking was done in a hole, paved and lined with flat stones. A fire was built in the hole and, when burned out, the ashes were removed or covered with leaves and grass, and the fish or meat was placed between layers of leaves and heated stones, over which water was poured. The whole was then covered with leaves, seaweed, and earth, to confine the heat and steam. Fish might remain an hour, but meat was usually thus cooked for half a day. In camp, I have seen Chilkat hunting parties cook goat meat by putting it in a hole dug under the fire after it had died down. The hole was lined with skunk cabbage leaves and the meat was covered with leaves and ashes. Then hot coals were hauled over the pit and the fire was rebuilt with heavy logs and left until morning. I have also seen goat meat stuffed and boiled with blueberries.

Editor's note: Information in this chapter was originally part of "Chapter V: Domestic Life."

**Editor's note:* I have added a paragraph about mealtimes, and information from Beresford, Portlock, Suría, Marchand (Fleurieu), Lisiansky, von Langsdorff, and von Kotzebue.

[A number of the early explorers have left observations on Tlingit foods and methods of preparation. For the whole Northwest Coast in general, Beresford (1789:244–45), who had been with Dixon to Yakutat, Sitka, and the Queen Charlottes in 1787, wrote:

> Food in the winter season consists chiefly of dried fish, but when the time of hunting comes on, they have greater variety, amongst which broiled seal seems to be reckoned a most delicious repast; they sometimes offered us pieces of it, and on our refusing this dainty, always looked at us with a mixture of astonishment and contempt. In the spring, or rather summer, here are [a] variety of herbs which the natives eat with great relish; and in Norfolk [Sitka] Sound, we saw the wild lilly root in abundance. [This is the Kamchatka lily.]

[At Yakutat, in June 1787, Beresford (1789:175) noted stone boiling: "They dress their victuals by putting heated stones into a kind of wicker basket, amongst pieces of fish, seal, porpoise, &c. and covered up close; sometimes they make broth and fish soup by the same method, which they always preferred to boiling, though we gave them some brass pans, and pointed out the mode of using them."

[That same year, Portlock (1789:290–91, 293–94) observed the Tlingit eating and cooking, and after visiting Hawaii was interested to see men, women, and children sitting down together, and eating the same food. He reported that their meals

> chiefly consist of fish of different kinds; such as salmon, which they have in the greatest abundance, mussels, and various other shell-fish, sea-otters, seals, and porpoises; the blubber of the porpoise they are remarkably fond of, and indeed the flesh of any animal that comes in their way. [Since he failed to see any quantity of fish being put up for the winter, he believed that the natives may have had to eat land animals; or, he wrote, probably] the principal part of their provision at that season is confined to the inner fine bark of the pine-tree. Any tin kettles they get from us they make use of to drink out of. They boil their victuals in wooden vessels, by constantly putting red-hot stones into the water.
>
> . . . [He went on to report:] They have a great number of curiosities amongst them, many of which shew them to be a people of great ingenuity and contrivance. They make a curious basket of twigs [spruce roots], in which they frequently boil their victuals, by putting red-hot stones into them. [pp. 290–91, 293–94]

[At the insistence of the natives, Portlock (1789:285) let the seaman, Woodcock, sleep on shore, as a hostage, while some of the Tlingit slept on board. Woodcock did not enjoy the experience:

> Except for their watching him so closely, they treated him with great kindness; and at their meals always gave him what they considered as choice dainties, mixing his fish with plenty of stinking oil, which in their opinion gave it an additional and most agreeable relish; and he found it no easy matter to persuade them to let him eat his fish without sauce.

[Suría (Wagner 1936:254, 257) found the Yakutat still cooking in the primitive manner in 1791:

> Their sustenance and daily meal is as follows: they catch a fish and pass a stick through it from the tail to the mouth which they fasten in the ground. They keep turning it towards the fire. [So far this is the ordinary way of roasting a fresh fish over the fire. But the next words suggest that it is a dried fish which is being softened by heat:] As soon as it is softened they place it in a straw [spruce root] basket which is very flexible and is so closely woven that not a drop of water can come out. In this they put it to cook with seawater, and so that the basket may not burn underneath they have various red hot stones which they throw inside, according as necessity demands, always maintaining the heat until the dried fish in small fragments forms a mess and then they eat it with some long deep spoons made of horn. . . . The pots and jars in which they cook are those already referred to. Their food consists of fish: salmon, smelts [longfin and surf smelt, and eulachon] and another which looks like a conger eel [Pacific lamprey].

[At this same period, 1791, Captain Marchand visited Sitka, and observed the native diet (Fleurieu 1801, 1:337–40):

> The principal food of the natives of TCHINKITÂNAY is fish, fresh or smoked, the dried spawn of fish, of which they make a sort of cake, and the flesh of the animals that they kill; to these they add, in the intervals of their meals and in their excursions, the use of a farinaceous legume, the taste of which may be compared to that of the sweet potatoe, and which Surgeon ROBLET believes to be the *saranne*. [A footnote by Fleurieu identifies this as the Kamchatka lily.] Wild fruits, and berries which are found in abundance in the woods, with the tender root of the fern, likewise afford them an occasional supply. [pp. 337–39]

[But the Sitkans had already abandoned their old cooking boxes and baskets in favor of iron pots and pans:

> . . . but, taught by experience, they no longer expose to the fire the tin and pewter vessels which they have received from the Europeans; they gave the French to understand that the former were unsoldered, and the latter, melted: they make use of both for serving up their food when dressed; and they employ them jointly with the wooden dishes and bowls which they manufacture themselves. Their travelling utensils are become much more

Drying fish. (Photograph by G. T. Emmons. AMNH.) Herring strung and hung on drying racks, Sitka, 1889. USS Pinta *at anchor (in background).*

cumbersome than they were before their intercourse with strangers: they begin to experience the embarrassment of riches.

They always mix train-oil with their broth. [Although this is offensive to European taste, it is a necessity for people living on the northern coasts, and Fleurieu went on to develop a complex theory about how the "fish-oil" concentrates and then drives the body heat to the extremities!] [pp. 339–40]

[Lisiansky (1814:239) had a little information on the food of the Sitkans in 1805:

The common food of these islanders consists, during the summer, of different sorts of berries, fresh fish, and the flesh of amphibious animals [sea mammals]. During the winter they live on dried salmon, train oil, and the spawn of fish, especially that of herrings, of which they always lay in a good stock. On the first appearance of these fish in the spring, the people assemble on the coast, and are active in catching them. For taking the spawn, they use the branches of the pine-tree [hemlock], to which it easily adheres, and on which it is afterwards dried. It is then put into baskets, or holes purposely dug in the ground, till wanted. To this list we may add a particular sort of sea weed, and cakes made of the rind of the larch-tree, which are about a foot square and an inch thick. They roast their meat on sticks, after the Cadiack [Kodiak] manner; or boil it in iron, tin, and copper kettles, which they purchase of the Russian settlers, or of chance traders. The rich have European stone-ware, such as dishes, plates, basons, &c.: the poor, wooden basons only, of their own manufacturing, and large spoons, made either of wood, or of the horns of the wild sheep.

[Von Langsdorff (1814, 2:111, 130–31) was at Sitka also in 1805, and was entertained by the Tlingit, so had a better opportunity than most to note their food:

It is astonishing how much, and what a variety of things these people will eat [when Baranov entertained them]. They are very fond of rice, berries, the flesh and fat of sea-dogs [seals], fish, &c., &c., but will not touch the fat or train-oil of whales, and always intreat that it may not set before them. [The Aleuts in Russian employ relished whale blubber.] . . . [p. 111]

Their principal objects of food are fresh and smoked fish, fish-roes, sea-dogs, and in spring and summer several sorts of sea-weed; the latter when cooked make a bitterish sort of soup. They eat besides muscles [*sic*], the *pinna mytilus* and *mya* [blue mussels and small clams], the *sepia* or cuttle-fish, and a sort of square cake made of the bark of the spruce-fir, pounded and mixed with roots, berries, and train-oil. Rice and molasses, which are brought them by the Americans, they consider as choice objects of *gourmandise*; instead of salt they use sea-water. Whale-fat they never eat; it seems from some prejudice to be forbidden to them: they shew the same kind of horror at it that a Jew does at the idea of eating swine's flesh: they sometimes, however, bring large pieces of the whales that are occasionally cast upon their coasts to the Russian settlement for the benefit of the hungry Promüschleniks and Aleutians. [pp. 130–31]

[There is evidence (see section entitled "Sea Mammals," page 150) that the Tlingit did not always or uniformly despise whale meat.]

SALMON

The men caught the salmon and the women prepared and cured them. The fish were always cut from the vent, along the belly to the throat. This was believed necessary, lest the fish or their spirits feel offended and desert the stream. There is a tradition among the Stikine that once, in a salmon stream up the river [Stikine River], a fish was cut along the side by mistake. Whereupon all of the others immediately disappeared. The people were then assembled, and the shaman directed them to man a large canoe in which he seated himself in the middle, covered over with bark mats. They paddled down the river until they reached a stream crowded with fish, where they put the canoe across its mouth. Then the shaman's spirit went out to the fish and begged them to follow the canoe. This was headed upstream, and the fish complied, so that the home stream was again filled and has ever since been a favorite resort of the salmon. [For other supernatural regulations about cutting salmon, see de Laguna 1972:400.]

When the cut up the belly was made, the entrails were removed. Then the head was cut off, the backbone taken out, and the body opened up to the back. The split fish was then hung to dry over the cross sticks on the drying frame, the skin side out; then it was turned and dried for several days, depending on the weather. The larger fish were cut in half, or even quartered if very thick. The tails were cut off to be processed separately.

The drying frame consisted of four upright posts, in pairs, the tops of which were mortised to receive the ends of two horizontal poles. Sometimes the latter were lashed to the uprights. Across these poles were laid the rods or saplings upon which the fish were hung. A roof of boards, bark, or brush served as protection against the rain; in an emergency, mats or the canoe sail might be thrown over the rack. In rainy weather, the fish might be dried indoors, but this was not considered desirable. At *Indastahka* [Yandestake, the Chilkoot village on the Chilkat River] the frames were like an old-fashioned post-and-rail fence. The posts were cut at intervals of eighteen inches and through [these holes] were passed the rods that carried the fish.

After two to five days, the partly dried fish were taken down and laid in turn over a triangular block, the center of the back along the ridge and the halves falling on either side. The flesh was then split lengthwise at a sharp angle along each side, once or twice according to the thickness, so that it might cure more readily. The fish was then hung in the smokehouse.

Here a smoldering fire was kept up night and day. Cottonwood and alder, with a certain proportion of rotten wood, gave the best results. At the four corners of the fireplace were posts, about five feet high, which supported two beams. Over these was laid a platform [or "table"] of slightly spread planks that acted as a smoke spreader. Outside of this stage, more posts, several feet higher, supported two beams upon which rested the cross rods on which the fish were hung, and above this there might be one or two sets of staging suspended by ropes from the roof beams for hanging fish. The fresher, partly dried fish were first hung below, and when partly smoked were hung higher up, until they were finally taken down and corded in bundles of ten or twenty.

The tails of the larger fish were cut off, strung up, dried and smoked separately. Fish heads were strung on small sticks, dried and smoked for winter use, or they were tried out for the oil in which they were rich.

After a sufficient amount of fish had been prepared and stored for winter, the subsequent catch was made into grease. To prepare the grease, a small canoe was buried and staked firmly at the sides [see Krause (1885) 1956, pl. III]. The salmon, and particularly the heads, which may have been preserved in a half decayed state, were put in the canoe with water. A fire was built nearby, and smooth boulders of moderate size that could withstand the heat [without cracking] were put in the fire. When heated, these were picked up with wooden tongs and dropped into the mass of fish, fish heads, and water in the canoe. The mixture was continually stirred and, as the water boiled, the oil rose to the surface and was skimmed off with wooden or bark spoons and poured into boxes. As the stones cooled off they were removed, washed with warm water over the canoe, and reheated. When all the oil possible had been obtained [in this manner], the mass of fish was put into bark or root bags, placed on slats laid over a box; a flat board was laid on top of the bags, and the remaining oil was pressed out by weighting the bags down with boulders or by a heavy woman sitting on them. Water and all impurities were eliminated from the oil by a second heating, after which it was poured into bladders or boxes, where it hardened and assumed the consistency of grease. Berries and salmon spawn were preserved in this grease and the dried fish was eaten with it.

Cooking techniques. (Pen and ink sketches by G. T. Emmons. AMNH.) (a) Interior of a smokehouse at Yakutat, showing racks for hanging fish and a set of planks for spreading the smoke. (b) Roasting salmon on a spit, tseak [cí̓k]. *(c) Roasting trout,* qwat [x̣ʷá·t̓, *"Dolly Varden"], on a spit. (d) Salmon, split and spread, roasting on a divided spit,* qwa nah [x̣ʷé·na·].

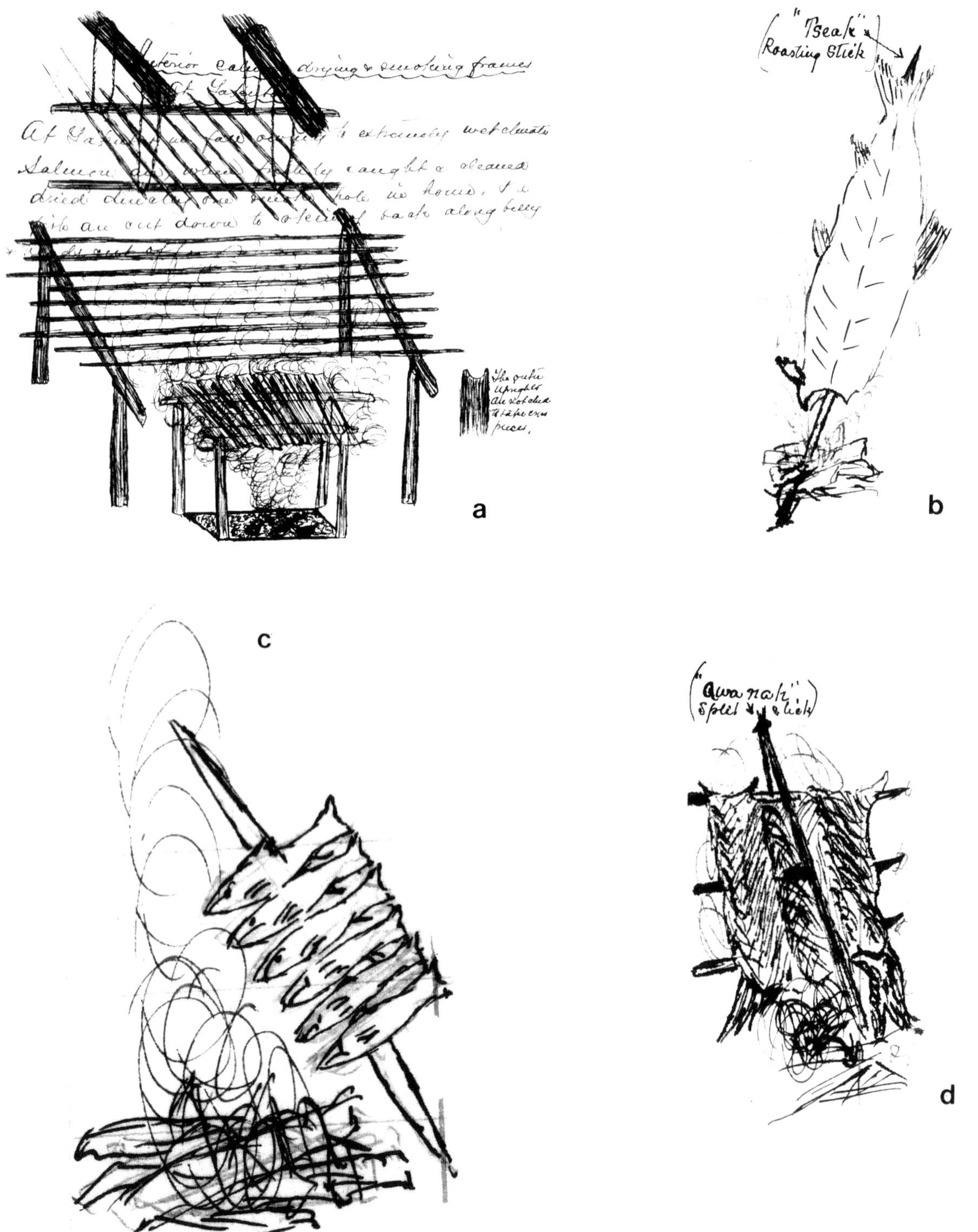

Herring, eulachon, and seal blubber were treated in the same way [to extract their oil], and these oil products formed the most nutritious food of the Northwest Coast.

As long as the salmon ran, they were eaten fresh. The favorite method of cooking was by boiling. This was formerly done in boxes or closely woven baskets, with a little water and hot stones. In camp, the fresh fish were spitted whole, head down, on a stick, *tseak* [cí·k, "spit"], that was inclined over the fire. Or the fish was split [down the back?], opened out and enclosed between the halves of a partially split stick, *qua-nah* [x̣ʷé·na·, "forked spit"], with two or three cross sticks to keep it distended.

If the dried fish became moldy, it was freshed by soaking in salt water. At Hoonah, on the pebble beach in front of the houses, just above the low water mark, holes three feet deep were dug, and lined with stout stakes. In these fish were placed, covered over, and weighted down, and allowed to remain over a tide.

All varieties of salmon were used, but the dog salmon, of little or no commercial value, was a favorite [in southeastern Alaska, not at Yakutat] for drying, because it contained relatively little oil.

Salmon spawn was eaten fresh, and was also dried, cooked, or stored in grease for winter food. Sometimes the head and spawn were put in holes in the beach below the high tide mark. These holes were lined with flat stones and skunk cabbage leaves, and were covered with weighted boards. The contents were allowed to remain for five or more days until they became a putrid mass, salted by the sea. This was eaten with great relish. The spawn was also prepared in a number of ways: beaten up with water; boiled and put up in grease; or mixed with seaweed or berries. For winter use it might be mashed to a jelly and preserved in seal bladders. This was done by the Yakutat. It was also mashed and mixed with cooked huckleberries, and stored in boxes to be eaten with grease. It is said that in former times the spawn was prohibited to boys who had not reached maturity.

HALIBUT

Halibut came next to salmon in importance as food. It was dried and smoked in the same manner as described for salmon. The head, tail, and dorsal fin were particularly esteemed as the choice portions. [Just as the halibut had to be hauled aboard the canoe, belly up, if the fisherman was to retain his luck, so it had to be laid in that position when it was sliced for curing.] The cut was made from under the mouth, along the stomach and around the gills, laying the flesh bare to the backbone. The entrails were removed and thrown away; the stomach was squeezed out and put aside. Then a deep cut was made just above the narrow part of the tail, the bone was cracked by bending, and the tail removed. The head was then cut off. The fish was cut down its length along the backbone on the under side. It was turned over and a similar cut was made down the back, and the two sets of halves were separated. These were cut in lengthwise strips, an inch thick and three or more inches wide, that were hung over the drying frame. When cured they were taken down and done up in bundles for winter use.

HERRING AND EULACHON

Eulachon and herring were the only other fish that were cured for winter use, but only in limited quantities, for their importance as oil producers was paramount, and only the surplus was preserved for winter food. Both were also eaten fresh.

[It will be remembered that the herring which were caught in the fall were fat and so were used for their oil.] This trying out of herring oil, both for home consumption and for trade, was carried on only by the *Hootzah-tar Qwan* [Hutsnuwu tribe] who built very substantial houses all along the shores of the lagoons of Kootznahoo Inlet where they spent the fall. The fish were tried out in canoes with heated stones in the manner previously described for salmon. But since this was more of a commercial industry, several special implements were used. Thus, a long-handled wooden straining spoon with slits and holes in the bowl was used to remove the mass of fish from the canoe. This was emptied into a long, open-weave, spruce root bag. When half filled, the bag was folded over and laid on a slat frame over a large box half filled with water. On top of the bag a heavy slab of wood, two feet square and two inches thick, with a handle at one end or corner, was placed and pressed down. The oil was skimmed off the water in the box with a wooden ladle, often finely carved, and was put in boxes about one foot square and eighteen inches high, or in seal bladders. Under ordinary temperature it solidified as yellow grease. It was eaten with all dried foods: fish spawn, berries (except for the soapberry), potatoes, and seaweed—in fact with every kind of food, and if it were rancid, this added rather than detracted from its quality. It was largely used in trade and had a fixed value. With the establishment of the Killisnoo Oil Company [probably the

Processing fish. (Photographs by G. T. Emmons. AMNH.) Top. *Tlingit man with salmon taken in the Taku River, 1889. [Soaking the fish for a day is said to remove some of the slime and makes the fish easier to cut.]* Bottom. *Trying out salmon (or eulachon) oil in a canoe, Chilkat River, 1889.*

Strips of salmon and halibut drying on racks in front of the houses at the Hoonah summer village, Khart Heenee [Ǥat-hí'ni], *"Salmon Water," at Bartlett Cove, near the entrance to Glacier Bay, 1889. Note the canoes covered with blankets or canvas to prevent cracking in the sun. (Photograph by G. T. Emmons. AMNH.)*

Alaska Oil and Guano Company that had acquired the old whaling station at Killisnoo in January 1887, and was processing herring oil], the natives gave up its manufacture, since they could procure a better product [from the company] with a minimum cost of time and labor.

A limited amount of herring was cured for home consumption. The woman preparing the fish held it in her left hand just below the head, belly up and head to the left, and with a knife cut the fish from the gills along the stomach. With the thumb of the right hand she pushed out the entrails and this was all the cleaning done. The fish were strung on a small alder stick or line, passed through one gill and the mouth, alternate fish being strung through the right and through the left gill, so that the fish stood out from each other when the string was placed over a rod, and thus had a better opportunity to dry. After being sun dried for a day or two, they were hung under and about the smokehole of the house, and so cured. Or, they might be strung together with lines, fastened alternatively around the head and small of the tail and crossing between each fish; or the fish might be opened lengthwise and strung through the head. Like all other dried fish, they were dipped in oil when eaten.

Herring eggs [procured in the spring] were considered a luxury rather than a regular article of diet. When eaten fresh, they were dropped into boiling water for an instant. [To cure the eggs], the moss, seaweed, or boughs to which the eggs adhered were hung on the fish racks, or on lines, trees, and bushes, and sun dried. They were temporarily put in bags, or boxes, as the [spring] season when the herring spawn is very short, and the cleaning process was not attempted until later [when as many herring eggs as possible had been obtained]. To prepare the eggs for winter use, they were put in a box of water, together with the material to which they were attached, and when the eggs swelled, they were stripped from the broad leaves of the seaweed or from the moss. Spawn on sea moss was often packed away as gathered, since the moss does not decay and is tasteless. The eggs on hemlock branches had to be stripped very soon, before becoming impregnated by the pungency of the needles. This was done by breaking the twigs, rubbing them together, and dropping them in water,

Herring spawn that has been deposited on moss and broad seaweed leaves is drying on lines in front of the houses. (Photograph by G. T. Emmons. AMNH.)

where the eggs separated and sank, while the needles and woody particles floated to the surface and were easily removed. After the eggs had been separated and cleaned, they were sun dried on boards, canoe covers, or so forth, and then packed away in boxes for the winter.

Cured eggs were allowed to boil in a little water for a few minutes, and were generally eaten with oil or grease. Herring spawn constituted an article of trade, and in 1882 were worth $3 for the amount contained in a hardtack box.

[Eulachon caught in the spring was most highly valued for its oil and its delicate flesh. The runs on the Chilkat River were the only ones in Tlingit territory of importance, except for those of the Alsek River at Dry Bay.]

On the sandy shore of the Chilkat River, a few feet from the water, oblong pits, two or three feet deep, were dug. These were boarded around, and sticks were laid across the bottom and covered with rushes or coarse grass, through which the water drained as the fish were thrown in. The oil was tried out with hot stones in an old canoe, half sunk in the ground. It was carefully cleaned before being put into boxes. As the fish were kept too long [in the pits, by white standards, not by those of the natives], the oil was very rancid and offensive to us, but was doubly appreciated by them. [The Tlingit report that fish and seal fat from which oil is to be rendered should be slightly rotten, or the oil will not keep. On the other hand, oil is also rendered from fresh fish and seal fat for certain purposes.] Eulachon oil forms a thick grease when kept, and has the consistency of soft butter. It was the greatest food luxury and was more often obtained from the Nass River [in trade with the Niska Tsimshian, than made locally], since the runs of eulachon were not general throughout southeastern Alaska. In use, it was beaten up with an equal amount of water. Salmon spawn, berries, seaweed, tree bark, and meat were all preserved in or eaten with grease.

Fresh eulachon were spitted on sticks inclined over the fire and roasted.

OTHER FISH AND SHELLFISH

All varieties of fish, such as cod, rock fish, bass, flounder, sculpin, eel, smelt, whiting, trout, were eaten fresh, but not

Food preparation. (Photographs by G. T. Emmons.) Top. *Seaweed cakes drying in the sun, Sitka. (AMNH.)* Bottom. *Roasting porcupines, Chilkat River trip, 1902. (BCPA.)*

cured. They formed an unimportant part of the diet as long as fresh or dried salmon or halibut were to be had.

Devilfish were considered the best bait for halibut, but the tentacles were also boiled and eaten.

The skate was not considered fit to eat. [In fact, it was believed that the canoes used by the dreaded Land Otter Men were skates.] Sharks and dogfish were never eaten, although they were taken for the oil in the liver which was used only for crafts or for trade with the whites.

[Many varieties of shellfish were eaten fresh] or were strung up and dried for winter. Clams, cockles, scallops, abalone, chiton, and mussels were eaten freely from fall to spring, but were generally avoided in the season of growing plants. Mussels, in particular, should not be eaten with salmonberry shoots, wild celery stalks, and fresh berries, but if this were done and sickness ensued, the scalp should be cut on top of the patient's head and poulticed with skunk cabbage leaf, or woman's milk should be applied.

[The reason for the seasonal prohibition is that mussels and some types of clams may become poisonous during the summer months, or on certain beaches at all seasons, as a result of ingesting a dinoflagellate, *Gonyaulax catenella,* closely related to the microorganism that causes the so-called red tide or bloom. The poisons accumulated in the shellfish attack the autonomic nervous system of the eater and may bring death through paralysis and suffocation (pers. comm., Dr. Seton H. Thompson, chief of the Branch of Alaska Fisheries, U.S. Fish and Wildlife Service; see de Laguna 1956:6–7). This was why death came to the Aleut party who ate mussels at Poison Cove, on Peril Strait, in 1799.]

Sea urchins were eaten where they were found, by scooping out the insides with the forefinger [or with a wooden spatula (nı́'ṡa·). It was the ovaries that were eaten.]

Boiled crabs were greatly enjoyed.

[Emmons neglected to discuss the category of "beach food"—that is, edible sessile tidal shellfish and seaweeds. Perhaps because this food was so easily gathered by women and children, it became associated with poverty, particularly with that caused by laziness. Eating beach food was therefore circumscribed by a number of taboos, particularly for the shaman and his family. See Table 17.]

LAND ANIMALS

The flesh of such animals as bear, deer, marmot, porcupine, and beaver was eaten fresh, but occupied a secondary place as compared with fish. The liver of the deer was most esteemed [and ground squirrels, when obtainable, were also relished]. The porcupine was eaten fresh and also dried. It was not skinned, but the hair and quills were singed over the fire and the flesh was boiled or roasted on a spit. The skeleton [presumably with the flesh] was also dried and hung in the house, or preserved in grease for the winter.

The leaf fat of the mountain goat was melted and molded into cakes, which were traded by the mainland tribes to those on the islands, where the goat was not found. The fat might be eaten [it was, in fact, regularly served at feasts by the Yakutat people, who killed many goats], but it was universally used to grease the face before blackening or painting it. The fat and flesh of the deer [found only in southeastern Alaska proper] was mashed to a pulp with the stone hand hammer in a wooden dish, then boiled, and the grease skimmed off to be molded into cakes that were used like goat fat. The Tlingit, however, neither made nor used pemmican [dried, pounded meat and berries, preserved in fat.]

The dog, wolf, and fox were not considered edible. The marten, mink, weasel, rat, mouse, and in particular the land otter, were animals of mystery connected with the practice of shamanism [or witchcraft], and were absolutely tabooed as food. Figures of these animals appear on the shaman's costume and paraphernalia. [But so do the mountain sheep and the tentacles of the devilfish, which were eaten when available.] It is said that the land otter was never hunted for its pelt before the increased demand for furs by Europeans allowed cupidity to overcome superstition. The lynx, rarely found within Tlingit territory, was expressly forbidden to women.

SEA MAMMALS

Sea lion and hair seal were of much more value than any land animal. The greatest amount of oil was obtained from the seal, and this was universally used and traded along the coast.

The seal was cut open along the belly, with the skin and blubber taken off in one piece. The flesh was divided in halves, and the backbone [with the skull] was discarded. The flesh was spitted over the fire when eaten fresh, or was dried and hung up for winter use. [Seal meat was also boiled for eating when fresh.] The bladder was used as a float for the halibut line and also as a receptacle for oil. The skin and blubber were laid over an inclined board, and separated by means of a crescent-shaped iron blade, set in a wooden handle, a knife which superseded that made of a large blue mussel shell, and was called by the same name, *yease* [yí·ṡ]. The blubber was tried out in boxes with hot stones, and was poured into boxes for storage. On the upper edges of these boxes were placed fine strips of the flesh on which the cover was set and corded down to prevent leakage. The Yakutat, who made a business of seal hunting [as did the Hoonah], carried on a lucrative trade in seal oil with the Sitka and Chilkat.

The whale was never hunted by the Tlingit, nor was it eaten by the more northern tribes, but the flesh was eaten by the Haida and by some of those associating with them. However, in late years, when a whale was found stranded, the oil was tried out and sold.

[This statement should be qualified. It would appear that stranded whales were eaten until relatively recently at Yakutat and Dry Bay, and also at Angoon (Viola Garfield, pers. comm.; de Laguna and McClellan, field notes 1950; de Laguna 1972:398–99). This was, however, not always from choice, but more often when there was little else available. The porpoise was also eaten by the Northern Tlingit, but at Yakutat was considered food fit only for the poor families of unlucky hunters, since it was said to cause a disagreeable body odor (de Laguna 1972:398). The Southern Tlingit, according to Drucker (1950:243, Trait 150), said they did not eat porpoise because it caused nosebleeds.

[Khlebnikov, who was at Sitka as early as 1817 (1976:29), reported that the Sitka Tlingit ate seals, dolphins (porpoise?), sea lions, and whale fetuses that had washed ashore, and drank the oil from these animals at feasts. Marchand, it will be remembered (see Chapter 5, the section "Porpoise, Sea Lion, and Whale"), reported that the Sitka Tlingit even hunted whales, and esteemed the oil from their blubber as a delicacy. Von Kotzebue (1830, 2:53–54), who was at Sitka in 1825, wrote: "Their food, sufficiently disgusting in itself, is rendered still more so by their manner of eating. It consists almost exclusively of fish, of which the whale is the chief favorite, and its blubber an especial dainty. This is sometimes cooked upon red-hot stones, but more commonly eaten raw." A Sanya informant told Drucker (1950:243, Trait 178): "When they were lucky enough to find a beached whale, they cut it up and rendered out the grease. They ate a little of it themselves, but not much—'they didn't care for it.' However, they could always sell whale grease to the Haida and Tsimshian, which explains their eagerness to get it."

[The oft-cited revulsion of the Tlingit to whale meat and fat thus would seem to be exaggerated. Most of the Tlingit probably avoided whale meat, like porpoise flesh, as a matter of preference, associating it, I suspect, with poverty. The flesh and fat of the stranded whale may have been in a category similar to that of "beach food," the injudicious consumption of which could lead to poverty. The traditional abhorrence of whale flesh at Sitka was apparently due to the teachings of the shamans, according to Veniaminov ([1840] 1984:400); but he was unable to discover the reason for this taboo. When did the Sitka shamans announce it? And did not some Tlingit continue to enjoy whale meat and blubber?]

BIRDS

Waterfowl and land birds were eaten, except for the albatross, oyster catcher, raven, crow, owl, hawk, [and small song birds]. The eagle was eaten only when necessity demanded. [Drucker (1950:175, 247, Trait 238) was told that the Sanya occasionally ate eagle, the Chilkat never, but that the Yakutat ate eagle. This last is not confirmed by Yakutat informants.]

In preparation for cooking, birds were only partly plucked, and the down and smaller feathers were singed off over the fire. The eggs of all seabirds were gathered in spring on the outer rocks and were eaten fresh, but not preserved.

BERRIES AND OTHER PLANT FOODS

With the coming of spring and the growth of plants, the Tlingit craved fresh food after a steady diet of dried fish and oil, and whole families of women and girls went out in parties to gather the tender shoots [ke̦·t] of the salmonberry and the stalks of the wild celery, which they brought back in great packs, and ate sitting in groups in front of the houses as they discussed social gossip. The wild celery was often skinned with the fingernail and eaten raw, or sometimes the stalks were mashed to a pulp and mixed with grease.

[Young wild celery stalks are still (1980) a favorite with Tlingit children, who gather them along the paths in the villages. They are eaten raw, but their mothers warn them to peel off the astringent outer skin or they will burn their mouths.]

Alaska is the land of berries [ƛé·qʷ]. These form a most necessary and acceptable article of diet, eaten fresh, or cured and pressed into cakes, or preserved in oil. [For the principal berries listed by Emmons, see Table 18. In addition, he recognized the tiny crab apple, *Malus fusca* (Raf.) Schneid., *kwuts* (x̌á·x̌), as a "berry." He omitted the "low bush" or trailing black currant, *Ribes laxiflorum* Pursh., kane·ƚc̓ákʷ; the gooseberry with prickles, *R. lacustre* (Pers.) Poir, x̣a·he·wú; and a few others. The salmonberry and the blueberry seem to be most important to the Tlingit.]

Berry fields, like salmon streams, were hereditary property in families [lineages, or clans]. The gathering and preparation of berries was woman's work. In berrying, she carried a small spruce root basket, *sahk-kah ton-nar* [se·gatá·na·] or *su-yet* [saye̦·t], "to hang from the neck" or "thing under the neck." It was suspended from her neck and hung in front, and the berries were dropped into it. On her back was a much larger basket, *yah-nah,* "to pack on the back" [yá·na·, "burden"], or *dsu-na* [c̓áne·], or *kah-tihk-ka´r-r* [possibly qa· dex̌ ká?a·], into which the smaller basket was emptied. Among the Chilkat, where berry picking was an important economic occupation, still larger baskets, *kluck-tar-tu´n* [perhaps ƛakt da-tá·n], "stationary," or *kah date tu-see-ar* [possibly ka·dé· k(a)dus?i· ?a·], "to empty into from the packer," were filled from the pack baskets and were carried by two people by means of loop handles of heavy roots or hide. [In 1950, such a large basket, said to have been made at Yakutat, was seen at Angoon (de Laguna and McClellan, field notes, 1950).]

Berries were eaten fresh as gathered, with oil, or cooked, and most varieties were prepared for winter use. For preservation, the berries were hung in bags under the smokehole and slightly dried, then boiled and mashed, or simply mashed, and formed into cakes about ten inches square and one inch thick. These were placed on slat frames, on wild celery leaves, set on crosspieces over a very slow-burning fire where they were allowed to remain two days. Then they were turned over for two days more, sun dried for a week or more, and then packed away in boxes for later use. Or, the cakes might be placed in a stone-lined oven in the ground in which a fire had burned out. If the soil were clay, the stone lining was not necessary, and only wild celery leaves were used. The berry cakes were then put into the oven on slat frames, packed one upon another with a layer of leaves between; the top was covered with leaves and tamped down with earth, which excluded the air and kept the heat in.

Cranberries, huckleberries, and blueberries were preserved fresh in grease. Some berries were slightly mashed with salmon spawn and put away in grease. The small wild crab apple was cooked and preserved in grease.

The soapberry was cooked, mashed, and pressed into cakes as described above. It was found only on the mainland and in limited quantities, and was the greatest luxury food known to the Tlingit. It was not eaten like other berries. A small piece of the cake was broken into water, and beaten to a light froth in a dish absolutely free of grease, by the hand of a virgin, otherwise, it would not rise. In later years, sugar was mixed with it. It was eaten with a special long-handled paddle-shaped spoon of maple, generally carved in animal design [the host's crest]. When not in use, such spoons were kept in a special deep, cylindrical, spruce root basket, *chetle tar-káte,* "spoon bag" [šáƚ da·ke·t], that hung on the wall.

The Kamchatka lily, *kuh* [kú·xʷ], known as "wild rice" or "Indian potato," which is found in open patches, was dug in midsummer with a digging stick, or potato digger. The roots were picked over, washed, cooked in open-work baskets in boiling water, and eaten with grease. Or they were mashed with the blue or red huckleberry, mixed with seal oil, and stored in boxes. The roots were also hung up

Chilkat berry picker, 1900. (Photograph by G. T. Emmons? BCPA.)

and dried. The cooked and mashed root was used like putty to fill the seams and corners in the sides and bottoms of the oil boxes to prevent leakage. [In this account, Emmons had erroneously applied the popular name, "Indian potato," to the Kamchatka lily. It more properly designates the *Hedysarum alpinum* L., or cé·t (see Table 18). Or he has combined the two food plants.]

A fern root, *qwutch* [k̓ʷáłx̣], was dug in the fall and cooked in the earth oven or under the fire. Another root, *tset* [cé·t, the true Indian potato], that grows on the sand flats, was cooked and eaten, or dried for winter use. [In addition to the lady fern, k̓ʷáłx̣, the Tlingit also ate the root of the licorice fern, s̓a·č, although this is not mentioned by Emmons.]

The inner bark of the hemlock, spruce, and pine was gathered in the spring and eaten fresh with oil, but that of the hemlock alone was prepared and preserved for winter. [The inner bark or cambium is called sáx̣.] The tree trunk was debarked in slabs one or two feet wide and four or five feet long by means of wedges made of the limbs of hemlock, spruce, or cedar, pointed at one end and sharpened to a flat edge at the other. The wedge used by men was six feet long, the woman's but half that length. The bark [to be detached] was cut across at the bottom with the pointed end, and pried off upwards with the wedge-shaped end of the stick. Then the woman scraped off the fine inner bark with her crescent-shaped knife, originally of mussel shell, later of metal. These shavings were dried or steamed in the earth oven between layers of skunk cabbage leaves, then mashed in wooden dishes with the woman's hand hammer, or rubbed soft with her hands. Then they were formed into cakes and pressed between pieces of hemlock bark, sun dried on the canoe cover, and stored in boxes or strung up on the wall. The preserved bark was softened in boiling water and then mixed with oil before being eaten.

The Tlingit obtained their salt from seaweed which the women gathered in the spring on the outer rocks below the high tide line. There are two [edible] varieties [see Table 17]: the purple-black seaweed, ***klark-ish*** [ła·q̇ásk], and the lighter colored [ribbon] seaweed, ***kartch*** [q̇á·č̓]. These were pressed into flat cakes like those of berries or bark, sun dried, and packed in boxes, or were rolled up in bundles the shape and size of a large sweet potato and dried. To prevent mold, the cakes or bundles of seaweed were spread out on boards [in the sun] on bright days. Like the bark cakes, they were softened in boiling water and eaten with oil.

Potatoes were introduced by the Russians and are now [post-1867 to ?] generally grown on old village sites where the soil has been enriched through generations by the refuse from the fireplace, and this is further fertilized by covering with seaweed and burning it. The soil is light, and both easy to work and fertile. The gardens are fenced with brush, the beds are made long and narrow and high, being built up from eight to twelve inches above the trenches, and at the top are not more than two feet wide. Potatoes are planted in the early spring in April, and are visited and weeded several times during the summer. The potatoes are dug up by the middle or end of September. The cultivation is done by the women, their only implement being a stake about four feet long, the end sharpened and hardened in the fire. They also use paddlelike sticks [with a leaf-shaped, pointed blade and a crutch handle] and an imitation of our spade [with a crutch handle and the blade expanded on one

Digging sticks, Angoon, 1892. (Pencil sketches by G. T. Emmons. AMNH.) Straight digging stick, a paddle-shaped digging stick, and a wooden spade with step for the foot, all used for potato cultivation.

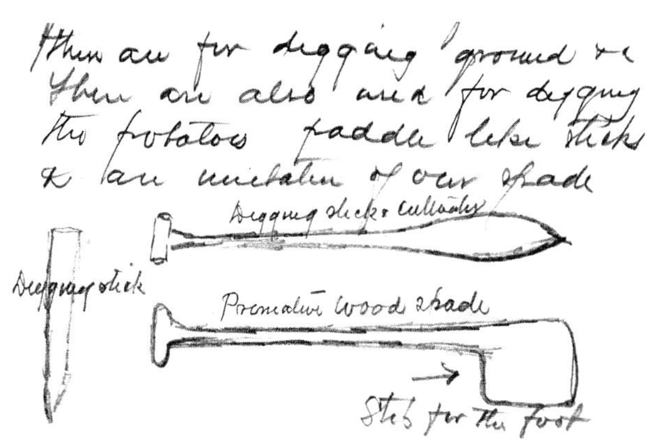

side to make a step for the foot, according to sketches and notes made by Emmons at Angoon, 1892, in AMNH]. After being gathered, the potatoes are stored in cellars under the floor, or in root houses. They were generally cooked by steaming in the ground oven, or on a hearth of heated stones, and covered with seaweed which not only confined the steam but contributed salt, and were eaten with grease. [Although the Indians of Killisnoo and Angoon were famous for their potatoes, these were described by Muir in 1879 (1915:130) as "the size of walnuts."]

[Krause (1885) 1956:109, reported that the Tlingit chewed the root of the lupine, *kantak* [kantáqʷ or gantáqʷ, *Lupinus nootkatensis* Donn], which produced a mild form of intoxication, but this report remains unverified.]

TOBACCO*

The Tlingit and Haida cultivated, used, and traded a native tobacco long before the coming of Europeans to the Northwest Coast and the introduction of commercial tobacco. They neither smoked nor chewed the plant, but compounded it with lime and ash to form a product that was sucked. [Both the native plant and the imported tobacco were called *gunge* (gánč), although the former is sometimes specifically designated as "Tlingit tobacco," Łingí't ganči.]

There has been some discussion of the true character of the native plant. [Emmons evidently refers here to the article by R. B. Dixon (1933), who came to the conclusion that the plant in question was not a true tobacco, *Nicotiana,* but some other species, since the early explorers, Captain Dixon at Yakutat in 1787, Marchand at Sitka in 1791, Ingraham and Hoskins on the Queen Charlottes between 1790 and 1793, and Vancouver's party at Angoon in 1794, all speak of a plant similar to tobacco, but not identical. R. B. Dixon could find no evidence that any specimen of true tobacco had ever been collected from the Northwest Coast. The authors cited by Emmons are taken from this article.]

I would state that, in 1883, Mrs. George Dickenson, the Tsimshian wife of the agent of the Killisnoo Trading Company's post at Haines, Alaska, gave me an envelope containing broken leaves and stems of the native tobacco, which she had been given by her people many years before. These plants had been raised by the Haida of the Queen Charlotte Islands and brought to Port Simpson in earlier days. I sent this sample to Professor Frederick V. Coville, of the Division of Botany, United States Department of Agriculture, in Washington, D.C. In reply he wrote:

> The plant you thought was tobacco, I soaked up carefully and dissected, and as a result there is little doubt in my mind that the thing was a real tobacco, possibly the species known as *Nicotiana multivalvis* or *N. quadrivalvis*.

In the summer of 1900, in Victoria, B.C., Mrs. Roderick Finlayson, the daughter of John Work (Factor of the Hudson's Bay Company post at Fort Simpson, B.C., from 1835 to 1849), told me that, as a girl, she had seen native tobacco brought by the Haida to Port Simpson as an article of trade. It had a narrow leaf and was said to be very mild.

Vancouver (1801, 5:441) stated, from the report by Whidbey, who in July 1794 stopped on the Chatham Strait shore of Admiralty Island, off Kootznahoo Inlet where the old village of Angoon stands today:

> On each side of the entrance some new habitations were constructing, and for the first time during our intercourse with the North West American Indians, in the vicinity of these habitations were found some square patches of ground in a state of cultivation, producing a plant that appeared to be a species of tobacco; and which, we understood, is by no means uncommon amongst the inhabitants of Queen Charlotte's islands, who cultivate this plant.

**Editor's note:* The authors cited by Emmons are from the article by Ronald B. Dixon (1933). In addition to checking and adding the quotations from these which Emmons wanted to use—Captain Dixon (Beresford), Marchand, Ingraham, Vancouver, and Dawson—I have added information from Tikhmenev, Colnett, Malaspina, and Beresford, as well as the references to Heizer (1940), de Laguna (1972), and Meilleur (1979) on the nature of the plant and its cultivation. I was not able to check the reference to Hoskins. The last paragraph is mine.

[R. B. Dixon (1933:148) stated: "This latter information [Vancouver] must have secured from Alexander Menzies, a member of that expedition, who had been among the Haida with Colnett in 1787." He also reported (p. 149) that a botanical specimen, supposedly collected by Menzies on the Northwest Coast, and originally published as *Nicotiana,* was later proved to be *Hesperochiron,* which does not grow on the Pacific coast.]

Dr. George Dawson, in a report on the Queen Charlotte Islands (Dawson 1880:144B–15B), stated that the Haida had previously grown tobacco, not only for themselves but for trade to neighboring tribes, and that the plant was still cultivated in 1878 by one old woman at Cumshewa. [R. B. Dixon (1933:148) added: "Dawson, however, doubted that the plant called tobacco was really such," and suggested (p. 150) that the Tlingit and Haida plant was a lupine.

[The Russian writer, Tikhmenev ([1861–63] 1978:84) stated (as of 1803):

> On the coast of the mainland, near Sitkha, a small-leafed plant about the height of tobacco and somewhat like laurel grew, which the natives mixed with lime calcined from shells and used for smoking and for chewing. This mixture was not strong, but when burned, it gave out a pleasant odor. The natives did a good trade in it.]

The statement that this mixture was smoked is quite misleading, for the Tlingit never smoked before they had commercial tobacco.

[Emmons here forgets that the Tlingit were probably smoking by 1803. There is evidence that even the Yakutat used snuff and grew the plant before the arrival of Europeans. Colnett (manuscript 1788) reported "a house and garden neatly fenced in, & European plants growing"[!] at a site within Hoonah territory on the Gulf Coast, perhaps Palma Bay. Since this was before the Russians had attempted to introduce garden crops anywhere on the Northwest Coast, it seems that this must have been a tobacco patch (de Laguna 1972:131–32). Malaspina, who was at Yakutat in 1791, reported patches of "cultivated ground" (1885:164–65) on Knight Island in Yakutat Bay and on the mainland, which I interpreted as tobacco gardens. In 1787, Beresford (1789:175) reported the use of this plant at Yakutat:

> The Indians are particularly fond of chewing a plant, which appears to be a species of tobacco; not content, however, with chewing it in its simple state, they generally mix lime with it, and sometimes the inner rind of the pine-tree, together with a rosinous substance extracted from it.

The growing and preparation of native tobacco was described by Yakutat informants in 1952 and 1954 (de Laguna 1972:410–11).

[Emmons also cited Marchand's report of the Sitkans in 1791 (Fleurieu 1801, 1:340–41) in notes that he intended to incorporate in this book:

> Their custom, like that of almost all the nations of AMERICA and ASIA, is to chew habitually a species of herb; and as soon as they were acquainted with the tobacco leaf, they gave it the preference to that which they had before employed to satisfy the same want.

[Emmons also planned to include, if he could, the following passages summarized in R. B. Dixon (1933:149–50). The first was from Ingraham, who was in the Queen Charlottes in 1791 (Ingraham 1971:150). A copy of his manuscript in the Library of Congress was in the library of the Provincial Archives in Victoria, where Emmons worked. Ingraham wrote:

> The natives chew a plant (as many among us do tobacco) which perhaps may be worthy of attention. It appeared to me to possess some of the properties of tobacco. Whether the natives consider it as our tobacco chewers do (a luxury) or make use of it to benefit by its medical qualities I am not able to say. However, I have procured a good quantity of the seeds and shall send them home for investigation of some friend whom botanical knowledge may enable to point out the good properties of the weed (if any there are) and to describe it with philosophical propriety. I can only lament it is not in my power to do so.

[The other passage Emmons wanted to cite, like the one above, was used by C. F. Newcombe (1923) in editing *Menzies' Journal* of his voyage with Vancouver, and in turn were cited by R. B. Dixon (1933:147–48). As summarized by Emmons:

> Hoskins (with Capt Gray) went ashore at Rose's Hbr, at the head of the Sound they found a meadow containing some tobacco plants, wild celery, etc. Hoskins states that the men here "chew tobacco in a green state, with which they mix a substance resembling lime. They put quids of this plant into their mouths as big as a hen's egg."

[The manuscript of the Narrative of J. Hoskins, 1790–93, is in the library of the Massachusetts Historical Society, but has not been consulted for this book.]

The tobacco plant cultivated by the Tlingit and Haida was unquestionably an annual that disappeared when its cultivation ceased. The only story I ever heard about its origin was that it was discovered by some bear hunters in the interior country back of Yakutat and that the seed procured was distributed and cultivated along the coast.

[In a later version of this manuscript, Emmons referred to two Haida myths that trace the origin of tobacco to the upper Stikine River (Dawson 1880:152B, and Swanton 1905b:233), both cited by R. B. Dixon (1933:149–50), and Emmons added the Chilkat belief that tobacco was the gift of Raven.

[That Emmons was correct and R. B. Dixon wrong was established by Robert F. Heizer (1940:704–6), but too late for use by Emmons. Heizer cited the botanist, Alice Eastwood, who examined the plants collected by Menzies and Captain Dixon, explained the confusion caused by the mislabeling of a species of *Hesperochiron* collected by William Bird in the Rockies, and identified the specimens from the Northwest Coast as a *Nicotiana,* but not *N. attenuata,* and not *N. multivalvis,* although it resembles the latter. It is now recognized as *N. quadrivalvis* Pursh., var. *multivalvis* (Lindl.) Mansf. See Meilleur 1979.]

After the arrival of the Russians at Sitka, commercial tobacco became an article of trade, in the form of bundles of leaves in a twist, which the natives called *gunge* [gánč, and the cultivation of the native plant ceased, so that the present generation do not know it.

[Tobacco was originally used in the form of snuff.] To prepare this, the shell of the large horse clam, *Saxidomus giganteus, gatle nuku* [gá·ł nú·x̌u], was roasted or calcined, and then pulverized in a stone mortar, a utensil found in every Tlingit home. An old Sitkan said that sometimes a strong decoction, made by boiling the bark of the crab apple, might be mixed with the calcined shell, but this seems to have been a local, not a general practice. To the lime was added the ash of the inner bark of the willow or of the yellow cedar, and the crisped leaf of the native tobacco that had been dried before the fire. All of these ingredients were reduced to a fine powder in the mortar, and were bound together with a particle of gum from the spruce or cedar to form a thick paste.

[According to an informant at Angoon (de Laguna and McClellan, field notes, 1950), it was the yellow cedar bark ash that gave the desired "kick," but that too much of this could bring tears to the eyes. He had been told that ash from the inner bark of the hemlock was much stronger.]

When commercial tobacco was introduced in trade, this also was made into snuff, mixed with bark or leaves, but lime was omitted since the imported tobacco was much stronger than the native plant. About this time, wooden mortars also came into use. They were generally hollowed out of a hard root or knot, and often had a flattened and expanded base [with two planklike projections] to give greater stability.

Snuff, in the form of a paste, was shaped into a cake that was carried in a little woven spruce root case like a double basket, or in a cylindrical box of birch bark, bone or ivory. Copper cases of Russian manufacture came into general use later. The woman carried the case in a skin pouch suspended around the neck, this was called *tuck-tar-kate* [tax̌ da·ke·t], "bite bag"; the double basket for snuff was called *wus-shut-káte* [waš ʔát da·ke·t], "cheek box." Tobacco bags, like those of the interior, were not used.

For use, a small amount of the tobacco mixture was rolled into a pellet about the size of a large pea, called *wash at* [waš ʔat], "cheek thing." It was placed between the lower lip or cheek and the gums, and was sucked with frequent expectorations. A misapprehension generally existed among the early explorers as to the use of this tobacco mixture. They speak of "chewing it," a natural conclusion from seeing the movement of the mouth in sucking and spitting. But in this they were mistaken. The tiny pellet, loosely bound, could not possibly have been chewed, for it would have been dissipated at the first attempt. [Yet the snuff bag was called "bite bag," tax̌ da·ke·t, from -tax̌, "to bite or chew."]

The pellet was an article of luxury, offered to a guest as a gesture of hospitality. At potlatches, feasts, or ceremonial councils little pellets were distributed to those assembled. I witnessed this being done at a potlatch at Sitka as late as 1885.

Smoking was not practiced by the Tlingit or by other tribes of the Northwest Coast until it was introduced by the early traders in the last quarter of the eighteenth century. After it was taken up, the older use of the snuff pellet was gradually abandoned and the smoking feast became an important ceremony, especially after a cremation, at later meetings in memory of the dead, and at potlatches. On these occasions, the imported leaf tobacco was handed around to the assembled guests, and was also cast into the fire for the deceased as the latter's name was called out. The gift had more than symbolic significance for, like food sacrificed on memorial occasions, the tobacco was believed to be received and enjoyed by the spirit in the other world.

The Tlingit was a very moderate smoker. While smoking was universally practiced by men, few women smoked. [Women apparently used snuff at commemorative ceremonies or "smoking feasts" for the dead, until cigarettes were

"Prior to the coming of the European the Thlingit used implements of stone, shell, bone, ivory and copper. What we commonly call a pestle, seems from the greater numbers obtained to have been the most common." (*a, b, c, d, e, [and g]*) Kar-tihk-r [kaṫíx̣a˙ / ku˙ṫíx̣a˙] *used for smashing bones, salmon eggs.* (*f*) Tihk-r [ṫíx̣a˙] *used in manufacture of tobacco and snuff in conjunction with* (*h*) Tihk-r ate [ṫíx̣a˙ ye˙t (?)]: *stone mortar used in manufacture of native tobacco.* (*i*) Ka-tu [ké˙ṫu]: *stone war pick or club [two views of clubs with wooden handles and stone heads; views of two stone heads]. (Pencil sketches by G. T. Emmons, on page from notebook in BCPA.)*

Stone Implements

Prior to the coming of the European the Thlingit used implements of stone, shell, bone ivory & Copper. What we commonly call a pestle, seems from the greater numbers obtained to have been the most common.

a) b) c) D E "Kar-tihk-r", used for mashing bones, salmon eggs

"Tihk-r" used in manufacture of tobacco and snuff in conjunction with —

"Tihk-r ate" Stone mortars used in manufacture of native tobacco;

"Ka-tu" Stone war pick or club.

introduced. Ordinary commercial brands of cigarettes have become more common than pipes. Although most Tlingit women did not smoke in 1950, yet when cigarettes were passed around at the smoking feast in memory of the dead, all guests, regardless of sex or age, or personal inclination, were obligated to smoke.]

The tobacco most esteemed [in the last century] was the plain black leaf, which had a fixed trade value before money was used. With its introduction, the pipe came into existence, and the smoking feast became an important ceremony after cremation, and at other commemorative ceremonies for the dead.

Pipes, *suck-ta-kate,* "smoke case" [s̓e·q da·ke·t, "smoke container"], may be divided into those for general use and those for ceremonial occasions. The former were small and plain, generally commercial articles [obtained from the whites]. With the increased importance of the smoking feast, the trade pipe gave place to fine specimens of native manufacture. A chief might have a number of such pipes that would be handed to the more honored guests at ceremonies. Pipes of stone, ivory, or bone were rare. The crudest pipe I ever saw was a large piece of pumice, picked up on the beach, hollowed out and fitted with a stem of elderberry. [The bowls of ceremonial pipes] were generally made of foreign wood, usually in the form of driftwood or the stocks of discarded muskets. These were elaborately carved and painted, usually in animal form representing the totemic crest of the family, and were often overlaid with copper plates or inlaid with haliotis [abalone] shell and opercula. The bowl was lined with copper or with an inserted section of a gun barrel. The stem was a section of some pithy [hollow] wood, three or five inches long. No other article gave the carver such freedom in artistic conception and execution.

[Keithahn (1962, fig. 5) has illustrated plain and decorated stone pipes from southeastern Alaska, including a tubular pipe from near Klukwan (fig. 5*a*), presumed to be of interior manufacture.

[In judging the amount of smoking by the Tlingit in different periods, allowance should be made for the marked differences noticeable in whites at the same period. In the 1930s, smoking by white women in public was accepted in the East but not in Alaska until later. Now the easterner is impressed by the amount of smoking among both sexes in the western states, while heavy smoking by both men and women is common in Alaska despite the warnings of the surgeon general.]

DRINK*

The Tlingit drank fresh water to quench their thirst, and salt [sea] water for medicinal and for ritual purposes in connection with fasting.

"Hudson's Bay tea" was made by boiling the green leaves of the swamp laurel, *sick-shel-teen* or *sick shult* [s̓ikšaɫdí·n, *Ledum palustre* L., ssp. *groenlandicum,* (Oeder) Hult.]. Some say that an intoxicant was made by boiling the roots of a berry bush, *sick-ga-kow thlaku ka-ha-ge* [s̓igi· qá·wu ƛ́é·g̣u (and) kaha·gu, "dead people's berries" and "dried berries," *Streptopus amplexifolius* (L.) DC., or clasping twisted-stalk], but this is generally disclaimed. The root of a mountain plant, *scht* [s̓íkš, *Veratrum viride* Ait., ssp. *Eschscholtzii* (Gray) Löve & Löve, American white hellebore, or "Skookum root"], when eaten, produced a deep sleep, like liquor. [This was, however, a very potent medicine.]

Distilled liquor was introduced by Europeans and became a prime necessity in ceremonies and trade, until an attack on the Hudson's Bay Company post at Wrangell (1846) led to an agreement between that company and the Russian-American Company to prohibit its use, though this restriction was observed only at the main posts. [See Tikhmenev (1861–63), 1978:354.]

[At first, however, the Indians did not like liquor, or at least were cautious in their use of it. Marchand (Fleurieu 1801, 1:340) reported of the Sitkans in 1791: "It is not known that the Tchinkitanayans make use of any fermented drink, or any strong liquor; and the brandy of which they were prevailed on to make a trial, appeared to be not to their liking: it were to be wished, for their tranquility and happiness, that their communication with Europeans may not introduce into their forests, this fatal liquor which has carried confusion into those of the savages of the EAST part of NORTH AMERICA, and which, on the coast of AFRICA, is paid for by the freedom of men."

[Von Langsdorff (1814) reported from Sitka, as of 1805–6: "Though they would like brandy very much, they reject it because they see the effect that it produces, and are afraid that, if deprived of their senses, they should fall into the power of the Russians" (2:111). "Brandy, which is sometimes offered them by the Russians, they reject as a scandalous liquor, depriving them of their senses" (2:131). Unfortunately, it was not long before they avidly accepted liquor from the traders.]

**Editor's note:* I included information from Marchand, von Langsdorff, and Howard, as well as an explanation of the word "hooch."

When I was passing through the eastern entrance of Peril Strait in 1881 [*sic,* Emmons was not in Alaska until mid-1882], some of the older natives who were with me pointed to "Trader's Island" [the largest of the Traders Island group] and said that each spring, at about the same time, a Hudson's Bay Company trading vessel came to trade with the neighboring people [Hutsnuwu] who had assembled with their winter catch of pelts. When a gun was fired, the natives flocked on board, and each one was given a bottle of liquor, a pipe, and tobacco. That night a debauch followed, and in the morning when they were still drunk and groggy, their furs were taken from them for more liquor or trifles. When they sobered up, the ship had sailed, and they found themselves with nothing to show for their season's work. [See Chapter 2, "Trade."]

[In 1867, when Captain Howard took the USS *Lincoln* on a tour of southeastern Alaska, "to show the flag," some of the Indians became very angry when he refused to give them the whiskey they demanded. A party of Hoonah (?) replied to his refusal, "You come to Icy strait, we give you good fight!" (Howard 1868:207).]

The distilling of *hootchanoo* from hops, potatoes, and molasses or brown sugar was taught them by a discharged soldier after the withdrawal of our troops. [The word "hootchanoo" or "hootznoo," from which our word "hooch" is derived, is a corruption of xú·c nu·wú, "brown bear fort," or Hutsnuwu, the name for Admiralty Island, where the soldier taught the Tlingit (see James G. Swan, 1875, in Morris 1879:146; and Krause [1885] 1956:108).] The ingredients were boiled with water in a tightly covered iron kettle, from the top of which a tin coil led to a closed vessel, generally a five-gallon kerosine can. A section of giant kelp was substituted when the metal coil could not be obtained. The worm [or coil] was enclosed in a box filled with snow, which condensed the vapor that dripped into the vessel [placed to receive it]. This produced an almost colorless strong liquor that made the natives wild, and thus caused many quarrels and killings at the feasts where it was consumed. It constituted the most valuable article of trade with the interior people, although fortunately only very small quantities were so employed.

FIRE MAKING

In the childhood of the world, according to ancient myths, the elements were jealously guarded by supernatural beings. When the creator and transformer, *Yehlh* [Yé·ł], Raven, appeared to make the world habitable for human beings, his first endeavor was to release these natural forces. Fire existed far out in the sea, and Raven persuaded the Sparrow Hawk to get it. At that time, the Hawk had a long, straight, black bill. But while he was carrying the ember in it, the end was almost burned off, which accounts for its present recurved shape and changed color [black tip and yellow base]. When he reached the land, he dropped the spark, which fell on wood and rock, to each of which its power was given [of kindling fire]. Since that time, man has been able to produce fire, through the rubbing together of wood and the striking together of rocks. Both methods of making fire were practiced by the Tlingit.

[According to the version of this myth recorded by Swanton (1909:11, Tale 1), Raven put the fire in red cedar and white beach stones (presumably quartz), for the benefit of mankind.]

The wooden outfit [fire drill] was preferably made of the heart of the red cedar, although when traveling with the Chilkat in 1890 I saw cottonwood utilized with equally good results. The spindle [drill], *tul-thlee ekh ghon* [tu·łí "drill," ?, x̣̓a·n "fire"], was about twelve inches long and three-fourths inch in diameter at the lower, rounded end, and tapered toward the upper end. The bed piece [or hearth], *tulthlee ekh tini* [tu·łí "drill," and ?] was a flat piece of wood, about twelve to eighteen inches long, and from one-half to one inch in thickness. Just at the edge, a groove or notch was cut out, about one-fourth inch wide and of the same depth, to allow for the exit of the sawdust produced by the drilling, since these narrow channels were connected with the slight depressions on the face of the hearth in which the spindle was turned. This bed piece was often slightly charred to make it more combustible. To make fire, the larger, rounded end of the spindle was pressed down in the depression at the end of one of the notches, and was revolved rapidly back and forth between the palms of the hands, by a person kneeling in front. A constant downward pressure was maintained, because when the hands approached the base of the spindle, they were slid upward with a quick twirl, so that the pressure was never relaxed. Sometimes the spindle was rotated by two people, relieving each other by turns.

[The Tlingit also made fire by means of the strap drill, which required two operators, as reported by informants at Angoon and Yakutat (de Laguna and McClellan, field notes, 1950, 1952) in addition to the ordinary drill. Drucker's Sanya and Chilkat informants also reported the bow drill for fire making, as did ours at Yakutat, although Drucker (1950:269, Trait 955) suspected that it was not aboriginal.]

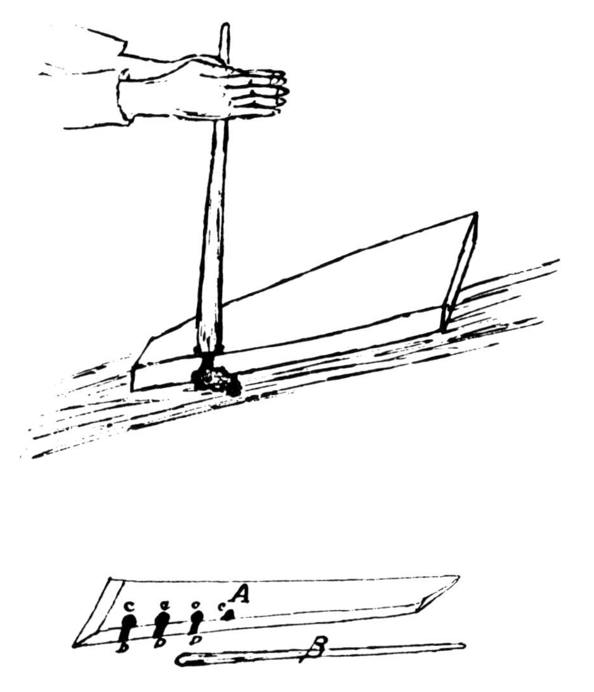

Fire drill. "A" is hearth; "B" is drill; "C, C" are holes in hearth for the drill; "D, D" are grooves cut for sawdust. (Pen and ink sketch by G. T. Emmons. AMNH.)

With the friction exerted, a fine sawdust would be worn out of the hole into the channel, and the accumulated heat would cause the sawdust to glow like a coal. A wisp of finely divided cedar bark, or fungus, *tchon-e-he* [?], hemlock fungus *charl-eh-ka* [?], might be placed in the groove to act as a slow match. If more heat were needed, a few grains of sand or grit might be dropped in the hole in which the spindle was rotated. Or a few grains of gunpowder might be mixed with the sawdust.

Dick [Satan or Se·tá·n, of Sitka] said that the heartwood of the red cedar was preferred for both parts of the fire drill because it was very compact. It had to be thoroughly dry. If fire did not come soon, some wax from the ear was put in the drill hole to increase friction. [Yakutat informants said that earwax was put on the tinder to make it catch fire more easily (de Laguna 1972:307).]

The primitive strike-a-light, *tdart-see* [dá·ʒi], consisted of pyrites and some hard stone, such as quartz, since the Tlingit had no steel and little flint. An interesting and very old fire [making] bag was found in a shaman's dilapidated gravehouse at Dry Bay near the mouth of the Alsek River. [The grave was that of an unnamed shaman of the Raven 17; see de Laguna, 1972:686–87.] This bag was some six inches square, made of black bear skin with some of the hair still adhering, and had a long flap [to close it] and a hide strip to go over the shoulder, so that it hung under the arm. Inside were several pieces of pyrites and dried tree fungus. Another bag from a shaman's gravehouse at Dry Bay contained pieces of iron. From a very old Chilkat man at *Kloquan* [Klukwan] I obtained a small bag, four and one-half to five inches square, containing small splinters of pitch wood for fire kindling on trail trips inland.

Which of the two methods of fire making was the older is not known. While the use of the twirling stick and bed piece [fire drill] was universal among the coastal tribes as far as the Copper River delta, the strike-a-light seemed to be confined to the Northern Tlingit who did not have red cedar, and [appeared to be] borrowed from the interior people. [Drucker (1950:269) reported: "Stones for this type of firemaking were imported from the interior."] With the coming of Europeans, flint and steel were introduced and became generally used, for I have seen these in boxes in different localities. [Of course, matches later replaced all such appliances.]

[In an earlier version of this monograph, Emmons stated his belief that the fire drill was older among the Tlingit than the strike-a-light, as use of the drill "was more generally practiced and suitable woods were ever at hand, while pyrites occur only in [certain] localities, and flint was more rarely met with." Other notes stated that a piece of flint and iron ore or pyrites for kindling fires was "used by the northern tribes more, the southern people adhering to the stick drill more."]

Since the Tlingit traveled by canoe and camped at night or under stress of bad weather, certain favorable camping places became well known, and here the spruce trees were barked so that a flow of gum was always at hand to give a ready blaze. Fire was laid between two logs placed parallel to the direction of the wind.

DOMESTIC UTENSILS

Before the acquisition of kettles, [stone] boiling was done in boxes and closely woven spruce root baskets, using only a little water. For this primitive form of cooking, and also for trying out fish and seal oil, and for preparing the sweat bath, small boulders of fine-grained, heavy rock were selected that would neither disintegrate nor explode when heated and plunged into water, or when water was thrown on them to produce steam. The general name for such stones among the Southern Tlingit was "solid," *eetch* [ʔí·č̓, "heavy round stone"], referring to the uniform close texture of the rock. But the Northern Tlingit named the stones used for cooking *dog-ta-ye* [da·k te·yí], "heating stones," and those for the sweat bath were called *char-le-ta-ye* [x̣a·y te·yí, "bath stones"].

Hot rocks were handled with wooden tongs, *eena* [ʔí·na·]. The same word was used for the split stick for broiling fish and a split stick used for barking spruce root, but the tongs for hot stones are longer, wider, and heavier than the spit or the barking tool. [Tongs are also called łáṫa·]. The split stick for roasting is also known as *qua-nah* [x̣ʷé·na·], while the simple spit for roasting fish is *steak* [cí·k].

Any vessel used for stone boiling is called *ta-yet* [té ye·t or taye·t], whether of wood or basketry, and vessels made of stone may be called by the same word. When using a basket for cooking, kelp leaves are put in the bottom [presumably to protect it from the hot stones].

[In "Notes to Use" (BCPA), Emmons indicated another form of cooking with hot rocks. These are covered with leaves; then potatoes, fish, or other food is laid on top; and this, in turn, is covered with leaves. Water is poured on to make steam.]

Food dishes and spoons were of wood and horn, and in elegance of form, design, and technique of carving exhibited the highest order of native art. Dishes were mainly of alder but also of such nonresinous woods as maple and birch, and were more often procured in trade from the Tsimshian than Tlingit-made. Birch and maple of sufficient size were interior woods. Such dishes were of four distinct types, including the oil dishes into which dried fish was dipped when eating. These [oil dishes], the smallest in size, were the most varied in shape, representing in miniature all of the other three types, as well as representing animal forms in which the body was hollowed out to form the receptacle. They became so permeated with grease and smoothed through use that they had every appearance of being of ebony. [See Krause (1885) 1956, pl. I, *-7, -9.*]

One of the other types of food dish, *kah-kon-na* [q̇a·kané·, "deep dish"], was made like all food [storage] boxes and chests: by shaping, steaming, and bending a single length of board around three corners, and sewing or pegging it at the fourth, to form the sides, to which the bottom was secured in like manner. The sides were hollowed out on the inside, showing a very graceful rounded exterior which was carved in low relief in conventional animal figures, and was often painted or inlaid with haliotis or opercula. This was a large dish. [See Krause (1885) 1956, pl. I, *-4.*]

The other types of food dish, varying in size, were cut out of solid blocks of wood, and were used not only to eat from, but in preparing all kinds of food. The commonest type of dish, of medium size, rather longer than wide, three to four inches high, and carved at the ends with an animal's head in low relief, was cut out of a block of wood. [This is probably what Archy Hoonah told Emmons was called *tsikh shee-ou.*]

Tsek, tsikh, or even *tsick* [ṡíx̣, "bowl, dish"] is the general name for any food dish. One kind was rectangular in form, with low, convex sides, the ends slightly higher. Sides and ends were rounded, and carved in low relief to show an animal's head bisected and spread out to fill the entire field. In the more ornamental dishes, one half of the body was shown on each side, and the rim was inlaid with opercula. These were attributed to the Tsimshian, although they were found along the coast from Vancouver to Yakutat. [See Krause (1885) 1956, pl. I, *-8.*]

Sho-hun-cut-tor, or *sho-hun-cut-to-r tsikh* [?, ?- ṡíx̣], was a much rarer type of dish, most graceful in its oval shape, with high canoelike ends, deeply curved sides, and slightly convex outer surface. This was ornamentally carved like the *tsek* [ṡíx̣] and, in addition was more frequently painted. [See Krause (1885) 1956, pl. I, *-5, -6,* of horn.]

The largest dish, *kithlar* [q̇éła· or q̇íła·, "platter"], was a long, low, shallow tray, hollowed out with a narrow rim along the sides and slightly raised solid ends. The latter were generally carved in low relief to represent a bear's or a bird's head. The rim was usually painted, inlaid with opercula, or ornamented in parallel ridges. [See Krause (1885) 1956, pl. I, *-1.*] Such trays were more characteristically Tlingit, and were of spruce or cedar. They were used only on feast occasions, when they were placed before a number of guests. The largest and most celebrated feast dish among the Tlingit is the property of the *Con-nuh-ta-de* [G̣a·nax̣te·dí, Raven 3] of the Chilkat. It was named *Thluke-hotsick* [ƛ̣úkʷ ṡíx̣], "Woodworm Dish," and is fourteen feet six inches long, two feet six inches wide, and one foot high. It is painted, inlaid with opercula, shaped and carved to represent an important family [clan] crest, the Woodworm, that, according to legend was responsible for the division of the original clan [G̣a·nax̣ʔádi, Raven 1], then living on Prince of Wales Island. This division resulted in the northern migration of that body [Raven 3] that settled at Chilkat. The dish was used only on the most important family occasions. [See Swanton 1909:151–52, Tale 31, for the story of the girl who suckled the Woodworm.]

Two Raven chiefs, Angoon, ca. 1901. (Photograph by Vincent Soboleff. BCPA.) The De·ši·ta·n *chief,* Kennel-ku, *on the left, wears the Raven Hat; the Beaver Feast Dish is at his feet. An unidentified chief wears a headdress* (šaki´at) *and a woven tunic.*

Food preparation. (Pen and ink sketches by G. T. Emmons. AMNH.) (a) Seal bladder filled with oil and hung on hook on wall. (b) Wooden tongs, Elar [ʔí·na·], *for heated stones,* tuk-kut tar-ee [-?- te·yí]. *(c) Apparatus for straining eulachon oil: wooden strainer, spruce root bag in which the fish are put, wooden block that is pressed down on the mass of fish, and frame over wooden box on which the bag of fish is placed. (d) Small spoon made of a clam shell set in a cleft stick. (e) Wooden mold for shaping a horn spoon,* chetle *(spoon)* [šáł, *"spoon"*] con-nuck-kar *[?]. (f) Wooden mold for shaping horn spoon,* Shish-shar con-nuck-kar *[?].*

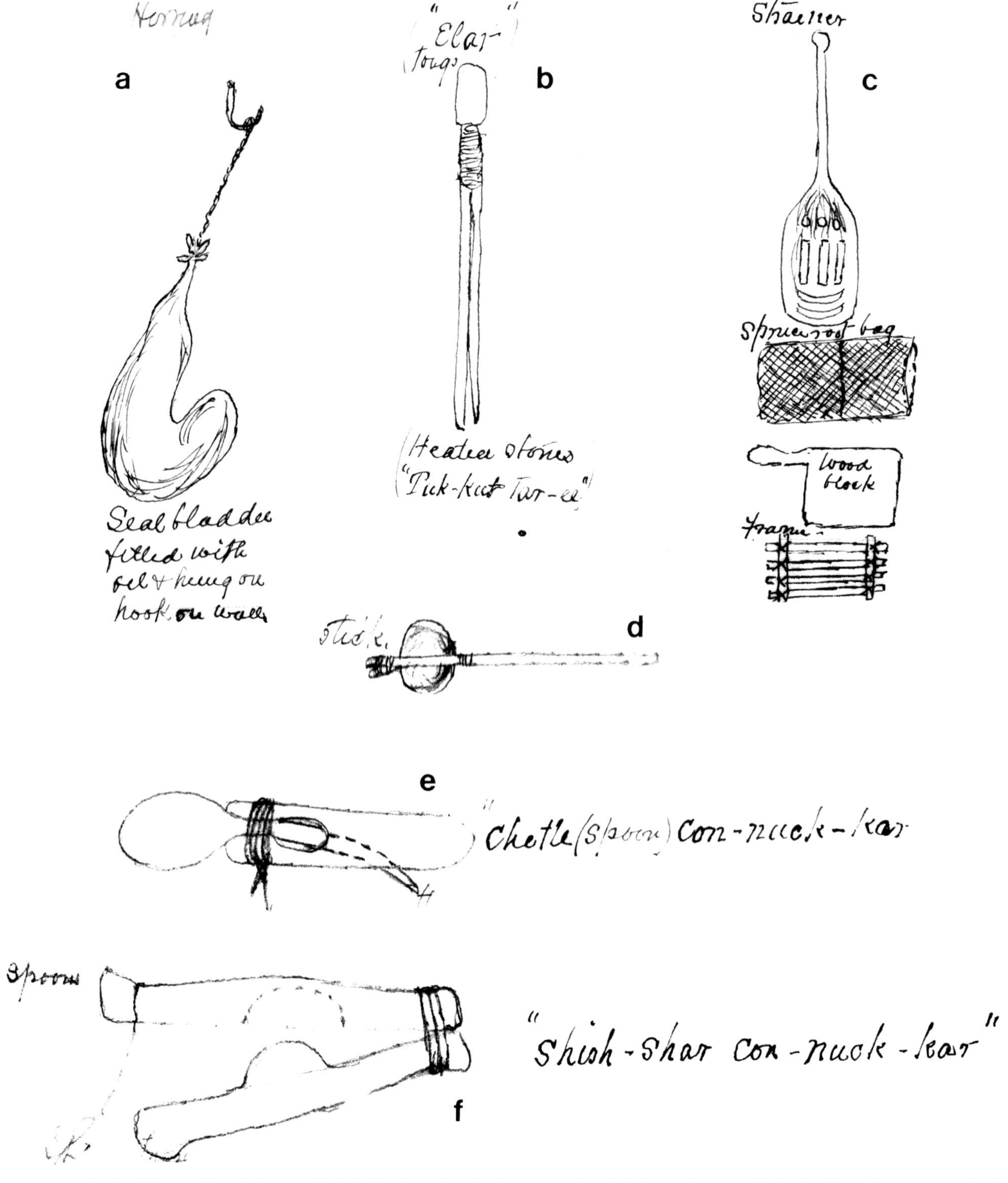

I saw only one large stone bowl among the Tlingit. It was used as a feast dish upon ceremonial occasions by the Chilkats of Klukwan. [Drucker (1943:54) has argued that many of the stone bowls found on the Northwest Coast were used as feast dishes, and is skeptical that tobacco preparation or the smashing of berries for drying would have required so many hollow stones as have been labeled "mortars."]

From the horn of the mountain sheep [Dall sheep] were fashioned the most graceful of oil receptacles. These were often carved and inlaid with haliotis. The finest specimens were from the Haida. A favorite design showed a mouse at each end, in the act of crawling in, representing their fondness for grease. They are most destructive in eating into winter supplies.

Ladles and spoons were made of the horn of the mountain [Dall] sheep and of the mountain goat, and of maple wood. The ladle, *sheen* [ší·n and xʷéna·], was often beautifully carved and inlaid with haliotis, and when used at feasts, was filled with oil and handed to the most honored guests. Large wooden ladles, often carved with the family crest, were used as skimmers in the manufacture of fish oil. Spoons, *chetle* [šáł], were generally of goat and sheep horn, though sometimes of wood, maple being preferred. Probably the earliest type of spoon used by the Tlingit was a simple mussel shell which was later mounted to a wooden handle, made by splitting the end of a stiff stick and lashing the split with spruce root. In an old deer hunting camp I once found an improvised spoon consisting of a clam shell secured in the split end of a stick. This type of spoon is still [1900?] used by hunting and traveling parties, and by the poorest people.

The general eating spoon of sheep horn or wood was larger than the goat horn spoon, and had a broad, flattened handle, usually plain, but sometimes terminating in a single figure or in a bird's head. Among the Southern Tlingit and Tsimshian the spoon of maple wood was often painted on the inside of the handle and bowl in a very conventionalized bird or animal form. [See Krause (1885) 1956, pl. I, *-11, -12,* wooden spoons.]

The spoon used in eating the soapberry was of maple among the Tlingit, though the interior people often made it of horn or bone, and I have seen several of whalebone [baleen] from the Tsimshian. They were paddle shaped with a long slender cylindrical handle. The finer specimens were beautifully carved over the face in conventional animal figures in low relief, with a naturalistic figure at the end of the handle.

All spoons were kept in open-work spruce root baskets that were fitted with a root handle to hang on a peg or on a deer antler hook on the wall. The spoon basket was called *chetle tar-káte* [šáł da·ke·t], "spoon bag."

The Tlingit ate out of the side of the spoon, sucking the more liquid food, and picking out the solid particles with the thumb and forefinger of the other hand [not holding the spoon]. Large clam shells were sometimes used as dishes or as spoons for dipping into the box or basket of boiled fish.

Eating dishes, wooden spoons, and ladles were made from maple or alder, as the wood of any conifer would contain more or less resin and would give a bad taste.

[Emmons does not mention the small wooden knife, ní·s̓a·, used for opening sea urchins, ní·s̓, and scooping out the ovaries to eat.]

A drinking cup, *ku-quor* [gúx̣ʷa·, "dipper"], carried when traveling, hung from the belt by a hide string, was made of sheep horn, circular in form [presumably this refers to the bowl?], and shallow like a saucer. This was procured from the interior people in trade, and was generally ornamented with lines or geometric figures filled in with red ochre.

The food box, *thlukt* [łáqt], was practically square in cross section, had higher sides than ends, and was painted with conventional figures on two sides and with a simple figure on the other two. The finer boxes were both carved and painted, and were ornamentally inlaid with opercula.

Boxes and chests for clothing, *kook* or *kuke* [qú·kʷ], were oblong in form, but were more elaborately carved, painted and inlaid. Some were double, the outer larger box, with a solid top, fitting over the smaller inner box, as a cover or lid. These were called *wush-tar-ku-gu* or *usht-toe-kook-gu* [wu·š da· qú·gu or wu·š tu qú·gu. The lid was called há·t. A small covered box for oil was called x̣ał da·ke·t; a large box for grease was dane·t.] These were procured in trade from the Tsimshian and Haida. [In notes (BCPA) made at Sitka, dated 1892, Emmons wrote: "Boxes are made of yellow cedar bark, bent around as old boxes are, sewed with root, and the bottom sewed on. Filled with grease and covered with bark of yellow cedar."

[Other objects to be found in the house would be sacks of various kinds and sizes to hold small implements and bulky clothing. Such sacks were called gʷé·ł.]

The Tlingit broom was a bunch of switches tied at the upper end to form a handle. An eagle's wing was also used.

[To provide more light in the house than was furnished by the open fire and smokehole, stone lamps were used, cobblestones roughly hollowed out and provided with a wick.] The lamp, *tsu-nar-yet,* or *te tse-na,* or simply *se-na* [té s̓i·ná·, "stone lamp," or s̓i·ná·, "lamp"] can be distinguished by a slight groove on the rim, leading from the basin. Seal or other oil was put in the basin and wisps of inner cedar bark or moss were twisted and laid up in the groove as a wick. The stone lamp was of rare occurrence [except in the Yakutat area where they were very common (de Laguna et al. 1964:117–21), although they are known as far south as Wrangell. Krause (1885) 1956:109, commented on "the meager light of fish-oil lamps."].

The mortar and pestle, *tik-har-yate* [t̓íx̣a· ye·t (?), "grinding or pounding place"] and *koo-tich-a* [kat̓íx̣a· or ku·t̓íx̣a·, "masher, grinder"], or *kar-huk-ha* [ka-xágʷa·, "pestle to grind with"], sometimes of wood, more often of stone, were common articles in the equipment of every Tlingit household. The mortar was made of a compact rock, generally circular in form, neatly finished, and often ornamented with a ridge or groove encircling the outside just below the rim. The finest ones were carved in animal form, such as a squatting bear or frog, with the back hollowed out for the bowl. This household article was used in the manufacture of the native tobacco compound [snuff]. [See Keithahn 1962, fig. 4.]

The pestle used with the mortar was the least worked of any article of stone. It generally consisted of a cylindrical waterworn beach cobble, some eight or ten inches long, with one end ground rounded to fit the concavity of the mortar. Among the southern tribes I have found several finely worked cylindrical pestles, sixteen or more inches in length, that had been traded north from Washington and Oregon.

The abundance of stone mortars and pestles found in all Tlingit villages bespeaks the general manufacture of snuff, for which alone they were used.

In addition to the plain cylindrical pestle, *tihk-r or tikr* [t̓íx̣a·], there were more elaborately shaped pestles or mashers, *kar-tihk-r* [kat̓íx̣a· and ka-xágʷa·]. These were the most numerous of all stone implements and varied greatly in material, shape, and finish. [See Keithahn 1962, fig. 3, except *g, h, i.*] They were essentially the woman's hammer, with many uses in the preparation of food, for smashing bones, salmon eggs, and berries, for example. They were generally made of a carefully selected fine-grained stone, such as marble, limestone, or an igneous rock. The prevailing form was cylindrical in the main shaft, with a heavy expanded base, and tapered upward to a reasonable body to grasp, with a small expansion at the top to keep the hand from slipping. This terminated in an ornamentally rounded, pointed, or nipple-shaped head. Another type had a crutch-shaped handle with pointed ends at right angles to the cylindrical body. But the rarest and most elaborately shaped type, which must have taxed the skill of the maker with hammer and pecking stone, had a heavy cut-out handle [stirrup shaped].

CHAPTER 7

Arts and Industries: Men's Work

DIVISION OF LABOR

The industrial life of the Tlingit was fairly shared by the two sexes, and the division of labor very clearly established. The man did the heavy work, and was the provider of the staple foods in fish, marine, and land animals. The woman supplied berries, roots, plant stems, and crustaceans. She was the housewife and took care of the small children, but when necessary each aided the other.

The man was the worker in stone, bone, metal, and wood. He built the house, fashioned the canoe, chests, utensils, and all the implements and tools used in the labor of both sexes. He was the carver and painter. He made all of his weapons, the frames for skin dressing and blanket weaving, and the frames for snowshoes, as well as ornaments of ivory, bone, and shell. He made the musical instruments [drum, rattle, tapping sticks], gambling devices, and wooden hats, helmets, and headdresses used in ceremonies. He supplied firewood and the large slabs of cedar bark used for various purposes.

The woman cared for the little children and trained the girls. She tanned and dressed the pelts, made the clothing, spun the goat's wool for blankets, prepared the roots, grass, and plant stems used in sewing, weaving, and making blankets, baskets, and nets. She received, prepared, smoked, and cured the fish [perhaps her most important contribution], but often assisted in hanging them on the drying frames and in packing them for transportation. She gathered berries, edible roots and plants, clams and other shellfish and seaweed, cured or prepared them for use. She prepared the food at meals and apportioned what was served. She worked in split porcupine quill and bead embroidery. Medicinal plants were also within her province, since she was the leech and midwife. The manufacture of fish and seal oil was principally her work, but the man assisted. She planted, cultivated, and dug the potatoes when these were introduced by Europeans. [There is no information on who cultivated the aboriginal tobacco.]

The woman's position in the household was assured. She was the treasurer and carried the keys of the chests that contained the blankets, clothing, and in later years, money. Formerly the Tlingit had only wooden chests and boxes which might be corded for safety, but after the advent of the Russians, whose fur trade was exclusively with China, camphor wood trunks with locks found great favor with the Tlingit, and so the housewife carried a bunch of keys suspended from her neck on a hide or beaded cord. [Her role in trade has already been indicated. She not only could veto any bargain made by her husband, but also made the goods which she traded herself or gave away at potlatches.]

A distinctive feature of the life of the Northwest Coast was the artistic sense of the people as expressed in all of their industries. Everything they produced, from the great communal house with its wealth of carving, tooling, and painting, down to the least important article of use, was ornamented in animal design, which greatly impressed the explorers, who found it difficult to reconcile this excellence with their savagery, rude manner of living, and primitive tools.

[Men were responsible for realistic or conventionalized representations of birds, animals, and anthropomorphic figures on crest objects and shamanistic paraphernalia, and women produced weaving in geometric designs; nevertheless, there was collaboration even in these productions, since the women in weaving Chilkat blankets copied the crest designs from patterns prepared by the men.]

WORK IN STONE

The earliest European explorers who reached the Northwest Coast in the last quarter of the eighteenth century

---

Editor's note: This chapter and the next, planned by Emmons as one, gave Emmons, and me, great difficulties in organization. This was not only because of the many different drafts and notes that had somehow to be included, but because the same artifact might be described both as the product of work and as a tool with which to make something else. An attempt has been made here to separate the two approaches. Emmons left many drafts of the table of contents for these two chapters, and was still agonizing over the problem in his last years, as is evidenced by scraps of paper in the trembling hand of old age. I have finally selected the present arrangement, one that Emmons had earlier discarded, which separates men's and women's work. The present text includes everything substantive from the various typed manuscripts and handwritten notes.

found the natives depending upon implements of stone for general working purposes, supplemented by tools of shell, bone, and wood. Copper was used for blades of spears, arrows, and knives, and for personal ornaments, but there was no other metal except for a very limited amount of iron [drift iron?]. As soon as more iron was made available through trade, it was used especially for daggers, knives, and axes [adzes], although the forms of the original tools were copied in iron. As late as 1883 the Tlingit were still a very primitive people, for, except for the edged tools of iron or steel, they still made use of stone for mauls, hammers, mortars, pestles, paint dishes, pipes, charms, and doll heads. The discarded stone adzes were preserved as heirlooms.

The common types of Tlingit stone implements, judging by those found in possession of the people and preserved as mementos of their ancestors, or as curiosities dug up on old living sites, were similar to those of the Tsimshian and Haida. Continuous trade between these peoples contributed to uniformity, not only in distributing the finished tools but in disseminating ideas. Nevertheless, certain characteristics mark the work of particular localities, and each people had some pieces peculiar to themselves. [For a summary and illustration of these artifacts, see Drucker 1943:34–62, 120–24; Keithahn 1962.]

[Among implements, utensils, weapons, and other objects made of stone, Emmons listed the following, the shapes and functions of which are described in appropriate sections and chapters: strike-a-light, cooking stones, stones for the sweat bath, hammerstone, mortar and pestle for making snuff, woman's hand hammer or pestle, lamp, whetstone, sinker for fish line, anchor for canoe, adzes, chisels, skin scrapers, knives, war clubs, stone saw, weapon points, doll's head, paint dish, paint, rubbing amulets, and spinning tops for gambling.]

Methods of Tlingit stone working must be inferred from those specimens treasured by the natives or found at archaeological sites, since stone implements have not been manufactured within the memory of the present generation. Those in use until recently were handed down from the past. Processes of manufacture are indicated by partially worked specimens which had been thrown away after breaking.

Since southeastern Alaska is a land of rocks and boulders, the native had only to go outside his door to find all manner of stone. He selected rocks which in size and shape corresponded as closely as possible with the dimensions of the intended implement. In fact, he sometimes found what would answer his purpose without any alteration, as is shown by some pestles and mortars [which are simply unshaped hammerstones and naturally hollow beach boulders]. Anchors and sinkers, *go-wor-ta* [gu·waté], were unworked stones, generally oblong, that were of suitable size to tie a line about. I have seen only two grooved pebbles used for such a purpose. For anchoring the canoe a suitable boulder could always be found on the beach.

The selection of the material was also contingent upon its use. For cutting tools, the finest texture combined with toughness was required, while for the maul and hammer weight and density were necessary. [Since not all varieties of rock were at hand, the Tlingit had to travel to localities where the needed rock was available, or secure it in trade.]

When the stone was to be worked, the first step was to shape it roughly by breaking it with a harder stone. Probably any convenient [tough] cobble was used as a hammerstone, for no regular implement made for this purpose has ever been found with the hundreds of stone tools that have been preserved or dug up at village sites. When satisfactorily shaped in the rough, the implement was worked down by pecking. This is plainly shown on many pieces where it was not necessary to carry the work any further, as in the case of mauls or the sides of adz blades. In most instances, however, implements were finished to a smooth surface all over by rubbing with a piece of sandstone. The hand hammer, war club, and some other pieces were smoothed with sandstone and polished with pumice stone, dogfish skin, and the hand. Some implements of minor practical use might be patiently worked into animal form.

There is no evidence that the Tlingit practiced the art of chipping [except for the rough shaping by percussion of some tools, such as slate scrapers]. The occasional flint or obsidian spear or arrow blade found [in Tlingit territory] may be referred to trade [with the interior]. These were preserved as curiosities, rather than for use.

[Thin slabs of sandstone were occasionally used for sawing harder rock, especially greenstone or "jade," but such saws were evidently not common.] The only examples of cutting saws of stone, similar to those of the Interior Salish to work jade, were several broken pieces dug up on Strait Island in Sumner Strait, but no jade was found thereabouts, and these saws might have been brought here by travelers, for no Tlingit tools show evidence of having been worked by such tools.

[In 1923, Emmons wrote (1923:18–19): "Among the Tlingit, throughout southeastern Alaska, during a period of more than twenty years the writer observed no saws or other

Stone utensils, implements, weapons, and other objects. (Pencil sketches by G. T. Emmons, on page from notebook in BCPA. (a) [No sketch], Ta suck-tar-kate *[té š̓eq- da·ke·t, "stone smoke case"]. (b)* Tukch *[táqɬ]: stone hammer [hafted maul] fitted with one or two grooves on sides and bottom over which lashings of spruce root, seal, or bear thong wet and stretched are bound around end of handle and stone and then later when necessary wedged. (c) A stone hammer with a pointed or cutting head is called* kutz *[x̣ús̓] or club and used as a war club, but I believe all were used indiscriminately as hammers or war clubs as the occasion demanded [hafted specimen; three heads; two complete clubs of stone]. (d)* Ti-esse *[té yi·s or tayi·s, "stone wedge"]: stone axe [splitting adz] [hafted specimen; five heads].*

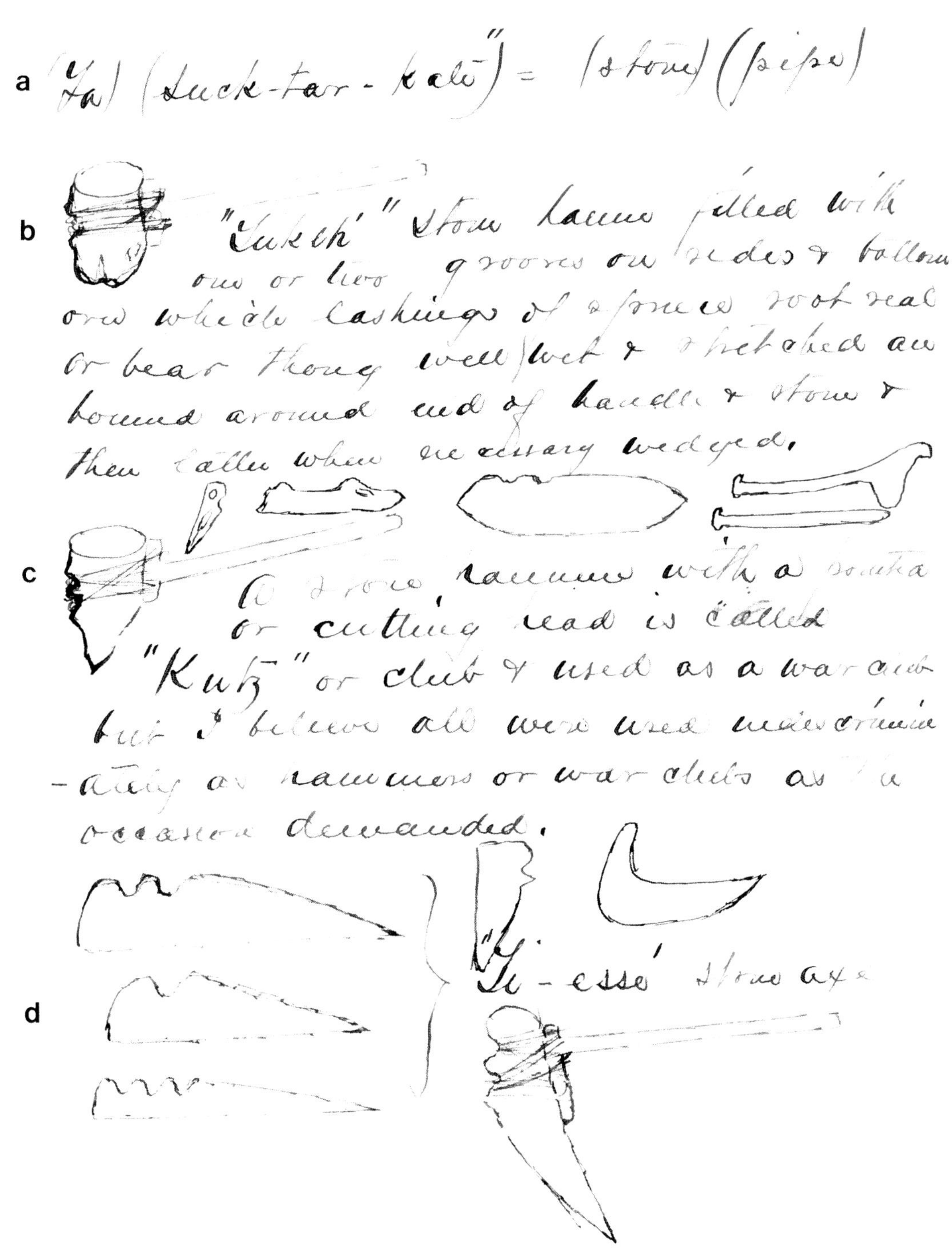

Stone implements. (a) Hoot-tar [x̣úƚ̇a·, *"chopper"*]. *What might be termed an adz. It is flat and for finer work [planing adz]. (b)* Ta Kin-tar-kar [té x̣enƚ̇á·ẋa]: *stone, a large labret. (c)* Ta can-noh [té q̇a-nu·x̣ʷ]: *stone, a small labret [two examples]. (d)* Nukt Thlinget [né·ẋ̣, *"marble," or* nú·ẋʷ, *"shell, china"*; ƚingít]: *stone doll's head for children. (e)* Which-r [xʷáǯa·, *"scraper"*]: *stone skin dressers. "a" is used in hand, "b" attached to pole handle. In first place "a" is used to soften skin, "b" for scraping down. (f)* "Goo-war-ta / go-war-ta" [gu·waté]: *sinkers for fishing line.*

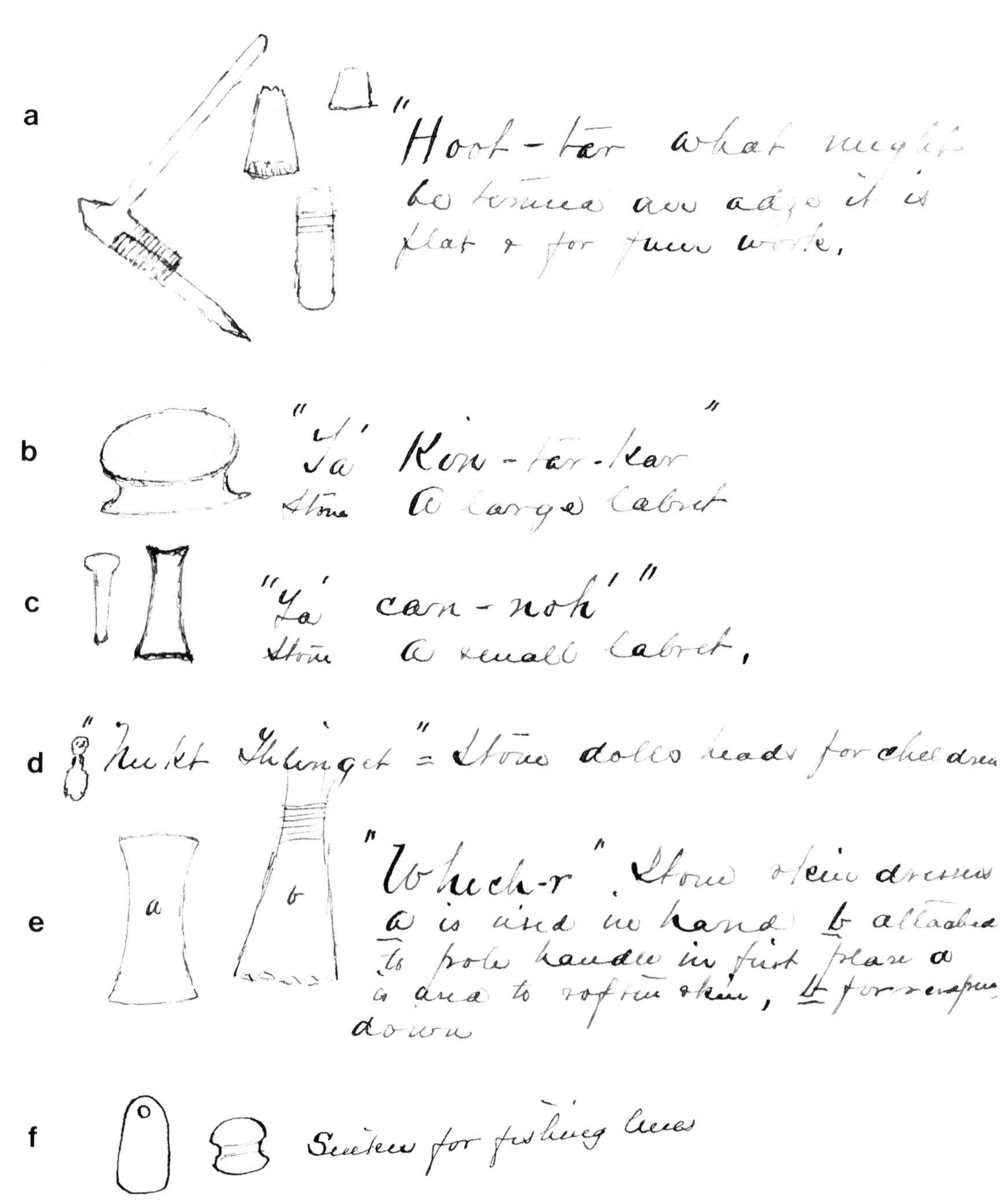

Stone implements. (a) Thluk-we-ta *[possibly* ċáqɬ yi-te·yí ?, *"rock under paint"]: any stone on which paint is mixed or pulverized [front and side views of two specimens].* Thlaok *"paint"* [ɬé·x̣^{w}, *"paint, red ochre"*], ta, *"stone"* [té]. *(b)* Tsu-nar-yet [ši̓ná·, *"lamp,"* ye·t, *"container"*]: *stone lamp can be distinguished by slight groove on the side leading from basin. Seal or other oil is put in the basin and wisp of inner cedar bark or moss is twisted and laid for a wick. (c)* Tsik [šíx̣, *"bowl, dish"*]: *small stone dish for eating grease from. (d)* Klar-te-hone-yet [ɬa·-tu-x̣$^{(w)}$án, *"breast-in-milk,"* ye·t, *"vessel"*]: *a small stone dish in which a woman having a nursing baby milks herself before going off in the woods after berries. (e)* Kuk-qwart-kli-ate [kaq^{w}á·ƛ̓i ye·ṭ, *"melting receptacle"*]: *stone bullet mold.*

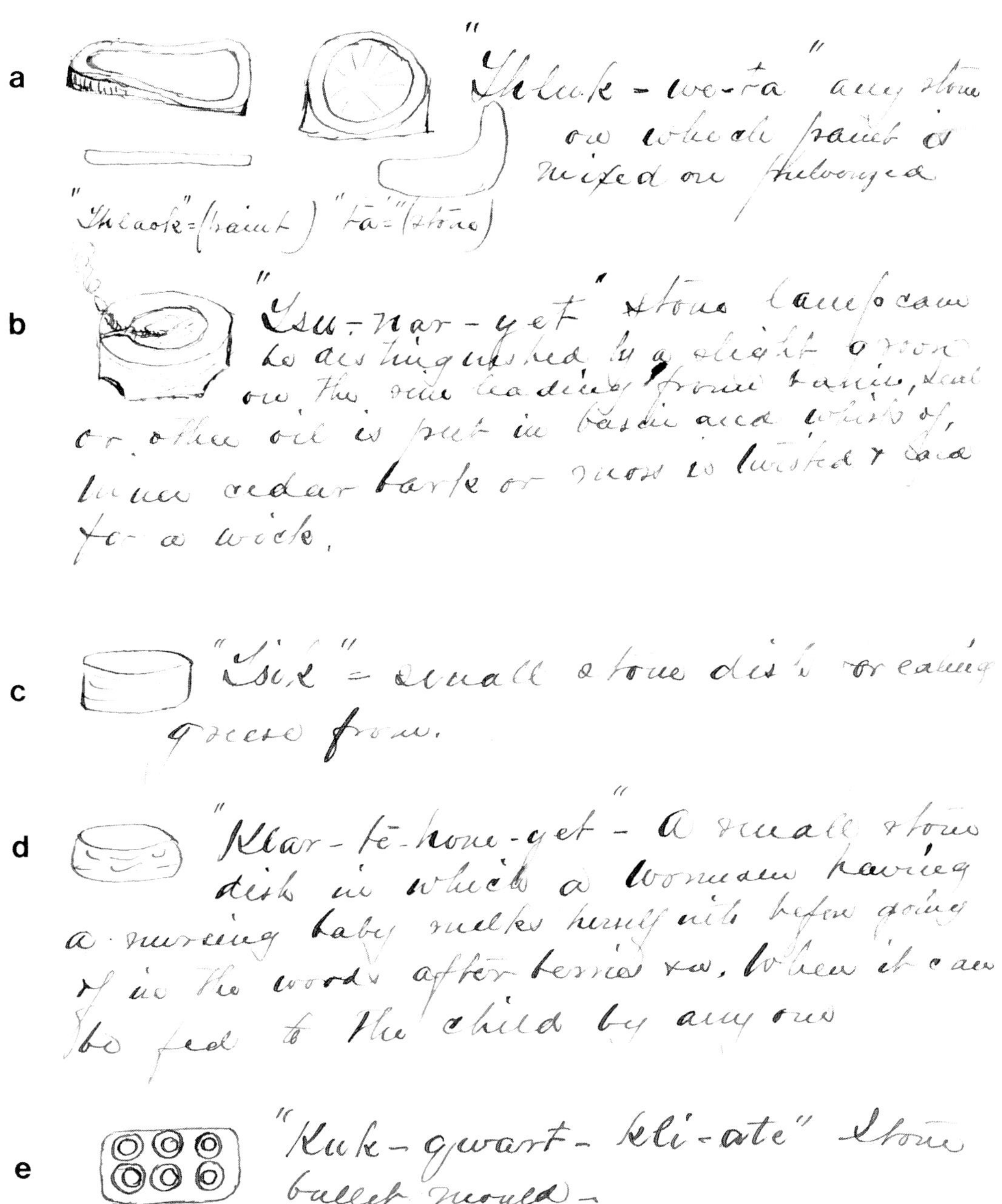

tools for working the raw material, and but two cut boulders of jade." Although a few nondescript stone saws have been found in Tlingit territory: in the Yakutat area, in the Angoon area, and at Mole Harbor on the east coast of Admiralty Island, it may be significant that the present-day natives did not recognize these implements (Keithahn 1962:72; de Laguna 1960:105; de Laguna et al. 1964:113–14). Other methods of cutting or sawing stone were evidently preferred.]

Jade and other of the denser pebbles were cut in pieces by means of twisted cord of sinew or rope of cedar inner bark and black sand and water, or with small pieces of flint.

Slate was little used by the Tlingit. I collected a double-bladed slate dagger at Chilkat. In a cave at Hot Springs, on the west coast of Baranof Island, below Sitka, a cache of some eight long slender slate spear blades with wooden foreshafts was found. These were certainly never used by the Tlingit, but might have belonged to the Aleut [more likely Koniag] sea-otter hunters brought here by the Russians.

[For the last type of spear blade, see Birket-Smith (1941, fig. 16). We should note, however, that narrow weapon blades of slate, including the same kind of "bayonet" points as those mentioned by Emmons, have been found at Sitka and Angoon and Yakutat (Drucker 1943, fig. 7*a, b, d, e*; de Laguna et al. 1964, fig. 14, pp. 125–30). But the Tlingit evidently preferred ulos made of large shells, or made with copper blades where copper was available, rather than women's knives with slate blades (de Laguna et al. 1964, fig. 10, pp. 99–104).]

The whetstone, *ya-ye-nar, yayeena* [yayé·na·], was a homogeneous white stone [a fine-grained shale, claystone, or limestone *"suck-nuh"* (siknax̣?)]. This was used for sharpening knives. Sandstone was used as a grindstone [gíła·, "sharpener"] to sharpen adz blades.

"JADE"

In former times nephrite or jade was the most valued stone and this had to be procured in trade from the south, for there is no evidence that nephrite was found on the coast of southeastern Alaska, and the nearest sources of supply were the upper Fraser and Thompson River valleys. Nephrite, or rather celts, chisels, and knives of nephrite, were traded by the Interior Salish to the lower river people and southern coastal tribes. The only piece of unfinished jade that I ever saw or heard of in Alaska was a worked boulder dug up in 1885 at the native village of Sitka, under the foundations of an old house. Although the natives could give no information about it, it must have been brought here comparatively recently, for this village site was first occupied in 1821, [when the natives already had iron and steel tools]. [Notes left by Emmons in BCPA described this piece: "The stock piece from which two or more knives had been taken . . . weighs 19¾ lbs., gives evidence of having been a vein or seam of jade, the sides worn smooth as if by water, although the ends show fracture. It is . . . somewhat wedge-shaped. . . . It is of a yellowish mottled green, and two or three adzes or knives have been already taken from it and another cutting commenced. . . . [It was found] some 3 feet underground."

[In these notes, Emmons listed all the objects made of "jade" that he knew of from the Tlingit:

Adzes	45
Axes	2
"Katu"	5 [These are war picks. See Chapter 12.]
Pipe	1
Charms	2 shaped, 2 rough [Scratching amulets.]
Pestle	1
Pebble with cut in it.	1

The pipe referred to had been buried with a Chilkat chief and is therefore partly decomposed. . . . I have one piece shaped as a bear's tooth, but larger, which was a charm of an old Angoon *Icta* [ʔíx̣t̓, shaman]. I once obtained from a very old man a very fine homogeneous piece of jade, worn smooth; he was wearing it as a charm or scratcher, and he said way far back it had been an adze, which statement its general shape corroborates.

[This piece is also described in Emmons 1923:16: "Among the Tlingit of both sexes it was the custom to wear . . . a small object, generally of carved stone, for scratching the head and body, and in three instances pieces of jade so worn were found which the wearers regarded as of greater value than like articles of other stone. One of these was a small, broken adze, in bargaining for which a year was spent." (See Chapter 13 for the use of such amulets.)]

A few very beautiful weapons for war or ceremonial use, ***katu***, or ***kinda kha-too*** [ké·t̓u, "pick," or kínde ké·t̓u, "upward (turned) pick"], with a long picklike, highly polished, jade blade, hafted through the end of a stout wooden handle, have been found among the Tlingit as family possessions [lineage or clan heirlooms]. Similar weapons are known from the Tsimshian and the Haida, although the latter lashed the blade to the end of the handle. No finished piece of jade of this form has ever been found among the Fraser River Salish, and the question as to who made them must be solved in the future.

That jade tools were not abundant is evidenced by their great value and the superstition connected with their use.

A large piece like that dug up at Sitka [twenty pounds] was worth four slaves. An adz blade three inches long was worth one or two slaves, and so not within the reach of the common people.

[The adz or knife with jade blade was used for fine wood carving. Notes by Emmons, BCPA, also state:

> It was valued from a utilitarian standpoint on account of its toughness and the fine edge it would take. They worked out the canoes with it, the ornamentation of boxes, carved interior [house] posts, etc., and it is even claimed that they worked other stone implements with those of jade.
>
> In working an adz or ax [of jade], they believed in very old days that they must work without eating for four days, or the stone would grow so hard that they could do nothing with it. [This probably reflects the knowledge that such hard, fine-grained rocks like greenstone and flint must be worked while they are still fresh, for when exposed to the air the stone dries out and becomes hard; but I do not know if this is true of what Emmons called "jade."

[If a "jade" adz was broken during use], the owner would blame his wife for some frivolity or indiscretion. [That is, she would be blamed for the breach of a taboo similar to that which she had to observe when her husband was hunting.]

Jade was called *tsu* [š̓u·w, "green"], because of its color, and the name was also applied to a translucent, bright green serpentine found on the Chatham Strait side [eastern side] of Baranof Island, at a place called *tsu quaddy,* "greenstone bay."

[This was probably Redbluff Bay, claimed by Raven 13, although anyone could obtain greenstone here. The name was probably š̓u·w ge·yí, "bay of greenstone"; *quaddy* would be x̣̓a·t̓í, "island of." The native name (š̓u·w) is, as a matter of fact, applied by the Tlingit to any hard green stone, such as green basalt or green chert; and they evidently had many local sources of supply, since Tlingit adz blades are usually made of some form of greenstone, some of which is of rather fine quality. Emmons may be in error in supposing that the "nephrite" or "jade" pieces that he saw in southeastern Alaska came from as far away as the Fraser and Thompson rivers. In any case, their provenience could only be determined through careful mineralogical comparisons. Notes in BCPA also indicate other local proveniences:

> [Jade] is also known to the more northern tribes as "Klukheen" for it is said to be found in natural state in the bed of a small glacial stream known as "Kluck-heen" [ł̓ux̣ʷ hí·n, "milky (with milt) water or stream"], which flows into the Pacific about thirty miles to the northward of *Lit-tu-ah* [Lituya] Bay, from which the name comes. [This stream was later covered by advancing ice, according to Emmons 1923:19–20.] It is also said to come from north and west of Yakutat. . . . A single worked adz was exchanged for one or two slaves, with the Haida who had no jade, but were the pirates of the North West Coast, gathering their prey [slaves] as far south as Puget Sound. . . .
>
> A Kehk [Kake] Tradition of Jade: In the first days of Thlingit life when they made fire with two stones, they had no axe. [When] they wanted canoes, they would burn down a tree, burn off the ends, and then burn out a hole along one face of the tree, but this was a clumsy affair. It was launched, and two young men started out in it, but it soon upset. One went down, and at the bottom of the water he saw the Halibut chief, *Narthl* [ná·ɬx̣]. And he had a slave, *Thlakh* [?], who was chopping wood with an axe [adz]. The slave said it belonged to his master. Then he went to the chief's house, and said, "Chief, I would like to have that thing your slave uses to chop wood with." And the chief asked him what it was. He repeated his request again, and the chief said that it is called *Kluk-heen.* Then the chief gave him *Kluk-heen,* and he [the Tlingit youth] said "My name is *Narthl* [ná·ɬx̣, "large halibut"], and my family [clan] name is *Narthl-hut-tee* [ná·ɬx̣ʔadi], the same as *Goutch* [g̣u·č, "wolf"] family, a Tongass family [not among Emmons's lists of clans]. Then he returned to his family and showed them the axe and they went off and found the same kind of stone, and made axes.

[The word for flint, *een* (ʔín), was also applied to other hard stones, such as greenstone and chert, or jadeite.]

Among the earliest legends of the Tlingit relative to the wanderings of Raven, the Creator and Transformer, is mentioned the jade adz, *tsu hootar* [š̓u·w x̣úta·, "green [stone] small adz"], with which he induced the king salmon to jump ashore near Yakutat [so that he could kill and eat it]. This story is illustrated on a beautifully carved house post in the Whale House at Klukwan [Emmons 1916a, pl. 4 *a.* For a version of this myth see Swanton 1909:5. Raven pretended that the greenstone was insulting the salmon, and when the fish came ashore to fight the stone, Raven clubbed him.].

Perhaps the earliest reference to jade cutting tools occurs in the narrative of the Spanish pilot, Mourelle, who in 1779 saw Tlingit [Klawak] in Port Santa Cruz, Bucareli Bay, on the west coast of Prince of Wales Island, and described their implements [quoted in La Pérouse 1799, 1:247]. These included "little hatchets of flint, or of a green stone, so hard, that it cleaves the most compact wood without injury to the edge."

MEN'S TOOLS

Of all stone implements the adz was the most important, for the Tlingit was primarily a worker in wood. Adzes were made in two main sizes and shapes. The larger [splitting] adz, *ta yese* or *ti-esse* [tayí·s or té ỵí·s] "stone wedge," was in fact wedge-shaped, with one, two, or even three deep grooves near the rear of the back, over which passed the lashing that secured it to the handle [see Drucker 1943, fig. 9; Keithahn 1962:67–69, fig. 1; de Laguna 1960, pl. 5 *a, b*; de Laguna et al. 1964, pl. 5]. These heavier blades varied from six to fourteen inches in length, and were generally finished throughout, although sometimes they were smoothed only toward the cutting edge. They were made of the toughest, densest stone obtainable, and were used in the heaviest woodworking. The short, bent [T-shaped] handle was made of a stout tree limb with a small section of the trunk left attached, to which the blade was secured with [cords of] twisted spruce root or strips of seal or bear hide, put on wet [to shrink] and later tighten with [little wooden] wedges at the sides. Handles for adzes and hafted mauls were of alder wood.

The smaller [planing] adz, *hootar,* "chipper" [x̣útʼa·, "chopper"], consisted of a plain celt, from three to six inches long, which was hafted like the larger adz, except that the butt rested against a shoulder or step in the T of the handle. [The planing adz had an elbow handle which might more properly be described as shaped like an inverted L.] This was the principal and favorite tool of the man with which he hollowed out the canoe, finished the house timbers [smoothed the planks with a dimpled finish], shaped and carved the totem pole and the elaborate interior house posts, and so expert was he with this rude blade that the tooling of the canoe, house beams, etc., was in its perfection considered as ornamental as the shaping of animal forms. [See Drucker 1943:46–47, "celts"; Keithahn 1962:68, "chipping adz"; de Laguna 1960:100 196101, "planing adz"; de Laguna et al. 1964:93–95.]

The Tlingit also made stone chisels, *ta-ya* [tíya·, "patcher"], for finer woodwork. One was a blade of nephrite seized to the end of a short handle. Two were splinters of nephrite held in the hand and used more like knives.

[It is not clear whether Emmons ever mentioned a stone chisel which was driven by a hammer or maul (see Keithahn 1962:68–69; de Laguna et al. 1964:97; Niblack 1890:282, fig. 78). Such tools were rare. We should also note small woodworking tools made of slate, some of which were shaped like small splitting adz blades, others like small planing adz blades, or even like chisels or knives (see de Laguna et al. 1964:95–99, pls. 7, 8). These were evidently used for gouging and cutting, like burins. Keithahn (1962:68) mentions "micro bits" of nephrite, serpentine, or greenstone which he believes were hafted and used in shaping bone or antler harpoons. These fine cutting tools seem to be related to the rubbing tools, so common at Hutsnuwu sites, and evidently were used to finish wood carvings (de Laguna 1960:106–8).

[We should note that in addition to splitting adzes, the Tlingit occasionally made double-bitted adzes, and even an occasional stone ax. Keithahn (1962) distinguished various subtypes.]

The man's maul, *tukle* or *tachtl* [táqɬ], consisted of a heavy cylindrical dense boulder, slightly flattened on one face to fit the T of the wooden handle, and deeply grooved on the opposite side for the lashing. It was hafted like the grooved [splitting] adz head. It was used for heavy woodworking, such as splitting tree trunks with crude wedges, *yease* or *yese* [yi·s], of hemlock or spruce, or in driving stakes of the fish weir. It was generally neatly finished, and was often shaped like an animal's head. [See Drucker 1943, fig. 12 *b*; Keithahn 1962, fig. 2; de Laguna et al. 1964, fig. 21 *b*.] The man's maul was also used as a war club, carried hidden under the blanket for an attack without warning.

[This last may not have been a maul, but a pick-shaped weapon, hafted like a splitting adz (see Keithahn 1962, fig. 1 *e,* "ice pick"). At any event, the usual maul had the head and handle shaped from one block of wood, according to Tlingit at Angoon, and was used with wooden wedges for splitting out planks. Keithahn (1962, fig. 3 *o–q,* p. 70) believes that the elaborate hand hammers with T-shaped grip were used with wedges. No doubt many of the heavy hammerstones, so common on Tlingit sites, were used by men.

[Other tools made and used by men are described or mentioned in Chapter 4, the sections "Manufacture and Repair of Canoes" and "Snowshoes"; Chapter 5, "Firearms"; and Chapter 6, "Berries and Other Plant Foods." These are the planing adz, hand drill, wooden gauge to measure the gunwales of a canoe, awl as marker, crooked knife, molds of wood and stone for making bullets, and long wedges for stripping bark. Other tools are described under "Work in Wood" and "Art" in this chapter.]

WORK IN HORN, IVORY, SHELL, AND INLAYS

Spoons were made from the horn of the mountain goat, and both dishes for grease and large spoons were made from the horn of the mountain [Dall] sheep. Dishes, ladles, and spoons were all made the same way. The horn was put into boiling water and allowed to remain there until softened. Then it was split the length of the hollow space, and opened out. While still warm it was soaked in oil. Then, while soft and pliable, it was put into a wooden mold and allowed to cool. The mold for spoons was like a lemon squeezer, the hinge being a couple of turns of rawhide. After the horn was introduced, the lashing was passed around the other end of the mold. When cool the horn retained the shape of the mold. The roughly shaped spoon was then pared down and shaped; in the case of the heavy sheep horn it might be again boiled and molded.

The natural curve of the goat horn was generally satisfactory for the curve of the spoon handle, but if some other shape was desired, it was again softened in boiling water and put through an oval, slanting hole in a piece of wood, bent as desired, lashed down and allowed to cool. Or, the handle could be shaped at the same time as the bowl of the spoon by passing the end through one of the arms of the mold and lashing it. The carving of the handle was done when the horn had been softened by putting it into warm water, and the finish was given by rubbing it with dogfish skin in lieu of sandpaper, or equisetum, and polishing with the hand. However, the high polish of an old spoon is the result of constant use and grease. The sheep horn was similarly treated.

The exquisite carving on the handles of the horn spoons in human and animal figures is more realistic than the conventionalized relief figures on the dishes, for the rounded field allows the whole body to appear. Indeed, spoon handles may be considered as totem poles in miniature, since they frequently represented family crests or illustrated a legend by the context of the principal figures, although some of these may be employed purely as ornaments to fill in vacant spaces.

In the larger spoons when the entire length of the goat horn was required for the handle, the separate bowl was attached with copper rivets. When the bowl was of sheep horn, colored a rich yellow with oil, its contrast with the dark goat horn was very pleasing. The [bowl of] the small goat horn spoon of the Tlingit was generally plain, in contrast to that of the Haida, which was carved on the back of the bowl, or of the Tsimshian, ornamented throughout the inside of the bowl in parallel ridges.

From the teeth of the sperm whale, the finest of ivory, were made shaman's charms, knife handles, and smaller articles, while the baleen of the bowhead whale was used for similar purposes, and was also bent around to form circular boxes used by the women for trinkets. The bone of all species of whale was used for such articles as war clubs, tool handles, mortars, and so forth.

[Animal teeth were used, among other things, as pendants, and bear canines were cut and worked for their "ivory" (see de Laguna 1960, pl. 10, *a* through *d, g, h, m, n*). Some of the ivory charms and long, rattling pins of the shaman's necklace were evidently of walrus ivory, traded from the Eskimo (see de Laguna 1972, pls. 170, 171, 173, 182, 183), some of the pieces in the necklace still bearing Eskimo incised patterns. Fossil shark teeth (šax̣daq ʔu·x̣ú), traded from southern tribes, were used for earrings, and the shape was even sometimes copied in other materials. Bear teeth were also used by women to smooth their basket work. The incisors of the beaver were used for knife blades. There is no need here to enumerate the many articles, useful or ornamental, that were made of animal bone and horn.]

The larger blue mussel shell, *yeese* [yí·s̓, *Mytilus californiensis]*, was used as a knife in skinning, dressing, and cutting skins, in cutting fish and meat, while the mussel shell of medium size [ya·ḳ, *M. edulis*] was the universal tool of the basket maker and mat weaver. Even after the introduction of metal knives of crescentic shape, the shell knife remained the favorite for half a century.

To obtain a mussel shell, the seeker drew a blanket over his [her?] head, and going to the shell bed at low water, covered the shell selected with the blanket and worked it loose and, concealing it, returned to the house. If the sun should see it, bad weather would follow. [This belief seems to apply to the handling of most objects from below the tide "line."]

Large clam shells, *gartle nuku* [gá·ɬ̓ nú·x̣u, *Saxidomus giganteus?*], were used as dishes for paint and for spruce gum, and also as spoons. Smaller shells were secured to the split end of a wooden handle to serve as spoons. Clam shells were burned to furnish the lime which was mixed with tobacco in making snuff.

The pecten or scallop shell [x̣ʷe·na?] was the universal primitive rattle on the entire Northwest Coast. The half shells were strung on circular withes of cedar through a hole near the hinge [rather like the rattles of puffin beaks and deer hoofs (see de Laguna 1972, pl. 205)]. The whole pecten shell was also used as a rattle by enclosing it within the split ends of a stick [and presumably putting pebbles inside the closed shell]. Whole pecten shells and broken shells were commonly found in shamans' grave boxes and burial caves.

Dentalia [táx̣x̣i], used for personal ornaments and to decorate blankets, were procured in trade from the west coast of Vancouver Island [from the Quatsino Kwakiutl and the Nootka]. They were, however, more valuable in trade to the interior people, and were therefore often called "the

Chief Shakes and another Nanya'a·yi *(Wolf 18) chief in dance costumes, Wrangell, 1895. The man in the doorway wears a complete brown bear skin. Chief Shakes (left) wears the "bear's ears" headdress and a tunic ornamented with haliotis shell to represent bear's head, and holds the "Killerwhale Cane." (Photographer unknown. AMNH.)*

shell money," since there were fixed trade values for a certain number of standard lengths and colors.

[According to Lütké (1835, 1:137–38), in 1827, the Russians were trading to the Sitka Tlingit woolen blankets, various copper utensils, sea lion whiskers to ornament their hats, ermine skins, and so forth, receiving in exchange *tsouklis* or dentalia, shells found on the Queen Charlotte Islands, for which the Russian American Company paid about thirty rubles for one hundred. They were needed for the company's trade with northern Americans.]

Opercula, also from Vancouver Island, were universally used for inlaying masks, food dishes, chests, and carvings, especially where they represented the teeth of a figure. [They were obtained from the red turban shell, especially by the Haida.]

But by far the most valued of all shells was the beautiful California haliotis [or abalone, gúnx̣a·] that showed a brilliant iridescent blue-green color. It was the jewel of the entire Northwest Coast for personal wear and for inlaying the most valued carvings. The natives claim that they had it long before the white man was known on the coast. Oblong pieces, standardized in size, had a fixed value in early days. The local [Alaskan] shell, thin and pale in color, had no value and was not used for any purpose. For inlaying shell, heated spruce gum was used as glue.

[Drucker (1948:395) wrote about abalone shell: "The use of abalone-shell inlays is more easily understood as the transfer of the inlay technique from sea-otter teeth and the opercula of a sea snail, which was noted by the earliest voyagers on the Northwest coast, to a new and attractive material. The shells themselves seem to have been imported from California by the Spanish—not from the 'South Seas'—they are usually referred to in the accounts as 'Monterey shells.'"]

[Hair and feathers were also used for decoration, and may be mentioned here.] Tufts of human hair were pegged into holes on the head and upper lips of old masks, and often this hair is more red than black. (And here I might say that I have seen in several instances Tlingits, men only, with red hair, who did not seem to have any mixture of white blood, but at so late a date this, of course, could not be stated definitely.)

[I was told (field notes 1949) that red or reddish hair was a sign of Tsimshian ancestry or of predestination to the profession of shaman, but in either case (if true) this would make such hair particularly appropriate for masks.]

The fur of black and brown bears was often used in the ornamentation of masks [especially when showing a drowned man turning into a Land Otter Man (see Chapter 10, the last section)]. Such hair or fur was secured with wooden pegs or metal tacks, or was fastened with spruce gum.

[Human hair was also used as fringes on dance paddles, rattles, and other objects. Keithahn (1954:17) has written about Tlingit use:

> In decorating wooden objects with hair the usual procedure was to drill rows of small holes at uniform distances varying from one quarter inch to two inches or more apart depending on the size of the object being decorated. The tuft of hair to be inserted was then bent in the middle across the end of a short wooden peg which, when driven flush, held the tuft upright securely. When thus properly set, all were clipped to a uniform length. These clipped tufts appear so coarse and bristly they have sometimes been described as "horse tail." [And, in fact, two in the Alaska State Museum, a baton and a rattle, are decorated with hair from horse's tails.]
>
> In decorating ceremonial batons in the typical killer whale fin and paddle designs, the hair embellishment appears only on the back edge. In this instance the hair is not clipped but drapes gracefully, the locks being six inches or more in length.
>
> [On a few specimens] the hair tufts had been stitched down the middle as through the hair were parted, and then glued to the wood. In decorating cloth or felt hats and caps the hair was sewed on with cotton thread.

[Although such human hair is said to have come from slaves, it is far more likely, Keithahn argues (1954:19–20), that such hair came from the Tlingit themselves: slain chiefs, noble women on betrothal, or when widowed or dead.

[Sea lion whiskers, traded from the north, and flicker feathers, rare on the coast and perhaps traded from the interior, were set into the tops of carved wooden headdresses (šaki·-ʔát).]

On some masks, thin strips of copper [instead of hair] covered the lips and eyebrows, and even the eyes, nostrils, and the bills of birds [if the masks included these].

WORK IN COPPER*

Objects of native copper were seen in the possession of the Tlingit by the earliest explorers. It was never very abundant and was highly valued for daggers, spears, and arrowheads, for personal ornaments such as neck rings, nose rings, ear ornaments, bracelets and anklets, and for decorations on ceremonial dress; it was occasionally used for masks and rattles. The most valuable copper object was the hammer shield-shaped "copper."

[Emmons quite possibly consulted the study published in 1939 by T. A. Rickard on the use of iron and copper by the Indians of the Northwest Coast, especially since it was the author's presidential address, given to the Victoria Section of the British Columbia Historical Association, October 14, 1938, which Emmons might even have heard. Emmons refers to many of the original sources consulted by Rickard, as well as to others. The first draft of this section was evidently written much earlier. Evidence of the use of native copper by the Tlingit and their immediate neighbors is found in the quotations below, cited by Emmons and here included.]

Fray de La Peña, on the First Bucareli Expedition in 1774 (in Griffin 1891:132), noted near Nootka Sound that the natives had "some implements of iron and copper." Fray Juan Crespi, on the same ship, referred to "some pieces of iron and of copper" in the possession of the Nootka (in Griffin 1891:203), but was evidently more observant of the Haida (Kaigani) encountered off Dall Island, with whom

---

Editor's note: This section combines several versions left by Emmons. Although he mentioned the reports of many early explorers who had seen native copper in the hands of the Indians, and quoted from their reports or cited their observations, Emmons did not leave exact quotations or full bibliographic citations. These I have supplied, arranging the observations in chronological order; but I have bracketed only my comments, not the introductory remarks or summaries. Many of these sources had been used by Rickard (1939), with whom I believe Emmons was acquainted, or at least with whose work he was probably familiar. They are: de la Peña and Juan Crespi (in Griffin 1891), Mourelle (1920, and in La Pérouse 1799), Riobo (in Thornton 1918), and Bodega y Quadra (concerning metal seen on the Bucareli expeditions).

I have added a discussion of trade routes for Tlingit copper, and have cited Rickard (1939) and Hayes (1892) concerning its source. I have also added a paragraph on the settlement of the Gulf Coast by the Tlingit, and on copper in archaeological sites.

the Spaniards traded. He wrote (in Griffin 1891:194): ". . . the women wore rings on their fingers and bracelets, of iron and of copper. These things I saw on several women, and the sailors who saw them nearer assured me that there was a woman who had five or six rings of iron and of copper on the fingers of her hands. We saw these metals, though not to any great amount, in their possession, and we noted their appreciation of these metals, especially for large articles and those meant for cutting which are made of them."

[That metal for weapons was not common is indicated by the fact that at Kalinin Bay, near Kruzof Island, Salisbury Sound, in Sitka territory, the Tlingit who threatened the Second Bucareli Expedition the following year had "long and large lances pointed with flint" (Mourelle 1920:45).]

In 1779 the Third Bucareli Expedition spent some time in Port Santa Cruz, Bucareli Bay, Klawak Tlingit territory. Here Fray Juan Riobo (in Thornton 1918:224), noted that some of the Tlingit arrows had heads of copper and iron, as well as of flint and bone, and that the Indians were anxious to obtain copper, but especially iron. The leader of the expedition, Juan de la Bodega y Quadra [mentioned especially by Emmons], noted bracelets of copper, iron, and whalebone; "and on their neck sundry rows of the beads they make of bone, and necklets of extremely fine copper; and in their ears, twisted wires of the same metal" [Barwick translation, manuscript in BCPA, also cited by Rickard 1939:27].

Mourelle (in La Pérouse 1799, 1:246), a pilot on the expedition, wrote: "On the wrists they have bracelets of copper or iron, or, for want of these, of whalebone; and round the neck rows of small pieces of bone of fish or other animals, or sometimes copper collars two fingers thick. They wear ear-rings of mother-of-pearl, or plates of copper, on which are embossed pieces of resin the colour of topaz, with grains of jet." And again (in La Pérouse, 1799, 1:248): "[The Indians offered in trade, among other items] . . . collars of copper, and bracelets of iron, for which they asked extravagant prices. . . ."

The previous year, among the Nootka, Captain Cook had seen iron knives and spears pointed with copper, while John Ledyard with him observed [cited by Rickard 1939:25, 29]: ". . . a few copper bracelets and three or four rough wrought knives with coarse wooden hafts. . . ."

La Pérouse, in 1786, observed that the Tlingit (Hoonah) of Lituya Bay (1799, 1:369) all wore daggers, mostly of iron: "Some were of copper, but they did not appear to give a preference to these. This metal is pretty common among them: they use it chiefly for collars, bracelets, and various other ornaments; and they also point their arrows with it. . . . The arrows are commonly headed with copper . . ." (p. 407). And La Pérouse correctly speculated that the copper was native copper from some local source (La Pérouse 1799, 1:369).

Meares, who was at Nootka in 1788, saw "pure malleable lumps of copper ore," as well as "necklaces and a sort of bracelets worn on the wrist, which were of the purest [copper] ore," and the natives indicated that the copper came from the north [cited in Rickard 1939:30–31].

Beresford (1789:237), supercargo with Captain Dixon on the Northwest Coast in 1787, reported: ". . . we frequently saw large circular wreaths of copper both at Norfolk Sound [Sitka Tlingit] and Queen Charlotte's Islands [Haida], which did not appear to be [of] foreign manufacture, but twisted into that shape by the natives themselves, to wear as an ornament about the neck."

Copper was procured by the Tlingit in trade with the interior Athabaskans of the Copper River and White River [Atna and Southern Tutchone]. It was found in the form of flat nuggets on the headwaters of these rivers or dug out of veins. ["The Indians on the White River, which flows eastward from the range in which the Copper River also has its source, used caribou horns to dig the copper nuggets out of the stream gravel," wrote Rickard (1939:37–38), citing A. H. Brooks (1900), the geologist who surveyed this area.] These rich copper deposits formed a source of wealth to the interior natives in trade with the coast, long before the coming of Europeans, and the Russians throughout their long occupation of Alaska were never permitted to reach the copper deposits. [The first whites to discover this source of copper on the upper White River and on the Nizina, a tributary of the Chitina and Copper rivers, were Frederick Schwatka, Mark Russell, and Dr. Charles Willard of the U.S. Geological Survey, in the summer of 1891 (see Hayes 1892).]

[In the several versions of his manuscript, Emmons credited first the Hoonah and then the Chilkat with having originated or developed the trade in copper, though in general he favored the Chilkat. He also recorded a number of legends about the origins of shield-shaped "coppers," the most valuable form supposedly taken by this native copper. There are several routes by which copper is known to have reached the Tlingit: (1) down the Nizina, the Chitina, and the Copper River to its mouth, or from the Chitina over the glaciers to the Gulf Coast near Kaliakh; thence via the Eyak-speakers of the Gulf Coast; (2) from the White River to the headwaters of the Alsek River, and down the latter to Dry Bay; and (3) from the White River to the headwaters of the Chilkat

River, and thence to the shores of Lynn Canal. For the first trade route, the Atna carried the copper to the coast and the Eyak (or Eyak-speakers) acted as middlemen; for the second the Athabaskans at Dry Bay or on the Alsek (Southern Tutchone?) presumably acted as carriers and middlemen; for the third, the Chilkat themselves made trading trips nearly to the source of the copper, which they presumably obtained from Southern Tutchone middlemen near Lake Atlin.]

The Copper River was the principal source of supply [of copper] for the coast as far south as Vancouver Island. The discovery of copper is credited in a Hoonah story to *Ka-kakh-ta* [Qaké·x̣ʷte?], a *Thluke-nuh-ut-de* [Łukʷnax̣ʔádi, Raven 6] man, who lived at a small village *Nook-kook-heen* [?, a village or sea otter hunting camp, in a narrow bay two miles above Cape Spencer, no trace of which remained when Emmons heard this story. He hazards that this was *Tah-an,* "Sleep Town" (ta ʔa·n), where the Ṫaqde·nta·n, Raven 16, originated.] While in his canoe one night, *Ka-kakh-ta* killed the "Spirit of Sleep," *Tah* [ta, "sleep"], in the form of a small bird that flew about the canoe. In consequence, all of the people of his village died, and he became a wanderer. He traveled north along the coast to Dry Bay and then up the Alsek River until he met the interior people. He taught them how the Tlingit took animals and fish, what roots, bark, and plants they ate, and how they prepared food for the winter. Here he first saw copper, in the form of knives, spears, and arrow blades, and the copper shield or "copper." Upon leaving, he was given copper which he carried back to his people. From this time, the Hoonah made trading trips to the Alsek country and procured native copper which they traded to the southern coastal tribes.

[This is a well-known story, versions of which have been recorded at Wrangell, Sitka, and Yakutat (Swanton 1908, Tales 32 and 104; de Laguna 1972:270–72). It seems evident that the protagonist, Qaké·x̣ʷte, or Kakē´q!ʷtÊ or Qakē´q!ʷtÊ (Swanton), belonged to a Wolf clan, while his Tlingit wife, to whom he gave the Sleep Bird as a crest, was a Łukʷna-ša·, a Raven 6 woman. According to the Sitka version, the Wolf man came from XAkAnuwū´, perhaps the same as *Hook-nu-wu,* "Dry Fort" (xakʷ nu·wú, "sandbar fort"), supposed to be in Dundas Bay, north shore of Icy Strait.]

[In a later version of his manuscript, Emmons stated:] From all native accounts the Chilkat at the head of Lynn Canal were the first to discover and develop the trade in copper. Nuggets of reasonable size for packing were carried over the hundreds of miles of interior trails and over the coast mountains during the annual fur-trading trips of the Chilkat. I believe this was the earliest introduction of copper to the coast. It is most probable that the first copper was brought out by those who crossed the mountains [over the Chilkat divide] and followed the lakes and rivers in the spring, to meet by appointment the more nomadic interior people with their winter catch of furs. The copper in pure nuggets came from *Klitsan* [Kletsan] Creek, a tributary of the White River, and were gathered at low water along its banks.

[Although a few monster nuggets weighing several tons have been found on the White River—and across the pass on the Nizina River side—"most of the copper was in the form of lumps weighing about 5 or 6 lb., such as were suitable for immediate fabrication" by the Indians (Rickard 1939:38). According to Hayes (1892:143), the Pelly River Indians at Fort Selkirk, Yukon, called copper *kletsan,* and the tributary of the White River where it was found *Klet-san-dek,* "copper creek," or Kletsan Creek.]

A later [?] source of supply was from the Copper River [from the same mineral district], and was brought to the coast by the interior people [Atna]. I say later, for the Chilkat had established themselves at the head of Lynn Canal and were trading inland long before the outer coast north to Yakutat was settled.

[This last statement can be accepted only if it means "settled by the Tlingit from southeastern Alaska." This process was probably taking place during the eighteenth century, begun after the Yakutat received a migration of Atna, the Kʷá·šk-qʷá·n, from the interior, and was later stimulated by the loot from the Russian post at Yakutat. Hoonah Tlingit from Lituya Bay who moved to Dry Bay must have been the first contingent. Archaeological evidence indicates that native copper was already at Yakutat in late prehistoric times (de Laguna et al. 1964).]

The Tlingit word for copper was *e-ak* or *ik* [ʔi̒·q], and old weathered or "dark copper" was *ik-yatze* or *ik-yatz* [ʔiq-yé·s̀, a term also applied to "iron"]. When the Tlingit procured brass in trade they called it *e-ak-natch* [ʔiqná·č̓], "light-colored copper." Iron was called *ga-yatze* [gayé·s̀, derived from ʔiq-yé·s̀], which some say was associated with or derived from *ik-yatze,* and in the minds of the people was considered a harder, darker copper. The Atna word for copper is *chiti* [čedi] and for river is *na* [naʔ]. The Chitina, the tributary of the Copper River on which native copper was principally found, is therefore "copper river" [čedinaʔ], in Atna. The Tlingit, however, called the main river *eek heene* or *e-ak heene* [ʔi̒·q hí·ni, ʔiqhí·ni], "water of copper," the name we have translated as Copper River.

Copper was never very abundant [on the coast] and increased in value as it was traded southward. The natives learned to work copper by heating it and beating it with stone hammers which gave it increased hardness, but artificial tempering was unknown. [A note in BCPA reads that the Tlingit "claim to have tempered it by dropping it when hot in old urine which was strong . . . had been allowed to stand for some time."]

[Archaeological specimens from the Yakutat area, dating from late prehistoric times, indicate that copper was cut or scored with chisels, bent, pounded repeatedly, and apparently pulled (?) or shaped into wires that were twisted like rope or coiled into spirals. Native Yakutat informants ascribed the discovery of copper and the knowledge of how to work it to a poor, outcast Atna boy who became respected and wealthy because of his work in copper, and the Atna have similar tales. Although the Yakutat believed that their ancestors could make the soft native copper "almost as hard as steel," this obviously was not possible (de Laguna 1972:412–13). Archaeological specimens from Yakutat were arrowheads (de Laguna et al. 1964:141, pl. 14, *a–e*), pins or awls (fig. 18, *d, e*), small knife blades (fig. 10, *c, d*; pl. 14, *h*), ulo blades (fig. 10, *a, b, e*; pl. 14, *l, m*), tiny nails used in making small boxes (fig. 23), rings for the finger or nose (pp. 161–62, fig. 19, *c*), bracelets (fig. 19, *a, b, d*), conical danglers (fig. 19, *g, i*), and cylindrical coiled wire beads (fig. 19, *h*). No copper barbed heads for sea otter harpoon arrows, barbed heads or blades for harpoons, spears, or daggers were found in the Yakutat sites explored, nor any trace of copper plates (tiná·); see below. Only the Yakutat and Chilkat Tlingit seem to have had enough native copper for this to have been the preferred material for the woman's ulo blade (de Laguna et al. 1964:101–2).]

Copper masks were rare. The oldest ones, possibly of native copper, are very crude. Later ones made of ship's sheathing were hammered over wooden forms and show the ingenuity and technical skill of the native artist.

For ornamenting masks, headdresses, pipes, knives, and dance paraphernalia, copper was greatly prized and has been used up to recent days.

COPPER NECK RINGS

The commonest type of metal bracelet was of copper or brass wire, twisted into a two-stranded open ring, but more valuable were broader bands etched in animal design or inlaid with haliotis shell. Very heavy rounded bracelets and anklets of copper were received in trade [and were] not of native workmanship.

Heavy neck rings were worn upon ceremonial occasions and were indicative of rank and wealth. One of these figured in an old legend about the son of a chief who was captured by the Salmon people and turned into a salmon. He was later speared by his father, and when his mother was cutting off the head of the fish, she encountered the copper neck ring which she at once recognized as that worn by her son. The fish later came to life [in human form] and became a great shaman.

[This is the well-known story of Salmon Boy, or "Moldy-End," versions of which I heard at Angoon and Yakutat (de Laguna 1972:889–90), and which were recorded by Swanton at Sitka, the locale of the story (Swanton 1909, Tales 99 and 100). The transformed boy was a Kiksʔádi, Raven 10, who not only taught all the people the proper treatment of salmon but obtained Fish Spirits for the shamans of his clan. See also Chapter 14 (in the section "Stories about Shamans") for another version.]

The copper neck ring worn by the natives was particularly noticed by the early explorers, such as Bodega and Mourelle (at Bucareli Bay in 1779), La Pérouse (at Lituya Bay in 1786), and Beresford with Dixon (at Sitka and the Queen Charlottes in 1787), [whose accounts have been quoted above].

[Marchand (Fleurieu 1801, 1:331), who was at Tchinkitanay or Sitka Sound in August 1791, said of Tlingit men:

> Most of them are adorned with a necklace, composed of copper wire interwoven; and this ornament appears not to be of European manufacture; it might be taken for a work of their own hands. They therefore possess mines, whence they extract this metal; and nothing contradicts this first supposition: but it would be necessary to suppose too that they possess the art of melting metal, of drawing it into wire, of working it; and what we have been able to learn of their industry, does not favour the idea that we can grant them this knowledge. What seems most probable, is, that these necklaces, fabricated in some European settlements of the interior, come to them ready made, from tribe to tribe, through the channel of the intermediate nations.]

In 1906 I purchased at Kincolith, Nass Harbour, B.C., one of these very old copper neck rings, which the old Niska chief said had been in his family for four or five generations when his people lived on the upper Nass River before the white man was known. These personal ornaments were among the rarest possessions of a family. (This specimen is now in the Museum of the American Indian, Heye Foundation, New York City.)

I sent this to Doctor Wirt Tassin [Dr. Wirt de Viviert Tassin, 1869–1915], Chemist of the U.S. National Museum, for examination. His statement was:

A qualitative test of the metal shows the presence of silver. Examination of an etched surface shows that the strands are each made up of two other strands, made up apparently of hammered sheets. These observations give rise to the following conclusions:

The copper is perhaps "native," since silver is a constant of the copper of the Copper River and Lake Superior regions. The sheets composing the individual strands taper from the centers to the ends, and vary greatly in thickness at different points, a condition which would arise when hammering a nugget into a sheet with the idea of getting as great a length as possible with a minimum width.

My idea of the method of manufacture is somewhat as follows: The native nugget was heated to a full red and quenched to make it soft, and then hammered from the ends to the middle. It was then reheated and worked in the same manner, except that the work was applied along the edge. These two processes were repeated alternately till the desired flat was obtained. Two of these flats were placed side by side, one end fastened, and both were then twisted together, but not "laid up." When a certain amount of work had been done, the twist was heated, cooled, and rounded up by hammering, thus forming a strand. Two such strands were thus twisted to form the necklace.

[Emmons evidently included this description because he felt that it could be taken as illustrative of Tlingit methods of working copper into similar articles.]

"COPPERS"*

The most valued of all worked copper pieces, however, was the shield-shaped object known as *tinneh* [tiná·], which represented wealth far beyond its intrinsic value as copper. It was possessed only by chiefs, but was more the property of the family [lineage] than an individual possession. It might be bought and sold, displayed or given away at a potlatch, and its value increased each time according to the amount of property distributed at the potlatch. Or, it might be broken into pieces and given to the more honored guests, or wholly destroyed, in order to humiliate a rival or to wipe out an insult, and such an act would require an equal or greater destruction of property by the opponent. The "copper" might be placed on the gravehouse or mortuary column to honor the dead. The face of the shield was ornamentally carved, or it was covered with a mixture of spruce gum, grease, and powdered charcoal, or smoked over a resinous slow-burning fire, through which the animal [crest] design was scraped, to bring out the design in bright copper against the dark field. Each of the larger "coppers" was given an individual name.

In the old folktales, the interior people are credited with the origin of the "copper," but this shield-shaped object was certainly made by the Tlingit, since the etching and painting on all that have been collected are clearly of coastal origin.

[One reason for the erroneous belief that the "coppers" were made by the Athabaskans may be due to the frequent confusion in old accounts between the metal, ʔiq, and the shield-shaped object made from it, tiná·. Keithahn (1964:75) has pointed out that Swanton's Tlingit informant, Q!ādustin (X̣a·dustí·n, "Sitting between") or Sitka Jack, a Kʷá·šk-qʷá·n, Raven 19 man, from Yakutat living at Sitka, used the terms *yutînná*, "the copper," and *yū'ēq*, "the piece of copper," interchangeably. This referred to the object left behind on the Tana River in the Copper River drainage; it took six men to fetch it to Yakutat, when the Atna immigrants wished to buy the Humpback Salmon Stream. This object, which Keithahn thinks was a nugget, is described in the story as very long, with eyes and with hands that pointed in the direction in which its owners had gone. The latter cut it in two down the middle (suggesting that it was thin). It was worth ten slaves (Swanton 1909:347–56, Tale 105).

[In an early version of the Qa·ke·x̣ʷté story, among the notes by Emmons in BCPA, this hero came to the Athabaskans of the Alsek River:

> There he saw lots of copper ("eakh") "Tin-nah" which had come from "Eakh-heene" [Copper River]. He finally returned to Hoonah (Cross Sound) and brought "Tin-nah" with him, *the first introduced to Thlingits to Southward*. . . . Copper was found as [nuggets? (illegible)] in possession of Stick Indians but the "Tuk-tain-ton, Kut-kow-ee," and "Thluk-har-hut-tee" [Raven 16, 7, and 17, especially associated with Dry and Lituya bays] traded with the "Eakh-kar-qwan" ["copper digger tribe," Atna] for copper and "Tin-nah" (copper shields from small to large size) which was traded with Southern Thlingits [and more southern Northwest Coast tribes]. . . . The "Tin-nah" were worked into shield shape by Interior or Sticks. A piece from tip of finger to neck in length was valued at two slaves, and from fingers to elbow one slave, while the small pieces passed as current money, four small pieces — in X — in [figures were omitted] were worth a moose skin.

[In the same notes is the recording under the name "Dick Satin" (Se·tá·n, a Raven 6 sub-chief at Sitka):

**Editor's note:* In addition to verifying the citation of Lisiansky, I have added quotations from Colnett, Niblack, Keithahn (including the letters by Emmons), and Rickard on the origin of "coppers."

> Copper, "eakh" obtained by the people living far up the Alseck river. They were Stick Indians known as "China-ko-qwan" [?] who travelled by foot to Copper River, traded for copper and brought it down to Dry Bay "Kehl-kar" [?] and the Thlingit came up coast and traded for this copper and took it south. Tin-nah made by Copper River people. Could not temper copper.

[An entry in these notes indicated that the Chilkat traded for copper or "coppers" both by water along the coast and by an inland trail, presumably via the Alsek River drainage.

[That "coppers" were available in the Akwe-Dry Bay area is indicated by the tradition that the Drum House Te·qʷe·dí (Wolf 32), who were first living there, were able to buy the rich hunting lands of the Ahrnklin River (ˀA·n ƛe·n) east of Yakutat, for a copper worth ten slaves (de Laguna 1972:241). Emmons believed that the original people who made this purchase were an Athabaskan clan that became extinct and were replaced at Ahrnklin by Tlingit Te·qʷe·dí from the south. The tradition which he follows here again links the shield-shaped "copper" with the interior.

[Oberg (1973:9) suggested that the raw copper was already partly shaped by the interior natives before they traded it to the Tlingit: "Native copper was used only for making the large copper shields which were used as potlatch goods. These shields were beaten out of raw copper found in the interior and brought to the Tlingit by the Athapascan traders." And again (p. 108): "Many of the interior groups [Athabaskans] were near sources of placer copper which they hammered into sheets and traded to the Tlingit. The best-known sources were in the valleys of the Copper and White rivers."

[Emmons evidently accepted the tradition of an interior origin for the "coppers," at least for those of small size. A note in AMNH indicates: "Coppers three or four inches were attached to *Kate* [ke·t, the shaman's skin apron], like deer hoofs or puffin beaks; longer ones five to seven inches worn on headdress of fur [of the shaman?]. The larger ones a foot or more to four feet long were valued at eight or ten slaves and were shown at potlatches. The coast people, who were always ready to accept something foreign if it were to their advantage, immediately began to hammer similar pieces out of malleable copper nuggets, and placed fictitious values upon them."

[It is now probably impossible to discover the values of "coppers" of various sizes. It is interesting to note the dimensions of the smaller ones, since these are rarely reported, and were perhaps the only ones made of native copper.

[The farther from the supply of copper or of "coppers," the more mysterious the origin, as is evident from the myths. Emmons reported a story from Wrangell that deals with the origin of "coppers." It is a variant of the stories recorded by Swanton at Wrangell and Sitka, although in these the monster killed by the widow's son was her father's miraculous brown bear canoe, which was made of copper plates (Swanton 1909, Tale 31, pp. 132–33; Tale 89, pp. 252–61).]

In early days in a more southern Tlingit village there was a widow and her son. She was a malicious gossip and in her evil talk created much trouble that culminated in a conflict in which many were killed. This led to her exile and she wandered far away with her son. He was a hunter and supported them both. One day before he went out, his mother told him that when he saw an animal he should shoot his arrow and call like a raven. [This cry was common magic to avert evil.] When he came to a lake, he saw a large fishlike monster coming toward him. Shooting and calling as he had been told, he killed it. Upon returning home, he told his mother he did not know what he had killed but that it looked like a huge shark and was covered with great scales or plates. The mother told him to take these off and to keep them, as they would make him rich. With his stone tools he cut down the middle of the monster's back and removed all the heavy plates which he stacked like wood by the house. When this was done, a visiting Tsimshian stopped, and, seeing the pile of shining plates, evidently of copper, bought one for twenty blankets, one mink skin, and one [sea] otter skin. Later, others came to buy and the hunter became wealthy. The plates were bright at first, but later turned almost black. The plates were used as ornaments on or in the house [of the hunter?], which was given the name *Ik-yatz hit* [ˀiqyé·ṡ hít, "dark copper house"], and the lineage became the *Ik-yatz hit-tan*, "Copper House Family." In some unexplained way the *Ga-yatze hit-tan* [gayé·ṡ, "iron," derived from ˀiqyé·ṡ], "Iron House Family," was looked upon as the same line. [The latter was listed by Swanton (1908:406) as a Ka·gʷa·nta·n lineage at Sitka, but Emmons considered them to be a branch of the Ču·kane·dí, Wolf 5, of Hoonah, who had moved to Sitka.]

[The earliest published description and illustration of a "copper" is that by Lisiansky (1814:150, pl. I, *f*, upside down), who was in Sitka in September, 1804. The "copper" was among objects that Baranov had taken from Tlingit houses he had destroyed. The "copper" was described as:

> . . . a thin plate, made of virgin copper, found on the Copper River, to the north of Sitca (Plate I. Fig. *f*): it was three feet in length, and twenty-two inches in breadth at one end, and eleven inches at the other, and on one side various figures were painted. [The illustration shows what may be a bear.] These plates are

only possessed by the rich, who give for one of them from twenty to thirty sea-otter skins. They are carried by the servants before their master on different occasions of ceremony, and are beaten upon, so as to serve as a musical instrument. The value of the plate depends, it seems, in its being made of virgin copper; for the common copper ones do not bear a higher price than a single skin.

[These "coppers" were certainly not used as gongs. That the beating on them was to indicate their value by their tone is suggested by the following description written by Niblack (1890:336), a naval officer in Alaska, 1885–87:

> To be of great value these plates must be large, of virgin copper, worked by hand, of native manufacture, of uniform thickness, except at the edges, where they should be thicker than elsewhere; and, finally, when struck should give forth a dull sound and not ring. Totemic etching on the outer surface also adds value to them. Modern "coppers" of European manufacture are not very highly prized, as compared with the ancient ones. [Presumably they ring when struck, although Bill Holm informs me that no "coppers" really "ring."]

[Commenting on the remarks of Lisiansky, quoted above, Emmons continued:] From the last paragraph it is clear how quickly the early traders learned the value placed on this object [the "copper"], and took advantage of it, for scarcely twenty-five years after trade relations had been established they so flooded the market with the manufactured imitation plates that had little value, although in size and workmanship they were superior to the native product. Their distinguishing features were greater thickness, cut edges, smooth surface and color, while the native-made specimens showed the hammered marks, but few if any of the latter can be identified with certainty.

The value varied with the size and increased on the southern journey [of the traded "copper"], and with each time that it was displayed or sold. An old Sitka native [Dick Se·tá·n] reported that one in length from the tip of the finger to the elbow was worth one male slave, one measuring from the finger to the neck two slaves, and that small ones had a current value of four moose skins. Miniature ones of traded copper were used as ornaments attached to ceremonial dress.

[Keithahn has argued that none of the natives encountered by eighteenth-century explorers possessed any of the large "chief's coppers" and that these were not made until the natives had acquired commercial sheet copper. Of 135 known "coppers" in museums, none is claimed to be of native copper. And Keithahn (1964:67) supposed "there should not be a single chief's copper in any of the museum collections of the world today that is made of native copper." In support of his argument he quoted two letters from Emmons. The first, dated June 18, 1941, was addressed to his Tlingit friend, William L. Paul:

> Now one more question about the old copper shield (Tinnah or Denah) what does this name mean[?] Copper in Tlingit is "Eek." The ones made of native copper from the White and Copper rivers were pounded out of copper nuggets of small size probably 3 to 6 to ten pounds—pounded into thin plates which were rivetted [*sic*] together to make the tinneh shape for they could not have hammered out a larger nugget to shape. I have seen smaller ones one or two feet in height of thin riveted plates but never a really large one. When the early explorers saw the great value far beyond size or weight of metal placed on these, they had made all sizes and flooded the coast with them—heavy commercial copper that would ring when struck while the native copper ones gave only a dead sound. But these commercial coppers were engraved in animal crest figures [by the natives] and can be had today. Do you know of any really old native made pieces? [p. 73]

[On February 8, 1942, Emmons wrote to Keithahn:

> I have never seen an identified *native* copper "tinneh." I have seen smaller ones 15 or 20 inches long of very thin copper, some another looking much like ship's sheathing, others more uneven that might have been hammered out, and one or two of plates riveted as the larger older ones must have been made. But all of the larger ones must have been so made of thin plates riveted together for it would seem impossible to have hammered one out with stone boulders from a single nugget. [He then referred to the story of the Kʷá·šk̓-qʷá·n migration to Yakutat (Swanton 1909, Tale 105, mentioned above) as "the story of the first 'tinneh.'"] When I first went to Alaska in 1882 I never saw any large coppers at Chilkat, Hoonah, Sitka among the Northern Tlingit, but south among the Haida at Kasaan there were many, but all of them commercial coppers brought by European traders, when they saw the value the natives placed on such objects. . . . What became of the primitive native coppers I do not know. The ceremonial use of the copper was more a feature with the Tsimshian, Haida, Kwakiutl and possibly the Southern Tlingit (this simply my belief). . . . Now, we *really* know practically nothing about the origin of the tinneh in its Interior home even the name itself whether Interior or Coast. . . . The thing I want greatly to find out from some native source in the Interior, are any of these shields to be found today. . . . [pp. 74–75]

[In discussing a Haida myth about making "coppers" from a copper fish, Rickard wrote (1939:34–36):

> . . . the Indians on this coast do not appear to have understood how to anneal, therefore the prehistoric *tinnehs,* made of native copper, are small—from 5 to 7 inches long, and patched. The

larger ones are of later date and were made out of pieces of copper sheathing derived from vessels that came to grief on the shores of Alaska and British Columbia.

. . . The estimation in which the "coppers" were held is indicated by the fact that when they were sold they could be exchanged for ten slaves or for a thousand blankets [the last by the Kwakiutl?]. When, however, the Indians began to buy sheet copper from the Russians at Sitka and the English at Victoria, their value decreased promptly, and, subsequently they were completely debased when several natives on the coast began to manufacture spurious, or commercial, "coppers." These glutted the market, and, as Mackenzie [an anthropologist] says ([1891] . . . p. 52), "destroyed the romance of the idea that the copper was one of earth's rarest and choicest treasures, fit only to be purchased by great chiefs who desired to squander away their property for the sake of gratifying their self esteem."

[The puzzle in all this—beyond the one of who made the first native "coppers"—is who were the "early explorers" who saw "coppers," large or small, that were made of the native metal? The "copper" described and illustrated by Lisiansky was said to have been made of native copper, but its large size (three feet in length and over one foot in breadth) would seem to make that impossible. It was most probably native made, but was it from commercial copper sheeting?

[The very first report and sketch of a "copper" is that made in August 1787, in the *Journal* of Captain James Colnett (manuscript 1786–88) when anchored in "Port St. James," probably Rose Passage or a nearby bay on Kunghit Island, the southernmost of the Queen Charlottes. Here the natives (Haida) reminded him of those at Nootka in most manners and dress, except that they were apparently more warlike. He sketched a suit of wooden slat body armor, not unlike that published by Lisiansky (1814, pl. I, *a*), and alongside it (but to a larger scale?) a typical "copper," which he described as "their Copper Breast plate which is their under armour & the wooden stays wch is the second case." (Bill Holm gave me a beautiful reconstruction of this "copper" from the sketch in the manuscript; the design seems to me to be that of a bear, the head above the cross ridge, and the front "hands" and hind paws on each side of the vertical ridge below. I am indebted to Mr. Stephen Wilson of London for a photocopy of the original manuscript.)

[A number of anthropologists and art historians have speculated on the original shape and function of the "copper" or of its prototype (MacDonald 1981, Widerspach-Thor 1981, Lévi-Strauss [1979] 1982), often arguing backward from its resemblance to masks, human figures, houses, mirrors, and so forth, or using its (assumed?) symbolic meanings as clues to its origins. The last approach is risky, since various meanings may become attached in the course of time to any object or symbol, a process Boas called "secondary associations." And the shape of the "copper" can be copied for amulets (de Laguna 1972, pls. 136, 178), or as petroglyphs (de Laguna 1960, pl. 11 *f*). Keithahn (1964:77–78) believed that the prototype was an Athabaskan-made copper arrowhead, used as a charm, which was expanded in size when sheet copper became available. I have suggested (de Laguna 1972:137) that the copper or brass medals and coats of arms given by the Russians to native chiefs or buried to claim the land for the tsar might have furnished a prototype. But these objects do not seem to have had the traditional "copper" shape, with its widened top ("head"), and T-shaped ridge dividing the bottom ("body") and separating it from the top.

[There may be more justification for taking Colnett's word that the "coppers" he saw in 1787 were, in fact, "under armour." He was not only an accurate and interested observer of the native scene, but also, on several occasions during the ten days he was at "Port St. James," he saw the natives donning and taking off their armor in attempts to intimidate the Englishmen with their military equipment. The outer armor he described as "their wooden stays & Leather Jackets which are made like a Wagoner's Frock & of a thickness sufficient to protect their Bodies from spears & arrows" (Colnett manuscript 1786–88). He would have seen the copper plates under them. He further noted that European beads, some iron and copper, had been made into ornaments for the neck, wrists, and ears (some collars and bracelets of twisted iron and copper strands). Most of their iron had been made into weapons: "None of the small pieces of copper seem'd to be held in any Estimation, but their breast Plates nothing would Induce them to part with; their Iron & Beads Captn Dixon supplyd them with [earlier that year], but their Copper must be procured from some distant tribe for I saw not the least sign of any mineral among them" (Colnett manuscript 1786–88).

[Even though small ornaments, charms, weapon blades, and points were being made of native copper in the late eighteenth century, there is as yet no hard evidence that "coppers" appeared before commercial copper sheets became available for their manufacture. Yet the late eighteenth century was the period in which the Tlingit, Haida, and Tsimshian were learning the power of firearms and were eager to acquire their own. Some of the southermost Haida that Colnett encountered were still ignorant until his demonstration, as were the southern Coast Tsimshian.

[By 1804, the Sitka Tlingit had strengthened their aboriginal armor to meet the new form of warfare, for Lisiansky wrote (1814:238): "Their war habit is a buck-skin, doubled and fastened round the neck, or a woolen cuaca [a sleeveless vest obtained from U.S. traders], to the upper part of which, in front, iron plates are attached, to defend the breast from a musket-ball." This was, I suggest, an improvement made on the earlier plates of native (?) copper that had been used as protection against aboriginal spears, daggers, and arrows, and also perhaps the first guns. Already in Lisiansky's time (1814:238, pl. I *a*), wooden slat armor had become obsolete at Sitka, and the associated wooden helmet was being worn at festivals. And as the latter evolved into the wooden clan hat, so I suggest the small earliest "coppers" expanded in size as they assumed ceremonial functions.]

WORK IN IRON*

Iron, *ga-yatze* [gayé·s̓], was not a product of Alaska. The earliest knowledge of it by the natives came from the wreckage of Asiatic vessels and drift carried eastward to the American shores by the Japanese current. This is also the traditional belief of the Tlingit, which in one instance is substantiated by a rude knife blade I saw in 1888 at Klukwan among the Chilkat, and which they claimed was made from an iron spike taken from a piece of wreckage on the Yakutat shore by a party of adventurers long before the white man was known in Alaska. This knife is today in the University of Pennsylvania Museum.

[Emmons refers here to the knife called "Ghost of Courageous Adventurer," described by Louis Shotridge (1920:11–26), who collected it. The specimen is fifteen and one-half inches long, with a single double-edged blade of iron with medial ridge and tang, and iron guard. The grip is padded with goat hair, and the pommel is of walrus ivory carved in the shape of a human skull, inlaid with abalone shell. It was an heirloom of the Thunderbird House of the Šangukʷe·dí, Wolf 8, of Klukwan. According to the story recorded by Shotridge, a group of Wolf men, lead by Eagle Head, Č̓á·k̓ Ša·yí, ascended the Tlehini River and went overland across the Chilkat Pass to the headwaters of the Alsek River. From "Chan-you-ka" (Čanukʷa?), somewhere on the upper Alsek, they passed via one of the "through glaciers" (perhaps Nunatak Glacier) to Russell Fjord. They saw here no sign of habitation, so they pushed on. Two men were lost in crevasses of the (Malaspina?) glacier. On the shore Eagle Head found a drift log with queer "spurs" sticking out, which were so hard that one broke the edge of his greenstone adz when he struck it. When pounded with boulders, the "spurs" bent but did not break. When the log was burned in a fire, the "spurs" remained like red hot coals. It was from one of these that the knife was later made. From this place the Chilkat party went along the shore until they came to the banks of a great river, which Shotridge thinks was the Copper River, but which was probably a stream much closer to Yakutat Bay. Here they found a village of G̣unana·, an inland people speaking an unknown tongue. They kindled fire with a fire drill, so Eagle Head gave their chief his flint and pyrites. A return gift was a piece of walrus ivory, up to that time unknown to the Tlingit. This was later used for the pommel of the knife. It was from this place that the Tlingit in later years obtained copper. (One gathers that these people were Eyak.) After the return of the party to Klukwan, "Kah-oosti" (a Ka·gʷa·nta·n leader of Killerwhale's Dorsal Fin House) made the spike into a war knife with the ivory on the handle. The iron was rough; it was not smoothed until the people acquired a grindstone. He called together the men of the Ne·sˀádi (Wolf 23), Šangukʷe·dí (Wolf 8), and Ka·gʷa·nta·n (Wolf 1), and then awarded the knife to Eagle Head in memory of the men who had died on the trip.

[The Yakutat also have traditions of similar finds of iron in driftwood, even of a whole ship wrecked on the beach west of Yakutat, long before the appearance of the Russians themselves (de Laguna 1972:233, 412). Drift iron was very precious, and the finder became a rich and important man. Archaeological evidence indicates that iron was used in later prehistoric times (that is, prior to the presence of any other objects of civilized manufacture or origin) but was not known as early as native copper (de Laguna et al. 1964:88–90). Drucker has written (1950:256):

> The types and materials of knives in pre-iron times is a mystery to most informants. Many natives, particularly in the north, maintain that their people had iron long before Europeans appeared on the scene and for corroboration cite any number of traditions relating how some ancestor found a "log" with iron in it along the beach. (The "log" they interpret as a mast of a wrecked vessel.) This traditional motif of the finding of drift iron, if it be

*Editor's note: This section required considerable editing. I had to check and amplify the original references made by Emmons, and have also included information from other pertinent sources. All of these had to be arranged in a more logical order than that adopted by Emmons, which necessitated writing new introductory or connecting remarks for these citations. But this made it possible to detect and correct Emmons's confusion of Trinidad Bay in California and "Rada de Bucareli" in Washington with places in Kaigani and Tlingit territories in Alaska. The first paragraphs on the evidence of drift iron in Alaska before Bering are mine. Later citations made by Emmons are not enclosed in brackets, even though I am responsible for some of the wording.

a myth, has a wide distribution on the Northwest Coast, or else the event occurred rather often, for the Tolowa of northwest California claim their forefathers got iron in the same manner. It is difficult to retain one's skepticism in the face of the plausibility and constant reiteration of this story, although what these vessels with timbers so laden with iron could have been is hard to say.

[We should also note that Steller in 1741 saw iron knives among the Aleut of the Shumagin Islands (Steller in Golder 1925, 2:97–98): "Two [of the Aleuts] had hanging on their belt, like the Russian peasants, a long iron knife in a sheath of very poor workmanship, which may have been their own and not a foreign invention. . . . From the distance I observed the nature of this knife very carefully as one of the Americans unsheathed it and cut a bladder in two with it. It was easy to see that it was of iron and, besides, that it was not like any European product."

[Steller discussed the possibility that the natives knew how to smelt iron, or that they had obtained iron knives from the Chukchee, who had acquired these from the Russians at Anadyrsk, and in turn traded them to the Americans for furs. In a footnote (216, p. 97), Golder cited corroborative evidence that by 1759–63 the Russian hunters among the Aleuts of Unimak and Unalaska had reported that the natives knew how to make knives of iron which they obtained from the eastward, in exchange for furs and clothing. He added: "It is not likely that the natives to the eastward knew how to smelt iron. They probably obtained this metal in some indirect way either from the white men or from wrecked vessels. In a report of a Russian hunter (about 1765) a statement is made that the Aleuts told him a large ship had been driven ashore to the eastward."

[Holmberg (1855:101, 135) and Jochelson (1933:22) also cited traditions from Kodiak that drift iron was obtained long before the Russians, and it is also possible that the westernmost Aleut even may have traded with Chinese, Japanese, or Russian adventurers before Bering. Evidence for the early appearance and use of iron has been summarized by Rickard (1939:38–50), whose work Emmons evidently consulted, and also by Jochelson (1933:21–24), and by de Laguna (1956:60–64). There is no question but that the natives of southwestern and southeastern Alaska possessed iron in the eighteenth century, before direct contact with traders or explorers, and that they knew how to work it in primitive ways, perhaps copied from their experience with copper, but that they could not smelt it from ore.

[Emmons rejected the idea that this early iron had come to the Tlingit and other tribes from Russian sources, and discounted the possibility that some pieces might have passed from group to group and so crossed from Siberia to the New World, through intertribal trade.]

Iron was certainly not first procured from the Russians, for while Bering reached the Alaska coast in 1741, he had no intercourse with the natives, beyond the disappearance of Chirikov's two boats, which has ever since remained a mystery. [Some authors had speculated that the iron had come from them.] The eastern expansion of the Siberian adventurers through the Aleutian Islands to Cook Inlet was marked by brutality and murder in which trade had no place. The Tlingit were not westward traders, and from their outpost at Yakutat they went only as far as the Copper River delta to get copper from the interior people. Zaikov reached Prince William Sound in 1781 [*sic*]. [According to Bancroft (1886:190, note 31) this erroneous date was copied from Dall. It should be 1783. But the first Russians, a party of Zaikov's men in a skin umiak from Cook Inlet, visited Prince William Sound in 1779 (Bancroft 1886:219); and Zaikov himself wintered there in 1783–84, when he traded at Kayak Island and in the sound (Bancroft 1886:189–90).] In 1783 Nagaiev discovered the mouth of the Copper River, and Ismailov reached Yakutat in 1788 [Bancroft 1886:268–70]. From all of these iron might have been obtained, but it had already by this time become well known on the Northwest Coast.

In 1774 Juan Perez in the *Santiago* sailed north from Monterey to the vicinity of Dixon's Entrance. Off the Islands of Santa Margarita [probably Langara Island, northwest of Graham Island] he met two canoes of Haida. As Fray Crespi wrote (in Griffin 1891:188): "In these canoes we saw two very large harpoons for fishing and two axes. One of these seemed, on account of the shining appearance of the edge, to be of iron; but I could not verify this. We saw that the head of one of the harpoons was of iron, and it looked like that of a boarding-pike." [It was a gaff?]

Off Dall Island, the Spaniards traded with the Kaigani and Crespi noted (in Griffin 1891:192): "It is apparent that they have a great liking for articles made of iron and of copper, if they be not small. For the beads they did not show a great liking." He also noted (p. 194) finger rings and bracelets on the women that were of iron and copper. Fray de La Peña (in Griffin 1891:123), who was also aboard, noted of the Kaigani: "It was apparent that what they liked most were things made of iron; but they wanted large pieces with a cutting edge, such as swords, wood-knives and the like. . . ."

So it is a fact that they knew about iron and could fashion it to their own use. Returning south, Perez put in, at or near

Nootka, and there Crespi noted (in Griffin 1891:203): "Some pieces of iron and of copper and of knives were seen in their possession."

[The reference cited by Emmons for iron seen at "Cross Sound" in Tlingit territory in 1775 by the Second Bucareli Expedition under Hezeta is confused. The passage refers to California Indians near Trinidad Head. See below.]

In 1779 another Spanish expedition sailed north under Juan Francisco de la Bodega y Quadra from San Blas, that reached as far northwest as Prince William Sound. At Port Santa Cruz, in Bucareli Bay, Klawak Tlingit territory, Mourelle, Bodega's pilot, noted bracelets of copper and of iron [quoted above under "Work in Copper"], and also in La Pérouse 1799, 1:247, 250:

> . . . lances, four yards long, headed with iron; knives of the same metal, longer than an European bayonet, but not common among them. . . . [p. 247]
>
> In some of the Indians the desire of procuring iron, cloth, or other stuffs, was stronger than parental affection: they sold their children for a few yards of cloth, or pieces of iron hoops. The Spaniards purchased in this manner three boys, one of four years old, one of five or six, and the other of nine or ten, not to make slaves of them, but Christians. . . . Two little girls were also bought with the same views, one very ordinary, about seven or eight years old, the other younger, and handsome, but ill, and almost dying. [p. 250]

Father Riobo (Thornton 1918:224, 226), on the same expedition, also noted that the Tlingit arrows were sometimes pointed with iron:

> They are extremely fond of iron of which they possess many lances and knives. [Some lance heads were twenty-four inches long; the short knives had double-edged blades.] . . . They are very desirous of obtaining copper and iron but they are chiefly anxious for iron, so much so that as soon as they see a piece of barrel hoop they care no longer for glass beads, mirrors, rings or anything else that is presented to them. [The women wore hanging from the neck a little knife, used in woodcarving, and in fighting with each other. These knives were of iron.]

Captain Cook noted in April 1778 that the natives of Nootka Sound had weapons with blades or points of bone or stone, except that (1784, 2:324, 329–300):

> Some of the arrows are pointed with iron. . . . [p. 324]
>
> Their great dexterity in works of wood, may, in some measure, be ascribed to the assistance they receive from iron tools. For, as far as we know, they use no other; at least, we saw only one chisel of bone. And though originally, their tools must have been of different materials, it is not improbable that many of their improvements have been made since they acquired a knowledge of that metal, which is now universally used in their various wooden works. The chisel and the knife, are the only forms, as far as we saw, that iron assumes amongst them. [The largest chisels had blades eight to ten inches long, three to four inches wide, although most were smaller. The handle was of wood, and they were struck with a stone mallet.] The knives are of various sizes; some very large; and their blades are crooked, somewhat like our pruning-knife; but the edge is on the back or convex part. Most of them that we saw were about the breadth and thickness of an iron hoop; and their singular form marks that they are not of European make. Probably, they are imitations of their own original instruments, used for the same purposes. They sharpen these iron tools upon a coarse slate whetstone; and likewise keep the whole instrument constantly bright. [He also mentions a polisher of fishskin.] [pp. 329–30]

[Although Captain Cook admitted that the Indians had some things, such as iron and brass, that must have been derived from some civilized source, he did not believe, or was loath to believe, that the Nootka had had any direct contact with traders. He was convinced that the natives had never seen ships like his before, and that the Spanish expeditions of 1774 or 1775 had not come to Nootka Sound. Yet he had heard of at least one of these expeditions before sailing from England, and must have suspected that they had already claimed Nootka Sound for Spain, otherwise why would he not have claimed it for England? Two silver tablespoons, he conceded, must have come from Mexico; but the Nootka had so much iron—and evidently knew how to work it—that it could not have been derived from "an accidental supply from a ship" (p. 332). And the Spanish could not have represented a constant and regular source of the metal. He was inclined to believe that the brass and iron came to the Indians through intertribal trade, the ultimate source being the British colonies of Hudson Bay and Canada. Cook maintained the same theory with respect to the beads and iron he saw among the Chugach Eskimo of Prince William Sound and the Tanaina of Cook Inlet, even though the word for iron, "goone," was derived from the Russian "chugun." (See citations and arguments in de Laguna 1956:60–62.)]

La Pérouse, who entered Port des Français or Lituya Bay in 1786, was a close observer of native life. He wrote (1799, 1:369–70):

> Of all our articles of trade, they appeared to have no great desire for any thing but iron: they accepted indeed a few beads; but these served rather to conclude a bargain, than to form the basis of it. We at length prevailed on them to take pewter pots and plates: yet these had only a transient success, iron prevailing over every thing. They were not unacquainted with this

> metal. Every one had a dagger of it suspended from the neck, not unlike the criss [Kris] of the Malays, except that the handle was different, being nothing more than an elongation of the blade, rounded, and without any edge. This weapon had a sheath of tanned leather, and appeared to be their most valued moveable. [Some daggers were of native copper.]
>
> Gold is not an object of more eager desire in Europe, than iron in this part of America, which is another proof of its scarcity. Every man, it is true, has a little in his possession; but they are so covetous of it, that they leave no means untried to obtain it.

La Pérouse bought sea otter skins (1799, 1:371) "bartered for hatchets, adzes and bar iron. At first they gave us salmon in exchange for pieces of old hoops; but they soon became more difficult, and would not part with this fish unless for nails, or small implements of iron." He also noted (p. 401): "They make scars on the arms and breast with a very keen iron instrument, which they sharpen by rubbing it on their teeth as on a whetstone." [And (p. 407) they had lances of wood, hardened in the fire, or] "pointed with iron, according to the wealth of the owner. . . ."

La Pérouse believed that the Indians "know how to forge iron" (1799, p. 406). But that this metal, as well as "necklaces of beads, and some little articles of brass" (p. 370), probably came from the Russians, less likely from the Hudson's Bay Company, from the Spaniards, or from American merchants.

Dixon, who anchored in Port Mulgrave near the entrance of Yakutat Bay in 1787, made the first known exploration of this area. Beresford, his supercargo, indicated how well established iron was here (1789:168, 176; pl. opposite p. 188, nos. 3 and 4): "They [the natives] shewed us plenty of beads, and the same kind of knives and spears we had seen in Prince William's Sound [i.e., of iron]. . . . Toes [small iron adz blades] were the article of trade held in the first estimation here, and next to these, pewter basons were best liked."

The Sitka Tlingit of Norfolk Sound also had particular preferences in trade goods (Beresford 1789:182):

> Toes are the article of traffic held in the first estimation at this place; but they always refused small ones, wanting them in general from eight to fourteen inches long. Besides these, we traded with pewter basons, hatchets, howels, buckles, rings, &c. Of these the basons were best liked; for though the hatchets and howels were obviously the most useful tools these people could possibly have, yet they were only taken in exchange for furs of inferior value. Beads of every sort were constantly refused with contempt, when offered by way of barter, and would scarcely be accepted as presents. [In summary (p. 192):] . . . iron, however, may justly be reckoned the staple commodity, every thing else depending, in great measure, on fancy and caprice.

[The next year, 1788, the English trader Colnett, and the Russian exploring expedition under Ismailov and Bocharov, both called at Yakutat Bay, and both reported some iron. Colnett wrote (quoted in de Laguna 1972:130): "All the European articles I saw was a file with Hunsberg [?] on, & a pair of Russian or Dutch scissors. They shewed us very little iron, but from the familiar method of receiving us, should suppose European visitors were common."

[Ismailov and Bocharov had been sent in the galliot *Trekh Sviatiteli* (*Three Saints*) by Shelikhov, with orders to explore the coasts of Alaska from Prince William Sound and southeastward and to claim these lands for the tsar. In Yakutat Bay, the natives traded eagerly for clothing, iron, kettles, and copper stills (for the metal), but were not very eager for beads. As reported in Coxe (1803:328): "We saw in their possession several hatchets, which from their shape, we supposed to be procured from some European ship [presumably Dixon's]." At Yakutat the Russians met the Ga·naxte·dí, Raven 3, chief from Klukwan, "Ilchak" (Yé·ł xá·k, "Raven's Smell"), who had come with his two sons and a large trading party. To this impressive individual the Russians gave a brass medal with the imperial coat of arms, and a portrait of the crown prince. In return, the chief gave them, among other presents, "an iron image of a crow's head, which he considered as sacred" (Coxe 1803:332). From a rather obscure passage in the report, we gather that the "iron images of crows" were actually barbed spear heads used to take sea otter, seal, and salmon (pp. 326–27), although they were also used as ornaments, and probably as amulets, because of the valuable material of which they were made.

[Etienne Marchand visited the Tlingit of Norfolk (Sitka) Sound in 1791 and observed (Fleurieu 1801, 1:342–43) that the men were all armed with double-edged daggers of metal [iron?], fifteen or sixteen inches long, worn in a sheath on a shoulder belt. They also had pikes with iron heads of European manufacture, and lances with iron heads like halberds. Their adzes had thick iron blades. Fleurieu (p. 341) hazarded that the first iron must have come via intertribal trade from either the "English settlements of HUDSON'S BAY, or from the Spanish *presidios*," but that for the past fifty years there had been native trade with the Russians.

[Malaspina visited Yakutat Bay also in 1791. He found the natives eager to acquire clothing and iron, either by trading or pilfering, the most desired items being warm seaman's clothing or uniforms and iron axes. The rate of one nail for one salmon was also accepted. The natives were certainly familiar with European ships, for Malaspina noted hatchets, cooking pots, silver spoons, items of clothing, and even three books, which he believed had been left by Captain Dixon (summarized in de Laguna 1972:143–46).

[From 1791 on, iron became plentiful, as trading vessels increasingly engaged in the fur trade, the Russians established posts in Prince William Sound (1793), Yakutat (1795–1805), and Sitka (1799–1802, 1804); the Spanish establishment at San Francisco had been founded in 1776.

[Indians were encountered by the Second Bucareli Expedition of 1775 at what they called "Puerto de la Santísima Trinidad," at approximately 41°03′ north latitude, or Trinidad Bay, just south of Trinidad Head, northern California. These Indians were presumably the Yurok, and their village visited by the Spaniards was perhaps Tsurau (see Kroeber 1925:8–9, fig. 1). These Indians had arrows, some of which had heads of copper and iron, which Mourelle understood "were procured from the N. and one of these was thus marked $C_{///}$." These arrows are carried in quivers of wood or bone, and hang from their wrist or neck. "But what they chiefly value is iron, and particularly knives or hoops of old barrels, . . ." (Mourelle 1920:28–29).

[Fray Campa, a chaplain on the expedition, added some interesting observations (quoted by Sierra, in Wagner 1930:218, n. 4): "A few of them had also some pieces of sword-blades about a span long which they told us by signs came from the north. On our asking them if they obtained any from some other part they answered no and that they only obtained them from the north where there were larger ones. One of them gave us to understand by very expressive signs that he had made his from a nail which he had found in a piece of wreckage and had beaten out with a stone." According to Sierra (1930:221), the Indians told Padre Campa that no ships had come there, but they knew large ships like the two of the Spaniards came "lower down (indicating the direction of Monterey). . . ."

[Later in the voyage, the Spaniards lost seven men and their longboat to the treacherous Indians of "Rada de Bucareli." They were probably the Quinault, or perhaps their neighbors, the Queets or Hoh to the north, south of Point Grenville on the coast of what is now Washington State. The attack was evidently made for the purpose of securing iron, for Sierra reported (1930:228)]: "After satiating their sanguinary instincts by murdering our men, the savages set to work to smash up the boat, carrying off with them every piece of iron it contained. Iron is what the Indians most prize, because iron articles are what they always ask for first when bartering."

[Since each of the boat's crew had taken a gun and a pistol, and some also had a cutlass, and some hatchets (Mourelle 1920:37), the plunder of the Indians must have been impressive.

[Emmons evidently knew of the encounter of the Spaniards with the Indians of Trinidad Bay, for he quoted part of the same passage from Fray Campa as that given above, in which the Indians indicated that the pieces of iron swords had come from the north. Because Emmons seems not to have known where these Indians were, or even to have confused the place with Cross Sound, Alaska, he evidently missed the clue as to the provenience of the iron. Ignoring the evidence of early trade with Asiatic sources, or with Russians in Siberia, as summarized by Rickard (1939), and misinterpreting the evidence from Fray Campa, Emmons was inclined to think that (some?) of the iron seen by explorers on the Northwest Coast had been traded northward from Spanish settlements. Thus:]

Iron may have reached Puget Sound in Indian barter, along the inland trade route, for it is traditional with the Tlingit that the much prized iridescent California haliotis shell came to them through native exchange long before [*sic*] the white man was known on the coast [implying that Spanish iron from Monterey or even farther south may have followed the same route].

That iron was not obtained from eastern sources is answered by Alexander Mackenzie. On 9 June 1793, near the headwaters of the Peace and Fraser rivers, Mackenzie ([1801] 1903, 2:88–91) met Rocky Mountain Indians [Sekani], who informed him that they had heard of white men but have never seen any before. They also told him that they obtained iron, in exchange for beaver and moose skins, from a people [the Carrier], who lived on the banks of a river and lake, eleven days journey to the west. The latter traveled for a moon, to the country of another tribe, who live in houses, and from whom they traded the skins for iron. The latter also "extend their journies in the same manner to the sea coast, or, to use their expression, the Stinking Lake, where they trade with people like us [Europeans], that come there in vessels as big as islands." In this way (pp. 97–99), the inland people obtained a few white beads, evidently dentalia, and an "ample provision of iron weapons," consisting of blades for arrows, spears, adzes, and knives, which they shaped themselves.

On the Upper Fraser, Mackenzie ([1801] 1903, 2:160–61) met Indians who also obtained "iron, brass, copper, and trinkets, from the Westward; but formerly these articles were obtained from the lower parts of the river, although in small quantities. [There was a knife that had come from that quarter, derived from white men,] long before they had heard that any came to the Westward. [One old man said he had been told of white men to the southward. The Indians also indicated that] They had been informed by those whom they meet to trade with, that the white people, from whom these articles are obtained, were building houses at the distance of three days, or two nights journey from the place where they met last fall."

[Rickard (1939:41–44) summarized this report as evidence that the iron found on the Pacific Coast in Cook's time could not have come from Hudson's Bay Company posts, and Emmons may have taken this argument from him. Rickard believed that the whites who had been building houses were Spaniards who were building on Vancouver Island in 1789 and 1790. He added the information obtained by Simon Fraser in 1806, to the effect that the Indians of the Finlay, a northwestern tributary of the Peace River, received iron from the Tsimshian-speakers of the upper Skeena, who in turn had secured it from their coastal kinsmen. This was corroboration of Mackenzie's report.]

From these statements of the first explorers [Emmons concluded], it is evident that the natives of the Northwest Coast had some iron when first encountered, could work it into shapes and tools suitable for their purposes, and in trade demanded it above all else. They desired iron in forms like their own tools, and so the *toe* [or *tohis*, the Hawaiian word for "adz" (Krause [1885] 1956, chap. 1, n. 36 by Gunther)] became a standard article of trade, made abroad or fashioned from bar iron by the ships' smiths. It took the place of the stone adz that was the principal woodworking tool, and was similarly hafted to a short, bent wooden handle. Its great value can be readily understood, since the felling, shaping, and hollowing out of great trees to make canoes was a time-consuming labor which the iron blade simplified. Also the artistic sense of the people had long been held in abeyance by the want of material means of expression, and the exchange of their stone, beaver teeth, and shell for iron blades gave us the wealth of animal figures and designs which are the wonders of our museums today.

[In the BCPA version of the manuscript, Emmons wrote:] From the noticeably fine carved masks, boxes, tools, and household articles collected from them when first met and from other objects seen and described, it is evident that they must have had iron for generations, to have mentally and artistically perfected their animal art, especially in the forms in which the animals are represented symbolically under the least favorable conditions. So it is unreasonable to date their art from their contact with Europeans and the trade in iron of the eighteenth century.

[It is curious that Emmons does not mention the crooked knife, yu· ka-tan łíta·, of necessity made with a metal blade, as an important tool of the native artisan.]

While iron ore is found in Alaska, the natives had no means of reducing the ore to precious metal. It would seem that before the coming of trading vessels toward the close of the eighteenth century, the coast natives had already procured small bits of manufactured iron, either from wreckage or from inland southern trade from Mexico, and knew its use. From their knowledge of copper they soon learned to work it into weapons, tools, and even ornaments, and almost invariably followed the original forms, as may be observed in their manufactured spear heads, adzes, knives, etc., which are exact replicas of the primitive stone implements. In nothing was their ingenuity better displayed than in the ornamentation of the upper blade of the dagger and in the fine temper of its edge. Although La Pérouse did not believe that the natives of Lituya Bay in 1786 "are acquainted with the method of reducing iron ore to the state of metal," the samples of iron which he procured from them were "as soft and easy to cut as lead" (La Pérouse, 1799, 1:369–70), and he stated (p. 406): "The Americans of Port des Français know how to forge iron. . . ."

In working steel and iron, they learned to soften it by heating it with charcoal, enabling them to work it more easily, and then bringing the temper back by plunging it in a bath of oil and water when hot. The blades of the short single-bladed knife and the spear were often worked down from files, and this may readily be seen by the cross cuts still remaining on the blades.

That the Tlingit learned to work iron is reasonable, [first] from his experience with copper, and [later] from watching the ships' smiths, but trade gave him so exactly what he required that his work was largely confined to shaping by grinding rather than by hammering. Certainly the animal designs on the upper blades of the war knives and the fluting of the lower blades must have been worked by grinding.

Iron nails were not employed in the construction of the old-style communal house. The timbers and planking were dovetailed, grooved, and fitted. In canoe making and repairing, sewing with spruce root ever held its place over metal fastenings. [Therefore, the Tlingit had no need to make bolts or nails; when manufactured ones were obtained, they were turned into more useful tools or weapons.]

[In discussing the occurrence of wreckage with iron and brass from Japanese and Russian vessels, Rickard (1939:44–50) also pointed out that survivors of such vessels, as well as men from ships that had been pirated by the Indians, sometimes included men who knew how to work iron, and that the natives may have learned the craft from them. Emmons cited one of the examples given by Rickard of a Spanish(?) ship that was wrecked at the mouth of the Columbia River, furnishing the Indians with both iron and a survivor who could work it. This was perhaps in 1745. (See Rickard 1939:48–49; Emmons mixed up the bibliographic citations.)

[The problem of determining the date and provenience of the earliest iron on the Northwest Coast has again been raised by the occurrence of iron tools at the Ozette site in Makah territory, Washington, in contexts dated to the fifteenth century. If iron had come from Siberia and been slowly traded southward along the American shore, "This could possibly account for the woodworking tradition in the north being more highly developed than in the south [of the Northwest Coast]" (Stewart 1984:36).]

WORK IN SILVER AND GOLD*

In primitive days copper had been valued for personal ornaments, but it lost its place when the early traders flooded the coast with cheap trinkets of copper and brass. It was during the period of Russian occupation that coin silver came into use for jewelry. The Tlingit claim that it was the Mexican dollar that was first used, which seems very reasonable, since [Rezanov made the first voyage from Sitka to San Francisco in 1806, and] Baranov established a farming colony at Fort Ross in 1812, which led to the exchange of products between California and Alaska. Silver was also known to the natives from medals presented to chiefs by the Russian government. Later, the United States silver dollar came into circulation on Puget Sound and eventually reached the northern coast. This must have been before the middle of the last century, although silver was not used as a medium of exchange in Alaska until after the purchase of the country by the United States. [The Tlingit word for money or silver is dá·na·, clearly derived from "dollar."]

I do not know whether the Haida or the Tlingit were the first silversmiths in the north, but both were pioneers in this craft and have remained the most skilled. As only coin silver was to be had, the silversmith was restricted in the size of his product. The jeweler's outfit consisted of a heavy close-grained boulder for an anvil, a hammer, a wooden mold, two or three engraving tools rubbed down from pieces of files or knife blades, a whetstone, a piece of dogfish skin for smoothing, and fine clay and deerskin for polishing.

In 1882 there were not more than four silversmiths in Alaska, at Sitka and Wrangell. One had obtained a small [commercial?] anvil, another used a large iron wedge driven into a section of tree trunk as an anvil, and a third used a heavy piece of iron wheel, evidently part of a machine, as a bed piece on which the silver coin was beaten into a bar or flat piece. One jeweler in Sitka had a large lignum vitae sheave [hardwood pulley wheel] of a ship's block, placed on a section of tree trunk [and suitably hollowed out to serve as a mold].

[It has been possible to identify only two of the four jewelers. One of these was "Jim," mentioned by Emmons as a Sitka man who gave him information. The other was "Charlie Gunnock," or "Tim nook," Gú·n-wa·q or "Golden Eyes," a Raven 25 man, Suqʷti·ne·dí, who had left Kake in disgrace and was living in Wrangell. He had refused to contribute to a potlatch, so his relatives had "sold him for thirty blankets." He eventually returned to Kake and redeemed himself. Young (1927:220–21) identified him as a jeweler at Kake in 1878 who was accidentally shot in the knee and crippled for life during the "war" between the Stikines and the Hutsnuwus.]

With these tools were made small articles such as rings for the ear, nose, and finger, hair ornaments, labret pins, and later shawl or blanket pins, but the most important article was the bracelet. The first bracelets were wide ones for native use, but with the coming of white settlers and industries, and later tourists, the native silversmiths could not supply the demand, and so made very narrow bracelets that could be manufactured in a shorter time. [These were, incidentally, very similar to the prehistoric copper bracelets.] After tourist travel began, the Sitka silversmiths began to make small spoons, the handles of some of which were hammered out to represent animal heads in repoussé.

Gold came sparingly into use after silver [1900?]. There was an old woman from Yakutat living in Sitka who was known as "Princess Tom." She wore three wide gold bracelets on each wrist, but was more noted for having two brothers as her husbands, all of whom lived happily together.

Editor's note: This section necessitated the fitting together of several versions dealing with the same topic.

[She was a Raven 19 woman, Kʷá·šk̓-šá·, whose name I recorded as Qaǯínt and Swanton (1909:405) as Gadji'nt. She later was known as Mrs. Emeline Baker. She was a wealthy woman who used her Yakutat connections to advantage in trading. Her husband (or chief husband), Tom (or Thom), was the ranking Wolf leader of the Ka·gʷa·nta·n when they were invited to a potlatch at Sitka shortly before 1904 (see de Laguna 1972:191–92). At present, all the bracelets treasured by the Tlingit are of gold, probably dating from the prosperous last decade of the nineteenth century and the early years of the present century.]

An innovation of the twentieth century was the inlaying of old [silver] bracelets with abalone or gold, to the disadvantage of both metals, [and these inlays] destroyed the perfection of the animal figures [with which the old bracelets were engraved].

[Emmons left conflicting versions as to how silver was worked, specifically how the bar or piece used for a bracelet was shaped from a silver coin. This discrepancy may be because the methods were observed in different years at different places. In the most complete version (notes in BCPA) he wrote:]

Silver bracelets, spoons, nose rings, and [indecipherable] are made from coin. If the amount of metal required is more than that contained in a dollar, several pieces of silver are smelted in a crucible, consisting of a piece of brick lined with potash and glazed with potash. And upon reaching a molten state [the silver] is poured into a wooden mold and allowed to cool. If the piece to be made is of a size to allow the use of a piece of coin (a half dollar is a favorite size), or if it is preferred to cut a dollar in half [instead of using a fifty-cent coin?], this is heated on a piece of hoop iron, the handle end of which is insulated with a wrapping of bark or cloth. The coin [or half coin] was placed on edge [on the other end of the iron], and this is shoved in among the coals of fire in a stove today, but in the past, when the old-fashioned fireplace was in use, was put in among the coals. Upon being slightly acted upon by the heat, it [the silver] is removed, taken between a pair of pincers and laid on an improvised anvil. [This] consists of a sited piece of old iron, let into a piece of wood. The partially softened silver is beaten out a little, reheated, and so beaten until it has been shaped to [desired] dimensions, [a bar or a flat shape].

[In another version (AMNH), Emmons stated:] As the native had no means of melting the silver and molding it into shape, he resorted to continued heating and hammering. [To heat, the coin was placed on a piece of hoop iron, as above.]

[Emmons evidently did not understand that nonferrous metals, like copper and silver, must be worked cold. I am indebted to Bill Holm for this information, and for the following reference to *Silversmithing,* by Finegold and Seitz (1983:1, 13). These authors point out that silver and most other metals, except pure gold, become harder and more brittle when worked, and that they must be annealed (heated and quenched in cold water) at intervals as they are pounded, stretched, or bent, otherwise they will shatter.

[In still another version (in BCPA), headed "268 Bracelet Making Silver," Emmons wrote]: "Run coin in wooden mold in bar in assayer's retort. Then beat out to required size for bracelet on piece of iron as anvil with hammer."

[In a typed version of the manuscript in AMNH, Emmons wrote:] I saw a Sitka jeweler beating into shape a bar of silver the size of a finger. This must have been made by melting a coin in an iron spoon or ladle and running it into a wooden mold. This bar he placed on the end of an iron hoop [piece of hoop iron] a foot or two long, the other end of which was wrapped with spruce root and hide. With this he held the bar over the coals to heat it, and then transferred it to the anvil and hammered it. Heating and hammering were alternated until the silver was reduced to the required shape, a thin parallelogram.

[In the first two versions quoted above, the bar is formed by pounding. The first is the more specific:] If a bracelet of the smaller type of cross section [is to be made], it is beaten into a uniform bar in a uniform groove filed across the anvil. If a wide bracelet, or a spoon, is to be made, it is beaten into a flat band or a partially shaped flat piece. [Presumably the silver is alternately pounded and annealed.]

[The final shaping of the object made use of wooden molds and forms, according to the various versions.] To make this [the band or bar] into a bracelet, the silver was shaped over a circular block of wood, slightly greater in diameter in the middle, which gave the bracelet the curved exterior. [This wooden mold or form is also described as "a wooden ring or oval with rounded edge."]

The raised heads, bowls of spoons, and half-rounding (hollow on the underside) of bracelets are beaten into shape by means of wooden curved sections fitting into corresponding concavities in hard wood. The sheaves [pulley wheels] of blocks of lignum vitae are greatly in demand for hollows. These are burnt in and worked out, and even lead is used, while the convex sections fitting into same are of ax handles or iron, and when beaten down with a wooden maul into place, assume shape. [Of the Sitka jeweler's sheave of lignum vitae, Emmons wrote:] In this were cavities hollowed out in the shape of an animal or a bird's head or a small bowl of a spoon. In or over these the piece of silver was placed, and was hammered into shape with a correspondingly shaped convex piece, which produced a repoussé ornamentation. [Elsewhere Emmons simply stated:] Such raised parts as heads, eyes, etc., were formed in corresponding cavities in the face of the lignum vitae block by driving the thin plate [of silver] into the hollow with a knob of hard wood.

The object was then smoothed with pumice stone and fine dogfish skin, the design cut with the graving tool, and then polished with a fine clay and a piece of soft deerskin. The engraver relied entirely on his eye in marking out the design on the bracelet. Some designs were copied from older bracelets, but some silversmiths made drawings to which they could refer. There were comparatively few figures and these were representations of crest animals [see below]. The carving knives are points [burins] made from old files or a razor blade, with short points, and kept extremely sharp and kept in a case of skin. [When the decorating or carving work is done, it] is finished up with dogfish skin [a dogfish tail]; now emory paper and polishers are used. [In the first BCPA version, it was specified:] When the desired shape is obtained, it is filed off, the edges smoothed down and burnished with smooth iron, and it is ready for carving. The filings are saved, melted in a retort, and run into molds. Soldering is done with copper paint tinned as we solder, as they have learned the art from us (and some used modern soldering irons).

WORK IN WOOD*

While the house and the canoe constituted the most important work in wood, the ornamental carvings of the interior house posts and partitions, and the smaller and more delicate house furnishings and ceremonial objects better displayed the artistic sense of the people. The early navigators expressed admiration for their workmanship. [This is not altogether true. In the manuscript, Emmons cited only the most favorable opinions, omitting others which I have added below.]

La Pérouse (1799, 1:397, 406, 407) wrote of the Tlingit of Lituya Bay in 1786: "Their arts are considerably advanced, and their civilization in this respect has made great progress; but in everything that polishes and softens the ferocity of manners, they are yet in their infancy" (p. 397). "[In contrast to Eskimo, the Indians] are very unskillful in the construction of their canoes, which are formed of a trunk of a tree hollowed out, and heightened on each side by a plank" (p. 406). "These Indians have made much greater progress in arts than in morals, and their industry is farther advanced than that of the inhabitants of the Southsea islands [except for agriculture and its civilizing effects]" (p. 406).

[After praising the weaving and basketry, he added:] They likewise carve all sorts of figures of men and animals, in wood or stone, in a very tolerable manner; make boxes of a tolerably elegant form, and inlay them with the opercula of shells; and cut serpentine into ornaments, giving it the polish of marble" (p. 407).

[Captain Portlock (1789:292) wrote of Sitkan woodworking: "It is very surprising to see how well they will shape their boards with the shocking tools they employ; some of them being full ten feet long, two feet and a half broad, and not more than an inch thick. [And p. 294:] They have tolerable ideas of carving, and indeed almost every utensil they make use of has some kind of rude carving, representing one animal or other." The Indians gave seaman Woodcock a wooden comb carved to represent an eagle. The captain forbade trading for such things, fearing it would end the trade for sea otter furs.

[Suría (Wagner 1936:253), who was with Malaspina at Yakutat in 1791, was not much impressed with the native manufactures. He wrote of their square wooden boxes: "All their ornament is reduced to a mask on the four fronts with the mouth open, badly carved with the teeth inverted and in others by way of ornament they have placed them in a parallel line."]

The observations made by La Pérouse were at a period when the natives were just acquiring metal tools. The two types of stone adz [large splitting adz and smaller planing adz; see the section "Men's Tools," above], though differing in form and size, were similarly hafted and used, and constituted the principal woodworking implements. When iron was procured, the old forms and haftings were retained. The early knife was a splinter of jade used in the hand, although sometimes seized at the end of a handle, as a chisel; a beaver tooth similarly hafted, or a mussel shell, and possibly from the shape of these [the beaver tooth and the shell] the curved steel-bladed [crooked] knife was evolved. The drill was a small stone point set in the end of

**Editor's note:* To the reference made by Emmons to La Pérouse, I have added quotations from Portlock and Suría.

Painted canoe paddles. (Pencil sketches by G T. Emmons on pages of field notebook. R: *red paint;* B: *black paint. AMNH.)* Top. *Killerwhale.* Bottom. *Whale (with one jaw).*

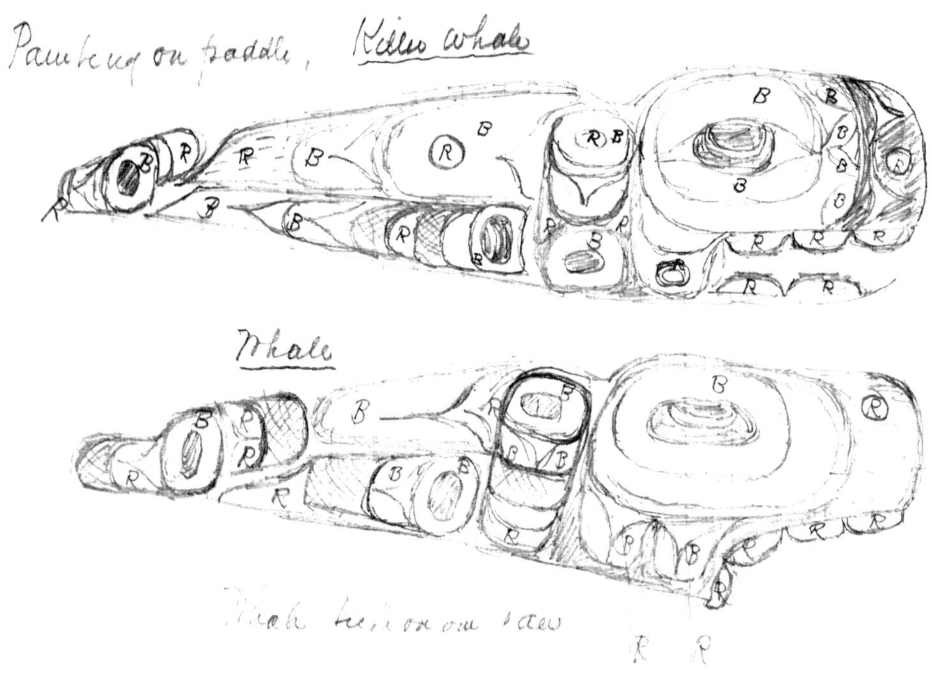

a twirling stick; later a sharpened nail was substituted for the stone point. In splitting wood or driving stakes, a heavy stone maul, hafted like the ax, was used in conjunction with a wedge of hemlock or spruce, some two inches in diameter, about one foot long, from a small tree trunk. In carving with the knife, the man was seated with legs extended in front, and the knife edge was always drawn toward the body.

The construction of storage boxes for food and clothing might be described here. Both types were made after the same manner. The sides of one length of thin board were partly cut out on the inner face [at what were to be the corners], steamed until pliable, bent around, and sewed at the meeting place with spruce root, countersunk. The bottom was partly hollowed out and neatly grooved within the outer face into which the sides were fitted, and [these] were sewed or pegged with root. The top was fashioned like the bottom, and when in place was secured with a two-stranded twisted cedar-bark cord. [See also "Domestic Utensils," in Chapter 6. The process of making a bentwood box is well illustrated by Stewart 1984:84–92.]

MEASUREMENTS*

The Tlingit possessed no mechanical lineal measure. His rule was the human body, with the tip end of the second finger as the zero point. [The following are the lengths used.]

1. *Ka dlekh* [qa· ƛ̓e·q], "a [human] finger," from the tip of the second finger to its third joint.
2. *Ka dlekh woddy* [qa· ƛ̓e·q wa·dí], "a span," from the tip of the second finger to the tip of the outstretched thumb.
3. *Ka tdee* [qa· ṫi·y, "elbow"], "where the arm breaks," from the tip of the second finger to the elbow.
4. *Ka kikee* [qa· kígi, "half the body," or "half of something symmetrical or paired"], from the tip of the second finger to the middle of the body ["half a fathom, half a man"].
5. *A wot* [ʔa wa·t; from wat, "to stretch the arms"], "a fathom," from the tip of the second finger of the left hand to the tip of the second finger of the right hand, both arms outstretched.

**Editor's note:* This short section has been placed here for want of a more logical place, since it refers primarily to measurements made by men in woodworking. Emmons had put it and a section on "Count" (see Chapter 17, the section "Count") at the end of his original "Chapter V: Domestic Life."

In carving, painting, and weaving, depending so generally on the eye, the Tlingit formed habits of accuracy unknown to those relying on artificial means, but when necessary for accurate copying, or as a matter of comparison, they measured by means of a length of grass stem, a piece of bark, or a line. [The measures listed above would be ones primarily used by men in woodworking. The gauges used in making the canoe have already been mentioned in Chapter 4.]

TOTEM POLES*

The distinctive feature of the Northwest Coast villages in the last century was the elaborately carved memorial columns standing in front of the houses that proclaimed the heraldry and the social standing of the family [lineage]. These carvings followed the few rude figures seen by the early explorers and were made possible by the general use of iron tools from trading vessels toward the close of the eighteenth century.

[Garfield and Forrest (1948:2) have expressed a similar opinion:

> Before tempered iron and steel blades were introduced into Alaska . . . intricate carving was a slow and laborious process, even on soft wood. It is probable that in this epoch the largest sculptures attempted were those on house posts and short mortuary columns.
>
> The acquisition of metal cutting blades in the latter part of the eighteenth century facilitated more complex carving and increased the production of individual artists. The tall totem pole, set in front of the owner's house, was a late product, made possible by more efficient tools and the greater wealth brought by the fur trade of the early nineteenth century.

[The same authors point out (1948:7) that new wealth came to the natives in the latter part of the nineteenth century, from commercial fisheries, mines, and other industries: "Many of the newly rich invested their earnings in carved columns. The dignity of the older symbolic legendary history [illustrated in the carvings] degenerated in the course of competition for the tallest poles or for the most lavish expenditure at dedicatory feasts."

[Emmons in general followed Barbeau in his discussion of the recency of the totem pole, citing a number of the same sources as those quoted by Barbeau (1929 and 1951, vol. 2), although the latter work was published too late for Emmons to have read it. Drucker (1948) has discussed the problem of the antiquity of the Northwest Coast totem pole and Barbeau's ideas at length, pointing out, among other facts, that the early explorers seldom saw the winter villages where such poles would have been erected, and had so poor an opinion of native art that they usually neglected to describe the carvings they did see. Such negative evidence, therefore, cannot be used to prove that no totem poles were made before European contact. Large carved poles were, in fact, observed among the Central Nootka or Clayoquot in 1788 and 1799, in 1790 and 1791 among the Haida of Cloak Bay, and in 1791 at Yakutat (see sources in Drucker 1948:390–91). These were memorial or mortuary poles, portal or doorway poles, and some were free-standing poles. Drucker (p. 397) concluded that "Northwest coast art, and the carving of totem poles themselves, antedated all European influences in the area." And presumably the first iron used was obtained indirectly from "some Asiatic source long before the entry of Europeans or Russians into the North Pacific." In view of this extensive review, I have omitted all the quotations used by Emmons that deal with totem poles among tribes other than the Tlingit.]

The earliest notice of carved figures standing out of doors in villages occurs in Meares (1790:364), from a report by Captain Douglas off North Island [Haida] on 23 June 1789. Captain John Bartlet on 25 June 1791 described and sketched a totem pole in Cloak Bay, off North Island [see Barbeau 1951, 2:803], and Captain Marchand in August 1791 described a house and totem pole there most minutely (Fleurieu 1801, 1:400–403). [Also that same year, at Cloak Bay, Captain Ingraham (1971:103), mentioned two carved posts through one of which the doorway was cut], and Vancouver described Nootka carved wooden images in 1793 [see Barbeau 1951 2:806–8].

The preceding citations to the journals of the early explorers show how few there were of these outside carvings, whether figures, house entrance poles, or grave posts, all of which were memorial or heraldic in character. That the first evidence of this sculptural art was found upon the Queen Charlotte Islands would give precedence to the Haida as its originator, and this is further borne out by the seaward position of their coast, so directly influenced by the drift of the Japanese Gulf Stream which brought the first iron to these shores in the wreckage of Asiatic ships driven overseas. [Drucker (1948:397, n. 25) argued that Spanish galleons in the Manila trade were a more likely source of spars with iron.] While it may have been possible to have

**Editor's note:* I have introduced the opinions of Garfield and Forrest, Barbeau, and Drucker on the age of totem poles, and a description of Yakutat grave monuments. Emmons had originally planned to put this section in his Chapter III, after "Graves."

Deserted Henya village of Tuxekan, west coast of Prince of Wales Island, showing old-style houses and grave posts, 1888. (Photographer unknown. BCPA.)

worked out these carvings with stone adz and knife, yet it is not probable that it was accomplished without iron, which Cook and others found already in possession of the natives upon their arrival. Whether the elaborately carved, graceful column which features the old villages was the conception of the Haida or the Tsimshian is of little moment, as both contributed equally to its highest development. It was the product of the early half of the nineteenth century and resulted mechanically from the use of iron tools obtained from the early trading vessels, financially from the fur trade, and socially from the extreme jealousy and rivalry of the chiefs to outdo one another in any public exhibition.

The Southern Tlingit, from intimate association with the Haida and Tsimshian, adopted many of their customs, among which the most visible was the totem pole, but as copyists they did not approach the consistent conventionalism of the Haida nor the versatile delicacy of the Tsimshian, and so added nothing to this art.

From the Tongass and Sanya, the totem pole spread to the neighboring tribes: the Stikine, Henya, and Kake, until it reached Frederick Sound, the artificial [?, natural] boundary between the Northern and Southern Tlingit. Here it lost its significance [?, importance], and throughout the entire area extending to Yakutat, within the territory of the nine Northern Tlingit tribes were to be found only an odd pole here and there, altogether eleven in 1882.

[Emmons was evidently not aware of the large carved grave monuments sketched by Cardero at Yakutat in 1791. Although the artist has surely exaggerated their height and failed to reproduce adequately the crest carvings, they would qualify for consideration as "totem poles." (See de Laguna 1972, pls. 60–61, pp. 540–42; Henry 1984, pls. on pp. 162–63.) The most famous of these monuments was a carved Bear, holding a box for ashes in its paws; another consisted of two boxes, the upper carved to represent the face of a Bear, the lower was surmounted by a crest hat or helmet representing a Wolf. The upper box was supported between two tall poles like dance leaders' wands, carved to represent the dorsal fins of Killerwhales, and decorated with hair. The style of the carving was like that on a Bear house post carved at Yakutat in 1875, and like a carved stone petroglyph with a Bear's face, commemorating the defeat of the Russians at Yakutat in 1805. Curiously enough, Captain Dixon, who had visited this cemetery in 1787, did not notice or record these grave monuments, for it seems hardly possible that one or another of them was not already there at the mouth of the Ankau, especially since similar grave monuments were seen by Malaspina's men on the southern shore of Knight Island, farther up Yakutat Bay, and included the same monstrous carving of a Bear. Although there was a copy of Malaspina's report in the Archives Library in Victoria, possibly the manuscript translation had not yet been made, and so Emmons did not see it. And probably, too, these pictures had not been reproduced in publications available to him.

[Both Emmons and I (de Laguna 1972:316–17) heard of a now abandoned Tlingit site at Diyagunaʔet, a few miles east of Yakutat. This was a prehistoric-historic site, at which one house, Bear House, had the doorway cut just below the carving of a large, threatening bear. This house, and some others in the village, belonged to the Bear House Te·q^{w}e·dí, Wolf 32, and I believe that the Bear and Killerwhale grave monuments seen by Malaspina, as well as the Bear petroglyph (de Laguna et al. 1964, pl. 3, *b*), were associated with the Te·q^{w}e·dí. This Tlingit clan was recognized as having originated among the Tongass, and members had moved north to Sitka and eventually to Yakutat. Although not all those at Yakutat who called themselves Te·q^{w}e·dí were Tongass Tlingit, still it is reasonable to suppose that the leading aristocrats of that clan were of Tongass descent, and that the immigrants had brought to Yakutat the typically Tlingit heraldry and the totem pole. House posts and carved grave monuments on a smaller or simpler scale were undoubtedly much older, not only among the Tlingit but among all the tribes of the Northwest Coast.]

The whole idea expressed on the totem poles was the honor of the dead and glorification of the family [clan or lineage], in exhibiting the crest and such other figures as were definitely associated with some particular member of the family. In every feature of Tlingit life, in every ceremony, on every object from the house and canoe to the smallest charm, ornament, or implement, the crest figure was the dominant feature, and these columns offered only another field for its display.

Totem poles may be divided into two kinds, those that told stories and those that exhibited the crest, the latter being more particularly confined to the mortuary column. But both types so often came to perform both functions that it is difficult to distinguish between them, and both were really at basis crest poles. The story-telling pole proper stood in front or at the corner of the house, but never in contact with it and consequently never formed the doorway, as was the custom with the Haida. This pole was always the taller and generally the more ornamented, both in the number and elaboration of human and animal figures. These were always surmounted by the lineage crest, or by a human figure with the crests below. Unlike the Haida, who often introduced the wife's crest, the Tlingit rarely showed that of the opposite moiety unless this was necessary to illustrate the story. These poles were always memorial in character, since they were erected by the new house master to his predecessor, whose cremated remains might or might not be placed in a receptacle at the back of the pole.

The second class of poles were much lower in height and simpler in ornamentation, and more often consisted of a rounded pole surmounted by a single crest or a human figure. These were placed among the gravehouses and frequently contained the cremated remains of the deceased. At Tuxekan, on northwestern Prince of Wales Island, a Henya village, such poles formed striking groups at either end of the village, and were exceptional in their more elaborate carvings and numbers of figures.

[Garfield and Forrest (1948:4) pointed out that the Tuxekan poles were all grave markers or held boxes containing the ashes of the deceased, or were memorials of the dead, and that in contrast to those of Tongass they were very slender, measuring ten to thirty feet in height and only two to three feet in diameter. In 1916 there were 125 poles at the then already deserted village. And (p. 100), of all the poles in the area, none was known to have been carved before 1865. It is interesting that no carved house posts were found in this village.]

The mortuary column containing the ashes of the dead, or representing them [the deceased] at the base, were fifteen or more feet in height, and were essentially individual monuments, similar in meaning to those in our cemeteries. The typical totem pole was also a memorial in honor of the dead, but was much more important in a heraldic sense as the glorification of the clan in its presentation of the crest which occupied the most prominent place. The pole, according to the wealth of the family, might be a simple, barked cedar tree surmounted by the crest, or one elaborately carved from base to summit, but in either case, the dominant figure was the animal crest which indicated the origin of the clan. The column was supplied and carved by the clan of the owner's wife, if possible by a member of her direct family [house, lineage]. The raising of the pole was

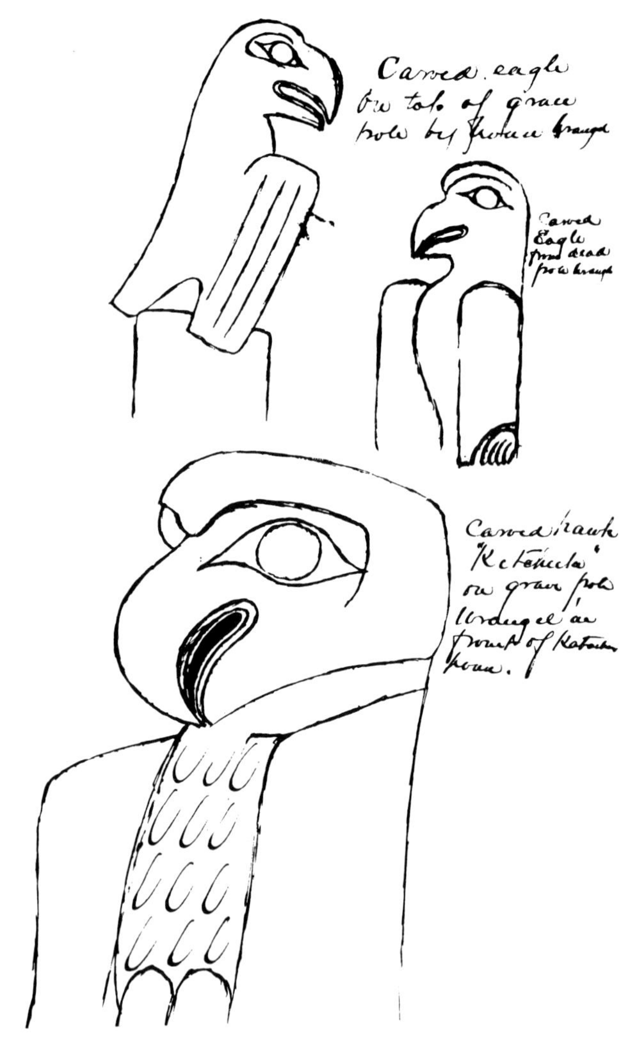

Mortuary posts, Wrangell. (Sketches by G. T. Emmons. AMNH.) Top. *Two posts with carved eagles.* Bottom. *Carved hawk,* Ketchuke [kiǯu·k / giǯu·k], *on mortuary pole in front of Kadashan's house, Raven 32.*

followed by a potlatch, "the feeding of the tree," when the carver and all of those who had assisted in the labor were paid. While the pole was in memory of the dead, yet it reflected equal honor on the successor, who had given away his accumulated savings and thus increased the prestige and social standing of his clan. [See Chapter 11, "Ceremonies."]

[Emmons does not discuss the carved house post in this connection.]

The general name for totem pole is *ka da ka dee* [qa·da·ke·dí], "man's grave pole," which indicates the purpose.

[The Tlingit word means literally "man's container," and seems to be applied both to the coffin and to the grave post that hold the body or the ashes. The totem pole that has no such function is simply called ku·tí·ya· ("carved figure or emblem"), a word applied, I believe, to any representation of the crest.]

All poles were partly decorated with paint, traces of which can still be detected in the cracks, however much weathered. The only colors used were black and red, native mineral paint mixed with salmon egg, which proved an excellent preservative. The blue-green paint so attractive on masks was too expensive to use on such a large surface. The painting of figures was in the recognized conventional art of the coast [see below].

PAINTING*

While every man might paint, as every man might carve in wood or bone, to fulfil his own needs, yet as a business such industries were practiced by individuals whose excellence was recognized, and they were paid accordingly. [Since artwork of this kind involved making or decorating objects with crest designs, to be dedicated or used on ceremonial occasions, the artist was supposed to be a member of the opposite moiety from that of the future owner who had commissioned him. If this was not the case, the fiction was preserved by paying the wife of the artist, who would be a member of the proper moiety.]

The artist's outfit consisted of brushes, [painting] sticks, stencils, paint dishes or stones, mineral paints, salmon or trout spawn, and cases or boxes in which to keep these.

The brush, *ku-hee-tar* [ku·xí·da·, or ku·xʷí·da·, from ǯ-xi·t, "to paint"], was of fine porcupine hair, *hut-thur-kutch* [x̣ałak̓áč̓] "porcupine," *how-oo* [x̣a·wú] "hair". The handle was generally of wood, preferably cedar wood, or in rare instances of bone or ivory. The lower end of the handle was slightly tapered for just the thickness of a wrapping of bark, so that the size, after wrapping, was uniform. At this end the wood was split, and the porcupine hairs or bristles were arranged evenly in the split, to project one-fourth to one-half inch; the ends were enclosed in the split for one or two inches and brought out, and a neat wrapping of split spruce root, the rounded outer surface outside, was wrapped tightly around, binding the split and holding the hairs in

**Editor's note:* In this section and in the following one, "Art," I have tried to reconcile and combine the different versions of the text and the many notes left by Emmons, but elimination of all repetition was impossible.

Carvings representing the sandhill crane, dulth [dúˑƚ], *(a) on a dancing headdress, Wrangell, and (b) on a mortuary post in front of Kadashan's house, Raven 32, Wrangell. Stikine tribe. (Sketches by G. T. Emmons. AMNH.)*

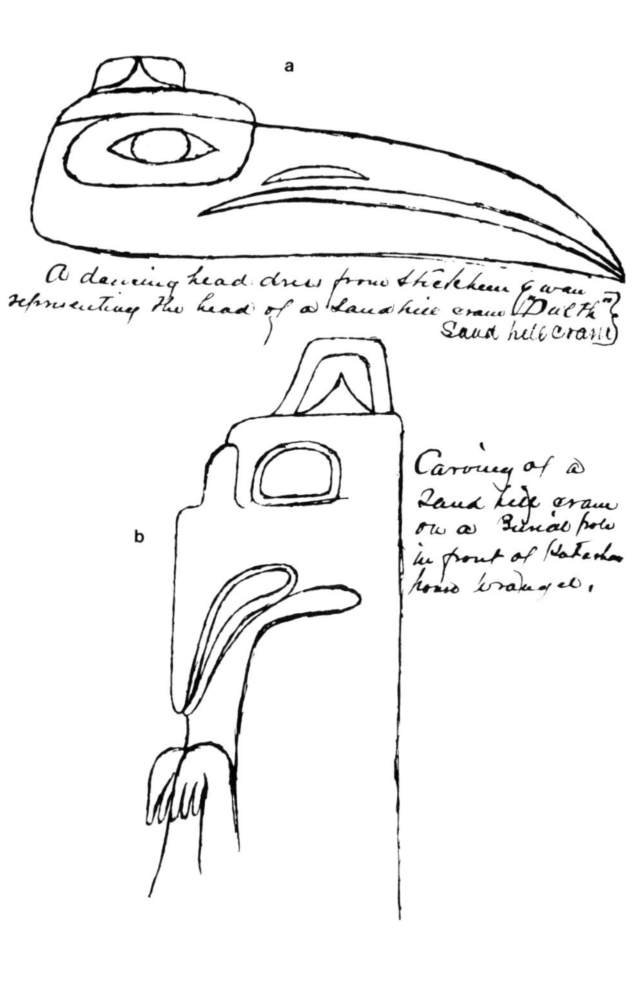

place. The wrapping is put on from the end upwards. [Since Emmons mentioned both a seizing of spruce root and a wrapping of bark, it is not clear whether one or both might be used.] In some cases the hairs are placed on the flattened side, or in the case of a double brush on both sides, of the lower end of the handle and wrapped with spruce root. The brush is always flat except for those of the largest size. The handle, four to eleven inches long, was often finely carved in animal designs, such as the head, tail, fin, or some other characteristic feature, or sometimes the whole figure. Sometimes the handle tapered to the upper end, which was pointed or flattened to an edge, and served both as a pencil to draw in color and to use in work too fine for the brush. The artist might have half a dozen to a dozen brushes of different sizes. For painting the old wooden gambling sticks, on which are traced colored parallel lines and sometimes figures, sharpened sticks were used instead of brushes. These were short cylindrical sticks, pointed at one or both ends, but beveled so that a broad band as well as a narrow line could be drawn.

Paintbrushes were kept in flattened boxes of bark, basketwork, fishskin, or seal intestines, or in boxes often ornamented in totemic or general designs. [Emmons did not explain what were "general," nontotemic designs.] These containers were called ***ku-hee-tar tar-kate*** [kuˑxíˑdaˑ daˑkeˑt]. The paint box was not of any particular pattern, but was long enough to take the brushes, paints, and stencils. The stone dishes for mixing paints were not kept in these boxes.

Only mineral colors were used for painting, and among the Tlingit were confined to red, black, and blue-green. Red was obtained from hematite and cinnabar, but principally from an oxide of iron, a reddish rock found throughout the coastal region, which was fired to give a deep brownish red. Red paint was called *tlaok* or *thlaok* [ƛ̓éˑx̣ʷ]. Black was obtained from coal, *Yehlh hoots-see* [yéˑƚ xuˑʒí, "Raven's embers"], or charcoal. Black paint, charcoal, or the color black was called *tooch* [ṫuˑč̣]; black paint was also called *tsukl* [c̓áqƚ]. The green-blue paint was made from azurite, ***na-hin-ta negwat*** [neˑxinté or neˑxíˑntá níˑgʷáƚ], an oxide of copper found in sea caverns and overhanging cliffs particularly on the outer shore of Kruzof Island, beyond Sitka. The people went to get it with great fear, believing that it was protected by some supernatural power [see Swanton 1909, Tale 17; de Laguna 1972:416]. It was also found in the Queen Charlotte Islands. This mineral gave a deep blue-green and was the most esteemed and expensive color, and was sparingly used. A small piece the size of a walnut was valued at $10 to $20 at Sitka as late as 1890. This color withstood the weather like the other colors, but in contact with grease the blue changed to green or was lost.

[Emmons consulted Alexander H. Phillips, Department of Geology, Princeton University, about two samples of paint, and received the following letter from him, dated February 19, 1929:

> (1) . . . the green specimen is a mixture of the two carbonates of copper, the green portion being malachite and the small blue areas being azurite. [This may be the sample listed as "1708. Piece stone used as source for blue color employed by Tlingit; broken

Set of ornamentally carved paint brush handles. (Pencil sketches by G. T. Emmons. AMNH.) (a) Shark's tail. (b) Killerwhale dorsal fin. (c) Crane's head. (d) Raven's head. (e) Killerwhale dorsal fin. (f) Whale. (g) Not identified.

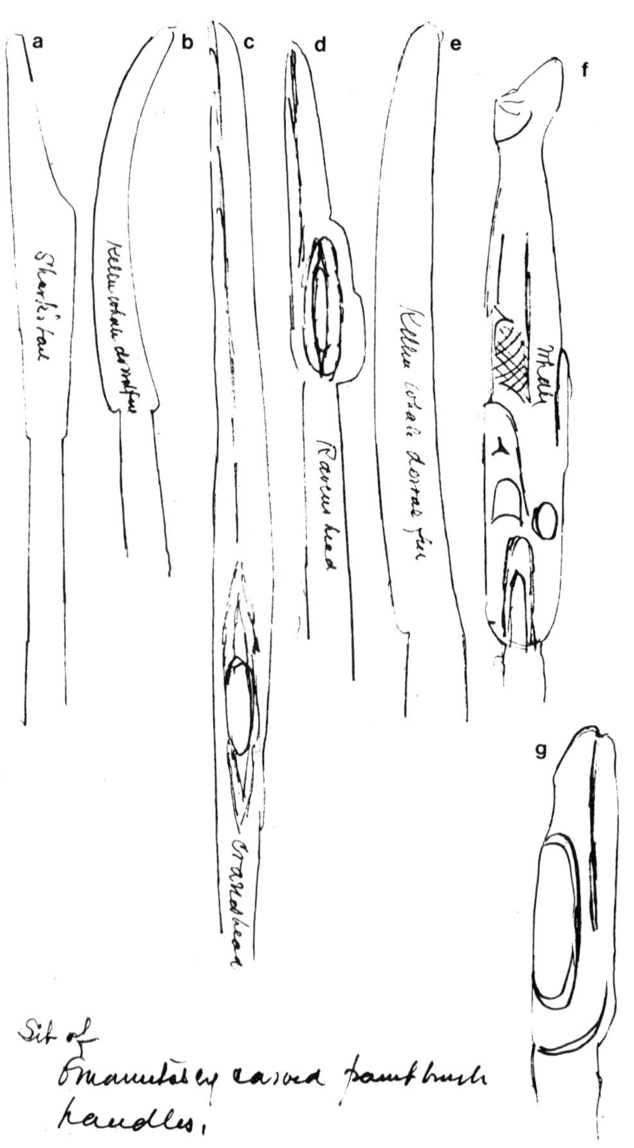

from piece actually in use. (Chrysocolla, silicate of copper.)" This note was with the letter in BCPA.]

(2) The reddish-colored specimen is rather a decomposed piece of igneous rock which contains considerable iron and is reddened by the oxide of iron. If this is burned in a reducing atmosphere it will turn out black; and if burned in an oxidizing atmosphere, it will turn out a red pigment. I suppose the Indians had acquired this knowledge by experiment.

[The black oxide of iron, or magnetite, was used as black paint, at least on some masks from Yakutat. (See paint colors listed in Table 19.) Hematite or red ochre was used for painting objects and the face, and in addition were used some pieces of clay stone which had been burned to produce red paint (de Laguna 1972:416).

[Emmons's notes in BCPA also mention "yellow paint which is also a native mineral, and a brown paint made from a darker ochre." The brown paint or color was *tsu gart* (s̓agʷá·t). "White paint was produced from a clay resembling kaolin." White or yellow was called *klate* (ƛe·t, "snow"), and the white clay was wé·na·, "whitener." It was, I believe, sometimes mixed with red ochre for painting boxes (de Laguna 1972:416).

[Emmons, and many others, may well be mistaken about the nature of the blue-green pigment used on the Northwest Coast. It was not apparently derived from copper, or copper sulfite, copper carbonate, or copper impregnated clays, but came from green earth, or greensand (*grün erde, terra verde,* or *terre verte*). This is an iron potassium silicate, of which glauconite and celadonite are examples. This pigment occurs naturally in many areas, and the Northwest Coast Indians could have obtained it aboriginally, and/or later in the form of a commercial European trade pigment. Green earth was probably the "blue clay-stone" sought by the Tlingit as ne·xinté from Kruzof Island, and used by them for painting, and by the Tsimshian as a dye, but it was not copper (azurite) as Emmons supposed (Emmons 1907:336). With the exception of a northern Wakashan specimen collected in 1893 (date of manufacture unknown), none of the nineteenth-century specimens that have been analyzed have green or green-blue paint derived from copper. More recent specimens from the Tlingit and Tsimshian have been painted with commercial Scheele's green (an acid copper arsenate). Prussian blue and chrome green (a mixture of Prussian blue and chrome yellow) were commercial pigments available in the early nineteenth century. I am indebted for this information to Judi Miller, Canadian Conservation Institute, Ottawa, 1986.]

Blending of colors was never practiced nor shading attempted. Red varied from bright to brownish shades, according to the several iron stones used. A white clay found on Prince of Wales Island, and yellow ochre and graphite [for black paint], traded from British Columbia, were sometimes used by the Southern Tlingit. With the coming of Europeans, vermilion replaced the duller native red paint, but the black and blue-green were retained for use on paddles, canoes, and articles painted for tourists. Later commercial oil colors came into general use.

Native paint [ní·gʷáɬ, c̓áqɬ] was ground in shallow stone dishes or on flat stones of a hard, fine texture, and mixed

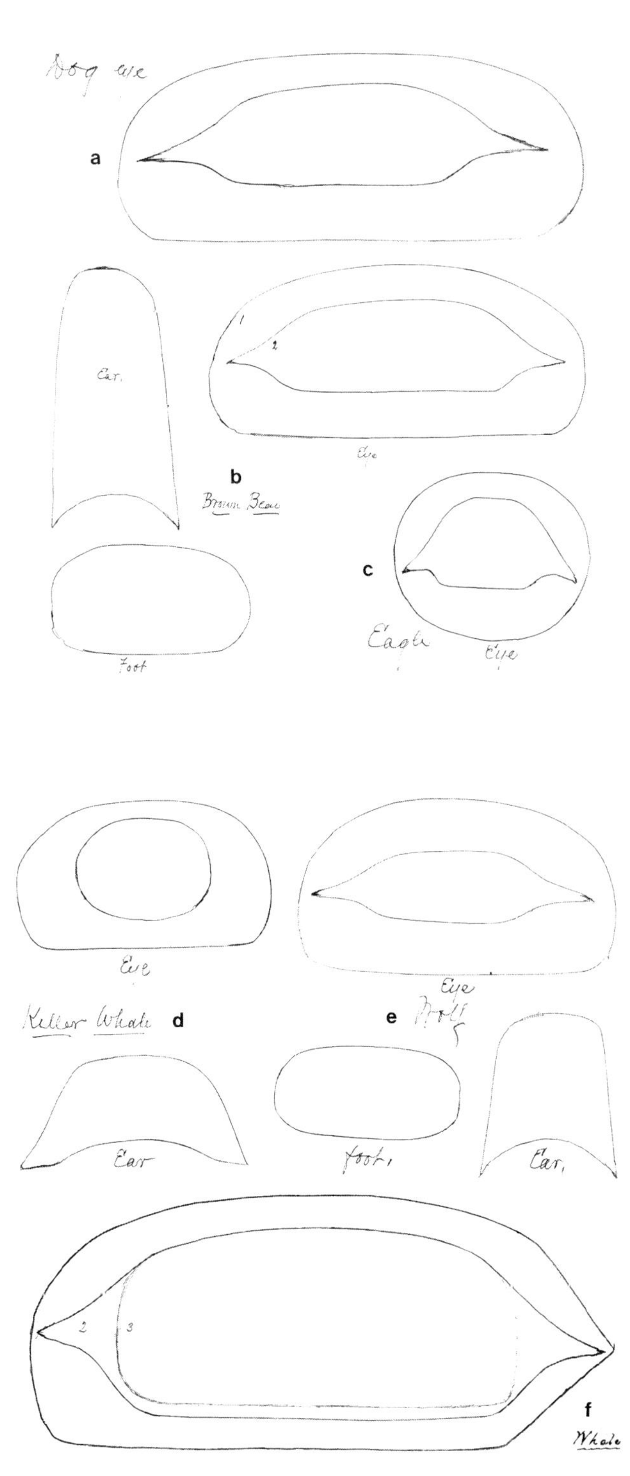

Outlines of cedar-bark stencils, used by Tlingit artists for laying out designs for carving or painting, Sitka. (Pencil tracings by G. T. Emmons. AMNH.) (a) Dog eye. (b) Brown bear eye (two stencils superimposed), ear, and foot. (c) Eagle eye. (d) Killerwhale eye and ear. (e) Wolf eye, foot, and ear. (f) Whale eye (three stencils superimposed).

with salmon or trout eggs, ***ka hawk*** [ka-há·kʷ], and water. The paint stone or paint dish was called ***tsukl ye-ta-ya***, "to rub off stone with salmon eggs" [c̓áqɬ ỵi-te·ỵí, "rock under paint," (?)], or *ya gha yate* or *wo ta ge yate* [?-ỵe·t, "something ?-dish"]. [The fish eggs might be fresh, but] if dried, were chewed with a little cedar or maple inner bark and spat out into the dish. The natural oil of the spawn acted as a fixative that withstood water and the elements as well as [does] commercial oil. If a large amount of paint was desired, the paint stone was reduced in a stone paint mortar with a stone pestle, but when painting small objects the paint stone was dipped in water and then rubbed in the paint dish or on a stone. The paintbrush was dipped in mashed salmon eggs (or better still, in mashed eggs of salmon trout), or the brush was dipped in the small dish in which the paint had been mixed with the mashed egg. [Old notes in BCPA indicate: "Graphite is used by rubbing on dry for coloring masks among Southern Tlingits." In other words, it was not mixed with water and eggs.]

The paint dish was a low, shallow, hollowed-out piece of fine close-grained stone, and often natural formations could be used without any work. But some were carefully shaped in oblong form. One of the most perfectly worked stone objects was carved as a brown bear's forepaw which I procured from an old Chilkat chief. Sometimes the dish had twin hollows for black and red paint, the two colors most used. The paint stone might also be rubbed on smooth flat pebbles or small boulders.

Paintings of animal and human figures were in no sense freehand drawings, although in the beginning they must have followed natural lines, largely in profile. But in an advanced stage, art became highly conventionalized and, except for the emphasis placed on the symbolic features [see below], the figure in its distortion, elimination, and separation of body parts would have been unrecognizable. Figures now became patchwork, made up of exact geometric forms, representing eyes, mouths, jaws, ears, noses, beaks, wings, tails, fins, and other specific features of human and animal bodies, with eyes for all the joints. These were laid off with stencils of thin yellow cedar bark cut to shape. Most stencils, *uh to wark koya* [?, *wark* or wa·q means "eye"], were for the eye patterns which marked the joints of limbs, wings, tails, fins, and even supposedly internal organs.

The stencil was placed over the exact space to be painted, and outlined with the pointed stick in the color that was to be used. Often one stencil was placed inside the outline drawn from another, particularly for eyes. In this way the whole design was built up of stenciled parts. But the figure as a whole might be first outlined, and then the separate stenciled figures placed in position.

While the artist always had on hand a variety of stencils, yet for specific paintings, particularly for those of large size, on the house front, interior screen, canoe, or skin clothing, complete new sets had to be made to fit the figures. This I saw done in preparation for the decoration of a canoe in Sitka in 1890. [This was probably the Haida canoe purchased by Brady, and painted or repainted by "Jim," as the Killer-whale Canoe.] The wonderful exactness of these [stencils], without measurements, attests to native skill through generations of labor with primitive tools.

The same system obtained in painting carvings as in painting flat surfaces. A figure was seldom entirely covered with a single color. As mentioned above, the figure was made up of a number of conventional geometric forms representing the different parts or members, and these were outlined in black or red, and connected with one another by broader lines of these colors in order to present the whole as a complete form. [These were evidently the structural outlines described by Holm as "formlines" (1965).] A general color scheme prevailed for animal and human faces: the hair, eyebrows, eyeballs, and generally the bills of birds (except those of the eagle and oyster catcher) were black; the nostrils, lips, and ears were red, and the cheeks were blue-green. But individual variations often interchanged the black and the red. In separate figures, or in those carved in the round, as on totem poles or house posts, the bodies of human beings were generally red, while animals were black. In many cases, however, the natural color of the wood was retained, and only the joints, hands, feet, or bony structure were shown in color. In painting on flat surfaces, such as house fronts, interior partitions, wooden boxes, or skin clothing, the figure was generally outlined in black, sometimes in red, and the features or details within the figure were outlined in red. Blue-green was used around the many eyes and for some of the outlines of the eye patterns, or for filling in small circles or figures.

All colors were laid on flat, without attempts at blending or shading, so that any apparent differences in depth of color must be attributed to wear or weathering. [In some more recent paintings made with commercial paints, Tlingit artists have attempted to indicate the coats of animals or feathers of birds by shading, but these efforts have not been very successful.] The Tlingit never used meaningless lines, curved figures, or natural objects such as flowers or plant forms. If a rock, mountain, stream, or other natural object came into the picture, it was represented by a human or animal figure, a head, or by the conventional geometric figures used in the body construction.

ART*

The cultural center of the Northwest Coast was about Dixon Entrance, where the Haida, Tsimshian, and Tlingit met. The unit of their social organization was the clan, which was represented by an animal crest [or crests], to which every member had a right, and around which their whole religious [?], social, and political life revolved. It was shown on everything they possessed, the house, totem pole, canoe, implements, ceremonial dress, facial painting, and tattooing. It was their figurative way of recording and transmitting their myths, beliefs, and family [clan] history. This distinctive art was born of their social system and was continually stimulated through the intense clan rivalry of an extremely vain, sensitive people, in their endeavors to outdo one another on all ceremonial occasions, particularly in the most elaborate display of the crest.

They believed that their crest had come to them from a hazy past, when in the childhood of the world all life was on the same plane, and was marked by the sexual or beneficent relations between some remote ancestor with a member of an animal family [species] whose form was taken totemically [as a crest]. But this did not imply actual descent from the animal, nor relationship with the species in later days. [The last is not quite true, since old-fashioned Tlingit believed that they could influence the animals that were represented by the crest of a relative, and which they addressed by the same kin term that they would use for that relative. (See de Laguna 1972:825–26.)] In addition to the two phratral crests of the Tlingit—Raven and Wolf—they had assumed many others through time, through marriage, seizure for debt, capture in war, feast giving. [These events and crests were] localized among the different branches.

**Editor's note:* The diagnostic features used by the Tlingit artist to indicate the species represented, the distortions and dissections of figures to fit the field to be decorated, and similar problems of Northwest Coast iconography were apparently being investigated by Emmons and Boas at about the same time. Boas's first work in this field was published in 1897, although his interest had been aroused by an exhibit of Bella Coola masks that he saw in 1884 in Berlin; and Emmons was collecting examples, in different media, of representations of animals and birds in the early summer of 1896, to judge by sketches made at Wrangell. Since he later that year left Sitka for Princeton, Emmons might well have discussed these problems with Boas at AMNH. Even though Emmons's observations may have been used by Boas, the discussion in this section seems clearly to reflect the influence of Boas.

Pencil sketches of crest animals by Rudolf, a Tlingit artist, Raven 10, Sitka. (In G. T. Emmons's field notebook. AMNH.)

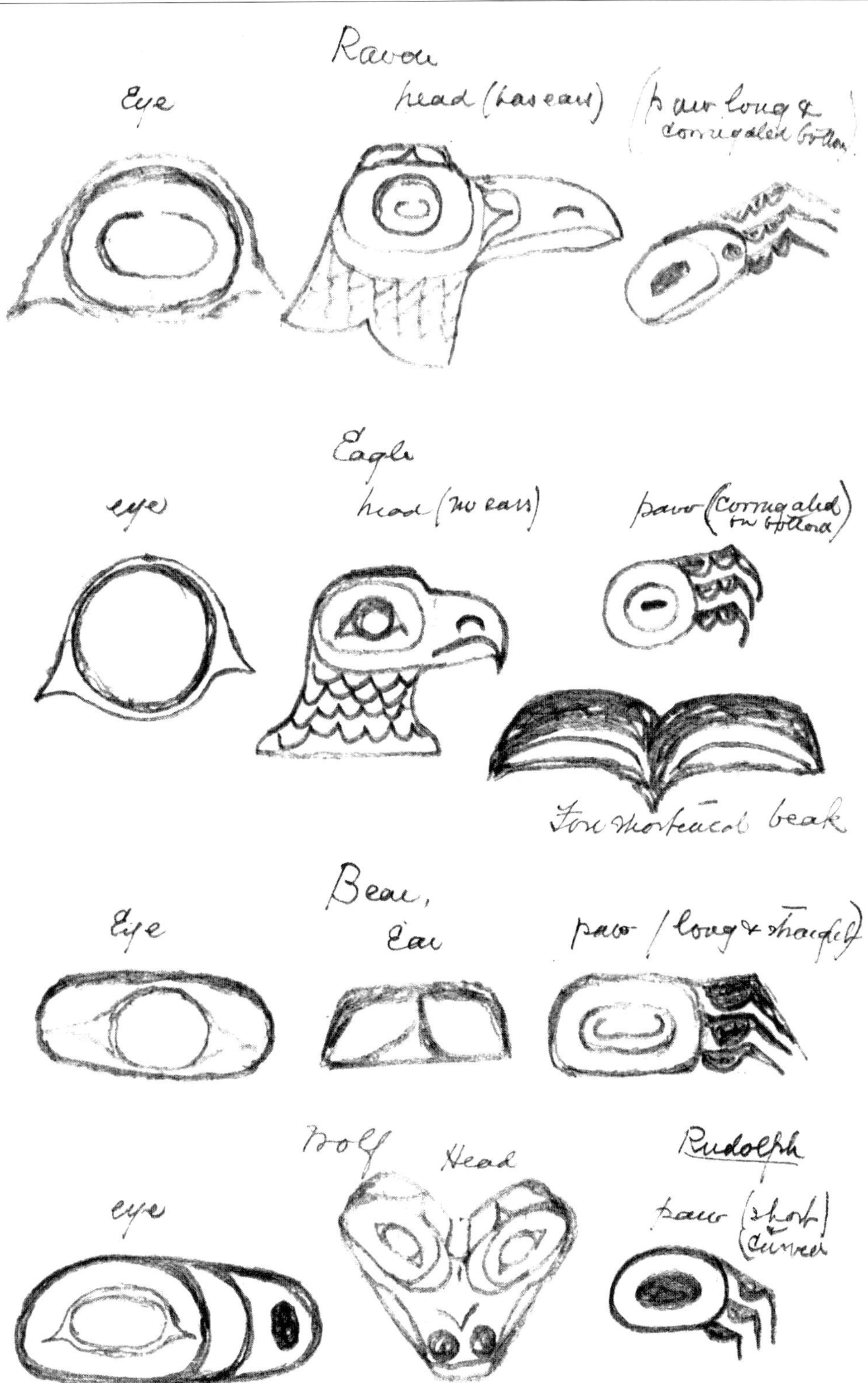

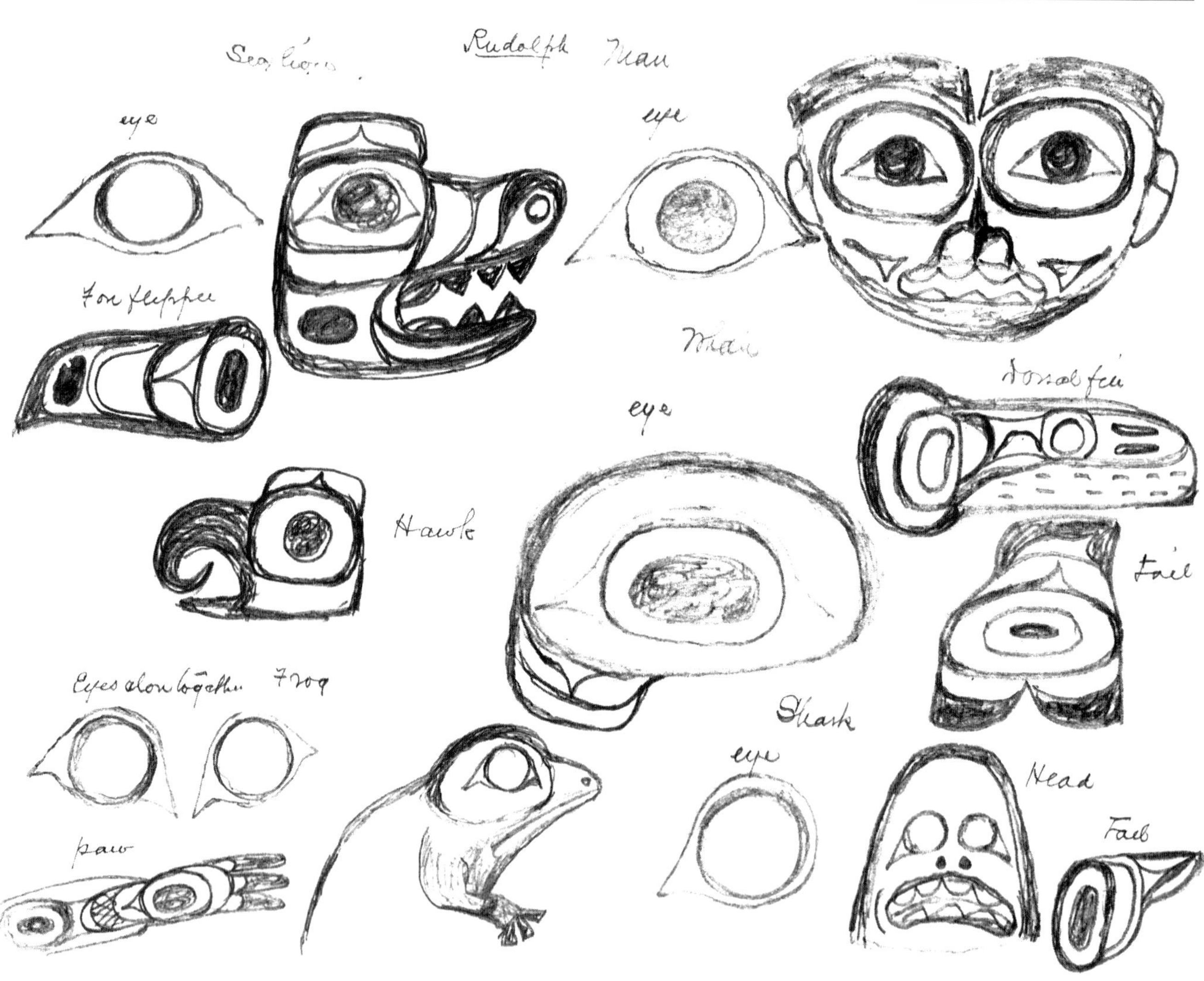

Sketches by Rudolf. (AMNH.)

In the presentation of animal forms, the native artist was on very sure ground. His intimate contact with nature [rendered him] fully capable of realistic representation [of animals] when he was permitted perfect freedom, as on separate [detached] figures. But this was seldom the case, owing to the various shapes of the decorative field, to which he must subordinate his subject. So he resorted to the most ingenious distortions, dissections, and even the elimination of the ordinary bodily features in order to give increased emphasis [to others]. [These became] exaggerated characteristics [of the species], which in time were conventionalized into symbols as intelligible as the whole figure [would have been]. The following list includes the symbolic features of the principal animals used as crests or for decorative purposes. [Some of these were found on old notes in BCPA, in which the particular feature used for recognition was underlined. This procedure is followed below.]

Brown Bear: is indicated by broad head, wide mouth, canine teeth, pronounced nostrils, small erect ears, and generally protruding tongue often overlapping the lower lip. (The Tlingit make no use of the Black Bear as a crest, while the Brown Bear occupies a first place in story and representative art.)

Wolf: head is longer and narrower than that of the Bear; he has a long nose, canine teeth, long ears, and a protruding tongue, extended or turned up, often over the upper lip. The tail is long.

Beaver: has prominent incisors (two or four), and the crosshatched tail is unmistakable. The animal is generally shown sitting up with a stick in the mouth, grasped on each side by the forepaws.

Mountain Goat: has horns, and the characteristically long head and hoofs when the whole body is shown.

Land Otter: has a long, narrow body, terminating in a tail of equal length, short front legs, and the tongue always protruding, generally turned up over the nose. The Land Otter is so intimately connected with the shaman and his practice that it rarely occurs elsewhere [than on his paraphernalia], and is not symbolized but is presented as a complete figure.

Mink, Rat, and Mouse: are much alike and are indicated by their long narrow tail. They are more or less associated with the practice of the shaman.

Ground Hog or Whistler [hoary marmot]: is seldom shown, but is indicated sitting up, but never with a stick in the paws like the Beaver. [It may appear as the prey of the Golden Eagle.]

Sea Otter: is used simply as an independent carving, as for a pipe or figure, and is unmistakable lying on its back with short legs and triangular tail, as it sleeps on the water.

Sea Lion: has a broad head, with or without teeth or ears, the fore and hind flippers enclosing a triangular tail.

Hair Seal: is hardly distinguishable from the Sea Lion, omitting the teeth, although these are sometimes shown.

Whale: is more often shown in the whole figure, but may be indicated by the blunt head, blowhole, and tail.

Killerwhale: is symbolized by the dorsal fin of great length, generally with a circular hole through it and often with a face at the base. Also shown are the large blunt head, blowhole, and teeth.

Sea Bear, a mythical monster: is represented with a bear's head and forepaws and a whale's, or more often a killerwhale's body, with long dorsal fin, and tail.

Shark and Dogfish: represented with a blunt pointed, extended nose, crescentic mouth, with or without teeth, and depressed at the corners, with two or more crescents beyond the corners of the mouth representing gills, and other crescents over the forehead with two circles. The two prominent symbols are the heterocercal tail and pointed nose.

Halibut: has a flat, rhomboidal body, with mouth at one side and two eyes just beyond, and an extension of fins around the body.

Sculpin: two spines, generally triangular in shape and rising above the mouth, are the particular features, although in the complete body, the continuous dorsal fin extending down the back is always present.

Squid [octopus]: has tentacles with sucking cups, also a parrotlike beak when the head is shown.

Skate: unmistakable in its angular body.

Salmon: always shown in profile like the Halibut, but is distinguished by the characteristic hooked nose.

Starfish: the complete figure is unmistakable.

Birds are indicated by wings and tail, and symbolized by their bills; ears may or may not appear.

Raven: has a long bill, gradually curving to the end.

Eagle: has a broad or stout bill, turned down at right angles [i.e., a hooked bill].

Thunderbird: is little used by the Tlingit and [its] bill is difficult to distinguish from the turned-down bill of the Eagle. Or it is more like the Osprey which is considered its present-day representative. The Tsimshian mythical Mountain Hawk found on Skeena River totem poles, particularly at Kitzegulka [see Barbeau 1929, pls. xix–xxi], with the long bill turned down at right angles and then returning to the mouth, is wholly foreign to the Tlingit.

Owl: has a bill, broad and curved down close to the face. The large round eyes and ears are generally shown.

Puffin: has a parrot-shaped bill.

Crane: has a long slender bill, more often for convenience shown extending down close to the whole length of the body, and slightly curved toward the end and painted red (its natural color).

Oyster Catcher: has a perfectly straight bill, blunt at the end, and painted red (its natural color).

Dragonfly: has a large head, bulging eyes, and a segmented, extended body, and double wings.

Frog: has a broad, low head, rounded over the eyes and depressed between [them], a wide, toothless mouth (although I have seen teeth in rare cases), and the webbed feet of the water frog.

Woodworm: a long segmented body, blunt head, and rarely shown feet.

Sun: a face within a circle surrounded by triangles representing rays.

Moon: a human face within a circle, or a crescent with a human figure seated on the horn.

"Painted figure of a raven on hewn boards which formed the decorated sides of an old Thluke-nar-huttee [Łukʷnax̣ʔádi, *Raven 6*] *house, at Sitka, Alaska. The totemic emblem of the family being the Raven. Painted in red and black." (Pencil and ink sketch by G. T. Emmons. AMNH.)*

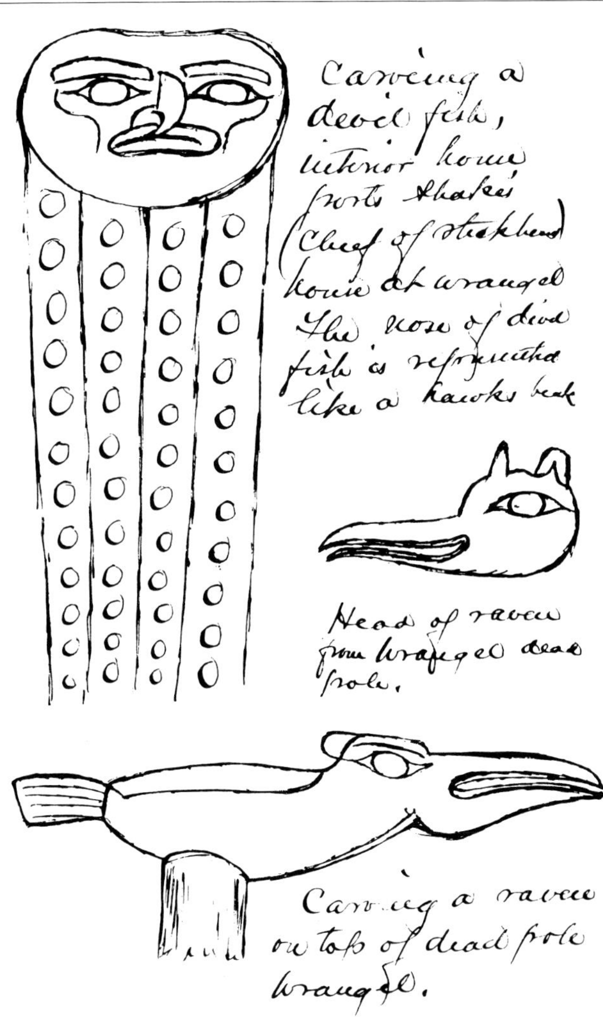

Carved posts, Wrangell. (Sketched by G. T. Emmons. AMNH.) Top. *Carving of a devilfish; the nose is like a hawk's beak; interior post in Chief Shakes's house, Wolf 18.* Bottom. *Ravens on mortuary poles, Wrangell.*

Star: has a human face in a circle surrounded by four or five triangular rays.

Rainbow: is a bent bow, enclosing a figure or face; if colored, at least three alternating colors are shown.

[From the old notes, BCPA:] The habits of animals were represented in connection with others, as in a Sea Lion eating a seal, its natural food; a Bear eating a salmon; a Beaver and its home; a Kingfisher or a Crane with a frog in its bill; a Beaver eating a piece of stick.

While the symbol identifies the species, the human being and the animal are distinguished from each other by the ears. The human ear is natural in shape and position, but those of animals (including birds, but rarely fish) are shown in a rounded form, placed above the head. But even with this feature as a guide, the human forms with animal faces, and animal bodies with human faces, that appear on totem poles and house posts, are very confusing, and can be read [interpreted] only through an intimate acquaintance with the myths about the beginnings of life, when transformation was in practice and the animal could cast aside its coat and appear in human form.

Masks that play such an important part in the social life of the whole coast, while human in form, could become animal in character by the substitution of a symbolic feature, such as the bill of a bird [or mosquito] for the nose, [the prominent] canine [of the wolf] and incisor teeth [of the beaver], or an animal symbol painted on the cheek. The creature symbolized was personified [impersonated] by the wearer in action, or honored as his crest.

[Some masks were made for or by the shaman, for his exclusive use, and worn when he was possessed by the spirits they represented. At potlatches, copies of the shaman's masks might be worn by laymen of his clan who imitated his dancing. Other masks, representing the clan crest, might be worn by noble dancers; and some masks, Tlingit made or imported, were used for dramatic performance, like those copied from the Tsimshian.]

Many masks are so true to native type that they might be considered portraits. Sex is shown by the labret in the lower lip of the female (even in animals), while the male was indicated by hair (or painting) on the upper lip and chin. There seems also to be an indication of sex by the form of the face: the male is more square and heavy jawed; the female more oval and pleasing, the child more round. Old age was indicated by wrinkled cheeks and forehead, singing and speaking by open lips, anger by the expression of the mouth, and the agony of death (as illustrated by two realistic masks in the museum [AMNH] by the half-closed eyes and the relaxed muscles of the mouth and tongue, the highest sense of technique in the art. [One of these, AMNH E-2501 (Boas 1897, fig. 2; 1927, fig. 155), was found in the gravehouse of a shaman at Chaik Bay, Admiralty Island. This was the home of the famous Daqławe·dí, Wolf 27, shaman, *Klee-a-keet* (X̌iya·kí·t), although we cannot prove that the mask was his. See Chapter 15, the section "Witches, Shamans, and the Authorities."]

The whole desire of the artist was to present his work understandingly [intelligibly], and so long as he was able to show the figure separately, in profile, [in] bas-relief or painting, he had no trouble. But restricted as he was by the many decorative fields, he systematized the construction of

Goose Drum, Tar-wark Gough [ṫa·wáq ga·w], *painted in black, green (1), and red (2), a family drum of the* Con-nuh-ta-di [G̣a·nax̣te·dí, *Raven 3*], *Klukwan. (Pencil sketch in field notebook, 1902, by G. T. Emmons. AMNH.)*

Eagle Drum [čá·k̇ ga·w] *of the* Kah-gwan-tan *family* [Ka·gʷa·ta·n, *Wolf 1*] *family at Sitka.* (R: *red paint; outline in black*). *(Pencil sketch in field notebook, 1902, by G. T. Emmons. AMNH.)*

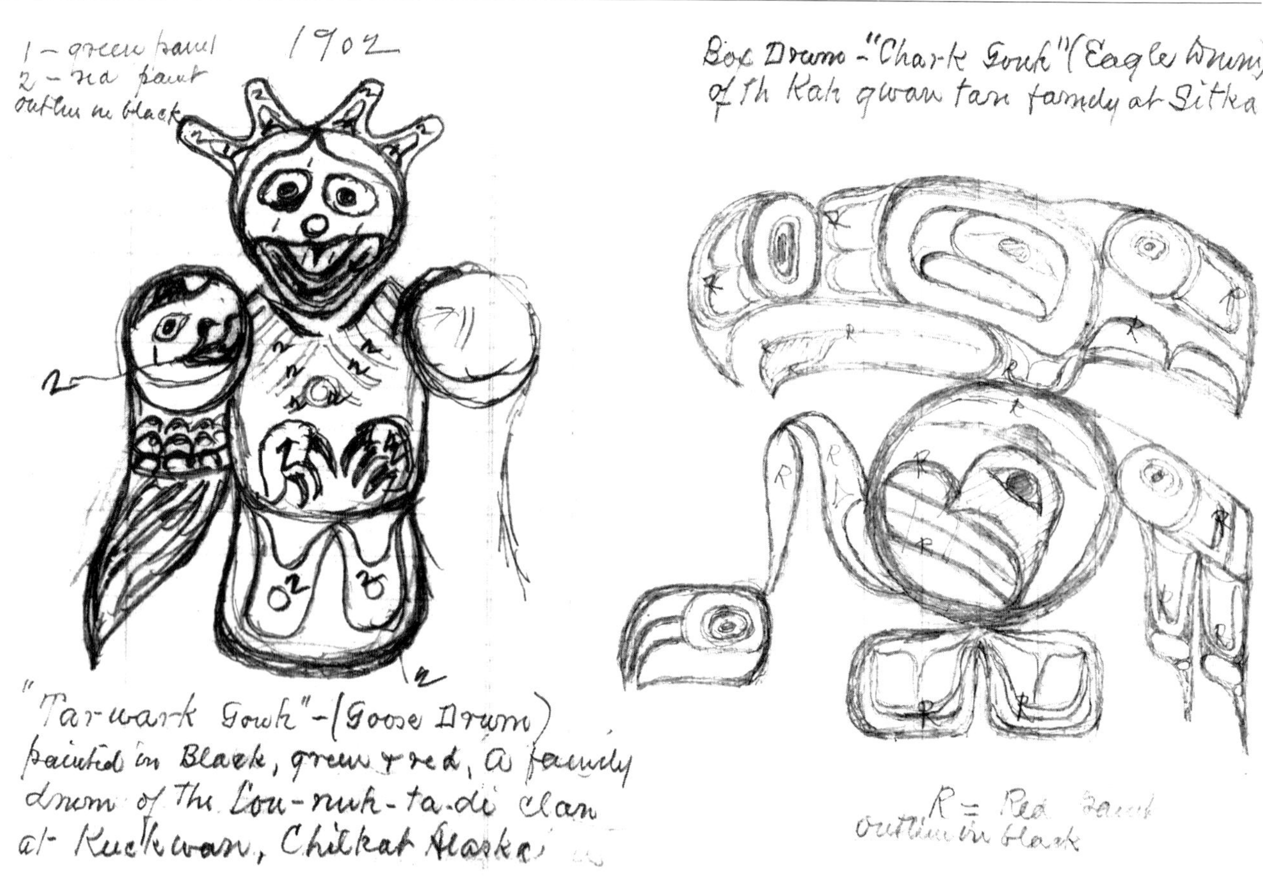

his figures as best suited to the three principal forms, cylindrical, circular, and plane.

Of these, the cylindrical form is the most important, as it includes not only the large figures, but totemically the most important, on the crest pole and the house and grave posts. These present only a front view, since the back is either the rounded tree trunk, or is shut in by the walls, so that if the figure were carried completely around, more than a third of it would be invisible, to the loss of the symbolic [identifying] features. To remedy this, the perpendicular figures can be visualized as split down the back, and the two parts unrolled to the sides, and so spread out to show the complete form. In fish, the cut is made along the underpart, since the symbols are on the back and sides.

The circular form is best shown in the wide metal bracelet and the crest hat in wood and/or woven spruce root. In decorating the silver bracelet with crest figures, the bodies of animals, fish, and birds are shown as if split in two down the middle of the back, but forming two profiles, with half of the body extending on each side to the ends of the bracelet or clasp. The bodies are joined at the nose and mouth, which results in an exaggeratedly broad face and head. An exception is made in the case of the shark, where the head remains intact in front, although the body is cut through the back and stretched out on each side. In most cases the bodies of animals were left to the imagination, since only the members [legs] were shown, and the symbolic features which identified the figure were illustrated in the head. This [the head] was placed to best advantage in the middle of the bracelet, and was the most elaborately carved part. Bird figures were treated differently. The head was bisected from the point of the bill upward, so that the two halves adhered at the back of the head; but sometimes the two parts were entirely separated, so that they formed two complete profiles facing outward. The species was identified by the shape of the bill, since the bodies of all

Top. *Painted Raven canoe paddle*. Bottom. *Wolf paddle. (Pencil sketches by G. T. Emmons.* R: *red paint;* B: *black paint. AMNH.)*

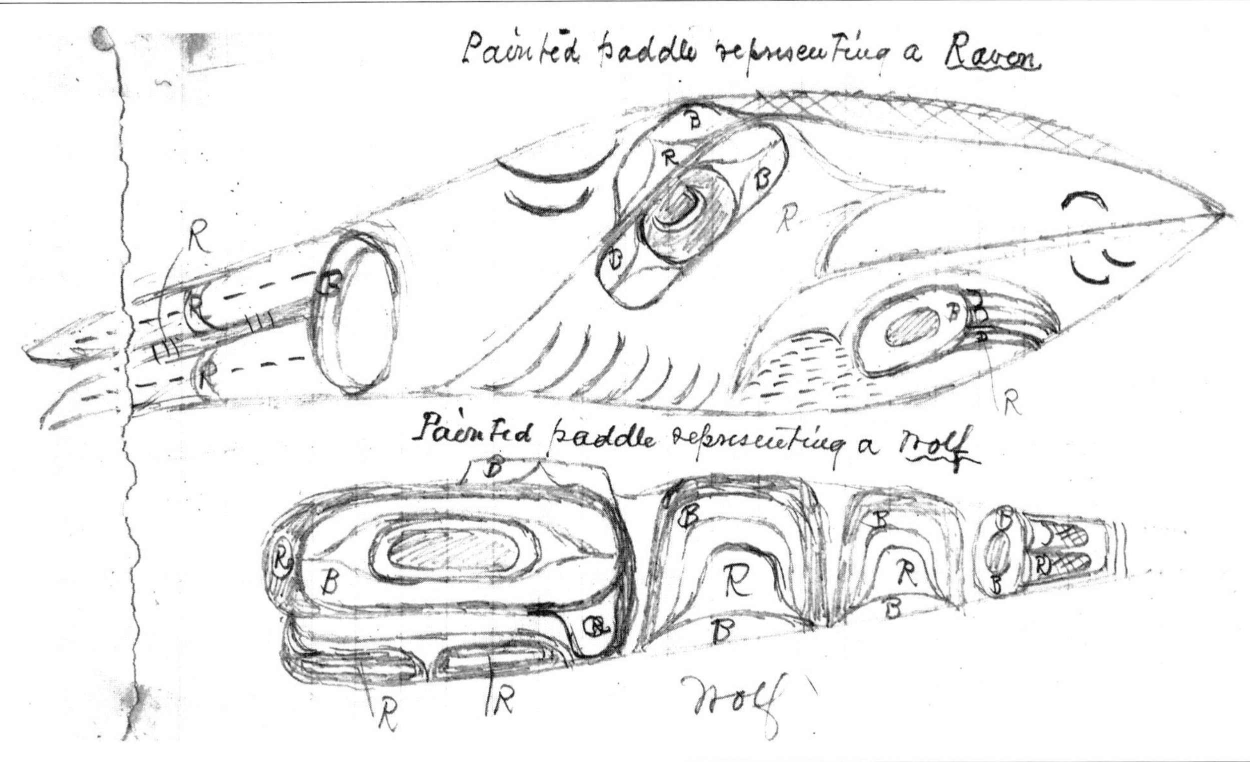

birds were alike, and the wings, tails, and talons were placed indiscriminately at the will of the artist, without any regard for their anatomical relationships. I saw but one bird portrayed on a bracelet as standing in profile. This illustrated the myth of Raven in the Whale [see Swanton 1909:12–13]. Here the body of the whale extends in profile from end to end of the bracelet, and the raven stands in relief with the bill open as if speaking. Sometimes the animal body was shown in profile, with the head at one end of the clasp and the body extending around [the bracelet] with the tail at the other end, meeting the head. This simplest form, however, was not as satisfactory as the divided body with head in the middle, for the central part of the body [in a single profile], which would then fall in the middle of the bracelet, is without characterizing symbols or details.

The crest hat, in the form of a truncated cone, presents two distinct ornamental fields: the central one, comprising the small cylindrical top which is surmounted by a series of superimposed cylinders of woven spruce root that are most important in indicating social standing. [The outer brim of the hat is the second field.] The animal crest figure surrounding this [the top of the hat] is treated as if it were draped over this [the brim or second field]. It is lying on its lower side around the rim, in two symmetrical profiles opened out along the under side, and split from head to tail down the back so that it could go over the cylinders.

Food dishes representing complete animal figures are perfectly natural [in shape], except that they are flattened along the belly to form the stand, and the back [of the animal] is hollowed out to form the bowl. Square food dishes, carved or painted, follow the same idea. The head is at one end, the tail at the other, while the sides represent the body in two profiles, and the interior the hollowed out back of the figure. The square or oblong bowl, breaking the joints at the corner, is not so pleasing as those in the natural figure.

Painting, I believe, was the mother of art on the Northwest Coast, for the application of color was so much simpler a process than the labor of carving with stone and shell tools. [This thesis is debatable.] The artist had no idea of perspective, and [in painting] rarely presented the full front view. Carvings were generally painted, as the oldest pieces, now weathered and decayed, still show some evidence of

Ends of food dishes. (Ink and pencil sketches by G. T. Emmons. AMNH.) Top. Left. *Eagle.* Top. Right. Kone-ko-tate, *"mythical sea monster"* [Ģuna·kade·t, *the wealth-bringing water monster*]. Bottom. Left. *Shark.* Bottom. Right. *Hawk (one of four different designs).*

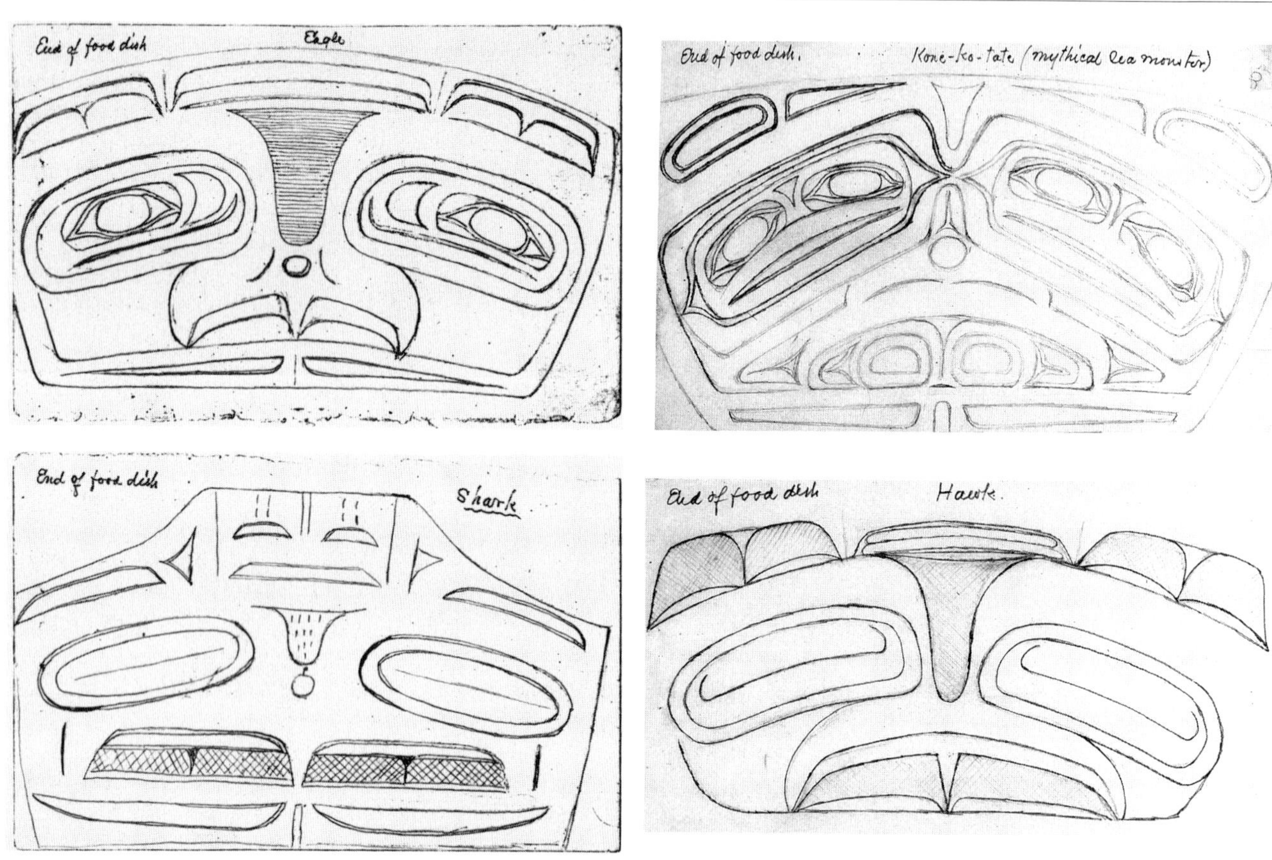

color. A general color scheme prevailed among the Tlingit. Animal, bird, and fish bodies were wholly or partly black; the human figure, and sometimes animals, were painted red, or the limbs and features were so painted, while the body was left in the natural wood. The human face, particularly in masks, followed certain lines: The eyebrows black (and standardized, since the natives trim their own), and the eyeballs black; the lips, tongue, nostrils, and ears red; and the face around the eyes and cheeks blue-green, with geometric figures or crest designs in different colors, applied according to the fancy of the wearer.

One ornamental feature that characterizes the carvings and paintings is the ever-present eye. This is usually represented by two curves and a round eyeball between them, but fish generally have completely round eyes. The eye indicates all joints of limbs, wings, tail fins, and even supposed internal organs. I once handed an elaborately carved eagle to an old man and asked him the meaning of the eyes at the wing and tail joints, and he said: "The eyes on the wings told how to fly, those on the tail how to steer, those on the head where to go." Thus each controlled certain parts of the body, and all were necessary to complete the whole.

The flat surface was probably the original decorative field for painting, bas-relief, weaving, petroglyphs, and tattooing. It included not only the largest and most important crest objects: the painted house and grave fronts, the great interior rear screen that set apart the house chief's quarters, the war (or chief's) canoe—but also the ceremonial skin blankets, aprons, leggings, hide armor, box and skin drums, chests, food boxes, and numerous smaller articles for personal use, all of which bore the family crest. Here [on the flat surfaces of these objects] animal forms were presented largely in profile, because this view was most intelligible. But since the decorative field often did not lend itself so well to the shape of the figure, every form of bisection, distention, dissection, exaggeration, and elimination was practiced, even to the placing of bodily members without any regard to their proper position. But every representation always kept in view the presentation of the distinguishing symbols for the ready recognition of the animal form.

Household furnishings consisted wholly of receptacles for ceremonial dress and articles, for furs and later blankets, food boxes, [serving] and eating dishes, spoons, and baskets. The pride of every chief were the large carved and painted chests. Their shape, slightly longer than high, offered no field for either the profile or the upright bisected figure. So the artist, to avoid a meaningless jumble of small features, selected the head, partly bisected and forming two profiles, to fill the greater part of the whole field. The body was partly or wholly omitted, and the outstanding parts, such as legs, arms, wings, tail, or fins, were shown separately, with little or no regard to their true connection. But they served, nevertheless, to distinguish the figure symbolically. These chests, in their fine carving and color, with the great head [face design], represent the height of native originality in art.

The wholly original and beautiful Chilkat robe, and the associated pieces of clothing [apron, shirt or vest, leggings], woven with the wool of the mountain goat, must be considered from an artistic point of view, since the figures are copied from a painted board. [The men paint these boards and the women do the weaving. This weaving of goat's wool is treated in the next chapter, as are basketry and matting on which the ornamentation is geometric.]

[Emmons (1907 and here) and Boas (1897, 1927), each influencing and learning from the other, though sometimes disagreeing, have shown the general principles underlying Northwest Coast art: the identifying symbols of the creatures (animal, bird, fish, and human) portrayed, the details of their several parts, and the ways in which these subjects were adjusted to fit the objects decorated. A fuller understanding of the style, of how the design elements were held together, has been developed by Holm's masterful study of form (1965). Meanwhile, Surrealists and other artists in New York and abroad were discovering Northwest Coast art as Art (Carpenter 1975, 1976), and Lévi-Strauss was interpreting these "speaking" objects, which he correctly recognized as endowed with a life of their own (witness their personal crest names), although they spoke to him in "confused words" (Lévi-Strauss 1943, 1963, 1982). Jonaitis (1986) has carried on this search for a (subconscious) meaning, applying structural principles to the art of the Tlingit, and stressing differences between secular and shamanic art. We must remember, however, that both crests and shaman's spirits were derived from the same kind of religious experiences, and their representations followed the same artistic cannons. Holm (1983) can recognize the fine distinctions in style, not only between the work of different Northwest Coast tribes, but between different periods, and even that of individual artists.

[As yet, however, we have not explained the deeper meanings of this art for the natives themselves, beyond their identification of the subjects portrayed, the clan myths illustrated, the potlatch wealth spent for each display, or the particular shaman's spirit (yé·k) invoked. We assume that the decorations on crest objects enhanced the sense of pride and self-worth in the hearts of the owners, but what else? Did the Woodworm in the arms of the G̣a·nax̣te·dí girl on the post in Whale House at Klukwan evoke sympathy for the misguided "mother" of this all-devouring monster? jubilation that the creature was dead? sorrowful remembrance for the kinsmen left behind in the south? Did the inhabitants of the house, on returning from a difficult journey, see these houseposts with the Woodworm Girl, Strong Man violently rending the sea lion, Raven overcoming the king salmon with lies, or peering from the whale he had killed, as scenes of violence or as comforting symbols of home? What sensations did guests entertain on entering Whale House? Were they supposed to be frightened, overcome with a sense of their own inferiority, or honored? Did the images of bound witches, land otters, octopus tentacles, dead or dying men on the shaman's paraphernalia and masks evoke only awe and terror? Or did they also inspire faith and hope? We cannot rely only on our own reactions. What a pity we did not secure more information from the natives themselves while these wonderful objects still held their full aboriginal meanings.]

CHAPTER 8

Art and Industries: Women's Work

SKIN DRESSING*

[Preparation of skins was women's work.] Animal pelts, whether of the land or the water, were removed, stretched, dried, and dressed as required for further use. There were two general methods of skinning animals, and these determined the ways in which the skins were stretched and dried. Bear, deer, goat, beaver, sea lion, hair seal, and fur seal were skinned by making a straight cut down the belly from the head to the base of the tail. Cuts were made on the inside of the legs, and the skin was rolled off on each side, as a flat surface. Slits were cut along the edges of the green skin through which the lacings passed that stretched it to the drying frame. [These frames of poles or saplings were made by men.] Sometimes stout saplings passed through the side slits, and the lacings rove around these and the frame. The frame consisted of two stout wooden bars or uprights and two crossbars that were lashed together at the corners. The frame could be adjusted by changing the [spacings between] the uprights, or the crossbars, to accommodate any size or shape of skin. In the case of some skins, particularly that of the seal, one upright was used with temporary crosspieces at top and bottom, or simply with three or four rough slats with notched ends that fitted in the slits at the sides of the skin and extended it. Or, saplings were passed through the slits along the sides and these were held apart by the notched crossbars. [The stretching frame was called ṫí·š or ṫí·ša·.]

The more valuable and delicate skins were removed by cutting a slit across the rear of the animal and drawing the pelt off over the body and head [like a bag]. This was stretched and dried, fur inside, on a flat, pointed board [inserted in the skin]. Sometimes two stout rounded poles were used that met at the nose and were stretched apart at the bottom. This was done with the valuable sea otter pelt. The forepaws were held out by a short stick, the broad tail was stretched out and corded down to one of the poles. Skins so treated were of the sea otter, land otter, lynx, fox, mink, marten, ermine, muskrat, and wolf. All of these skins, except that of the wolf [and land otter], are thin and tender. They required little dressing other than removing the grease [and adhering flesh], and softening. Marmot and squirrel skins were sometimes stretched, sometimes simply dried.

Birds were skinned by a cut down the back [since this left the soft breast feathers intact].

The only skins that were dehaired before dressing were those of the deer used for clothing, the hair seal used for leggings and moccasins, and the bear and sea lion which were hard-tanned for armor. Moose and caribou skins traded from the interior were already tanned. If green skins were to be plucked or dehaired at once, they were simply rolled up and sweated, which loosened the roots of the hair. Dried skins when required for use were thoroughly wetted and put in a bag to remain until the hair was loosened. An old Angoon woman stated that sometimes the wetted pelt in the sack was buried in the ground where a fire had burned out, for when it was removed the hair would fall off.

The graining [dehairing] was done with a deer metapodial, split and sharpened, and used with both hands [as a beaming tool], *ut-har-ou kh-hun-nah,* "hair take-off" [ʔat x̣a·wú, "its hair," kahéna· or kahána·, "take-off"]. The skin was placed over a slightly rounded log, four to six inches wide, set at an angle convenient for the worker who was seated in front of it. The log was called *klah shar* [?]. [The woman removed the hair by scraping downward with the beamer.] It was sufficiently sharp to remove the hair without injuring the skin.

After the hair was removed, the skin was washed in fresh water and wrung out around a post, being twisted from left to right. Then it was hung over the fish rack, or hung up in the house away from the fire, and when partly dry, was

---

Editor's note: This chapter was originally part of the preceding chapter, but they have been separated because of their length. Here, as before, the main problems I had to solve involved collating different versions of the same topic or section and including notes from AMNH and BCPA material.

**Editor's note:* I arranged Tables 20 and 21 from notes left by Emmons. While all Tlingit women presumably followed the same principles of dressing skin, each had her own individual method, and these could not be reduced to a standardized procedure, as Emmons was attempting in arranging the lists of actions in these tables.

Skin stretching and drying, Sitka, 1895. (Pencil sketches by G. T. Emmons. AMNH.) Above. *A land otter skin.* Below. *A bear skin laced into a frame.*

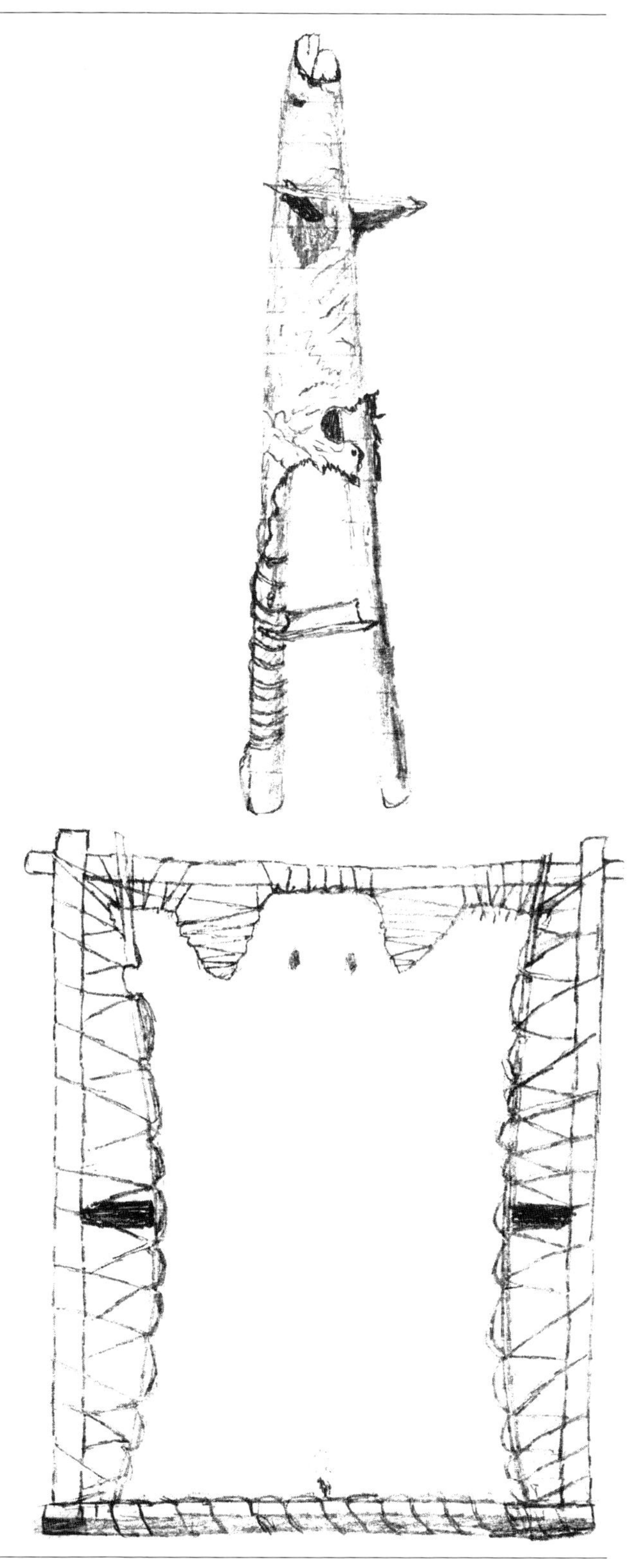

rubbed over with fish grease (eulachon preferred), and pulled and stretched by two women. If no grease were available, the brains of a deer or other animal would be substituted. When the grease had taken hold, and the skin had become soft and pliable, it was hung up in a cool place for a couple of days. But if the grease had not softened it, the skin would be again well greased. The skin, now thoroughly softened, was again soaked in fresh water, and then put in a tub containing human urine for one day, to cut the grease. It was then taken out, and rinsed in fresh water. Then the edges of the skin were slit, so that it could be stretched on a frame. [Sometimes] this was a framework of sticks which ran through the slits at the edges of the skin. [Sometimes this was a rectangular frame, as described above. The frame is called t̓í·ša·.]

Then the women worked on the skin with a mussel shell scraper, *yeese* [yí·ṣ̓] to press the water out of the skin. The outer skin, *ah-chart-too* [ʔat č̓á·t-wú, "its outer surface of skin"], must all be taken off, for if any were allowed to remain, and the skin should get wet after being tanned, the outer skin would become hard; but if all had been removed, the skin would always remain soft, even after wetting. So the skin would be worked down with a rough stone scraper attached to a pole or handle by a lashing of hair seal or bear hide. [A sketch in the original manuscript shows a paddle-shaped stone blade, *ta-hwa-tcha* (té xʷáǯa·), *ta-ku-hun* (probably té kahána· or kahéna·), or *thu-clalk* (probably té, "stone," ƛá·q, "sharp-edged").] This was a chipped stone blade, set and lashed in the split end of a stout wooden handle, some four feet long. [This long-handled end-scraper was used with both hands.] Sometimes a [semi-lunar] stone scraper, ***kloh-shar*** [xʷáǯa·], often a split cobble, or the mussel shell scraper was used. In later days, an iron scraper was lashed to the long handle. Both sides of the skin were worked down, until the hide was of the desired thickness. Deer brains, burned powdered clamshell, or soft white clay was rubbed into the skin.

If the dressed skin was to be smoked, it was turned inside out, with the hair side inside, and sewed up to make a long bag, with the bottom end open. It was hung over a smoldering fire of rotted wood, decayed spruce or pine, which does not blaze but gives off much smoke, like punk. If the skin was to be used for clothing, it was not allowed to smoke long enough to become discolored, but if it was for moccasins, it would be smoked yellow.

The lighter pelts of the fur-bearing animals were taken off very carefully, so that no particles of flesh remained. [For this purpose, the split deer leg bone, with sharpened

"Hair seal skin. Sketch from nature, Wrangell, July 1888." (Pen and ink sketch by G. T. Emmons. AMNH.) *"Hair seal skin curing. The frame, A, A, is of rough spruce sticks from 1½ to 2 inches in thickness. These are lashed together at the corners with lashings of seal skin, rope, or spruce rope or cedar bark, and the framework is put together a little larger than the skin to allow for hauling out. The green skin is slit along the edges, and through these slits, spruce limbs ½ inch in diameter to ¾ inch, B, B, etc., are run through either side and smaller pieces, B′ B′, etc., are likewise passed through slits. And this framework is hauled out to the outer framework by means of spruce rope, rawhide, thongs of seal, or as in this case sinew rope and the inner bark of the yellow cedar; and put out in the sun to dry, skin side out, or on crosspieces above but not over fire, skin side down."*

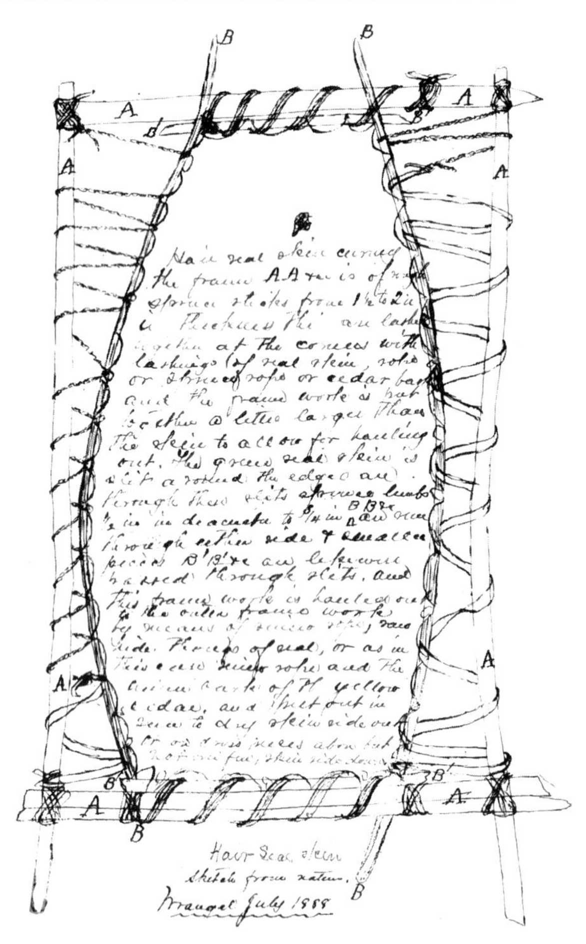

blade at one end, *hilchar* (x̣íša·, "skinning knife or scraper") was used.] If the pelts were to be used for clothing, they were lightly treated, cleaned of grease, and made pliable. Those for trade purposes remained in the raw state. Fur seal for commercial purposes were salted and rolled up. Bear and mountain goat skins used for bedding were seldom treated beyond removing any adhering particles of flesh, although they were sometimes scraped to render them more pliable.

The moose skins obtained by the Tlingit were more liable than not to be poor skins, full of holes where the grubs had buried themselves under the hair. They were of little value in commerce, so were used principally for shoes, and as rawhide for plaiting snares, since the moose hide is heavier and stronger than that of the caribou.

Caribou skins were used for clothing and robes, and were the ordinary skin of commerce. Although not as heavy as the moose skin, it wears better. Elk hide is the heaviest of these three skins.

SINEW AND INTESTINES

All skins were sewed with sinew of deer, caribou (traded from the interior), or [stranded] whale. The thread was split from the strand with the thumbnail, scraped smooth, and then passed between the lips to moisten it. [Field notes by Emmons in BCPA suggest a somewhat different procedure: Sinew was divided with the thumb and first finger of each hand. It was first smoothed along with the thumbnail of the left hand. The tiny thread worked off was drawn through the mouth and moistened.] Then it was held between the thumb and forefinger of the right hand, and twisted with the palm of the left hand on the right thigh. [This was done] by rubbing down the leg from halfway from top of the leg [hip] to the kneecap, three or four times, which formed the thread used for sewing. The sinew or thread is called *tuss* or *tussee* [tás, tási, "sinew, sinew thread, string"].

The Sitka, Hoonah, and Yakutat used small bags of bear and seal intestines, made of strips sewed with sinew from the tail of the whale, or of deer or caribou sinew. In these bags the women kept their finer basket materials and other things. The [ordinary?] woman's workbag of skin was oblong, the opening or mouth closer to one end than the other, so that the long awl or knife could be entered. The bag was closed with a flap and tie string. It contained the sinew thread, the awl [used in sewing] stuck through a piece of hide, the knife, mesh sticks for netting, and often bird quills, a bear tooth [used for smoothing baskets], and other things.

When weaving a Chilkat blanket, the women kept the balls of spun mountain goat wool and the warp of the blanket in bags of mountain goat intestines, to keep them clean.

Fancy beaded cloth bags, worn in dances, were of the type used by the interior people, and were either traded or copied from them, for the Tlingit were not workers in beads to any great extent.

[It is significant that the decorations on the "finger bags," as they were called, and on other beaded items of the dance costume, were floral, suggesting remote links with the Algonkian double-curve designs which had been transformed into conventionalized floral patterns under missionary influence. Of course, some beaded garments and regalia were in Northwest Coast crest style.

[Emmons left no description of sewing. He had evidently planned sections on Bead Work and Porcupine Quill Work,

"*Woman removing hair from deerskin, Sitka, December 12, 1888. (Pen and ink drawing by G. T. Emmons. AMNH.) "Skin had been well wet, rolled up, hair in, for several days. Skin a greenish tinge. Skin placed on half rounded piece of wood, A, 3¼ feet long and 4½ inches wide, wood resting in inclined position, upper end against rock. Woman sitting in front and scraping down with half-curved bone dressing knife [B], the ends of B covered with rags to protect hands. Another woman had just washed skin in hot water after it had. . . .*"

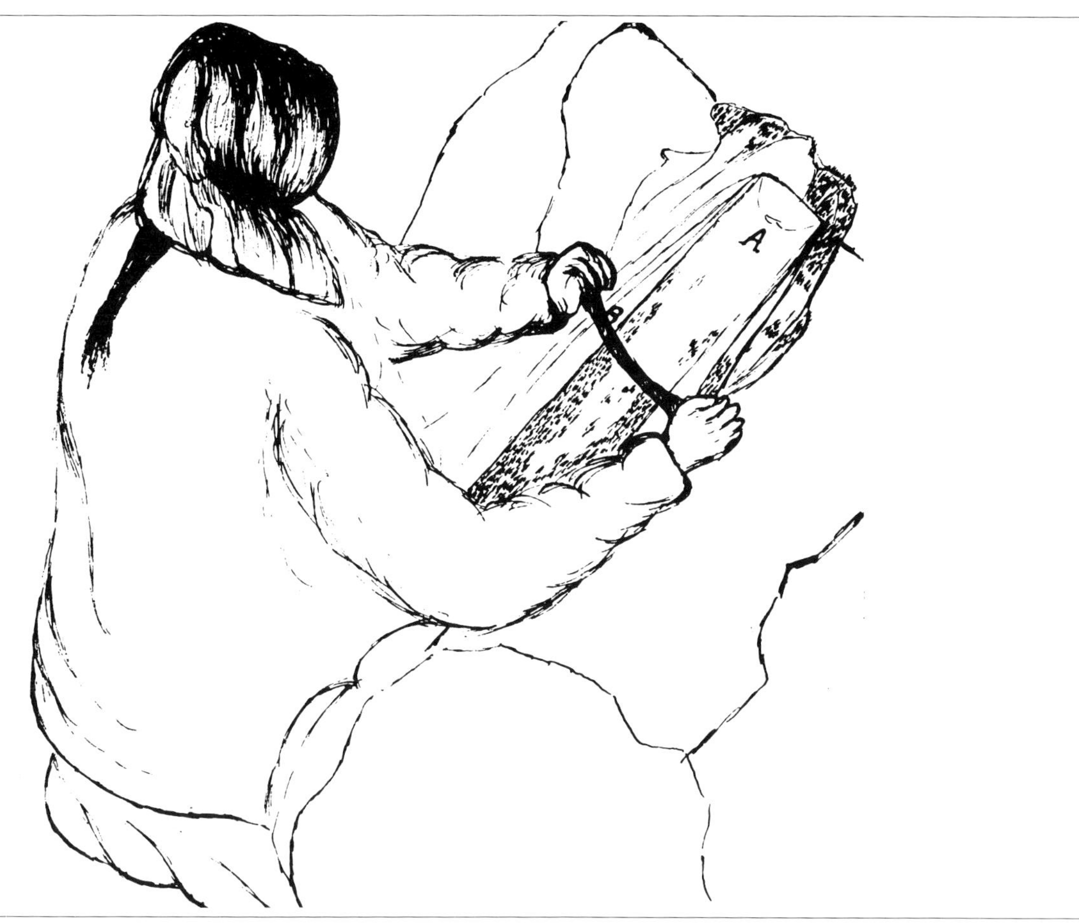

as evidenced by a note in AMNH archives, but these sections were never completed. In sewing, a hole was first made with the awl, qé·na· (from -qa, "to sew"), and the sinew thread was pushed through this. The woman's knife used for cutting skins was like an ulo, and was called wé·kš or *yeese* (yí·s̓). The snowshoe netting needle was *tchar-tchee ug-gah* (ǯá·ǯi ʔá·ga·). A small flat-faced awl was *tuth-ku* (perhaps túɬx̓u, "drill bit"), and the awl used in making snowshoes was *tsu-ar* (possibly s̓úwa·, "chopper"?).]

BASKETRY*

The Tlıngit north of Frederick Sound lacked the red cedar, and in its place used the spruce. While the wood is inferior, the root is far superior, and it is with this that the Northern Tlingit produced the most elaborately beautiful basketry of the entire coast, in perfection of weave, decorative embroidery, variety of geometric designs, and wealth of color.

While all of the northern tribes wove in spruce root, not all were equally expert. The intimately related *Gu-nah-ho* [Dry Bay tribe] and Yakutat tribes produced the finest larger baskets, and have commercialized this industry since early days, so that their work is found from Kodiak to Vancouver Island. But for fineness of weave in smaller baskets, the Hoonah of Cross Sound excelled. The Sitka people were equally expert, and in later years, spurred by the tourist trade, took the most prominent place. The Chilkats wove large baskets, but exclusively for their own use in berry picking and in storing winter food. These were neither ornamented in embroidery or color, but were distinguished by a geometric figure in the weave, below the border. The

**Editor's note:* Data in this section have been checked against Emmons (1903), and some information from that publication is summarized and included here. I compiled Table 22.

"Wringing out a wet skin." (Drawn by G. T. Emmons. AMNH.)

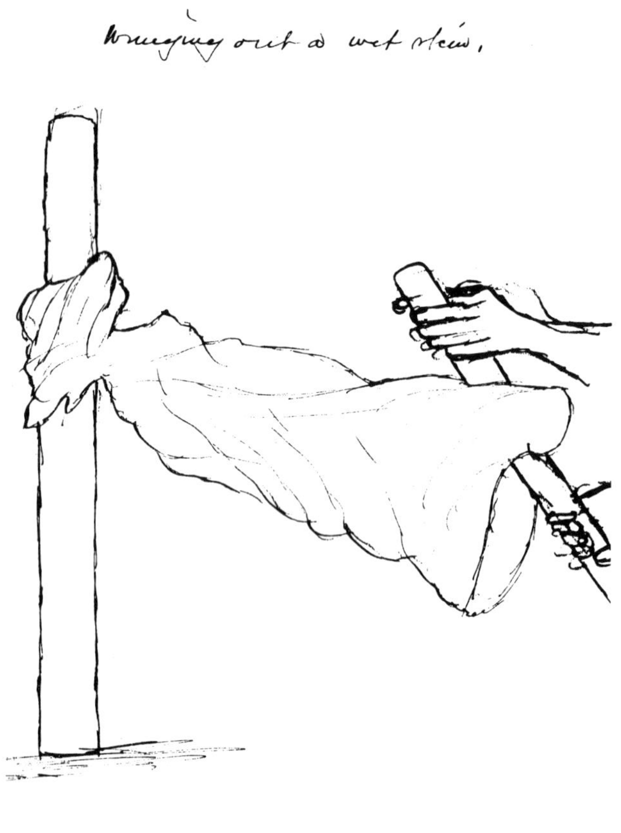

basketry of the other northern tribes, the *Hootz ah tah* [Hutsnuwu], Auk, and Taku, was coarse and made simply for local use.

The root was gathered by the women in the late spring, from carefully selected young mature trees. It was best barked while green, before the sap dried. This was done by slightly charring the root over the coals of a dead fire, and then drawing it through a split stick, *eena* [ʔí·na·], held in the left hand, which regulated the pressure to meet the size of the stem, when the loosened bark was readily peeled off without injury to the smooth outer surface [of the root]. The barked root was then tied loosely in a coil and dried. It might be split at once, but generally it was packed away for several months, since the summer was spent in gathering and preparing food [and making baskets was a winter occupation]. The coils of roots were known as ***khart shuc-kar-tdu'ke*** [x̣a·t šakadú·x̣].

Roots, as well as the plant and grass stems employed for ornamental purposes, were kept wet to render them pliable, as all were very brittle in a dried state. The root was split into sections according to its size, each of which (known as a "split," ***khul katst*** [kaɬqášt, "she is splitting"?]), furnished three distinct parts. Of these, the outer layer, ***khart ku'h-kne*** [x̣a·t káx̣i], "root outside," which included the smooth polished surface next to the bark, was most valued, and supplied the woof strand[s] that gave the weave its polished, ornamental exterior surface. The next section, ***thlart thla'r-tu*** [x̣a·t ɬ̓á·twu or ɬ̓á·du], "root inside," that showed a fibrous, uneven surface, but was of good color and strength, constituted the warp, which was the body of the weave. The innermost section, including the heart, was discarded, as its name signified, "root thrown away," ***khart tu-qwu't-see*** [x̣a·t-tu x̣ʷášiʔ].

The sections of root were then divided into working strands, and when dried the fine woof was done up in skeins, the coarser warp in coils, which were carefully packed away in boxes and baskets to be kept clean until needed.

The only tools used in basketry were the knife, awl, and bear's canine tooth. The primitive knife was a blue mussel shell, ground to a keen edge the length of the lower curved side. Blades of iron, copper, and tin, shaped like the shell, were later introduced, but they found little favor with the older weavers. The bear's tooth was used to smooth any irregularity in the weave.

The characteristic ornamentation of baskets was accomplished by means of an overlaying twined embroidery in grass stems, both natural and colored. Of the several varieties [see Table 22], the *Glyceria striata* (Lam.) Hitchc. *var. stricta* (Scribn.) Hult., or *G. borealis* (Nash) Batchelder, was known as ***kha'-kar shark*** [x̣é·ga·, "true," šá·k, "grass"], "true straw." It was most esteemed on account of its uniform pale straw color, its delicate texture, and its glossy exterior. This was never colored, but was used in its natural state, and brought out to advantage the colored designs.

All grasses and plant stems were gathered in the early summer, before ripening, as the matured stem was more brittle. They were pinched off with the thumbnail just above the ground, and divided into lengths of single sections between the joints, done up in loose bundles, and carried to camp. There they were stripped of leaves or outer growth, and plunged into boiling water, where they were allowed to remain until the color faded to a greenish yellow, when they were spread out to dry, and were later strung in lengths of several feet and bleached in the sun for several

Twined spruce root baskets with false embroidery of colored straw, all from Yakutat. (a) Basket for screening berries, 8.5 inches in diameter. (USNM.) (b) Fine old basket, 8.5 inches in diameter, with the false embroidery almost worn off. (Burke Museum.) (c) Small open basket, 5.4 inches high. (USNM.) (d) Rattle top basket, 7.6 inches high. (USNM.) (e) Basket in rather coarse weave and false embroidery of straws colored with commercial dyes of green, yellow, and orange; 7.6 inches high. (USNM.) (f) Rattle top basket, 4 inches high and 6.8 inches in diameter, with false embroidery of brown and yellow native-dyed straws. (PAM.)

days. This was done before splitting the straws, whereas the spruce root was dyed after the strands had been prepared. Both roots and straws were colored alike [in the same way, with the same colors]. In primitive days, judging from the older baskets, the standard colors were black, purple, and red, with evidences of yellow and green-blue. The depth of color was dependent upon the strength of the bath and the period of immersion. [See Table 19.]

Black was obtained generally by soaking in the mud of sulphur springs, or boiling with the mud, salt water, and hemlock bark, in a bath of powdered charcoal. The *Equisetum* stem sometimes used for ornamentation was black [but it is unclear from the notes whether it was used for black dye].

The blueberries and huckleberry [see Table 22] furnished different shades of purple from almost black to reddish.

Red, the dominant color, was obtained principally from the alder and the bark of the western hemlock, by steeping or boiling the bark or the wood in urine. The color red, *qwus* [kʷás, "urine"], was derived from the name of the alder urine tub. A lighter shade of red was "red like the sky at sunset," *qwus kus-su´ck-ho* [kʷás kaséq̓ʷx̣u], and a deeper color was known as "fire red," *kha-ghón kus-su´ck-ho* [ka-x̣̓a·n kaséq̓ʷx̣u]. [The verb łi-séq̓ʷ means "to stain or to dye," and ka-di-séq̓ʷ means "to be stained." According to notes made at Sitka, now in BCPA, a reddish pink was obtained from salmonberry leaves (?), and purple from the cranberry. The maidenhair fern stem was also purple.]

Yellow, *kut-thlark* [ka-λ̣á·λ̣, "like the yellow warbler"] was named for the color of the "wild canary," and was derived from the yellow lichen, *Evernia vulpina,* obtained in trade from the interior. [Notes indicate that light brown may have been derived from some variety of tree moss, and a golden brown from dock root.]

Green-blue, *kuh-khashsk* [ka-x̣é·šx̣ʷ, "like the bluejay"], named for Steller's crested jay, came from oxide of copper and hemlock bark.

[Emmons (1907:336) specified: "The greenish-blue, the most esteemed of all the colors, came from the oxidation of copper in urine and the boiling of the same. The yarn is introduced and boiled, removed, well washed in fresh water, and dried in the sun. The Tsimshian tell me that a blue clay-stone was used to produce this shade. The Tlingit use this same stone for the decoration of masks, houses, robes, etc., as a paint, but not as a dye." (The blue claystone was probably "green earth"; see the section on "Painting" in the previous chapter.) He also (p. 337) referred to the blue coloring as due to "the copper mordant," but this was not correct (see page 226).]

Other colors were obtained from various other berries and plants. In later days, colored cloth and aniline dyes were used, but these had little permanency and were not to be compared with the native plant colors.

The Tlingit wove only in the twining stitch in which one or more warp strands or splints were enclosed by a cross twining of the [double] woof, the work progressing from left to right, and the outer woof strand crossing from up to down and around. The standard weave, *wush tookh a´r-kee* [probably wu·š tú·xʷ ʔá·gi], "close together work," from the closeness of the texture, was perfectly watertight, and consisted of the twining of two woof strands around each warp splint. The open-work bag or basket "strainer," *khart* [ka·t], "will not hold water," that was used in trying out fish oil and in cooking, was in a similar weave, except that the spirals of woof were distanced from one another. Another open-work weave was named "eye holes," *wark kus-ka´rt* [wa·q kaska·t, "eyed basket"], from the polygonal meshes of the crossed warp, which are drawn aside from the perpendicular at a fixed angle, the odd numbers trending one way and the even ones the other, as they are enclosed in the woof twining. This weave was used for spoon baskets and flat cases.

Another arrangement of weave, "rough or uneven, like the skin of the frog's back," *hiktch hee-ha´r-see* [xíxč xá·ši, "frog's skin"], was formed by twining the two woof strands over a pair of warp splints, that, in the successive spirals of weave, break joints perpendicularly, giving a diagonal appearance to the surface.

A combination of weaves, known as "between" or "in the middle of," *khark-ghee-su´t* [probably x̣á·kisat], was formed by the introduction of a single coarse plaited strand between the close-twined woof spirals. This strand passed over and under each alternate warp splint, or, putting it plainly, this strand alternated with the close-twined woof spiral to give a broken, irregular surface effect. It was economical in material and saving in time. It was generally employed by the Chilkat in their large baskets used in preparing the high-bush cranberry for winter use, in the basinlike basket for berry screening, in the basket maker's own workbasket, and in the bottoms of coarser baskets. [Yakutat informants specified that this plain wicker weave was used for undecorated, plain baskets for packing.]

In the long, cylindrical fishwier traps of spruce slats the twining in spirals or circles was of the two-strand spruce root, as in basketry.

A strengthening weave, *uh ta´hk-ka* [possibly ʔat té·x̣], "twisted," was more like a braid, in which three woof strands were employed, each one of which made a part of a turn over the preceding two, enclosing two warp splits on the outside, and only one on the inside, which gave a winding, ropelike appearance on the surface. It was used as a strengthening twist in one, two, or three spirals of weave on the bottom or sides of heavy or large baskets, and was generally placed at the turning up of the bottom warp to form the sides. It constituted a very fine ornamental weave in the crown and in the superimposed series of cylinders of the ceremonial hat, *shar-dar khuke,* "around the head" [šada·, "around the head," kú·x̣, "cylinder" or "wild celery"].

In weaving, the woman sat with knees drawn up to her chin, the feet together, shoulders bent over and arms around the knees, a characteristic position of Tlingit women generally. By her side was a low basinlike, plain basket, *tarlth* [tá·ƚ], "spread out, flattened," holding bunches of warp, skeins of woof, finely divided splits of grass and plant stems (kept in grooved cedar sticks, *shark ku-see-a khars-see* [šá·k x̣usyi· ʔa· qá·ši]), the shell knife, bear's tooth, and awl. She also had a small basket of water, into which she dipped her fingers continually in order to moisten the root that she was working. All baskets, regardless of type, were begun in the same way. Half a dozen or so warp splints were evened up and bent over at the middle, where a single strand of woof thread was carried around and half hitched, binding them together. They were then opened out as radii, and the twining of the two woof strands proceeded. Extra warp splints were continually introduced between the others [as the circle grew], and when necessary, those reaching their end were backed by others. As the weave progressed, an occasional colored woof strand was employed to test the accuracy of the circle of weave. At the periphery of the bottom, where the warp splints were turned up to form the walls, an increase in the number of warps was required, and was provided for by an extra strand and backing of the warp before reaching this point, and here a strengthening circle of three-ply woof was used. The process of weaving was carried on with the thumb and first two fingers of the right hand, which manipulated the twining of the woof, while the thumb and fore and middle fingers of the left hand separated the warp and kept the weave taut. With practiced weavers, the movement of the fingers became automatic, and in their regularity and swiftness could hardly be followed by the eye.

The border was the life of the basket, and that this was fully appreciated is shown by the means used to protect it. Two principal methods were employed in the finish of the border edge: (1) by twining off the warp ends flush with the last spiral of weave, and (2) by doubling the warp over and twining it down to the standing part. But whether the warp was cut off or turned down, the last few spirals of weave were strengthened by additional twining, embroidery over the weave, or an increase of woof to form a braided ridge along the edge. Unquestionably, the turning down of the warp and twining it to its own part gave the most protection to the finish, and this occurred on all better woven, open cylindrical baskets, and is particularly found on the oldest specimens of the best Yakutat work. Weaving in root was very trying on the thumb and forefinger, and the constant wetting of these possibly augmented the trouble and kept them sensitive. Practically all open baskets made for use were fitted with handles of two-stranded twisted root or hide, let into the weave with the awl and knotted on the inside.

The characteristic ornamentation of Tlingit basketry was executed *on* the weave, rather than *in* it, and so was considered as an embroidery by the weaver. If the overlaying strand was of colored root in one or more spirals of weave, it was called *tahk* [probably té·x̣̓], "twist," and while ornamental, was employed more as a strengthener. But if the extra filament was of grass or plant stem, the work was known as *ut-tah yark tu-twage* [possibly ʔada-yax̣-tut-yaʔá·gi], "outside lifted up and put over," or *yudah-shark* [y̥ada· šá·k] "outside grass" ["grass around the side"]. In this weave, the narrow plant strip was introduced from the outside and twined around the outside woof, and so not enclosing the warp, did not appear on the inside of the basket. Sometimes the embroidery stitch was elongated, passing over every other unit of woof, giving a broken appearance to the embroidery.

Form in baskets was determined by their use, dependent upon the material and construction methods. The more pliable lighter spruce root lent itself best to the cylindrical shape with a broad base. Occasional odd shapes, more experimental, at the fancy of the weaver, are found, but the cylindrical has ever remained the standard form, and it seemed to satisfy the requirements of the life of the people in their preparation of food, storage, and packing.

Baskets took their names from their function and shape: *kuhk tar-yee* [qákʷ tayi̇·, "underside of basket"] was the primitive cooking pot, long since obsolete, in which heated stones were used to boil fish or meat. [It was probably so named because the height was one-half the diameter. Emmons glossed the name as "half-basket."] It was also known as *ta-yet* [té y̥e·t or tay̥e·t, "any vessel used in stone boiling"] from the method of cooking. It was a low basket of heavy weave, with slightly flaring sides, and was reinforced around the bottom and sides in spirals of the three-stranded ropelike weave.

Kuhk kish-shar, "basket bucket" [qákʷ x̣̓ïšá·, "basket pot"], a medium sized tightly woven, cylindrical basket, unornamented, was used, as its name implied, as a water bucket, the close weave making it perfectly watertight. It was also called *tchook-ate* [ču· (?) ke·t], "a vessel between," because of its size.

Kish-shar yat-kee [x̣̓ïšá· y̥átx̣̓i, "baby basket"] or *athle yet* [ʔé·ł̓ y̥e·t, "salt-water cup"] or *athle-thlu-ottee* [ʔé·ł̓ łuʔádi(?)], "belonging to salt water," was a drinking cup. It was an elongated cylinder, with a root handle, for when not in use it was always hung on a peg on the wall. It was a personal article, woven for a man, and used by him to drink salt water to purify his body. This was a primitive custom, strictly followed by the men in early days, when they rose early, "before the Raven cries," as the Tlingit say, went down to the shore and filled the basket with salt water. Then, secreting it under their blankets, they went into the forest and drank four swallows. This was done on four successive mornings, sometimes every morning for a period, in order to acquire good fortune in hunting, fishing, gambling, [or other chancy pursuits], to guard against sickness, and as part of fasting. It was sometimes prescribed by the shaman. The weave and the ornamentation, in design

Tlingit basket makers, Sitka, 1890. (Photograph by Winter and Pond? AMNH.)

and color, marked the perfection of the weaver's art. An additional ornamentation was seen on several shaman's basket cups from very old gravehouses; these were flicker tail feathers, dentalium shells, and beads, attached to the border, a feature absolutely foreign to any other type of basket.

Three different kinds of basket were used in picking berries [see Chapter 6, the section "Berries and Other Plant Foods"]. These were the small basket hung in front from the neck, the larger basket on the back, and the very large stationary basket with heavy hide or twisted root handles, carried between two people.

Tchu-qwelth [čugʷé·λ] was the name given to any large, open-top, cylindrical basket, in general use, especially for packing, or to hold household articles, food, or clothing. It often had a cloth lining.

Son-nay [c̓ané·, a Tsimshian word], is a general name for any plain spruce root basket of medium size, and means "rough," referring to the coarse quality of the weave.

Tarlth [tá·ł], "spread out," was a low, flattened basinlike basket, some fifteen to eighteen inches in diameter. The bottom was flat, the sides curving upward and outward from it. It was generally made in the mixed rough weave with a single plaited woof strand between the twining woof, and was seldom ornamented. The border was generally finished by turning down the ends of the warp and weaving them in on the outside. This was the basket maker's workbasket, and held her materials and tools.

The plaque used for screening berries was called *kut-tuts-ar yate* or *kut-tuts-ar yet* [kada·ʒá· or kadáʒa· yẹ·t], "beating or shaking under." It was similar to the workbasket, *tarlth,* in weave and shape, except that the bottom was not so flat, and the upward trend of the warp was continuous from the center. It was thus more basinlike, with no dividing line between bottom and sides. This type of basket was largely in use among the Chilkat, where berries were abundant. These were shaken into the basket held under [the berry bush], or the hand stripped the branch of leaves and all. Then the basket was held up, shaken, and blown through to get rid of the trash. It was fitted with two or four loop handles. This was essentially a Chilkat article, and when the berrying season was over, it was wetted, folded in half or quarters, and put away.

The strainer, *khart* [ka·t, glossed by Emmons as "will not hold water"], was more of a bag than a basket, and was made in both a conical and cylindrical shape. It was of coarse root, the woof in the regular twining but distanced apart as the spiral wound around [i.e., the spirals of twining were not pushed together]. At the contracted bottom was a loop of braided strands, so that it could be picked up and emptied. It was used when trying out fish oil, in pressing the cooked fish.

Another [open-weave] type of strainer, was more like a basket with a root handle, and was used in scalding and cooking berries by dipping them into boiling water in a wooden vessel. The weave was in a crossing of the warp strands, enclosed in the woof just after crossing, thus forming the polygonal mesh called *wark-kus-kart* [wa·q kaska·t, "eyed basket"]. Bands of close weave alternated with the open weave to give the walls rigidity and strength.

The spoon bag, *chetle tar-ka´te* [šáƚ da·ke·t], also had a similar cross warp and open work, with alternating bands of close twining. It was fitted with a twisted root handle, to hang on the wall. As its Tlingit name indicates, it held the horn eating spoons.

A long, elliptical, flattened baglike container, of varying size, was named *thleete* [ƛi·ṫ(?)], for a flat sea worm that lives under the boulders along the shore. It was a very old type, and the few specimens found among shamans' effects in old gravehouses were very fine in weave and were covered with delicate embroidery in colored designs. They were receptacles for valuable articles used by the shaman, particularly his carved ivory spirit charms, and also for the eagle down used in dancing.

Large covered baskets were of rare occurrence among the Tlingit and may be recent. Those of smaller size became very popular after tourist travel reached the coast, but very old specimens, found occasionally in the rubbish of old houses, indicate that they were formerly used by women as workbaskets or to hold trinkets and small articles. [Such a basket] was the *tu-dar-huck* [tu-da-xákʷ or tuqʷ-da·da-xákʷ], "noise inside," or *tu-dar-hook ah-yhum-r-r tun-ee* [probably tudaxákʷ, "rattle-top," ˀa yaná·ṫani, "its lid"]. The name referred to the small chamber in the top of the cover that was filled with tiny pebbles that rattled. The walls and the cover were elaborately ornamented in embroidery with plain and colored straw.

A very tiny covered case, in two parts, one fitting over the other, or with a rather deep top, was used to hold the native tobacco, and was carried in a skin bag suspended from the neck. This was called *tuck tar-káte* [tax̌ da·ke·t], "bite bag," or *wus-shut tar-káte,* "chewing or cheek bag" [waš ˀát da·ke·t, "cheek-thing (i.e., snuff) container"], since the snuff made from the tobacco was placed between the gums and the lower lip, and sucked.

[A globular covered basket was called *qwutle qwut,* "egglike belly" (probably x̣uƚ k̇ʷá·t, the last word meaning "egg"). This is mentioned by Emmons (1903:255) as possibly derived from the "familiar preserve-jar of the Chinese," brought in by traders.]

There were double baskets, like cases with one part fitting over the other. The larger one was called *yun-nah kar-ar-kee* [yana· kaˀá·gi(?)], "top to lap over," or *wush-tu-ku-gu* [wu·štu qágu], "one inside the other." This consisted of two slightly tapering cylinders; the inner one, of the finest possible weave and elaborate colored embroidery, was protected by the outer case, which was in the close root twining and was seldom ornamented, except in circles of the three-ply twining. These baskets were found among the shaman's effects in old graves, which may account for their extreme fineness. Such baskets were used to hold his charms, or the bird's down with which he dressed his hair. It is said that he drank from the basket during his periods of fasting.

A smaller case, of similar weave and decoration, came into use after the introduction of firearms, as a shot carrier. It was called *ut-tu-qwu´n-see tar-kate* [ˀat tux̣únši, "pellet," da·ke·t, "container"]. This was worn in a skin wallet hung from the neck by the Hoonah, Sitka, and Hutsnuwu tribes; the others preferred shot pouches of skin, gut, or horn.

A very small cylindrical basket, made for children, but embroidered, was called *kuhk ku´hkee* [perhaps qákʷ qakʷ k̇ʷ (?)].

[Basketry and baskets are described in great detail in Emmons 1903. A shorter but well-illustrated booklet about Tlingit spruce root baskets is by Frances Paul (1944).]

SPRUCE ROOT HATS

Several varieties of hats were of basket weave. The common type, *sarh* [sá·xʷ], was really of two kinds. The first was a hat for bad weather, rain, and canoe travel. It was coarsely woven and was usually smeared with paint to render it waterproof. The second was a finer one of excellent weave. The rim in the close-twined woof was interspersed at regular intervals by enclosing two warp splints, thus forming geometric zigzags, triangles, and so forth, while the upper half or crown was in the three-ply ropelike twining, and the whole was like the frustum of a cone in shape. An inside band was woven to fit the head, and this was found on all hats. Persons of rank might have these hats painted with a crest figure.

A much larger, finer hat was called *sark klin* [s̓á·xʷ ƛe·n], "large hat," or *kwon-tu-gee-hit sark* [kawduǯixidi s̓a·xʷ or kanduǯixidi s̓á·xʷ], "painted hat." It had a very wide, more outward curving brim, and was made in the finest weave and painting in animal design. Such hats were rare and very valuable.

The smaller, but finest, and most beautifully woven and ornamented hat was the *shar-dar khuke* [šada· kú·x̣̓ʷ], "around-the-head cylinder," referring to the cylindrical ornament woven with and surmounting the crown. This was named for the dried, hollow stem [ku·x̓ʷ] of the wild celery. The lower half or rim was in the close weave, with the skip stitch extending across two warp splints at regular intervals, forming geometric figures on the surface. The upper half was in the finest possible thread of woof in the three-ply ropelike weave. This field was beautifully painted in a conventional animal figure, the clan crest, and in addition to this there was sometimes attached a raven's bill or animal's head of wood, to further represent the totemic emblem of the wearer's family. But the special feature which gave this hat its name was the ornamental top, which consisted of a series of superimposed cylinders with narrow connecting necks, rising from the top of the hat and woven with it. In the necessary expansion and contraction of the weave, the greatest ingenuity of the weaver was shown. The cylinders varied in number, according to the rank of the wearer, and were woven over hollowed out blocks of dead cedar for lightness, which gave substance to the cylinders as they stood upright. From the hole in the top an ermine skin was hung.

The rarest type of hat was a shaman's headdress, called a war bonnet, not that he wore it in actual war, but in his struggles with hostile spirits during his practice. This was called *shar-dar yar-ar-kee* [šada· yaʔá·gi], "around-the-head work." It was rectangular, made of two flattened, broad sides, connected at the front and at the rear. In fact it was a continuous woven band, open at top and bottom, with an outward flare, higher in the front [than at the sides or back]. The entire surface was embroidered, or largely embroidered, in grass stems in designs [often or usually zigzags]. Unlike any other article of primitive Tlingit basketry, there was usually a tiny crude stiff animal figure, woven in color. (I say specifically "primitive basketry," for after the tourist trade became established and commercialized basket making, animal figures were introduced, and the old, simple designs became mixed, but the fancies of the later weavers were without meaning.) The top of the headdress was ornamented with fur: a wolf or fox tail, or the mane of a mountain goat. [This type of "war bonnet" or shaman's hat was probably related to the folded birch-bark headgear, like an army barracks cap, worn by the Atna and Upper Tanana Athabaskans in former days (de Laguna and McClellan, field notes, 1960; de Laguna and Guédon, field notes, 1968).]

BASKETRY DESIGNS

The antiquity of basketry ornamentation certainly goes back to before Europeans reached the coast, as the published narratives of the early explorers not only speak in admiration of this art, but the illustrations show the embroidery stitch and color in the shaded figures, and the oldest specimens found today excel in fineness anything now being produced.

The different weaves and the colors used in ornamentation have been described. Their adaptation to the cylindrical walls was best employed in encircling bands, on which single or combined figures are shown. In the open-topped baskets of large and medium size, the standard baskets, the decorative bands are arranged in three zones: the upper and lower are broader and alike in design, and enclose a narrower middle one, showing a different figure. In the finest old baskets, two or four vertical figures, below the encircling ornamental zones, stood out in bold relief against the uniform, plain root background of the walls. This same ornamentation is found on the small personal drinking basket-cup. The walls of baskets with lids were entirely covered with a broad band of colored embroidery, as was the top, but in a different design adapted to the circular shape. The narrow design around both the lower edge of the basket and the overlapping of the cover were always alike, which identified them if separated. Generally, the inner case of the double basket and sometimes the cover were wholly covered with colored embroidery, as was the shaman's bonnet.

Design in basketry was geometric, and constituted a noticeably fundamental exception to the characteristic art of the Tlingit, who, in carving, painting, and weaving in animal fabrics [see "The Chilkat Blanket" section, below], employed only realistic or symbolic animal figures, totemic in character and connected with their social organization. It would, therefore, seem reasonable that this geometric character of design was borrowed, and, as none of the

Side and top views of a crest hat, with four cylinders on top (the ermine panache is missing), and a Killerwhale design painted in red, black, and blue over the textured weave. Collected by William S. Libbey at Yakutat in 1886. (Photographs by Donald Baird. Princeton University Museum.)

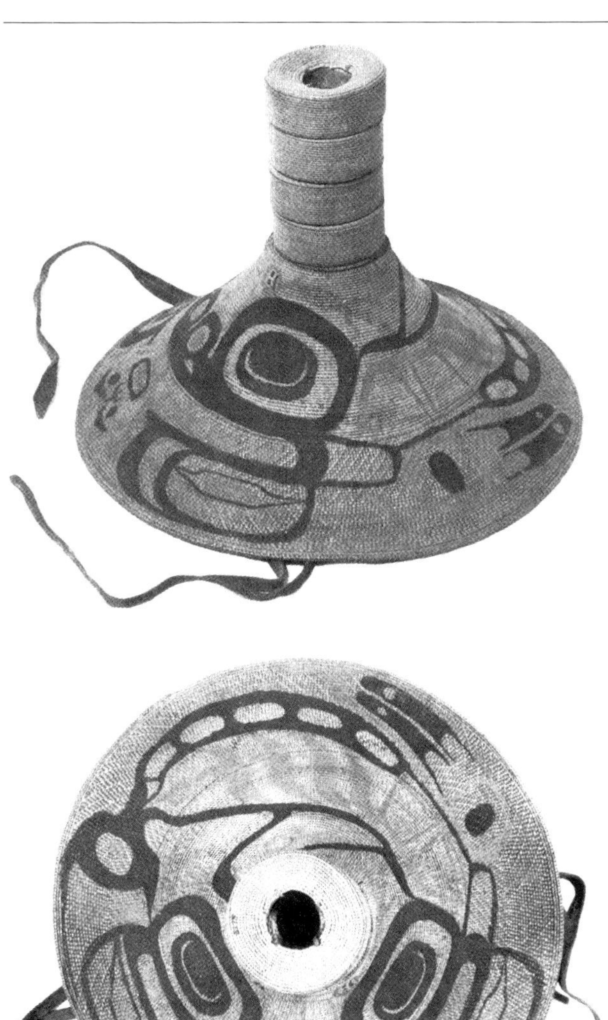

neighboring people employed such figures in any of their work, we may go beyond to the Athabaskan porcupine quill embroidery. This was similar in simpler figures, and was well known to the Tlingit through [a common?] origin, intermarriage, and trade. Possibly it was practiced by them to some degree, since old skin clothing ornamented with quill work was not uncommon among them.

Naturally designs would increase through accident or in the course of experiment, but by far the majority [of basketry designs? or designs in general?] were so realistic in outline that they justify the belief that they were the result of a desire to represent an object, or some characteristic feature, as clearly as possible in geometric form. The Tlingit seldom applied a design singly to a plain field. It generally was placed within a decorative zone in conjunction with other motifs. Now the idea existed with the people that originally the main figure (that we consider the design and that gave its name to the basket) was that which was embroidered in the fine natural straw on a field of root, often colored to show it [the straw figure] to advantage. Under this condition, the intervening spaces, or complementary figures, were of secondary importance, without meaning. But later, at the fancy of the weaver, these complementary figures were likewise embroidered [with colored straws], and became the design proper, while those first so considered [in the natural straw] became a background. Then came the work in colored straw [i.e., multicolored straws], until today each line in root or straw has its meaning for one versed in the art. Nevertheless, the pattern in the fine natural straw remained paramount.

All designs were not equally well adapted to the decorative field. While some lend themselves to all sizes and shapes of baskets, others admit of expansion or contraction only within certain limits, which accounts for the more frequent appearance of certain motifs on certain types [of basketry] to the exclusion of others. Designs were neither tribal nor individual; they were common to all. It is true that preference for certain patterns existed in localities, and that individual weavers should have their favorites. Indeed, this was very common and worked to the best advantage, producing better results at less cost of time and labor, as the process of weaving became almost mechanical. Color in design had no significance, except in one motif representing the rainbow, and this was seldom used. It was indicated by the close arrangement of three or four colors in bands. Again, in the use of colors, individual preference was a factor. In the late 1890s the most experienced and artistic weaver at Sitka wove all her baskets alike in size, shape, design, and color, greatly to her own advantage.

The accuracy with which designs were preserved and transmitted through generations, as seen by comparison of the work of different periods, was largely due to copying or to the conservatism of primitive people [wishing] to preserve the past. But sometimes one finds an old piece of weave in a long forgotten motif.

As might be expected, a people living so close to nature, in their rather restricted simple life, drew upon their surroundings for decorative motifs. So we find that these are largely representative of natural objects, features of animals, and their own manufactures. While most of the [designs] carry their own interpretation, yet others are differently understood in different places.

[It could be better argued that the geometric designs of basketry were named for fancied resemblances to objects than that they were intended to represent those objects. Of the designs figured by Emmons (1903), six were named for features of crests (Killerwhale teeth, Raven tail); twenty-seven for other animals or natural features (shark tooth, fern fronds); twenty-five for manufactured articles (labret, shaman's hat). Except for the animal figures woven on the shaman's headdress, only an occasional basket has woven representative designs. Such a one is that collected by Emmons, now in the Alaska State Museum, which copies the painting on the front of Snail House at Hoonah, showing Raven carrying a king salmon (Paul 1944, pl. XXXVI). Curiously, Emmons did not list a Snail House at Hoonah, although he did for Kake (Table 14). Swanton (1908:404) noted a Slug House, "TAq! hît," of the Hoonah Slug House People, and (pl. LVII, *a*) illustrated a basket with a geometric design "representing a mountain called Tsaɬxā'n"—that is, Mount Fairweather, a crest of Raven 16.]

With the influx of tourists in the late 1890s, the demand for baskets increased beyond the normal supply, and weaving became an important commercial industry. In the competition [between weavers] to outdo each other, the old designs gave place to individual fancies and animal forms became popular, while aniline dyes supplanted the old native colors. [Bottles covered with twined spruce roots belong to this period.]

The ornamentation of all hats, except that of the shaman, was never in colored root or in embroidery with grass stems. It followed the characteristic [crest] art of the coast in conventional animal forms in paint.

SPRUCE ROOT MATS

Spruce root mats, beautifully ornamented in colored embroidery, were made in two shapes. Both were small. The first, called *tarlth* [tá·ɬ], "flat," was oval, and is said to have been originally used as a dish from which dried food, such as dried berries or roots, was eaten, or was placed by guests at feasts on which they could put their horn spoon. The other was a circular mat, like the bottom of a basket, and was so named, ***kuhke too-gu*** [q̓ákʷ tú·g̣u], and is a modern product.

CEDAR BARK WEAVING

The Tlingit south of Frederick Sound, like all of the tribes southward to the Straits of Juan de Fuca, might be termed "people of the red cedar," as their industrial life was so dependent upon this tree. Of the wood they built their houses, fashioned their canoes, domestic articles, and carvings. The bark furnished the material for clothing, baskets, mats, fishing lines, and cordage of every kind. The Northern Tlingit, lacking this tree, made use of the Sitka spruce for like purposes, and might be called "people of the spruce."

Cedar bark was gathered about June. [This was man's work, and should, perhaps, have been included in Chapter 7.] A healthy tree was selected, and it was climbed by means of an apparatus consisting of a wooden footrest and a broad woven backstrap of cedar bark. Both were fitted with long rope ends that went around the tree. The footrest, two feet long, with a concave edge on the tree side, was fitted with a two-inch, three-strand cedar bark rope, knotted through a hole in the rounded end; this, after going around the tree trunk, was rove through a hole in the other end of the board and hitched over the forked handle at that end. The five-inch broad backstrap of woven sennit was formed into a loop at one end, and [at the other] terminated in a length of three-stranded cedar bark rope, that tapered from four to one and three-fourths inches in thickness. These two parts were connected at the ends.

The climber adjusted the backstrap under the shoulders, and, with his feet on the wooden rest, ascended the trunk by bracing his back [against the strap], pulling up the footrest. Then he slipped up the rope of the backstrap. The use of this apparatus gave complete freedom of the hands in cutting the bark, which was done with a curved bone knife, about a foot long, of deer rib, which was also used to pry off the bark. The pieces thus obtained were folded into convenient strips for packing.

[Bill Holm informs me (letter of May 22, 1986) that while southern tribes, such as the Kwakiutl and Nootka, have a tree-climbing rig similar to that described by Emmons (Stewart 1984:164), he doubts that it was used to get bark for mats or like use, since cedar bark can be easily secured by standing at the foot of the tree and stripping the bark upward. The rig may have been used for getting roof slabs.]

The raw bark as taken from the tree supplied several layers for weaving, wrapping, and cordage. It was split [by the woman] with a bone knife or mussel shell. The deep yellow inner layer next to the trunk is of the finest quality in texture and color and was used for baskets and mats. It was separated into long, thin ribbons, five to eight or more inches wide, or wrapped in loose bundles about two feet long, and hung up or stored in baskets for future use. In all work with bark it was necessary to keep it pliable by continued wetting to overcome its natural brittleness.

Baskets of cedar bark were but rude, plain receptacles in comparison with those of spruce root. They were cylindrical in shape and open at the top, unornamented except in black lines or squares, and in their pliable material were more like bags than baskets. They were all in plain plaiting or checker weave. The warp and woof were of the same width, ranging from less than one-fourth to one inch, depending on the size of the basket.

The large baskets, used for storage purposes in the house, and as containers of food or clothing in the canoe, were fitted with an open weave at the mouth that terminated in a twisted ropelike border, so that the basket could be corded and closed at the top. Small baskets of twisted bark in the close-twined weave were rare. Long baglike containers of maple splints and bark [called c̓ané·] were used for storing potatoes. [Woven cedar bark bags were called g̣á·č gʷé·ł.]

Painted food boxes were often protected by a close fitting cover of woven bark. The finely woven painted spruce root hat had a cover of loosely woven bark.

The cedar bark weavers, however, excelled in making the mats which were of great economic value in their lives. The mat [g̣á·č] served for bedding, floor covering, as a lining along the inside walls against the weather, as a wrap for clothing and bedding in canoe travel or to cover the cargo, and, when old and worn, as protection over the canoe in bright weather. The corpse was wrapped in it for cremation. Very small, fine mats were used as a table cloth for dry food, and were also placed between players when gambling.

For weaving mats the more southern tribes used a frame of two uprights, and a crossbar over which the warp was hung. The Tongass and Cape Fox [Sanya] people sometimes followed this method, but the Tlingit generally spread the ribbons of warp on a broad board, like a table, raised by logs or boulders a foot or two from the ground. The weaver sat before this, with knees drawn up to her chin or with legs extended underneath. This was not as convenient as the upright frame. The bark strips, four to eight inches wide, cut to the length of the proposed mat, were laid side by side the width of the mat. As the mat was woven in separate halves from the middle to each end, the half not being worked was folded and weighted down with flat boulders at the middle.

Beginning at the right [and working toward the left], the worker split the bark into strips of the required width of the warp, either with the shell knife or with the thumbnail of her right hand which was grown to a length of one-half inch for this purpose. [She held the strip taut with the left hand.] In the incision made at the middle, the forefinger of the right hand was inserted, and, guided by the thumb and second finger holding the bark, was run down to the weaver at the end. The average width of the strips was one-fourth inch, although it might be much finer for a very small mat. When all of the warp had been split in width, it was split in thickness from the end to the middle. The strand was opened and separated, the outer half taken between the teeth and held taut, while the under half was separated, drawn up to the middle, and nipped off with the thumbnail. This piece later served as a woof strand.

When the warps were all split, they were held in place by a two-strand twining of twisted cedar bark cord across the middle of the mat. [This might or might not be removed when the mat was finished. Emmons was inconsistent in the several versions of the manuscript.]

The weave was in the plain or checkerboard pattern, made by laying back alternate warps and introducing the single woof between them and those lying flat on the board. In the next line of weaving the warps were reversed. The end of the woof was looped over the outer warp and then laid back against its own part for several divisions of weave. To strengthen the border, a continuous double or heavier strand was carried around the entire mat. The ends of the warp were looped around this, laid back against their own part, and woven in with the last three or four woof strands. [When half of the mat was finished, it was turned end for end, and the other half was worked like the first.]

The ornamentation of these mats was wholly in geometric figures: squares, lines, angles, zigzags, in black. Either the warp or the woof strands might be dyed black. In later years, other colors, pink or green, were sparingly used. If the warp were colored, it constituted one whole ribbon or width. The woof was colored in single strands and so could be introduced at any point by nipping off the plain strand and entering the end of the colored one under the weave. This same method was used to introduce a fresh strand if one broke. A wooden dish or box containing water always stood at the right side of the weaver, in which she continually dipped her fingers and drew them along the strands.

[According to a note in BCPA, headed "248. Mat making": "The black color is obtained by putting the bark in to soak with a soft black mud found in wet ground, and salt water is added. The bark is allowed to soak for five or more days until it is perfectly dyed. The black mud which comes from a grindstone, after working down iron, is saved and used as a black dye. Alder bark would give the pink or red."]

Cordage, canoe cables and lines, fish lines, seines, and nets were of two-stranded cedar bark rope laid up right-handed.

THE CHILKAT BLANKET*

The most original and pleasing ceremonial robe of the Northwest Coast tribes was known commercially as the Chilkat blanket, because it was produced in later [historic] times only by this Northern Tlingit tribe [or by Chilkat-born women who had married outside their tribe, provided the materials were available, and the art may have been learned by other women who married Chilkat men].

This variegated blanket, woven from the wool of the mountain goat, was found among the Haida and Tsimshian, as well as the Tlingit. According to Tlingit tradition, the art of this type of weaving originated among the Tsimshian [who no longer practice it], and was carried to the Chilkat, through marriage or migration from that tribe in early days. It was noted by the earliest Europeans, and there is nothing in the coloring or manufacture of the blanket which is not wholly indigenous to Chilkat country. The Chilkats claim, as told me by Chief Chartrich [chief of Wolf 1, Ka·g^{w}a·nta·n of Klukwan], that they owe the knowledge of manufacture of this blanket to an old woman who, having obtained a blanket from the Tsimshian, took it to pieces and studied out the system of workmanship. The blanket is known to the Tlingit as *nar-kheen* [na·xe·n], a word said to be of Tsimshian origin. The ordinary Tlingit word for blanket is *thlou* [x̣ú·x; or ƚí· if it is a new blanket, used as potlatch wealth].

Weaving was confined to the woman. The man furnished the pelt of the mountain goat, the cedar bark, the frame, the painted pattern board, and the few tools required. The woman prepared and wove the materials. In early days, when superstition was rife among the people, the woman could not have intercourse with a man for two moons before she prepared the materials, otherwise the dyes would be uneven and the result would be a failure. She fasted throughout the first day of preparation. But of late years these customs have fallen into disuse.

For the manufacture of one blanket, three goatskins were necessary, and the wool was thickest and in best condition toward the close of winter, although the goat was hunted in both the fall and spring. The pelt consisted of a heavy coat of fine white wool covered by long coarse hair. [It would appear from notes in BCPA that if the pelt was not to be used at once, it would be dried in the sun or in the house, and put away. Then it was wetted or moistened on the skin side for several days, when it would be ready for picking.] The green skin [of the freshly killed goat] was rolled up and sweated until the roots of the hair and wool were loosened, and easily removed. This was done by the woman, seated with the skin flat on her lap, fur side uppermost, the hair and wool being removed with both hands. Large patches were separated and put [carefully] aside, until the whole skin had been picked. Then the hairs were separated by hand from the wool or fleece [and the wool was divided into conveniently sized bundles]. The process of spinning now began.

The woman, seated with bundles of finely divided wool in easy reach, took a handful in her right hand, and, drawing it out with the thumb and forefinger of the left hand to the required thickness, spun it, with the palm of the right hand on the side of her left leg. The loose thread or strand was spun by rubbing the hand from the hip toward the knee, and as spun, was rolled up into balls of different sized thread, as required. (The border of black and yellow, and the warp, are coarser, while the field in black and white patterns reach the greatest degree of fineness.) The yarn is formed by twisting together two strands [of the loosely spun wool], and these all-wool yarns form the woof. To give substance to the blanket, the warp consists of a heart [core] of cedar bark surrounded by wool.

The cedar bark was gathered in long strips in the spring [see above, "Cedar Bark Weaving".] The bark of the yellow cedar was preferred, although the bark of the red cedar was also used, [both? or only the latter?] imported from the Southern Tlingit, or Tsimshian. The outer bark was removed, and the inner bark dried. When required for use, it would be boiled in water for half a day, or even two days, to remove the resinous sap; then it was washed in cold

Editor's note: In addition to typed manuscripts in AMNH and BCPA, which contained only very short descriptions of the blanket, this section is based largely on the much fuller account in BCPA, entitled "245. Nar-^{kh}Heen. Chilkat Blanket 1891. From personal observation and information from a Chilkat blanket weaver of great experience." A few additions have been taken from the published memoir (Emmons 1907). I have added the comparative and historical information pertaining to the development of the classic Chilkat blanket from its geometric predecessor. The most recent studies of woven woolen blankets of the Tlingit are those by Cheryl Samuel (1982) and Bill Holm (1982), and Samuel's work on geometric patterned blankets (1987). I am indebted to both for their help with this section.

Hutsnuwu Raven leaders in ceremonial garb, at potlatch given to Wolf-Eagle clans, Angoon, c. 1901. Left to right: Youth wearing an abalone-incrusted "bear's ears" headdress and a Chilkat blanket; Mrs. Chief Mitlakettle in black (as a mourner?); Chief Mitlakettle of Basket Bay; and two unidentified younger men. (Photograph by Vincent I. Soboleff. BCPA.)

water, often weighted with stones in a stream and left until soft and pliable. It was then shredded by twisting and bending with the hands, to separate the fibers, and was dried on the fish drying rack. When needed, these bundles were softened by wetting, and the fibers made into a continuous strand by twisting between thumb and forefinger of the right hand. Then it was covered with loose wool, and again twisted, or spun on the leg, when the wool would take hold of the bark cord. All this was rolled into balls. A strand of double the length of the warp was cut from the ball, middled [folded in the middle], and twisted together and rolled on the leg as before. When done, this formed the thread of the warp. These warp strands were rolled into balls.

[This statement is confused, as Bill Holm has pointed out to me. I found it difficult to decipher, and may have misquoted. In his published work on the Chilkat blanket, Emmons (1907:335–36) indicated that the core of the warp thread was made up of two bark cords, each two-stranded, twisted, and covered with wool, then "laid up together," and rolled into balls. This was later cut up into lengths determined by wrapping it around the notched measuring stick.]

The warp was never colored; it was entirely enclosed by the woof, except for the side rolls and bottom fringe. The woof, in addition to the natural white, was dyed black, yellow, and blue-green. ["The only colors used in these blankets are or rather were in aboriginal days all of native dyes and were black, yellow blue or green and the natural wool"; Emmons's 1891 notes, BCPA.]

The black was obtained by steeping hemlock bark in old strong urine which had been kept in the common tub for several weeks and then allowed to stand for a week, and in another vessel a piece of copper was allowed to stand an equal period. Then boil the wool in the urine with the

Tlingit woman weaving a Chilkat blanket from a pattern board, Sitka. (Photograph by G. T. Emmons? BCPA.)

hemlock bark for a whole day. Then remove wool to pot of urine containing the copper and boil for a short time, half an hour or so. Then the wool was removed and washed and soaked in fresh water for a whole day, and then dried. During the day that the wool was being boiled, the woman had to abstain from food. [This rule was followed for each color used.] Black was [also] obtained from a marsh mud, or black soil from around the roots of decayed stumps, which was boiled with the fresh hemlock bark.

[Samuel (pers. comm., 1986) informs me that she has tried the local black mud, but this causes the yarn to disintegrate. She has been successful in using spring hemlock bark boiled in stale urine as a first dye bath, producing a red-brown color, followed by an overdye of copper oxidized in stale urine. If there is iron in the hemlock bark, as occurs around Klukwan and Haines, the wool instantly turns black with the copper-urine overdye; without iron, the black color comes more slowly, or remains a reddish-brown. Unfortunately this black dye makes the wool harsh and rather brittle, so that it sheds.]

The yellow dye was obtained from a tree moss (wolf moss, *Evernia vulpina*) known as *say-ho-nay* [ṡ̓é·x̣ʷani, a tree lichen], which is traded from the interior people and comes from the valley of the Yukon and is highly valued and expensive. The day before dying the wool, fresh urine (of children) was saved. The yellow moss was boiled for half an hour in this, until the color was extracted, then the yarn was added and boiled for a short time, and then left to steep. It was removed, washed in fresh water, and dried.

[Samuel (pers. comm., 1986) has verified this method, but reports that the yellow dye thus produced fades away quickly in the light, and will disappear in ten years. There are also other lichens, traditionally used by basket weavers, which will produce the same color as the wolf moss. She suggests these might not have been used because a sufficient quantity was perhaps not available. But claiming an imported origin for the dye material, even if untrue, would be a good excuse for charging a high price.]

The greenish-blue was obtained from an oxide of copper, again boiled in urine with the yarn, which was afterwards washed and dried.

[Emmons was here mistaken, as Bill Holm warned me: Copper and urine will not produce the green-blue color. In attempting to follow the lead he gave me, I sought information from both Judi Miller at the Canadian Conservation Institute, in Ottawa, and Cheryl Samuel. The latter confessed that for years she had been led astray by Emmons's copper-and-urine formula. The older yellow-green color was apparently produced by first boiling the wool in a copper-urine bath (producing an olive green), and then overdying it in a wolf moss yellow bath to get the desired yellow-green. While all of the older samples of Tlingit blanket tested positive for copper, the more recent ones with "Chilkat blue" had no copper. Then Samuel read Emmons's notes of 1891 in BCPA (which I myself had sorted in 1959 and of which I had obtained a photocopy!), in which he stated: "Latterly, this color [blue or green] has been obtained from blue blankets, boiling the wool with pieces of blanket." Samuel has since worked out the method of reproducing the correct "robin's egg blue" by overdying the trade cloth blue with wolf moss yellow.

[For a time in the late nineteenth century, trading stores flooded the country with colored wools, which the natives used to satisfy the tourist demand for Chilkat blankets. Later they returned to the original wool and dyes, according to Emmons. There are now [since 1980] a few women attempting to revive the art, but they are using commercial colored yarns, probably because mountain goat wool cannot be procured and they lack the time or skill to produce native dyes. Cheryl Samuel, who has mastered eighteenth and nineteenth century weaves, is now teaching the natives to make beautiful blankets.]

The material having been prepared, the loom was set up. It consisted of two slender uprights of maple which sometimes were elaborately carved [in the crest of the weaver's clan]. They each had two or three rectangular holes in the sides, above the middle, through which crossbars passed. The uppermost one, from which the warp was hung, was a broad flat board [or batten], pierced through its lower edge with tiny holes through which was rove a continuous sinew thread. This supported a hide thong over which the warp strands were middled and hung. Their lengths increased from the sides to the middle to give the blanket its pointed [or rounded] bottom. The other two crossbars were light narrow rods that were used only to support the frame or hold the weave in place as the work progressed. The weaver was seated on the floor in front of the loom, with her legs drawn up in front of her, and wove from left to right in a close twining of two woof strands over each warp strand in succession. [For cutting the warp strands to the proper lengths, a measuring staff with notches near one end was used.]

The design to be woven was taken directly and in exact size from a painted pattern board close at hand, on which [a little over] one half of the figure was shown in black. This figure was always an animal form, conventional and symbolic, very like that shown on all flat surfaces, such as house fronts, skin robes, and the sides of chests. But here it was divided perpendicularly into three fields: the larger central one presented the figure, opened out, while the narrow side divisions were [merely] decorative, although filled with conventional symbols and sometimes small forms. This arrangement of the blanket design was to show the figure to the best advantage, for as the blanket was worn over the shoulders, the main figure was spread out over the back, while the sides draped themselves in folds over the arms. At dances, when entering the house, the performers so dressed came in singly through the doorway, and danced with their back to the audience before each took his place in the line. In a few blankets, a single figure extended across the field without the divisions [or side panels]. Again, in a very old blanket, the body parts were placed without reference to their true connections with each other. [On the whole, the blanket designs resemble those of carved or painted boxes, on which the two profiles of a conventionalized head meet at one corner, while other parts of a body are fitted into the available spaces.]

[The pattern boards were painted by men.] These boards were highly valued; the painting of one was worth $5.00, and the boards themselves were valued at from $10 to $60. In working the blanket, the weaver made frequent reference to the board, [measuring the design elements] by means of a small piece of cedar bark marked with the right thumbnail. [To space out the fields and keep the blanket design properly centered, the weaver usually counted the warp strands carefully.] The woman in weaving worked the woof with the thumb and first two fingers of the right hand. The left hand was passed between the warp and the woof, and separated the warp strands, the first fingers of the left hand in the rear and the thumb in front. A practiced weaver used her fingers with great rapidity, and from the time of commencing a blanket, it would be finished in five to six months. The private mark of each weaver was worked in on each lower corner where the fringe begins, and generally consisted of two colors.

The blanket was woven from the head [top edge] down. The woof was made of two strands that were twined alternately over and under two warp strands. [For variations in the weave at the top and sides, see Emmons (1907) and Drucker (1950:263–65).] The warp threads were kept rolled up in bags of goat bladder and allowed to hang down. The blanket was worked parallel with the head, and when the figures were reached, a section between raised divisional lines was woven, then another one to the right of it was worked, leaving small eyes [along each edge], and the two sections were drawn together by sinew or fine wool thread, later cord, run through the eyes or small loops. The raised vertical lines separating divisions were obtained by letting in a number of yarns, generally of two colors, and these were worked as an extra warp by plaiting, half passing under and half over the woof. As the blanket was worked, the finished part was carefully kept clean by a covering of bear intestines, which was extended down as the weaving increased.

The color scheme of all blankets, regardless of pattern, is practically the same. The field is the natural white wool of the goat, and the figure is outlined in black bands or lines, while particular parts were filled with yellow and blue. These last colors were wholly for ornamental purposes, to give life to the picture, and their introduction certainly fulfilled this purpose, for the robe offered one of the most attractive examples of primitive decorative art of any people.

The finished blanket was used as a ceremonial robe by the wealthy, and every chief or prominent Tlingit possessed one or more. [It was owned and worn by men, women, and even by children for whom small blankets were woven.] They were used at ceremonies and dances, worn over one, or generally over both shoulders, and secured by thongs sewed to the head [top] of the blanket. Often they were

George Shotridge (Ye·ł gu·x̣u, "Raven's slave"), Emmons's friend, wearing a Chilkat blanket, Klukwan, 1900. (Photograph by Winter and Pond? AMNH.)

ornamented along the upper border with a strip of fur, such as sea otter, land otter [?], or mink. Blankets might be given to the more honored guests at potlatches, or cut into two or three strips to be given away. Such pieces were especially valued, as they could be later combined and made into [dance] aprons, leggings, or caps. Such aprons and leggings were ornamented with hide fringes with deer claws and puffin beaks. After a death, the blanket would be thrown over the body while it lay in state; others [belonging to the lineage] might be hung up and displayed. After cremation, or in the case of the shaman, after his burial, the blanket might be hung up over the gravehouse.

In addition to the blanket, a sleeveless robe that reached from the shoulders to the ankle was woven in the same way, of the same materials [with a design copied from a special pattern board. Some coats with sleeves were also made.] There were also aprons, leggings, and caps, but these smaller articles were more often made of pieces of blanket.

[The Chilkat blanket has been described in detail by Emmons (1907), with notes on the designs by Franz Boas, which, incidentally, illustrate the difficulties experienced by the Tlingit in interpreting the designs. There are further descriptions by Drucker (1950:263–65), Hirabyashi (1955), and most recently by Samuel (1982). Its origin, or rather its development from earlier forms, has been discussed by Carolyn Osborne (1964) and myself (de Laguna et al. 1964:170–72, 180–81), and most authoritatively by Holm (1982). Samuel (1986, 1987) has made definitive studies of the wool blankets in geometric style that preceded the classic Chilkat robe, and also of specimens that exhibit intermediate styles and techniques.

[Blankets of wool have a wide distribution in the Northwest—from the Alaska Peninsula to the Salish—and represent the transfer of weaving techniques (twining) from the ancient and more widely distributed mats of shredded bark or grass to wool. Both Holm (1982) and Samuel (1987) see the classic Chilkat robe as a nineteenth-century development from eighteenth-century antecedents, made possible by the invention of tapestry techniques needed to produce the formline crest patterns with rounded outlines. Also characteristic of Chilkat blankets are the use of yellow cedar bark as the core of the wefts, and the rounded bottom of the robe.

[The earlier blankets, in contrast, were rectangular, made of mountain goat wool and hair, without the addition of bark, and typically had heavily tasseled designs in black against the naturally white background, with "touches of yellow, sparingly applied" in horizontal bands (Samuel 1987:46). These designs of the Northern Geometric (Holm 1982; Samuel 1986) or Raven's Tail style (Samuel 1987) are clearly derived from those of Tlingit twined basketry, but, unlike the continuous twining of basket making, each row of weft twining in the blanket is done separately. It begins at the left selvage edge and ends at the right edge in a fringe (a corresponding fringe is added on the left side). Warp strands form the bottom fringe. These fringes are white. Patterns carried by black weft strands may form secondary fringes on the sides. Other black wefts may be introduced in the upper left corners of designs in the central field. There was nothing primitive about the weave, for these blankets utilized nine variations of two- and three-strand twining, whereas the classic Chilkat used only three (Samuel 1987:16). The top of the blanket was finished with a binding of sea otter fur.

[One group of seven known blankets—I retain the roman numerals assigned them by Samuel as useful guides to her illustrations and analyses (1987)—have very narrow borders of white with a black line, but wider inner borders patterned in vertical zigzags, horizontal zigzags and vertical bars, diamonds, "eye" lozenges, or diagonal lines in alternating directions to produce nested V-figures. The side borders are alike; the top and bottom borders differ from them and from each other. The white central field is decorated by black rectangular elements, woven in five to nine horizontal bands and aligned in five or six vertical columns. These may be nested ("concentric") rectangles ("one within another," to use the Tlingit name for the basketry design); "lazy" H-figures, lying on the side ("tattoo" design), similarly nested; and nested, squared C-shaped figures (one-half of "double around the cross"). All have long, black tassels falling from the lower left corners, where the introduced black wefts end. Blankets in this style are represented by fragments from a shaman's grave on Knight Island in Yakutat Bay, early postcontact (Osborne 1964; de Laguna et al. 1964:35–36; Samuel 1982; 1987, Robe III); also by fragments of a very similar blanket wrapped around a skull in a cave on Kruzof Island, near Sitka, said to be a shaman's grave also (Holm 1982, fig. 8; Samuel 1987, Robe II); the blanket worn by Chief "Kotlean" (Katlian) of Sitka, painted by Mikhail Tikhanov in 1818 (Shur and Pierce 1976, fig. on p. 43; Henry 1984, pl. on p. 46; Samuel 1987, Robe IV); a blanket sketched at Sitka (?) in 1827 by Pavel Mikhailov (Shur and Pierce 1978:36; Samuel 1987, Robe V); and three blankets (Samuel 1987, Robes I, VI, and VII) in Leningrad, originally believed to have been collected by Captain Cook (Gunther 1972:260–61; Kaeppler 1978:265; Rozina 1978:3, 10), they are now (Kaeppler 1983 and pers. comm.) identified as Tlingit, and were perhaps collected by Lisiansky (1804–5) or Golovnin (1818), presumably at Sitka. Two of these blankets (Robes VI and VII) were fur lined, achieved by introducing strips of fur, probably sea otter, among the wool and hair warp strands, and keeping the fur strands to the back in alternate slip-stitch twining.

[A second group of four blankets have wide borders of solid white, black, and yellow (suggestive of Chilkat style), and narrow inner borders patterned in black and white; the central field has an overall pattern, even though woven in bands. These are the "Lattice Robe" (Samuel 1987, Robe IX), in Copenhagen now but originally in the Leningrad collection, with bands of alternating diagonal lattice design, alternating with bands of zigzag-and-bars; the "Diamonds Robe" (Samuel 1987, Robe XI; Holm 1982, fig. 6), in the Cook-Banks collection of the British Museum, but also supposed to have been collected in 1792 (!), with a pattern of black and white diamonds, nested in black zigzags, giving a diagonal effect. The "Lattice Robe" has tassels that are not functional; the "Diamonds Robe" lacks them. The most beautiful robe of all is the famous "Swift Blanket" (Samuel 1987, Robe XV; Holm 1982, fig. 1), named for Captain Benjamin Swift who collected it about 1800, provenience unknown, on which the central field is divided in two, with differently patterned halves that would create the illusion that the wearer had mysteriously changed garments, as he turned around. The left side has bands of tasseled "lazy" H-figures, separated by bands of zigzag-and-bars; the right side has lattice bands (with nonfunctional black and white tassels) separated by bands of triangle-zigzag-and-bar units. Narrow bands of yellow running across the whole field give it a shimmer. Lastly, the "Three Panelled Robe" (Samuel 1987, Robe X), in the Leningrad collection, has the central design field divided vertically into three parts (as are many Chilkat blankets); these are decorated with nine horizontal bands of lattice, diamonds, zigzag-and-bar, and triangle-zigzag-and-bar motifs, the two sides alike and differing from the middle section.

[There are four more blankets that Samuel classes among the Raven's Tail robes because of the overall design arrangements and the lack of cedar bark in the warp, although they make use of Chilkat motifs, executed in Chilkat twining, and two add the yellow-green color used in the older Chilkat blankets. One of these blankets is the Lynn Canal robe (Samuel 1987, Robe XII; Holm 1982, fig. 9), which had been cut up and the pieces distributed at a potlatch. The larger piece was made into a tunic, collected in 1873 (now at Ottawa), and two smaller pieces into leggings (now in MAI, New York). Others are the "Single Eye Robe" (Samuel 1987, Robe XIII), known only from a photograph believed taken at the Kaigani Haida town of Howkan, 1884–1902; "Aichunk's Robe" (Samuel 1987, Robe XIV; Shur and Pierce 1976, upper fig. on p. 42), which belonged to a Koniag chief on the Alaska Peninsula, who was painted by Tikhanov in 1818 (although the blanket was probably traded from the south); and lastly, "Skatin's Robe" (Samuel 1987, Robe XV), now in Toronto but obtained from this Nishka Tsimshian chief by Marius Barbeau in 1927 when it was already one hundred years old.

[The central field on the first three blankets has horizontal bands of squared, nested, inverted U-figures ("double around the cross"), from the lower outer corners of which hang long tassels. Chilkat formline weaving outlines in black the perfectly round white circles in each arm of the U. The simplest in composition is Aichunk's blanket, on which the areas between the circles and the U outlines are bright yellow. The Lynn Canal and Single Eye blankets (XII and XIII) have formline motifs below the inverted U-figures, consisting of one or two eyes and several smaller U-elements or crescents, the whole suggesting an inverted face. In Robe XII, and probably in Robe XIII, yellow alternates with yellow-green in these spaces. The background of the central design area is white on Robe XIV, and probably on Robe XIII; that of the Lynn Canal robe (XII) is filled with zigzag-and-bar patterns. The Single Eye blanket (XIII) has a rounded bottom, like a Chilkat blanket, as has the last in the group, the Nishka chief's robe (XV). The central white area of this blanket has highly conventionalized formline motifs, in yellow, yellow-green, and black, vaguely suggestive of animal heads with ears at the top, a single "eye," and wide toothless mouth. The wide black border is broken by rectangular insets in Chilkat formline technique, five on the top and bottom, four on each side. These represent inverted human faces with black hair (fringes) falling from the forehead; the outlines of the faces and eyes, the nose, eyebrows, lips, and checkerboard teeth are worked in black. The faces were painted blue (presumably in imitation of the later, classic Chilkat blue dye). This blanket is most clearly transitional.

[Square inverted faces, alternating with octagon-in-a-square elements, fill the central area of a robe, which also has a border of formline motifs like those in Robes XII and XIII; this is in a sketch made by Sigismund Bacstrom in 1792 of a Sitkan (?) chief (Vaughn and Holm 1982, bottom center fig. on p. 208). Inverted faces continued through classic Chilkat style, as is shown in an apron collected before 1833 (Holm 1982, fig. 14); and was even reproduced on a painted board, worn hanging down the back of one dignitary at a Sitka potlatch, 1904 (de Laguna 1972, pl. 210 dd).

["The movement of weft strands out of the warp, and the weaving of these strands vertically by using the underlying horizontal wefts as their base, is the kernel of genius behind Chilkat weaving" (Samuel 1987:158). This made possible curved outlines and the copying of painted formline designs by the weaver, who now had not only to master weaving techniques but also to understand the complexities of the men's crest representations, since the pattern boards furnished to them lacked necessary, fine details. Except for top and bottom borders, no wefts run from selvage to selvage as in the Raven's Tail robes. The design elements are woven in separate blocks, joined together by drawstring and dovetail joins. Other critical changes in the Chilkat blanket were the use of yellow cedar bark in the warp strands, the heavy fringes, and the curved bottom edge.

[The Chilkat themselves have the tradition that they learned the techniques for making Chilkat blankets from the Tsimshian, who originally wove dance aprons. A Chilkat woman, married to a Tsimshian chief, learned and wove one of these, which was sent back to her relatives after her death. Her kinswomen carefully studied the apron and then rewove it; afterward they began to make blankets in the same style, the designs copied from those of the Tsimshian (Drucker 1950:263).

[Yet no early Tsimshian example exists to support this account, and the blanket (Samuel 1987, Robe XV) of the Nishka Chief, Skatin, is too uncertain in age to offer proof. The five blankets collected by Captain Cook in 1778 at Nootka Sound (Samuel 1987, figs. 434–38), obtained from "strangers" (Haida?), are accepted as transitional, yet overlap in time the geometric style robes. These blankets are of wool and cedar bark with patterned borders of zigzags and/or stylized eyes. The most famous of the five is the Vienna Blanket with stylized human faces, as well as rectangular figures in its top and bottom borders. Holm (1982:36, fig. 5) identifies it as "the earliest known formline twined textile from the Northwest Coast," although Samuel (1987:157–58, figs. 438–42) finds it "not totally successful" but representing a "step towards the solution" of weaving curved forms.

[Perhaps the earliest references to woven woolen blankets are to be found in the reports of Fray Tomás de la Peña and Fray Juan Crespi, who were on the First Bucareli Expedition of 1774. In the vicinity of Dall Island they encountered twenty-one canoes of natives, presumably Kaigani Haida, who came to the ship to trade. Fray de la Peña wrote (in Griffin 1891:122–23):

> [The natives in the canoes] brought a great quantity of mats, skins of various animals and fish, hats made of rushes and caps made of skins, bunches of feathers arranged in various shapes, and, above all, many coverlets, or pieces of woven woolen stuffs very elaborately embroidered and about a yard and a half square, with a fringe of the same wool about the edges and various figures embroidered in distinct colors. [Both men and women wore garments of the woven cloth or of skins.]

[Fray Crespi (in Griffin 1891:191–92) described these "coverlets" in more detail:

> [Among the trade goods offered the Spaniards were blankets of skins sewn together, and] coverlets, or blankets, of fine wool, or the hair of animals that seemed like wool, finely woven and ornamented with the same hair of various colors, principally white, black and yellow, the weaving being so close that it appeared as though done in a loom. All these coverlets have around the edge a fringe of some thread twisted, so that they are very fit for table-cloths, or covers, as if they had been made for that purpose. They gave us, also, some little mats, seemingly made of fine palm leaves [cedar bark], wrought in different colors. . . . They gave us, also, some girdles very closely woven of threads of wool or hair. . . .

These Indians also wore cloaks of woven wool "of different colors in handsome patterns" (p. 192), as well as skin garments, and the women were similarly dressed.

[Mourelle (in La Pérouse 1799, 1:246) wrote that the Tlingit of Bucareli Bay in 1779 were wearing:

> over their shoulders a kind of mantle, a yard and half long, and a yard wide, of the same texture as the *peillons* of Peru [presumably woolen serapes], round which is a fringe four or five inches deep, made of threads regularly twisted. [And he further reported (p. 248) that the Indians wanted to trade] coverlets [or mantles] of coarse linen [!], white clouded with brown, very well woven, but in small quantity: broad ribbands of the same, which might be compared with the covering of the *matrasses* of the Spanish officers. [He also mentioned (p. 247)] stuffs well woven, and clouded with different colours.

[Potap Zaikov, who was in Prince William Sound in 1783, wrote in his journal (in Tikhmenev [1861–63] 1979:4–5) that he took from a Chugach summer camp "a rug made of white wool resembling sheep's wool, with ornaments made of the same wool and dyed yellow and brown." Petroff (manuscript in Bancroft Library, Berkeley; in de Laguna et al. 1964:180) translated this passage to mean that the blanket was "plaited and fringed, [and] ornamented with yellow and coffee color."

[Captain Cook (Cook and King 1785, 2:368) in 1778 saw, in Prince William Sound, "one or two woollen garments like those of Nootka," from which we may infer that these had only simple geometric decorations. James Strange, who visited Prince William Sound as a trader in 1786 (1928:42–43), saw

> . . . a most excellent Substitute for our thickest and warmest Bath rugs. I used my Endeavours to procure a piece of this Cloth, without however succeeding; although the Price I offered for it was equal to what would have purchased half a Dozen good otter skins; it was presumable therefore that the material wherewith it is made is very scar[ce] and the possession only of the principal Men. I procured a Skin of the Animal of which it is made, which has more the Appearance of a Sheep Skin, than any other Animal I know.

[La Pérouse, who was in Lituya Bay in 1786, wrote (1799, 1:406):

> The Americans of Port des Français know how to forge iron, fashion copper, spin the hair of diverse animals, and form with the needle, of the thread thus procured, a stuff not unlike French tapestry. They intermingle with this slips of otter-skin, which gives their cloaks a resemblance of the finest silk plush.

[Beresford, who had been with Captain Dixon at Port Mulgrave (Yakutat), Norfolk Sound (Sitka Sound), Cloak Bay on North Island (Queen Charlottes), and King George Sound (Nootka) in 1787, wrote of the Northwest Coast Indians in general an appreciation of their skills, citing first how they bent the iron knives received from the Russians into what were apparently crooked knives, and their skill in carving (1789:244):

> The ingenuity of these people is not confined to devices in wood, or drawings on bark; they manufacture a kind of variegated blanket or cloak, something like our horse cloths; they do not appear to be wove [on a loom], but made entirely by hand; and are neatly finished: I imagine these cloaks are made of wool collected from the skins of beasts killed in the chace [*sic*]; they are held in great estimation, and only worn on extraordinary occasions.

[The Russians, Ismailov and Bocharov, who came to Yakutat in 1788, described the dress of the Indians as consisting, in part, of an "upper garment, the outside of which is woollen," which suggests that it may have been fur-lined. It was worn "thrown over the shoulder," like a blanket. Among the goods offered in trade by the natives were "woollen clothes of their own manufacture" (Shelikhov in Coxe 1803:326, 328).

[Malaspina, who was at Yakutat in 1791, wrote (1885:348 in Spanish): "Finally among the woven materials, special attention is merited by the blanket of pine (cedar) bark, spun and woven, on which is inserted on one part with good symmetry the fur of the skin of an otter." A blanket of this type was collected for the Royal Cabinet at Madrid. Suría and Cardero, Malaspina's artists, sketched Indian men wearing long robes that fell from the neck to the ankles, or to the bulge of the calf. These seemed to have been of woven materials, with up to seven rows of dark tassels hanging down, as well as fringes at the bottom and sides (de Laguna 1972, pls. 50, 59, 60), clearly showing blankets of the northern geometric type.

[In 1792, Captain Caamaño described a robe (quoted in Holm 1982:43) as "made of the inner wool of the wild goat. This wool is very fine in the thread; well spun, and well woven. Narrow strips of sea-otter fur are worked into this; and are so neatly sewn that the outer side of the garment has the appearance of a whole skin, while nothing is noticeable on the inner side. . . . The back part is decorated with various figures or patterns in a purple colour. Altogether, this cloak is quite the best piece I have seen by them." (The designs were evidently worked in the rich, reddish black of hemlock bark

Raven's tail geometric-type blanket of twined mountain goat wool, 70½ inches long. Collected by Captain Benjamin Swift, 1800. (Photograph by Hillel Burger. Courtesy of the Peabody Museum, Harvard University.)

dye, without iron; and the wearer had turned the cloak inside out, to display the fur lining.)

[Marchand (in Fleurieu 1801, 1:344), commenting on the industry and skills of the Sitka Tlingit in 1791, mentioned with approval, "cloaks of spun hair, woven in a workman-like manner, intermixed with pieces of otter-skin, and extremely well calculated as a preservative from the cold. . . ."

[Vancouver's Lieutenant Whidbey, on an exploration of Lynn Canal in 1794, encountered a party of Chilkat, led by a chief of consequence, of whom Vancouver wrote (1801, 5:430): "His external robe was a very fine large garment, that reached from his neck down to his heels, made of wool from the mountain sheep, neatly variegated with several colours, and edged and otherwise decorated with little tufts, or frogs of woollen yarn, dyed of various colours."

[Lisiansky, at Sitka 1804–5, commented on the native costume (1814:238): "The rich wrap themselves up sometimes in white blankets, manufactured in the country, from the wool of the wild sheep, which is as soft and fine as the Spanish merino. These blankets are embroidered with square figures, and fringed with black and yellow tassels. Some of them are so curiously worked on one side with the fur of the sea-otter, that they appeared as if lined with it, and are very handsome."

[Von Langsdorff, at Sitka in 1805–6, also wrote (1814, 2:132): "A principal employment of the women is to make a

Late prehistoric pebble amulet, Old Town, Knight Island, Yakutat Bay. Obverse and reverse views to show design representing a masked shaman, wearing a Raven's tail geometric blanket and apron of similar weave (de Laguna et al. 1964, fig. 21.)

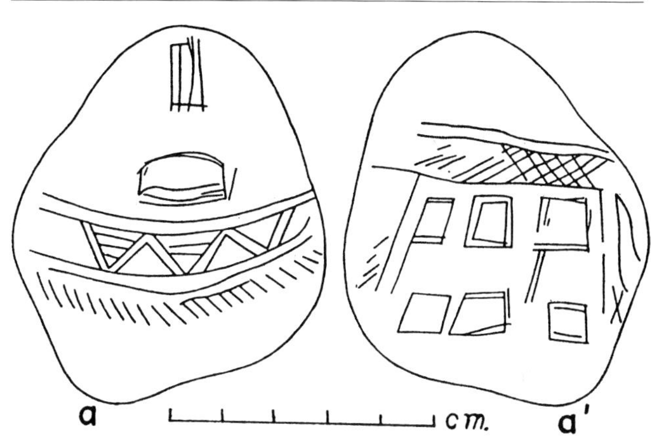

sort of carpeting of the wool of a wild sheep, which, to the best of my knowledge, is not yet included in any Natural History."

[The wool in every case was not that of the mountain (Dall) sheep, but that of mountain goats, as Lütké (1835, 1:213) and Caamaño recognized. "Variegated colors" may mean no more than the use of yellow and black (or dark brown) in addition to the white of the natural wool. The classic Chilkat blanket has an additional color: the blue-green which replaced the yellow-green of some of the oldest examples. The only designs specifically mentioned in the accounts quoted above are the "square figures" and the "black and yellow tassels" of Lisiansky's account, and consequently we have no evidence yet for the developed Chilkat dancing robe.

[Fortunately, Lütké in 1826–29, on his voyage around the world, took with him two artists, A. F. Postels and Baron Kittlitz. The former is believed to have made the first known sketch, in watercolor, of a Tlingit chief wearing a Chilkat blanket (Holm 1982, fig. 11; Henry 1984, pl. 4). According to Henry, "The Tlingit chief . . . is clothed in a Chilkat blanket, spruce root hat [painted on brim and crown in red and black crest designs], and Athabaskan leggings [combination boot-trousers] traded from the mainland interior. [He also wears an apron in Chilkat weave.]" The chief's costume, including the dagger and sheath, is now in the Anthropological Museum of the Lomonosnov University in Moscow (Bill Holm, pers. comm.). Holm (1982:46) wrote of this painting that it is "so carefully drawn that both blanket and apron designs can be identified with existing pieces of the same pattern." One of these is the apron in Vancouver (Holm 1982, fig. 12); others are in Leningrad and Chicago. A blanket like that in Postel's painting is of much later date (Holm 1982:46), showing the constancy of design patterns, once established. We can conclude that the classic Chilkat blanket of the Tlingit had appeared by 1827, the date of Lütké's and Postel's stay at Sitka, but that it was worn contemporaneously with blankets of fully geometric and transitional types. A blanket woven and decorated in Chilkat style, but with two "coppers" as major elements in the somewhat empty side panels, was given in 1832 by Captain R. B. Forbes to the Peabody Museum in Salem, and is hailed by Samuel (1982:81, fig. 85) and Holm (1982, fig. 15) as the earliest documented, and one of the finest, examples of the classic Chilkat robes.

[That the northern geometric blanket with fringes, zigzag or diamond border design, and tasseled rectangles in the central design field is as old as late prehistoric or protohistoric times among the Northern Tlingit (or Eyak?) is shown by the figure incised on both sides of a pebble amulet, from the site of "Old Town" on Knight Island, Yakutat Bay (de Laguna et al. 1964:171–72, fig. 21 *a, a'*). This I have interpreted as representing a masked shaman, wearing such a blanket and also a heavily fringed apron with zigzag decoration. The blanket must have been like that found in the grave on the island (Osborne 1964; Samuel 1987, Robe III), but considerably older, since the site contained no evidence of direct contact with whites.]

CHAPTER 9

Dress and Decoration

PERSONAL CLEANLINESS*

In habits of personal cleanliness, the Tlingit have unquestionably improved, and soap has taken the place of urine which was formerly the only solvent for grease. As late as 1885 I saw at Klukwan large tubs of urine just within the doorway that were used for washing the body and clothes, tanning skins, and fixing colors used in basket weaving.

The sweat bath was taken after a hunting trip or travel, and hot springs at several points throughout the islands were resorted to in case of disease, as a tonic or luxury. In cold weather, when in the vicinity of these natural basins, the Indians might sit in the water all night and sleep comfortably with the head just out of the water, when too lazy to build and keep up a fire.

Washing the face and hands was generally practiced upon rising. The women took great care of their hair, which was considered a feature of beauty, although it was not an unusual sight to see one carefully going over another's head for vermin. But from personal experience, living in their houses and sleeping with my hunters in camp, I have never suffered the slightest inconvenience from this source.

Strangers judge their cleanliness from the general untidiness of their houses, the odor of smoked fish and rancid oil, and their faded clothing, but the latter they wash continually, and when blankets were universally worn, a soiled one was the exception.

I once made a canoe trip of several hundred miles, my crew consisting of a fine old native and two younger men, and an Irish sailor brought up in all of the cleanly habits of the Navy. The first morning out my sailor introduced the old man to a thorough scrub that was regularly followed afterwards. When upon the return trip within two days of my destination, we took on board the old wife of the steersman. Early the next morning we were disturbed by a great row in their tent which resulted from his insistence that the old wife should strip and bathe as he had been taught to do. This simply illustrates the adaptability of the Tlingit to accept our ways, and accounts for the changed conditions that the past few years have brought in their manner of living.

To harden the body and make one's spirit indifferent to discomfort and suffering, the men and boys over eight years of age used to plunge into the cold water of the sea in the winter mornings an hour or so before dawn. This custom was still practiced at Sitka as late as 1883. The village was awakened by a loud shout which was immediately answered from every house as the men rushed out naked and plunged into the sea, uttering piercing shrieks as they crouched in the ice cold water while others beat them on the backs with bunches of switches, to increase circulation. This might last for ten or more minutes, when all would return to their beds, and quiet was restored.

[Since the hair was often dressed with grease, the smell was offensive to European noses. In addition, the dark paint that was used to protect the face from sunburn and from insect bites was often regarded as dirty. For example, Dixon's men persuaded one young woman at Yakutat to wash her face and hands, and then were surprised to see her beautiful healthy skin (Beresford 1789:171), which would not have reminded them of an English milkmaid's if it had not been protected.

[Von Langsdorff, who was at Sitka in 1805–6, wrote (1814, 2:112):

> . . . They [the Tlingit] have black hair and dirty complexions, which are rendered worse by the earths, the coal, and the different coloured ochres with which they besmear themselves. . . . Some of the women and girls, who live chiefly with the Russian Promüschleniks, when their skins are clean, and purified from the dirt, which they consider as ornamental, have complexions as fair as those of many Europeans, and by no means unpleasing features.

Editor's note: Most of the material in this chapter was originally in "Chapter IV, The Tlingit People," where Emmons had also placed sections on "Physical Type," "Character," "Disease," and "Music."

**Editor's note:* This section was moved from the original "Chapter V, Domestic Life." To it I have added observations by Beresford and von Langsdorff on washing, and Crespi, Portlock, and Marchand on lice.

[We should probably here call attention to the lice with which the natives were infested. Captain Portlock, reporting on the experiences of the seaman, Woodcock, who was sent as a hostage to stay with the Tlingit of Portlock Harbor, when the *King George* was anchored there in August 1787, wrote (1789:286):

> These poor wretches [the Tlingit], by living in so filthy a manner, were intirely [*sic*] covered with vermin; but this they seemed to consider as no kind of inconvenience; for at any time when the lice grew troublesome they picked and ate them with the greatest relish and composure: sometimes indeed, when they were greatly pestered, and had not an opportunity of ridding themselves of their guests in that manner, they would turn their jackets, and wear the inside outwards, by way of giving them a few hours respite.
>
> Poor Woodcock soon became as much incumbered with vermin as his companions, but use had not as yet reconciled him to such troublesome guests, and he felt his situation extremely disagreeable. The Indians endeavoured to persuade him to dispose of them in the manner they did; but this was so totally repugnant to his feelings, that they soon perceived his dislike to their proposal. At length he persuaded one of the women to rid him of the vermin, and she (probably considering them as a peculiar dainty) accepted the offer with pleasure, and entirely cleared him from everything of the kind.

[A reason for eating the lice may have been similar to that requiring that a log destined for a canoe or house post should be burned with fire made from its own chips, thus returning the strength that had been taken from it. Were mosquitoes that had drawn blood also eaten to return the blood to its rightful owner? More likely, the Indians were simply killing lice by cracking them with their teeth, not actually eating them.

[Captain Marchand, at Sitka in 1791, also commented on the lice (Fleurieu 1801, 1:327–28):

> The individuals of both sexes, children, whether young and old, are covered with vermin: they assiduously hunt those devouring animals, but in order to devour them themselves; and they appear so keen after them, that one might be tempted to believe that it is for the purpose of husbanding themselves the pastime of hunting in the *vale of pleasure,* that they suffer them to multiply. The furs which they sell to strangers are so infested with them, that whatever pains be taken to rid the skins of those insects, they soon increase to such an excess, that it becomes impossible for the crew of a ship to escape their pursuit and voracity: it may be said, that, in taking a cargo of furs, a vessel takes a cargo of lice.]

CLOTHING*

The primitive clothing [na· ʔát] of the Tlingit can best be described as detailed in the narratives of the early explorers. Since their expeditions were largely in the interest of trade in furs, they tried to discourage the use of furs by the natives, and, in their place, supplied blankets and manufactured materials, which, though accepted, did not entirely displace the original articles of dress which could be seen in use as late as 1885.

[Reports of eighteenth-century explorers and traders show clearly that the Tlingit were avid receivers of European dress, especially naval uniforms, or exotic materials. This love of uniforms lasted all through the nineteenth century.

[The clothing of the Haida encountered off Dall Island in Alaska by the First Bucareli Expedition of 1774 was presumably very similar to that of the nearby Tlingit. Thus, according to Fray Crespi (in Griffin 1891:192):

> All appeared with the body completely covered, some with skins of otter and other animals, others with cloaks woven of wool, or hair which looked like fine wool, and a garment like a cape and covering them to the waist, the rest of the person being clothed in dressed skins or the woven woolen cloths of different colors in handsome patterns. Some of these garments have sleeves; others have not. Most of them wore hats of reeds [spruce root], such as I have described. [These were (p. 191) "some coarse and others of better quality, most of them painted, their shape being . . . conical with a narrow brim, and having a string which passing under the chin keeps the hat from being carried away by the wind."] The women are clothed in the same manner. [And they wear the labret.]

[Fray de la Peña (in Griffin 1891:123) also described the Kaigani dress seen off Dall Island:

> [The women's] dress consists of a cape with a fringe about the edge and a cloth reaching to the feet, made of their woven woolen stuff, or of skins, and covering the whole body. . . . The men are also covered, with skins or with the woven cloths of wool, and many have capes like those of the women; but they do not hesitate about remaining naked when occasion for selling their clothing offers.]

**Editor's note:* This section was intended by Emmons to be made up largely of quotations from appropriate sources. I have corrected and in some cases amplified his quotations from Mourelle, La Pérouse, Marchand, Vancouver, and von Langsdorff, adding to these the necessary introductory phrases. In addition, I have provided quotations from Crespi and de la Peña, Portlock (summarized), Beresford, Ismailov and Bocharov, Malaspina, Suría, Lisiansky, von Kotzebue, Golovin, and Krause.

Mourelle, in Bucareli Bay in 1779, reported (in La Pérouse 1799, 1:246):

> The women evince in their dress the modesty and decency of their manners. . . . Their principal garment is a long robe of smooth skin, girded about the loins, and not unlike that of our monks, covering them from the neck to the feet, and with sleeves reaching down to the wrists . . . [with other robes on top during cold weather].

And referring to the dress of the men, he wrote (pp. 245–46):

> Their clothing consists of one or more raw skins (with the hair probably) of otters, seals, benades (a species of deer), bears, or other animals, which they take in the chace [*sic*]. With these they are covered from the neck to the midleg; and many of them wear boots of skin without the hair, much resembling English boots, except that they are laced up before. On their heads they wear hats made of narrow slips of bark woven together in the shape of a funnel, or of a cone. . . . [They also wear a fringed and presumably woven woolen mantle or cape (see "The Chilkat Blanket" in Chapter 8).]

La Pérouse spent almost all of July 1786 in Lituya Bay, and described the summer clothing of the Tlingit men (1799, 1:401):

> A simple skin is thrown over their shoulders, and the rest of the body is left naked, except the head, which they commonly cover with a little straw hat, curiously woven. . . .
>
> Some of the Indians had complete shirts of otter-skins; and the common dress of the grand chief was a shirt of tanned elk-skin, bordered with a fringe of deer's hoofs and beaks of birds, the jingling of which when he danced was not unlike that of sheep's bells. [Although this is called his "common dress," this Athabaskan type costume was probably reserved for special occasions, like visits to the French ships. (p. 401)] . . . Though they go barefoot, the soles of their feet are not callous, and they cannot walk over stones. . . . [p. 400]

[Although Captain Portlock was interested in the ornaments worn by the Tlingit of Portlock Harbor and Sitka Sound, he said only of their dress in 1787 (1789:289): "Their [the women's] apparel is the same kind as wore by the men. . . ." This description is not very helpful, since he never attempted to describe the dress of the men. We gather that it was of skins, made into a frock, loose enough so that some of the men were able to hide under it the things they wanted to steal. One of the chiefs who visited the ship for ceremonial trading wore an old European coat of scarlet that had once had gold or silver braid on the shoulders, a garment obviously reserved for very special occasions (Portlock 1789:282). We also gather that Tlingit women went barefoot, at least when they had occasion to go into the water (p. 292).

[Beresford, who was with Captain Dixon in 1787, described the clothing worn by the Tlingit of Norfolk (Sitka) Sound (1789:189)]:

> The cloaths wore universally on the coast are made of skins sewed together in various forms, . . . [A chief happened to see a piece of Sandwich (Hawaiian) Island cloth (tapa?) which he wanted and which was given him. He reappeared early next morning] dressed in a coat made of the Sandwich Island cloth given him the day before, and cut exactly in the form of their skin-coats, which greatly resemble a waggoner's frock, except the collar and wrist-bands. . . . the coat fitted exceedingly well; the seams were sewed with all the strength the cloth would admit of, and with a degree of neatness equal to that of an English mantua-maker.

[And later Beresford wrote (p. 191):

> Besides their ordinary dress, the natives at this place have a peculiar kind of cloaks made purposely to defend them from the inclemency of the weather. I had no opportunity of examining them minutely, but they appear to be made of reeds sewed very closely together [twined cedar bark?]. . . . [like the rain capes of the New Zealand Maori].

[Beresford also had observations about the Northwest Coast in general, having visited Cook Inlet, Prince William Sound, Yakutat, Sitka, the Queen Charlottes, and Nootka (1789:239):

> In their dress, there is little variety; the men generally wearing coats (such as I have already described [see above, at Sitka]) made of such skins as fancy suggests, or their success in hunting furnishes them with, and sometimes the loose cloak thrown over the shoulders, and tied with small leather strings. Besides this, some of the more civilized sort, particularly those in Cook's River [Cook Inlet], wear a small piece of fur tied round the waist, when the heat of the day causes them to throw their coat aside, or they are disposed to sell it. [We gather that the Tlingit and Haida men were not so modest!] The dress of the women differs in some respects from that of the men: their under garment is made of fine tanned leather, and covers the body from the neck to the ancle [*sic*], being tied in different parts to make it fit close: over this is tied a piece of tanned leather like an apron, and which reaches no higher than the waist; the upper garment is made in much the same manner as the men's coats, and generally of tanned leather, the women not caring to wear furs, as they were always unwilling to be stripped of their garments, which, should they happen to be worth purchasing, their husbands always insisted on their being sold; indeed, the deportment of the women in general was decent, modest, and becoming.

[Ismailov and Bocharov, reporting on their visit to Yakutat in 1787 (in Coxe 1803:326), also mentioned the native dress:

Their upper garment, the outside of which is woollen, is thrown over the shoulder, and like the Tunguses they sometimes tie round their necks a kind of apron [dancing bib?], ornamented with beaks of birds, and other trifles, which make a rattling noise. [The Chilkat chief who had come to Yakutat gave the Russians six shirts of sea otter fur, but the cut is not described, nor is there any information about women's clothing, except (p. 327):] The dress of the women is similar to that of the men.

[Fortunately, Malaspina (1849:286–87) has left us a more complete description of Yakutat clothing in 1791:

The clothing of the men is regularly a cape of nutria [otter] pelts, of wolves or of martens over the body, with a band (sash) on the lower part of the abdomen. They cover their heads with hats of straw [spruce roots] in the form of a truncated cone. The women are decently clothed with a kind of under tunic of tanned skin, and on top wear a cape of nutria or marten which is very well sewn together with thread.

[Suría, the artist, not only has left us his sketches of Yakutat men and women (see de Laguna 1972, pls. 44–57), but a fuller description of dress and decoration (in Wagner 1936):

They [the men] were dressed in skins of various colors, well-tanned, large and flexible. With one which hangs from a skin tied around their waist [i.e., an apron or breech clout] they cover their private parts and the other which reaches to the knees they hang from the shoulder like a cape. The skins seem to be those of bears, tigers, lions [brown bear?], and some of deerskins, and of marmots, with the hair outside. [p. 247]

. . . The dress of the women is very modest. It consists of a robe of tanned skin and without hair which covers them from their throat down to their feet, and the breast and arms, down to the wrist. There is a sleeve which is wide but modest. In all, this tunic has the same form as that which they put on the effigy of Jesus Nazareno and tie around the waist. Besides this robe they wear a cape or square cape also of skin which is held on the right shoulder by a piece of leather and some living on the banks of the sea wear [only] a fringe. Some use these cloaks made strictly of marten skins.

The dress of the men is as I have stated, of various skins, the most ordinary being of black bear, and very hairy. When it rains and they have no hats they cover their heads with the same skin of the head of a bear, which makes them look like some Hercules. The rest of the skin they gather in at the waist by means of a piece of leather and what is left of the animal, claws and tail, etc., hangs down to the middle of the leg. From this it may be inferred that the arms, breast, stomach and belly are uncovered except the shoulders and the rump. In order that this skin may not get loose they sustain it on the right shoulder by means of another connecting piece of leather. Some besides this wear another skin which we can call a cape or cloak, as it serves the same purpose. Others go entirely naked with a breech clout. [p. 255]

[Children at Yakutat went naked. And so, at times, or virtually so, did the men, for Suría wrote of the chief (in Wagner 1936:249):

A large lion [brown bear] skin for a cape was gathered in at the waist and left entirely bare his breast, arms, thighs, and endowments, very muscular and strong. . . . [And his older son] was dressed in a black bear skin and very hairy, also in the form of a cloak which he fastened with some ornament, leaving bare at times all his nakedness, and passing to and fro over the quarter-deck, very proud and straight, his look full of ire, arrogant, and condescending.

[Marchand, who was in Sitka Sound in 1791, reported on Tlingit dress (Fleurieu 1801, 1:330–31):

The dress of men and women of TCHINKITÂNAY consists of a sort of shirt of tanned skin, sewed at the sides, the wide sleeves of which reach only a little below the shoulder, and a fur cloak which is worn with the hair on the outside. Over this, the women wear, besides, an apron of the same skin which comes no higher than the waist, and another otter cloak over the former. . . . When the cold is not sharp, the men throw off the skin shirt, and content themselves with the skin cloak, which admits of part of their body being seen naked. . . . Both sexes make use of a small hat, made of bark, plaited, and in the form of a cone truncated at a fourth or a third of its height: but, most frequently, the men have the head bare; their thick hair, mixed with ochre and down of birds, forms a natural head-dress, which, in ordinary weather, must be sufficient to protect the head from the injury of the air.

[By this date, however, both Malaspina and Marchand remarked on the avidity with which the Tlingit men sought European clothing.

[Von Langsdorff, who visited Sitka in 1805–6, after the Russians had retaken the area, wrote about the native costume (1814, 2:112–13):

The cloathing of these people is very simple, consisting of a covering round the waist, and an outer garment made of a piece of cloth, or skin, about five feet square, two ends of which are either tied round the neck, or fastened together with a button and button-hole. In latter years, since they had so much intercourse with the people of the United States of America, they have obtained from them a sort of carter's frocks, made after the European fashion, of woollen cloth, so that it is no uncommon thing here to see Indians dressed like Europeans. Red and blue are the colours which they prize the most. These garments are, however, only worn in their visits to the town, or in severe cold;

Dress of inhabitants of Port Mulgrave, Yakutat, 1791. Left. *Woman with baby.* Right. *Man in fur robe, and man in woven blanket and hat. (Sketches by Tomás Suría. Courtesy of Yale University Library.)*

> when employed in their domestic concerns, in felling timber, in fishing, in making canoes, &c. &c., they commonly go quite naked. Little children at the breast, though the cold is at eight or ten degrees, are scarcely covered, having only something of an old rag or mat wrapped round them. It cannot but excite the astonishment of people accustomed to warmer climates or more cloathing, to see how much the bodies of these people are proof against cold; scarcely will any other nation be found where they are so hardened against the effects of a very rough climate.

[And later (p. 114):

> The women never go naked; their whole bodies, and even their breasts, are at all times covered: many of them wear a sort of long shift, but their feet are always bare.

[When von Langsdorff with Captain D'Wolf went to visit the group of Sitkans who had fled the Russians to establish themselves in a fort near Chatham Strait, they were surprised by the welcome given them, when "Some hundred naked men armed with muskets, and others carrying large fire-brands, thronged to the landing-place . . ." to receive their visitors (von Langsdorff 1814, 2:125).

[Lisiansky (1814:237–38) adds little to our knowledge of dress at Sitka at this period, reporting only:

> The men cover their body with square pieces of woollen cloth, or buck-skin: some dress themselves in a kind of short pantaloon, and a garment resembling a shirt, but not so large. [And in winter, the rich wore goat wool blankets, as reported in Chapter 8.]

[Lisiansky also wrote (p. 241): "The use of the needle is said to be but little understood by the women. I have seen, however, some of their dresses that were neatly sewed, and extremely well made."

[Von Kotzebue (1830:49–50), described the Tlingit dress at Sitka in 1825:

> Their usual clothing consists of a little apron; but the rich wear blankets, purchased from the Russians, or from the American ships, and tied by two corners round the neck, so that they hang down and cover the back. Some of them wear bear-skins in a similar manner. The most opulent possess some European garments, which they wear on great occasions, and which would have an absurd effect were they not so disgusting as to extinguish all inclination to laugh. They never cover the head but in heavy rain, and then protect it with round caps of grass [spruce root hats], so ingeniously and closely plaited as to exclude every drop of water.
>
> Whatever the degree of heat or cold, they never vary their costume; and I believe there is not a people in the world so hardened against the weather. In winter, during a cold of 10° of Reaumur, the Kalushes walk about naked, and jump into the water as the best method of warming themselves. At night they lie without any covering, under the open sky, near a great fire, so near indeed as to be sometimes covered by the hot ashes. The women whom I have seen were either dressed in linen shifts reaching to their feet, or in plaited mats.

[By 1860, the Tlingit were generally wearing "a shirt and a woolen blanket, but many like to dress in European clothes" (Golovin [1862] 1979:28).

[Aurel Krause ([1885] 1956:101–2) had to report that in 1881:

> The aboriginal costume can no longer be found anywhere among the Tlingit. Not only European materials but also ready-made garments are found everywhere, as we learned from the accounts of the fur traders, since very early times. . . .
>
> The place of the skin shirts has been taken today by calico shirts of white and blue, and the fur cape which consisted of a blanket of skins sewn together is being crowded out by the woolen blanket. Blankets of marmot skin though are still being worn by the Chilkat.
>
> A woolen blanket now is the most indispensable piece of clothing of an Indian.

[Trousers had been introduced by Europeans, and in 1881 were almost universally worn by the men. The Indians still went barefooted and bareheaded, except that in winter the Chilkat wore moccasins copied from or obtained from the interior, and during the summer fishing season the spruce root hat might be worn to protect the face from the sun. The only survivals of the aboriginal costume seem to have been reserved for ceremonial occasions: funerals, potlatches, and shamanistic performances.]

A general agreement of the foregoing sources indicates that the women were wholly clothed in a long shift [or dress, ƛ̓a·k] of dressed skin, reaching from the neck to below the knee, either sewed up on both sides with short wide sleeves, or as a loose robe fastened over the shoulder and tied around the body, an apron of dressed skin about the waist, and one or two mantles of fur over the shoulders, as the weather demanded. The men wore a dressed skin shirt [gu·dáṡ or k̓udáṡ] and a square mantle of fur, but when at work were completely naked. Moccasins [tí·ƚ] of tanned skin and sealskin boots [x̣ʷán] reaching halfway to the knees, were worn when hunting, but generally hunters were barefooted. Ordinarily neither sex wore any head covering, but in canoe travel, to protect them from the heat of the summer sun to which they were particularly sensitive, and from the glare from the water, or from rain, they wore the woven spruce root hat. Little children were scantily clothed in a single loose skin garment, and in a loose shirt or dress for a girl (in later days of cotton). I have seen them so dressed, barefooted in the snow, and seemingly indifferent to the cold. Indeed, I remember seeing a little boy almost naked strap a skate on his bare foot and play on the ice in winter.

The tanned skin dress was ornamented with fringe strips and bands painted red. Beadwork was not employed on the dress, and porcupine quill work was only on clothing procured in trade from the interior tribes. The early adoption of our dress consisted in discarding the tanned deer or caribou skin dress and shirt for that of wool or cotton, and in using the trade blanket [x̣ú·w], as well as that of fur, as an outer covering in cold weather. Mining and fishing enterprises later gave employment to the natives, and with an abundance of money and with access to trading stores, the natives adopted our clothes, retaining the native dress only for ceremonial occasions.

Moccasins were worn in the house principally by women, and by men with snowshoes and on the trail on dry snow. Generally the men went barefoot, on account of the prevailing wet [which would rot skin footgear]. Moccasins were ordinarily of tanned deer or hair seal skin, in the latter case, the hair remained intact on the outside; but the best quality moccasins were made of caribou or moose hide procured in trade from the interior. The moccasin consisted of three parts: the footing (which included the sole, sides, and body) cut in the shape of a parallelogram, the tongue of skin or cloth, and the extension top of a softer skin that was folded around the ankle and was secured with tie strings. There was a middle front seam from toe to tongue;

Little girl with a black silk kerchief, beaded dance bib, and ground squirrel (?) robe, Sitka, 1889 or 1890. (Photograph by G. T. Emmons? AMNH.)

the T-shaped sewing of the heel formed a horizontal seam or a flat trailer. The primitive moccasin was plain, but with the acquisition of colored cloths and beads, it became ornamented over the tongue, and today [1885?–1900?] for the tourist trade this is beautifully beaded in fancy designs.

[The Chilkat needed more protection when going on snowshoes.] For hunting and winter travel on the cold mainland, a legging which reached to just below the knee took the place of the extension top [on the ordinary moccasin]. Leggings were called *khuse-kate* [probably ẋ̣us-ke·t, "foot cover"].

[The Tlingit seem to have made distinctions between the moccasin, tí·ł, the short boot or warrior's boot, ẋ̣u·ske·t or "foot cover," and the tall boot, ẋʷán. The belt was called sí·k, and the apron ("lap or thigh cover") was g̣u·š-ke·t.

[Ceremonial costumes and shamans' regalia will be described in connection with the occasions on which they were worn.]

HAIR DRESSING*

When first seen by Europeans, both sexes wore the hair long, that of the men straggling or tied up on top of the head and matted with grease, red ochre, and adhering birds' down. The powdering of the hair with eagle down was done on all dance or ceremonial occasions. The women wore the hair in one plait, or confined at the neck and hanging down the back, in which manner they continued to wear it up to the beginning of the present century.

The hair of the shaman was never cut. When practicing, he wore it hanging down, but at other times it was tied in a knot on top of the head and fastened with a comb, bone pin, or string. [At Yakutat, shamans might wear their hair in long, thin braids (de Laguna 1972:446).]

Long hair was considered beautiful on women. It was carefully combed, washed, and kept free of grease and paint. Young women of the higher class wore ornaments attached to the plait when the hair was confined at the neck. The conventional type [of hair ornament, *tcheene* (č̓í·n)] was made of deer skin, in size and shape like a made-up four-in-hand necktie, and was ornamented on the outer side with four or five parallel rows of dentalium (one above the other), and was fringed with spun goat wool and beads at the bottom. Later it was decorated with beadwork in geometric designs. This enclosed the plait at the neck and hung down over it. [At Yakutat the ornament might be made of bamboo driftwood, through which the braided hair was drawn, like a napkin ring (de Laguna 1972:446).] Attached to this near the top, or if the ring were absent, secured to the hair at the nape of the neck, was a peculiar half-moon shaped ornament of copper, iron or silver. Such pieces certainly originated with the interior people. I have seen them of copper taken from old sand graves on the Fraser River about Lytton in British Columbia [see Harlan I. Smith 1900, fig. 84, and also fig. 85, iron, Chilkat, and fig. 86, copper, from near Wrangell]. Those of iron were fluted and often inlaid with a small piece of haliotis shell in the middle of the curled ends. This peculiar form [two spirals joined at the base] occurs as the head of the dagger of the Déné

Editor's note: I have added the quotations from Suría, Portlock, Marchand, and Mourelle.

Hoonah Indians of the Wolf-Eagle moiety in dance costume, in front of Snail House (Raven 16), Hoonah. (Photographs by Case and Draper. BCPA.) (Top) *Six men and* (bottom) *six women, posed in the same place. Of these, five men and five women are wearing the same costumes. The exceptions are the second man from the right, in a shirt embroidered with two Wolves and carrying a Wolf dance staff, and the woman on the extreme right wearing the traditional button blanket. (Identification of moiety and of locale by Kristin Barsness.)*

[Athabaskan] tribes from the Babine through the Yukon valley, and particularly among the Copper River people [Atna]. Other ornaments of horn or wood, carved in crest designs, might be attached to the plait and worn by women of the higher class when dressed for particular occasions. All hair ornaments were known as *tcheene* [čí·n].

For mourning the dead, both sexes cut the hair short. In primitive days this was done with a sharpened mussel shell knife, the hair being placed against a block of wood.

Young men and older women plucked out any facial hair with tweezers of copper, bone, or two pieces of wood. Those of metal were often worn suspended around the neck of the women, or carried in the tool box by the men. Old men wore straggling beards, but I never remember seeing a Tlingit with a fine beard such as the Haidas had.

[Suría (in Wagner 1936:249) described the chief at Yakutat in 1791:

> The chief was an old, venerable and ferocious looking man with a very long gray beard, in a pyramidal form, his hair flaccid and loose on his shoulders. False hair over it in various locks, without any order or arrangement, made him look like a monster. . . . [The chief's older son also] had his hair loose which, on account of its thickness, seemed like a horse's mane. It was very black like that of his beard.

[Portlock (1789:290) commented that among the Tlingit of 1786:

> [Both men and women were] very fond of long hair, which is considered as a great ornament. At the death of a friend [relative] the hair is cut off pretty short, which seems to be the general mourning of all Indian tribes. The women wear the hair either clubbed behind or tied up in a bunch on the crown of the head; the men wear theirs either loose or tied at the crown. The method of dressing the hair with birds-down is only practiced by the men. The women in general are hair-dressers for their husbands, which office they seem to perform with a great deal of dexterity and good nature.

[Marchand (Fleurieu 1801, 1:322–23), reported of the Sitka Tlingit in 1791:

> Their coarse, thick hair, covered with ochre, down of birds, and all the filth which neglect and time has accumulated in it, contributes to render their aspect still more hideous [than the dirt and paint on the face]. They wear their beard only at a certain age; the youths carefully eradicate it: adults suffer it to grow: and it is at this day well proved, by the unanimous account of the different voyagers who have visited the NORTH-WEST coast of AMERICA, that all the Americans have a beard, in contradiction to the opinion of some of the learned, who have refused it to the men of the New World, and wished to make of this want of hair a variety in the human species. . . . The women, more fair, or less dark than the men, are still more ugly. . . . [Their] hair, or rather a mane, thick, bushy and coarse, [is] tied behind with strips of leather, either in the form of a cue or a club. . . .

[The hair was dressed by means of bone or wooden combs (xé·du), some of which were very nicely carved (Niblack 1890, figs. 11c, 11d, 11e; and de Laguna 1972, pl. 136 *top,* pl. 178 *left*). They were also used in prehistoric times (de Laguna et al. 1964, fig. 20c).

[Mourelle (in La Pérouse 1799, 1:246), wrote of the men at Bucareli Bay in 1779:

> Their hair is long and thick. They use a comb much like ours to gather it into a little tail from the middle to the end, tying it with a narrow ribband of coarse linen woven for the purpose. . . . [The hair of the women] which they wear braided, [is] long.

[The bunch of feathers, stuck into a turban made of a black silk handkerchief wound around the head, was admittedly copied from hackles on the Scottish bonnets worn by many of the Hudson's Bay Company men. This headdress was worn by Tlingit men and women at ceremonies in the nineteenth century, and the bunch of dyed chicken feathers was called (in English) "Canadian feathers."]

EAR AND NOSE ORNAMENTS*

Shortly after the birth of a child, when the baby was three to ten days old, it was customary to pierce the septum of the nose and the lobe of the ear. This was done by the paternal aunt with a bone awl. The hole was allowed to heal around a small bone peg.

At a later period, two or three holes, one above the other, were made in the rim of the ear, but the third hole was made only when a chief gave a great feast and freed a number of slaves; some say eight, others say four [slaves freed?] when children of both sexes were presented to the guests by their father or grandfather and were given honorable names. This latter ceremony not only ennobled, but permitted them to wear an ornament through this upper hole. Slaves were not permitted to have the ears pierced.

[Emmons recorded the following names for the four holes in the ear, or rather for earrings: The hole in the lobe was *suck ta ho hoo* (?, see shark's-tooth earrings, below), or *kah guke thleete* (probably qa· gukʷ-ƚí·t, "human ear-tail"). The three

**Editor's note:* In addition to the bracketed observations on nose rings, I have appended information from Portlock and Suría.

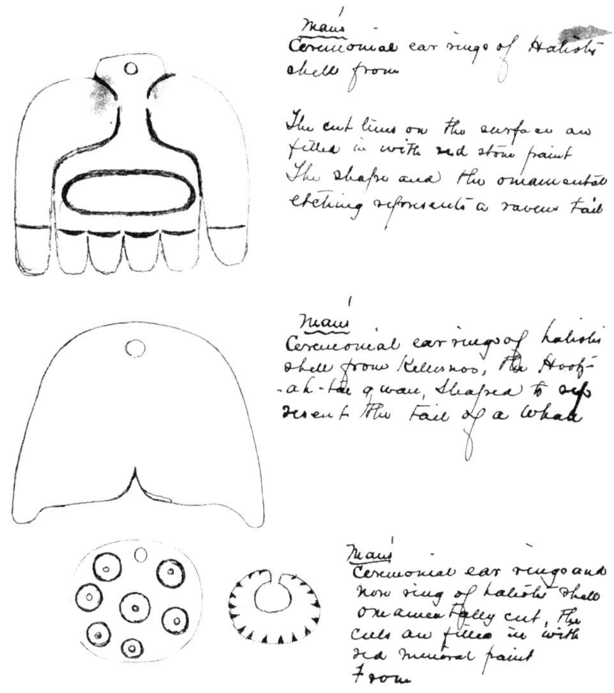

Men's ceremonial earrings and nose rings of haliotis shell. (Pen and ink sketches by G. T. Emmons. AMNH.) Top. *Earring, the grooves on the surface filled with red hematite, representing a raven's tail.* Middle. *From Killisnoo, and representing a whale's tail.* Bottom. *Earring and nose ring, the cuts filled with red hematite.*

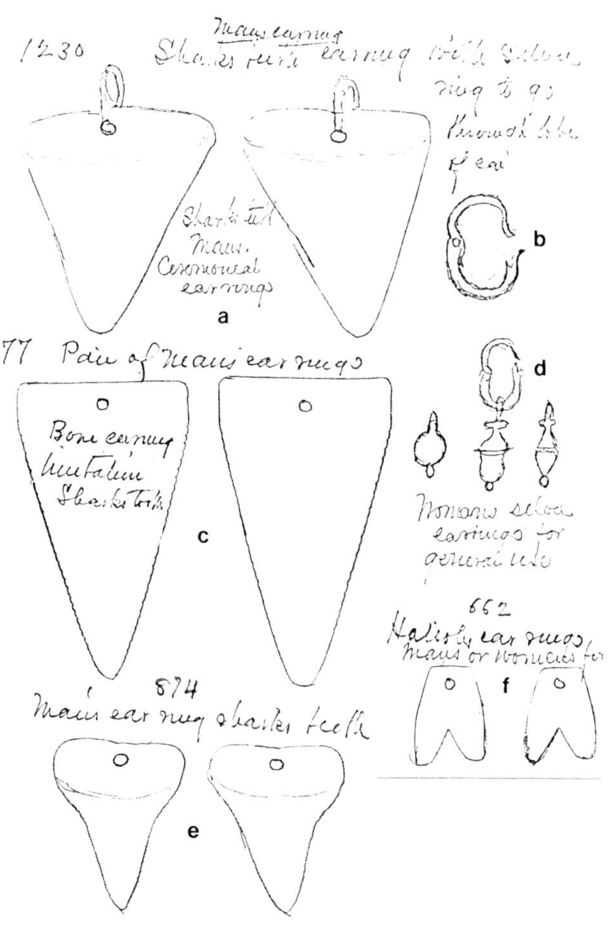

Earrings. (Sketches by G. T. Emmons. AMNH.) (a) Man's ceremonial earring of (fossil?) shark's teeth, with silver ring to go through the ear lobe. (b) Silver earring. (c) Bone imitation of shark's tooth earrings. (d) Women's silver earrings for general wear. (e) Man's earrings of shark's teeth. (f) Man's or woman's earrings of haliotis shell, for general use, from Sitka.

holes in the rim were all called *koon kla* (?). In addition, the lowest on the rim, and second to be made, was *ka guke* (possibly qa· guk^w, "human ear"). The next was *ka dute (guke?) thleet,* like that in the lobe. The highest on the rim and fourth hole, reserved for members of a chief's family, was called *ka guke she kou* (?). Although the number of holes indicated rank, there was no difference between the numbers for boys and for girls.]

Children of both sexes of the higher class above the age of eight years, and even younger, and generally all women and most men, wore some ornament in the lobe of the ear. For adults these might be divided into two classes: those for general use, and those for ceremonial occasions. The former, in primitive times, were alike for both sexes, and consisted of small pieces of haliotis shell, stone or bone pendants, or very small shark's teeth [šax̣dáq ʔu·x̣ú; earrings in general were known as guk^{w} ʔát, "ear thing," or guk^{w}-ka-ǯa·š]. After the acquisition of silver, the older ornaments were generally discarded; and as the Tlingit became expert metal workers, small silver, and later gold earrings were universally substituted. The typical man's earring was known as *dis yar kuku* [dís yi-gágu ?], "half moon," from its shape; the curved ornamental portion representing a woodworm, wolf, squirrel, or raven. But as late as 1890, some of the older men still wore haliotis shell in squares or in crest figures. The women's silver earring for general use consisted of a fine hinged circle to which was hung a globular or fancy shaped, ornamented pendant.

The man's ceremonial earring consisted of a large square of haliotis shell or a piece carved in crest design. The incised lines on the outer face were filled with red ochre or vermillion. The most highly valued earring, possessed only by chiefs, was the larger shark's tooth, which like the haliotis and dentalium, was procured in trade from the south, at great cost. This [the shark's tooth] was imitated in bone. Haliotis shells, because of their great value, were sometimes backed with copper, which not only protected them but enhanced their value. Under ordinary circumstances, the holes in the rim of the ear were not decorated, but for

Little boy, dressed for dance, with head scarf, cockade, silver nose ring, and button blanket. He holds a rattle of puffin beaks, Sitka, 1889 or 1890. (Photograph by G. T. Emmons? AMNH.)

ceremonies they were hung with dentalia, squares of haliotis, or tied with bits of colored yarn.

The women's dress earring was very different from the men's. It was originally a strip of hide ornamented with dentalia or haliotis shell, tufts of human hair, or ermine tails or skins. The modern earring was of red worsted or yarn in skeins, about eighteen inches long and three inches wide. About one-third of the distance from the top it was separated into four or six tightly wrapped cylindrical divisions (sometimes these were in black), and over them was fastened a large square of haliotis, a shark's tooth, or sometimes a long switch of woman's hair, or ermine tails. In the dance, these long pendants were very effective, swaying from side to side with the movement of the body. [These ear ornaments were called gukʷ ƛ̓é·nxʷ, "big earrings."] The handsomest older pendants that I ever saw were of strips of finely tanned deerskin, wider at the bottom than at the top, ornamented with five oblongs of haliotis shell down the middle, increasing in size with the width of the hide. The bottom was hung with twisted strands of mountain goat wool, dyed black and strung at the top with beads of broken dentalium.

The septum of the nose was pierced at the same time as the ear, when the baby was three to ten days old. Ordinarily no ornament was worn, but, when dressed for dances, adults and older children of both sexes wore a ring of haliotis or copper, or of silver in later days. The shaman wore a bone pin when practicing, but no nasal ornament at other times. After death, when the corpse was dressed, these nose ornaments were used. [The nose ring was called łunás.] The silver nose ornament was a ring with an opening so that it could be slipped through the hole in the septum of the nose, to hang down over the upper lip.

[When piercing the nose was abandoned, the same type of ring could be worn by simply fitting it over the septum, since the latter is wider at the bottom, where the two ends of the ring hung, than at the top; see the portrait of Charley White, who was wearing such a nose ring (de Laguna 1972, pl. 1). While Niblack (1890, pls. VI, VII) illustrated the various ornaments worn on the Northwest Coast, he offered no explanation of which groups favored the nose ring or which the nose pin. Suría [in Wagner 1936, pls. V, VI, VIII], with Malaspina at Yakutat in 1791, showed the chief wearing a large nose pin with flaring ends, possibly made of dentalia, and his son, or another man, with a very slender pin like a nail (de Laguna 1972, pls. 44, 45, 47, 50); and one young woman wore dentalia hanging from four holes in each ear and a dentalium nose pin (de Laguna 1972, pl. 56). Some Yakutat Tlingit as late as 1916 were wearing a nose pin, as well as nose rings that did require the pierced septum (de Laguna 1972, pl. 214a). The nose pin in modern times seems to have been worn only by shamans among the Tlingit and Haida (Drucker 1950:261, Trait 632), which suggests that it may have been an older type of ornament than the nose ring. The nose pin was also mentioned by Emmons as worn by male members of the Kʷá·šk̓-qʷá·n clan, Raven 19, at Yakutat, a group descended from Copper River Athabaskans (de Laguna 1972:444).

[When not wearing an ornament in the nose, Tlingit men often found the hole in the septum a handy place in which to put "a needle or nail that they purchase in trade" (Portlock 1789:288). According to Suría (in Wagner 1936:254) the septum was pierced by a "delicate feather," or quill.]

Silver ornaments, Sitka. (Pencil sketches by G. T. Emmons. AMNH.) Left. *Silver bracelets, with shark and eagle designs, made at Sitka, 1887.* Right. *Nose rings worn by adults and children of both sexes on ceremonial occasions.*

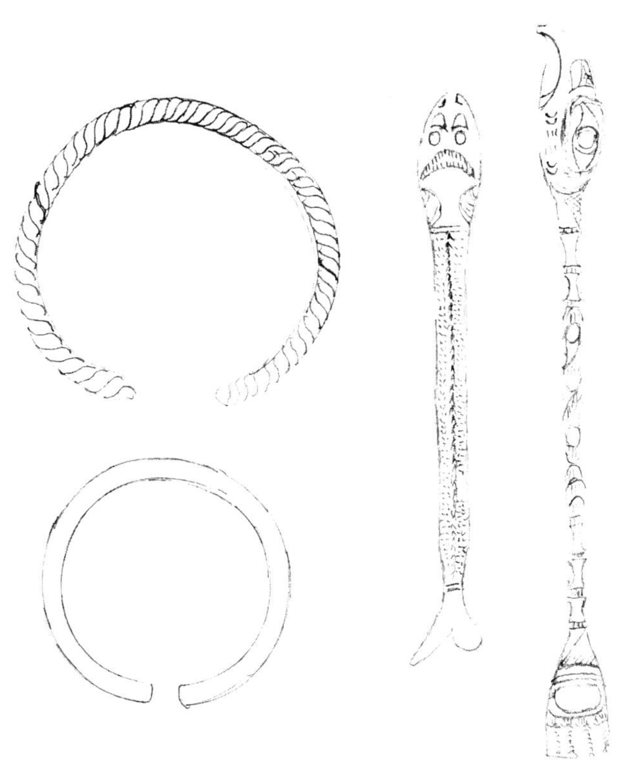

LABRETS*

Upon reaching the age of puberty, a girl was considered unclean, and was therefore secluded for a period dependent upon her rank. When released, she was dressed in festival clothes and brought out in the evening before the family and guests. A small feast was given at which her lower lip was pierced and a bone plug was inserted in the cut, around which the hole healed. From time to time, after marriage, the hole was enlarged by means of a larger labret, until with age, it might measure three or more inches in length. Two large labrets that I have measured were respectively 2 7/16 inches long, 2 7/16 inches wide, 7/8 inches thick.

The smallest size labret called *kanoh* or *kan-noh* [q̇a-nu·x̣ʷ] was shaped like a nail; that of medium size was longer than it was wide and oval in cross section, the largest, called *kintaka* or *kantakar* [x̣e·nṫá·x̣a·], "mouth stone," was flattened, saucer- or platterlike, grooved around the circumference but deeper on the outside surface. The smallest labret projected well from the lip; it and the plug first used were generally of bone, though occasionally of stone. [When labrets had all but gone out of style, small ones of silver, "smart pin," were worn (de Laguna 1972:444).] The medium sized ones, shaped like a spool and universally worn by women of middle age and low rank, just filled the aperture in the lip, and projected very little. These were of bone, ivory, and marble [de Laguna 1960, pl. 10*z, aa, bb*]. The largest labrets were generally of wood for the sake of lightness, and in some instances were elaborately inlaid on the upper surface with haliotis shell. These were worn only by older women of high rank. The labret was never removed in the presence of strangers. Slaves were not allowed to wear labrets.

[Emmons reported that the Yakutat women of the Kʷá·šk̓-qʷá·n clan, Raven 19, and of the Drum House Te·qʷe·dí and the now extinct Łux̣ʷe·dí, Wolf clans 32 and 30, which were either of Eyak or Athabaskan derivation, did not wear labrets. All of the women that Suría sketched at Yakutat seemed to be wearing labrets, however, although one young girl did not (de Laguna 1972, pls. 52–57).]

Large stone labrets were rare among the Tlingit, but several, dug at Killisnoo on Admiralty Island, were of highly polished, dark green serpentine, circular in shape. A remarkable large labret of crystal was dug up at Wrangell. [Keithahn (1962:75) described four stone labrets, only one of which was very large: 8 cm long.] Silver pins were universally used later [from perhaps 1875?], until the custom of wearing labrets disappeared. [Tlingit informants of the twentieth century believe that high class women wore labrets so that they would not become talkative, and cause wars.

[Labrets were noted by almost every explorer on the Northwest Coast, and their use was deplored because they rendered the native women repulsive in European eyes. A few examples of their comments are of interest.

[Father Riobo, who was in Bucareli Bay in 1779, wrote (in Thornton 1918:226–27):

> These women have fine features and some are exceedingly white but all make themselves hideous by a little tablet, two fingers wide, which they carry on their under lip. There is a horizontal incision for that purpose and they insert the wooden tablet through the opening until it rests against the teeth. It is considered a distinctive mark of married women. The unmarried women have only an incision in the lip from which they hang a small stick or a copper needle.

**Editor's note:* This section has been taken from the discussion of girls' puberty in Chapter 10, where Emmons commented on information from Portlock, Vancouver, and Lisiansky. To the quotations from these authors, I have added those from Riobo, Mourelle, La Pérouse, Beresford, Marchand, von Langsdorff, von Kotzebue, and Lazarev.

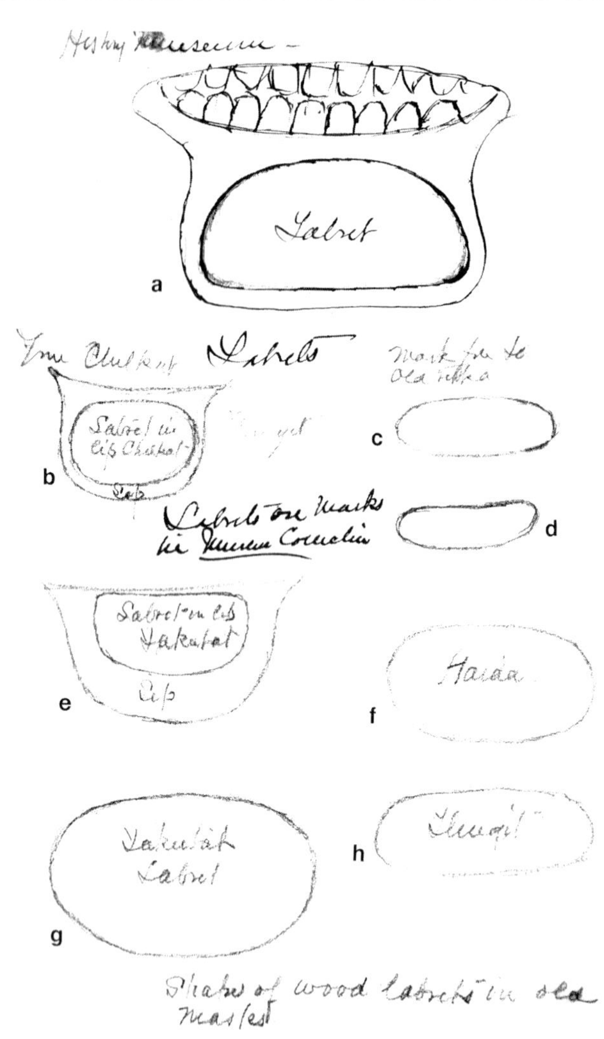

Labrets in masks, presumably representing shamans' female spirits. (Sketched by G. T. Emmons. AMNH.) (a) Shows mouth with teeth, and the lip stretched around the edge of the large labret. (b) Lip and labret on Chilkat mask. (c and d) Outlines of labrets on masks from island, Old Sitka. (e) Outline of lip and labret on Yakutat mask. (f) Labret in Haida mask. (g) Labret in Yakutat mask. (h) Labret in Tlingit mask.

[Mourelle (in La Pérouse 1799, 1:246–47), who was on the same expedition in Bucareli Bay, praised the natural beauty of the Tlingit women, many of whom

> . . . might dispute the prize of beauty with the handsomest of our women in Spain [if they were better dressed, and if they had not disfigured themselves with the labret]. All the married women have a large opening in the lower lip, filled up with a piece of wood, of an oval shape, and near an inch wide in it's [*sic*] smallest diameter. The older a woman is, the greater the extent of this elegant ornament; which renders them frightful, the aged particularly, whose lip, robbed of it's natural elasticity, and dragged down by the weight of this precious jewel, necessarily hangs in a very disagreeable manner. The girls wear only a copper needle, which crosses the lip, where the ornament is hereafter to be placed.

[All the women seen by La Pérouse (1799, 1:402–3), in Lituya Bay in 1786, wore the labret:

> All without exception have the lower lip slit close to the gum the whole width of the mouth, and wear in it a kind of wooden bowl without handles, which rests against the gum, and which the slit lip serves as a collar to confine, so that the lower part of the mouth projects two or three inches. . . . The young girls wear only a needle in the lower lip: the married women alone have the right to the bowl. We sometimes prevailed on them to lay aside this ornament; but it was with difficulty; and they made the same gestures, and testified the same embarrassment, as an European woman on discovering her bosom. The lower lip dropped on the chin, when the piece of wood was removed, and this second exhibition was scarcely more agreeable than the first.

[Beresford, with Captain Dixon at Yakutat in 1787, was surprised and revolted by this ornament (1789:172). He described it as about a half inch thick, elliptical in shape, and hollowed out on each surface like a spoon. The edges were also hollowed "in the form of a pully, in order to fix this precious ornament more firmly in the lip," and the latter extended at least three inches horizontally.

> This curious piece of wood is wore only by the women, and seems to be considered as a mark of distinction, it not being wore by all indiscriminately, but only those who appeared in a superior station to the rest.

[The wearers were, perhaps, the Tlingit aristocracy in the originally Eyak and Athabaskan population. Beresford also noted (pp. 186–87) the same labret worn by the women of Sitka Sound, where

> . . . it should seem, that the female who is ornamented with the largest piece of wood, is generally most respected by her friends, and by the community in general.
>
> . . . When the girls arrive to the age of fourteen or fifteen, the center of the under lip, in the thick part near the mouth, is simply perforated, and a piece of copper wire introduced to prevent the aperture from closing; the aperture afterwards is lengthened, from time to time, in a line parallel with the mouth, and the wooden ornaments are enlarged in proportion, till they are frequently increased to three, or even four inches in length, and nearly as wide, but this generally happens, when the matron is advanced in years, and consequently the muscles are relaxed; so that possibly old age may obtain greater respect than this very singular ornament.

[Captain Portlock (1789:289) also commented on the labrets which he saw at Portlock Harbor and Sitka Sound in

1787, and noted also that the older the woman, the larger the labret:

> . . . one old woman, I remarked particularly, having one as large as a large saucer. The weight of this trencher or ornament weighs the lip down so as to cover the whole of the chin, leaving all the lower teeth and gum quite naked and exposed, which gives them a very disagreeable appearance. When they eat, it is customary for them to take more in the mouth at a time than they can possibly swallow; when they have chewed it, the lip-piece serves them as a trencher to put it out of their mouths on, and then they take it occasionally.

The hole was bored when the girl was about two years old, when a piece of copper wire was inserted, to be replaced by the wooden lip plug at the age of thirteen or fourteen: "its first size is about the width of a button."

[Captain Marchand (in Fleurieu 1801, 1:324–25) reported that the labret worn by Sitka women in 1791 made them appear as if they had "*two mouths,*" and that the shape and size of this ornament were those of "the bowl of a table-spoon," and that its weight exposed "a set of yellow and dirty teeth." After quoting Captain Dixon's journal (actually Beresford's, cited above), to the effect that the first incision was made when a girl was fourteen or fifteen years old, Fleurieu cited Captain Chanal and Surgeon Roblet (both of whom were with Captain Marchand) to the effect that (p. 327):

> . . . the operation is begun from the most tender infancy; and they saw girls at the breast who already had their lip slit, and adorned with a wooden skewer.

The age at which the first incision was made might, in some cases, depend on the wealth of the father, since payment to the operator was expensive.

[Vancouver (1801, 4:253–54), in September 1793, met several canoes full of women and girls near the mouth of the Stikine River, and reported:

> . . . most of the full grown women wore very large lip ornaments, and as we were now visited by all ages, an opportunity was afforded of seeing the progress of this horrid piece of deformity in its several stages. In their early infancy, a small incision is made in the centre of the under lip, and a piece of brass or copper wire is placed in, and left in the wound. This corrodes the lacerated parts, and by consuming the flesh gradually increases the orifice, until it is sufficiently large to admit the wooden appendage. The effecting of this, if we may be allowed to judge by the appearance of the young girls who were undergoing this cruel treatment, was attended with the most excruciating pain; and which they seemed to endure for a great length of time.

A girl wearing nose pin and earrings of dentalia, and a large labret, Port Mulgrave, Yakutat, 1791. (Sketch by Tomás Suría, courtesy of Yale University Library.)

[It seems clear from Vancouver's accounts of the hostile Tlingit parties encountered by his exploring boats, that the women of rank, who not only steered the native canoes but directed the attacks, were all older women wearing very large labrets.

[Lisiansky (1814:243–44), who was at Sitka in 1804 and 1805, reported that the labret of a grown woman might be six inches long and at least four inches wide, and that "women of consequence" strove to wear as large a one as possible, in spite of its disadvantages.

> The piece of wood is so inconveniently placed, that the wearer can neither eat nor drink without extreme difficulty, and she is obliged to be constantly on the watch, lest it should fall out, which would cover her with confusion. [p. 244]

[Von Langsdorff (1814, 2:115–16), reporting on the Sitkans in 1805, wrote:

When a girl has attained her thirteenth or fourteenth year, a small opening is made directly in the center of the under-lip, into which is run, at first, a thick wire, then a double wooden button, or a small cylinder made somewhat thicker at each end. This opening once made, is, by degrees, enlarged, till at length it will contain an oval or elliptic piece of board or sort of small wooden platter, the outward edge of which has a rim to make it hold faster in the opening. The women thus all look as if they had large flat wooden spoons growing in the flesh of their under-lips.

. . . All the women, without distinction, have it, but the circumference of the piece of board seems to mark the age or rank of the wearer: the usual size is from two to three inches long, about an inch and a half or two inches broad, and at the utmost half an inch thick; but the wives of the chiefs have it much longer and broader. I have even seen ladies of very high rank with this ornament, full five inches long and three broad; and Mr. Dwolf [D'Wolf], who is very far from being likely to exaggerate, . . . assured me, that at Chatham Street [Strait] he had seen an old woman, the wife of a chief, whose lip ornament was so large, that by a peculiar motion of her under-lip she could almost conceal her whole face with it. It will be easily conceived, from this account, to what a horrible and deformed size the lip must be extended.

[Although von Langsdorff was unable to suggest why Tlingit women wore the labret, he remarked] . . . one disadvantage that it has must strike everybody, that it is wholly impossible for the fair-sex, on the north-west coast of America, to receive a kiss.

[Von Kotzebue (1830, 2:51–52) also wrote of the disadvantages suffered by the Sitka women of 1825 in wearing the labret:

The outer rim of the lip surrounding the wooden button becomes by the violent stretching as thin as a packthread, and of a dark blue colour.

In running, the lip flaps up and down so as to knock sometimes against the chin and sometimes against the nose.

. . . the lips of the women, held out like a trough, and always filled with saliva stained with tobacco-juice, of which they are immoderately fond, is the most abominably revolting part of the spectacle.

[And later (p. 61): A party of Tlingit men and women were entertained with] a favorite mess of rice boiled with treacle. They lay down round the wooden dishes, and helped themselves greedily with their dirty hands. During the meal, the women were much inconvenienced by their lip-troughs; the weight of the rice made them hang over the whole chin, and the mouth could not contain all that was intended for it.

[By this period, however, many women were beginning to abandon the labret, "especially the young Koloshi women who probably had learned the advantage which good looks gives them with sea-faring visitors," as observed by Captain Lazarev, who visited Sitka in the course of a voyage around the world in 1822–24 (1861:129, Petroff translation).

[It should be noted that shaman's masks intended to represent female spirits were carved with large labrets. It was, of course, the popular (Aleut) name for the labret, *kaluga,* "wooden dish," from which the designation of *Kalosh* was derived and applied by the Russians to the peoples of the Northwest Coast.]

BRACELETS AND NECKLACES

Bracelets [kí's] of copper and bone were worn by both sexes. The former, plain or ropelike, were always flat on the inner side, but the anklet of copper was circular in cross section. Flat pieces of caribou horn, incised with geometric figures and lines, were worn only by the shaman. These, I believe, were procured in trade from the interior people. The geometric character of ornamentation is Athabaskan in every line. Iron, when first obtained, was so highly valued that an ornament made of it was an indication of wealth and could be worn only by a chief or his wife. In later times, silver came into general use and took the place of all other materials. Broad bands, worked from coins, and beautifully engraved in animal designs came into general use, the wealthier persons wearing five or more that covered the arm from wrist to elbow.

The oldest silver bracelets of the Tlingit and Haida were of equal width throughout, while those of the Vancouver [Island] tribes were narrowed slightly from the middle to the ends. The description of silver working indicates that the traditional Tlingit bracelets were fairly wide, although narrower ones were later made to satisfy the increased demands from both natives and tourists. The bracelets were hammered over a form which produced a rounded surface, the greatest diameter being in the middle. [See Chapter 7, the section "Work in Silver and Gold."] The bracelet was not a complete circle, but was rather a metal band bent into an oval shape with an opening on one side which could be forced wider to insert the wrist. The ends were often fastened together with a clasp to make the bracelet fit snugly and securely. These bracelets were decorated in incised or repoussé crest figures.

The older explorers noticed a neck ring of copper twisted like a two-stranded rope and of native manufacture [see Chapter 7, the section "Copper Neck Rings"]. The sea traders, seeing the great value the natives attached to these ornaments, and also how much more they valued iron than copper, flooded the market with similar neck rings of iron, specimens of which may be seen in the collections of the American Museum of Natural History. [They were introduced by Ingraham (1971:105, 143, 192), among the Haida in 1791, 1792.]

Finger rings [ƛ̓eq-ka-kí·s] of stone and copper were women's ornaments which were later supplanted by those of silver and gold.

[Beads of stone or bone, and later imported glass beads, were worn, presumably as necklaces, as ear ornaments, as hair ornaments, and so forth. The bead was called kawú·t. The necklace was saka?át "anything for the neck," while a necklace of small elements was se·t. A bone necklace was ṡa·q se·t; a bead necklace was sakakawú·t.]

An amulet called *ta-sate* [té se·t], "neck stone," was worn suspended about the neck, and consisted of a small stone, selected for the color (green, brown, or black), generally flat, one or two inches long, and shaped or incised in animal or geometric design. This was used by both sexes to scratch the head or body, since the use of the fingernail for this purpose was considered very harmful [tabooed]. In several instances I found other materials substituted [for the ordinary stone]: the prized blue-green California haliotis shell, wood, or most valued of all, small pieces of nephrite. In one case the latter was a very small chisel blade, another a piece ground and shaped to represent the canine tooth of a brown bear—the only ornamentally worked piece of nephrite I ever saw or heard of among the Northwest Coast natives. The superstition in regard to the use of a scratcher was still alive in the early 1880s, and the older people still wore the amulet around the neck. It was believed, in early days, that if the wife of a man who was away for war should forget and scratch herself with the fingernail instead of a neck piece, the arrow or blade would pierce the body of her husband at the very spot she had scratched.

[Scratching amulets of slate were obtained at Yakutat in 1886 by Professor William S. Libbey for Princeton University (see de Laguna 1972, pls. 136 *bottom,* 137 *left*). Incised pebbles, some of which have designs suggestive of a human figure, were found in an early historic site near Angoon, and may have been scratching amulets, although they lacked a suspension hole (de Laguna 1960:122–25, fig. 15). A similar pebble with an incised design probably representing a shaman came from a protohistoric level on Knight Island in Yakutat Bay and may have had a similar function (de Laguna et al. 1964:168–72, fig. 21*a, a'*). The bone necklace and other paraphernalia worn by the shaman are described in Chapter 14.]

FACE PAINTING

The painting of the face in black and red was done in several different ways, in different designs, according to the occasion or the purpose for which it was required. Vancouver (1801, 4:133) mentioned the use of white paint by the people he met in Portland Canal, whose faces were colored red, white, and black. But this [the use of white paint] was characteristic of the Haida, who used a soft white clay, which may have been procured in trade from them and used by the southern Tlingit tribes. [The Indians encountered in Portland Canal may have been either local Tlingit, Tsimshian, or Haida come to trade for eulachon oil.]

For protection against the sun and wind when on the water in canoes, or against snow blindness when hunting or traveling in winter, against mosquitoes and gnats in summer, and for mourning, both sexes covered the whole face with fine wood powder applied with a preparation of spruce gum and animal fat that hardened and remained for several months until it gradually wore off. As a luxury, women of the higher class followed this practice to improve and bleach the complexion. The basic material consisted of *sukqwart* [ṡagʷá·t], a fungus growth on hemlock. [At Yakutat it was said to be red cedar bark.] This was prepared by charring it in the fire, and rubbing it off as a fine reddish-black [or brown] powder on a hard, rough stone, lava often being used for this purpose. Spruce gum was liquefied by heating it in a clam shell plate at the fire. If necessary the liquid gum was strained through moss placed over a small hole in the bottom into another, larger shell. To a little of this was added a large proportion of goat or deer suet, preferably the former. This was well mixed and rubbed over the face, upon which the fine wood [fungus] powder was puffed on with a piece of soft skin. It dried hard, showing a reddish black color, and was impervious to water. This mixture was also prepared in the form of a soft paste and was preserved in small wooden or metal boxes to be used with stencils [stamps].

Common charcoal, giving a blacker effect, was used for temporary purposes, particularly when angry after a quarrel or insult, when suddenly attacked, and also for mourning. A piece was taken from the fire and rubbed over the face to serve both as a disguise and to prevent an opponent from seeing any change of color or expression that might indicate doubt or fear.

[In 1949, I was told about an Angoon woman who woke in the night, realizing that she was dying. Because she was a daughter of the Te·qʷe·dí, Wolf 32, who pride themselves on

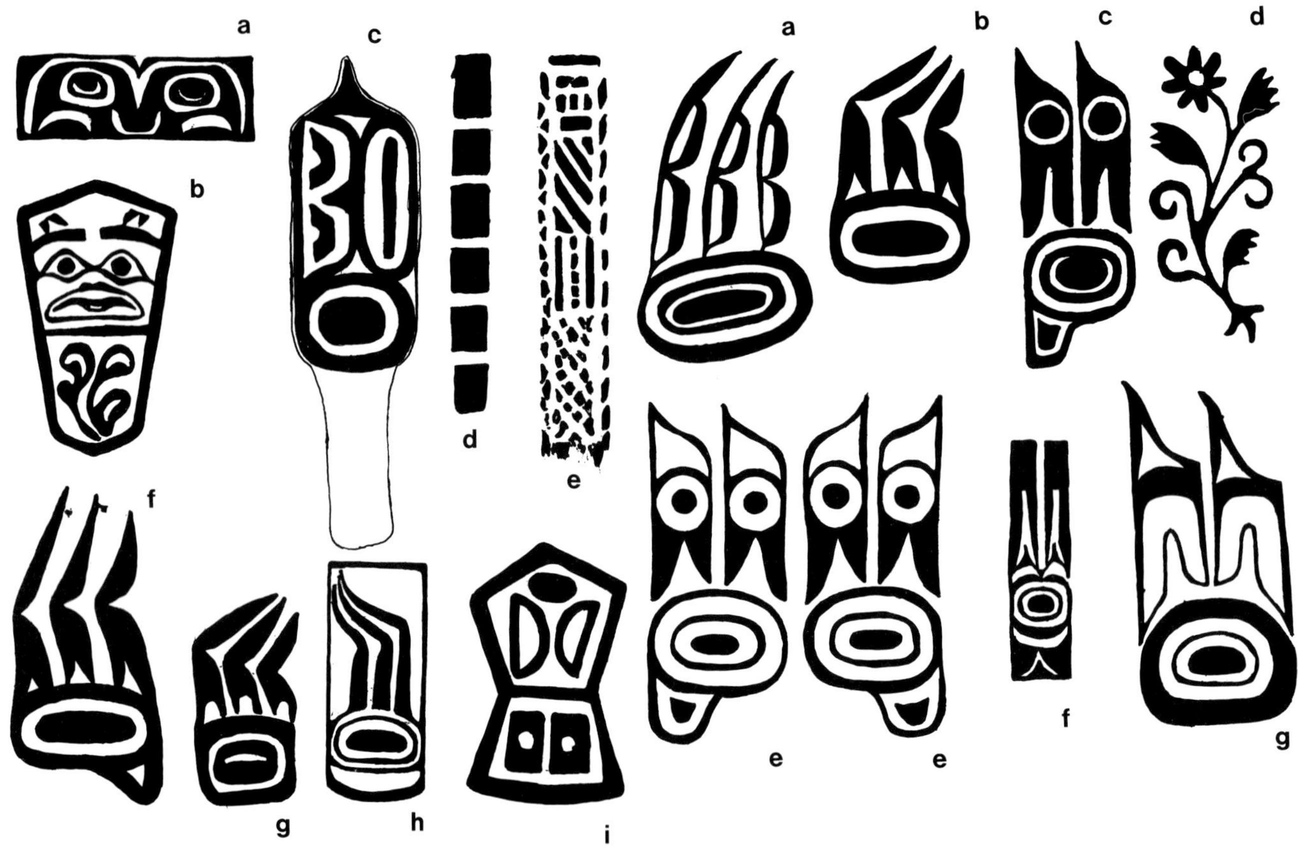

Face stamps used for dances and ceremonies. (AMNH.) Left. *(a) Frog, Raven 3, Chilkat. (b) "Copper," with face of the wealth-bringing sea monster* [G̣una·kade·t] *above, and flowers [magic "medicine"?] below; belonged to* Qa·ǯaqʷti, *chief of Raven 14, Angoon. He had appropriated some crests of the Wolf 1 for an unpaid claim; the* G̣una·kade·t *was probably one of these. (c) Salmon tail, Raven 7, Sitka. (d and e) No meaning, Klukwan. (f and g) Frog's foot, Raven 3, Klukwan. (h) Raven's foot, Raven 3, Klukwan. (i) "Copper," Wolf 1, Klukwan.*

Right. *(a) Raven's foot, Raven 19 (from Yakutat), Sitka. (b) Raven's foot, Raven 3, Klukwan. (c) Raven's wing, "very old, belonged to Jacob," Raven 10, Sitka; used for right cheek. (d)* Kayanee, *"a flower"* [kaẏa·ní, *"leaves," probably a magical "medicine"]; used on left cheek, to go with* c. *(e and e′) Both sides of a double stamp, Raven's wing, Raven 10, Sitka. (f) Raven's wing, Raven 17, Chilkoot. (g) Raven's wing, Raven 6, Sitka. "Used by Bean at great feast of Coudewots [of Raven 3], at Klukwan in 1901."*

courage, and did not want to disgrace her father's clan, she took charcoal from her stove, rubbed it on her face to show that she was not afraid, and lay down to die. Next morning her neighbors found her with blackened face and knew what she had done.]

Black face paint was universally used for death, sorrow, anger, and war. Black and red were both used for ceremonial occasions, dances, and some say for war parties. The red was from powdered ochre procured in trade from the interior Déné; later vermilion was substituted.

For dances, the face was ordinarily daubed over with both black and red, in every conceivable pattern; sometimes one half of the face was red, the other half black; or there might be alternate streaks of color, or spots of one color on a field of the other. The principal idea was to produce a startling effect.

Chiefs and persons of the higher class generally used crest designs, in either color, that were stamped with small wooden stencils [carved stamps] on the cheeks or forehead. These sometimes showed the whole animal form, but more often represented some pronounced feature, such as the foot, tail, fin, or wing. In applying the stencil, the face was rubbed slightly with suet and the stencil [stamp] was covered with the [colored] paste preparation. In addition to these very exactly stenciled patterns, each family [clan] used a number of ruder figures, worked [drawn on the face] with bits of skin and sticks. These were supposedly totemic or legendary in origin, but were too conventionalized to be definitely representational. It is said that on war parties the chiefs and leaders painted the face in their crest designs.

The most exact, valued, and interesting facial paintings were those used on the dead when they were prepared for cremation, or were painted on one's face when one offered his or her life to another clan in payment for a life taken by one's own clan. Facial paintings used on these occasions were absolutely totemic in symbolism, conventional in

Left. *(a) Wolf's ears, Wolf 32, Angoon. (b) Killerwhale, Wolf 27, Klukwan, used in 1902. (c) Shark's tail, Wolf 1, Sitka. (d and d') Two sides of a double stamp, with scroll for one cheek and Wolf's foot on the other; Wolf 1, Sitka. (e) Halibut eye, Sitka [probably Wolf 1]. (f) Whale's tail, Raven 13, Angoon; one side of a double stamp, with the same design for the other cheek on the other side.*

Right. *(a) Bear's eye, Wolf 1, Sitka. (b) Bear's foot, Wolf 1, Chilkat. (c) Bear's ears, Wolf 1, Klukwan, Chilkat. One side of a double stamp for the left cheek; the other side is similar. (d) Bear's foot, Wolf 1, Sitka. (e) Bear's foot, Wolf 1, but appropriated by* Qa·ǯaqʷti, *chief of Raven 14, Angoon, because of an unpaid debt. (f) Bear's foot, Wolf 32, Angoon. (g) Bear's foot, "front paw," Wolf 1, Sitka. One side of a double stamp for the left cheek; the other side is similar. (Emmons inked all the stamps and pressed them in a notebook. AMNH.)*

design, few in number, and were unquestionably of great age. Many were phratral in character. Members of the Raven phratry painted their faces in the Raven's Nose design, *Yehlh lhluou* [yé·ɬ ɬu·wú], which was an acute isosceles triangle, with the apex at the bridge of the nose and the base at the chin. The Wolf phratry painted the *Goutch ku gu* [g̣u·č gúgu], Wolf's Ears, in which the characteristically shaped animal's ears rose above the eyes and sometimes extended in a broad band down to the chin. Another phratral design was the Eagle's Nest, *Chak-quaddy* [č̓á·k̓ kúdi], of the *Nahutte* [Ne·x̣ʔádi, the Eagle people among the Sanya]. Almost all the Raven clans used the Raven's Nose, but for the Wolf clans the uniformity of pattern was not so general, for while the Wolf's Ears was most often used, some clans preferred the Bear's Den [x̣ú·č kúdi], the Killerwhale's Dorsal Fin [kí·t gu·ší], or the Killerwhale's Breath or Spouting [kí·t dasé·kʷ]. These other designs [both Raven and Wolf] I believe had originated in the same way that the crests have increased from the two original phratral emblems, the Raven and the Wolf.

[These designs, or perhaps only their use on the corpse before cremation, had been abandoned long before Emmons came to Alaska. When used at funerals, they were painted in black, but on other occasions they were in black or red, according to notes by Emmons.]

In addition to painting the face, it might be decorated with very thin squares or parallelograms of haliotis shell, fastened on with spruce gum, or by a string of such pieces tied behind the head.

[On his sketches of clan and moiety face paint designs, Emmons indicated that these were called *Ka gha ou she na*, "face paint" (qa· ỵá, "someone's face," ʔawsiná·, "dampened one's face"?), and specified that "*Ou-she-nai*, simply meaning 'painting,'" should be added after the name of each design. Emmons also wrote that pattern sticks for marking off (the design) when decorating the face were called *Oó-she-nar*,

Design for tattooing, drawn by an old Sitka artist. (The original drawing, in pencil, on lined notebook paper, was preserved in separate pieces: head, body, and the two hands; but are here reassembled in what must have been the original sketch. The whole figure is about 40 cm long; see centimeter scale. The parts are labeled.) Face of a man with two killer-whales. Right hand (on left) is tattooed with figure of a raven; left hand (on right) with figure of an eagle. The man appears to be wearing a Chilkat sleeveless vest, woven to represent a bear. His own feet, however, have been drawn like the hind paws of a bear. (AMNH.)

evidently the same word, presumably referring to "dampened one's face."]

TATTOOING*

Tattooing was practiced by the North Pacific Coast people to a limited extent, as was noted by the earliest European explorers and corroborated by the testimony of the natives and the evidence remaining on the persons of a few very old people. The Haida unquestionably used this kind of body ornamentation for both sexes to a greater degree than did any of the other coast tribes, and applied it to the breast, arms, hands, and legs [see Niblack 1890, pls. IV, V, pp. 257–58]. The Tlingit along their southern border, who came into intimate contact with the Haida, probably followed this practice, but those beyond the reach of Haida influence generally confined tattooing to the back of the hands and the forearms of the women. This is born out by La Pérouse (1799, 1:402), who wrote: "I saw no appearance of tatooing, except on the arms of some of the women." Marchand (in Fleurieu 1801, 1:323) noted that in Norfolk (Sitka) Sound in 1791: "*Tattooing* is little in use among the Tchinkitanayans; a few men only are *tattooed* on the hands, and on the legs below the knee; almost all the women are tattooed on the same parts of the body."

Captain Portlock, when in Portlock Harbor in 1787, noticed (1789:271) a man marked by smallpox. The latter gave him to understand that he had suffered greatly from this disease, which Portlock correctly inferred had been introduced by the Spaniards. This man had lost ten children in the epidemic, and "he had ten strokes tattooed on one of his arms, which I understood were marks for the number of children he had lost." In following up this subject through many years and visiting all of the tribes, I was unable to find any marks on men, save a ring on a finger, or a star or circle on the back of the hand. [Niblack (1890:257) reported tattooing rare among the Tlingit and Tsimshian, but highly developed among the Haida, where both men and women were tattooed in crest designs.

[In 1889 Emmons sketched the designs tattooed on the hands of three women then living in Angoon. One was tattooed in blue-black, representing the Raven's Tail, *Yehlh ku ou* [yé·ł ku·wú], the crest of her moiety. Another design was the representation of a Killerwhale on the back of the left hand of a woman from Kake. The third, and most elaborate, was the tattooing in dark blue on the arms and the back of the hands of a very old woman. The fret design on the back of her hand had been copied from the border of a Hudson's Bay Company trade blanket, and was called *Klee kaah je ji* (ƛ̓í·ka ǯá·ǯi, "blanket-on snowshoes"?] The design on the back of her thumb was *Kurl-saak nah-si*, "squirrel tail" (kał̓čá·k na·sí, "gray squirrel intestines," not "tail"). The lines on her wrist represented a bracelet, and the rows of dots from the wrist almost to the elbow were *Kah kal chee ut* (qá· –?–ʔat, "human –?– thing").]

Editor's note: In addition to correcting the quotations from La Pérouse, Marchand, and Portlock, I have added an analysis of the sketches made by Emmons of tattooed women's hands, and also a note on tattooing. These were among the manuscripts in AMNH, the sketches drawn on paper of the Rangeley Lake Hotel, Maine, evidently copied from a field notebook.

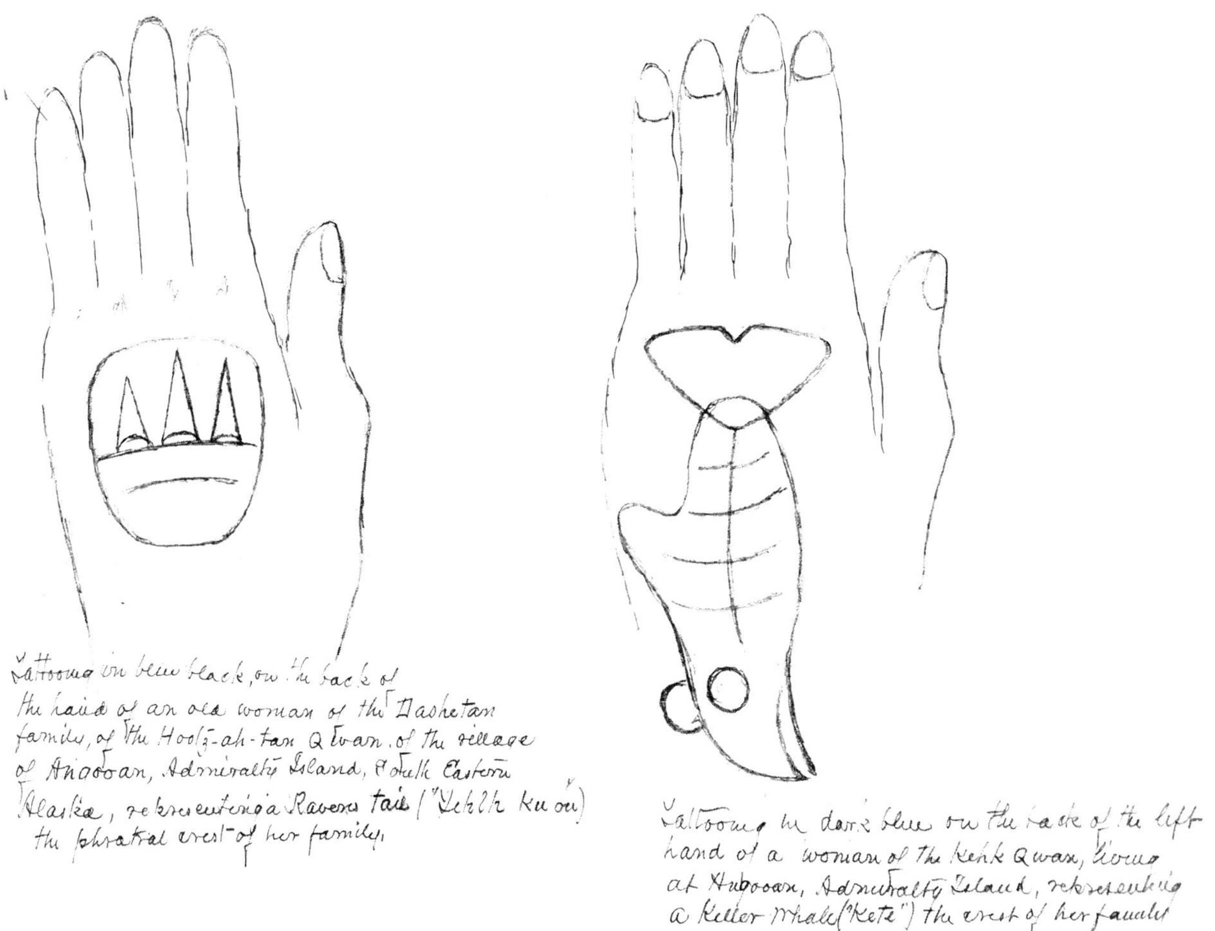
Tattooing in blue black, on the back of
the hand of an old woman of the Dashetan
family, of the Hootz-ah-tah Qwan, of the village
of Angooan, Admiralty Island, South Eastern
Alaska, representing a Ravens tail ("Yehlh ku ou")
the phratral crest of her family
Tattooing in dark blue on the back of the left
hand of a woman of the Kehk Qwan, living
at Angooan, Admiralty Island, representing
a Killer Whale ("Kete") the crest of her family

Tattooing seen at Angoon, 1889. (Sketched by G. T. Emmons on stationery of the Rangeley Lake Hotel Co., Rangeley, Maine. AMNH.) Left. *Tattooing in blue black, on the back of the hand of an old woman of the* Dashetan [De·šı̆·ta·n, *Raven 13*] *family, of the* Hootz-ah-tah Qwan *[Hutsnuwu tribe], of the village* Angooan *[Angoon], Admiralty Island, representing a Raven's tail,* Yehlh ku-ou [yé·ł ku·wú], *the phratral crest of her family.* Right. *Tattooing in dark blue on the back of the left hand of a woman of the* Kehk Qwan *[Kake tribe], living at* Angooan *[Angoon], Admiralty Island, representing a Killerwhale,* Kete [kí·t], *the crest of her family.*

Tattooing was prohibited to slaves. It was, in fact a sign of rank and an expensive luxury which only the wealthiest could afford, since its completion entailed a feast to the opposite phratry [from that of the tattooed person] and a payment of blankets to the operator. The latter was a woman of the opposite phratry, and generally connected through marriage. Blue-black was the only color used, and while this might be from common charcoal, the best color was obtained from the ash of the blueberry bush, *con-nah-tah* [kanataá]. It was said to have been mixed with mother's milk and was pricked into the skin with a bone awl. After the acquisition of trade needles, a pricker was made with four of these placed close together in the end of a wooden handle.

The figures tattooed generally represented the whole body or some part of the crest animal. The young girls of the family [clan, lineage] were tattooed at a great potlatch when property was distributed and slaves liberated.

The general name for tattooing was *kuh karlh,* "mark" [?], but it is said that at Yakutat it was called *kuh kay chul,* "sewing on the body" [kaqé·čáł, "stitches"], as it was done by passing a needle threaded with stained sinew under the skin. This must have been practiced at a later date, since the Tlingit had no needles until they procured them from

Tattooing seen at Angoon, 1889. (Sketched by G. T. Emmons on stationery of the Rangeley Lake Hotel Co., Rangeley, Maine. AMNH.) Tattooing in a very dark blue color on both hands and arms of a very old woman of the Hootz-ah-tah Qwan *[Hutsnuwu tribe]. The figure on the back of the hand was taken from the ornamental border of a Hudson's Bay Co.'s trade blanket,* klee kaah je ji [ƚ̓i-ká ǯá·ǯi, *"new blanket—on snowshoes"*]. *That on the back of the thumb is called* kunl-sark na si, *"squirrel tail"* [ka(na)ƚ̓šá·k na·sí, *"gray squirrel intestines"*]. *The two lines represent a bracelet. The two rows of dots extending from the wrist almost to the elbow were called* kah kal chee ut [qá· -?- -?- ʔat].

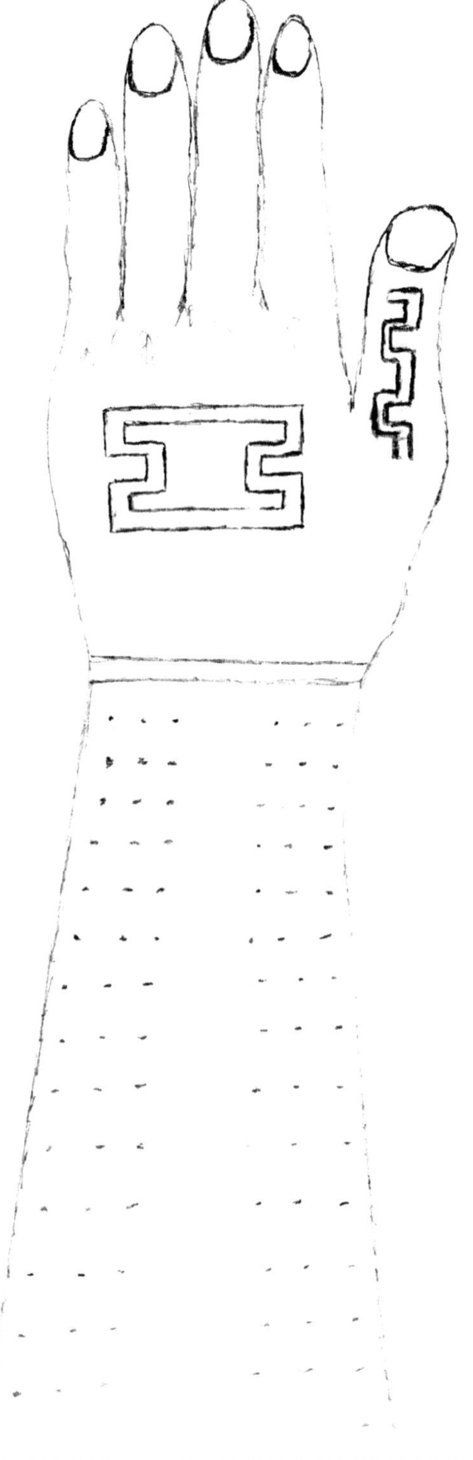

Europeans, but sewed by means of an awl and a separate thread of sinew. [Emmons overlooked the possibility that the Yakutat word reflects an old Eyak method of tattooing, similar to that of the Eskimo, and that the Eyak-speakers of the Gulf Coast might have had bone needles like those of the Chugach.

[An old note, written in ink and later crossed out, was among the manuscripts of Emmons in the AMNH. It was numbered "33," evidently referring to the lists of questions or topics Emmons intended to use in his ethnography, and in which is recorded the Yakutat word for tattooing. The note read: "Tattooing was unknown in olden times. The face, back, chest, arms (forearm), back of hands and legs are tattooed now-a-days. The white man introduced tattooing. Men, women, and children are tattooed *now.* Only the high caste are tattooed. The Tlingit word for tattooing is *Kuh-kay-chul,* meaning "sewing on the body.'" I am not sure that the writing is Emmons's, nor what to make of this text.

[Olson (1967:68–69) reported that tattooing used to be done only to the children of the most wealthy and aristocratic, at a festival or potlatch "for the children," no longer held even in Veniaminov's day, because of the expense. Presumably, tattooing and ear piercing were later done at minor potlatches. See Chapter 11, especially the sections "A Major Potlatch" and "Ceremony for the Children."]

CEREMONIAL GARMENTS*

[While Emmons described at length the garments, charms, and headgear worn by shamans (see Chapter 14), he did not attempt any orderly description of what was worn by men and women at potlatches, occasions for the display of crest insignia. It will be pointed out that the mourners, the hosts of the four "crying feasts" for the dead, would be dressed in old, ordinary clothing, a rope around the waist, hair cut or singed short, the face blackened. It was not until the successor of the dead house chief was ready to give the great potlatch to repay the "opposites" who had built the new house, that he and his clan would appear in their crest regalia, and that the guests would also wear their dancing costumes during the festivities.

[The leading man of lineage or clan wore the crest hat of twined spruce root, less often of wood or copper, painted in totemic design or with carved crest figures attached. The number of woven or copper rings on top reflected the inherited prerogative of the kin group, or number of potlatches given. The noble men and women might wear the headdress

**Editor's note:* This section is mine, to remedy an obvious omission.

Chief Kochteech [Qučtí·č], *of Ketchikan, wearing a wooden hat with copper plates, representing a golden eagle or fish hawk* [kiǯu·k / giǯu·k], *a crest of the Raven 1 of Tongass. (Photograph by Milotte Studio. BCPA.)*

with frontlet mask, carved and inlaid with haliotis to represent the crest, surmounted by flicker feathers and sea lion whiskers, and trailing ermine skins down the back. (Called "something on the head," šaki·ʔát in Tlingit, it was copied from the *amhalait* worn by the Tsimshian chiefs in their religious capacity as *simhalait,* bestowers of "power" to child initiates.) The crown was filled with down which flew about the house when the wearers moved. Other headgear worn by dancers might copy that of shamans; the host might don the "bear's ears" when receiving his guests on the beach, to show how bravely he was going to sacrifice wealth. Both men and women commonly wore a black silk kerchief on the head into which was stuck a bunch of "Canadian feathers," dyed different colors. Earrings, especially long ones for women, nose rings, and face painting in clan designs would be worn, except when a dancer donned a mask to give a "spirit dance," like a shaman.

[Chiefs and their near relatives wore Chilkat blankets, sometimes with the shirt, apron, and leggings of the same weave; or the long Chilkat tunic could be worn without the blanket. Such persons might wear heavy dark blue woolen blankets, beaded with crest designs, often on red felt appliqué. Others, chiefly women and girls, wore "button blankets" of similar dark wool cloth, trimmed with a border of red felt outlined with rows of buttons of mother-of-pearl, across the top and down the front on each side. Men also wore these, or coats of ermine or tanned skin, cut like our coats, but decorated with beadwork of Athabaskan floral patterns at neck, wrist, bottom, and down the front. Jackets to slip over the head were similar, or had beaded crest designs. Over the blankets, coats, jackets, and shirts, men and women often wore cloth bibs at the neck, with crest beadwork, or one or two "octopus finger bags," bandoleers of cloth with floral beadwork.

[Because some novelty in costume and performance was highly prized, it is impossible to detail what might be featured at a potlatch. I should note, however, that the heavy materials of these costumes made the natives very hot, especially when a fire was lit or the house crowded, and the weight of the button blankets would perhaps partially account for the swaying "dances" of the women.]

CHAPTER 10

The Life Cycle

BIRTH*

A pregnant woman was careful in her actions and manner of life, for if she suffered fright or trouble, this might react on the child. She was restricted to dried fish and land food, and could not eat anything fresh from the sea [i.e., no "beach food"]. No food restrictions were placed on the husband.

Birth was never permitted to take place in the house, as it would bring misfortune to the residents. A temporary bark structure was built back of the dwelling to which the woman went when the first symptoms were felt. In this hut was dug a shallow hole, measured from the elbow to the wrist, which was filled with soft moss, into which the child was to drop. The mother squatted over the hole and grasped with both hands a heavy stake driven into the ground in front of and inclining toward her. She was attended by two to four experienced women or midwives who were paid for their services. They supported her and rubbed her stomach with hot water or urine, to assist the delivery. Whether or not the delivery was painless in early days [Emmons is referring to the popular notion that women in primitive societies gave birth without pain (see Jones 1914:46)], I am assured by an experienced midwife that today labor is more or less severe, lasting from some hours to four days, and even causing death.

[Holmberg (1855:36–38, free translation) gave his impressions of the horror of Tlingit childbirth:

> . . . when Tlingit women are going to give birth, when they consequently most need the help of others, they are left helpless to their own fate, yes, even sent away. Accounts do not completely agree about this. According to some statements, Tlingit women give birth with the help of midwives. The newborn child is usually washed with cold fresh water and is kept in a cradle of moss. After childbirth the mother is brought out of the house into a specially prepared shelter and is there confined for ten days, because she is considered to be a most unclean being during this period. This is the account of Veniaminov about the confinement of women. [Birth took place in the hut, not the house—FdeL.] As I was leaving Sitka for California, at the end of December 1850, and because of storms and bad weather had to spend several days on board the ship which lay at anchor off the Tlingit settlement, I often heard from the wooded hill above the settlement a most pitiable cry, and that indeed from several directions; and when I asked several Tlingit who were serving as sailors for this trip to inform me about these cries of the women, they answered that there were several women out in the woods, who with pain and misery awaited their delivery, and they added, as if it were an excuse, that no one could help them because they were at present unclean. So, abandoned by their own people, they lay in the severe winter, with rain, storm, and cold, without being able to move a single heart to pity by their cries of distress.]

Immediately after delivery, the woman was placed on a bed, and if the placenta [du ki'gí] was not ejected, her stomach was rubbed with heated urine, and heated stones covered with a dressed deerskin were placed under her. Upon removal, the placenta was immediately burned. Nothing was done to staunch the usual bleeding. She was given only hot water mixed with a little oil to drink, and later, boiled dried salmon with a little oil. A band of woven bark was bound around her abdomen, and replaced after ten days by a broad band of hide, enclosing perpendicular strips of stiff cedar bark, which she wore for a month or more. After ten days she could return to the house, and in about a fortnight she would be at work again.

[A fuller account of pregnancy, childbirth, and care of the newborn than this, I was able to publish because a native midwife, concerned about her first white patient, came to consult with my mother, the late Dr. Grace A. de Laguna, when she was with me at Yakutat in the spring of 1954 (de Laguna 1972:500–507).

[Lütké (1835, 1:211) wrote about the Sitka Tlingit in 1827 (free translation):

Editor's note: This chapter was originally titled "Birth, Children, Marriage, Death." Aside from some changes in the titles of the sections, this chapter remains essentially as Emmons had planned it. The section on "Labrets" was, however, transferred to Chapter 9, "Dress and Decoration"; "Mummy" was included in a section I titled "Various Older Forms of Disposal of the Dead," and I followed this by "Recent Graveyards." The last part of the final section on spirits I moved to the beginning of Chapter 14, "Shamanism."

**Editor's note:* I supplied the quotations from Holmberg, Petroff, Lütké, and Khlebnikov, and the information from Veniaminov. This section had earlier been titled "Childbirth."

After the birth of a child, the mother remains lying down for a whole month, without leaving her hut. At the end of this time, she washes herself, and also her child, puts on new clothing, and with a kind of solemnity, accompanied by a festival to which the relatives are invited, a name is given to the newborn, ordinarily in memory of some relative of the mother. Tlingit women often have six children, even eight, but never more than ten.

[Khlebnikov, writing in 1817–32 from Sitka, reported (1976:27):

> When a boy is born, his mother stays in bed in the hut for a month. After this period of time she bathes herself, bathes the infant, washes all of her clothes, and dresses in fresh clothing. Then the relatives are called in to celebrate, at which time the mother gives the newborn son his name, which she takes from one of her dead relatives. With this, the ceremony ends. [A woman may have six to eight children, but rarely ten.]
>
> The mother nurses the infant until such time as he begins to walk; she places half-chewed morsels of dried salmon into its mouth until the child's teeth come through and he can feed himself.

[Veniaminov ([1840] 1984:415) indicated that the new mother and infant were confined for ten days after birth in the same hut as that used for menstruation. The baby was not nursed until it had expelled all the "pollution" in its body, and also at intervals during the first few months its abdomen would be massaged to achieve this. The baby was breast-fed for ten to thirty months.]

INFANCY AND CHILDHOOD*

As soon as the child was delivered, it was wiped with soft moss or finely shredded cedar bark, wrapped in soft dressed deerskin, and placed in a cedar-bark cradle, *duke* or *tooke* [ṫu·kʷ], filled with soft moss. If the baby was of high caste, it was taken to the house of the paternal grandfather [who was of the same moiety, and preferably of the same clan, as the baby], and placed across the doorway, where ashes were thrown outside over the child to drive away the spirits of the dead and to prevent their entrance. Babies [of commoners?] were taken into the house [of their parents?], and laid by the fire, where ashes were thrown over them four times to drive away any evil spirits.

**Editor's note:* This section was originally called "Children." To the text I have supplied the passages from Beresford, Suría, Marchand in Fleurieu, Khlebnikov, Veniaminov, Holmberg, Lütké, and von Kotzebue. I pieced together the paragraphs on children's toys and games from notes by Emmons and from the sources cited above.

[Presumably the baby was returned to the mother in the birth hut, and was brought home with her at the end of her confinement.]

[Holmberg (1855:38), continuing his account of childbirth, reported (free translation):

> The newborn child may not taste mother's milk until he has vomited up the uncleanliness which, according to the ideas of the people, would start all possible kinds of sickness if it remained in the body. If vomiting does not take place of itself, the child's tiny stomach is pressed and squeezed in every way until the desired result follows.

[Von Kotzebue (1830, 2:49), who was at Sitka in 1825, observed further manipulation of the infant:

> Immediately after the birth, the head of the child is compressed, to give it what they consider a fine form, in which the eyebrows are drawn up, and the nostrils stretched asunder.

[As explained by a Yakutat informant in 1954, this molding was done by the midwife, who put her hands inside the baby's mouth and pushed against the soft bone and cartilage at the roof of the mouth.]

The umbilical cord, *ka tu-nu* [qa· ta·nú, "human umbilical"], was cut with a stone knife if the baby was a boy, but for a girl the woman's blue mussel shell knife was used, so that she might grow up to be an industrious woman. The [end of the] cord was tied with a sinew thread, and mucus [ge·x̣̌] was put around it, and it was kept moist for several days. When the cord dropped off, pitch from the white pine was warmed in the mouth, put in the navel, and covered with soft moss to heal. The umbilical cord that had dropped off was sewed up in a little ornamented, circular case of skin, later of cloth, which was attached to the front of the cradle. Sometimes, in addition to the cord, the little case contained miniature paddles, bow and arrows, an arrowhead, or an earring; sometimes also attached to the cradle was a tiny rude carving, given by the shaman as a protection against evil spirits. When no longer used on the cradle, the bag [with the umbilical] might be suspended around the child's neck for several years, after which the mother would hide it in a cave, or a crack in a rock, or some place where it would not be found, since someone evilly disposed [a witch] might use it, like a bit of hair, or any other part of the body, or a secretion, to cause sickness or death.

The primitive cradle, it is claimed, was made of a length of cedar bark, but in later days it was a large spruce root pack basket, cut in half, and the halves sewed together lengthwise, and strengthened with a thin wooden slat

Left. *Baby in a skin pouch, Sitka, 1888.* Center. *Tlingit baby buttoned into a cradle, Sitka, 1900.* Right. *Tlingit child in fawnskin dress. (Photographs by G. T. Emmons. AMNH.)*

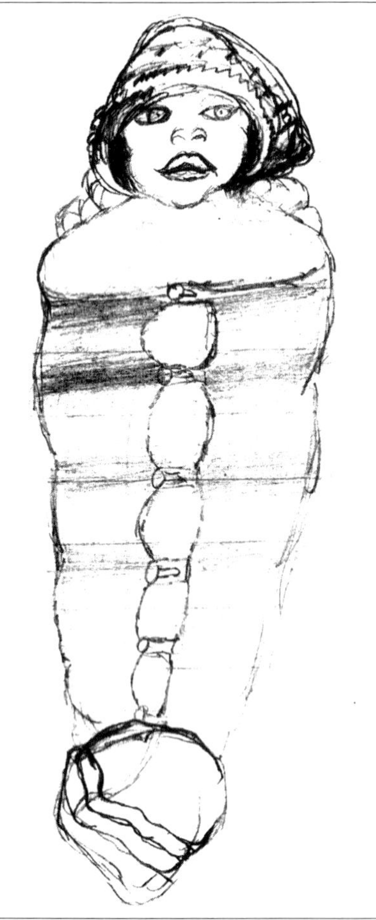

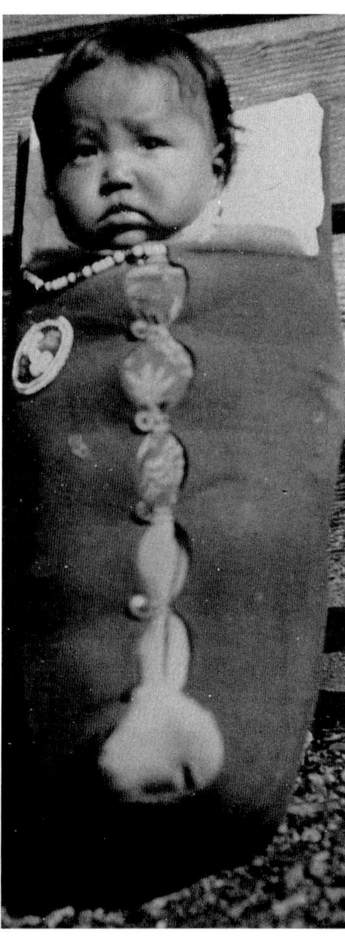

sewed to the outside. This formed the body of the cradle. The front consisted of a skin sewed to the edges of the basket, laced or togged down the front, to confine the baby [see de Laguna 1972, pls. 53, 54, 55 after Suría, and pl. 63 taken 1886]. A cradle was used but one time. When the child had outgrown the cradle, it was carefully hidden in a hollow tree, a deep cleft in a rock wall, or weighted down with stones, because it was believed still to have some influence on the well-being of the child.

[According to Suría (in Wagner 1936:254), writing about the Yakutat of 1791:

> When the Indians are newly born they put them in a cradle made of a kind of reed [spruce root] very well worked. Two skins hang down from each side of this which they fold over the breast of the baby and which covers it down to the knees. These are joined by a skin which through various holes extends from one side to the other. The creatures are dressed with their arms inside, all with skins, and thus they put them inside the cradle, and cover them very well down to the feet as stated. Thus they manage the affair, giving them to suck and leaving them stretched out on the ground.

[According to Fleurieu (1801, 1:361–64), who "blended" together the observations of Captains Marchand and Chantal, and of Surgeon Roblet, who were at Sitka in 1791:

> The good understanding which reigns in their families is manifested, in an affecting manner, by the general expression of their fondness for their children; and the cares which nature seems to have allotted exclusively to the mother, the father is often seen to take a delight in sharing. The situation of the children at the breast is, however, deplorable. They are packed up in a sort of wicker cradle, somewhat like one of our chairs, the back of which has been cut at a small height above the seat. This cradle is covered outwardly with dry leather, and lined with furs in the place where the child is to rest. There it is that the

little sufferer experiences a sort of continual torture, and all the evils that can be produced by filthiness and confinement. Placed in a sitting posture with its legs extended, and stuck one against the other, it is covered to the chin by an otter-skin, and tied down, in order to fix it on its bed of pain, by leather straps which leave it no liberty except for the motions of its head; and most frequently, it moves that only to express its suffering. The care which is taken to cover with dry moss the seat on which it sits, and to place some between its thighs, also turns against it: its urine and excrements soon convert this moss into dung; and the fermentation which there takes place, produces, in those delicate parts of the body, excoriations, the scars of which it preserves for life. When the unfortunate little creature is taken from its case in order to be cleaned, an idea may be formed of what it must have suffered: all its limbs appear furrowed by the deep marks imprinted on them by the strong pressure of the straps which bind it, of the folds of the skin which envelops it, and even of the wood of the cradle in which it is carried.

The effects of this state of continual constraint are manifested in all the children at the breast; their leanness and weakness sufficiently indicate that, although the mothers are, in general, excellent nurses, the good quality of the milk which they suck, is unable to give to their fettered members, the spring and the strength which motion and exercise can alone maintain and increase. But as soon as, released from the bonds of the fatal cradle, they can crawl on the ground and walk on all-fours, there takes place, throughout every part of their body, a sudden and rapid expansion; gaiety, that charming gaiety of childhood, soon succeeds to cries and tears; and health, which diffuses over their plump cheeks a brilliant carnation, announces that Nature has again laid hold of her work in order to bring it to perfection. [Fleurieu goes on to argue that the constraints of the cradle serve to protect the child from the cold and from accidents.]

[Beresford (1789:239–40) wrote about the Northwest Coast in general that:

. . . three pieces of bark are fastened together, so as to form a kind of chair, the infant after being wrapped in furs, is put into this chair, and lashed so close, that it cannot alter its posture even with struggling; and the chair is so contrived, that when a mother wants to feed her child, or give it the breast, there is no occasion to release it from its shackles. Soft moss is used by the Indian nurse to keep her child clean; but little regard is paid to this article, and the poor infants are often terribly excoriated, nay, I have frequently seen boys of six or seven years old, whose posteriors have born evident marks of this neglect in their infancy.]

Cradle songs were composed for the occasion as desired, which can be observed in the following examples. To girls this song was sung:

Like a bluejay
I'll sing like a bluejay
When I see the berry blossoms bloom on the hillsides
When I see the berry blossoms ripen on the hillsides.

For boys this song was sung:

Bring me my arrow
My bow and arrow
And I'll shoot a little bird
For my sister's little dollie
For my sister's little dollie.

[Why should this song seemingly encourage the boy to break the taboo against needless killing of small animals?]

As previously noted, shortly after birth, both the septum of the nose and the ear lobe of the baby were pierced by a woman of the opposite phratry [i.e., the father's sister, or clan sister].

[Emmons left a sketch, "Framework for baby's head to protect from mosquitoes and striking," but failed to describe it. The framework was, probably, made of willows or similar flexible sticks, bent around and fastened together to form an openwork, inverted basket, which was placed over the baby's head when it lay in the cradle or was carried on the mother's back. In modern times this was covered with cloth or mosquito netting.]

Children nursed for one year or more. I have seen children over two years of age at the mother's breast. I was told by the older people that a mother leaving a young baby might milk herself into a small cuplike stone dish called ***klar te hone yet*** [ƛ̓a·-tu-x$^{(w)}$án ye·t, "breast-in-milk vessel"], so that the baby might be fed in her absence. This type of dish was also used to mix grease and spruce gum in for facial painting, and by children as a plaything.

[Emmons did not mention the use of a hammock [gi̹·gáč̓], made by folding a blanket over two lines of rope, in which the baby might be placed, although this was in use while he was in Alaska.]

Babies and little children were wonderfully quiet, patient, and good, and though strapped in the cradle for a year or even longer they made no complaint. When able to walk, their movements were restricted by a length of line attached to a broad band around the waist and secured to some fixed object. Corporal punishment was rarely administered, regardless of age. Their sense of obedience and helpfulness seemed to be inherent, and they learned through observation without any system of instruction. The older children took care of the younger ones; gentleness and good nature prevailed in their play. Loud voices and quarreling were foreign to their nature. Little girls played with dolls, and boys with bows and arrows, but their greatest pleasure was to get into a canoe and paddle about in front of the village. Thus they became very expert watermen at an early age, although few or none could swim. They were taught the family [clan] history and songs during the winter evenings spent about the fire, and, when quite young children, they were dressed and participated in the ceremonial dances.

And so, without instruction in our sense, they acquired the knowledge necessary to fit them for their future life, through absorption and observation.

[Emmons had no section specifically describing children's games or playthings. We gather, however, that model canoes were made for them which faithfully copied the decorations of the house chief's war canoe (see Chapter 4, the section "Canoes"). They were given a light pack to carry about every day for an hour or so (see "Bags, Packs, Boxes, and Sleds" in the same chapter). In a letter to his son (see Chapter 5, "Land Animal Hunting: Aboriginal Weapons"), Emmons described the whip sling with which the Indian boys were playing. And in the same chapter, he mentioned catching hummingbirds and playing with the them (see "Bird Hunting").]

The doll with which little girls played was called by the Northern Tlingit *Neckt Tlingit* [né·x̣ łingí't] or *neck tsi* [né·x̣ sí·, "white-rock daughter" or "doll"], because they were made of marble or white limestone for the head and neck, to which clothing was attached. It was a child's plaything quite common at Chilkat, [and when found elsewhere] could be traced to that locality.

[Such white stones for doll's heads were also obtained by the Dry Bay people from the upper Alsek, and were known at Angoon from local sources, especially from Limestone Inlet, in Taku territory. Suría (in Wagner 1936:256) noted at Yakutat in 1791: "For their children they make some toys with heads of marble for them to play with."

[Boys, too, were given dolls, for Emmons collected from the Chilkat (AMNH, catalogue no. 358) a "Small medicine man with complete outfit, and although some superstition is attached to it, it is given to boys as a plaything as dolls are given to girls." Because such dolls were more common among the Chilkat and Chilkoot than among other groups, Emmons speculated that the trait may have been borrowed from interior peoples.

[Continuing Khlebnikov's account of childbirth, infancy, and childhood (1976:27):

> They make clothing from animal pelts for little boys. And when the child starts to talk, his relatives, uncles and others, must bathe him every morning either in river water or sea water, regardless of the frost, until the young boy becomes accustomed to the cold. Fathers and mothers stay completely away from the whole custom, because the tears and weeping of the children would cause them grief. It is customary however for the uncles to beat children with sticks if they are insubordinate or shriek. In all stages of their growth children are obedient to their parents, and even more remarkable, the aged and the infirm are attended with great care. [Author's note:] Orphans and children without relatives, who are unable to take care of themselves because of illness, are cared for by those who have means and who will be responsible for bringing them up.

[Veniaminov ([1840] 1984:415) mentioned that the child was first bathed in the sea when he began to walk. This was done by the father and mother; later they left this to the maternal uncle.

[Lükté (1835, 1:211–12) continued with his description of the Tlingit child as follows (free translation):

> The child is suckled until he can walk and has teeth. In the meantime, he is early made accustomed to nourish himself with fish, by putting into his mouth some dried fish which has already been chewed. When he begins to talk, one bathes him each morning in the cold water of the river or of the sea; this is done, as has already been said, by one of his close relatives. . . . [pp. 211–12] The Kalosh also have some good qualities. Their affection for their children is remarkable, and is pushed to the point that the fathers do not take upon themselves the bathing of their children in salt water (which, to accustom them to the cold, is carried out every day, winter and summer), but leave this task to the uncles [mother's brothers of the children] and other relatives, who, less tender than the fathers, beat the intractable children who won't stop crying. The children, for their part, show at every age obedience and respect for their relatives, especially for the aged and infirm for whom they care with the greatest attention. . . . [pp. 200–201]
>
> The whole education of a Kaloche from the moment of birth, is directed toward the goal of fortifying his body against every kind of suffering. [p. 201]

[Marchand (in Fleurieu 1801, 1:365–66) expanded upon the education of boys and girls:

> But if the Tchinkitanayans have thought proper to restrict Nature in the attentions which they pay to infants, they preserve to her full liberty in the education of adults, and, by daily exercise, hasten the progress and development of their physical faculties. Male children share the fatigues of the father: trained, from their youngest days, to hunting and fishing, it is they who go and harpoon fish in the river, and there seek, with basins, kettles, and other vessels which they have obtained from the Europeans, all the water necessary for the consumption of the family: they also go and cut wood for fuel and cooking; [they also kindle fire with flint and steel, but before these were obtained, doubtless could

make it in some other way]; here are no little boys even, who, though scarcely yet able to walk, do not begin to exercise themselves with a piece of wood fashioned like a lance, and try the strength of their young arm against the trunk of the trees that are within their reach. The education of the girls allows them not to go far from the habitation: sedentary like the mother, they share her peaceful labours and occupations; and, in sharing equally with her the attentions which young infants require, they are, betimes, instructed in the duties that will one day be imposed on them by conjugal union and maternity.]

NAMING*

Personal names belonged to the family [lineage] and clan. In most instances they referred to the crest and generally to some animal used as an emblem. While several clans might have the same crest, yet the names [referring to it] differed so that not only the clan, but the social position was indicated, for names had different values. Names of the chiefs and house chiefs were hereditary, and could not be used by others, and these largely referred to the highest animal crest [of the clan or lineage. Because the highest of these names were not given at birth, like ordinary names, but were assumed only when the recipient achieved chiefly or advanced status, they were more like *titles.*] Again, some [names] have been given to mark some event and have been perpetuated in the direct family line, and have increased in value through use, but such names were confined to direct descendants and could not be used by others of the clan. Such was *Gin-ko-teen* [ǯín qu-tí·n], "Hands See," given to a successful hunter of the *Chu-con-na-de* family [Wolf 5, Ču·kane·dí] of Hoonah, who killed many animals at night when it was difficult to see. Towyot [Ṫawyá·ṫ], the Tlingit name for the "Flatheads" or Kwakiutl of Vancouver Island, was a chief's name of the *Ka-yash-ka-hit-tan* [Wolf 25] of Wrangell, because he had so many slaves from these people, and being a chief's name [title] it was taken by his successor. [A Christian chief of this name was killed in 1880; see "Interclan Warfare" in Chapter 12.]

A man might also take the name of an enemy killed in war, and such a name would become a family possession. [This was the case with "Shakes," or Šé·kš, a Tsimshian name meaning "splasher" (referring to a whale), which was captured in a war, "six generations ago," and was assumed as a title by the chiefs of the Stikine Na·nya·ʔa·yí, or Wolf 18.] For an unpaid debt, a name as well as a crest might be taken, even one of the opposite phratry. This would be announced at a public ceremony to shame the debtor, but when the obligation was discharged the name was dropped.

The names of the sexes were different, although a woman might take the name of a dead man if there were no male heirs, or upon assuming the chieftainship [i.e., in default of a male heir, a woman might become house or clan chief and take the title associated with the position (?)], but rarely was a man given a woman's name. The name *Ka kah yeach,* "Ruler over men," [Qá·ka–?–], was once given as a nickname to a very beautiful woman of the *Ka-qwan-tan* clan [Ka·gʷa·nta·n, Wolf 1], on account of her dominance over men. It became an [inherited] family name for men, and was later given to a boy [apparently at birth, for he received another name at a potlatch when he was seven. See below].

Names [honorable appellations used at potlatches, as distinct from birth names or nicknames] were conferred by the paternal grandfather at feasts [at Yakutat by either paternal grandfathers or paternal grandmothers, to grandchildren of both sexes]. When the grandfather was of a different clan from that of the grandchild receiving the name, although of the same phratry, this might occasion some confusion in correctly placing the recipient. Ordinarily such names were not transmitted; yet, if given by a clan of great prominence, every effort was made to retain them. Among the higher class *Nan ya-yi-ee* [Na·nyaʔa·yí, Wolf 18] of the Stikine are found some *Ka-gwan-tan* [Wolf 1] names which are highly valued because the givers were socially esteemed. The *Kau-a-kon* [quwaka·n or guwaka·n], "deer," the hostage in a peace dance, was always given a name by the opposite party [i.e., by the clan that had been adversaries of his own; this does not refer to the opposite moiety. The name always (?) referred to the crest or some important possession of the captors' clan.] This name was only for the duration of the dance, and though considered an honor was never used afterwards. [At Dry Bay and Yakutat some guwaka·n names were retained by the receivers and used instead of their ordinary names.]

The Tlingit never spoke his own name except to his opponent in battle. If asked, a third person might give it, but the owner remained mute. The name was considered almost as a part of the person, like hair or body secretions, which, if given away [or taken] might be used to produce sickness or misfortune by someone evilly disposed. Nick-

**Editor's note:* To the text of this section, originally called "Personal Names," I have added information on "Chartrich-Shotridge," "Ononistoy-Kho-na-nest-ta," "Kanaut-Klanott"; I incorporated a note left by Emmons on names, and commented on the statements by Veniaminov and Holmberg on naming.

names were common and were given for some physical or personal characteristic, but were more confined to family use.

The first name was given immediately after birth and was announced by the father. It was a name belonging to the mother's family [lineage, clan], generally that of a lately deceased [maternal] uncle or aunt, or [maternal] great-uncle or great-aunt, whose spirit [consequently?] was said to be born again in the child. Such a name might be agreed upon beforehand between the mother and her brothers and sisters. The father, being of the opposite phratry, had no voice in the selection. But, again, the name might be determined later from some peculiarity or resemblance to a dead [maternal] relative, whose spirit was believed to live again in the child. This was the commonest [type of] name and was given without any attending ceremony, and was largely used throughout life.

The next name was given by the paternal grandfather and was also one belonging to the mother's family. [The paternal grandfather belonged to the same moiety as the mother and child, but not necessarily to the same clan.] It could be bestowed only upon the occasion of the feast accompanying the building of a new house, raising a crest or mortuary pole, or at a special potlatch. The recipient, generally an older child or even an adult, was dressed [in ceremonial garments] and brought out before the guests, while the name was announced by the host or the oldest man or leader giving the feast. Thus, at a certain *Ka-qwan-tan* [Wolf 1] potlatch, celebrating the rebuilding of the family [lineage] house by the paternal grandfather of seven-year-old *Ka-kah yeach,* the boy was brought before the assemblage, and as each blanket was given away [to guests of the opposite moiety], it was rubbed against his head, and the grandfather named him *Ou-ow-ed'h'l-karch* [ʔa·ʔawuɬxa·č, "giving it up"], "We give it up." This referred to an Eagle crest hat, which was held by a stronger branch of the clan and which for many years he had tried to get; now he gave it up, and the bestowal of this new name commemorated this voluntary release.

The most honored of all names [titles] was both taken and conferred. It was that of one recently dead. The family met and decided on the successor, who, in assuming the name [title] took upon himself the obligations of the deceased and received the family insignia [lineage crests] and property which he held in trust. The assumption of the name might be delayed for many years until the recipient [heir] had accumulated sufficient property to give an appropriate feast. Other members of the family contributed, and such an occasion was usually selected to coincide with [the potlatch for] the rebuilding of a house, or the raising of a crest or mortuary pole. With each major potlatch, other names [additional titles] might be assumed [by the host], and the last one taken was always the most honorable.

Chartrich, Sha-trich, or Shotridge (or even "Chatsquit"), leading chief of the Ka·gʷa·nta·n, Wolf 1, of Klukwan, received this name, [(Ł)ša·tx̣íčx̣], from his [paternal] grandfather, a prominent *Nan-yi-ee* [Na·nya·ʔa·yí, Wolf 18] man of the Stikine, and is abbreviated from *Klato-sha-to-which,* "Do not strike a shark on the head" [ɬ-ša·-du-x̣ič-x̣, "One that is customarily not to be clubbed on the head"]. It refers to the Shark, which was the crest of the donor's clan. In its abbreviated form it means "Very powerful, not to be trifled with."

[It is taboo to club a shark to death, and indeed it cannot be killed by clubbing, but is said to die only if snot from the nose is thrown on it. The donor of the name may well have been the father-in-law of Chief Chartrich, for the latter was married to "the daughter of the great chief of the Stikines" (Howard 1868:308), and this clan was the leading Wolf-moiety clan at Wrangell. Chartrich was the Klukwan chief who led a party of Chilkat to plunder the Hudson's Bay Company at Fort Selkirk in 1852. Davidson (1901a) knew him in 1869 as Koh Klux (also spelled "Klotz Kutch," "Klo-kutch," or even "Clacach"), from the Tlingit ƛaɬkic. This may well have been his birth name, or a name used before he was given the name Chartrich. He was the father of George Shotridge, Yé·ɬ gu·x̣ú ("Raven's Slave"), a chief of the G̣a·nax̣te·dí, Raven 3, the friend of Emmons; and George was the father of Louis Shotridge. According to his tombstone at Klukwan, Chief Chartrich died March 1, 1889, at the age of seventy, so he would have been born in 1819. His English nickname was "Hole in the Head," from a bullet wound in the cheek.

[The endurance of important names or titles is evidenced by the Raven moiety name, G̣una·ne·stí or G̣una·ne·sté, spelled by Emmons as *Kho-na-nest-ta,* "Wandering in a strange country," referring to the wanderings of the Raven Creator in early days. Since it is a Stikine name, we may infer that it belonged to the Kiksʔádi, Raven 10. Vancouver (1801, 4:209), in August 1793, was visited by the important Stikine chief, "*O-non-nis-toy,* the *U-en-Smoket,* of *U-en Stikin,*" when Vancouver's ships were anchored in Port Stewart, Behm Canal. We note that šəmʔó·git is the Tsimshian word for "chief." A 1867 "G̣una·ne·sté" or "Ononistoy" was known as "Con-mis-ta, son of Shakes, the principal chief of the Stikine tribe" (Howard 1868:211); in a report on the bombing of Wrangell in 1869, the name is given as "Qu-naw-is-tay Kosh-

Young boy with deerskins drying in frames. A number over the house door was a method devised by Commander Henry Glass, USN, to keep track of all the children of school age. Each child was issued a round tin badge, to wear around the neck, on which was stamped the child's sex, number within the household, and house number. The oldest man in the house was fined one blanket and confined for one day in the guardhouse for each child absent from school. (Photograph by G. T. Emmons. AMNH.)

Keh" (Colyer 1870b:9); Young (1927:89) reported that "Thomas Konanisty" was a prominent native Christian and policeman at Wrangell in 1880.

[Along with the prominent chief named above, Vancouver's ships were also visited by "Chief Kanaut," of lesser distinction (Vancouver 1801, 4:214). This name is probably "Klanott," or "Clan-ott," more properly Ł?una·ṫ, "They never die." This was also the name of a Chilkoot subchief of the Łukʷa·x̣?ádi, Raven 17, who killed a Sitka chief for trespassing (i.e., packing on the Chilkoot Pass), and in consequence gave himself up to death; this was in 1888 (see Chapter 2, the section "Laws"). But there was also a prehistoric shaman of the Tongass, named Klanott, who was involved in the war on the Ka·g̱ʷa·nta·n of "Grouse Fort," Hoonah (see Chapter 14, the section "Stories about Shamans: Ko-qunk").

[Emmons left in BCPA the following notes, evidently written with the clumsy hand of the elderly. Some of the topics mentioned in them he did not cover in his draft of this book:

> *Name*—generally received names from children—Father of- [a reference to teknonymy].
>
> *Prerogative*—personal names, houses, canoes, even articles of use [i.e., the lineage or clan had the right to give crest names to objects, as well as personal names to their members].
>
> Some names belonged wholly to chief.
>
> Reincarnation—born always in own clan and generally in own family [lineage; inheritance of the name accompanied reincarnation, which is why this item appears in this list].
>
> Man received name from paternal grandfather who was of same crest, or from [maternal] granduncles.
>
> Girl received name from paternal grandfather['s] clan and family.
>
> After assuming [maternal] uncle's position, could take one of the uncle's potlatch names ["big name," or title], and could take new name every potlatch—not necessarily the uncle's but [a name that would] commemorate some old man [of the clan].

[Veniaminov ([1840] 1984:415–16) stated that a Tlingit might have two names: the first, a birth name, bestowed by the mother on her newborn child, a name formerly borne by a deceased relative in the maternal line. The second name he calls a "clan name," that came from the father's side and was given by the father only at a great remembrance feast or

Woman of Port Mulgrave with baby, 1791. She wears a large labret, and the baby in the cradle wears a nose pin of dentalia. (Aquatint by Suría. Courtesy of Museo Naval, Madrid.)

memorial potlatch, in order to preserve the name. Because of the great expense involved, not all Tlingit had such names. A father might, if he were rich enough, give even his own "clan name" to his newborn son, but later would have to give great potlatches to his own kinsmen, his son's "opposites."

[This statement about a name "on the father's side," echoed by Holmberg (1855:38–39), has greatly puzzled ethnographers, because Tlingit names seem to be restricted to those owned by one's clan or moiety, unless it was one seized in war or in default of payment for a debt. The great feasts given to the father's own kinsmen were almost certainly the potlatches called "[Ceremonies] For the Children" (see Chapter 11). The motive alleged, that the paternal relative's name was given to the child in order to preserve it, would indicate that the earlier holder was deceased and not yet reincarnated. Was the name like the "potlatch name" of the Eyak (Birket-Smith and de Laguna 1938:156)? This was a name regularly used to call each guest in the opposite moiety when they were to smoke or eat for the benefit of the hosts' deceased relatives. Something of this kind is suggested by the statements of Shukoff and Katishan in describing the smoking or tobacco feasts (see below, in the section on "Death").

[Holmberg (1855:39) added a third name to Veniaminov's two, one that might be given to a man after his son had in some way distinguished himself (i.e., teknonymy). Actually, both parents might have such names for their first or for a favorite child, and be known as "Father of So-and-so," and "Mother of So-and-so." A teknonymous name was like a nickname, but might be inherited, as well as given. Both Tlingit men and women had such teknonymous names. If a man had inherited a teknonymous name, but had no child of the right clan or sex to receive the birth name to which the teknonymous name referred, he might name a dog after himself. This was more common than to name a man for his dog (here Holmberg is in error, I believe), although there have been nicknames of this kind referring to a pet. Though used in a somewhat joking manner, such names do not seem to have been given "in derision" as Petroff (1884:170) interpreted the case. (See Table 23.)

[A Tlingit man or woman, but more often a chief, might exchange names with another person, often a white captain or officer. In this way, "Merriman" and "Schwatka" were adopted by the Tlingit. (For further information on names, see de Laguna 1972:781–90.)]

GIRL'S PUBERTY*

At the first signs of puberty, the girl was confined in a small outhouse or in a partitioned space near the parents' sleeping place inside the house, for a period of four months. This might be increased, according to her social position, to a year and even longer. As she was considered unclean, this confinement was intended to appease the spirits [?]. The whole procedure was discussed and arranged beforehand. The girl fasted for the first four days, drinking water only in the evening. She ate on the fifth day, and then fasted for four more days. During this period her fingers were bound; she was not allowed to wash, comb her hair or do any work; only her mother or her attendant was allowed to see her. After this fasting period was over, however, she

**Editor's note:* I have checked and corrected the citations from Vancouver, Portlock, Dixon (Beresford), Fleurieu, von Langsdorff, and Dall, and have added Veniaminov, Holmberg, Petroff, and Grant on the age at which the labret hole was cut and on what dates this and other puberty customs were observed. The descriptions of labrets were moved to Chapter 9.

was visited by her female relatives and playmates. Throughout her confinement, her food was restricted to dried fish and meat, oil, and berries; and no fresh sea food was permitted. She drank water slowly through a bone tube, made of the leg bone of a swan or goose. Around her neck she wore suspended a stone charm with which she scratched her head or body; fingernails were never used.

Throughout her confinement, she was encouraged to keep herself occupied with those industries common to women, and she was instructed in those procedures and manners of her future life which she had not already learned through observation. She never went out in the daylight, but at night, with her face almost covered by a hat or hood, she might be taken out by her mother or aunt. [If she looked at the sky, it would storm.]

At the conclusion of her confinement, if the family were of high caste, her father gave a feast at which time she was bathed and dressed in new robes, and the confinement hat [puberty hood] was exchanged for one smaller, which was hung with a fringe of fur that partly concealed her face. She was seated in the place of honor opposite the doorway. Her lower lip was pinched until it was numb and then was pierced by her father's sister or a female member of his family [lineage] with a sharpened bear claw or bone awl, and a small bone plug was introduced to keep the hole open. In honor of this occasion and as a demonstration of the position and wealth of the family, a slave might be freed.

The first labret, *kan-noh* [q̓a-nu·x̣ʷ], was of bone or ivory, pinlike in form, put through from the inside, and this was worn until after marriage. This custom of piercing the lower lip and the introduction of the labret unquestionably marked maturity and introduced the girl to the public as marriageable. This is the explanation given by the Tlingit themselves, which makes it difficult to understand exceptions noted in the narratives of several early explorers. [See the quotations in "Labrets," Chapter 9. They were originally placed here in the manuscript, but have been included in the previous chapter.]

The statement made by Vancouver (1801, 4:253–54) that the cut was made in early infancy, and enlarged by laceration throughout girlhood, must have been made without sufficient knowledge, for no attempt was made to increase the size of the labret until after marriage. Portlock (1789:289) said that children have the lip bored when about two years old, and the hole is enlarged when they are thirteen to fourteen. Lisiansky (1814:243) wrote that the hole was made when they reached puberty, but in describing the wife of a Sitka chief in 1805, added (p. 225):

> She had a child with her, that was carried in a basket. Though it could not be more than three months old, it had the nose and lower lip pierced and hung with strings of beads.

[Fleurieu, citing evidence from Captain Chanal and Surgeon Roblet, with Captain Marchand at Sitka in 1791, wrote (1801, 1:326–27) that infant girls already wore wooden skewers in the lower lip (quoted in Chapter 9, the section "Labrets").]

Contradicting these observations are the statements of Dixon [Beresford] (1789:186–87) and von Langsdorff (1814, 2:115–16), [also de Laguna 1972:522], as well as of Dall and Holmberg, that the labret hole was cut at puberty [after release from puberty confinement].

[H. J. Holmberg, who followed Veniaminov ([1840] 1984:416), and who was himself at Sitka in 1850, wrote (1855:21, 40) that the maiden's lower lip was pierced at puberty, her first labret being a pin of bone or silver. At marriage this was replaced with a larger ornament of wood or bone, with repeated enlargements over the years.]

Dall (1884) wrote:

> The labret (formerly a slender bone or wooden pin, now generally of silver) among the Tlingit now means, and has long meant, maturity only. . . . The marriage of a girl was followed by the substitution of a larger plug, which was gradually enlarged, and typified the power, privileges, and respect enjoyed by the real head of the family [the married woman]. This practice has now gone out of date entirely, owing, no doubt, to the influence of the adverse opinion of the whites upon the younger people of the tribe. [p. 82] At present a silver pin, manufactured out of coin by the Indians themselves, replaces the bone pin with unmarried girls. The large labret, or kalushka, is entirely out of use, unless with some ancient dame in some very remote settlement. Many of the women from Sitka south have abandoned the practice entirely. [p. 88]

And Harmon [reference not available or found] reported that the lip of the daughter of a chief at Yakutat was pierced when she was twelve years old. [Harmon had apparently seen her when] she was lying, well dressed, in view on a shelf in the house, in an insensible condition from the operation, while the other children were running around, badly clad.

In personal conversation with the older people, from 1885 to 1900, it was unanimously stated that the piercing of the lip took place at the end of puberty and marked the girl as mature. The natives could not account for the previously quoted statements that the operation was performed at an earlier age.

[We have the testimony of Portlock (1789:289), of Marchand (Fleurieu 1801, 1:326–27), Vancouver (1801, 4:253–54) and Lisiansky (1814:225) that the lips of infant girls might be pierced. All other observers, especially in the nineteenth century, when perhaps the custom of wearing labrets was already declining or about to decline, report that the lip was cut at puberty, often specifying that this was done when the girl emerged from her confinement. The first labret was only a copper wire (or a wooden pin), inserted to keep open the hole. (Later this became the only labret.) At marriage, the wooden labret was inserted, to be replaced by larger and larger ones with increasing age, according to the testimony of all observers. It is possible that the time of lip cutting varied with the wealth of the father, and that when it was done at puberty, payment to the operator could be combined with the distribution of gifts at the girl's "coming out party," and so be less costly. In that case, the infants with labret pins must have been the daughters of wealthy chiefs.]

Von Langsdorff (1814, 2:133) also discussed the confinement of girls at puberty, as practiced in 1805:

> It is not uncommon when a young girl is grown up to shut her up, even for a whole year, in a small house by herself, at a distance from her family and acquaintance, where she is kept constantly employed: the idea is, that by this means she acquires habits of industry and diligence, reserve and modesty, which will afford the better chance of her becoming a good wife, and lay a solid foundation for wedded happiness. It is certain that industry, reserve, modesty, and conjugal fidelity, are the general characteristics of the female sex among these people, and form a most valuable distinction between them and the women of the more northern parts of the coast.

[Holmberg (1855:39–41) wrote that at the first signs of puberty a girl was confined in a dark, cramped place; because she was considered unclean, she must not look at the sky, to prevent which she had to wear a hat with a wide brim. Confinement was formerly (before 1850) for a year, but the Sitkans had cut it to six or even three months. At the beginning of this period, her lip was bored for the labret. All Tlingit women had a limping, crippled gait, in comparison to the proud, upright carriage of the men, which Holmberg could not explain. Rich Tlingit would give a feast when the girl was released. She was dressed in new clothes, the old ones were destroyed, and the slaves who had dressed her were freed. (This was taken from Veniaminov [1840] see 1984:416.)

[Whit. M. Grant, district attorney, writing from Sitka in May 1888 (p. 169), mentioned among the old customs that were being abandoned, the seclusion of Tlingit girls:

> They have a small house, about six by six feet and eight feet high, in which is a small door and one small air hole six by six inches in one side. In this they lock up and keep their maidens, when showing the first signs of womanhood, for six months, without fire, exercise, or association. All of the world they see is through that six by six inch hole, and all they get to eat and drink is through it. It makes no difference to them whether it is summer or winter. How the poor creatures survive the ordeal I can't understand. When let out, if alive, they are free to get married, and are often sold when in prison, to be delivered when their term of probation is over.

Although this account is exaggerated and inaccurate in some details, it indicates how late this custom survived.

[According to Petroff (1884:170) slave girls were not confined at puberty, a point which one can question. He also reported, apparently based on Holmberg (1855:40) and Veniaminov ([1840] 1984:416), that female slaves were not allowed to wear the labret.

[In addition to stressing puberty as a time for learning the skills demanded of adulthood, the Tlingit would not seem to have considered the girl only as unclean or "polluting" (Veniaminov, p. 416), but also as filled with power, dangerous to others, to the environment, and to herself.]

MARRIAGE*

Marriage could take place only between members of opposite phratries, because the exogamic law governed the life of the people. Intermarriage between members of groups that had the same phratral emblems came under the same law; but in other cases, even though the Tlingit phratral crest occurred only as a minor family [lineage] crest of the other people, that crest determined their position. This is particularly shown in the case of the two Haida families [clans] among the Stikine, the *Kas-quoir-qway-tee* [Ka·sx̣̓agʷe·dí, Raven 32] and the *Tahl-qway-de* [Ta·łqʷe·dí, Raven 33], that belonged to the Eagle division of the Masset Haida. But, since the Raven was a subordinate crest of the [Haida] Eagles, these clans took their places as Ravens among the Tlingit. [See Boas 1916:519–22, for the equation made on the basis of shared crests between the Haida Ravens, the Tlingit Wolves, and the Tsimshian Wolves and Bears; the Haida Eagles, the Tlingit Ravens, and the Tsimshian Ravens and Eagles. The controlling factors were the crests, not the phratral name.]

**Editor's note:* Toward the end of this section I added the quotations from von Langsdorff, Khlebnikov, and von Kotzebue; summaries from Lütké, Holmberg, and Shotridge; and references to Veniaminov and Marchand.

Intermarriage with the *Na-hut-di* [Ne·x̣ʔádi, "Eagles" of Sanya], who had no phratral standing with the Tlingit [and were outside the two Tlingit moieties], was in the same category as intermarriage with whites. The *Na-hut-di* claimed the Eagle crest, although this was not considered a phratral emblem by the Tlingit, but simply a subcrest [clan crest], so the children of such a union would belong of course to the mother's clan. But should the mother be a *Na-hut-di,* her children would have no phratral standing among the Tlingit, unless they were adopted as "opposites" of their Tlingit father. [Lack of phratral standing would be very awkward in ceremonial life, for the individual would never know whether to act as host or as guest at potlatch time (see Olson 1967:33–34).]

Polygyny and polyandry were both recognized practices among the Tlingit. The former was common, the latter exceptional. Yet as late as 1895, there was living at Sitka a Yakutat woman, Mrs. Tom or Thom [Kʷá·šk̓ ša·, Raven 19 woman], who had two husbands (brothers), and all lived happily together. [One husband, Thom, was the ranking Wolf 1 chief invited to a potlatch in Klukwan shortly before 1904 (Swanton 1908:439, de Laguna 1972:191–92)]. A man could have as many wives as he desired, but these seldom exceeded two, or possibly three. The wife brought to her husband certain privileges of trade, hunting, and fishing, belonging to her own clan. The trading rights with the interior people of the Yukon basin were of great value to many of the Chilkat who had Athabaskan wives. *Klanott* [Ƚʔuná·t̓, "They never die," Chilkoot], the second chief of the *Thlu-quoir-ut-di* [Ƚukʷa·x̣ʔádi, Raven 17], had three wives, two of whom were interior women, a mother and a daughter [see Olson 1936:214].

In the matriarchal system succession followed directly in the totemic line, which precluded the widow from sharing in the estate of her husband. In order that she might not be cast adrift, but might retain her place in the household, it was incumbent upon the husband's successor to take her to wife, regardless of her age or any additional wives he might have. When such a marriage was absolutely impossible, the widow could be bought off, but only by an older man having property of his own. But this seldom occurred. If a brother succeeded, he might release his wife in favor of the widow if the latter were of higher caste. But the succession more often fell to the nephew, the son of a sister of the deceased, who had been brought up in the house [of his maternal uncle]. While frequently this heir was only a mere boy, the disparity in age made no difference. Later, he would select a wife of more suitable age. And so, as a man's sister's son was brought up to marry his aunt (mother's brother's wife), a woman often chose her sister's daughter to take her place when she died. Or, a step-grandchild might be brought up as the logical successor to the grandmother [if of the same clan]. I knew of a case of this kind at Sitka, where the wife was so much older than her husband that it might reasonably be supposed that he would survive her. Even the oldest men seldom remained unmarried after the death of their wives.

[Polygyny posed problems for both the missionary and the convert. When *Tow-a-att,* t̓awyá·t̓, head of Wolf House at Wrangell, became converted, he was married to Eve, and to her daughter Julia by a former marriage. He solved the problem by keeping the younger woman as a wife, while the old woman remained in his house as his mother-in-law (see Young 1927:160).]

All Tlingit married: boys after sixteen, and girls after twelve or fourteen, upon reaching maturity. The parents often arranged for the marriage of their children in their infancy. The mother, [maternal] aunt, or sister of a young man would go to the mother of the girl to ask for her and would state the amount of property they would give. If, after several days of consideration, this was accepted, the property was delivered by the suitor's family. If the offer were not considered adequate, more might be added after much controversy, or negotiations might end and the property be returned. When acceptance had been signified, and the day appointed, the families [lineages?] of both parties fasted and assembled at the house of the bride. The guests were seated on either side of the house, the host with his brothers and friends [clansmen or lineage-mates] in the front space, while the groom, in ceremonial dress, occupied the place of honor opposite the doorway, seated on a new mat. The bride was hidden in a back corner of the house. Speeches were made by the head men of both families. Then the accumulated property was distributed to the host's [bride's] family and some to the groom's family. Then the bride was called. Taking her hand, her father led her to the groom and seated her at his side; or, while the family [clan] song was chanted, she might come forth and approach the groom, singing and dancing. She was covered from shoulders to feet in a ceremonial blanket, wore moccasins on her feet, while a woven spruce root hat covered much of her face. More property was then distributed, of which the host gave some to the groom as a token of good will, thus ending the ceremony.

An older man who had his own house would then take his bride home, but a young man would live with his father-in-law and work for him. If a man and wife separated, he gave her a certain amount of property, and either could remarry. Upon the death of a wife, the husband could take her unmarried sister to wife without further payment, but under the same circumstances he could not take her married sister without the consent of her husband.

[There is relatively little information on marriage in the reports of the early explorers, undoubtedly because they did not understand the principles of Tlingit social organization, and lacked opportunities for witnessing a wedding.

[Thus, von Langsdorff (1814, 2:133) reported only that:

> The Kaluschians have commonly only one wife: a few among the chiefs, who are in their way very rich and substantial men, have two wives, an old and a young one.

[Fortunately, Khlebnikov ([1817–32] 1976:28) was more specific:

> A man who enters into marriage must be strong enough to undertake any kind of work, and be able to use weapons. He asks and receives permission of the parents [of the intended bride—Translator] to go to their settlement where he wishes to marry; he sends a man with his proposal to the woman he plans to marry. If the bride and her father agree, he then brings gifts to the parents of the bride, and to her close relatives, and is given his bride. Later he and his wife go to her parents and receive gifts from them, which must be more valuable than the initial gifts from the groom. These gifts consist of animal pelts, items from Europe, weapons, and frequently slaves.

[This form of marriage was evidently that practiced by wealthy, established men—house owners. Khlebnikov went on to explain that the intended bride had the right to reject the marriage, citing the case of a woman who refused to marry a chief, "toion," because he refused to send his first wife back to her relatives.

> Wealthy and influential Kolosh may have as many as five wives, and sometimes more. They try to receive large dowries through these ties, and to acquire a large number of relatives in order to strengthen their position thereby. In some tribes [of Tlingit?] it is the custom to marry before puberty. There are cases of jealousy among wives which often lead to a quarrel and sometimes to fights with knives and cudgels. If a wife is unfaithful, and is caught, then the husband kills her and her lover, with no vengeance on the part of the relatives, to whom he may pay something in the line of clothing or other items of value. This punishment applies to a man who has no blood ties with the husband.

[In the latter case, the husband could force his relative to take the woman as a concubine, Khlebnikov explained, but the insulted husband might attack the lover in anger. We should also note that infidelity of the wife with a clan-brother of her husband is cited by the Tlingit as a reason for emigration of part of the clan.

> There are some indulgent husbands who will allow an elder wife to have a young male assistant who lives with them in the hut and takes care of all the work, and in the absence of the husband takes his place in bed. [Such a secondary husband, or "future husband," as the Tlingit call him, would be the nephew or other heir of the husband—FdeL.]
>
> . . . A wife is always selected from another tribe [clan, moiety]. However, one must note that after the death of an uncle, the nephew is supposed to take his wife [widow] regardless of age difference. It is possible that two sisters may become wives of the same man.

[Lütké (1835:209–11) copied Khlebnikov's account almost word for word, but did identify the chief who was rejected by his intended because he refused to divorce his first wife, as Naouchket, or Naouchketl or Naouchkekl, who was baptized about 1826 (Lütké 1835:210, 145, note 11).

[Marchand (in Fleurieu 1801, 1:367–70), in commenting on the apparent harmony in the Tlingit family, noted the modesty and decorum of the women in the presence of the men. One man indicated with gestures that, if he suspected that the baby his wife was suckling was not his own, he would stab the woman and devour the child, which last threat the Frenchman deemed exaggerated. A woman who thought the white man's question implied that her baby was not by her husband, snatched up a dagger and was ready to strike the Frenchman. However, when their husbands were absent, these same women came running to the French with eagerness and smiling affability, which proved "that ugliness is not always the pledge of chastity: perhaps too the French demonstrated to them, that it was not always doomed to experience a refusal" (p. 370).

[Von Kotzebue (1830, 2:56–57), who was at Sitka in 1825, reported that wars or feuds might start over Tlingit women, "similar to that of Troy for the fair Helen," and that while he was in Sitka:

> A girl had four lovers, whose jealousy produced the most violent quarrels: after fighting for a long time without any result, they determined to end the strife by murdering the object of their love, and the resolution was immediately executed with their lances. The whole horde assembled round the funeral pile, and chanted a song, a part of which was interpreted by one of our countrymen, who had been long resident here. "Thou wast too beautiful—thou couldst not live—men looked on thee, and madness fired their hearts!"

Indian family, Chilkoot, posed for their picture, late 1870s or 1880s. Note "camphor" chest and boxes on the elaborately adzed bench on which the boy is sitting. The doorway leads into a sleeping room. (Photograph by I. W. Taber. Courtesy of SNM.)

[Their weddings were celebrated merely by a feast given to the relatives of the bride.

[Holmberg (1855:33–35), largely following Veniaminov ([1840] 1984:416–18), wrote that marriage was without religious ceremony, but was forbidden within the same "race": a Raven must marry a Wolf and vice versa. Polygyny was common among the wealthy, although the first wife had authority over the others. When a young man had selected his bride, he would send a spokesman to her parents or relatives; if the answer was favorable, the man would send gifts to his future father-in-law. On the set day, when all the guests were assembled, the groom would enter and sit down with his back to the door. The guests then sang a special song, accompanied by a dance, as if to call the bride out of her dark corner. Then the floor was covered with utensils, furs, and weapons from the corner to the groom's place, and over these his bride walked to sit beside him. She had to keep her head bowed throughout the whole proceedings. Then came dancing and singing by everyone except the young couple, to be followed by feasting, in which they also could take no part. In fact, the bride and groom had to fast for two days to ensure a happy marriage for life. After this time, they were allowed a very small portion of food, and then had to fast for two days more. The marriage would not be consummated for four weeks. If the groom was rich, he would be at liberty either to stay with his parents-in-law or to return to his home. The bride brought a dowry at least as valuable as the gifts of the groom.

[Holmberg further specified that if the marriage proved unlucky, the pair were free to separate, in which case neither dowry nor gifts were returned. If the husband was not pleased with his wife, he could send her home, but he had to surrender the dowry and would not get back his presents. If the wife had been unfaithful, the husband had the right to demand the return of his gifts, without giving up the dowry. In all cases of separation, the children remained with their mother.

[Louis Shotridge (son of "Raven's Slave," and grandson of Chief Chartrich) of Klukwan was married in the traditional fashion (Shotridge 1929). Early marriage between equals, arranged by the parents on both sides with due regard to the morals, character, and industry of the couple, to ensure a long married life, was still practiced, so that Louis knew whom he was to marry. All of his maternal relatives, and the immediate male relatives of his father, collected money and valuables, and took these to the bride's family, leaving Louis and an elderly uncle alone. In a reasonable time, the intermediaries returned with the bride, accompanied by her relatives. They were Louis's "brothers-in-law," or men of the bride's clan (Raven 3); "fathers-in-law," or men of the bride's father's clan (Wolf 1); the bride's "sisters-in-law," women of the groom's clan (Wolf 1); and the bride's "fathers-in-law," men of the groom's father's clan (Raven 3). All contributed in one way or another to the marriage.

[On the day following the feast given to the bride's relatives, Louis was led from house to house by his "brothers-in-law," and from each received clothing, guns, and other things necessary to a man. About four months later, Louis and the young men of his clan carried a gift of firewood to the bride's father, who was the elder of his clan. Louis was seated near the fire, and his "fathers-in-law" came to express approval by warming their hands at the fire. Then food was set before Louis, and, beginning with the youngest, the "fathers-in-law" in turn brought money and gifts to him; then an equal amount, representing the main dowry, was given him. Eight days after the marriage (in this case there was also a church wedding), the bride's father distributed to all his fellow clansmen the gifts contributed by Louis's party. Eventually twice the amount received would be contributed to the married pair by the bride's father's clansmen.

[Holmberg (1855:36–36) wrote that the authorized lovers of married women, the substitutes for their husbands, were regularly the brothers or other close relatives of the husbands. This statement was based on the report by Veniaminov ([1840] 1984:418). We believe that this "vice-husband," to use Petroff's expression, was the man already selected to be the woman's husband when she became widowed. (See Petroff 1884:169.)

[Marchand (Fleurieu 1801, 1:370) reported that there were a few male homosexuals among the Tlingit. They remained, apparently, outside of all marriage alliances.]

DEATH*

Upon the approach of death to a man, when all hope had been abandoned, his family assembled and chanted their clan war songs. The dying man was placed behind the fire, facing the door, and was dressed in clean clothes and surrounded by the family's ceremonial paraphernalia. It was a fixed belief of the Tlingit that at this time the dying person was in direct communication with the spirits of the departed, and that they talked to him, telling him to have no fear, that they would guide and protect him on his journey to the future life [land of the dead] where all his ancestors awaited him. And thus death was made easy and there was no struggle. The Tlingit had no fear of death.

Death was announced by the wife's [widow's] brother, who called out loudly outside the house. In 1885 [1882?], the death of a chief at Sitka was announced by the firing, in the night, of a small Russian cannon mounted in front of the house. The family [the deceased's clan-mates] then moved out of the house, while the brothers-in-law [of the deceased], or men of the opposite moiety, took charge of the corpse. They washed, dressed, and placed it in a sitting position; the knees were drawn up to the body and bound, and the hands were placed on the knees. Sometimes a sharp knife was placed in the right hand, [so that the ghost could] combat the powerful animal spirits to be met on the narrow trail to the spirit land. Strong moccasins were placed on the feet and heavy mittens on the hands, for the trail was rocky and led through a tangle of devil's club and bushes. The face was painted red with the clan crest design used especially for the dead. For most of the Raven clans this was a solid inverted V with the apex at the bridge of the nose; for the Wolf clans there were usually red bars down each cheek. Eagle down was blown over the hair, a head-

Editor's note: I added information and a quotation from Shukoff about the funeral and the smoking feast, as well as the longer account written for Emmons by an unknown Chilkat Indian, the quotations from Petroff, and information from Swanton. The death and wake of a chief at Sitka were witnessed by Emmons, and the cremation of what was presumably the same chief is described in the next section. Emmons has given the dates of 1882 and 1885 for the two events, but his memory for dates is known to be faulty.

Coudawot, a chief of the Raven 3 clan at Klukwan, dressed for death, after a severe hemorrhage. He displays his ceremonial blanket, headdress, and other heirlooms. (Photograph by G. T. Emmons. AMNH.)

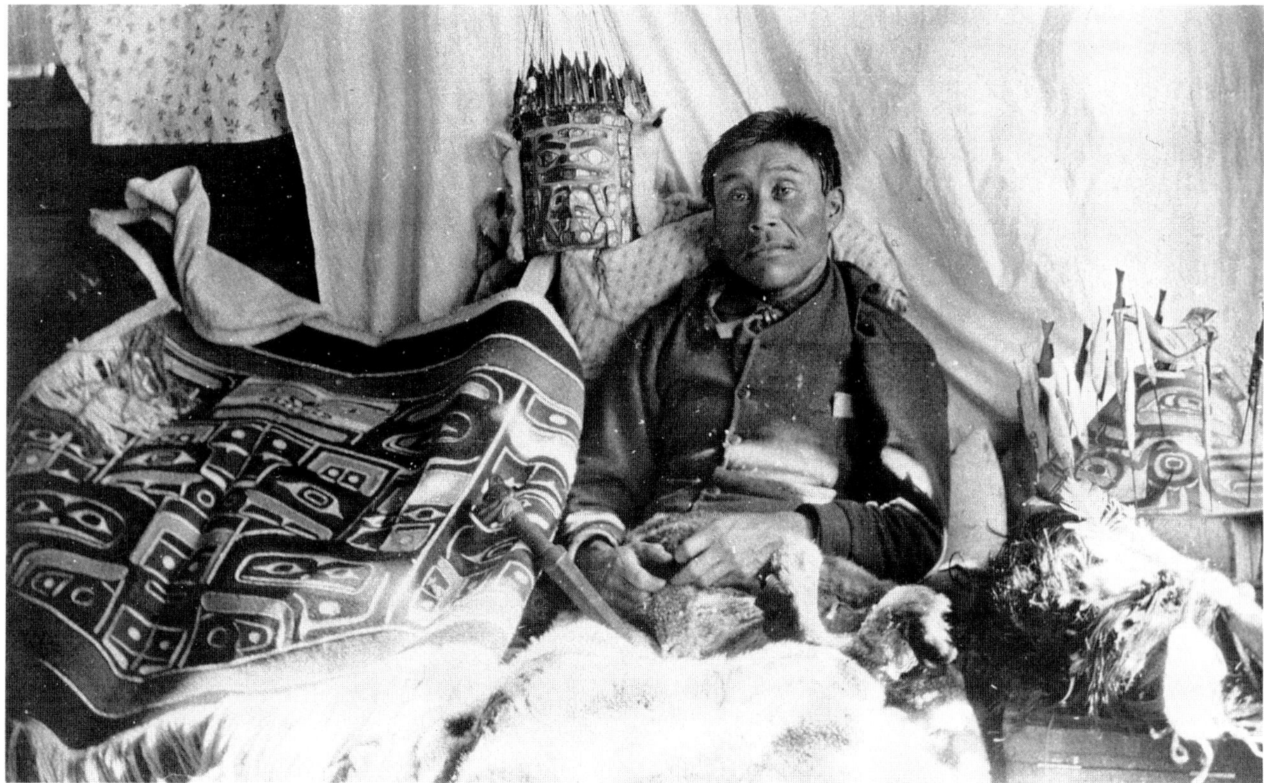

dress was placed on the head, and the body was covered with ceremonial robes or a Chilkat blanket reaching to the chin. For a chief, all the family headdresses and ceremonial paraphernalia were crowded around the body.

The hair of the widow was washed and then cut or burned off; her face was blackened, her right arm and the fingers of her right hand were bound [because of the taboo against doing any work]. In some extreme instances, she cut and bruised her breasts, and bit her body, and it has been claimed that she even threw herself against the funeral pyre during the cremation of the corpse and might be slightly burned, but not to death.

Throughout the eight days of mourning, the widow was not allowed to do anything; all her wants were supplied by attendants. She was dressed in her oldest clothes, with a bark rope around the waist. While the corpse remained in the house, she sat beside it and cried. She fasted throughout the day, and ate a little at night. But the old customs required her to fast during eight days and only on the evenings of the second, fourth, sixth, and eighth day, to partake of the food which was placed on a flat stone. She threw a little of everything she ate into the fire for the spirit of the dead.

Upon the death of a man [according to Dick Satan of Sitka], his mother, wife, brothers and sisters, and his sister's children, but not his own children who belonged to the "opposite clan," blackened their faces with the hemlock fungus.

Upon the death of a woman [he also said], her father [!], brothers and sisters, and sister's children, but not her own sons [!], blackened their faces.

[This second note is incorrect. The only "opposite" to blacken the face was, in both cases, the spouse. The other mourners belonged to the clan of the deceased, and included the mother, brothers and sisters, sister's children, and the dead woman's children of both sexes, but not her father.]

As will be seen, everything was done by the widow's family [especially her lineage], and for these services they were paid at the feast given later. At the death of a chief, one or more slaves might be killed, since it was believed that their spirits would attend to their master's wants in the spirit world. But if he had so signified, the slaves might be

Chief Shakes V, Kow-ish-te, Wolf 18, lying in state, surrounded by crest heirlooms of his clan, Wrangell, May 1878. (Photograph probably by George Davidson. USNM cat. no. 4780.)

set free, in which case a crier would go through the village, calling their names.

While the corpse lay in state, no cooking was done in the house, but food was prepared elsewhere and brought in. Every day, morning and evening, while the corpse remained in the house, the men of the lineage, dressed in old robes with a bark rope around the waist, chanted four weeping songs. They were led by an older man who beat time with staff in hand. Singing these mourning songs was supposed to make the trail easier for the ghost to travel. In the interval, women mourners, sitting in front of the corpse, improvised crying songs and wailed. It was believed that at this time the spirit remained in or near the corpse until after cremation, and that it was instructed by the spirits of former friends how to avoid the many dangers that beset the trail over which it had to pass.

[Shukoff, the Tlingit half-breed, who provided information in 1882, gave a slightly different account of the Tlingit funeral. For example, when a chief died he was dressed in a button blanket (blue cloth trimmed with red and mother-of-pearl buttons), or a Chilkat blanket, and his face was painted red, so that it wouldn't look as if he were dead. They put the wooden headdress (šakiˑʔát) on his head and covered his face with a handkerchief. The women sat before the dead chief for hours, facing the corpse and talking to him: "When you were alive you used to look after us and help us, and liked us so. Now you have left us forever, you will never see us again, but you will see your fathers in another world who have been waiting many long days for you, but don't forget us, for we will see you in the future."

[The talk was low and like a song or chant. Shukoff repudiated the idea that women were paid to wail; some may come to sit and cry, but they cry remembering their own troubles. The men of the deceased's lineage would come to the house, each wearing a rope around his waist, and would sing, standing near the door. One led, and all joined in the chorus, keeping time by pounding long sticks on the floor. This was done early in the morning and late at night. The body of a chief or important person might be kept for five or six days. On the last day of the wake, before cremation, the smoking feast was held.]

After the introduction of tobacco, the smoke feast, *sakis ko-eek* [ṡe·q-yís, "smoke-for," qu-ʔí·x̣, "an inviting"], replaced the primitive chewing feast, when a little pellet, composed of a native nicotine plant, lime, and bark ash, was sucked. This feast was held in the evening preceding the cremation.

The invitations were delivered by the "brothers-in-law," the men married to the "sisters" of the deceased, to their own clan. That is, supposing the dead man were a Wolf, only Ravens would be invited and entertained. The house was straightened up and swept with eagle wings; great cedar logs were laid in the fireplace and oil poured over them. After dark, the guests began to assemble and were silently shown to their places by two or more ["brothers-in-law"], members of the opposite clan (Ravens) [from the deceased]. The chiefs and principal men were seated on mats in the space back of the fire and facing the door, other men [also guests] on each side, and the women behind the men. The mourning lineage, in mean dress and with blackened faces, occupied the front space of the house. The master of ceremonies, a head man of the lineage (Wolf), stood a little to one side, in front of the fire with a dance staff in hand, and near him was a long dish containing black leaf tobacco which had been contributed by all the members of his clan. This was presided over by one of the lineage (Wolf), who crumbled it and filled the carved pipes of the lineage and those of the guests. [All but guests of high rank were supposed to bring their own pipes with them.]

As the pipes were handed to the guests, commencing with the most important, the name of some ancestor was mentioned [by the Wolf master of ceremonies], as the pipe and the gift of tobacco were supposed to come to the guest from the dead, and honored both giver and guest. They smoked in complete silence. Women often received a little pellet to suck, but more recently pipes were handed to them which they passed from one to another, since they did not smoke continuously as did the men. After all the guests were provided with tobacco, the family [lineage] of the deceased smoked in silence. Then some strands of tobacco were placed at each corner of the fireplace and were burned as an offering to the dead. The names of members of the Wolf lineage were called out as tobacco was cast into the flames with the words *tok a dy* [du x̣é·de·], "for his mouth." The spirits of even those long dead were invited to attend this feast, and they were believed to receive the spiritual equivalent of the tobacco thus offered, which came to them through the fire, just as their spirits had passed through the fire when their bodies were cremated.

[As explained by Shukoff:

> They invited guest[s], *ku-neyet-kar-nar-gu* [gune·tkana·yí, "members of the opposite moiety"], who are supposed to bring their own pipes with them, each receive a small piece of tobacco, the relatives of dead chief light pipe and give to guest, calling man's name who died long since. For instance, suppose *Kat-lean* [Q̇ałyá·n, Raven 10 chief in Sitka] a dead ancestor, then as they hand pipe they would say "from Katlean," *Katlean che-ta* [Q̇ałyá·n ǯí·-dé, literally "to Katlean," rather than "from".]

This perhaps means that the guest was conceived as sitting in for the departed. It would be interesting to know whether the Tlingit always gave the same dead person's name to the same guest at such smoking feasts, as did the Eyak with their "potlatch names" (see Birket-Smith and de Laguna 1938:156).]

> Guests silent smoke, then when all have received pipes, one elder relative appoints six or eight guests to go after wood for cremation. Later one head man makes a very mournful speech, and owner of house replies. Then after owner of home replies, he talks to dead, "Stand on one side and let your fathers go by you." [The "fathers" are the guests in the opposite moiety.] They suppose that the dead man's spirit lives in house [until body is] cremated.

The family [clan] songs were sung to the accompaniment of the drum and the beating of the chief's staff on the floor. Speeches were made first by the host, thanking his guests for honoring the dead and the clan, then by the chief guest for the entertainment, during which he mentioned the names of his host's family who responded with "Ah, ah." At this meeting the names of those who would build the funeral pyre and carry the corpse were announced. [The choice was made by the bereaved from among those most closely related by paternal or affinal ties to the deceased, and were called out by the chief.]

A song sung when the body is lying in state:

I am sorry, my brother
  When you go.
I will see you again, my brother.
  Maybe I die soon.

A chant song at first mourning:

Come back, come back,
  My brother.
From the spirit land,
  Come back. (Repeated)

Photograph by G. T. Emmons of a man a few moments before his death, taken at the request of his relatives, Sitka, 1889. (AMNH.)

Chant song at second mourning:

As if it were possible to hear thy voice
Once more in thine house,
My brother,
I listen for thee in the early morning. (Repeated)

[Such songs were among the most treasured prerogatives of clans; but Emmons did not identify the clan owning these.]

[The following manuscript, written for Emmons by an unknown informant, was found in BCPA, and is entitled: *Death Ceremonies, All About Chilkat Natives.* Here, some of the information is consolidated in the interest of brevity.

> The tribe [clan of deceased?] gathers together at the announcement of death at the house where the dead lay. Natives, the sex of the dead but of a different clan, that are invited guests, wash and dress the corpse in undergarments and put over the body a blue blanket decorated with a red border and the border is covered with small white pearl buttons, which may belong to the dead body or to a relative.
>
> The body is placed in a sitting position, facing the door. The invited guests are generally dressed in their dancing costumes. Should the dead happen to be a chief, he has two red marks painted across both cheeks, and his fancy dancing hat is put on his head. He is surrounded by all that has dancing costumes [all his own? or all of those of his lineage?]. The natives that wash the body of a male, they also wash the widow's hair, then cut it. The natives that wash and dress the corpse must also gather the boughs for the burning.
>
> In the presence of the dead body after he is dressed, the feast begins. Natives of the totem of which he or she belonged furnish the potlatch or the presents to be given away. The widow has to sit near the corpse and is compelled to cry until the whole business is over. The mourners [lineage? of deceased] cannot cook their meals, but the neighbors bring the food to the house to eat. The mourners and the members of the totem to which the dead belonged must not handle a thing during the ceremonies, only when the service is over.
>
> It takes from three to five days according to the wealth of the dead, as the gifts are distributed to the invited guests from the friendly tribes [clans?] as long as they last. While the body lies in state the invited guests dance and chant, and when tired they rest and others of the invited guests take their place. That is kept up day and night, and some of the women sit around and beat little sticks to keep time. The smoking and chewing feast begins with the passing of *Konge* [gánč] or Indian black native leaf tobacco to smoke, and ground leaf tobacco like snuff, mixed with a little ashes, is given to the women to chew.
>
> The building of the funeral pyre [is] by them that helped wash and dress the corpse. Four or six of the invited guests carry the corpse to the place to be cremated. The body is wrapped in a clean white blanket, usually a Hudson Bay blanket that the natives call "King George blanket."
>
> At death of a chief one or more slaves are killed and buried [?], but not too close to where the ashes of the chief rest. Sometimes one or more slaves are set free, according to the wish of the chief before he dies. One of the guests with a bell in hand goes around and calls it ordered by the former chief before his demise that the name of the slave is set free [*sic*]. If the chief left more slaves, they go to the new chief. A nephew, son of a favorite sister of the dead chief, is generally named by the old chief to be the coming chief.

[Ivan Petroff wrote in the census report of 1880 (1884:165):

> The former custom of killing slaves on the death of a chief in order to furnish him with servants in the other world has become obsolete or exists only nominally, as for long years previous to the sale of the territory the Thlinket of Alaska were in the habit of accepting presents from the Russian authorities in consideration of releasing the intended victims of this practice. They resorted to the same extortion during the first year of American occupation, when the military commander at Sitka, with 200 or 300 soldiers at his back, was weak enough to comply with it, and to bribe the insolent chiefs into abstaining from murder.

[Petroff (p. 171) also stated, on the authority of Holmberg (1855:44; see also Khlebnikov 1976:27, 29, 31–32) that:

> No certain time is set for the cremation or for the festivities; this depends altogether upon the magnitude of the preparations, and it frequently occurs that the corpse is in an advanced stage of putrefaction when the time arrives.

[Swanton (1909:372–73) reported a hypothetical "tobacco feast," as dictated by Katishan [Qá·daša·n], of the Raven 32, Ka·sx̣agʷe·dí, of Wrangell. S. Hall Young (1927:185–86) described him as "the shrewdest and most diplomatic of the Stickeens. . . . [He was] a master of metaphors. . . . His family was the tribal custodian of the funeral songs and ceremonies, which must be executed after the death of every native of note." He died in 1916.

[In this account, Katishan's wife, a Na·nya·ʔa·yí, Wolf 18, woman had supposedly died. Her clan would hold the tobacco feast before the cremation, inviting the widower's clan, the Raven 32. The hosts were quiet, because they were mourning. Katishan would speak to the mourners, to offer comfort, addressing them as "my grandfathers."

> We are not smoking this tobacco for which you have invited us. These long dead uncles of ours [mother's brothers—FdeL] and our mothers are the ones who smoke it. . . . Our [dead—Translator] chief has come back because he has seen you mourning. Now, however, he has wiped away your tears. [Swanton 1909:372]

[Then a spokesman for the mourning Wolves would thank their "grandfathers" for their words, and would say to the dead woman:

"Get up from your husbands' path [so that they may pass out—Translator]" [referring to all the Raven men as her "husbands"—FdeL]. Katishan also explained (Swanton 1909:373):

> The spirits of the dead of both phratries are supposed to be smoking while their friends on earth [fellow clansmen] smoke, and they also share the feast.]

CREMATION*

On the fourth day the body was cremated. [Shukoff said that the body of a chief or of someone of high rank might be kept in the house for five or six days before cremation. This was expensive, since all this time the guests were being fed from the supplies of the bereaved.]

The funeral pyre was built by members of the opposite phratry, who gathered yellow cedar logs for it, and who performed all the work: removing the body from the house, placing it on the pyre, burning it, collecting the ashes and depositing them in the gravehouse.

I can best describe the entire ceremony from the cremation of a chief that I witnessed at Sitka in 1882 when the Tlingit practiced the old customs in every particular. The body had lain in state for four days. On the afternoon of the fourth day since death, it was placed in a woven cedar-bark mat and carried by four men of the opposite phratry through the side of the house, where a plank had been removed. As it passed out, an old woman gathered some of the ashes from the fireplace in a small basket which she cast through the opening. Then she picked up a dog and threw it out, to cleanse the house of the spirit of death, which some claimed would enter the dog.

[Shukoff said that the corpse might be taken out through the smokehole, as well as through a hole made in the side wall; and that, if the dog were not thrown out after the corpse, death might return to the house. At the Christian funeral of the wife of chief Anahootz, at Sitka in 1881, the body was carried out through an opening made in the side of the house, after a dog had been led out ahead of it (Mrs. Willard 1884:18).]

The rectangular funeral pyre of yellow cedar logs, eight feet long by four feet wide, was built up about three feet high to support a platform. The sides and one end were extended upward for three feet, thus forming a boxlike receptacle with one end open. The corpse was entered through this end; then the end was closed and a roof of cross logs was laid on top. Over this a gallon of seal oil was poured, and the whole ignited. The male members of the family [lineage] of the dead man were grouped a short distance from the pyre. They were dressed in old robes tied about the waist with cedar-bark rope, their faces blackened and hair disheveled. At their head was an old man of high rank who beat time with a long baton in his hand, as he led the slow death chant. This was taken up in a shrill key by some thirty women of the widow's clan, who stood in a semicircle on the opposite side of the pyre. They were dressed in blue blankets with wide red borders and rows of pearl buttons ["button blankets"]. Their faces were blackened, heads bound with black handkerchiefs; silver rings were pendant from the septum of the nose and long earrings of red worsted ornamented with plates of haliotis shell

**Editor's note:* I have included information about the whites' attitudes toward cremation and their efforts to prevent the practice. This is based on information and quotations from Wardman, Young, Mrs. Willard, Olson, Krause, and Veniaminov.

Cremation of a Tlingit, Sitka, 1886. (Photograph by G. T. Emmons. AMNH.)

hung from their ears. They wore moccasins. In her right hand each woman carried a hemlock sapling ten to twelve feet long, stripped of its branches to within a foot of the end, and as they sang they swayed their bodies from side to side, in a movement which is called *co-ta-ceh,* "dancing with the knees" [?-łe·x̣, "? – dance"]. To the right of the men of the lineage, seated on the ground, dressed in old clothes, with faces blackened and hair cut short, were the widow and female members of the lineage who kept up a continuous wailing.

Two men, brothers of the widow, tended the fire with long poles, and at intervals valuable pieces of property, such as guns, robes, and clothing, were cast into the flames. After the fire had burned down, the charred bones and ashes were gathered up and placed in a handsomely carved, oblong chest which was corded and deposited in the family [lineage] gravehouse behind the dwelling. According to old custom the family used to cleanse themselves by going into salt water, but in this case the men and women repaired to separate houses to bathe, in preparation for the invitation feast which always followed cremation. [Shukoff specified that all the male members of the deceased's clan or lineage, not simply their leader, carried long sticks with which to beat time.]

When the remains had been consumed, the women of the widow's clan who had taken part in the occasion in ceremonial dress, now marched through the village in single file, chanting for the dead. They entered each house of their clan and invited their clan-mates to the coming feast.

[According to Shukoff, it was the duty of members of the opposite moiety to gather up the ashes and charred bones of the deceased in an expensive blanket and to put this in a wooden box, *tlak* [łáqt]. This was kept in a tent until a gravehouse was built to hold the box. Then the bereaved gave a potlatch and gave away torn pieces of blanket and other presents to the guests who had worked at the funeral.]

At the cremation of a chief, sometimes one or more slaves were killed to attend to his wants in the next world. [A slave was always killed for a dead chief, according to Shukoff.] It is generally stated that the body of a slave killed at this time was cast into the sea, but Lisiansky (1814:241) wrote that the slave's body was cremated with the master's, and I know of one case in which the body of a slave was cremated.

[It should be remembered that inhumation was almost the universal method of disposing of the dead in the United States in the 1880s. Cremation was regarded as a heathen practice by the missionaries, who did everything they could to eradicate it (Willard 1884:129–30; Wright 1883:98, 135–36; Young 1927:135). Perhaps the first cremation in the United States took place in 1879, when Dr. LeMoyne celebrated the completion of his crematorium in Washington, Pennsylvania, by cremating the body of Baron von Palm, an event which attracted tremendous public interest, with journalists from New York City and Philadelphia "to report the wonderful ceremony" (Wardman 1884:62). Even the Reverend S. Hall Young (1927:134–35) who was to take "a stand against this horrid heathen ceremony [cremation] and [try to persuade] the people to adopt Christian burial," had been present at the funeral of a friend whose body, at his own request, was "cremated in a Le Moyn furnace. Of course there was nothing revolting in that ceremony. But the gruesome sight of a Thlingit burning brought a change in my feelings."

[It seems worthwhile, therefore, to add descriptions of two Tlingit cremations that were witnessed by whites. The first was that described by Young, which took place at the "Foreign [Indian] Town" at Wrangell, apparently in 1879. He wrote (1927:134–35):

> The deceased woman was the daughter of a chief of the Raven phratry. I arrived just after the funeral pile of logs had been erected and the naked body of the woman laid upon it. The Indian women were all wailing in their peculiar doleful minor singsongs, and a large crowd of natives surrounded the pile of logs. At a given word the family of the deceased surrounded the bier, and one of them applied the torch. The logs were of dry yellow cedar, and quantities of pitch wood had been distributed among them and gallons of seal grease poured over the body and pile of wood.
>
> The flames sprang up quickly, and black smoke flooded the whole scene. Then the mourners began to circle around the funeral pyre, and the songs grew louder and faster and the move-

ments more rapid. It resolved itself into a frantic dance; the natives screeching and crying and invoking the spirit of the dead in loud tones. Then they began to snatch burning embers from the fire and as they circled around would thrust these fagots into the flesh of the corpse; then long splinters of spruce pitch were thrust into the flesh, and these soon were on fire until great flames enwrapped the body; the fierce heat from under it roasted and charred the flesh. It was a most revolting sight, and it continued for over an hour before the body was reduced to ashes.

[George Wardman (1884:63–64) observed a cremation at Sitka in 1879 and described it:

> The funeral pyre consisted of a crib of dried logs, each about six inches in diameter and six feet in length, arranged four at the ends and three upon each side, supported by green stakes.
>
> The arrangements were very simple. The body of a squaw, who had died on Sunday (this was on Wednesday), was hoisted out of the smoke-hole in the center of the house. Dead bodies are never permitted to go out through the doorway, among these Indians. If they were taken out that way, the spirits would be almost certain to return to plague their surviving relatives. The body in question was wrapped in a common bark mat, such as these Indians make, and laid in the crib, the top being covered with logs laid crosswise. The fire was then started and the mourners, who consisted of female relatives, sat around upon the ground to the windward and slightly to the right of the burning pile. Their hair had been cut short, their faces were all blackened, and as the tears from their weeping eyes cut channels through the lampblack, the effect was exceedingly touching. The squaws, who numbered fifteen or twenty, sobbed, sniffled, and whined with every evidence of genuine grief. To the left of the women a number of male relatives of the deceased put in the time chanting continually and keeping time with staves about five feet long, with which they rapped pieces of boards. The men stood erect all this time and were led in the chant by an old man who held a crow totem in one hand, which being shaken, produced a rattling noise, by pebbles within the hollow instrument. [This was a chief's Raven rattle.]
>
> The ceremony continued for about three hours and a half, when the remains were consumed, with the exception of some of the larger leg and arm bones and a portion of the skull. As soon as the residuum was cool enough to be taken up, the mass, along with some of the wood ashes, was placed in a box, which was deposited in a sort of small hen-coop on stakes, scores of which dot the hill behind the village.
>
> After the cremation the tired Indians turned in and slept during the afternoon, and at night had their customary dance in honor of the successful issue of the enterprise. [This was a feast to feed the dead; see below.]

[Emmons consulted Mrs. Willard's *Life in Alaska* and took notes on her description of the funeral of a baby boy at Haines

Old funeral pyre back of Klukwan, 1889. (Photograph by G. T. Emmons. BCPA.)

(Chilkoot), but he does not seem to have incorporated this in his account. Mrs. Willard (1884:249–61) noted that the baby was dressed in all the good clothing he possessed, with a turbaned handkerchief on the head, the face painted with vermilion, and mittens on his hands. "In a little bag hung about his neck were charms for his safety and a paper containing a quantity of red powder for use on the way" (p. 251). The body was placed sitting up, the knees drawn to the chin and tied in place. All around him were beautiful white woolen blankets. The body would lie in state for several days, while preparations were made for the cremation. The night before this, all of "the friends of the tribe" (the baby's "opposites") would be called to a feast; the highest ranking clan chief would be invited first. The logs for the fire would be stacked up, "log-house fashion," so that the flames roared up through the smokehole. One man by the fire would fill the pipes, which a little boy lit and passed to all the guests in turn, who smoked in silence. Occasionally some one would give a slow, solemn speech. Then the invited chiefs beat time on the floor with their staves, while the men sang, and the women with blackened faces and short hair would break out with shrill cries.

[At sunrise, the body wrapped in blankets was hoisted out of the house through the smokehole with skin ropes. "Some of the other tribes [clans] take out a board from the back of the house, and after removing through it the body a dog is led through, that any attending evil may fall upon it" (p. 255). Cremation took place on a little hill, some distance from the houses. Here the ashes were put into a box and the latter was set in a miniature house on four high stakes. The graveyard looked like a village of such small houses. On the night after the cremation, a feast for the dead was held (see below).

[According to Olson (1967:59), the clan "brothers-in-law" start the fire, a man of the "opposite moiety" beats the drum,

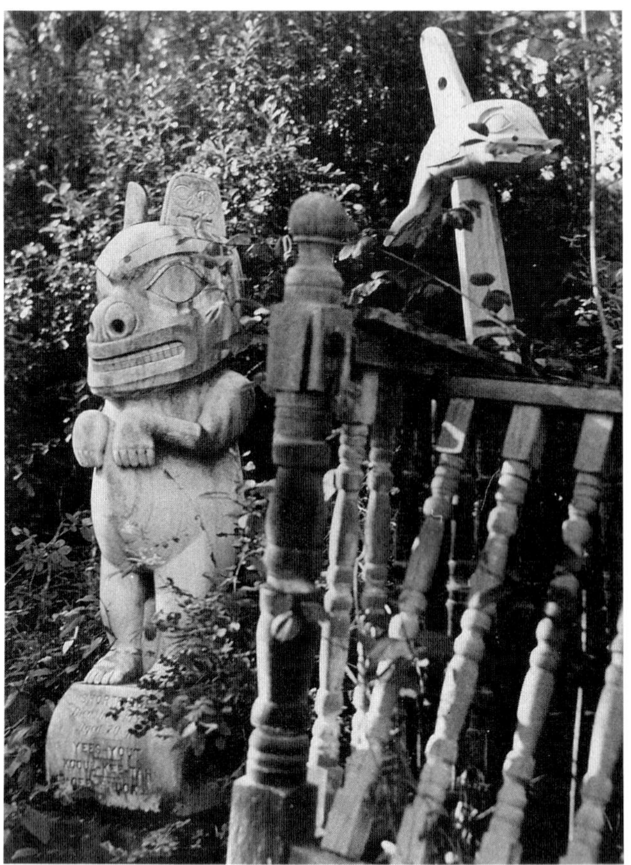

Ka·gʷa·nta·n, *Wolf 1, grave monuments, Klukwan, 1949. (Photograph by Frederica de Laguna.) The marble monuments were carved in Portland, Oregon, from wooden models supplied by the family of the deceased. The inscription on the bear figure reads: "SHORTRIDGE/ Died March 1, 1887/ Aged 70 years/ YEES-YOUT/ KOOUL-KEE-TAR/ ———?" "Shortridge" is evidently the chief of the Chilkat Wolf 1,* Łša·tx̣íčx̣, *or Chartrich.*

and the mourning clan sings four songs. These, with the four songs sung at the wake, make up the ceremonial eight "for the 8 bones of the body."

[Krause ([1885] 1956:155–59) reported several cremations and funerals among the Tlingit. These all conformed to the pattern described above, although he stated that the four days of mourning before the cremation need not be consecutive; at the funeral of a woman, he further stated, the potlatching of gifts took place for four days or nights before the cremation, and not after it, although this is not clear. What is important is that not only did her own clan give gifts but the widower also gave away almost all his possessions, reserving only enough to pay for the twelve-year-old girl who was to be his future wife. At the funeral ceremonies of a Sitka chief, it was reported that the widow was not allowed to speak for eight days, nor could anyone speak to her during that time. In addition, Krause quoted the report by Schabelski (1826) to the effect that at the cremation of a rich chief, some of his slaves might be burned alive on his pyre, to serve him in the next world.

[If the deceased was poor and came from a poor lineage or clan, the cremation took place some distance from the house, and the whole ritual was shortened, to avoid the costly returns to the "opposites" who had assisted (Holmberg 1855:44; Petroff 1884:171).

Cremation was deemed necessary that the spirit or ghost might be warm in the future life. [The wrapping of the ashes and bone fragments in a blanket or cloth was to protect the soul from the cold (Krause [1885] 1956:157). But some men were not cremated, because they were so brave they would not mind the cold (Swanton 1908:430).] Burial or the putting away [in a cave] of the body was sometimes accorded to a great chief. Chartrich, the last of the chiefs of any importance among the Chilkats, and one or more of his predecessors, were buried, not cremated. [He died in 1889, and on his tombstone are also engraved "Yees-yout" and "Kooul-kee-tar," and "Gee-Shuckl," presumably the names of his predecessors or other relatives. Yet in 1881–82, the severe winter was blamed by the Indians at Haines (Chilkoot) on the fact that a child had been buried, not cremated; in consequence, they exhumed the body and burned it, after huge bonfires on the beach and burning the child in effigy had failed to improve the weather (Krause, [1885] 1956:161).]

In the Auk village, below Juneau, a woman with an unborn child died, and an American doctor was called in to remove the foetus, which was cremated separately from the mother. [In earlier days, this postmortem caesarean would have been performed by the natives; neglect was believed to bring death to the deceased's lineage.]

The shaman's body was never burned, but was laid away intact in a small house on a prominent headland or island, or in a cave, the idea being that fire could not destroy it.

Cremation was seldom accorded to slaves, and cremation ceased entirely with the Christianizing of the natives.

[Because the memorial feast for the dead (see the next section) began on the evening of the day on which the body was cremated, Veniaminov ([1840] 1984:420) reported that the cremation might be delayed for a good many days, until the relatives were ready for the ceremony; and by that time the corpse might be entirely decomposed.]

CEREMONIES AFTER THE FUNERAL*

The first night after cremation [or burial], or at such time as sufficient property and food to be given away had been collected, members of the other ["opposite"] clan [the

**Editor's note:* This section was originally titled "Feast After Death." To the text I have added notes from Rudolph of Sitka and quotations from Veniaminov and Mrs. Willard.

gune·tkana·yí] were entertained by the family [clan or lineage] of the deceased, and were paid in gifts for all the services which they had performed.

As described for the tobacco feast, at the beating of the drum, the guests assembled in the evening at the house of the deceased. They were seated according to rank, their chief and those of high status opposite the door, the others on each side of the fire, the men in front and the women behind them. Members of the hosts' clan were in the front part of the house, on each side of the doorway, the chief and several principal men standing to one side. The blankets and material to be given away, contributed by the whole clan, were piled in the left front corner. The brothers-in-law [the deceased's sisters' husbands] were the ushers.

When the guests had been seated, the chief or spokesman for the clan of the deceased recounted the family achievements and thanked the guests for coming. Then he started a mournful song in which his family [clan] all joined. The piles of blankets and property in one corner were presided over by an old woman of the family. Each piece was given away in the name of a dead person [member of the hosts' clan], who received proportionate spiritual comfort from the gifts. [The spirit of the object went to the dead person.] The master of ceremonies who stood with the chief [the chief's speaker, or du x̣é·tx̣ yu· x̣a tángi] called out the name of the recipient who would answer "This way," "*Ar-tay*" [ha·dé, or ha·ndé], when the article would be held up for exhibition by the ushers before being passed to him. The chiefs and those who performed services for the dead received the greater gifts, but practically every member of the guest family would receive something. The distribution concluded, the host might thank his guests, or they merely rose and left the house.

The next day they again assembled and were fed. Carved boxes, dishes, and spoons were furnished [by the hosts] as far as possible, but the guests usually brought their own. Native food, meat, fish, grease, seaweed, berries, were provided, but in later days hard bread and store produces were added. Food was put into the fire not only for the newly deceased, but for others, long dead [members of that clan], who were supposed to receive the spiritual equivalent. The brothers-in-law or [fraternal] nephews in the opposite phratry waited on the guests, and when the feast was over, all that was not eaten was given to the guests to take home. Of late years, the old carved dishes were replaced by china wash bowls. Seal and fish oil in large sheephorn ladles was handed to certain [selected] guests, and they most honored those who drank the most, even though they might be able to retain it only a few moments. [This account of the two days' ceremonies Emmons based on Shukoff's report.]

While all potlatches and feasts were made in payment for services rendered or benefits received, the religious aspect was ever present and the dead were always remembered. The close communion between the living and the dead was shown by the offering of clothing and food at feasts in which both participated equally. Ancestor worship entered into every important feature of Tlingit life.

[In addition to such offerings made at feasts or potlatches], products of the hunt or fishing are often thrown in the fire [at meals] and the name of the dead mentioned. Sometimes this is a voluntary offering, but very often it represents the discharge of a debt, for the strictest law [demands] the return of a present or a debt. Gifts to the dead are necessary for their happiness and comfort.

Water is sacrificed to the dead spirit but is not thrown on the fire, but is buried in a vessel in the earth.

[Notes in BCPA, probably from Rudolph, the Kiksʔádi artist of Sitka, indicate that at the death of a shaman, no public announcement is made (see, however, "Death of a Shaman" in Chapter 14), but women of "both families . . . come out and mourn. Other family dress corpse and take charge." On the first night after death "smoke other family. No talk no dance. Family of dead fast all day." "Night of cremation–smoke feast. Next night or second night—potlatch feast to other family."

[The following account by Veniaminov ([1840] 1984:420–21], on which were based those of Holmberg (1855:43–45) and after him of Petroff (1884:171), gives a better idea of the sequence of events at a funeral, and at the ceremonies following the cremation. It will be remembered that there was no set day for the cremation, since this depended on the wealth of the bereaved clan. Veniaminov wrote:

> Following the rite of the cremation of the corpse, all guests are invited into the barabora [dwelling] of the deceased and are seated in a circle. With them sit the wife (or the husband) of the deceased, as they, too, are members by birth of the other moiety.
>
> After the guests have assembled, the kinsmen [of the deceased] enter the barabora. Their hair is singed and their faces are smeared with soot. In their hands they carry staffs. Taking up a position in the center, heads bowed, they begin to lament the dead and sing [an appropriate] song. The guests provide an accompaniment. This lament may take place four evenings in a row following the rite of cremation.
>
> During the [period of] lamentation, the deceased's kinsmen, if they so desire, also kill slaves: one or two (to provide servants

for the deceased in the other world); but the slaves killed are not of the number belonging to the deceased, but those belonging to the kinsmen. The slave loses his life in the same manner as did the deceased whose memory is celebrated. If the deceased has drowned, the slave is drowned also. However, if the deceased died of illness, the slave is throttled by means of a stick pressed against the neck.

When the lament ends, that is, on the fourth evening, the deceased's kinsmen wash their faces and decorate themselves with various pigments [paints] and begin to begift the guests, especially those who worked at the cremation of the corpse. Afterwards, the final meal [feasting] begins, which concludes the entire festival.

The entire estate of the deceased falls to his kinsmen. A wife inherits after her husband's death almost nothing of his estate, though she keeps her dowry. If the deceased has a nephew (his sister's son) or a younger brother, the latter inherits the deceased's wife. In such a case, he is the main sponsor of the memorial feast [potlatch—FdeL].

[I have omitted Russian words put in brackets by the translators, but have retained all other brackets.

[Mrs. Willard (1884:255–58) described the feast after a cremation. It followed the description of the funeral of a boy in 1881, although the deceased individual in this case was evidently not that child:

On the night after the burning of the body is celebrated the "Co-ek-y"—the feast for the dead. Another tribe [clan] is invited. Red paint is used with the black. There is much noisy music and dancing. Great quantities of berries and salmon-oil are brought out in hugh dishes and placed on the floor before the guests (or among them, rather, as every bowl is surrounded); then, as they eat together, wooden dishes of similar food and of flour, sugar, and whatever else they are able to obtain, are placed in the fire and burned; so that, being thus spiritualized, as they think, it may be partaken of by the spirit of their friend, so lately freed from the body by fire, and which is still hovering about before starting on the journey. After this the music and dancing are again resumed, and then comes the display for which the entire family has been saving and gathering—it may be, many years—and for which they generally suffer in absolute want for years to come. Great heaps of blankets, all new and good, webs of cloth, muslin and calico, are brought out and laid before a man appointed to dispose of them. With two assistants he cuts and tears all these things into small strips. This being done with a peculiar carved and inlaid hook kept for that purpose, they are distributed among the people, who treasure them as precious possessions, and by sewing them together construct a garment after the style of Joseph's coat of many colors. Sometimes we see a coat made of three pieces obtained at different times, when the body will be striped red, yellow, purple and green, one sleeve of blue, the other of brown. Dresses are gotten up in the same unique fashion—it may be, of a dozen different patterns and colors.

This feast ends the ceremonies, which, according to their belief, are participated in by the dead. Afterward, if the deceased be a male of high class, the heir or heiress must build a great dwelling-house with feasting and dancing, to stand an empty monument to the departed.

[It is difficult to establish the "usual" order of ritual events and ceremonies connected with death, disposal of the corpse, and rewarding the "opposites" for their assistance. Emmons evidently had trouble, for he left confusing notes on the sequence of events; one list was evidently based on information given by his informant, Rudolph of Sitka, who unfortunately also gave the sequence of events for other occasions (building of a lineage house, major potlatch), and confused these with the funeral sequence. Probably there was no set program for the funeral, the actual events varying according to the wealth and status of the deceased and his clan. In any case, house building, totem pole raising, and repair of graves were also conceived as honoring the dead, and were part of the grand ceremonial cycle which climaxed in a major potlatch (see Chapter 11, "Ceremonies"). Table 24 outlines the funeral events, as nearly as they can be deduced from the original notes given by Rudolph, and Table 26 (also from Rudolph, in Chapter 11) shows how these events were carried on at the potlatch that ended the funeral cycle.]

SHAMANS' GRAVES

Shamans were never cremated, but their bodies were wrapped in skins and mats, and laid away in houses similar to those to be described. These were generally ornamented with paintings or carved corner posts, or might be surmounted by animal figures, totemic in character or sacred to their profession. Shamans' gravehouses were never with the others, but might be beyond the end of the village, and, if possible, always on an elevation overlooking the water. Often they were on some distant island or bluff point. Caves were often selected, and among the Chilkat, caves and rock shelters far up the mountains were used. A canoe was hauled up by the side of the grave, and sometimes large and small carved human figures, supposed to possess supernatural power, were placed nearby to guard their master from the spirits of evil that lived in the air.

[Refurbishing these graves, which sometimes involved putting the bones in new boxes, might be done as a preliminary to a great potlatch in honor of the dead. Handling of the remains was done by the opposite moiety, but all fasted, including the younger clansmen of the deceased, for this was a time when one of them might receive the shamanistic call, it was hoped; and for the same purpose, perhaps, the shaman's scalp was sometimes saved. Further information on the death and funeral of shamans is found in Chapter 14.]

VARIOUS OLDER FORMS OF DISPOSAL OF THE DEAD*

It was an old custom, especially for those who fell in war, and sometimes for chiefs, to cremate the body but preserve the head wrapped in furs and placed in a chest. La Pérouse, Dixon [Beresford], and Lisiansky all mentioned this custom, and described the disposition of the body or of the ashes in a box supported on posts, and the separate preservation of the head.

Thus La Pérouse (1799, 1:389–90), who was in Lituya Bay in 1786, wrote:

> Our travelers [exploring party] saw likewise a morai [burial place], from which they learned, that these Indians were accustomed to burn the bodies of the deceased, and preserve the head. They found one wrapped in several skins. This monument consists of four tolerably strong posts, supporting a little chamber of planks, in which are reposited the ashes of the dead, enclosed in chests. They opened the chest, unfolded the skins in which the head was wrapped, and, having satisfied their curiosity, replaced everything with scrupulous exactness, adding presents of iron instruments and beads. The savages, who witnessed this visit, showed a little uneasiness; but they did not fail to take away the presents left by our travellers without delay. [And did the same with gifts left the next day.]

Ismailov and Bocharov, who visited Yakutat Bay in 1788, reported only (Coxe 1803:327) that the natives "burn their dead, place the ashes in a chest, and suspend it on poles, called Imilasaby [?]."

The previous year, however, Beresford with Dixon (1789:175–76) described in greater detail the sepulchers at the mouth of Ankau Creek, Port Mulgrave, on Yakutat Bay, to which they were attracted "by the sight of a number of white rails . . . constructed with order and regularity," and reported:

> The manner in which they dispose of their dead is very remarkable: they separate the head from the body, and wrapping them in furs, the head is put into a square box, the body in a kind of oblong chest. At each end of the chest which contains the body, a thick pole, about ten feet long, is drove into the earth in a slanting position, so that the upper ends meet together, and are very firmly lashed with a kind of rope prepared for the purpose.
>
> About two feet from the top of this arch, a small piece of timber goes across, and is very neatly fitted to each pole: on this piece of timber the box which contains the head is fixed, and very strongly secured with rope; the box is frequently decorated with two or three rows of small shells, and sometimes teeth, which are let into the wood with great neatness and ingenuity; and as an additional ornament, is painted with a variety of colours; but the poles ["rails"] are uniformly painted white. Sometimes these poles are fixed upright in the earth, and on each side [of] the body, but the head is always secured in the position already described.

[But did the explorers actually see a decapitated body, or was a complete body in each chest—that of a shaman, for example? Notes by Emmons in BCPA indicate that at this place in 1883 there were only shamans' gravehouses.]

Near Sitka, Beresford (1789:181) described a large cave in which was

> a square box, with a human head in it, deposited in the manner already described at Port Mulgrave; the box was very beautifully ornamented with small shells, and seemed to have been left there very recently, being the only one in the place. This circumstance seems to shew, that the natives of this place dispose of their dead in the same manner as at Port Mulgrave, but probably make choice of caves for that purpose, in preference to the open air.

[No mention is made of calcined bones or a body in this cave.]

Portlock, when exploring Norfolk (Sitka) Sound, in 1787, discovered a native burial (1789:280):

> In this bay, and not more than ten yards from the beach, there was a kind of monument erected probably to the memory of some distinguished chief. This edifice was composed of four posts, each about twenty feet long, stuck in the ground six feet distant from each other, and in a quadrangular form. About twelve or fifteen feet from the ground there was a rough boarded floor, and two of the sides were boarded four feet higher up, the other sides were left open. In the middle of this floor an Indian chest was deposited, which most likely con-

*Editor's note: This section and the following one on "Recent Graveyards" were organized to deal with the wealth of material in the text and notes by Emmons and in reports of the early travelers. This section includes the discussion of a mummified body which Emmons had treated in a separate section, "Mummy." For this section on older forms of disposal of the dead, I checked Emmons's references to La Pérouse, Ismailov and Bocharov, Beresford (as "Dixon"), Portlock, Vancouver, and Lisiansky; and I added information from Malaspina, Lütké, a letter from Rasmussen, and various notes by Emmons and others among his papers in BCPA.

> tained the remains of some person of consequence; and on that side of the edifice to the Westward, and which pointed up the Sound, there was painted the resemblance of a human face.

[This structure was evidently very old, and the Indians had more recently added braces to the uprights, and had retouched the painting several times. Portlock wanted to see what the chest contained, but refrained, fearing that the whole edifice might fall down. In 1885 Emmons saw two very old individual graves back of Klukwan that were on high supports, and which he compared to this.

[Members of the Spanish exploring expedition under Malaspina in 1791 visited on Ankau Creek, Port Mulgrave, what they determined was the same cemetery as that described by Beresford. Here there were three monuments in a group, in front of which were ditches with half-burned timbers where the dead had been cremated. At a distance of two musket shots was an isolated monument. All of these were painted by Suría and Cardero, and described by Suría and Malaspina (see de Laguna 1972:540–42, pls. 59, 60, 61; Malaspina, 1849:289; and 1885:161, 164, 346; Suría in Wagner 1936:257–58).

[The central monument of this group was the wooden figure of a monstrous Bear, about ten and a half feet high, holding under its claws a box, in which the Spaniards believed were the ashes of some personage, and also a bowl-shaped basket, the crown of a European hat, a wolf skin, and a piece of board. The box was inlaid with small shells. The figure was painted with red hematite, except for the teeth, claws, and the upper part of the head, which were painted black and white. The figure faced east, and the Spaniards reported that it was called *Iukitchetch* (yu ki·t- –?–). (I believe that it was the grave post of some member of the Te·qʷe·dí, or Wolf 32.)

[Flanking this Bear were two other monuments, that on the left apparently older than the other, but otherwise very similar. Each consisted of a box, or open-sided shelter, raised on four posts about seven and a half feet high, with another box on the ground below. These structures were supposed to contain the ashes of the Ankau's two sons; since he was a Raven, they would have been Wolves. The elevated box on the left was painted (?) with masklike faces, and both boxes contained two baskets, one larger than the other, and presumably the cover. The lower boxes on the ground were covered over with loose boards, and one at least contained bits of calcined bone, among which the Spaniards recognized fragments of a cranium and of the first two vertebrae of the neck. They collected one (the upper?) box from the older monument. This was inlaid with opercula, and contained a smaller box (basket lid?) that held a small basket with a few bits of calcined bone.

[Identical monuments, including the Bear, were also seen on the south side of Knight Island, farther up Yakutat Bay.

[The fourth monument on Ankau Creek (de Laguna 1972, pl. 159) was supposed to hold the ashes of the chief's father and/or of his wife (both of whom would have been Wolves). This consisted of two supports, about eight feet high, carved to represent Killerwhale fins and decorated with hair. These held up a small box, while another box rested on the ground between them. The upper was carved with the face of the Bear; the lower box seems to be capped with a crest hat, representing a Wolf, and surmounted by a tall pile of cylinders.]

Vancouver described a number of sepulchers seen by his exploring parties in southeastern Alaska in 1793 and 1794. For example, Lt. Whidbey reported that on the north shore of Cross Sound, near Dundas Bay (Vancouver 1801, 5:417–18):

> Here were erected two pillars sixteen feet high, and four feet in circumference, painted white; on the top of each was placed a large square box; on examining one of them it was found to contain many ashes, and pieces of burnt bones, which were considered to be human; these relicts were carefully wrapped up in skins, and old mats, and at the base of the pillars was placed an old canoe in which were some paddles.

Near Mud Bay, on the north shore of Chichagof Island, Lt. Whidbey also saw (Vancouver 1801, 5:448):

> a box . . . about four feet square, placed upon wooden pillars about six feet from the ground. This box contained the remains of a human body very carefully wrapped up, and by its side was erected a pole about twenty feet high, painted in horizontal streaks red and white; and colours were fresh and lively, and from the general neatness of the whole, it was supposed to be the sepulchre of some chief.

[This last is more likely to have been the grave of some shaman, since these persons were not cremated.]

Mr. Johnstone (Vancouver 1801, 6:47–48) saw graves in Hamilton Bay, near the eight deserted Kake villages or forts.

> In the vicinity of these ruins were many sepulchres or tombs, in which dead bodies were deposited. These were made with a degree of neatness seldom exhibited in the building of their habitations. A wooden frame was raised about ten feet from the ground, the upper half of which was inclosed, and in the open part below in many, but not in all of them, was placed a

canoe; the flooring of the upper part was about five feet from the ground, and above that the sides and top were intirely [*sic*] closed in with boards, within which were human bodies in boxes wrapped up in skins or in matting. These repositories of the dead, were of different sizes, and some of them contained more bodies than the others; in the largest there were not more than four or five, lying by the side of each other, not one appearing to be placed above the rest; they were generally found near the water side, and very frequently on some conspicuous point. Many of these sacred monuments seemed to have been erected a great length of time, and the most ancient of them had evidently been repaired and strengthened by additional supporters of more modern workmanship. Hence it would appear, that whatever might be the enmity that existed between the several tribes when living, their remains when dead were respected and suffered to rest quietly and unmolested.

[Persons of a different clan would certainly never approach the place where the corpse of a shaman was entombed, unless requested by his clan-mates to repair his gravehouse. These graves seem to have been those of shamans, although the numbers of bodies they contained suggest that formerly ordinary persons were entombed in a manner later reserved for shamans.]

On what was probably Vancouver Island, south of Annette Island, Vancouver saw "on a high detached rock . . . the remains of a large village," and a grave (Vancouver 1801, 4:190):

> Here was found a sepulchre of a peculiar character. It was a kind of vault, formed partly by the natural cavity of the rocks, and partly by the rude artists of the country. It was lined with boards, and contained some fragments of warlike implements, lying near a square box covered with mats and very curiously corded down. This we naturally conjectured contained the remains of some person of consequence. . . .

[Although naturally curious, Vancouver refrained from opening the box, out of respect for the feelings of the natives.]

When in Smeaton Bay, on the eastern arm of Behm Canal, Vancouver (1801, 4:157–58) found another grave:

> Not far from the spot on which we had dined, and near the ruins of a few temporary huts of the natives, we found a box about three feet square, and a foot and a half deep, in which were the remains of a human skeleton, which appeared, from the confused situation of the bones, either to have been cut to pieces, or thrust with great violence into this small space. One or two other coffins, similar to this, had been seen in the excursions of the boats this season; but as we had met with so few of this description, I was inclined to suppose that this mode of depositing their dead is practiced only in respect to certain persons of their society, since, if it had been the general usage, we should in all probability have more frequently noticed them.

[Did this grave represent the reburial of the remains of a shaman? Such reburial was common, with refurbishment of the coffin or gravehouse.]

Writing about the Sitka Tlingit in 1804–5, Lisiansky 1814:240–41) reported:

> The bodies here are burned, and the ashes, together with the bones that remain unconsumed, deposited in wooden boxes, which are placed on pillars, that have different figures painted and carved on them, according to the wealth of the deceased.
>
> On taking possession of our new settlement [Sitka], we destroyed a hundred at least of these, and I examined many of the boxes. On the death of a toyon, or other distinguished person, one of his slaves is deprived of life, and burned with him. The same inhuman ceremony is observed when a person of consequence builds a new house; with this difference, that on this occasion the unfortunate victim is simply buried without being burned. The bodies of those who lose their lives in war are also burned, except the head, which is preserved in a separate wooden box from that in which the ashes and bones are placed. This mode of destroying dead bodies originated, I was informed, in the ridiculous idea, that a piece of the flesh gave to the person who possessed it, the power of doing what mischief he pleased [witchcraft]. The body of a shaman is interred only; from another absurd notion, that, being full of the evil spirit, it is not possible to consume it by fire.

In 1885, when hunting on one of the many small islands in Sitka Bay, I came upon a shallow rock cave where I found some human bones, and a small box with the head.

[A similar find (de Laguna 1933) was made by a resident of Petersburg, on an island some thirty miles south of that town. In a narrow cave or rock shelter were the remains of six boxes that had evidently been deposited there over a long period. The three oldest boxes were in fragments, and it was impossible to determine their contents. The fourth box, represented by painted fragments and the lid decorated with "stones" (opercula), contained a human head and lower jaw, and had been wrapped in matting. The fifth box was intact. It was wrapped in matting, corded with a double-strand rope of cedar bark. The sides (made of a bent plank sewed together at one corner) had been elaborately carved and painted in red and green. Inside was the well-preserved head of a woman, with long reddish hair, and labret hole plugged by a tightly rolled strip of hide. The inside of the skull had been cleaned out, and sticks inserted to hold out the cheeks. The sixth and youngest box was similarly wrapped and corded. The fine matting, made with a diagonal weave of brown (black?) and red, was waterproof. The sides of the box were painted with crest designs. Inside was a mummified human head, wrapped in a soft woolen cloth (mountain goat wool?), and packed in cedar-bark shavings. The skull had been cleaned out but there were no sticks in the mouth. Next to the head were the remains of a knife with iron blade, and under the box were about 200 beads, some reportedly of sections of hollow bone, the others ordinary glass beads. This I interpreted as a deposit of trophy heads, but am now less sure.]

The mummified remains of a woman were found in 1905 in a cave in the rock not far from Old Sitka. The mummy was in a sitting position, with knees drawn up to the breast and the arms close around them. Surrounding it were a number of skulls placed with great precision. Nearby was a cubical wooden box about three feet high, the sides made of one thin plank bent around three corners and sewed with hide at the juncture of the ends [fourth corner]; the bottom was sewed to the sides, and the top was separate. The outer sides bore the remains of ornamental painting. The corpse showed evidence of having been wrapped in a covering. The long hair was of a reddish color. The natives could give no data regarding this find. As is so often the case when something old is found with which they are not familiar, they at once attribute it to a race that preceded them. But in this case, the chest, which appeared to have some connection with the mummy, pointed to the Tlingit themselves: in size, construction, and decoration, it corresponded exactly to modern Tlingit boxes. As to cave burial, the shaman's body was often hidden in a cave. Of this I have seen two instances near Sitka. [This description seems to be based on the report of the finder and on photographs by Merrill.]

[In a letter (in BCPA) to Emmons, November 18, 1932, written by Axel Rasmussen, superintendent of Wrangell Public Schools, the latter reported:

> There was found recently about 25 mi. south of Wrangell an Indian burial rather different from any I have previously heard of. The body probably had been cremated and the ashes and bone fragments deposited in a box which was carved and painted. This box was cached in a dry cave in a rocky cliff facing the sea. The finder brought in the box which is shown in the enclosed photos, #1 and #2. The bottom was so decayed that when the box was lifted the bottom and the contents remained. He [the finder] brought in only the box but will get the bones etc. if it is worth while. He states that the bones and ashes adhere in one mass which can readily be removed intact. Part of a small skull and other bones were visible. The box is 19 × 13 × 8 inches, carved and painted in red, black, and blue-green. It is peculiar in having double walls as one picture shows. There is no cover.
>
> In the same cave was another double-walled box with a cover as shown in photo #3. This also seems to have been disturbed, some bones and a skull lying near by. This box is 23 × 14 × 8 inches, plus a 6½-inch cover. The design is painted but not carved and the bottom has rotted away.

[With this letter in BCPA were several notes, in Rasmussen's hand (?), on "Head-in-Box Burial," evidently based on questions sent by Emmons and addressed to Indian informants and others at Wrangell. For example:

> Mrs. Shakes, Mrs. Clark. Mrs. C. had no knowledge of the practice. Mrs. S. at first did not quite understand. She told of the massacre of Sitka people [Ka·gʷa·nta·n, Wolf 1, by the Na·nya̧·ʔa·y̧í, Wolf 18] at the Stikine mouth. The bodies lay for a year, when Chief Shakes had the skulls collected and buried on an island in the Stikine. When I insisted it was a single mummified head with the hair intact, placed in a food box, she *guessed* it was a doctor's burial. The custom is one she doesn't know about.

[Another note was "Head-in-Box Burial, Mrs. Don Miller":

> When a warrior who was a leader was killed far from home there was no way to bring back the body. There were no gas boats and no lumber for a casket. Therefore the head was cut off, placed in an empty food box and brought back to the relatives. When they reached home the head was kept for five days and then put away, usually in a natural cave or crevice in a rocky cliff. After one year, five slaves, sometimes ten, were killed and their bodies placed on the beach. A cairn of stones was erected. People would come and seeing the pile of stones would ask "What is that?" "That is in memory of the great warrior——," would be the reply. Mrs. Miller says she has seen many such piles of stones.

[The third note was "Head-in-Box Burial, Tom Ukas," and read:

> Mr. Corser (Rev. H.P.?) told me a year ago that Mr. Ukas told him such burials were of the heads of warriors who fell in battle far from home. Their friends took home the heads.

[Whole heads or scalps were taken as mementoes both of one's own dead and of the enemy. A war party would try to bring home the ashes and heads of their dead comrades, but usually only the scalps were saved, perhaps because they were easier to carry, and also could be kept. Sometimes the heads of the enemy were held until they could be ransomed by their relatives (see de Laguna 1933:744; 1972:584).

Tlingit graves, Sitka. (Pencil sketches by G. T. Emmons. AMNH.) Top. *Three native graves in the Russian cemetery.* Center. *Grave within inclined fence.* Bottom. *Older type of gravehouse for chests or boxes containing ashes of cremation.*

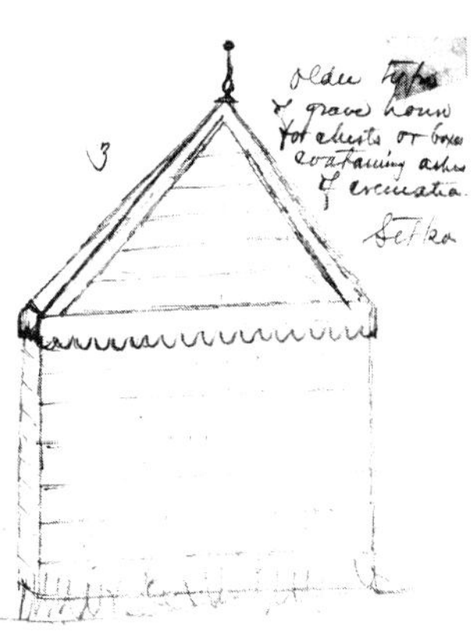

[Chase (1893:52) reported:

> The custom of scalping was once customary among the Tlinkits, though now it has fallen into disuse. When the chief died he was scalped before cremation.
>
> The scalp, together with the most showily decorated blankets of the deceased, was deposited in a most elegantly carved box, to be removed only on some festival of importance from the place of sepulture by the nearest living relative of the dead chief. On such an occasion the relative takes from the box these relics of the dear departed, and discourses upon his many virtues, while the surrounding friends are expected to lament according as their grief is revivified.

[Emmons summarized in a note in BCPA:] It was also a custom to take the scalp for a chief or man killed in war of the family [i.e., a clansman], and preserve it very carefully, and bring it out at great potlatches and when blankets were torn up. [This information was corroborated by Shukoff.]

RECENT GRAVEYARDS

[Within more recent times, but while cremation was still practiced,] the ashes were placed in boxes or trunks of every description, and these were deposited without order in the family [lineage] gravehouses that stood directly in the rear of the dwelling houses, the terrain permitting. Otherwise the graveyard was at one end of the village, or, as at Hoonah and Tuxekan [in Henya territory], on an island opposite.

The oldest type of gravehouse—and some of those that I examined were so decayed that they must have dated back well to the early half of the nineteenth century—were low structures of logs from six to twelve inches in diameter, some in the rough and others squared, notched at the ends and tightly fitted and joined. The houses were about eight feet square, and slightly higher in front so that the [shed type] roof made of several layers of split planks might carry off the rain. The front side might be covered with boards. Gravehouses of later construction were wholly of planks, and in all cases there was a floor raised above the ground. Often the front was painted or carved with the family crest, or over it might be hung a Chilkat blanket.

Dall (1895:126) described the graves at Sitka, as they were in 1865:

> On the bank, which rose behind the houses, densely covered with herbage of a vivid green, were seen curious boxlike tombs, often painted in gay colors or ornamented with totemic carvings or wooden effigies. These tombs sheltered the ashes of their cremated dead.

Later, gravehouses followed no particular pattern. They were built of boards, with high pitched [gable] roofs, windows, and rude attempts at ornamentation. With the advent of missionaries and conversion of the people, burial [inhumation] replaced cremation; fenced enclosures, crosses, and tombstones took their places among the old gravehouses. [Cement slabs over the graves, presumably copied from those characteristic of nineteenth century cemeteries in British Columbia, or small houses, were also sometimes built over the graves. (These various types were illustrated by Krause [1885] 1956:159–60.)]

The Southern Tlingit who borrowed the totem pole from the Haida placed the ashes of the dead in a hollow at the back of the post, and this custom was also practiced in some of the Northern Tlingit villages. At the entrance to Nakwasina Sound in Neva Strait, where the Sitka people lived when the Russians first came, there were as late as 1885 several old decayed mortuary columns hollowed out in back. [These were evidently at the site of *Kasta-ah-de-an* (?), on the south point of Halleck Island, supposed to have been the first settlement in the Sitka area of the Kiksʔádi, Raven 10.] At Icy Strait in several of the old Hoonah villages were similar posts. As most of the Tlingit [clans] claimed a southern origin, this custom is readily explained. But in time it was abandoned and the carved post was superseded by the family [clan or lineage] gravehouse. Later tombstones, some of which were carved in crest designs at great expense, were used to mark the graves. [The latter evidently took the place of the mortuary columns in the graveyards.]

INHERITANCE OF PROPERTY*

Inheritance of property was in the direct totemic family, which naturally followed from the succession of the brother or sister's son of the deceased. The widow received practically nothing from the estate of her husband. That she might retain her place in the house and not be thrown back on her own family in a state of poverty in her old age, the custom of marriage with the heir was required, in lieu of which a compensatory gift of property was made to her. Since children belong to the mother's clan, they would inherit nothing from the father. Similarly, the property of a woman was inherited by her totemic family [lineage], though her children would receive more than the others if they were old enough to protect their rights. More often, however, her brothers took the greater portion. Slaves were inherited like [other] personal property.

[Shukoff reported:

> If man loses his wife he must live among her relatives for five or six days until all her property is distributed among relatives. After a wife dies, not only her property but the husband's goes to her relatives. [It was probably for this reason that in a similar case reported by Krause ([1885] 1956:156) the widower had to hide some of his blankets with the white trader, in order to have the bride price for his future wife, a twelve-year-old girl.] If the husband has been good to his wife, her relatives give him the necessary articles to begin a new life with, and if he is a good hunter and will become rich soon again, they try to get him to marry some one of his wife's relatives. If he goes against his wife's relatives and marries in another family [clan, lineage], the women of former wife's family try to make trouble for him and his new wife. If chief dies, widow must marry husband's nephew in order to retain property, and if she fails to do so she loses everything. If she names husband's nephew [i.e., selects the nephew as her husband], the property is all kept and some presents only are made to dead husband's relatives. Nephew of chief inherits everything upon death of chief. New husband tries to get together as much money and property as possible so that he can give large potlatch which is held in fall or winter after salmon is dried and packed. [This establishes him as the chief's successor; see Chapter 11 for this great potlatch.]

[A note left by Emmons in BCPA stated that a man might inherit from his father "such temporary houses as fishing houses. [They] could be given by a father to his son, as they had nothing to do with the crest." Another field note in BCPA stated that: "Upon death of a member of family it is considered highly honorable to burn or bury with corpse any property, the more the high honor of the family." Emmons also prepared a number of questions in advance, leaving a small space for the answers. One of these was taken to the *Tar-ku Kwan* (Taku tribe), and reads:

> *Inheritance of Property upon death of husband?*
> Succeeded by brother or nephew who had to marry wife even if he had a wife himself. The wife received a certain amount of property, say wife gets a fifth or less of blankets and etc. but the greater portion goes to the family of man and all old family heirlooms as dancing headdresses and so forth which must remain within the tribe [clan, lineage]. House goes to family of man. Slaves divided as property going to widow, rest to totem [clan]. [It will be remembered that the former owner might have bequeathed their freedom to certain favorite slaves.]
> *Death of Wife?*
> All her property goes to totem her children sharing with others but receiving more than outsiders. The same with slaves, but the

**Editor's note:* To the text by Emmons I have added the quotation from Shukoff, a number of notes by Emmons, and information from Mrs. Willard.

Wooden mortuary poles with receptacles for the ashes of the dead, in front of Chief Shakes's house, Wrangell, ca. 1890. The pole on the left represents the Bear, that on the right the wealth-bringing water monster, Ģuna·kade·t, *both crests of Wolf 18. (Photographer unknown. AMNH.)*

house is always the man's and goes to opposite totem [from the wife's].

[The field notebook with an entry on the *Sum dum Quan* (Sumdum tribe) indicated that a chief's property would be inherited and a feast given in his honor:

> just as soon as Chief is disposed of the family elect chief if there is suitable relative left and feast is given at once by family all together and then the successor takes name and honors of chief.
>
> In *Chartritch* case [was added], election deferred as there are many applicants but none suitable.

[The teachings of the white missionaries and the imposition of our legal system caused the greatest confusion, often with bloodshed and misery, when the old matrilineal rules of succession and inheritance were shifting to our patrilineal inheritance with the widow's rights to a share in her husband's property. These difficulties were particularly disruptive when clan or lineage heirlooms were involved. Thus sons took the clan or lineage property that their fathers had held in trust, and sold it as if it were private property; widows held on to their husband's clan regalia and sometimes were beaten by those who claimed it; or old men and old women were left destitute and without the new spouses who would formerly have supported them. Some of the confusions, however, had a slightly humorous side, as reported by Emmons in a notebook dated 1892:

> In Feb 29th Mrs Hollywood's father, an old Kagwanton [Wolf 1] died, and left her one of the old family headdresses or helmets. The whole tribe [clan] rose at once and carried the case before the judge, claiming that these old pieces (they were numerous) belonged to no individual but to the whole tribe [clan], and therefore could not be willed to any one person. One of the family or tribe [lineage or clan] could keep them and for this honor it would in itself be expensive, for when shown at a feast of one of the family when a new house was built, then there would have to be a proportional distribution of property. They [the heirlooms] are displayed around a dead chief. They said in arguing the case that these articles had no intrinsic value, or rather, they were above value. They were to the Tlingit what the flag was to America, Russia, or England.

[There was no indication as to how the case was decided. Emmons noted that this case showed that the Tlingit were "recognizing the power of the white man's law." The woman was married to a white man.

[Mrs. Willard (1884:135–39, 306–10, 368), the missionary's wife at Haines and Sitka in the early 1880s, has indicated the unhappiness and domestic discord attending the forced marriages of the young girl or youth to an older man or woman, dictated by Tlingit rules of inheritance, and of the sororate and levirate.]

AFTERLIFE: SPIRITS, SOULS, REINCARNATION*

Every child possessed a spirit [or soul] at birth, and the Tlingit belief is that the spirit enters the child before birth. The fact that the fetus was taken from a dead mother at Auk

---

**Editor's note:* Emmons had originally titled this section "Spirits," but I felt that this was not sufficiently specific, especially since the concluding paragraphs pertained to spirits in general, and this information I have transferred to Chapter 14 on Shamanism. I have added the references to and quotations from Lütké, Mrs. Willard, and Veniaminov.

in 1903, and cremated separately, would signify the belief that the spirit already existed, for cremation was for the good of the spirit. The spirit may be new [?], or that of a dead member of the family, for reincarnation could take place only in the clan [and then normally involved only close relatives]. While it is generally believed that the spirit can return but once [?], some claim that it may be reborn three or more times, and that some spirits die and others never return nor are reborn.

The recognition of a preexistent [and now reincarnated] spirit was usually because of some physical peculiarity or birthmark. A Mrs. Clark of Wrangell [a native woman from whom Rasmussen (?) obtained information for Emmons], who is well versed in the beliefs of her people, says that a Tongass woman during pregnancy had dreams of her [maternal] aunt, a woman of high caste who had many perforations in the rims of her ears—a sign of her social standing. The child, when born, had a number of scars and holes about the edges of the ears, which at once indicated that the spirit of the aunt had returned and entered the child. Mrs. Clark saw these marks, but attributed them to the constant thought of the aunt by the pregnant woman.

Again, Mrs. Wigg [another Wrangell informant], equally interested in her people, tells of a relative to whom the spirit of his grandfather returned. The grandfather was a famous warrior who had died from a wound in the left breast which made a hole through the left side of the back. Fred, the boy, was born with large marks in the two spots where the bullet passed through the body, which clearly indicated that he possessed the returned spirit of his ancestor.

In 1932, Esther Johnson's aunt, of Wrangell, continually dreamed that her sister, Esther's deceased mother, was in spirit returning as Esther's son. Upon birth they were positive that it was her spirit, as she always said she would come back as a man. It was common for a relative to say to another, "When I die I shall come back in your child." Babblings, traits, and tendencies of young children would bespeak some ancestor, for the preexistent spirit would at first be conscious of its earlier life, but this knowledge would gradually be lost. No reason was given to explain why some spirits return while others fail to come back. The Tlingit had no idea that the spirit increased in power or goodness with each rebirth. That the spirit became dissatisfied because of the neglect of the living to provide the comforts so necessary to its spiritual well-being has been suggested, but this is hardly reasonable [it does not occur?], for ancestor worship is founded on provision for the dead, the most sacred obligation of the Tlingit. [For beliefs of the Tlingit about reincarnation, see de Laguna 1972:498–99, 758, 765–81; and for modern Tlingit beliefs, see Stevenson 1966:191–240.]

According to an old Taku, rebirth takes place always in the same family [clan] and can happen only once to the same spirit whose sex is arbitrarily interchangeable and sometimes not permanently decided until after birth. Hence people often find it difficult to determine the sex of a newborn child[!]. At times, actuated by certain unknown forces, the spirit returns to and isolates itself on the bank of a rising river, sitting sheltered under the overhanging branches of trees, with the chin resting on the knees drawn up to the breast. It sinks into total unconsciousness, not heeding the gradual rising of the water, until it is completely covered, whereupon a terrestrial birth takes place. [See the stories of ʔAskadut and of ʔAsdjiwan in de Laguna 1972:767–69 and 774–75. The nine days spent by the spirit on the banks of the river are the nine months of gestation before rebirth.]

The spirit, although sexless, retains in some unexplained manner its life's individuality. The human spirit never dies. It cannot enter an animal. Each species has its own spirits. That the spirits of animals live after death is shown by the propitiatory observances of the hunter after bringing in the skin of a bear so that its spirit may not be offended.

The Tlingit idea of the soul and spirit is difficult to reconcile [understand?], for while they say that the spirit is eternal and simply inhabits the body during life, yet they speak of the spirit leaving the body, which is indicated by sickness, when the shaman's [assistant] spirit [yé·k] catches it and restores it to the body. Again, when a dog is thrown out after a body is removed from the house for cremation, the dead spirit would enter the dog instead of some human being to cause death, while the living spirit or soul would go on to the spirit world. [The spirit or ghost cannot enter the dog (see above); the dog is probably to frighten it away.]

As explained by an old native of the *Hootz-ah-ta* tribe [Hutsnuwu], the Tlingit recognize three entities in man: (a) the material body [qa· da·]; (b) the spirit, a vital central force through which the body functions during life and which, leaving the body, causes death; and (c) the soul, a spiritual element that has no mechanical connection with the body, and is eternal, dwelling in spirit land or returning from time to time to live in different bodies. The only knowledge man has of this [entity b] is the breath, *ka sa-go* [qa· ẋ̣a-sé·gu; ẋ̣a-sé·k^w, "breath, life"]. [A person's mind, thoughts, feelings, are "his insides," du tu·wú. After death, naná, the body becomes a corpse, qa· na·wú.]

The spirit of one living was called *ka yu-ha-yee,* "shadow" [qa· ya-ha·yi, "human shadow, reflection, picture"]. After death this spirit was called *ka yu-ha-yee wha-goo,* "man's shade" [qa· yakʷgʷahé·yagu, "ghost," or "reincarnated spirit"]. The spirits of the dead [those who died from ordinary causes: accident, disease] are called *sick-ka-kow, sick-yi-ka-woo* [šigi·qá·wu, from šiq-yi-qá·wu, "smoke-under-man or men," obviously referring to cremation]. The spirits of warriors killed in war are *ka-ya-ka-woo* [ki·waqá·wu, "people of Sky Land," Ki·waʔa·]. An idiot is believed to have the soul of a slain man who has returned from the land of the dead [in the sky], and is therefore called *kee-wah-kah-woo yuk-ha-yee* [ki·waqá·wu yaha·yí].

[We should not confuse the "spirit" as indicated above, whether it be the "spirit" or "soul" of a living person, or the "ghost" perhaps lingering by the grave, or the reincarnated "soul" or "revenant," with the spirit, yé·k, which is the assistant spirit controlled by the shaman. There is some evidence, however, that the "spirit" of a man *can* come back as a yé·k, as in the case of the slain Yakutat warrior, Łušwaq, who vowed to "come back as a yé·k" against his enemies. That yé·k was known as "Łušwaq's shadow," Łušwaq ya-ha·yi· (see de Laguna 1972:267). In addition to the shaman's familiar spirits, each human being had a personal guardian spirit, or qa· kiná yé·k, "a person's Above Spirit," the loss of which meant death (see Chapter 14, under "Spirits").]

The future abode of the spirit [soul] depends upon the manner of death. Those who die from natural causes go to *Sick-ka-kow-anee,* "Sky-eaves land" [šigi·qá·wu ʔa·ní, "smoke-under people's land," or dead people's land, not "sky-eaves"!]. The sky is believed to be an inverted dome over a flat earth and the horizon is likened to the eaves of a house, and here the spirits live. [Horizon is se·ʔí·t, and this is where the fish live; but it is not a land of the dead. Emmons relies on a faulty etymology.]

The belief in and knowledge of the future existence was given to the Tlingit by one who returned to life after having made the journey to the land of the dead [šigi·qá·wu ʔa·ní]. The narrator [protagonist of the story] is localized at many points under different names. When released from the body at cremation, the spirit traveled a rough, narrow, rock-strewn, bush-tangled trail. [This belief] accounts for the care of clothing and the covering of the hands and feet [of the corpse] with strong mittens and moccasins. The trail gradually widened and terminated on the shore of a green water, across which in the far distance could be seen moving about what appeared like human forms, but were no larger than mosquitoes. He called to these to no avail, and gradually fell asleep. Upon waking he saw a canoe approaching. In this he was carried over [the lake] to a beautiful country, where he was surrounded by relatives who had preceded him in death. Those whose bodies had been cremated were sitting about great fires, comfortable and happy, but those who had not been accorded this rite shivered in the cold, bewailing the neglect of their [living] relatives. [See the story of Łxakunuk, de Laguna 1972:775–76, for a similar tale.]

Those who were killed in war or had been murdered went to *Kee-wa-kow-anne,* "above people's country" [ki·waqá·wu ʔa·ní, or ki·waʔá·], which they reached by means of the rainbow. They were visible to men in the scintillations of the Aurora when the warrior spirits came out to play. This was the highest abode and so greatly to be wished for that the Tlingit had no fear of death in battle. The Aurora [gišú·qʷ, or Northern Lights] was in itself a sign of war, an omen of future bloodshed.

A warrior's spirit might be returned to earth by a sharp stroke across the back by the spirit chief, which would be indicated by a black mark on the [baby's] body [Mongolian spot?].

A very few bad people, whose Spirit Above had deserted them, went to an immense open space between the winds and have no rest, as it [they?] are blown hither and thither. The shaman's spirit [ghost or yé·k?] lives about his grave-house and is guarded by carved and painted figures, to which people passing in canoes make a small offering. [The witch spirits that cause sickness and death are described in Chapter 14.]

Since cremation was not only a religious rite but a sacred duty, necessary to the happiness of the dead, drowning and the loss of the body was the most dreaded death. The body of the drowned, if not recovered, might be "rescued" (captured) by the Land Otter People and would become a *Koushta ka* [kú·šda·-qá·], or "Land Otter Man." The transformation was slowly accomplished: first hair grew over the body, speech became confused, he began to walk on knees and elbows, a tail grew out, and, in time, he became more otter than human. Upon seeing anyone, he would try to be recognized, and if so he would be saved. Should he sink, however, he would go to *hi-ye quanee* [ha· yi· qʷa·ni, "Spirits of Below"] at the bottom of the water. But if at any time the body was recovered and cremated, the soul would go to the [regular] spirit land [daganqú, "way back," or šigi·qá·wu ʔa·ní, "smoke-under people's land"]. Again it is claimed that the drowned were sitting in deep muddy water under an overhanging cliff and were kept down by a great cascade pouring its water over them. In this case, food [and tobacco] was cast into the water to sustain and comfort them until such time as they might escape and follow the trail to the spirit land, when the body might be cremated. Children who drowned were believed to be imprisoned on the earth.

[Land Otter Men also kidnap or "rescue" those who die of exposure on land. Sometimes a shaman is able, through his yé·k, to find a lost child and to save him by removing the land otter taint. For stories about Land Otter People, see de Laguna 1972:744–55.]

Some years ago a man and his wife were drowned at the mouth of Indian River, just below Sitka, and as the bodies were never recovered, they were believed to have been turned into *Koushta ka* [kú·šda· qá·], Land Otter People, and their spirits were thought to inhabit the nearby shore. In 1887 a relative passing by in a canoe thought that he saw a Land Otter Man on the point at the river. That he might be recovered and restored, or his body cremated, a network of bark ropes was stretched among the bushes [to capture the Land Otter Man], but to no avail. Later a dance and feast were given in which the capture of the otter spirits was enacted. The performers, dressed in dance blankets and headdresses, each with a paddle in the hand, entered the house of the family [lineage] of the lost man in single file, and, forming two columns, made the motion of paddling, as if in a canoe. In one corner of the house was secreted a man who, from time to time, imitated the call of the otter [a shrill piping or whistle]. Then all motion would cease, and each actor would put his hand up to his ear. Concealed under an improvised platform were two crude stuffed half-human otter figures. These were suddenly cast out on the floor. All of the dancers formed around these and broke into a low, wailing chant, keeping time with the paddles, and pretended to have recovered the drowned man [and his wife?] and to be bringing them in a canoe to the village.

[This performance is very similar to one reported by Olson (1967:98–99). It was given by the head of Raven's Hat House of the Ga·nax̣ʔádi, Raven 1, when the Tongass tribe were living at Fort Tongass (about 1865–1900). This "spirit dance" (or secret society performance) given in connection with a potlatch, involved sleight of hand tricks and impersonations, dramatizing the supposed capture and taming of the drowned chief who had become a Land Otter Man.

[Mrs Willard (1884:260–61) reported eloquently on Tlingit beliefs about drowning:

> More than any other form of death, more than the most excruciating torture, the Indian dreads drowning. Going through the water, he is never utterly freed from the clogs of earth; he is unequipped for the journey through a land of mystery; for ages he must wander hungry and cold, with scarcely a possibility of at last finding the great green water which lies between every soul and heaven[?]. When a soul has gained for itself the right to eternal happiness, it sees, upon approaching the great river, a canoe in waiting to convey it to the happy land; a sure entrance and everlasting security are assured. The wicked also gain the shore, but are doomed to eternal waiting.

[Mrs. Willard (1884:305–6) also described the Tlingit belief about the journey to the afterworld:

> The straight road to their spirit-world is over two high mountains and the intervening valley. When the shore of the great water is reached, the rocks are seen to be crowded with spirits waiting to be taken over to the beautiful island, which, though so far away, is plainly visible, with its inhabitants, whose attention these waiting souls vainly try to gain by shouting. But, wearied with watching, one no sooner begins to yawn than the faintest sound of it is heard and heeded in the island, and a canoe is immediately sent to carry the sleeping spirit to its final home. It is circulated throughout the country that during the past winter [1882–83] a man who died in Sitka came back long enough to tell the people that they must burn more food and clothing and turn out more water on the fire when their friends die, that they may have more comfort in the other world, and that all who adhered to the traditions of their fathers were the favored ones in the next life; they sat close about the warm, bright fire, while those who follow the new Christ-religion were their slaves and sat back in the dark, cold corners.

[We should not expect much information about Tlingit beliefs in souls or the afterlife from the earliest explorers. Such information becomes available to us unfortunately only after missionaries have been active. Nevertheless, Lütké (1835, 1:193) was able to write something on the aboriginal beliefs of the Sitka Tlingit in 1827:

> The Kaloches [Tlingit] believe that the soul lives on after death, without, however, receiving in another world recompense for good, or punishment for evil. The souls of chiefs do not mingle with those of their inferiors, but the souls of slaves who were sacrificed on the tomb of their master remain eternally the slaves of his own [free translation]. [Khlebnikov ([1817–32] 1976:27) says exactly the same.]

[The earliest full account of Tlingit beliefs, on which the statements of so many others have been based, is of course that of Veniaminov (1840). His account has been translated in large part by Holmberg (1855), and from the latter's German into English by Petroff (1884). Although the last could and did translate Russian sources for H. H. Bancroft, he apparently found it easier to translate Holmberg than Veniaminov. The most recent and most authoritative translation of Veniaminov is that by Lydia Black and R. H. Geoghegan (1984). To avoid confusion in the spelling of Tlingit words, which were rendered in the Popular Orthography by Norah Dauenhauer, I have here retranscribed them according to the phonetic system used in this book. The ending *-i* on some Tlingit words, as explained in a note (p. 396) by Richard Dauenhauer, is the Russian plural. (Tlingit has no true plural.) Veniaminov failed to distinguish between this Russian plural and the Tlingit possessive, *-i,* "of, belonging to." In the examples given below, note the shift from the surd *k* to the sonant *g* in the Tlingit, as in yé·k, "spirit(s)," to kí· yé·gi, "spirit(s) of above." I have omitted almost all the Russian words included by the translators, and where alternative translations are offered, I have chosen that which makes for the easiest reading.

[Veniaminov ([1840] 1984:397) began by identifying the three classes of spirits: The first was the spirits of above, *Kiyeiki* (kí· yé·gi); the second class were the *Takiyéki* (dá·gi yé·gi, "spirits of over there"), those living over there, on the mainland, to the north; and the third class were the water or sea spirits, the *Tekiyeki* (de·kí· yé·k, or dé·kí· yé·gi), spirits out to sea. The spirits of above or sky spirits are the souls of those who have been killed, and they "always appear to the shamans as warriors in full battle gear." If anyone sees the sky open to receive such a soul, he will die, and this person is called *Kiyaqáu,* meaning "he will travel up" (derived by Richard Dauenhauer from kina "above," ya "will travel," qau "person"). Some souls of dead persons, but not all, may return as yé·k to the shamans (like that of Łušwaq).

[The way to the land of the dead is not the same for everyone. For those whose relatives weep a lot, it is wet; for those whose relatives mourn less, the way is dry and smooth.

[Veniaminov continued (pp. 398–400):

> The Koloshi believe also that the souls of all people do not and shall never die. . . . However, it is necessary to add here that the *tskeqau* [šigi·qá·wu] or the souls of people who died the ordinary death, do not live in the Tankanku [Daganqu, "over there, way back," Land of the Dead] all in the same conditions.
>
> The souls of those whose bodies had been burned are warm, easy and dwell in light, as they are always able to approach the fire; the souls of those whose bodies were not burned dwell in the dark, are cold and burdened as they always stand behind the others and are not able to come close to the fire.
>
> The souls of those for whom or in whose name no kalgi [slaves—Translator] were killed, live there without any servants and thus must labour for themselves. On the contrary, the souls of those for whom kalgi were killed have servants over there.
>
> The Koloshi believe in the transmigration of souls but not into animal [form—Translator], but exclusively into [other—Translator] humans. To put it differently, they believe that the souls of the dead always return to this world, but not otherwise than to their own kin by inhabiting [the bodies of—Translator] women. It is for this reason that women become pregnant. If a woman, in the course of her pregnancy, often dreams about one of her deceased kin, she believes that this same kinsperson took up his/her abode within her. When they find on the body of a newborn some distinctive similarity to one of the deceased kinsmen, such as a birthmark, or some bodily defect, in common with the deceased, they become convinced that precisely this kinsperson has returned to earth. The newborn then receives this person's name.
>
> The poor, observing the wealth status of the Toens and the differences to which the latter's and their own children are subject, say: "when I die, *I shall without fail return into the family of such and such a Toen,* the one whom the speaker prefers." [He must, of course, be a relative, for there is not a free choice, as Veniaminov would imply.—FdeL] Others say: "*Ah, the sooner I get killed the better. . . . Then, the sooner I can return here.*"
>
> One may infer from the latter [statement—Translator] that the Koloshi consider that it is immeasurably better to be killed than die a natural death and that those who are killed have a better life over there and are also able to return sooner. [A footnote by Veniaminov indicates that this means "*to bring back their youth* and to begin a new and better life. . . ."]
>
> The souls of those killed in war, or the souls Kiuaqau [Ki·waqá·wu] often manifest themselves in the form of the Northern Lights. To put it differently, the Koloshi consider the Northern Lights (kitsuq [gis̓ú·q^w]) an apparition or a maneuver of the Kiuaqau [Ki·waqá·wu]. Especially that kind of the Northern Lights which appears in the form of columns or sheaves [of grain—Translator] which usually shift from one side to another, moving rapidly around, or replaced by new ones are held to be very similar to military exercises [maneuvers—Translator] of the Koloshi. Strong Northern Lights are held to presage a great bloodletting because the Kiuaqau [Ki·waqá·wu] desire [new—Translator] companions.]

CHAPTER 11

Ceremonies

MUSIC AND DANCE

The love of music is a strongly marked feature of the Tlingit. Music is characteristic of all their ceremonies. Their feasts, dances, cremations, gambling—all are marked by singing and rhythmic motion. The legends, family traditions, in fact their history is transmitted in song, and knowledge of the clan songs—for each clan has its own songs—is a matter of common general education, and a want of this knowledge would be a sign of gross ignorance, and a public disgrace. Small children of five or six years may sometimes be seen together, imitating the singing of the grown people, one child leading. (This I have seen at Klukwan, and the execution was not bad.) The little children are instructed in the winter evenings, and the whole family may sing at this time. At the age of eight to ten, boys and girls attend and often take part in dances with their seniors. They are introduced in the dances, and in that way are trained. The old conventional chants are transmitted through generations until, in the case of some of their songs, the people do not understand the words they sing. When questioned, the singers would say that the words were in the old tongue, no longer spoken. Some songs have been taken [copied] from the neighboring tribes: Haida, Tsimshian, [and Athabaskan]; or certain dances represent [imitate] a foreign people, and the songs [for the dances] are in the language [of the foreigners]. The families [clans] who originated elsewhere, and had originally a different language and death feast song, may use another tongue than Tlingit [that is, use their original language].

The songs, or more naturally, chants [these are the clan mourning songs], consist of a few words long drawn out. In some instances men or women sang alone, but both generally sang together in harmony; the female voices pitched an octave higher than those of the men. A song leader led, and gave the pitch, and beat time with a staff on the floor. The song ended suddenly on a high note. Songs are generally accompanied by the drum, the striking of dance sticks [tapping sticks] on the floor, or the rattle.

In practically every instance, dancing or some movement of the body, even when seated in gambling, kept time with the song, accompanied by the drum and rattle. In dancing, the men jumped up and down in place with stiff legs and a spasmodic movement of the body. The women, standing in place, swayed from side to side.

The only musical instruments were drums, the chief's [or song leader's] staff, beating sticks, and the rattle. Hollow wooden pipes, calls, bellows-shaped instruments, are sometimes found among the Tlingit, but they belong to the southern tribes, Haida and Tsimshian. I have seen a call or whistle used at Killisnoo [Hutsnuwu tribe] by a Chilkat man in a dance with a drum. [Rattles were called še·šú·x̣ʷ; or a ceremonial rattle was *Chuck-ah-hut-tar* (ǯi-ka-x̣áda·). The leader's staff or cane was wu·ca·g̣á·, often named for its totemic carving: such as "Wolf Staff" (g̣u·č wu·ca·g̣á·).]

Drums, *gouh* [ga·w], were of two kinds. One was of wood in the form of a high, narrow box, open at one end, and made of red cedar. The sides were of a single dressed plank, cut in the corners, steamed until softened, bent into shape, and sewed with spruce root at the meeting at the fourth corner. The solid bottom was likewise sewed or pegged to the sides. At each end, well toward the top, were loops of hide by which it could be handled or hung from the roof beams. The sides were generally painted in animal designs representing the clan or house crest, and the drum was named according to the figure, as, for example, "Raven Drum." These box drums might properly be called potlatch drums, although they might be used generally. I have seen them carried in the canoe during the ceremony of towing the frame timbers for the chief's house to the village shore. This drum was beaten with the hand.

The more ordinary drum in common use was of tambourine type, with a single head. The circular frame of poplar, or maple, was steamed, softened, and bent around, and was secured at the meeting with root or hide ties. Such drums were from two to two and a half feet in diameter. Over the frame was stretched a hard, tanned skin of moun-

Editor's note: This chapter corresponds somewhat to that originally envisaged by Emmons when he was collecting information in the 1890s, and which he had called "Feasts, Dances, & Amusements." It was omitted, however, in the later manuscript that he had prepared, the contents scattered in other chapters. It seemed better to bring them together here.

Raven guests at a potlatch given by the Wolf 32 clan at Sitka, December 1904. (Photograph by Merrill. AMNH.)

tain goat, seal, or deer; strips of the skin crossed at the back by which it could be held. This drum also might be painted on either side in animal design. It was beaten with a short stick, the head of which was wrapped in hide.

[Sketches by Emmons in his notes at BCPA show the strands of skin crossing each other at right angles; the drum stick is shown as bent into a loop at the striking end. If the drum was beaten on the outside of the head, any painting on the inside would have been protected from wear.]

The box drum was found less frequently among the Tlingit than the skin-headed tambourine, but may have been more common in the past. There were two in the Sitka tribe, one at Hoonah, three at Angoon. Wooden box drums were received in trade from the Haida and Tsimshian. The skin drum was more recent [?], according to Pete [a shaman?]. The wooden drum properly belongs to the shaman and is used by him when he gives exhibition dances. The skin drum is alone used in his practice about the sick.

The primitive rattle on the entire Northwest Coast was made of half shells of the pecten, strung on circular withes of cedar by a hole near the hinge. The whole shell was also enclosed within the split end of a handle as a ceremonial rattle. Whole shells and pieces of the pecten shell were commonly found in the shaman's grave boxes and burial caves.

[For other rattles, tapping sticks, and sounding boards, see de Laguna 1972:697–99, pls. 62, 176, 177, 178, 187. The hollow oval rattle of wood was the typical shaman's rattle, but they also used wooden rattles carved in the shape of birds, with subsidiary figures carved on them to illustrate their practice or their familiar spirits, yé·k. The "chief's rattle" was of this type, but carved to represent a raven; a shaman could use this also.]

The Tlingit display much musical talent by readily picked up airs, which many hum and whistle, very soon after hearing them once or twice. They also readily learn to play on the more common instruments, mouth organ and accordion; and some play the piano, flute, and violin very creditably after instruction.

[Fuller information on songs and dances may be found in de Laguna 1972:560–77, the music of the songs transcribed by Dr. David F. McAllister (pp. 1149–1367). These songs, ší, represented potlatch songs, na·g̣a ší, "songs about the clan," most of which were mourning songs, and very precious. There were also "walking songs" sung by potlatch guests, ya̱· naˀát da·ši·y̱í; "house doorway songs," hít ẋ̣awu·ł da·ši·y̱í, sung by the guests as they entered; and "dance songs," łe·x̣ da·ši·y̱í·, sung when they danced to thank their hosts. Songs for other occasions were peace dance songs, funny songs, songs for children, shaman's spirit songs, and songs about one's feelings ("Haida mouth songs"). Some of the last were "sad songs," tu·wu nú·kʷ da·ši·y̱í·. Other songs that have been reported were addressed by the hunter to the animals he had killed; there was a separate song for each species, but the songs are no longer known. Emmons left a list of dances; the songs which they accompanied would be called by the same names (see Table 25). The information seems to have been supplied by Rudolph, the Kiksˀádi (Raven 10) artist of Sitka. There is some confusion in the list, since potlatches and dances are not clearly separated. An old note in BCPA reports: "Amusement dances generally connected with animals in which they use whole skin and represent very exactly the movements and actions of the animal." These were not for slain animals, but represented the crest animal of the clan dancing.]

TLINGIT CEREMONIALISM IN THE EIGHTEENTH AND EARLY NINETEENTH CENTURIES*

[The early explorers and traders and the later visitors did not usually observe ceremonies that were carried out inside the house, and most of what they reported was the ceremonialism that accompanied trading, or the signals given that peaceful trading was desired. Thus, La Pérouse (1799, 1:365), at Lituya Bay in 1786, noted that signs of friendship were the "displaying and waving white mantles, and different skins."

[The Indians were at first rather cautious in their approach, but the chief of the principal village visited the ships the day of their arrival and La Pérouse wrote (p. 370):

> Before he came on board, he appeared to address a prayer to the sun [to his personal Spirit Above, see Chapter 14]. He then made a long harangue, which was concluded by a kind of song, by no means disagreeable, and greatly resembling the plain chaunt of our churches. The Indians in his canoe accompanied him, repeating the same air in chorus. After this ceremony, they almost all came on board, and danced for an hour to the music of their own voices, in which they are very exact.

[Later, when the chief came with an offer to sell Cenotaph Island, this proposed trade required even more ceremony, and "the chief came on board better attended, and more

---

**Editor's note:* I am responsible for this whole section, for although Emmons had assembled and used a few scrappy quotations from early observers, he did not attempt to arrange them chronologically or to analyze the ceremonies observed.

Wooden drum with painted decoration representing an owl, with inlaid eyes of haliotis shell, a crest of the Raven 17 clan, Yakutat. (Courtesy of MAI, Heye Foundation.)

ornamented, than usual. After many songs and dances, he offered to sell me the island . . ." (p. 375).

[La Pérouse also observed (1799, 1:401, 408):

> On occasions of high ceremony, they wear their hair long, braided, and powdered with the down of sea-fowl. [White bird down symbolized peace and absence of evil.]
>
> [Although the Indians were made solemn by gambling] . . . yet I have often heard them sing, and when the chief came to visit me, he commonly paraded round the ship singing, with his arms stretched out in form of a cross as a token of friendship. He then came on board, and acted a pantomime expressing either a battle, a surprise, or death. The air that preceded this dance was pleasing, and tolerably melodious. [The score is reproduced by de Laguna 1972:560, with the footnote: "They who have the strongest voices take the air a third lower, and the women a third higher, than the natural pitch. Some sing an octave to it, and often make a rest of two bars, at the place where the air is highest."]

[Beresford (1789:187), reporting on trade at Yakutat in 1787, wrote that the natives conducted such trade "with great order and regularity;" beginning at daylight in the morning after singing for at least a half hour, would break off at noon to eat, and return in the afternoon. Trade for each group [lineage? household?] was carried out through its chief. And, "When the traffic of the day is pretty well over, they begin to sing, and never leave off till the approach of night; thus beginning and ending the day in the same manner" (p. 188).

[Colnett noted that same year at Yakutat that the tails of birds fastened to a canoe mast or a skin similarly hung signaled a desire for peaceful trade (in de Laguna 1972:131). Beresford (1789:180) reported that the natives of Norfolk Sound who wanted to trade hoisted a tuft of white feathers on the top of a long pole when they paddled out to the ship.

[Beresford (1789:242–43) wrote about the Northwest Coast Indians in general:

> . . . the Indians are very fond of masks or visors, and various kinds of caps, all of which are painted with different devices, such as birds, beasts, fishes, and sometimes representations of the human face; they have likewise many of these devices carved in wood, and some of them far from being ill executed.
>
> These curiosities seem to be greatly valued, and are carefully packed in neat square boxes, that they may the more conveniently be carried about.
>
> Whenever any large party came to trade, these treasures were first produced, and the principal persons dressed out in all their finery before the singing commenced. In addition to this, the Chief (who always conducts the vocal concert) puts on a large coat, made of the elk skin, tanned, round the lower part of which is one, or sometimes two rows of dried berries [?], or the beaks of birds, which make a rattling noise whenever he moves. In his hand he has a rattle, or more commonly a contrivance to answer the same end, which is of a circular form, about nine inches in diameter, and made of three small sticks bent round at different distances from each other: great numbers of birds beaks and dried berries [?] are tied to this curious instrument, which is shook by the Chief with great glee, and in his opinion makes no small addition to the concert. Their songs generally consist of several stanzas, to each of which is added a chorus. The beginning of each stanza is given out by the Chief alone, after which both men and women join and sing in octaves, beating time regularly with their hands, or paddles: meanwhile the Chief shakes his rattle, and makes a thousand ridiculous gesticulations, singing at intervals in different notes from the rest; and this mirth generally continues near half an hour without intermission.

Beresford (1789:243) also published here the score of a Norfolk Sound (Sitka) song (see de Laguna 1972:562, where it is also reproduced). The rattle and the form of the song are typically Tlingit.

[Portlock (1789:282) was similarly entertained in Sitka Sound in 1787. He had met a chief who indicated that he would soon return with excellent sea otter skins:

> . . . and perhaps he thought that on his last visit we were not impressed with a sufficient idea of his importance; for now he

came along-side with his party in great pomp and solemnity, all of them singing; and in addition to the vocal concert, they entertained us with instrumental music, which consisted of a large old chest, beaten with the hands, by way of a drum, and two rattles. The rattles were two feet long, about two inches round, made of hollow pieces of wood neatly joined together, and a number of small stones being put in, they were closed at both ends. The chief held one of these rattles in his hand, which he frequently shook with an air of meaning intelligence, and the rest of his tribe seemed to follow his directions, in singing in the most exact manner.

[After presenting Captain Portlock with an otter skin, the chief went ashore, presumably to sort out his skins; then came out to the ship again (Portlock 1789:283):

. . . and now I expected our trade to begin to good earnest; but in this I was again disappointed; for the singing again commenced, and by way of varying our amusement, the chief appeared in different characters during the time his people were singing; and always changed his dress when he varied his character; in doing of which some of his companions held up a large mat, by way of scene, to prevent us from seeing what was going on behind the curtain. At one time he appeared in the character of a warrior, and seemed to have all the savage ferocity of the Indian conqueror about him. He shewed us the manner in which they attacked their enemies, their method of fighting, and their behaviour to the vanquished enemy. He next assumed the character of a woman, and to make his imitation more complete, he wore a mask, which represented a woman's face with their usual ornaments; and indeed it so exactly resembled a woman's face, that I am pretty certain it was beyond the reach of Indian art, and must certainly have been left by the Spaniards in their last visit to this part of the coast[!].

Was the chief dancing in imitation of a shaman possessed by a female spirit, as may be done at potlatches?

[Portlock further reported (1789:282, 290) that the chief, on this occasion, had come in an old uniform coat, and

His hair, after being well rubbed with oil, was entirely filled with down taken from gulls, and which is always worn by the Indian chiefs when in full dress. . . . The method of dressing the hair with birds-down is only practiced by the men. The women in general are hair-dressers for their husbands, which office they seem to perform with a great deal of dexterity and good nature.

[Marchand (Fleurieu 1801, 1:354), who was at Sitka in 1791, noted the "regulated songs, at the rising and setting of the luminary of the day," which he believed religious. And (pp. 350–51):

The Tchinkitanayans have a decided taste for singing, and it appears to be among them a sort of social institution: at fixed periods of the day, in the morning and evening, they sing in chorus; every person present takes a part in the concert; and they all exhibit a composure which might suggest the idea that the words of their songs carry with them an interest that fixes their attention.

[Fleurieu then quoted Beresford (1789:242–43), as "The Editor of DIXON's Journal," about singing. (See above.) They have, adds that Journalist, a great variety of tunes, but their method of performing them is universally the same. The French observe, in like manner, that all the singers beat time, and that they have so true an ear, that never more than a single stroke is heard. Our voyagers [Captain Marchand and ship's company], taking a pleasure in their singing, which is melodious, frequently requested them to sing, and they did so without suffering themselves to be pressed; nor did they endeavour to make a favour of shewing their talent by a resistance which is not always a proof of modesty or diffidence. In their turn, they requested the French to sing, and appeared particularly to enjoy the slow tunes, the movement of which comes near to that of their songs [especially the prized clan songs]; an opera of LULLY would be heard with rapture at TCHINKITÂNAY; and, no doubt, its success would be complete, if it were terminated by a ballet of devils, in which the natives might recognize themselves.

[Malaspina, the officers, and specialists on his two ships had probably the most favorable opportunities for hearing Tlingit songs when they were at Yakutat in 1791. Suría, the artist, described the singing, and Dr. Haenke, the scientist, transcribed several songs, although his manuscripts have been lost. As the two Spanish ships approached, Yakutat natives in two canoes, with the chief, "Ankau," in a kayak, came out to meet them. When they were close, as reported by Suría (in Wagner 1936: 247–48):

. . . all except the steersman stood up, and at the sound of a stentorian and frightful voice which the ugliest one, who was in the center, uttered [as song leader], they all extended their hands together in the form of a cross with great violence, and turning their heads to one side intoned a very sad song in their language, which, however, preserved tune and time. It was composed of only three notes although the measure varied. [This may have been a clan song, na·ga ší·.] Soon they continued with other songs in this style, but very agreeable and sonorous. Amid all that confusion the one in the middle could be heard dictating the words with a loud voice and carrying the measure, making various contortions and movements for this purpose, now to one side and now to the other, with his right arm extended and at times looking towards the sun. The others understood him perfectly, keeping good time. On other occasions, after a short pause, they continued with a great shout, repeating it three times, and, striking the palms of their hands against those who were carrying the tune and those of the rowers, finished by extending their arms in the form of a cross.

Malaspina's ships at Port Mulgrave, Yakutat, in 1791, are visited by the Tlingit in their canoes. (Drawing by José Cardero. Courtesy of Museo Naval, Madrid.)

> [The canoes escorted the ships into Port Mulgrave], . . . always singing songs which, although harsh on account of the pronunciation, were not very disagreeable.

Malaspina (1885:155–56) also reported:

> [As the ships were nearing Port Mulgrave, two large and one small canoe came out to meet them.] From a great distance a harmonious hymn of peace resounded, which they accompanied by the clear signal of open arms to demonstrate that they came disarmed and sought only peace and friendship from us. [As the ships entered Port Mulgrave, and were about to anchor] . . . many canoes came out to meet us, repeating several times the hymn of peace, other times a general harmonious call, of invitation or admiration, [and brought salmon and wooden carvings for trade].

The natives were familiar with Europeans and their vices, and some of the younger men and women could sing English sea chanties (see de Laguna 1972:146).

[In restoring friendly relations, after trade had been suspended by the Spaniards because of thefts, the Tlingit chief or leader was paddled out to the ships, holding up the stolen garment with wide-stretched arms, singing "the hymn of peace," and requesting the Spaniards to sing it also. (See Suría, in Wagner 1936:252, 258; Malaspina 1885:166; de Laguna 1972:151.) This was done, both on the ships and on shore, "not without a certain harmony and with the expressive gesture of the open arms," as Malaspina wrote. And that night the natives danced and sang happy songs at bonfires on the beach. Suría also described this reconciliation (p. 258):

> They also make use of others [songs] of this style in order to ask for peace as we found out as the result of having suspended commerce with skins with them for a day. Believing that we were very angry they did not stop singing all afternoon and night and as this song is interesting, I find it necessary to give an account of it.
>
> They divided themselves into three parties . . . on the beach in front of the ships. At the end of each song they finished with a kind of laugh which jointly and in measure they sustained on this sound, Xa Xa Xa Xa Xa. In others they ended with another sound which cannot be described but it was like the barking of a dog. Thus they went on all night, leaving us unable to sleep.

Happy Tlingit songs were often accompanied by animal cries, such as the cawing of the raven or sounds suggestive of a whale spouting; and such cries were said to be Tsimshian. Sad songs were often accompanied and followed by sobs or wails (de Laguna 1972:567).

[Suría (in Wagner 1936:250; de Laguna 1972:150) had a frightening experience when, left by his companions, he was surrounded by natives in a house. Because this seemed something like the experience of a hostage in a peace ceremony, it will be described in Chapter 12, "War and Peace."

Suría (in Wagner 1936:258) also described the way in which native visitors were received at Port Mulgrave:

> We noted that whenever some canoe from the neighborhood whose Indians are subject to some other chief come to this island [Khantaak?] they make a salute to it which is worth describing. As soon as they see them [as the residents see the visitors] they go down to the beach and all together in unison kneel until they remain on their knees and on standing up they utter a great cry, very ugly, and ferocious, on a *gangora* which sounds something like an N [evidently a nasal sound]. This they repeat three times and at the last end with a very sharp and quavering shriek. On the occasion of receiving foreigners they make use of many songs all different . . . [as when the Spanish ships entered the port].

[Malaspina (1885:160) described such an event (see also de Laguna 1972:146–147): Early on the morning of June 30 or July 1, the "Ankau" and another dignitary came to Malaspina, to inform him with some anxiety that two canoes were coming, already only a mile or so away. They did not know if these were friendly or hostile, and wanted the Spanish to fire a volley, so that the newcomers would have to show their intentions. So, while the Spanish went to the outer beach, the Yakutat men armed themselves and launched two canoes, and the women hid.

> . . . we fired a rifle and then let ourselves be seen by the people in the canoes [i.e., the strangers, as Malaspina wrote]. With this sign the men in the canoes (about 40) broke into a hymn of peace. . . . The *Ankau* was still fearful [or pretended to be] and took precautions as he continued to shout that we were his allies and that they had better be careful. Almost all the fears of a breach were dissipated and the inhabitants of the port were unarmed [disarmed themselves?]. They waded out to bring in the chiefs to the beach without getting wet. They were immediately presented to the *Ankau*. This ceremony was followed by general peace and later all of the natives embraced, and amid joy and conversation they all went together into the huts . . . they all mingled and appeared to be one tribe even though an hour before they were ready to destroy each other.

This was not a narrowly averted fight, but the warlike, ceremonial reception of visitors, as at a potlatch, when one group of guests at the hosts' village apparently opposes with arms the landing of the other guests, invited from another tribe. McClellan (1954:96) has analyzed the war and peace-making symbolism employed in Tlingit potlatches. Although the visitors to Port Mulgrave had come to trade, they seem to have been received as if they had come to a potlatch.

[When Purtov and Kulikalov came to Yakutat in 1794 with a party of Kodiak Island hunters, they experienced a reception similar to those described by Suría and Malaspina. To establish peaceful relations with the newcomers, the Yakutat chief sent his own son as a hostage, and also according to the Russians' report (Tikhmenev 1979, 2:49): "As a sign of friendship they sent us also three staffs decorated with eagle feathers, and sea otter skins." The Russians sent one of their Koniag men as a hostage, "and staffs decorated with beads." When the two Russians went to the Tlingit village in Port Mulgrave,

> The taion came out of his yurt [house] with many of his people and after a ceremonial dance they asked us to come ashore. About twenty of them ran to our baidarka and carried us to the village situated on a hill. Then the taion invited us to his yurt and offered us a meal, which consisted of halibut and berries with fat, served on fir bark. For a present he gave me two sea otter skins, and I gave him beads and brass rings.

[As reported by Lieutenant Johnstone, commander of the *Chatham,* which entered the harbor soon after (Vancouver 1801, 5:402–3], a large canoe with twelve local natives visited the Russians' camp on Khantaak Island, "and were welcomed to the shore by a song from the Kodiak Indians; this compliment being returned in the same way," and the conference began. The Indians told Purtov their grievances, that the Koniag hunters were taking sea otters in their territory, and gave Purtov a sea otter skin. They were delighted when he accepted it, no doubt thinking that it meant recognition that their claim was valid. "[A] loud shout was given by both parties: this was followed by a song, which concluded these introductory ceremonies." Later, more Tlingit came and landed "after similar ceremonies of song and dances," until their numbers frightened the Russians.

[Captain Vancouver had experienced Tlingit ceremonialism the year before (1793), when his ships were anchored in Port Stewart, on the western arm of Behm Canal, in Stikine territory. While he was still off Camano Point, Cleveland Peninsula, bound for Behm Canal, a party of natives visited the ships. Their leader, "who bore the character of an inferior chief," was *Kanaut* (Ł ʔuná·ṫ, "They never die," a Wolf name). He "said that he belonged to a powerful chief whose name was *O-non-nis-toy,*" and had Vancouver fire a gun which would call this great chief to trade. (It will be remembered that the name of the chief, Ģuna·ne·sté, referred to the wanderings of Raven, so the name belonged to the Raven moiety, and had been borne by a series of Stikine chiefs; see Chapter 10, the section "Naming." Quite possibly Vancouver's *O-non-nis-toy* was the leader of the Stikine Kiksʔádi, Raven 10;

and *Kanaut* may well have been his Wolf son, perhaps Na·ṇya·ʔa·ỵí, Wolf 18, for the two leading clans of the Stikine would have been united by marriages.) At any rate, Vancouver gave the "inferior chief" some blue cloth for *O-non-nis-toy* (Vancouver 1801, 4:209–10).

[Two days later (August 23, 1794), the same party visited the ships in Port Stewart, and the "inferior chief" made arrangements for the great chief's visit, and solicited more presents for him (p. 213).

[As Vancouver (1801, 4:214–15) reported, at midnight, August 25–26,

> . . . we were disturbed by the singing of a party of the natives, as they entered the harbour. [It was a single canoe with seventeen persons] who, after paddling round the vessels with their usual formalities, landed not far from the ship, where they remained singing until day-break. It appeared that much time had been bestowed on the decoration of their persons; their faces were painted after various fancies, and their hair was powdered with very delicate white down of young sea fowls. With the same ceremony they again approached the ship, then came along side with the greatest confidence.

[The leader of the party, *Kanaut,* came on board and presented Vancouver with a sea otter skin, to which the latter made "a proper acknowledgment," and trade began. The natives proved themselves keen but honest traders, and spoke "in the highest terms of *Ononnistoy*; who they acknowledged as their chief, and the head of a very numerous tribe."

[On the afternoon of August 30, twenty-five natives, in three canoes, came from the south. They were complete strangers to the English, and were led by two chiefs, neither of whom was Ononnistoy. As Vancouver wrote (1801, 4:223–25):

> They approached us with the same formalities as those observed by our former visitors . . . [and their deportment was that of] people of some importance; and I was consequently induced to compliment them with presents suitable to their apparent rank. They accepted them with indifference. . . .

The next day they returned and were more friendly; they gave Vancouver a sea otter skin and indicated that they desired to trade. So Vancouver purchased from them a lot of salmon, and the two chiefs stayed on board all morning. They were fed on bread and molasses, which Kanaut had indicated was Ononnistoy's favorite food. In return they offered Vancouver some "whale oil," and on his refusal drank it themselves, and also a large glass of rum, "a luxury to which they seemed by no means strangers."

[That afternoon (Vancouver 1801, 4:225–27), there came "a large canoe full of men singing a song, and keeping time by the regularity of their paddling" (p. 225). The Indians already present at once put on their war garments and took up their spears from the bottom of their canoes, and laid them with their points toward the newcomers.

> Thus prepared they advanced slowly to meet them, making most violent and passionate speeches, which were answered in a similar tone of voice by some persons who stood up in the large canoe. They continued to paddle with much regularity towards each other; yet those who had now entered the harbour, did not appear to be so hostilely inclined as those who had already occupied the port; as the lances of the former, though in readiness for action, were not disposed in a way so menacing. On a nearer approach they rested on their paddles, and entered into a parley; and we could then observe, that all those who stood up in the large canoe were armed with pistols or blunderbusses, very bright and in good order. [p. 226]

They seemed to reach a peaceful agreement, for both parties came on together:

> . . . but just as they came alongside the Discovery, one of the chiefs who had been on board, drew, with much haste, from within the breast of his war garment, a large iron dagger, and appeared to be extremely iritated by something that had been said by those in the large canoe, who again with great coolness took up their pistols and blunderbusses. [But a satisfactory explanation was evidently made, and they all put away their arms] . . . a perfect reconciliation seemed to have taken place on both sides.

[This warlike reception of another group of visitors reminds us of what Malaspina had observed at Yakutat. Since Ononnistoy and his group lived in the northwest, and the other party had come from the south, the two groups may have come from different tribes (Stikine, and Sanya? or Tongass?) or from different clans.

[Ononnistoy, the chief in the large canoe, was accompanied by a man who seemed to be his minister, someone who was not a chief, but a wise man to whom his chief appealed for advice, and who spoke for him, du x̣̓$^{(w)}$é·tx̣ yu· x̣̓$^{(w)}$atángi, "from-his-mouth speaker."

> [Kanaut now] arrived in a small canoe, and was received by the tribe in other canoes with similar ceremonies, but in a manner not quite so fierce and hostile. [p. 227]

All were now friends (Vancouver 1801, 4:227–29), and Ononnistoy came on board, but without the "distant formalities shewn by the chiefs of the other party." The other chiefs came on board also, but Ononnistoy with two or three companions stayed on board for the night, after dining on bread, molasses, and dried fish, with rum and wine, and after Vancouver had exhibited some fireworks. This was indeed a reception given by one chief to another!

> Early the next morning, . . . Ononnistoy with his friends joined the party on shore, where they were very busily employed in adorning their persons in the manner already described; which being accomplished by breakfast time, he, attended by all the other chiefs, came off in his large canoe, and, according to their custom, sang while they paddled round the vessels. This ceremony being ended, they came alongside the Discovery, and exhibited a kind of entertainment that I had not before witnessed. It consisted of singing, and of a display of the most rude and extravagant gestures that can be imagined. The principal parts were performed by the [five] chiefs, each in succession becoming the leader or hero of the song; at the several pauses of which, I was presented by the exhibiting chief with a sea otter skin; and the Indian spectators seemed to regret the performance was at an end, from which they had apparently derived great amusement. [pp. 228–29]

[They now all came on board and trading began. It would appear that the chiefs had been demonstrating clan prerogatives, and, as was customary, were paying Vancouver for witnessing and thereby approving them. It was like the behavior of hosts at a potlatch.

[Other Stikine Indians, met on the south shore of Clarence Strait, between Zarembo and Prince of Wales islands, "performed their ceremonies, indicative of friendship, [like those already described, and] conducted themselves very orderly," and the next day returned with many songs and two or three medium-sized canoes of women (Vancouver 1801, 4:253).

[In 1794, Mr. Whidbey, leading a boat party that was exploring Lynn Canal, encountered a Chilkat chief, who at first behaved in a very friendly manner, apparently with intent to delay the boats until a war party could overtake them. The Englishmen were lucky to have been able to escape such a superior force. Vancouver (1801, 5:429–31) described the chief and his party of about twenty, who were in one large canoe, as if going to a potlatch, wearing ceremonial clothes.

> This chief Mr Whidbey represented as a tall thin elderly man. He was dressed in a much more superb style than any chief we had hitherto seen on this coast, and he supported a degree of state consequence, and personal dignity, unusual to be found amongst the chiefs of North West America. His external robe was a very fine large garment, that reached from his neck down to his heels, made of wool from the mountain sheep, neatly variegated with several colours, and edged and otherwise decorated with little tufts, or frogs of woollen yarn, dyed in various colours. His head-dress was made of wood, much resembling in its shape a crown, adorned with bright copper and brass plates, from whence hung a number of tails or streamers, composed of wool and fur wrought together, dyed of various colours, and each terminating by a whole ermine skin. The whole exhibited a magnificent appearance, and indicated a taste for dress and ornament that we had not supposed the natives of these regions to possess. [pp. 430–31]

He was wearing a geometric patterned (?) blanket and a type of headdress known as šaki·ˀát, "something on the head," with frontlet mask.

[Von Langsdorff (1814, 2:110–11, 113–14), who was at Sitka in 1805–6, described the visits to the Russian fort by the Tlingit who came to trade:

> Their visits are commonly made in large companies of both sexes; they come in canoes . . . singing and rowing [paddling] to a measured time. When they have reached the landing-place they stop, and one from the midst of them makes a long oration; nor do they attempt to land until Nanok, as he is called by them, that is the Commandant Von Baranoff, or somebody deputed by him, comes down to invite them on shore, and assures them that they will meet with a friendly reception. I was informed by the interpreters that these speeches are composed with method, and even rhetorically; they consist of long periods, the great art of which appears to be repeating the same thought over and over again under different words. "We were your enemies, we sought to do you injury, you were our enemies, you sought to injure us;—we wish to be good friends, we would forget the past, we no longer wish to molest you, forbear to injure us, be henceforward good friends to us." These orations will sometimes last half an hour.
>
> When the proper assurances of friendship are given they venture on shore, and the commandant, who has studied their humours, orders a tent to be pitched for them, and a profuse dinner to be prepared. [They reject the offer of brandy, knowing its effects.] [pp. 110–11]
>
> These visits usually last some days, during which the visitors are entertained with eating, drinking, and dancing. It is only the men that dance, and in their preparations for it, which consist of painting their faces, and ornamenting their heads, as much time is spent as by any European lady at her toilette. The hair is powdered over with the down feathers of the white-headed eagle, *falco leucocephalus,* and ornamented with ermine: many regular figures are painted on the face with coal-dust, chalk, ochres, and cinnabar: these latter ornaments seem to supply the place of tattooing, which I never saw practised among these people. Small looking glasses are become a necessary article to them for their toilettes, and numbers are brought here every year by the ships of the United States. Before they were acquainted with this invention, the people used to be *coëffeurs* to each other, since it

"The Kaluschians of Sitka dancing," ca. 1805. (Von Langsdorff, 1814, Part 2, pl. opp. p. 114. Courtesy of the Bancroft Library, University of California, Berkeley.)

was impossible for any one to paint his own face, or arrange the ornaments of his own head.

The dance itself consists chiefly in a very eager spring, in executing which the dancers scarcely remove at all from one spot. They are all barefooted, and wear a single garment only, commonly the woollen carter's frock mentioned above. One of the dancers seems, as it were, to lead the rest, carrying in his hand a thick sort of staff ornamented with the teeth of sea-otters; with this he strikes upon the ground to mark the measure. All, without exception, hold in their hands either the tail or wing of the white-headed eagle, or a piece of ermine. The latter is valued by them very highly as an article of luxury; they not only ornament their heads with it, and hold it in their hands, but sew it about their garments. The women sit upon the ground at the distance of some paces from the dancers, and sing a not inharmonious melody, which supplies the place of music. [pp. 113–14; the plate opposite page 114 illustrates the dance.]

[Lazarev ([1832] 1861:128–29, Petroff's translation), who had visited Sitka in the 1820s, received a party of natives on board his sloop, the *Ladoga*. The Indians were led by "*Na-oosh-ket,* the Chief of the Sparrow tribe" [Ná·wuške·ƛ (?), a Raven], and came in ceremonial dress, sang, and danced on board.

> The Toyoun [chief] and his nearest relatives had not smeared or painted their faces, but wore various articles of clothing given to them by the official at the Fort, over which they wrapped blankets of different patterns and some had skins of wild sheep over their shoulders and others, however, powdered with feathers, wore entire skins of wild animals and had their faces daubed with vermilion and soot, the men having the partition of the nose pierced and the women the lower lip, through which opening they wore rings made of beads and other ornaments [and the women wore wooden labrets].

[The chief went to the quarterdeck and made a speech to Captain Lazarev, which he did not understand, and the other natives began to dance:

> Standing in rows along the bulwarks of the quarterdeck they sang with hoarse voices, and beating upon drums, they stamped their feet and jumped, accompanying these moves by various gestures and savage contortions. Finally they began to advance toward each other with knives in their hands, flourishing them in the most dangerous manner, and as they generally keep up their dances for a long time we thought it would be difficult to make them end this amusement, when it happened to rain and interrupted their performance; and after that we began to entertain our savage visitors at the table.

[Von Kotzebue (1830, 2:58–61), who was at Sitka in 1825, described a visit of the Kalosh to his ship. Native chiefs liked to take their whole family and attendants.

> Before coming on board, they usually rowed round several times the ship, howling a song to this effect: "We come to you as friends, and have really no evil intention. Our fathers lived in strife with you, but let peace be between us. Receive us with hospitality, and expect the same from us." This song was accompanied by a sort of tambourine, which did not improve its harmony. They would not climb the ship's side till we had several times repeated our invitation, as it was not their custom to accept the first offer of hospitality, perhaps from a feeling of distrust. On these visits, the Kalushes were more than usually particular in the decoration of their persons. Their faces were so thickly smeared with stripes of red, black, and white paint, that their natural colour could not be known. [The author had earlier (p. 51) explained that the "different races distinguish each other" by their face painting.] Their bodies were painted with black stripes, and their hair with a quantity of white down and feathers, which were scattered around with every motion of their heads. Ermine-skins are also frequently fastened into the hair. A wolf or bear-skin, or a blanket, tied round the neck, covers their bodies, and they use an eagle's wing or tail as a fan [to mark time as they sing]. Their feet are always bare. [pp. 58–59]
>
> [After looking over the ship] they assembled upon deck to dance. The women did not dance, but assisted as musicians. Their song, accompanied by the dull music of tambourine, consisted of a few hollow and unconnected tones, sent forth at intervals to keep time with the stamping of their feet. The men made the most extraordinary motions with their arms and bodies, varying them by high leaps into the air, while showers of feathers fell from their heads. Every dancer retained his own place, but turning continually round and round, gave the spectators an opportunity of admiring him on all sides. One only stood a little apart; he was particularly decorated with ermine-skins and feathers, and beat time for the dancing with a staff ornamented with the teeth of the sea-otter. He appeared to be the director of all the movements. [p. 60]

The Russians gave them tobacco at every pause in the dancing, and when they finally stopped from exhaustion, gave them their "favorite mess of rice boiled with treacle," and at parting a dram of brandy (p. 61).

[So far, the explorers and Russians have described only the ceremonies attending trade, in addition to those involving the reception of visitors or guests, and a few incidents that suggest shamanistic dances or peacemaking, and the meaning of the ceremonies to the Tlingit themselves has not been apparent. Captain Lütké and Father Veniaminov form the only exceptions during this period.

[Lütké (1835:215–17), who was at Sitka in 1827, wrote, apparently following Khlebnikov ([1817–32] 1976:31; free translation):

> The Kaloches are great lovers of fêtes, which means for them eating without limit and dancing afterwards. Pretexts for this are never lacking: new liaisons, new recognitions, peace and war, every unusual event, commemoration in honor of relatives or friends who have died, all become a motive for these reunions, which are here designated, as we have already said, by the word *igrouchki,* the games. [The Sitka interpreter had used this Siberian expression, *igrouchka,* for the ceremony at which slaves were sacrificed (p. 193).] They are of all kinds: the particular ones, which are held several times during the year only between the nearest neighbors, and the general, to which are invited acquaintances and distinguished personages from the farthest regions.
>
> The first are celebrated in autumn, when they make the winter's stores. The oldest taïon [chief, toyon] in the tribe treats his neighbors at his house for several days, during which they alternately eat and dance without interruption. Finally the host presents gifts to his guests, of furs, caribou [tanned hides?], blankets, etc., and moves on with the whole group to another, then to a third, and so forth. They know, on these occasions, how to allocate with great finesse, the quantity and quality of their gifts, so that the distribution is not too much in anyone's favor.
>
> It is no longer families, but whole tribes that give the general games, to which guests from far away take part during more than a month. In the village in which the festival is given, each hut is distinguished by a sculptured figure, representing some animal, a bird, or something completely different, and during the whole time that the reunion lasts, the hut is no longer called by the name of the owner, but by that of the insignia [crest] that it bears. After having been treated at the sign of the Eagle, they go to that of the Crow, of the Bear, of the Sun, of the Moon, etc. The invited guests receive everywhere presents proportionate to the rank of each person, and to the more or less sound hope of receiving from him in the future an equivalent gift.
>
> It seems that in these games one sometimes sacrifices slaves, as has been said above.
>
> The savage dance of the Kaloches, the bedaubed faces of the dancers, the rattles, the tambourines, etc., have been often de-

Ka·g^{w}a·nta·n, *Wolf 1, guests from Sitka, attending potlatch at Klukwan, given by George Shotridge* [Yé·ɬ gu·x̣ú, *"Raven's Slave"*] *and other* G̣a·nax̣te·dí, *Raven 3, to dedicate the new Whale House, 1901. (Photograph by Blankenberg, no. 159. AMNH.) Enlarged details of this photograph (AMNH and BCPA) have been identified by Emmons as taken at Sitka in 1890 or 1900, and at Killisnoo in 1902 by Vincent Soboleff.*

scribed by earlier voyagers, and there is nothing to add to what they have said.

[Lütké (1835:193–94) also mentioned that:

> . . . [The Tlingit] have a ceremony which is linked to their religious ideas, which they celebrate from time to time, now in one tribe [clan], now in another, and in which they sacrifice slaves. [The interpreter called this ceremony *igrouchka*.] A short time before our arrival in Sitka, there had been such a game in the tribe of Naouchket, who lives near the fort, to which all the neighboring tribes came, and in which a *kalga* (slave) was offered in sacrifice. They suffocated the victim by putting a plank on his neck. Doctor Mertens, who was making a collection of skulls of the peoples we were visiting, discovered, from the description given him, the place of sacrifice in the thick woods, and also the corpse of the victim, from which he took the skull at the peril of his own life.

And Lütké further specified (p. 196) that the slaves chosen for sacrifice were always those who were too old to be good for anything else and that one could neither sell nor give away.

[Later writers, such as Holmberg (1855:46–50), Krause ([1885] 1956:162–68), and Petroff (1884:171–72), have based their descriptions of Tlingit ceremonials largely on the report by Veniaminov ([1840] 1984:419–25). The latter specified that there were three major festivals or ceremonies: the wake, held "to nourish the dead" (see the section "Death" and "Ceremonies after the Funeral" in Chapter 10); the second, called "to raise up the dead," which we would consider as the major house-building potlatch; and the third, "for the children," at which the ears of the noble children were pierced. In addition, there were lesser ceremonies held at a birth, when a girl emerged from her puberty seclusion, at a wedding, and at a house-warming "to dry out the house," as well as shamanistic performances. Some of these have already been mentioned in connection with the life cycle (Chapter 10); information from Veniaminov about the others will be given in the following pages.

[Olson (1967:58–69) has described in rich detail these major potlatches, and also a variety of minor ceremonies, including the symbolism involved.]

HOUSE-BUILDING CEREMONIES*

The building of the house was the most important event in the life of the Tlingit, for, aside from the enormous labor of getting out, working down, and fitting the great timbers with the crudest implements, the ceremonies attending each step, so exact in procedure, went back to the fundamental principles of their social organization. The attending potlatch, while regarded as an investment and used as a means of payment, was in every sense a religious observation in honor of the dead. The food and property distributed or put in the fire was believed to be received in spirit form by those dead whose names were called with each gift. The named houses, totem poles, and graves were all memorials to ancestors, besides serving practical purposes. It was the ambition of every man to build or rebuild a house, and to this end he saved throughout his life, and if he died before being able to accomplish this, it was a solemn obligation to be carried out by his successor. [Emmons should have indicated, however, that it was only a wealthy house chief, or a nephew succeeding to that position, who could build or rebuild a lineage house. He was the chief mourner of the one to whom the house was a memorial.]

All of the builder's household and members of his clan contributed to this end. The first step was a family council to take stock of their means, and if a new house was to be built, to select the site. [Olson (1967:60) specified that the chief went at dawn to each house of his clan to summon them to this meeting, appealing for their help.] At this gathering every detail was discussed, and it was settled which members of the opposite moiety, particularly from the wife's family, were to be selected to do the work. If, as was so often the case, the construction of the new house, erection of a totem pole, and making a gravehouse were to be undertaken by the successor to the deceased, the ceremonies attending this work should be considered as forming part of the funeral series, even though such a memorial might not be built for some years after the death, since it might take a long time for the host (chief mourner, or new chief) to collect enough for the necessary potlatch. [Olson (1967:61) referred to this potlatch as the "joy feast," which followed the four "crying feasts" of the funeral. This might be four years later, although the chief mourner might indicate by a riddle at the last mourning feast that he intended to build a new house.]

Sometimes the beginning was made a few days after the weeping feast.

The new house master [that is, the chief mourner and builder], dressed in his poorest clothes, would go out early in the morning before the crow flies, to plead with those of the opposite moiety, and to invoke the departed spirits of his own family.

[Emmons here adapted the manuscript written for him by William Paul, Sr., of Wrangell, in which this Ti'y hít-ta'n, or Raven 11, man wrote as if he were the chief builder. It seems better to quote the original manuscript although the spelling and punctuation have been corrected.

> After the cremation and the weeping feast, a few days after, the leader goes around the village before any one is up, and sings pleasing songs, and pleads with the widow's tribe [the "opposite" clan or gune'tkana'yí]. He makes his long dead relatives talk to the tribes, or to the spirits of their dead relatives. [It seems that he appeals to the dead who are ancestral both to himself and his clansmen, and also to the "opposites," the widow's "brothers and sisters."] This is the speech:
>
> If he was the son of *Nin-ye-ah-yee* [Na'nya'ʔa'yí, Wolf 18. Paul, a Raven, was presumably such a "son"], he says:
>
> "My great father, Shakes, thy child is shivering with cold. ["Shakes" was the title of the head chief of Wolf 18, and therefore a "father" to Paul. "Great father" is *not* "grandfather."] No shelter, nothing to cover my head. I am in the middle of a large river; the current is carrying me down to the great sea, and there was no one to save me. The bridge is broken down with me. Who, oh who, will come with his canoe to deliver me from the mouth of the great sea? My father, Shakes, will the old Shakes heed to my wailing? Will he not come and deliver me from the hands of my enemies? I plead with the spirits of thy dead relatives.
>
> "They are responding to my call now, and are saying to thee, 'Go, Shakes, go and help thy uncle's son in his great distress!' Oh my father, Shakes, heed them, and come with thy men and help me!"

[According to Olson (1967:60), the plea with the simile of drifting helpless toward the ocean was made in the speeches of the chief mourner-host to his fellow clansmen when he wanted their contributions to the feast or potlatch he was to give.

> Responses from Shakes: "Ye ah, ye ah! My son, the spirit of my long dead relatives heard thy cry. As of old when thou wert a child, thy father and great uncle will take thee in their arms

**Editor's note:* I have substituted William Paul's more specific account, including speeches, for that of Emmons, which is based upon it. When Emmons wrote, it was the style to present ethnographic descriptions in as generalized a way as possible, even though they might have been derived from a few, or even one, specific observation. Yet the speeches by Paul cannot be fully understood without knowing the identities of the speaker and those addressed and their clan affiliations and relationships. I have also added statements from Chase, Shukoff, and Paul on slave sacrifice, and observations by Olson.

Ceremonies at Sitka, 1889. Canoes towing the structural timbers for the new house of "Annahootz" [ʔAnaxú·c], *chief of the Sitka* Ka·gʷa·nta·n, *Wolf 1. (Photograph by G. T. Emmons. AMNH.)*

and will hush to sleep. Will also give thee things to play with and keep thee quiet. The toy is the Bear Hat, and the Killerwhale hat."

[It is characteristic of Tlingit oratory in such situations for the speaker, in this case supposedly Shakes, to offer the clan's greatest treasures to comfort their "opposites" (see Swanton 1909:374–89).

The meaning [of the last speech] is that Shakes and all his tribe will help him bring his trees for totem poles and for crosspieces and four great posts for the corners of the house.

The leader [mourner-host] goes to the next house and delivers the same speeches.

If the chief of the house does not respond to the leader's call, then he would know that the tribe [clan] was offended at something. They either got offended at the first weeping feast, or the leader did not treat the widow right. [She belonged to their clan.] In this case, the leader with his friends or his tribe [clansmen] take their emblems, Raven Hat or Frog Hat, or whatever emblems may be. [This display of the Raven clan's most sacred emblems is mollifying, I believe, because the offended Wolf clansmen are descended from Ravens who treasured these hats.]

Almost the same speech is delivered at the offender's house [the house of the offended chief?].

After much pleading and coaxing the spirits of his ancestors, he responds and says, "Ye ah, Ye ah." To return the courtesy that has been shown him, he tells some of his men to tear up some blankets. Whole blankets are given to the leader, strips of blankets to the others, meaning payment [will be made] for their coming.

Next day, whole tribes [both clans?] are ready to go after trees for the totem pole, posts and crosspieces. All the guests are dressed in their best. The leader [host] goes before them; he fasts on that day.

[To continue with Emmons:] Then the trees were selected by the builder [future owner of the house], and a fire was built nearby. Oil or other food was thrown on it as an offering to the other trees, *As qwan-ee* [ʔa·s qʷá·ni, "spruce-tree indwelling-spirits"], "tree friends," as they were all looked upon as members of one family, having spirit life the same as animals' people. So they must be treated with proper respect. Eagle down was scattered around as a sign of peace, so that the trees cut, in falling, might not injure their neighbors.

In former days the felling of a tree with stone axes was a great labor, and it was an old belief that in this people had been taught by the beaver. They scored the trunk, burned a little and cut a little, until the tree fell; then they cut the trunk to the required lengths with burning and the adz.

The heavy timbers, including the corner posts, interior supports and stringers, might be fashioned in the woods but were more often brought to the village to be finished. All of this work was done by those selected from a clan of the opposite phratry, who then towed them [the logs] in behind the central canoe, while the other canoes were in line on either side, and they all sang to the accompaniment of a drum as they approached the village. The canoes drew up in a line [abreast] in front of the [future] housemaster's house [site?]. Two or more head men in ceremonial dress danced in the stern of the canoe. [Paul specified that these head men wore the headdress called *Shu-ke-ut* (šaki·ʔát) trimmed with ermine skins. The leader (future house owner) tore more blankets and calico and these were distributed among the guests in the canoe and those on land.] Then followed speeches of thanks by the housemaster who was answered by those in the canoes.

That night invitations were again sent to all the very same clans of the opposite phratry who had done the work, and they were fed. This feast is called "Feeding the Trees," for as soon as the guests were all in, some food was put in the fire for this purpose. [Paul: "The trees, totem pole, crosspieces, and the post [are fed]. Berries and oil are given to the

Ceremonies begin for new house construction for Wolf 1 chief at Sitka, 1889. (Photograph by G. T. Emmons. AMNH.)

guests, in large bowls. Nothing particular is done at this feast, simply food is put into the fire for the trees, and the guests are fed."]

Then followed short speeches, and a distribution of food. [Paul: "The guests go home with their bowls of oil or berries."] After the departure of the guests, the housemaster, who has fasted for two days, may eat. During the time of building he must practice abstinence and eat no food from the sea. [Paul: "During the months he is building a house, he does not approach his wife, and does not eat anything from salt water. If he does not keep these laws, he is sure to die. He keeps himself from all uncleanness before the house is built and after it is built."]

He then selected those who were to build the house. These were generally or largely of his wife's family.

[According to Paul, these were:

> . . . the widow's nearest relatives—brother, [maternal] uncle, or cousins [mother's sister's sons]. [The house is evidently to be a memorial to the builder's deceased kinsman whose title he will assume.] It may be 10 or 20 men, depending on how well off he is. During these times, or before these times, his [the builder's] wife makes presents to all of her relatives' wives [her "sisters-in-law"], anything by way of clothing, or boxes of berries. These presents are called *kēhh hiss,* meaning pay back more than it's worth. [Hi·x̣ is payment to a shaman, from the verb -si-hi·.]

In aboriginal days when slaves were sacrificed, the first one was killed on the ground selected for the building; others were killed as each corner post was erected. This was done by knocking them on the head with a ceremonial club, or by laying them on the ground with a stone under the neck and placing a stout pole over the neck on the ends of which several men bore down. But the greater chiefs killed the slave with a ceremonial pick, called *ka tu* [ké·t̓u], "turned up," which was the most prized of all weapons. It sometimes had a long, slender, finely worked blade [or head] of jade, set through the end of a stout wooden handle that was carved in animal [crest] design. The body of the dead slave was cast out on the beach to be washed away by the tide. The killing of slaves was an indication of wealth and a sacrifice of property that greatly added to the prestige of the builder.

[Chase (1893:51) described what he believed to have been the ceremonies attending the building of a Tlingit house, as practiced prior to 1867:

> The rectangular space for the building is then cleared, a spot for the fireplace designated, and four holes dug, wherein the corner posts are to be set, and then comes the most shocking part of the performance. A slave, either man or woman, who has been captured in war, or is even a descendant of such a slave, is blindfolded and compelled to lie down face uppermost on the place selected for the fireplace. A sapling is then cut, laid across the throat of the slave, and at a given signal the two nearest relatives of the host sit upon the respective ends of the sapling, thereby choking the unhappy wretch to death.

But the corner posts must receive their baptism, so four slaves are blindfolded, and one is forced to stand in each post hole, when, at a given signal, a blow on the forehead is dealt with a peculiar club ornamented with the host's coat-of-arms. [The Russians had to permit "the barbarous part of the ceremony" for fear of provoking a war with the Tlingit that would have interrupted the fur trade, Chase concluded. Details of this account were denied by Paul, see below.]

[In describing slave sacrifice at the time of house building, Shukoff wrote that when the ground was selected and the name of the future house had been determined, for example, "Bear House," Xú·c Hít, the owner

> . . . asks one of [the] carpenters to carve a bear's head on [a] heavy club about two feet long. Then after club is finished, he invites relatives and friends [own clansmen and the "opposites"] and kills him [slave] with the club, and kills another one after they finish house. During performance chief makes speech and tells people his family history, what [that] of his ancestors, and that he is trying to follow their lives as much as possible. They take [the] slave and lay him down on [his] back, and put small stone under [his] neck, and lay [a] pole, six or seven feet long, across neck, and two Indians sit at either end of pole and press down. Then they throw [the] slave on the beach for dogs to eat; often the tide washed [the] body away. . . . Then after this performance, . . . they commence putting up the building, for if things are left some misfortune will happen.]

The ground was now cleared. [Paul indicated that the old house was torn down, so the new house could be built on the same site.] The earth and debris were thrown far out on the shore, otherwise some misfortune would happen during the building. The wife of the builder went to her family and collected property which was actually a loan and would be returned at the ensuing potlatch with interest. This was merely to make the distribution of property appear greater than it actually was. The workers were fed every night by the builder.

[Paul wrote:

> [When the old house is torn down], and the posts [for the new] are put up, the totem pole is beginning to be carved. Almost every evening he [the future house owner] invites the builders and the totem pole carvers for their supper. When they used to kill slaves, years ago, a slave is killed just as soon as they brought home the tree for the totem pole. More slaves were killed when putting up the posts and crosspieces. They do not put the bodies of slaves under the four corners of the house, [as] reported by some visitors. The Tlingits are afraid of the evil spirits and of dead bodies. Of course, I do not know anything about the other tribes of Alaska—I mean Wrangell, Tongass, and Chilkat tribes.

[Shukoff stated also:

> After the building is finished they kill [a] second slave. They knock him in head with club, and if this does not kill him, they stab him. When they knock him in head, they try to just knock him down and hurt him severely, without killing; and while he thus suffers, the builder of [the] house makes a speech which may last some time, at [the] conclusion of which he kills [the] slave with spear. [See Swanton 1909:343–44.]
>
> Most of [the] chiefs own many slaves, and [the latter] don't know who will be killed. All these things are told through women; the women generally do their talking through whispering. During this time, [the] owner of slaves keeps strict eye on them, keeps them close together guarded like sheep in corral. They kill another slave when four house postholes are dug, and another fourth slave when they give potlatch and guests are invited to attend.]

[Emmons wrote:] When the house was near completion, the brothers-in-law, *Ah-qwan-ee* [ʔax̣ ká·ni, "my brother-in-law"] went around the village and entered each house of the opposite phratry; and, commencing with the chiefs, invited them to the potlatch, calling out each name: ". . . I have come for you. You are invited by . . . ," saying the name of the one giving the potlatch.

[Paul continued:

> When the house is completed and the totem pole carving finished, the leader goes around the village, and again delivers the same kind of speeches [as before]. He pleads with the tribe [opposite moiety or clan] to come and help him. Everyone, children, women and all, go to help raise the totem pole. After a great deal of shouting and excitement the pole is raised.
>
> If a woman chief is putting up this totem pole, her daughter will be made higher by giving her a new name. This daughter dances outside, and a slave is made free because of her appearing in public for the first time. More blankets and calico are torn in strips and distributed. The guests go home.]

[Emmons omitted the above details, but reported only:] With the building of a house, a new gravehouse was prepared, or among the more Southern Tlingit a totem pole might be raised.

[Olson (1967:46–47) indicated that each pole, like each house, had its proper name, and that the person who erected such a memorial to the dead should secure the approval of his clan elders, and that, *in theory,* no totem pole should be erected that had not previously been erected by an ancestor from whom the present builder had inherited the privilege. Grave, pole, and house were all memorials to the clan dead.

[The second part of Rudolph's list of Funeral Ceremonies (see Table 26) seems to fit the potlatch given after the house was built. This potlatch could be either a minor one, involving only local guests, or a major one to which one group of guests was invited from another town or tribe. The minor form of the ceremony is described in the next section, and the major potlatch later. Possibly a wealthy house head might give both: a minor potlatch when the gravehouse or pole had been finished, and a major potlatch when he had had his house repaired or had built a new one. Even more likely, the ceremonies listed by Rudolph may have included so little in the way of distributed gifts by the hosts, especially if a major potlatch were planned, that Rudolph did not list the "potlatch" proper (i.e., the distribution of gifts and repayment for services) nor the "gratitude dances" held afterward by the guests, for such thanks would be reserved for an occasion at which they received more than food and a few tokens of the payment to come.]

DEDICATION OF THE HOUSE AND RAISING A TOTEM POLE*

When the house was ready, the owner and his family [lineage] would enter, the men standing near the door in ordinary clothes, the women dressed in dance blankets [button blankets] and ornaments were ranged on each side near the walls. Then the drum was beaten four times four, and they swayed the body with it. [Paul specified that the men swayed.] This dance is called *Ah-ketch,* "putting it together with wings" [yaduwakíč, "they had a housewarming ceremony," from kítč, "wings"]. [Paul: "The four corners of the house are put together with their wings. It takes less than an hour to go through this performance."] This procedure may have originated at a very early period when the walls of the house were constructed by lashing planks together and each side was raised in one section. This is the only ceremony in which no guests were present. [Paul: "When this dance is over, another invitation is sent out to the same guests."]

In the evening, the clans of the opposite phratry assembled for the Smoking Feast, *Sa-kesk-ko-eek* [ṡe·q-ẏís quʔĭẋ; see Table 26].

> [Paul: This feast is called *Wō da hūn,* "Rising," [wudaha·n, "is standing"]. The black is taken off their faces, and their clothing is changed [this refers to the mourning hosts]. So this is called *Ya da klatch (Ya da Keetch)* [possibly yá-da· łe·ẋ̣ʷ], meaning "reddened face," or "red painted face." Red paint is put on the widow above the forehead, just where the hair parts. That means taking off mourning.]

The host, with one of his family who acts as a leader, and other men of his family [clan, lineage?], all poorly dressed, with dance staffs in hand, stood in front, just to one side of the doorway; the women of the family, wearing ceremonial blankets [button blankets] and ornaments were ranged along the walls on either side. The guests were seated in the body of the house around the fire, those most important opposite the door.

The host welcomed his guests and related his family history. He was answered by the guest chiefs [heads of houses]. The *Na-ka-nee* [na·-ká·ni], "[clan] brothers-in-law," separated the tobacco leaves, pieces of which were put into the fire as the names of the dead were called; they were believed to be present in spirit and to receive the gift as it was consumed by the flame with the same satisfaction as felt by those who were present in the flesh. The host might furnish pipes to the most honored guests, but the people generally brought their own. The *Na-ka-nee* [na·-ká·ni] filled them and lit the pipes for the guests.

Then the leader started the family songs [of the host clan], and called on members of the family to start other songs. The women of the family sang and swayed their bodies in unison with the song. At this feast there might be a small distribution of property for those who helped with the gravehouse.

[Paul added a number of details:

> The leader calls on each man to start up a song. After each song, blankets and calico are distributed. Each woman is called upon to start a song. At this feast they take new names, any name of their dead relatives. They are called by their new names at this feast. [Is this simply a device by which the dead may smoke too? Are these "potlatch names" permanent?]
>
> During this time, the *Na-ka-nee* are like waiters on the *Queen* [a ship] when there are crowds of tourists on her. They do all the waiting on the guests, lighting the pipes for the guests, tearing blankets and calico [to be distributed], and starting up songs for those that have no husbands [these must be women of the host clan, not guests]; and the wives are scolding them, or telling them not to forget one particular person who had helped to dress the [dead] chief, or who had helped to put moccasins on his feet, and so forth; and the poor *Na-ka-nee* are sometimes bewildered, and don't know hardly what to do! But they always take it so good-naturedly; they seem to be proud to be *Na-ka-nee.*
>
> "*Na-ka-nee*" is used as a by-word. Anyone that has not any modesty is spoken to: "Are you *Na ka nee,* that you have no shame? [No proper modesty?]." . . .

**Editor's note:* As in the previous section, I have used Paul's account in place of the description by Emmons that is based on it. Swanton's observations on rival groups of guests have also been used, as has Golovin's report of a quarrel between such rivals.

Poles identify Na·nya·ʔa·yí *clan houses, Wrangell, 1888. (Photographer unknown. AMNH.)*

At this dance the women sway themselves sideways. No sticks are used [?], The faces are painted red and black: Raven's Wing, Raven's Tracks, Raven's Bill, or Frog's Footprints. These are the face paints.

After this feast, the next day is for food.]

The next day, about ten o'clock in the morning, the drums were beaten and the guests assembled in ordinary dress and filled the body of the house. As before, the host, with the men of his family [clan], stood at the left of the door, poorly dressed and with dance staff in hand. The women of the family were dressed [in ceremonial clothing, as before] and were ranged along the side walls. This meeting was called *Ut-keh-yes-ko-eek,* "calling for food" [ʔat-x̣a-yís quʔí·x̓, "inviting to eat"], or "calling together for food." The host spoke of the dead, and as food was put in the fire by the *Na-ka-nee,* the names of the dead were called out, for it was believed that their spirits were present and that they heard their names and benefited by the gift [of food], not only spiritually, but in some material way that cannot be explained. The leader might sing the songs of the old shamans of the family [lineage] at this time, asking for good weather.

Then the feast dishes were brought out and placed before the guests and filled with food: dried salmon and grease, berries in grease, seaweed, salmon or herring spawn in grease; and beaten-up soapberry was always served last and was most esteemed. The two sides [rival groups of guests] might eat in competition with each other; individuals might be selected to do so, and he who ate the most, however sick it might make him, honored the host the most. Often the leader might call upon certain ones to drink a set quantity of oil, or to eat a whole dish full. In some cases, when the dishes were filled, the guest [guests?] rose, with spoon in hand, and danced while standing in place, with motions of the body, to honor the host. After the food was consumed the guests left.

[This is the first time that Emmons has mentioned the two rival groups of guests. Swanton (1909:375) explained that at Wrangell, if a Na·nya·ʔa·yí (Wolf 18) woman had died, her clan would be the hosts, and the Kiksʔádi (Raven 10), Ti·y hít-ta·n (Raven 11), and Qa·čʔádi (Raven 28) would "dance on one side" and the Ka·sx̣ag^{w}e·dí (Raven 32) and Ta·łq^{w}e·dí (Raven 33) would dance on the other. These were like two teams that "dance against each other," wu·š yá·ʔadułe·x̣. In the example cited by Swanton these two groups were all residents of Wrangell, and the occasion was the evening of the day that a totem pole had been erected. This had been done by the Na·nya·ʔa·yí (Wolf 18) chief, presumably in honor of his dead kinswoman. Swanton specified:

> Each side had two song leaders, a head song leader and a second song leader, who bear dancing batons.
>
> All this is done only when a chief or one of his family had died, not for a common person, and the first side to dance is that to which the widower [as in this case], or the widow of the deceased belongs. [1909:375]

[This rivalry between two groups of guests, belonging to different clans, or to different groups of lineages, is a crucial feature of every potlatch. The alignment of lineages and clans was traditional, as Swanton (1908:435) has indicated. Thus, at Sitka, the Box House People (Quˑkʷ hít-taˑn, Wolf 3) danced against the Wolf House and Eagle's Nest lineages, both sides being considered as branches of the Kaˑgʷaˑntaˑn (Wolf 1). At Sitka, the Kiksʔádi (Raven 10) were rivals of the Łukʷnax̣ʔádi (Raven 6) and X̣at̓kaʔaˑyí (Raven 7), when invited by Sitka Wolves to a potlatch. At Wrangell, the Kiksʔádi, Qaˑčʔádi, and Tiˑy hít-taˑn (Ravens 10, 28, and 11) were grouped opposite to the Kaˑsx̣agʷeˑdí and Taˑłqʷeˑdí (Ravens 32 and 33). There the Naˑnyaˑʔaˑyí (Wolf 18) and Šiknax̣ʔádi (Wolf 19) were rivals of the X̣uˑx̣ʷeˑdí (Wolf 26), Kayáˑška hít-taˑn (Wolf 25), and probably also the X̣eˑł qʷáˑn (Wolf 31) when the latter joined the Stikine tribe. In somewhat similar fashion, the clans from the home village and those from another tribe's village, when invited as guests to a potlatch, were traditional rivals (see below, "A Major Potlatch").

[As indicated by Swanton (1909:375), in speeches of the host to the opposite clans, he addresses them by kinship terms, based upon his relationship to them, actual or traditional. Thus, a Wolf chief at Wrangell might address the five Raven clans there as: "My father's brothers, my grandfathers, people that I came from, my ancestors, and my mother's grandfathers."

[Paul explained the feast and the later dancing:

> When all the guests are in, there are speeches, talking to the spirits of the dead. Food is put into the fire, calling out each name of their dead relatives. *Na-ka-nee* do this. When all the dead relatives are named and remembered, the food is passed around to the guests. When everything is passed around, and every person's dish is full up to the brim, the guests get up and dance with the spoons in their hands, meaning this dance [to] show their gratitude.
>
> Before putting any food in the fire, the leaders [of the hosts] sing *Ict's* [ʔix̣t̓, "shaman"], or *Yake* [yéˑk, "shaman's spirit"] songs; and the women sometimes dance, shaking themselves. When through singing, the leader says he calls out the head chief of each family [clan, lineage] of his guests, and says, "I have sung these songs of my dead doctors that I may have good weather, that it may not rain on me, that it may not storm upon me. . . ." [For the exchange of meticulously polite speeches, full of the symbolism of the crests, see Swanton (1909:374–89).]
>
> After the closing speeches, the leader [of the hosts] always the very last thing he says was to the head men of his guests, to arise and go in peace. And the head man gets up, and all follow him.
>
> After this feast, the guests are divided in two parties. One of the parties going to dance first, the other party afterwards the same evening. It is called Gratitude Dance.]

In the afternoon [after the feasting], the guests dressed and returned [to the house of the host]. They divided into two sides, one dancing in the afternoon, and the other in the evening. These dances were to show respect to the host and gratitude for the food. They were theatrical and were usually copied from foreign peoples, whose dress and movements were imitated, and the words to the songs were in their languages. Each side sang four songs. Great care had to be exercised not to exceed this number, nor to offend their rivals in referring to their crests, for all were highly excited, and a minor incident was likely to cause a clash resulting in bloodshed and a feud.

[Emmons here referred to the following incident recorded by Paul:

> One instance at Wrangell—while dancing Gratitude Dance, one party, *Wo-way-tee* tribe [probably Wolf 26, X̣uˑx̣ʷeˑdí], sang more than four songs. *Nin-ye-ah-ye* [Naˑnyaˑʔaˑyí, Wolf 18] got insulted, and they began to fight, right while at the dance.
>
> It happened that their [host's] emblem, the Raven Hat, was not anywhere near at hand [to place between them as a symbol of peace, Emmons explained.] So one of the leaders, a woman, got up. In her excitement she says, "Caw, Caw, Caw," just like a raven [the cry of her clan]. The whole party quieted down just as soon as that was heard. Another woman shouts and says, "When a raven is hard up for something to eat, the raven crows upon killerwhale, and the killerwhale dies. Now that Raven has crowed upon you, upon the Killerwhale."
>
> Both parties' emblem was the Killerwhale. The emblem is more like their flag. The party broke up and went home for fear of further trouble. The Raven tribe [moiety] got together, Kadashan [a Raven 32 leader] among them, and they went to each house of the guests and sang the *Ict's* [ʔix̣t̓, shaman's] songs for them, and pleaded with them. Three days after that, all the Raven women dressed up in their best and went to the guests' houses and invited them for a light lunch. Their faces were painted Raven's Wing, Raven's Bill, Frog's Footprint, etc. [in ceremonial crest designs].
>
> When the guests came, [there was] coaxing, singing, etc. . . . Then the *Wo-way-tee* tribe [Wolf 26] got up and one man danced with *Shu-kē-ut* [ceremonial headdress, šakiˑʔát]. One of the *Nin-ye-ah-ye* [Wolf 18] danced in like manner, so both parties made up.
>
> The reason why the leader always seems so anxious about his guests, for fear of any trouble among themselves. If there is serious trouble among the guests, the leader [host] is to be blamed for it.]

[Emmons ended the story:] Peace was finally made by the head man of each family [the two Wolf clans] who dressed in ceremonial costume as *Kau-a-kon* [quwakaˑn, "deer," or hostage-ambassador], the customary method of settling trouble between clans or tribes after war.

"Grave Dancers," Sitka (?) (Photograph by Vincent Soboleff, no. 621. Courtesy of the Alaska Historical Library.) The inscription on the monument reads: "In memory of KEE-NE-GNACK, Wife of Koo-sa-tan, a famous chief of Sitka tribe. Died at Sitka at an advanced age and highly respected, July 3, 1899." The persons in costume are chiefs and song leaders invited to the dedication of the monument; the hosts, in ordinary clothing, stand behind them. The photographs at the foot of the monument are probably of men also being memorialized at the same potlatch. Where this took place is uncertain, for while the inscription on the monument would suggest Sitka, Soboleff's negative "no. 151," a slightly different view of the same scene, is identified as "Dance at Killisnoo, 1902." Emmons identified the guests as chiefs of the Ka·gʷa·nta·n, *Wolf 1, of Sitka: To the right of the monument is "Paddy" wearing the Eagle Hat, and "Klantich" (or "Klantach")* [Ła·nti·č] *with the Killerwhale Hat and a chief's "Raven" rattle. The Bear Hat is worn by the song leader with baton just to the left of the monument.*

[Golovin (1860–61) 1983:103–6, reported on a brawl or quarrel of this sort while he was at Sitka. It was between the Yakutat and Sitka guests of a chief named Alexandr. The reason for the quarrel was that a year before, during a potlatch, the Sitkans had outsung the Yakutats, because they knew more songs than the latter. Vexed by this "defeat" the Yakutat had sent men to the Copper River and farther north to learn new songs. They also resolved that if the Sitkans again outsang them the following year, they would kill the Sitkans. So they had come armed to the house of the toion Alexandr, who was giving a house-building potlatch. At first all went smoothly, the Yakutats able to sing and dance along with the Sitkans, but when the latter started an Aleut song, the Yakutats were astounded. They had not known that the Aleuts had songs! Humiliated, they attacked the Sitkans and probably would have killed them all, if a woman had not knocked out two boards from the house with her ax, permitting the Sitkans to escape. At that point the Russian governor Furuhjelm appeared and stopped the fighting. The host, Chief Alexandr, had been seriously injured. Several chiefs brought out their clan hats and helmets, inherited from their ancestors, to demand a truce until peace could be made by payments for each of the injured. Since it was the Yakutats who had caused the injuries, they would have to pay, and it was feared that if any of the wounded Sitkans died, the Yakutats would be too poor to pay the price, and then the feud would begin in earnest, with killings on each side. Fortunately, the Yakutats agreed to the Sitkan terms, and under threats from the governor a peaceful settlement was reached.

[The only questionable detail in this account is the statement that the Yakutats had not known that the Aleuts had songs. Surely, the Aleut parties brought by the Russians to Yakutat on their way to Sitka would have sung; possibly they had forgotten the Aleut songs they once knew and had learned no new ones after the destruction of the Russian posts at Yakutat. The potlatches in question were major ones, since out-of-town guests had been invited to Sitka.

[To continue with the description of a house-building potlatch by Emmons:]

The feasting and dancing that preceded the distribution of property might continue for several days. The dancers, dressed in ceremonial blankets or skin clothing, carried rattles, eagle tails, bows, spears, etc., and wore spruce root hats or the ceremonial headdress, *Shack-ee-et* [šakiˑʔát, "something on the head"]. This was a hat covered with swan skin with a mask in front, a crown of sea lion whiskers filled with bird down, and several rows of ermine skins pendant behind. After dressing in their houses, each family formed a separate procession, and, headed by a drum, marched to the feast house where, one at a time, they danced into the house in a stooping posture, jumping up and down in quick jerks and shaking the rattle, or moving their arms spasmodically. The dancer moved his head very slowly after entering and danced to one side of the house, where all were finally assembled in many lines. The song accompanied by the drum, the rapid movement of the bodies in varied dress, the air filled with light eagle down, the nervous expectancy of both the host and his guests that some old feud might break out through intention or want of control, all combined to make a never-to-be-forgotten scene.

[Paul wrote:

> After the Gratitude Dance, the next day, comes Potlatch, feast. The drum is sounded early in the morning. It means that every relative that received presents, or *ke hiss* [qéˑhíˑx̌, "ceremonial fee"] from the hands of the leader's [host's] wife, is now being called to remember these gifts that she made to their wives. [These wives would belong to the same moiety as the host.] Each relative opens his [?, her] trunk and takes out blanket after blanket: five blankets, ten blankets, fifty blankets. It is very interesting to watch. Sometimes whole tribe [clan? moiety?] going to the new house; they carry the blankets as you have seen Chinaman carrying his water pail—two men with a long pole, shoulder to shoulder. Upon it the blankets are thrown. No ceremony. When they bring it into the house, the leader says *gonacheese* [gunaˑƛ̓číˑš, "thank you"], as each *Na-kah-nee* comes in with the blankets.]

Those of the opposite phratry—the family of the host's wife—brought the property in blankets, including the loan. These were counted, piled, and marked by the host's wife. These, together with the property that the host and his family expected to distribute, were placed in piles to one side of the entrance.

[Meanwhile] the host was dressed by his slaves, with the crest headpiece and the family robes that had descended to him through a long line of ancestors, and carried in his hand a long staff. Sometimes a new wooden hat was carved for the occasion. This headpiece [hat or helmet] was the most valued article in the possession of a family [clan] and was always in the keeping of the head chief. It was never exhibited except at potlatches when property was distributed, or at death, when it was placed by the side of the corpse that was lying in state. The "grandchildren" of the host's clan were also dressed by slaves. [These slaves were freed after the potlatch.]

[Paul continued:

> When that is all settled [bringing in the blankets], the old drum is sounded again. It is to call the workers [on the house or pole, now guests] together, to receive payment. When that is done, the leader's wife, with a f . . . [?] look on her face, gets up from the corner of the house where all the blankets were piled up. She takes it [them] out and hands it down to *Na-ka-nee,* and there is made pile upon pile in the center of the room.
>
> [When] the people assembled, the more honored guests, usually men, were seated opposite the door, and the women on either side. The host, the leader, and the principal men of his family [clan] stood to the left of the doorway where the blankets and other property were piled in the corner. The women of the family, in ceremonial dress, were ranged along the side walls of the house, and joined in the songs.

[The blankets were counted and made into separate piles in the middle of the room, according to the designated recipients. This was done, I believe, in the presence of the guests, and Paul specified that "all is silent."]

After the host, in a long speech, had related his family history, and had taken a new name, that of his predecessor if a chief, or of some ancestor on his mother's side [i.e., in his own line], he would likewise give new names to his "grandchildren" from the same source, and give the end of his staff to the slaves he was freeing [because they had dressed him and the "grandchildren"].

[As explained by Paul, the "grandchildren" might be anyone in a clan of the same moiety as the host's: preferably his son's son's clan. These new names were honorable names, those of men referring to a crest of the host's clan (possibly used previously), while those given to women were made up for the occasion and usually referred to the new house or pole for which the potlatch was given. Paul did not, however, make clear whether any member of the host's clan who was contributing property had a right to give a name to a "grandchild," as was the case at Yakutat.]

The distribution of property was [then] made by the *Na-ka-nee*. The giver [contributor of specific blankets or other goods] was privileged to select the recipient [among the guests of the opposite moiety] and to name the particular dead person in whose honor the gift was made. The property was held up by the *Na-ka-nee,* who called out the name of the recipient. The latter answered: *Artay,* "this way" [ha·dé·, ha·ndé·]. This distribution served to discharge all obligations to those who dressed the dead, carried out the corpse, performed all the offices of cremation, carved the totem pole, built the gravehouse, or the house. All of these were paid, and old debts of long standing might likewise be discharged.

[As enumerated by Paul, in the hypothetical potlatch:

> . . . 20 blankets for each carver, house builders 10, 15, 20; it depends upon how much work they did. A blanket or two for the person who had drawn the deerskin mittens upon the chief's stiffening hands, and those that dressed him. Two blankets for carrying him to the gravehouse. The widow's brothers or [maternal] uncles carved the totem pole. The bones and ashes of the chief are put behind the totem pole, [in a cavity] which had been hewed for them.
>
> Great deal of loud talking! Some persons are not satisfied with their payment. In this case the leader [host] is not very courteous. He tells them, that when *they* had built *their* house and he himself had worked hard, but hardly received any pay. And he had also helped dress or helped cremate their relative, but hardly got anything for it. "You better be satisfied with the blankets."
>
> The builder or the carver is very much insulted. He goes home without the blankets. A relative comes up to the leader [host] and says, "Gun, chū kāh, "Hear, my fellow man," [G̣an, ča·qá·, "Look, moiety-mate:"], I will help you pay that man. It is not right that he should take our brother's name."
>
> The totem pole carver declares [had declared] that he will take the name of the deceased chief for his name, if they do not pay him any more than those 20-odd blankets. He is sent for. Ten more blankets are added to it. "*Go na scheese*" [guna·ƛ̓čí·š, "Thank you"].]

To take a name of the host's family would result in a future debt [for the host would have to redeem it with more property].

It was often arranged that two or more houses of the same family [clan] were built about the same time and the celebrations would then continue through several days, and a separate distribution of property was held in each.

After the potlatch, the guests gave exhibition dances as a mark of respect to the host, and they were feasted in return.

DICK *SA-TAN'S* POTLATCH, 1891*

In March, 1891, Dick *Sa-tin* or *Sa-tan* [Se·tá·n], head chief of the Łukʷnax̣ʔádi (Raven 6) of Sitka, rebuilt his house, upon the completion of which the following ceremonies were enacted. [Emmons evidently witnessed them, or part of them, and later received explanations from Sa-tan, in answer to his questions. The following account is compiled from two manuscript versions in BCPA and from the typed manuscript.]

The old house was pulled down, and Sa-tan had the ground cleared early in the winter and the erection of a new house by men selected from the opposite phratry [Wolves] was begun [on the same site]. As sawed timber was used, the labor of cutting down trees and fashioning the heavy posts and beams, and the ceremony of towing them in, were not necessary, otherwise the old customs were observed. The building was completed as far as the walls and roof, but was unfinished inside; the windows and doorway were hung with sailcloth, and all was ready for the celebration in which Sa-tan entertained all the members of the opposite phratry then resident at Sitka, or visiting it at that time. [Because no guests from a foreign village were invited, this ceremony could be classified as a minor one, despite its lavishness.] By giving this potlatch, Sa-tan honored himself and his family [clan], the *Thluke-nar-hut-tee* [Łukʷnax̣ʔádi, Raven 6], a part of the Raven clan [moiety] or *Kla-a-din-nar* [Ła·y(a)ne·di].

On the morning of Saturday, March 7, Sa-tan invited some members of the "opposite clan [moiety]" or *Shen-ku-qwa-tee* [Šankukʷe·dí, Wolf 8] to build a new clan gravehouse in place of the old one where rested the ashes of his departed relatives. Those who had prepared the gravehouse assembled and, attended by the family [Raven 6], pulled down the old structure without any ceremony, and replaced it with the new, and transferred to it the boxes and trunks that contained the ashes of the dead.

When this work was done, Sa-tan called to a council in his house his "brothers-in-law," or *Na-kah-nee* [na·-ká·ni], to the number of eight or ten. This general term includes all men of the opposite moiety who have married women of *Thluke-nar-huttee* [or Łukʷna-šá·], that is [the husbands of] his "sisters, cousins, or aunts"; and who consequently were of the opposite moiety. Sa-tan instructed them whom to invite and when (although the time is fixed by convention). So the "brothers-in-law" invited their relatives, the

Editor's note: This section was made up from notes by Emmons, but he had not included it in his text.

Kar-gwan-tons [Ka·gʷa·nta·n, Wolf 1], the *Ki-yatz-hit-tons* [Ǥayé·ṡ hít-ta·n, Wolf 6], *Kuke-hit-ton* [Qu·k hít-ta·n, Wolf 3], and the *Kut-ar-qwut-tee* [Kadagʷʔádi, Wolf 2], to the smoking feast that night. The last three clans were believed to have separated from the *Kar-gwan-ton* at an early date. [Among the guests were also some visiting Wolves from Chilkat.] In all the ceremonies following, the *Thluke-nuh-ut-die* [Raven 6] were assisted by the *Khart-kow-ee* [X̌aṫkaʔa·yí, Raven 7] and the *Kuse-ka-de* [Qu·sḳe·dí, Raven 8], that were closely related to them [Raven 6] in the same way.

Both men and women [of the invited clans] came in after dusk, bringing their own pipes with them, although the host served out pipes to the most honored guests as long as his supply lasted. The *Na-ka-nee* told them where to sit. The chiefs and men of the higher class were placed opposite the door, the women and others were on either side, filling the body of the house, all sitting on the floor. The host, in poor clothes, stood in the front place to the left of the door, and behind him were members of his own and the assisting families [clans]. He welcomed his guests in a few words, telling them that his forefathers and theirs were warm friends. But many years have passed and now his family, once so many and wealthy, have gone to the land of the spirits, and he is left poor and with few people. But it warms his heart to see his friends doing honor to his house, and he hopes they may come again and again to make his heart glad.

To this, the principal chiefs or chief answered in a short speech, mentioning the friendships between their clans. The head chiefs all wore their family headdresses. Tom [or Thom, a chief of high rank among the Ka·gʷa·nta·n] said, "In old time we very good friends. Your grandfathers our friends."

Then the *Na-ka-nee* separated the bunches of tobacco leaves, and as pieces were put on the fire, the names of the dead were called. After this, the pipes of the guests were filled, and lighted by the *Na-ka-nee* with coals from the fire. For at least half an hour to an hour, they smoked in silence [while leaves or bundles of tobacco were distributed by the *Na-ka-nee*]. Then the host told them that tomorrow he invites them to a dance and potlatch, naming the hour. Then the guests rose and returned to their houses.

Early next morning [or on the morning of Monday, March 9], before daybreak, Sa-tan went out of his house, and standing in front of his doorway, called out in a loud voice, so that all could hear and rousing the village, proclaimed the deeds of his ancestors.

Soon after 10 o'clock the drum was beaten, and the guests began to assemble, and were shown by the *Na-ka-nee* where to sit: as before, the most honored guests opposite the door, the men in the center of the house, and the women on either side along the walls. The host and his clan were assembled to the left of the doorway, and behind them were the piles of blankets and goods to be distributed. These had been contributed principally by the host and by members of his clan [Raven 6], and also by other families [clans] of the same totem [Raven].

The principal contributors were:

Thluke-nar-hut-tee [Ł̓ukʷnax̱ʔádi, Raven 6, the host's clan]

Khart-kow-ee [X̌aṫkaʔa·yí, Raven 7]

Kuse-ka-de [Qu·sḳe·dí, Raven 8]; all three having been originally one clan at *Kook-noo-oo* [Kax̌ nu·wú, "Grouse Fort" on the north shore of Icy Strait, a Hoonah village site].

Tuck-tain-ton [Ṫaqde·nta·n, Raven 16]

Kake-sa-tee [Kiksʔádi, Raven 10]

The host, Sa-tan, was dressed in old clothes with no attempt at decoration, although he held a ceremonial Tsimshian dance rattle in his hand, and on a low stand or small table beside him was the family [clan] heirloom, a carved wooden hat, with a Raven's head, ornamented with copper (said to be native copper) and abalone shell. This hat belonged really to the whole clan, but the chief kept it carefully put away in a box. It was shown only on great ceremonial occasions, for when it was displayed much property had to be distributed.

[Bill Holm has informed me (pers. comm. 1986) that this hat, and the blanket worn by Chilkat Dick at this potlatch, were collected by Louis Shotridge at Sitka, and are now in the University Museum, Philadelphia. They are illustrated in Miller and Miller (1967:208), although the wearer is not identified. The wooden hat was called "Barbecuing Raven Helmet" by Shotridge (1919:45–56, pl. I), referring to the myth in which Raven cooked and ate the king salmon he had lured ashore. The hat is surmounted with a carved Raven's head, topped by two woven cylinders because it had been "carried through only two ceremonies," according to Shotridge, and an ermine skin. The carved tail sticks out behind, and the face of a "hawk" is on the front. The wings at the sides are of painted rawhide. It was the display of this hat by the Ł̓ukʷnax̱ʔádi, Raven 6, of Sitka and Dry Bay that provoked the Ǥa·nax̱te·dí, Raven 3, of Chilkat to war (see Swanton 1909:161–65; de Laguna 1972:273–75, and pl. 210 *z*, showing it worn by Q̓ex̱i·x̱, chief of Sitka Whale House of the Raven 6 clan, at a potlatch at Sitka, December 9, 1904.) I am indebted to Susan Kaplan for this identification.]

Tobacco pipes. (a) Wooden pipe bowl, 3 inches high, in the shape of an eagle or Thunderbird, belonging to a Dry Bay chief of the Raven 7 clan. (b) Wooden pipe representing the Spirit of Lituya Bay as a frog with a bear at the other end. They are shaking up waves at the mouth of the bay and capsizing a canoe with two occupants. 10 inches long. (c) Pipe carved to represent a bear, with a brass cap as a mouthpiece. (d) Pipe in the shape of a ship's cannon, 9¼ inches long. (All items collected by G. T. Emmons. Courtesy of MAI, Heye Foundation.)

Mrs. Dick, the wife of Dick Sa-tan, in ordinary dress sat among the blankets behind her husband.

The leader of the ceremonies was a subchief of the *Thluke-nar-huttee* [Raven 6, the host's clan], Chilkat Dick, who stood beside the host. He was dressed in a dance blanket of deep blue [broadcloth] with a deep border of Chilkat blanket weave [presumably woven especially for this blanket, according to Holm], his head was tied up in a black silk kerchief, and in his hands he held a long carved baton, representing a Raven.

Behind the host and the master-of-ceremonies were the head men of the *Thluke-nar-huttee* [Ł̓ukʷnax̱ʔádi], *Kut-kowee* [X̱at̓kaʔa·yí], and the *Kuse-ka-de* [Qu·ske·dí], Andrew, Percy, and a dozen others, all poorly dressed, but carrying dance batons in their hands. The faces of some were decorated in black paint. [This may have stood for mourning, worn in public by bereaved persons who had not yet given (or contributed to) a smoking feast.]

Along the two walls on either side were seated some forty women of the *Thluke-nar-hut-tee* [the host's clan], dressed in full dance costumes: dark blue Hudson's Bay blankets ornamented with strips of red cloth and small pearl buttons. They wore black silk handkerchiefs like turbans around their heads, into which were stuck vertically some white feathers from an eagle's tail. Their hair was plaited and hung down the back, generally in one braid, occasionally in two. Their faces were painted in red and black, some in geometric or fanciful figures, others with crest patterns representing some part of Raven, stamped on the cheek or forehead with a wood die. From the lobes of their ears hung earrings of shark's teeth, squares of abalone from one to three inches square, or pendants of twisted worsted, twelve to eighteen inches in length, and three inches wide. In some instances these earrings of red yarn were ornamented with abalone or shark's teeth. They wore nose rings of silver, copper, or abalone. With the women were children, girls seven or eight years old, and dressed similarly.

In the corner of the house, to the left on entering, and suspended from a beam, was an old-fashioned, wooden box drum, beaten during the singing by a young man of the host's clan, who struck it on the inside with the soft side of his fist by the little finger.

When all the guests were assembled, the host addressed them, saying,

"In years long past my family were like the trees on the mountain side, and they had many houses filled with skins and many slaves. But today we are like a dead forest with only a live tree here and there. We are very poor, but you are my best friends. You come and honor my poor house. I give you all the entertainment I can, so do not look down on my efforts."

Then *Kutsin-ish* [Kuči·n-ʔí·š], "Father of Mice," an old Kagwantan man of high class who was always selected as spokesman on such occasions, rose and spoke in reply, saying that the clans were of one heart and all had assembled in good friendship, then he dwelt on the former greatness of his own clan, its force and strength in early days, and how it had wasted away.

After these formal addresses, Chilkat Dick, the leader of ceremonies, started the family song [of the Łukʷnax̣ʔádi], which was joined in by all of the clan, and all of the Raven totem, and was accompanied by the drum and the tapping of the dance batons on the floor. The women of the clan, sitting along the side walls, rose in their decorated blankets, to sing and dance in their places, by swaying their bodies from side to side and bowing in time to the music. [Dick later told Emmons: Only the women of the host's clan dance at the distribution of property.] In these songs, the leader would sing and give out only a few words at a time; these would be taken up by the singers and long drawn out. This first song related to Raven, since the clan was a Raven clan.

> The first time I came to this country
> I dreamed that Yehlh [Yé·ł] showed me where the alders grow.
> The first time I came to this country
> I dreamed that Yehlh showed me the chief's house.

Such songs belong entirely [exclusively] to the clan and have been handed down through generations. [Dick Sa-tan told Emmons that sometimes they might know the words, but not understand their meaning.] The song ended with a loud beat of the drum.

After this song, another song was started by one of the other head men assembled by the host. Four separate songs were sung.

When the songs were ended, each of the blankets was handed by the contributor, a man or woman of the clan or totem of the host, to one of the *Na-kah-nee*. The blanket was opened out to full length and measured by extending the arms, and passed from one hand to the other. If it was to be cut into strips, it was held by two *Na-kah-nee,* and torn down the breadth in strips about twelve to eighteen inches in width. The name of the person (man or woman) to whom it [the blanket or a strip of blanket] was to be given, would be called out, and he or she would answer, when the *Na-kah-nee* would hand it over. The donor had the privilege of saying to whom the whole blanket is to go, but the strips are distributed evenly to all the guests. One or more whole blankets were given to chiefs and the more important people, and to those who had assisted in building the grave-house and the house, but some gift was given to every person present who was of the opposite moiety. Sometimes money might be given by relatives [clansmen] of the host to be distributed. In the old days, instead of blankets, they distributed skins of caribou, moose, or elk, and furs of sea otter, beaver, and marten, and also *Tinnah* [tiná·, "copper shield"], either the whole or pieces of copper. While the distribution was going on, snuff was distributed to the women guests by a woman [also a na·-ká·ni?], and tobacco [to smoke] was distributed to the male guests by a man.

At this time nothing was given to the *Na-kah-nee* [even though they were men and women of the guest clans], but the host may make presents to them afterwards.

The two following days were devoted to feasting. The guests assembled in the morning and were fed. And they were also given a surplus to carry away. In return for this, the guests dressed up and entertained their hosts with spectacular dances in the afternoons and evenings.

A MAJOR POTLATCH*

[Some of the potlatches described in the preceding sections I would call minor ceremonies, because only "opposites" within the village of the host clan were invited. A major potlatch, quʔí·x ƛe·n, "big invitation," was one involving guests from another tribe, as well as from the home village, and was therefore a more lavish and expensive affair. This was the potlatch called *Qkhatasi,* "to raise up" or "to glorify the dead" (x̣áda· ši·yí; or possibly qa·da· ši·yí, "song" or "singing about the dead people"), by Veniaminov ([1840] 1984:421–23; Holmberg 1855:46–49; Petroff 1884:171–72). This potlatch was the last of what Olson (1967:61–63) called the four "joy feasts," following the four "crying feasts" and so ending the funeral cycle of eight feasts, "to finish the body" of the deceased—eight, because of the eight bones of the body. This

**Editor's note:* For this section I have used the text of Emmons's article on the potlatch (1910c), Shukoff's description, information from Swanton and Veniaminov, as well as observations by Olson and Kan.

great potlatch was to pay the members of the opposite moiety who had built a new house or refurbished an older one as a memorial to the dead predecessor of the new house chief, and to all the dead of the lineage. The ceremony was held in the new house. The "opposites" might also have built one or more gravehouses for the host clan. During their labors, they had been feasted and given gifts, at the "three joy feasts" that preceded the great potlatch. (Any potlatch, however, to pay for erecting a grave monument, pole, or house, would be called a *qkhatashi,* even if no guests were invited from another town, I believe.)

[Emmons wrote (1910c:230):

> Preparations for the function may occupy the lifetime in the accumulation of material to be given away, and the invitations are personally delivered months or a year in advance. The guests, including generally two tribes or two village clans, if living at a distance get ready as soon as they return from the summer camps. The canoes are repainted and decorated, dancing paraphernalia is unpacked and gone over, a sufficient food supply for the travel is put aside, and a programme of dances and songs with which to honor their host is arranged. Households embark together in the largest canoes and as in war parties are under the direct supervision of their chief. They travel and camp together and practice their dances and songs en route. From time to time the host receives notification of their progress and when they are within one camp of their destination, he sends out envoys and food to them.]

When families from another tribe are to be asked, the wife or *Na-ka-nee* [na·-ká·ni], "brothers-in-law," including those that have married sisters, aunts or cousins [mother's sisters, and mother's sister's daughters of the host], go in canoes and extend the invitation, collecting property [to be given away at the potlatch], and [later, at the designated time] they accompany the guests, bringing up the rear during the entire travel, so that none may straggle.

Those invited select two leaders for the songs and dances which they practice every night when they camp [on the way to the potlatch]. These leaders must fast for two days and keep away from women. It was the invariable custom that visitors, whether invited or not, should never come directly to a strange village, but should land and camp the preceding night at some distance, the place being designated by the host's friends, who met them bringing food.

That night the guests might man their canoes and pretend to attack the village with loud cries and the beating of their paddles on the gunwales of the canoes, and then return after the [host] village had been thoroughly aroused, for in early days villages were attacked at night, and even when expecting such a play, the people would become greatly excited.

The next day the guests would don their dance costumes, paint their faces in red and black, and [Emmons 1910c:230–34:

> The men and women . . . have the hair dressed with red ochre and bird's down. With drum, rattle, and dance staff they [the principal personages among the guests] take their places in the sterns of the canoes which now follow each other in column. . . .]

The line would slowly paddle toward the village of their hosts, the occupants singing. [Emmons 1910c:234:

> [Near the village] . . . they form in line abreast and holding gunwale to gunwale stand in slowly to the shore, the occupants singing and dancing to the accompaniment of the drum. When nearing the beach those paddling hold water, the bow and stern men get out the poles and the line of boats is kept in position, while speeches are exchanged through several hours.]

Stopping in front of the chief's house, the canoes would be held afloat, just clear of the shore, by paddles and poles, and families of their phratry, residents of the village, who were likewise guests, would assemble on the beach in ceremonial dress, dancing and singing their family [clan] songs, in honor of the host and in part as a welcome to the visitors. [When finished], they would retire.

[The local guest clans and the clan or clans from away formed the two rival groups that "danced against each other." Some of the songs they sang were "peace songs" to each other, in which the others were addressed as "clan children" of their hosts, flattering the latter, or the singers expressed their love for the clan-children of their rivals (persons of the opposite moiety, actual or potential sweethearts).]

The host would then appear and a pantomime would be enacted by him or his family. This pantomime was highly spectacular and generally illustrative, both in dress and action, of the crest animal. After this, the chief of the visitors, standing in the stern of his canoe, would speak, and when finished, would be answered from the shore by the host, who would end with an invitation to land. Then the canoes would separate, turn, and back in [stern first] in front of the houses designated for their reception, when those on shore would rush into the water and unload them. In old times the chiefs would be picked up and carried to shore.

[Shukoff described the coming of the guests (I have corrected the translator's text—FdeL):

> Before potlatch is given, the owner [of the new house] practices the ceremony of reception beforehand, his speech, how to

Dancers at a Klukwan potlatch. Photograph by Winter and Pond, no. 208, in 1895. (AMNH.) Note that there is snow on the ground, and the house is different from that on page 293. The dancers are in Athabaskan costume, or wear Raven moiety crests, so presumably are members of Raven 3, at some earlier potlatch at Klukwan.

receive the guests, and what songs and dances the hosts will use. The people make different hats out of wood to be used in dances.

When guests come, they camp one or two miles from the village and wait until night then they go to the village to scare the hosts; when they approach the house they halloo and strike their canoes with paddles, and sometimes they do scare the village. Then they go back to camp again; they don't land that night. A little while afterwards, the chief sends relatives with provisions to the guests: berries, *karh-weh* [kax^{w}é·x̣, "highbush cranberries," *Viburnum edule*], preserved in seal oil, herring oil. Then he sends another canoe after wood to make his guests warm. He then takes his costumes out of his trunks, fur, buckskin clothes, and necklaces of bird noses, *kuhn har,* "sea parrot" [łu-gán, literally "nose-red," the tufted puffin].

The next morning the guests come in canoes and before they land the owner of the house comes out and, with hand shading his eyes, looks at them as if they were strangers. And he asks the people around who they are and where they come from. And someone will tell that they see a certain chief from some village. Then this chief asks [the] one in the canoes who they are and where from. Then the [guest] chief answers them that they are his guests, and gives the names of his village and of himself. "We came here by the road or travel of the sun," the guest answers. "They [We] came with good faith. We came to have a joyous time."

Then they make speeches. [First] the guests call the people on shore, they call them each one by name, and they answer "Aye." Then they make speeches concerning their ancestors, their pursuits and customs. The owner of the house makes a speech and says that he has just been out hunting and has killed several hair seal and has not had time to skin them. And he turns to his people and tells them to throw out hair seal bones on the beach. And instead, two men lead out a slave, holding him by the hand, and after they bring him before the guests, they kill him and leave the corpse on the shore. They then wipe blood off the trail so the guests won't dirty their feet. Then they bring out another slave, and kill him instantly, striking him on the head with a club. And after they killed the slave, they drag the corpse along the trail where the first slave was killed, and thus the trail is killed; and they throw the [second] body by the side of the former corpse.

Then he [host chief] invites the guests, and they come into the house. He lays down the club, *katu* [ké·ł̓u], and the guests enter house and examine the club and praise the carving. If a bear's head is carved they call it *hootz katu* [xú·c ké·ł̓u], "Bear Club." They look at the spear with which the slave is killed [or had been killed?], called *tsar karkle* [ca·gáł̓]. If it has killed people they call it *nan-nar quar-tlar* [na-ná, "death," gwáła·, "dagger"], the old double-bladed knife. After examining knives and spears and clubs, they [the weapons] are put away, and all slaves are locked up in a room in the house, waiting for freedom or death.

Then after the potlatch is over, the spears, *katu,* and knives are put away and not taken out until someone dies, when more slaves may be killed. When any of the children die, the chief asks one of his slaves to take out *katu* and examine it, then put it back in box. Then he asks if he put it back nicely, and he answers "Yes." Then he is freed with a great deal of noise.

Now they tear blankets and cotton [cloth], instead of killing slaves.

Festivals and potlatches begin in the evening when the chief dresses himself in clothes inherited from his uncle. They used to wear buckskin pants and shirt, and before a potlatch he dresses in clean clothes, wears a carved wooden hat, such as Bear [Hat], Beaver, Wolf, etc. Those hats generally have sealion whiskers above, and around; the center of the headdress is filled with eagle down. [This is the headdress called šaki·ˀát, not a hat.] He wears a blanket of goat [wool], *nar-ghen* [na·xe·n], "Chilkat blanket"; and he wears earrings of abalone, very large 2½ inches square. Then he puts a long stick of bone or ivory through the septum of his nose, takes a carved dancing stick in hand; and friends or relatives all dressed to suit themselves. The chief is dressed by his children or his slaves, and he must have the same number of slaves to assist in dressing as there are children, and the children are dressed each by one of these slaves at the same time.

[This last statement indicates a blending of the major house-building potlatch with the major potlatch for honoring children, either a confusion in Shukoff's mind or an accurate statement of the conduct of potlatches in his day. Shukoff continued:

When the chief is dressed, he comes to the door and addresses the guests, *viz.,*

"You all know that my uncle was a great hunter, also my ancestors all were great hunters, they killed a great many wild animals and wounded a great many. The latter have gone back to the woods and are alive at the present time." And that he himself does the same as his ancestors, and that's how he became rich and owned many slaves.

After he has finished speaking he calls the slave that dressed him and gives him the end of the stick, and he tells him he is free and he can go, and so he frees all who dressed himself and his children.

After this they have a dance. They have no musical instruments save drums, and they keep time to singing. Head of drum [is] of deerskin. They start in to dress the guests by giving them pieces of blankets, and call each one's name as they make the gift. And the guest answers "*Ar-táy,* This way!" [ha·dé, or ha·ndé].

They don't eat this day, but eat next day: hair seal, berries preserved in oil, eulachon grease, dried fish; and with feasting the festival ends. After [Often] the guests eat so much that they vomit, for the host tries his hospitality by making guests sick, and then it is to his honor afterwards that all got sick. And if no one should get sick, it would speak badly for the food. And those who vomit and get sick are made extra presents of blankets. All guests bring their own spoons and dishes, and they carry away all the food their dishes hold.

[The kind of reception given the guests, and the particular symbolism in the theatrical show and speeches made to greet the guests, vary from clan to clan, and lineage to lineage, depending on the ceremonial prerogatives of the host and the history of his house (see McClellan 1954). Some of the Southern Tlingit clans owned the right to display "Secret Society" spirit dances (yé·k ṡa·ti), which they had obtained from the Tsimshian and Haida, and even at Sitka the Kiksˀádi clan put on copies of such Kwakiutl-derived shows (Olson 1967:98–100, 118–21). The dramatic simulation of recapturing and restoring a man who had drowned and been rescued by Land Otter Men, reported by Emmons as having been given at Sitka about 1887 (see Chapter 10, the section "Afterlife: Spirits, Souls, Reincarnation") was such a display by the hosts at a potlatch. Emmons cited other examples, more typically Tlingit, of the reception and entertainment of guests:]

In 1891, when the *Ka gwan tan* [Ka·gʷa·nta·n, Wolf 1] of Sitka invited the *Tuck dane tan* [Ṫaqde·nta·n, Raven 16] of Hoonah, the latter, in six canoes abreast, approached the village slowly, just dipping the paddles in the water. Stopping in front of the chief's house, two chiefs standing in the stern of their canoes made long speeches, telling of their family. After they had finished, the *Ka-gwan-tan* house master, *Kut-sin ish* [Kuči·n-ˀí·š], "Father of the Mice," opened the door and looked out, shading his eyes as if surprised. Hesitatingly he came hopping out sidewise, imitating the movements of an eagle, which was his crest and which he impersonated. Reaching a high boulder on the shore, he perched upon it, and moved his head slowly from side to side, like an eagle. He wore the family crest hat of wood representing an eagle [the "Eagle Hat"], and over a ceremonial blanket was a robe of plucked eagle skins. He had on a pair of ornamentally embroidered caribou skin trousers, his feet were bare, and in each hand he carried an eagle's tail of white feathers. After remaining in this position for some minutes, he launched into a long speech, relating his family history, his delight in being honored by his visitors, and finally invited them to land.

In 1888, the *Da-she-tan* of *Hootz-nu-wu* [De·ši·ta·n, Raven 13, of the Hutsnuwu] invited the *Ka-gwan-tan* and associated Wolf families of Sitka to a great potlatch, to celebrate the building of four family [clan] houses.

[This must have been to celebrate the rebuilding of houses destroyed in 1882 when Angoon was shelled by the Navy. According to notes in BCPA, the Wolf clans invited were the

Ka·gʷa·nta·n, Wolf 1; *Ky-yaz-hit-tan,* Ǥayé·s̓ hít-ta·n, or "Drift-iron House People," Wolf 6; and the *Koke-hit-tan,* Qu·kʷ hít-ta·n, "Box House People," Wolf 3. The two latter groups have also been considered as lineages of the Ka·gʷa·nta·n.]

These Sitkans to the number of over four hundred, in twenty large canoes, followed by the canoe bearing the invitation [that is, of the na·-ká·ni], stopped at Kenasnow Island before reaching Angoon, and put on their dance dress. Crossing the narrow waterway, they came abreast in front of the village, where they were welcomed by the *Tuck-cla-way-de* [Daqławe·dí, Wolf 27], the *Nush-kee-tan* [Wu·škí·ta·n, Wolf 17], and *Ta-qway-de* [Te·qʷe·dí, Wolf 32]. These were [local] villagers of their own phratry, and likewise guests of the *Da-she-tan* [Raven 13]. They were all in full costume, singing and dancing. When through, they retired to their houses. Then *Ken-al-kow,* the chief of the *Da-she-tan,* came out of his house. Seeing the canoes, he feigned great fear, and went from house to house crying "*Ats ka na*" [ʔa·t skiné·!], which one cries in fright, and having called all of his people, he returned to his house.

Then a subchief of the *Da-she-tan* came out with arrow in bow, crying "Ko-ho-ho!" which one cries when about to die, and those of the opposite phratry on shore called to him to attack the canoes. He went down to the water's edge and suddenly, as if just discovering who they were, he threw down the bow, saying he would not hurt any *Kagwan-tan.* Then another *Da-she-tan* came out and invited the visitors to land. That evening the visitors dressed in dance costume and entertained their hosts with dances and songs they had learned the previous year from Vancouver Island natives who had been taken and interned at Sitka for illicit sealing.

[According to notes in BCPA] the potlatch lasted a number of days. On the second day, the guests were called together in the morning and given food: dried salmon, potatoes, beans and rice, "all in grease." During the morning, when the meal was over, the Sitkan guests danced in the new house. That afternoon the Angoon Wolves danced. That evening, the guests were fed again: dried salmon and grease, potatoes, and soapberry. The Sitkans danced, then the Angoon Wolves danced. [It should be noted that the potatoes served were a "speciality" of Angoon.]

On the third day, the *Dashetan* fed their guests in the morning. In the forenoon, the *Dashetan* women dressed and danced until supper time. The guests in ordinary dress were spectators in the body of the house. The guests were fed their evening meal, after which the Sitkans danced, followed by the Angoon Wolves.

The same took place on the fourth, fifth, sixth, and seventh days. There was a potlatch for each house. There were four new houses, and it took one day for each to give blankets and food. [A note indicates that these days were the equivalent of the potlatch given on the third or fourth day of Rudolph's outline, Table 26.] The guests dance the last evening, ending the potlatch. The givers of the feast never dance, and eat only after the guests have gone each day.

In later years, the *Da-she-tan* again entertained the Sitka [Wolf] families. When the canoes were just off shore and after the speeches had been made, a man costumed as a beaver suddenly sprang out of a hole on the shore [that had been] covered with light boards and neatly concealed. Impersonating the Beaver, he ran along the shore and disappeared. The Beaver was the principal crest of the *Da-she-tan.*

[A Beaver had led the founders of Angoon to their village site (de Laguna 1960:130–33). At a potlatch given at Angoon about 1948, a De·ší·ta·n woman danced behind a blanket held up as a screen, only the Beaver Hat showing, as she made the hat imitate the movements of the animal (de Laguna field notes 1949).]

In 1899, when the *Con-nuh-ta-de* [Ǥa·naxte·dí, Raven 3] gave the last great feast at Chilkat [Klukwan], when the visitors from Sitka reached the village front, ***Yehl cock*** [Yé·ł xá·k, "Raven's Fragrance or Odor"], the second chief, came out of the house with drawn bow and arrow, as if to attack those in the canoes. Then followed ***Yehl gou-hu*** [Yé·ł gu·x̣ʷú, "Raven's Slave," George Shotridge], wearing the family crest, the Raven Hat, and leading a number of women.

[This potlatch was described to Swanton (1908:438–43) by one of the guests from Sitka, Dekinā´k!ᵘ (De·ki-na·k̓ʷ, "Little Haida," or "Far-out-to-Sea People"). The belligerent gestures with the bow and arrow were made "because he was about to spend a great deal of money and [he] wished to show how brave he was" (p. 439). For the same reason, the host might wear the warrior's Bear's Ears. Swanton's account is particularly valuable for explaining how the wife of "Raven's Slave," a Wolf woman, went as na·-ká·ni to invite the Sitka Wolves to the potlatch, and how she collected over $2,000 worth of property from them, her people, as their contribution to the coming potlatch, because they had not built her husband's house at Klukwan. The reckless behavior of the guests on the way to the potlatch, their rowdy fun and eating feats at the potlatch, and other details are well described.

[We might also note that a Chilkat chief by the name of Yé·ł xá·k, "Raven's Odor," visited Yakutat in 1788, and that Swanton (1909, Tale 32, pp. 161–65) recounted how a chief of the same name, or title, perhaps the same man, was killed in a war between the Chilkat G̣a·naxte·dí and the Łukʷnax̣ʔádi, Raven 6, of Yakutat and Dry Bay, over rights to the Raven Hat.]

Two or more families of the opposite phratry, either of this or another tribe, were always invited to a potlatch. They were divided into two sides that competed with each other in songs and dances, and so keen was this rivalry that it took the greatest tact on the part of the leaders to prevent clashes ending in bloodshed. [Perhaps because rivalry between two groups of guests was most acute at the major intertribal potlatches, Emmons discussed guest rivalry only in this connection.]

[McClellan's study of Tlingit ceremonialism (1954, esp. pp. 86, 96) has made clear the warlike character of Tlingit potlatches. Rivalries between the two groups of guests are present, no matter whether they both live in the same community or one group comes from another town. As she wrote:

> . . . the guest competition is often symbolized as warfare, and sometimes leads to real fights. Each sib constantly watches the other for mistakes, and if one is detected, immediately begins to "make fun" of the erring group. A woman song leader told how she barely averted a riot when one of the opposing song leaders sang the same verse of a song twice. If one side sings more songs or does more dances than the other, this too means trouble. The institutionalized way of halting a resulting fight is for the hosts to run forward with their own crests. This act recalls to the guests the need for proper respect for the hosts' emblems, which probably have added emotional significance as the crests of the guests' grandfathers, fathers, wives, or children. [p. 86]

[Veniaminov ([1840] 1984:421–23) wrote that the major potlatch, the *Khatashi* (x̣áda· ši·yí, "to raise the dead"), was given very rarely, and only by wealthy chiefs. Since 1828 there had been no such festivals, he wrote, because of the ruinous expense. The host would give away all his property, including his wife's dowry, and the Tlingit had a saying or proverb for the man who had fallen into poverty: "You must have held a *Khatashi*." Veniaminov specified that when the messengers were sent to different villages to invite the guests, they did not invite persons individually, but all, including wives and children, could come. (It is thus clear that the invitations given to house heads were understood as including their lineage mates, and all the members of their households.) They (the local guests) would erect new gravehouses for their host, and they would clean out the house in which the festival was to be held, and sometimes build a new house. Outside and inside would be displayed the clan emblems: the *Kukhontani* (Wolf 1), the Wolf or the Eagle; and the *Takuyati* (Wolf 32), the Bear.

[When the guests were assembled, the festival would begin with songs and dances, from the evening until dawn, followed by an excellent feast for the guests only. Singing, dancing, and feasting continued for several days, as long as the host could feed his guests. On the last evening, the chief of the hosts would retire and don the "sacred regalia" of his clan, which were reserved for such occasions, and could never be worn at other times, except when the Sitka natives danced onboard Russian ships. Veniaminov further specified that the Tlingit of the "Wolf Clan" had as their "sacred regalia" the skin of a wolf, complete with tail, paws, and head, and with teeth made out of wood or even copper. The Frog Clan (Kiksʔadí, Raven 10) had a wooden hat with a frog on it and a cloak (blanket) with the figure of a frog.

[As the chief, wearing these things, stepped forward, accompanied by several slaves, someone outside would howl like a wolf or croak like a frog (i.e., utter the cry of the totem), the tone indicating whether slaves were to be freed or killed, and how many would die, matters already settled in advance. The slave who dressed the chief was always freed, so the chief would select this favorite. Then the hosts sang their clan songs, telling their clan history and the deeds of their ancestors. After this, the chief would be seated, the presents for the guests brought out. These were not distributed equally, for the most honored and wealthy received the most and the best, even slaves, while common people were given less.

[Next day the same festival would be held at the next house, and after that at the next, if the festival had been organized by the whole village (by houses of the same moiety in the village). At such potlatches, men of the host clan had the right to assume the name or title of deceased kinsmen. (We suppose they had to be wealthy men who had made significant contributions.) Chief's wives also could take new names.

[This same information is summarized in the account by Petroff (1884:171–72), which is based on Holmberg's translation (1855:46–49) of Veniaminov.

[Olson (1967:64–65) reported that formerly the Tlingit gave additional feasts in honor of the dead. One might be given years after a potlatch, in order to add to the gifts previously given. It was called *gauwuta'n*, "drum taking up to beat" [ga·w wuduwata·n, "drum has been taken up"?]. Other feasts or potlatches might be given when the host had dreamed of the dead; for example, a drinking feast might be given in answer to the request of the dead as conveyed in a dream. The guests were to get drunk so that the dead might enjoy the liquor. Of course, food and drink for the deceased were put into the fire on many other occasions. Some potlatches were given to enhance the prestige of the donor and his clan, the house being rebuilt to justify the occasion. Kan's (1983) observations of recent potlatches, 1979–80, and his analysis of potlatch oratory would indicate that no great change has occurred, except for substituting modern goods for the old, and perhaps a further shortening of the ceremonial cycle; the basic meaning remains the same. There is only a difference in the time at which the host would exchange his ordinary, old clothes of the mourner for his full clan regalia.]

CEREMONY FOR THE CHILDREN*

[Veniaminov ([1840] 1984:424) listed a third major festival, "for children," the other two being the wake ("to nourish the dead") and the major potlatch just described ("to raise the dead"). The festival for the children was very expensive and was rarely given. Whereas the expenses of the wake and of the potlatch could be recovered when the donor was a guest of his "opposites," at the children's festival he was giving to members of his own clan, his children's "opposites," and therefore could never hope to recover his outlay. Slaves were not killed, but those who had dressed the children being honored were set free, and there had to be as many slaves as there were children. For this festival a new house was always built, but the workers were from both moieties, and all were paid; and at the ceremony held in the new house the ears of the children were pierced. True nobles, *Angashi* [ʔa·nqá·wu, ʔa·nyạ́dɨ] were those who had had their ears pierced at such a potlatch, but only the most wealthy could attain four holes in each ear (eight for the "eight bones"), since this would require four such expensive festivals. Veniaminov noted that almost all the Indians at Sitka had pierced ears, but these were only pretenders to nobility.

[Olson (1967:68–69) explained this children's potlatch in detail. Not only must the donor be very wealthy and high-born, but he must have inherited the right to give the celebration; that is, someone in his lineage must have given one previously. The songs sung by the host were those sung by his predecessors, whose names he would recite to justify his right to hold the ceremony. All the houses in the village would be invited, both from the donor's moiety and from the other. For a really big potlatch, a clan from another tribal village would be invited. (Olson referred to it as a "clan of the father's moiety," which might mean that it was a clan in the donor's moiety, although this is not clear.) Eight men selected by the host from his own clan acted as na·-ká·ni. The ceremony would be given in the name of the host's oldest child (boy or girl), but the rest of his children would be included, as well as others from the same matriline. The ceremony might be given to console a wife for the death of a child.

[The ceremony (except for the potlatch proper) would last a minimum of four days. The out-of-town guests would arrive the first day. The children to be honored would be placed at the rear of the house, the host's clan-mates in the center, the visitors on the right side, the local guests on the left. Each group would sing two songs, go out to dress, and return to dance two dances. Then the host would feast them, his clansmen acting as waiters.

[On the night of the second day the host would lead eight songs. The two groups of guests each danced twice.

[On the third day was another feast, and that night all the groups, the host's clan, visiting guests, and local guests, might each give special theatrical performances.

[On the fourth day the ears of the children were pierced by the highest ranking chiefs among the guests. If the children were tattooed—girls on the hands, boys on the hands and chest—this might take several days.

[A few days later some or all of the children would be given new names, the history of which would be explained. Then followed the distribution of gifts: the chiefs who had done the ear piercing or tattooing would receive the most, but something went to each person who had sung or danced.

[A ceremony of this kind was no longer given when Emmons was in Alaska. Ear piercing seems to have been accomplished at a lesser affair, one in which the operator was a father's sister or similar relative, and tattooing was becoming obsolete.]

THE BERRY POTLATCH DANCE

[Notes left by Emmons in BCPA contain information about a ceremony he called the "berry potlatch dance," an event illustrated by photographs in AMNH that were taken at Sitka on August 6, 1889, but are now somewhat faded; there is also a brief account of the same festival by Isabel S. Shepard (1889:169), but this is not a ceremony mentioned by other visitors to the Tlingit, as far as I know. On a scrap of paper, in pencil, Emmons wrote: "Berry feast a memorial for the dead. Yearly. G. K."]

On the evening of August 5th, two large canoes containing some forty women, a few children of both sexes, and some six or eight men, left Sitka for the islands to northward; one canoe [belonging to] *Kar-qwanton* [Ka·gʷa·nta·n,

**Editor's note:* In order to make the account of Tlingit ceremonies more complete, I have added this section, based on information in Veniaminov and Olson.

Canoes coming in with dancers for the berry feast. (Photograph by G. T. Emmons. BCPA).

Wolf 1], and one canoe *Chuconnatee* [Ču·kane·dí, Wolf 5], both being *Shen-qu-qway-tee* [Šangukʷe·dí, the clan name used for all the Wolf-Eagle moiety]. On the following afternoon, the *Kake-sa-te* [Kiksʔádi, Raven 10] and *Thluke-nar-hut-tee* [Łukʷnax̣ʔádi, Raven 6], both *Thlar-har-na-tee* [Ła·y(a)ne·dí, Raven moiety], decorated their houses with whole pieces of colored calico [i.e., with the whole, uncut bolts].

At 4 PM the canoes approached Sitka and passed along the village front, close inshore and very slowly, being held together and paddled only in bow and stern. The masts were stepped and dressed rainbow style, and bright pieces of calico hung from the mast heads. The occupants of the canoes were in dance costumes, the women in dark blue blankets with red borders, faces painted both red and black, black handkerchiefs over the head, nose rings and earrings. Men with headdresses of cedar-bark rope, dance sticks. One man led the dance and song. The dance was in the usual style, swaying the body, turning from side to side, and jumping up and down hard. In front of the decorated houses, the canoes stopped, the occupants danced, and spokesmen in the canoes made short addresses.

Then an old woman dressed in a white blanket and with blackened face, came out of a door and danced on the upper step. Three men took the decoration off the houses, which was secured to poles, and carried this down to the canoes. They commenced to tear up this calico, and just slashed it at distances of one to two yards. Blankets were also torn, and a general distribution commenced from —— to —— [times? or donors and recipients?—left blank]. Then the canoes backed in, and their decorations were pulled down and also torn and distributed. People from the canoes landed and brought out berries.

[Isabel S. Shepard, wife of the captain of the USS *Rush,* described part of the Berry Feast held at Sitka on August 1, 1888 (1889:169):

> At [Sitka] the first day of August the Indians term "Berry Day"; the berries are then all ripe. It has its appropriate celebration.
>
> On the first day of August last year [1888] a friend, Mrs. E—[Kitty Emmons?] and myself pulled over to one of the pretty little islands in the harbor of Sitka. As we roamed around, busily picking the many berries we found there, we heard a faint sound of singing resembling a chant, of a strange weird character. It was a beautiful day, the sky and air clear, the sea blue and the sky blue. All else was still, and we listened, fairly holding our breaths as gradually the sounds approached nearer and nearer. At last out from behind the island on which we were shot a large canoe filled with Indians, and gaily trimmed with strips of white and red cloth extended over a rude frame, erected somewhat like a canopy. They were still singing in their strange and monotonous song, keeping in time with their paddles. We stood as if entranced, watching them as they drifted away out of sight, their song growing fainter and fainter in the distance.]

CHAPTER 12

War and Peace

EARLY ENCOUNTERS WITH EUROPEANS*

The early European explorers on the Northwest Coast of America were united in their testimony as to the warlike character of the Tlingit. They described the natives as courageous, daring, alert, and never without their arms in readiness for instant use.

The first meeting of Europeans with the Tlingit was by Chirikov's men in 1741. Having made the entrance of what appeared to be an extensive bay in latitude 57°15′ N, he dispatched an armed boat's crew to make a reconnaissance. The party not returning after five days had elapsed, a smaller boat was sent to render any necessary assistance, and to direct an immediate return. The following morning, two canoes filled with natives put off from shore. Nearing the ship, they called "*Agai, agai,*" evidently meaning "Come, come," several times, and quickly put about for the shore. As no sign of the boats was seen, after standing off and on for several days, Chirikov sailed without making any further effort to land, concluding that his men had been killed by the natives. No evidence ever came to light as to their fate. It is possible that they were lost in the tide rips and swirls of Sergius Narrows [at west end of Peril Strait, 57°24′20″ N, 135°38′00″ W (Orth 1967:854–55)], for the latitude given, which at best was only approximate, suggests the entrance to Salisbury Sound which leads directly to Peril Strait, and without local knowledge, they might have been drawn into the rapids which at the full run of the tide are avoided by the largest steamers. No evidence of the killing of these boats' crews was ever learned from Tlingit stories.

Editor's note: Emmons outlined this chapter with only three sections—Peace Dance, Arms, Armor—but these were inadequate for the data he had collected. The section titles and their arrangement here are my own.

**Editor's note:* Because Emmons had entertained two different interpretations of Chirikov's loss of two boats and their crews, I have had to add more detailed information, taken from Golder's publication of Chirikov's Report. References to the numbers of sea otters taken in 1793–95 were checked against Bancroft and Tikhmenev, and details were added. I have also included quotations from Rezanov, Khlebnikov, and Lisiansky about the Tlingit attack on the Russian fort at Sitka, and raise the question as to which clans may have been involved.

[It is not clear why Emmons chose to introduce his discussion of Tlingit warfare with this episode, especially since no one knows what happened to these men. The story was more complicated than Emmons has here indicated, and in another account Emmons suggested that the boats were lost in tide rips at Lisianski Strait, farther north (see below).

[Golder (1922–25) has published a translation of Chirikov's Report (1:312–48) and of the Journal kept on the *St. Paul* (pp. 283–311), and also gathered opinions from experts as to the probable fate of the lost men. The following account of the episode is summarized or quoted from Golder.

[According to Chirikov's Report, on July 18 he sent ashore Fleetmaster Dementiev with ten armed men in the larger ship's boat to explore a bay at 57°39′ N latitude. According to Captain Ellsworth P. Bertholf of the U.S. Coast Guard (Golder 1922–25, 1:343–44), Chirikov's vessel, *St. Paul,* was five miles WSW, true, from the entrance to Lisianski Strait. The ship was forced by bad weather to leave this locality, but returned to the same place on July 23. Smoke was seen on the beach, and though guns on the ship were fired as a signal, no boat appeared, although after each shot the fire grew larger. The next day Chirikov was able to take an observation close to the mouth of the bay, in clear weather, and the latitude was 57°50′ N, the true latitude of Lisianski Strait, according to Captain Bertholf.

[Since their boat had still not come off, the Russians believed that it might have been damaged, so the remaining small boat, with the carpenter, calker, and materials for repairs, as well as provisions, was sent ashore in the same bay. The boatswain was ordered to build a fire as soon as he landed, and to return with as many men as he could, leaving the carpenter and calker ashore. Although the day was clear, the water was rough. There was no signal for a long time, but later that day a fire was seen on shore. The Russians fired guns, but no boat returned.

[The next day, July 25, the Russians saw two boats coming from the bay, one large and one small. At first they believed that these were their own boats, but as Chirikov reported (Golder 1922–25, 1:296–97):

> When the small boat drew close to us we became aware that it was not our boat, for it had a sharp bow, and those in it did not

row with oars but paddled. The boat did not, however, come near enough so that we could see the faces of those in it. All that we did see was that it contained four persons, one at the stern and the others at the paddle. One of them had on clothes of red material. Being that far away they stood up and shouted twice "Agai, Agai," waved their hands, and turned back to shore. [Were they crying "ha·dé!—This way!"?] I commanded my men to wave white kerchiefs and to invite those in the boat to come to our ship. Many of my men did that but it did no good; the boat proceeded on its way to shore. We could not pursue them because in the first place we had no wind, in the second place the small boat went very fast, and the large one had stopped a considerable distance from us. They continued to pull away and finally disappeared in the bay from which they had come. We then became convinced that some misfortune had happened to our men. . . . The fact that the Americans did not dare to approach our ship leads us to believe that they have either killed or detained our men.

[All that day the ship kept close inshore and in the afternoon] steered for shore where we observed a fire, also two boats which came out and, after keeping close to land, put back and disappeared. This is the last of boats and signals that we saw, except on the spot where we formerly observed fire we now had smoke.

[On July 27, the officers concurred in the decision to leave, since they no longer had any small boats to go to shore, and did not have much fresh water.

[In an attempt to discover what might have happened, Golder (1922–25, 1:311 note) consulted a number of Northwest Coast ethnologists, but none had heard of any native tradition about Chirikov's lost men. George Davidson was also unsuccessful, although he noted the latitude 57°15′ N, as that of the scene of Chirikov's disaster (Davidson 1901:19), a reading which Emmons accepted. The latter, consulted by Golder, suggested (Golder 1922–25, 1:311 note):

. . . Chirikov's two boats may have been swamped in the strong tidal rips that occur at the mouths of such narrow fiord arms as Lisianski Strait, especially if they entered with the strength of a flood tide. That this might easily happen to small boats is evidenced by the fact that today even powerful steamers, as he states, enter Peril Strait, a similar passage somewhat farther south, only at slack water. The assumption that the boats were swamped and their occupants drowned would seem to be borne out by the fact that the two native canoes put off from shore and approached the *St. Paul*. If the Russians had landed and if, in spite of Chirikov's admonitions to his men, there had been a fight, and natives, after this first experience of firearms, even if they had overpowered the landing parties, would certainly not have exposed themselves to the greater risk of facing the main body of the Russians. The fact that they approached the ship would rather prove their innocence. Also, the similarity of their call of "agai," as reported by Chirikov, to the Tlingit "agou," which means "come here," would seem to imply friendly intentions. [The Tlingit word may be ha·dé, "this way," as called out by a guest whose name is announced at a potlatch.] In most later instances the first meetings of natives of this coast with Europeans, before the Russians commenced to appropriate their hunting grounds, says Lieutenant Emmons in conclusion, were friendly; indeed the Tlingits were rather ready to trade.

[It is impossible to tell which explanation—a fight resulting in death or enslavement, or drowning in the tide rips—was the final judgment made by Emmons, or whether he believed the men were lost at Lisianski Strait or Sergius Narrows, for we do not know whether he wrote this chapter before or after he offered his opinion to Golder.]

Early European and American traders who visited the Northwest Coast in the last quarter of the eighteenth century found the Tlingit generally friendly, suspicious although not actively hostile. The Russians, brutal and ignorant in an age of lawlessness, came not to trade but to possess, and their total disregard of any sense of justice forced the natives into open hostility. This resulted in the destruction of the first two posts established among the Tlingit, at Sitka and Yakutat, and the attack on hunting parties wherever found. The most valuable fur-bearing animal of the North Pacific was the sea otter upon which the natives depended for their trade with Europeans, and when the waters to the westward had been depleted, Russian expeditions were formed in which thousands of Aleuts were impressed, to seek new fields along the continental shore. This brought them into competition with the Tlingit, who saw their favorite sea-otter hunting grounds appropriated and exhausted by the more skillful Aleut hunters, who, in their light skin bidarkas, could keep the sea, when the less seaworthy wooden canoes of the Indians were stormbound.

To show to what extent the valuable hunting rights of the Tlingit were infringed, we may cite the reports of the Russian leaders of these expeditions:

In 1793, an expedition of 170 bidarkas, escorted by Shields, secured 2,000 sea otter skins in or near Yakutat Bay (Bancroft 1886:344 note 19; Tikhmenev [1861] 1978:35). The next year, a fleet of over 500 bidarkas under Purtov and Kulikalov, with upwards of 1,000 natives from Kodiak, Kenai, the Alaska Peninsula, and Prince William Sound, hunted along the Gulf Coast as far east as Yakutat Bay, procuring 400 sea otters at Icy Bay and 515 at Yakutat (Tikhmenev [1863] 1979:46–52, Report by Purtov and Kulikalov, August 9, 1794). Although this Russian-led

Indian of Port Mulgrave, Yakutat, 1791. He wears a spruce root hat and bearskin robe, and clutches a dagger, ready to strike. (Aquatint by Suría. Courtesy of the Museo Naval, Madrid.)

party was at first received with friendly courtesies, bad feelings were soon aroused because the local Tlingit wanted to trade, not to watch the strangers take all the sea otter which they claimed as their own, especially since the skin bidarkas could venture where their wooden canoes dared not go (Bancroft 1886:347). Only the arrival in Yakutat Bay of Vancouver's *Chatham* under Lieutenant Puget, and shortly after of the *Jackall,* Captain Brown, prevented real trouble. Although the local Tlingit promised the Russians many sea otters the following year (1795), the chief failed to keep his word, and the Russians had to send out their own native hunters, in spite of the obvious hostility of the Tlingit. The hunters killed 400 sea otters, and there might have been a clash with the local natives, but just then two Aleuts came down with smallpox, and the whole party fled in a panic (Bancroft 1886:350). In 1796 Shields, in the *Orel,* convoying a fleet of 450 bidarkas, visited Lituya Bay where he took 1,800 sea otters, and proceeding southward to Norfolk Sound, added 2,000 more to this number (Bancroft 1886:356–58).

So it can readily be seen why the Tlingit, with their established sense of law and property rights, should have conceived for the Russians such a hatred that it confined them to the limits of their stockaded posts during their entire occupation of Alaska.

[The imperial envoy, Rezanov, wrote to the directors of the Russian American Company, on November 6, 1805, from Sitka (Tikhmenev ([1863, II] 1979:156–57):

> The Kolosh, or Koliuzh, as the Kadiak Americans call them, have become peaceful, I do not know for how long. They are armed by the Bostonians with the very best guns and pistols and have falconets too. They have built forts everywhere in the Straits. Having more than six hundred Russians and Kadiak Americans in the hunting crew, we were awaiting their return about September 1st . . . [with] great anxiety as to their safety. . . . [But they returned safely September 17 with 1,700 sea otters.]
>
> The brutal massacre committed by the Americans has taught us to take precautions. Our cannons are always loaded; not only are sentries with loaded guns everywhere but even in our rooms weapons are considered the best and most valuable part of our furnishings. Every night after sounding taps the signals are continued till morning and the patrols are on guard. In short, strict military discipline is upheld and we are ready to receive our "dear guests" at any minute. They are used to making their attacks at night and in rainy weather. Up to the present, by God's mercy, everything is quiet. The Sitka Kolosh came here during my sojourn, danced as usual, not sparing strength, and assured us of their friendship, something that we know we cannot rely upon. In the Straits there are villages of many thousands of inhabitants,

who seem to be peaceful but who do not give us hostages. The manager by chance seized toions' sons from Sitka and Akoi-koknout. They live here now.]

Thus it can be seen that while the Russians claimed Alaska through discovery, they exercised no control over the Tlingit, who lived independently after the manners of their forefathers, acknowledging no alien authority, trading with whom they pleased as a matter of convenience, a position they owed to their courage and manhood.

[The attack on and destruction of Fort Sv. Mikhaïl at Sitka in 1802, as told by Khlebnikov ([1833] 1861b:65–67); and Tikhmenev ([1860, I] 1978:65–67; [1863, II] 1979:134–39) based on accounts of the survivors, was an unusual example of Tlingit military strategy. (See also Bancroft 1886:410–12; de Laguna 1972:170–73). It was the climax of a long-planned attempt, involving clans from many tribes: Henya, Stikine, Kuyu, Kake, Hutsnuwu, Hoonah, Sitka, Chilkat, and even Yakutat and the Kaigani Haida, to rid themselves of the Russians and their Aleut sea otter hunters. The Russians believed it had been instigated by British and American traders who furnished the natives with arms and ammunition, including some small cannon with grape and canister, and who hoped thereby to secure the sea otter trade for themselves. The leader of the plot seems to have been a Henya chief, *Kaniagit,* from an island near Port Bucareli. The secret was kept because only the principal chiefs were informed.

[The first and inconclusive blow came in May 22–25, 1802, when a party from Kodiak, under Ivan A. Kuskov, was attacked near Dry Bay; a hunting party from Sitka of some two hundred Aleuts in ninety bidarkas under Urbanov was all but wiped out in Frederick Sound, on June 20–21, while the embers of the whole installation at Sitka were still smoking; but the planned attacks on the Yakutat posts were postponed for three years (till August 1805). In addition to assembling over one thousand men and a fleet of over sixty large canoes, to launch simultaneous attacks from both land and sea, the Tlingit had learned from some of their women who lived with the Russians all about the routine of the Sitka garrison and their defenses. The foreman at Sitka, Vasilii Medvednikov, foolishly confident in the goodwill of the natives, despite plenty of warning signs, had not only dispatched the large party of sea otter hunters who were virtually destroyed, but on the fatal day, June 18 or 19, had even sent others to hunt sea lions, and to fish, and some women to pick berries. So there remained at the fort only fifteen Russians, a few sickly Aleut, some women and children, including a few Tlingit women.

[On this holiday, after the midday meal, the men at the barracks saw the Tlingit warriors suddenly and silently emerge from the woods. Khlebnikov wrote (1861b:46, Petroff translation):

> [They were] armed with guns, spears, and daggers. Their faces were covered with masks, representing the heads of animals and smeared with red and other paint, their hair was tied up with feathers and eagle plumes. Some of the masks were shaped in imitation of ferocious animals, with gleaming teeth, and other monstrous beings. They were not observed until they were close to the barracks which they quickly surrounded, and with wild and savage cries, opened a heavy fire from their guns at the windows. [Their cries were] in imitation of the animals that were represented by their masks [i.e., their totemic crests].

[The two-story barracks had a balcony on the upper floor, reached by outside stairs; there were no stairs on the inside. The defenders were able to fire one or two shots from the cannon on the lower floor, which temporarily balked the assailants. But the men at the guns fell, and when the others on the ground floor cut through the ceiling to get the ammunition stored above, they found the barracks set on fire, allegedly by a few renegade American seamen who were living with the Indians. Meanwhile the Tlingit managed to break into one of the doors, and through the hole "kept up a wild, but continuous fire" (Khlebnikov 1861b:46). The women and children, crazed with terror, crowded onto the balcony, and when the trapdoor gave way, fell down the stairs, only to be seized by the Tlingit and carried off to their canoes. The Russians who had been fighting on the upper floor jumped from the balcony and ran for the woods, only to be speared and beheaded. Other Indians rushed into the building and carried off everything they could: sea otter pelts, trade goods, and personal possessions. All of the buildings were looted and burned.

[*Ska-oushle-oot* (leading chief of the Kiksʔádi, Raven 10, whom the Russians called "Mikhaïlov") directed the assault from the top of a knoll, and also signalled the sixty canoes full of warriors, that were hidden behind a point, when to join in. His sororal nephew, Katlyan, led the actual attack.

[The only survivors of the massacres at Sitka and Frederick Sound were three Russians, two Aleuts, and eighteen women and children. Some of them had been warned by friendly Indians, for not all the Tlingit, even at Sitka, joined the attack. These survivors were picked up by Captain Barber and taken in his ship to Kodiak, where he exacted a large ransom in furs for them.]

Knowing that the Russians would return in force (which they did in 1804), the Sitkans deserted their nearby villages and established themselves some six miles distant, in a fort on top of a hill, at the mouth of a small stream (Indian River), where shoal water prevented the too near approach of ships. [Here, in 1804, Baranov with the *Alexander Nevski,* and *Ekaterina, Ermak,* and *Rostitlav,* met Lisiansky in the *Neva.* At first the Russians offered peace to the Indians, but when this was rejected, an attack on the Tlingit settlement was ordered.] Here, within strongly fortified walls, defended by several of the cannon previously captured, the Tlingit for six days withstood and repulsed the Russian attack with slight loss. After their supply of ammunition had given out, and they failed to receive the expected reinforcements from their neighbors, the Sitkans fled. Crossing Baranof Island, they settled at the eastern entrance of Peril Strait.

[Meanwhile the Russians destroyed the Indian fort, and erected their own, Novo Arkhangelsk (present Sitka). The Tlingit fort is described in Chapter 3, under "Forts," where their new fortified village on Peril Strait is also described and its location discussed.]

The exiled Sitkans remained unmolested until, at the invitation of the Russian governor in 1821, they returned to the site of their present village at Sitka, below the Russian fort. No great friendliness, however, ever existed between the Russians and the Sitkans. They traded with each other for mutual convenience, but attacks, ambuscades, and murders constantly occurred, and the Russians were never safe outside the limits of the post.

While at first the Tlingit considered all foreigners as the same, single people, yet in time, with a better acquaintance, they learned to differentiate the several nationalities, and the offenses of one were not attributed to another. This is shown in several instances. Captain Sturgis of the American ship *Caroline* stated [reference unverified] that seven seamen deserters from the American ship *Jenny* were living with the Russians at the time of the destruction of the Sitka post in 1802. They were invited by the natives to visit them, when it was proposed that they join with the Tlingit in attacking the Russians. Since they [some of them] refused these overtures, they were, as a matter of safety, held until after the assault, when they were liberated and placed on board visiting ships. [See Bancroft 1886:408–9 note 3; Howay 1973:56 and 72 on William Sturgis.]

[Mention has already been made (see Chapter 4, the section "Handling the Canoe," of encounters between Vancouver's boat parties (1793, 1794) and the Sanya and Chilkat. In these, the Indians were evidently organized as in a war party, with a chief near the bow of the canoe, and an old woman of rank at the stern steering paddle. It was only with difficulty that the English were able to escape from these native "pirates."]

INTERCLAN WARFARE*

Because of the peculiar political and social organization of the Tlingit, foreign wars, in which all of the people might be engaged, were unknown. The Indians unquestionably resented the coming of the Russians, with their arbitrary abuse of native hunting and territorial rights, but even then, there was no attempted combination of [all Tlingit] forces, and opposition was offered only by those who came directly in contact with them. Again, when Vancouver's surveying parties explored the inland waterways and channels in 1793 and 1794, the *Hootz-ah-tas* [Hutsnuwu], Hoonahs, Stikines, and Tongass were most friendly, while for no specific [obvious] reason, the Chilkats, Auks, and Sanyas were hostile. Evidences of cooperation and of any national spirit were likewise absent both in intertribal and foreign relations.

[See Olson 1967:69–98, for accounts of feuds, raids, wars, and peacemaking, in which a single clan or several clans might be on one side, the alliances depending largely on family relationships.]

Intertribal wars in which all the clans [of one community] made common cause against an enemy were the exception, for while marriage, association, and economic interests were strong factors for [tribal] unity, yet the coexistence of the same clans in different tribes prevented their joining with other clans against each other, for the clan was the unit of Tlingit life. It recognized no superior tribal authority. All its members were brothers, and while they might have differences with each other, they would never join with others against each other. This lack of any national spirit or even tribal sympathy was shown when the Haida from Massett crossed Dixon Entrance and dispossessed the Tongass of their villages and country (which included the southern portion of Prince of Wales Island [and adjacent islands]), and later, when the Tongass had settled on Annette Island and the Stikines attacked them, destroying their villages at Port Chester and Tamgas Harbor,

**Editor's note:* I have added passages from Holmberg and von Langsdorff, as well as summaries of the war between Wolf 18 of Wrangell and Raven 13 of Angoon in 1880, of the war between Chilkat and Chilkoot clans in 1880, and of the averted war between the Hoonah and Tsimshian. Brief references to the policies of Commanders Beardslee, Glass, and Lull are also included.

and driving them away from Annette Island. In neither of these instances was any assistance offered by other Tlingits.

Clan stories are largely those of wars, feuds, and disagreements between the Tlingit clans and their southern neighbors, the Haida and Tsimshian [but even more of fights between Tlingit clans]. Tlingit relations were uniformly peaceful with the interior people, except for the Taku Tlingit who raided the upriver people with whom they were closely connected.

On a rock cliff on the west bank of the Chilkat River, some eight miles above Klukwan, is a rude painting of a head in red, called *Kuw-tche-hit ka-yah,* "Painted Face" [kawǯixidi qa· yá], which is said to have been painted with the blood of Hoonahs who had attacked the Chilkat. It was a bad season for salmon and the Hoonah had been unable to put up their winter supply, so they formed a war party and came north. [Elsewhere Emmons identified the attackers as Łukʷnax̣ʔádi (Raven 6), and the Chilkat as G̣a·nax̣te·dí (Raven 3).] The Chilkat deserted their village and fled up the river to this point, where they held a truce with the invaders and offered them food. The latter accepted and pretended to leave, but shortly after turned and attacked the Chilkat. They were defeated with great slaughter. The headless bodies of the slain were cast into the river, and floating down, were grounded on "Bull Island" [not listed in Orth], which was consequently named in Tlingit *Ka shawee ghart ee ku,* "Head or Headless Island" [qa· ša·yí x̣á·ti ká]. The painting on the cliff commemorates this victory. [See also Chapter 3, the section "Petroglyphs."]

Of greater wars, those between the *Ka-gwanton* [Wolf 1] of Chilkat, Hoonah, and Sitka, and the Stikine [Na·nya·ʔa·yí, Wolf 18], seem to have been the most serious and to have continued through several generations. On one occasion [1852], the Stikine were invited to Sitka to make peace. They were seated in a long row at a feast, when a cannonade loaded with slugs and concealed under a blanket, was fired, killing most of the guests, while those uninjured were knifed. Then years afterwards [before?] the Sitkans went to the Stikine where they were ambushed and slaughtered.

[For other versions of these events, see de Laguna 1972:279–84; Olson 1967:78–79. On March 31, 1881, Commander Henry Glass, senior naval officer in Alaska, brought about a "Treaty of Peace between the Stickeen and Sitka Tribes." For the former, the signers (who affixed their marks) were "George Shckes" (i.e., Shakes, Na·nya·ʔa·yí) and "Jake Sha-kach," (probably Wolf 18 or a closely related clan); and for the Sitkans the signers were "Annahortz" (ʔAnahú·c, Wolf 1), and "Woosh-kina" (Wu·š-kiná·, "Above Each Other," probably Wolf 17). It was evidently an uneasy truce, and a "final" peace treaty was signed on the day before the United States entered World War I (de Laguna 1933:744).]

Wars were carried on in this way and peace could be established only by adjudging the loss of lives on each side as equal, or by payment for the excess to the losers.

The early explorers frequently mention the belligerency of the natives, as well as their jealousy of each other. Wars were generally between clans. One or more clans might be engaged on each side, but other members of the tribe would be simply spectators [or acted as peacemakers]. As conducted by the Tlingit, warfare consisted of sudden descents on villages or unprotected camps, and equally quick retreats before the attacked could gather their forces. Treachery and murder marked these conflicts. The hunter's training, upon which life depended, taught him cunning to outwit his opponent, patience to bide his time, and, above all, self-protection. The idea of fighting in the open did not appeal to him. This implied no deficiency in personal courage, for when called upon to offer his life for the honor of his clan, for an act that another had committed, he unhesitatingly went forth without [apparent signs of] fear, unarmed, to die by the spears or guns of those awaiting him. [See cases in Chapter 2, the section "Law."] Or recourse might be had to a duel, in which, arm to arm, the two opponents stabbed with the long bladed knife [dagger] until one or the other fell.

[The duel was described by Holmberg 1855:42–43, free translation, as:

> The single or private wars are only quarrels between single clans and families, which usually, unless they degenerated into undeclared wars, were settled by single combat. In this case, each party selected from their midst one man to fight. The ranks were positioned on each side in order of battle; the chosen champions were dressed in thick armor of moose or bear hide, and wore wooden helmets which, while protecting the whole head, depicted the animal of their family crest. The only weapon on such occasions was the afore-mentioned dagger [p. 28], and the whole combat was accompanied by dance and song, ever adjusted to victory or defeat. [Then followed the Peace Ceremony, see below.]

[Von Langsdorff (1814, 2:130) has also commented on Tlingit warfare:

> Single families, as well as single tribes, have contentions sometimes with each other. The inhabitants of the Archipelago of King George the Third [the islands west of Chatham Strait; i.e., Chirikof and Baranof islands], for instance, are often at variance with those of Admiralty Island, which lies to the

Left. *Powder horn collected by G. T. Emmons at Yakutat in 1886. (AMNH.)* Right. Top to bottom. *Powder measure, bullet and bullet mold, and powder measure of mountain goat horn, carved to represent an eagle, a crest of the owner, a* Te·qwe·di *Wolf 32 man, collected at Yakutat by William S. Libby in 1886. (Photographs by Donald Baird. PUM.)*

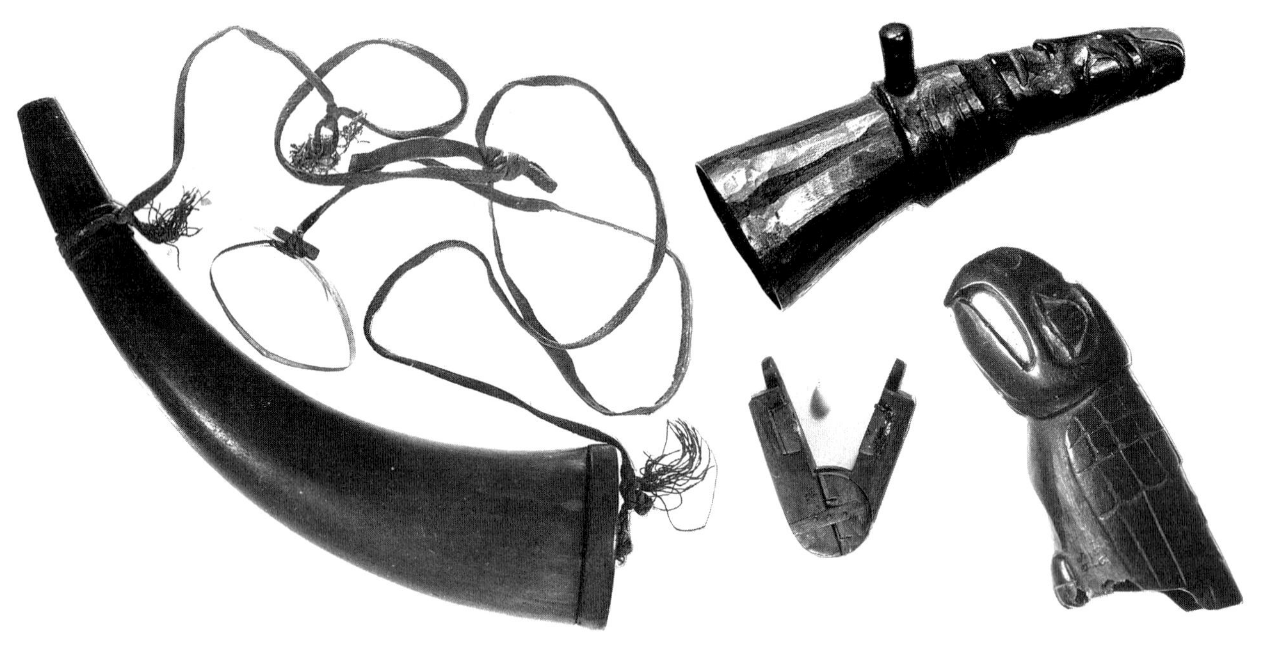

eastward of them; but if attacked by a common enemy, suppose the Russians, they unite for their common defence. All private quarrels are decided by the right of the strongest; if in the contest any one be taken prisoner, he must serve as slave to his conquerors till a price is agreed upon for his ransom; this is commonly fixed at a certain number of sea-otter skins.

[The clan histories published by Swanton (1909) and by Olson (1967) are filled with accounts of feuds, raids, and wars.]

The frequency of clan warfare developed from the lack of individual responsibility, for every act of an individual involved the whole clan, and intent had no bearing on the case. As far as the settlement was concerned, an accident and a premeditated act were considered alike. This hostile arraignment of clans frequently acquired the character of feuds, marked by individual killings, rather than actual warfare, although at any time war parties of considerable size might combine for surprises or reprisals. While the old law of a life for a life might even up affairs, yet the different values placed on the lives of individuals, based on their social status, made it difficult to equalize the results. The life of a chief was equal to several lives of those in other social ranks. The extent to which this rule was carried out may be seen in the following instance:

[The "Kake War," cited by Emmons, as well as the troubles between the whites and the Tlingit which resulted in the bombardment of Wrangell in 1869 and of Angoon in 1882, all turned upon the Indians' notions of evening the score, or retaliation. These incidents are discussed below in "Encounters with Americans." See also the cases discussed in Chapter 2, under "Law."

[Another war of long standing, but not cited by Emmons, was that between the Na·nya·ʔa·yí, Wolf 18, of Wrangell, and the De·ši·ta·n, Raven 13, of Angoon. It began (?) with the siege of the Ravens on their fortified island, Daxatkanada, in Kootznahoo Inlet near Angoon, in which the Wrangell Wolves were victorious. This was followed by a victory for the Ravens, either when their enemies were drowned in the treacherous waters of the inlet, or when the Angoon people fought them in a "sea battle" off Wrangell. The memories of these old fights undoubtedly played some part in the subsequent trouble at Wrangell in 1880 (de Laguna 1960:150–54).

[Several incidents led to the bloody fighting at Wrangell, in addition to the bad feeling between the Hutsnuwu and the Stikine. Both sides had been making "hooch" and were drunk. The self-appointed missionary, Dr. Corlies, whose zealous and "imprudent act" was blamed by Commander Beardslee (1882:52–53) as "the true cause of the trouble and the bloodshed," insisted that two Christian policemen, go to the "guest houses" where the Hutsnuwu were staying and break up their stills. These policemen were Matthew Shakates and Aaron Kohnow, both relatives of the Christian chief, *Tow-a-att* (Ṫawyá·ṫ, "Flathead Indian"), and members of a Wolf clan (25 or 26?). In the skirmish which naturally erupted, Aaron received a deep cut in his face, a deadly insult.

[Two days later some thirty unarmed Stikine went to the Hutsnuwu camp, demanding redress. This was obtained when a young man came out and received a blow on his face. This would have ended the trouble (since both sides were now even), but he was struck a second time. This precipitated a fight, in which the arms of the Stikine were turned against them. Seven men were injured, and the Hutsnuwu vowed revenge.

[The next day, the Hutsnuwu rushed, well-armed, to the Stikine village. The Reverend S. Hall Young and Dr. Corlies attempted to prevent bloodshed by telling the Stikine to stay indoors, an action which their enemies interpreted as cowardice. The Hutsnuwu broke into the house of "Moses," or Jim Coustateen (Ģuš-du-tí·n, "Visible Dorsal Fin," probably Daqławe·dí, Wolf 27), and broke up his valuable furniture. This enraged the Stikine, and Jim Coustateen, Aaron Kohnow, and Matthew Shakates, took up arms. Meanwhile, some thirty to forty white men remained interested spectators, one who was a distiller saying, "Let them alone, and let's see the fun!" (Young 1927:223). Old Ṫawyá·ṫ, the chief, came out bearing "a curious carved spear, made of some solid, heavy wood, which had floated from the East Indies and stranded on Alaskan shores. He used the spear as a sign of chiefly authority" (Young 1927:223). This was probably considered a clan heirloom, or emblem, and was therefore being used to try to make peace between the two sides (see Chapter 11, the section "Dedication of the House and Raising a Totem Pole").

[But the old chief was shot dead, as was his brother, *Kitch-gow-ish* (Kič-ga·w-ʔí·š, "Wing-Drum's Father"), and Jim Coustateen. Two of the attackers were also killed. Eventually, the Angoon natives retreated, but refused to give up a chief to match Ṫawyá·ṫ. Skirmishing and firing went on for several days, until the Hutsnuwu finally slipped away on a dark night. Colonel Crittenden, deputy collector of customs, who had organized the native police force at Wrangell, had the "guest houses" destroyed, and fenced in the area for a garden. The natives resented this, and for a time none came to Wrangell to trade.

[Meanwhile the Stikine feared that the Hutsnuwu might return with reinforcements. To keep the peace and relieve the fears of the whites, Commander Beardslee sent a large Indian canoe with fifty rifles, a Gatling gun, and a gunner to instruct the whites, plus fourteen of his hired Sitka Indians. The latter made a great impression at Wrangell. They marched ashore in sailors' uniforms, and gave an exhibition of "small-arm and broadsword drill, substituting sticks for arms, they having become quite expert at these drills, through watching our sailors and marines." Their military skills came as an unwelcome surprise to Commander Beardslee (1882:58).

[Beardslee's replacement, Commander Glass, on March 22, 1881, brought this "war" to an official conclusion when a peace treaty was signed in his presence by the Angoon chiefs, An-ti-nat (ʔA·nde·nʔa·t, De·ši·ta·n, Raven 13) and Joe Kennel-ku, of the same clan. Signing for the Wrangell natives were chiefs Shakes (Na·nya·ʔa·yí, Wolf 18) and Kadashan (Qá·da·ša·n, of the Ka·sx̣ag^{w}e·dí, Ṙaven 32). It is not clear why the latter was involved.

[During the fight, Tacoo Charley, "Chief of the Taku," a Yanye·dí, Wolf 16, man, who had been visiting in Wrangell, maintained strict neutrality, inviting Young to safety in his house, to which the minister brought the body of Ṫawyá·ṫ.

[Another "war" that was settled by the naval authorities at Sitka was that between the Chilkat and the Chilkoot, in August 1880. The "Lower Chilkat Village," or Yandestake (Yánde·sṫaqyé) at the mouth of the Chilkat River, was inhabited by about an equal number of Chilkat and Chilkoot. The chief, Danawak (Dá·na·wa·q, "Dollar (Silver) Eyes," Łuk^{w}a·x̣ʔádi, Raven 17), was a Chilkoot. The trouble started because Yakekoko, a nephew of Klotz-Kutch (Chartrich), and probably Ka·g^{w}a·nta·n like the old chief, got drunk and wanted to kill a French trader who was then visiting Klukwan. "Yakekoko has what is termed a 'blood feud' with the whites, he having been stabbed last winter in Wrangell by a white man named Currie, and in consequence has sworn to kill a white man to 'get even'," Beardslee (1882:71–72) reported. The young Indian had been drunk, and when turned out of the store, he had received a wound in the face, "which by Indian logic is, until atoned for, a great disgrace" (Beardslee 1882:65–66). Although Currie had paid him the sum he demanded, it later appeared that he was still angry, and therefore wanted to kill a white, Pierre Erassard being apparently available. The attack on this man was prevented by Chief Klotz-Kutch (Chartrich), but then the Indians all got drunk on "hootch" from a barrel of molasses, probably sold by the same Frenchman; and in the resulting fight Yakekoko shot and killed a Chilkoot named Kootsnatz, the same man who had wounded Klotz-Kutch in a drunken brawl in September 1879. (This injury may have been the one that earned for the chief the nickname of "Hole in the Head.") Kootsnatz was a Łukʷa·x̣ʔádi (Raven 17), and all the Indians of the Lower Village sided with the Chilkoot. Chief Dá·na·wa·q sent to the main Chilkoot Village where his younger brother, a shaman and his probable successor, Karskarz, was chief.

[There were also at the same time problems with the Chilkat because some whites who had attached themselves to an "authorized" party of prospectors had violated the agreement made with the Chilkat, by trading with the interior Indians. This agreement was one that Commander Beardslee had negotiated. This trouble was settled by one of the prospectors involved.

[Meanwhile Commander Beardslee, accompanied by Major Morris, collector of customs, arrived at Haines on the schooner *Favorite,* on which the Chilkat and Chilkoot leaders were asked to meet. They did so, all in full uniform: Klotz-Kutch and Colchica from Klukwan, Dá·na·wa·q from Yandestake, and his brother Karskarz from Chilkoot village. Commander Beardslee addressed them, saying that he was mortified to find the Chilkat and Chilkoot at war, and couldn't the four chiefs stop it? Although the Indians then asked him to arbitrate, he cannily refused, knowing that if he did so he would be blamed if anything went wrong. Finally, Klotz-Kutch promised to pay what the council decided, since it was a member of his clan who had taken a life. He had come with a bale of blankets and furs, knowing that these would be needed. So all the chiefs agreed to stop the fighting. They were then edified by a speech about smuggling and whiskey from Major Morris, an exhibition of the Gatling gun and howitzer on the *Favorite,* and the promise by her owner, Mr. Vanderbilt, that he would build a schoolhouse by the trading post; the Indians promised to build houses for themselves on each side. So was Haines founded.

[Just as killings or injury, for which no restitution had been made, led to further feuds and "wars," so such conflicts might be caused by intrusion onto the hunting grounds held by another clan or another people. This was the case in 1880 when a war between the Hoonah and the Tsimshian was averted only at the last minute. A somewhat similar fight nearly broke out between the Tsimshian and the Yakutat people, when a Tsimshian hunter tried to take the otter that was the rightful prize of the Yakutat Chief George (de Laguna 1972:284–86). In these cases, it was particular Tlingit clans that were involved; at Yakutat it was the Kʷa·šk̓-qʷá·n, Raven 19; but for the Hoonah, the clan or clans were not identified (see Beardslee 1882:57, 66–69, 74–77).

[Whereas it was Beardslee's policy to interfere as little as possible in interclan disputes, Commander Glass and the latter's successor at Sitka, Commander Lull, took more active parts in achieving settlements. For example, in 1881, a Chilkoot Indian who had been confined on the charge of trying to murder his wife committed suicide. According to native rules of justice, the "other man," a Sitka Indian, was responsible for the suicide, and the Chilkoot demanded compensation in blankets. Commander Lull was inclined to forbid such payment, but did permit it, because the Indians of both the clans involved felt it to be just (Glass 1882:29–30; Lull 1882:47). Such action led to the custom of appealing to naval authorities to settle claims of one Indian group (clan) against another, as well as cases in which the Indians had grievances against white men. In this way "a long standing feud between the Auke and Hoonya tribes" was settled by officers under Commander Glass (Glass 1882:3; 1890:14–15).]

ENCOUNTERS WITH AMERICANS*

In 1857 a party of Kakes visited Puget Sound to engage in hop picking. When the season was over, they camped on the outskirts of Port Gamble and went on a debauch until, being a menace to the neighborhood, the authorities appealed to the commander of the USS *Massachusetts* that was anchored offshore. In the encounter that followed, the chief of the Kakes was killed. The party of Indians left immediately, returning north.

The following spring a war party, consisting of ten men and one woman of the immediate family of the chief, came south 1,000 miles to the scene of the trouble. Upon inquiry, they learned that Colonel Ebey, the collector of customs, was the principal official, or, in their estimation, the chief of this community. They killed him and, taking his head, quickly returned to Alaska, satisfied that his life was the equivalent of that of their own chief. In after years, the scalp that had been removed from the head and retained as a war trophy was recovered by the Hudson's Bay Company, and sent to his family.

[Fuller (1931:236–37) has written an account of the murders in Puget Sound which puts these events in historical perspective. There had been a series of clashes between Indians and whites around Puget Sound, with Canadian and U.S. naval forces collaborating in keeping the peace. These involved the Hudson's Bay Company's *Beaver* and *Otter,* and the USS *Jefferson Davis, Active, Massachusetts,* and *John Hancock.*

**Editor's note:* The greater part of this section is mine, for I have added details about the "Kake (-Kuyu) War," from Fuller, Howard, Louthan, Thomas, and Beardslee, and have summarized Colyer's account of the shelling of Wrangell in 1869.

(Such collaboration set the precedent for dispatching the Canadian ship *Osprey* to Sitka, when the local residents there felt threatened by the Indians in 1879.) The settlers around Puget Sound were especially fearful of a possible alliance between the local Coast Salish and the Haida, for the latter made long piratical raids for plunder and slaves. Then, as Fuller wrote (1931:237):

> A large band of the northern savages camped at Port Gamble and refused to leave. Captain Swartwout of the Massachusetts sent a howitzer ashore. After the Indians had been driven into the woods, with heavy losses, their canoes and provisions were destroyed. They surrendered and were taken to Victoria, where they were left to find their way home. . . . The savages felt obliged to strike a few blows in revenge, though they showed no further desire to match strength with the army or navy. They captured two schooners and murdered the passengers and crews. Their code required that they should take the head of a white chief in recompense for the loss of one of their chiefs at Port Gamble. So a party from Kake visited Whidby island, August 11, 1857, called Colonel Isaac N. Ebey to the door of his house, killed him and took away his head. United States Marshal George W. Corliss and his wife, who were in the house at the time, escaped, together with Ebey's wife and children, but were murdered by the northern Indians at a later date. In 1860, the legislature thanked Chief Trader Charles Dodd for recovering Ebey's head, after a two years' hunt, while on northern trips in the Beaver and the Labouchère.

[Unfortunately Fuller did not identify the particular tribes that were involved in these bloody exchanges. We do not know which group captured and killed the crews of the two schooners, for the Kake are not specifically mentioned. It was reported (Howard 1868:263) that both Stikine and "Kaki" (Kake) Indians had been killed at Port Gamble by fire from the howitzer of the *Massachusetts,* and that shortly after that,

> some of the sub-tribes, twenty or thirty miles west of the Stakeen, captured the English trading schooner Royal Charlie, murdered her crew, and plundered and scuttled the vessel.

Were these Indians Kake, Kuyu, or Stikine?

[At any event the Kake continued to be embroiled with the Americans, although not without provocation, and these incidents culminated in the so-called Kake War of January 1869.

[In October and November 1867, the U.S. revenue steamer *Lincoln,* commanded by Captain J. W. White, visited the principal Tlingit villages, to show the flag, inform the natives of the purchase of Alaska, and to attempt to win their friendship. Captain W. A. Howard, U.S. Marine Corps, reported on the trip (1868:209–10):

> [A stop was made at the Kake village on Kupreanof ("Kake") Island], the residence of a tribe well known for their ferocity and thieving propensities. It was this tribe that murdered Mr. Eby [*sic*] (formerly collector of customs) on Puget sound some years since; a whiskey trader was captured last year, and three men murdered (English). I was desirous of treating with these Indians, particularly as their villages are at the very entrance of the passage [Prince Frederick Sound] from [the] sea, entering our new possessions on the main and eastern shores.
>
> [The chief, like most of the Kakes, had traded with the Hudson's Bay Company and was loyal to "King George." Angered at being refused a drink of whiskey, he countermanded the sale of potatoes which the Kakes had arranged with Captain White.] This chief was laboring under the suspicion that we had visited them to retaliate for the death of Mr. Eby. . . . I of course made no allusion to the affair, being well aware they were justified in killing Mr. Eby, in accordance with their laws of retaliation. One of their chiefs was killed by Commander Swartwout, of the United States ship Massachusetts, by a shot fired from that ship, which was not approved by the community of whites in Puget sound—hence the death of Mr. Eby, previously the collector of customs, and supposed by the Indians to be at that time a "chief of the Bostons."
>
> ["Papers" were promised to the principal chief, recognizing him as "chief of the Kakes," as soon as he showed himself friendly to the Americans.]
>
> I am confident this tribe will cause us no trouble, and will be very happy to be unmolested and allowed to trade. The ship having left them in a friendly manner, has convinced them of our good intentions.

[Unfortunately trouble came soon, probably due both to hotheads among the Kake and to the rigid code imposed by the U.S. forces in Alaska, under Brevet Major General Jefferson C. Davis. As explained by the trader, F. K. Louthan (1869:17), who argued that peace could be kept only by settling the natives' claims according to *their* law (see Chapter 2, the section "Law"):

> Last New Year's eve a difficulty occurred at the market-house in Sitka, between a Chilkaht chief and a soldier, a sentinel, which resulted in the imprisonment in the guard-house of the chief, and through some unaccountable manner the death by shooting, in a day or two afterward, of three Indians. . . .
>
> Among the Indians killed was one Chilkaht, one Kake, and one Sitka. The Kakes very promptly sought the usual remedy [compensation in blankets], but, failing to satisfy themselves, adopted their extreme remedy, "an eye for an eye, a tooth for a tooth;" meeting two white men near their village, promptly dispatched them, thereby lost all their village, burned by order of the general commanding; hence the so-called "Kake war." [Since the general refused to listen to the Chilkat delegation,

Louthan, in the interests of trade, paid them the indemnity asked: thirteen blankets, worth about $50.]

[Major General Thomas, USA, reported on September 27, 1869 (pp. 115–16):

The Indians are treacherous, warlike, and, until recently discontented with the change of governments. It will be necessary to maintain a large garrison at this place [Sitka], to protect the traders from the Indians and preserve order and good behavior among the whites and half-breeds. In January last, a party of Kake Indians attempted to leave Sitka in violation of orders: in resisting the attempt, one of the Indians was killed by a sentinel. After they were permitted to return to their homes, they killed, in revenge for the loss of their companion, two white men who had left Sitka in December on a trading expedition in Chatham Straits. Upon hearing of these murders, General Davis proceeded in the United States steamer Saginaw to punish them; upon his arrival at their village, finding it deserted, it was destroyed. He did not succeed in finding any of the murderers. Since then this tribe has been very quiet.

In my personal interview with General Davis I became satisfied his course was right and necessary in that instance.

[Commander Beardslee (1882:54), senior naval officer at Sitka, 1879–81, gave further information:

In January, 1869, they [the Kakes] murdered without provocation two white men named Ludwig Madger and William Walker, who were encamped for the night at a small cove [Murder Cove] near Port Gardner, the southwest point of Admiralty Island [in territory frequented by the Kake], and after murdering these men, mutilated the remains. For this offense they received prompt punishment, for on the 14th and 15th of January, Lieutenant-Commander Meade, commanding the United States steamer Saginaw, burned and destroyed one town and three villages (thirty-five houses in all), and a number of their canoes, at Saginaw and Security Bays, Kou [Kuiu] Island [actually Kuyu villages, not Kake]; also, two stockade forts which were "about 100 feet square and from 15 to 17 feet high, and built of logs from 9 to 15 inches thick" [quoting from Meade's report of February 24, 1869].

[Apparently at this time no distinction was made between the Kuyu and the Kake.]

They have not rebuilt these villages, but have since led wandering lives, forcing themselves upon the hospitality of other tribes, who both dislike and fear them.

[Beardslee added (1882:180):

I attribute this wholesome fear of the whites [by the Tlingit in general] to the thorough punishment given by Lieutenant-Commander Meade to the Kake Indians in 1869, the story of which, greatly exaggerated, has spread throughout the country, and has produced most beneficial results.

All of the other tribes dislike the Kakes and admit the justice of the punishment, and are disposed to be careful to never themselves incur similar treatment.

[There seemed still to be difficulties with the Kuyu-Kake, however, for Commander Beardslee (1882:54–55) reported that in March, 1881:

a large delegation of Kake Indians from Kou Island, came to Sitka in four large war canoes, entering the habor in line abreast, with flags flying and all singing a war [?] song. These were caused to remain in their boats until they gave satisfactory assurances of good conduct. This tribe has for many years been justly considered troublesome and dangerous. . . . Their object in the present visit was to settle a dispute between their tribe and that of Sitka Jack [Raven 6].

[This dispute was settled peacefully, but in subsequent potlatches and feasts in the Kiksʔádi (Raven 10) part of town, the visitors became drunk and disorderly. They were punished by imprisonment on bread and water, made to compensate all persons injured, and the Kakes were ordered to leave Sitka and not return, but were permitted to camp a short distance away, to await their incarcerated companions.

[Although the action against the Kuyu-Kake was considered a police matter by the whites, the Indians concerned regarded it as a war. Unfortunately we do not know what clans were involved. A similar incident: accidental death of an Indian, refusal by the whites to pay the indemnity demanded, and seizure of white hostages, led to the bombing of Angoon in 1882 (Morris 1882:1–2; Merriman 1883:2; de Laguna 1960:158–72.) Two house chiefs, Joe Kennel-ku of Raven House, and "Lonigan," later known as "Killisnoo Jake," or "Saginaw Jake," of Steel House, both De·ši·ta·n, Raven 13, told Captain Merriman they "were glad I had burned the village," and that they had tried to restrain the young men. Merriman rewarded them with letters carrying big seals.

[The shelling of Wrangell in 1869 by the Army at Fort Wrangel (Colyer 1870a) was ordered to force the surrender of an Indian named Scutdoo or Scutdor (probably a Wolf 17 man), who had shot and killed a white trader (probably already hated for his racial prejudices), in retaliation for the "wanton and unjustifiable killing of an Indian named Si-wau by Lieutenant Loucks, the second officer in command of the Post" (p. 1). Si-wau (or "Lowan") was drunk at the time, and had been drunk when he bit off part of the finger of a sergeant's wife, for which offense Lieutenant Loucks had come to arrest him. Scutdoo Wish-Tah (probably Wu·ški·ta·n, Wolf 17) was a cousin of Si-wau, and the latter is presumed to have belonged to the clan of Ťawyạ́·ť (Wolf 25 or 26). Scutdoo surrendered himself after his mother and a sub-chief had been held as hostages by the Army, and was tried, convicted, and hanged for murder. In this case the Army escalated a drunken assault into a "war." Before execution, the prisoner said "Very well; that he had killed a tyhee [chief], and not a common man; that he would see Mr. Smith [the slain trader] in the other world, and, as it were, explain to him how it all happened; that he did not intend to kill Mr. Leon Smith, particularly; had it been any one else it would have been all the same" (p. 9).]

ABORIGINAL WARFARE*

Questions of war and peace were settled by a council of the men of the clan, presided over by their head chief. If war were determined upon, those selected to participate prepared themselves by keeping away from women and by fasting at intervals. The war leader, the head chief if physically able, was advised by the shaman who, in communion with his spirits, not only learned in advance of the enemy's movements, but contended with the spirits of the opposing shamans. When the canoe was prepared [for the war party], each person was assigned his place, the chief in the stern. In each canoe sat a bowman who had to sit with his legs crossed, facing ahead, and could never look back. On landing, he acted as a scout.

The wives of the warriors met in the leaders' houses each day. They placed stones around to represent the canoe and sat within these boundaries in the same order as their husbands sat in the canoe, the wife of the bowman with her legs crossed, looking ahead. Suspended from their necks they wore *ta sate* [té se·t], "neck stone," with which they scratched themselves, for if one used her fingers, the arrow or spear of the enemy would penetrate the same spot on the body of her husband. They blackened their faces and carefully restrained from any levity. At the supposed time that the war party would camp and eat, they ate and then returned to their houses for the night. They continued this procedure until the war party returned. [The war party might include a shaman, who lay in the canoe, covered with his cedar-bark mat, and from time to time made ambiguous prophesies.]

[Tlingit youths and men were supposed to keep their bodies in condition for warfare and for the rigors they might encounter on any hunting expedition. This they did by bathing in cold water and switching their bodies. When war was imminent, this regimen was vigorously pursued.

[Veniaminov ([1840] 1984:418–19) wrote how such beatings were carried out. Before the Russians came and before the Tlingit had learned the deadly power of guns, they used to beat themselves "to demonstrate their bravery and to strengthen their body and spirit," but later this was done less often. The time for such beatings was on winter mornings, when the men would bathe in the sea. The house chief or oldest man would wait at the edge of the water to whip the emerging bathers with switches. The bravest man would present his chest first, and would be beaten until the leader tired, or another bather pushed him aside. In addition, brave men might cut their own chests and arms with sharp rocks or knives, and then go back to the water, where they would remain until numb. The cold of the water dulled the pain of the beatings and lacerations. But the *evening* beatings, when the men's bodies were warm from the fire, were much more severe and therefore more rare. This was done without prior warning, when the senior of the clan ordered the switches to be brought. As Veniaminov wrote (p. 419):

> An eyewitness told me that the evening flagellation is so dreaded that even the rustle of the switches being brought into the barabora [dwelling—Translator] makes the flesh of even the bravest creep because to refuse this torture, not to stand up and present oneself to the blows, means to become known as a coward; to acquire the fame of a brave man, on the other hand, is most unpleasant [*sic!*—FdeL]. In general, both kinds of flagellation are offered at one's own will. No one is ever compelled or called upon by name [to accept the ordeal and to endure it—Translator].

[A Yakutat story tells how a house chief at Controller Bay (Tribe XVII, Kaliakh) punished his little nephews when they hid in order to avoid the morning bath and beatings (de Laguna 1972:714–15, "The Female Shaman, Cak^{w}e [ša·k^{w}e], and the Chief who Stabbed His Nephews").]

Slain enemies were decapitated. If this occurred in a raid, the heads were put under the stern thwarts of the canoe. On approaching their home village, the warriors raised the heads on poles in the bow, while everyone stood and shouted, "Oh" eight times. As they neared the shore all sang. After landing, the poles with the heads were planted in front of the houses of the slayers. Later, the scalp, which included all the hair and the ears, was removed. It was treated with hot stones to remove the flesh, but was never tanned. It was preserved with the ceremonial garments and might be worn by one of the family upon par-

**Editor's note:* I have added the quotations from Veniaminov, Lisiansky, von Kotzebue, and Lütké.

ticular occasions. I examined some six scalps, all of men, for the Tlingit took neither the scalps of women nor of children. One was decorated with an ermine skin, another had squares of haliotis tied through holes in the ears. In later years the people did not like to show these trophies. They were considered too valuable and were displayed only upon special family occasions. A strange custom is said to have been practiced: the scalp of one of their own chiefs, killed in war, was removed and carefully preserved, and shown on the most important family occasions when great feasts were held and much property distributed. [Such scalp trophies apparently included those of great shamans; the scalps of unimportant enemies were not preserved.]

Prisoners taken in war were considered as slaves, but could be ransomed at any time for an agreed price.

On the return of the war party, besides displaying the heads of the slain on poles in the bow of the canoe, they indicated their own losses by lashing the paddles of the dead [upright] in their places in the canoe. As soon as the war party landed, they took a steam bath to cleanse themselves.

Except for cutting off the head, no other mutilations were practiced. The Tlingit had a horror of personal disfigurement. Even in their hand-to-hand duels, they delivered their blows only to the body, and this was also the case even in minor altercations. They never struck each other in the face. [Such blows precipitated the war between the Stikine and the Hutsnuwu in 1880.]

[Lisiansky (1814:238–39) wrote:

> Though the Sitca people are brave, they are extremely cruel to their prisoners, whom they torture to death, or consign to hard labour for life. Their cruelty is chiefly exercised against Europeans. If a European is so unfortunate as to fall into their hands, he will, in general, receive no mercy. On these occasions, men, women, and children, fall upon the poor wretch at once. Some make gashes in his flesh, others pinch or burn him, others cut off an arm or a leg, and others again scalp the head. This last cruelty is also practiced upon an enemy, when killed and left on the field of battle. It is performed by the shamans, who first cut the skin round the head, and then pull away the scalp by the hair. The head is then cut off and thrown away, or stuck up anywhere as a mark.

[Lisiansky added (p. 241) that the bodies of their own people who lose their lives in war, are burned, "except the head, which is preserved in a separate wooden box from that in which the ashes and bones are placed."

[Von Kotzebue, who was at Sitka in 1825, also noted some features of Tlingit warfare (1830, 2:54–56):

> The continual wars which the different races [tribes?] carry on against each other, with a ferocious cruelty uncommon even among savages, may account for the scanty population of this district; the fire-arms with which, to their own misfortune, they have been furnished by the American ships, have contributed to render their combats more bloody, and consequently to cause renewed and increased irritation. Bows and arrows were formerly their only weapons; now, besides their muskets, they have daggers, and knives half a yard long; they never attack their enemies openly, but fall suddenly upon them in moments of the utmost fancied security. The hope of booty, or of taking a prisoner, is a sufficient motive for one of these treacherous attacks, in which they practise the greatest barbarities; hence the Kalushes, even in time of peace, are always on their guard. They establish their temporary abodes on spots in some measure fortified by nature, and commanding an extensive view on all sides. During the night, the watch is confined to women, who, assembled round a fire outside the hut, amuse themselves by recounting the warlike deeds of their husbands and sons. [pp. 54–55]
>
> . . . The slaves are required to assist the women [in their domestic work], who often treat them in a most merciless manner. The females take an active part in the wars; they not only stimulate the valour of the men, but even support them in the battle.
>
> Besides the desire of booty, the most frequent occasion of warfare is revenge. One murder can only be atoned by another; but it is indifferent whether the murderer or one of his relations fall,—the custom merely requires a man for a man; should the murdered person be a female, a female is required in return. [pp. 55–56]

[Lütké, who was in Sitka two years later (in 1827), also reported on the Tlingit motives for war and on their conduct of hostilities (1835, 1:196–98, free translation):

> The quarrels of the Kaloches are, like those of all peoples, interior [domestic] and exterior [foreign]. We call the first *assaults* and the latter *wars*. But the Kaloches do not make this sharp distinction between them as we do. Women are usually the cause [of these fights].
>
> When Kaloches of two different tribes [clans] fight each other, and one of them, of one side or the other, is killed, his relatives demand compensation, and in case of a refusal by the other party, they call them to a public combat. Then they do not use firearms and are careful to make only wounds that are not mortal. If the offended party wins, then the other agrees to the payment which is always fixed by negotiation; in the opposite case, the first party, yielding to necessity, makes peace for a time, but only while waiting for the occasion to avenge blood with blood, which may not be until after several years.
>
> Revenge for injuries is the usual cause for the exterior quarrels of the Kaloches, though vanity and hope of booty also may sometimes play their part. If a Kaloche is killed in another village

than his own and by men of another tribe [clan], then the latter expect revenge and prepare themselves to repulse it. Those injured carefully hide their plans and their projects until they are able to execute them with success, and because of that they do not admit to their meetings and to their discussions the women who, linked to other villages by bonds of relationship, would not fail to warn their relatives of the danger which menaces them. When their preparations are entirely made, they set out in their canoes, and take care to reach the enemy village at dawn. Before the attack, they put on a cuirass of wooden slats strongly interlaced with whale sinew, which protects their breast and their back; they cover their faces with masks on which are carved the faces of monsters of terrifying aspect, and their heads with a thick wooden bonnet [helmet] covered with similar figures, the whole tied together by thongs. Falling suddenly upon the enemy, they kill without mercy all the men who are unable to escape, and take into slavery the women and children. From this moment the roles are reversed, and it is now the turn of the vanquished party to look for and await the chance of avenging themselves on the victors through the deaths of an equal number of theirs; and he who does not live until that day, leaves as heritage to his children [sororal nephews] the duty of revenge. It is exactly like the bloody vengeance of the Bedouins and of our mountain folk.

[Lütké's account seems to have been based, in part, on that by Khlebnikov ([1817–32] 1976:30–31), who distinguished between "intertribal" and "intratribal" wars. Khlebnikov also specified that armor was worn by members of a party attacking at dawn.]

ABORIGINAL ARMS AND ARMOR*

The primitive arms of the Tlingit, as described by the early explorers, were the bow and arrow, the spear, the club, and the dagger.

The bow, as far as can be determined from the oldest specimens collected, differs in no wise from the bow used for sea otter hunting up to 1900. [See Chapter 5, the section "Sea Otter Hunting." Its manufacture has been described in the section "Land Animal Hunting: Aboriginal Weapons," which also includes descriptions of native arrows, and the observations about these weapons made by eighteenth-century explorers.]

The arrow was of hemlock, spruce, or cedar. The few old specimens that have been collected may represent either those used for hunting or for war. They are very crude, consisting of rudely finished shafts, feathered at the nock, and tipped with heads of copper, mussel shell, or iron. These heads are leaf-shaped blades with long tangs for insertion in corresponding holes in the head of the shaft, or have the split rear end that is drawn together [over the wedge-shaped end of the shaft], and held in place with a sinew seizing. I do not believe that the bow and arrow were used as extensively in war as in hunting. Conflict was largely confined to personal contact with spear, club, or dagger, since warfare was carried on through surprises, ambuscades, and murders.

[The bow and arrow could, of course, have been used very successfully in daylight fighting when the enemy could be seen, but not in the dark, and most surprise attacks were made just before dawn. Furthermore, it is possible that the Tlingit felt that the valor of the warrior ought to be displayed in hand-to-hand conflict. Note that the bear was "fought" with spears when emerging from its den, not "hunted," and in this was treated like a human adversary.]

The same spear was used in war and in hunting, as can be judged from those found in the possession of the people as late as 1885. The spear consisted of a leaf-shaped blade of stone or metal, inserted in the end of a stout pole six or eight feet long.

[According to the Yakutat account of the war between the Sitka Ka·g^{w}a·nta·n and the Stikine Na·nyạ·ʔa·ỵí (de Laguna 1972:282), the hero cut down the shaft of his spear to make it handier for fighting.] A fine example of a stone spear blade was found at Chilkat. Metal blades, first of copper and later of iron, were similar in shape, but after the introduction of iron all others were discarded. The primitive spear, as described by the natives, consisted of a wooden shaft, the end hardened in the fire, like that observed by La Pérouse at Lituya Bay in 1786 (1799, 1:407). Marchand (Fleurieu 1801, 1:342) and Vancouver (1801, 4:136) gave the length of the spear as from sixteen to eighteen feet, but since the latter mentioned barbed points, the observation refers to the sea mammal and salmon spear, not the war spear. [The spears with which the Indians at Traitor's Cove threatened Vancouver's party were not described (Vancouver 1801, 4:171–73).] The spears reported by Dixon [Beresford 1789:244] for the Northwest Coast in general were "fixed to a pole six or eight feet long. . . ." The war or bear spear was thrust, but never cast. The longer seal or salmon spear was either thrust or cast. The spear alleged to have been used in the fight between the Sitka and the Stikine [collected by Emmons] is said to have been driven with such

**Editor's note:* Two versions by Emmons on arms had to be combined. I added information on spears from La Pérouse, Beresford, Marchand (in Fleurieu), and Vancouver, and also references to Hough and the latter's explanations of Tlingit armor.

Bow and arrows used in hunting land animals and in war. Bow collected by G. T. Emmons at Yakutat. The arrows, with iron points, are 35 inches long. Although they were in the cedar wood quiver, the latter would not have been carried on land. Collected by Fred Harvey at Yakutat. (MAI, Heye Foundation.)

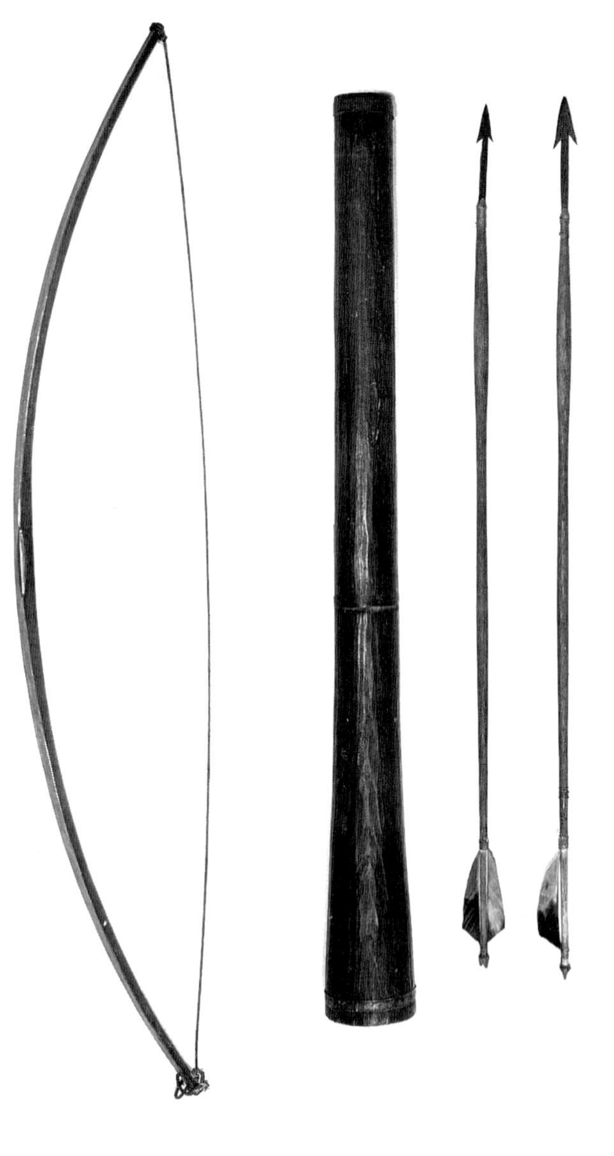

force that it passed through one man and impaled another Stikine with a single thrust. [Spears are discussed at greater length in Chapter 5, the section "Land Animal Hunting: Aboriginal Weapons."]

Clubs, ranging in material, shape, and size, were among the least common of all arms found [among the Tlingit in the late nineteenth century], which is not surprising, for, like the bow and arrow, they were discarded after the introduction of firearms. They are not mentioned by the early explorers in their descriptions of native arms. Two very rare [monolithic] stone specimens were found at the old Chilkat village of Klukwan. Although somewhat broken, the part missing in the one was intact in the other. The head [striking end] was carved to represent that of a raven, with sharp-pointed, projecting bill. Between this and the short handle was a broad lip-shaped [or axlike] blade. Such clubs were said to have been the property of a chief, and were carried concealed under his blanket, to be used in private attacks rather than in war. These two examples had been preserved as heirlooms, and were called ***qweese*** or ***qwuse*** [possibly x̣úṡ, the common name for "club"]. A commoner type of club, in the form of a pick, was known as ***kinda kha-too*** or ***ka-too*** [kínde ké·t̓u], "turned up," and consisted of a slightly curved, narrow blade of fine grained, hard stone, sometimes jade, that was hafted or set through the end of a short, stout wooden handle. This is said to have been a chief's weapon, used to kill slaves. The finest of these heads for ceremonial war clubs or slave-killers were rare, but have been found among the Tsimshian, Haida, and Tlingit, preserved as family heirlooms. They were made of the most homogeneous deep green mineral, finished throughout and highly polished. They were slightly curved, fifteen to seventeen inches in length, terminating in a dull point at the smaller end and a cutting edge at the other, being almost oval or hexagonal in cross section. Those of the Haida were lashed with hide to the end of the handle, not set through the wood as with Tsimshian and Tlingit specimens.

Among the Tlingit have been found a few stone club heads, grooved around the middle and pointed at each end, resembling the Plains war club head in form, except that they were flattened at the sides [see de Laguna et al. 1964, pl. 5*c*]. It is generally believed that these were procured in trade from the interior. None of them has ever been found hafted.

The stone maul, used in general woodworking, and very often carved in the form of an animal head at one end [see de Laguna et al. 1964, fig. 21 *d*], is said by the older natives to have been also used as a war club in an emergency.

Short heavy clubs of bone, carved in conventional animal designs similar to those on seal or fish clubs, were sometimes used. Metal clubs appear to be rare. A very beautiful copper specimen from the southern part of Prince of Wales Island, whether Tlingit or Haida [Kaigani], represents a very old type. Its broad swordlike blade is notched along the striking edge; the butt end of the handle termi-

Maul, pick, and clubs. (AMNH.) (a) Stone maul with wooden handle, for ordinary use. (b) War pick with jade head. (c) War club of elk or caribou antler, from the interior. (d) Old war club, of stone, carved to represent a raven, from Klukwan. Emmons has sketched in the broken bill. (Not to scale.)

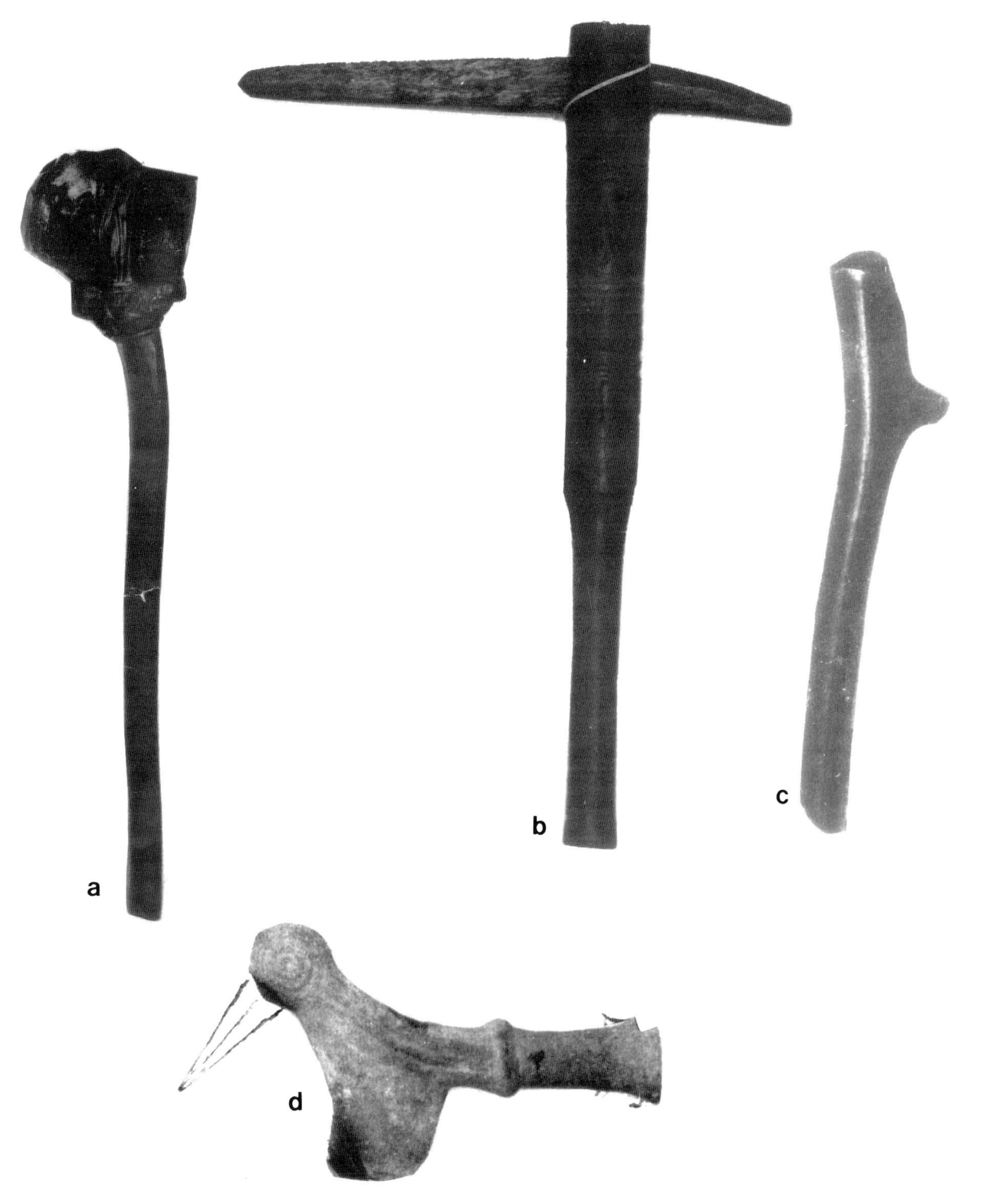

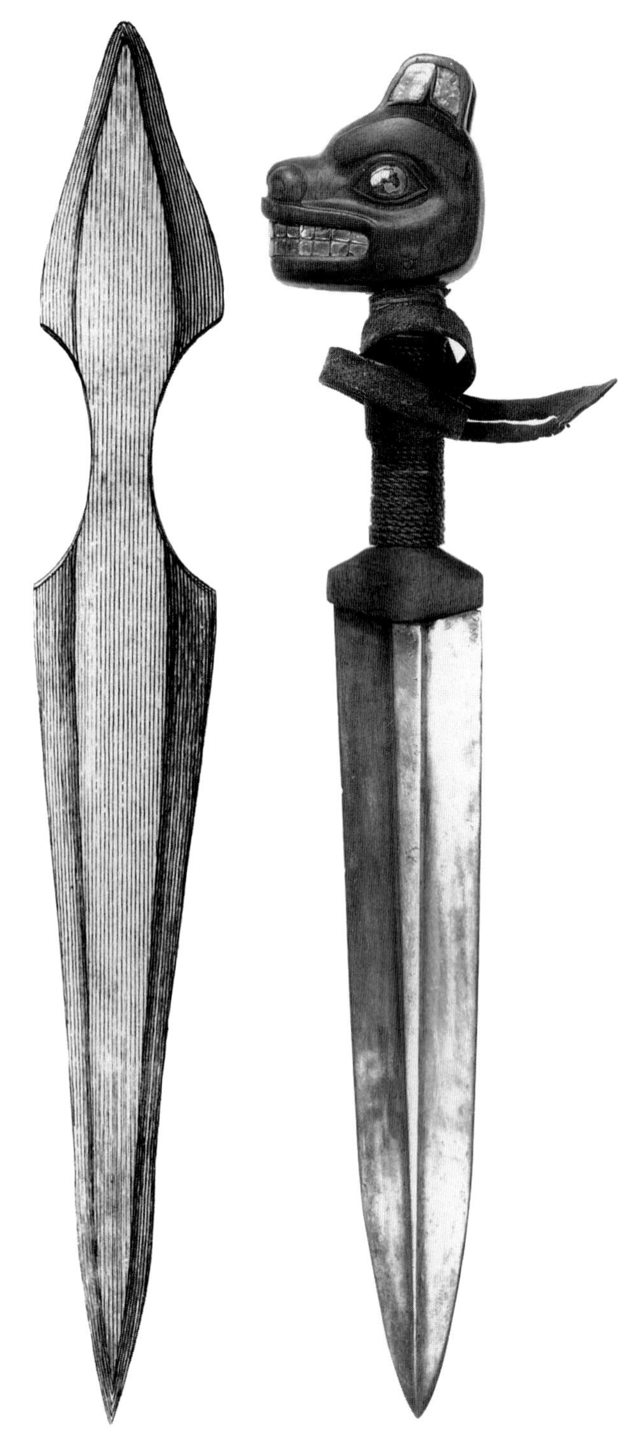

Left. *Iron dagger from Port Mulgrave, Yakutat, 1787. (Beresford 1789, pl. opp. p. 188. Courtesy of the Bancroft Library, University of California, Berkeley.)* Right. *Tlingit dagger collected at "Kootznahoo" (Killisnoo or Angoon), Admiralty Inlet, by J. J. McLean, 1881. (USNM.)*

nates in an eagle head. On an old mortuary column at the Henya village of Tuxekan, on the west coast of Prince of Wales Island, is carved a human figure holding such a type of club. Elk and caribou horn clubs were more frequently found and were unquestionably procured in trade from the interior people since these animals were not found on the coast. When such clubs were ornamented, the geometric designs were clearly Athabaskan. Of heavy two-handed clubs, two or three examples were collected [by Emmons]. One is of whale bone in a rich yellow-brown color, polished from long use. The other, of wood, is much longer and heavier, and was ornamentally carved in conventional animal designs on both sides in low relief. Both clubs are oval in cross section and must have been most effective weapons in the hands of a powerful man against an opponent in Northwest Coast armor.

The general name for club was *khootz* [x̣úṡ]. [For discussions of war picks and war clubs at Yakutat, see de Laguna 1972:588–89].

The commonest weapon, possessed by every Tlingit man, and particularly noticed by early visiting Europeans, was the dagger. This was a double-bladed knife, pointed at each end and sharpened on both edges, fifteen or more inches long. The upper blade was about a third or fourth the length of the lower; the grip between them was wrapped with hide, twisted root, bark, or braided human hair. Secured or seized to it was a hide strap. When the knife was grasped, the strap was wrapped twice around the wrist and the middle finger was passed through a slit near the end, so securing the weapon to the hand that it could not be dropped, and even in death it could not be snatched away. The sheath, which was suspended from the neck by a broad band, was of heavy hide (moose or other animal), the lower end seized to or around a hollowed-out guard of ivory, horn, or wood, that covered the point of the [lower] blade. The sheath for the upper blade was secured to the main case by a length of hide with sufficient play to allow it to be slipped off. I collected two stone knives of this type. One of slate, the smaller specimen, with double blades, was procured from an old Chilkat shaman of Klukwan, and was highly valued [by the natives] because of its antiquity. A much larger specimen, more representative in form and proportion, was excavated in an old house site at Angoon, Admiralty Island. Copper, and later, iron, was substituted for stone, and with increased proficiency in metal working, the lower blade was ridged or fluted and the upper was cut and shaped in conventional totemic animal figures and inlaid with haliotis shell. Such knives were important as

Daggers for war. (AMNH.) (a and b) Old type of war knife, 15 inches or more long, with a blade at each end. (c) More recent type with crest design on handle. (d) More recent type. (e through h) More recent type with separate blade and handle, the latter of wood or bone, with crest designs.

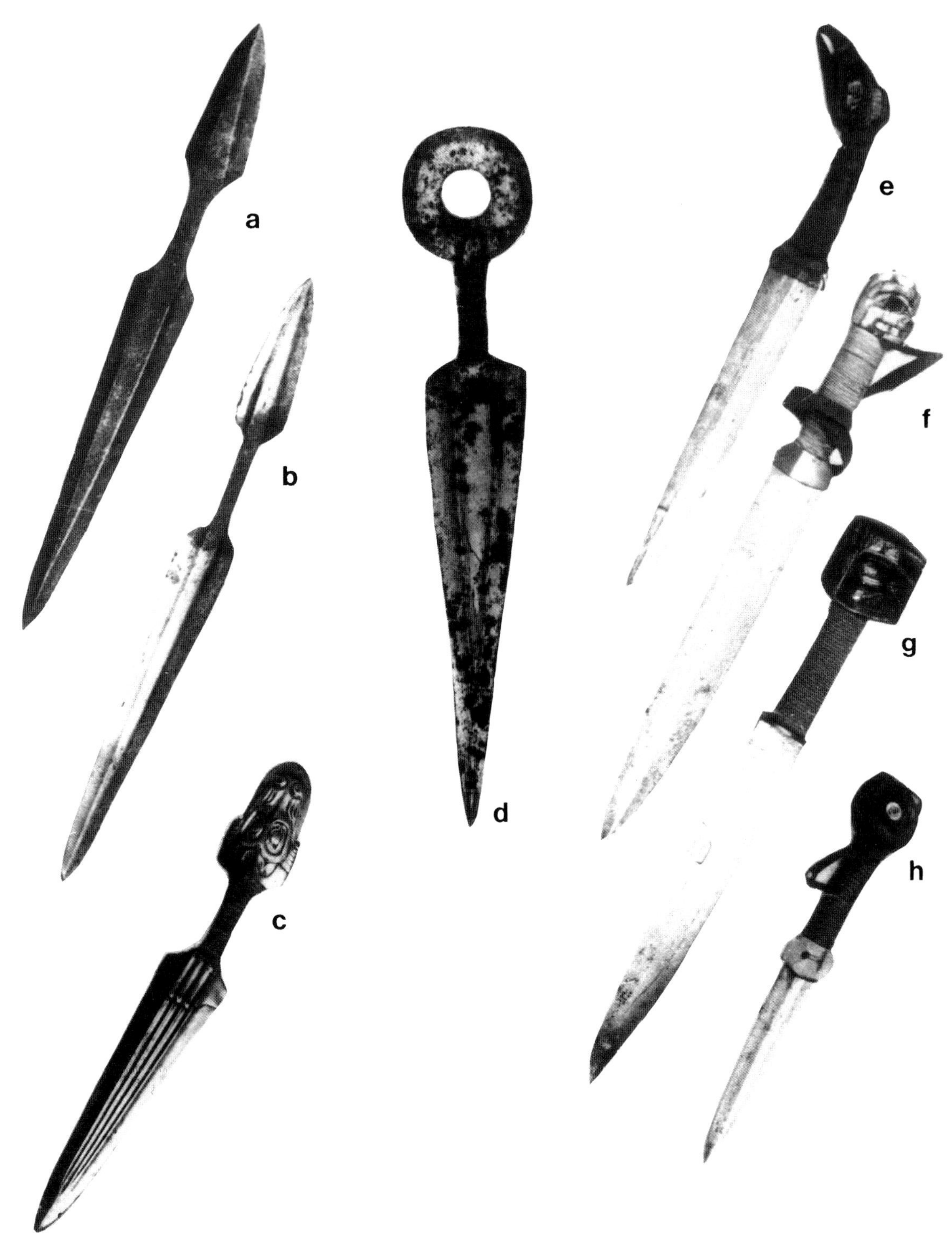

clan property that passed from a chief to his successor, and they might be kept in specially made wooden boxes. [Usually, however,] they were worn throughout the day and hung by the bed at night, and so were called *chuck-har-nut,* "right by me, always ready" [ǯix̣an?át, "thing near the hand." Another name for the double-bladed dagger was šak'áč.]

A more recent type of knife, *quoth-lar,* "to strike with the fist" [gwáɬa·, from -gwáɬ, "to strike"], had a single blade, the place of the upper blade being taken by a head of wood, bone, or ivory, carved in animal or human form and elaborately ornamented with opercula, haliotis, or copper. Sometimes the hide strap at the grip was replaced by a hide loop through which the hand was slipped. The sheath and the band that suspended the knife from the neck were of elaborately beaded cloth.

[Personal names were given to daggers and knives, and also to firearms, like the names given to houses and canoes, designating the clan totem. An example from Angoon, was kí·t· gwáɬa·, "Killerwhale Dagger." See Holm 1983, fig. 167.]

The Tlingit warrior was well protected against the dagger, spear, or bow and arrow, by armor which covered his body completely, though it was cumbersome and greatly impeded the movements of the wearer. It consisted of a helmet and wooden collar that protected the head and neck, and sleeveless coats of heavy hide, some of which reached just to or just below the hips, and some extended to below the knee. These coats were sometimes reinforced by a wooden slat or rod cuirass that covered the body, while greaves of slats or heavy hide boots or leggings extended from knee to foot. After the use of firearms became general, such armor was gradually discarded, for Lisiansky stated that even in 1804 the defensive masks or helmets, formerly worn in war, were then used principally at festivals, and that iron plates were used over the breast as a protection against musket balls [Lisiansky 1814:149–50, 238, pl. I *a, b, c*]. The head piece, often made of a tree knot or root, was generally carved like a human or animal face, painted, inlaid with shell, or decorated with copper or real hair. It fitted over a fur cap, worn for comfort, and was secured under the chin with hide straps. It rested on a wooden collar which covered the neck and the face to the height of the eyes. The collar was likewise ornamented. On its upper edge, at the level of the eyes, shallow grooves were cut out to enable the wearer to see. The collar was held in place by a loop of twisted bark or hide, or by a toggle held between the teeth. This collar was formed from a single heavy piece of wood, first shaped [inside and out], then cut on the inside perpendicularly in triangular grooves an inch or more apart, steamed and bent, and the ends drawn together with hide lashings; when cool it retained its shape. [The helmet was called ɬu·wú šada·, "wooden headpiece," but the word for the collar is not recorded.]

The body armor, *ne-art* or *khe-ka,* is named for the hip which it protects. [Possibly the first word is niya·?át, "protecting thing."] This consists of one or more thicknesses of sea lion, elk, moose, or caribou hide, and may also be called *sun-kate* [sanke·t, the common, general term for armor]. In one instance it was made of walrus skin. [See Hough 1895, pls. 16 through 19, and 22.] The outer piece was made of a single skin folded over, the shoulder pieces sewed or attached with toggles, leaving a hole for the head and the left arm. The edges meeting down the right side were fastened together with tie strings, loops, or slit bands and toggles, thus leaving both arms free. The unbroken left side that was presented to the enemy, particularly in duels with the knife, gave perfect protection to the wearer. Extra shoulder flaps were sometimes attached. The inner pieces were not always continuous, but were sewed with sinew or tied with hide to protect the more vulnerable parts and at the same time to give flexibility. In front, the armor extended in a curve below the stomach, and was cut out on either side to leave the legs free. The back was square across the bottom. Some pieces enveloped the whole body, reaching below the knees. Totemic figures were sometimes painted on the outside of the front, and again on one of the inside folds where they did not show. The edges of the right side were often fringed. Some pieces were decorated with horizontal bands of split colored porcupine quillwork, ornamentation that indicates an interior origin, as the Tlingit were not given to such work. [In a catalogue of the collection sold by Emmons to AMNH in 1888, he has listed under no. 1210, "Armor of skin-Kehk keh"—belonged to the chief of the "Tuck-tan-ton" (Raven 16)—Hoonah kow—but represented by him to have originally come from the Copper River country . . ." with ornamentation of porcupine quills.]

Worn with the hide were two kinds of wooden armor, one a jacketlike cuirass, *wonda* [wanda·, "about the edge"], and the other a broad rectangle of narrow rods, *sinkate,* literally "waist-apron," or *sun-kate* [sanke·t; Emmons also gave this word for leather armor made of elk skin]. The former [wanda·] was neatly constructed of slats, or of slats and rods combined, of the hardest wood available [see Hough 1895, pls. 6, 7 and 8, from Sitka]. These slats were drawn together with finely twisted strands of sinew in twined weaving. The front and back were separate, fastened to each other with hide ties; and narrow bands of

A warrior of Port Mulgrave, Yakutat, 1791. Redrawn from a sketch by Tomás Suría. (Wagner 1936, pl. II.)

similar slats at the top, front, and rear, were attached with a hide lacing. In front, the shape corresponded with that of the hide armor, but a V-shaped projection extended below the center of the bottom to protect the stomach and genitals, and was cut away on each side to allow free action of the legs. The back was straight [across the bottom], with the lower corners beveled. The slats were pared down in the wake of the weaving [inside or between the bands of twining], which did not cover the whole surface but was in a broad upper and lower horizontal band, and enclosed a certain number of slats on either side, leaving a plain square or rectangular space, front and back, that was ornamentally painted. Hide bands or straps passing over the shoulders held the cuirass in place. In some pieces, small rods were combined on the sides that made it more flexible. Early explorers describe this as being worn both [either] inside and [or] outside of the hide armor, and possibly it might be used alone.

In 1883 I procured at the old village of *Suska* [Ṡú·ṡ-ka, "on the turnstone," i.e., Port Mulgrave village, Khantaak Island], at Yakutat, a complete suit of armor of heavy hide, with the slat cuirass fitted and secured between the two folds of hide, so this is absolute proof that it [the cuirass] was so used. As to its being used over the outside fold of the hide, we can take only the rather indefinite statement of Maurelle that a skin robe was worn over the cuirass (see below).

The other type of wooden armor, *sinkate,* referring to the waist ["waist" is kasán; ke·t is "cover"; sanke·t is "armor"], consisted of a number of small wooden rods laced together with horizontal bands of fine sinew thread or two-stranded twisted cord of mountain goat wool, rectangular in form, with tie strings in the middle of each side. Several of the middle rods are bunched, while the rest of the rods are flexible. How this was worn the oldest natives did not know, but it appears that it was secured about the waist outside of the skin jacket. This type was, I believe, of interior origin and make, as the few pieces known can be referred to the Taku people about the mouth of the Taku River who were in intimate relations with their interior relatives [see Hough 1895, pl. 13].

At least two types of greaves for the protection of the leg from the knee to the instep have been collected. These are of slats like the cuirass. The finest specimen, in the U.S. National Museum, is of slats and rods combined, bound together with twisted sinew thread, cut out below the knee and beveled on the inside here and at the instep [Hough 1895, pl. 10 from Taku]. The other, cruder and more modern, was of slats secured together by means of wires through holes in the sides.

A more modern type of hide armor was in the form of a waistcoat with collar sewn on with sinew. It was fastened in front with cut straps [tabs with button holes] and buttons. Several of these vests have been found with perpendicular rows of Chinese or Japanese coins sewed on with sinew or hide. On some, the coins are made to overlap in each perpendicular row. This type came unquestionably after the Russian occupation, when Russian [European, and American] vessels traded with China and brought the brass coins to Alaska. [A "waistcoat" of three layers of tanned hide, closed with English sailors' brass buttons, and a second, similar vest, with Chinese coins in vertical rows down the front and over the shoulders, and English brass buttons, were collected in 1870 at Sitka (Hough 1895, pl. 21 *1, 2*).]

Hide armor, slat armor, and greaves were often painted in totemic design.

ARMS, ARMOR, AND TACTICS, DESCRIBED BY THE EARLY EXPLORERS*

[The descriptions given by early explorers of spears and bows and arrows used in fighting have been quoted and discussed in Chapter 5, sections on "Sea Otter Hunting" and "Land Animal Hunting," and in Chapter 7, sections on "Work in Copper" and "Work in Iron." The equipment of the Tlingit warrior that most impressed these observers and of which they often procured specimens were the daggers and the suits of armor.

[Father Riobo (in Thornton 1918:224), who was among the Klawak of Bucareli Bay in 1779, reported:

> The Indians have a kind of armor something like that of the ancients with buckler and spear; they have even protection for their thighs and legs, very skilfully made from pieces of hard wood joined and fastened together with a kind of very strong cord. On their heads they carry the figure of a ferocious beast rather skilfully and artfully carved from wood. They are extremely fond of iron of which they possess many lances and knives. [Some lances had] a spear head twenty-four inches in length. . . . The knives are short with double cutting edges like a carpenter's plane.

[Mourelle (in La Pérouse 1799, 1:247), who was also on the same expedition, mentioned the lances and knives with iron blades, and described the armor at greater length:

**Editor's note:* I compiled this section in order to carry out what I have interpreted as Emmons's own intentions.

In war these Indians wear cuirasses and shoulder-pieces, made not unlike the whalebone stays of European ladies. Very narrow slips of wood form the warp of these, and threads the woof, so that the whole is very flexible, and gives the arms sufficient liberty for handling their weapons. Round the neck they wear a gorget covering them up to the eyes; and their head is defended by a morion, usually made of the head of some ferocious animal. From the girdle to the feet, they wear a kind of apron, of the same manufacture as their cuirasses: and lastly they have a fine skin* hanging from the shoulder almost to the knee. The armour is impenetrable to the arrows of the enemy; but with such an encumbrance they cannot change their position so readily as if they were less loaded. [There is a footnote: "*The manuscript has *quera,* which I do not believe is a Spanish word; and I suppose we should read *cuera,* the name of a kind of garment of leather."—Translator]

La Pérouse (1799, 1:369), at Lituya Bay in 1786, noted:

Every one had a dagger of it [iron] suspended from the neck, not unlike the criss of the Malays, except that the handle was different, being nothing more than an elongation of the blade, rounded, and without any edge [i.e., it was single-bladed]. This weapon had a sheath of tanned leather, and appeared to be their most valued moveable. As we examined these daggers very attentively, they informed us by signs, that they made use of them only against the bears and other wild beasts. [The Indians were trying to allay any fears which the Frenchmen might have of them, for later (p. 397) La Pérouse remarked of the Indians: "Choleric and prompt to take offence, I have seen them continually with the poignard unsheathed against each other" [clearly indicating that the dagger was used in combat].

[The Tlingit of Lituya Bay evidently had armor, although La Pérouse did not describe it, because, he wrote (1799, 1:372) that in order to demonstrate the superiority of the French weapons:

. . . I fired a cannon, to show them, that I could reach them at a distance, and pierced with a musket-ball, in the presence of a great number of Indians, several doubles of a cuirass they had sold us, after they had informed us by signs that it was impenetrable to arrows or poignards.

In describing the natives' costumes, La Pérouse (1799, 1:401) mentioned that the Indians "sometimes wear on their heads caps with two horns, eagle's feathers, and entire heads of bears fitted on a skull-cap of wood." The last suggests the wooden helmet.

[Beresford (1789:244, pl. opp. p. 188, figs. 3 and 4), who was with Dixon on the Northwest Coast in 1787, was probably referring to the Tlingit of Yakutat Bay and Sitka Sound when he wrote:

Besides the skin coats and cloaks wore in common, they have large coats purposely for war, made of the elk skin, tanned, and wore double, sometimes threefold. Their weapons are spears fixed to a pole six or eight feet long, and a kind of short dagger, which is wore in a leather case, and tied round the body: to this dagger a leather thong is fastened, at the end of which is a hole for the middle finger, the leather is afterwards twisted round the wrist, in order to fix the dagger firm in the hand; so that the warrior loses his weapon only with his life. [Two daggers, presumably of metal (iron?), were illustrated from Port Mulgrave: the first with two double-edged blades, the second with a single blade, and the handle ending in two divergent prongs, like ears.]

[Portlock (1789:260–61), who was on the Northwest Coast the same year, saw similar daggers at Portlock Harbor. The Sitkans there indicated to him that they had fought with the Chugach Eskimo of Prince William Sound and with the natives of Cook Inlet (Tanaina or Kenai Peninsula Eskimo?). They had daggers they had bought at *Wallamute* (i.e., from the Eyak-speakers of the Kaliakh-Controller Bay area, the *Qwelthyet Kwan,* or tribe XVII, of Emmons).

The daggers which the people hereabouts [Portlock Harbor] use in battle are made to stab at either end, having three, four, or five inches above the hand tapered to a sharp point; but the upper part of those used in the [Prince William] Sound and River [Cook Inlet] is excurvated [i.e., the handle ends in two spiral (?) ears].

[Colnett in 1787 was the first of the explorers and traders to sketch native armor (see Chapter 7, in the section "Coppers"). Although this was among the southernmost Haida of "Port St. James," their armor seems to have been similar to that worn by the Tlingit. Thus he mentioned (*Journal* 1786–88):

. . . wooden stays, & Leather Jackets which are made like a Wagoner's Frock & of thickness sufficient to protect their Bodies from spears & arrows; [they] have great Confidence of their security when dressed in them; from what Animal they procure this Leather Armour it is hard to say.

The "wooden stays" represented the usual suit of slat armor, which he sketched as opened out: straight across the top edge, but scalloped along the bottom to give play to the wearer's legs. It was painted, on the front and back, with an anthropomorphic face. The "copper" that he sketched he identified as their "under armour." The natives, he reported, believed in "their superiority of arms & armour, frequently shewing me their Bows & spears of twenty foot Long, with Iron fix'd in them. . . ." This was before they had discovered the efficacy of muskets and cannon.

Wooden helmet, originally with an 8-inch plume, carved to represent a man with partial facial paralysis (probably Bell's palsy). Collected by G. T. Emmons at Dry Bay, before 1887. (AMNH.)

[Suría, the artist with Malaspina at Yakutat in 1791, not only described the outfit of the Tlingit warrior but sketched such a fully accoutered brave (Wagner 1936:255–56, pl. III; de Laguna 1972:586–87, pl. 51). He wrote:

> The fighting Indians wear all their arms, a breast-plate, back armor, a helmet with a visor or at least what serves that purpose. The breast and back armor are a kind of coat of mail of boards two fingers thick, joined by a thick cord which after being *berbirlis* [twined, twisted?] by *as* [front] and *embes* [back] with much union and equality joins them. In this junction the thread takes an opposite direction, it being the case that even here the arrows cannot pass through, much less in the thickest part of the boards. This breast plate is bound to the body by the back. They wear an apron or armor from the waist to the knees of the same character which must hinder their walking. Of the same material they cover the arm from the shoulder to the elbow, on the legs they use some leggings which reach to the middle of the thigh, the hair inside. They construct the helmet of various shapes; usually it is a piece of wood, very solid and thick, so much so, that when I put on one it weighed the same as if it had been of iron. They always have a great figure in front, a young eagle or a kind of parrot[!], and to cover the face they lower from the helmet a piece of wood which surrounds this and hangs from some pieces of leather in the middle of the head to unite with another one which comes up from the chin. They join at the nose, leaving the junction for the place through which to see. It is to be noted that before they put this armor on they put on a robe like that of the women but heavier and thicker, and with certain kinds of work. [The skin robe hangs to the ankles.] They hang *catucas* [quivers] and the bow they put over the arm to which it hangs back of the shoulders. They clasp a short lance, a knife, and a hatchet. Such is the equipment of a warrior. The lance is a heavy stick of black wood, very well worked, and at the point they tie on the blade of a great knife which they obtain from Englishmen in exchange for their skins. The knife which they carry in their belt is the same as ours for the same reason. The hatchet is a black stone of the size, figure, and edge of our iron hatchet. They fasten it to a heavy stick and make use of it in war and in their other necessities. The bows and arrows are the same as those of all other Indians. All this I know because an Indian who armed himself for us to see it, pointed it all out to us by signs.

[The helmet, as sketched by Suría, seems to have had a tuft of feathers or fur at the top, and is carved to represent a human face. The sleeves of the robe reached the wrists and the fringed hem the ankles. The dagger in its skin sheath is shown hung from a strap that passed over the right shoulder, ready to the left hand; in battle it was tied to the left wrist. Malaspina collected at least four suits of armor at Port Mulgrave, Yakutat. The Indians evidently also had hide armor, for one man tried to make his impervious to shots by soaking it in water and was angry when the Spanish demonstrated that their bullets could pierce it.

[The next year, 1792, Baranov's party in Prince William Sound were attacked by a war party of Indians from Yakutat and from the Kaliakh-Controller Bay area. These Indians were prepared to face musket fire and apparently attacked with daggers or possibly spears. Baranov described the fight in a letter to Shelikov, July 24, 1793 (Tikhmenev [1863, II], 1979:29, translation by Krenov. See de Laguna 1972:587 for translations of the same passage by Petroff and by Ginsberg.).

> During the darkest hours of the night, before daybreak, we were surrounded by a great number of armed men. They began to stab and cut down the natives who were with me. They also stabbed two of us when we jumped up from sleep. We had 5 sentries out, but the natives came up so stealthily in the darkness that we saw them only when they began to stab at our tents. They were about 10 paces from us, but we shot at them without any result because they had on thick armor made of three or four layers of hardwood and sinews, and on top of that had heavy mantles made of moose hides. On their heads they had thick helmets with the figures of monsters [crest animals?] on them, and neither our buckshot nor our bullets could pierce their armor. In the dark, they seemed to us worse than devils. The majority of them kept a perfect order, advancing toward us and listening to commands given by one voice [one man?—Translator] and only a part of them ran back and forth doing damage to us [Russians—Translator] and to the natives in our party. [The Russians had one cannon with them, and were able to hold off

> the enemy for two hours until daybreak, when reenforcements were sent to Baranov from Izmailov onboard ship nearby. The natives with Baranov could not penetrate the enemy's armor with their spears and arrows. When the Tlingit and Eyak fled, Baranov took two complete outfits of armor from the dead and wounded who were abandoned in the retreat.]

[One is impressed by the preparation, strategy, and discipline of the Tlingit and Eyak, who at first mistook the Russian party for their enemies, the Chugach, but bravely continued the attack even after they discovered their mistake. They were expecting reinforcements in the form of ten more canoes from the Copper River, and after exterminating the Chugach had planned to go on to Cook Inlet. In their retreat, they managed to carry away four Chugach hostages that Baranov had taken, as well as most of their wounded (Tikhmenev [1863, II] 1979:30).

[Captain Marchand, who was at Sitka Sound in 1791, observed Tlingit weapons, but has left us no description of their armor (Fleurieu 1801, 1:342):

> The Tchinkitanayans are all armed with a metal dagger, fifteen or sixteen inches long, from two and a half to three broad, terminated in a point, and sharp on both sides: this is the weapon which they are the most careful to preserve, and which they take a pleasure in keeping polished and bright: a grenadier is not more proud of his sabre, than a Tchinkitanayan is of his dagger; he wears it in a shoulder-belt, in a leather scabbard, and is never without it, either day or night. It is with this weapon, which never ought to have been turned against our fellow-creatures, that sometimes he engages the bear in close combat, and rips open its belly when the furious animal is ready to stifle him in its paws. It is not known how long this dagger, which originally must have been of hard wood, has been made of a metal the use of which man has not limited to his wants and conveniences, but which, in his hands, is become, for his species, the instrument of destruction.

[The passage continues (pp. 342–44) with a description of iron-tipped "pikes" and "lances," a mention of the adz, bow and arrow, and a clear indication that the Indians were already receiving their first muskets.

[In 1793, Vancouver (1801, 4:136–37) and his boat parties encountered several canoes of natives, Sanya or Niska (Tsimshian-speakers) in Observatory Inlet, on the present Alaska-Canada border:

> Their weapons seemed well adapted to their condition; their spears, about sixteen feet long, were pointed with iron, wrought in several simple forms, amongst which some were barbed [for fish and seals]. Their bows were well constructed, and their arrows, with which they were plentifully supplied, appeared but rude, and were pointed with bone or iron. Each man was provided with an iron dagger, suspended from his neck in a leather sheath, seemingly intended to be used when in close action. Their war garments were formed of two, three, or more folds, of the strongest hides of the land animals they are able to procure. In the centre was a hole sufficient to admit the head and left arm to pass through; the mode of wearing them being over the right shoulder, and under the left arm. The left side of the garment is sewed up, but the right side remains open; the body is however tolerably well protected, and both arms are left at liberty for action. As a further security on the part which covers the breast, they sometimes fix on the inside thin laths of wood; the whole is seemingly well contrived, and I doubt not answers the essential purpose of protection against their native weapons.

[This party of natives had apparently come from the vicinity of the Niska settlement of Kincolith in two canoes, ready to trade some very poor sea otter skins, to pilfer, or to fight. Their faces were painted in red, black, and white; they had with them a woman with an enormous labret, who apparently steered one of the canoes. One Indian, who seemed to be very influential, if not the leader, had six or eight spears which he arranged in menacing fashion in the bow, with bow and arrows near by. When he rejected the articles offered by Vancouver in trade (1801, 4:134), he

> put on his war garment, and drew his dagger. Some in the other canoe made similar preparations, either to menace an attack, or, what seemed to us more likely, to convince us they were upon their guard against any violence we might be inclined to offer them.

Eventually they were willing to accept the trade goods offered them, and Vancouver came to the opinion that they had been offended by his refusal to visit their village. They put aside their arms and war garments, traded peaceably, then began to pilfer, until Vancouver signaled that they should leave, which they did reluctantly. (For the whole account of this episode, see Vancouver 1801, 4:133–37, here summarized as indicative of native tactics.)

[A few days later, Vancouver's parties encountered another group of the same tribe (?) in Portland Canal (1801, 4:140–43). The first meetings with the small number of Indians were friendly; the chief gave them some sea otter tails in return for gifts; but the next day Vancouver and his men were visited by a second large canoe as well as by the first, and the natives now refused all trade goods, demanding fire-arms and ammunition, which were not given them. The second canoe was steered by an authoritative woman with an impressive labret, who took the lead in rejecting the profferred trade goods, and directed a man in the bow to arrange his dozen spears in two groups, one on each side of him, but no further aggressive move was made.

[The most dramatic encounter with the Indians during that survey occurred at Traitors Cove, on the western arm of Behm Canal (Vancouver 1801, 4:169–83). This area, according to Olson (1967:4), once belonged to the Kiksʔádi, or Raven 10 of the Stikine, but was later given to the X̣e·ł-qʷá·n ("Foam Tribe"), or Wolf 31. Probably the latter were the Indians involved in the fracas, for they had not yet moved from Behm Canal to Wrangell. The Indians, at first in small numbers, seemed interested only in peaceful trade; then more canoes joined the first few that were crowded around the yawl, forcing Vancouver to order his boat off from the shore where he had been attempting to make observations. The other boat of his party, the launch, was some distance away. Four or five Indian canoes, one steered by an old woman with a very large labret, pressed around the yawl; the old woman snatched up the lead line and lashed her canoe to the boat,

> whilst a young man, appearing to be the chief of the party, seated himself in the bow of the yawl, and put on a mask resembling a wolf's face, compounded with the human countenance. [Was this really a war helmet? The Wolf crest would seem to identify the wearer as X̣e·ł-Te·qʷe·dí, as the X̣e·ł-qʷá·n, or Wolf 31, were also called.] [p. 171]

When Vancouver advanced with his musket to force the young chief back into his canoe, "the surrounding Indians, about fifty in number, seized their daggers, brandished their spears, and pointed them towards us in all directions" (p. 171).

[Twice the Indians seemed to lay down their arms, but again took them up, urged on by the old woman, while an old man seized all the oars on one side of the yawl. As soon as Vancouver turned toward the bow:

> the Indians near the stern of the boat became very troublesome; and, as I was passing back along the boat, a general commotion seemed to have taken place; some spears were thrust, one or two of which passed very near me, and the Indians, in all directions, began to seize all the moveables in our boat that they could possibly reach, and to commit other acts of violence. [They had already stolen at least one loaded gun, and now took possession of most of the firearms in the yawl.] [pp. 171–73]

Vancouver was sure that had not the launch come within pistol shot at this time, he and his men would have been lost. Now, however, he ordered both boats to fire on the Indians, which effectively routed them.

> Those in the small canoes jumped into the sea, whilst those in the larger ones, by getting all on one side, raised the opposite sides of their canoes, so that they were protected from the fire of the yawl, though they were in some measure exposed to that of the launch; and in this manner they scrambled sideways to the shore. [pp. 173–74]
>
> The Indians, on reaching the shore, ascended the high rocky cliffs of which it is composed, and from whence they endeavoured to annoy those in the launch by stones, some of which fell into her at the distance of thirty or forty yards from the shore, and from whence also they fired a musket. [p. 175]

[Vancouver believed that they had not only the firearms they had stolen but also ones of their own, but that these were at first not loaded (or were defective). One at least had misfired when the trigger was snapped, and Vancouver had understood from the first Indians met that they had been sold defective guns by white traders. Had the attack been planned for retaliation? For it had evidently been planned, either when the English boats were first sighted or later when the English forbearance was mistaken for fear, or their lack of defensive preparations were interpreted by the Indians, correctly, as "want of caution."

[The boat maneuvers of the Indians are worth noting. Both the main large canoe that attacked the yawl and the similar canoe that attacked the launch were steered and commanded by authoritative women; each was attempting to immobilize the boat under attack by putting her canoe across the boat's bow. The first woman was successful, and held the yawl by lashing her canoe to it, but the second was frightened off by menaces with a musket. The trick of tipping the canoe in order to shelter behind the raised side must have been a maneuver practiced often against enemy arrows. Vancouver also noted that the Indians who had been, near the launch were so anxious to come quickly to the yawl, ostensibly to trade, that they threw overboard their dogs (this is the first specific mention that dogs were carried in such canoes).

[While two of Vancouver's men were dangerously wounded by spears, some of the Indians were hit by gunfire. They were seen to fall as if dead or severely wounded, and great lamentations were heard from the Indians retreating into the woods. Later these same Indians, encountering Vancouver's Lieutenant Whidbey in the large cutter, attempted to make peace in a ceremonial fashion (pp. 217–19), suggestive of the Peace Ceremony (see below).

[The following year, 1794, Lieutenant Whidbey encountered and escaped from a Chilkat war party in Lynn Canal (Vancouver 1801, 5:429–35). The tactics were similar. At first there was only one canoe, with a friendly, courteous chief who exchanged gifts with Lieutenant Whidbey, and followed the latter's boats. The next morning, more and more canoes of armed natives appeared, until there were at least five large canoes as well as a few smaller ones, with upward of two hundred Indians. This flotilla was commanded by three chiefs, and the five large canoes were each steered by an aristocratic woman. As the warlike intentions of these Indians became apparent, the canoes split up to go against the three English boats, to prevent them from joining together or escaping. The Indians were well armed, for in one large canoe the men

> were well provided not only with spears, but with seven muskets, and some brass blunderbusses, all in most excellent order. [The chief in it had a speaking trumpet with which he hailed the yawl, and a spyglass in the other hand. He also had a clean bright blunderbuss and powder horn.] . . . [B]eside the arms already mentioned, each man was provided with a short handy dagger, very conveniently tied round his wrist. Had they with these weapons assailed our boats, and got possession of them in the night by surprize, which was evidently what had been meditated, their project might possibly have been attended with serious consequences, if they had possessed sufficient courage to have maintained a contest. . . . [p. 433]

[The Indians' plans were defeated by the vigilance of Whidbey and his men, and the Indians were afraid to attack them when the three boats halted to await their assault. The whole party of Indians followed the boats for several miles before they gave up. On this occasion, no mention was made of armor or of bows and arrows.

[On that same trip, Lieutenant Whidbey also had trouble with the Auk (Vancouver 1801, 6:22–23). He had to fire on the canoes that were following his boats, and apparently hit the largest,

> . . . as the Indians all fell back in the canoe, and were quite out of sight; they, however, managed to bring their canoe's stern in a line with the boat's [*sic*] sterns: in that situation they paddled backwards with all their strength, and at the same time screened every part of their persons, by the height and spreading of their canoes' bows, excepting their hands, which, in the act of paddling only became visible, so very judiciously did they provide for their safety in their flight. . . .

To use the protection of the bow of a canoe must have been a common naval maneuver on the Northwest Coast.

[When the Tlingit destroyed the Russian post at Old Sitka in 1802, they were armed, according to Khlebnikov ([1833] 1861b:46), with guns, spears, and daggers, making their successful attack about midday. They apparently did not wear body armor, evidently because they needed freedom of movement, or possibly because they knew it was scanty protection against bullets. It will be remembered (see the section "Early Encounters with Europeans") that they wore wooden masks (or face paint?) representing their clan crests, roared, and yelled their clan cries. It is possible that some of the men were wearing helmets, not masks.

[When the Russians returned in 1804 to retake the place, they found the Tlingit established in a fort on a hilltop, defended by two small cannon. Despite the superior Russian force, the Tlingit in the fort repulsed an attempt to storm it, by withholding their fire until the Russians were close, then firing "with an order and execution that surprised us," as Lisiansky reported (1814:158). After skillful prevarication, delays, false promises to give more hostages and make peace, the Tlingit silently escaped from the fort one night, leaving behind many valuable possessions, including a store of provisions and twenty large canoes which they could not take with them, as well as the bodies of babies and dogs they had killed, lest their cries betray the whereabouts of those who fled. This fort, as well as the one on Peril Strait built by the refugees, has been described in Chapter 3, in the section "Forts." The Russians who had established themselves in a fortified position on a hill nearby, which they named Fort New Archangel, burned down the abandoned Indian fort.

[Lisiansky also described and illustrated articles that Baranov had previously taken from the houses of the Tlingit on Cross Sound (Hoonah?), Stephens Passage (Auk), and Chatham Strait (Hutsnuwu). Baranov destroyed their houses to punish these Indians for helping the Sitkans assault the Russian post in 1802. The objects taken (Lisiansky 1814:149–50, pl. I) included

> a number of masks, very ingeniously cut in wood, and painted with different colours (See Plate I, Fig. *b*). [This is actually a helmet.] He had found them in the habitations he had destroyed. These masks were formerly worn by the Colushes in battle, but are now used chiefly on festivals. They are placed on a neck-piece of wood (Plate I, Fig. *c*), that extends from the lower part of the neck to the eyes, with indentations, *o*, at the edge, to see through, and fastens behind. Some of them represent heads of beasts, others of birds, and others of imaginary beings. They are so thick, that a musket-ball, fired at a moderate distance, can hardly penetrate them.

[This whole outfit was illustrated by Niblack (1890, pl. XIV) and by Hough (1895, pl. 9), as shown by Lisiansky, and as actually worn. The neck piece or visor is turned upside down in Lisiansky's illustration; Hough turned it to show its correct orientation with the eye grooves uppermost. The inside view, with the loop to be grasped between the teeth,

Objects found by Baranov in Tlingit houses, Sitka, September 1804. (Not to scale.) (Lisiansky 1814, pl. I. Courtesy of the Bancroft Library, University of California, Berkeley.). (a) Wooden slat armor [not described in the text]. (b) Wooden helmet. "These masks were formerly worn by the Colushes in battle, but are now used chiefly on festivals" (Lisiansky 1814:150). (c) Collar (here shown upside down), or "neck-piece of wood [on which the helmet rests], that extends from the lower part of the neck to the eyes, with indentations, o, at the edge, to see through, and fastens behind." (d) Halibut hook [not described in the text]. (e) A "rattle which is used in dancing, and was very well finished, both as to sculpture and painting." (f) A "thin plate, made of virgin copper, found on the Copper river, to the north of Sitca. . . ." (here shown upside down).

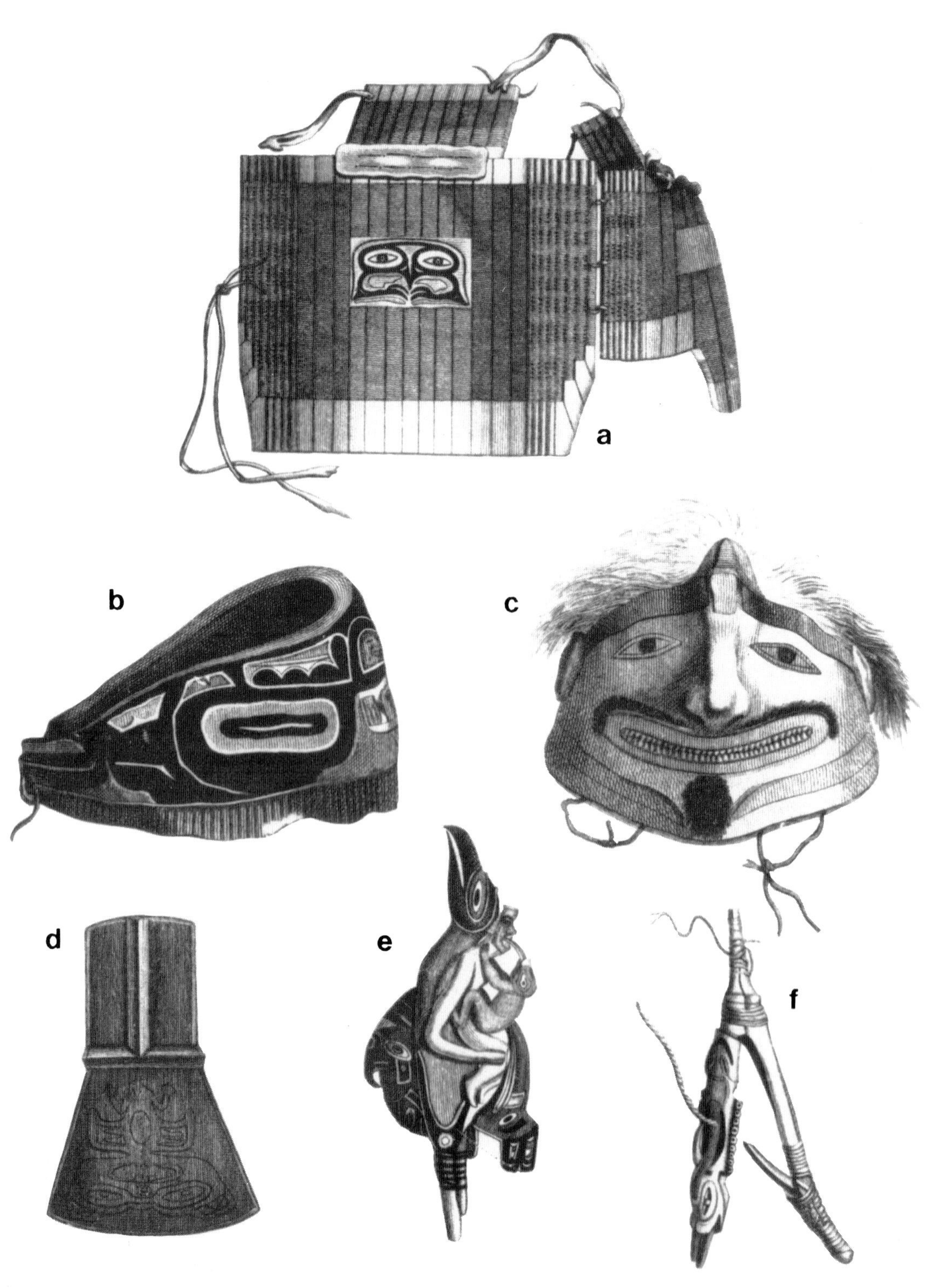

is also shown, as taken from a similar specimen collected at Sitka.

[Of warriors in 1805, Lisiansky wrote (1814:238):

> Their war habit is a buck-skin, doubled and fastened round the neck, or a woollen cuaca [vest, shirt?], to the upper part of which, in front, iron plates are attached, to defend the breast from a musket-ball. Formerly a sort of coat of arms was worn, made of thin pieces of wood nicely wrought together with the sinews of sea animals, as represented in Plate I, Fig. *a*. The cuacas are not made by the natives, but are furnished by traders from the United States in exchange for sea-otter skins.

[A painting made by Mikhail Tikhanov at Sitka in 1818 (Shur and Pierce, 1976, lower fig. on p. 42) purports to be of "Kolosh (Tlingits), Baranof Island, dressed for battle." Only the heads and a few shoulders are shown. The faces are painted and the hair is bound up on top of the head with what look like ribbons and ermine furs. The painting outlines the faces as if they were masks. One man wears a fur garment which leaves bare his outstretched right arm. Another wears a cloth mantle that is tied together over the right shoulder to leave the arm bare. There is no evidence of wooden armor.

[There is another painting by Tikhanov (Shur and Pierce 1976:46; in color, Golovnin [1822, I] 1979, frontis.) showing a Tlingit leader in hide armor that reaches from his neck to his ankles. It is simply a fold of hide, stitched together with thongs at each shoulder, with a hole cut through the fold for the left arm, and is open down the right side, exposing what appears to be an undergarment of softer skin. The hide is fringed down the opening on the right side and across the bottom, and is painted with a design suggesting a circular face in a square, repeated four times on front (and back?), with painted borders at the neck and bottom. The warrior's hair is tied in a topknot. His face is bare with a zigzag line of paint across his forehead. His feet are bare, as are his legs. He carries a gun in the right hand and a double-bladed(?) dagger in the left, lashed to his left wrist.

[Holmberg (1855:28) added nothing new to earlier descriptions of Tlingit weapons, except to corroborate such reports. The dagger and lance were both furnished with iron blades in 1850. The double-bladed dagger was the constant companion of the Tlingit, worn both on journeys and in the marketplace at Sitka. The lance was used only for war. Holmberg also described Tlingit fighting (1855: 42–43; see Petroff 1884:170). His account of duels or "private wars" between two armored champions, armed only with daggers, has already been quoted in the section "Interclan Warfare." "General" or "public wars," involving whole clans, were fought with ferocious cruelty through sudden surprise attacks. The captured enemy were enslaved, the dead scalped, and the scalps kept as war trophies, to be worn at ceremonies as leg ornaments, the number of scalps attesting the wearer's heroism. (Holmberg was not able to learn if the Tlingit ate their enemies!)

> When the Tlingit arms himself for war, he paints his face red, powders his hair with the same color and decorates it with white eagle down. The last especially indicates the solemnity of [his] purpose. [Then follows the description of the private war or duel, and the making of peace.] [p. 42]

[For the relative advantages and disadvantages of guns, chiefly muskets (up to about 1850), against the native with bow and arrow, spear, club, and dagger, and protected by native armor, see Townsend's illuminating discussion (1983).]

MAKING PEACE

The sign of peace was the display of white feathers on a pole or in the hand. Both Lisiansky and Vancouver mentioned the picking of bird's down and blowing it in the air, and the latter mentioned the carrying of green boughs in the hands. [Fuller references to these and similar instances will be found below.] Of late years a white flag was displayed. This I saw at Sitka in 1883 when a false report was circulated that the sloop of war *Enterprise* was about to bombard the native village, and on or from every house a piece of white clothing or sail was displayed. [A white flag was hoisted by the Sitkans in their fort, in answer to that on the *Neva* in 1804, when the Sitka Tlingit pretended to surrender, and also when they were exchanging hostages (Lisiansky 1814:157, 159).]

After a war or following a period of estrangement, peace overtures might be made by one party, either on a basis of equality, or on an offer of, or demand for, compensation. But whatever the conditions, the terms were settled in council. Should the participants be from different tribes and travel by water be necessary, the visitors never came directly to the village, but camped at a distance the day before [their expected arrival], and sent word of their movements. Under no circumstances would any strange party or canoe approach a village other than its own after nightfall. [The same overnight halt and announcement of expected arrival was observed by guests coming to a potlatch.]

The next day, if possible at high tide, the visitors' canoes, decked with flags or white feathers at the mastheads, approached the village in a single column, the occupants keeping time with their paddles to a slow song. Upon nearing the shore, the canoes formed a line abreast and stood in for the chief's house; here headway was checked, and the canoes were held by poles in the bow and stern. The visiting chief in the stern then rose and recounted the past trouble from its beginning, enumerating the losses sustained, and the desire [of his own people] for peace. He named the hostages offered, and finally called the names of the principal men of the opposite clan, and as each name was called it was answered. [The most common peace ceremonies would seem to have been between clans in opposite moieties, but clans in the same moiety made peace in the same way.] Then the chief or spokesman of those on shore replied in like manner, ending by inviting the guests to land. His people rushed into the water and carried the hostages to shore, and to the houses in which they were to be entertained. Then the canoes were unloaded and hauled up, and the visitors were assigned to their quarters.

The hostages, two, four, or eight, but in later years generally two from each clan, were termed *kuwakon* [quwaka·n], "deer," since the deer is a gentle animal and represents peace. They were chiefs or headmen, and their selection was considered an honor. This custom of exchanging hostages was universally demanded by the Tlingit in their earliest intercourse with Europeans, and was acceded to as a safeguard, and proved most satisfactory.

[The peace hostages were taken in a mock battle, and were carried, feigning death, into the house of their captors. Here the whole ritual of growing up was enacted, from helpless babyhood when they had to be fed, to the restrictive taboos and magical exercises reminiscent of a girl's puberty. (See de Laguna 1972:596–603.)]

The "deer" [quwaka·n] were not permitted to do anything for themselves. One or more attendants were appointed for each one, whose duty was to bring food and water, dress and make their toilet, paint the face, dress the hair with eagle feathers, and supply every want. The hostages lay on piles of furs, in the place of honor, back of the central fireplace and facing the doorway. Each had a rope tied around the waist, and the first three fingers of the right hand were bound together. They used only the left hand in eating, for the right hand was blood guilty. [See also Holmberg 1855:43.] They masticated their food on the left side, and after eating, wiped the mouth with the neck stone [rubbing amulet] wrapped with frayed cedar bark. They fasted the first four days, drinking a little salt water in the early morning "before the Raven cries." On the evening of the fourth day, they were washed, dressed in clean clothes, and feasted. They were not permitted to eat seaweed or shellfish ["beach food"], a prohibition which continued for two months. They feasted again on the fifth and seventh days, and on the ninth day returned to their families.

They took new names from some object or idea, which was impersonated in their dress, and in acting [and dancing] to the songs composed for the occasions. [The hostages were given honorific titles by their captors, who also composed the songs alluding to these titles. The names were derived from some valued possession of the captors, including their crests, that might symbolize goodwill. These titles became so closely associated with the peace hostages that they sometimes were used instead of the regular name. (See de Laguna 1972:599–600.)] The hostages danced with the opposite clan [their captors], and were honored guests when their own people danced.

[The fine costumes of the hostages, preferably including Chilkat blankets, were furnished by the captors. The hostage also wore two feathers in the hair as a sign of peace, and afterwards could use these feathers to make peace in time of quarrels. (See de Laguna 1972:600–601.)]

If the reconciliation had been arranged on a common basis of no indemnity, the first four days of the Peace Ceremony would be devoted to mourning [sacred clan] songs, each clan alternating with the other. They dressed poorly, wearing cedar-bark rope around the waist, their hair was covered with bird down, and one or two eagle feathers were stuck in the hair; their faces were blackened. On the fifth day, the guests were feasted and the songs of sorrow gave place to more joyful ones. In full ceremonial dress, they entertained each other with dance and song on alternate days, each side endeavoring to outdo the other. If, however, an indemnity was to be paid, the potlatch [i.e., this payment] preceded the feast. The ceremonies took place in the following order: the smoking feast, the distribution of property, the feast of food, and the dancing alternatively by each clan.

[Negotiations for peace, including the restitution to be paid and the hostages to be selected from each side, were carried out by neutral "clan brothers-in-law," na· -ká·ni, that is, by men who were married to women of the clan they were to represent, provided that they were not members of any clan that might be embroiled in the war. They also were supposed to be persons of rank, since they had to supervise the peace ceremonies. Because the exchange of hostages invoked supernatural sanctions against anyone breaking the peace, one party might initiate the procedures by seizing

Both sides of a silver feather, one of two worn by a Wolf 32 "deer" in a peace ceremony at Yakutat, ca. 1900. On one side is incised an owl, on the other a raven and a humpbacked (pink) salmon, all crests of the Raven 19 clan at Yakutat. (Photograph by Frederica de Laguna at Yakutat, 1952.)

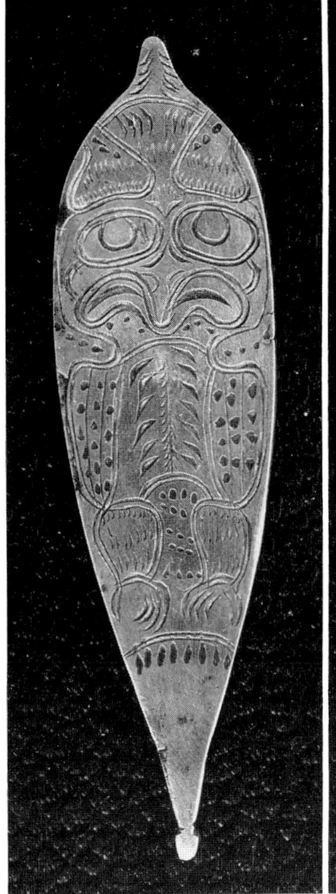

hostages from their enemies, and offering their own instead, hoping that the latter would not be harmed. (See de Laguna 1972:592–97.)

[Emmons gave the following as a peace song, but was in error when he wrote that it was "addressed to the *Nan ya a yi* family of the *Stick-heen Kwan*." Rather, since peace songs have the same form as love songs or other songs of personal feelings, this song addresses the Raven children-of-the-Na·nya·ʔa·yí (Wolf 18) *men*, the group from which was drawn the hostage who danced to this song, and the group in which the composers (Wolves) would find their spouses and sweethearts.

[The words are:

From the land of spirits
Will I come for you,
Will I come for you,
Oh, daughters of *Nan ye i ee*
  [Na·nya·ʔa·yí-yátx̣i, "N-children,"]
Then will not the daughters of *Nan ye i ee*
Look with mercy,
With mercy upon me?]

EARLY ACCOUNTS OF PEACE CEREMONIES*

[The early explorers had few chances to witness a full Tlingit peace ceremony, although they often reported the signals used by the Indians to indicate their peaceful intentions and desire to trade. Much of this trade was ceremonially conducted by a chief, as described in Chapter 11, the section "Tlingit Ceremonialism in the Eighteenth and Early Nineteenth Centuries." The display of white feathers, birds' tails, or pelts on poles set up like masts, the singing and dancing, and especially the extension of both arms in the form of a cross, have been cited by La Pérouse, Portlock, Beresford, Colnett, and Malaspina as signs of peace commonly used by the Tlingit. Malaspina (1885:155, 160, 166) and Suría (in Wagner 1936:247–48, 252–53, 258) have also described how the same "sign of peace" and the "harmonious hymn of peace" were employed by the Yakutat Tlingit when they wanted to restore amicable relations with the Spaniards after a barely averted fight. This was particularly effective when the men on the two ships joined in the singing. The same type of singing was used by the Yakutat and by their visitors, after the latter had been greeted with mock animosity.

*Editor's note: This section represents my own compilation and comments, made to carry out the author's plan.

[Suría (in Wagner 1936:250) had a terrifying experience when he was treated somewhat like a peace hostage. He had been left by the other Spaniards alone in a house at Port Mulgrave, while he was making sketches:

> I had scarcely commenced to work when with a great cry the cacique [house chief] spoke to me in his language in an imperious tone and a threat that I should suspend my work. Engrossed in my work I paid little attention to him when the third time there was a grand chorus of shrieks by all the Indians. I came to myself and suspended my work which was well started. They caught hold of me and pushed me. I began to shout for my own people, but when I turned my face I did not see a single one. They formed a circle around me and danced around me knives in hand singing a frightful song, which seemed like the bellowing of bulls. In such circumstances I resolved to carry out their mood and I began to dance with them. They let out a shout and made me sit down, and by force made me sing their songs which according to the gestures which they made I understood as ridiculing me. [These may have been only the funny songs appropriate to part of the Peace Ceremony.] In such a situation I feigned ignorance and

> shouted louder making the same contortions and gestures. They were very much pleased at this and I was able with my industry to gain their good will with a figure which I sketched for them with a coat etc., and dressed like ourselves.

The Indians pointed at it, exclaiming "ʔá·n qá·wu!" or "Chief!" They then insisted that Suría eat some fish, threatening him when he tried to refuse. They next offered him some women, but at that moment a sailor appeared, and the Indians let Suría escape. It is uncertain whether eating fish was or was not what a "Deer" would be expected to do. Possibly the Indians were testing him, as they most certainly were the women, since sexual activity was prohibited to a peace hostage.

[When Ismailov and Bocharov came to Yakutat in 1788, they were met by two large canoes; in the middle of each boat was a pole to which sea otter skins were fastened (Coxe 1803:322; see also de Laguna 1972:133). The reception of Purtov and Kulikalov at Yakutat in 1794 has been described in Chapter 11, the section "Tlingit Ceremonialism in the Eighteenth and Early Nineteenth Centuries," as has Vancouver's report of the visit to his vessels of the Stikine chief, when they were anchored in Port Stewart, Behm Canal, and the ceremonial mock hostility with which the Stikine party received other Indians from the south. All these illustrate the ways in which the Tlingit manifested friendship or established peaceful intercourse.

[In 1794, Mr. Johnstone's boats were in Kake waters, when about a hundred Indians, with their chief, appeared from the head of a bay. The Englishmen fired muskets into the air to force them to keep their distance. The Tlingit were well armed, some with guns, but were apparently eager to trade. As reported by Vancouver (1801, 6:49):

> One of the canoes now advanced before the rest, in which a chief stood in the middle of it, plucking the white feathers from the rump of an eagle, and blowing them into the air, accompanied by songs and other expressions, which were received as tokens of peace and friendship.

He was allowed to come alongside, and instantly gave Mr. Johnstone a sea otter skin, for which the latter returned suitable gifts.

[The attack on Vancouver's boats by the Indians of Traitors Cove, Behm Canal, has been cited already in this chapter. Later that same year, Lieutenant Whidbey's boats again encountered what they believed to be the same Indians (Vancouver 1801, 4:217–19). A single man was first seen, who invited the party to stop and come ashore. Then four canoes came out of a little cover, and one of these came within musket shot but could not be induced to approach nearer. The Indians in it were singing and making speeches. When the boats began to leave, the canoe followed at a distance, then crossed the bay and landed on a point that the boats would pass. Although the English set out small gifts fastened to floating wood and the Indians retrieved these, the latter refused to come closer. Then as the boats approached the place where the Indians had landed, all, except for three who were guarding their arms and one old man who sat apart (pp. 218–19),

> advanced unarmed to the water side, each bearing a green bough, and singing and dancing in a most savage and uncouth manner. [The English boats stopped to watch], after which one of the natives made signs that two persons should land from the boats, and immediately they laid down on the rocks a long twist of white wool, which was considered as an additional token of peace. . . . [p. 218]

But the English judged it more prudent to refuse, even though Mr. Whidbey believed that the Indians were making "a supplication for mercy and forgiveness" (p. 219). This was certainly an invitation to a formal Peace Ceremony, with exchange of "deer."

[The same exploring party later met seven Indian men in a bay on the west side of Behm Canal, who seemed ready to oppose any landing of the English, near a "small miserable hut" (Vancouver 1801, 4:219–20). The Indians put on their war garments, and advanced to meet the boats, armed with bows and arrows, one musket, and one pistol.

> Beside these, an elderly person made his appearance at a little distance; he was without any weapon, or his war garment, and whilst he made long speeches, he held in one hand the skin of a bird, and with the other plucked out the young feathers and down, which at the conclusion of certain sentences in his speech, he blew into the air. [p. 220]

Since these acts were judged as "overtures of peace" by Mr. Whidbey, his men threw some presents to him and indicated that they wanted some food. So some salmon were fetched, and the boats came to the rocks to pick them up. The old man, according to Vancouver (1801, 4:220–21):

> received in return such articles as appeared to be highly acceptable, still continuing to blow the down into the air, as he plucked it from the bird's skin.
>
> This custom I had before noticed with the inhabitants of this coast, but had never so good an opportunity of seeing it practised, nor have I a clear idea to what particular end it is directed, but as it has generally been accompanied by pacific measures, it is fair to presume that it is intended to display an hospitable disposition.

[Von Langsdorff (1814, 2:110–14), who was at Sitka in 1805–6, and von Kotzebue (1830:58–61), who was there in 1825, described the formal visits made by the Tlingit to the Russian post, to trade or to show their peaceful intentions. These were accompanied by singing and dancing, and have been described in Chapter 11, "Tlingit Ceremonialism in the Eighteenth and Early Nineteenth Centuries."

[Lisiansky (1814:165, 221–25, 230–31) was in Sitka in 1804 when his ship took part in the Russian reconquest of the area, and returned again in 1805, when he observed and described the visit of a Sitkan ambassador to settle terms of peace, and how this gentleman and his suite were received ashore by Baranov and on the *Neva,* and how Kotlean (Q̇ałyá·n, who had been a leader in the attack on the Russian post in 1802) came with gifts to make his peace. During the actual campaign of 1804, Lisiansky (1814:156–61) described the exchanges of hostages, the signal of a white flag from the *Neva,* which was answered by one from the native fort. Finally, the Tlingit sent more hostages under the protection of a white flag, and cried "Oo oo oo!" or "End!" when they left the parley. When ordered to surrender their fort, they were to signify their acceptance of the Russian demand by giving the same cry. This they did, but secretly abandoned the fort during the night.

[Khlebnikov ([1817–32] 1976:31) was perhaps the first to describe a typical, aboriginal Peace Ceremony, although Lütké (1835:198–99) copied this almost word for word. Khlebnikov explained that when a quarrel was resolved through negotiations,

> the defeated receive payment for the dead; at such a time peace hostages are exchanged. A strange ceremony is performed during this exchange. Both sides gather together on level ground, carrying daggers, both men and women. First the men try to seize a hostage (the top man of the adversaries, one most respected by virtue of family ties as well as age); they look as if they were attacking and lash out with lances and daggers; they yell and penetrate into the midst of the enemy and seize the selected hostage who hides in the midst of his party. Then with shouts which express joy and the fulfilling of their desires, and the end of war, they lift him on their hands and carry him to their side. Another similar exchange having also taken place, each side keeps its hostage in good condition, providing him all possible service; they do not permit him to walk, but always carry him on their hands, etc. The peace ceremony is concluded with dancing from morning to night and with feasting.

[Lütké (1835, 1:198–99, free translation) added:

> The hostages are finally conducted to the home of their new friends, and after having spent there a year or more, they return home, and the alliance is cemented by new festivities.

[After describing a formal duel between armored champions (see the preceding section, and Khlebnikov 1976:30–31), Holmberg (1855:43, free translation) wrote that the fight would be settled by a Peace Ceremony, in which hostages on each side were exchanged. Further

> . . . for several days [they] could eat only with the left hand, since they had carried weapons in the right hand during the fight. For each of them, were chosen from the enemy side two companions to guard him, and who ought not to be inferior to him in esteem.

[Mrs. Willard (1884:92), the wife of the missionary at Haines, reported briefly in September 1881 on the ceremony that ended the bloody feud between the G̣a·nax̣te·dí, Raven 3 or "Crows," and the Daqławe·dí, Wolf 27 or "[Killer] Whales." This feud, described in Chapter 2, under "Law," with all its killings was the result of a drunken brawl.

> The Crows took into their houses the young man in whose house we held service for the Whales, treating him to the best of everything they possessed, having him both eat and sleep with them; and the Whales took into their homes, in the same way, the great Crow terror, "The Murderer." This is their way of expressing perfect satisfaction, confidence and peace, and now the feasting and dancing are going on. The lower [Chilkoot] villages have joined them in this; and if only molasses (for the distillation of ardent spirits) can be kept from them, we hope for a new era.]

PEACE CEREMONIES IN 1891 AND 1877

I witnessed a peace dance in Sitka in 1891. A feud of long standing had existed between the two principal Raven families of the Sitka, the *Kiksade* and the *Thluke-nuh-ut-de* [Kiksʔádi and Łukʷnax̣ʔádi, Raven 10 and 6, respectively]. So bitter were their feelings that they took every opportunity to shame each other.

It seems that some years previously a *Kiksade* took some liquor to the *Hootzah-ta* [Hutsnuwu] village of Angoon on Admiralty Island. In the debauch that followed, a man of one of the resident families was killed. The responsibility for his death was laid upon the one who had introduced the whiskey. As no indemnity was forthcoming, the case rested until, many years after, several canoes manned by the family [clansmen] of the man who had died came to Sitka. Stopping abreast of the house of Katlean [Q̇ałyá·n], the chief of the *Kiksade* [Raven 10], the chief of the Hutsnuwu rose in the stern of his canoe and recounted the wrong that had been done them and demanded immediate payment. Great excitement ensued, and Katlean rushed out of his house, refusing to receive them or accept any responsibility. The canoes quickly turned and started homeward, but they were stopped at the upper end of the village by the *Thluke-nuh-ut-de* [Raven 6], and invited to land. This was done to shame the *Kiksade*. Furthermore, the debt claimed from the latter was paid by the *Thluke-nuh-ut-de,* consisting of eight blankets, one bottle of whiskey, and eight yards of cloth. This placed the *Kiksade* [Raven 10] in a very humiliating position. In order to reestablish themselves and to place a greater debt upon the *Thluke-nuh-ut-de* [Raven 6], they paid fifteen blankets to a Yakutat woman who had a claim against the *Thluke-nuh-ut-de*. This, as a greater payment, placed shame upon the *Thluke-nuh-ut-de* [Raven 6].

In 1891 two canoes from Taku suddenly appeared off Sitka. Stopping in front of Katlean's house, they demanded payment for the life of one of their people who had lately died, having been wounded by a *Kiksade* [Raven 10] many years before. Katlean indignantly repudiated the claim. As before, when the canoes started to turn away, the *Thluke-nuh-ut-de* [Raven 6] invited the visitors to land. Because of this act, a fight between the two Sitka clans [Raven 6 and 10] was nearly precipitated, but in the end a reconciliation was agreed upon, and a peace dance followed.

Each family [clan] selected two of their principal men to be given to the other as hostages [quwaka·n]. They were called out in front of their houses and told to go down and jump into the salt water. When they appeared, they seemed afraid to come out and cried "Ho! Ho! Ho! Ho!," as a Tlingit does when wounded.

[The peace hostages are traditionally taken in a mock battle, in which they are apparently killed or mortally wounded. Since the realistic performance could, in the heat of the excitement, lead to actual blows, it is not certain that the fear displayed by these unarmed hostages was completely feigned.]

The hostages were then taken into the houses of the opposite clan [their captors] and led to the place of honor back of the fire where beds had been prepared for them, and eagle down was put on their heads.

To each *kuwakon* [quwaka·n] was assigned an attendant who washed him and dressed him, made his toilet, and fetched his food. [The hostage is supposed to be as helpless as a newborn baby.] The two *Kiksade* [Raven 10] *kuwakons* were quartered in *Yough hit* [Yá·y hít], "Whale House," of the *Thluke-nuh-ut-de* [Raven 6]. In their dress, song, and dance they impersonated "Fort *Kuwakon*" and "Schooner *Kuwakon*" [Nu·w Quwaka·n and ʔA·n Quwaka·n], the latter referring to the first Russian ships to come to Sitka. The two *Thluke-nuh-ut-de* [Raven 6] hostages were quartered in the house of the *Kiksade* [Raven 10] chief, and had the names "*Thluke Kuwakon*" [Łu·kʷ Quwaka·n], "Fall, or Coho Salmon" hostage, and *Ya-se-ta Sha* [Yaṡé-ṫa-ša· Quwaka·n], "Mount Saint Elias *Kuwakan,*" which they personated.

[Emmons evidently has the names incorrectly assigned, for each clan would give a name referring to its *own* crest or to a landmark in its *own* territory, or to something claimed exclusively by that clan; and they would compose the song to which their hostage danced, wearing something emblematic of his new name. The Kiksʔádi, as "original" inhabitants of Sitka, would naturally claim the first Russian ships to Sitka, and probably the first Russian fort which they had destroyed, and would give these names to their captives. The Łukʷnax̣ʔádi, represented by so many members from Yakutat and Dry Bay, would naturally try to claim Mount St. Elias, even though this was the crest of an older Yakutat clan, the Kʷá·šk-qʷá·n or Raven 19, and would certainly have the salmon for which they were named, as honorific designations for their captives.]

These *Kuwakon* or "Deer" danced with the family [clan] that held them as hostages, and as guests were given seats of honor when their own family danced. When eating, they used the left hand; for the first three fingers of the right hand were tied together, since the right hand had [or would] hold the war knife. When dancing, they held the right hand open. They wore a stone charm suspended around the neck. In dancing, they always turned to the right, as the sun moves. Early in the morning, before the raven cried, they sang their clan songs of grief ["sorry songs"].

After four days, the *kuwakon* were taken by the master in charge [hít ṡa·ṫi] to the woods and washed. Rocks were put under them as a sign that they would have a long life, and a small drinking basket of water was passed around their heads four times from left to right, as the sun moves. Everything used in the washing was put in or under a stump to give them a long life. The *kuwakon* must carefully observe every rule laid down for his practice and must never ask for water. He fasted and ate on alternate days.

By ten o'clock on the morning of the Deer or Peace Dance, *Ko-wa-la-kank* or *Ko-wa-la-klank* [Quwałakánx̣], that was to be held in Whale House, the village was astir, and the *Kiksade,* who were to dance, assembled in several of their own houses, where they dressed in ceremonial robes, painted their faces in red and black, and powdered their hair with eagle down. The faces of the men were very much covered with color, with little regard for design, while those of the women were neatly stamped with a crest pattern in black or red. The men were dressed in Chilkat blankets, or [robes of] caribou skin with fringed and painted borders, beaded shirts, skin aprons painted in animal [crest] figures, or cloth ornamented with buttons, beads or shell, and hung with puffin beaks or pieces of metal. They wore the ceremonial headdress, *sheckiette* [šakí·ʔát], the crown of which was filled with bird down which, in the dance, was distributed like a fine cloud, hats of woven spruce root, wood or fur, imitation scalps, circlets of cedar-bark rope, or eagle feathers. [Two feathers in the hair was the sign of the peace hostage.] In their hands they carried rattles, spears, bows and arrows, wood carvings [possibly the wooden "tassels" mentioned at Yakutat (de Laguna 1972:601)], or white eagle tails. While some wore moccasins or leggings, they were more often barefooted. Others were costumed to represent animals or to impersonate a hunter or some foreign dancer. The women were generally dressed in the blue-black Hudson's Bay Company's blankets, bordered with a broad stripe of red cloth and ornamented with pearl buttons. They wore long earrings of red worsted, their foreheads were bound with black silk handkerchiefs, their hair was neatly arranged in a single braid falling behind, and they wore silver nose rings. Some carried carved wooden rattles or the white tail of the bald eagle. All wore moccasins.

The *Kiksade* [Raven 10] assembled at the beat of a drum, and in a procession of twos, headed by a man with a skin drum, singing, they marched to the Raven 6 Whale House. The guests, [from] *Kagwanton* [Ka·gʷa·nta·n, Wolf 1], *Kusekade* [Qu·sk̓e·dí, Raven 8], and *Khart-kow-ee* [X̌at̓kaʔa·yí, Raven 7], had previously arrived and had been seated in the rear and left spaces of the house, the men in front, the women behind them. The *Kiksade kuwakon* [Raven 10 hostages] were seated on a raised platform to the left of the fireplace and in front of the guests. The *Thluke-nuh-ut-de* [Raven 6] host and other members of his clan occupied the right front of the house, considered the place of least honor.

Upon reaching the house, the [Kiksʔádi] drummer entered and discarded his skin drum. He took possession of a wooden box drum in the corner to the left of the doorway, and commenced beating it as the *Kiksade* women entered singing, and took their places along the left wall of the house. Then the *Kiksade* men entered, dancing slowly, one at a time, with a long interval between them, for this was the most important spectacular feature of the performance. They danced up and down in spasmodic jerks, with legs stiff and feet apart, turning from side to side. They presented the more ornamental side of their dress to the audience, many entering backwards and singing as they danced along the right space to the farther end. Each dancer was freely criticized by the spectators.

While many simply danced, others enacted a pantomime. One, completely enveloped in a bearskin, was led in by another man holding a rope. He walked on hands and feet, swaying from side to side, rising at intervals, and moving his head in exact imitation of a brown bear. A boy representing a porcupine was wrapped in a blanket [to which were fastened] wooden sticks representing quills. One man with a spear went through the motions of spearing salmon. Another in war dress, knife in hand, rushed as if to attack; still another with a raven headpiece, robed in a black blanket with arms outstretched like wings, hopped in sideways as a raven walks. There was a song leader and a master of ceremonies. Men and women sang in different keys [part singing, probably an octave apart], keeping time to the beat of the drum, the stamping of feet, and the shaking of rattles. The songs recounted the history of the family [clan].

After the dancers had all entered and taken their places next to each other, filling the whole right side of the house, the songs continued and, in time, the theatrical effect gave place to intense clan feeling, as the mythology and heroic deeds of the past were unfolded. As darkness approached, the central fire lighted the excited, streaming faces of the performers, who, packed together, formed a moving mass of color. The air was filled with eagle down. The great chorus of hundreds of voices rose and fell in rich cadence until the singers were completely exhausted. Then with one loud shout the chant stopped, and guests and performers rushed out of the house to rest until the next day.

In all such entertainments the host and his side were poorly dressed, since they humbled themselves in the presence of their guests. Each clan danced [in this manner] four days [in each other's houses?], and the ceremony closed with a feast. On this [final] occasion the two clans danced opposite each other, and passed around in the house four times from left to right as the sun moves.

[Yakutat informants gave a somewhat different description of the taboos observed by the "deer," the names given to him

Although unfinished (the masts, sails, and rigging of the ship are omitted), Suría shows the Tlingit of Port Mulgrave, Yakutat, approaching the Spaniards with ceremonious offers of peace, after the Spaniards had suspended trading because of the theft of some pants, here being returned, 1791. (Aquatint by Suría. Courtesy of Museo Naval, Madrid.)

or her, and stressed the humorous character of many of the songs and dances. The "deer" also danced within the arms of his or her captors. (See de Laguna 1972:596–604.)]

The following account of the settlement of many years of warfare between the Nishka [Niska] of the Nass River in British Columbia and the Stikine tribe of Tlingit of Alaska was given to me by Dr. A. Green, an eyewitness, then in charge of the Methodist mission at Greenville on the Nass River. It is interesting because of its authenticity.

In the spring of 1877, thirty-five war canoes containing several hundred Stikine came to the mouth of the Nass River to conclude a permanent peace with the Niska people, with whom they had been on unfriendly terms for many years on account of numerous raids and conflicts. One canoe ascended the river to Greenville, the principal lower village of the Niska which had been built on the site of an older settlement, *Lagh-ul-zap,* "Lake of Bones" [Lax̣qalt̓sa´p in Tsimshian (Sapir 1915a:3)]. This, in early days, was the main village until a fatal disease carried off so many of the inhabitants that the dead could be disposed of only by being cast into the lake; the survivors moved away and founded *Kit ikx* [Kitgige·´nix, "people further upstream," Tsim. (Sapir 1915a:3)].

Finding the villagers [Niska] ready to meet them, the remaining Tlingit canoes came up the river. A great council was held, during which every question connected with their past troubles was discussed, and the count of the killed was compiled by each side. This was done by [making] red paint marks on hides, different symbols indicating men, women, and children of each sex, and the relative value of each, for the computation for indemnity, a life counting according to the rank of the individual. Pregnant women were specially marked, since each one counted as two lives.

After a satisfactory computation had been made, it was announced that the Niska were a number of lives ahead. Then, for half an hour, both parties sat in silence, their heads bowed, and half buried in their blankets as was the native custom. After a slight consultation, the Niska arose en masse and, going to their homes, got Hudson's Bay Company's trade blankets, then the standard of value, and arranged them in separate piles for each life in the count against them. When completed, each pile was inspected by the Stikine, who consulted together and announced their acceptance of the compensation. Then, with a mighty shout, both parties rushed together and grasped hold of each other, cementing a peace that has ever since been maintained.

CHAPTER 13

Illness and Medicine

DIAGNOSIS OF ILLNESS

The Tlingit had a very indefinite [sketchy] knowledge of anatomy in connection with the practice of surgery and medicine. Amputation was never attempted.

[Perhaps to explain this alleged lack of anatomical knowledge, Emmons then mentioned the highly conventionalized eyes (and also faces) that appear on all carvings and paintings of animate creatures (man included) to indicate the joints, and also the life, movement, or "intelligence" of the parts (see Chapter 7, the section "Art"). But he failed to show how this artistic convention might be related to Tlingit ignorance of anatomy, a point which I suggested (de Laguna 1960:15–16) in contrasting Eskimo and Tlingit abilities to identify animal bones. Tlingit midwives, however, were often very skilled; formerly when a pregnant woman died, the fetus had to be cut out and burned separately. This must indicate at least some gynecological knowledge (see de Laguna 1972:535–36, 655).]

Wounds, cuts [as well as burns, sprains, fractures], and other hurts which could be seen were understood to be naturally caused. On the other hand, a slow wasting sickness, or a hidden internal ailment, was usually attributed to supernatural causes, especially witchcraft, and could be treated only by the shaman. The latter utilized incantations and charms to remove the evil spirit, for he had no other means.

[The shaman certainly had some surgical skills in addition to his magical powers, and might supervise the treatment of wounds or burns, as well as himself undertake the lancing of an infection (especially if the patient were a member of his family; see de Laguna 1972:655). Any ailment was likely to be treated at first with "home remedies"; then, when lack of improvement or deterioration indicated the serious nature of the affliction and a supernatural etiology was suspected, an appeal would be made to the shaman for diagnosis and cure. In effect, only minor illnesses were explained by natural causes, and the shaman dealt almost exclusively with supernatural ones.

[Supernatural causes included retaliation by an animal or its spirit to an insult; aggression by evil spirits or ghosts; intrusion of a spirit (yé·k) or of some shamanistic object; refusal of the shamanistic call, or failure to follow the prescribed regimen; seeking excessive power; and, above all, witchcraft.]

The abuse or want of respect shown to many animals caused bodily infirmities. At Sitka in 1899, there broke out a bitter feud between the *Kik-sa-de* [Kiksʔádi, Raven 10] and the *Thluke-nuh-ut-de* [Łukʷnax̣ʔádi, Raven 6] over the right to use the Frog as a crest. [See also de Laguna 1972:288–91.] A group of *Ka-gwan-tan* [Ka·gʷa·nta·n, Wolf 1] were carrying the grave fencing for a member of the latter family [Raven 6], when the leader stumbled and fell in a hole. On looking down, he found that he had disturbed and possibly hurt a little frog—the disputed crest of the family [clan] that they were honoring. He was so frightened that he became paralyzed and was carried home, speechless. His affliction was attributed to his breaking into the frog's home. To appease its wrath and to restore the old chief to health, his family made a tiny ceremonial blanket, similar to that worn by themselves. They formed a procession, and with offerings of food marched to the frog's hole. With appropriate speeches they tied the blanket around the frog's body, and slipped a small silver ring on its hind leg. After covering it over, they retired, trusting that the offended spirit might give back speech and health to their chief.

It was believed that insanity from birth might result from [the pregnant mother's] fright at sudden contact with an animal, particularly a bear. Or, it might be caused by ridicule [by the mother? or by any maternal ancestor?] of an animal, an insult for which the animal's spirit retaliated by influencing the unborn child. [While the Yakutat might ascribe the malformation of a baby to the mother's sudden fright at an animal during pregnancy, they did not, apparently, believe that the animal was retaliating for a slight or injury. The cause for the malformation was thus a "natural" one. (See de Laguna 1972:500.)]

Editor's note: I have here assembled as a separate chapter the loosely organized notes and short texts that Emmons had intended to be placed partly in "Health and Disease" in Chapter 1 and partly in the chapter on shamanism. Because of its resultant length, the latter has been divided into three chapters: Chapter 13 on illness and methods of cure, plus magical "medicines"; Chapter 14 on shamanism; and Chapter 15 on witchcraft.

There was at Killisnoo a young man, imbecile from birth, deaf and dumb, who was believed to possess [be possessed by] a bear spirit, for the noises he made were said to be in the bear's tongue. His infirmity was believed the result of some disrespect shown to the bear family by his mother or one of his family [clan]. To be born dumb was an inheritance from an ancestor who had offended some animal.

An idiot was believed to possess the spirit of one who had been killed. Since the spirits of all persons killed in war were believed to go to an abode in the sky known as *Kee-wah-kah-woo* [ki'waʔá·, "sky land," qá·wu, "people of"], an idiot was therefore called *Kee-wah-kah-woo Yu-ha-yee* [ki'wa qá·wu yahá·yí], the last word meaning "spirit" or "picture" [also "shadow" or "reflection"], to indicate the reincarnated soul of the slain person. [A reincarnated person was called qa· yakʷgʷahé·yagu.]

Insanity might come in later life [as a result of] cutting out the tongue of a land otter or some other animal sacred to the practice of shamanism, when the spirits were not in accord, or when the shaman wanted to obtain undue power.

["Cutting the tongue" of an animal was the culminating act of the novice shaman, by which he gained or secured his power; but it should never be attempted without having received the shamanistic call or without observing all the contingent rules and taboos. It is not clear whether insanity came as an automatic consequence of an unauthorized attempt to acquire power, or whether it was a punishment sent by the shamanistic spirits (yé·k). Even a shaman might be similarly stricken for attempting to gain too much power by cutting too many tongues; eight was the limit.]

A case of this kind occurred at Yakutat in 1897. A sea otter hunter, the brother of the chief of the *Quash-qua-kwan* [Kʷá·šk-qʷá·n, Raven 19] cut out the tongues of certain birds which he carried with him on his hunting trips. His wish to become a great hunter was granted and his success in sea otter hunting was great. But in time he lost his reason as a punishment, and as insanity is looked upon as a family disgrace, he was threatened with death [by his fellow clansmen] unless he gave up and hid the tongues in the forest.

[The chief was Chief George who died in 1903. His younger brother was George Second Chief, or Kandestí·n, "Kun Da Stein." Of him a Yakutat informant said, "He would have become a chief. He was brother to Chief George, but he went Bible crazy and was sent Outside (to an insane asylum in the United States) before he was ever made chief" (de Laguna, field notes, 1954).]

Insanity might also be caused by a particularly bad act. This was the case with a man of the Hutsnuwu at Angoon who killed his wife while attempting to change the course of their canoe in the rapids [of Kootznahoo Inlet]. [The wife's death, presumably by drowning, was an accident, but the husband, we may infer, was guilty of stupid bad seamanship.] He lost his reason and, though harmless, was avoided, while he would sit in his doorway and talk to the spirits throughout the day.

[It should be noted that insanity, šká·di, was an affliction that even the shaman could not cure. In some cases, sudden fright was given as the cause. In this there is a suggestion of soul loss, although it was mentioned only once by Emmons. Drucker (1950:226–27), however, cited soul loss, especially from fright, as a cause of illness, and recovery of the soul by a shaman as a mode of curing among the Tlingit. Being "crazy" is a euphemism—at least in speaking English—for being bewitched or being a witch. Witchcraft (see below) was not curable by the shaman, for only the witch could undo his own spells, and witchcraft represented the illicit use of unauthorized powers, somewhat similar to the case of George Second Chief. The resemblances between insanity and bewitchment may explain both why his "craziness" was a family disgrace (as witchcraft would be) and why such insanity could not be cured, according to Tlingit informants.]

Fits were called *Kuckro* [x̣áx̣ ?] from a small saltwater animal which, if touched, would produce them, since it possessed an evil spirit. Fits could even be caused by contact with anything touching the creature.

There was much superstition about the land otter, and an indefinite idea existed that a small otter spirit lived inside some or all persons. This is exemplified when one faints, which is called *yea-taok gootz-ch* [ye· tex̣ k̓úcč, "heart breaks repeatedly"] or *taok wu-gootz,* "heart broke" [tex̣ wu·k̓u·c], "had a heart attack," the expression suggesting the belief that the heart is hung by cords, and that when touched by the otter spirit, these cords slacken and the heart drops.

[Emmons here has confused or combined several separate ideas. The land otter was the animal form most often assumed by a shaman's spirit helper (yé·k), the tongue of which he cut and preserved as part of his "outfit." The land otter, or more correctly, the Land Otter Men, were those who had drowned or died of exposure, and who later came to rescue or capture the drowning or those lost in the woods, in order to transform these into creatures like themselves.

"Skun-doo," a "defrocked" shaman, ministering to the sick. He is posing for the photographer, wearing a crown of bear claws, a necklace of rattling bones, and a tunic ornamented with buttons, and he shakes an oyster-catcher rattle. (Photograph by Winter and Pond, ca. 1894.)

[Lastly, there was a belief in a spirit (or object?) intrusion, called ʔanaƛsi·n or ʔaneƛsi·n, "hiding inside," and sometimes this "shifting ailment" was called "land otter." It was caused by approaching too closely to a shaman's grave or to his paraphernalia. The spirit intruder was either one of the shaman's familiar spiritual helpers or the counterpart of something in his "outfit." Women and girls, especially, were likely to become "infected" if frightened by inadvertently discovering and handling the shaman's things. For anyone who was not of the shaman's own clan, this ailment was likely to be fatal. The intrusion could be removed only by a shaman, or by an assistant who had acquired some of his power. In one instance, a girl at Yakutat was infected by the dead shaman's own spirit or ghost. She recovered because she was a "child" of the shaman's own clan (her father was a member of that clan) and because her parents appealed to the dead shaman and left offerings at his grave. Yet twenty-four years later, this woman developed a tumor that had to be removed surgically in a hospital. It was reported to have resembled the links of the shaman's necklace, which she had unknowingly put on (de Laguna, 1972:699–700).

[Epidemics of infectious diseases (introduced by white men) were believed to be caused by disease spirits that traveled in a "boat of sickness," accompanied by the ghosts of all who had died of the disease; or else the "disease spirits" were such ghosts, invisible to all but the shaman. The latter could advise what precautions to take against them.

[The most terrible of the introduced diseases was smallpox, k^{w}a·n, first brought to the Tlingit by the Spanish in 1775. The greatest epidemic was that of 1836–40, the disease spreading northward from California along the Northwest Coast and also affecting natives in the interior, on the Aleutians, and on the Arctic coast. At first the Tlingit resisted vaccination, relying on their shamans, but later became convinced of the superiority of Russian medical practice and religion, when they noted that those vaccinated had escaped the smallpox. This not only led to voluntary acceptance of vaccination but to conversion to the Orthodox faith

(Veniaminov [1840] 1984:434–35; Tikhmenev [1861, I] 1978:198–200). This did not mean, however, that the Tlingit abandoned their magical precautions against the "disease spirits." Pieces of the spiny devil's club were nailed around windows and doors of the house, as late as the present century, to keep out the "disease spirits."]

CURES FOR EXTERNAL AILMENTS*

Medicinal baths, sea water [taken internally or applied externally], mineral substances, and plants were used to treat wounds and minor ailments. First in importance were the natural hot springs with their strongly impregnated mineral waters which were freely used for rheumatic ailments and skin troubles. Here the rocks were hollowed out to accommodate the bathers. Aside from their curative properties, the hot spring baths were considered a great luxury. [Geographical distance from such hot springs obviously limited their use.]

Salt water was drunk as an emetic and to purify the system, especially in connection with fasting.

Broken limbs were set between two splints of cedar bark, and bound. This was done by someone with special skills (not a shaman), called ***koolth nook sa tee*** or ***koolth nuk sah-tee*** [quɬnu·kʷ ṡa·tí, "feeling-about expert," or rubbing doctor.]

Burns and scalds, ***ka wuh ghon*** [ka·waga·n, "it burned up," or wudix̣íx̣, "burned"], were covered with mud to exclude all air. [At Yakutat, the blisters from burns were drained, and the raw flesh was greased with fresh seal oil and covered with fresh chiton skins (de Laguna 1972:655).] A lichen (probably *Peltigera aphthosa*) was dried, powdered, and applied to the hurt.

Inflammations and swellings were covered with wet clay and dressed daily. Rotten spruce [na·qʷ] was rubbed off on a stone, mixed with a little water, and used as a poultice. But if this treatment was not effective, the part was punctured with the only surgical instrument used by the Tlingit. In aboriginal days this was a sharpened piece of shell or bone. Later a lancet [tága·] was made of a small steel blade with a wooden or wrapped handle, from which it extended barely a quarter of an inch. The cut was kept open and drained every day, with finely twisted seabirds' down pressed into the wound. For dropsy, they also punctured.

Wounds and cuts, *stalth* [ṡé·ɬ, from the verb "to rip"], and ***tsu kalth etee*** [ca·g̣áɬ̓ ʔi·tí, "spear former-place-of"], were treated in several ways, as follows:

(a) The inner bark of the spruce and pine were pounded to a fine powder on a hot rock, mixed with oil, and applied as a poultice that was changed every three days.

(b) Bear gall was applied.

(c) Powdered rotten spruce was applied [as for swellings and inflammation].

(d) Dried inner bark of the yellow cedar was reduced to a powder. Dogfish oil was applied to the wound and covered over with the powder.

(e) Deer or goat tallow was mixed with spruce gum and applied.

(f) The leaves of the *Arabis hirsuta* (L.) Scop., or hairy rock cress, a plant of the Mustard family, were pulverized in a mortar, mixed with water, and applied.

(g) A medicine, applied locally, was called ***ka-kuk-tleaty nak*** [kag̣ak-ɬ̓i·dí ná·kʷ, "rat's tail medicine"]. It was made from a small, strong smelling "fern" [probably *Achillea borealis* Bong., a yarrow]. This was heated on a hot rock, mixed with the milk of a woman of the opposite moiety [from the patient], and applied to the wound.

[Presumably these different procedures were alternatives, but Emmons does not report what determined the choice among them. The intervention of a woman of the opposite moiety in preparing and administering medicines of great power was secured whenever possible (see de Laguna 1972, 2:657), but Emmons reported only:]

The use of medicinal herbs was generally known, but their gathering and preparation was more confined to older women, who were likewise the midwives, and for their services they were paid accordingly. [Of course, any member of the opposite moiety would be paid for services rendered in a life crisis.]

The devil's club, *sauthkt* [ṡáxt̓, *Echinopanax horridum* (Sm.) Decne. & Planch.], was used for cuts, abcesses, sprains, and inflammations. For external application, the outer bark was scraped [off], the inner bark was cut in long strips and roasted, put in a layer of skin, and pulverized. It was then mixed with the gum of the white pine and a little grease. This was melted, spread on a piece of skin, and put over the parts affected. As an antiseptic, the bark was chewed and applied locally.

Skin diseases, *geetsi* [gi·c], were treated by bathing with ***kan-guairth wozee*** [kaxʷé·x̣ wáṡi], a lotion made by boiling the bark of the highbush cranberry, *Viburnum edule*.

**Editor's note:* In this section and the next all identifications of plants were made by Alix Wennekens. These two sections were organized from scrappy notes; the division into two is an attempt to clarify the material.

Hair was strengthened with oil mixed with mashed skunk cabbage leaf.

MEDICINES FOR INTERNAL USE

[A number of medicines (see Table 27) were used both externally and internally, and a few were used externally for ailments we would consider to be internal.]

The kidneys, ***kah gah-ha-goo*** [qa· kahá·gu], were treated by a person's dipping his hands in hot water and rubbing over the part affected. The person giving the treatment was called ***koolth nuk sah tee*** [quɬnu·kʷ ṡa·tí, the rubbing doctor].

For stomach trouble:

(a) The roots of ***ginnee nak*** and ***koushta nak*** [ɬičani ná·kʷ, "smelly or stinking medicine," from a wild heliotrope, *Valeriana sitchensis* Bong.; and "land otter medicine," kú·šda· ná·kʷ, from a gentian, possibly *Gentiana Douglasiana* Bong.] were rubbed off on a rough stone or chewed and spat out, boiled in hot water, and drunk for trouble arising from constipation, ***kah-gun-day-nach-goo-dee*** [qa· gánde nagu·dí, "one's going outside"]. The leaves [of both plants?] were also heated and applied as a poultice.

(b) The inner bark of the devil's club was dissolved in water and used both as a purgative and an emetic.

(c) Rotted wood of the spruce was rubbed off on a rough stone, mixed with a little water, and used as a stomach poultice. The fine particles were put in oil and taken internally, or boiled and the water drunk. The bear is said to use this medicine. [Knowledge of curing wounds with poultices was often said to have been learned from the animals.]

(d) The root of the skunk cabbage [x̣á·ɬ (to which Emmons erroneously applied the native name for devil's club), or *Lysichton americanum* Hult. & St. John] was dried, the outer bark scraped off, boiled in water and drunk. The root was also used as a poultice.

(e) The root of the false Solomon's seal [*Smilacina racemosa* (L.) Desf.] was dug in the spring, rubbed off on a stone, steeped in hot water, and drunk to produce vomiting.

For bowel troubles, the following were used:

(a) The seaweed, ***klark ish*** [ɬa·q̇ásk, *Porphyra perforata*], gathered from the sea rocks in the spring, was chewed fine or cut in small pieces and boiled in water and eaten, or dried by the fire, reduced to powder, cooked, and eaten.

(b) The bark of the devil's club was scraped, dried over the fire, and reduced to a fine powder. About two tablespoonsful of this was put in a cup of water and drunk before eating in the morning. This is likewise used for [treating] syphilis, and for constipation, which latter complaint in extreme cases was attributed to witchcraft and referred to the shaman.

For heart disease, the root of the Western sweet cicely, a species of wild parsnip [*Osmorhiza chilensis* Hook & Arn.], was eaten.

Eye trouble of any kind was treated as follows:

(a) The leaves of a wood fern [*Dryopteris dilatata* (Hoffm.) Gray], the leaf bud of a shield fern [*Gymnocarpium dryopteris* (L.) Newm.], [the needles of ?, or bark of?] the Sitka spruce (***Picea sitchensis***), [the leaves of?] the large-leaved avens (***Geum macrophyllum*** Willd. [called ʔa·n-ka ná·gu, "town-on medicine"]), were mixed together, pounded in a mortar, mixed with human milk, and applied locally.

(b) The leaf of the lily of the valley (***Maianthemum dilatatum*** (How.) Nels & Macbr.) was wetted, heated, and put over the eye.

Fever, ***yah ta yee neauk*** [yaṫa·ỵi ní·kʷ], was treated with the sweat bath, after which the patient was wrapped in blankets. He also chewed the small green leaves of a swamp plant, [which were then] set in cold water. If the leaves floated, the patient would recover; if they sank, he would die. This medicine was called ***koo-see yun-nee nak*** [unidentified].

Syphilis and venereal disease [introduced by the whites] were treated by bathing in hot springs, and by drinking a tea made by boiling together spruce needles and gum and the bark of the devil's club.

The root of the yellow violet [probably *Viola glabella* Nutt.] and of the mountain gentian [*Gentiana platypetala* Griseb.] were used medicinally. So was the root of a mountain plant, ***scht*** [ṡíkš, American white hellebore or "Skookum root," *Veratrum viride* Ait., *ssp. Eschscholtzii* (Gray)] that produced a deep sleep like the effect of an intoxicant. [It is generally regarded by the Indians as a sovereign remedy, though dangerous.]

Rheumatism [ṡa·g̣í tuní·kʷ, "sickness of the bones"] was believed due to witches, and was referred to the shaman, but [presumably in milder cases, or at first] was treated with the starfish, ***suckh*** [ṡáx; less likely to be ṡu·k, "barnacle"]. This was dried before the fire, ground to a powder in the stone mortar, mixed with grease, and applied locally. It was also treated with a species of jellyfish, ***teh-yah-tah-yea*** [té yata·yí, "rock face fat," or sea anemone] that is found adhering to the rocks, and which was applied directly to the parts affected.

Consumption, ***whooh too neekoo*** [wu·w tu ní·gu, "sickness in the chest"], was also attributed to witchcraft and was

Shaman's bundle (shutch, šu·č?) *of spruce twigs, devil's club roots, and a brown bear jaw, enclosing the tongue of a land otter or other animal, tied with spruce root cord. Collected by G. T. Emmons before 1888 from a gravehouse on the Alsek River. (Photograph by Richard A. Gould. AMNH.)*

properly referred to the shaman, but in milder cases was medicinally treated with the following:

(a) A tea made of the maidenhair fern, *shar-ah-thlee-tee* or *sha yar thleetee,* "on the side of the mountain" [*Adiantum pedatum* L., probably ša·ya̧ łí·t̓i, "mountainside vine," less likely to be šayá̧ łi·dí, "mountainside tail"].

(b) A tea made by boiling the dried leaves and stems of the swamp laurel, *sick shult* or *sick-shel-teen* [ṡikšałdí·n, Labrador or Hudson Bay tea, *Ledum palustre L., ssp. groenlandicum* (Oeder) Hult.]. This was generally used as a drink.

(c) A tea made by boiling the scraped bark of the devil's club in salt water, and drunk hot.

(d) A drink made by boiling spruce and hemlock gum in fresh water.

(e) A tea was made by boiling the leaves of a berry bush, *thlu kut ta.* [Is this possibly the red huckleberry, elsewhere written as *kla-kat-tunk* (ƛ̕e·katánk), or *Vaccinium parvifolium* Sm.?]

(f) For hemorrhage of the lungs, a tea made from the leaves of a small evergreen shrub that grows high up on the mountain, ***thluk kut*** [probably *Loiseleuria procumbens* (L.) Desv.].

(g) For a cough, drink a tea made from the "***Lipidodendron***" [unidentified plant. *Lepidodendron* is a genus of fossil tree ferns that grew in the Carboniferous, named for the scaly surface of its bark where the leaf stalks separated!]

OTHER "MEDICINES"

Besides the medicinal substances mentioned above that were believed to have curative value, there were other potions or medicines that were used to produce supernatural results not connected with disease or illness. These were more like philters or charms, designed to secure success in gambling, trading, or hunting, or to cause desire in another. The knowledge and preparation of these were not generally known but were confined to a very few individuals in each tribe.

[These "medicines" were sometimes called na·kʷ (like curative medicines); sometimes they were known as kaya̧·ní, "leaves," even though it was the root that was considered effective. In English, they may be called "dope." Even though the general public might be ignorant of the particular plant used for a particular magical effect, the knowledge that such a "medicine" existed and was probably being used would give confidence to the one for whom the "medicine" had been prepared and who was using it, while the individual against whom it might be directed would be frightened. Such a "medicine" might be used against a dangerous animal, like the bear, as well as against a human rival. There were evidently many "medicines" of this type, more than seem to have been recorded by Emmons. (See Swanton 1908:445–48; de Laguna 1972:659–67.) Overuse of such "medicines" could bring disaster.

[In the examples discussed below, Emmons described only one class of such "medicines," those that might be classed as rubbing amulets.]

Don nak [da· ná·kʷ], "body medicine," which was used to bring good fortune in hunting, gambling, and trade, was individual, something used in secret and never shared with another, although it might descend to the next person in line of inheritance. It consisted of a miniature wooden chest, five by four by three inches. [It would be more correct to say that the contents of this chest constituted the "medicine."] The chest was often carved and inlaid with shell, and would be wrapped with skin and sometimes tied around with laid up [doubly twisted] human hair. It was generally hidden in the rocks or woods, or if kept in the house, it was secreted from others of the family. [No one but the owner was supposed ever to see the contents.]

It contained odd objects, such as an Asiatic bean which might have been carried over by the Japanese current and picked up on the shore—I have seen at least three of these in such boxes that I have examined—a stone from the stomach of a deer or seal, or one of peculiar shape or color, bits of fur, decayed wood, small claws, dried tongue of bird or animal, bits of cloth, and what seemed to be excrement—all of which were believed to have had some connection with the supernatural and retained something of it. But these objects had to be treated with great thought, and were never to be seen by another, or they would lose their power.

The formula for the use of *don nak* [da· ná·k^{w}] was the same in general practice, but individual in detail. It consisted in bathing, drinking salt water, rubbing the body with the articles in the box, fasting, and abstinence from connection with women. As given me by an old Tlingit, the procedure was as follows:

Before any important undertaking, or when seeking good fortune on general principles, the possessor of *don nak* goes into the salt water early in the morning before the Raven calls. Then he seeks a place deep in the woods where, unobserved, he opens the box and with one or more articles rubs the eight parts [joints] of his body; the shoulders, the elbows, the hips, and the knee joints. He drinks four swallows of salt water from his personal drinking basket [cup], and takes eight nibbles of devil's club bark. He then fasts for four days. On the fifth day he eats morning and evening. Then he fasts four more days. During this time and for a period variously stated as from four to eight months, he must practice continence, and was prohibited such food as shellfish and seaweed ["beach food"].

I have been told that during this time a number of men would live together, but this I question, for we have no evidence that the Tlingit had any public or community house like the Eskimo. [A group of men may, however, have slept on the house platform in front of the sleeping cubicles of the women, as shamans were reported to have done at Yakutat.]

The origin of *don nak* [da· ná·k^{w}] and its use, as told me by another source, is attributed to the Tsimshian:

There was a chief, *Yah shute,* who, while going in canoe to *Jin heen* [possibly ǯín hí·n, "hand water," unidentified place] saw a strange looking animal ahead in the water. His slave, a very brave man, steered directly toward it and discovered that it was *Heen tark hootzee,* "brown bear under water" [probably hintak xú·ʒi, the Sea Bear], that is, the slave of the greater mythical animal, *Go ne ko date* [Ģuna·kade·t]. It was believed that to see this mythical animal would bring good fortune. The slave obtained some hairs of the *Heen tark hootze* [hintak xú·ʒi] for his master, and after offering food to the larger animal, they went ashore. The chief bathed and required his household to do likewise. They fasted for four days and then bathed again, and the hairs which were like the whiskers of the sea lion were put in the box made for them, and were treasured by the chief's descendants for generations.

Other objects also used [as da· ná·k^{w}] were pieces of meteorite, but I never saw a carved charm or object in one of these boxes.

In hunting, the Tlingit carry charms—little bundles of roots and leaves, and think these will make them invisible to bear and seal, and make the bear afraid. One bundle I examined [contained] two kinds of roots and other leaves, and small pieces of shell.

Khart tuk tchene [ł-qa·-tu·ƛ̓či·n, "no strength inside"] was a medicine plant [unidentified]. When a man has this, he holds it in his hand when he shoots, and the bear will not fight.

OMENS AND AMULETS*

[Emmons left some scattered notes on signs of good luck and of bad luck, and of additional sources of amulets, but these were not organized, and a number were scribbled in his notebooks in BCPA.]

"Signs of Luck, Wrangel"—[To see] *Kone ko tate* [Ģuna·kade·t, "Wealth-bringing sea monster"] is a sign of luck.

Kleu-nar-khee-tuck ["Property Woman," ƛ̓anaxí·dáq^{w}, or ƛ̓enax̣hí·duq^{w}]—in old times a woman living in woods. Had a little babe, and when one hears the little thing cry, they follow it, and before getting it, they throw off all their clothing, and bathe. *Kleu-nar-khee-tuck* carrying babe on [her] back in cradle of *Tinnah* [sketch of "copper," tiná·]. Then take something belonging to child, and keep it in box, *Don nock* [see above]. And at new moon bathe and rub *Don nock* over body and wish for what is wanted.

**Editor's note:* This section was put together from notes and from entries in the catalogue of the Emmons Collection at AMNH because there seemed to be no other logical place for them.

Paraphernalia of an unidentified Raven 7 shaman, collected by G. T. Emmons before 1888 from the gravehouse at Dry Bay. Left. *Bundles* (shutch, šu·č?) *of spruce twigs, wrapped around land otters' tongues.* Right. *Pair of wooden ornaments, representing the fins of killerwhales, worn on the shoulders of the shaman's dancing robe. (Photograph by Richard A. Gould. AMNH.)*

[A somewhat different tradition specifies that the baby is stuck to the woman's back, and when the man reaches her and tries to tear the child off, she scratches him. These scabs are the amulets he saves. "Property Woman" is believed to be gathering "beach food" at the New Moon low tides, the only time when shamans or ritual fasters may eat it. This is probably why her "medicine" was effective at this time.]

[The "Wealth-bringing woodchopper"], *Tah qwutsk* [Tax̣gʷáṡ "—?—"], the husband of *Kleu-nar-khee-tuck,* can never be seen, but one can see foot tracks and can hear him chopping wood in the forest, and this is sign of good luck. Any piece of wood or bark chopped by him is kept for *don nak,* and they fast, bathe, and rub with it.

Good luck signs are called *thluh hate* [ɬaxé·t ?], "blessing."

"Bad luck signs"—[The field notes are mutilated.]

1. *Juck-tee sth.* . . . "murdered person ghost" [probably ǯáqʷti, "murdered corpse" —?—] a bird something like a bat, makes a noise like dropping water, and you see blood dropping on ground before [you]—a sign of misfortune for self or relative [of yours]. A sign of war or bloodshed. The bird can never be seen.

2. *Gin-nar-har,* "something bad to happen, misfortune" [ǯinahá·, bad luck at some future time].

The hooting of the owl is a sign of misfortune. It tells of war and trouble.

Kush-tar-ka [kú·šda· qá·, "Land Otter Man"]—a sign of trouble or misfortune.

[In answer to the question written in a field notebook about observances to be followed for good luck in hunting and fishing, Emmons recorded:] "Fast four days at a time and sleep out of doors on board away from family."

There was a general belief in dreams [ǯu·n]. They were sent as warning by the spirits from the other world, and each person interpreted his own dreams, although the shaman was sometimes believed to receive such warnings

Ivory charm representing a shaman's dream. Above is a raven's or frog's head (?); in the center is a bear biting one man and holding another; below is a bird's head surrounded by octopus tentacles. Length: 4½ inches. Collected by G. T. Emmons at Dry Bay before 1888. (AMNH.)

from his spirits which in some way he transmitted in dreams [to others. See de Laguna 1972:759, for an instance in which a shaman "put" the witch's spirit into the victim's dream as a way of revealing the witch.] As generally understood, dreaming of silver salmon, eulachon grease, the moon, the sun, or stars signified good luck. Dreaming of the bear, devilfish, blood, or fat forecast accident or misfortune. Dreaming of clams indicated poverty. ["Beach food" was connected with poverty, perhaps because it was easy to get; eating it at certain times or under certain circumstances was taboo, because to do so would bring poverty.]

Persons who sneezed were thought to have the power of prophesy to a limited extent. If induced by the left nostril, calamity, war, murder, was predicted; if from the right, it was a good omen.

The twitching of the left side of the upper lip was a bad omen.

The amulet, *ta-sate* [té se•t], was worn suspended about the neck, and consisted of a small stone, generally flat, an inch or two long, and shaped or incised in animal design. It was used to scratch the head or body, for the fingernail was considered harmful. In several instances, I found other materials substituted, such as the prized blue-green California haliotis shell or wood, but most valued of all were small pieces of nephrite: in one case a small chisel blade, in another a ground piece representing a brown bear's canine—the only ornamentally worked piece of nephrite I ever saw or heard of among the Northwest Coast natives. The superstition in regard to the use of a scratcher was still extant in the early 1880s when the older people wore the amulet around the neck. In early days, in the absence of men on a war party, if a wife should forget and use her fingernail instead of the neck piece, it was believed that an arrow or weapon blade would pierce the body of her husband at that spot.

[Such rubbing amulets resembled "body medicine" (da•ná•k^{w}) in part, and in part were similar to the wooden, stone, or ivory charms worn by shamans around the neck, and given by them to a patient. For example, no. 208 in the Emmons Collection at AMNH is described as a shaman's charm of wood, carved to represent a "yake" (shaman's spirit) and a devilfish. It was transferred from the neck of the shaman to the patient or to a child to keep sickness away. This specimen came from the grave of an old shaman, at "Hootznahoo," probably Angoon. The shaman also wore charms fastened to his dancing robe.

[Emmons collected a number of stone amulets from Chilkat, Sitka, "Hootznahoo," "Yindestaky," Auk, and other places. They were carved to represent various animals, although there were also some plain ones. The designs were: 6 killerwhale, 5 eagle and eagle's head, 1 bear and 2 bear's head, 1 crow eating dead bear, 1 shaman and bear, 1 bear catching salmon that is leaping up a waterfall (represented by an anthropomorphic head; fish below signifies salt water), 4 copper shield, 2 porpoise, 2 worm, 1 head of dogfish, 1 small saltwater fish "wako," and 1 representing a child to be worn by an expectant mother. These amulets are numbered 263 to 307.]

The most unusual "amulet" belonged to an old shaman of the Qu•sk̓e•dí, Raven 8, named *Karsh-tock-tu-oo* or *Kash-took-two,* who lived in the Yakutat or Dry Bay area. He named a large stone [boulder or outcrop?] for his spirit, and it was therefore known as *Karsh-tock-tu-oo Don-nok-ku ko yagee* [K-? da•ná•k^{w} qu-yé•gi, or "K's amulet spirit"]. If one fasted for two days, drinking salt water beside this stone, he would become strong. [Emmons secured the grave guardian of this shaman, from a man named Andrew. It was a carved wooden figure with land otter heads on the body.]

CHAPTER 14

Shamanism

SPIRITS*

[A human being has a body (qa· da·), a vital force, "breath" or life (qa· x̣a-sé·gu, or x̣a-sé·k^{w}), and a soul or "shadow" (qa· ỵa-ha·ỵí). It is the "breath," or life, that leaves the body during illness or fainting and which can be recovered by the shaman, or by his helping spirit (yé·k). After death, the "soul" or "shadow" (now a "ghost") travels to a land of the dead, the place depending on the manner of death, and it may later be reincarnated in a living person (qa· ỵak^{w}g̣^{w}ahé·ỵagu). (See also de Laguna 1972:765–66.)]

In addition, there is believed to be a personal guardian spirit, *Ka kin-ah yage* or *Ka-ken-a yake* [qa· kiná· yé·gi, or qa· kiná· yé·k], "up above spirit." This spirit tries to protect and guide its ward aright. But the spirit may desert its charge if offended, and it can be killed through great wrongdoing, which would likewise react upon its mortal charge. The only prayer made by the Tlingit is to this spirit. [This is not entirely correct.] When in danger, the Tlingit would say, "*Kluw-kut-hut thlar-tin uh khen-nah ya-gee*" [ƛu·wk^{w}át x̣at ɬi-tín, ʔax̣ kiná· yé·gi, "Carefully me watch, my above spirit"], or "Watch over me carefully, my Spirit Above." [See de Laguna 1972:812–13.]

[Veniaminov ([1840] 1984:398) reported that a person's *Tukinayeik* always hovered above him, but the yé·k of a crooked person would leave or kill him. Hence they would say (or swear), "If I do evil, then my ʔax̣ kiná· yé·gi will kill me."]

The Tlingit endowed all nature with spirit life. Each species had its own particular spirits and there was no exchange [between species]. Natural phenomena and inanimate objects all possessed something which made itself felt or became visible under certain conditions. The wind, whirlpool, thunder and lightning, or a glacier, were controlled by spirits. The spirit of a tree was the shadow made visible by sunshine. The air, the earth, the water were all peopled by both good and bad spirits. The former, being harmless, were little thought of and were not appealed to, but the latter were greatly feared, and were propitiated through gifts and observances. All living creatures have spirits. [It will be remembered that the spirit of the tree cut for a house post or canoe had to be propitiated, as did the nearby trees that might be injured in the felling. In the same way the spirit of a dead animal had to be appeased.]

In early days, when the glaciers of Glacier Bay were advancing, the Hoonahs threw a slave into a crevasse and so propitiated the Ice Spirit, and the glacier retreated. On another occasion, the Takus killed a slave and threw his scalp into a crevasse. [In these instances the dead slave and the slave's scalp represented offerings. But other informants would hold that corpse and scalp were unclean and disgusted the ice so much that it retreated.] When hunting among icebergs, the Hoonahs throw a pinch of tobacco to the ice spirits and talk to those living in each berg. The spirit of the glacier, *sith tu yage* [siṫ tu yé·gi], was manifested in the cold wind.

[Oscar von Engeln, photographer for the U.S. Geological Survey during its study of Yakutat glaciers in 1906, reported (1907:176):

> The Indians have a superstitious terror of the glaciers, calling them "ghosts"; and whenever they come to any of the numerous gloomy arched cave passages which lead under the ice, they will not go on without hurling a number of large boulders into the opening, hoping to harm "Father Hoo," the evil spirit who dwells under the ice.]

Any spirit was known as *yehk* or *yage* [yé·k, yé·gi; the last meaning "spirit of"]. Spirits of the air were *Ki yehk* [ki· yé·k, "above spirit(s)"]; spirits of the earth were *Tah-ke yehk* [da·g̣i yé·k]; and those of the sea were *De-ke yehk* [de·kí· yé·k]. Spirits from below were known as *Hi-ye yehk* [ha·ỵi· yé·k].

[It is uncertain whether Emmons meant that these were a fourth class, or if this name was applied to one of the other

---

Editor's note: The original sections for this chapter were titled: The Shaman, Who May Be a Shaman, Novitiate, Dress and Implements (Articles) of Practice, Practice, Witchcraft (see the next chapter: Emmons was uncertain whether to include this larger section in this chapter, or to treat it as a separate chapter), Death, Death of "Scar-dun-na," Graves, Legends: Legend of the Salmon Shaman, Legend of the Man Stolen by the Land Otter People, Legend of the Ka-ghan-tan Ict Ko-qunk.

**Editor's note:* The first two paragraphs of this section were transferred from the end of Chapter 10, "The Life Cycle." I have added information from von Engeln and from Veniaminov.

three. He also mentioned a "spirit of the water," *tuk-hah yage* (? yé·gi); possibly this was another name for the sea spirit(s).

[Apparently the spirits that came to a shaman would belong to one or more of these groups. Thus, Veniaminov ([1840] 1984:396) (and after him Holmberg [1855:63–65] and Petroff [1884:174–75]) wrote: "Strictly speaking, there are no demons or devils in the Koloshi Spiritology. There are, however, spirits called yeiki, which are called upon by the Shamans. [A footnote by Richard Dauenhauer explains that the ending -i is the Russian plural, applied to the Tlingit word.] There is an innumerable multitude of these spirits so that every Shaman has his own, generally several, spirits." Because they like purity, the shamans must be chaste for three or four months before calling them. The house in which the séance is to be held must be cleaned and fresh sand put around the fireplace.

[There are three classes of *yeik* (yé·k), as described by Veniaminov. The first class of spirits are the spirits of the above, the *Kiyeiki* (ki· yé·gi), from the word *Kina,* "above." The second class of spirits are the *Takiyeiki* (da·gi yé·gi), which Veniaminov translated as "those living over there, somewhere on the mainland, to the north side." The third class of spirits are the *Tekiyeiki* (de·kí· yé·gi), the "water or sea spirits."

> The spirits of the above . . . [*Kiyeiki,* ki· yé·gi] are the souls of valiant people killed in war. . . . Their dwelling is conjectured to be in the above and in the sky, which from time to time opens up in order to receive new souls. Many happen to see this, but it happens only to one's own misfortune, as the one who observes the opening up of the heavens shall soon die (therefore, such a person is called *Kiyaqáu* [ki·wa qawu]. . . . The *Kiyeiki* . . . always appear to the shamans as warriors in full battle gear. . . .
>
> The *Takiyeiki* [da·gi yé·gi], or the land [earth—Translator] spirits, are always recruited from among the souls of those people who died the ordinary [natural—Translator] death, or those who were not killed in war. . . . [p. 397]

Veniaminov was not certain that he had understood the Tlingit correctly on this last point. At any event, the Tlingit could not explain why some of the ordinary dead could not appear as spirits. Probably only those who had been prominent in life would have been welcomed by the shamans as their spirit helpers.

> The Takiyeiki [da·gi yé·gi] . . . appear to the Shamans in the guise of land animals, while the Tekiyeiki [de·kí yé·gi] . . . or water spirits appear as sea mammals, for instance, whales, killer whales and so on. The spirits receive their names after the animals in whose guise they appear, the spirit of the wolf or wolf Yeik; . . . spirit of the killer whale or killer whale Yeik and so on. [The last would be rendered in Tlingit as kí·t qu-yé·gi, or kí·t yé·k.—FdeL]

"Skun-doo" [Sx̣anduˀú·, *from* yís x̣á·n duwaˀú·], *a celebrated shaman of the Wolf 7, Chilkoot. His hair was forcibly cut in 1888, so he had to renounce his profession, but later gave information to Emmons, and posed, presumably for a fee, for photographers. He wears a feather headdress* (yé·k č̓i·ni) *with small round maskette in front, a necklace of rattling bones* (ṡa·q se·dí), *a skin apron with rattling fringe, and he wields a rattle in each hand. (Photograph by Winter and Pond, ca. 1894. AMNH.)*

> But whence did come or how are recruited the Tekiyeiki . . . [de·kí· yé·gi, "spirits far out to sea"]? . . . The Koloshi are not able to explain this satisfactorily, though some think that these are the souls of the animals themselves. [p. 398]

[Emmons recorded the terms *Hi-ye yehk* (ha·yí· yé·k), "spirits from below," and *hi-ye quanee* (ha·yi qʷá·ni), "spirits (or ghosts) at bottom of water, those drowned." The similarity of these terms suggests that the yé·k of the sea, or "from below," were the souls of those who had drowned.

[It would appear that any spirit, except possibly the individual's Spirit Above, might become the helping spirit of a shaman, and such helping spirits could include human ghosts. Others were nature spirits? It is uncertain, however, if the human souls that became a shaman's familiars did so by appearing to him in the guise of animals or birds, the tongues of which he cut to secure his powers (see below). The Tlingit denied that human souls could be reincarnated in animals. Yet, since both certain animals and certain men, under certain conditions, might change their forms, the line between animals and men, at least on a spirit level, was hazy. If the spirits of the air or sky were the ghosts or souls of those who had died by violence, might they not appear in the shape of birds? Was the land otter that usually appeared to the novice shaman, and from which the latter cut its tongue to secure power, simply an animal? Or was it not the form taken by the ghost of a drowned person, a Land Otter Man? Was the spirit obtained from it that of an animal or that of a human being? As Olson wrote (1967:113, note 299): "As is usual in much of North America there is no sharp distinction between animals, animal spirits, animals in human form, or humans in animal form." The Tlingit themselves should not be expected to give completely consistent accounts of the various kinds of spirits and their manifestations.

[In addition to yé·k, or perhaps included in the group of yé·k possessed by a shaman, was something termed his "power," or "fighting spirit," łékʷa. His assistant spirit would be called ʔíx̣ṫ x̣an yé·gi, and his human assistant was called ʔíx̣ṫ x̣an qá·wu. When the shaman cried out to invoke his spirits, this was termed ʔat šuła ʔax̣č.

[Veniaminov ([1840] 1984:400) further reported that in time of misfortune or illness, a Tlingit might pray or appeal to the principal yé·k belonging to some famous shaman.]

THE SHAMAN

The worst feature of Tlingit life was the practice of the shaman, *ict* [ʔíx̣ṫ], and the associated belief in witchcraft, which made the people suspicious of each other and fearful of all natural conditions that they could not understand They endowed all animate life and inanimate objects with spirits: some good and harmless or others evil and hurtful. The former were disregarded, but their inability to contend with the latter brought into existence a class [of persons] which, through supernatural power, was believed able to combat the witch spirits that caused sickness, to discover and name those responsible for the illness.

The shaman might be of either sex, though among the Tlingit there were comparatively few women shamans. While it was claimed that the latter could not practice until after they had passed the age of child-bearing, yet, in 1888, at Hoonah there was a young woman, not over twenty-five, who was an accepted *Ict* [ʔíx̣ṫ].

The shaman was not a healer in any physical sense. He gave neither medicine nor bodily treatment, but through the power of the spirits he controlled, he exorcised and contended with those who caused sickness. When these were too powerful for him [to accomplish a cure], he proclaimed the witch [responsible]. The latter was tortured and confessed [thereby lifting the curse], or was killed. [In the last event, presumably the patient had died.]

Besides practicing about the sick, the shaman was the adviser of the chief when on war parties. At night, when all were assembled, he would appear naked, except for the waist robe [apron] and a fighting headdress [a woven rectangular bonnet]. Crouching on the floor by the fire, he would remain silent for half an hour or more, while his spirit went out to the enemy's camp to see their strength and learn their secrets. In one hand he grasped a spirit knife, wand, or club. Only the soft beating of the drum [by his assistant] broke the silence until his spirit returned, when he jumped up. The drum beats sounded quick and loud as he announced that he had conquered the opposing spirits. He used to accompany the war party, and at night would "spy" on the enemy, and advise his leader.

He might sometimes dance to celebrate the new moon. He fasted during the day. When all were assembled, he impersonated each of his spirits, singing its song, accompanied by his followers who chanted to the beat of the drum. At times, he would set a fast day for his family, to give him strength. Early in the morning, they [members of his family] drank salt water to wash away all evil in the body, and at night he impersonated his different spirits in dress and song.

He also performed to bring the run of fish, an abundance of berries, or good weather. The shaman was appealed to in almost every extraordinary occurrence. For example, in

Taku shaman with two wives, 1909. (Photograph by G. T. Emmons? AMNH.)

a case of an obstructed childbirth, he sent for the stake which the woman grasped, spat on it, put eagle down on it, and told the messenger to drive it into the ground, head first [blunt end down?].

[Perhaps because the shaman almost always had the Land Otter as one of his spirits, he was able to rescue those who had been captured by the Land Otters, provided they were found before their transformation into Land Otter Men.]

A man at a fishing village on the Chilkat River lost $50 that had been paid to him the day before. He gave *Skun-doo* [Sx̣anduʔú·], the shaman, ten "one-point" blankets to recover the money which was presumably stolen. Skun-doo dressed himself, and built a fire on the beach into which he spat fifty times. Then he jumped across it three times, took a stick, notched it, and stuck it in the sand, announcing that at night when it fell, it would point to the house of the thief. But when it was found still standing in the morning, the people laughed. But Skun-doo picked up the stick, swung it around his head and, after spitting on it, threw it into the water, saying that the thief would soon follow. It so happened that shortly after, one of the villagers was drowned. His family [lineage] had to pay the $50 with interest, believing the shaman was right.

This same shaman, when once called upon to determine the perpetrator of another theft, assembled all the villagers. Standing in front of them and holding a mouse, he said that when he released the animal, it would run into or under the house where the thief lived. [A mouse was associated with witchcraft; witches were guilty of all kinds of wrongdoing, including theft; the mouse was a notorious thief, and also could be used to detect thieves.] Later, Skun-doo was found guilty of having caused the death of a woman whom he had denounced as a witch. [This event and its consequences will be described later in this chapter.]

This same sinister looking, red-haired Skun-doo held sway in the tribe [Chilkoot] both by virtue of his natural shrewdness and by his native cruelty. While he was unquestionably a rank imposter, working for personal gain, yet some of his actions and divinations are not susceptible of any explanation. For example, I met a Chilkat who had passed through the [Protestant] mission at Sitka, and had little faith in the native beliefs and customs. He told me that one day at Klukwan, Skun-doo met him with the information that his brother at Skagway had just met with a serious accident. He [the Chilkat] looked at his watch, and it was just noon. While quite free from the old prejudice [superstition], yet he could not wholly satisfy his mind. So he took his canoe and went down the Chilkat River, then crossed the isthmus to Haines, and by canoe to Skagway, which he reached the following day. He found his brother in the hospital, suffering from an injury received at noon the previous day. Now Klukwan and Skagway are separated by an impassable mountain ridge, and there was at that time no air communication between them. The journey by canoe is fully twelve hours, and as the Indian said, "How did Skun-doo know of this the moment it happened?"

[*Skun-doo* or *Skundo,* Sx̣anduʔú, from yís x̣á·n duwaʔú, "One is enraged at him," was a famous shaman of the Dagisdina·, Wolf 7, and also a chief of the Chilkoot. He is buried at Yandestake.

[He was not, however, the only Tlingit to combine the offices of chief and shaman. Another was Chief *Cowee,* or *Kow-ee,* of the Auk, who became a friend of Emmons. He was Łi'ne·dí, Raven 15, and a rival of *Klee-a-keet,* Łiya·-kí't, (Daqławe·dí, Wolf 27), a notorious shaman of Angoon. Cowee told Emmons the Tlingit story of La Pérouse in Lituya Bay (Emmons 1911c). A predecessor, of the same name, was also shaman and chief of the Auk, who died about the middle of the last century, and whose outfit Emmons obtained for the AMNH (catalogue numbers E-2683 to E-2703, listed in Table 31).

[In his field notes Emmons also mentioned Ben Fox as "Donna-wak's successor" and listed his shamanistic paraphernalia. Dá·na·wa·q, "Silver/Dollar Eyes," was a chief of the Łukʷa·x̣ʔádi, Raven 17, at Yandestake, a Chilkoot. While Ben Fox was certainly a shaman, we do not know in what capacity he succeeded Dá·na·wa·q, for Emmons and Mrs. Willard knew the latter primarily as a chief. Ben Fox's professional outfit included "Drs. carved double box, mask eagle, mask mosquito, mask woman, 1 other mask [land otter, apparently], Tsimshian Chilkat blanket, bag Dulthlee [dú·ƚi] crane, containing old chief Drs. scalp." A note in the feeble hand of advanced age indicates that all these masks were burned up in 193? or later.

[Mrs. Willard (1884:50–55, letter of August 1881) met a Chilkoot shaman, Karskarz, the younger brother of Chief Dá·na·wa·q ("Silver Dollar Eyes") of Yandestake, "and himself a chief in Chilkoot village." See Chapter 3, the section "Domestic Life." These brothers were Łukʷa·x̣ʔádi, Raven 17.]

BECOMING A SHAMAN*

The question of who might become a shaman and at what age was not under human control. The spirit which had previously served a shaman selected the medium [i.e., a succeeding shaman], always within the same family, even though generations may have elapsed between the death [of the former] shaman and the return of the spirit. It may be born in a child and be recognized by some similarity to the deceased, or by some peculiar physical characteristic, like a twisted lock of hair, in which case the child was brought up with that end in view [i.e., as a future shaman]. The hair was never cut, but was matted with spruce gum and grease. The shaman was not allowed to partake of certain sea foods, such as clams and mussels, as these are offensive to the spirit.

[Yakutat informants stated that the shaman and his immediate family could eat beach food only during the one month when "Property Woman," ƛ̓enax̣hí'duqʷ, went down to the beach to gather and eat such food; to eat beach food at other times would impoverish him (de Laguna 1972:683).]

Otherwise, his life did not differ from that of others in the group until he reached maturity, possibly eighteen years of age. Then he had to comply with certain forms and prove that he was truly possessed of the spirit, before he was accepted and allowed to practice.

In 1888, I saw a boy eight or ten years old, at Killisnoo [Hutsnuwu tribe], Admiralty Island, who was considered to have inherited the spirit of a dead shaman of his mother's family [her clan and his own] because he had similar features. His hair had never been combed and was matted with spruce gum. Some years ago, at Chilkat, a baby so born was

**Editor's note:* I have here combined two sections of the original manuscript, and have included information from Shukoff, Mrs. Willard, Veniaminov, and Krause.

believed to have possessed such great power that he sent an evil spirit to Sitka and killed his sister who was visiting there. This explanation, like many superstitions, was simply advanced to account for her death, but was believed by many.

The spirit may come to an adult regardless of any desire on his part to possess it; again, one may acquire it through fasting, continence, or actually seeking it; but in any case, the family [clan] must be convinced of its coming. The spirit usually took possession of the novice in the evening and was instantly recognized by a vibrant buzzing in the ears, when the recipient fell to the floor in a trance and so remained apparently lifeless, for hours. At this time, he saw an opening in the sky and lights streaming down as the spirit descended and entered his head. To test the truth of the condition, a small feather was placed between his lips, and a watcher sat near the body, for if any sign of movement stirred the vanes it was proof that the aspirant possessed no spirit, but was an imposter. Upon regaining consciousness, the new shaman fasted for four or eight days, ate the bark of the devil's club, and drank no [fresh] water the last two or four days. During this initiatory period, he was wholly or partially unconscious and was carefully watched and attended by his family. Upon the termination [of this period], he resumed his usual life, but ate sparingly of salmon and berries, and abstained from grease.

This mode of living might last as long as eight months, or until the family [clan] were satisfied that the spirit had come to him. Then he was sent off in a canoe with four or more male members of the family. He sat in the bottom of the canoe, knees drawn up to the chin, head bowed, and completely covered by a blanket, and he sang to his spirit in a language known only to himself. Upon reaching some uninhabited island or shore, the canoe was beached. The entire party landed and made camp, and all fasted for four days, eating only the bark of the devil's club. At night, accompanied by his guards [assistants], the would-be shaman entered the woods and, as foretold, a land otter would appear. He [the novice] made a peculiar sound, "ha, ha," similar to that made in war when overtaking an enemy, [more like "wu·, wu·"], and with a crosslike club, *Ka-tu* [kétu], made several passes, and the otter fell dead, with tongue protruding. The shaman collected a bundle of twigs over which he cut out the otter's tongue, which he then enclosed in a longer bundle of twigs bound around with spruce root or cedar-bark cord. The twigs on which the blood had dripped were likewise wrapped up. Both of these were believed to possess strong spirit power and were known as *shutch* [probably šú·č]. They were worn attached to a twisted root cord, hanging around the neck over the breast. Now the shaman was believed to possess or command the land otter's spirit, which was considered the most powerful of all animal spirits.

All animals, in fact all nature, inanimate and animate, is possessed of a spirit, and the shaman through the same procedure accumulated as many spirits as possible, or were considered necessary to his practice. While the spirit of the land otter [kú·šda· qu-yé·gi] seems to have been essential and the most powerful, yet others, such as those of the mink, marten, weasel, squirrel, hawk, owl, bluejay, loon, kingfisher, cormorant, crane, and others, were most desired, and their tongues, skins and/or other parts of their bodies were enclosed in the *shutch*. I have found parts of most of these creatures wrapped up in bundles of twigs, and in the case of the smaller animals the whole skin with the skull intact was kept, especially that of the weasel and the small hawk. In one instance I found the jaws of a bear. Such animals as were generally eaten, such as the deer, porcupine, marmot, some birds, and fish, were regarded as possessing harmless spirits of no strength.

Each shaman was, in fact, quite individual in his spirits, although he certainly inherited or acquired some of those that had belonged to the shaman whose spirit had come to him when he used the masks and paraphernalia that represented them. [Does this imply that the predecessor's ghost came as a spirit?] Upon cutting out the land otter's tongue, the novice voiced his wishes as to his future power. He then fasted four or eight days, at the expiration of which time he returned with his followers, took a sweat bath, partook of food and, in the evening, gave an exhibition dance to honor his spirits. Any menstruating woman had to leave the house during this performance. Then the shaman was accepted as a practitioner. But to obtain great power, he must have no contact with a woman for eight months to four years. I was told that to obtain the masks and spirit charms of the one whom he would succeed, he must lie down beside the corpse in the gravehouse at night. No animal whose tongue he cut or whose spirit was taken could ever be eaten by the shaman or he would become crazy.

All space is the abode of spirits visible only to the shaman. Those he has acquired hover about him, ready to be summoned when needed. One who possessed the spirit of the bear had no fear of fire and could walk on the live coals without harm. What differentiated the shaman from others was his possession of a spirit besides that which all

Shaman in ordinary dress, with matted locks tied up. "Ek-kass" or "Ekass" ("Moose under the World"), Wolf 27, was the last shaman of the Chilkat tribe, Klukwan, 1888. (Photograph by Winter and Pond? AMNH.)

had [the guardian Spirit Above]. It is not clearly understood by the Tlingit themselves whether this was really a spirit or a power capable of calling outside spirits and demanding their aid, for upon their arrival they dominated and took possession [of the shaman], or, rather, the shaman became the spirit which he represented in appearance and impersonated in word and act, and through this medium his [own?] spirit was transported through space and saw the invisible. Again it is uncertain whether the shaman could send the spirit out to do his will. It was rather believed that his spirit and the one he had summoned were merged and went off together during the period when his body was in a trance. [At times the shaman sent a spirit, not his own, to discover something at a distance, and on its return the spirit is said to report to "his master."]

An old legend related that when the salmon failed to appear at the mouth of the Stikine River one summer, the spirit of *Ka-ja-du* [Qaǯadu?], an old shaman, went out to their country [that of the salmon], and brought them to the coast.

All shamans were believed to possess the power of levitation. The legend of the crane tells of the spirit of the grindstones that appeared as shoes that could outrun any game. When pursued by any supernatural monster, one could take them [stone shoes] off and throw them back, when they would be transformed into mountains. This was one of the most powerful legendary spirits.

The spirits that transport the shaman's spirit through space are known as *ko-see* "foot," *yage* "spirit" [qa· x̣̊us-yi yé·gi, "person foot-under spirit"]. In carvings they were frequently represented as bottom fish, like the devilfish, or sculpin, but more particularly the halibut. These transported his spirit, unseen, through space, and kept him informed of all that occurred about him.

[Emmons evidently based this account partly on the following statement by Shukoff:

> Ancestors used to keep customs strictly as possible, and they kept diet and fasted for some reason always. Now I will mention some few things about their fasting. First, anyone that wishes to become a shaman he refuses to eat anything that belongs to the sea or lives on the beach, especially devil fish, because that is very disgusting to future yake [yé·k]. If any shaman would eat anything that belongs to sea, he won't have same strength, or it will take him a long time to become one, or won't become at all, for he had dirtied his stomach with the filthy food which is disgusting to his yakes. . . .
>
> There are three grades of shamans.
> First grade [or kind], those born to be or become a shaman
> Second grade, those who are trying to become a shaman
> Third grade, those who inherit from a dead ancestor, a shaman
>
> Those born to be shamans are most respected, although when [the others become] shamans, they [the people] have confidence in all. Often a baby shortly after birth, through some peculiar twist of hair, his parents and relatives see that he will become a shaman, they never allow his hair to be combed, and never allow him to eat anything [from the] sea[:] clams, mussels, as no shamans eat these things, the reason is that "Yakes" dislike anything from sea and if he disobeys this injunction yakes will leave him and he will lose all power. Boy born to be shaman after reaches seventeen years of age his parents make him fast for eight days.
>
> Many wish to be shamans, and these are the most unscrupulous and lazy who are not fond of work but want an easy living. Before becoming shaman go down to shore and take salt water bath during the night, and then fast for two days, and after fast is over goes into woods early in morning with a knife, some go to ancestor's grave and pray for power through their yakes. In evening return home, eat dry salmon and drink water, the next morning does same, and he sees a land otter which comes up to him and dies at his feet, and puts tongue out and shaman quickly cuts tongue out and eats it [!]. (George [Shukoff's interpreter]

told of would be shaman in 1887). After that fasts eight days again, and then he composes songs[,] for each shaman has his own songs, and then he gets or makes wooden masks which are images of his Yakes, and having everything ready he gives out that his yakes are more powerful and he is ready to practice, and that all his relatives may have long life, he requires them to fast four days. He also tells them that his yakes through him make this request and any who disobey will be killed by his yakes.

[The rest of Shukoff's statement will be quoted in sections dealing with the shaman's practice and death.

[Mrs. Willard, wife of the missionary at Haines, wrote in December 1881 (1884:133, 132):

> In speaking of these medicine men . . . a little daughter (four or five years of age) of him whom we consider the worst man among them was born with curly hair; so of course she was destined to the profession, and her hair left uncut, uncombed, to become a matted, repulsive mass like her father's, while she was adorned with necklace of teeth and charms of green stone. . . .
>
> [All the medicine men] (so far as I have observed and there are about two in the Chilcat [and Chilkoot] tribe) have a most peculiar, cunning, and yet weird expression. They are hollow-eyed, but the pupil protrudes and rolls, and there is a keenness, a furtiveness, about them that is most unpleasant.

[According to Veniaminov ([1840] 1984:400), the Tlingit had great faith in their shamans and accepted whatever the latter told them as true: "Thus, for instance, the Shamans forbid them to eat whale, and the Koloshi do not touch it." He believed that this faith would endure a long time, even though in his day there were fewer great shamans than in the past, and some believed that the modern practitioners were not as powerful as their predecessors because they were "intemperate" (that is, did not obey the strict rules of their regimen). Veniaminov reported that only two great shamans remained: one at Yakutat who was credited with preventing the spread of smallpox to his people, and the other at Chilkat. The latter was famous because he had a land spirit one side of which had turned to stone; at the same time one-half of the mask that represented it had also turned to stone, while the other side remained wood. A third shaman, who had lived at Sitka, had died recently (Veniaminov, pp. 403–4). "To be a Shaman," explained Veniaminov, "means to have under one's own control several spirits (the Yeik [plural—Translator]), to call them and know how to make proper contortions when summoning them. To discern the unknown, to avert misfortune and calamities through the Yeik [plural—Translator], is the goal of Shamanism. The healing of sicknesses, however, is not always the business of a Shaman" (p. 400).

[Veniaminov (pp. 400–402) also explained how one becomes a shaman (see translations by Holmberg 1855:68–71) and Petroff (1884:175–76). This may be summarized:

[Shamanism is almost always hereditary—that is, it is inherited by the son or grandson of a shaman, together with all his masks, drum, and songs. (But since some spirits seem to be associated with certain clans, these would more likely be inherited by a sororal nephew, not a son, and only by a son's son in the same clan as the grandparent.—FdeL) But not all of a shaman's descendants can become shamans. No matter how hard they try, they cannot see a single yé·k. And on the other hand, sometimes the spirits force themselves on someone who does not want them. This was the case with the Yakutat shaman mentioned above. He did everything to drive them away, even going to a menstruating woman—the greatest pollution—but the spirits made him a great shaman. His brother, who wanted to become one, was not able to do so.

[The one who desires to become a shaman goes off into the forest or mountains, away from people, where he stays from two weeks to a month, eating only the bark of the *nazamainik*. (This is identified by Holmberg and Petroff as the devil's club, "*Panax horridum*," a powerful purgative and emetic.) He stays until he "is filled" with yé·k and the chief spirit among them has given him a land otter, "an absolutely necessary appurtenance of every shaman" (Veniaminov, p. 401). This animal comes of its own accord to the shaman, who cries "Oh!" four times in different keys. At this terrible cry, the animal falls on its back and dies, its tongue protruding. This the shaman cuts off, reciting incantations to ensure that he will be successful in his calling and never shamed before the people when holding a séance. The tongue is put in a special box with scraps of cloth, fur, or skin, and this is hidden in an inaccessible place, for if it were found by an uninitiated person, he would go insane. (While it is not clear in Veniaminov's account who would suffer, I believe that the shaman was the one who would lose his mind and the finder would be infected with a spirit-object intrusion.) The amulet is called *Kushtaliute* (kú·šda· ł̣ú·ṫi) "land otter's tongue." The skin of the otter is removed whole, and kept by the shaman as a sign of his profession; the flesh is carefully buried.

[Before the Russians came, the Tlingit did not dare even to touch a land otter; now (1830? 1840?) they kill them to trade the fur.

[The unlucky aspirant who fails to call together the spirits and get a land otter from them visits the graves of shamans and sleeps with their corpses. Or he takes a tooth, or cuts off the end of the little finger from one, and keeps this in his mouth, in order to receive the spirits and the land otter. (I think that here Veniaminov is confusing the shaman with the witch.)

[At the end of this fasting, the shaman leaves his retreat and returns to his people, so weakened that his face appears waxlike. He then at once conducts a shamanistic séance, in order to demonstrate his power and skill. His reputation depends upon the number of spirits (yé·k) he can control. Powerful shamans, with many yé·k, may become very rich. An unskillful one may be poor, and if he doesn't maintain his purity, his own yé·k may kill him. Each shaman has his own spirits, and each of them has his (or her) own name and songs. Only after some time has elapsed do the yé·k of his ancestors begin to appear to a shaman, usually at a séance. He is very happy to have a yé·k from his father or (maternal) uncle, and gives presents to his opposites, gune·tkana·yí.

[The shaman is never allowed to cut his hair. Only in deep mourning may he cut the front part of his hair, but the braid is untouchable.

[Krause ([1885] 1956:201–2) described the initiation of a new shaman among the Chilkat that he had observed at Klukwan in January 1882. The deceased and his successor belonged to the "Raven clan," presumably the G̣a·nax̣te·dí, Raven 3. The funeral had been held a short time previously and the youthful successor had been acknowledged.

[For four days the adult members of the clan fasted, the children for two days, the new shaman for eight (except for a morsel on the fifth day). In the evenings, all gathered at the house of the deceased for ceremonial dances. The leader of the ceremony and several old men, including two shamans, stood to the right of the door, near which the outfit of the deceased was displayed. Women and children of the clan were ranged along the left wall; spectators from the other clans were at the right; and the dancers, the men and boys of Raven 3, in clean clothes with evergreens round the neck, stood near the central fire. Many songs were sung, accompanied by beating sticks and by a wooden drum with a skin head that was pounded with the feet. The Raven men and boys moved toward the fire and back again in time to the song. Two boxes containing masks, rattles, and drums were lowered into the house during one of the dances, and the masks were held close to the fire. During the fourth song, the young shaman rushed out from the crowd and fell unconscious on the floor. One of his predecessor's necklaces was thrown over his head. When he regained consciousness, the ceremony was ended; the paraphernalia in the chests was hoisted out of the house, and bird down was blown about.

[The Ravens again fasted for four days. On the evening of the third, the new shaman danced about the fire with a sharp knife. The fourth and last night was a repetition of the first, but without much of the nervous tension and excitement evident on the first.]

THE SHAMAN'S OUTFIT*

The dress and implements [professional paraphernalia] of a shaman were never handled by others, nor were they brought into the house except when required for use. They were stored in chests that were generally kept on the house roof, but otherwise on platforms in the woods, in caves or outside shelters. Everything used or connected with the practice of a shaman had a spirit value, representing exactly what he had seen in his dreams or trances, what was worn or carried by each particular spirit he possessed. So when a particular spirit entered and took possession of him, he impersonated it in dress and speech, or rather he was the spirit himself. [While the identification of shaman and spirit may be disputed by some Tlingit, it is true that some shamans were known by the personal name of their principal spirit (de Laguna 1972:672).]

The objects [professional outfit] may be made by [the shaman] himself or by anyone else according to his direction. They possessed no power until used by him. It is clear, therefore, that in the routine practice of all shamans certain articles were considered necessary and were of common occurrence in each outfit, yet no two objects were actually identical. There was no duplication in all of the shaman's sets I have examined, except in one or two instances where the successor had taken the mask of one [of his predecessors] whose spirit had come to him, and an old mask had been used as a model. This originality is to be expected, for each practitioner was individualistic, depending largely upon the impression he exerted on his audience, an impression which was entirely spectacular. In addition to four masks, a rattle, skin waist apron, bone necklace, crown or headdress, and carved ivory or bone neck charms, which seemed to be absolutely essential, there are many other objects, such as medicine charms, wands, carvings, skin breast robes, blankets, and headdresses which may be found in any outfit.

The following list includes the principal and customary articles of dress and implements of practice that I have found in the numerous outfits and grave boxes of shamans

*Editor's note: The title of this section is mine. I compiled Table 31, the outfit belonging to the predecessor of Shaman-Chief Cowee from the catalogue of the Emmons Collection, AMNH, E-2683 to E-2703; and I added the description of a shaman's costume from Fleurieu.

Shaman's skull and paraphernalia from a gravehouse near Port Mulgrave, Yakutat. Collected by Professor William S. Libbey, 1886. (Photograph by Donald Baird. PUM.)

that I have examined, although no single shaman possessed all of them. [See Table 28; see also Jonaitis 1986:107–8 for the list of articles from a shaman's grave at Dry Bay, now in the Field Museum.]

[According to an entry by Emmons in his notes, Wolf moiety doctors wore eagle feathers; Raven doctors wore raven feathers.]

The mask, ***klah-kate, klo-ket*** [ƛ̓ax̣ket], was the most important part of the shaman's outfit. It alone represented the particular spirit in feature, but necessary with it were the skin waist robe, the bone necklace, the carved neck charm, and the spirit rattle. Numerous other articles of dress as well as implements were used as accessories, but were less important. Every shaman had four masks representing the four spirits he controlled, but the most powerful shamans possessed eight [spirits and eight masks]. These were generally of wood; the finest were of maple, birch, alder, and cedar; the commoner were of spruce and poplar [aspen]. The older masks were the larger, covering the face without any apertures for the eyes, ***wake kut dar took,*** [waqkadadú·kʷ, "eyes solid"]. Then followed those with holes burned through the eyeball, ***klo-ket*** [ƛ̓ax̣ke·t, from ƛ̓e·x̣ "dance" plus ke·t "cover"], or under it. What seems to have been the latest type (although it might have been the mask with eye holes) was the small maskette over the forehead, fastened to the headdress of eagle feathers and swan's down.

The mask exemplified the perfection of Tlingit art in carving. The realism of the features in their expression of feeling, the elaboration of ornamentation, and the technical excellence of workmanship and finish gave it a superiority over all other masks of the Northwest Coast. In the

Masks belonging to the Port Mulgrave shaman. Upper left. *Representing a man singing; painted red and black. Collected by G. T. Emmons from an old gravehouse near Yakutat, probably the same as that opened by William Libbey, since they were both present in 1886 (although Emmons's share cannot be identified with certainty). (Burke Museum.)* Top center. *Representing a man with face paint symbolizing an octopus. (PUM.)* Top right. *Representing a man singing. (PUM.)* Lower left. *Representing the spirit of a shark, with copper eyebrows and lips. (PUM.)* Lower center. *Representing the spirit of a hawk (?), with small faces in the ears. (PUM.)* Lower right. *Representing the spirit of a very old woman with large labret. Collected by G. T. Emmons, probably from the gravehouse opened by Libbey. (Burke Museum.)*

shaman's mask the Tlingit excels in originality, truthfulness, and elegance of carving. Each mask was named [given the personal name of the spirit it represented]. It might represent a human, animal, or half-human half-animal face. Except for the head of the bear, with its breadth, extended mouth with teeth, and enlarged nostrils, and that of the wolf, with its elongated nose, the faces are human in form, mouth, eyes, and cheeks, while the animal feature is represented by a bird's beak for the nose, eyebrows by the tentacles of the squid, or the whole figure of a mink or rat, or that of a frog or land otter may be shown coming out of the mouth, or may be on the cheek or forehead. Sometimes the painting is of some animal form or feature, and if it expresses an animal the ears are over the forehead [of the mask]. The carved designs on masks are generally supposed to represent some *yake* [yé·k] or spirit, often some bird or animal spirit. The carving is at the will of the doctor who seems generally desirous of producing the image of some foreign spirit. For with the Tlingit, the carving of the mask will often represent the spirit of a dead Stick [Athabaskan] or Haida Indian, or some animal or mythical spirit. (See Tables 29 and 30.) [Tlingit shamans often had Tsimshian-speaking spirits and when possessed by them could speak in Tsimshian. Presumably they were also represented in masks.]

The mask was always painted, sometimes in a solid color, but often in geometrical figures or in ceremonial designs in red, black, and blue-green, all native mineral colors. After the advent of Europeans, vermilion displaced the native red. While the coloring of the features varied somewhat according to the artist, there was always a prevailing color scheme: the lips, tongue, nostrils, and ears were red; the eyeballs [i.e., the iris and pupils], eyebrows, and hair were black; and the general flesh color was indicated by the native blue-green mineral paint. The indigo blue, red-brown, and grass green of the Tsimshian and Kwakiutl and the clay flesh color of the Haida were not used by the Tlingit; neither were the extremely large masks or those with movable parts ever found in the outfits of the Tlingit shaman. In addition to painting, masks were ornamented with copper for lips, nostrils, eyes, and eyebrows; teeth were of opercula and haliotis, human hair in tufts or locks was pegged in over the forehead, the lip, or chin; or bear fur was glued on with spruce gum. The mask was held in place by a span and tail of hide from each side.

[Masks with movable parts (eyelids, eyeballs, jaws, lips, or beaks) have been collected from the Tlingit, but it is not known whether the Tlingit had made them. Emmons reported in the catalogue of his collection sold to AMNH in 1888 that "in some instances the Tlingits purchased their masks from the Haidas and Tsimshians." Such a specimen was number 19-898:

> General dance mask of wood—represents a crane's bill and head so constructed that the bill can be opened and closed by means of strings, of Haida origin and workmanship and used in general dances for amusement. [From] Prince of Wales Island.

[Emmons collected several other Kaigani Haida masks of this type, used for "general dances" (AMNH E-1535, 1536, 1538), representing men, with movable eyes, or upper lip and nose, or both lips, all operated by fine strings on the inside. In the University (of Pennsylvania) Museum are several masks with movable parts, collected from the Chilkat of Klukwan and from the Snail or Slug House of the Ṫaqde·nta·n (Raven 16) of Hoonah. Although the names given some of these masks—"The Weeping Man," "The Controller of the Tides," and "Ģuna·kade·t" (the wealth-bringing sea monster)—suggest the names of shamans' spirits, this is not proof that they were used in a doctor's practice, or even in one of his exhibition dances. These masks were undoubtedly used in dramatic performances at potlatches—perhaps as demonstrations of the host chief's prerogatives—and may have been imported. This is suggested by the fact that they usually have a projection on the inside to be gripped by the wearer's teeth, a feature absent on Tlingit-made masks.]

A few copper masks have been collected from the Tlingit; the older ones representing human faces are very crude, and are supposed to have been beaten out of native nugget copper from the White and Copper rivers. But a very beautiful specimen of very thin metal, fashioned over a wooden mold, I found in the loft of an old house in Shekan, on the north coast of Prince of Wales Island, in 1888. [This was probably Shakan, a former Henya village, on the northwest coast of Kosciusko Island, the name perhaps derived from that of the famous Stikine chief, "Shakes," as Šéks ʔa·ni or "Shakes's village," (Orth 1967:858).]

After the establishment of Skagway as a railway point [White Pass and Yukon Railway, construction begun in 1897 and section finished between Skagway and Lake Bennett in 1899], several Chilkat, expert metal workers, obtained copper plating and made wonderful masks, rattles, spoons, and bracelets [of this copper], following the old designs, and aged them to a dark, dull green. But they were excessively heavy and so much finer and more artistic than any of the known pieces that I traced their history and found that they were all in the hands of a curio dealer in California who had formerly been in the same business in Skagway.

Through an agent there, he had delivered both the metal and the haliotis for inlaying. But the workmanship showed no deterioration of native skill and artistic sense. Some whale bone masks, equally misleading, were made at Hoonah and Sitka about 1890. While such may have been used, I never found a trace of one in the many shaman's outfits I examined.

The waist robe, ***ka-date*** or ***kade*** [ke·t, guš-ke·t, or k̓ide·t, "cover," "lap cover," or "buttocks cover"], or apron, was made of deerskin, painted in animal and supernatural figures, with a fringe at the bottom hung with puffin bills, deer dew hoofs, or bits of ivory. After trade with Europeans was inaugurated, brass thimbles as pendants became very popular, because of the noise they made in movement. This [apron] was generally the only piece of clothing worn in practice, and it was retained by the shaman, regardless of the change of mask during the séance, although sometimes it was dropped during frenzied movements.

A long oval skin, ***took*** [t̓u·kʷ] or ***tark*** [te·q], covering the breast and back, the head going through a slit in the middle [like a poncho], and a caribou shoulder blanket or robe, ***at-shick kuku, al-shick kuh-ku*** [?], both painted in figures similar to those on the waist robe [apron], were sometimes worn, but were of rare occurrence.

A necklace of ivory or bone pendants, ***sark-sate*** or ***sark sati*** [s̓a·q se·dí] was the ornament of every shaman. While some were of bone, the finer ones were of walrus tusk—long, slender, rounded, beautifully polished [rods of ivory], sometimes carved. [These ivory rods or pendants must have been imported from the Eskimo, because the walrus is rarely seen south of the Alaska Peninsula, and such ivory pieces often bear typical Eskimo incised designs, though others were carved by the Tlingit.]

Neck rings of twisted cedar-bark rope and shoulder girdles were both used. The bundle of twigs, *shutche* [?], containing the tongue or some portion of a bird or animal possessing a spirit commandeered by the shaman, were hung over his breast by a twisted rope of spruce root. But the most powerful charm, hanging over the breast, was a carving of horn, bone, baleen, or ivory, representing mythical animals, headless bodies, etc., which had been seen in dreams and trances, and were known only to the wearer. The most beautiful of these, exquisitely carved and richly colored through long use, were made of the split tooth of the sperm whale.

Next to the mask, the most important article [used by the shaman] was the wooden rattle, *sha-shough* [še·šú·x̣ʷ]. Each shaman had one of the bird type, with long neck and bill, representing a crane or an oyster catcher. On the back [of the rattle] were figures of spirits, or witches tied up, or of the land otter, or of the devilfish. Near the handle was generally the head of a mountain goat or a land otter. The sides [of the rattle] were ornamented with ermine skins. This type of rattle must not be confused with the conventional, ceremonial one, which was also in bird form, but had a short neck and bill like a raven, and had a recumbent figure on the back ["chief's Raven rattle"]. Often the shaman had minor rattles, circular or oval or cylindrical, plain or carved. As a rattle the pecten shell was often found in outfits; it was fitted with a wooden strip enclosing it and terminating in a handle [small pebbles were inside the two halves of the shell]. Or a number of pecten shells would be strung on a circle of root or hide. Any or all of these rattles might be used on less important occasions, but the large bird rattle was employed in cases of witchcraft or of extreme importance.

Headdresses were individual, according to the fancy of the wearer, but three types [Emmons named four] were possessed by almost every practitioner. These were:

[1] the crown of mountain goat horns, ***ut-har-gu*** [ʔat x̣a·gú, "its claws," since real bear claws were sometimes used], or of wooden spikes shaped like the horns [or claws] and sometimes covered with copper.

[2] the oblong hat, ***sha-dar-yar-ar-kee*** [šada· ya̤ʔá·gi, "around-the-head work"], of woven spruce root and colored grass stems in geometric designs. [The name refers to the stepped pattern, to which Paul (1944:64) gave the name *shu-dah-yay-ghee* [šada· yé·gi], "spirit around the head."] This was less frequently worn, but was remarkable in generally displaying a small animal figure on each side [in addition to the zigzag design]. This is the only example of any figure, human or animal, on old spruce root twining. [Such "shaman's hats" were also war bonnets, donned by men on a war party (Swanton 1908:450). I suspect that these rectangular Tlingit hats were related to the bark hats worn at potlatches by the Atna and Upper Tanana Athabaskans.]

[3] The ears of the brown bear, ***con-goush*** [gangú·š], or similarly shaped pieces of wood, hide, or copper, painted, etched, or ornamented with haliotis shell and human hair.

[The shape of this headdress has sometimes been compared to that of a bishop's miter (compare Henry 1984, pl. on p. 146, the original sketch by de Vancy, with pl. on p. 147, as published in La Pérouse). The bear's ears ("a hat provided with ears") might be worn as a sign of courage, when going into battle or giving away great wealth at a potlatch (Swanton 1908:439; de Laguna 1972:591, 694).

Left. *Shaman's crown of mountain goat horns, carved to represent bear claws, belonging to Qadjuse, a Raven 7 man of the Akwe River. Obtained from his heirs by G. T. Emmons before 1888. (AMNH.)* Right. *Shaman's wooden rattle representing an oyster catcher, with a dead shaman on its back, lying between the ears of a bear. Collected by G. T. Emmons before 1888 from an old shaman's grave at Yakutat.* Inset. *A wooden comb, carved to represent a bear, is used to pin the hair up on the shaman's head. Collected by Emmons from a gravehouse at Dry Bay before 1888. (AMNH.)*

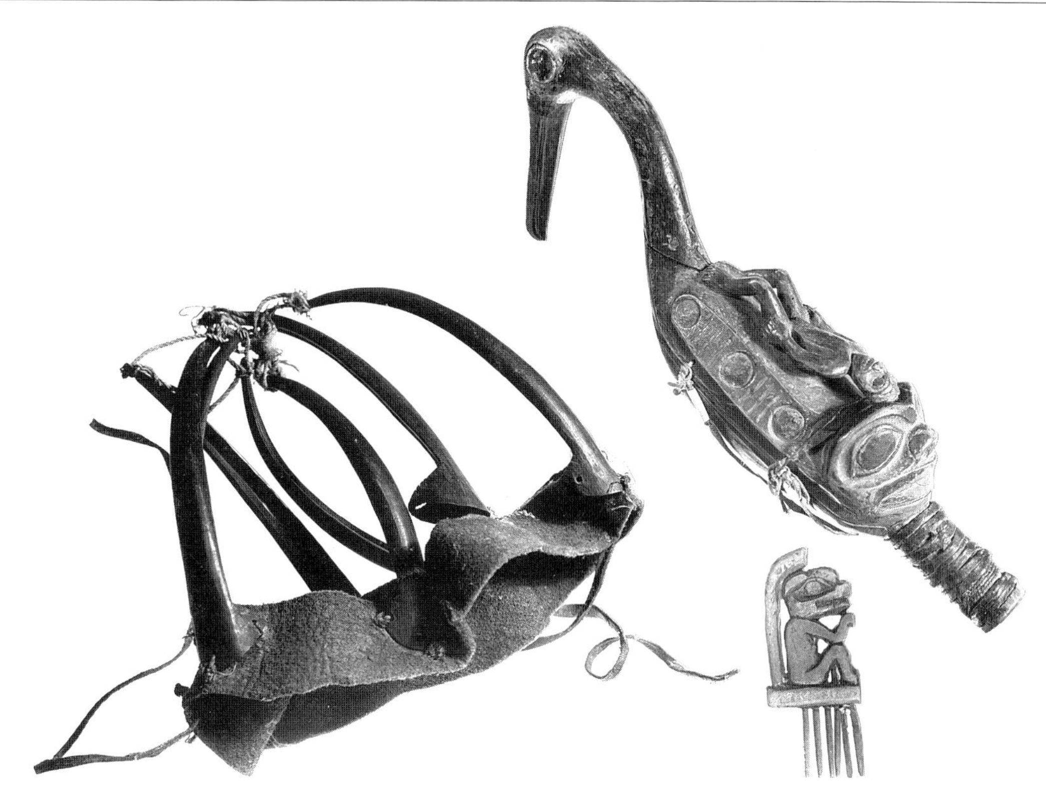

[Colnett, when anchored in what I take to have been Sitka Sound, described and sketched in his journal (1786–88)

> . . . a kind of cap thus:—was a favorite ornament [sketch of bear's ears]. The two uprights a skin of a Black seal, hair out, & studded with Copper Buttons. To the outer edges & tops are fixed human hair, the band for the forehead a piece of white leather, chequered with red stripes, with two large pieces of Round Copper in Front. I have seen this worn by natives at other parts of the Coast when drest for a visit. . . .

[4. Emmons also mentioned as shaman's wear the *sha-dar-kuke* (šada· qú·kʷ), or conical hat with woven cylinders on top, but this would have been owned, I believe, only by a shaman who was also a chief.]

On the arms and wrists, circles of ermine skin or etched bone were worn like bracelets. The latter were clearly of interior origin and workmanship, as shown by the incised geometric figures filled in with red paint. Wands of every description in size, shape, and ornamentation: animal forms, bows, spears, clubs, knives, all painted and carved in animal and spirit figures, were carried as the shaman fought with hostile spirits. The most beautiful wands were made of walrus tusk, shaped as daggers, and carved.

A drinking basket or cup for salt water, *alth-yet* [ʔé·ł̓ ye·t, "salt (water) container"], used when fasting; a double basket or bag for holding birds' down, *yun-nah kar-ar-kee,* "top to lap over" [yana· kaʔá·gi, "—?— work"], or *wush-tu kugu,* "one within the other" [wu·š tu qágu, "each-other within basket-of," from qákʷ, "basket"]; and a repair bag containing paint stones and odds and ends to supply missing parts, were to be found in any outfit.

Both the box drum and the skin drum were used by the shaman and by his family [lineage] indiscriminately. I never saw any evidence of either type of drum being deposited in the gravehouse. [But Emmons had evidently forgotten that he had sold to AMNH (numbers E-1195 to E-1197) a drum of goatskin stretched over a wooden hoop, a drumstick ornamented with eagle down, and a bundle of beating sticks, all from an old Chilkat shaman's grave.]

The beating sticks [tapping sticks, x̣í·č̓a?], about fifteen inches long, sometimes with otter heads carved on the ends, were used by the men of the shaman's party [male lineage mates] to accompany the drumming and singing, and these were always placed with the shaman's body. [The men held one in each hand and struck them together crosswise (de Laguna 1972:697), or beat with them on a plank. There were also slender wands, about three or four feet long, used to pound the floor (de Laguna 1986 field notes).]

In only one instance I saw a carved wooden pillow, *she-gate* [ša ye·t, "head container"], with a head carved at each end. [Emmons in AMNH catalogue (no. 19-259) noted that it had been used during the shaman's first communion with the spirits, and later while fasting. The faces at the ends represented *yakes* or spirits that were instructing the shaman. The open mouth indicated talking or singing, and also anger. The specimen is reminiscent of a Japanese neck rest.]

[While La Pérouse at Lituya Bay in 1786 and Colnett near Sitka in 1788 have given us the earliest sketches of the "bear's ears" headdress, it was probably Captain Chanal, with Captain Marchand, at Sitka in 1791, who wrote the earliest description of a shaman's costume (Fleurieu 1801, 1:332–36):

> As far as we are able to judge, the dress of which Captain CHANAL gives us the description, is reserved by the natives of TCHINKITÂNAY, for particular ceremonies or functions, for characters of buffoons or jugglers: to the object of war it appears to be quite foreign. It is remarked, however, that the use of this dress is not confined to old men; for the American to whom the French addressed themselves to see one of these dresses of character, appeared to be not more than twenty-five years of age [according to Dr. Roblet]. It was not without some difficulty that they prevailed upon him to display part of his wardrobe which he kept carefully put by in a little box, and in which, through great condescension towards strangers, he was pleased to muffle himself up in their presence. The first piece of this whimsical attire is a sort of grenadier's cap, or rather the fore part of a mitre [the shaman's woven bonnet? Emmons's *thlu-gu*?], which is placed on the forehead, and fastened by strings tied behind the head; the sides of it are bordered with long hair of men and beasts. On the exterior part of this head-dress, are represented figures of men, quadrupeds, and birds, painted [woven?] in a grotesque manner; and braids, composed of hair of beasts, and filaments of tree or shrub-bark, like flax, hang down behind as a long trailing tail [additions to the shaman's own hair?]. The breast is covered with a sort of plastron or cuirass, made of a tissue of spun hair, and trimmed with slips of skin, which are shaped like the skirts of a corset [a Chilkat-woven apron or poncho, shortened in front], the lower extremities of which are cut into little fringes to which are suspended, in infinite numbers, small shells, spurs and bills of birds: on the middle of this plastron, are painted various irregular figures. On each thigh, and knee, are placed pieces nearly similar, with this difference, that that of the knee presents a grotesque head with a wooden nose, moveable and hooked, three or four inches in length. These last-mentioned pieces are, like the cuirass, garnished with shells and dried extremities of birds, which, by striking against each other in the motions of the body, imitate, though very imperfectly, the sound of our little bells. The Tchinkitanayan, muffled up in his garb, holds, in one hand a hoop of plaited osier, eight or nine inches in diameter, the radii and circumference of which are decorated with the same gew-gaws as the other parts of the dress. [This is a rattle.] In the other hand, he carries the representation, made with osier or bark, of a human head, terminated in a point, and fixed at the end of a stick about eight inches in length; this head is filled with dried and sonorous seeds, and may be compared, though on a large scale, to those wicker-rattles which the village-nurses shake in the ears of their nursling. As soon as the actor had finished his toilet, the piece began. . . . [pp. 333–35]

[The Frenchmen could not understand the performance but noted that:

> [The shaman] confined himself to agitating his body in every way, and to endeavouring, by a universal contortion of his limbs, to find motions that might multiply the shocks of the sonorous gew-gaws with which his dress was loaded, in order to increase and diversify their sounds. At the same time, he made horrible grimaces. . . .
>
> This character-dress was not the only one that he possessed; his wardrobe contained a great number, no doubt for different parts, and was remarked, above all, for a varied collection of caps. [p. 335]

[While the French assumed that he had shown them his most impressive or valued costume, they were anxious to see the others, " but he would not permit them to be examined; and whatever entreaty they made, whatever price they offered, they could never prevail on him to part with any article of his wardrobe" (pp. 335–36).]

THE SHAMAN'S PRACTICE*

The general practice of the shaman was quite uniform throughout southeastern Alaska, although each one introduced certain minor individual features to impress the layman. [The séance was called ʔasá·n.] I feel that I cannot describe this better than by giving the testimony of the last

**Editor's note:* To the text of this section I have added a note left by Emmons in BCPA and information from the catalogue of the Emmons Collection at AMNH, as well as quotations from Veniaminov, Emmonds [*sic*] and Miles, Shukoff, von Langsdorff, Lisiansky, von Kotzebue, Lütké, Khlebnikov, and a summary of a passage in Krause.

shaman of the Sitka tribe, as related by him in 1888. [This man was probably the informant that Emmons called "Dr. Pete, Sitka, shaman of Iron House Family," Wolf 6, Ǫayé·s̊ hít-ta·n.] He had been proscribed [by the whites], and had fled the country some years before. Upon receiving permission to return, he foreswore his practice, and gave an exhibition performance, dressed only in his waist cloth [apron], with spirit mask, necklace, and charms. Rattle in hand, he danced, and chanted to his spirits, renouncing their aid. Cutting off his long hair, dressed with eagle down, he rushed out of the house and into the water, in the same way that a confessed witch would give up his practice. But I believe this [renunciation] was merely for effect, to satisfy legal conditions, and that at heart he remained the shaman, for he kept all of his paraphernalia and retained much of his influence.

[Dr. Pete posed in 1889 for a photograph taken by DeGroff. The plate was lost, but a sketch made from the print, "The Shaman and the Sick Man," appeared in the Sitka newspaper. An accompanying picture, posed by DeGroff, showed a shaman torturing a witch. Dr. Pete does not seem to have posed for this, for the print shows a white man as shaman. Dr. Pete also gave Emmons information about Yakutat and other places.]

When someone was sick [according to the Sitka doctor], a man of his family [lineage], generally a brother, would go to the shaman's house, and, standing in the doorway say: "A Tlingit is sick." He would turn and quickly run away, for the *ko-see-yage,* "under-foot spirit" [x̊us-yi̦· yé·gi], possessed by every shaman, would tell him everything that took place in the life of the village. Unseen, it visited every house, saw everything that was being done and heard everything that was said, and told everything to its master. Later the shaman, accompanied by one attendant, usually his nephew, would go to the house of the patient, enter without a word or greeting, and walk around the patient who would be lying on the floor behind the fire, opposite the entrance. He would go from left to right, as the sun moves around the world and as his spirit directed him. He then would seat himself near the patient's head; bowing his head and shutting his eyes, he would call his spirit in a spitting articulation. Its coming would be evidenced by a trembling of the body, when it lay open the life before him as a vertical, transparent cord, hanging in space, entering through the patient's mouth, and turning in his throat. The shorter the cord, the nearer the end, and the less inclined he [the shaman] would feel to hold out any hope. But should the cord be extended, he would say, "The spirits call, but I can give him life," which is a signal for the family to place before him property in blankets, etc. He would examine these critically and consult his spirit. If considered inadequate, more property would be demanded. If the fee was considered satisfactory, the shaman would rise and say that he would return at night.

[Field notes taken by Emmons at Chilkat (in BCPA) read:

> "Scundu" says when Dr is first consulted as to attending a sick man he asks [for a] number of blankets, then he consults his charms (spirits) and they either agree or turn from him. In the latter case he demands more blankets. In the use of his charms, masks, and dress each piece he puts on requires more blankets to be paid.]

When the spirit came to the shaman at such times it did not speak, but communicated through signs. As it approached, it would grow smaller and smaller. Its appearance would be copied in the shaman's dress and mask in practice. The payment was retained by the shaman's family [lineage], and even if given to him later, it would be returned if the patient died.

The house would be cleaned and dressed up, a fire laid and lighted. Early in the morning, the shaman arrived, accompanied by eight or more men of his family [lineage or clan], carrying a drum (either the older wooden box type or one of stretched skin), and the shaman's box of clothing and implements which they placed on a mat near the patient's head. They then would seat themselves in a line on one side of the house (as I have seen, generally to the right upon entering). Each one would have one or two beating sticks with which to strike on a long board or the floor, to accompany the drum and chant.

The household and visitors crowded around the side walls and front space. The shaman would stand on the mat, drop any clothing he might have on, and put on the painted skin apron, the bone necklace, any other neck ornaments, armlets, headdress or crown, and let down his long tangled hair, and cover it with bird down. Then with rattle in his right hand and possibly some charm or wand in his left, he would put on a mask representing the first spirit that he had called. Its coming was manifested by a convulsed movement of the [his] body. Suddenly he would start [running] around the patient and the fire. To the accompaniment of the rattle, drum, and beating sticks, he and his followers would sing in the voice and words of the indwelling spirit, "My master, I have come at your bidding to give health to the sick," [a phrase which would be] repeated again and again.

Taku shaman dressed for practice, Gastineau Channel, near Juneau, 1888. He wears a necklace of rattling bone or ivory pendants, and protective armbands with bear claws; he grasps rattles in his hands, and has sprinkled himself with bird's down.

At any time the shaman might suddenly stop, pass his hands on the affected part [of the patient's body], and then holding his hands high, as if grasping something tangible, blow through them, signifying that his spirit had caught and drawn out the sickness which he blew away. Or, at times, he might touch the patient with one of his charms, or take the patient's hands and put them to his own body. In all of these different movements, each shaman would practice as his spirit might direct. With a sudden stop and sharp cry from the shaman, the drum and song would cease, and with a change of mask, another spirit would come. The song would change, and so on, through four scenes as four spirits would appear. The more measured movements and the slower music would increase in action [tempo], until it became a frenzied race to keep step with the wild clash of drum, beating sticks, and rattle. Often the dancer [shaman] would loosen his single waist robe, and fall exhausted in a faint near the patient, and have to be rubbed and bathed to restore him to action. At the end, he would leave some charm or article possessing a spirit to guard the patient in his absence.

[According to the catalogue notes with the collection sold by Emmons to AMNH, there are a number of shaman's charms which he would wear and then hang around the patient's neck, for example number 19-209, of wood, carved to represent a *yake* [yé·k] and a devilfish, which would be transferred from the neck of the shaman to that of a patient or child to keep sickness away. This specimen was from a shaman's grave at Hootznahoo [Hutsnuwu]. From an old shaman's grave at Shakan, number 19-334, is a carving representing a *yake*. The shaman was said to have held it toward the fire to warm it and then rubbed it on the affected part and left it with the patient. The bundles of sticks with animal parts which the shaman wore hanging from his neck, *shutche,* were often touched to the patient's body.]

This practice was an extravaganza, beyond anything on this earth in its conception and acting, which we criticise but do not understand. The wild naked figure in all its contortions, with head thrown back and half-closed glazed eyes, flowing locks encircled in a cloud of down, the patient, the shadows cast by the fitful burning logs, the confusion of sounds, the atmosphere of smoke-dried salmon and human bodies, the tense expectancy of the crowd, all served to keep alive the belief in the unknown and in this juggler of life. When we consider that from childhood the Tlingit were reared in this atmosphere, is it any wonder that after a rudimentary education they should still revert to the past?

Should the patient fail to improve after one or two nights, with additional compensation the shaman might return and the same scene be enacted with the same four spirits, or with four new ones, should he possess that extra power. Eight spirits, as represented by eight masks, were said to be the maximum possessed by any practitioner. In several grave boxes I have, however, seen more than eight masks, but the extra ones might have been taken from older sets and be used only in exhibition dances. [Such dances or displays of power were often the only motive for a shamanistic séance.]

[As usual, Petroff (1884:176) and Holmberg (1855:72–74) based their descriptions of the shamanistic séance on Veniaminov ([1840] 1984:405–7), who wrote:

> The shamanistic seances among the Koloshi may be either major or minor ones. The first take place only during the winter months, and only on the 7th or 8th day of the moon, that is, at the first quarter, and the full moon. Such shamanistic seances are held for the purpose of, as the saying goes, *repairing the residence* . . . or of the settlement, i.e., at such a time the Shamans, solemnly summoning their Yeik [plural—Translator], order them to send happiness [good fortune—Translator] in everything to their kinsmen and the entire settlement; but most of all to themselves; they also ask that the epidemics be driven away from the shaman's village to another one.
>
> The Shamanistic seance . . . is performed by the Shaman together with his kinsmen who assist him in everything but especially through the singing of songs.
>
> On the day when the shamanistic seance is to be held, no one of the kinsmen either eats or drinks, beginning at the very [early—Translator] morning until the next one. Above that, on this same day, just before the Shamanistic seance, they take an emetic in order to purify themselves, i.e., after taking a bit of water, they introduce into their throats a feather, made especially for this purpose, and through its motion induce vomiting.
>
> The beginning of the shamanistic seances takes place at sunset and the end of dawn.
>
> When the sun begins to set, the Koloshi assemble in the barabora [dwelling—Translator] where the shamanistic seance is to be, which, as has been mentioned above, has been cleaned as best as possible and near the fireplace fresh sand is sprinkled. As soon as the appointed time approaches, they begin to sing, men and women singing together, while one of the singers beats the drum. The drum always hangs in the front, to the right of the entrance. The Shaman, having dressed himself in his ceremonial costume, begins to run around the fire (always with the sun) grimacing and making all sorts of unnatural bodily movements, in time to the beat of the drum and of the songs, until he reaches such a state of frenzy that his eyes roll under. His face is always turned up, toward the smoke vent. Prancing thus for some time, the Shaman stops and looks above the drum and occasionally shouts something. At this moment the drum and songs stop [cease—Translator]. All eyes are turned to the Shaman as to a prophet.
>
> The Koloshi believe that during the shamanistic seance it is not the Shaman himself who acts but one of the Yeik [plural—Translator] who entered into him.
>
> [The translator has scrupulously indicated every time when the word *Yeik* is used in the plural. I shall omit this whenever the plural is sufficiently clear from the context.—FdeL]
>
> It is said that when the drum and singing harmonize well, the shamanistic seance proceeds better than when the accord between them is poor.
>
> The Shamans assert that during shamanistic seance[s—Translator] they see a multitude of various Yeik [yé·k] . . . or spirits in different forms and of different classes. However, the Yeik . . . appear not all together at once, but singly and there is no fixed schedule which Yeik . . . or which class of Yeik is to appear first [or in what order—Translator]. Consequently, sometimes the

> Kiyeik [kiˑ yéˑgi] . . . appear first, at other times the Tekiyeik [deˑkíˑ yéˑgi] . . . or Takiyeik [daˑg̣i yéˑgi] . . . but most often the Kiyeik. . . .
>
> During the shamanistic seance, the Shaman frequently changes the masks he wears. . . . First of all he wears the mask of that particular Yeik whom he sees first, and then changes the masks in the same order as other Yeik . . . appear to him, as these masks represent particular Yeik. . . .
>
> After the shamanistic seance a feast begins, first of all with tobacco, followed later by various foodstuffs.
>
> Beyond these great and solemn seances, minor and private ones take place also. There is no specific appointed time when these ought to be held, but they occur whenever there is need for them. This type of shamanistic seance occurs for various reasons and at various occasions, for example, either in order to discover sorcerers or those who spoil people; or when a new Shaman appears, or at the order of the Yeik . . . themselves, to say it differently, when the Yeik . . . bother the Shaman with often apparitions, he, in order to be rid of them, conducts a shamanistic seance; and also for other causes. There is no feasting at such shamanistic seances, or if there is, then of a most mediocre kind.

[Veniaminov also wrote (p. 403) that the Tlingit believed that a shaman had the power during a séance to throw the yéˑk into anyone who did not believe in them. Such a person would faint, become rigid, and remain unconscious for a long time. The Tlingit individual who reported this to Veniaminov had been a song leader and assistant to a shaman but had himself never witnessed such an event. Fear obviously made believers out of the most skeptical.

[G. T. "Edmonds" (*sic*) and Miles 1939:33–34) published a most spirited description of a shamanistic curing session, probably embellished by Miles from the notes accompanying the collection of charms acquired from Emmons:

> The carved ivory objects [neck charms] herein described are thus not merely decorative but have functional social value in addition and are consequently all the more prized. A full appreciation of this social value and of the power obtained by the spectacular practices of the Shaman can be realized only by a visualisation of the stage setting in the communal house, with its somber smoke-stained walls, hung with arms, spears, nets, furs and bundles of raw and coloured weaving materials. The great adzed tree trunks supporting the roof structure rest on the heads of giant figures still colourful in deep vermilion and pale azurite—each one a legend in itself of some ancestral deed: overshadowing the back the crest figure of a raven with outstretched wings and [or] a conventional standing bear or a mythical sea monster.
>
> The central fire of yellow cedar logs like an immense incense burner spreading its fragrance through the air and just beyond—opposite the entrance—the patient on a bed of furs. Around the walls the many coloured, blanketed figures seated with knees drawn up to the chin, expectant and silent: the Shaman's followers with beating sticks in hand, seated before a long board ready to accompany him in song and movement. The Shaman, his long matted locks hanging down over his shoulders, dropping his robe—a weird figure—standing naked save for a narrow skin apron hung with deer hoofs, puffin bills and bits of bone, vibrant to the slightest movement, a necklace of pendants and carved ivory charms and one large carving, the most potent of all his medicines, suspended around his neck and hanging over his chest; a rattle in his hand and a mask over his face which is supposed to represent the human or animal features of the spirit he impersonates, that is his slave to summon but his master and guide when in control.
>
> When the spirit enters his body he breaks into song or commences to circle the fire and the patient to the accompaniment of beating sticks which become faster as the dance progresses. He may stop by the sick man, touch him or make passes over the body, each practitioner using different methods in locating the evil object, source of sickness or what would in modern medicine be called the septic focus. The dance may stop suddenly or another mask be put on to the accompaniment of a new song calculated to invoke a fresh spirit. Thus one spirit may succeed another, each one more insistent in action than the last.

[Shukoff had relatively little to say about actual séances:

> When an Indian gets sick he send for shaman, when shaman comes to see him, relatives ask how many blankets to cure him, and he answers giving number, and if sick man lives three or four months after doctor practices ("Ah son") [ˀasáˑn "séance"] doctor keeps all; if he only lives two or three weeks doctor gets half. But if he dies within a few days, doctor returns all payment.
>
> Each shaman has his own followers or singers, he composes his own songs and teaches them to these men. When he dances around fire his language is only known to singers who answer him. [It should be noted that many Tlingit shamans had Tsimshian spirits that spoke and sang in that language.]

[Very little information about shamanism is given by the early explorers and Russian officials. Thus, von Langsdorff (1814, 2:134) who was in Sitka in 1805–6, reported only: "All severe diseases are ascribed to the sorcery of their enemies, and the root of a particular valerian [wild heliotrope, *Valeriana sitchensis* Bong.] is considered as the most effectual remedy that can be administered."

[Lisiansky (1814:238–39, 243), who was at Sitka at the same time, offers little more. The shamans, he reports, took the scalps of enemies killed in battle, as trophies. Disease is supposed to be sent down by a Creator in heaven. "They also believe in a wicked spirit, or devil, whom they suppose to be cruel, and to inflict them with evils through his shamans."

[Von Kotzebue (1830, 2:58), at Sitka in 1825, wrote that the Tlingit had only a "confused notion of immortality," and seemed to lack any kind of religion or worship,

> but they place great faith in witchcraft; and the sorcerers, who are also their physicians, are held in high estimation, though more feared than loved. These sorcerers profess to heal the sick by conjurations of the Wicked Spirit; they are, however, acquainted with the medicinal properties of many herbs, but carefully conceal their knowledge as a profitable mystery.

[Lütké (1835:192–93, 217–18), who came to Sitka in 1827, recognized that the religion of the Tlingit was a form of shamanism related to that of northeastern Asia, and wrote that the "Kaloches" believe

> in wicked spirits that live in the waters and spread sickness on men by means of the fish and mussels that make up their food. They don't render any homage to them. The duty of the shamans is to predict the future, and sometimes to cure illness by invoking the devil.
>
> [Although most shamans inherit their position], everyone can of himself make himself such. The one who chooses this profession submits to a novitiate that lasts several years, and which consists of strict obligatory abstinence and chastity. He isn't recognized as a sorcerer until he has passed this test. . . . [pp. 192–93]
>
> Sickness of the eyes caused by the smoke in the houses, headaches and stomachaches caused by excessive eating, are the most common ailments among them; but it is rare that grave illnesses don't end in death. About the year 1770, according to the testimony of the elderly, this coast was ravaged by smallpox, which left only one or two individuals in each family. The Kaloches therefore believed that this sickness had been sent to them by *the crow* [Raven], in punishment for the wars which they used to wage continually among themselves. Old women treat maladies with herbs and roots; but the Kaloches do not have much confidence in this method of curing. Several shamans are also occupied in regular treatment of maladies, which brought them a large consideration; but their ordinary business on these occasions is to predict by magic whether the patient will recover or not, and to determine if the illness is due to sorcery or poison; and the guilty party whom they designate is cruelly beaten and often killed by the relatives of the patient. One can imagine the power of such a method in the hands of a clever imposter for satisfying his hate or his cupidity. [pp. 217–18]

[Lütké had obtained this information from the reports of Khlebnikov ([1817–32] 1976:29–30), but the former had stated:

> Shamans do not take part in curing sickness; they only are asked whether the sick person is going to recover from the illness or is going to die. For a good answer they receive various presents. There are, however, shamans who do engage in curing persons, and they deserve mention because they are so rare.

This should correct the common assumption that the shaman's séance was exclusively or even primarily curative.

[Aurel Krause ([1885] 1956:202–3) described a curing ceremony witnessed by his brother in September 1882 among the Hoonah. The patient, a boy of five, sat on a mat; beside him was the elderly shaman with gray hair to his knees, and a crown of rattling wooden "claws" on his head. He was naked except for a "brightly colored dancing blanket" (a Chilkat woven apron, probably) and a neck ornament or charm. He sang to the accompaniment of a wooden rattle in the shape of a crane, which he held in his right hand, and moved the upper part of his body so violently that he was soon bathed in sweat. He had a pair of wooden tongs with which he gripped the feet and head of the boy. After a while he put the boy's hands on his own hips and abdomen, and calling out the names of various animals (summoning his yé·k?), he led the boy several times around the fire, first in one direction, then in the other. Several men who sat in a circle round the fire sang a monotonous song, beating time on a board with small tapping sticks, and also answered the sporadic questions of the shaman (as encouragement to increase his power?). The women spectators were completely silent. After an hour, the shaman announced that the power of the bad spirits was broken and the boy cured. The father of the patient had already paid him in advance.]

STORIES ABOUT SHAMANS*

[Emmons had planned to include the following three tales in his chapter on Shamanism, but without commentary. Since these are not very good, complete, or well-told versions, they might have been left with the other myths that Emmons decided not to publish. Yet they are of a certain interest because they suggest that the events by which these three characters became shamans were the same kind of supernatural adventure by means of which a clan obtained a totem. There is really nothing in the incidents themselves to determine whether the clan thereby was to acquire a shamanistic spirit which its shamans would inherit, one after the other, or whether the clan had obtained an animal or fish or some

**Editor's note:* This section was originally titled "Legends about Shamans" and was placed at the end of the chapter. I have retitled the three stories with more familiar names, and have added the first three paragraphs of this section, as well as references to other versions of the legends.

other being as a crest, to be "displayed" in designs on house, canoe, clothing, implements, in inherited names, and in "copyright" songs and myths.

[The last two stories are of special interest in that they deal with Land Otters or Land Otter Men and their relations with human beings. In addition, the last one exhibits something of the shaman's role in war. Neither of these topics has been discussed at any length by Emmons.

[The first story, the well-known myth of Mouldy-End or Salmon Boy, is particularly interesting since Emmons believed he saw the remains of this famous Sitka shaman in 1888, when a native guide had taken him to the supposed grave.]

Salmon Boy

The legend of the boy who was carried away by the Salmon and was turned into a salmon, and afterwards resumed his human form and became a shaman, is a story told all over the coast of southeastern Alaska, but is localized by each tribe as its own. As told by the Sitka:

There was a *Kik-sa-de* [Kiksʔádi, Raven 10] whose hunting and fishing ground included the head of Nakwasina Bay, *Ta khate* [Daxe·t], where he had a summer house and took and cured his winter supply of salmon. [Since this man is the father of the boy who became a famous Kiksʔádi shaman, the father should have been a Wolf, and the mother Raven 10. This is a typical inconsistency in Tlingit legends, which the Tlingit themselves cannot explain.]

He had a little boy, who, one day, came to the mother for something to eat. She cut off a piece of dried mouldy salmon and gave it to him. But he threw it away, which angered the Salmon People so that they determined to punish him. Since he never went near the water, they were powerless, until they conspired with the Sea Gull that walked along the shore, eating salmon eggs. He made a snare of the membrane of the spawn and watched the little boy until he stepped into the loop. Then the Sea Gull took the leader in his bill and dragged him into the water. Then the Salmon took him and carried him away to their country, far out to sea.

The following spring, when the sun's heat was felt in the waters, the Salmon People got their canoes ready and set out for their favorite streams. With them was the boy who had now been transformed into a silver salmon, and he was sent up the stream where he had been taken. The mother standing by the water, grieving for her lost son, for whom a death feast had already been given, saw in the clear water at her feet a beautiful salmon, motionless in the pool. She called to her husband who, with his gaff, quickly took the fish and gave it to her to cut up. When she attempted to sever the head with her blue mussel shell knife, she found a copper neck ring which she recognized as the one she had fastened about the neck of her lost son. She called her husband who said, "Yes, our son has been turned into a salmon."

He wrapped the salmon in a cedar-bark mat and laid it away in the outhouse. Returning to their fire, the father and mother seated themselves with heads bowed and buried in their blankets. When night came, the people were aroused by a low "Ah-ah-ah-ah," such as a shaman sounds when practicing. They traced the sound to the bundle in the outhouse. Upon opening it, they saw that the salmon had disappeared. In its place lay a tiny child which grew larger and larger and by morning had become a man with long hair like a shaman. He said that the Salmon People had sent him back as their shaman and named him in their language *Ah-ko-tarts heene* [ʔa·k̓ʷ ta· ci·n, "Alive or moving at the bottom of a little lake"] or "Frog swimming in a lake." [The Frog was a Raven 10 crest.]

Calling upon four young men of his family [clan], he went with them to the mountain lake above the waterfall, where they built a sea lion canoe of branches. They embarked in it and floated down to the waterfall. They dove under it and were finally stranded on a rock at the mouth of the stream which is known as Sea Lion Rock, *Tawn each* [Ta·n ʔi·č]. By this act, he established himself as a powerful shaman.

I saw his remains in 1888, when [where] they had been laid on a bed of devil's club stems under a cavelike overhanging rock on the southern shore of Nakwasina Bay. At his side were a bow and two arrows, a rattle, several masks, wands, and charms, all more or less decayed.

[For other variants of this story, see Swanton 1909, Tale 99, Sitka version of Mouldy-End, and Tale 100, Wrangell version, both recorded in Tlingit; and for three Yakutat-Dry Bay forms, see de Laguna 1972:889–90. All these versions ascribe the adventure to a Sitka Kiksʔádi boy who became a shaman, and the last three use the story to explain how the Kiksʔádi shamans acquired Salmon or Fish People, xá·t qʷa·ni, as their yé·k.]

Qa·ká·

On the eastern shore of Kruzoff Island was a favorite fishing stream of the *Kik-sadi* [Kiksʔádi] clan of Sitka, that has descended from uncle to nephew in the same family [lineage?] for many generations. Here, long ago, *Ka-kah* [Qa·ká·, "Man on top"?] had a summer bark house where, with his family, he caught and put up his winter supply of fish. His wife, however, was unfaithful. Wishing to take another husband, she gave him to the Land Otter People [kú·šda· qá·] by working into his ear ornament a sinew thread from the tail of an otter.

One day when he was returning home in the evening, after working in the woods, he saw approaching over the trail a woman who seemed to be his wife. But he was under a spell cast by the Otter People, and the woman was really an otter. She led him into the woods to her hole that appeared to him to be his own house. Later, two otters took him to a small island off Biorka Island, and from there by sea to the Queen Charlotte Islands, and it seemed to him that he traveled in a canoe. Upon reaching the Otter village, he met an aunt who had been drowned and, like all drowned people, had been transformed into an otter. [She had been "saved" or "captured" by the Land Otter People.] She told him the trick his wife had played upon him, and that when he removed the otter sinew from his earring the spell would be broken and that his eyes would be opened to his surroundings. Doing so and becoming himself again, he begged the Otter People to take him back to his country.

Finally they consented, and summoning a skate, which was their canoe, they started and traveled by night; but before the raven called at daylight, they hid in the deep woods until darkness came. Upon reaching Biorka Island, [the westernmost of the Necker Islands], they cast Qa·ká· on a log in an unconscious condition. Some sealers hunting in the bay heard the voice of one singing like a shaman. They headed in that direction and found Qa·ká·, rescued him, and took him home. Later, he became a powerful shaman.

[Other variants of this story are recorded by Swanton 1909, Tales 5 (Sitka), 31 (pp. 87–88), and 46 (Wrangell); see also de Laguna 1972:749–50 (Yakutat).]

Ko-qunk

Before the coming of the white man, the Tlingit were constantly at war with one another, even within the tribe and the village; war parties also made sudden descents upon neighboring settlements and camps and carried away a few prisoners to be held as slaves or redeemed later [by their clan]. So in early days, the Tanta tribe [Tongass] had raided *Kooknoo-ou* [Kax̓-nu·wú·, "Grouse Fort"], the stronghold of the Ka-gwan-tan family [Ka·g^{w}a·nta·n, Wolf 1], in Icy Straits. In addition to killing many of them [Hoonah Ka·g^{w}a·nta·n], they carried away a woman of high caste. At this time the Tongass had a shaman named *Klanott* [Ł?una·t̓, "They never die"], who was possessed of great power, and against whom the Ka·g^{w}a·nta·n shaman, *Ko-qunk* [Ga·-g̣ánk̓?], was powerless.

But one night when Ko-qunk was keeping vigil in the deep woods, there came to him a female Land Otter that appeared to him as a beautiful woman. So he left his natural [human] wife, and went to live with the Land Otter Woman in a rock cave by the water. In a short time, eight children were born to them, four male and four female, all Land Otters, but to him they appeared human, since he lived under the spell of the Otter People.

One day his brother-in-law, the chief of the Otter People, came to him, bringing with him a valuable fishhook, carved to represent a woman with a headdress, and which gave the Otter People their supply of halibut. Then he [Ko-qunk?] called together the young men of the family and told them to prepare the canoe. When all was ready, Ko-qunk stepped into the middle of the canoe, knelt down with bowed head, and was completely covered with his caribou skin blanket, which was painted in spirit figures. [Tlingit shamans who wish to foretell the future or aid their party are often described as crouching in the canoe, their heads covered with their mat.] The four sons in human form paddled through the waters of Icy Strait, until, nearing a rocky island off Point Couverden, the shaman, who could see through the bottom of the canoe down into deep water, told them to lower the halibut hook. No sooner had the line run out, than a strong jerk almost upset the canoe. They were told to haul in the line. The surface of the water became alive with bubbles and an immense whirlpool was drawing the canoe down, when one of the paddlers, in his fright, cut the line. This want of faith cost the Ka-gwan-tan the support of the great spirit of the deep, but it assured Ko-qunk that [enough] power had come to him to contend with the spirits of the Tongass shaman.

A war party was formed to go south against the enemy. As they approached Tongass country, the Otter children, four on each side, in the form of low fog banks, hid the canoes. When they camped for the night, the Otters called for food. Wooden trays filled with salmon, berries, and dishes of grease were carried over and left on a projecting point [for the Land Otters], and after being emptied, the dishes returned of their own volition.

The shaman, "Little Stone's Father" (1830–90?), on the steps of Bear House, Port Mulgrave, Yakutat. He wears the "Sun's Ears" headdress, and holds a Russian sword cane. His long matted locks, perhaps artificially lengthened, indicate his profession. Photograph taken about 1888. (Courtesy of Minnie Johnson.)

Early in the morning they approached the stockaded village of Klanott [Łʔuna·t̓], and though they were enveloped in fog, that shaman with his great spirit power saw them approach. He warned his people to provide plenty of water in their reservoirs, and summoned the Rain Spirit from the clouds, but Ko-qunk pointed his wand to the southeast and drew it slowly along the horizon. The clouds broke, the sun came out, and dried up everything. The eight Otter children, invisible to the enemy, crawled into the stronghold and drank up all the water supply. After a few days of thirst, the besieged sent back the captured woman, and a little later they gave up the fort. As they [the Ka·g^{w}a·nta·n war party] pursued Klanott, he disappeared in an old decayed stump.

Had they not cut the line in the beginning when the canoe was drawn into the whirlpool, they would have had sufficient power to capture Klanott.

[A Yakutat version of the first part of this story was recorded in 1954. It was told to explain the origin of the design being carved on a modern hook. It was the Land Otters who gave such a hook to "Gagánk," the shaman, whereby people learned how to make such hooks. See "The Land Otter's Halibut Hook," de Laguna 1972:897–98.

[Although this version of the story does not identify the clan of the Tongass shaman, Klanott [Łʔuna·t̓] was a name belonging to the Łuk^{w}a·x̣ʔádi, Raven 17, among the Chilkat. The Rain Spirit he summoned may be the Being portrayed on the Rain Screen of the Whale House at Klukwan.]

DEATH OF A SHAMAN*

[When a shaman died], his body was tightly wrapped in a skin, the legs extended, the arms to the elbows held close to the sides, the forearms up over the breast and the hands folded below the chin, though often they grasped a war knife or some other article. [For example,] in an old log gravehouse on the mainland shore of Frederick Sound was the body of a shaman from which the wrappings had disappeared. It was grasping an old copper dagger in one hand and an old type of liquor bottle in the other, both held on the breast. The hair [of a dead shaman] was drawn to the top of the head and secured with an ivory or bone pin, and a similar pin was passed through the septum of the nose. The body was laid out on its back on a board to which it was lashed with root or bark. The face was covered. It rested one night in each corner of the house, commencing with that toward the rising sun, and was moved from corner to corner in a sunwise direction. During this interval, the gravehouse was prepared by a party of men of the opposite moiety—the wife's clan—and the household of the dead fasted, and there was neither ceremony nor mourning. On the fifth day the body was taken out of the house and deposited in the gravehouse by men of the wife's clan. The head was laid toward the rising sun, *Ko-ghan de-sha* [gaga·n-de šá, "sun-toward head"]. The box with the masks and paraphernalia connected with his practice was placed alongside, generally on the left. A faggot of devil's club was placed under his head, and broken stalks were scattered over the corpse and the floor [presumably to keep away evil spirits, as devil's club branches tacked around doors and windows keep away the evil spirits of infectious disease]. The head was completely covered, generally with cedar-bark matting. His canoe was drawn up beside the gravehouse and the mast was stepped, with a streamer at the head.

In 1870 the death of a very old shaman was foretold by his most powerful spirit, *Ha-ye ko ghon*, "Beneath Fire" [Ha· ỵï· g̣aga·n, "Down-below Sun"?; "fire" is x̣̓a·n]. This spirit was represented by the mink. He told his master that he [the shaman] would die in the following spring, and that his family must, in the meantime, eat nothing from the salt water, and the one who was to succeed him [as shaman] must keep away from all unclean things and must not approach his wife or any other woman. The shaman died in the spring, as foretold. The body was prepared, wrapped in blanket and mat, and kept one night in each corner of the house. On the fourth day [*sic,* fourth night], it was carried out and placed in the gravehouse with all of the shaman's implements of practice. While the body remained in the house the family had fasted, but they ate the night after the body was removed.

When I reached the Hoonah village of *Ghau-de-kan* [ga·w-t̓aq-ʔa·n, "Town beside the drum/bell"], or Hoonah, on Chichagof Island, a very old and widely known shaman, *Scar-dun-nar* [?], of the *Ka-gwan-tan* family [Ka·g^{w}a·nta·n clan, Wolf 1] had just died, and since I was an invited guest I witnessed the attending ceremonies. His death had been expected for some days. Every evening a man of his family [clan] had come out to the shore in front of the house, and called to his [the shaman's] spirits to give him life, but if they would not do so, it would be accepted as a sign that

**Editor's note:* This section combines the original sections "Death, Death Ceremonies of 'Scar-dun-nar' or 'Shaman Sca-dun-na'" and "Graves." To the text I have added information from notes and the catalogue of Emmons, as well as a quotation from Shukoff and a summary of information from Veniaminov.

they were tired of him [the shaman] and favored a successor. Death, which occurred late at night, was announced by the firing of a small Russian cannon in front of the house, bringing all the villagers to the scene, but since nothing was done [at that time], they soon returned to their beds.

As soon as possible, the body was laid out straight on a flat board stretcher, with spruce root handles at the sides. The body was wrapped tightly in a blanket, the elbows close to the sides and the hands brought up over the breast. The whole body, with legs extended, was tied down with spruce root to the stretcher. The hair was drawn up on the head in a knot and confined with a long ivory pin, and a similar pin was put through the septum of the nose. Under the head was a faggot of devil's club stalks. Over the body was thrown an old painted mooseskin blanket, a piece of the dress he had worn in his practice, while a cedar-bark mat covered the head and shoulders. Surrounding it were all his clothing and paraphernalia, consisting of skin aprons, masks, rattles, crowns, headdresses, wands, necklaces, and charms. Over the doorway several branches of devil's club were hung. The body was placed in the eastern corner of the house, toward the rising sun, where it remained one night. Then it was placed in each of the other corners for one night, going from left to right, as the sun appears to move. After the fourth night the body was placed in the gravehouse on an island opposite the village.

[During the period before burial], in front of the house [in which the shaman's body lay], was improvised a fence of boards and rope, extending from the doorway to the low tide mark. No woman suffering from her monthly sickness could cross, for should one so affected cross, it was believed that the earth would open, the corpse would be swallowed up, and his spirit would be wholly lost. [Therefore, it could not come to a successor.]

Before daylight each morning, the drum would sound in the shaman's house. Then those who were building the gravehouse, to the number of ten or twelve, would assemble and dance and sing to the accompaniment of the drum, for about twenty minutes. Then they would rush out, launch a canoe, and cross over to the island, where they remained throughout the day preparing the gravehouse, returning in the evening just before sunset. Upon approaching the village, they would shout at intervals "Ah! Ah!" and a master of ceremonies from the wife's clan, *Tuck-dane-tan* [T̓aqde·nta·n, Raven 16], would come out of the door with a cedar bough in his hand and make motions of sweeping the doorsill outside. When the canoe landed, one of the crew, acting as leader, would approach the house, and turning, speak a word or two to those on shore, then rush into the house. The others would follow, and the drum would commence to beat, and the workers would sing and dance for twenty minutes.

After being fed, they would dance in the evening, naked except for the waist apron. Thus, every day while the gravehouse was being built, the same routine was followed. These workers were all of the *Tuck-dane-tan* [Raven 16], the widow's clan. Whether for a shaman or any other person, the preparation of the corpse, the building of the funeral pyre or the gravehouse, removal of the corpse, cremation or interment of the body, were all done by members of the opposite moiety, the clan of the widow.

In the afternoons there would appear some ten or twelve principal women of the clan of the deceased, dressed in the ceremonial blue blanket trimmed with red cloth and ornamented with pearl buttons, with a cedar-bark rope around the waist. The head was tied around with a black silk handkerchief. Large silver or haliotis shell earrings and nose rings were worn; the face was blackened. In the left hand each carried a balsam pole six feet long, stripped of needles and branches except at the head [tip], and there tied with streamers of colored cotton or blanket. In the right hand each held a number of pebbles. [These mourning women, with blackened face, were called gáxni.]

Under the leadership of a man of the opposite moiety, they would march in single file, commencing at one end of the village, and enter every house. Their coming would be announced to the household in advance. In anticipation of this visit, the body of the house would have been put in order, and the head of the household would be seated on the far side of the fireplace, opposite the door. Following the leader, these women would file in silently. They would march around the fire square five times, from left to right as the sun moves. Then they would stop, form a circle around the fire square, and face each other. The leader would lift both hands; the women holding the poles in the left hand would raise the right hand. Then the leader would give a long "Sho-o-o," bow his head in his hands, and the women would follow by dropping their hands and bowing their heads in their right hand and so remaining for several seconds. This act would be repeated three times, and then the women would file past the house master, each giving him one pebble, and wishing him many riches, the leader bringing up the rear. The latter would make numerous passes over the bowed head of the house master, and then, as if holding something, would raise his hands, open them, and blow through them. Then all would file out and go

Top. *Shaman's gravehouse, just below Indar stakha, 1889(?).* Center. *Shaman's gravehouse of Killerwhale totem, Sitka, Alaska, 1888. The front is painted to represent the crest of the dead.* (AMNH.) Bottom. *Gravehouse of the Henya shaman, "Dr. Skah-owa, the fire-eater," near Tuxekan, Prince of Wales Island. Spirit guards are at the corners. The letters were painted some years after ensepulture. (Photograph by W. H. Chase. AMNH.)*

through the same ceremony at the next house, and so on from house to house through the village.

Then the women, unaccompanied, would go to an open space, all lie on the ground close to one another, and then the leader would throw one of the poles across the line of figures. This would be done four times. If the poles touched anyone, sickness would result; if untouched, they would have good health. This ceremony would be repeated every day the shaman's body remained in the house. After it was placed in the gravehouse, the poles were collected, taken to the woods, and tied upright to the bushes, and the women bowed their heads toward the gravehouse, and asked the shaman's spirits to help them. Then they returned to their homes, and resumed their normal routine.

At 9 P.M. on the fourth [fifth?] night after the death, the shaman's body was carried out of the house without ceremony, placed in the canoe and taken across the channel, and deposited in his gravehouse with his box of paraphernalia, and the house was then closed. The shaman's canoe was carried ashore and placed under the gravehouse. This structure was a square built of spruce logs, neatly fitted together and notched at the ends; it rested on four heavy corner posts, and was elevated two feet above the ground. The flooring and roof were of split log shakes, the roof being higher in front and sloping to the rear, and weighted down with cross logs.

During the period that the body remained in the house the family [clanmates, widow, and children?] fasted during the day, eating only a little at night. In earlier days they would have fasted absolutely, and if a death occurred while they were fasting, they would have chewed devil's club bark and drunk water to cleanse the stomach of all food.

The next night after the interment, the shaman's clan, *Ka-gwan-tan* [Wolf 1], gave the smoking feast to the wife's clan, the *Tuck-dane-tan* [Raven 16]. The body of the house was cleared and the floor swept with eagle wings. The fire was built of yellow cedar logs [laid] across one another. It was lit about 6 P.M. as the guests began to arrive. As they entered, they were shown to their places by two head men of the wife's clan [na·-ká·ni], those of highest rank being seated on the floor space back of the fire, the principal chief of the *Tuck-dane-tan* in the center, the other men in front and the women in the rear. The shaman's family and clan occupied the right front corner and were crowded about the doorway. No word of welcome was spoken to the guests. They simply took the seats indicated to them by the ushers.

When all had assembled, bunches of the long, black leaf tobacco, *gunge* [gánč], were handed to the ushers by members of the dead shaman's family [lineage?]. The donor's name was called out when it was handed to the brother of the deceased, who, in turn, handed it to an old man at his side, who cut it up for smoking. After all the tobacco had been received, four or more strands were put in the fire at each corner and burned as an offering to the spirit of the dead who was believed to receive it as it was given. The box of old family pipes, carved in animal figures claimed as family [lineage?] and as clan crests, representing bears, eagles, sharks, whales, etc., was brought out. [These animals, if the "whale" was the Killerwhale, are all Wolf moiety crests.] The pipes were filled, lit, and handed to the most honored guests, commencing with the women who smoked only a little while and then handed them to their men [clan brothers]. Most of the guests provided their own pipes, which were already filled, or tobacco was given them.

For some time they smoked in silence, some having their pipes refilled. Then a *Tuck-dane-tan* [Raven 16], standing by the fire, broke off pieces of tobacco and, throwing them into the fire, called out "A gift to ——," giving the names of those long dead, the most honored of the family [clan]; he [who made the gift] had been prompted by the brother of the deceased. The remainder of the tobacco was distributed by the ushers to the guests, the amounts being proportional to the social standing of the recipients. When this distribution was finished, the chief of the guests made a speech of thanks in short sentences, mentioning the name of practically every male member among his hosts, even to boys of eight and ten. As each name was mentioned, the holder answered "ah." The older brother of the deceased replied, after which the assemblage broke up.

[Emmons evidently obtained some pipes used in this smoking feast, for the catalogue of his collection in AMNH carries this entry:

> These pipes were the property of the family of "Scar-tin-r," a "Kar-qwan-ton," the last of the Hoonah Doctors, who died November 1888, and on the evening following the placing of the body in the gravehouse, when all the guests had arrived to hold the smoking feast, these pipes were filled and presented to the most distinguished guests, [E-] 812–817.
>
> 812 Wooden pipe carved to represent a young eagle coming out of the egg.
>
> 813 Wooden pipe carved to represent a bear's paw.
>
> 814 Wooden pipe carved to represent an eagle.
>
> 815 Wooden pipe, ornamented with brass bowl.
>
> 816 Wooden pipe, carved to represent the old "Kar-qwan-ton" village of Kook-noo-oo [Kax̂-nu·wú·, "Grouse Fort"], which stands or stood on a bluff rocky point in Icy straits.
>
> 817 Wooden pipe carved to represent two bears and a raven with a bear's body. This pipe illustrates the old legend [myth] of the Raven . . . [the episode in which Raven and Bear go halibut fishing, and in which Raven kills Bear and his wife by tricks, and eats them].

All of the animals, except the Raven, are crests of the Ka·gʷa·nta·n, Wolf 1, and Grouse Fort is the site where the original house burned down, from which this clan derives its name.]

The next evening the family [clan] of the shaman feasted the clan of the wife. One year afterward a feast for the dead was given, at which time those who had performed the various services for the dead and built the gravehouse were potlatched in payment for their work.

[A version of these ceremonies for the "dead doctor" was written in what we have called Notebook 4, in BCPA. Between the entries for the funeral and for the smoking feast, Emmons had a list of native articles, together with what he had evidently paid for them. The list included shamanistic items, which may have belonged to the deceased shaman. See Table 32.]

Cremation was practiced by the Tlingit for everyone except the shaman [not counting slaves whose bodies were simply thrown out in the water, on the beach, or in the woods.] The charred bones were placed in a chest which was deposited in the family [clan or lineage] gravehouse directly in the rear of the dwelling. The body of the shaman was laid away intact in a gravehouse, a short distance beyond the village, near the water and, circumstances permitting, on a bluff point, as seen at the Sitka, Chilkat, Auk, and Hootz-ah-ta [Hutsnuwu] villages, or on opposite and adjacent islands as at Hoonah and *Tuxshi-kan* [Tuxekan, a Henya town]. Or, the deceased shaman might have selected some distant prominent headland, to which the occupants of passing canoes would offer sacrifice in the form of a pinch of tobacco or food, which they believed would be received by him in a material, rather than a spiritual sense. If children were among the occupants of the canoe, bird down would be blown over their heads to protect them.

Cave interment was also practiced for shamans. It may have antedated the introduction of steel, which so facilitated woodworking. The caves I examined were actually only overhanging rock shelters, giving protection from the

Board from a shaman's grave near Angoon, Admiralty Island, painted in red and black to represent a shark's head at the bottom, two crane's heads and a decapitated man in the middle, and a spirit above. Redrawn from tracing on four pieces of toilet paper, glued together, by G. T. Emmons. Original 44 cm long. Screened areas are red; solid areas are black.

elements. In one on a small, land-otter infested, rocky island in Sitka Bay, the bones and rotted wooden bed remained, while the skull was separately encased in a much decayed carved wooden box. Another very similar rock chamber in Naquasena [Nakwasina] Bay, across from the original village of Sitka, contained a layer of decayed bones and wood. Through Peril Straits on Admiralty Island, back of Whitewater Bay and elsewhere, such old burial caves were pointed out by local natives. [See de Laguna 1960:49, for such a cave burial near Angoon.] On the mountainsides bordering the Chilkat River, miles distant from the nearest villages, shaman's bodies were deposited in caves and wooden structures, with all their paraphernalia. One in particular, far up the *Yehlh heene* [yéˑɬ hí·ni], "Raven's Water" [a small tributary entering the Chilkat River from the west, just above Mosquito Lake], the burial place of a very celebrated, old shaman was pointed out, 1,000 feet or more up the steep rocks. On Mount Calder on Prince of Wales Island, overlooking the entrance to Sumner Straits, a shaman's interment is said to be located far up toward the summit.

The ordinary gravehouse was of rough or squared logs, eight or ten inches in diameter, notched and fitted over each other near the ends, thus forming a permanent crib work that only the elements and time could obliterate. It was about six feet wide, seven feet deep, and six or more feet high in front. The roof of two or more overlapping layers of heavy split boards and bark, laid lengthwise from front to rear, with an incline to shed water, was often weighted down with heavy logs and boulders. Whether built up from the ground or resting on four stout corner posts, the heavy split flooring was raised a foot or more from the foundation. Often the front was covered with perpendicular, smoothed planks on which was carved or painted an animal figure, or such a figure surmounted the structure. Sometimes carved corner posts acting as spirit guards were placed in front; sometimes a Chilkat blanket was hung over the face of the hut. The gravehouse always faced the water, wherever it was placed, either on shore or mountainside.

The shaman's spirit after death was believed to go to the land of the dead [? There are words missing in the manuscript]. But the body was believed to be guarded always by the spirits belonging to him in life, or friendly to him. In some cases carved figures represent these spirits, or in fact possess the spirit itself, and these were placed in contact with the gravehouse or near it. The best example of this is shown in a photograph taken in 1889 of the grave of

Carved wooden figures, guarding the grave of Date-hun (Date-khoon?) [De·txú·n?], *a Chilkat shaman of Killerwhale House, Wolf 1, in the woods below Klukwan, "1885" (possibly 1889). The full-length figure on the left is that of* Geese-teen, *or* Gease tene *[?], a supernatural spirit helper. The large figure on the right is* Gou-ghe yah-tee [ga·w yịʔádi], *"drum holder," for the drum of the shaman was hung on the outstretched arms. Such figures were known as* ut nuh teen [ʔat wutí·n], *"he sees something," and were made for very special occasions. (Photograph by G. T. Emmons or Winter and Pond? AMNH.)*

Date-hun [also written as *Date-khoon,* De·txú·n], an old ***Kagwan-tan*** [Ka·g^{w}a·nta·n, Wolf 1] shaman of the Chilkat tribe, in a grove of cottonwood on the riverbank just below the village of Klukwan. The four well-carved figures, all of which had been painted, were grouped about, leaning against a large tree trunk, a few feet from a crumbling log gravehouse with a very primitive type of canoe, much decayed, by its side. The large torso with the uplifted arm is ***Ghou ghe-a-de*** [ga·w yịʔádi, "drum thing-under"], depicted as beating the shaman's old type of wooden box drum. The full-length figure, painted a dark red, and partly covered with a cedar-bark mat, the hands at the breast as if holding rattles, was *Geas-tine* or *Geese-teen,* a supernatural being that lived above and was greatly dreaded. It is said that he sometimes descended and killed Tlingit people. The two small figures are *Khart-she-tar-woon yagee* [ga·t or x̣á·t ša-ṫa·wú yé·gi], "Salmon Head Feather Spirit," and *Shakarl yeelth* [ša·ka yé·ł], "Mountain Raven," and were likewise protecting spirits. All of these were regarded with much superstitious fear by the people, who never approached the vicinity of the tomb. [Krause ([1885] 1956:204) mentioned these figures, but was unaware that they guarded a tomb. See Jonaitis 1986, fig. 36.]

[Field notes evidently written by Emmons at Chilkat, and now in BCPA, mention:

> . . . [so] great was fear of Doctor that years after his death when remains had crumbled away to dust, no one would approach

depository. No touch implement. Charms carried in moss [to avoid contact] when sold to me at Inds—— (?), [perhaps Yandestake]. During life no one was exempt from his power and exactions even the chief might be laid under his law and I have known of a chief of power who when accused by Doctor of being a witch, deserted by his family and followers and tied up by Doctors orders.

[Shukoff gave an informative description of a shaman's death and entombment:

> Before shaman dies he sends for the man he likes most and gives him all things [all his outfit] and tells him if he wants to become shaman to come to his grave and he will teach him secrets and his yakes will come, and he will be just as powerful [as his predecessor. The man chosen should be a close relative of the dying shaman in the maternal line, and he may well have been the shaman's assistant, ʔíx̣ṫ x̣an qá·wu.] He designates his burial place, generally a high bluff or elevation. The man who inherits all later becomes a shaman by going through same ordeal [fasting, thirsting, continence, quest in the woods].
>
> When shaman dies, relatives black[en their] faces, and tie rope around waist. When shaman dies, one of relatives goes on house and cries out, tells all his [the deceased's] yakes to come, as their master has fallen down, and is now fast asleep. Then they bring in a board and make eight holes [in it, then] lay body on board, dress him and cover with skin mantle used in practice. Put headdress or crown on head and rattle in hand. Then they strap him down to board through holes in board. Keep body in house four days; first night in left corner back; second night right corner back; third night left corner by door; fourth night right corner by door. During [these] four days, built [grave]house on point or elevation near beach, so that he can see Indians passing by him, for reception of body.
>
> On fifth day, carry directly to [grave]house, no ceremony. After leaving grave and returning home, relatives fast for eight days. Not only relatives, but other women of village blacken face, put on dance blankets, go in woods and cut spruce poles about seven feet long. Trim all branches, leave top and tie colored ribbons [to the end], and walk Indian file everywhere about village where shaman went when alive. And they do this to live long and be healthy, [and believe] that the dead shaman's yakes will protect them.

[Veniaminov's description ([1840] 1984:404–5) of the death of a shaman, from his fatal illness to the sacrifices offered to him by those passing his gravehouse, corroborates the accounts by Emmons and Shukoff, and makes clear that the shaman's body is in his own corner of the house on the day of death, the front right-hand corner from the door; and that entombment takes place on the fifth day. The plank with eight holes for lashing the body, the pin through the nose and another to hold up the hair, the use of a large basket of twigs to cover his head, are all mentioned. It is also believed that the shaman's gravehouse rots all at once, so that it collapses evenly. One of his chief spirits remains with the body, which is why it dries up without rotting. A tree never falls on the grave. The dead shaman is honored at a mourning potlatch like any other person. No one passes his grave in a canoe without throwing a little tobacco into the water and praying to him for good luck.]

CHAPTER 15

Witchcraft

THE WITCH SPIRIT*

Witchcraft dominated Tlingit life. It not only kept the people in constant fear of the supernatural, but also made them so suspicious of one another that the simplest words or acts were subject to misconstruction. The whole cult resulted from the shaman's efforts to retain his prestige when his incantations had failed to save his patient. In other words, to "save his face" he denounced as a witch someone who had hated [? writing not clear] the sick person and poisoned his life. Generally this was some poor person, either old or young, with few friends or no following. Sometimes he even selected a personal enemy [to denounce]. So great was the dread of witchcraft and so deep the shame, extending to the family [lineage] of the accused, that the nearest relatives were the first to lay hands on the poor victim and tie him or her up to starve to death. [Traditionally the sick person and the witch belonged to the same clan or lineage, but the shaman to another, and preferably to another village (see de Laguna 1972:736–37).]

Aside from ordinary sickness produced by evil spirits in general, a much more fatal form of disease was directly attributable to witchcraft, when the body was poisoned as it were, not by an indwelling spirit, but by the evil practice of one who possessed the black art. This was accomplished by secretly procuring from the person whose death was desired some bodily secretion, a lock of hair, a drop of blood or what not [or a bit of clothing], which was then incorporated in the make-up of a little image supposed to represent that person. This was placed inside [or beside] the corpse of some shaman. The well-being of the person it represented was dependent upon this doll, and as it rotted away, so was afflicted its living counterpart, unless the witch was discovered and denounced by the shaman, when he or she was forced to confess [and undo the evil charm], or be put to death. These dual powers, representing good and evil (although unfortunately both were very evil and even antagonistic) dominated Tlingit life and were responsible for all the cruelty and suffering that have blinded these people from their infancy. The belief in the one that does not exist has created a powerful class of spiritual fanatics whose influence has retarded the development of a people, kindly in disposition, industrious in habits, and naturally intelligent.

The witch spirit lived in space, unobserved until the approach of darkness, when it descended to earth and sought the burial ground. There it might assume human or another form, and with many kindred spirits dance wildly or hold high revelry, until the first streak of light appeared in the eastern sky, when it vanished as it had come. To certain people this spirit [hí·xʷ] came like the power of the shaman. The latter permitted no refusals, but the witch spirit was gained only after long vigils and renunciations. Like the shaman, *Ict* [ʔíx̣t̓], the witch controlled a spirit under the foot which carried him invisibly through space, gave him the power of flight, or sustained him so that he could walk on water. This spirit was generally represented by a bear, wolf, mountain goat, mink, marten, sculpin, or devilfish, and was known as *ko-see yage,* "underfoot spirit" [x̣̓us-ỵi yé·gi]. These spirits were believed to be stronger than those of the shaman.

The witch spirit was sought. It was neither born in one, nor came of its own accord. It was obtained or induced by contact with dead bodies, handling their bones, spending nights around the gravehouses, and associating with the spirits that visited thereabouts in the dark. Then, when finally possessed of the spirit, the one who had sought it could visit all the houses invisibly and learn what was happening.

[Emmons may be incorrect in reporting that the witch spirit was sought. The first witch alone may have done so, or tried too hard to become a shaman (see "The Origin of Witches," below), but all later witches came from him, their evil propensity passed on, I believe, like a malignant infection. Olson (1967:116) reported that witches and novices went to

---

Editor's note: Emmons apparently wavered between including Witchcraft as a topic under Shamanism, or making it into a separate chapter, as it is here. His topics under Witchcraft were "Origin of Witches" and "Practice in Witchcraft."

**Editor's note:* The last five paragraphs of this section have been compiled from notes left by Emmons, information from Yakutat, and my comments on Veniaminov.

the graveyard because they were "impelled by a 'feeling' or a spirit within them," and that witchcraft was "inherited in the same way as hereditary traits." Since the strong-willed, according to Yakutat informants, might resist, to be a witch or a bewitched accomplice seems to "involve some element of consent or of moral weakness, and hence of guilt" (de Laguna 1972:735. See also de Laguna 1987:91–92).]

He [the witch] had the power of mesmerizing [bewitching or recruiting] children and the weak-minded. [This was often done by touching the victims with a dog skin.] With their assistance, the witch could obtain something bodily from the one to be destroyed: a hair, a nail, or any secretion. This was placed in a crudely made figure like a doll that was put away in the dead body of a person or a dog, usually in the part to be affected. As the doll decayed with the corpse, so the body of the victim wasted away. [The bewitched assistants, unless forced to confess, would become full-fledged witches in their turn.]

[Scrappy notes, probably made in the field and now in both AMNH and BCPA, shed a little further light on witches and their spirits. Thus we gather that the rat, *kut-sin* (kuč̓i·n), mouse, *kok-karkh* (kag̣á·k), mink, *nukshean* (nuk^{w}šiyá·n or łuk^{w}šiyá·n), skate (č̓i·g̣á·), sculpin, *wake* (wé·x̣̓), and crab (ṡ̓á·w, "Dungeness crab," or x̓é·x̣, "spider or king crab"?) are all associated with witchcraft. Of these animals' spirits, that of the mouse is strongest—stronger than a doctor's (Emmons queried). Witch spirits live in lakes; yet to get rid of the evil spirit, the witch and his deadly charms must be immersed in water.

[At Yakutat, the witch was said to be "crazy" and guilty of antisocial behavior, such as stealing, lying, disregarding avoidance rules for certain relatives, and committing incest. These were signs of witchcraft that the shaman saw as "water" of different kinds (de Laguna 1972:735–38). The drink of water offered a suspected witch was used as a test of his guilt. The association of the mouse with witchcraft may be in part due to acquaintance with the Haida belief that the witch owes his powers to a mouse inside his body, or in part because the mouse steals, especially the scraps that a witch would use in harming someone, and because witches are thieves.

[No other authority (Veniaminov, Lütké, Krause) mentioned witch spirits, even though their accounts of the activities of witches and of the measures taken to detect them and to make them undo their work agree with the account given here by Emmons. The Tlingit word for "witch" (*kolduny* in Russian, but translated as "sorcerer") Veniaminov rendered as "nakutsati" (Veniaminov [1840] 1984:407). This would be na·k^{w} ṡ̓a·tí·, "master of (herbal) medicine." The use of this term is euphemistic; it should apply only to the healer; or is the implication here that the practitioner is a "master of bad medicine"? A related term is "kunakutsati," or qu-na·k^{w} ṡ̓a·tí·, also meaning "healer."

[The witch was more properly called ní·k^{w} ṡ̓a·tí·, "master of sickness," from ya-ní·k^{w} "to be sick," and si-ní·k^{w} "to make sick." Or, more likely, the witch was called nú·k^{w} ṡ̓a·tí·, "master of pain." The witch's spirit was hí·x^{w}, by means of which he practiced "witchcraft," du hí·xu; "to bewitch people" is ya-hix^{w}. Inasmuch as the practitioner was controlled by his own evil spirit, he was truly a witch, not a sorcerer.

[Veniaminov further stated ([1840] 1984:407) that most human illnesses, including all external (?) ones, especially the festering of wounds, and tuberculosis (consumption), pain in the limbs (arthritis?), and loss of mobility in the arms and legs, and other ailments, were ascribed to witchcraft. The witch "spoiled" his victims through corruption—those who had injured, cheated, or offended him. But he could cure them, if forced to confess and wash away the corruption, as is described below.]

THE ORIGIN OF WITCHES

All witches sprang from the first.

I will relate the origin of the first of these demons, from whom, according to Tlingit belief, all others sprang, as told me by my old Chilkat shaman friend.

In the early days there lived a young man, a great hunter, with his young wife and his son. They were happy until one day, while gathering sticks in the woods, she met the son of the chief. They loved each other at once. After that they met in the woods every night. Later, she feigned sickness. Telling her husband that the spirits of the departed had appeared to her, which meant death, she made him promise that he would not have her body burned, but would instead put it in a large chest and place it in the gravehouse. After her apparent death this was done, and a death feast was given. However, with the assistance of her lover, she was released and went with him to live in the chief's house, where she remained throughout the day, never coming out until night.

Returning from hunting one evening and finding his fire out, the husband sent the little boy to get some coals. When he entered the chief's house he recognized his mother before she could cover her face. Upon returning, he told his father, who told him not to say such things but be quiet. The boy was, however, so persistent in his story that, at last, the father's suspicions were aroused. He stole quietly to the chief's house, and looking through a crack in the wall, saw his wife sitting by her lover in the firelight.

To avenge himself, he determined to possess himself of a witch spirit. So the following night he went to the gravehouse of a shaman and slept by the corpse, but the evil spirit did not come to him. Then he killed a dog and after skinning it, slept in the skin one night, but with no better results. [Witches are supposed to bewitch others and recruit them as helpers by touching them with the skin of a dog (see de Laguna 1972:734).] Then he took the skull of a dead shaman from the gravehouse and used it as a drinking cup, upon which he fell down in a trance. When he woke up he felt that the witch spirit had come to him. [For a somewhat similar incident, see de Laguna, p. 733, and Swanton 1909, Tale 85.]

That night, he sought the dead houses. He was able to see all the witch spirits, and he danced and played with them and learned their secrets and practices. He took the bones of a shaman's corpse and strung them together for a necklace, made a waist blanket of dog skin, and took two shaman's skulls filled with pebbles for rattles. He continued to visit the dead houses at night and by associating with witches learned to fly. With a rattle in each hand he flew to the chief's house, and putting the occupants to sleep, he entered through the smokehole, and found his wife and her lover asleep in each other's arms. The next morning the people all reported how soundly they had slept. He then cut a short pole and sharpened it to a fine point. At night, after again putting the household to sleep, he flew down the smokehole and drove the pole up through his wife, killing her without a sound.

Now he possessed the witch spirit, and wanting to give it to his son, he hung a shaman's skull about his neck. The boy fell down in a trance and was immediately possessed by the witch's spirit. With his father, he played with the witches at night. The man now sent the little boy out to watch the chief's son, and to wipe up his tracks, or his spittle, and cut off an edge of his blanket that had absorbed perspiration. [Witches' "dirt" is called qa· da·ʔit se·dí, and people that supply it, like the boy, are qa· da·ʔit se·dí qʷá·ni.] The man took these things and put them into a little figure which he placed inside the corpse of a shaman. As it rotted so did the body of the one from whom the small body particles had come. He was bewitched and could not be cured unless the witch spirit was driven out. So the lover died. Now the hunter made witches of all his family and this was the beginning of witchcraft.

[This same story, in slightly different phrasing, was quoted by Boas (1888:215–17) from the original catalogue by Emmons in AMNH. According to Veniaminov ([1840] 1984:407) witchcraft came from Raven (was learned?) and was nearly always hereditary. In Swanton's version (1909, Tale 85), the deserted husband and first witch was an ʔA·nx̣a·k hít-ta·n of Killisnoo, a member of a clan with reputed Haida ancestry. In Tale 31 (Swanton 1909:134–35) the origin of witchcraft is ascribed to the Haida. A Yakutat informant said that witchcraft came from the Tsimshian (de Laguna 1972:733). Swanton (1908:469–71) gives further information about the activities of "wizards and witches." In a tale from Wrangell (1909:134–35) the Haida were the first witches, nuks!ā´tî, taught by a female mouse; witchcraft also came to the Tlingit (1909:90–91) from the sons of Ayā´ỵî, a cannibal in what I believe was Eyak country; the sons made the first skin-covered boats from human skin.]

SHAMAN AND WITCH*

When a shaman was first called to examine a patient, his spirit gave him the power to look through the body. If it appeared transparent, like bright light, the ailment was of minor importance. But should the body be cloudy or opaque like a jellyfish, then a witch spirit was at work. This fact the shaman confided only to the family [of the patient], and left immediately, returning to the house [the shaman's] to await the offer of payment they would give him for denouncing the witch. When his demands were satisfied, two men, preferably brothers of the patient, would come to his door, one standing directly behind the other, and would cry out, "Let the spirit come!" which they repeated four times, and then returned [to their lineage house?].

[Emmons wrote in a Chilkat notebook:

> *Scundu* [a "reformed" Chilkoot shaman, see below] says when Dr. is first consulted as to attending a sick man, he asks number of blankets [that will be paid.] Then he consults his charms (spirits) and they either agree or turn from him. In the latter case, he demands more blankets. In the use of his charms, masks, and dress, each piece he puts on required more blankets to be paid. [Each change of costume signified a new spirit come to the shaman, and the fiction was held that it was the spirits that were paid, even though the shaman received the actual blankets.]

In the evening, the shaman came with his followers [assistants from his own clan], carrying his paraphernalia [and entered the house of the patient]. He took one turn, from right to left, around the patient who was laid out back

*Editor's note: Information from notebooks left by Emmons and my comments are clearly indicated by brackets. I have added the last three paragraphs on Land Otter Men and on data from Veniaminov and Olson.

Shamans practicing. Newspaper clippings made from posed photographs taken by George de Groff, Sitka, 1889. (Photographs and clippings, AMNH.) Left. *"The Shaman and the Witch." The "witch" here wears the long, unkempt hair of a shaman. The "shaman" is a white man.* Right. *"The Shaman and the Sick Man." This picture represents Dr. Pete, Sitka, dressed, treating sick . . . (?)" Dr. Pete was a Wolf 6 shaman, but the "patient" is the same man who posed as the "shaman" in the picture on the left.*

of the fire in the space opposite the door. He dropped what clothing he wore, and donned the skin waist apron, the necklace of bone pendants, and a crown of goat horns. His hair was dressed over a toggle of devil's club and covered with bird down. In his right hand he carried the crane spirit rattle and in the left a carved knife or wand. Trembling violently, he gave a peculiar cry to indicate the presence of the spirit, and his followers took up the song [associated with that spirit], beating time, as he commenced to run around the patient. The song was rendered as if sung by the witch spirit about itself:

He is a long way off.
He is on the beautiful point (referring to a far-reaching grassy headland without trees).
The witch has a den like the beaver.
The witch has gone into his den.

When he stopped [running], the song ceased. When he growled like a wild animal, another spirit came to him, while the first one remained. Another song was started, sung as if by the second spirit, which was also a witch spirit. For when a human witch had been tied up and tortured, and the spirit tried to escape, it was caught by the shaman and made his slave.

I am very glad that I have something,
Something belonging to the sick. [The reference is to witches' "dirt."]
Look for me, my friends,
Someone might come and see me.

And as the shaman was possessed by the two spirits, he lost all sense of his surroundings. He staggered and trembled violently, as he tore around and around, often falling, his body glistening with sweat. Then one of his attendants filled a spruce root hat with clear spring water, and placed it at the corner of the fireplace nearest the rising sun. This represented a lake where the witches live and paddle in their spirit canoes and so escape the pursuing shaman. The

Dance wand or implement carried by the shaman, carved and painted to represent a wolf with protruding tongue at one end, and a bear's head at the other. From an old shaman's gravehouse near Yakutat, possibly that opened by William Libbey. (Photograph by Richard Gould. AMNH.)

shaman came to a stop near the hat. He was given a length of bark rope, intertwined with the intestines of a land otter. This he trailed in the water as he made the motions of paddling a canoe. As he drew the end of the rope toward himself, he caught the witch long enough to see his face, but released him. With this knowledge he was able to demand more payment. He might either name the witch at once, or return home and do so later. Instead of announcing the name directly, he might offer a riddle for the family of the patient to solve, by referring to the name in a general way. [Shamans were reputed to speak in vague language; they would pronounce the names of witches in punning fashion, or indicate them by some descriptive phrase (de Laguna 1972:702, 736).] For example, if the witch's name had some connection with an eagle, the shaman might say, "An eagle is sitting on its nest, drying its feathers."

But, in any case, when the witch was identified, all friends, as well as his nearest relations [in his lineage] deserted him or her in terror and shame, and were the first to bind and torture the witch.

[This was because the witch traditionally bewitched members of his own lineage against whom he bore a grudge or of whom he was jealous. And when the witch was discovered and forced to undo his evil spells, he would not be able to undo any that he might have made against members of his lineage who had supported him in his ordeal. For this reason, and because his relatives did not know whether he had made any magic against themselves, they would abuse the witch—just to be safe. Confession under duress was necessary to save the patient and any other potential victims of his magic, and also to free the witch himself of his evil spirits. A voluntary confession would be ineffective.]

The witch's arms were tied behind the back at the wrists with the palms out; the hair was wound around a toggle of devil's club with sinew or hide cord woven in, and with it, stretching the head as far back as possible, it was brought down to the wrists and secured to a low stake driven into the ground as the body was forced into a kneeling position. Or the knees were drawn up to the chin and the legs bound at the ankles. The witch just secured, generally in some deserted house, was abandoned to starve to death, and the body was later cast into the water as unworthy of cremation, unless the witch [Emmons consistently calls him "victim," which is confusing] were secretly released or made a confession renouncing all communion with the witch spirits. [The confession, not his death, was desired, since if dead, he could not save the patient. Many accused witches, however, were killed in a rage.]

Upon the fourth day of torture he was supposed to communicate with the shaman who came to him at night. He would ask for water from a stream or spring near the gravehouses and thus, by drinking the water, acknowledge his crime.

[In one witchcraft case at Yakutat, the suffering witch was offered a drink of apparently clear water, but the evil spirit knew it had been taken from a footstep, and "told" the witch, who then betrayed himself by refusing to drink it. It would appear that drinking polluted water would exorcise the witch spirit? (see de Laguna 1972:738, 741).]

Then the family of the patient tied a rope around the witch's waist and he led them to the gravehouse where he had deposited the witch figure representing the patient. He would take this secretly, hide it in a leaf or fold of his blanket, go down to the shore, and walk into the salt water up to his waist. Bowing four times in the direction of the rising sun, he held the image in front of him, and threw it under the water. He plunged in himself, and then rushed ashore, cleansed of all power of witchcraft forever. He then went back to the house of the patient and wished him good health. If the latter recovered soon, he might feast the witch and his family.

[This account would seem to be that of an eyewitness to a particular witchcraft case. Yet it seems unlikely that an officer in the U.S. Navy, an organization active in suppressing shamanism and in freeing alleged witches, could have permitted this case to go as far as torturing the witch without interfering. Perhaps what Emmons witnessed was an enactment staged by a "defrocked" shaman like Skundu (Skundoo), or Dr. Pete, who both posed for pictures of shamanistic séances and who gave information to Emmons. The methods used to extract a confession he could have deduced from the condition in which the alleged witches were found, and from their statements.]

Sometimes the shaman made a mistake and denounced someone too strong for him. Such a case occurred at Angoon in 1863 [*sic*, more probably 1868]: *Kenalkow* or *Kenalku*, the head chief of the *Da-she-tan* clan [De·ši·ta·n, Raven 13], was ill with consumption and the treatment by the shaman's spirits had availed nothing, so Jake, a subchief of the same clan and unfriendly to him, was named as witch [the classic case]. In the excitement of the moment, he was seized and tied up. Shortly afterward, he was released by the coming of the U.S. man-of-war *Saginaw*. He then proclaimed that he would kill Kenalkow, not as a witch, but as a chief. [Persons who knew they were suspected of witchcraft might seek to clear themselves by offering a physical attack on the person they were believed to be witching, since a true witch would not resort to violence.]

Unquestionably, he would have done this, had not branches of the clan united in appealing to him to permit compensation for the injury. [It is very usual for damages to be paid for an intraclan injury. Perhaps the two men belonged to different lineages, or subclans?] Old Jake, besides being a knife-scarred warrior, was also a particularly sensible, practical, and acquisitive person. So, smiling to himself, he allowed his family to carry him to Kenalkow's house, for being at enmity with him, he could not, with dignity, step over the threshold. As he was placed on the floor in the seat of honor, he spoke no word, made no sign, but buried his head on his breast. Then Kenalkow's family brought piles of blankets, boxes, guns, and other property which they placed before him. But all these were insufficient to offset the great indignity [of being accused of witchcraft], so he jumped up and ran out of the house. But when he was carried back, more property was added, and he signified that his honor was satisfied. Wise old Jake, who, to bring shame to Kenalkow's family, then took the name of "Saginaw Jake"!

In 1883 there occurred a case of witchcraft at the *Hootz-ah-tah* [Hutsnuwu] village of *Neltooch-k-an* [Neltushkin, Nałdú·šgánt], on Admiralty Island. On account of the sickness of the old chief, a poor older man was accused by the two principal shamans of having bewitched him, and he was tied up and left to starve in a deserted house. Upon information received, the U.S. Sloop-of-war *Adams*, then patrolling these waters, went to the scene, released the victim, arrested the two shamans, and brought them on board. All hands were called to muster on the Quarter Deck, and upon assembling, some twenty-five Sitka Tlingit who were enlisted in the crew were placed in the front rank. The shamans, between guards, were held on chairs, while their heads were shaved by the ship's barber. One submitted to the ordeal without a struggle, but the other tried to use a knife which he had concealed. Failing in this, while forcibly handled, he appealed to his spirits for aid and for the destruction of the ship and crew. The Tlingit sailors, an excellent lot of men accustomed to civilized ways and ship discipline, were still greatly affected by his appeal, and fear was plainly written on their faces as the superstitions of their earlier environment eliminated [wiped out?] their later conversion. After the shamans' heads had been shaved, their long matted locks of hair were cast into the ship's furnace in their presence; they were then released and put ashore. This indignity of losing their hair, without any action by their spirits, broke their power, and, while they may have practiced in secret later, they gave no more trouble.

[Emmons himself was serving on the *Adams* at the time, so the above is an eyewitness account. An entry in one of his notebooks indicates that the loss of their hair did not in fact destroy their powers for good: "Two shamans at Killisnoo both belong to Neltooshkin, practice yet although hair was cut in past."]

Several years later another shaman of this tribe was involved in a similar case. He was taken by the civil authorities, his hair cut off and his head painted with red lead, an incident which ended his shamanistic career. But notwithstanding these drastic punishments, which were quickly heralded to the most remote communities, the practice [of shamans denouncing witches] continued into the present century, when the breaking up of the old communal life separated the households into small families. [The outbreak of witchcraft fears and accusations at Angoon in 1957 (de Laguna 1960:200, note 56) proves that such fears long remained below the surface, even though they came to reflect unfocused anxieties and generalized stress, rather than the anxieties and strains of life in the lineage houses.

[It is interesting that Emmons did not discuss the role of the shaman in rescuing persons who had been "captured" by Land Otter Men and were being turned into otters. Perhaps witchcraft fears were so strong in the 1880s and 1890s that the fear of Land Otter Men was easily overlooked, or perhaps the fear of land otters and their transformed victims, so pronounced in the twentieth century, developed only after witchcraft beliefs and fears had been largely overcome. A note by Emmons reads:

> 477. The Mink. The mink in early days was believed to be in league with land otter to save indians upset from canoe. [The canoe was the skate, the paddles were the mink.]

[The account given by Veniaminov ([1840] 1984:407–11), of the activities of witches, and of how they are detected by shamans and forced to confess and undo their evil, agrees very closely with the account given by Emmons. We may cite only the following special points. If the accused witch had a powerful chief as "patron," he might be released from torture; sometimes, however, the witch's own kinsmen would eventually kill him (after he had affected the cure?) because of the disgrace he had brought to the lineage. On other occasions, the accused was not seized at all, because he had rich and powerful kinsmen; rather, they came to him secretly and begged him to cure his victim.

[In addition, Veniaminov (p. 410) described the marvelous things that Tlingit witches were supposedly able to do: assume the shape of a bird, escape from a locked and guarded place, frequent cemeteries where they consorted with the dead, and fly through the air—just as the witches of Kiev are supposed to do! According to Olson (1967:116–17), Tlingit witches frequented graveyards in order to have sexual relations with the (spirits of the) dead, and for this reason relatives of the deceased might hold an armed watch over the graves for several days after a funeral. Other accounts of these and similar activities may be found in Krause ([1885] 1956:202, 203–204; and de Laguna 1972:738–44).]

WITCHES, SHAMANS, AND THE AUTHORITIES*

[As we might expect, the missionaries and the authorities in Alaska, the latter being the U.S. Navy in the 1880s and 1890s, were united in their determination to stamp out shamanism. This was not only because it represented superstition, but especially because of the shaman's power to denounce and persecute others as witches. Scidmore (1893:46–47) has summed up the success of this attack, and the whites' attitude:

> In illness the Tlingit sent for his *shaman* or medicine-man, who, continuing his fasts alone in the forest throughout life, continued to receive inspiration from his guardian and familiar animal spirits. In frantic parades and dances about a village, a shaman bit live dogs [not shamanism, but a Southern Tlingit copy of a Tsimshian "secret society" act, of Kwakiutl origin] and ate the heads and tongues of frogs, which contained a potent medicine. He performed his miraculous cures under the spell of his special totemic spirit, and an emetic of dried frogs and sea-water gave him a vision to perceive the soul leaving a man's body, ability to catch and replace it, and cast out the evil spirits which had possessed the patient. When the chant, dance, and hocus-pocus failed to cure, the shaman denounced some one for charming or bewitching his patient, and demanded his torture or death. Usually the infirm or the aged poor, slaves or personal enemies, were denounced and subjected to fiendish tortures. Captain E. C. Merriman, U. S. N., broke the power of shamanism in the archipelago by repeated rescues of those charged with witchcraft, by fine and punishment of tribe and shamans, and finally by taking the shamans on board his ship, shaving off and

**Editor's note:* I prepared this section not simply to round out the roster of witchcraft cases in the 1880s and 1890s and to show how they were treated by the shamans and the authorities, but because these accounts contain information not included in the descriptions of contemporaneous events written by Emmons.

Headdresses belonging to a Lukʷaʔxádi *(Raven 6) shaman named Wolf-Weasel* (G̣u·č-da·)*, collected by G. T. Emmons from a gravehouse on Dry Bay, before 1888.* Top. *A headdress made of swansdown and eagle tail feathers, and three headless figures representing guardians.* Bottom left. *Crown made of the pads and claws of a brown bear paw. (Photograph by Richard Gould. AMNH.)* Bottom right. *Necklace from a shaman's gravehouse near Port Mulgrave, Yakutat. (Photograph by Donald Baird. PUM.)*

> burning their long sacred hair and sending them out bald-headed, to be met with roars of Tlingit laughter. There have been few cases of witchcraft since.

Of course, Captain Merriman, who assumed command of the naval forces at Sitka in January 1882, was not the only naval officer to take action in witchcraft cases. He had been preceded by Commander L. A. Beardslee, USS *Jamestown,* June 1879–September 1880; Commander Henry Glass, USS *Jamestown,* October 1880–June 1881; and Commander Edward P. Lull, USS *Wachusett,* June 1881–January 1882. All of these men had to deal with shamans and witches; even as late as 1893, the U.S. gunboat *Pinta* meted the same punishment to a shaman at Shakan, in Henya territory.

[S. Hall Young (1927) and Mrs. Willard (1884), as missionaries, give us the most vivid accounts of their experiences with witchcraft cases, the first at Wrangell, the second at Haines. Young's accounts are worth quoting, for he actually witnessed the shaman's séance, the denunciation of the witch, and the torture.

[Just before Young arrived at Wrangell in 1878, the Tlingit wife of a trader, Charley Brown, was accused of witchcraft because "somebody dreamed" she was a witch (Young 1927: 114–15). *Kohlteen* (possibly Q̓aƚyá·n, Kiksʔádi), Raven 10, a subchief of the woman's clan, seized her and tied her up.

> The manner of binding a witch was very cruel. The victim was first stripped of her clothing, her hands tied together behind her back with a thong of deer sinew, then the hard rope was passed around her ankles and her feet drawn up to her hands and tied so tightly that the thin sinew tendons cut into the flesh. Then the victim's braid of hair, if a woman, was pulled down and bound to the hands and ankles so that feet, head and hands were made to meet behind the back; a horrible posture of constant agony. The victim was then thrust into a dark hole under the upper platform of the Indian house, and left to roll helplessly on the hard ground.
>
> She would be visited at intervals by the medicine-men who accused her, and by her enemies whose "dreams" had brought about her accusation, and she would be whipped with "devil's-club" (a thorny cactus-like shrub), which left its poisonous barbed needles in the flesh at every stroke. She would be given no food at all, but compelled to drink large quantities of salt water to increase her thirst; and if obdurate in her refusal to confess herself a witch and throw away her "bad medicine," other more strenuous tortures, such as sticking the flesh full of fat spruce splinters and setting them on fire, dragging the victim sideways across sharp stones of the beach to lacerate her naked body, and other devices too foul and revolting to record would be resorted to. All of these operations were superintended by the *Shaman* or *Iht.* The family of the man or woman whom she was supposed to be bewitching would gather in full force, helping with the torments and taunting the victim with jibes and obscene mirth, exhorting her to "confess" and throw away her "bad medicine." [pp. 114–15]

[Of course she would have to confess, and would also have to name her accomplices, on whom the same tortures were repeated, and in this way four more women were seized; all had attended the Christian meetings held by Mrs. McFarland.

> One of these was found dead, hanging by the neck to a log under the floor of the house where the witches were kept. Whether the woman was put to death by her accusers, or in her agony and despair had committed suicide, was never ascertained. Four or five other victims were named and seized, two of them being old men of low caste, and the others children of tender age. [p. 115]

The Christian Indians could not stop this, but when Charley Brown returned, he cut loose his wife and the women with her, and threatened Kohlteen with his pistol.

> An old medicine-man who had been a leader in this outrageous torture took to his canoe and fled to distant parts, but there were from thirty to forty accused persons, or those who expected to be named as witches, hiding among the islands and up the rivers afraid to come to town for fear that they would be seized and meet a like fate.
>
> We estimated that during this wave of superstition which swept over the Archipelago that summer of 1878, at least a hundred victims lost their lives, while two or three times that many had been cruelly tortured. [pp. 115–16]

[That dreaming of a man "making medicine" was evidence that he was a witch is illustrated by the accusation that Richard, one of the Wrangell converts, brought against "our Christian chief, Tow-a-att" [Ṫawyá·ṫ, Wolf 25 or 26], and the latter took the usual violent action to refute the charge by physically attacking his accuser. Young (1927:116) finally made peace between them, of an uneasy sort.

[That same summer, Young was the helpless witness to a shaman's denunciation of a witch (1927:121–26). The famous shaman, *Klee-a-keet* (ƛiya·-kí·t, "Far-away Killerwhale," Daqƚawe·dí, Wolf 27), had been called from Angoon to cure a Taku chief who lived in a large house near the Stikine settlement of Wrangell. This man had become wealthy from his trade with the Tahltans and was now dying of tuberculosis. Since the shaman had announced that he could cure him, the dying chief and his people had assembled great wealth in "blankets, Indian boxes, beads, guns and ammunition . . . at least two thousand dollars' worth of goods," as a fee. Young was anxious to witness the conjuring.

Rattle in the shape of an oystercatcher, on the back of which are carved the figures of a shaman torturing a witch, placed between the horns of a mountain goat head. There were formerly ermine skins fastened to both sides of the rattle, now reduced to bare white skins. It came from the shaman's gravehouse and was collected by William Libbey at Yakutat in 1886. (Photograph by Donald Baird. PUM.)

[The séance took place at night, and was attended by almost all the Indians in town: Stikines and visitors. Every inch of the house was packed, except for a space by the fire, reserved for the shaman. The dying man, with his wife, children, and close relatives, lay on the lower platform behind the fire, which was kept bright by handfuls of grease thrown on from time to time.

At last, far away, was heard the sound of Indian drums. . . . Louder and louder it grew, nearer and nearer, while the crowd inside the house held their breath in suspense. Now the weird minor strains of the medicine song blended with the drumming—a solemn, mournful measure. Suddenly broke in upon the singing the long tremulous wail of a wolf, and instantly every dog in the village responded with a discordant chorus of howls. [p. 122]

Now the door swung open, and four young men fantastically garbed, with faces painted in rings and streaks of black, white, red and yellow, holding their flat drums [tambourines] by their handles before them, drumming and singing, keeping time by the jerking and posturing of their bodies, marched in. After them came eight men with wooden masks on their heads, carrying two long carved wooden boxes and in their hands round sticks, with which they beat upon the boxes, in time with the songs. [pp. 122–23]

[These twelve young men squatted, took the lids from the boxes, on which they beat rapidly with their sticks. Inside were the rattles, aprons, masks, and charms of the shaman.] The songs grew more frenzied, their time more rapid. . . . Every eye was turned towards the door.

The wild, maniac cry of the loon quivered through the air; all gave exclamations of wonder and fear, as into the room rushed Klee-a-keet with frantic gestures and horrid cries. He leaped over the heads of those on the lower platform and landed on the cleared space by the fire. Close after him rushed two of his slaves. Their business was to keep their master out of the fire and prevent him from hurting himself. [We can assume that the eight young men with beating sticks wore masks with eyeholes, while the masks of shamans often lacked eyeholes, although Klee-a-keet does not seem to have worn a mask on this occasion.]

Klee-a-keet had made himself as hideous as it is possible for a human being to be. He was naked, except for a short apron of buckskin, hung with small clinking shells, and anklets of swansdown, ornamented with puffins' bills. His body, legs, arms and face were painted all over the totemic figures and grotesque devices. Green figures of his family totem, the frog, covered his chest and abdomen. [Since the shaman was a Wolf 27 man, the frog could not have been one of his totemic crests, but must have represented one of his spirits. We note the Tlingit belief that frog slime is poisonous.] Goggling eyes in black, white, and ochre stared from his arms and legs. His face was a jumble of red, blue and yellow rings and streaks. His hair, which never had been cut or combed in his life, surrounded his head in ugly bunches like a mass of brown seaweed. In each hand he held a rattle, with carved frogs chasing each other over its surface; these he rattled furiously as he howled and danced. [pp. 123–24]

This dreadful figure was never still. It crouched and sprang; it writhed and bent and swayed; it pitched towards the fire, only to be thrown back by the slaves; it dashed itself on the floor, rolling over and over, tying itself in knots and convolutions like a bundle of snakes; it turned somersaults and cramped backward until heels touched head; it rolled its eyes, clutched with its claws, frothed at the mouth and steamed with sweat. It lost all semblance to a human being and seemed a demon from another world.

[The shaman uttered cries of animals: wolf, bear, eagle, lynx, whale, and] hissed like a serpent [*sic;* none live in Alaska]. Prayers to the demons of the mountains and the sea and to his *Yakes,* and curses upon his enemies, including the missionaries and the witches, followed each other ceaselessly.

The ordinary *Shaman* had only one *Yake,* or familiar spirit. Klee-a-keet boasted of six, and in his incantations invoked each in succession, calling it by name, and selecting different rattles and aprons and amulets to please each spirit. . . . [The songs also changed with each spirit invoked, but increased in tempo. After two hours, the shaman fell, stiff in every muscle and exhausted, his eyes rolled up.] This was his trance when his soul was in the spirit world communing with his *Yakes* and the spirits of other great *Ihts* [ʔíxṫ]. [p. 124]

[After lying unconscious for two hours, the shaman suddenly] bounded to his feet . . . talking rapidly in short, explosive sentences:

"I have been in the spirit world. I have talked with my ancestors. My medicine is strong. My *Yakes* are omniscient. They tell me everything. I know all secrets. I can speak all languages. Nothing is hidden from me. I could make your chief well in a

> minute. But a bad spirit is here. He is in this room. The chief is *nooksatty* (bewitched) [*sic;* nú·kʷ ṡa·ti· means "witch."]. Somebody has a *heehwh* (evil spirit) [hí·xʷ]. He is killing our brother. I must find him; I must find him!" [p. 125]
>
> [He sprang up and rushed around the room, while the Indians recoiled in horror. Suddenly he jumped into the crowd and] quickly snatched at an invisible rope; then, straining back with all his strength, while the sweat poured from his face, he made the motions of gathering in the rope. Yelping like a dog on a hot trail . . . snarling like a dog . . . [he at last reached] a little group of poorly clad Tacoos [Taku] who stood huddled together, their eyes staring, their bodies shivering. They were poor slaves, and knew that from their number the *Iht* would choose his victim. . . .
>
> [The shaman stared at the group. Then with a shriek, he seized a slave.] "It is he; it is he!" screamed the *Shaman,* and fell upon the floor in convulsions.
>
> [After a moment of stunned silence,] Excited voices cried: "The witch! The witch! Take him! Tie him up! Kill him!"
>
> The friends of the sick chief, led by his brother, came storming up and laid violent hands upon the slave, jerking him hither and thither. One of them struck him in the face. A Tacoo woman called him a foul name and spit upon him. They flung him on the floor. They tore all his clothes from him. Two men took him by his feet and dragged him across the sharp gravel which surrounded the fire, tearing the flesh of his back and staining the stones with his blood. Men and women sprang to the fire as he passed, and snatching burning brands stuck the live coals against his body. The horrible smell of scorching flesh filled the room. Then the attendants of the *Iht* brought thongs of sinew, and he was bound as Mrs. Brown had been, the rope in this case being passed around the man's throat and drawn so tight behind his back that he could breathe only with great difficulty. Some one pried up two planks from the upper platform and the victim was thrown to the ground eight feet below, and the planks replaced. [pp. 125–26]

[Although Young had attempted to protest and go to the man's rescue, he was restrained by men of his own Christian group who knew that this time he could do nothing.

[Young eventually eradicated shamanism and the torture of accused witches by boldly facing down the shamans and the assembled natives and freeing the accused victims. The first was *Kah-tu-yeatley,* a lowly member of the clan of Tow-a-aat (Wolf 25 or 26). He was denounced by Klee-a-keet for bewitching the aunt of Chief Shakes (Na·nya·ʔa·yí, Wolf 18), who was married to Chief Shustaak (Raven 33, Ta·łqʷe·dí). Young simply went to Shustaak's house, where the accused witch was hidden under the platform, denounced the assembled natives for having broken the law of the United States, and demanded and secured the release of the poor old man. The latter and his wife felt it prudent to leave Wrangell for good, and Young's courageous stand began to win adherents (Young 1927:134).

[Soon fears of witchcraft were again revived when a human skull, with the flesh half gone—surely the property of a witch—was found under the house of Jakob Ukotsees, a relative of Kah-tu-yeatley's. Chiefs Shakes and Shustaak demanded to know if Young would tolerate the witches that were making people sick (Young 1927:137–39). At a meeting of all the principal leaders of the Stikines, Shakes called for testimony of the natives to convince Young that witches really existed. As the latter wrote (Young 1927:140–42):

> The testimony of practically all present was then heard. Of late years I have made a study of the Salem witchcraft cases and have compared the testimony given in the press by our enlightened New England forefathers with the testimony of the Stickeens in that notable council of ours. A comparison of this evidence shows a surprising resemblance. . . . [T]here were in both the same positive statements of the transformation of the persons accused into the form of wolves, ravens and demons; the same mysterious convulsions, trances and painful seizures of their victims; the same jumble of piety and malice, of falsehood and delusion; the same *hysterics.* . . . [p. 140]
>
> One by one stories of incidents which were told as coming under the personal knowledge of the speakers were related with seeming truthfulness. . . . The mass of testimony, if it could be dignified by that name, was overwhelming. But while these men claimed to be eye-witnesses of these mysterious events, the "witnesses did not agree together"; . . . [and Young became convinced that] the unscrupulous and avaricious medicine-men were at the bottom of it all. Many of these tales were put into the mouths of the witnesses by their *Ihts.* [p. 141]

As Young (1927:146) wrote later:

> I firmly believe that all of the medicine-men in Southeastern Alaska at that time and since were *conscious frauds.* They were in the business simply for the profit that there was in it. They did not believe in their own powers. In fact, one of the most noted of them, when I pinned him down, confessed as much. I said, "You know yourself that you are simply fooling these people; you have no *Yake,* and never had one. You cannot do anything you profess to do. Why do you do it?"
>
> He grinned at me with that aggravating insolence that those fellows possessed in superlative degree, and said: "I do it for the same reason that you come and preach about your God—for *pay.*"

[Young succeeded in getting the Wrangell natives to form a council, with Chief Shakes as the head (although Young himself retained great power as "manager"), with authority to try all cases of alleged witchcraft, practicing black arts, or frightening people. The Indians pledged that there was to be no more tying people up for witchcraft, no medicine man was allowed to practice in the Stikine town, and that "the old feasts and potlatches which led to so much robbery and disorder were to be done away . . ." (p. 143). All the principal men signed. "Then there was a general handshaking and the presentation to me of a multitude of old dance implements, pipes, stone axes and other relics of their past life, and the Council adjourned with prayer and benediction" (p. 144).

[Thus the Indians of Wrangell pledged to give up all the ceremonies symbolizing crest and clan, and gave away their clan heirlooms. Henceforth they were to be modern United States citizens.

[Young knew of course that superstition died hard. Shamans continued to practice in the "Foreign Town" where visiting natives from other areas lived. Shakes engaged Klee-a-keet to cure his younger brother, whom Young had been treating. When the missionary broke into the house where the shaman was holding his séance, Shakes was embarrassed but pleaded that the shaman be allowed to continue (there was evidently no witchcraft accusation). Young agreed, but told Klee-a-keet that if he failed and the youth died, neither he nor any other shaman would be allowed to perform in the town. And when the young man did die, the whole family of Shakes took back all of the wealth that had been given as fee to Klee-a-keet, and left him nothing but his canoe. The shaman in a rage tried to stab the missionary, but was prevented by the outraged Stikines. And Mr. Young acquired the knife, "a beautiful trophy! The handle was of crab-apple wood, carved in the semblance of a wolf's head with abalone shell eyes and teeth" (Young 1927:151–52).

[Shakes and Young together dealt with another witchcraft case, this one in the Foreign Town, where a little girl had been hidden under the flooring of a house occupied by a Kake couple. When they got the trap door open:

> Down in a hole under the floor, about three or four feet deep, lay a naked child, some five or six years of age, sobbing. . . . Her hands were tied tightly behind her back, and we found on her body marks or stripes, as if she had been cruelly beaten. . . . She was apparently starved. When we asked how long since she had eaten anything, she said: "Many days." When questioned why she was put down in that hole she did not know. Shakes had been informed, however, that a medicine-man had named her as bewitching the [Kake] woman, and they had begun to torture her. They might have put her to death had we not interfered. [p. 153–54]

[There were few cases of witchcraft accusation at Wrangell after this, because the shamans were afraid, and the town became known as a haven of refuge. "At one time," wrote Young (1927:154), "there were seven girls and six boys in our school under our care, who had been accused, and in some cases tied up, as witches," but who had escaped to Wrangell.

[Furthermore, Young (p.155) reported:

> When a Stickeen *Iht* made an incantation in a house on the outskirts of the village our Council was called. We summoned the offender, made him return the fee he had collected and talked to him so severely that he voluntarily cut off his long hair and presented the ugly mop to me as a sign of his surrender . . . [and Mrs. Young burned it!].
>
> Another *Iht* of the Hoonah tribe was less tractable. He was performing in full blast when I went up and stopped him and sent the crowd home. He made such a fuss that we summoned him before the Council. Not proving amenable to reason, we laid hands on him, and while he was cursing us and calling on his *Yake* to come and blast us, three strong Stickeens held him fast while I cut off his tousled hair. He threatened to kill himself in order that his family might collect damages, but when, instead of imploring him to remain alive, I encouraged him in his suicidal intention, saying that the country would be better without him, he concluded to spite me by continuing to exist.

[According to Young (p. 156), the most troublesome shamans were Klee-a-keet from Angoon, who committed suicide when the missionary failed to die as he had predicted, "Kowee, the Tacoo *Iht*" ("Cowee," or "Kowee," chief and shaman of the Auk tribe, Raven 15, Ł̓ïne·dí), "and the red-haired Chilkoot doctor, Skundoo-oo" (Sx̌andu?ú·, Wolf 7, Dagisdina·).

[Mrs. Willard, wife of the missionary at Haines, mentioned a number of witchcraft cases, but did not see any shamanistic séance and believed that there would be no denunciation of witches so long as the Navy was at hand (Willard 1884:131, letter of December 1881). She mentioned two boys, Allan (no last name) and Moses Jamestown, both from Hoonah, who had found refuge in the Sheldon Jackson Institute home in Sitka. The first had freed his mother, who had been tied up for witchcraft, and paddled with her and her baby some ninety miles to Sitka. Moses, who took the name of the USS *Jamestown* as his surname, had been an orphan, treated as a slave at Hoonah, and had escaped to Sitka, but was accused of witchcraft. His torture had already begun when rescuers came from the ship and freed him (Willard 1884:280–81, letter of March 1883).

[Mrs. Willard (pp. 300–305, letter of May 1883) told the story of an old Chilkoot woman who had not only been accused and tortured as a witch, but who admitted the charge.

Mrs. Willard got the story from Mrs. Dickinson, who had befriended the woman.

[She had been accused of causing the death of a little boy. She confessed to the charge and named a man in "the lower Chilcat village," Yandestake, as her accomplice. Both were put to the torture. (It should be noted that witchcraft cannot be undone, it was believed, without the suffering of the witch; see de Laguna 1972:737.) "Don-a-wok [Dá·nawa·q, "Silver/Dollar Eyes," chief of Raven 17, Łukʷa·x̣ʔádi], our good chief," compelled the release of the man, but the relatives of the old woman kept secret her confinement for eight days, when some school children told Mrs. Dickinson. The latter went down to the house where the poor old woman had been confined, and took her into her own home. "She is a weird old crone," she reported, probably senile or confused. When Mrs. Dickinson asked her why she had lied in confessing that she had killed the little boy, she answered, "It was no lie, I did make him die. And plenty more people I make die too." When questioned further, she explained that she felt old, tired, and sick. She had heard the missionary preach about God, but to her this was nonsense. She went outside and the spirits told her that "God no good; he not strong. Devil very strong; he make all people do bad; he make people die. It better you work for him." And she began to think of another world where everyone could "begin all over again" (Willard 1884:302–3).

[Urged by these spirit voices, she promised to work for the devil.

> I take dirty string off somebody's neck, and little bit of salmon somebody spill out of mouth; take little rag off little woman's dress; cut little hair off somebody's head. All easy, quiet, so nobody see; nobody know anything. I hide it quick. By and by nobody knows. I steal away to medicine-man's dead-house. Devil strong then; he take me. I put on just one old ragged skirt, and bit of blanket on shoulders; then I go inside. I hide all bits of string, fish, rag, hair, in blanket. Now all these people going to die. Maybe in one year; maybe two, maybe five, years. By and by boy dies; I know I make him die. Then my heart looks very wicked. [And she prayed God not to let others see so much wickedness in her heart. But next day they knew all about how she had witched people, and she then believed a little bit that God was strong because he had revealed her wickedness.] I say, "Yes, I make him die. You go with me to dead medicine-man. I take all pieces out; I show you." We all go to dead house. I say, "Devil very strong. I go in; [if] you no tie me[, y]ou never see me any more. Tie strong rope round me: hold fast." I show the people all the pieces. Then everybody 'fraid: many people going to die; and they tie me strong on thistles [devil's club]. They give me nothing to eat, nothing to drink. By and by I 'most die. [pp. 303–4]

And in that condition she saw a little light: that it was no good to work for the devil; God was stronger.

[Even though Mrs. Willard was recording the woman's words at second hand, what she reported is the classic behavior of a witch in securing "witch's dirt," and the old woman's readiness to adopt this role and to confess is what we might expect from a person who felt worthless and unworthy of attention. But a young girl of sixteen, who was supposed to have killed a small boy and caused a man's arm to shrivel, confessed to these accusations "because of the torture." And since she had nothing to pay for her release, the injured family of her victims took her as a slave (Willard 1884:368–69, letter of November 1883).

[The U.S. Navy was, of course, able to use physical, as well as moral, force to put down the shamans. Commander Beardslee, assigned to the USS *Jamestown,* June 1879–September 1880, was perhaps the first officer to deal with such a case. He had sent Stickeesh, a wealthy Indian of Sitka, to Klukwan to mediate in the war between the Chilkat and the Chilkoot, but the man returned with serious rheumatism (Beardslee 1882:58–59). The shaman whom he consulted was unable to cure him, but had been paid ten blankets to discover the witch responsible for the ailment. A "simple young Indian, belonging to an unimportant family," was denounced, caught, and bound for torture, when the Indian policemen, led by Annahootz (ʔAnaxú·c, chief of the Sitka Ka·gʷa·nta·n, Wolf 1), stopped the proceedings and reported the case to Beardslee. They did not dare to do more because of their fear of the shaman's powers. Beardslee had the shaman, witch, and invalid brought to the guardhouse, where, after vain persuasions, the shaman was sentenced to a cell until he should return the ten blankets to Stickeesh. The latter was given treatment by the medical officer of the *Jamestown,* and the accused witch returned to his family.

> Many Indians being present, I availed myself of the opportunity to weaken, if possible, their faith in witchcraft, and gave the shaman full permission to exercise upon me all of the sorceries of his profession while occupying a cell to which he was assigned until he should restore to Stickeesh the blankets he had received from him; and to this end he was permitted to carry into his seclusion such implements of his art as he had with him. Whether he tried or not I do not know; the sentry reported that he saw no such attempt; but after release, which took place when the blankets were restored, he told the other Indians that his spirits had no power over the white man—which was a good point gained, as it lessened the possibilities of any white man being suspected of witchcraft.
>
> Upon release, the shaman was assured that upon repetition of the offense his head would be shaved and his person subjected to a Russian [sweat] bath; which, as they never wash themselves,

nor comb or cut their hair (by which process, it is believed, they would lose their supernatural power), so frightened him that he at once left Sitka, with the threat that he would never again return; and neither he nor any of his professional brethren ever again attempted to practice in Sitka. The experiment involved a serious risk, and such Indians as were friendly to me personally expressed great grief and apprehensions for my safety. And had any misfortune occurred to me the belief in witchcraft and the powers of the shaman would have been greatly strengthened. As nothing did happen to me, I have hopes that the result was a weakening of this superstition. [p. 59]

[Commander Glass, who succeeded Beardslee, reported as of June 6, 1881 (1882:30):

> On May 29, an Indian from the village of Hootz-Na-Hoo [probably Angoon] came on board [the *Jamestown*] and reported his escape from confinement in that village, where he had been denounced as a witch by the native medicine-man, and held a prisoner to be burned alive [?] in case of the death of one of the tribe, the wife of one of the leading men. As this was the first authentic case of the killing, or attempted killing, of a supposed witch that had been brought to my notice I decided to punish the persons attempting such a crime, and at once sent a boat expedition under Lieut. E. P. McClellan, to Hootz-Na-Hoo to arrest the medicine-man and the leading men of the village, and bring them here [Sitka] for an investigation, and the punishment of the guilty parties.

The Lieutenant returned with two chiefs, but the shaman had left for Chilkat country, and was never apprehended. After investigation, Glass punished one chief with a fine and imprisonment, and hoped to get the shaman through the other chief.

[Glass (1890:13) also reported "a case of witch-denouncing" at Sitka, in January 1882. The witch was rescued by miners before he was killed.

> An investigation left no doubt of the guilt of the leading Shaman of the village, and he was arrested and confined in the guard-house just as he had about completed all his preparations for leaving Sitka in a very hurried manner. All the Indians were assembled in front of the guard-house, the witch-doctor was brought out, and the case and the absurdity of his pretensions explained through an interpreter. It was announced that the Shaman's hair would be cut off close to his head, that he would be scrubbed thoroughly, to deprive him of the supernatural powers he claimed, and then be kept at work for a month, and afterwards banished from the Sitka settlement. He was first invited, however, to test his powers, in the presence of the Indians, in bringing any plagues he chose on the commander and his officers and men. The sentence was carried out, to the delight of all the Indians present, but banishment was not found necessary, for the Shaman was not proof against the ridicule to which he was subjected, and left the village of his own accord at the expiration of his confinement. The case seemed to have a good effect in breaking down the witchcraft superstition, and no more cases occurred for some time; none, at, least that were made public.

[Admiral, then Ensign, Coontz (1930:123–24) reported how he went to Portage Cove, near Haines, with the *Pinta* in July 1888, and here some Indians came on board with the Chilkoot chief, "Donawauk":

> Donawauk informed us that a red-headed Indian witch doctor [was this Skun-doo? also a Chilkoot] had accused an Indian girl about fourteen years old of being a witch and had tied her up in an Indian hut where she was starving to death. Our doctor and an officer went ashore to ascertain the facts, and found the poor child in a cabin on her knees suffering intensely. Her hands were lashed and her black hair was tied to her feet. They cut her bonds and the doctor chafed her hands while the officer gave her a small quantity of food. The captain [John S. Newell] decided to order all Indians on board for a feast and consultation, hoping by this means to get the red-headed Indian witch doctor. [The latter, however, had fled the country and the party from the ship pursued him in vain.] [p. 123]
>
> Several years elapsed before the Indian witch doctor was captured. After a fair trial he was convicted and sent to the Washington State [*sic*, Federal] penitentiary at McNeil's Island where Federal prisoners from Alaska were received. His sentence was for twenty years.
>
> [Before the *Pinta* left, Donawak brought] a pretty Indian girl on board and presented her to the captain with his compliments for having rescued the victim of the red-headed witch doctor. The captain thanked him but declined to accept his gift. [p. 124]

According to Tlingit custom, whoever saves the life of another person becomes his owner. That is why Land Otter Men that "save" a drowning person are said to "capture" him.

[In 1893 the *Pinta*, under command of Lieutenant Commander William T. Burwell, made a cruise to all the ports of southeastern Alaska. As Coontz related (1930:164):

> One of our ports on this cruise was Shakan [a Henya village]. There we discovered that another witch doctor had been practicing. We decided to arrest him and give him a hearing. When it was over we erected a small platform on the quarter deck, brought out the barber's chair, and, while two sturdy bluejackets held him fast, his long, black, flowing hair was removed with the barber's clippers. The inhabitants thronged on the nearby beach and watched the operation. When shorn of his locks, the power of the witch doctor vanished!

[Skun-doo was probably the best known of the late nineteenth-century shamans, and conflicting accounts are given of his downfall at the hands of the authorities in Alaska. According to Emmons, in 1888 he was found guilty of causing the death of a woman whom he had denounced as a witch. She had been tied up for eight days without food or water, in order to force a confession. Skun-doo was imprisoned for three years. On his release with his hair cut, he gave up his title of shaman, *Ict* [ʔíx̣t̓], and assumed the white man's title of "judge," acknowledging that the whites had the more powerful spirits since they had been able to imprison him. Although he had lost his power with his hair, he posed as a shaman for the photographers, Winter and Pond (who erroneously called him a "Taku"), and he provided Emmons with information. The Reverend Young (1927:156) called him "the red-haired Chilkoot doctor, Skundoo-oo," and rated him one of the worst in his profession.

[Keithahn (1963:18) published a photograph of "Skun-doo-ooh, a famous Chilkat [*sic,* Chilkoot] shaman," and wrote:

> Physical divergences from the normal such as crossed eyes, hunched backs, a double crown, or red hair were taken as signs of innate occult powers and such individuals were trained from boyhood for the medicine man role. Skun-doo-ooh not only was born with a double crown but had red hair so his destiny was manifest. He became so famous that another shaman, stricken ill, engaged his services for the price of 40 blankets. The suspected witch died of torture and so did the patient a few days later. Skun-doo-ooh was reported to white authority for not refunding the blankets [as he was obligated to do under Tlingit law] and got a three year term in San Quentin. At Sitka they cut off his hair wherein lay his "power" but it grew out again in prison. There he composed his famous "San Quentin Song" and came back to Alaska more powerful than ever.

[Skun-doo was a brother to the Indian who served as guide and packer to a number of expeditions into the interior, especially to that of Frederick Schwatka in 1883, in consequence of which he adopted the name "Schwatka" as his own. (This would have involved giving the explorer his own Tlingit name.)

[A wooden mask, painted green, red, tan, brown and black, with inlays of opercula and copper (now in Saint Joseph Museum, Missouri) was published in *The Far North* (1973:247, no. 312). The mask had formerly belonged to Skundoo but seems to have been collected from his brother. It represents a bear, somewhat anthropomorphized, though the erect ears indicate that it is an animal, one of his spirits.

[Sackett (1979:77–80, pls. 18 and 19) has published portraits of "Skondoo" and of his brothers, "Schwatka" and "Monkey John," in ordinary clothes and in traditional costumes (both photographs taken in the 1890s) and has described his grave at Yandestake. It was a ruined gravehouse, with his canoe at one side. His wife is buried nearby in an ordinary grave surrounded by a balustrade. Military personnel from nearby Fort Steward had taken the doctor's paraphernalia. According to Sackett:

> In July, 1894, he [Skun-doo, Skundu] was arrested for causing the death of an Indian woman, Ches Oqhk, while practicing shamanism. A death had occurred in the village, and the relatives of the deceased employed his services, at a fee of 20 blankets, to determine the cause of death. As a result of his divinations, Skondoo settled on Ches Oqhk, suspected of being a witch, as the cause of death. Under his direction, the deceased's family bound the woman for 10 days, and she died from lack of food and water. Because she had died, she was declared to have been a witch, establishing her guilt (The Alaskan 1895). Gleh-Naw, a member of the woman's family, made a complaint to the white authorities and Skondoo was arrested for murder and taken to Juneau to stand trial (U.S. Court Records 1894; Alaskan Boundary Tribunal 1904). As an outcome of the trial, he was found guilty and sentenced to 3 years at San Quentin for manslaughter (The Alaskan 1895).

[The Tlingit, too, have their own tales of cutting, or rather of attempts to cut, the hair of shamans. Their spirits were so strong that the barber's shears were turned aside, or broke in his hands, or the matted braids writhed so that they could not be held, it is said.]

CHAPTER 16

Games and Gambling

The Tlingit were keen gamblers, in proportion to their opportunities for play. During much of the year they were scattered in small families at their fishing and hunting grounds, and during the winter their potlatches and ceremonies took up much of their time. Their principal games of chance were the stick and the toggle [better known as "hand"] game, played only by men. The latter was known over a large area of the continent and may have come to the coast of British Columbia from the interior, and then spread northward through Tlingit country. The stick game was the older, and was superseded among the Tlingit in the first half of the nineteenth century by the toggle [hand] game. In 1882 only a few of the older men at Sitka could explain the stick game. The toggle [hand] game when introduced spread coastwise very quickly, because of its greater simplicity in manipulation and in materials, and because any number could participate in it; it also appealed more directly to the excitable temperament of the people, with the singing to the accompaniment of the beating sticks and drums.

The minor games, dice, spinner, and checkers, were played more for amusement than profit.

[Other games, not mentioned or described by Emmons, were races (on foot or by canoe), shinny and other ball games, and cat's cradle. Swanton (1908:445) mentioned several games for boys that involved hitting a mark with an arrow or spearlike stick.]

THE STICK GAME*

The stick game, *ahl-kar* [ʔaɬqá·], was played by two men, seated opposite to each other, about three feet apart, with a mat between them and the implements of play close at hand. Each player had his own sets of sticks, and he played with one or another as he thought his luck required. The stake of blankets, furs, etc., was placed between them to one side; friends and others stood behind the players and made individual bets, placing their stakes opposite each other. Their bets were governed by the same rules as those of the players. Counters were bunched to one side in the middle within easy reach.

The game was played with an indeterminate number of small cylindrical sticks, from twenty-five to eighty odd. These were beautifully fashioned of fine-grained hardwood: yew (from the Queen Charlotte Islands), maple, crab apple, alder, and birch. In each set the sticks were all of the same kind of wood, averaging four to five inches long, and a quarter inch in diameter. They were absolutely true in circumference, for each was tested during manufacture to barely pass through a hole in a bone gauge, *Alkar-kon-wolth-lah* [ʔaɬqá· x̣̓awu·ɬ, "stickgame doorway"]. They were smoothed with pumice stone, dogfish skin, or Equisetum stem, and hand polished. The ends were rounded, dull pointed, nipple shaped, flattened, or sometimes hollowed out and inlaid with haliotis shell. All or almost all were painted with red or black encircling lines, bands, or spirals, and these designs were named for animals, manufactured articles, or natural objects, and so forth, and in one set there might be several with the same decoration. Sometimes the sticks might also be decorated by burned lines, as in a set reputed to be of Haida origin, but obtained at Wrangell and identified by an old Hutsnuwu Indian, "Jim" or "Kilisnoo Jake" (AMNH 16/9383). Some sticks might be inlaid with square, rectangular, triangular, or circular pieces of shell, bits of bone, or circles of copper wire. Common names and marks, found in different sets, were mostly of birds and fish; others in a set seem to have been named at the will of the owner. These marks and the corresponding names were simply to identify the sticks, and gave no value in play. [See Table 33.]

The marked sticks were called *scheest*, "painted" [ši·št?]; the plain sticks were called *wu-de-shutch-yar-ka*, "washed clean" [wudišuǯi qá·, "man who has bathed"]. One or more [marked] sticks in every set was known as *naq* [ná·qʷ], "devilfish" or "bait," for the devilfish [squid] was used as bait in halibut fishing, so this, the trump stick, was the bait in the game. The exceptionally fine sticks, particularly those carved and burnt in animal designs and those most

*Editor's note: In the interest of clarity, I have combined the two versions of the manuscript and have had to rearrange somewhat the paragraphing of the text. The last section is mine.

elaborately inlaid with shell, were of Haida workmanship. All bone sticks and the equally slender ones of maple were from the interior, particularly from the Carrier of the upper Skeena River, and from the Babine.

A complete gambling outfit was kept and carried in a hide bag, *al-kar takar qwelth* [ʔałqá· da·kagʷé·ł], and consisted of several sets of sticks in skin pouches with extension flaps, often painted on the inner side, which were wrapped around to confine the sticks. The bag was secured by a string with a toggle at the end. There was also a bundle of finely divided inner bark of the cedar, kept in the leg skin of a deer or caribou with the hair intact on the inside; and a square of stiff, flat leather, generally cut on the face in animal design. In later years this leather square was procured in trade from Europeans, but originally it was of the heavier hide of the neck of the moose and was traded from the interior. The paint stick with which the sticks were colored in black and red was often in the pouch, also. It was sometimes carved, but ordinarily was a three-inch stick like a pencil pointed at both ends. The colors were from an oxide of iron which gave both red and black; the mineral was rubbed off on a stone with crushed salmon egg and saliva. In the pouch was also carried a bone gauge with several circular holes, graduated in size, through one of which a certain set of sticks was required to pass. A set of counters, *al-kar kah-khartsee* [probably ʔałqá· kaqá·ṡi] or *ku-nee na* [?], "tied together," were also contained in the bag and consisted simply of sixteen to twenty small, unfinished, split sticks, less than a foot in length and pointed or flat at the ends.

Each player arranged his sticks with one or more trump, "bait," sticks, *naq* [ná·qʷ], at his left and a corresponding number of painted sticks, *scheest,* in sets of three on his right. When the game commenced, the player took one *naq* and three *scheest,* and wrapped each one in cedar bark, making four piles in front of him, the relative position of which he would constantly change. The player opposite watched every move, and when the piles of sticks were finally placed, he pointed to one pile, with his right forefinger and arm extended, saying "There is *naq.*" The dealer would then take fifteen to twenty sticks from the main pile, and holding them end up in his left hand, insert the covered stick selected through the bark wrapping into the middle of the other sticks, and rolled the sticks around with his right hand. The opposite then signified another pile which was likewise forced into the bundle.

The player then drew one stick at a time out of the bundle and threw it down on the square of leather in front of him. Should one of the *scheest* appear, it was set aside, and the other sticks already thrown down were gathered up and manipulated as before, and cast down. And again should the other [next?] selected stick be a *scheest,* it was placed by the other one, and the player won one counter, which he placed on his left side. Then holding the bundle of sticks, he waited for his opponent to select one of the two remaining piles in front of him. The same operation was carried through again, and should the third *scheest* be produced, the player won another counter, and then took up the fourth bundle which contained the *naq,* and cast it down on the leather. However, in this second selection, should the *naq* be first displayed, the deal passed [to the opposite man]. When one player had accumulated all the counters but one, three piles were made, containing two *scheest* and one *naq,* and the sticks were manipulated as before, but the opponent guessed two piles at once, which gave him an advantage of two out of three. If he lost, the game was finished, but if he won he took the play.

Some played the game in a different way: when in the odd and even guessing, only one *scheest* and one *naq* were used in two piles instead of in four; and toward the end of the game, the loser was given a three to one chance in guessing.

For success in this game a gambler drank a swallow or two of salt water and ate the bark of the devil's club every morning for a month and fasted four days before playing.

[Swanton (1908:443–44) described this game, which he called *cīs* (šì·s), not ʔałqá·, naming the ordinary sticks *cīct* (šì·št) and the bait or devilfish nāq (ná·qʷ). He also gave the names of all the sticks in a set obtained by Emmons (provenience not given), and of a second set which Emmons obtained at Kake; both now in AMNH. For the names of the sticks in a fine set of Haida origin, but collected at Wrangell, see Table 33.

[Stick games of this type that were played on the Northwest Coast are described and illustrated by Culin (1907:227, 243–46, 259–63). The clearest explanation of the complex rules for playing and scoring are those by Swanton (1905b: 58–59) for the Haida.]

THE TOGGLE [OR HAND] GAME

This guessing game of odd and even [the hand game] came to the Tlingit from the Haida and Tsimshian. It is generally known throughout the Northwest Coast as *lehal* or *lahal*; although the Tlingit call it *ne han* [nahé·n]. It required only two ivory or bone toggles, less than three

Decorated sticks for the Stick Game, part of a set of sixty-eight pieces, said to be of Haida origin but obtained from Killisnoo Jake, a Hutsnuwu man. Pencil sketches by G. T. Emmons; red (R), black (B). The numbers correspond to those listed in Table 33. Top to bottom. Sea otter *(nos. 28 and 45; but listed as "precipitous rock" and "guillemot"),* Wolf *(no. 29),* Sculpin *(no. 30),* Land Otter *(no. 31),* Squirrel *(no. 32).*

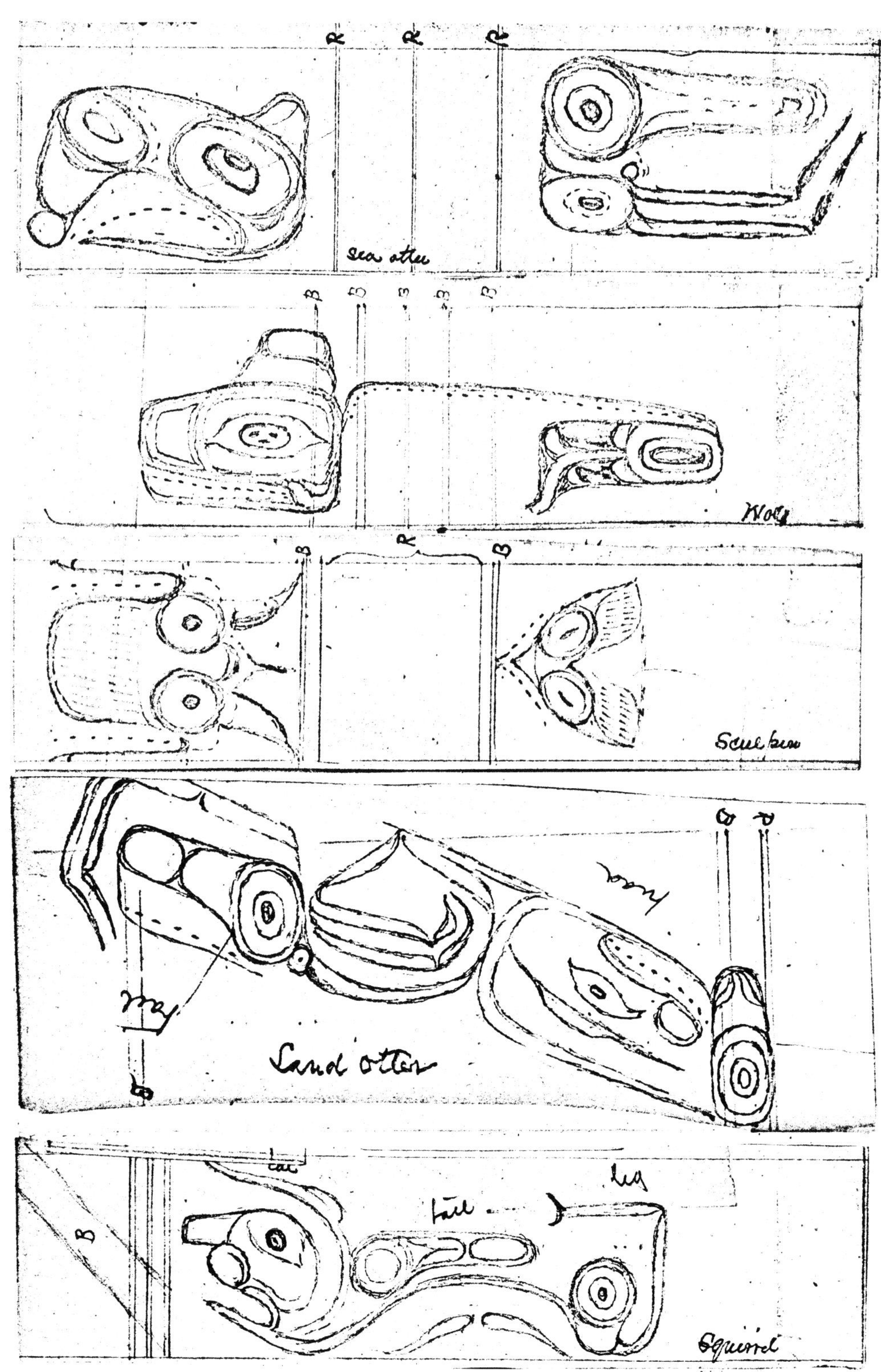

Decorated sticks for the stick game. Top to bottom. *Crab (no. 33), Thunderbird (no. 34, but listed as "raven"), Leech (no. 35), Brown Bear (no. 36), Brown Bear (no. 38).*

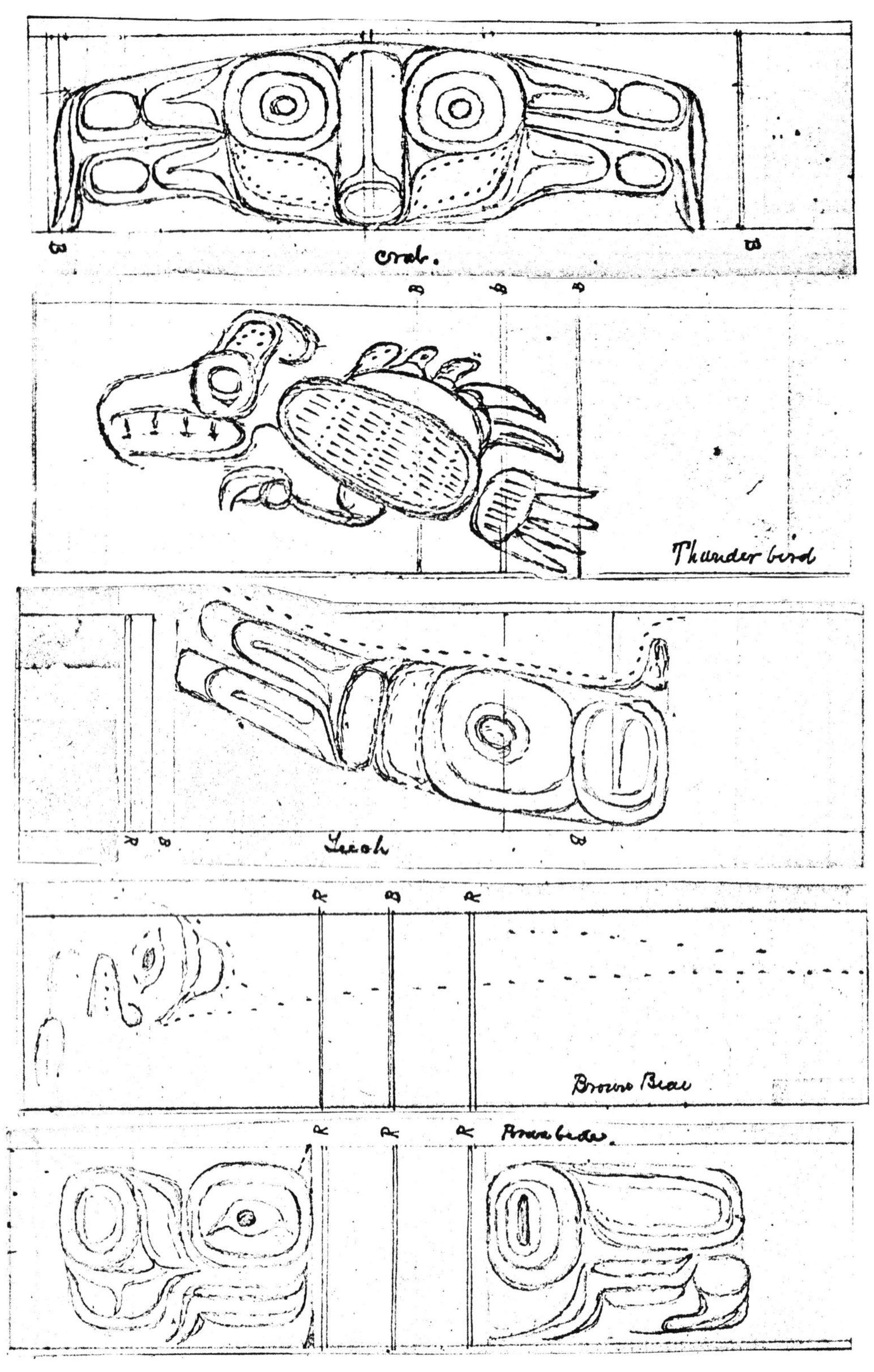

Top to bottom. *Small owl (no. 48, but listed as "Butterfly"; looks like "Man Cooking Eels" in Whale House, Klukwan), Young Raven (no. 49), Butterfly (no. 50, but listed as "Crab"), Butterfly (no. 51), Sea Lion, head and tail (no. 54).*

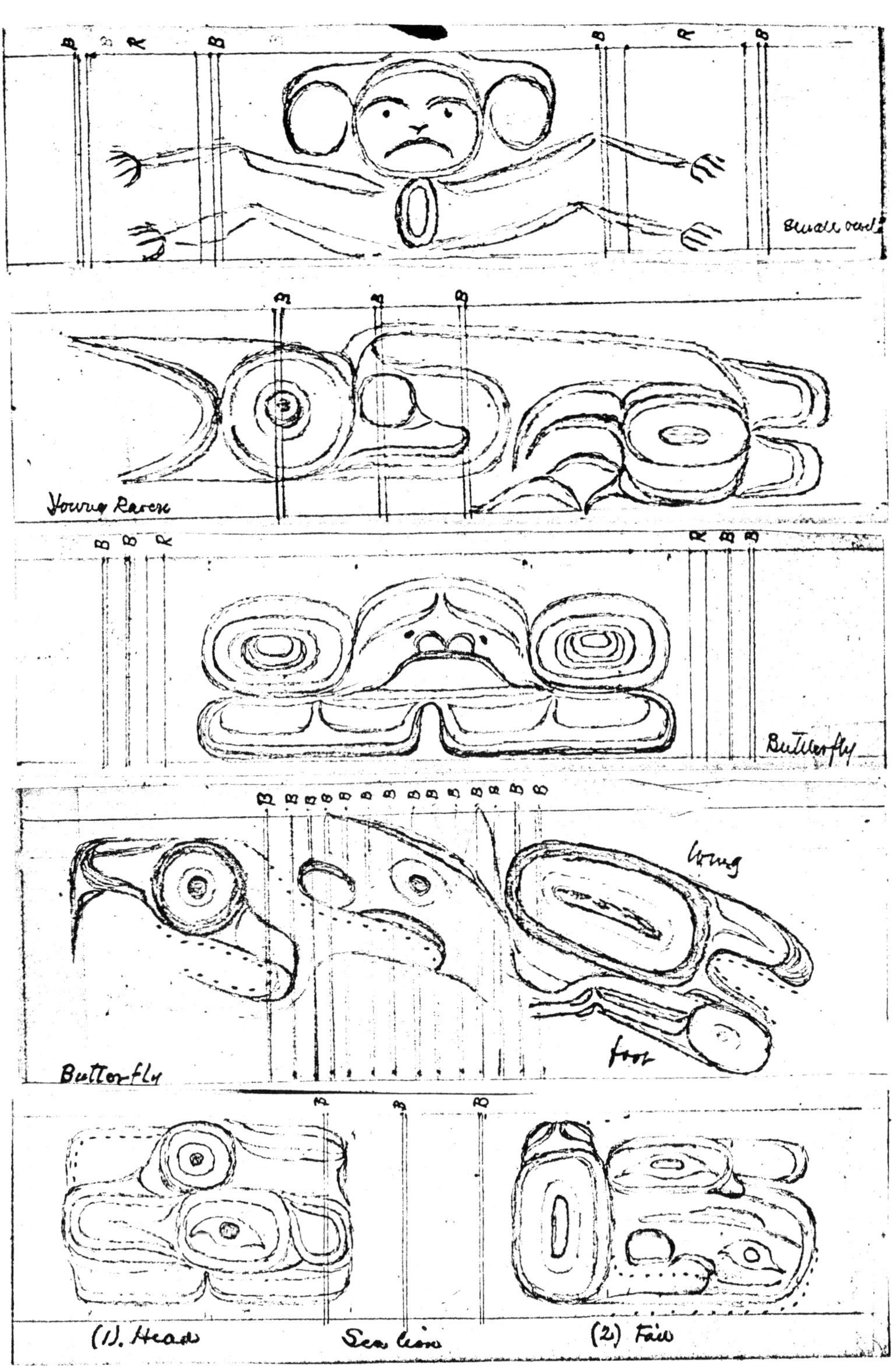

Decorated sticks for stick game. Top to bottom. *The three successive platforms in a chief's house (no. 62), Owl (no. 64), Eagle (no. 66), Wolf (no. 67).*

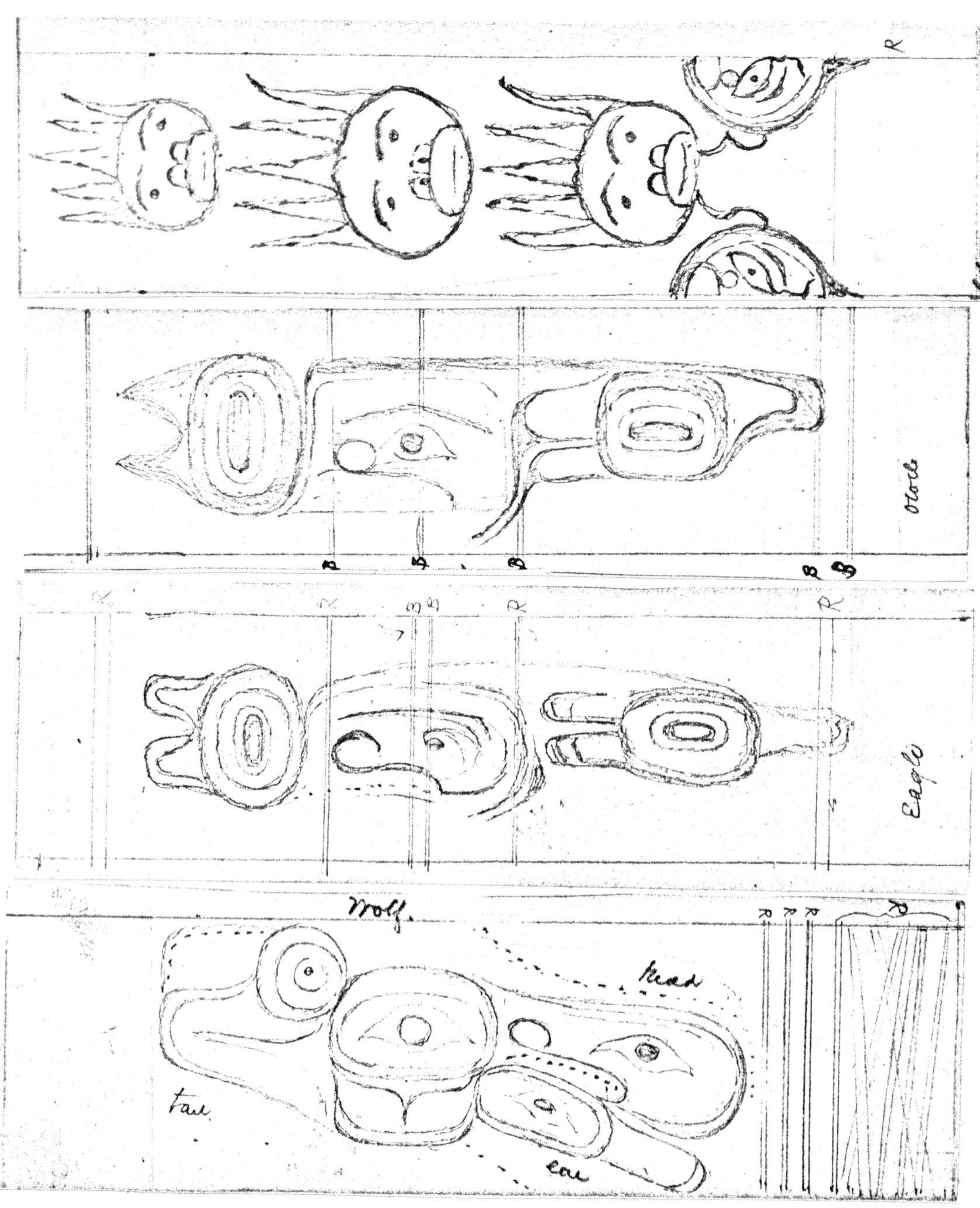

Carved wooden chessmen or checkers collected by W. H. Dall at Port Mulgrave, Yakutat, in 1874. Three pieces out of twenty-two are missing. (Culin 1907:793, fig. 1089.)

inches long so that they could be easily concealed in the hand, cylindrical or slightly larger in the middle and tapering to the rounded ends. One was plain, *na-han* [nahé·n], giving its name to the game; the other, *na gan* [nagá·n], was grooved and blackened around the middle or tied with hide.

The game was played by two groups of the same number, each having its leader who handled the toggles and made the guess, although another might be substituted at any time. The players sat in two lines, opposite each other and about three feet apart, the leaders in the middle of their lines. The stakes were placed between the sides, [with each man's stake in front of him]: each player had a vis-à-vis with whom he made his wager on the game. The counters, also placed between the two sides, consisted of ten to twenty small split sticks, about ten inches long. The leader [of one side] commenced the play by taking a toggle in each hand, one plain, the other marked, and extending both fists toward his opponent. He then would shift the toggles from one hand to the other, in the open, behind his back, under a robe, mat, apron, blanket, or a quantity of finely beaten cedar bark. Sometimes he tossed them in the air and caught them. During all this time, the two leaders looked directly into each other's eyes, as the side that was playing sang to the accompaniment of beating sticks and drum which became louder as the excitement increased. At a word from the opposite side, the player [with the toggles] brought his closed hands stretched out in front of himself. The guesser, looking the player directly in the eye for the slightest movement, might say, "I can see it in this (or that) hand,"

and then point to one hand with extended forefinger and outstretched arm. Then the player opened his hand, and if the hand held the na gan, or marked toggle [*sic,* the unmarked toggle], the play passed to the opposite side [of the one guessing], and that side got one of the counters; but if they were mistaken, the playing side took one counter from the central pile. [The aim was to guess the *unmarked* toggle.] The play continued until one side had won the whole number of counters, taking them first from the central pile and then from the pile won by their opponents, so deciding the game; and each player on the winning side took the stake put up by his opponent.

The songs had only a few words, long drawn out and repeated, and were usually in Chinook Jargon, sometimes in another language. In June 1892 when a number of Canadian sealing schooners were seized in Bering Sea and brought into Sitka, the crews of Vancouver Islanders and the Sitka Tlingit inaugurated a season of gambling that lasted for several weeks, playing daylong from morning to evening, although they did not speak each other's language and could communicate only in a few words of English or Chinook. But they played the same game without difficulty.

The Sitkans sang in Chinook Jargon:

We have a good heart,
You cannot catch us.
We will not cheat you.

[Emmons recorded in notes, BCPA: "The gambling toggle of the Tlingit was of solid bone and smaller than that of the Kwakiutl or Salish, which was of hollow bone."

[Swanton (1908:444–45) described this game, and recorded that the signal given by the guesser was "Hands out! (da´kdê djīn [dá·kde ǯín])," and that he would indicate the hand with the marked toggle by saying "This one (he´do)." "Sometimes a man would wager a $50 canoe, value the games at $10 each, and make his opponents win five times before getting up." Swanton here makes the same mistake as Schwatka (1893:70–71)—and most whites, according to Bill Holm (pers. comm.)—in assuming that the aim is to pick the marked toggle. As Culin wrote (1907:267), "The object is to guess the unmarked one." Southern tribes (Salish, Kwakiutl) more often played with two pairs of toggles, two marked and two plain, and the Tlingit also occasionally used two pairs (Culin 1907:287–89, 299–303, 318–23).]

Like all Indians, the Tlingits are inveterate gamblers, and when coming in contact with the white man, they began to discard their own games [stick game and toggle game] in favor of cards, which they learn readily, and play unceasingly. In the mining camps they may be seen sitting along the roadside or by the shore, staking their hard-earned wages on the spots.

[Emmons did not raise the question of cheating in these games. Yet this was common among the Haida. Culin (1907, fig. 417) published a pair of Haida bones for the hand game, one of which was made in two parts that fitted together so that it could be shown as either plain or marked—that is, in order to cheat. And in writing about the stick game, Swanton stated (1905b:58): "It is not so true to say that cheating was fair in Haida gambling as to say it was part of the game. If one could conceal or get rid of the djil ["bait" stick] temporarily, so much the better."]

THE DICE GAME

The dice game was considered a woman's game among the Tlingit. Although it was a gambling game, it was played more for amusement than for gain. It was played with a small die, *kitchu* [gic̓̌ú· or k̓ic̓̌ú·], "buttocks-shaped," of ivory, bone, or wood, about one inch high, with a base three-quarters by one-half inch. The upper front half of the piece was cut out in a curve which left a narrow flange [hence the common name "chair die"]. The die was sometimes ornamented with incised parallel or crossing lines or holes plugged with lead, "loaded" in a gambling sense, to the advantage of the player. The game is also called *anal tu chuc* [?], "they throw" in Haida.

The game was played by two persons, sitting opposite to each other with a flat smooth surface between them. This was sometimes a square piece of heavy leather, plain or ornamentally cut in animal design, upon which the die was thrown. The narrow flange or top ["chair back"] of the die was held between the thumb and forefinger of the right hand, and flipped up with a twist of the wrist. As it fell the count was taken. I found that count rather arbitrary. If the die falls on either side, there is no count, but the play passes to the other player. [If it balances] on one of the four edges, the count is 1, 1, 2, or 2, and an appropriate number of counters, small sticks or pebbles, are taken from the pile of ten or twenty in the center. The game continues until one player has won them all.

A peculiar wooden die much larger than the ordinary bone dice was found at Wrangell. It was shaped to represent a murrelet, and the count depended on how it fell: 0 on either side, 1 if upright, 2 if standing on its tail, 4 if upside down.

The primitive form of these dice was the astragalus of the deer, which was also used to foretell luck in hunting. But the shoulder bone [humerus] of the seal or sea otter

Chair dice. Top. Ordinary chair die, with points as scored at Yakutat. X wins the game. (Sketch by Frederica de Laguna.) Bottom. *"Fig. 1" Chair die in the form of a bird, and "Fig. 2," tally stick. (Sketches by G. T. Emmons. BCPA.)*

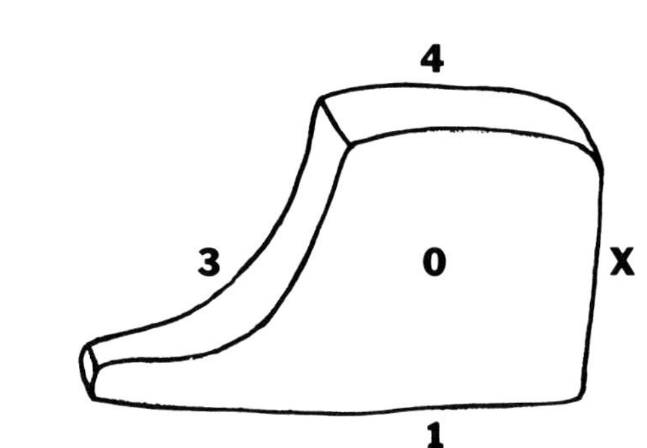

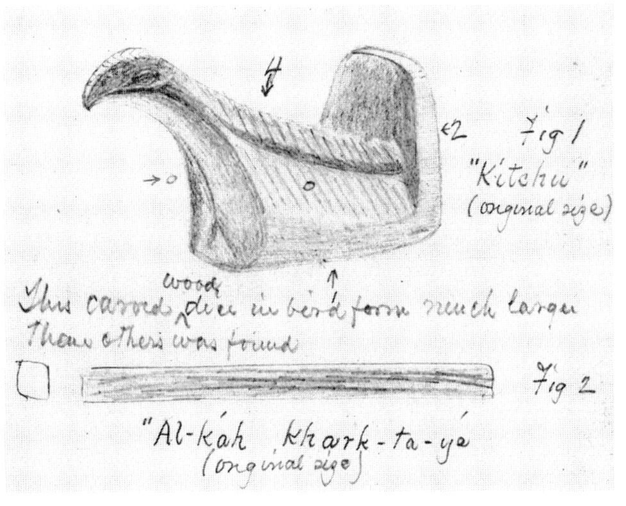

was preferred and even in recent times could be found in the canoe boxes of the older men. Before a hunting trip or other expedition, the man would put the bone to his lips, whisper his wish through the natural hole [in the distal end], and toss it up. As it fell, it foretold the future and the outcome of his wish.

SPINNER

A gambling device was a spinner, *tohl-khon* [tu·ƛ̓čán, "top"], made of a disk of stone or bone, two to three inches in diameter, with a hole through the center, in which was fitted a bone or wooden spindle, three to four inches long and pointed at the lower end. The two teetotums [one for each player] were spun between the palms of the hands, and the one that spun the longer won the stake. I found these spinners only among the Yakutat and Chilkat [but they are used by other Tlingit tribes, according to a personal communication from Jeff Leer]. Both of these disks were of stone, the one from Yakutat a bright green stone, two inches in diameter and fitted with a pointed bone spindle three inches long. The Chilkat specimen of black stone is somewhat larger.

CHECKERS

The Yakutat play a game of checkers which they evidently learned from the Russians so long ago that the Indians have forgotten its origin and believe it to be native. The game is called *alth dar-war* [ʔaɬ dá·wa·], and the individual pieces are *dar-war* [dá·wa·, from the Russian word for checkers].

The board, *dar-war tar-yee* [dá·wa· ṫá·yi, "checkers underboard"], is divided into sixty-four squares [eight to a side], and the pieces are named for and carved to resemble natural and manufactured objects, living things, and persons, and therefore have more of the character of chessmen. The set I procured at Port Mulgrave, Yakutat, included the board and twenty-five pieces, divided between twelve "men" and twelve "women" [with one extra piece, in case of loss?]. In playing the game, two people sit on opposite sides of the board, and each place twelve pieces, "men" on the one side, "women" on the other, on the white squares in the three parallel rows nearest each player. The play resembles our checkers, except that when a move is made, the player names the particular piece he intends to move. When a pawn is taken, he would say, "*dar-war chuck*," "I kill *dar-war*" [dá·wa· ǯaq, "Kill the checker!" (second person imperative)].

[In Table 34, the names of the set of twenty-five pawns are listed by their former Yakutat owner.]

GAMBLING IN THE RUSSIAN ERA*

[There were undoubtedly many games or amusements played by the Tlingit in remote times: shinny, racing, especially in canoes, shooting at a mark, string figures, to name only a few that were probably aboriginal. The early visitors to the Tlingit commented on their love of gambling.

[La Pérouse (1799, 1:397) observed that the natives in Lituya Bay (1786) could catch more than enough fish in one hour to satisfy the needs of the family.

**Editor's note:* I added this section in order to include full information from the authors cited by Emmons as well as La Pérouse and Suría.

The rest of the day they remain idle, spending it on gaming, of which they are as passionately fond as some of the inhabitants of our large cities. This is the grand source of their quarrels: and I do not hesitate to pronounce, that this tribe would be completely exterminated, if the use of any intoxicating liquor were added to these destructive vices.

[And later (p. 408):

Of the passion of these Indians for gaming I have spoken above. The kind to which they are addicted is altogether a game of chance. They have thirty little sticks, each marked with a different number. [Translator's note: "'Differently marked like our dice,' in the original. But this cannot be, because our dice are all marked in the same manner. 'Like the different sides of our dice,' is probably the meaning of the author. T."] Seven of these they hide. Each plays in turn, and he who guesses nearest to the number on the seven sticks, gains the stake, which is commonly a piece of iron, or a hatchet. This game renders them grave and melancholy. . . .

[Beresford, who was with Dixon on the Northwest Coast in 1787, wrote in summary about the inhabitants in general (Tanaina, Chugach, Yakutat, Sitkans, and Haida), yet seemed to have especially in mind the Yakutat and the Sitka Tlingit of Norfolk Sound (1789:245):

Though these poor savages are in their general manners truly in a state of uncultivated barbarism, yet in *one* instance they can boast of a refinement equal to that of more polite nations, and that is *gaming,* which is carried on here to as great a pitch (comparatively speaking) as at any of our moderate fashionable clubs. The only gambling implements I saw, were fifty-two small round bits of wood, about the size of your middle finger, and differently marked with red paint. A game is played by two persons with these pieces of wood, and chiefly consists in placing them in a variety of positions, but I am unable to describe it minutely. The man whom I before mentioned our having on board at Port Mulgrave, lost a knife, a spear, and several toes [iron shaped like an adz blade] at this game in less than an hour: though his loss was at least equal to an English gamester losing his estate, yet the poor fellow bore his ill-fortune with great patience and equanimity of temper.

[Suría, with Malaspina at Yakutat Bay in 1791, also wrote about gambling (in Wagner 1936:256–57):

They gamble with some little sticks, about eight or nine fingers long, and a finger in thickness, very well made. They count up to fifty with various signs, which differ one from the other. They shuffle them and then stretch one or two on the ground. From what we could make out the companion [opponent] must pick out from these two the one which has been hidden by the one doing the shuffling, which he recognizes by signs. If he succeeds the little sticks pass to his companion and if not the same man continues the same shuffling. There is sufficient reason for thinking that with this game they put up their persons and whoever loses has to be at the disposition of the other, because one of our sailors went to play with one of them, and having lost as usual, because he did not know the game, the Indian became very contented and made a sign to the sailor to embark in his canoe, because he was now his, and on being resisted the Indian insisted, indicating by signs that he had won.

[Von Kotzebue (1830, 2:61–62), writing about the Sitkans in 1825, reported:

That no vice may be wanting to complete their characters, the Kalushes are great gamblers. Their common game is played with little wooden sticks painted of various colours, and called by several names, such as crab, whale, duck, &c., which are mingled promiscuously together, and placed in heaps covered with moss; the players being then required to tell in which heap the crab, the whale, &c. lies. They lose at this game all their possessions, and even their wives and children, who then become the property of the winner.

[Lütké (1835, 1:205–20, free translation) corroborated these observations of gambling at Sikta in 1826–29:

Many are passionately fond of the game of little sticks, played on the whole northwest coast of America, even as far as New Albion. . . . they lose in this sometimes all their clothing, their furs, their guns, their slaves, and there are even instances in which they have lost their wives.

[The game, as sketchily described by these authors, was probably the stick game; the natives in the eighteenth and early nineteenth centuries were as obsessed by it as they were later by the toggle game or cards. These accounts also indicate that the Tlingit had debtor slavery.]

CHAPTER 17

Time, Tides, and Winds

COUNT*

[We have seen that the Tlingit easily kept score in gambling games by using stones or sticks as counters. These counters, however, were insufficient for preserving a record.]

Count [for a record] was kept by knotting a string, ***kuh-qwoir duke*** [ka-, or x̣̓a- dú·x̣̓^{w}, "tied knot"] or by means of pebbles in a little skin bag or tied in the end of a piece of skin. Another method was by means of small sticks, ***kuh-du-war-tsik-khart*** [?], in a parallel row, enclosed by a twining of sinew thread near each end of the sticks, so that they could be added to or subtracted from the group without disturbing the others. Counts were also kept by wrapping a string around a stick, ***karts-dar-arh*** [qá·s̓ da·ʔá·x̣^{w}, "stick wrapped"].

At Yakutat I found two old counting sticks from six to eight inches long and half an inch square, with notched edges. I believe that these had been procured from the westward, or at least the idea had been borrowed and was not originally Tlingit. With the introduction of pencils and paper such methods were abandoned.

[La Pérouse (1799, 1:409–10) recorded the Tlingit words for numbers, showing clearly that the basic numbers were 1 through 5, 9(?), and 10; that 6 through 8 seem to combine 1, 2, 3 with something which must mean "five"; and that numbers 11 through 19 looked as if formed by similar combinations of "one" through "nine" with something which must mean "ten." "Twenty" looked like something based on "two" and "ten"; 30, 40, and so on seemed to be "3 tens," and 100 looked like "10 tens." The difficulties of writing Tlingit in French spelling, and the untrained ear of the recorder, should caution us, but since the Lituya Bay Tlingit could count to 100, it is clear that they could count anything they wanted.

[La Pérouse's vocabulary differs from that of Veniaminov ([1840] 1984:446–47), who recorded cardinal numbers up to 200, and wrote: "The Koloshi system of numeration has not a decimal but a *quinary* base." He indicated, as we had suspected, that 6, 7, and 8 are formed by adding "one, two, three" to the "syllable *tushu*" (du·sú). Above 10, the numbers 11 through 19 are formed by adding, as "ten and one, ten and two," etc. ("Twenty" looks to me like a combination of "one" plus "human being," ƛé· qá·.) Veniaminov pointed out that "thirty" is "twenty plus ten," 40 is "two 20s," and so on. One hundred is "five 20s," and 200 is "ten 20s." Veniaminov also wrote that higher numbers can be formed only by addition, such as "*two hundred and another hundred added,* and so on." Since the fundamental base for 20 is "human being" (qá·), I believe that the base in 5 (ke·ǯin) and 10 (ǯinka·t) is "hand" (ǯin), which suggests counting on the fingers, just as "one human being" for 20 suggests counting on all digits. "And" or "plus" is qa, not to be confused with qá·, "human being."

[A device for counting the days of the month, "like a cribbage board," is described in the next section.]

TIME: SEASONS AND DAYS*

The Tlingit had no definite conception of time as reckoned in years, and kept no records of years, yet memory alone was an uncertain dependence. Important happenings such as wars, epidemics, great feasts, or unusual natural conditions were the milestones in the past to which everything relating to time or to the age of a person was referred. Such standards were naturally local. Among the Sitka, the coming of the Russians and their several ensuing conflicts, the introduction of smallpox, wars with the Stikines, and later the transfer of Alaska to the U.S. marked the principal events of the last century, beyond which family [clan] and legendary history were much confused.

Years were reckoned as winters, with the same word, ***tak*** [tá·k^{w}], applying to both. Four seasons were generally recognized:

Editor's note: This chapter was originally titled "Calendar, Tides, Winds." I have compiled it from short, often scrappy notes and short passages of text.

**Editor's note:* The section on "Count" was at one time placed at the end of the original "Chapter V: Domestic Life." I have chosen to put it here, for want of a more logical place, and have added references to La Pérouse and Veniaminov.

**Editor's note:* The original section, "Calendar," obviously needed to be broken into two sections and retitled. To the first section I have added a discussion of the relative ages of the twelve- and the thirteen-moon year, reintroducing a first draft by Emmons on this question, and on the length of time covered by Tlingit oral traditions.

Winter—*tak* [tá·kʷ]
Spring—*tak eta,* "after winter" [tá·kʷ ʔi·tí, "where winter was"?]
Summer—*kootan* [quta·n]
Autumn—*yass,* "change to winter" [ye·s]

Of these, winter and summer really constituted the year. Spring and autumn, as their Tlingit names imply, were separating periods between summer and winter of no definite duration, which agrees with the climatic conditions of this region, for toward the close of September the milder weather gives place to heavy southerly gales, snow covers the higher mountains, and winter begins, to continue until well into mid-"spring." The Chilkat who lived farther inland, and were less influenced by the milder seaward climate, reckoned two seasons: ten months of winter and three of summer.

The year was divided into twelve or thirteen periods termed *dis,* "moons" [dís, -dísi], corresponding to lunar months. These were named from natural conditions depending on seasonal changes, mostly in the animal world, upon which the economic life of the people depended. That some calendars contained thirteen months and others twelve seems to have been local. The Haida and some of the Tsimshian introduced the intercalary moon in their reckoning, while the Tlingit recognized it by an extension or overlapping of the seasonal periods between summer and winter. A comparison of the several calendars of the Tlingit, except those of the Chilkat, shows a general agreement, with such local differences as might be expected to arise from climatic and locational variations. The Chilkat introduced the thirteenth moon in their enumeration. This may have been borrowed from their interior neighbors with whom they met and traded at fixed seasons.

[It would seem from the variety of calendars, and the multiple names for the same lunation, that each town, sometimes each informant, had its own calendar! The thirteen-moon count is more likely to have been an ancient Athabaskan-Tlingit calendar, rather than something new that the Tlingit had borrowed. One also wonders whether Russian influence may have affected the twelve-moon count. This is, in fact, what Emmons suggested in the first draft of this chapter:

> The fact that some calendars contained twelve periods and others thirteen can only be accounted for by the belief that the former has in later years, since the advent of Europeans, been made to coincide with the artificial Julian calendar [of the Russians], while the primitive reckoning included the exact number of moons, for there would be no more practical reason to eliminate one than two or three moons. The other coast tribes and their interior neighbors have very similar calendars, in some of which the intercalary moon appears, as with the Haida, Gitksan, but in a majority of cases only twelve moons are given and a large number of similar names are common to all.]

The year began in or about July, and in one instance I heard this moon called *yeese disi* [should be yí·s dís, "new moon." (See Tables 35 to 37 for examples of the lunar calendar.)]

[Beresford (1789:245), who was on the Northwest Coast with Captain Dixon in 1787, seems to have been thinking of the Tlingit of Norfolk (Sitka) Sound, when he wrote: "Time is calculated by moons, and remarkable events are remembered with ease for one generation, but whether for any longer period is very doubtful."

[Chief Kowee's account of the meeting between La Pérouse and the Tlingit in Lituya Bay (Emmons 1911c) proves that the Tlingit oral tradition could last one hundred years. At Yakutat, traditions of geological changes go back to a period before the last advance of the glaciers in the eighteenth century (de Laguna 1972:25–28, 286–87), and the same is doubtless true of Hoonah traditions about Glacier Bay.]

The divisions of the day were general in time [loosely judged or defined?]. *Tak* [ta·t], "night," is derived from *ta* [ya-ta·], "sleep" [an uncertain etymology]. While we include the night in enumerating days, the Tlingit count days' travel as so many nights or sleeps. "Day" or "daylight" is *yuk-ye-e* [ỵagiỵi·, which Emmons tried to derive from the bow of a canoe, because one should arrive at a strange village only in daylight to avoid being mistaken for an enemy in the dark!]. "Daybreak," *ka-a-ga* [probably qe·x̣é], is literally the "mouth of daylight" from *ka* [x̣é], "mouth," as anything beginning is spoken of as showing its mouth. [The various times of day may be summarized as follows:]

Dawn	[qe·x̣é or qi·x̣é] [qe·-ʔá or qi· -ʔá]
Daybreak	*ka-a-ga* [qe·x̣é]
Morning, Early Morning	*tsu-tart* [ṡu·ta·t or c̓u·ta·t]
Day, Daylight, Mid-day, Noon	*yuck-e-ya, yuk-ye-a* [ỵagiỵi·]
Evening, Darkness	*khana* or *khohner* [xá·na·]
Night	*tak* [ta·t]

[Other expressions involving concepts for day or for various times of day are:]

Now	*andai* or *e-dūt* [ỵi·dát]
Today	*yah-yuck-e-ya, ya yuk yea* [yá· ỵakỵi·, or yá· ỵagiỵi·]

This morning	*yat-tsū-tārt* [yá· c̓u'ta't]
Last night	[nisda't]
Yesterday	*tut-kuh* or *tut ga* [tatgé]
Day before yesterday	*tut kuh clea-r-cut* [tatgé ƛiyaʔa· kát]
Tomorrow	*sa-cum* or *sagun* [se·gán]
Day after tomorrow	*sagun kleh ar* [se·gán ƛiyaʔa· (kádin)]
Days beyond tomorrow	*Sagun nar thla* [apparently "tomorrow is far," se·gán na·ƚé·]

[For additional distinctions in the time of day, and a count of days, see de Laguna 1972: 801–2, in which a calendar board, with pegs for day and month, set in three rows of ten holes each, to make a thirty-day month, is described. This device, undoubtedly adopted from the Russians, was used by a wise chief at Yakutat.]

"MOONS" OF THE YEAR*

The following calendar was compiled from information given by several of the more intelligent, older people of Sitka in 1888–1890, although there were differences of opinion as to several spring and summer months. The enumeration [calendar] commences with July, the period of abundance, which is considered the beginning of the year.

SITKA CALENDAR

July	*Khart disi* [x̣á·t dísi], "salmon moon-of."
August	*Shahayi.* A number of meanings are given, derived from *sha* [ša·], "mountain," such as berries ripe on mountain, or new snow on mountain [ša· xe·yí, "mountain shadows"?].
	Sha, "hair," shedding of hair by animals [šax̣a·w, "hair"].
	Shawut, "woman," female animals ready to conceive [ša·wát, "woman"].
	[Presumably dísi, "moon-of," is appended to these designations.]
September	*Dis Ya-ti,* "child or little moon" [dís yádi]. Weaning of young, or less abundant food.
October	*Dis Tlin,* "big moon" [dís ƛe·n]. Animals in prime condition, wild fowl abundant, people returning to winter villages with summer stock of food.
November	*Ko-ka-har dis* [qu-ka-ha· dís], "digging or scratching moon," when bears dig and prepare their winter dens.
December	*Sha-nagh dis,* "head or hair moon," when hair shows on head of young seal in the womb [? šá·náx̣ dís, "through the head"?, or ša·náx̣ dís "valley moon"?].
January	*Ta-wak disi* [t̓a·wáq dísi], "goose moon," geese are flying and calling; also named for the saltwater plant, *tsate* [?], that geese feed on, and is now grown.
February	*Tseek disi* [s̓i·k dísi or s̓ikdísi], "black bear moon-of," black bear cubs are born.
March	*Heen ta na kayani disi* [hí·n ta·náx̣ kaya·ní dísi], "underwater plants begin to grow moon-of."
April	*Khe ka kayani disi* [x̣é·ga·, "true," kaya·ní dísi], "budding or flower moon-of," referring to land plants.
May	*At-ka-ta-hate etna disi* [ʔat gadax̣it yina· dísi], "month before pregnancy, before giving birth," referring to animals [-x̣it means "breed"].
June	*At-ka-ta-hate disi* [ʔat gadax̣it dísi], "month of mating," "birth moon."
	Kho-ko-wuk disi [–?– x̣a·wáqʷ], "moon of shedding" of winter coats.
	Ey-ta-tlitle disi [–?– ʔat ƚiƚ dísi, "? moon-of defecate"], "diarrhea moon," because of change of food, or hair seals "evacuate freely."

*Editor's note: Although Emmons originally included in the text all the calendars he had obtained, I have placed all but the Sitka example in Tables 35 to 37.

[The calendars of the Hutsnuwu, Stikine, Chilkat, Chilkoot, and Yakutat are given in Tables 35 to 37. Other calendars for Sitka, with thirteen months, and Wrangell, with twelve, can be found in Swanton 1908:426; and further Yakutat variants are in de Laguna 1972:800–801.]

In some calendars, it should be noted, some, or even all, of the moons may be designated by ordinal numbers. Thus, the calendar given by *Yehl kock* of the *Con-nuh-ta-de* at Chilkat [yé·ƚ x̣a·k, "Raven's smell," of the G̣a·nax̣te·dí, Raven

Counting board, probably for calendrical use, collected at Yakutat by G. T. Emmons before 1889. (AMNH.)

3], includes thirteen moons, those between March and July being expressed in numerals and including four months. Otherwise, the months agree with the Sitka calendar, except that September is the "Groundhog [marmot] moon," and February is the "moon of the North wind." The year begins *about* July. The calendar given by a man of the Chilkoot branch of the Chilkat tribe is an entirely different calendar from any other Tlingit one, and would seem to be idiosyncratic, except that the names of the months express very accurately the climate and activities of the people in this colder, more inland country. The two calendars from Yakutat were obtained [by Hendrickson, the missionary] from two of the older people. In the first, the year begins with August, and in the other, in July.

[We should note that the moon is counted from its first appearance, yí·s dís, "new moon," wuʒiqi·n, "it begins," not from the dark of the moon, which we recognize as the "new moon."]

TIDES

The Tlingit conceptualized tides as currents of moving water.

[The notion of a river is applied to the directions "north" and "south," which appear as "up river" (na·-, na·kí·, nánde, or náná) and as "down river, seaward" (ʔí·x, ʔixkí·, or de·kí·, or dak-), respectively. There are no other designations for the cardinal directions. Thus the Haida are the "southern tribe," "the people out to sea," de·ki-na·; and the true, "westward, further-up Aleut" are na·kí· ʔa· k̓uṫé·x̣, "up-stream or northward enemies."]

The tide in general is *Hat* [ha·t], or *Hat-tlie-ziu* [probably ha·t łici·n, "tide is-strong"].

Flood tide is *Daht-gonna-tehu* [da·q kanadé·n, "from-the-shore (back-up) is-flowing-up"].

High water is *Yen-kud-ow-ah-tah* [yan-kát, "onto shore," ʔuwadá·, "it has flowed"].

Ebb tide is *Yen-ah-thleen* [ye· nałé·n, "tide is going out"].

Low water is *Yenow ah-thlah* [yan ʔuwałá·, "it is low tide." Another expression is wu·ła·, "tide has gone out."]

The spring tides at the full and change of the moon were of special importance because they laid bare the clam beds so that ["beach food"] could more readily be secured. Therefore they were designated by the addition of the word "moon" or *dis* [dís] to their names:

Full moon tides: High water was *Dis yah-keet-zeh* [dís ya-qí·ši, "moon face-flood," from qí·š, "flood"]. Low water was *Dis yah-thlee-neh* [dís ya-łé·ni, "moon face-tidal flats," from łé·ni, "tidal flats" or "low tide"].

The new moon tides: High water was *Dis etah keet-zeh* [possibly dís ya-da·-qí·ši, "moon face-around flood"]. Low water was *Dis etah-thlee-neh* [dis ya-da·-łé·ni, "moon face-around low tide (or tidal flats)." At this time one might say that the tide "becomes small," wudix̣ú· or wudiwúx̣ʷ.]

WINDS*

The principal seasonal winds recognized throughout southeastern Alaska are *Hoon* (north), *Tuck-da-ut* (east), *Son-nah hate* (southeast), and *Yunda ut* (south-southwest-west). Besides these, every tribe has names for winds from different directions that are diverted from their true course by mountains, valleys, or through channels. Of course, the directions given here only approximate the compass points.

Hoon [xú·n] is the cold winter wind that comes from the north, over the snow-capped mountains from the interior. It is the breath of the Spirit of the Cold. The Sitka and Chilkat apply this name also to both north and northeast winds; the Chilkat also include the northwest wind; the Kake and Tongass recognize only the northwest wind by this name.

Tuck-da-ut, or *Tuck-ta* [dák-de ʔat, "out-to-sea one"], is the strong wind from the east or northeast that blows through the mountain passes and down the river valleys, toward the sea. The Kake call it *Har-goon con-nah-hate* [hagu·n, "over there," ka·ná-x̣e·t, "it blows"?]. The Stikine call the northeast wind *Tchune* [?]. Some of the Hutsnuwu may call the northeast wind *Tuck-huck ha-hate* [łagakáx̣e·t, "–?– blows"?], applying this name also to the north wind; and others call the northeast wind *Taku* [ta·qú], because it blows from the Taku River, or *Tuck-ta-ut* [dák-de ʔat, "out-to-sea one"]. The Stikine call the east wind the Nass.

Son-nah-hate [sá·náxe·t] is the southeast wind that blows in heavy and continued gales in the fall. The Yakutat use this name for both east and southeast winds, as do the Henya. The Chilkat may call the southeast wind *Son-nah* [sá·nax̣] or *Keel-tchar* [ki·łǯá·, "storm wind"], or *Kluck-ka-kuk* [unanalyzable]. The Hutsnuwu may call the wind *Sa-qwan ah hate* [ca·gʷá·nax̣e·t, from ca·, "seal"], because it blows from Hood ("Seal") Bay, or they may use the ordinary name for the southeast wind, *Son-nah-hate.* This wind represents a spirit that lives on an island in the sea, and when he puts on his hat, rain follows. [According to Hendrickson, a missionary at Yakutat who supplied Emmons with information], it was a man who drowned that turned into the east wind.

Yunda-ut or *Yunda* is the south to southwest wind from the sea that brings good weather in the summer, but rain and hail in the fall, the name [yánde ʔat, "this-way one"] meaning "everything comes ashore." The Hutsnuwu may apply *Son-na-hate* to a strong southwest wind, *Eh-nah hate* [ʔíxnáx̣e·t (?), "down-river it blows"?] to a medium southwest wind, and call a mild southwest wind *Nou-nah hate* [ná·náx̣e·t, "up-river it blows"?]; and they apply the name *Yun da ut* to the south wind. The Stikine call the south wind *You gu nah* [possibly yán ka·náx̣, "shore surface along"?]. The Yakutat name the southwest wind *Ta dar da nook,* "because it blows against the mountains" [–?– da·dé nú·kʷ, "–?– toward-circumference (of mountains) breeze"]. The Stikine and the Kake call the southwest wind *Da kee nah* and *Da keen ah hate,* respectively [de·kí·náx̣, de·kí·nax̣e·t, "from out-to-sea (it blows)"], and say it is a "strong winter wind."

The west wind, when distinguished from the southwest wind, is called *Klar ka ker quate* [probably łagakáx̣e·t?] at Yakutat: "It blew Raven's blanket back to him." The Hutsnuwu call it *She-ehlh-quar-nuh* [perhaps ša·ʔé·ł ka·náx̣?, suggesting that it is blowing from the "sea," ʔé·ł]. At Sitka it is *Tuck ta ut* [dákde ʔat, "the one out to sea"], *Kate suke* [?] at Wrangell, and for the Tongass it is *Tan nuh* [tá·n-náx̣, "Prince of Wales Island (literally tá·n, "sea lion") along"].

The northwest wind is called *De yar na hate* [diyá·náx̣e·t, "other side along"], "from back of the mountains," by the Yakutat; *An na e ya-ka hit* [?] by the Sitka; and *Tluh-kuh-kut-hate* and *Thluk kuk-kar* by the Hutsnuwu and Stikine, respectively [łagakáx̣e·t, łagakáx̣?]. The Henya call the

**Editor's note:* The information in this section Emmons had expressed chiefly in the form of a large table. Unfortunately, since this chart could not be reproduced adequately, I have been forced to transfer the data in it to the text, and have organized the latter primarily according to the major winds. In the latter part of the section I have brought together various notes by Emmons about the weather, and added Swanton's discussion of the spirit or spirits controlling the winds. The wording of this section is therefore largely mine.

northwest wind *Neh hate* [náx̣e·t, "it blows"]. The Chilkat, Kake, and Tongass group the northwest wind with the north wind, *Hoon* [xú·n].

To bring a fair wind, the Tlingit would whistle and strike the water with their paddles, throwing it [the spray] in the direction they wanted it to blow.

In order to bring favorable weather a large fire was built. Food was sometimes thrown into the fire, and a form of prayer was said. In the act of throwing in the food, a person might say, "Here's for favorable weather."

To walk into the house with snowshoes caused storms and unfavorable winds.

The Tlingit believed that to kill a fish with a stone will bring rain and storm. The rainbow is a ladder or trail for dead warriors to ascend to their house in the highest heaven.

Snow was but the chips made by a mighty man who lived in the sky and spent his time in winter chopping a great block of ice.

[Among notes left by Emmons in BCPA was the following:

> 698. To Drive away Fog
>
> 1889 when enroute to Hoonah from Sitka encountered much fog. Frank a "Chuconnatee" of Hoonah Kow [Ču·kane·dí, Wolf 5, of Hoonah] tried to drive it away. He took a mitten and placed it on end of sprit and stepped sprit in bow of canoe palm forward. He also reached out in all directions and made the motion of grasping the fog in his hand and then at each effort put his hand under his hat which was placed opening down in the canoe. Also put piece of dried sal[mon?] in mouth chewed it up fine and lying on back blew it out in the air.

[Swanton (1908:453), in writing about the limitless numbers of spirits believed to be in the world, mentioned the Tlingit belief that there were spirits in the sun, moon, sea, salmon streams, glaciers, and also:

> It was thought that there was some being in the wind, so people always talked to it kindly to induce it to moderate, and offered it a piece of fish. The wolverine (nūsk) [nú·sk] was said to have control over the north wind, and when a story is told about one the north wind will blow. The same thing is said when one told a story about the Athapascans, because they live toward the north, and about the wolf. Winds from the north and east blow very persistently out of Silver bay [on Baranof Island, near Sitka], but when people once complained because Silver Bay blew so much, he said, "It is not I, but my children," meaning the smaller inlets.

[The beliefs and practices of the Yakutat Tlingit concerning the weather and the winds, and how to control them, supplement the reports of Swanton and Emmons (de Laguna 1972:803–7).]

Tables

TABLE 1

Climatic Data

	January Mean (degrees Fahrenheit)	July Mean (degrees Fahrenheit)	Maximum Recorded (degrees Fahrenheit)	Minimum Recorded (degrees Fahrenheit)	Average Annual Precipitation (inches)
Annette Island (1962) 55°02′N, 131°34′W	34.6	56.8	90	1	96.85
Ketchikan (1941) 55°20′N, 131°38′W	32.6	57.5	96	−8	150.89
Wrangell (1941) 56°28′N, 132°22′W	29	58.2	92	−6	82.95
Petersburg (1962) 56°40′N, 132°57′W	28.6	55.7	84	−19	105.08
Sitka (1941) 57°03′N, 135°20′W	32.4	54.9	87	−5	87.13
Killisnoo (1943) 57°28′N, 134°34′W	28.4	55.1	84	−10	76.8
Juneau (1941) 58°22′N, 134°35′W	27.5	56.6	89	−15	83.25
Juneau (1962)	26.2	54.7	84	−21	56.05
Haines (1941) 59°14′N, 135°26′W	22.9	57.6	90	−15	56.43
Haines (1962)	23.2	57.6	90	−16	60.64
Skagway (1943) 59°27′N, 136°18′W	21.4	57.6	92	−22	26.40
Cape Spencer (1954) 58°12′N, 136°38′W	34	52	75	4	108.76
Yakutat (1941) 59°31′N, 139°40′W	29.3	52.8	82	5	129.13
Yakutat (1954)	28	53	81	−23	131.98

Note: This table has been compiled by the editor from data gathered by the U.S. Weather Bureau, published in Kincer (1941:1211, 1215), *U.S. Coast Pilot, Alaska, Part I* (1943:439), *U.S. Coast Pilot 8* (1962:194–95), and *U.S. Coast Pilot 9* (1954:575, 599).

TABLE 2

Most Important Trees

Tree (in general), evergreen, especially spruce [ʔa·s]

Alder, red or Oregon, *shaok* [šé·x̣̓ʷ], *Alnus oregona* Nutt.

Alder, small or Sitka, *kashah* [ke·šíš], *Alnus crispa* (Ait.) Pursh, ssp. *sinuata* (Regel) Hult.

Birch, *ut daye* [ʔat da·yí̱, "its bark"], probably *Betula papyrifera* Marsh. ssp. *humilis* (Regel) Hult.

Cedar, Alaska yellow [cypress], *haee, hya* [x̣á·ỵ], *Chamaecyparis nootkatensis* (Lamb.) Spach

Cedar, western red, *tlah* [ła·x̣], *Thuja plicata* D. Don

Cottonwood, black, *duk* [dúqʷ], *Populus balsamifera* L., ssp. *trichocarpa* Torr. & Gray (Hult.)

Crab apple, Oregon, *hah* [x̓á·x̓], *Malus fusca* (Raf.) Schneid.

Fir, Pacific silver, *klayees* [łe·ỵís], *Abies amabilis* (Dougl.) Forbes

Hemlock, western, *yun* [ỵán], *Tsuga heterophylla* (Raf.) Sarg.

Maple, Douglas, *kahlka, khalka* [x̣a·łx̣̓é·], *Acer glabrum* Torr. ssp. *Douglasii* (Hook.) Wesmael

Spruce, Sitka, *seet* [sí·t], Picea sitchensis (Bong.) Carr.

Willow, *ktchalh* [č̓á·ł̓], probably *Salix scouleriana* Barratt, or *S. sitchensis* Sanson

Yew, Pacific, *saks, saqs* [sáqs, same as "bow and arrow"], *Taxus brevifolia* Nutt.

Note: This table was compiled by the editor from information in the Emmons manuscripts and notes. All scientific botanical names in this table, and elsewhere in this book, have been supplied by Alix Wennekens, based on the botanical nomenclature of Hultén (1968). Jeff Leer has checked the Tlingit orthography.

TABLE 3

Tlingit Tribes

Outer Islands and Coasts		Mainland and Sheltered	
	GULF COAST TLINGIT		
XVII	Kaliakh (Controller Bay) [mixed Eyak-Tlingit]		
XVI	Yakutat [formerly Eyak]		
XV	Dry Bay [formerly Athabaskan]		
	NORTHERN TLINGIT		
XIV	Hoonah	XI	Chilkat-Chilkoot
XIII	Sitka	X	Auk
XII	Hutsnuwu (Angoon)	IX	Taku
		VIII	Sumdum
	SOUTHERN TLINGIT		
VII	Kake	III	Stikine
VI	Kuyu	II	Sanya
V	Klawak	I	Tongass
IV	Henya		

Note: This table was prepared by the editor to show the major divisions of the Tlingit, except for the Inland Tlingit (McClellan 1975), who are not included. The others are Southern Tlingit (Dixon Entrance to Frederick Sound), Northern Tlingit (Frederick Sound to Cape Fairweather on the Gulf Coast above Lituya Bay), and Gulf Coast (Dry Bay through Controller Bay). The tribes are roughly divided into those who live mostly on sheltered waters or along the mainland and those of the outer coasts and islands. It should be noted that the Kuyu and Kake, here listed among the Southern Tlingit, are linguistically intermediate between that group and the Northern Tlingit (Leer, pers. comm.). The Hoonah are now essentially a southeastern Alaskan tribe, but formerly had settlements on the Gulf Coast through Lituya Bay. The northwestern-most group (Kaliakh), listed by Emmons as Tlingit, were really Tlingitized Eyak. The tribes may be read from the bottom (south) upward.

TABLE 4

Estimate of Kolosh in 1834 by Veniaminov

Tangasskoe	[Tongass I]	150 souls
Sanakhskoe[a]	[Sanya II]	100 souls
Stakhinskoe	[Stikine III]	1,500 souls
Genuvskoe[b]	[Henya IV or Auk X]	300 souls
Kuyutskoe	[Kuyu VI]	150 souls
Kekuvskoe	[Kake VII]	200 souls
Takutsskoe	[Taku IX]	150 souls
Akutskoe	[Auk X]	100 souls
Chilkatskoe	[Chilkat-Chilkoot XI]	200 souls
Kutsinovskoe	[Hutsnuwu XII]	300 souls
Sitkhinskoe	[Sitka XIII]	750 souls
Ledianoprolivskoe[c]	["Icy Strait" Hoonah XIV]	250 souls
Ltuiskoe or Akvetskoe	[Lituya and/or Dry bays XV]	200 souls
Yakutatskoe	[Yakutat XVI]	150 souls
	TOTAL	4,500 souls

Note: This table is from Veniaminov ([1840] 1984:382), although the tribes have been rearranged according to their order in Table 3 and given their modern names. There are no entries for Klawak (V) or Sumdum (VIII), probably because these small groups were not recognized as distinct tribes, or were not known. Veniaminov included two Haida groups, omitted here: the Kaiganskoe (1,200 souls) and Chasinskoe (150 souls), making a grand total of 5,800. (His editor, R. A. Pierce, has corrected this figure to 5,850.) Veniaminov further stated that the total number had been 10,000 in 1833, before the smallpox epidemic. Petroff (1884:35) reproduced what was essentially the same table, but with anglicized names, finding it "remarkably accurate in its total."

[a] This group was placed by Veniaminov at the end of the list, right after the Haidas, thereby suggesting that this group was also Haida. Petroff (1884:35) designated them as "Sanakhan," which is close to Sa·nyạ· q^{w}á·n, the Tlingit name. They were probably the Sanya Tlingit, who were otherwise not represented.

[b] Petroff rendered the name of this group as "Henu," and suggested that they were the "Hunya or Hanega," that is, the Henya. The translators of the Tlingit in Veniaminov ([1840] 1984), Nora and Richard Dauenhauer, indicate that the tribal name refers to Dzantik'i Hí·ni, or Gold Creek, Juneau; this would make the inhabitants Auk. Henyu seems to be the more likely identification, especially since this tribe was not otherwise mentioned.

[c] The name refers to an unidentified settlement on Icy Strait (according to Nora and Richard Dauenhauer), so the inhabitants were Hoonah.

TABLE 5

Census of Native Tribes of Russian America between Latitude 59° and 54°40′ N., Exclusive of the Sitka Tribe on Baranof Island, in 1839

				Free				Slaves	
Trader's Name	Tribal Name	Location	Total	Men	Women	Boys	Girls	Male	Female
Tourgass [Tongass]	Kitahoonet	Clarence strait	315	85	90	60	65	6	9
Cape Fox [Sanya]	Lukhselee	Cape Fox	177	45	50	39	43	—	—
Stikeen [Stikine]	Stakhin river		1,586	502	455	256	229	55	89
Anialt [Wolf 31]		Port Stuart	186	50	45	42	49	—	—
Liknaahutly [Wolf 19]		Stakhin river	118	31	24	30	27	2	4
Ta-ee-teeton [Raven 11]		Stakhin river	93	38	29	10	9	3	4
Kvaskaguatee [Raven 32]		Stakhin river	135	59	41	10	6	6	13
Kukatu [Wolf 26?]		Stakhin river	234	97	67	36	32	2	—
Naaniagh [Wolf 18]		Stakhin river	390	83	117	60	46	32	52
Talguatee [Raven 33]		Stakhin river	169	52	51	27	23	2	4
Kiksatee [Raven 10]		Stakhin river	99	31	21	21	18	4	4
Kadi-ette [Raven 28?]		Stakhin river	172	61	60	20	19	4	8
Hanega [Henya]	Henega	Prince of Wales island	269	82	80	29	27	27	24
Kake	Kehk	Kehk archipelago	393	109	106	70	64	24	20
Tako Samdan [Taku, Sumdum, and Sitka]		Takoo and Sitka rivers	493	127	110	71	66	59	60
Auke [Auk]	Auke	North of Takoo river	203	72	61	35	31	2	2
Chilcat [Chilkat]	Chilkhaat	Lynn canal	498	167	116	71	66	42	36
Hoochenoo [Hutsnuwu]	Hootznoo	Hood's bay	729	247	240	85	76	40	41
Cross Sound [Hoonah]	Hoonyah	Cross sound	782	258	234	108	88	40	54
		TOTAL	5,445[a]	1,694	1,542	824	755[b]	295	335

Note: Census by Sir James Douglas, Hudson's Bay Company (from Petroff 1884:36–37). The order of the tribes has been rearranged to correspond to that in Table 3. The Stikine clans have been identified that were listed by Douglas as separate villages. The "Ahialt" were evidently still living in Port Stewart as an independent tribe, and the other Stikine clan groups were not yet at Wrangell ("Fort Stikeen"). The totals have been recalculated, excluding the six villages of Kaigani Haida, which had a total population of 1,735 (excluding slaves). The grand total for the native population in the leased territory is given as 7,190 persons, of whom 5,455 would be the Tlingit and their slaves.

[a] If all the separate totals in this horizontal line are added, the grand total would be 5,445 persons living in Tlingit territory: 4,815 Tlingit and their 630 slaves. The same total is reached by adding the Tlingit figures given by tribes. But if 1,735 Kaigani are subtracted from the grand total of 7,190, the resultant figure is 5,455 for the Tlingit area. The error seems to lie in the calculation of the number of Tlingit girls.

[b] If a total of 436 Kaigani girls is subtracted from the total of 1,201 girls, this figure would be 765.

TABLE 6

Estimate of Kolosh in 1861

Settlements, Tribes		Totals	Free		Slaves	
			Males	Females	Males	Females
Tanga	[Tongass I]	333	154	154	13	12
Stakhin	[Stikine II]	697	308	308	41	40
Genu[a]	[Henya IV? Auk X?]	411	195	197	10	9
Kuiuts	[Kuyu VI]	262	126	126	5	5
Kek	[Kake VII]	445	210	210	13	12
Taku	[Taku IX]	712	335	337	20	20
Asanka Harbor[b]	[Auk X?]	118	56	56	3	3
Chil'kat	[Chilkat XI]	1,616	728	728	80	80
Khutsnov	[Hutsnuwu XII]	600	280	280	20	20
Sitkha	[Sitka XIII]	1,344	715	535	51	43
Icy Strait	[Hoonah XIV]	331	154	154	13	10
L'tua Bay	[Dry Bay XV]	590	265	267	29	29
Yakutat	[Yakutart XVI]	380	163	168	25	24
		TOTAL 7,839	TOTAL FREE 7,209		TOTAL SLAVES 630	

Note: This table, the tribes or settlements arranged according to the order in Table 3, is taken from the census of Lieutenant ("Wehrman") Verman of the Russian Navy, published by Tikhmenev ([1861–63, I] 1978:428). The Kaigani Haida with 280 free men and 280 free women, plus their 90 male and 90 female slaves, have not been included here. Petroff (1884:38), who also published the same figures, remarked that Verman had "obtained only the totals at each place and divided them subsequently." He also corrected the totals for Tlingit free men and women as published by Tikhmenev. The corrected totals are given here.

[a] There is again the difficulty in identifying the "Genu." Petroff calls them "Hoonyah," but does not add them to the Icy Strait Hoonah ("Cross Sound Settlements").

[b] Asanka Harbor ("Assan Harbor" of Petroff) is probably Freshwater Bay, on the east coast of Chichagof Island, where the Wolf 17 settled, coming from Hoonah to Hutsnuwu country. It may have been Auk territory in 1861.

TABLE 7

Estimate of Tlingit in 1880

Group	Village	Total
Tongas [Tongass], Island mouth Portland canal		173
Cape Fox [Sanya, not Tongass] "Prince of Wales island"		100
Stakhin [Stikine]		317
Shustak's village, Etholin island [Raven 33]	38	
Kash's village, Etholin island [Raven 11]	49	
Shakes' village, Etholin island [Wolf 18]	38	
Towayat's village, Etholin island [Wolf 25 or 26]	82	
Kohltiene's village, Stakhin river [Raven 10]	28	
Hinauhan's village, Stakhin river	31	
Kadishan's village, Stakhin river [Raven 32]	27	
Shallyany's village, Stakhin river	24	
Hanega [Henya], Prince of Wales island, west coast		500
Klawak, Prince of Wales island, west coast		27
Kouyou [Kuyu], Prince of Wales island, west coast		60
Kehk [Kake]		568
Klukwan [Kake village] Kuprianof island	261	
village, Kuprianof island	82	
village, Koo island	100	
village, Port Houghton	50	
village, Seymour's channel	75	
Takoo [Taku]		269
Tokeatl's village, Takoo river and inlet	26	
Chitklin's village, Takoo river and inlet	113	
Katlany's village, Takoo river and inlet	106	
Fotshou's village, Takoo river and inlet	24	
Auk		640
village, Stephens passage	290	
village, Admiralty island	300	
village, Douglas island	50	
Chilkhat [Chilkat-Chilkoot]		988
Yondestuk, Chilkhat river and bay	171	
Kutkwutlu, Chilkhat river and bay	125	
Kluckquan, Chilkhat river and bay	565	
Chilcoot, Chilcoot river	127	
Khootznahoo [Hutsnuwu]		666
Augoon [Angoon], Admiralty island, Hood's bay	420	
Scutskon, Admiralty island, Hood's bay	246	
Sitka		721
Sitka, Indian village, Baranof island	540	
Silver Bay [Baranof island]	39	
Hot Springs [Baranof island]	26	
Indian River [Baranof island]	43	
Old Sitka [Baranof island]	73	
Hoonyah [Hoonah]		908
Koudekan [Hoonah], Chichagof island	800	
Klughuggue, "Chichagof island" [N shore Cross Snd]	108	
Scattered villages between cape Spencer and Bering [Yakutat] bay [Not Yakutat tribe, but Lituya Hoonah and Dry Bay]		200
Yakutat, Bering bay		300
[Tlingitized Eyak, Kaliahk]		328
Yaktag villages, foot of Mount Saint Elias range	152	
Chilkhaat villages, Comptroller bay	170	
Cape Martin, Mouth of Copper river	6	
TOTAL		6,765

Note: These figures are from the Tenth Census of 1880 (Petroff 1884:29, 31–32). The groups are identified as far as possible, and are listed in the same order as the tribes on Table 3. Some of Petroff's groupings are corrected. Thus the Tongass and the Cape Fox groups do not form one tribe; nor do the Kuyu, Henya, and Klawak form a "Prince of Wales Island tribe."

TABLE 8

Estimate of Tlingit ("Koluschan") in 1890

Tribe	Males	Females	Totals
Tongass	137	118	255
Stakhin [Stikine]	135	120	255
Hanega [Henya]	152	110	262
Kake [and Kuyu?]	114	120	234
Taku [and Sumdum?]	114	109	223
Auk	145	134	279
Chilkat [and Chilkoot]	420	392	812
Hutznahu [Hutsnuwu]	235	185	420
Sitka	427	387	814
Huna [Hoonah]	283	309	592
Yakutat	169	176	345
Totals of "Thlingit in Southeastern District"	2,331	2,160	4,491
Sitka	1	—	1
Yakutat	3	6	9
Yaktag [Kaliakh]	44	38	82
Totals of "Thlingit in Kadiak District"	48	44	92
TOTAL	2,379	2,204	4,583

Note: These figures, taken from the Eleventh Census of 1890 (Porter 1893:158), omit the Kaigani and Tsimshian in southeastern Alaska and the Eyak ("Ugalentsi") of Controller Bay and the Copper River delta, but include the Tlingitized Eyak of the Gulf Coast (Kaliakh or Tribe XVII) and Tlingit from Sitka and Yakutat living among them or among the Eyak proper.

TABLE 9

Tlingit Clans

	Raven Clans		Wolf Clans
1	Con nuh ut de	1	Ka gwan tan
2	Tark an a de	2	Kut a gwat de
3	Con nuh ta de	3	Kuke hit tan
4	Tihk a de	4	Tchis qway de
5	Ish kee tan	5	Tchu con na de
6	Thluke nuh ut de	6	Guyasz hit tan
7	Khart kow ee	7	Tuck es te na
8	Kuse ka de	8	Shen ku ka de
9	Kulch heen na de	9	Ka kuse hit tan
10	Kik sa de	10	Sha ah kwan
11	Tee hit tan	11	Nass ta de
12	Tee na de	12	Nass ah ut de
13	Da she tan	13	Khoon hit tan
14	An kark hit tan	14	Kah qwoir hit tan
15	Tlee na de	15	Neh ka hut de
16	Tuck dane tan	16	Yun ya de
17	Thlu qwoir ut de	17	Nush kee tan
18	Nu shuck ah ah ye	18	Nan ya i ee
19	Quash gae kwan	19	Sick nuh ut de
20	Wake heen na de	20	Klin tan
21	Yes qwoir na de	21	Tsa te na de
22	Thluke heen na de	22	Wash heen na de
23	Ku ya de	23	Na sat de
24	Teetle hit tan	24	Sit gae de
25	Souke tee na de	25	Kayash ka hit tan
26	Ketchuke qwit tan	26	Hook qway de
27	Tun na de	27	Tuck cla way de
28	Kartch hut de	28	Tsar gae de
29	Koke hit tan	29	Gau hit tan
30	Kah yah ut de	30	Tlu quay de
31	To ku a de	31	Helh kwan
32	Kas qwa gua de	32	Ta qway de
33	Tahl qwa de		
34	Hu-yahk-hut-tee [Not on list; appears on charts]		

Eagle People = Na ut de

Note: This list was prepared by Emmons as a table of contents for Part 1 of his projected *History of Tlingit Clans and Tribes.* The indentations and spacings of the clan names indicate his conceptions of the relationships between the groups. To facilitate identification I have added Arabic numbers, so that a given clan in the Raven moiety, such as the *Kik sa de* of Emmons, may be designated as "Raven 10." The phonetic transliteration, Kiksˀádi, will be found on Table 10 under the same number. Several spellings for the same clan may be found in the text. I have added hyphens where Emmons has omitted them in many cases. The same system of numerical designation is used in all tables and in the text.

TABLE 10

Phonetic List of Tlingit Clans

	Raven Clans		Wolf Clans
1	G̣a·nax̣ˀádi	1	Ka·gʷa·nta·n
2	Tá·kʷˀa·ne·dí	2	Kadagʷˀádi (?)
3	G̣a·nax̣te·dí	3	Qu·kʷ hít-ta·n
4	T̓í·ẋˀádi	4	ǯi·šqʷe·dí
5	ˀIški·ta·n or ˀIška hít-ta·n	5	Ču·kane·dí
6	Ł̓ukʷnax̣ˀádi	6	G̣ayé·s̓ hít-ta·n
7	X̓ał̓kaˀa·yí	7	Dagisdina·
8	Qu·sk̓e·dí or Xa·s hít-ta·n	8	Šank̓ukʷe·dí or Šangukʷe·dí
9	X̣̓ałčane·dí	9	Qa·x̣̓us hít-ta·n
10	Kiksˀádi	10	Ša·ˀa· qʷa·n (?)
11	Ti·y hít-ta·n	11	Na·ste·dí
12	Ti·yine·dí	12	Na·sax̣ˀádi (?)
13	De·ši·ta·n	13	Kú·n hít-ta·n
14	ˀA·nx̣̓a·kíta·n or ˀA·nx̣̓a·k hít-ta·n	14	Kagʷax hít-ta·n (?)
15	Ł̓i·ne·dí	15	Nika·x̣ˀádi
16	T̓aqde·nta·n	16	Y̨anye·dí
17	Ł̓ukʷa·x̣ˀádi	17	Wu·šk̓i·ta·n
18	Nu·wšakaˀa·yí	18	Na·nya·ˀa·yí
19	Kʷá·šk̓iqʷá·n or Kʷá·šk̓-qʷá·n	19	S̓iknax̣ˀádi
20	Wéx̣̓hine·dí	20	ƛenta·n
21	Yí·s̓qane·dí (?)	21	Ca·ti·ne·dí or Ca·t̓ine·dí
22	Ł̓u·kʷhine·dí	22	Waši·ne·dí or Waš-hí·n-ˀádi
23	Kuye·dí	23	Ne·sˀádi
24	Tí·ł̓ hít-ta·n	24	S̓i·t̓qʷe·dí
25	Saqʷti·ne·dí or Suqʷti·ne·dí	25	Kayá·ška hít-ta·n
26	Kiǯu·kʷ hít-ta·n or Giǯu·kʷita·n	26	X̣u·ẋʷe·dí (?)
27	Tane·dí	27	Daqł̓awe·dí
28	Qa·čˀádi	28	Ca·gʷe·dí
29	Ku·qʷ hít-ta·n	29	Ga·w hít-ta·n
30	Kaya·ˀádi	30	Ł̓ux̣̓ʷe·dí
31	Tuqʷye·dí or Tuqʷwe·dí	31	X̣e·ł-qʷá·n
32	Ka·sx̣̓agʷe·dí	32	Te·qʷe·dí
33	Ta·łqʷe·dí		
34	Quyé·q̓ˀádi		

Eagles Clan = Ne·x̣ˀádi

Note: This list follows that of Emmons, Table 9, but the clan names have been transcribed, whenever recognized, into phonetic characters, thanks to Jeff Leer. No attempt has been made here to explain the meaning of these names, nor to equate the clans or lineages listed by Emmons with those enumerated by Swanton (1908).

TABLE 11

The Composition of Tlingit Tribes

I TONGASS

Emmons: Tan-ta Kwan, Ton-ta Kwan, "Sea lion tribe," from Prince of Wales Island, which was called *tan,* "sealion." Tangash, Tongass is the name in more general use.
Phonetic: Ta·n (ya-)ƛa qʷá·n, "people from behind (i.e. inland side of) Prince of Wales Island." Ƭanga·s or Ƭanga·š, from ta·n, "sealion," the name for Prince of Wales Island.
Swanton: TAngā´c qoan
Raven 1 Con-nah-hut-tee [Ga·nax̣ˀádi]
*Wolf 8 Shen-ku-qway-tee [Šankukʷe·dí]
*Wolf 27 Tuck-clar-way-tee [Daqƛawe·dí]
*These seem to be alternate designations for the same clan.
Wolf 32 Tay-qway-tee [Te·qʷe·dí]

II SANYA

Emmons: Son-nah Kwan, Sa-niya or Sa-nya Kwan, "Southward tribe," from *sa-nuk* "south."
Phonetic: Sa·nya· qʷá·n, from sa·-niya·, "southern direction."
Swanton: Sā´nya qoan
Raven 10 Kake-sat-tee [Kiksˀádi]
Wolf 32 Ta-qway-tee [Te·qʷe·dí]
Eagle Na-ah-tee, Na-ah-hut-tee [Ne·x̣ˀádi]

III STIKINE

Emmons: Stick heen or Stikheen Kwan, "Bitter, unwholesome water tribe," from *stahk* "glacial mud in the river."
Phonetic: Štax̣ hí·n qʷá·n, from š datax̣ hí·n, "water (so silty) that (it) must be chewed."
Swanton: Staq!hī´n qoan, or Cq!At qoan [Šx̣at qʷá·n]
Raven 10 Kake-sat-tee [Kiksˀádi]
[Raven 14 Arn-kark-hit-ton. An obvious error for Raven 11.]
Raven 11 Tee-ton or Teete-ton [Ti·y hít-ta·n]
*Raven 25 Souk-heen-a-tee [Suqʷti·ne·dí]
*Raven 28 Kartch-hut-tee [Qa·čˀádi]
*These appear to be alternative designations for the same group.
Raven 32 Kas-qwoir-qway-tee [Ka·sx̣agʷe·dí]
Raven 33 Tahl-qway-tee [Ta·ƛqʷe·dí]
Wolf 18 Nan-ya-i-ee [Na·nya·ˀa·yí]
Wolf 19 Sick-nar-hut-tee [Šiknax̣ˀádi]
Wolf 26 Hook-qway-tee [X̣u·x̣ʷe·dí(?)]
Wolf 31 K'Hithlh-qwan or Hethe[l]-qwan [X̣e·ƛ-qʷá·n]

IV HENYA

Emmons: Hen-yeh Kwan, contracted from Hay-nuk-a-koo-oo-woo Kwan, "people from the other side," referring to the outer coast of Prince of Wales Island.
Phonetic: He·nya· qʷá·n, from he·-niya·, "this direction (over there)."
Swanton: Hē´nya qoan
Raven 2 Ƭar-qwan-a-tee, or Tark-an-a-tee, or Tsar-wan-ee [Tá·kʷˀa·ne·dí]
Raven 12 Tee-hee-na-tee, or Tee-heen-a-tee [Ti·yine·dí]
Raven 21 Yes-kah-na-tee or Yes-qwar-na-tee [Yí·šqane·dí (?)]
Raven 24 Teetle-hit-ton [Tí·ƛ hít-ta·n]
*Raven 20 Wahke-heen-a-tee [Wéx̣hine·dí]
*Raven 34 Hu-yahk-hut-tee [Quyé·q̇ˀádi]
*Raven 20 was omitted from one chart, perhaps because extinct; Raven 34 added on the other chart.
Wolf 8 Shen-ku-qway-tee [Šankukʷe·dí]
Wolf 14 Kah-qwoir-hit-ton [Kagʷax hít-ta·n (?)]

V KLAWAK

[Added by Emmons as an afterthought to one chart. The constituent clans, of which there seem to be only two, are difficult to read.]
Emmons: Klawak Kwan, "place of wrath." Or "people from the other side."
Phonetic: Ława·k qʷá·n (etymology unknown)
Swanton: Ławāk, a Henya town.
Raven 30? Ka-yah-ut-de (Ka-ya [otter]) or Ka-ya-te [Kaya·ˀádi] ?
Raven 31? Toke-ku-a-de (beaver) [Tuqʷye·dí]?

VI KUYU

Emmons: Kuyu Kwan. Name said to be derived from "stomach," referring to the shape of either Kuiu Island or some bay where they first lived.
Phonetic: Kuyu qʷá·n, Possible derivation from stomach, yu, needs to be checked.
Swanton: Kuiu qoan.
*Raven 20 Wahke-heen-a-tee [Wéx̣hine·dí]
*Raven 34 Hu-yahk-hut-tee [Quyé·q̇ˀádi]
*These different names seem to designate the same group.
Raven 22 Thluke-heen-a-tee [Łu·kʷhine·dí (?)]
Raven 23 Ka-ya-tee or Ku-ya-tee [Kuye·dí (?)]
Wolf 10 Sha-ah-qwan [Ša·ˀa· qʷa·n (?)]
Wolf 11 Nas-ta-tee [Na·ste·dí]
Wolf 12 Nas-sah-hut-tee or Nas-ah-hut-tee [Na·sax̣ˀadí (?)]
Wolf 13 Khoon-hit-ton [Kú·n hít-ta·n]

TABLE 11 (Continued)

The Composition of Tlingit Tribes

VII KAKE

Emmons: Kehk Kwan. More properly *gak,* said to be derived from a stream on Kupreanof Island, where the sand blistered the toes (*geka*); pronunciation shifted to *kaka* or *kake*.
Phonetic: Qí·x̣ or Qé·x̣ qʷá·n. Etymology uncertain, although -x̣í·x̣ is the stem for "(flesh) burns."
Swanton: Kēq! qoan
- Raven 9 Kultch-heen-a-tee [X̣ałčane·dí]
- Raven 25 Sook-heen-a-tee or Souk-te-heen-a-tee [Suqʷti·ne·dí]
- Raven 26 Kitchuke-qwit-ton or Ketchuke-qwit-ton [Kiǯu·kʷ hít-ta·n or Giǯu·kʷita·n]
- Raven 27 Tun-na-tee [Tane·dí]
- Raven 28 Kartch-hut-tee [Qa·č?ádi]
- Wolf 8 Shen-ku-qway-tee [Šankukʷe·dí]
- Wolf 22 Wis-heen-a-tee or Wi's-heen-na-tee [Waši·ne·dí]
- Wolf 23 Na-sat-tee [Ne·s?ádi (?)]
- Wolf 28 Tsar-qway-tee [Ca·gʷe·dí]

VIII SUMDUM

Emmons: Sum-dum Kwan, named for Holkham Bay, which is called *Tsu-dan,* "the hunting ground."
Phonetic: Śawdá·n (?), "Holkham Bay."
Swanton: S!aodā´n qoan
- Raven 1 Con-nah-hut-tee [G̣a·nax̣?ádi]
- Wolf 16 Yun-yeah-tee [Yanye·dí] [Only on one list.]
- Wolf 24 Seet-qway-tee [Śi·tqʷe·dí]

IX TAKU

Emmons: Tar-ku or Taku Kwan, from inlet, derived from runs of *ta* "king salmon" and *ku* "nest." Or inlet was named *Tawak thla ku,* "geese nesting place," contracted to *Taku*.
Phonetic: Ṫa·qú, from ṫa·waq gałaqú, "flood of geese."
Swanton: T!āq!ᵒ qoan
- Raven 1 Con-nah-hut-tee [G̣a·nax̣?ádi]
- Raven 5 Ish-kee-ton [?Iški·ta·n or ?Iška hít-ta·n]
- Raven 29 Kok-que-ton or Ko-kee-ton [Ku·qʷ hít-ta·n]
- Wolf 16 Gun [Yun?]-yeah-tee [Yanye·dí]

X AUK

Emmons: Auk Kwan. "Little lake Tribe," from lake at end of Auke glacial moraine.
Phonetic: ?Á·ḳʷ qʷá·n, from "lake-little tribe."
Swanton: Āk!ᵘ qoan
- Raven 15 Clee-na-tee [Ł̇i·ne·dí]
- *Raven 4 Tihk-ah-dee [Ṫí·x̣?ádi]
- *Raven 30? Kah-ya-tee [Kaya·?ádi]

*These are on one list; not on the other. Probably only two Raven clans.
- **Wolf 17 Nush-kee-ton [Wu·ški·ta·n]
- **Wolf 20 Klin-ton [ƛenta·n]

**Since each of these is on one list and not the other, they may designate the same clan.

XI CHILKAT-CHILKOOT

Emmons: Tchil-kart or Chilkat Kwan, "Salmon storehouse tribe." Chilkoot—No "*kwan*" added. "Yields to power," or "abundance of salmon."
Phonetic: Ǯiłqa·t qʷá·n
Ǯiłqu·t
Swanton: Djîłqā´t qoan; Djîłqo´t, a town.

Chilkat Clans
- Raven 3 Con-nah-ta-tee [G̣a·nax̣te·dí]
- *Raven 34 Hu-yahk-hut-tee [Quyé·q̇?ádi]

*On only one list. Probably mentioned in error.
- Wolf 1 Kar-qwan-ton [Ka·gʷa·nta·n]
- Wolf 7 Tuck-es-tee-nar [Dagisdina·]
- Wolf 27 Tuck-clar-way-tee [Daqławe·dí]
- **Wolf 8 Sheen-ku-qway-tee [Šankukʷe·dí]

**Mentioned as residents, but without clan houses.

Chilkoot Clans
- Raven 17 Thluke-r-hut-tee or Thu-kah-hut-tee [Łukʷa·x̣?ádi]
- Raven 18 New-shuck-ar-ar-ee [Nu·wšaka?a·yí]
- Wolf 7 Tuck-est-tee-nar [Dagisdina·]

XII HUTSNUWU

Emmons: Hootz-a-ta Kwan, Hootz nu-wu Kwan, "Brown bear fort tribe," named for the shore of Admiralty Island (near Angoon).
Phonetic: Xuc-nu·wú qʷá·n
Swanton: X̣ūts!nuwū´ qoan
- Raven 13 Dash-she-ton [De·ši·ta·n, from De·šú hít-ta·n]
- Raven 14 Arn-kark-hit-ton [?A·nx̣a·kíta·n or ?A·nx̣a·k hít-ta·n]
- Wolf 17 Nush-kee-ton [Wu·ški·ta·n]
- Wolf 27 Tuck-clar-way-tee [Daqławe·dí]
- Wolf 32 Tay-qway-tee [Te·qʷe·dí]

TABLE 11 (Continued)

The Composition of Tlingit Tribes

XIII SITKA

Emmons: Sitka Kwan, from She-ka or Sheet-kar Kwan, "People of Baranof Island." The island is called *she* or *she-ee* "limb of a tree," referring to its shape. Full name is *She-tika Kwan,* "people from outer edge of Baranof Island."
Phonetic: Šiʼtká, from šiʼy "knot, limb," ṫi-ká "outer (seaward) side" of Baranof Island (šiʼy).
Swanton: Cīt!ka´ [qoan]
Raven 6 Thluke-nar-hut-tee [Łukʷnax̣ʔádi]
Raven 7 Kut-kow-ee [X̣aṫkaʔa·yí]
Raven 8 Kuse-ka-dee [Qu·sk̓e·dí]
Raven 10 Kake-sat-tee [Kiksʔádi]
Raven 14 Arn-kark-hit-ton [ʔAnx̣a·kíta·n]
Raven 16 Tuck-tane-ton [Ṫaqde·nta·n]
Raven 19 Qwash-qwa-qwan [Kʷá·šk̓-qʷá·n]
Wolf 1 Kar-qwan-ton [Ka·gʷa·nta·n]
Wolf 2 Kat-oh-qwot-tee or Kut-ah-qwot-tee [Kadagʷʔádi]
Wolf 3 Ko-kee-ton or Kuke-hit-ton [Qu·kʷ hít-ta·n]
Wolf 5 Chu-con-na-tee [Ču·kane·dí]
Wolf 6 Ki-yatse-hit-ton [Ġayé·ṡ hít-ta·n]

XIV HOONAH

Emmons: Hoonah Kow, from *hoon-ya ka-woo,* referring to exposure to strong north wind.
Phonetic: Xuna· qá·wu, "Hoonah man," from xú·n niya·, "north-wind direction-of."
Swanton: Hū´na qoan
Raven 8 Kuse-ka-dee [Qu·sk̓e·dí]
Raven 16 Tuck-tane-ton [Ṫaqde·nta·n]
Wolf 1 Kar-qwan-ton [Ka·gʷa·nta·n]
Wolf 5 Chu-con-na-tee [Ču·kane·dí]
Wold 6 Ki-yatse-hit-ton [Ġayé·ṡ hít-ta·n]
Wolf 17 Nusk-kee-ton [Wu·šk̓i·ta·n]

XV DRY BAY

Emmons: Gun-na-ho Kwan, "Tribe among strangers," from *gu-na-nah,* "strange or foreign nation."
Phonetic: Ġuna·x̣u· qʷá·n, from guna-na·-x̣u·, "other-tribe-among."
Swanton: Gonā´xo, a Huna settlement.
Raven 7 Kut-kow-ee [X̣aṫkaʔa·yí]
Raven 8 Kuse-ka-dee [Qu·sk̓e·dí]
Raven 17 Thluke-r-hut-tee or Thlu-kah-hut-tee [Łukʷa·x̣ʔádi]
Wolf 7 Tuck-est-tee-nar [Dagisdina·]

XVI YAKUTAT

Emmons: Yakutat or York-tat Kwan, from *yak-dw-dal,* "the dam of the ocean," applied to the narrow barrier of land ending at Ocean Cape. Or it is corrupted from *Ya-ook-dot* or *Ya-ook-da-teet,* "waves splashing about the canoe." Call themselves Thla-ha-yeek Kwan, from *Thlaka* or *Hlaha,* a river on coast with many dead cedar trees; or reference may be to icebergs in Disenchantment Bay: "People of the red cedar within"; or "People of the iceberg within."
Phonetic: Ya·kʷdá·t qʷá·n; Łax̣a·-yík qʷá·n. Names are derived from Eyak words or names (see de Laguna 1972:58–59).
Swanton: Yaqᵘdā´t qoan; Łaxayî´k qoan
Raven 19 Qwash-qwa-qwan [Kʷá·šk̓ qʷá·n or Kʷá·šk̓iqʷá·n]
Wolf 1 Kar-qwan-ton [Ka·gʷa·nta·n]
Wolf 29 Gou-hit-ton [Ga·w hít-ta·n]
*Wolf 30 Thluke-way-tee [Łux̣ʷe·dí]
*On both charts erroneously identified as a Raven clan with silver salmon, *thluke* [łu·kʷ], as crest; corrected in MS.
Wolf 32 Tay-qway-tee [Te·qʷe·dí]

XVII KALIAKH

Emmons: Qwolth-yet Kwan, Gut-leuhk Kwan, or Guthle-uk Kwan (mixed tribe).
Phonetic: Ġałyé·x̣ or Ġałyax̣ qʷá·n, referring to Kaliakh River, derived from Eyak word gałyAx̣, "the lowest" of a series (de Laguna 1972:101, information from Michael Krauss).
Swanton: Not recognized as a Tlingit tribe, probably because predominantly Eyak.
Raven 3 Con-nah-ta-tee [Ġa·nax̣te·dí]
Raven 8 Kuse-ka-dee [Qu·sk̓e·dí]
Raven 19 Qwash-qwa-qwan [Kʷá·šk̓ qʷá·n]
*Raven 31 Toke-ku-a-dee (beaver) [Tuqʷye·dí (?)]
*This clan appears (in error?) on one list; writing unclear.
Wolf 1 Kar-qean-ton [Ka·gʷa·nta·n]
Wolf 4 Tchis-qway-tee [Ǯi·šqʷe·dí]

Note: Emmons prepared several lists and charts to show the composition of the different Tlingit tribes, usually listing them from north to south along one side of a large sheet of paper, with the various clans indicated in vertical columns, together with their main crests and face painting designs. The chart in BCPA appears to be older than that in AMNH. The latter omits or corrects a few entries in the first and adds a few. In BCPA there is also a list of clans in which Emmons compared those he had recorded with those published by Swanton (1908), but he did not attempt a concordance of clan names. The table here combines the information in Emmons's several lists, including Emmons's often faulty etymology of tribal names, and also gives Swanton's tribal names (1908), as well as the best phonetic transcriptions that Jeff Leer could supply. Michael Krauss has supplied the Eyak meanings. I have not attempted to supplement Emmons's lists of clans with those reported by Swanton (1908), or Olson (1967) from southeastern Alaska, or by myself from the Gulf Coast Tlingit (de Laguna 1972).

TABLE 12

Kin Terms

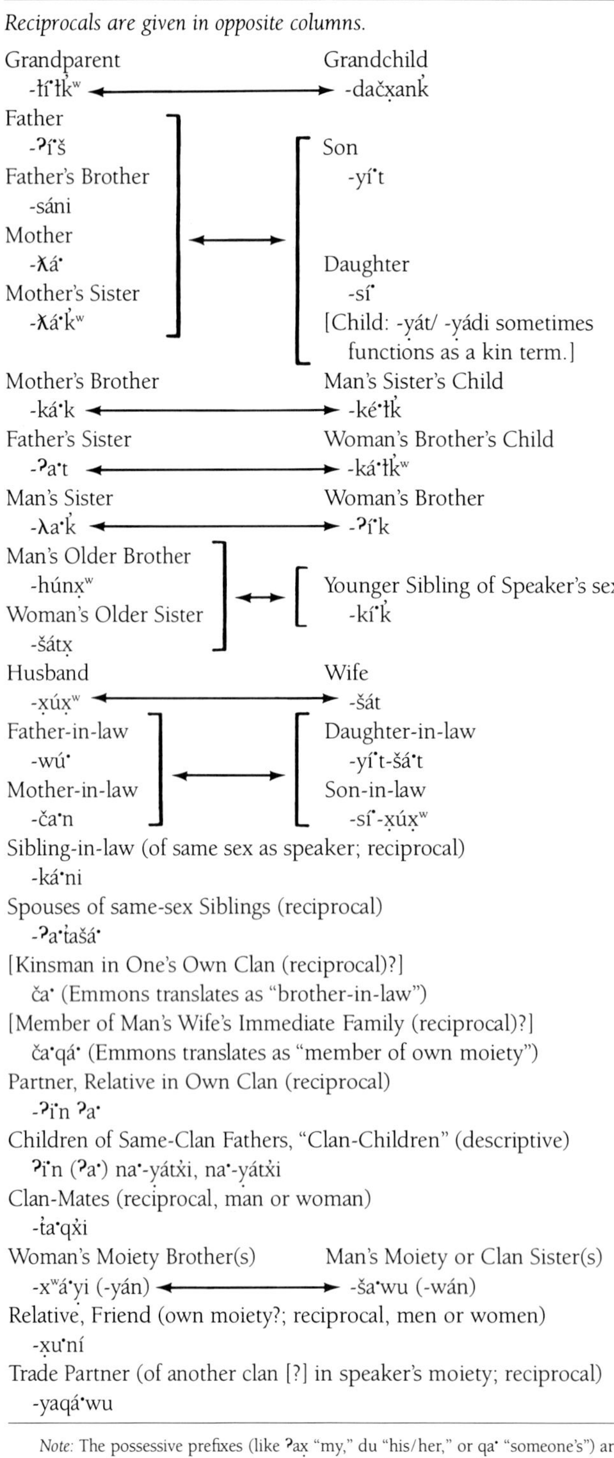

Reciprocals are given in opposite columns.

Grandparent -łí·łk̓ʷ ↔	Grandchild -dačx̣ank̓
Father -ʔí·š Father's Brother -sáni Mother -ƛá· Mother's Sister -ƛá·k̓ʷ ↔	Son -yí·t Daughter -sí· [Child: -yát/ -yádi sometimes functions as a kin term.]
Mother's Brother -ká·k ↔	Man's Sister's Child -ké·łk̓
Father's Sister -ʔa·t ↔	Woman's Brother's Child -ká·łk̓ʷ
Man's Sister -λa·k̓ ↔	Woman's Brother -ʔí·k
Man's Older Brother -húnx̣ʷ Woman's Older Sister -šátx̣ ↔	Younger Sibling of Speaker's sex -kí·k̓
Husband -x̣úx̣ʷ ↔	Wife -šát
Father-in-law -wú· Mother-in-law -ča·n ↔	Daughter-in-law -yí·t-šá·t Son-in-law -sí·-x̣úx̣ʷ

Sibling-in-law (of same sex as speaker; reciprocal)
-ká·ni

Spouses of same-sex Siblings (reciprocal)
-ʔa·t̓ašá·

[Kinsman in One's Own Clan (reciprocal)?]
ča· (Emmons translates as "brother-in-law")

[Member of Man's Wife's Immediate Family (reciprocal)?]
ča·qá· (Emmons translates as "member of own moiety")

Partner, Relative in Own Clan (reciprocal)
-ʔi·n ʔa·

Children of Same-Clan Fathers, "Clan-Children" (descriptive)
ʔi·n (ʔa·) na·-yátx̓i, na·-yátx̓i

Clan-Mates (reciprocal, man or woman)
-t̓a·qx̓i

Woman's Moiety Brother(s) -xʷá·yi (-yán) ↔	Man's Moiety or Clan Sister(s) -ša·wu (-wán)

Relative, Friend (own moiety?; reciprocal, men or women)
-x̣u·ní

Trade Partner (of another clan [?] in speaker's moiety; reciprocal)
-yaqá·wu

Note: The possessive prefixes (like ʔax̣ "my," du "his/her," or qa· "someone's") are omitted here. They are always necessary, except in a few vocative forms or usages, not here included. Tlingit lacks true plurals, but groups of relatives may be indicated by appropriate collective suffixes: -hás, -x̓í, -yán, or -wán.

TABLE 13

Incomplete List of Tlingit Crests

Raven		Wolf	
Raven	*Yehl, Yehlh* [yé·ł]	Eagle	*Tchak* [č̓á·k̓]
Hawk	*Ketchuke* [kiǯu·k/giǯu·k]	Murrelet	*Tcheet* [č̓i·t]
Crow	*Tsu whelh* [ċaxʷe·ł]	Petrel	*Ganuk* [ganu·kʷ]
Puffin	*Hick* [x̣ík]	Cormorant	*York* [yu·q̇ʷ]
Seagull	*Tats la ta* [ku·ƛ̓é·ṫa(?) or ké·λadi(?)]	Owl	*Cisk* [ċísk̓ʷ/ ʒísk̓ʷ]
Goose	*Ta wak* [ṫa·wáq]	Flicker	*Khun* [ku·n]
		Thunderbird	*Hehl* [xe·ƛ]
Beaver	*Sigadi* [ṡige·dí]	Wolf	*Goutch* [gu·č]
Land Otter	*Koushta* [kú·šda·]	Brown Bear	*Huts, Hootz* [xú·c]
Mouse	*Kutesin* [kuċi·n, red-backed rat?]	Mountain Goat	*Genou* [ǯánwu]
Moose	*Khars* [xa·s, cow; císk̓ʷ]	Dog	*Katle* [ke·ƛ]
Sea Lion	*Tan* [ta·n]	Hair Seal	*Tsar* [ca·]
Whale	*Yai* [yá·y]	Killerwhale	*Kete, Keet* [kí·t]
Dog Salmon	*Teetle* [ṫí·ł̓]	Dogfish	*Toos* [tú·ṡ, shark]
Coho Salmon	*Thluke* [ł̓u·kʷ]	Ground Shark	*Kutku* [x̣átgu]
Halibut (very large)	*Narlh* [ná·łx̣, riches]	Porpoise	*Tcheech* [či·č]
Herring	*Yar* [ya·w]	Halibut	*Tchartl* [ča·ƛ]
Sculpin	*Wake* [wé·x̣]	Codfish	*Sarkh* [ṡá·x̣]
Starfish	*Sach* [ṡáx]		
Clam	*Crakl* [gá·ł̓]		
Frog	*Hiktch* [xíxč̓]	A very small saltwater bug	*Suck-war* [ṡu·kʷ(?), barnacle, ref. to swimming larval stage?]
Woodworm	*Tluke* [ƛ̓úk̓ʷx̣ʷ]		
Seaweed	*Danih* [da·-né; né, hairy seaweed]		
Sun	*Kaghan* [gaga·n]		
Moon	*Dis* [dís]		
Great Dipper	*Yaxte* [Obviously from Swanton, yax̣té]		
Mythical character of Strength "skin-black," Black Skin]	*Duck Tool* [Dukʷ-ł̓u·ƛ,	Mythical Sea Monster [Wealth Bringer]	*Gone ka tate* [G̣una·kade·t]
Spirit of Sleep	*Ta* [ta, sleep, Sleep Bird]	A carved cane captured from Tsimshian	*Arnk* [perhaps ˀank̓?]
Rock in the Stickheen River near Glenora	*Klone* or *Thlone* [ƛ̓u·n(?)]	Glacial iceberg	*Khartl* [x̣á·ƛ]
[Same as above, or] a nearby mountain	*Ta nass sha yuh, Tar-nass-shen yur*[?]	[Indecipherable]	*Sku da chete* [possibly -?- da-č̓i·t, "-?-around-murrelet" (?)]
A mountain on Baranof Island, [near Pybus Bay?]	*Tark sha* [da·x̣ ša·(?)]	Rock west of Kuiu Island	*Dake nu*, "Far out Fort" [de·ki-nu·w, "out to sea fort"?]
A mountain on mainland back of Frederick Sound [Devil's Thumb]	*Thlku na ka sha, Tahl ku na sha*, "mountain that floated up" in the Flood [probably ta·ł-qu-nax̣-k̓ʷuša·]	Monster of *Talqw Bay* [southeast arm of Thomas Bay]	*Heen tark hootsee* [hí·n-tá·k-xú·ʒi, "bear of the water's bottom," or "Sea Bear"]
Mount Fairweather	*Tsahchan* [całx̣a·n]	[Added notes:]	
Mount Saint Elias	*Tar sa te sha* [yaṡe·ṫa ša· or waṡe·ṫa ša·]	Swan used by *Thluke nah ot di* ? [Raven 6; swan is guq̇ʷł̓]	
		Take qway di [Wolf 32] crest mountain?	
		Nas ta de [Wolf 11] crest?—*Dake nu* [See Rock west of Kuiu Island, above]	

TABLE 14

Tlingit House Names

LAND ANIMALS

Bear, *hootz* [xú·c]*: Wolf 1 at Klukwan (Chilkat XI), Sitka (XIII); Wolf 5 at Hoonah (XIV); Wolf 32 at Tongass (I), Cape Fox (Sanya II), Tuxekan (Henya IV), Angoon and Neltushkin (Hutsnuwu XII), Port Mulgrave and Situk River (Yakutat XVI).

Bear's Den, *hootz kuou* [xú·c qu·wú·]: Wolf 32 at Cape Fox (Sanya II), Situk River (Yakutat XVI).

Bear's Nest, *hootz kudi* [xú·c kúdi]: Wolf 1 at Cape Fox (Sanya II), and Hoonah (XIV); Wolf 6 or 17 at Freshwater Bay (Hoonah XIV).

Wolf, *goutch/gouch* [gú·č]: Wolf 1 at Klukwan (Chilkat XI), Sitka (XIII), Controller Bay (Kaliakh XVI): Wolf 26 at Wrangell (Stikine III).

Wolf Den, *goutch kanlye/kanlyekat* [gú·č -?-]: Wolf 1 at Port Mulgrave (Yakutat XVI). [Probably the same as Wolf Sweathouse.]

Wolf Sweathouse, *gooch kha* [gú·č x̣a·y]: Wolf 1 at Yakutat (XVI).

Beaver, *sigade* [šige·dí]: Wolf 1 at Controller Bay (Kaliakh XVII).

Beaver Dam, *sigade shae* [šige·dí x̣a·yí, "beaver's lodge or sweathouse"]: Eagle at Cape Fox [Sanya II].

Marten, *kouh* [k̓ú·xʷ]: Unidentified Raven clan at Tuxekan (Henya IV).

Moose or Cow, *kars/karse* [xa·s]: Raven 1 at Tongass (I); Raven 8 at Sitka (XIII), Hoonah (XIV); "Moose House People" [probably Raven 8] at *Scar-ta-heen* (Dry Bay XIV); Wolf 9 at Tuxekan (Henya IV).

"Owl," *tsiskw* [probably "moose," císk̓ʷ/ʒisk̓ʷ]: Wolf 9 at Saxman (Sanya II).

Mouse, *kutsin/kutesin* [kuči·n, "red-backed rat"?], or Mouse Dish, *kutsin kithla* [kuči·n qíła·/qéła·]: Raven 8 at Hoonah (XIV).

Land Otter, *koushta* [kú·šda·]: Raven 3 at Klukwan (Chilkat XI) and Chilkoot (XI); Raven 27 or 28 at Kake (VII).

Frog, *hikth* [xíxč̓]: Raven 10 and 28 at Wrangell (Stikine III).

Frog's Den, *hikth kaye* [xíxč̓ x̣a·yí]: Raven 32 at Wrangell (Stikine III).

BIRDS

Raven, *yehl/yehlh* [yé·ł]: Raven 1 at Tongass (I); Raven 3 at Klukwan (Chilkat XI), and Controller Bay (Kaliakh XVII); Raven 12 at Tuxekan (Henya IV); Raven 13 at Angoon (Hutsnuwu XII); Raven 17 at Yandestake (Chilkoot XI); Raven 25 at Kake (VII).

Raven's Nest, *yehlh kudi* [yé·ł kúdi]: Raven 16 at Hoonah (XIV); Raven 18 at Kutwaltu (Chilkoot XI).

Raven's Bones, *yehlh sage* [yé·ł šaqí]: Raven 19 at Yakutat (XVI).

Eagle, *tchak/chak/chark* [č̓á·k̓]: Eagle at Cape Fox (Sanya II); Wolf 1 at Sitka (XIII), Wolf 4 at Controller Bay (Kaliakh XVII).

Eagle's Nest, *chak-qwaddy* [č̓á·k̓ kúdi]: Eagle at Cape Fox (Sanya II); Wolf 1 at Klukwan (Chilkat XI), Sitka (XIII).

Eagle's Tail, *chak kuou* [č̓á·k̓ ku·wú]: Eagle at Cape Fox (Sanya II).

Eagle's Foot, *tchak ka kosee* [č̓á·k̓ (qa·) x̣u·sí]: Eagle at Cape Fox (Sanya II).

Eagle Spear, *tchark kut* [č̓á·k̓ kát]: Eagle at Cape Fox (Sanya II).

Flicker, *khoon/khun* [ku·n]: Raven 13 at Angoon? (Hutsnuwu XII); Wolf 26 at Wrangell (Stikine III)—later erased; Wolf 27 at Tongass (I).

Hawk, *ketcuke* [kiǯu·k]: Raven 3 at Tongass (I); Raven 27 at Kake (VII).

Golden Eagle [same or different from Hawk?], *gitjuk* [giǯu·k]: Wolf 32 at Yakutat (XVI).

Murrelet, *cheete/chete* [či·t]: Wolf 27 at Klukwan (Chilkat XI).

Seagull, *kate-lahta* [ké·ƛadi]: Raven 16 at Hoonah (XIV).

Owl, *tchisk* [císk̓ʷ/ʒísk̓ʷ]: Raven 19 at Yakutat (XVI).

Bluejay Head, *sha cla-kash-ko* [šaɫax̣e·šx̣ʷ ?]: Wolf 31 at Wrangell (Stikine III).

SEA MAMMALS

Killerwhale, *kete/keet* [kí·t]: Wolf 1 at Klukwan (Chilkat XI); Wolf 26 at Wrangell (Stikine III); Wolf 27 at Tongass (I), Klukwan (Chilkat XI), and three houses at Angoon (Hutsnuwu XII); Eagle at Cape Fox (Sanya II), later changed to "underseas animal."

Killerwhale's Dorsal Fin, *kete gooshe* [kí·t gu·ší]: Wolf 27 at Klukwan (Chilkat XI).

Chief Killerwhale's Dorsal Fin, *tlegooshi* [ɫigu·ší, "it has a dorsal fin"]: Wolf 1 at Klukwan (Chilkat XI).

Killerwhale's Tongue, *kete klutee* [kí·t ɫ̓ú·ti]: Wolf 27 at Klukwan (Chilkat XI).

Killerwhale's Backbone, *kete todake* [kí·t-tu-déx̣, or -dix̣-ká, or -déx̣i?]: Wolf 27 at Klukwan (Chilkat XI).

Killerwhale Family, *kete qwannee* [kí·t qʷani·, "Chilkat-Chilkoot spirits"]: Wolf 27 at Klukwan (Chilkat XI).

Whale, *yai/yough* [yá·y]: Raven 2 at Saxman (Sanya II); Raven 3 at Klukwan (Chilkat XI); Raven 6 at Sitka (XIII); Raven 28 at Wrangell (Stikine III).

Sealion, *tan* [ta·n]: Raven 6 at Sitka (XIII); Raven 32 at Wrangell (Stikine III).

FISH

Dog Salmon, *teetle* [tí·ł]: Raven 14 at Angoon and Neltushkin (Hutsnuwu XII); Raven 18 at Auk (X); Raven 24 at Tuxekan (Henya IV).

Old Silver Salmon (changing color), *kark/khark* [x̣á·kʷ]: Raven 16 at Hoonah (XIV); Raven 17 at Yandestake (Chilkoot XI); Raven 28 at Kake (VII).

Coho Salmon, *thluke* [ɫ̓u·kʷ]: Raven 7 at Sitka (XIII).

Halibut, *chartle* [čá·ƛ]: Wolf 1 at Sitka (XIII).

Halibut (large), *natlk/narlh* [ná·ɫx̣, "riches"]: Eagle at Cape Fox (Sanya II); Raven 28 at Wrangell (Stikine III).

Shark, *tuse* [tú·š̓]: Wolf 3 at Sitka (XIII); Wolf 17 at Auk (X); Wolf 28 at Kake (VII); Wolf 32 at Port Mulgrave and Yakutat (XVI).

Shark's Fin, *toose guche* [tú·š̓ gu·ší]: Wolf 6 or 17 at Freshwater Bay (Hoonah XIV).

Shark's Backbone, *toose tihka* [tú·š̓ dix̣-ká ?]: Wolf 1 at Hoonah (XIV).

TABLE 14 (Continued)

Tlingit House Names

Dogfish (ground shark), *kut-gu* [x̣átgu]: Raven 21 [ought to be Wolf 8?] at Saxman (Sanya II); Wolf 18 at Wrangell (Stikine III); Wolf 22 at Kake (VII); Wolf 27 at Klukwan (Chilkat XI).

Dogfish Intestine, *kut-gu nasi* [x̣átgu na·sí]: Wolf 18 at Wrangell (Stikine III).

Sculpin, *waok* [wé·x̣]: Raven 10 at Cape Fox (Sanya II).

Herring, jumping, *kakatdj qwaktgw* [kax̣átǯa· "fish splashing"]: Raven 10 at Sitka (XIII).

INVERTEBRATES

Butterfly, *ka thlu* [ƛe·łú]: Wolf 27 at Klukwan (Chilkat XI).

Snail, *tahk* [táx̣, "slug," "snail out of its shell"]: Wolf 27 at Kake (VII).

Woodworm, *thluke/thluke quar* [ƛ̓úk̓ʷx̣ʷ]: Raven 3 at Klukwan (Chilkat XI).

Starfish, *sash* [šáx]: Raven 1 at Tongass (I).

Starfish, *tsukh* [same as above? or ṡù·k, "barnacle"?]: Raven 12 at Tuxekan (Henya IV).

Sea Bug, *yush* [possibly "tadpole," duš]: Eagle at Cape Fox, (Sanya II).

CELESTIAL AND METEOROLOGICAL

Sun, *ka-ghan/ka-ghon* [gaga·n]: Raven 10 at Wrangell (Stikine III), Sitka (XIII).

Bright Sun, *ghon it illa* [x̣an -?-]: Unidentified clan at Chilkoot (XI).

Moon, *dis* [dís]: Raven 19 at Port Mulgrave and Yakutat (XVI).

Star (Great Dipper), *yaxtah* [yax̣té]: Raven 15 at Auk (X).

Star, *kotha naha/kotka naka* [qutx̣ ʔa(ya)nahá·]: Wolf 1 at Sitka (XIII).

Rainbow, *kuhk kha on two* [kičx̣ ʔanaga·t?]: Unidentified clan at Tuxekan (Henya IV).

Thunder (a bird), *heith/hatl/hahtle* [xe·ƛ]: Raven 1 at Tongass (I); Wolf 7 at Klukwan (Chilkat XI) and Yakutat (XVI); Wolf 32 at Yakutat (XVI).

PLACES (Crest Sites and House Locations)

Mountain [unidentified], *kark* [x̣à·k, "valley"]: Wolf 14 at Saxman (Sanya II).

Mountain [unidentified], *sha* [ša·], or Hill, *ghuh kah* [gu·č-ka, "hill-on"?]: Unidentified clans at Tuxekan (Henya IV). There may be two or three houses.

Mountain (unidentified), *sha* [ša·]: Raven 25 at Kake (VII).

Mountain (unidentified), *sha* [ša·]: Raven 17 at Chilkoot (XI).

Tahlku Mountain [ta·ł-qu-nax̣k̓u ša·, the Devil's Thumb, above Thomas Bay]: Raven 33 at Wrangell (Stikine III).

Mountain, *sha* [ša·], Mount Fairweather, *Tsath hon* [catx̣a·n]: Raven 6 at Yakutat (XVI) and Raven 16 at Hoonah (XIV).

Mountain, *sha* [ša·], Mount Saint Elias, *Yar sa te sha* [yaṡé·-ta-ša·, "mountain in back of Icy Bay"]: Raven 19 at Yakutat (XVI).

On Top of Mountain [Mount Stoevkl?] on Unuk River, *tleete kah* or *tlute ka* [ƛ̓útk-ká ? or łukʷá ?]: Raven 32 at Cape Fox (Sanya II).

Mountain Back of Town, *Ghe son* [ge·sán, Mount Ripinski?]: Raven 17 at Yandestake (Chilkoot XI).

Valley, *kark/shanuk* [x̣a·k/ša·náx̣]: Wolf 32 at Tongass (I).

Valley or Middle, *kark* [x̣a·k]: Raven 3 at Klukwan (Chilkat XI).

Hillside, *tool see*[?]: Raven 17 at Chilkoot (XI).

Precipice, *ghitle* [gił̓]: Raven 33 at Wrangell (Stikine III).

Rock (Boulder) or Reef, *each* [ʔi̍č]: Wolf 1 at Sitka (XIII); Raven 6 at Situk River (Yakutat XVI).

Cave, *tatuke* [tatú·k]: Wolf 18 at Wrangell (Stikine III).

Waves Cavern, *teete tlasar* [ti̍t -?-]: Raven 10 at Cape Fox (Sanya II).

Waves, *teete* [ti̍t]: Raven 16 at Thlu-huggu (Hoonah XIV).

Iceberg, *khartle* [xá·ƛ]: Wolf 5 at Sitka (XIII) and Hoonah (XIV).

Treeless Island, *chil-cla* [ša-ł-ƛa·x̣]: Raven 25 and Raven 27 at Kake (VII).

On the Point, *katgun* [x̣ał̓-gú·n, "island-isthmus"]: Raven 3 at Tongass (I).

On Sandy Point, *klauwa-thluka* [łé·w łukʷá?]: Wolf 7 at Yandestake (Chilkoot XI).

On (Castle Rock) Point, *thluka* [łukʷá]: Raven 10 at Sitka (XIII).

Deep Salmon Hole, *ish ka* [ʔíš-ka]: Raven 3 at site on Chilkat River (Chilkat XI).

Log Jam (where salmon hide), *yon goon* [yanxu·n]: Raven 14 at Angoon (Hutsnuwu XII).

Spring (fresh water), *goon* [gu·n]: Raven 13 at Angoon (Hutsnuwu XII); Wolf 7 at Klukwan (Chilkat XI) and Yandestake (Chilkoot XI).

Salmon Stream near Dry Bay, *shada-yi* [šg̣a·da·yi?]: Raven 8 at Sitka (XIII).

Middle of Town, *an kark* [ʔa·n x̣á·k]: Raven 14 at Neltushkin and Angoon (Hutsnuwu XII); Raven 25 at Kake (VII).

[Lower] End of Town, *hina* [xina· from ʔixi-na·, "down-river"]: Raven 6 at Sitka (XIII).

End of Town, *ich dar* [ʔi̍č da·, "reefs around"]: Wolf 1 at Tongass (I); Wolf 27 at Klukwan (Chilkat XI).

Last House in Town, *an tchu ka* [ʔa·n šukʷá, "on town's end"]: Wolf 8 (erased) or Wolf 28 at Kake (VII).

House Back of Town, *tack-tane* [ṫaqde·n]: Raven 16 at Hoonah (XIV).

House Back of Town, *an-tark* [ʔa·n ṫá·k]: Raven 27 at Kake (VII).

Farther on Beyond, *nan-na* [na·na·, "up-river" ?]: Wolf 5 at Hoonah (XIV).

Town on Shore, *an-ar-kark* [ʔa·n ʔi̍gayá·k, "town on beach below"?]: Wolf 1 at Sitka (XIII).

Distant House, *an-tchu-kwa* [ʔa·n šukʷá], or Marble Cave House *kuke qwak* [kú·qʷ -?-]: Raven 13 at Angoon (Hutsnuwu XII).

Far Away (out to sea), *dikiná* [de·kina·, also "Haida"]: Raven 6 at Yakutat (XVI).

TABLE 14 (Continued)

Tlingit House Names

MATERIALS

Green or Young Tree, *shisk/shitz ka* [šíšq]: Wolf 7 at Klukwan (Chilkat XI).

Dead Wood, *shuck* [ša·q, "driftwood"?]: Wolf 23 at Kake (VII).

Brush, *kartch* [qa·č]: Raven 28 at Wrangell (Stikine III).

Bark, *tee, ti* [ti·y, "cedar bark"]: Raven 11 at Wrangell (Stikine III); Raven 12 at Saxman (Sanya II).

Yellow Cedar, *haee/hye/haye/haghee* [x̣á·y]: Wolf 2 at Hoonah (XIV); Wolf 28 at Kake (VII).

Iron, *guyasz* [gayé·š, "drift iron"]: Wolf 6 at Sitka (XIII).

Steel, *steen* [šdí·n]: Raven 10 at Sitka (XIII); Raven 13 at Angoon (Hutsnuwu XII); Raven 26 at Wrangell (Stikine III).

Copper, *tinneh* [tiná·, shield-shaped object]: Raven 10 at Sitka.

Clay, *sa* [šé]: Raven 10 at Sitka (XIII).

CONSTRUCTION

Big House, *hit klin* [hít ƛe·n]: Wolf 18 at Wrangell (Stikine III); Wolf 20 at Auk (X).*

Box, *kuke* [qú·kʷ]: Wolf 3 at Sitka (XIII); Wolf 8 at Kake (VII); Wolf 18 at Wrangell (Stikine III); Wolf 22 at Kake (VII).

Pit, *kough* [kú·qʷ]: Raven 13? at Chaik (Hutsnuwu XII).

Retaining Timber (around interior pit), *tak* [tá·x̣]: Raven 10 at Wrangell (Stikine III).

Flat, *koqwitch eta ton* [qákʷ "flat basket" -hít-ta·n "house people"]: Wolf 7 at Klukwan (Chilkat XI).

Shelf, *kayash* [ka-yá·š, "platform, shelf"]: Raven 7 at Sitka (XIII); Wolf 26 at Wrangell (Stikine III).

Sidewise, *kla dane* [ƛ̓a·dé·n]: Raven 13 at Angoon (Hutsnuwu XII); Raven 23 at Wrangell (Stikine III); Wolf 3 at Sitka (XIII); Wolf 22 at Kake (VII).

Red, *kan* [x̣a·n]: Wolf 19 at Wrangell (Stikine III).

Two Doors, *dehk kawoolth* [dé·x̣ x̣a-wu·ł]: Wolf 1 at Sitka (XIII).

Looking Out (reference to windows), *kotisse* [qutíš]: Raven 1 at Tongass (I); Raven 3 at Klukwan (Chilkat XI); Raven 28 at Kake (VII).

DEFENSE

Fort, *nu* [nu·w]: Raven 1 at Tongass (I); Raven 19 at Port Mulgrave and Yakutat (XVI); Wolf 17 at Kake (VII); Wolf 17 at Angoon (Hutsnuwu XII); Wolf 17 at Hoonah and Thluhuggu (Hoonah XIV).

Armor, *wanda* [wanda·, wooden armor "about the edge"]: Raven 14 at Neltushkin (Hutsnuwu XII); Raven 25 at Kake (VII); Wolf 5 at Hoonah (XIV); Wolf 32 at Wrangell (Stikine III).

Cannon, *anda una* [ˀa·nda· ˀú·na·, "guns around the ship"]: Wolf 26 at Wrangell (Stikine III).

SUPERNATURAL OR MYTHICAL

Picture or Shadow, *ki yah hi/ka hu hayi* [qa· yaha·yí, probably referring to ghost]: Wolf 1 at Yandestake (Chilkoot XI); Wolf 18 at Wrangell (Stikine III).

[Wealth-bringing water monster], *Gone-ko-tate* [G̣una·kade·t]: Wolf 8 at Saxman (Sanya II).

Water monster killed by *Thlayak* [Łq̇ayá·k̇ʷ], called *Kohk ka ou du wa* [káx̣-qu-ya-n-duˀá]: Raven 33 at Wrangell (Stikine III).

Katz [ka·c], the man who married a she-bear: Wolf 32 at Tongass (I).

Sleep, *ta* [tá, a bird]: Raven 6 at Sitka (XIII).

Coward (homosexual), *quhat han* [q̇atx̣á·n, a character in myth]: Wolf 32 at Yakutat (XVI).

Lowered from the Sky (reference to myth of Children of the Sun), *cough ye* [kawƛiya·yi]: Raven 28 at Wrangell (Stikine III).

Drifted or Towed Ashore (reference to a Raven myth) [spelling taken by Emmons from Swanton 1908:403], [yan wułihaši]: Raven 12 at Tuxekan (Henya IV).

Man's (amputated) Head (a shaman's spirit), *kah sha-ee* [qa· ša·yí]: Raven 16 at Hoonah (XIV).

Man's (amputated) Foot (a shaman's spirit), *ka koose* [qa· x̣u·sí]: Wolf 9 at Saxman (Sanya II).

(Named for a doctor's spirit), *anyaku ka yagee* [ˀa·n ya·gú qu-yé·gi, "ship's boat spirit"]: Wolf 26 at Wrangell (Stikine III).

OTHER

Drum, *gough* [ga·w, so-called because of reverberating noise inside]: Wolf 1 at Klukwan (Chilkat XI); Wolf 32 at Port Mulgrave and Yakutat (XVI).

Play, *kus hook* [qusˀu·k̇ʷ]: Raven 19 at Yakutat (XVI).

Gambling, *alka* [ˀałqá·]: Raven 28 at Wrangell (Stikine III).

High Class, *anyedi* [ˀa·n-yádi]: Wolf 1 at Sitka (XIII).

Burned Down, *kaghon/kow-ah-ghon* [ka·waga·ni]: Wolf 1 at Sitka (XIII) and Hoonah (XIV).

Bent Over Carrying a Heavy Load, *at ow-r-hitchee* [ˀat ˀuwaxiǯi, "exerted strength on something," may have mythical reference]: Raven 10 at Sitka (XIII).

Ank (Tsimshian cane captured in war) [ˀank̇?]: Wolf 19 at Wrangell (Stikine III).

Nu shuck ah ahye [nu·w ša-ka-ˀa·yí, "ones on the head of the fort"]: Raven 18 at Kutwaltu (Chilkoot XI).

Note: This list has been compiled by the editor from the house names recorded by Emmons at the various village sites described in his unpublished manuscript, *History of Tlingit Clans and Tribes*. Jeff Leer corrected the transcriptions. No attempt has been made to compare this list with any other published record of Tlingit house names, such as Swanton (1908:400–407), Olson (1967:3–4, 7–11, 110, and passim), de Laguna (1960:176–92), and de Laguna (1972:315–27).

*With the exception of Big House, hít ƛe·n, all the house names begin with the form in the list, to which is added "house" or hít (e.g., Bear House, xú·c hít, or House Drifted Ashore, yan wułihaši hít).

TABLE 15

Value of Native Products at Sitka, 1890

Herring grease per gallon	$0.50
Seal grease per gallon	.70
Eulachon grease per gallon	1.00
1 cake seaweed	.25
1 cake hemlock bark	.25
1 cake soapberries	from .25 to $1.00
1 biscuit box herring eggs	2.50
1 dried salmon	.10
1 gallon *ke-whahi* [ˀat kaxu·kʷ, "anything small, round, and dried," probably dried berries	.60
1 cake strawberries	1.00
1 cake mountain goat grease	2.00
1 cake deer grease	1.00 to $2.00
½ dried deer	1.50

Note: Emmons prepared this table.

TABLE 16

Trading Profits of the Chilkat Tlingit, 1890

	Cost to the Tlingit	Sale to Trader
marten	$0.50	$2.00 to $3.00
mink	.25	.25 to $1.50
lynx	.20	—
silver fox	1.25	4.00
cross fox	.25 to .50	1.00 to $2.00
red fox	.25 to .50	.75 to $1.00
wolverine	.37½	—
black bear	.50 to $1.50	1.50 to $3.50
brown bear	.50	.50 to $2.50
grizzly	.50 to $1.50	1.00 to $3.00
beaver	.20 to .40	.80 to $1.00 per lb.
land otter	.50	1.50 to $2.00
hair seal	—	.08 to .10
deer skins		.15 to .20
Cost of Trader's Goods		
Prints and sheeting		$0.25 per yard
tobacco		1.50 per lb.
molasses		1.00 per gallon
powder		1.50 per lb.
shot		.50 per lb.
blankets (assorted)		3.00 to $6.00

Note: This table was compiled by the editor from information given by Mahoney (1870:20), who reported also that "[The trading prices for skins] hold for the Indians from Chilkat to Portland Canal; also for the Taku."

TABLE 17

Edible Sea Resources

	MARINE INVERTEBRATES	
*	Devilfish (octopus), also "bait"	ná·qʷ
	Starfish, with arms, *sash/sach*	s̓áx
	"Starfish," probably barnacle, *tsukh*	s̓ù·k
*	Sea urchin	ní·s̓
*	Crab	s̓á·w
*?	Spider crab, king crab	x̓é·x̣
?	Shrimp	s̓í·x̓át
*	Clam [*Saxidomus giganteus*], *crakl/gartle*	gá·ł̓
	Giant clam	x̣í·t̓
*	Horse clam	ye·s/ỵi·s
*	Small butter clam	ʒ̣íx̓ʷ
	Large mussel [*Mytilus californiensis*], *yeese*	ỵí·s̓
*	Small mussel [*M. edulis*]	ỵa·k
*	Scallop	x̣ʷe·na
*	Cockle	sá·xʷ [Yakutat] ỵału·łe·t [SE Alaska]
*	Abalone, haliotis	gúnx̣a·
	Dentalium [imported]	táx̓x̣i
*?	Large chiton	ku·w
*	Small chiton	ša·w
	Sea cucumber	yé·n
	"Jellyfish," adheres to rocks, used as medicine, probably sea anemone, *teh-yah-tah-yea*	té ỵata·yí, "rock face-fat"
	Jellyfish	ta·kʷ-ˀa·nási
	Small saltwater animal, *kuckro* [believed to cause fits]	x̣̓áx̣̓?
	SEAWEEDS	
	Algae growing in rocks	ła·gák
	Kelp	gi·š̓
	Sea grass (hairy seaweed, a long black skeleton moss), *Nh, danih*	né (da·-né, "around seaweed")
	Broad-leafed purple seaweed, *dow*	t̓a·w, "feather"
*	Purple-black edible seaweed, *klark-ish* *Porphyra* sp., probably *perforata* J. Agardh.	ła·q̓ásk
*	Light-colored, red ribbon seaweed, *kartch*	q̓á·č̓

Note: This table was compiled by the editor from lists and notes by Emmons. Tlingit names were checked by Jeff Leer, and Alix Wennekens tentatively identified the black seaweed. Species marked with an asterisk (*) were eaten, and (with the possible exception of devilfish or octopus) were classed as "beach food." A few also had medicinal use.

TABLE 18

Edible Plants

ROOTS AND LEAVES

"Wild celery," cow parsnip [ya·na?e·t], *Heracleum lanatum* Michx. (raw stem eaten when young; dried stem kú·x̣ʷ]

"Wild rhubarb," dock or sorrel [ƛ̓a·q̓ʷáč̓], *Rumex* sp., probably *R. fenestratus* Greene (leaves boiled)

Lady fern, *qwutch* [k̓ʷáɬx̣], *Athyrium filix-femina* (L.) Roth., ssp. *cyclosorum* (Rupr.) Christens. (root eaten)

Licorice fern [ša·č], *Polypodium vulgare* L., ssp. *occidentale* (Hook.) Hult. (root eaten)

"Indian potatoes," bear root, *tset* [cé·t], *Hedysarum alpinum* L., ssp. *americanum* (Michx.) Fedtsch. (root eaten)

Unidentified plant with edible roots [cá·c] (possibly a beach pea, *Lathyrus maritimus*?); more likely Pacific silverweed, *Potentilla Egedii* Wormsk., ssp. *grandis* (Torr. and Gray) Hult.

"Wild rice," Kamchatka lily, *kuh* [kú·xʷ], *Fritillaria camschatcensis* (L.) Ker-Gawl. (white bulblets around root eaten)

"Labrador" or "Hudson Bay tea," *sick-shel-teen,* or *sick-shult* [šikšaɬdí·n], *Ledum palustre* L., ssp. *groenlandicum* (Oeder) Hult. (leaves used)

BERRIES

Red-berried elder, *yetle* [yé·ɬ], *Sambucus racemosa* L., ssp. *pubens* (Michx.) House, var. *arborescens* Gray

Strawberry, *shouk* [šúkʷ, šákʷ, šíkʷ], *Fragraria chiloensis* (L.), Duchesne, ssp. *pacifica* Staudt

Bearberry, kinnikinnick [tínx], *Arctostaphylos uva-ursi* (L.) Spreng., ssp. *minus* (Lodd.) Hult.

Sorrel berries [x̣ʷe·q], *Rumex* sp.

Soapberry, *huk klee* [xákʷɬi], *Shepherdia canadensis* (L.) Nutt.

Lagoonberry, "nagoonberry," mountain cranberry [né·gú·n], *Rubus arcticus* L., ssp. *stellatus* (Sm.) Boiv. Emend. Hult.

Salmonberry, *klaok mutsee* [ƛ̓é·qʷ wáši, "berry bush"; also wašx̣a·n ƛ̓é·gu, and č̓a?a·náx̣ ƛ̓é·qʷ], *Rubus spectabilis* Pursh

Thimbleberry, *chaok* [č̓e·x̣, č̓i·x̣], *Rubus parviflorus* Nutt., var. *grandiflorus* Farw. (This is probably the berry bush whose leaves were used for the medicine *thlukeet ta.*)

Raspberry, *klaok yuttee* [ƛ̓é·qʷ yádi, "baby berry"; sometimes called ke·ƛ gukʷ kʷaǯa·ší, "dog's earrings"], *Rubus pedatus* Sm.

Cloudberry, yellow [néx̣ʷ], *Rubus chamaemorus* L.

Currant, blue, black, gray, or highbrush, *sharh* [ša·x̣], *Ribes bracteosum* Dougl.

Currant, trailing black [kane·ɬčákʷ], *Ribes laxiflorum* Pursh

Gooseberry (currant with prickles) [x̣a·he·wú], *Ribes lacustre* (Pers.) Poir.

Cranberry, highbush, *kush whaokh* [kaxʷé·x̣], *Viburnum edule* (Michx.) Raf. (A skin lotion was made from the bark, *kan-guairth-wozee* [kaxʷé·x̣ wáši].)

Cranberry, small bog ("lowbush"), *kush ka hauk ku* [q̣e·škahá·gu], *Oxycoccus microcarpus* Turcz.

Cranberry, lowbush [dáxʷ, duxʷ], *Vaccinium vitis-idaea* L., ssp. *minus* (Lodd.) Hult.

Blueberry, in general, or smaller variety, *con-nah-ta, kon-nah-ta* [kanaɬá], *Vaccinium uliginosum* L., ssp. *alpinum* (Bigel.) Hult.

Blueberry, large blue-black, *nan-na kon-nah-tah-ee,* or *nan-na´r con-nah-ta´-ree* [na·na· kanaɬa·yí, "upriver blueberry"], *Vaccinium ovalifolium* Sm. (Also used for basketry dye.)

Blueberry used for dye, *Vaccinium membranaceum* Dougl.

Huckleberry, mountain blueberry, *see-kooch-koo* [či·káx̣k̓ʷ], *Vaccinium caespitosum* Michx.

Huckleberry, red, *kla-kat-tunk* [ƛ̓e·katánk], *Vaccinium parvifolium* Sm.

OTHER

Clasping twisted-stalk, *sick-ga-kow thlaku ka-ha-ge* [šigi· qá·wu ƛ̓é·gu, "dead people's berries"; omit kaha·gu], *Streptopus amplexifolius* (L.) DC. (Roots boiled as an intoxicant.)

Lupine, *kantak* [kantáqʷ, gantáqʷ], *Lupinus nootkatensis* Donn (Root reported as a mild intoxicant [Krause 1956:109].)

Tobacco, *gunge* [gánč], *Nicotiana quadrivalvis* Pursh, var. *multivalvis* (Lindl.) Mansf. (This native-grown tobacco was used for snuff.)*

Note: This table was compiled by the editor from manuscripts and notes by Emmons. The trailing black currant and the gooseberry were added, based on field notes (de Laguna and McClellan 1950, 1952). Jeff Leer corrected the transcriptions. Identification of the plants was made by Alix Wennekens, using Hultén (1968) as authority for the botanical nomenclature.

*This identification is according to Meilleur (1979).

TABLE 19

Colors, Paints, Dyes, and Stains

Paint, *negwat* [nı́·gwáƚ]; or *tsukl* [ćáqƚ]

Dye, stain, *kus-su´ck-ho* [kaséq̇ʷx̣u or ka-séq̇ʷa·]

Face paint, *ka-gha ou-she-na* [qa· ỵá, "someone's face," ʔawusiná·, "dampened"]

Color of, or Like in color, is rendered by the prefix ka-

Red paint [for wood or face], red ochre, or burned oxide of iron, *tlaok, thloak* [ƚ̓é·x̣ʷ]

Red dye from urine [kʷás]; also name for urine and for the urine tub of alder; red dye also made from alder and hemlock bark

Light red dye, from alder bark, *qwus kus-su´ck-ho* [kʷás kaséq̇ʷx̣u]

Red or fire color (a house name), *kan* [x̣a·n]

Deep, "fire"-red dye, *kha-gho´n kus-su´ck-ho* [gaga·n, "sun," or ka-x̣a·n, "like fire," kaséq̇ʷx̣u, "dye"]

Purple-red dye, from bog cranberry, *Oxycoccus mycrocarpus* Turcz., *kush ka hauk ku* [q̇e·škahá·gu, the name of the berry]

Reddish pink dye, from salmonberry leaves, *Rubus spectabilis* Pursh

Orange color or dye, *kush shaok,* "from the breast of the robin" [ka-šu·x̣ʷ, "like robin"]

Yellow color, *kut-thark,* "color of wild canary" [ka-ƛ̓á·ƛ̓, "like the yellow warbler"]

Yellow paint from a mineral (oxide of iron?)

Yellow-green or yellow dye from wolf moss, a tree lichen, *say-ho-nay* [ṡé·x̣ʷani], *Evernia vulpina;* now known as *Letharia vulpina* (L.) Hue.

Light brown dye, from a tree moss (unidentified)

Golden brown dye from root of dock or sorrel, *Rumex* sp.

Brown color or paint, *tsu gart* [ṡagʷá·t]; dark brown paint to protect the face, from hemlock fungus, *suk qwar ta, suk qwart* [ṡagʷá·t, the name of the paint and of the fungus]; brown paint also from a dark ochre (oxide of iron)

Blue paint or color, *gashgoo* [x̣é·šx̣ʷ, Steller's (blue) jay] or *kuh khashsk* [ka-x̣é·šx̣ʷ, "like the Steller jay"]. [Emmons gives this color as a blue-green; de Laguna as a purple-blue.]

Purple-blue dyes from the blueberries, *Vaccinium ovalifolium* Sm., and *V. membranaceum* Dougl.

Blue-green paint and dye "from azurite, an oxide of copper," *nahinta negwat* [ne·xi·nté nígʷáƚ, "blue claystone paint"]*

Green color or green paint, *tsu* [ṡu·w, "greenstone," or "jade"]; a green paint "from malachite"; a greenish-blue dye, *kut´-tsu,* [ka-ṡu·w, "like greenstone"]*

Black color, black paint, charcoal, *tooch* [ƚ̓u·č̓]; charcoal used for face paint

Black paint also from coal, *Yehlh hoot-see* [yé·ƚ xu·ʒí, "Raven's embers"]; and also from magnetite, a black oxide of iron

Black paint, or paint in general, *tsukl* [ćáqƚ]

Black dye, from black mud and iron filings [yéč̓]

Black, or discolored as in copper or iron [ye·ṡ (obsolete)]

White color, *klate* [ƛe·t, "snow"]; sometimes applied to yellow

White clay used as "whitener" [wé·na·]

*The blue-green pigment was probably an iron potassium silicate, not a form of copper. The blue-green dye (modern) was from commercial blue blankets and wolf moss. Earlier, only a yellow-green or olive green was obtained from the moss. (Judi Miller, Canadian Conservation Institute, and Cheryl Samuel, pers. comm.)

TABLE 20

Skin Dressing

1. Wet skin rolled up several days to loosen roots of hair.

    Wash salt water. Hang one day. Roll up hair side out. Skin half dry, put in bag. In old times in hole in ground where fire has been: wet a little; cover over [with] earth [and] sand for four days. Then hair shaves off.

2. [Skin] placed over rounded board, 4 to 10 inches diameter, hair side out, and hair is removed with bone scraper, *ut-har-ou kh-hun-nah* [ʔat x̣a·wú kahéna·, "its hair take-off" or beaming tool].

    Wet skin and put on stick and work with deer leg bone, split, *hilchar* [x̣̓íša·, "skinning knife"]. *Klah shar* [xʷáǯa·, "skin scraper to make soft"] used on flat board.

3. When hair removed, [skin is] washed with fish [fresh?] water.

    Dip in water and wash. Put end [of skin] on post; put hand stick through [slit in opposite end of skin], and wring out [until] dried.

4. Hung up to dry on fish frame [or drying rack, x̣a·náš̓].

    Take water salmon boiled in; put in skin one day to soften.

5. When dry, [skin is] rubbed over with grease.

    Herring grease heated and rubbed over both sides [while] skin still wet; or deer brain [used]; and pulled and rolled and softened.

6. When soft, [skin is] hung up for several days.

    Then hang up in sun or near enough to fire to keep warm. Then [when] half dry, ties (worm holes) [?], and stretch. When softened hang up in cool place seven days.

7. Again soaked in fresh water.

8. Then put in tub of urine for one day.

    Then soak in urine and work it around [?], and leave ten minutes or more. Then wring out. Then pull and stretch.

9. Then washed [in] fresh water.

10. Then put on stretching frame [fastened by cord or poles run through slit cut around edges of skin].

11. Work water out with shell [on] outside [of skin]. Side cut around edges and put on stretcher. Now on stretcher hair side out. [Stretching frame is t̓í·ša·.]

    Put on stretcher, and put on in sun [?] one day, and then one day in house. Outer skin of hair side *Ah-chart-too* [ʔat č̓á·t-wú, or č̓á·dú, "surface of skin"], which must all be scraped off for if wet becomes hard.

12. This is worked off with stone scraper [sketch of end scraper hafted at end of long handle, or of semi-lunar scraper].

    Thu-clalk [probably té ƛá·q, "stone sharp-edged"]; and work down with stone.

13. Then inside worked down same.

14. Made bag [with] *Ah-chart-too* [outer side of skin] inside, and smoked over decayed wood. If for clothing very little [smoking] but for moccasins browner.

    1 caribou skin [$]4 [In R margin of table.]
    1 moose skin 5

    Burn clam shell, animal brains, later chalk, today flour [for cleaning tanned skin].

Note: This table was drawn up by Emmons in an attempt, evidently, to combine two versions of skin dressing: that represented by the initial entries after each number, and the other by the indented portions. This last would appear to have been taken from Table 21. There is no orthodox method of skin dressing, since every woman is likely to have her own version, which differs in minor details from the methods used by others.

TABLE 21

Skin Dressing

. . . Then take dried salmon and boil it in kettle. And take out salmon and put skin in water, and leave one day (to make soft).

Salmon, herring grease is then heated, and when little warm is rubbed over both sides of skin, still wet.

Then hang up in sun or near enough to fire to just keep warm. Then when half dry, two women sit near each other, and pull hard [on skin] to stretch in all directions.

Then put more grease on and hang up in cold place, and leave four to seven days.

Then put skin in urine and work it around, and leave [it in] about ten minutes or more. Then wring skin out. The urine is to cut grease. And then pull and stretch.

Then cut [slits] around edge of skin, and put on stretch[er], and put out in sunshine and leave one day in sun, and one day in house, until dry.

Then work down with stone, having well chalked to make [??] thin and soft, and clean.

Then take off [frame], and cut off edges, and is finished.

If desired to smoke skin to make or keep [it] soft after being wet, smoke with old tree punk.

One caribou skin is valued at $4.00 at Chilkat, a moose skin is worth $5.

Note: This incomplete version, of which the first page is missing, was evidently what Emmons was trying to fit with the numbered sequence in Table 20.

TABLE 22

Plants Used in Basketry

STRAWS FOR OVERLAY TWINED EMBROIDERY

Fowl manna grass, *kha´-kar shark* [x̣̓é·ga· šá·k, "true grass"], *Penicularia nervata,* now *Glyceria striata* (Lamb.) Hitchc., var. *stricta* (Scribn.) Hult.; or *G. borealis* (Nash) Batchelder (since Hultén does not list *G. stricta* as appearing in southeast Alaska)

Blue joint grass, *Calamagrostis canadensis* (Michx.) Beauv., subsp. *Langsdorffii* (Link) Hult.

Tufted hair grass, *Deschampsia caespetosa* (L.) Beauv., subsp. *caespetosa,* var. *caespetosa*

Slender reed grass, *Cinna latifolia* (Trev.) Griseb. [šá·k, "grass"]

Alaska brome grass, *Bromus sitchensis* Trin.

Beach rye grass, *Elymus arenarius* L., ssp. *mollis* (Trin.) Hult., var. *mollis*

Maidenhair fern, *shar-ah-thlee-tee,* "on the side of the mountain," or *sha yar thleetee* [ša·ya ƛ̓idí, "mountain-side tail" ?], probably *Adiantum pedatum* L. var. *aleuticum* Rupr. [But see the native name for alpine club moss, *Lycopodium alpinum* L.]

Marsh horsetail, *Equisitum palustre* L. (sometimes used)

STAINS OR DYES

Alder, *Alnus oregona* Nutt., and hemlock, *Tsuga heterophylla* (Raf.) Sarg. The bark is boiled in urine for red.

Salmonberry, *Rubus spectabilis* Pursh. The leaves for pink.

Purple-blue from blueberries and huckleberries, *Vaccinium ovalifolium* Sm., and *V. membraceum* Dougl.; and bog cranberries, *Oxycoccus microcarpus* Turcz.

Yellow tree lichen, *say-ho-nay* [ś̓é·x̣ʷani], wolf moss, *Letharia vulpina* (L.) Hue. (Imported from the interior, especially for Chilkat blankets.)

Note: Identifications by Alix Wennekens. Hultén (1968) is the authority for the botanical nomenclature.

TABLE 23

Tlingit Personal Names

An-na hootz, "Brown bear country," a *Ka-gwan-tan* chief's name [ʔanaxú·c, "?- brown bear"], chief of Wolf 1 at Sitka.

Goutch sha-ee, "Wolf's head," a *Yun-ya-de* name [gu·č ša·yí, "wolf head," of the Yanye·dí, Wolf 16]

Ku-tcheeshe, "Bear's den easy to get at or enter," a *Duck-cla-way-di* name [possibly qučí·š, of Wolf 27, Daqławe·dí]

Cou da na ha, "Brown bear disappearing in den," a *Ka-gwan-tan* chief's name [qúdenaha·, "to move unseen," Wolf 1]

Yehlh gou ou, "Raven's slave," a chief of the Con-nuh-ta-di of Klukwan; upon building the new Whale House, "Raven's Slave" assumed the name *Tinneh tark,* "Bites the Copper," the copper shield, an emblem of wealth. [Raven's slave was yé·ł gu·xú, his clan Raven 3; his new name was tiná· tá·x̌, assumed in 1901 (see Emmons 1916a:33).]

Kleeny, "Starved himself in a good cause," referring to an individual occurrence in the *Con-nuh ta di* family [łé·ni, of the Raven 3, Ga·naxte·dí]

Goush di teen, "Dorsal fin of the killerwhale seen," a *Duck cla way di* name, the Killerwhale being their principal crest [Gu·š-du-tí·n, "visible dorsal fin," Wolf 27, Daqławe·dí]

Eh klas, "Moose under the earth," a *Duck cla way di* name [?; he was the last Chilkat shaman, Wolf 27]

Kootch-e-kow-nuh, "Beyond control," a Con-nuh-ta-di name [possibly qa·ǯika·náx̣; James Hatch (or Hotch) of Chilkat, Raven 3]

Yuh dah klaow, "Sand over or on the face," referring to a frog burying itself in the sand, a *Kik-sa-di* name, the Frog being the principal crest of the family. [ya-da-łé·w, "face-around sand," Raven 10, Kiksʔádi]

Note: Most, if not all, of these names are titles to be assumed at potlatches, not names given at birth or in early childhood. This table was compiled by Emmons.

TABLE 24

Funeral Ceremonies at Sikta (I), according to Rudolph

First Night [after death?]

Suck ik ko-eek, "smoke invite" [še·q-yís quʔí·x̌, "for-smoke invitation"]. Other family ["opposites"] come in night. Guests smoke. Take charge. Family of dead fast during day.

Second Night

Kok woo see de shee, "spirits passing on the trail, song" [qa·x̣us-ʔi·tí ši, "human footprints song"]. The spirit is passing on the trail [to land of the dead]. Guests give [are given?] tobacco and the deceased's family sing.

Third Night

Ut-huh yees ko-eek, "eat—invite" [ʔat x̣a-yís quʔí·x̌, "to eat invitation"]. Little food. Guests put food in fire for dead.

Kou nah ka a dee ko-eek, "feed the dead" [possibly qa·na·wú, "dead person," x̣^(w)é·-de, "to mouth," quʔí·x̌, "invitation"].

Cremation [on fourth day after death; for a great chief on sixth day]. Men of "opposite" clan attend to cremation; men of deceased's clan, in old clothes, beat time and sing "heavy" songs; women of "opposite" clan, with saplings, dance "with the knees," or *co-ta-ceh* [?].

Night after Cremation

Gou whit tan, "drum carried" [ga·w wuduwata·n, "drum has been taken up"]. "First dance after cremation." [This would appear to be the hosts calling the "opposites" to the feast.]

Wo tu nuk, "stand up" [wudana·q, "standing" plural], danced by the women of the "opposite" clan, standing in line, and swaying.

[Presumably this occasion is a "Smoke Feast," although Rudolph's lists are confusing.] Or, the dance is *woo-de-han,* "risen" [wudaha·n, "standing" singular].

Second Day[a] *after Cremation*

Wo-da-not, "stand up" [wudana·q, "standing" plural; see above]. Second dance, second day. Afternoon, by women of "opposite" clan.

Wo da hun, "rising" [wudaha·n, "standing" singular]. When take off black paint [from faces of mourning clanswomen of the deceased]. The dance is by women.

Ya da klitch [yá-da· łé·x̣ʷ, "face-around red-paint"], paint "face red." Women of deceased's family dance; sway from side to side.

Second Night[b] *after Cremation*

Kon nah ku a dee ko-eek, "feed the dead" [qa· na·wú x̣é·-de quʔí·x̌, "dead person's mouth-to invitation"]. The family of the deceased feed the opposite clan, and put food in the fire.

Note: This table was compiled by Emmons, evidently from an interview with Rudolph, perhaps after witnessing a particular potlatch. Rudolph was a native artist of Sitka, a Kisʔádi Raven 10, possibly the man called *Kawootk* (or Qawu·tk̓).

[a] Are these ceremonies of the "second day" really part of the ritual of cremation and therefore held on the same day? Or is there variation in the timing?

[b] This feast, "to feed the dead," corresponds with the text. Rudolph gave a second list of "Funeral Ceremonies at Sitka," but this seemed to correspond with those that would be given after a house had been built or repaired, a gravehouse built or totem pole erected as a repository for the ashes of the dead, or when a new gravehouse was built to which the contents of the old were moved, for all these acts were in honor of the dead. See the next chapter.

TABLE 25

List of Tlingit Dances

FUN DANCES

These are theatrical dances, with appropriate costumes; the words are in the language of the people from whom the song and dance were copied.

Gu-na-nah klah-ji, "Stick dance" [G̣unana· ł̓e·x̣í, "Athabaskan dance"]

Da-kee-nar klah-ji, "Haida dance" [De·kina· ł̓e·x̣í]

Tsuts-hun klah-ji, "Tsimshian dance" [C̓u·cxán ł̓e·x̣í]

Tom-yolt or *Tow-yote klah-ji,* "Flathead dance, Vancouver Island" [T̓a·wyá·ƛ̓ ł̓e·x̣í]

Kee-yak k̇wan klah-ji, "Newchuk [Nuchek, a former town in Prince William Sound] or Aleut dance [Chugach Eskimo]" [Giyaqʷ qʷá·n ł̓e·x̣í]

To-bee-at klah-ji, "Bella Bella dance" [?]

Eek-ka kwan, "Copper River dance" [ʔIqka· qʷá·n, "Copper diggers' dance," i.e., Atna]

Kal-ta-kee kwan klah-ji, "Naked dance" [Kałda·gi (?) qʷá·n ł̓e·x̣í, Translation (?) Kałda·gákʷ is "naked," but who are the naked qʷa·n?]

A-yon klah-ji, "Moon dance, Yakutat" [ʔAyá·n ł̓e·x̣í, "Down-river" Athabaskan dance, from Athabaskan word meaning "others," probably the Northern Tutchone]

Yeek-no-tee, "imitations of a doctor's spirit, Yakutat" [yé·k ʔuti·]. "A fun dance of one or two men for a visiting chief." [These included yé·k ša·ti, or Secret Society shows.]

Kat-so-war klah-ji, "Ptarmigan dance" [x̣e·sawá· ł̓e·x̣í]

Berry Dance, Salmon Dance, Herring Dance. [No Tlingit names were recorded.]

PEACE DANCES

Ko-wa-thurlh-kun, or *Koo-wa-la-kank,* "Deer dance, Jump deer dance, Peace dance" [quwałakánx̣, "Peace Dance" (refers to the "tassels" of wooden shavings carried by the dancers; see de Laguna 1972:601)]

Woosh yulth hun, "Yakutat peace dance" [wu·š yałkán (?), "causing each other to stand"]

POTLATCH DANCES

Ah ketch, "putting it together with wings." Held when the house is nearly finished, or is finished, involves four songs and four swaying dances [compare yawduwakíč, "they had a house-warming ceremony"].

Hit u is kake, "feeding it (the house)," first day of potlatch [hít yu· ʔisx̣é·k (?), "house causing-it-to-eat," a ceremony, rather than a dance]

Ut thlaok, "moving in different ways," dance by women on second night in the new house [? ?]

Tyeek-jach klah-ji, "Basin dance" [? ?]

Ut ka setlk te, "Tear up," Women of host clan dance [ʔat kašéł̓ti, "torn scraps," referring to tearing calico or blankets to distribute to guests]

Kark tla eekh at toolth, ? Feast dance in new house [? ?]

Nalth tah ua aht, "entrance to house" [ne·łdé ha·ʔa·t, "they are entering the house one by one," presumably referring to the guests' "doorway" song and dance]

Ya-ko klah-ji, "Canoe dance" [ya·kʷ ł̓e·x̣í]

Note: This list was prepared by Emmons, possibly from information furnished by Rudolph.

TABLE 26

Funeral Ceremonies at Sitka (II), according to Rudolph

A Week, a Month, or Months after Cremation

Gou whet ton [ga·w wuduwata·n, "drum has been taken up," meaning that the clan of the deceased are inviting their "opposites"]. Give property to those of opposite clans who assisted at ceremonies [of] cremation. Head men of deceased's family dressed in old clothes.

First Night

Suck ik ko eek, "smoke invite" [ṡe·q-yís quˀí·ẋ]. Head of family talks, guests smoke.

Second Night

Kowor sedih she, "spirit passing on trail to spirit land song," [qa· x̣us-ˀi·tí ši, "human footprint song"].

Third Night

Ut-huh-yees ko-eek, "eat invite" [ˀat x̣a-yís quˀí·ẋ, "something for the mouth invitation"].

Fourth Night

Konah hu a dee koo eek, "feed the dead" [probably qa· na·wu´ x̣é·-de quˀí·ẋ, "human dead to-mouth invitation"].

Note: This table was prepared by Emmons, based on information from Rudolph, perhaps after witnessing the ceremonies.

Although the actual distribution of property is not indicated, we assume it to have taken place on the fourth day (possibly the third). These ceremonies appear to have been those held at the dedication of a house, raising a totem pole, or making or repairing a gravehouse. These structures were memorials to the dead.

TABLE 27

Medicines, "Medicines"

Medicine, *nak* [ná·kʷ]

"Medicine" (magical amulet) [kaya·ní, "leaves"], (usually roots)

"Body medicine" (rubbing amulets), *don nak* [da· ná·kʷ]

Rotten spruce; inner bark of spruce, yellow cedar and "pine"; spruce gum, hemlock gum; spruce needles

Starfish, *suckh* [šáx]

Sea anemone, "jellyfish," *teh-yah-tah-yea* [té yata·yí, "rock face fat"]

Seaweed, *klark ish* [ła·q̇ásk], *Porphyra perforata* J. Agardh.

A lichen, *Peltigera aphthosa* (L.) Willd.

Maidenhair fern, *shar-ah-thlee-tee* [probably ša· yałí·ti, "mountain side vine," less likely ša·yə ƛ̓idí, "mountain-side tail"], *Adiantum pedatum* L., var. *aleuticum* Rupr.

A wood fern, *Dryopteris dilatata* (Hoffm.) Gray, ssp. *americana* (Fisch.) Hult.; leaves used

A shield fern, *Gymnocarpium dryopteris* (L.) Newm.; leaf bud used

"Labrador" or "Hudson Bay tea," *sick-shel-teen,* or *sick shult,* [šikšałdí·n], *Ledum palustre* L. ssp. *groenlandicum* (Oeder) Hult.; leaves used

A berry bush, *thlu kut ta* [?], perhaps red huckleberry, *Vaccinium parvifolium* Sm.; leaves used

Small mountain evergreen shrub, *thluk kut,* probably *Loiseleuria procumbens* (L.) Desv.; less likely, *Rhododendron lapponicum* (L.) Wahlb.; leaves used

Lipidodendron [*sic*] (Unidentifiable)

Highbush cranberry, *kan-guairth wozee* [kaxʷé·x̣, "cranberry," *wáši,* "bush"], *Viburnum edule* (Michx.) Raf.; bark used

Devil's club, *sauthkt* [šáxt], *Echinopanax horridum* (Sm.) Decne. & Planch.; syn. *Oplopanax horridum* (Smith) Miq.; bark and thorny stem used

Skunk cabbage [x̣á·ł. Emmons erroneously gives it the native name for the devil's club, *sauthkt*], *Lysichiton americanum* Hult. & St. John (formerly *Lysichitum kamtschatkense*); root used

False Solomon's seal, *Smilacina racemosa* (L.) Desf.; root used

American white helebore, "Skookum root," *scht* [šíkš], *Veratrum viride* Ait., ssp. *Eschscholtzii* (Gray) Löve & Löve

"A strong-smelling small 'fern,'" *ka-kuk-tleaty nak* [kagak-łi·dí na·kʷ, "rat's tail medicine"], probably the yarrow, *Achillea borealis* Bong.; probably stem and leaves used

Hairy rock cress, *Arabis hirsuta* (L.) Scop., ssp. *pycnocarpa* (M. Hopkins) Hult.; leaves used

"Land otter medicine," *kousta nak* [kú·šda· ná·kʷ], from a gentian, probably *Gentiana douglasiana* Bong.

Wild heliotrope, *ginnee nak* [łičani ná·kʷ, "smelly medicine"], probably *Valeriana sitchensis* Bong.; root used

Mountain gentian, probably *Gentiana platypetala* Griseb.

Yellow violet, probably "syphilis medicine" [šá·x̣ xasti ná·kʷ ?], *Viola glabella* Nutt.

Western sweet cicely, "wild parsnip," *Osmorrhiza chilensis* Hook. & Arn.; syn. *O. brevipes*

Large-leaved avens [ʔa·n-ka-ná·gu, "town-on medicine"], *Geum macrophyllum* Willd., ssp. *macrophyllum*; leaves used. (The same Tlingit name was given to the composite, *Arnica cordifolia* Hook., also used as a medicine.)

Swamp plant, the leaves of which were used for fever, *koo-see yun-nee nak* [x̣usi, "foot" -?- ná·kʷ]. Unidentified

"No strength inside medicine," used in bear hunting, *khart tuk tchene,* [ł-qa·tu·-łaci·n, or łqa·-tu·łči·n], unidentified; root used

A thick-leaved plant, "bone mending medicine" [šaq-x̣aš ná·kʷ]; possibly *Sedum rosea* (L.) Scop., ssp. *integrifolium* (Raf.) Hult.

Note: All plant identifications were made by Alix Wennekens. Hultén (1968) is the authority referred to for botanical nomenclature.

TABLE 28

The Shaman's Outfit [yé·k da·ˀádi]

Mask without eye holes, *Wake kut dar took* [waq kadadú·kʷ, "eyes solid"]

Mask with eye holes, *Klah-kate, klo-ket* [ƛ̓ax̣ket from ƛ̓e·x̣, "dance," ke·t, "cover"]

Small face mask in front of headdress of eagle feathers and swan's down, *Thlu-gu* [ƛu·gu? The word applies to the entire headdress?]

Bear's ears headdress, *Con-goush* [xú·c gangú·š or gangú·š]

Rectangular spruce root hat or bonnet, with zigzag decoration, *Sha-dar-yar-ar-kee* [šada·, "around-the-head," yaˀá·gi, "work"]

Shaman's headdress of ermine tails, feathers, etc., worn on top of hair, *Yake tcheeni* [yé·k čí·ni]

Crown of claws or of mountain goat horns, *Ut-har-gu* [ˀat x̣a·gú, "its claws"]

* Shaman's neck charm (twigs and tongue, etc.), *Sutch, shuche* [šú·č?]

Shaman's necklace of bone, *Sark sati* [ṡa·q se·dí, "bone necklace," or ˀíx̣ṫda·ˀit se·dí, "shaman's necklace"]

Shaman's bone nosepin, *Ka thlu saok* [qa· łu ṡa·q?, man's nose bone]

Shaman's bone hairpin, *Thou-too saok* [łutu ṡa·q, nose-in bone]

Shaman's bone armlet, *Chick-ar-ut* [ǯikaˀát]

Shaman's bracelet of ermine skins, *Chick-ut-duke* [ǯikadú·x̣ʷ, "knotted on arm/hand"]

Shaman's skin apron or waist robe, *Kate, ku dah kate, ka-date* [ke·t or k̇ide·t, "apron worn over buttocks"; Possibly "lap cover," guš-ke·t]

Shaman's skin back blanket, shoulder blanket, shoulder robe, *At-shick kuku, Ah-shick kuk-ku, Al-shich kuh-ku* [?] [Emmons translates this word as "rattles" on another list, perhaps because it had a rattling fringe.]

Shaman's covering of skin for breast and back (like a poncho), *Tark* [te·q]

Shaman's cedar-bark neck girdle, *Cos-sask* [?]

Scallop shell strung for rattle, *Whandr* [x̣ʷe·na, "scallop"]

* Rattle of bird bills and animal hoofs, *Thlar-kate see-dee* [?] [Ceremonial rattle, ǯi-ka-x̣áda·]

Shaman's rattle of hollow wood, shaped like crane or oyster catcher, *Shou-show, Sha-shough* [še·šú·x̣ʷ, "rattle" applied to any rattle]

* Drum, *Gouh* [ga·w]

* Tapping sticks [x̣í·č̓a]

* Carved whistle, *Yake-see* [yé·k sé; "spirit's voice"]

Shaman's wand or carving carried in his hand, *Keen, kutze* [probably "club" x̣úṡ. Some were in the form of a sharp pick, kínde ké·łu.]

* Shaman's war knife or dagger, *Chuck-har-nut* [ǯix̣anˀát, "thing near the hand," or gʷáła·]

Shaman's basketry water cup (for salt water), *Athle-yet* [ˀé·ł ye·t]

* Shaman's fine woven bag, *Thleete* (named for a flat sea worm) [ƛ̓í·ṫ is a fine basket; ƛ̓ukʷx̣ʷ is a "worm"]

Wooden pillow, *Shegate* [ša ye·t]

* Shaman's urine box, *Kwus* [k̇ʷás, "urine"]

Note: This list was compiled by Emmons, to which the editor has added items marked with an asterisk (*). Emmons wrote: "The following articles included all of the articles of dress and implements of practice I ever saw in numerous outfits and in grave boxes, although no one shaman possessed all of them," yet he overlooked these.

TABLE 29

Shaman's Masks Found in an Old Gravehouse (on the Alsek River?)

1. *Keel-char ku-yage,* "Cold wind comes down Alsek River [Spirit]" [ƙiƚǯá· qu-yé·gi]
2. *Shon ku-yagi,* "Old man" [ša·n qu-yé·gi, "old-man spirit-of"]
3. *Keeh-kah kah ku-yage,* "Spirit of an angry man" [x̌iga· qá· qu-yé·gi, "spirit of a warrior"]
4. *Kush-tar kah ko see-tee u kah,* "Spirit of a drowned man only half turned into land otter" [kúšda· qá·x̣ wusiti·yi qá, "land-otter like became man"]
5. *Tu-wilt-tu-kah (ku-yage),* "Spirit of peacemaker between angry families" that can cure sick [ʔadawú·ƛ tu-qá·]
6. *Gu cheetle ku-yage,* "Spirit of a young woman who lives on hump [Ɋaƚčí·nuwu] island in Dry Bay" [?]
7. *Har-gee-shon-e qwoir yake,* "Spirit of dead who lived underground" [ha·yi· ša·náƙu yé·k, or ha·yi· ša·ní qu-yé·k]
8. *At-too-wolt shon-uk-ku,* "Spirit of old warrior" [ʔadawú·ƛ ša·náƙu]
9. *Gin-tark ku-yage,* "Spirit that comes to shaman and rests in palm of hand" [ǯin-ta·k qu-yé·gi]
10. *Tuck-ah-see,* "Mythical water spirit like, but much larger than, devilfish. Has doctor's spirit" [?]

Note: This list was made by Emmons.

TABLE 30

Eight Masks Ascribed to a Klukwan Shaman

1. *Ickt ku-yage,* "Spirit of a shaman" [ʔíx̣ṭ qu-yé·gi]
2. *Gin-tark ku-yage,* "Spirit that comes to a shaman and rests in palm of hand" [ǯinta·k qu-yé·gi]
3. *Har-gee shon-o-qwoir ku yake,* "Spirit of the dead who live underground" [ha·yi· ša·náƙu quyé·k]
4. *Gu cheetle ku-yage,* "Spirit of a young woman who lives on small hump island in Dry Bay" [? The island, called "Bear Island" in English, is Ɋaƚčí·nuwu, "clam fort?"]
5. *Sha-wut ku-yage,* "Woman's spirit" [ša·wát qu-yé·gi]
6. *Klhu-nas ku-yage,* "Kingfisher's spirit" [ƛax̣ane·ṡ qu-yé·gi]
7. *Waok ku-yage,* "Sculpin's spirit" [wé·x̣ qu-yé·gi]
8. *Nook ku-yage,* "Devilfish spirit" [ná·qʷ qu yé·gi]

Note: This list was made by Emmons.

TABLE 31

Outfit[a] of the Shaman-Chief, Cowee or Kowee,[b] Raven 15, Ł̇i·ne·dí, of the Auk Tribe

E-2683[c] Wooden mask, *Ka-nah-nah tchitch ge yake* [possibly qa-na·ná· či·č qu-yé·k, ?-Up-river Porpoise Spirit ?], "a spirit of which I could learn nothing." The face is encircled by tentacles of the devilfish.

E-2684 Wooden mask, representing the spirit "Sun Dog," *Ka-ghon katle* [gaga·n ke·ƛ̣i, "dog of the sun"].

E-2685 Wooden mask representing a spirit living on a small island in the lake, *Ah-tah-guttee* [perhaps ʔá·-tá·k ʔádi, "on-lake-bottom being"?]

E-2686 Wooden mask representing the spirit of the Land Otter Man living in the woods along the rocky shores, *Kush-tar-kar* [kú·šda· qá·]. Lips and nostrils of copper; black bear fur on head.

E-2687 Wooden mask representing spirit of a porpoise, *Cheetch ko yake* [či·č qu-yé·k].

E-2688 Wooden mask representing the spirit of the Trout Canoe, *York quart* [ya·kʷ x̣á·ṫ, "canoe trout"]. This mask was held before the face as with all others. Lips, eyes, and nostrils of brass.

E-2689 Wooden mask representing the spirit living in the stars, *Kut-hun-ah-har ko-yake* [qutx̣ ʔaỵanahá· qu-yé·k, "star spirit"]

E-2690 Wooden mask representing the Deer spirit, *Kanah-kan ko yake* [quwaka·n or guwaka·n qu-yé·k, "deer or peace hostage spirit"]. Tongue of copper.

These eight masks represent the eight spirits possessed by this individual doctor and personated by him in his practice about the sick.

E-2691 Waist robe of caribou skin, ornamented with dew hoof of deer and bills of the crested puffin. Worn about the loins of the doctor in his practice.

E-2692 Shoulder or neck robe of moose skin, worn over the chest and back, painted to represent the whale.

E-2693 Crown of plain horns of the mountain goat, on caribou skin band, worn in practice.

E-2694 Bone bead which has been attached to dancing robe.

E-2695 Wooden ornament for a headdress, representing a killerwhale fin above and a bear's head below, ornamented with human hair. Worn on general [ordinary] dance occasions.

E-2696 Wooden carving representing a salmon, on which is carved a crab. This piece antedates the other material. At some early time this was sewed or pegged to a house post or a canoe; later it was carried in the hand of the Doctor (whose totem is the [dog] salmon), as an ornament or wand.

E-2697 Plain bone bracelet, worn in practice.

E-2698 Bone bracelet, ornamented in middle with cross lines; worn in practice.

E-2699 Stone carving of an eagle, worn as a charm suspended from the neck and hanging over the chest.

E-2700 Ivory carving representing the land otter, worn as a charm at all times.

E-2701 Wooden club, rudely carved to represent a [dog?] salmon, totem of the Doctor's clan, with a human head in its mouth. Carried by the Doctor in practice. [The field catalogue carries a pencil sketch labeled "sculpin with large eyes."]

E-2702, A & B Pair of bone earrings representing salmon.

E-2703 Ivory nose ring, worn through septum of nose.

[On the field notes:] "I think another box lost. Auk Drs outfit" waist robe, *congoush* [gangú·š], necklace of bone pendants, crown of brown bear's claws, head ring of ermine skins and red flicker feathers, hat [sketch indicates cylinders on top], hat of basket work, wolf tail, two bundles of braided human hair. "I think incomplete."

[a] This list is taken from the field catalogue made by Emmons and also from the catalogue in AMNH. Since the typist could not read Emmons's writing, the latter contains errors, which have been corrected here as far as possible. The heading in the catalogue for this list reads: "The set of Doctor's implements was originally the property of a chief Doctor of the *Tlee na dee* [Ł̇i·ne·dí, Raven 15] family of the Auk qwan, claiming originally the country about Berners Bay. This Doctor was the chief-hereditary, and also the Doctor; his name was 'Kow-ee.' He died between forty and fifty years since [ca. 1840?], but his implements of practice may go back several generations. The outfit has always been kept hidden in an old gravehouse in Berners Bay."

[b] The same name was born by the chief and shaman of the Auk, who was living at *Sinta-ka-heenee* [ʒánti k̇i-hí·ni], "Flounder base-river" at the mouth of Gold Creek, Juneau, in 1886 (Emmons 1911c:296).

[c] These are the AMNH catalogue numbers for that part of the second Emmons collection, purchased in 1893.

TABLE 32

Items, Some Shamanistic, Purchased by Emmons at Hoonah, 1888

87 pieces	$ 91.05
1 whale bone handle knife }	
2 salmon barbs }	6.50
1 bone berry smasher }	
1 iron salmon barb	
1 stone mouth wiper red cedar bark	.25
1 large wooden bowl	.50
1 small tobacco bowl ivory	.50
4 halibut hooks	.50
3 shell knives	.20
1 small plain powder charger	.10
1 very handsome ivory handle knife	15.00
1 finest Drs mask*	30.00
1 Drs fighting knife *bear* (?)	7.00
8 feast pipes	26.00
1 labret	.25
2 stone charms and bead band	1.00
117) 179 (1.53	178.85**
3 pieces Drs bag	2.00
7 pieces Drs *stalfs* (?)	8.00
1 stone charm	.25
	189.00
For house Hoonah	5.00
baskets	17
	211.
For canoe	32.
	243

Note: This list by Emmons, with amounts paid, is in a notebook between notes on the shaman's burial and those on the smoking feast afterward. Note the inaccuracies in his accounts.

*From this point on, the entries are in hasty writing.

**Emmons entered $179.85; the correct total is given here.

TABLE 33

Decorated Gambling Sticks

Names of Painted Lines		Names of Burned Designs
1. Shag (*youk*, yu·qʷ, cormorant)	N*	. . . .
2. Surf duck (*karkh*, gá·xʷ)	N	. . . .
3. Red rockfish (*thlaok*, ƚé·q̇ʷ, red snapper)	N	. . . .
4. (same as above)	N	. . . .
5. (same as above)	S*	. . . .
6. Hat with rings (*shut dar ku*, šada· kú·x̣)	S	. . . .
7. Crow (*tschu qwelth*, ċaxʷe·ƚ)	S	. . . .
8. Deer (*kaw-r-kon*, quwaka·n)		. . . .
9. Crane (*dulth*, dú·ƚ)		. . . .
10. Sea lion stomach (*tan you-wú*, ta·n yu·wú)		. . . .
11. Fire (red) shirt (*khon ku-tuss*, x̣a·n gu·dáṡ)		. . . .
12. Rattle (*chuck-r-hút-tar*, ǯi-ka-x̣áda·)		. . . .
13. Sea lion stomach [see 10]		. . . .
14. Robin (*shouk*, šu·x̣)	N	. . . .
15. Sea lion stomach [see 10]		. . . .
16. Feather (*t-r-m*, ṫa·w)		. . . .
17. Sandhill crane [see 9]		. . . .
18. Hawk feather (*ke-tchuke tar-wu*, kiǯu·k ṫa·wú)		. . . .
19. Fire (*ghon*, x̣a·n)		. . . .
20. Robin [see 14]		. . . .
21. Fire flame (*yeck klah*, yíqλa·, "spark carried up by draft from fire")		Hawk (*ketchuke*, kiǯu·k)
22. Sea gull (*take-lar-ta*, ké·λadi, or ku·ƛ̇é·ṫa·)		Surf duck (*khauk*, gá·xʷ)
23. Blue huckleberry (*con nar tah*, kanaṫá, blueberry)		. . . .
24. Gull (*tate-lar-ta*, ké·λadi)	N	. . . .
25. Gull (see above)		Hair seal (*tsar*, ca·)
26. Arrow barb (*gush*, gúƛ̣?)		Spiral shellfish (*klukkk*, -?-)
27. Gull [see 24]	N	Sea lion, head (1), hind flipper (2)
28. Gull [see 24]		Precipitous rock (*kihtlh*, gíƚ̣)†
29. Blue huckleberry [see 23]		Wolf (*goutch*, gu̇·č)
30. Fire (red) shirt [see 11]		. . . .
31. Mosquito (*tar-kae*, tá·x̣a·)		Land otter (*coushtar*, kú·šda·)
32. Raven's nose (*Yehlh thlu-u*, yé·ƚ ƚu·wú)		Squirrel (*khurl-sark*, kaƚċá·k)
33. Albatross (*kitche ótt*, -?-)		Crab (*s-a-mm*, ṡá·w)
34. Hawk (*ketchuke*, kiǯu·k)		Raven (*yehlh*, yé·ƚ)†
35. Osprey (*hahtle*, xe·ƛ, thunder)		Leech (*nalet*, -?-)
36. Blue mussel shell (*ghark*, ya·k)		Bear (*hootz*, xú·c)
37. Bear skin (*hootz tu-gu*, xú·c du·gú)		. . . .
38. Gull [see 24]		Bear (see above)
39. Albatross (*ketch-ee-ott*, -?-)		Eagle (*chark*, čá·k̇)
40. Fire drill (*tuhl thlee*, tu·ƚí)		Ground shark (*toose*, tú·ṡ)
41. Barnacle (*souke*, šu·k)		Eel (*thlute*, ƚú·ṫ)†
42. Barnacle [see above]		Sea lion head (*tan shaw-ee*, ta·n ša·yí)†
43. Salmonberry (*klaok*, ƛé·qʷ)		Skate (*cheet-gar*, či·tgá·)
44. Hawk [see 34]		Sea gull [see 24 left]
45. Hawk [see 34]		Gullemot (*cheete*, či·t, murrelet)†
46. Barnacle [see 41]		Snail (*tark*, tá·x̣, slug)
47. Gull [see 24]		Sea lion (*tan*, ta·n)
48. Standing dead tree after forest fire (*khun-ghun-tee*, qu-gánṫi?)		Butterfly (*kla-thlu*, ƛe·ƚú)†
49. Hawk [see 34]		Young raven (*yehlh yuttee*, yé·ƚ yádi)
50. Food tray (*kar-kar-la*, q̇a·kané·)		Crab (*s-o-m*, ṡá·w)†

TABLE 33 (Continued)

Decorated Gambling Sticks

Names of Painted Lines	Names of Burned Designs
51. Sand (*klaum*, ł̓é·w)	Butterfly [see 48 above]
52. Albatross [see 39]	. . . .
53. Earring (*koqwarjork*, gukʷ-ka-ǯa·š)	. . . .
54. Hawk [see 34]	Sea lion [see 47 above]
55. Hawk [see 34]	Mosquito eating a baby [see 31 left]
56. Earring [see 53]	Porpoise (*tcheetch*, čí·č)
57. Gull [see 24]	Hair seal [see 25 above]
58. Skin drying frame (*teesh*, t̓í·š)	Snail [see 46 above]
59. Hawk [see 34]	Tlingit inside whale
60. Starfish (*tar yish*, tayí·š?)	Devilfish (*nok*, ná·qʷ)
61. Hawk [see 34]	Mosquito [see 31]
62. Large devilfish (*tuck-kus-sar*, -?-)	The platforms in a chief's house (*woosh kee nar gars yar*, -?-)
63. Elderberries (*yatle*, yé·ł̓)	. . . .
64. Barnacle [see 41]	Horned owl (*cesk*, císk̓ʷ)
65. Mallard (*kinde tchu net*, kinde-ču·ne·t, "upward arrow")	. . . .
66. Drying frame [see 58]	Eagle sitting up
67. Fire [see 19]	Wolf (*goutch*, gu·č)
68. Robin [see 14]	. . . .

Note: A fine set of 68 gambling sticks, of Haida origin, collected by G. T. Emmons at Wrangell, Alaska. The designs, consisting of painted encircling lines and of burned-on figures, were identified by Jim or Killisnoo Jake, at Killisnoo, Alaska, about 1900. Figs. 158 to 165 are from pencil sketches by Emmons (AMNH, 16/9383), and the numbers on the legends refer to this list. "This is as far as I know the only set of ornamented gambling sticks from the Northwest Coast of America identified both as to designs of figures, and names of encircling lines in red and black" (signed G. T. Emmons). The sketches are natural size. Colors are red (r), black (b).

*N stands for *nok* or *naq* [ná·qʷ], "devilfish or bait," here used as the trump stick; S stands for *scheest* [ší·št?], "painted." There was supposed to be one "devilfish" or trump stick for every three painted sticks. According to Emmons's notes, the "devilfish" sticks in this set were numbers 1, 2, 3, 4, 14, 24, and 27; the "painted" sticks were numbers 5, 6, 7, 10, 13, 8, 12, 20, ?, 11, 15, ?, 17, but are not all so designated on the list.

† The names written by Emmons on his sketches do not correspond exactly to the list given above. Thus, no. 28 is clearly a sea otter, no. 34 a thunderbird, no. 41 a butterfly, no. 42 a whale, no. 45 a sea otter, no. 48 a small owl, and no. 50 a butterfly.

TABLE 34

Names of the Yakutat Checkers

1. *Yehlh hittee,* "Raven's House" [yé·ł hídi]
2. *Sheh-kwhl-kusht,* "Crossing X" [šakałq̓íšt̓, "2-point buck"]
3. *Ut-khart-ee,* "The root of a tree or bush" [ʔat x̣a·dí]
4. *Woush-ka-nast ut-lut,* "One on top of another" [?]
5. *Yough ku-wu,* "Whale tail" [yá·ỵ ku·wú, "baleen-whale, its tail (of fish)]
6. *Kart-ah-ka-dee ya-kla-kee,* "Dead house, mouldy, or a moth" [qa· da·ke·dí, "person's casket" or "gravehouse"; ỵa-ƛa·x̣í, "face-mould,"—a moth or butterfly]
7. *Gulth gha-yee,* "Clam bay" [gáł̓ geỵí]
8. *Guh-kut-tou-nut,* "Tying on top," or "at the top" [?]
9. *Ut-hah,* "Paddle" (for canoes) [ʔax̣á·]
10. *Yuht-uh-thlee-ut,* "A heavy thing," hence a "weight" [ỵadał̓i ʔát, "heavy thing"]
11. *Shaht-dar-kuke,* "Hat with cylinders" [šadakúx̣̓]
12. *Ut-wu-nah sucks-shu-ton,* "The cover for the smokehole" [ʔat yana·, "something covering"; s̓aq-šután, "smoke-is-located"]
13. *K̇ah thlas sha-dee,* "The muscles on either side of the back" [qa· łaša·dí, "a person's holders, or graspers"]
14. *Garst,* "House post" [gá·s̓]
15. *Kla-kah kah,* "Bad man" [ł ʔa·k̓e qa·, "not good man," ungrammatical]
16. *Shick-kheen tu tark,* "A scalp" [šaki·-datá·k̓, "a bird with a brown spot on head"]
17. *Shick-ee suk-r,* "Top or head, dish" [šakí· s̓íx̓]
18. *Shut-dar sarlkh,* "Headdress, small skate" [šada·, "head-around"; s̓á·x̣̓, "gray cod"]
19. *Sarh sar-tee,* "Hat keeper" [s̓á·xʷ s̓a·tí, "hat master-of"]
20. *Shick-ee ahk,* "Head, small lake" [šakí· ʔá·k̓ʷ, "mountain-top little lake"?]
21. *Shick-ee Sukh,* "Head, starfish" [šakí·, "head," s̓u·k ?, "barnacle"?]
22. *Shick-ee kunsee,* "Head, crown" [šakí· -?-]
23. *Shick-ee qwart you-wu,* "Head or top, trout, stomach-of" [šakí· x̣ʷá·t̓ yu·wú, "head, Dolly Varden's stomach"]
24. *Shut-dar sar-tee,* "Hat keeper" [šada· s̓a·tí, "Headdress master-of"]
25. *Shick-ee hit sartee,* "Head, house keeper" [šakí· hít s̓a·tí, "head, house master-of," or "house chief"]

Note: This list was made by Emmons.

TABLE 35

Calendars of the Hutsnuwu and Stikine

	Hutsnuwu	Stikine
July	*At-ka-ta disi,* "moon of prosperity" [ʔat ka-ta·, "animals in prime condition or fat"]	*At-ka-ta disi,* "fattening moon" *At-ye-na-tlath disi* [ʔat yina· (?) ƛeṫ dísi, "lick"], "eating moon" *Ya ga glea disi* [probably ẋé·ga·, "true," or -?- ʔa ɬ̇iɬ̇, "it defecates"], "diarrhea moon" *Har-ou-wak disi* [x̣a·wáq dísi], "shedding moon"
August	*Sha-ha-yi* [dísi], [ša·xe·yí, "mountain shadow"], "shedding moon"	*Sha-ha-yi,* [ša·-xe·yí], "berries ripe on mountain"
September	*Dis yati* [dís ỵádi], "child moon," referring to weaning of young animals	*Dis yiti* [dís ỵádi], "young [animals] moon" *Sarh disi* [ṡa·x̣ dísi], "groundhog moon" because they prepare winter nest
October	*Dis tlin* [dís ƛe·n] "big moon." People with abundant supplies of food return to winter village; animals are fat	*Dis tlin* [dís ƛe·n], "big moon"
November	*Ko-ka-har dis* [qukaha· dís], "digging moon," animals prepare winter nests	*Ko-ko-har dis* [qukaha· dís], "scraping moon," bears prepare winter dens
December	*Sha-nagh dis* [šá·náx̣ dís], "head or hair moon," as head of embryo in womb develops and hair grows [meaning is unclear]	*Sha-nagh dis* [šá·náx̣, "head-through," but meaning is unclear], "head moon," as hair appears on head of fetal seal
January	*Tah-wak disi* [ṫa·wáq dísi], "goose moon," referring to a contest between geese and crows [ravens], when the latter were worsted and had to disappear, while geese remained	*Tah wak disi* [ṫa·wáq dísi], "goose moon"
February	*Tseek disi* [ší·k dísi], "black bear moon," when black bears have cubs and throw them out in the snow	*Tseek disi* [ṡí·k dísi], "black bear moon," cubs born and thrown out on snow.
March	*Heen-ta-na ka-ya-ni disi* [hí·n tá·náx̣ kayạ·ní dísi], "underwater plants sprouting moon"	*Heen-ta-na ka-ya-ni disi* [hí·n tá·náx̣ kayạ·ní dísi], "underwater plants sprout"
April	*Khe-ka ka-ya-ni disi* [ẋé·ga· kayạ·ní dísi], ["true"] "budding moon," referring to shrubs and land plants	*Ka ya ni disi* [kayạ·ní disi], "budding moon" of plants and shrubs
May	*At-ka-ta hate eh-na disi* [ʔat gadax̣it yina· dísi, "month before breeding"], "ripening moon" referring to advanced pregnancies of animals	*At-ka-ta-hah eh na disi* [ʔat gadax̣it (?) yina· disi], "month before pregnancy"
June	*At ka-ta-hate disi* [ʔat gadax̣it dísi], "Birth moon," of animals	*At kata hate disi* [ʔat gadax̣it dísi, "breeding"], "Birth month"

Note: These calendars were recorded by Emmons.

TABLE 36

Calendars from Chilkat and Chilkoot

	Chilkat (Yé·ł x̣a·k)*	Chilkoot (Old Man)†
July 1st	*Us whook disi* (1st month) [ʔasxu·kʷ disi, "drying moon-of"], "Native tobacco drying moon"	*Atchan* [ʔat x̣a·n, "smoking salmon"], "eating smoked salmon"
August 2d	*Sha-ha-ye* [ša·-xe·yí], "new snow on mountains" [meaning unclear]	*Kakit* [qu-ḱí·t], "berry picking"
September 3d	*Sarh kla disi* [ša·x-ƛ́á· dísi, "mother of ground-hog moon-of"], "ground-hog preparing winter hole"	*Kachich* [kaxʷé·x̣, "high-bush cranberries"], "cranberry picking"
October 4th	*Dis tlin* [dís ƛe·n], "big moon"	*Kutzku koosiat* [qusiʔá·t, "it is cold," ḱácḱʷ, "small"; word order reversed], "little cold"
November 5th	*Ko-ka-ha dis* [qu-kaha· dis], "digging or scratching moon" when bears prepare holes	*Kutzku klate* [λe·t, "snow," ḱácḱʷ, "little"; word order reversed], "little snow"
December 6th	*Shanagh disee* [šá·náx̣ dísi, "through head"?], "head grows or hair shows" on young seal in womb	*Ko ka hit,* "digging or scratching house" [qu-ka-xí·t, "digging or scratching furrows"]
January 7th	*Tahwak disee* [ƚ́a·wáq dísi], "goose moon"	*She warchel* [?], "leaves falling"
February 8th	*Sha yana kluck* [?], "north wind blows strong"	*Kooti kutzku,* "little warm" [prob, qutí, "weather," ḱácḱu, "small"]
March 9th	*Heen ta na kayanee disee* [hí·n ta·náx̣ kaya·ní dísi], "sea plants begin to grow under water"	*Kooch* [ḱú·xʷ], "marten" trapping [Venus is "marten's moon," ḱú·xʷ dísi]
April** 10th	*Tchin-kat ah* [ǯinka·t ʔa], "10th thing" or "moon"	*Kauhkish,* "eulachon spawn" [possibly ġá·x̣ʷ, "herring eggs," -?-]
May** 11th	*Tchin-kat minah ka,* "11th thing" or "moon" [ǯinka·t wanák ʔa, "ten and-extra one"]	*Kiyanee,* "land flowers" [kaya·ní, "green plants"]
June** 12th	*Tchin-kat minah ka dak,* "12th moon" [ǯinkát waná·k qa dé·x̣, "ten and-extra two"]	*Khart,* "salmon" [x̣á·t]
extra** moon 13th	*Tchinkat min ah ka nusk a,* "13th moon" [ǯinka·t waná·k qa nášk ʔa·, "10 and another three things"]	

Note: These calendars were recorded by Emmons.

*Of the first, Emmons wrote: This calendar was given by "Yehl Kock" [Ye·l x̣a·k, Raven's Odor], the old chief of the *Kon na ta di* [Raven 3] at Chilkat. [He was chief of the old Whale House, (Emmons 1916a:23).] It includes thirteen months, those between March and July are expressed in numerals and include four months. Otherwise the months agree with the Sitka calendar except that September is the "Ground hog Moon" and February "the Moon of the North Wind." The year begins *about* July.

† About the Chilkoot Calendar Emmons wrote: This calendar was procured from an old man of the Chilkoot branch of the Chilkat tribe and is entirely different from any other Tlingit calendar, and would seem to be more individual than general, although it expresses very accurately the industries of the people at the seasons.

**At Chilkat, these moons are designated by ordinal numbers.

TABLE 37

Two Calendars from Yakutat

July	*Loot a klitle,* "when animals evacuate freely from change of food" [-?- ʔa· ɬiɬ, "defecates"]	*Ye-da klitle,* "hair seals evacuate freely at this time," [?-? -ɬiɬ]; *First Moon*
August	*Sha-ha-yi,* "when berries are ripe on mountain" [ša·xe·yí, "mountain shadows"]; *First Moon*	*Sha hayi*
September	*Dis yati* [dís yádi], "young moon"	*Dis yati,* "cradle moon," referring to young animals [dís yádi]
October	*Dis tlin,* "big moon" [dís ƛe·n], when the salmon are in the lakes	*Dis tlin* [dís ƛe·n], "big moon"
November	*Ko-ko-ha dis* [qu-ka-ha· dís], "when bear digs winter hole"	*Ko-ko-ha dis* [qu-ka-ha dís], "bear scratching winter hole"
December	*Sha-nagh dis,* "hair seal in womb grows hair on head," [šá·náx̣ dís]	*Sha-nugh dis,* "hair grows on head of hair seal in womb" [šá·náx̣ dís]
January	*Tah-wak dis* [t̓a·wáq dis], "goose moon"	**Kladashu ah* [ƛe·du·šú ʔa·], "6th one"
February	*Heen-ta-na ka-ya-ni disi* [hí·n ta·náx̣ kaya·ní dísi], "underwater plants grow"	*Heen-ta-nah ka-ya-ni disi* [hí·n ta·náx̣ kaya·ní dísi], "seaweed under water begins to grow"
March	*Yat-kut-leth* [?], "when seaweed grows on rocks"	*Nush-ka-dashu ha* [naš̓gadu·šú ʔa·], "8th one"
April	*Yar-harni disi* [ya·w, "herring," ? ʔa·ní, "land-of,"? disí "moon-of"], "when the eulachon [?] run in fresh water"	*Ku-shuck ha* [gu·šúqʷ ʔa·], "9th one"
May	*Ka-ya-ni disi* [kaya·ní dísi, "moon of green leaves"], "budding moon"	*Chinkat (ah)* [ǯinka·t (ʔa·)], "10th (one)"
June	*Kok-hoo wock,* "when animals are shedding" [x̣a·wáq (disi), "shedding"]	*At-ka-ta disi,* "calm, good moon," [ʔat katá·y, "?" dísi]

Note: Emmons writes of these: "Two calendars of the Yakutat tribe, procured from two older people at Yakutat. In one [on the left] the first month of the year corresponds with August, in the other with July."

**Some moons may be, or commonly are, designated by ordinal numbers, but the counts are not the same in these two calendars, in that on the right the count between the "First Moon" and the "6th" is inaccurate. (FdeL)

Bibliography

WORKS BY GEORGE THORNTON EMMONS

1886 Letter to the editor, *The Alaskan* (Sitka), June 19, p. l. [From Chilcoot, Alaska, May 20, defending the Chilkoot and Chilkat Indians from complaints of prospectors on their way to the interior.]

1893 "Alaska's Weather: Lieutenant Emmons on Our Great Northern Province." *Kate Field's Washington* (Seattle) 5:21–23 (July 12).

1902 "The Woodlands of Alaska." Unpublished manuscript. [Report to President Roosevelt on a national forest in southeastern Alaska.] National Archives, Washington, D.C., file 3841–02, record group 48.

1903 *The Basketry of the Tlingit.* AMNH Memoirs 3(2):229–77. New York. [Reviewed by O. T. Mason, *American Anthropologist* 5:700–701 (1903). Emmons left three or four copies of this review among his papers in BCPA.]

1904 Letter to the Secretary of the Navy (dated March 28, 1903, from Washington, D.C.), *Proceedings of the Alaskan Boundary Tribunal,* vol. 1, part 2: Appendix to the Case of the United States, pp. 402–6. S. Doc. 162, 58th Cong., 2d sess. (in *Senate Documents,* vol. 15).

1905 "Report on Conditions and Needs of Natives of Alaska." [In President Roosevelt's message to Congress, January 19, transmitting this report and urging legislation to meet those needs.] S. Doc. 106, 58th Cong., 3d sess., vol. 3. Serial 4765. 23 pp.

1906 "Conditions and Needs of Natives of Alaska." *Southern Workman* 35:306–10. ("Selections from the official report of Lieutenant G. T. Emmons, U.S.N., submitted to President Roosevelt in 1905.")

1907 *The Chilkat Blanket, with Notes on the Blanket Designs by Franz Boas.* AMNH Memoirs 3(4):329–401, pls. XXIV–XXVII. New York. [Reviewed by O. T. Mason, *American Anthropologist* 10:296–98 (1908). Emmons had five copies of this review among his papers at BCPA.]

1908a "The Use of the Chilcat Blanket." *The American Museum Journal* 8(5):65–70.

1908b "Petroglyphs in Southeastern Alaska." *American Anthropologist* 10(2):221–30.

1908c "Copper Neck-rings of Southern Alaska." *American Anthropologist* 10(4):644–49.

1910a "Niska." In *Handbook of American Indians North of Mexico,* ed. F. W. Hodge. BAE Bulletin 30, 2:75–76. Washington, D.C.

1910b "Tahltan." Ibid., 2:670–71.

1910c "The Potlatch of the North Pacific Coast." *The American Museum Journal* 10(8):229–45.

1911a *The Tahltan Indians, Illustrated by Specimens in the George G. Heye Collections.* University Museum Anthropological Publications 4(1):5–120, pls. I–XIX. Philadelphia: University of Pennsylvania Press.

1911b "Conditions among the Alaska Natives." *Lake Mohonk Conference,* Twenty-ninth Annual Meeting, 2d sess., Wednesday evening, October 19, 1911, pp. 57–67.

1911c "Native Account of the Meeting between La Pérouse and the Tlingit." *American Anthropologist* 13(2):294–98.

1912 "The Kitselas of British Columbia." *American Anthropologist* 14(4):367–471.

1913 "Some Kitksan Totem Poles." *The American Museum Journal* 13:362–69.

1914 "Portraiture among the North Pacific Coast Tribes." *American Anthropologist* 16(1):59–67.

1915 "Tsimshian Stories Carved in Wood." *The American Museum Journal* 15(7):363–66.

1916a "The Whale House of the Chilkat." AMNH Anthropological Papers 19(1):1–33, pls. 1–4. New York.

1916b "The Whale House of the Chilkat." *The American Museum Journal* 16:451–60.

[1916c] "History of Tlingit Clans and Tribes." Unpublished manuscript. "Part 1: Raven Clans, Wolf Clans, *Na-ahde* (Eagle Phratry of the Tsimshian, but a clan of the Sanya Kwan)." "Part 2: Tanta-Kwan, Sanya Kwan, Stikine Kwan, Hen-yeh Kwan, Klawak Kwan, Kuyu Kwan, Kake Kwan, Sum-dum Kwan, Taku Kwan, Auk Kwan, Chilkat Kwan and the Chilkoot, Hutz-nuwu Kwan, Sitka Kwan, Hoonah Kow, Gunaho Kwan, Yakutat Kwan, Qwolthyet Kwan." (Copies of manuscript in both AMNH and BCPA.)

1921 "Slate Mirrors of the Tsimshian." *Indian Notes and Monographs* [Miscellaneous series] 15:5–21. MAI, Heye Foundation, New York.

1923 "Jade in British Columbia and Alaska, and Its Use by the Natives." *Indian Notes and Monographs* [Miscellaneous series] 35:11–52. MAI, Heye Foundation, New York.

1925 "The Kitksan and Their Totem Poles." *Natural History* 25:33–48.

1928 "'Wings' of Haida Ceremonial Canoes." *Indian Notes* 5:298–302. MAI, Heye Foundation, New York.

1930 "The Art of the Northwest Coast Indians." *Natural History* 30:282–92.

Emmonds [*sic*], G. T., and G. P. L. Miles

1939 "Shamanistic Charms." *Ethnologica Cranmorensis* 14:31–35. Cranmore Ethnographical Museum, Chiselhurst, England. Issued for private circulation only.

For further sources on Lieutenant George Thornton Emmons, in addition to the reviews of his works cited above, see Boas (1888a, 1888b) about his first collection sold to AMNH and its catalogue; de Laguna (1972:187, 189, 192, 686–87) for his activities at Yakutat in 1887 and his collections from that area and from Dry Bay (evidently on a later occasion); Jean Low (1977) for a spirited account of his ethnographic work in Alaska; Polly and Leon Miller (1967:196, 211–13, 243–51 passim) for Emmons on the condition of the Alaska Natives and for his activities as a collector; Wardwell (1978:24–28) and Jonaitis (1988:87–113) for his relations with AMNH; and also Cole's outstanding study of collectors on the Northwest Coast and Emmons's role in the context of his predecessors and rivals, and of the museums that obtained the specimens (1985:80, 85–89 passim, 132, 142–51 passim, 208–28 passim, 236, 241–43, 255, 260–61, 264, 294, 308, 337, 350). Other writers who have treated Emmons may be mentioned, although their views or interpretations of events differ in particulars from ours: Carpenter in *The Far North* (1973:288, n. 12) and in Holm and Reid (1975:9–27; and 1976, excerpted from the last); Conrad (1977, 1978, and 1984).

SOURCES CITED

Alaska Geographic Society
1978 *Alaska Whales and Whaling* [Quarterly]. Vol. 5, no. 4. Anchorage: Alaska Northwest Publishing Co.

Alaskan Boundary Tribunal
1904 *Proceedings of the Alaskan Boundary Tribunal* (1902–3). S. Doc. 162, 58th Cong., 2d sess. Vol. 1, part 2: Appendix to the Case of the United States, pp. 1–1550. In *Senate Documents*, vol. 15. Washington, D.C.

Armstrong, Robert H.
1980 *A Guide to the Birds of Alaska*. Anchorage: Alaska Northwest Publishing Co.

Bancroft, Hubert Howe
1884 *History of the Northwest Coast*. 2 vols. San Francisco: A. L. Bancroft and Co.
1886 *History of Alaska, 1730–1885*. San Francisco: A. L. Bancroft and Co.

Barbeau, Marius
1929 *Totem Poles of the Gitksan, Upper Skeena River, British Columbia*. National Museum of Canada Bulletin 61, Anthropological Series no. 12. Ottawa.
1951 *Totem Poles*. 2 vols. National Museum of Canada Bulletin 119, Anthropological Series no. 30. Ottawa.

Bartholomew, John
1942 *The Oxford Advanced Atlas*. 7th ed. London: Oxford University Press.

Beardslee, Captain L. A., USN
1882 *Reports of . . . Relative to Affairs in Alaska and the Operations of the U.S.S. Jamestown under his Command, While in the Waters of that Territory*. S. Exec. Doc. 71, 47th Cong., 1st sess., vol. 4.

Belcher, Captain Sir Edward, RN
1843 *Narrative of a Voyage Round the World, Performed in Her Majesty's Ship Sulphur, During the Years 1836–1843. . . .* 2 vols. London: Henry Colburn.

[Beresford, William]
1789 *A Voyage Round the World; But More Particularly to the North-West Coast of America: Performed in 1785, 1786, 1787, and 1788, in the King George and Queen Chàrlotte, Captains Portlock and Dixon. . . .* By Captain George Dixon. [A series of forty-nine letters by "W.B.," Supercargo on the *Queen Charlotte*, ed. Captain George Dixon.] 2d ed. London: Geo. Goulding.

Birket-Smith, Kaj
1941 "Early Collections from the Pacific Eskimo." In *Ethnographical Studies: Published on the Occasion of the Centenary of the Ethnographical Department, National Museum*. Nationalmuseets Skrifter, Etnografisk Række 1:121–63. Copenhagen.
1953 *The Chugach Eskimo*. Nationalmuseets Skrifter, Etnografisk Række 4. Copenhagen.

Birket-Smith, Kaj, and Frederica de Laguna
1938 *The Eyak Indians of the Copper River Delta, Alaska*. Det Konglige Videnskabernes Selskabet. Copenhagen: Levin and Munksgaard.

Boas, Franz
1888a "Gleanings from the Emmons Collection of Ethnological Specimens from Alaska." *Journal of American Folk-Lore* 1(3):215–19.
1888b "An Ethnological Collection from Alaska." *Science* 11 (April 27):199.
1897 "The Decorative Art of the Indians of the North Pacific Coast." AMNH Bulletin 10:123–76. New York.
1916 *Tsimshian Mythology*. BAE Thirty-first Annual Report. Washington, D.C.
1917 *Grammatical Notes on the Language of the Tlingit Indians*. University Museum Anthropological Publications 8(1). Philadelphia: University of Pennsylvania Press.
1921 *Ethnology of the Kwakiutl*. 2 vols. BAE Thirty-fifth Annual Report. Washington, D.C.
1927 *Primitive Art*. Oslo: Instituttet for Sammenlignende Kulturforskning.

Bodega y Quadra, Juan Francisco de la
1865 "Expeditions in the years 1775 and 1779 towards the West Coast of North America." *Annuario de la Dirección de Hidrografia, Ano III*, trans. G. F. Barwick. (Manuscript in BCPA. Cited by Rickard 1939.)

Boursin, Henry
1893 "Additional to First District: The Natives." In *Report on Population and Resources of Alaska at the Eleventh Census: 1890*, pp. 54–63. Washington, D.C.: U.S. Bureau of the Census.

Brooks, Alfred Hulse
1900 "A Reconnaissance from Pyramid Harbor to Eagle City, Alaska, including a description of the copper deposits of the upper White and Tanana rivers." U.S. Geological Survey Twenty-first Annual Report, 1899–1900, 2:331–91. Washington, D.C. (Cited by Rickard 1939.)

Brooks, Charles Wolcott
1876 "Early Migrations: Japanese Wrecks . . . Ethnologically Considered." *Proceedings of the California Academy of Sciences*. March 1. San Francisco.

Carpenter, Edmund
1973 "Some Notes on the Separate Realities of Eskimo and Indian Art." In *The Far North: 2000 Years of American Eskimo and Indian Art,* pp. 282–89. Washington, D.C.: National Gallery of Art.
1975 "Introduction: 'Collecting Northwest Coast Art.'" In Holm and Reid 1975:9–27.
1976 "Collectors and Collections." *Natural History* 85(3):56–67 [excerpted from Holm and Reid 1975].
Chase, Walter G.
1893 "Notes from Alaska." *Journal of American Folk-Lore* 6:51–53.
Chinard, Gilbert
1937 *Le Voyage de La Pérouse sur les côtes de l'Alaska et de la Californie (1786).* Institut Français de Washington, Historical Documents 10. Baltimore: Johns Hopkins Press.
Clemens, W. A., and G. V. Wilby
1961 *Fishes of the Pacific Coast of Canada. Fisheries Research Board of Canada Bulletin* 68. 2d ed. Ottawa.
Cole, Douglas
1985 *Captured Heritage: The Scramble for Northwest Coast Artifacts.* Seattle and London: University of Washington Press.
Colnett, Captain James
(1786–88) "Journal, Prince of Wales, 16 October 1786–7 November 1788." Unpublished Crown-copyright manuscript in Public Record Office, London (Adm. 55/146). Quoted by permission of Her Majesty's Stationery Office, London.
Colyer, Vincent, Secretary, Board of Indian Commissioners
1870a "Bombardment of Wrangel, Alaska." Report of . . . to the President, March 31, 1870. [2 pp.] To which is attached the Letter of the Secretary of War, Wm. W. Belknap, March 19, 1870. [10 pp.] S. Exec. Doc. 67, 41st Cong., 2d sess.
1870b "Wrangel, Alaska, Previous to Bombardment," March 22, 1870, pp. 2–23. S. Exec. Doc. 68, 41st Cong., 2d sess.
Conrad, David E.
1977 "Creating the Nation's Largest Forest Reserve: Roosevelt, Emmons, and the Tongass National Forest." *Pacific Historical Review* 46(1):65–83.
1978 "Emmons of Alaska." *Pacific Northwest Quarterly* 69(2):49–60.
1984 "[Emmons] A Historian of the Tlingit." *Abhandlungen der Völkerkundlichen Arbeitsgemeinschaft* 37:2–11.
Cook, Captain James, and Captain James King, RN
1784–85 *A Voyage to the Pacific Ocean . . . performed under the direction of Captains Cook, Clerke, and Gore, in His Majesty's Ships the Resolution and Discovery, in the Years 1776, 1777, 1778, 1779, 1780.* 3 vols. London: Nicol and Cadell.
Coontz, Admiral Robert E., USN
1930 *From the Mississippi to the Sea.* Philadelphia: Dorrance.
Coxe, William
1803 *Account of the Russian Discoveries between Asia and America. . . .* 4th enl. ed. London: Cadell and Davies. [Translations from Russian reports. See Shelikhov for a more recent translation of the passages cited from Coxe.]
Crespi, Fray Juan (1774). *See* Griffin 1891
Culin, Stewart
1907 *Games of the North American Indians.* BAE Twenty-fourth Annual Report. Washington, D.C.
Dall, William H.
1884 *On Masks, Labrets, and Certain Aboriginal Customs.* B(A)E Third Annual Report, pp. 73–203. Washington, D.C.
1895 "Alaska as It Was and Is, 1865–1895." Annual Presidential Address. Philosophical Society of Washington, D.C. Bulletin 13:123–62.
Davidson, George
1901a "Explanation of an Indian Map . . . from the Chilkaht to the Yukon Drawn by the Chilkaht Chief, Kohklux, in 1869." *Mazama* (Portland, Ore.) 2(2):75–82.
1901b "Tracks and Landfalls of Bering and Chirikof on the Northwest Coast of America. . . ." *Transactions and Proceedings of the Geographical Society of the Pacific,* ser. 2, vol. 1. San Francisco: J. Partridge.
Davis, Horace
1872 "Record of Japanese Vessels Driven upon the North-West Coast of America. . . ." *Proceedings of the American Antiquarian Society,* April, pp. 65–82. Worcester, Mass.
Davis, Brevet Major General Jefferson, USA
1869 Letter of October 25, 1869. Report of the Secretary of War. H. Exec. Doc. 1, part 2, 41st Cong., 2d sess.
Dawson, George M.
1880 "On the Haida Indians of the Queen Charlotte Islands." Appendix A in *Reports of Explorations and Surveys, Report of Progress for 1878–79,* pp. 102B–171B. Geological Survey of Canada. Montreal: Dawson Brothers.
Dixon, Captain George. *See* Beresford, William
Dixon, Ronald B.
1933 "Tobacco Chewing on the Northwest Coast." *American Anthropologist* 35:146–50.
Drucker, Philip
1943 *Archeological Survey on the Northern Northwest Coast.* BAE Bulletin 133:17–142, pls. 5–9. Anthropological Papers, no. 20. Washington, D.C.
1948 "The Antiquity of the Northwest Coast Totem Pole." *Journal of the Washington Academy of Sciences* 38(12):389–97.
1950 *Culture Element Distributions: XXVI, Northwest Coast.* Anthropological Records 9(3). Berkeley: University of California Press.

1955a *Indians of the Northwest Coast.* AMNH Anthropological Handbook 10. New York: McGraw-Hill. Reprinted 1963.

1955b "Sources of Northwest Coast Culture." In *New Interpretations of Aboriginal American Culture History,* ed. Clifford Evans and Betty Meggers, pp. 59–81. Seventy-fifth Anniversary volume, Anthropological Society of Washington, D.C.

Dunn, John Asher
1984 "Tsimshian Grandchildren: Redistributive Mechanisms in Personal Property Inheritance." In *The Tsimshian and Their Neighbors of the North Pacific Coast,* ed. Jay Miller and Carol M. Eastman, pp. 36–57. Seattle and London: University of Washington Press.

Durham, Bill
1960 *Canoes and Kayaks of Western America.* Seattle: Copper Canoe Press.

Durham, George
1955 "Canoes from Cedar Logs: A Study of Early Types and Designs." *Pacific Northwest Quarterly* 46(2):33–39.

Durlach, Theresa Mayer
1928 *The Relationship Systems of the Tlingit, Haida, and Tsimshian.* American Ethnological Society Publications 11. New York.

D'Wolf, John
1968 [1861] *A Voyage to the North Pacific.* Fairfield, Wash.:Ye Galleon Press. (Also in *Tales of an Old Sea Port,* ed. W. H. Munro, pp. 100–201. Princeton University Press.)

Engeln, Oscar von
1907 "An Alaskan Wonderplace." *The Outlook* (New York) 86(4):169–80.

Engstrand, Iris H. W.
1981 *Spanish Scientists in the New World: The Eighteenth-Century Expeditions.* Seattle and London: University of Washington Press.

The Far North: 2000 Years of American Eskimo and Indian Art.
1973 [Illustrated catalogue for an exhibit, March 7–May 15. Articles by Edmund Carpenter, Henry B. Collins, Frederica de Laguna, and Peter Stone.] Washington, D.C.: National Gallery of Art.

Finegold, Rupert, and William Seitz
1983 *Silversmithing.* Radnor, Pa.: Chilton.

Fleurieu, Charles P. C. (editor)
1801 *A Voyage Round the World . . . during the Years 1790, 1791, and 1792, by Etienne Marchand. . . .* Translated from the French (Paris, 1789–1800). 2 vols. [All citations from vol 1.] London: Longman and Rees.

Fuller, George W.
1931 *A History of the Pacific Northwest.* New York: Alfred A. Knopf.

Gabrielson, Ira N., and Frederick C. Lincoln
1959 *The Birds of Alaska.* Illus. O. J. Murie and E. R. Kalback. Washington, D.C.: Wildlife Management Institute; Harrisburg, Pa.: Stackpole.

Garfield, Viola E.
1947 "Historical Aspects of Tlingit Clans in Angoon, Alaska." *American Anthropologist* 49(3):438–52.

Garfield, Viola E., and Linn A. Forrest
1948 *The Wolf and the Raven: Totem Poles of Southeastern Alaska.* Seattle: University of Washington Press.

Glass, Commander Henry, USN
1882 "Reports of . . . October 11, 1880, to June 8, 1881, [and] November 14, 1881, to January 10, 1882." In *Report of United States Naval Officers Cruising in Alaska Waters,* 2–45, 50–52. H. Exec. Doc. 81, 47th Cong., lst sess.

1890 "Naval Administration in Alaska." *Proceedings of the United States Naval Institute* 16(1):1–19.

Goddard, Pliny E.
1912 Review of *The Tahltan Indians* by G. T. Emmons. *Current Anthropological Literature* 1(1):109–11. (Published by the American Anthropological Association.)

Golder, Frank A.
1922–25 *Bering's Voyages: An Account of the Efforts of the Russians to Determine the Relation of Asia and America.* 2 vols. New York: American Geographical Society.

Golovin, Lieutenant-Captain Pavel N., Russian Navy
1979 (1862) *The End of Russian America: Captain P. N. Golovin's Last Report 1862.* Trans. Basil Dmytryshyn and E. A. P. Crownhart-Vaughan. Portland: Oregon Historical Society.

1983 *Civil and Savage Encounters: The Worldly Travel Letters of an Imperial Russian Navy Officer, 1860–1861.* Trans. Basil Dmytryshyn and E. A. P. Crownhart-Vaughan. Portland: Oregon Historical Society.

Golovnin, Captain Vasili Mikhailovich, Russian Navy
(1822) 1861 *Voyage Round the World, in the Sloop of War, Kamchatka, in 1817–19.* 2 vols. St. Petersburg. An extract is included in *Materials for the History of the Russian Settlements on the Shores of the Eastern [Pacific] Ocean* (in 4 parts), ed. P. Tikhmenev. Part 3, no. 4. Manuscript translation by Ivan Petroff in Bancroft Library, University of California, Berkeley. Quoted by permission.

(1822) 1979 (Part 1) *Around the World on the Kamchatka, 1817–1819.* Trans. Ella Lury Wiswell. Honolulu: Hawaiian Historical Society and University of Hawaii Press.

Grant, Whit. M.
1888 "Confining Maidens in Alaska." *Journal of American Folk-Lore* 1(2):168–69.

Green, Lewis
1982 *The Boundary Hunters: Surveying the 141st Meridian and the Alaska Panhandle.* Vancouver: University of British Columbia Press.

Griffin, George Butler (editor and translator)
1891 "Diary of Fray Tomás de la Peña, kept during the Voyage of the Santiago (August 26 to October 5, 1774)" and "Diary of Fray Juan Crespi, kept during the Same Voyage." Documents from the Sutro Collection. *Publications of the Historical Society of Southern California* 2(1):111–43, 177–213.

Gruber, Jacob W.
1967 "Horatio Hale and the Development of American Anthropology." *Proceedings of the American Philosophical Society* 111(1):5–37. Philadelphia.

Gunther, Erna
1972 *Indian Life on the Northwest Coast of North America, as Seen by the Early Explorers and Fur Traders during the Last Decades of the Eighteenth Century.* Chicago and London: University of Chicago Press.

Hall, Raymond E., and Keith B. Kelson
1959 *The Mammals of North America.* New York: Ronald Press.

Hallowell, A. Irving
1960 "The Beginnings of Anthropology in America." In *Selected Papers from the American Anthropologist, 1888–1920,* ed. Frederica de Laguna, pp. 1–90. Evanston, Ill.: Rowe, Peterson. Reprinted 1976, Washington, D.C.: American Anthropological Association.

Hanus, G. C., Master, USN
1881 "Reports of . . . , Chilkoot, Alaska, July 1, 188l." In Lull 1882:42–43; and in Porter 1893:41–46.

Hayes, Charles Willard
1892 "An Expedition through the Yukon District." *National Geographic Magazine,* 4:117–62, pls. 18–20.

Heizer, Robert F.
1940 "The Botanical Identification of Northwest Coast Tobacco." *American Anthropologist* 42(4):704–6.

Henry, John Frazier
1984 *Early Maritime Artists of the Pacific Northwest Coast, 1741–1841.* Seattle and London: University of Washington Press.

Hirabayashi, Joanne
1955 "The Chilkat Weaving Complex." *Davidson Journal of Anthropology* (Seattle) 1(1):43–61.

Hodge, F. W. (editor)
1907–10 *Handbook of American Indians North of Mexico.* 2 vols. BAE Bulletin 30, parts 1 and 2. Washington, D.C.

Holm, Bill
1965 *Northwest Coast Indian Art: An Analysis of Form.* Seattle: University of Washington Press.
1982 "A Wooling Mantle Neatly Wrought: The Early Historic Record of Northwest Coast Pattern-Twined Textiles, 1774–1850." *American Indian Art Magazine,* Winter, pp. 34–47. Scottsdale, Arizona.
1983 *The Box of Daylight: Northwest Coast Indian Art.* [Contributions by Peter L. Corey, Nancy Harris, Aldona Jonaitis, Alan R. Sawyer, and Robin K. Wright.] Seattle and London: Seattle Art Museum and University of Washington Press.

Holm, Bill, and Bill Reid
1975 *Form and Freedom: A Dialogue on Northwest Coast Indian Art.* Introduction by Edmund Carpenter. Houston: Institute for the Arts, Rice University. Also distributed as *Indian Art of the Northwest Coast: A Dialogue on Craftsmanship and Aesthetics.* Seattle: University of Washington Press, 1976.

Holmberg, Heinrich J.
1855 *Ethnographische Skizzen über die Völker des Russischen Amerikas.* Vol. 1: *Die Thlinkithen.—Die Konjagen.* Acta Societate Scientificae Fennicae 4. Helsingfors. [Translation of quoted passages by Frederica de Laguna.] (See also *Holmberg's Ethnographic Sketches,* trans. Fritz Jaensch. Rasmuson Library Historical Translation Series, vol. 1. Fairbanks: University of Alaska Press, 1985.)

Hough, Walter
1895 "Primitive American Armor." U.S. National Museum Annual Report for the year ending June 30, 1893, pp. 625–51. Washington, D.C.

Howard, W. A., Captain, USMC
1867–68 "Cruise of the U.S. Revenue Steamer Lincoln." In *Russian America,* pp. 195–361. H. Exec. Doc. 177, 40th Cong., 2d sess.

Howay, F. W.
1941 "The First Use of Sail by the Indians of the Northwest Coast." *The American Neptune* (Salem, Mass.) 1(4):374–80.
(1930–34) 1973 *A List of Trading Vessels in the Maritime Fur Trade, 1785–1825.* Edited by Richard A. Pierce. Kingston, Ont.: Limestone Press.

Hultén, Eric
1968 *Flora of Alaska and Neighboring Territories: A Manual of the Vascular Plants.* Stanford: Stanford University Press.

Ingraham, Joseph
1971 *Journal of the Brigantine* HOPE *on a Voyage to the Northwest Coast of America, 1790–1792.* Edited by Mark D. Kaplanoff. Barre, Mass.: Imprint Society.

Ireland, Willard E.
1941 "James Douglas and the Russian American Company, 1840." *British Columbia Historical Quarterly* 5(1):53–66.

Jochelson, Waldemar
1933 *History, Ethnology and Anthropology of the Aleut.* Washington, D.C.: Carnegie Institution.

Jonaitis, Aldona
1978 "Land Otters and Shamans: Some Interpretations of Tlingit Charms." *American Indian Art Magazine* 4(1):62–66.
1981 *Tlingit Halibut Hooks: An Analysis of the Visual Symbols of a Rite of Passage.* AMNH Anthropological Papers 57(1):1–48. New York.

1986 *Art of the Northern Tlingit.* Seattle and London: University of Washington Press.
1988 *From the Land of the Totem Poles: The Northwest Coast Indian Art Collection at the American Museum of Natural History.* New York: AMNH; Seattle: University of Washington Press.

Jones, Livingston F.
1914 *A Study of the Thlingets of Alaska.* New York: Fleming H. Revell.

Kaeppler, Adrienne L.
1978 *"Artificial Curiosities": An Exposition of Native Manufactures Collected on the Three Pacific Voyages of Captain James Cook, R.N.* Honolulu: Bishop Museum Press.
1983 "A Further Note on the Cook Voyage Collection in Leningrad." *Journal of the Polynesian Society* 92(1):93–98.

Kan, Sergei
1983 "Words that Heal the Soul: Analysis of the Tlingit Potlatch Oratory." *Arctic Anthropology* 20(2):47–59.

Kaplan, Susan A., and Kristin J. Barsness
1986 *Raven's Journey: The World of Alaska's Native People.* [Catalogue of an exhibition at the University Museum, University of Pennsylvania, for the Museum's Centennial, 1988.] Philadelphia: University of Pennsylvania Press.

Keithahn, Edward L.
1940 "The Petroglyphs of Southeastern Alaska." *American Antiquity* 6(2):123–32, pl. XI.
1954 "Human Hair as a Decorative Feature in Tlingit Ceremonial Paraphernalia." *Anthropological Papers of the University of Alaska* (Fairbanks) 3(1):17–20.
1962 "Stone Artifacts of Southeastern Alaska." *American Antiquity* 28(1):66–77.
1963 *Monuments in Cedar.* Rev. ed. Seattle: Superior.
1964 "Origin of the 'Chief's Copper' or 'Tinneh.'" *Anthropological Papers of the University of Alaska* 12(2):59–78.

Khlebnikov, Kyrill Timofeëvich
1861a "Notes on America." In *Materials for the History of the Russian Settlements on the Shores of the Eastern [Pacific] Ocean.* Part 3: Supplement to *Morskoi Sbornik,* no. 3. 171 pp. Manuscript translation by Ivan Petroff, in *Russian America,* vol. 3, Bancroft Library, University of California, Berkeley. [Quotations are all from the edition of 1976; see below.]
(1833) 1861b "The First Settlement of Russians in America." In *Materials for the History of the Russian Settlements on the Shores of the Eastern [Pacific] Ocean.* Supplement to *Morskoi Sbornik,* no. 4, pp. 40–56. Manuscript translation by Ivan Petroff, in *Russian America,* vol. 3, Bancroft Library, University of California, Berkeley. Quoted by permission.
1976 *Colonial Russian America: Kyrill T. Khlebnikov's Reports, 1817–1832.* Trans. Basil Dmytryshyn and E. A. P. Crownhart-Vaughan. Portland: Oregon Historical Soc.

Kincer, J. B.
1941 "Climate of Alaska." In *Department of Agriculture Yearbook, 1941,* pp. 211–15. Washington, D.C.

Knapp, Frances, and Rheta Louise Childe
1896 *The Thlinkets of Southeastern Alaska.* Chicago: Stone and Kimball.

Kotzebue, Otto von, Post Captain in the Russian Navy
1830 *A New Voyage Round the World in the Years 1823, 24, 25, and 26.* 2 vols. London: Colburn and Bentley.

Krause, Aurel
(1885) 1956 *The Tlingit Indians: Results of a Trip to the Northwest Coast of America and the Bering Straits.* Trans. Erna Gunther. Seattle: University of Washington Press for the American Ethnological Society.

Krauss, Michael E.
1970a "Eyak Texts." Cambridge: Massachusetts Institute of Technology Microphoto Laboratory.
1970b "Eyak Dictionary" (as above).
1982 *In Honor of Eyak: The Art of Anna Nelson Harry.* Compiled and edited by M. E. Krauss. Fairbanks: Alaska Native Language Center, University of Alaska.

Kroeber, Alfred L.
1925 *Handbook of the Indians of California.* BAE Bulletin 78. Washington, D.C.
1939 *Cultural and Natural Areas of Native North America.* Publications in American Archaeology and Ethnology 38. Berkeley: University of California Press.

de Laguna, Frederica (Senior)
1894 "A Voyage Northward." *Overland* 4 (July):30–38.

de Laguna, Frederica
1933 "Mummified Heads from Alaska." *American Anthropologist* 35(4):742–44, pl. 28.
1952 "Some Dynamic Forces in Tlingit Society." *Southwestern Journal of Anthropology* 8(1):1–12.
1956 *Chugach Prehistory: The Archaeology of Prince William Sound, Alaska.* University of Washington Publications in Anthropology 13. Seattle and London: University of Washington Press. Reprinted, 1967.
1960 *The Story of a Tlingit Community* [Angoon]: *A Problem in the Relationship between Archeological, Ethnological, and Historical Methods.* BAE Bulletin 172. Washington, D.C.
1963 "Yakutat Canoes." *Folk* (Copenhagen) 5:219–29. [Essays presented to Kaj Birket-Smith on his seventieth birthday, January 20, 1963.]
1972 *Under Mount Saint Elias: The History and Culture of the Yakutat Tlingit.* 3 parts. Smithsonian Contributions to Anthropology 7. Washington, D.C.
1975 "Matrilineal Kin Groups in Northwestern North America." In *Proceedings: Northern Athapaskan Conference,*

1971, ed. A. McFayden Clark, 1:17–145. Ottawa: National Museum of Man.

1983 "Aboriginal Tlingit Sociopolitical Organization." In *The Development of Political Organization in Native North America,* ed. Elizabeth Tooker, pp. 71–85. The 1979 Proceedings of the American Ethnological Society, Washington, D.C.

1987 "Atna and Tlingit Shamanism: Witchcraft on the Northwest Coast." *Arctic Anthropology* 24(1):84–100.

de Laguna, Frederica, and Francis A. Ridell, et al.

1964 *Archeology of the Yakutat Bay Area, Alaska.* BAE Bulletin 192. Washington, D.C.

Langsdorff, Georg H. von

1813–14 *Voyages and Travels in Various Parts of the World, during the Years 1803, 1804, 1805, 1806, and 1807.* 2 vols. [All citations from vol. 2.] London: Henry Colburn.

La Pérouse, Jean François de Galaup, Comte de

1799 *A Voyage Round the World, Performed in the Years 1785, 1786, 1787, and 1788. . . .* Trans. from the French by L. A. Milet-Mureau (1797). 2 vols. and atlas. [All citations from vol. 1.] London: Printed by A. Hamilton for G. G. and L. Robinson, etc.

1937 *See* Chinard, Gilbert

Lazarev, Captain-Lieutenant Andrei Petrovich, Russian Navy

(1832) 1861 *Voyage Round the World in the Sloop Ladoga in 1822–1844. . . .* Extracts included in *Materials for the History of the Russian Settlements on the Shores of the Eastern [Pacific] Ocean.* Part 4, no. 4. Manuscript translation by Ivan Petroff, in *Russian America,* vol. 3, Bancroft Library, University of California, Berkeley. Quoted by permission.

Ledyard, John

1783 *A Journal of Captain Cook's Last Voyage to the Pacific Ocean in Quest of a North-West Passage.* Hartford, Conn. (Cited by Rickard 1939.)

Lévi-Strauss, Claude

1943 "The Art of the Northwest Coast at the American Museum of Natural History." *Gazette des Beaux-Arts* 24:175–82.

(1956) 1963 "Split Representation in the Art of Asia and America." In *Structural Anthropology,* trans. Claire Jacobsen and B. G. Schoepf, pp. 239–63. Garden City: Doubleday.

(1979) 1982 *The Way of the Masks.* Trans. Sylvia Modelski. Seattle: University of Washington Press.

Lisiansky, Urey, Captain in the Russian Navy

1814 *A Voyage Round the World in the Years 1803, 4, 5, & 6. . . .* London: John Booth.

Loring, C. G.

1864 *Life of William Sturgis.* Boston.

Louthan, F. K.

1869 Letter of October 28, 1869. Appendix E, Colyer 1970b:16–18. S. Exec. Doc. 68, 41st Cong., 2d sess.

Low, Jean

1977 "George Thornton Emmons." *The Alaska Journal* 7(1):2–11.

Lull, Commander Edward P., USN

1882 "Reports of . . . June 28, 1881, to October 18, 1881." In *Report of United States Naval Officers Cruising in Alaska Waters,* pp. 45–50. H. Exec. Doc. 81, 47th Cong. 1st sess.

Lütké, Frédéric, Captain Lieutenant in the Russian Navy

1835 *Voyage autour du Mond . . . 1826, 1827, 1828, et 1829: Partie historique.* 3 vols. Trans. from the Russian by F. Boyé. Paris: Didot Frères. [Free translation of quoted passages from vol. 1 by Frederica de Laguna.]

1987 *A Voyage Around the World, 1826–1829.* Vol. 1: *To Russian America and Siberia.* Trans. from the French by Renée Marshall, supplemented with a parallel account by E. H. Baron von Kittliz, trans. from the German by Joan Moessner. Edited by Richard A. Pierce. Kingston, Ont.: Limestone Press.) [This translation appeared too late for my use.—FdeL]

MacDonald, George F.

1981 "Cosmic Equations in Northwest Coast Art." In *The World Is as Sharp as a Knife: An Anthology in Honour of Wilson Duff,* ed. Donald N. Abbot, pp. 225–38. Victoria: British Columbia Provincial Museum.

(1979) 1980 *Kitwanga Fort National Historic Site, Skeena River, British Columbia: Historical Research and Analysis of Structural Remains.* National Museum of Civilization, Manuscript Report 341. Ottawa.

Mackenzie, Alexander

(1801) 1927 *Voyages from Montreal on the River St. Laurence through the Continent of North America to the Frozen and Pacific Oceans in the Years 1789 and 1793 with a Preliminary Account of the . . . Fur Trade. . . .* Edited by John W. Garvin. Introduction by Charles W. Colby. Toronto: Masterworks of Canadian Authors. (1st ed., London, 1801.)

Mackenzie, Alexander (anthropologist)

1891 "Descriptive Notes on Certain Implements, Weapons, etc., from Graham Island, Queen Charlotte Islands, B.C." *Proceedings and Transactions of the Royal Society of Canada* 9:45–59. (Cited by Rickard 1939.)

McClellan, Catharine

1953 "The Inland Tlingit." In *Asia and North America: Transpacific Contacts,* assembled by Marian W. Smith. Society for American Archaeology Memoirs 9:47–52. Salt Lake City: University of Utah Press.

1954 "The Interrelations of Social Structure with Northern Tlingit Ceremonialism." *Southwestern Journal of Anthropology* 10(1):75–96.

1975 *My Old People Say: An Ethnographic Survey of Southern Yukon Territory.* 2 vols. Publications in Ethnology, no. 6. Ottawa: National Museum of Man.

Mahoney, Frank
1870 "Letter from . . . on the Indians and Their Trade in Eastern Alaska." Appendix F, Colyer 1870b:18–21.
Malaspina, Alejandro, Captain in the Spanish Fleet
1849 "Viaje de . . . ." In *Coleccion de Documentos Inéditos para la Historia de España*, ed. Miguel Salvá and Pedro Sainz de Baranda. Vol. 15: *Examen Histórico-Crítico de los Viajes y Descubrimentos Apócrifos del Capitan Lorenzo Ferrer Maldonado, de Juan de Fuca y del Almirante Bartolomé de Fonte*, ed. Eustaquio Fernandez de Navarrete, 6:268–320. Madrid: Imprenta de la Viuda de Calero.
1885 *Viaje político-científico alrededor del Mundo por las Corbetas Descubierta y Atrevida . . . desde 1789 á 1794*. Edited by Don Pedro de Novo y Colson. 2d ed. Madrid. [Manuscript translation by Sue Roark-Kalnak.]
Malin, Edward
1978 *A World of Faces: Masks of the Northwest Coast Indians*. Portland, Ore.: Timber Press.
Marchand, Étienne. *See* Fleurieu, Charles P. C. (editor)
Mason, Otis T.
1903 Review of *The Basketry of the Tlingit* by G. T. Emmons. *American Anthropologist* 5:700–701.
1904 "Aboriginal American Basketry: Studies in a Textile Art without Machinery." U.S. National Museum Annual Report for 1902, pp. 171–548. Washington, D.C.
1908 Review of *The Chilkat Blanket* by G. T. Emmons. *American Anthropologist* 10:296–98.
Maurelle. *See* Mourelle, Don Francisco Antonio
Meares, Lieutenant John, RN
1790 *Voyages in the Years 1788 and 1789, from China to the North West Coast of America, (with) a Narrative of a Voyage in 1786, from Bengal, in the Ship Nootka*. London: R. Griffiths.
Meilleur, Brien A.
1979 "Speculations on the Diffusion of *Nicotiana quadrivalvis* Pursh. to the Queen Charlotte Islands and Adjacent Alaskan Mainland." *Syesis* 12:101–4.
Merriman, Commander E. C., USN
1883 "Report to Secretary of the Navy, on Oct. 28, 1882." H. Exec. Doc. 9, part 3, 47th Cong., 2d sess. [On the shelling of Angoon.]
Miller, Polly, and Leon Gordon Miller
1967 *Lost Heritage of Alaska: The Adventure and Art of the Alaskan Coastal Indians*. Cleveland and New York: World.
Morris, William Gouverneur, Collector of Customs, Sitka
1879 "Report upon the customs district, public service, and resources of Alaska Territory." H. Exec. Doc. 59, 45th Cong., 2d sess.
1882 "Report to the Secretary of the Treasury, as of October 28, 1882." H. Exec. Doc. 9, part 2, 47th Cong., 2d sess. [On the shelling of Angoon.]
Morrow, James E.
1980 *The Freshwater Fishes of Alaska*. Illus. by Marion J. Dalen. Anchorage: Alaska Northwest Publishing Co.
Mourelle, Don Francisco Antonio
(1775) *Voyage of the Sonora in the Second Bucareli Expedition. . . .*
1920 The Journal Kept in 1775. . . . Trans. Daines Barrington. Reprinted with notes by Thomas C. Russell. San Francisco: Thomas C. Russell. (Kraus Reprint, 1975.)
1798 Extract from *The Account of a Voyage Made in 1779 by . . . Don Francisco Antonio Maurelle. . . .* In La Pérouse 1:242–56.
Muir, John
1915 *Travels in Alaska*. Boston and New York: Houghton Mifflin.
Murdock, George Peter
1949 *Social Structure*. New York: Macmillan.
1980 *Theories of Illness: A World Survey*. Pittsburgh: University of Pittsburgh Press.
Naish, Constance, and Gillian Story
1976 *English-Tlingit Dictionary: Nouns*. 2d ed. (1st ed. 1963). Fairbanks: Summer Institute of Linguistics.
Newcombe, C. F.
1923 *Menzies' Journal of Vancouver's Voyage, April to October 1792*. Edited by C. F. Newcombe. Biographical Note by J. Forsyth. Archives of British Columbia Memoirs 5. Victoria.
Niblack, Albert P., Ensign, USN
1890 *The Coast Indians of Southern Alaska and Northern British Columbia*. U.S. National Museum Annual Report for 1887–88, pp. 225–386. Washington, D.C.
Nichols, Ensign, USN
1882 In Glass 1882:44–45.
Oberg, Kalervo
1934 "Crime and Punishment in Tlingit Society." *American Anthropologist* 36(2):145–56.
1973 *The Social Economy of the Tlingit Indians*. American Ethnological Society, Monograph 55. Seattle and London: University of Washington Press.
Okun, S. B.
1951 *The Russian-American Company*. Edited by B. D. Grekov. Trans. from the Russian by Carl Ginsberg. Cambridge, Mass.: Harvard University Press.
Olson, Ronald L.
1927 "Adze, Canoe, and House Types of the Northwest Coast." University of Washington Publications in Anthropology 2(1):1–38. Seattle: University of Washington Press.
1936 "Some Trading Customs of the Chilkat Tlingit." In *Essays in Anthropology Presented to A. L. Kroeber*, ed. Robert L. Lowie, pp. 211–14. Berkeley, University of California Press.

1961 "Tlingit Shamanism and Sorcery." *Kroeber Anthropological Papers* 25:207–20. University of California, Berkeley.

1967 *Social Structure and Social Life of the Tlingit in Alaska.* Anthropological Records 26. Berkeley: University of California Press.

Orth, Donald J.

1967 *Dictionary of Alaska Place Names.* U.S. Geological Survey, Professional Paper 567. Washington, D.C.

Osborne, Carolyn

1964 "The Yakutat Blanket." In *Archeology of the Yakutat Bay Area, Alaska,* by Frederica de Laguna et al., pp. 187–99. BAE Bulletin 192. Washington, D.C.

Paul, Frances

1944 *Spruce Root Basketry of the Alaska Tlingit.* Indian Handicrafts 8, Education Division, U.S. Indian Service. Lawrence, Kans.: Haskell Institute. Reprinted 1982, Sheldon Jackson Museum, Sitka.

Peña, Fray Tomás de la (1774). *See* Griffin, George Butler (1891)

Peterson, Roger Tory

1941 *A Field Guide to Western Birds.* Boston: Houghton Mifflin. (2d ed., 1961, etc.)

Petroff, Ivan

1884 *Report on the Population, Industries, and Resources of Alaska, 10th Census: 1880,* vol. 8. U.S. Department of the Interior. Washington, D.C. (Also in *Compilation of Narratives of Explorations in Alaska,* U.S. Senate Committee on Military Affairs, pp. 53–281, 1900.)

Poole, Francis, C. E.

1872 *Queen Charlotte Islands: A Narrative of Discovery and Adventure in the North Pacific.* Edited by John W. Lyndon. London: Hurst and Blackett.

Porter, Robert E. (editor)

1893 *Report on Population and Resources of Alaska at the Eleventh Census: 1890.* Washington, D.C.: U.S. Bureau of the Census.

Portlock, Captain Nathaniel

1789 *A Voyage Round the World; But More Particularly to the North-West Coast of America, Performed in 1785, 1786, 1787, and 1788, in the King George and Queen Charlotte, Captains Portlock and Dixon.* London: Stockdale and Goulding.

Rickard, T. A.

1939 "The Use of Iron and Copper by the Indians of British Columbia." *British Columbia Historical Quarterly* 3(1):25–50.

Riobo, Fray Juan Antonio (1779). *See* Thornton, Very Rev. Walter, S. J. (1918)

Rozina, L. G.

1978 "The James Cook Collection in the Museum of Anthropology and Ethnography, Leningrad." In *Cook Voyage Artifacts in Leningrad, Berne, and Florence Museums,* ed. Adrienne L. Kaeppler, pp. 3–17. Honolulu: Bishop Museum Press.

Russian America

1725–1865 A collection of translations from various Russian publications and documents, ca. 1725–1865. Trans. Ivan Petroff. 7 vols. Manuscript, Bancroft Library P–K 1–6, University of California, Berkeley.

Russian America

1868 "Message from the President of the United States in answer to a resolution of the House of 19th December last. . . . February 19, 1868." H. Exec. Doc. 177, 40th Cong., 2d sess.

Sackett, Russell

1979 *The Chilkat Tlingit: A General Overview.* Anthropological and Historic Preservation, Cooperative Park Studies Unit, Occasional Paper 23. University of Alaska, Fairbanks.

Sacred Circles: Two Thousand Years of North American Indian Art.

1976, 1977 [Exhibition organized by Ralph T. Coe, in cooperation with the Arts Council of Great Britain with the support of the British-American Associates.] Kansas City, Mo.: Nelson Gallery of Art and Atkins Museum of Fine Arts.

Samuel, Cheryl

1982 *The Chilkat Dancing Blanket.* Illus. Sara Porter. Seattle: Pacific Search Press.

1986 "The Knight Island Robe." In Kaplan and Barsness 1986:91–95.

1987 *The Raven's Tail* [Northern geometric style robes]. Vancouver: University of British Columbia Press.

Sapir, Edward

1915a *A Sketch of the Social Organization of the Nass River Indians.* Museum Bulletin 19, Anthropological Series no. 7. Ottawa: Department of Mines.

1915b "The Na-Dene Languages, A Preliminary Report." *American Anthropologist* 17(3):534–58.

Schwatka, Frederick

1893 *A Summer in Alaska.* Philadelphia: J. Y. Huber; St. Louis: J. W. Henry. [An enlarged edition of *Along Alaska's Great River* (1885). New York: Cassell.]

Scidmore, Eliza Ruhamah

1884 *Appleton's Guide-Book to Alaska and the Northwest Coast. . . .* New York: Appleton.

1893 "The First District from Prince Frederick Sound to Yakutat Bay." In *Report on Population and Resources of Alaska at the Eleventh Census: 1890,* pp. 42–53. Washington, D.C.: U.S. Bureau of the Census.

Sessions, Francis C.

1890 *From Yellowstone Park to Alaska.* Illus. C. H. Warren. New York: Welch, Fracker.

Seton-Karr, H. W.

1887 *Shores and Alps of Alaska.* London: Sampson Low, Marston, Searle, and Rivington.

Shepard, Isabel S.
1889 *The Cruise of the U.S. Steamer "Rush" in Behring Sea: Summer of 1889*. San Francisco: Bancroft.
Shelikhov, Grigorii I.
(1787, 1793, 1812) 1981 *A Voyage to America, 1783–1786*. Trans. Marina Ramsay. Edited by Richard A. Pierce. Kingston, Ont.: Limestone Press. [Contains the material cited by Coxe.]
Shotridge, Louis
1919 "War Helmets and Clan Hats of the Tlingit Indians." *The Museum Journal* 10(2):43–48. Philadelphia: University of Pennsylvania Press.
1920 "Ghost of Courageous Adventurer." *The Museum Journal* 11(1):11–26.
1929 "The Bride of Tongass: A Study of the Tlingit Marriage Ceremony." *The Museum Journal* 20(2):131–56.
Shotridge, Louis and Florence
1913 "Indians of the Northwest" containing "Chilkat Houses" by Louis Shotridge, pp. 81–99, and "The Life of a Chilkat Indian Girl" by Florence Shotridge, pp. 101–3. *The Museum Journal* 4(3):69–103.
Shukoff
(1882) "A Glance at the First Customs of the Tlingit or Kolosh as the Russians Found Them at Sitka." Typed copy in AMNH; original handwritten copy in BCPA. ("Sketch of Thlingits by Shukoff, a half Russian and half Thlingit, who was educated for the Church by Russian Church in Sitka. Died in 1885, about sixty years old. He was in 1882–1885 employed by the U.S. Naval Commander and later by the Civil Authorities as a native policeman at Sitka, Alaska. This sketch of his people, the Thlingits of Alaska, was given in Thlingit, to a Russian interpreter and translated into English, in 1882." "These are the original notes as translated to me by George Kostrometinof of Sitka Alaska 1888. [Signed] G. T. Emmons.")
Shur, L. A., and R. A. Pierce
1976 "Artists in Russian America: Mikhail Tikhanov (1818)." *Alaska Journal* (Anchorage) 6(1):40–49.
Sierra, Fray Benito de la (1775). *See* Wagner, Henry R. (1930)
Simpson, Sir George
1847 *An Overland Journey Round the World, during the Years 1841 and 1842*. Philadelphia: Lee and Blanchard.
Simpson, J. D.
1907 "How Canoes Were Built." *Alaska-Yukon Magazine* (Seattle) 4(2):171–73. [Pages torn from magazine among Emmons's papers, BCPA, with the note in his hand: "This article by an Indian who knows the work."]
Smith, Harlan I.
1900 "Archaeology of Lytton, British Columbia." Jesup North Pacific Expedition 1(3):129–61. AMNH Memoirs 3. New York.
1909 "Archaeological Remains on the Coast of Northern British Columbia and Southern Alaska." *American Anthropologist* 11(4):595–600.
Steller, Georg Wilhelm
1925 "Journal of His Sea Voyage from the Harbor of Petropavlovsk in Kamchatka to the Western Coasts of America and the Happenings on the Return Voyage" (1741). In Golder 1922–25, 2:9–241.
Stevenson, Ian
1966 *Twenty Cases Suggestive of Reincarnation*. Proceedings of the American Society for Psychical Research, vol. 26. New York. Richmond, Va.: William Byrd Press.
Stewart, Hilary
1977 *Indian Fishing: Early Methods on the Northwest Coast*. Vancouver and Toronto: Douglas and McIntyre; Seattle: University of Washington Press. Reprinted 1982.
1984 *Cedar: Tree of Life to the Northwest Coast*. Vancouver and Toronto: Douglas and McIntyre; Seattle: University of Washington Press.
Story, Gillian L., and Constance M. Naish
1973 *Tlingit Verb Dictionary*. Fairbanks: Alaska Native Language Center, University of Alaska. (2d ed., 1976.)
Strange, James
1928 *Journal and Narrative of the Commercial Expedition from Bombay to the North-West Coast of America. . . .(1786)*. Edited by A. V. Venkatarama Ayyar. Records of Fort St. George, Madras.
Suría, Tomás de (1791). *See* Wagner, Henry R. (1936)
Swanton, John R.
1905a *Contributions to the Ethnology of the Haida*. Jesup North Pacific Expedition 5(1). AMNH Memoirs 8. New York.
1905b *Haida Texts and Myths: Skidegate Dialect*. BAE Bulletin 29. Washington, D.C.
1908 *Social Conditions, Beliefs and Linguistic Relationship of the Tlingit Indians*. BAE Twenty-sixth Annual Report, pp. 391–485, pls. XLVIII–LVIII. Washington, D.C.
1909 *Tlingit Myths and Texts*. BAE Bulletin 39. Washington, D.C.
Swineford, Honorable A. P. (Governor of Alaska, 1885–89)
1898 *Alaska, Its History, Climate and Natural Resources*. Chicago and New York: Rand, McNally.
Thomas, Major General George H., USA
1869 "Report of General of the Army, 27 Sept., 1869." In *Report of the Secretary of War*, 1:113–21. H. Exec. Doc. 1, part 2, 41st Cong., 2d sess.
Thornton, Very Rev. Walter, S. J.
1918 "An Account of the Voyage Made by the Frigates 'Princesa' and 'Favorita' in the Year 1799 from San Blas to Northern Alaska," by Father John Riobo. *Catholic Historical Review* 4(3):222–29.

Tikhmenev, Petr A.
(1861–63) 1978–79 [*Historical Review of the Russian American Company and Its Doings Up to the Present Time* (in Russian). 2 vols. St. Petersburg.] Vol. 1: A History of the Russian-American Company, trans. and ed. Richard A. Pierce and Alton S. Donnelly. Seattle and London: University of Washington Press, 1978. Vol. 2: *Documents,* trans. Dmitri Krenof; ed. Richard A. Pierce and Alton S. Donnelly. Kingston, Ont.: Limestone Press, 1979.

Townsend, Joan B.
1983 "Firearms Against Native Arms: A Study in Comparative Efficiencies with an Alaskan Example." *Arctic Anthropology* 20(2):1–33.

United States Coast Pilot
1943 *Alaska, Part I, Dixon Entrance to Yakutat Bay.* 9th ed. Washington, D.C.: Coast and Geodetic Survey, U.S. Department of Commerce.
1954 *9, Alaska: Cape Spencer to Arctic Ocean,* 6th ed. Washington, D.C.: Coast and Geodetic Survey, U.S. Department of Commerce.
1962 *8, Pacific Coast, Alaska: Dixon Entrance to Cape Spencer.* 11th ed. Washington, D.C.: Coast and Geodetic Survey, U.S. Department of Commerce.

Vancouver, Captain George, RN
1801 *A Voyage of Discovery to the North Pacific Ocean, and Round the World . . . Performed in the Years 1790, 1791, 1792, 1793, 1794, and 1795.* New edition with corrections. 6 vols. London: John Stockdale.

Vaughan, Thomas, E. A. P. Crownhart-Vaughan, and Mercedes Palau de Iglesias
1977 *Voyages of Enlightenment: Malaspina on the Northwest Coast, 1791/1792.* Portland: Oregon Historical Society.

Vaughn, Thomas, and Bill Holm
1982 *Soft Gold: The Fur Trade and Cultural Exchange on the Northwest Coast of America.* Portland: Oregon Historical Society.

Veniaminov, Ivan
(1840) 1984 *Notes on the Islands of the Unalaska District,* Part 3, section 2: "Notes on the Koloshi," pp. 380–451. Trans. Lydia T. Black and R. H. Geoghegan. Edited by Richard A. Pierce. Published jointly by the Elmer E. Rasmuson Library Translation Program, University of Alaska, Fairbanks, and the Limestone Press. Kingston, Ont.: Limestone Press.

Viereck, Leslie A., and Elbert L. Little, Jr.
1972 *Alaska Trees and Shrubs.* Agriculture Handbook 410. U.S. Forest Service. Washington, D.C.: U.S. Department of Agriculture.

Wagner, Henry R. (editor)
1930 "Fray Benito de la Sierra's Account of the Hezeta [Don Bruno Heceta] Expedition to the Northwest Coast in 1775." Trans. A. J. Baker; introduction and notes by Henry R. Wagner. *California Historical Society Quarterly* 9(3):201–42.
1936 "Journal of Tomás de Suría of His Voyage with Malaspina to the Northwest Coast of America in 1791." *Pacific Historical Review* 5(3):234–76.

Wardman, George
1884 *A Trip to Alaska . . .* [1879]. Boston: Lee and Shepard.

Wardwell, Allen
1978 *Objects of Bright Pride: Northwest Coast Indian Art from the American Museum of Natural History.* New York: The Center for Inter-American Relations and the American Federation of Arts. Distributed by the University of Washington Press, Seattle.

Wheeler, Arthur O.
1929 "How I Went to Alaska." *The Canadian Surveyor* 3(5):7–9.

Widerspach-Thor, Martine de
1981 "The Equation of Copper: In Memory of Wilson Duff." In *The World Is as Sharp as a Knife: An Anthology in Honour of Wilson Duff,* ed. Donald N. Abbott, pp. 157–74. Victoria: British Columbia Provincial Museum.

Willard, Caroline McCoy
1884 *Life in Alaska: Letters of Mrs. Eugene S. Willard.* Edited by her sister, Mrs. Eva McClintock. Philadelphia: Presbyterian Board of Publication.

Williams, Frank and Emma
1978 *Tongass Texts.* Transcribed and edited by Jeff Leer. Fairbanks: Alaska Native Language Center, University of Alaska.

Williams, Harry G.
1870 "The Stikine Indians at Wrangel," Fort Wrangel, October 30, 1869, Appendix B in Colyer 1870b:11–14.

Wood, Major E. S., USA
1882 "Among the Thlinkits in Alaska." *The Century Magazine* 24(3)323–39.

Wright, Julia McNair
1883 *Among the Alaskans.* [History of missions in Alaska, 1877–83.] Philadelphia: Presbyterian Board of Publication.

Young, Reverend S. Hall
1927 *Hall Young of Alaska, "The Mushing Parson": The Autobiography of S. Hall Young.* Introduction by John A. Marquis. New York and Chicago: Fleming H. Revell.

Index

Pages appearing in boldface type include illustrations; the names of individuals quoted extensively in the text are given in capital letters.

The editor and the publisher are grateful for the generous contributions of the following to the publication fund for this book:

David F. Aberle
Wendy H. Arundale
Marjorie Mandelstam Balzer
Karen I. Blu
John Bockstoce
Ernest S. Burch, Jr.
Maria G. Cattell
Donald W. Clark
J. Desmond Clark
Helen Codere
John L. Cotter
Nancy Yaw Davis
Christopher Donta
Nancy Dorian
Robert H. Dyson, Jr.
John C. Ewers
Jane Fajans
Ray Fogelson
George M. Foster
Charles Frantz
Ernestine Friedl
Ward H. Goodenough
Richard A. and Elizabeth Gould
Richard Graf
James B. Griffin
Jacob W. Gruber
Tadahiko and Hiroko Hara
William A. Haviland
Regina Herzfeld
Bill Holm
W. W. Howells
Frederick S. Hulse
Karl L. Hutterer
Richard H. Jordan
Susan A. Kaplan
Kenneth A. R. Kennedy
Sue Kenyen
Catherine Kernan
H. D. Kernan
Patricia Kernan
Igor Kopytoff
Samuel Noah Kramer
Michael E. Krauss
Margaret Lantis
William S. Laughlin
Emily B. Massara
Catharine McClellan
Mary P. McPherson
Machteld J. Mellink
Henry N. Michael
Richard E. Morlan
Michael Moulton
Fred Myers
Edward Norbeck
Sherry B. Ortner
Naomi B. Pascal
Diana Putnam
George I. Quimby
B. S. Ridgway
Sue Roark-Calnek
William Schneider
Judith Shapiro
Michael Silverstein
Melford E. Spiro
Alexander Spoehr
Wayne Suttles
Julidta C. Tarver
Holly Taylor
J. Callum Thomson
Marilyn Trueblood
James VanStone
Evon Z. Vogt
Mary M. Voigt
Anthony Wallace
Patty Jo Watson
Annette B. Weiner
Wendy Weiss
Frederick H. and Constance West
Gordon R. Willey
William and Karen Workman
Beth Ann A. Workmaster
H. H. Wormington

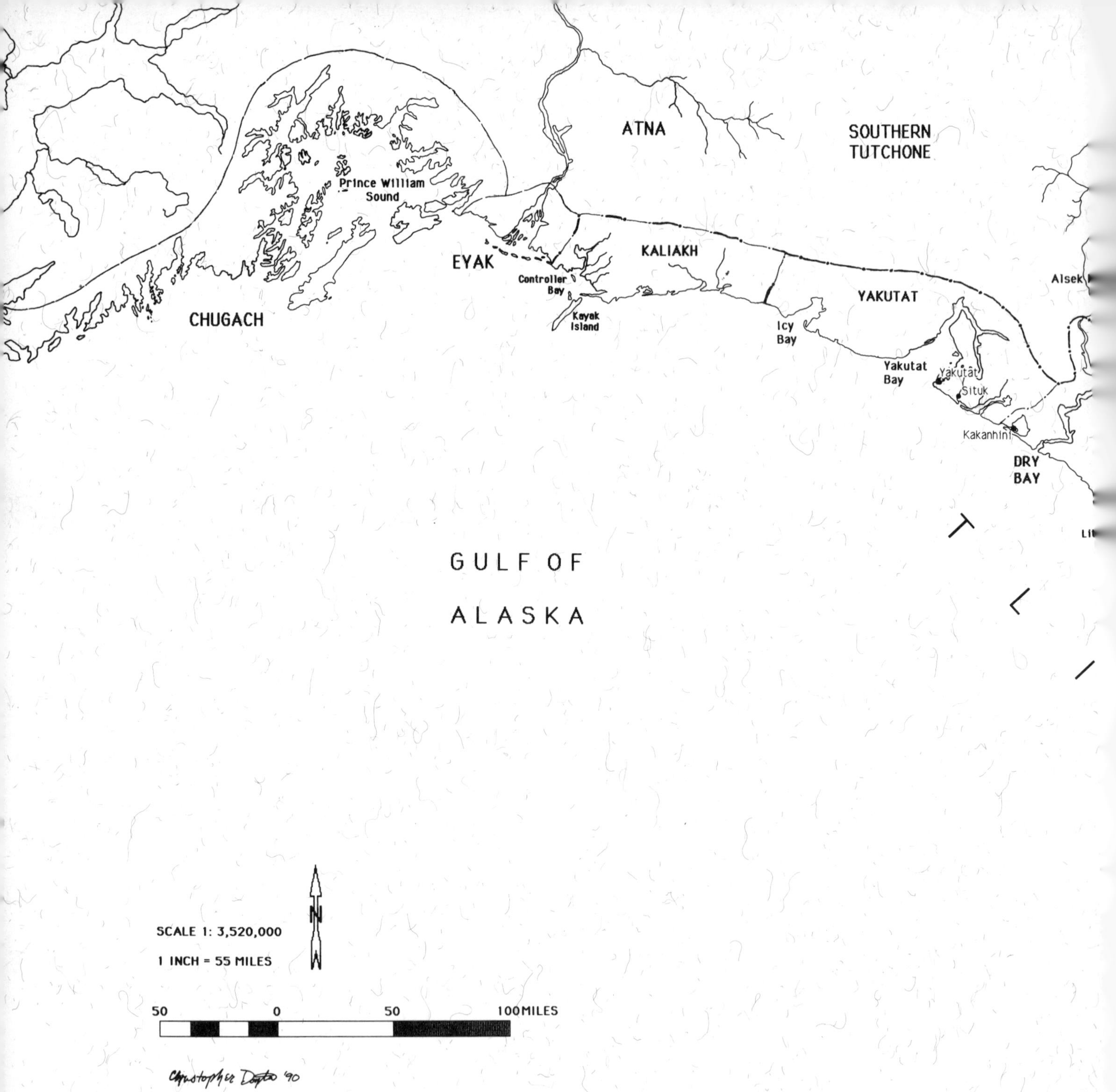

ATNA

SOUTHERN
TUTCHONE

Prince William
Sound

CHUGACH

EYAK

Controller
Bay

Kayak
Island

KALIAKH

Icy
Bay

YAKUTAT

Alsek

Yakutat
Bay

Yakutat

Situk

Kakanhini

DRY
BAY

T

L

I

GULF OF

ALASKA

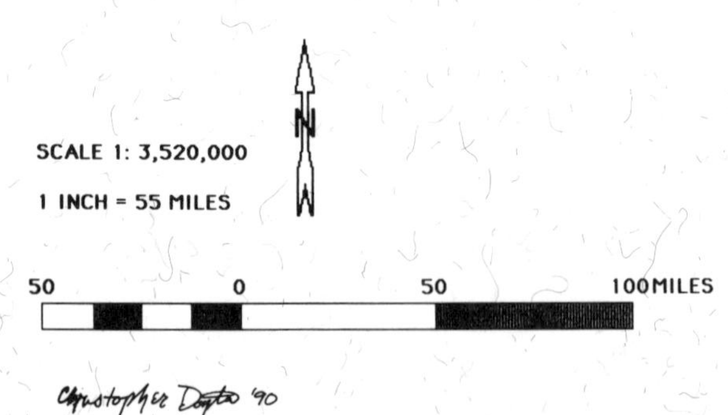